The Handbook of International Humanitarian L

The Handbook of International Humanitarian Law

THIRD EDITION

Edited by

DIETER FLECK

In collaboration with
MICHAEL BOTHE,
KNUT DÖRMANN,
HANS-PETER GASSER,
WOLFF HEINTSCHEL VON HEINEGG,
KNUT IPSEN, BEN F. KLAPPE,
JANN K. KLEFFNER, SANDRA KRÄHENMANN,
NILENDRA KUMAR,
MARY-ELLEN O'CONNELL,
STEFAN OETER, ROGER O'KEEFE, and
SILJA VÖNEKY

OXFORD
UNIVERSITY PRESS

OXFORD
UNIVERSITY PRESS

Great Clarendon Street, Oxford, OX2 6DP,
United Kingdom

Oxford University Press is a department of the University of Oxford.
It furthers the University's objective of excellence in research, scholarship,
and education by publishing worldwide. Oxford is a registered trade mark of
Oxford University Press in the UK and in certain other countries

© Dieter Fleck 2013

The moral rights of the author have been asserted

First Edition published in 1999
Second Edition published in 2008
Third Edition published in 2013
First published in paperback 2014

Impression: 4

Published in the United States of America by Oxford University Press
198 Madison Avenue, New York, NY 10016, United States of America

British Library Cataloguing in Publication Data
Data available

Library of Congress Control Number: 2013939373

ISBN 978–0–19–965880–0 (Hbk.)
ISBN 978–0–19–872928–0 (Pbk.)

Printed and bound by CPI Group (UK) Ltd, Croydon, CR0 4YY

Preface

The present revised edition of the *Handbook of International Humanitarian Law* responds to an increased interest in the international community. In a time of a continued need for clarifying the principles and rules described in this book and ensuring respect for their implementation, this interest deserves full support.

Substantive changes of the manual text include new developments in treaty law, such as the 2010 amendments to the ICC Statute, as well as new topics that have been extensively debated in recent years: *inter alia* the notion of direct participation in hostilities; air and missile warfare; belligerent occupation; operational detention; cyber operations; and the protection of the environment in armed conflict. The growing need to consider borderline issues of the law of armed conflict and the interplay of international humanitarian law, human rights, and other branches of international law has led to reconsidering certain approaches taken so far. Thus, Chapter 7 is no longer confined to the protection of prisoners of war under the Third Geneva Convention, but addresses all applicable legal standards that are relevant in contemporary practice. The commentaries both deepen reflection on such innovations and critically reconsider views expressed in earlier editions.

Some personal changes respond to the need for generational change which is necessary in any activity of this kind to remain relevant and influential in practice. I welcome the interest and active support by new contributors bringing their insight and experience from various aspects of international co-operation and academic research. At the same time I may express my gratitude to Professor Horst Fischer, Judge Sir Christopher Greenwood, CMG, QC, and Judge Rüdiger Wolfrum for their long-standing support and advice, accepting that they had to discontinue their co-operation in this project due to an increased workload in international co-operation, academic teaching, and jurisprudence. Their contributions to former editions which have been further developed in the present one are very much appreciated.

In order to facilitate the use of this Handbook, the manual text **printed in bold type** has again been made available as a separate document under <http://ukcatalogue.oup.com/product/9780199658800.do>. A comprehensive bibliography is no longer made available considering the ever-increasing number of relevant publications,* but an updated selection of sources used is provided in the footnotes.

I invite proposals and suggestions which will be considered for the preparation of further editions. Again, I must express my gratitude to Oxford University Press, in particular to John Louth, Merel Alstein and Barath Rajasekaran, for their professional support.

Dieter Fleck
Cologne, April 2013

---

* See the annual bibliographies included in *YIHL*. For former decades, see International Committee of the Red Cross & Henry Dunant Institute (eds), *Bibliography of International Humanitarian Law Applicable in Armed Conflicts*, 2nd edn (ICRC, 1987).

Contents

Introduction

During the past decades, international humanitarian law has been subject to a progressive development which culminated in the four 1949 Geneva Conventions, the 1977 Protocols Additional to these Conventions, the 1980 Weapons Convention, the 1997 Ottawa Convention on the Prohibition of Land Mines, and the 1998 Rome Statute of the International Criminal Court. These treaties have underlined and specified three general legal restrictions which are described in Section 132 of the present Handbook, as follows: an act of war is permissible only if it is directed against military objectives, if it is not likely to cause unnecessary suffering, and if it is not perfidious. While such legal restrictions are constantly challenged in armed conflicts, this is particularly true for the present time: the character of war has changed in the recent decades,[1] even if it is fair to state that many of the new wars are linked to historical legacies and many characteristics of current armed conflicts are known from history. The world today witnesses new war aims of belligerents, an increase of active participation in hostilities by civilians, privatization of specific military tasks, new forms of war financing by local-global networks, and criminal forms of diversion of funds and materiel at the expense of victims.

If globalization can be considered a common feature of this new reality, the same is true for efforts to improve knowledge of and education and training in international humanitarian law and to sustainably increase its public acceptance and level of implementation. Extensive international co-operation, which had been encouraged decades ago by the negotiations on the Additional Protocols from 1974 to 1977 and is today practised in close professional contacts between diplomats and military officers, scholars and practitioners, states and non-governmental organizations, and individuals, has contributed decisively to the worldwide dissemination of international humanitarian law. This co-operation has paved the way for a continuously progressing development of customary international humanitarian law in all cultures.[2] It has also underlined the significance of humanitarian protection for security and co-operation throughout the world. While many positive efforts have been made by states to implement their obligations under international humanitarian law,[3] fundamental work remains to be done at international and national levels.[4] This task poses a challenge to political decision-makers and to their legal and military advisers, many of whom must shoulder this workload in addition to their other duties and in spite of the pressure of other priorities.

---

[1] See Mary Kaldor, *New and Old Wars*, 2nd edn (Cambridge: Polity, 2006); Hugo Slim, *Killing Civilians: Method, Madness and Morality in War* (London: Hurst & Co., 2008); Hew Strachan & Sibylle Scheipers (eds), *The Changing Character of War* (OUP, 2011); Elizabeth Wilmshurst (ed.), *International Law and the Classification of Conflicts* (OUP, 2012).

[2] Frits Kalshoven, 'Applicability of Customary International Law in Non-International Armed Conflicts' in Antonio Cassese (ed.), *Current Problems of International Law* (Milan: Giuffrè, 1975), 267–85; Theodor Meron, *Human Rights and Humanitarian Norms as Customary International Law* (OUP, 1989), 246 *et seq.*; *CIHL*, with update at Customary IHL Database, <www.icrc.org/customary-ihl/eng/docs/home>.

[3] For relevant national legislation, see Vol. II/2 *CIHL*, 4208–85; for a list of military manuals on international humanitarian law, see Vol. II/2 *CIHL*, 4196–207.

[4] Bothe, in Michael Bothe/Peter Macalister-Smith/Thomas Kurzidem (eds), *National Implementation of International Humanitarian Law* (Nijhoff, 1990), 261 et seq.; for current activities, see in particular the work of the ICRC and its Advisory Service, <http://www.icrc.org/ihl-nat>; the process of reaffirmation

DIETER FLECK

Recent achievements of worldwide co-operation in this field are manifold: The inter-relationship between humanitarian law and the protection of human rights in armed conflicts is largely accepted and better understood today than ever before. A progressive development of international criminal law has led to increased jurisprudence on war crimes and crimes against humanity by national courts, international ad hoc tribunals, and finally to the establishment of the ICC. States and international organizations have shown a growing awareness of their obligation under Article 1 common to the Geneva Conventions to ensure respect of international humanitarian law, to better implement its rules, and to enforce compliance by state and non-state actors in all armed conflicts. The Geneva Conventions have reached global acceptance and Additional Protocol I to these Conventions is now in force for 173 states.[5] Member states of military alliances have ensured interoperability in the not so rare cases of their adherence to different treaty obligations, a work which for both legal and political reasons must clearly go beyond the lowest common denominator (see below, Section 1403). In multinational military operations, non-parties to AP I have applied its protection standards for policy reasons, thus demonstrating that the alleged 'great schism' between parties and non-parties to the Protocol which at times still dominates academic debates is not insurmountable in reality.[6] Despite various back falls in recent armed conflicts, including the ongoing 'war on terror', a term based on political rhetoric rather than legal expertise, international co-operation has convincingly shown that strict adherence to humanitarian protection standards in military operations is an essential prerequisite for professional effectiveness and lasting solutions.

Academic experts have reflected on these developments in most proactive forms. A proliferation of books and articles, courses, and research projects have demonstrated a widespread interest in international humanitarian law that is hardly to be observed in other branches of international law and at the same time has led to remarkable stand-ards of specialization. It may be due to this development that comprehensive treatises have widely been replaced by individual approaches to serve the needs of specific course programmes and increase understanding by means of presenting key issues of the topic.[7] Fully recognizing such approaches, the challenge prevails to present all relevant issues in context, assess the entirety of international humanitarian law in one publication,

and development of international humanitarian law started by Switzerland with the Harvard Program on Humanitarian Policy and Conflict Research, <http://www.hpcr.org>; the San Remo Round Tables and courses held over many years by the International Institute of Humanitarian Law, <http://web.iihl.org/>; and the Geneva Academy of International Humanitarian Law and Human Rights, <http://www.ucihl.org>.

[5] See <http://www.icrc.org/IHL.nsf/(SPF)/party_main_treaties/$File/IHL_and_other_related_Treaties.pdf>.

[6] As mentioned by L. C. Green, *The Contemporary Law of Armed Conflict*, 2nd edn (Manchester University Press, 2000), xv, during the 1991 war in the Gulf, which was fought by the US alongside a coalition of twenty-six states in which no common legal obligations as to AP I did exist, White House press releases on aerial bombardments extensively used language of Article 51(5) of that Protocol (one of the most controversial provisions in the perception of the US Administration which had been used as one of its arguments against ratification), to describe how precision strikes in Iraq had been planned and executed. The Chairman of the US Joint Chiefs of Staff, General Colin Powell, in his Report to Congress on Coalition operations in the Gulf, had gone even further in stating that the provisions of AP I were, for the main part, applied as if they constituted customary law: see Department of Defense, 'Conduct of the Persian Gulf War: final report to Congress' (1992), 696, 700–3.

[7] For a most recent excellent example, see Jean d'Aspremont/Jérôme de Hemptinne, *Droit International Humanitaire. Thèmes Choisis* (Pedone, 2012).

DIETER FLECK

and take a case-oriented approach in order to serve the need for continuing exchange between legal theory and practice.

Some terminological inconsistencies may still be a matter of discussion. In both academic and military courses 'international humanitarian law (IHL)' and 'the law of armed conflict (LOAC)' are widely used as synonymous terms, like 'fraternal twins'.[8] 'International humanitarian law' appears to be more precise, first due to the preference given to it by the ICRC and the UN, and second with respect to the fact that this term better conveys that there exist important peacetime obligations for dissemination, instruction and training, as well as binding commitments to ensure respect for existing rules. But such considerations should not be exaggerated. In fact, both terms comprise all aspects of the conduct of hostilities and the protection of war victims, aspects that must not be neglected, if international law is to be applied properly during armed conflict.

Achievements in the reaffirmation of international humanitarian law and its further development have not been reached without controversies. Many armed conflicts are dominated by asymmetries between rich and poor parties, between states and non-state actors, and between technologically advanced forces and those lacking even rudimentary equipment and logistics. These asymmetries are characterized by unlimited methods of fighting by the poor, and by excessive acts performed even during precision strikes by the rich. Humanitarian protection in such conflicts is too often neglected. This also leads to specific vulnerabilities of technologically advanced societies.[9] Types and amount of wartime atrocities in many cases are not contributing to the war effort and endangering post-conflict peacebuilding. It is, indeed, a timely task to stress again that in any armed conflict, the right to choose methods or means of warfare is not unlimited (Article 35 AP I).

There have been gross violations of international law which increased the awareness of the importance of humanitarian protection in the general public. The international Red Cross and Red Crescent movement has repeatedly, and with complete justification, launched appeals for humanitarian mobilization, to enhance protection in armed conflicts and other situations of armed violence, an objective as important as reducing the risk and impact of disasters and diseases.[10] The heavy task of improving compliance with international humanitarian law calls for new political initiatives, for more and better training, and for the use of international mechanisms.[11] The UN Secretary-General has underlined very convincingly that compliance with international humanitarian law, human rights law, refugee law, and international criminal law by all parties concerned provides the strongest basis for ensuring respect for the safety of the civilian population in armed conflicts.[12] The protection of civilians in armed conflicts agenda which was reaffirmed by the Security Council[13] must be further implemented to this effect. As

---

[8] Cf. Gary D. Solis, *The Law of Armed Conflict. International Humanitarian Law in War* (CUP, 2010), 23.

[9] Wolff Heintschel von Heinegg/Volker Epping (eds), *International Humanitarian Law Facing New Challenges. Symposium in Honour of Knut Ipsen* (Springer, 2007), vi, 11, 65.

[10] 31st International Red Cross and Red Crescent Conference, Strengthening legal protection for victims of armed conflicts, 31IC/11/R1, 2011; 4-Year Action Plan for the Implementation of international humanitarian law, 31/C/11/R2.

[11] ICRC, International Humanitarian Law and the Challenges of Contemporary Armed Conflicts, Report prepared for the 31st International Red Cross and Red Crescent Conference, 31IC/11/5.1.2, 2011.

[12] Report of the Secretary-General to the Security Council on the protection of civilians in armed conflict (UN Doc. S/2005/740 of 28 November 2005), para. 12.

[13] Aide Memoire for the consideration of issues pertaining to the protection of civilians in armed conflict, annexed to the Statement by the President of the Security Council of 22 November 2010 (S/PRST/2010/25).

DIETER FLECK

emphasized by the UN Secretary-General, even the right of self-defence must be carried out in accordance with international law. The repeated phenomenon of large numbers of civilian casualties from military operations is not acceptable. Also, the legal prohibitions protecting combatants against unnecessary suffering and perfidious acts are to be respected. Excessive use of force is unlawful and has often proven counterproductive, as it exacerbates existing resentments and fuels those who advocate hatred rather than providing conditions for long-lasting security and stable peace.

There is an urgent and continuing need for investigatory and punitive measures as well as for reparation and for activities to prevent future violations. Quite similar to human rights law, international humanitarian law includes obligations owed by states to individual persons. Yet, different from human rights law state practice and jurisprudence have denied so far that international humanitarian law also offers rights to individuals corresponding to the duties of states. The obligation of states has been endorsed by the United Nations and by regional organizations. As early as 1975, the Conference on Co-operation and Security in Europe Final Act signed in Helsinki had emphasized in Principle VII the right of the individual to know and act upon his or her rights and duties in the field of human rights. At the same time, it had stressed the duty of participating states constantly to respect these rights and freedoms in their mutual relations and to endeavour jointly and separately (including in co-operation with the United Nations) to promote universal and effective respect for these rights and freedoms. This duty of states is not only relevant during peacetime, but it extends to times of armed conflict. It is not limited to obligations under human rights law which continues to apply in armed conflicts, but fully includes obligations under international humanitarian law.

The first edition of the present Handbook, published in 1994[14] and 1995,[15] was prepared as a result of close co-operation between academic research and practice. It was designed to support not only further studies at universities but also the legal instruction of the armed forces. The key statements of that edition, printed in bold type, were identical with the *German Manual*, promulgated for the German Armed Forces in August 1992. Ever since its inception in 1956, the *Bundeswehr* has had a legal advisory organization, a service which is now mandatory worldwide under Article 82 AP I. Its tasks include advising military commanders and instructing the armed forces in relevant rules of international law. Owing to experiences in two World Wars, Germany has been particularly active in the implementation of international humanitarian law, not least because for several decades the country was divided by the line of confrontation between two opposing military alliances. Accordingly, and in view of the differences in the status of national ratifications of AP I even within the North Atlantic Alliance, German initiatives aimed to settle problems regarding the conduct of combined operations by reaching agreement on common standards for the application of the law, and to support legal co-operation in this area extending far beyond the membership of NATO. Hence, the publication of the *German Manual* was preceded by an intensive co-operation between practitioners and scholars, and an international conference of government experts.[16] Both the text of the *German Manual* and also the commentaries have greatly benefited from the results of

---

[14] Fleck (ed.), *Handbuch des humanitären Völkerrechts in bewaffneten Konflikten* (C. H. Beck, 1994).

[15] Id., *The Handbook of Humanitarian Law in Armed Conflict* (OUP, 1995; paperback 1999).

[16] Fleck, 'Military Manuals on International Humanitarian Law Applicable in Armed Conflicts. Consultations of Government Experts in Koblenz (Germany), 7–11 October 1991', HuV-I (4/1991), 213–15.

DIETER FLECK

this co-operation. The Handbook was well received in the growing community of international humanitarian law. Numerous reviews in many countries, its use in academic activities to support dissemination and research, the frequent references made to it by international and national courts, as by legal advisers in military headquarters, and the award of the renowned Ciardi Prize at the XVth Congress of the International Society for Military Law and the Law of War (Lillehammer, 2000) were encouraging for all contributors.

Since its second edition,[17] the Handbook is no longer connected to a single national manual, but aims at offering international best practice to assist scholars and practitioners worldwide. For this purpose the group of contributors has been expanded and both the manual text **printed in bold type** and the commentaries have been extensively revised. The Handbook is designed to support state practice and jurisprudence, academic studies, and the legal instruction of armed forces. It shows in context the importance of a by now complex branch of international law for both the conduct of military operations and international co-operation in peacetime.

To fulfil this task both legal and policy arguments are discussed in the Handbook, considering that fundamental values of humanity require a generalized approach which should avoid flawed interpretations and ensure operational standards of protection. For any military operation, law and policy are interrelated and must be seen in context. Policy principles are normally mandatory for those engaged in operations. They may increase, but not lower the standards set by international law, as expressed in rules of engagement. Hence, the role of rules of engagement for military operations is discussed in various respects, not only in the context of air, sea, and land warfare, but also in international peace operations.

In **Chapter 1** the historical evolution and the existing legal foundations of international humanitarian law are evaluated in the light of current practice. In this context the ethical and political prerequisites for legal development are discussed in their global relevance, as the origins of the fundamental principles of humanitarian law are not exclusively based on a single region, culture, or religion. At a time which is characterized by rapid societal changes and diminishing distances, the establishment of a multicultural basis for humanitarian rules is of the utmost importance.

Chapters 2 to 10 describe the law of the conduct of military operations in all theatres and at all levels. Here, the distinctions between Geneva Law and Hague Law, developed at different occasions in history, have lost their importance, as have those between the law of treaties and customary law. For the latter the *ICRC Study on Customary International Humanitarian Law*[18] provides excellent source material which has extensively been used and discussed in the Handbook. In **Chapter 2** particular attention is paid to law enforcement aspects, to the application of human rights in armed conflicts, to the continued relevance of rules of international law of peace during armed conflict, and to the relevance of humanitarian law in peacetime and post-conflict military operations. **Chapter 3** considers challenges for combatant status in recent conflicts and diplomatic negotiations. It includes a discussion of topical issues of 'unlawful combatants' or—what may be considered the better term: 'unprivileged belligerents'. **Chapter 4** offers an in-depth discussion of means and methods of combat, providing commentaries on current treaty law, a discussion

---

[17] Fleck, *The Handbook of International Humanitarian Law* (OUP, 2008; paperback 2009).
[18] *CIHL* (above, n. 2).

DIETER FLECK

of the progressive development of customary law, and borderline situations of law enforcement relevant for military operations. **Chapter 5** explains current aspects of the protection of civilians in armed conflicts including consequences for civilians directly participating in hostilities, further developments in the law of humanitarian assistance, and the present state of the law of occupation. It also underlines the increasing importance of human rights for the protection of civilians in occupied territories. In **Chapter 6** a systematic approach to the protection of medical personnel is undertaken in the light of recent state practice; likewise, the development which resulted in the adoption of a new protective emblem, the Red Crystal, is explained. In **Chapter 7** the protection of prisoners in any armed conflict and prisoner-of-war status in international armed conflicts are addressed on the background of recent state practice. **Chapter 8** offers a discussion of the protection of religious personnel and the legal significance of religious tolerance in armed conflicts. **Chapter 9** provides a commentary on the protection of cultural property in armed conflicts which covers recent developments in treaty law and international practice. In **Chapter 10** legal developments and practice with respect to armed conflict at sea are explained and further discussed.

    Chapter 11 contains rules of the law of neutrality concerning the protection of the victims of armed conflicts which must be considered as part of international humanitarian law. These rules have been challenged by state practice in recent armed conflicts, hence they are the subject of a continuing international development and exchange among experts. In **Chapter 12** the law of non-international armed conflicts is assessed in context with its progressive development. The legal distinction between international and non-international armed conflicts is explained and an important policy rule already included in the first edition of this Handbook reaffirmed and further developed: armed forces should comply with the rules applicable in international armed conflicts in the conduct of their operations in all armed conflicts; however, such conflicts are characterized.[19] The binding effect of these rules on armed opposition groups is discussed and specific means and methods to ensure compliance in internal armed conflicts elaborated. **Chapter 13** describes the law of international peace operations comprising both peacekeeping operations and peace enforcement operations conducted in support of diplomatic efforts to establish and maintain peace. This concept deliberately goes beyond traditional peacekeeping, as it combines elements of peacekeeping with peacemaking and post-conflict peacebuilding. While peace operations normally are not conducted in an armed conflict but rather in situations in which civil–military co-operation and law enforcement principles provide essential elements of rules of engagement, the relevance of international humanitarian law for peacekeepers cannot be underestimated. The final **Chapter 14** deals with the most important part of international humanitarian law, as it describes and evaluates national and international measures to ensure compliance with existing rules and to provide remedies for violations. Highlighting long-lasting legal developments which have eventually led to a strengthening of national and international criminal jurisdiction on war crimes and crimes against humanity, this chapter also evaluates the legal obligations of states and international organizations and appropriate measures to implement existing obligations, to prevent any violations, and take effective action where breaches are committed.

    The **Table of International Instruments** is supplemented by a **Table of Judgments and Decisions** which clearly shows an increase of relevant jurisprudence and policymaking

---

[19] See Sections 211 and 1216.

by intergovernmental and other organizations in recent years.[20] The **Annex** shows the relevant international distinctive emblems.

It is the common objective of the contributors of this Handbook not only to provide reliable information on the state of international humanitarian law and relevant legal developments, but likewise to encourage necessary new discussions. In this spirit the interrelationship between international humanitarian law and other branches of international law, in particular human rights law, is addressed in this book under various aspects. This interrelationship is not only of academic interest, as it has a distinct practical relevance for the conduct of hostilities and law enforcement operations, for example with respect to persons in detention, territories under belligerent occupation, and situations of domestic jurisdiction in non-international armed conflicts. The requirement for training tools is multifaceted and the need for specific approaches will be felt by many participants and course directors. Additional national rules and regulations will be required to ensure effective implementation of this field of international law, considering its progressive complexity and importance for military operations in armed conflicts and even in peacetime. A good perception of applicable international standards which are forming the contents of this Handbook is essential for lawful conduct of military forces and relevant training activities.

International humanitarian law is not, and never was, confined to issues of the conduct of hostilities. The legal difference between armed conflict and peacetime notwithstanding, many humanitarian law principles are relevant in a wider sense also for military operations in post-conflict peacebuilding.[21] There is a clear requirement for further developing adequate rules for the conduct of military operations. Proper conduct in armed conflicts may be key to relevant activities. States and international organizations, members of armed forces and civilians, practising lawyers, and academics alike remain challenged with the complex task of expanding knowledge of existing rules of humanitarian law, ensuring its application under ever-difficult circumstances, and co-operating in its further development.

---

[20] See also: National Case-Law and International Case-Law, *CIHL* Vol. II/2, 4286–307, 4308–34; Marco Sassòli/Antoine Bouvier/Anne Quintin (eds), *How Does Law Protect in War? Cases, Documents and Teaching Materials on Contemporary Practice in International Humanitarian Law*, 3rd edn (ICRC, 2011); Oxford Reports on International Law/International Law in Domestic Courts (ILDC), <http://www.oxford-lawreports.com>.

[21] See T. D. Gill and D. Fleck, *The Handbook of the International Law in Military Operations* (OUP, 2010; paperback 2011).

DIETER FLECK

List of Contributors

Professor emeritus Dr Michael Bothe, J. W. Goethe Universität, Frankfurt (Main), formerly President of the International Humanitarian Fact-Finding Commission (*Chapter 11*).

Dr Knut Dörmann, Head of the Legal Division, International Committee of the Red Cross (*Chapter 5*).

Dr Dieter Fleck, formerly Director, International Agreements and Policy, Federal Ministry of Defence, Germany; Honorary President, International Society for Military Law and the Law of War; Member of the Advisory Board, Amsterdam Center for International Law (*Introduction* and *Chapter 12*).

Dr Hans-Peter Gasser, formerly Senior Legal Adviser, International Committee of the Red Cross and Editor of the International Review of the Red Cross, Geneva (*Chapter 5*).

Professor Dr Wolff Heintschel von Heinegg, Europa-Universität Viadrina, Frankfurt (Oder); Stockton Professor, Naval War College, Newport, RI; Vice-President, International Society for Military Law and the Law of War; Member of the Council, International Institute of Humanitarian Law (*Chapter 10* and *Sub-Chapter 6 V*).

Professor Dr Dr h.c. mult. Knut Ipsen, Ruhr-Universität Bochum, formerly President of the German Red Cross (*Chapter 3*).

Colonel Ben F. Klappe, Director Administrative Law Department, Ministry of Defence, the Netherlands; formerly Chief of Staff, NATO Rule of Law Field Support Mission, Kabul; formerly Special Assistant to the Military Adviser, Department of Peacekeeping Operations, Headquarters United Nations, New York (*Chapter 13*).

Dr Jann K. Kleffner, Head of the International Law Center, Swedish National Defence College, Associate Professor of International Law (*Chapters 2* and *6*).

Dr Sandra Krähenmann, Research Fellow, Geneva Academy of International Humanitarian Law and Human Rights, formerly Staff of the Chief of the Swiss Armed Forces (*Chapter 7*).

Major General (ret.) Nilendra Kumar, AVSM, VSM, Director of the Amity Law School, Amity University, Delhi, formerly Judge Advocate General of the Indian Army (*Chapter 8*).

Professor Mary Ellen O'Connell, University of Notre Dame, Indiana, USA, Vice-President of the American Society of International Law (*Chapter 1*).

Professor Dr Stefan Oeter, Universität Hamburg (*Chapter 4*).

Dr Roger O'Keefe, Deputy Director, Lauterpacht Research Centre for International Law, University of Cambridge (*Chapter 9*).

Professor Dr Silja Vöneky, Universität Freiburg (*Chapter 14*).

Table of Abbreviations

ACHR	American Convention on Human Rights of 22 November 1969
AJIL	*American Journal of International Law*
AP I	Protocol I of 10 June 1977, Additional to the Geneva Conventions of 12 August 1949
AP II	Protocol II of 10 June 1977, Additional to the Geneva Conventions of 12 August 1949
AP III	Protocol III of 8 December 2005, Additional to the Geneva Conventions of 12 August 1949
ARSIWA	Articles on Responsibility of States for Internationally Wrongful Acts (2001) UN Doc. A/56/10
AVR	*Archiv des Völkerrechts*
BiologicalWeaponsConv	Biological Weapons Convention of 10 April 1972
BR-Drs	*Drucksache des Bundesrats*
BYIL	*British Yearbook of International Law*
CAT	United Nations Committee Against Torture
Chemical WeaponsConv	Convention on the Prohibition of the Development, Production, Stockpiling and Use of Chemical Weapons and on their Destruction of 13 January 1993
ChildConv	Convention on the Rights of the Child of 20 November 1989
CICR	Comité international de la Croix-Rouge
CIHL	*Customary International Humanitarian Law* [Jean-Marie Henckaerts and Louise Doswald-Beck (eds)], (CUP, 2005) with update at *Customary IHL Database*, <http://www.icrc.org/customary-ihl/eng/docs/home>
ClusterConv	Convention on Cluster Munitions of 30 May 2008
CPA	Coalition Provisional Authority
CSC	Geneva Convention on the Continental Shelf of 29 April 1958
CSCE	Conference on Security and Co-operation in Europe
CultPropConv	Cultural Property Convention of 14 May 1954
CultPropReg	Regulations for the Execution of the Cultural Property Convention, adopted on 14 May 1954
CUP	Cambridge University Press
DDR	Disarmament, demobilization, and reintegration
Decl.	Declaration
DPKO	United Nations Department of Peacekeeping Operations
ECHR	European Convention for the Protection of Human Rights and Fundamental Freedoms of 4 November 1950

ECJ	European Court of Justice
ECOWAS	Economic Community of West African States
ECtHR	European Court of Human Rights
ed./eds	Editor/editors
edn	Edition
EEZ	Exclusive economic zone
EJIL	*European Journal of International Law*
ENMOD	Convention on the Prohibition of Military or Any Other Hostile Use of Environmental Modification Techniques of 18 May 1977
ERWProt	Protocol on Explosive Remnants of War, adopted on 28 November 2003
EU	European Union
GA	General Assembly
GasProt	Geneva Gas Protocol of 17 June 1925
GC I	First Geneva Convention of 12 August 1949
GC II	Second Geneva Convention of 12 August 1949
GC III	Third Geneva Convention of 12 August 1949
GC IV	Fourth Geneva Convention of 12 August 1949
GenocidConv	Genocide Convention of 9 December 1949
German Manual	Bundesministerium der Verteidigung, ZDv 15/2 *Human-itäres Völkerrecht in bewaffneten Konflikten* (1992); English version: Federal Ministry of Defence, Joint Service Manual, *Humanitarian Law in Armed Conflicts* (1992)
GYIL	*German Yearbook of International Law*
HagueDecl 1899	Hague Declaration concerning Expanding Bullets (Dum-Dum Bullets) of 29 July 1899
HagueReg	Hague Regulations of 18 October 1907 concerning the Laws and Customs of War on Land
HC III	Hague Convention (III) of 18 October 1907 concerning the Opening of Hostilities
HC IV	Hague Convention (IV) of 18 October 1907 concerning the Laws and Customs of War on Land
HC V	Hague Convention (V) of 18 October 1907 concerning the Rights and Duties of Neutral Powers and Persons in Case of War on Land
HC VI	Hague Convention (VI) of 18 October 1907 concerning the Status of Merchant Ships at the Outbreak of Hostilities
HC VII	Hague Convention (VII) of 18 October 1907 concerning the Conversion of Merchant Ships into War Ships
HC VIII	Hague Convention (VIII) of 18 October 1907 concerning the Laying of Automatic Submarine Contact Mines
HC IX	Hague Convention (IX) of 18 October 1907 concerning Bombardment by Naval Forces in Time of War
HC XI	Hague Convention (XI) of 18 October 1907 concerning Certain Restrictions with regard to the Exercise of the Right of Capture in Naval War

HC XIII	Hague Convention (XIII) of 18 October 1907 concerning the Rights and Duties of Neutral Powers in Naval War
HCHR	United Nations High Commissioner for Human Rights
HPCR	Harvard Program on Humanitarian Policy and Conflict Research (HPCR), <http://www.ihlresearch.org>
HPCR Manual	*Manual on International Law Applicable to Air and Missile Warfare* with Commentary (Harvard 2010), <http://ihlresearch.org/amw/HPCR%20Manual.pdf> HRAW 1923
HRAW 1923	Hague Rules concerning the Control of Wireless Telegraphy in Time of War and Air Warfare, drafted 19 February 1923
HRC	United Nations Human Rights Committee
HSC	Convention on the High Seas of 29 April 1958
HuV-I	*Humanitäres Völkerrecht—Informationsschriften. Journal of International Law of Peace and Armed Conflict*
IACHR	Inter-American Commission on Human Rights
IACtHR	Inter-American Court of Human Rights
ICAO	International Civil Aviation Organization
ICBL	International Campaign to Ban Landmines
ICC	International Criminal Court
ICC Statute	Rome Statute of the International Criminal Court of 17 July 1998
ICCPR	International Covenant on Civil and Political Rights of 19 December 1966
ICDO	International Civil Defence Organization
ICESCR	International Covenant on Economic, Social and Cultural Rights of 19 December 1966
ICJ	International Court of Justice
ICLQ	*International and Comparative Law Quarterly*
ICRC	International Committee of the Red Cross
ICRC Commentary	Y. Sandoz/C. Swinarski/B. Zimmermann (eds), *Commentary on the Additional Protocols of 8 June 1977 to the Geneva Conventions of 12 August 1949* (ICRC, 1987)
ICRC Manual	B. Doppler (ed.), A. P. V. Rogers & P. Malherbe (authors), *Fight it Right. Model Manual on the Law of Armed Conflict for Armed Forces* (ICRC, 1999)
ICTR	International Criminal Tribunal for Rwanda
ICTR Statute	Statute of the International Criminal Tribunal for Rwanda of 8 November 1994, as amended
ICTY	International Criminal Tribunal for the Former Yugoslavia
ICTY Statute	Statute for the International Criminal Tribunal for the Former Yugoslavia of 25 May 1993, as amended
Id.	Idem
IDPs	Internally displaced persons
IHFFC	International Humanitarian Fact-Finding Commission

IHL	International humanitarian law
IllicitImpExpTransConv	Convention on the Means of Prohibiting and Preventing the Illicit Import, Export and Transfer of Ownership of Cultural Property of 14 November 1970
ILM	*International Legal Materials*
ILO	International Labour Organization
ILR	*International Law Reports* (since 1950)
IMPP	Integrated Mission Planning Process
IMT	International Military Tribunal (Nuremberg, 1945–1946)
IMTF	Integrated Mission Task Force
IncendiariesProt	Protocol on Prohibitions or Restrictions on the Use of Incendiary Weapons of 10 October 1980
InhumaneWeaponsConv	Convention on Prohibitions or Restrictions on the Use of Certain Conventional Weapons Which may be Deemed to be Excessively Injurious or to Have Indiscriminate Effects of 10 October 1980
IRRC	*International Review of the Red Cross*
ISAF	International Security Assistance Force
IsrYHR	*Israel Yearbook on Human Rights*
ItalYIL	*Italian Yearbook of International Law*
LandMinesConv	Ottawa Convention on the Prohibition of the Use, Stockpiling, Production, and Transfer of Anti-personnel Mines and on their Destruction of 3 December 1997
LasersProt	Protocol on Blinding Laser Weapons, adopted on 13 October 1995
Lieber Code	*Instruction for the Government of Armies of the United States in the Field*, prepared by Francis Lieber, promulgated as General Orders Nr. 100 by President Lincoln, 24 April 1863, text in: D. Schindler & J. Toman, *The Law of Armed Conflicts. A Collection of Conventions, Resolutions and Other Documents*, 4th edn (Nijhoff, 2004), 3; L. Friedman (ed.), *The Law of War. A Documentary History*, Vol. I (Random House, 1972), 158
LNOJ	League of Nations Official Journal
LNTS	League of Nations Treaty Series
LondonDecl 1909	London Declaration of 26 February 1909 concerning the Laws of Naval War
LondonProt 1936	London *Procès-Verbal* of 6 November 1936 concerning the Rules of Submarine Warfare
MercenaryConv	Mercenary Convention of 4 December 1989
MinesProt	Protocol on Prohibitions or Restrictions on the Use of Mines, Booby-traps and other Devices of 10 October 1980, revised on 3 May 1996
MIO	Maritime interception operations
MONUC	United Nations Organization Mission in the Democratic Republic of Congo

MoU	Memorandum of understanding
MPEPIL	R. Wolfrum (ed.), *Max Planck Encyclopedia of Public International Law,* 10 vols (OUP, 2012) <http://www.mpepil.com>
NATO	North Atlantic Treaty Organization
NethYIL	*Netherlands Yearbook of International Law*
NGO	Non-governmental organization
No.	Number
NonDetectableFragmentsProt	Protocol on Non-detectable Fragments of 10 October 1980
NPT	Treaty on the Non-Proliferation of Nuclear Weapons of 1 July 1968
NWP 1–14M	US Navy, *The Commander's Handbook on the Law of Naval Operations*, (Edition July 2007)
NZWehrr	*Neue Zeitschrift für Wehrrecht*
OAU	Organization of African Unity
OCHA	United Nations Office for the Coordination of Humanitarian Affairs
OHCHR	Office of the United Nations High Commissioner for Human Rights
ONUC	United Nations Operation in Congo
OSCE	Organization for Security and Co-operation in Europe
OUP	Oxford University Press
Para.	Paragraph
ParisDecl 1856	Paris Declaration of 16 April 1856 concerning Maritime Law
PBSO	United Nations Peace Building Support Office
PetersburgDecl 1868	St Petersburg Declaration of 29 November/11 December 1868 Renouncing the Use, in Time of War, of Explosive Projectiles under 400 Grammes Weight
Prot.	Protocol
ProtChildConv	Optional Protocol on the Involvement of Children in Armed Conflict, adopted on 25 May 2000
Prot1CultPropConv	Protocol for the Protection of Cultural Property in the Event of Armed Conflict, adopted on 14 May 1954
Prot2CultPropConv	Second Protocol to the Hague Convention of 1954 for the Protection of Cultural Property in the Event of Armed Conflict, adopted on 26 May 1999
RdC	*Recueil des Cours de l'Académie de droit international de la Haye*
RDMilG	*Revue de Droit Militaire et de Droit de la Guerre*

RefugeesConv	Convention Relating to the Status of Refugees of 4 November 1950
RegExCultPropConv	Regulations for the execution of the Convention for the Protection of Cultural Property in the Event of Armed Conflicts of 14 May 1954
Res.	Resolution
RGDIP	*Revue générale de droit international public*
RIC	*Revue Internationale de la Croix-Rouge*
ROE	Rules of engagement
San Remo Manual	International Institute of Humanitarian Law (L. Doswald-Beck, ed.), *San Remo Manual on International Law Applicable to Armed Conflicts at Sea, Prepared by a Group of International Lawyers and Naval Experts* (CUP, 1994), <http://www.icrc.org/ihl.nsf/FULL/560?OpenDocument>
SC	Security Council
TEZ	Total Exclusion Zone
TSC 1958	Geneva Convention on the Territorial Sea and the Contiguous Zone of 29 April 1958
UAV	Unmanned aerial vehicle
UCAV	Unmanned combat aerial vehicle
UK Manual	UK Ministry of Defence (ed.), *The Manual of the Law of Armed Conflict* (OUP, 2004), with amendment, available at <http://www.mod.uk/NR/rdonlyres/1FE28D1C-9FB7–4236–832A-C09E2B3B4FDF/0/20100929JSP383Amendment3NoterUpChs14Sep10.pdf>
UN	United Nations
UNAMA	United Nations Assistance Mission to Afghanistan
UN Charter	Charter of the United Nations of 26 June 1945, as amended on 17 December 1963, 20 December 1965 and 20 December 1971
UNCLOS	United Nations Convention on the Law of the Sea of 10 December 1982
UN Doc.	United Nations Document
UNEF	United Nations Emergency Force
UNESCO	United Nations Educational, Scientific and Cultural Organization
UNHCHR	United Nations High Commissioner for Human Rights
UNHCR	United Nations High Commissioner for Refugees
UNICEF	United Nations Children's Fund
UNMOGIP	United Nations Military Observer Group in India and Pakistan
UNOSOM I and II	United Nations Operation in Somalia

UNPREDEP	United Nations Preventive Deployment Force
UNPROFOR	United Nations Protection Force
UN SafetyConv	United Nations Convention on the Safety of United Nations and Associated Personnel of 15 December 1994
UN SafetyProt	Optional Protocol to the United Nations Convention on the Safety of United Nations and Associated Personnel of 15 December 1994, adopted by the General Assembly on 8 December 2005 (resolution A/60/42), open for signature from 16 January 2006
UNTS	United Nations Treaty Series
UNTSO	United Nations Truce Supervision Organization
US	United States of America
USC	United States Code
US Naval Manual	*NWP 1–14M (formerly NWP 9) Annotated Supplement to The Commander's Handbook on the Law of Naval Operations* (Vol. 73 *International Law Studies*, Naval War College 1999, new edition July 2007, <http://www.nwc.navy.mil/cnws/ild/documents/1–14M _(Jul_2007)_(NWP).pdf>)
USNIP	*United States Naval Institute Proceedings*
USV	Unmanned seagoing vehicles
VaJIntL	*Virginia Journal of International Law*
Vol.	Volume
WEU	Western European Union
WMD	Weapons of mass destruction
YIHL	*Yearbook of International Humanitarian Law*
ZaöRV	*Zeitschrift für ausländisches öffentliches Recht und Völkerrecht—Heidelberg Journal of International Law*

Table of International Instruments

Table of Judgments and Decisions

A. *Judgments of International and National Courts*

International Court of Justice

International Criminal Court

European Court of Justice

Inter-American Commission on Human Rights

Inter-American Court on Human Rights

Nuremberg and Tokyo Trials

International Criminal Tribunal for Rwanda

International Criminal Tribunal for the Former Yugoslavia

Eritrea-Ethiopia Claims Commission

UN General Assembly

UN Secretary-General

UN Human Rights Committee

Other UN Documents

European Union

International Red Cross and Red Crescent Movement

International Law Association (ILA)

1

HISTORICAL DEVELOPMENT
AND LEGAL BASIS

I. Definition of the Term 'Humanitarian Law'

The use of armed force is prohibited under Article 2(4) of the UN Charter. States   101
may resort to armed force only in the exercise of individual or collective self-
defence (Article 51 UN Charter) or as authorized by the Security Council (Articles
39–42 UN Charter). International humanitarian law (IHL) applies with equal
force to all the parties in an armed conflict irrespective of which party was responsible for starting the conflict. IHL comprises the whole of established law governing the conduct of armed conflict.

1. *Introduction.* Although the subject of this Handbook is the law applicable to the conduct
of hostilities that applies once a party has entered into armed conflict (the *jus in bello*),
that law cannot be properly understood without some examination of the separate body
of rules which determines when resort to armed force is permissible (the *jus ad bellum*).
The *jus ad bellum* has ancient origins but current law is founded on Article 2(4) and
Chapter VII of the UN Charter.[1]

2. *The Charter prohibition on the use of force.* Article 2(4) of the UN Charter states that:
'All Members shall refrain in their international relations from the threat or use of force
against the territorial integrity or political independence of any state, or in any other
manner inconsistent with the purposes of the United Nations.' By prohibiting the use of
force, rather than *war*, this provision avoids debate about whether a particular conflict
constitutes war. Although some writers have endeavoured to read Article 2(4) narrowly,
arguing that there are instances in which the use of force may occur without it being
directed 'against the territorial integrity or political independence of any state' or being
'in any other manner inconsistent with the purposes of the United Nations',[2] the prevailing
view is that Article 2(4) aims to restrict the first resort to significant armed force by a
state or states unless it can be justified by reference to one of the specific exceptions
to that provision. The UN Charter expressly provides for only two such exceptions:

---

[1] For more on the prohibition on the use of force in contemporary international law, see Olivier Corten,
The Law Against War: The Prohibition on the Use of Force in Contemporary International Law (Oxford:
Hart Publishing, 2010); Christine Gray, *International Law and the Use of Force*, 3rd edn (Oxford: Oxford
University Press (OUP), 2008); and M. E. O'Connell, 'The Prohibition of Force' in N. D. White and
C. Henderson (eds), *Research Handbook on International Conflict and Security Law* (Cheltenham: Edward
Elgar, 2013); Marc Weller and Alexia Solomou (ed.), *The Oxford Handbook of the Use of Force in International
Law* (OUP, forthcoming).

[2] For a discussion of this question by various writers, see Antonio Cassese (ed.), *The New Humanitarian
Law of Armed Conflict* (Oceana, 1979).

MARY ELLEN O'CONNELL

military action authorized by the Security Council and the right of individual or collective self-defence.[3]

3. *Military actions authorized by the Security Council.* The extensive limitation placed by the Charter upon unilateral resort to force by states is linked to, but not dependent upon,[4] the system of collective security in Chapter VII of the UN Charter. Under Article 39 of the Charter, the Council is empowered to 'determine the existence of any threat to the peace, breach of the peace, or act of aggression'. Once it has taken this step, Articles 41 and 42 give the Council power to take measures to restore international peace and security.[5]

a) Under Article 41, the Council may require member states to apply economic sanctions and other measures not involving the use of armed force, a power which it has used, for example, in relation to Iraq's invasion of Kuwait,[6] Libya's refusal to co-operate with investigations into terrorist attacks on aircraft,[7] the situation in the Former Yugoslavia,[8] and the controversy over Iran's nuclear programme.[9] Where the Council has imposed sanctions under Article 41, it may authorize states to use limited force to prevent ships or aircraft from violating those sanctions.[10] The power extends far beyond the imposition and enforcement of economic sanctions and has been used, for example, to create the international criminal tribunals for the Former Yugoslavia[11] and Rwanda,[12] and to authorize various measures to suppress piracy on the territory and off the coast of Somalia.[13]

b) Article 42 then provides: '... should the Security Council consider that measures provided for in Article 41 would be inadequate or have proved to be inadequate, it may take such action by air, sea or land forces as may be necessary to maintain or restore international peace and security. Such action may include demonstrations, blockade, and other operations by air, sea or land forces of Members of the United Nations.'

c) To give effect to this provision, Article 43 envisaged that member states would conclude with the UN a series of bilateral agreements under which they would make

---

[3] The previous edition of this Handbook suggested that support was growing for a 'right to use force in cases of extreme humanitarian need', citing Charlotte Ku and Harold K. Jacobson (eds), *Democratic Accountability and the Use of Force in International Law* (Cambridge: Cambridge University Press (CUP), 2002); J. L. Holzgrefe and Robert O. Keohane (eds), *Humanitarian Intervention: Ethical, Legal, and Political Dilemmas* (CUP, 2003); Christopher Greenwood, *Essays on War in International Law* (Cameron May, 2006), 593. Following the adoption of the World Summit Outcome Document in 2005, UN GAOR, 60th Session, UN Doc. A/60/L.1 (15 September 2005) at 22–3, and the Security Council's authorization of humanitarian intervention in Libya in 2011 (SC Res. 1973, paras. 1, 6, UN Doc. S/RES/1973 (17 March 2011)), consensus has developed that the right to use force in cases of humanitarian need is conditioned upon Security Council authorization.

[4] ICJ, *Corfu Channel* case, *ICJ Reports 1949*, 3.

[5] Decisions of the Council adopted under Chapter VII of the Charter are capable of creating legally binding obligations for states (see Arts. 2(5) and 25 of the Charter); by virtue of Art. 103, the obligation to carry out the decisions of the Council, as an obligation arising under the Charter, prevails over obligations under other international agreements; see the ICJ Orders in the *Lockerbie* cases (*Libya v UK; Libya v US*), *ICJ Reports 1992*, 3 at para. 39, and 114 at para. 42.

[6] Res. 661 (1990).

[7] Res. 748 (1992). See also the decisions of the ICJ in the *Lockerbie* cases (n. 5).

[8] Res. 757 (1992).

[9] Res. 1737 (2006).

[10] For example, Res. 665 (1990).

[11] Res. 827 (1993).

[12] Res. 955 (1994).

[13] Res. 2020 (2011). The resolution only cites Chapter VII in general, not specific articles within Chapter VII, as has been the practice of the Security Council by now for many years.

MARY ELLEN O'CONNELL

forces and other facilities available to the Council on call. Articles 46–47 provided that plans for the use of armed force were to be made by the Council with the assistance of a Military Staff Committee which was charged by Article 47 with responsibility, under the Council, for 'the strategic direction of any armed forces placed at the disposal of the Security Council'. Due to Cold War rivalries and different perceptions of the UN's military role, no Article 43 agreements were concluded and the Military Staff Committee has never functioned as intended.[14] Nevertheless, the Security Council has authorized a number of operations which have involved the deployment of military forces.

d) Until the 1990s, most of these were peacekeeping operations, in which UN forces, made up of units contributed on a voluntary basis by various member states, were deployed with the consent of the states in whose territory they operated. The sole purpose of these forces was to police a ceasefire line or to monitor compliance with a truce or deliver relief supplies. The UN forces in Cyprus, Cambodia, Croatia, Lebanon, and on the Iran–Iraq border are all examples of this kind of peacekeeping by consent. Although peacekeeping forces are not intended to engage in combat operations, they have sometimes become involved in fighting when attacked.[15]

e) Increasingly, however, the Council has gone beyond peacekeeping and has authorized enforcement action of the kind envisaged in Article 42. In the Korean conflict in 1950, the Council (which was able to act because the USSR was boycotting its meetings) condemned North Korea's invasion of South Korea, and called upon all member states to go to the assistance of South Korea.[16] Following Iraq's invasion of Kuwait in 1990, the Council adopted Resolution 678, which authorized those states co-operating with the Government of Kuwait to use 'all necessary means' to ensure that Iraq withdrew from Kuwait and complied with the various Security Council resolutions on the subject and to 'restore international peace and security in the area'. It was this resolution which provided legal authority for the use of force by the coalition of states against Iraq in 1991.[17] In the absence of Article 43 agreements, the Council was not able to require states to take part in these operations. Instead, it relied upon voluntary contributions of forces from a wide range of states.[18] Nor did the Council and the Military Staff Committee direct the two operations. In Korea, the Council established a unified command under the US and expressly left to the US Government the choice of a commander, although the contingents operating in Korea were regarded as a UN force and were authorized to fly the UN flag.[19] In the Kuwait conflict, the Council authorized the use of force, but command and control arrangements were made by the states concerned and the coalition forces fought as national contingents, not as a UN force. Following Kuwait, a number of other operations were organized in a similar way, for example in Libya, Somalia, Haiti, and the Former Yugoslavia.

f) It was at one time argued that neither the Korean nor the Kuwaiti operation constituted enforcement actions of the kind provided for in Article 42 of the Charter,

[14] D. W. Bowett, *UN Forces* (Praeger, 1964), 12.
[15] For example, in the Congo. On the application of international humanitarian law to UN forces, see below, Section 1309.
[16] Bowett (n. 14), 29.
[17] Greenwood, *Essays* (n. 3), 517.
[18] In Korea, sixteen states contributed forces. The coalition forces in the Kuwait conflict were drawn from twenty-eight states.
[19] Res. 84 (1950).

MARY ELLEN O'CONNELL

because neither operation was controlled by the Council and neither was based upon the use of forces earmarked for UN operations under Article 43 agreements. Yet there is nothing in Article 42 which stipulates that military enforcement action can only be carried out using Article 43 contingents, nor does Chapter VII preclude the Security Council from improvising to meet a situation in which military operations can effectively be conducted only by large national contingents contributed by states which wish to retain control in their own hands. Moreover, the Charter expressly envisages that the Council might authorize an ad hoc coalition of states to carry out its decisions, for Article 48 provides that: 'The action required to carry out the decisions of the Security Council for the maintenance of international peace and security shall be taken by all the Members of the United Nations or by some of them, as the Security Council may determine.' While the wording of the key resolutions in both Korea and Kuwait leaves room for argument on this point, both operations should be seen as instances of enforcement action authorized by the Council.[20] Moreover, these and other examples of Security Council authorization of ad hoc peacekeeping and peace enforcement missions amount to significant practice, which the Vienna Convention on the Law of Treaties indicates is appropriate to consider in properly interpreting treaty rules.[21]

g) The Security Council may authorize resort to force if there is a threat to the peace, breach of the peace, or act of aggression. States acting without Security Council authorization may only use force in individual and collective self-defence. Clearly, the Council may respond to a wider variety of concerns, but international law scholars continue to debate what the limits of the Council's powers may be under international law. Most would agree with Sir Elihu Lauterpacht's observation in the *Lockerbie* case that the Security Council must respect at least some limits in acting under Article 39. It could not, for example, authorize a coalition to commit genocide in responding to a use of force. Based on the consensus that there are some limits on Security Council authority, commentators have argued that the Security Council must observe the general principles on resort to force, in particular, necessity and proportionality.[22]

In the Kuwait case, for example military action authorized by the Security Council was limited under the principles of necessity and proportionality to liberating Kuwait and ensuring Kuwait's future security. Resolution 678 authorized the coalition to ensure that Iraq complied with all relevant Security Council resolutions and 'to restore international peace and security in the area'.[23] The coalition acted to move the Iraqi armed forces out of Kuwait and to create a security zone on Iraqi territory. The coalition did not go to Baghdad to attempt to end the regime of Saddam Hussein. This action would have been beyond the necessity of liberating Kuwait and providing enough security to prevent a repetition of the invasion.[24] As a Human Rights Watch report stated respecting military necessity that military planners have a certain degree of freedom of judgement about

---

[20] Oscar Schachter, 'United Nations Law in the Gulf Conflict' (1991) 85 *AJIL* 452; Eugene V. Rostow, 'Until What? Enforcement Action or Collective Self Defense?' (1991) 85 *AJIL* 506; Christopher Greenwood, 'New World Order or Old?' (1992) 55 *Modern Law Review* 153.

[21] The Vienna Convention on the Law of Treaties provides that treaties shall be interpreted in light of their context, object, and purpose. Context is to take into account 'any subsequent practice in the application of the treaty which establishes the agreement of the parties regarding its interpretation', Art. 31(3)(b).

[22] W. L. Reisman and D. L. Stevick, 'The Applicability of International Law Standards to United Nations Economic Sanctions Programmes' (1998) 9 *EJIL* 86.

[23] Res. 678, para. 2.

[24] J. Gardam, *Necessity and Proportionality and the Use of Force by States* (CUP, 2004).

MARY ELLEN O'CONNELL

the appropriate tactics for carrying out a military operation, '[but] it can never justify a degree of violence which exceeds the level which is strictly necessary to ensure the success of a particular operation in a particular case'.[25]

The Security Council then adopted additional resolutions focused on the threat that Iraq continued to pose, in particular, the danger of Iraq possessing weapons of mass destruction (WMD). The US, France, and the UK continued to use limited force to prevent Iraq from engaging in renewed armed conflict within Iraq or against neighbours. Other enforcement action was taken to force Iraq into complete WMD disarmament. Advisers to the US and UK governments argued in 2002–2003 that a ground invasion of Iraq was lawful under, among other resolutions, Res. 687 (1991) and 1441 (2002) because those resolutions made clear that the threat to international peace and security had not ended with the 1991 ceasefire. It was on the basis of this argument that the US, the UK, and a number of other states maintained in 2003 that the authorization to use force remained in being and provided a legal basis for the renewal of military action against Iraq.[26] The alternative view, that a new Security Council authorization for the use force was required in 2003, is now, however, the predominant view.[27]

h) Only the Security Council has the authority to authorize enforcement action,[28] but it may choose to make use of other organizations (or, as in Kuwait and Korea, ad hoc coalitions) to carry out such action. Articles 52 and 53 of the Charter provide that regional organizations may undertake enforcement action with the authorization of the Security Council. The decision of the Organization for Security and Co-operation in Europe (OSCE) to constitute itself as a regional organization under Article 53 makes it possible for the OSCE, with the consent of the Security Council, to undertake action of this kind in Europe. In such a case, there seems to be no legal obstacle to the OSCE using NATO or the WEU as the military vehicle for conducting such operations.

i) One feature of Security Council action in recent times has been the expansion of the concept of 'international peace and security'. Originally perceived as confined to 'inter-state' threats, it is now treated as covering the threat posed by human rights violations, WMD proliferation, international terrorism, and other categories of illicit conduct,[29] although the Security Council rarely points to the inter-state repercussions of the conduct to which it is responding.[30] This development also received support in the 2005 World Summit Outcome Document.[31]

[25] Human Rights Watch, 'Jenin: IDF Military Operations' [May 2002] HRW Report vol. 14, no. 3(E), <http://www.hrw.org/reports/2002/israel3/index.htm> (citing ICRC, Commentary on Protocol I, p. 396).

[26] C. Greenwood, 'The Legality of the Use of Force: Iraq in 2003' in M. Bothe, M. E. O'Connell, and N. Ronzitti (eds), *Redefining Sovereignty: The Use of Force after the Cold War* (Transnational Publishers, 2005), 387–416. For criticism of this position, see Lord Alexander of Weedon, 'Iraq: the Pax Americana and the Law', [2003] *Justice Annual Lecture*; V. Lowe, 'The Iraq Crisis: What Now?' (2003) 52 *ICLQ* 859; R. Wolfrum, 'The Attack of Sept 11, 2001, the Wars Against the Taliban and Iraq: Is There a Need to Reconsider International Law on the Recourse to Force and the Rules in Armed Conflict?', (2003) 7 *Max Planck Yearbook of United Nations Law* 1; T. M. Franck, 'What Happens Now? The United Nations after Iraq' (2003) 97 *AJIL* 607.

[27] The support for this view was strengthened by revelations that UK Prime Minister Tony Blair had been advised by the Attorney General that new authorization was needed. See R. Norton-Taylor, 'Revealed: The Government's Secret Legal Advice on the Iraq War', *Guardian* (London, 28 April 2005), 1.

[28] The General Assembly asserted such a power in its 1950 Resolution on Uniting for Peace, UNGA Res. 377(V), but this claim was questioned by the ICJ in the *Certain Expenses Advisory Opinion, ICJ Reports 1962*, 151, and has not been repeated in more recent times.

[29] See, e.g., Res. 1368 (2001) and 1373 (2001).

[30] See, especially, Res. 794 (1992), the preamble of which stated that 'the magnitude of the human tragedy caused by the conflict in Somalia . . . constitutes a threat to international peace and security'.

[31] World Summit Outcome Document (n. 3).

MARY ELLEN O'CONNELL

right of self-defence.[32] Article 51 of the Charter provides that: 'Nothing in the
~~t~~ Charter shall impair the inherent right of individual or collective self-defence
~~i~~rmed attack occurs against a Member of the United Nations, until the Security
~~c~~il has taken measures necessary to maintain international peace and security.
Measures taken by Members in the exercise of this right of self-defence shall be immediately reported to the Security Council and shall not in any way affect the authority
and responsibility of the Security Council under the present Charter to take at any time
such action as it deems necessary in order to maintain or restore international peace and
security.' The term 'armed attack' is not defined. In its decision in *Nicaragua v US*, the
ICJ held that armed attacks included 'not merely action by regular armed forces across
an international border', but also 'the sending by or on behalf of a State of armed bands,
groups, irregulars or mercenaries, which carry out acts of armed force against another
State of such gravity as to amount to [*inter alia*] . . . an actual armed attack conducted
by regular forces . . . or its substantial involvement therein'.[33] On this basis, systematic
terrorist attacks organized, or perhaps sponsored, by a state could constitute an armed
attack to which the victim state could respond in self-defence. However, the Court went
on to set a threshold by ruling that terrorist or irregular operations would constitute an
armed attack only if the scale and effects of such an operation were such that it 'would
have been classified as an armed attack rather than as a mere frontier incident had it
been carried out by regular armed forces'. In other words, the Court considered that the
concept of 'armed attack' in Article 51 was narrower than the concept of 'use of force'
in Article 2(4).

a) In addition to an attack upon the territory of a state, it is generally accepted that an
attack against a state's warships, military aircraft, or troops overseas will amount to an
attack upon the state itself. Again, however, the 'scale and effects' of such an attack must
be considered before resort to force in self-defence would be justifiable. It is certainly
unlikely that an attack upon a merchant ship could be treated as an armed attack upon
the state whose flag it flies.[34] During the Iran–Iraq War, for example, states deployed
naval forces to the Gulf making it clear that those forces would defend merchant ships
flying the same flag but such defence could only lawfully amount to protecting the
vessel at the moment of the attack. The US was found to have violated Article 2(4) during the Iran–Iraq War when it attacked oil platforms belonging to Iran. The US could
not prove that it had suffered a significant armed attack for which Iran was responsible.
In this situation, the US had no basis within Article 51 to use major military force on
the territory of Iran.[35]

There have also been a number of cases (of which the best known are the UK's
Operation Barras in Sierra Leone and Israel's Entebbe rescue mission in Uganda) in
which one state has used force to rescue its citizens being held hostage on the territory

---

[32] See generally M. E. O'Connell, 'The Right of Self-Defense in International Law' in A. Carty (ed.),
International Law, Oxford Bibliographies Online (OUP, 2012), <http://oxfordindex.oup.com/view/10.1093/
obo/9780199796953–0028>.
[33] *ICJ Reports 1986*, 14, at para. 195. The Court cites Art. 3 of the Definition of Aggression, annexed to
UN GA Res. 3314 (1975). See also T. Ruys, *Armed Attack and Article 51 of the UN Charter* (CUP, 2010).
[34] M. Bothe, 'Neutrality at Sea' in I. Dekker and H. Post (eds), *The Gulf War of 1980–1988* (Nijhoff,
1992), 209.
[35] *Oil Platforms (Iran v US)*, 2003 ICJ 161, para. 74, (6 November) (citing *Military and Paramilitary
Activities (Nicaragua v US)*, 1986 ICJ 14, para. 194); C. Greenwood, 'The Relationship Between *jus ad bellum*
and *jus in bello*' (1983) 9 *Review of International Studies* 221, 223.

MARY ELLEN O'CONNELL

of another state. The legality of such actions has been questioned. Nevertheless, when they involve the minimum amount of force necessary to effect the rescue, the use of force will fall below the Article 2(4) threshold. Force that is less than that prohibited by Article 2(4) is regulated under the principle of non-intervention. The non-intervention principle may, arguably, be violated as a countermeasure in response to a prior violation of an important obligation owed to the enforcing state or the international community as a whole.[36]

b) The military response by the US following the terrorist attacks of 11 September 2001 in the US has given rise to a debate as to whether an armed attack can emanate from non-state actors, such as terrorists, even if their acts are not attributable to a state.[37] The Security Council referred to Article 51 in Resolution 1368 without referring to the need to attribute the attacks to a state. Resolution 1368 has ever since provided the primary evidence to those who argue such attribution is not required.[38] The Resolution, however, is silent on the question of attribution. It only indicates that the 'armed attack' requirement of Article 51 had been meant. The Security Council made no specific statement about attribution, necessity, or proportionality. When the US and the UK undertook Operation Enduring Freedom against Afghanistan, they did so on the basis of a UK White Paper making a case that the Taliban, the *de facto* government of Afghanistan was responsible for the acts of al-Qaeda.[39] The UK made the case for attribution and provided significant state practice and implicit *opinio juris* that such a case must be made for the exercise of lawful self-defence.

It has been pointed out that nothing in the text of Article 51 requires that the concept of armed attack be limited to acts for which states are responsible in international law. Nor was such a limitation evident in customary international law prior to the adoption of the Charter; indeed, the famous *Caroline* incident in 1837,[40] which is widely regarded as the fountainhead of the modern law on self-defence, was itself about a military reaction to attacks by non-state actors. Nevertheless, the ICJ, in its *Advisory Opinion on Legal Consequences of the Construction of a Wall in the Occupied Palestinian Territory*, appeared to assume that an armed attack had to be in some way attributable to a state. Moreover, the Court has made clear that Article 51 is not a complete statement of the law of self-defence. Necessity, proportionality, and attribution are all additional conditions that exist in customary international law or in the general principles of international law, but are not mentioned in Article 51. The ICJ said in the *Nuclear Weapons* case: 'there is a specific rule whereby self-defence would warrant only measures which are proportional to the armed attack and necessary to respond to it, a rule well established in customary international law'.[41]

[36] See T. D. Gill, 'The Forcible Protection, Affirmation and Exercise of Rights by States Under Contemporary International Law' (1992) 23 *NethYIL* 105, 125.

[37] Greenwood, *Essays* (n. 3), 409.

[38] *ICJ Reports 2004*, 136 at para. 139. For criticism of the Court's approach, see the Separate Opinion of Judge Higgins at para. 33. See also the decision in *Case Concerning Armed Activities on the Territory of the Congo (DRC v Uganda)*, *ICJ Reports 2005*, para. 146.

[39] M. E. O'Connell, 'Lawful Self-Defense to Terrorism' (2002) 63 *University of Pittsburgh Law Review* 889, 889–904.

[40] R. Y. Jennings, 'The Caroline and McLeod Cases' (1938) 32 *AJIL* 82.

[41] *Legality of the Threat or Use of Nuclear Weapons*, 1996 ICJ at 245, para. 41 (quoting *Nicaragua* (n. 35) 94, para. 176). See also, E. P. J. Myjer and N. D. White, 'The Twin Towers Attack: An Unlimited Right to Self-Defense?' (2002) 7 *Journal of Conflict and Security Law* 5.

MARY ELLEN O'CONNELL

c) A particularly difficult question, left open by the ICJ in the *Nicaragua* and later cases, is whether a state must wait until it is attacked before it can respond in self-defence or whether it is entitled to act in advance of an attack by taking measures of 'anticipatory self-defence'.[42] The express terms of Article 51 appear to rule out any concept of anticipatory self-defence. Moreover, to apply principles of necessity and proportionality to any use of force in self-defence requires that the state acting in defence have actual knowledge of the nature of the attack. Before 1945, it was generally assumed that the right of self-defence included a right of anticipatory self-defence provided that an armed attack was imminent.[43] Since 1945, there are virtually no examples of states invoking a right of anticipatory self-defence as the legal basis of a use of force under Article 51; certainly there are no examples that have been widely accepted by states.[44] It is widely thought that Israel invoked this right in 1967 and received at least the Security Council's acquiescence. In fact, Israel claimed before the Security Council that Egyptian forces had already crossed into Israel when Israel attacked.[45] Israel did try to rely upon this argument in attempting to justify its destruction of Iraq's nuclear reactor in 1981. The debate in the UN Security Council, however, centred not upon whether there was a right of anticipatory self-defence but upon whether any threat to Israel was sufficiently close in time to meet the requirement of necessity in attacking in self-defence. The Security Council concluded that any threat posed by Iraq to Israel in 1981 was too remote to meet the requirement that there be a necessity to use force.[46]

In its 2002 National Security Strategy, the US asserted a right to use force in self-defence to pre-empt an inchoate future attack.[47] The claim was widely criticized,[48] but was, nevertheless, repeated in the 2006 National Security Strategy.[49] The claim did not appear in the 2010 National Security Strategy.[50]

d) A less controversial aspect of Article 51 concerns the right of collective self-defence. Collective self-defence means that one state may come to the assistance of another which has been the victim of an armed attack. In the *Nicaragua* case, the ICJ held that for a state to be able to justify going to the assistance of another state by way of collective self-defence, two requirements must be satisfied: the second state must have been the victim of an armed attack, so that that state is itself entitled to take action by way of individual

---

[42] Compare D. W. Bowett, *Self-Defence in International Law* (Praeger, 1958), with I. Brownlie, *International Law and the Use of Force by States* (OUP, 1963).

[43] See, e.g., the *Caroline* dispute between Britain and the US in 1837, Jennings (n. 40).

[44] For an assessment of this practice, see C. Gray, 'The Charter Limitations on the Use of Force: Theory and Practice' in V. Lowe, A. Roberts, J. Welsh, and D. Zaum (eds), *The UN Security Council and War* (OUP, 2008), 86–98.

[45] For a discussion of the facts and legal arguments surrounding the Six Day War, see M. E. O'Connell, 'The Myth of Preemptive Self-Defense', *ASIL Task Force on Terrorism* (2002), <http://www.asil.org/task-force/oconnell.pdf>.

[46] Debate of 12 June 1981, S/PV 2280, and Res. 487 (1981).

[47] Office of the President, 'The National Security Strategy of the United States of America' (2002), <http://georgewbush-whitehouse.archives.gov/nsc/nss/2002>.

[48] See, e.g., the statement by Lord Goldsmith, the Attorney General of England and Wales, that the UK's position was that 'international law permits the use of force in self-defence against an imminent attack but does not authorize the use of force to mount a pre-emptive strike against a threat that is more remote'. It is important to note, however, that he added 'those rules must be applied in the context of the particular facts of each case', House of Lords debate, 21 April 2004.

[49] Office of the President, 'The National Security Strategy of the United States of America' (2006) <http://georgewbush-whitehouse.archives.gov/nsc/nss/2006>.

[50] Office of the President, 'The National Security Strategy' (2010) <http://www.whitehouse.gov/sites/default/files/rss_viewer/national_security_strategy.pdf>.

MARY ELLEN O'CONNELL

self-defence, and it must request military assistance from the first state. In the absence of a request for assistance from the state attacked, the Court considered that the right of collective self-defence could not be invoked.[51]

e) The right of self-defence under Article 51 is preserved only 'until the Security Council has taken measures necessary to restore international peace and security'. It is not clear what action on the part of the Council will put an end to the right of self-defence. Purely verbal condemnation of an aggressor by the Council cannot be sufficient for, as the UK Representative at the UN stated during the Falklands conflict, Article 51 'can only be taken to refer to measures which are actually effective to bring about the stated objective'.[52] When Iraq invaded Kuwait, however, the Security Council reinforced its immediate demand for Iraqi withdrawal by imposing economic sanctions upon Iraq.[53] When the sanctions and negotiations did not succeed after five months in persuading the Iraqis to withdraw, the Security Council then authorized the use of force. This case indicates that Kuwait and its coalition partners needed Council authorization at that point to begin military action against Iraq.[54]

f) As mentioned above, not all the conditions for a valid exercise of the right of self-defence are stated in Article 51. It was accepted by both parties in the *Nicaragua* case, and confirmed by the ICJ, that measures taken in self-defence must not exceed what is necessary and proportionate. These requirements have been described as being 'innate in any genuine concept of self-defence'.[55] The exercise of lawful self-defence permits only the use of force to put an end to an armed attack and to any occupation of territory or other forcible violation of rights that may have been committed. This does not mean that the state using force in self-defence must limit the force used to the amount used against it. Such a rule would be wholly impractical. The UK, for example, could not have retaken the Falkland Islands after the Argentine invasion of 1982 using only the degree of force which had been used by Argentina. Argentina had placed a far larger force on the Islands than the small British garrison overcome in the initial invasion. Dislodging the Argentine force effectively required an even larger British force. The correct test is that stated by Sir Humphrey Waldock when he said that the use of force in self-defence must be '. . . strictly confined to the object of stopping or preventing the infringement [of the defending state's rights] and reasonably proportionate to what is required for achieving this objective'.[56] In the case of the Falklands, the UK was entitled to use such force as was reasonably necessary to retake the Islands and to guarantee their security against further attack. The limitations which the principles of necessity and proportionality impose upon the degree of force that may be used have implications for the conduct of hostilities, which are examined in the commentary to Section 132 below.[57]

5. *Humanitarian intervention.* It has already been suggested that the Security Council now treats some humanitarian emergencies as threats to international peace and security warranting enforcement action. However, claims by States that they had a right to use

---

[51] *Nicaragua* (n. 35).

[52] UN Doc. S/15016.

[53] Res. 661 (1990).

[54] For a view that Art. 51 must be referring to 'effective measures' by the Security Council, see D. W. Greig, 'Self-Defence and the Security Council' (1991) 40 *ICLQ* 366.

[55] Brownlie (n. 41), 434.

[56] H. Waldock, 'The Regulation of the Use of Force by Individual States in International Law' (1952) 81 *RdC* 451.

[57] For an excellent general overview of these two principles, see J. Gardam (n. 24).

MARY ELLEN O'CONNELL

force in extreme humanitarian cases, even without Security Council sanction, were generally rejected prior to 1990.[58] In the 1990s, support grew for unauthorized intervention to advance humanitarian goals.[59] The Economic Community of West African States (ECOWAS) attempted to get Security Council authorization for its intervention in Liberia in 1990. The Security Council endorsed the action after it began. Some NATO states also asserted such a right during NATO's intervention in the Kosovo Crisis in 1999.[60] A draft resolution which would have condemned the intervention as illegal was defeated by twelve votes to three in the Security Council. The UK government declared in 2004 that 'there is increasing acceptance of the view taken in 1999 that imminent humanitarian crises justify military intervention'.[61] In 2011 the Security Council authorized the use of force for humanitarian purposes in Libya. The Council passed Resolution 1973, which called for an immediate ceasefire and authorized the establishment of a no-fly zone.[62] The resolution also authorized all necessary means to protect civilians within the country.[63] The Council's action respecting Libya both consolidated the Council's role in humanitarian crises and weakened the claim that a right to unauthorized humanitarian intervention was developing in international law. Such a claim had already been rejected in 2005 in the World Summit Outcome Document.

6. *Other possible justifications for the use of force.* On occasions, a number of other possible justifications for military action have been advanced. Reprisals, the protection of nationals abroad, intervention to promote self-determination, and intervention in an internal conflict at the request of the government of the state have all been cited. Of these, intervention to protect nationals is properly regarded as a minimal or *de minimis* use of force, for the reasons given above. Armed reprisals, though once lawful, have been condemned by both the Security Council and the General Assembly, and their legal basis must now be regarded as highly doubtful. Intervention to promote self-determination is also of doubtful legality. Even if it might be said to exist in the classic case of a colonial people fighting a war of independence, it is unclear that it could be extended to more modern cases of pro-democratic intervention. Finally, intervention in a state with the consent of the government of that state has generally been taken as involving no use of force against that state, unless the state concerned was already in a condition of civil war.

7. *The equal application of international humanitarian law.* Once hostilities have begun, the rules of international humanitarian law apply with equal force to both sides in the conflict, irrespective of who is the aggressor. On the face of it, this seems illogical. To place the aggressor and the victim of that aggression on an equal footing as regards the application of humanitarian law appears to contravene the general principle of law that no one should obtain a legal benefit from his own illegal action: *ex injuria non oritur ius.*

---

[58] For example, India asserted such a right in the Bangladesh conflict in 1971, Vietnam in the case of Cambodia in 1979, and Tanzania in the case of Uganda in 1979. All three states also claimed self-defence, however. See generally, Simon Chesterman, *Just War or Just Peace? Humanitarian Intervention and International Law* (OUP, 2001).

[59] See Greenwood, *Essays* (n. 3), 593.

[60] Ibid.

[61] Lord Goldsmith (n. 48).

[62] SC Res. 1973, paras. 1, 6, UN Doc. S/RES/1973 (17 March 2011).

[63] Ibid. Germany abstained in the vote and from participation in the action because it did not meet the principle of necessity, in the German view. Germany was correct in that only a minimal attempt had been made to resolve the Libyan crisis through negotiation.

MARY ELLEN O'CONNELL

Yet the principle that humanitarian law does not distinguish between the aggressor and the victim is well established. In the Diplomatic Conference which adopted the two 1977 Protocols Additional to the Geneva Conventions,[64] the Democratic Republic of Vietnam argued that states which committed acts of aggression should not be allowed to benefit from the provisions of humanitarian law. This argument was roundly rejected and the Preamble to AP I reaffirms that: 'the provisions of the Geneva Conventions of 12 August 1949 and of this Protocol must be fully applied in all circumstances to all persons who are protected by those instruments, without any adverse distinction based on the nature or origin of the armed conflict or on the causes espoused by or attributed to the Parties to the conflict'.

A number of war crimes trials held at the end of the Second World War make clear that the provisions of the earlier Hague Conventions on the laws of war[65] are also equally applicable to all parties in a conflict.[66] The reason for this apparently illogical rule is that humanitarian law is primarily intended to protect individuals, rather than states, and those individuals are, in general, not responsible for any act of aggression committed by the state of which they are citizens. Moreover, since in most armed conflicts there is no authoritative determination by the Security Council of which party is the aggressor, both parties usually claim to be acting in self-defence, as Iran and Iraq did throughout the 1980–1988 Iran–Iraq War. Any attempt to make the rules of humanitarian law distinguish between the standards of treatment to be accorded to prisoners of war or civilians belonging to the aggressor and those belonging to the state that was the victim of aggression would thus almost certainly lead to a total disregard for humanitarian law. As Sir Hersch Lauterpacht said, 'it is impossible to visualize the conduct of hostilities in which one side would be bound by rules of warfare without benefiting from them and the other side would benefit from them without being bound by them'.[67] After initial hesitation,[68] similar reasoning has led to general acceptance that a UN force, or a force acting under the authority of the Security Council, is also bound to observe the rules of international humanitarian law.

> International humanitarian law constitutes a reaffirmation and development of the   102
> traditional international laws of war (*jus in bello*). Most rules of the law of war now
> extend even to those armed conflicts that the parties do not regard as wars. The
> term 'international humanitarian law' takes this development into account.

1. *The scope of 'international humanitarian law'.* The term 'international humanitarian law' (IHL) is of relatively recent origin and does not appear in the Geneva Conventions of 1949.[69] International humanitarian law comprises all those rules of international law designed to regulate the treatment of persons—civilian or military, wounded or active—in armed conflicts. While the term is generally used in connection with the Geneva Conventions and the Additional Protocols of 1977, it also applies to the rules

---

[64] See Section 128 below.
[65] See Section 126 below.
[66] See, e.g. *US v List*, (1948) 15 Annual Digest 632 and the *Singapore Oil Stocks* case (1956) 23 *ILR* 810. See also the moving argument for equal application of IHL in Telford Taylor, *Nuremberg and Vietnam: An American Tragedy* (Random House, 1970).
[67] H. Lauterpacht, 'The Limits of the Operation of the Laws of War' (1953) 30 *BYIL* 206, 212; see also C. Greenwood, 'Ius ad Bellum and Ius in Bello' (n. 35).
[68] Bowett, *UN Forces* (n. 14), 484; see Chapter 13 below.
[69] H. P. Gasser and D. Thürer, 'Humanitarian Law, International', *MPEPIL*.

MARY ELLEN O'CONNELL

governing methods and means of warfare and the governance of occupied territory, rules found in earlier agreements such as the Hague Conventions of 1907 and in treaties such as the Inhumane Weapons Convention of 1980. (For a list of many of these treaties, see Sections 126–129.) International humanitarian law also includes a number of rules of customary international law and general principles of international law. International humanitarian law thus includes most of what used to be known as the laws of war, although strictly speaking some parts of those laws, such as the law of neutrality, are not included since their primary purpose is not humanitarian. This Handbook, however, deals with all of the rules of international law that apply in an armed conflict, whether or not they are considered to be part of international humanitarian law.

A significant development in the law is that, whereas the older treaties applied only in a 'war', today humanitarian law is applicable in any armed conflict, even if the parties to that conflict have not declared war and do not recognize that they are in a situation defined under law as war.[70] This matter is discussed further in the commentary to Chapter 2.

2. *Reciprocity*. In contrast to human rights treaties, which usually require each party to the treaty to treat all persons within its jurisdiction in accordance with the treaty's requirements, even if they are citizens of a state not party to that treaty, humanitarian law treaties are binding only between those states parties to them.[71] In the 1991 Kuwait conflict, several of the coalition states (such as Italy, Canada, and Saudi Arabia) were parties to AP I, but they were not obliged to apply its provisions in the conflict because Iraq was not a party.[72] However, once it is established that a humanitarian law treaty is binding upon states on both sides in a conflict, the application of the treaty is not dependent upon reciprocity. As the *ICRC Commentary* to the Geneva Conventions puts it, a humanitarian law treaty does not constitute 'an engagement concluded on the basis of reciprocity, binding each party to the contract only in so far as the other party observes its obligations. It is rather a series of unilateral engagements solemnly contracted before the world as represented by the other Contracting Parties.'[73]

Thus, the fact that one side in a conflict violates humanitarian law does not justify its adversary in disregarding that law.[74] Moreover, it is not necessary today that all the states involved in a conflict must be parties to a particular humanitarian treaty for that treaty to apply in the conflict. If there are states on both sides of the conflict parties to a particular treaty, that treaty is applicable between them, even though it does not bind them in their relations with those states which have not become parties. In this respect, humanitarian law has changed since the beginning of the twentieth century.

---

[70] For a description of what constitutes 'war' or 'armed conflict under international law', see the International Law Association Committee on the Use of Force, Report on the Meaning of Armed Conflict in International Law (2010) <http://www.ila-hq.org/en/committees/index.cfm/cid/1022>. See also the book written to accompany the report, M. E. O'Connell (ed.), *What is War? An Investigation in the Wake of 9/11* (Nijhof/Brill, 2012).

[71] An important exception is some of the weapons treaties, notably the Biological Weapons Convention, the Chemical Weapons Convention and the Landmines Convention, impose absolute obligations on the states party to them.

[72] Many provisions of AP I are, however, declaratory of customary law or were general principles of law and as such applicable to all states in the Kuwait conflict (see commentary to Section 127); in the ISAF mission in Afghanistan, AP II, and all other provisions of Customary IHL applicable to a non-international armed conflict are in force, see Rule of Law in Armed Conflicts Project, 'Afghanistan: Applicable International Law' <http://www.geneva-academy.ch/RULAC/applicable_international_law.php?id_state=1>.

[73] J. S. Pictet, *The Geneva Convention of 12 August 1949, Commentary*, Vol. IV (ICRC 1958), 15.

[74] For the special case of reprisals, see Sections 485–488, and 1408.

MARY ELLEN O'CONNELL

Older humanitarian law treaties contained what was known as a 'general participation clause', under which a treaty would apply in a war only if all the belligerents were parties to that treaty.

3. *Humanitarian law and the law of human rights.* International humanitarian law obviously has much in common with the law of human rights, since both bodies of rules are concerned with the protection of persons.[75] Nevertheless, there are important differences between them. Human rights law is designed to operate primarily in normal peacetime conditions and within the framework of the legal relationship between a state and its citizens and those under the state's control. International humanitarian law, by contrast, is chiefly concerned with the abnormal conditions of armed conflict and the relationship between a state and persons associated with its adversary, a relationship otherwise based upon power rather than law. It is now clear that human rights law applies in armed conflict, though derogation from some human rights obligations may be permitted.[76] For example, during armed conflict, the ICJ in its advisory opinion on nuclear weapons held that the application of the right to life provision in the International Civil and Political Rights Covenant in time of armed conflict was subject to the relevant norms of humanitarian law as the *lex specialis* for such situations.[77] International humanitarian law decriminalizes the taking of life in some circumstances that would constitute a criminal offence in peacetime. Nevertheless, the fundamental human right to life continues in armed conflict as in peace. International humanitarian law and the law of human rights have been called 'complementary and mutually reinforcing'.[78] For further considerations concerning the relevance of human rights in armed conflicts, see below, Sections 249–255.

> **International humanitarian law sets certain bounds to the use of force against an   103 adversary. It determines both the relationship of the parties to a conflict with one another and their relationship with neutral states. Certain provisions of international humanitarian law are also applicable in the relationship between the state and its own citizens.**

1. International humanitarian law is centrally concerned with the legality of conduct in armed conflict, in contrast to the central focus of the *jus ad bellum*, which

---

[75] A. H. Robertson, 'Humanitarian Law and Human Rights' in C. Swinarski (ed.), *Studies and Essays on International Humanitarian Law and Red Cross Principles in Honour of Jean Pictet* (ICRC/Nijhoff, 1984), 793.

[76] This has been reaffirmed by the ICJ in its advisory opinions on *Nuclear Weapons, ICJ Reports 1996*, 226, at para. 25 and *Legal Consequences of the Construction of a Wall, ICJ Reports 2004*, 136, paras. 102–42 [106]. The ICJ also confirmed the point in contentious cases, *Armed Activities on the Territory of Congo (DRC v Uganda); ICJ Reports 2005*, 168, para. 216, *Application of the Convention on the Prevention and Punishment of the Crime of Genocide, (Bosn & Herz v Serb & Mont) ICJ Reports 2007*, 43, para. 147 and *Application of the International Convention on the Elimination of all Forms of Racial Discrimination (Georgia v Russia) ICJ Reports 2008*, general list 140, para. 182. The same finding has been made by regional human rights courts, most notably by the European Court of Human Rights in *Al-Skeini and Others v UK* Application no. 55721/07 (ECtHR, 7 July 2011). See also, L. Doswald-Beck, *Human Rights in Times of Conflict and Terrorism* (OUP, 2011). Doswald-Beck discusses Israeli arguments against concurrent application of international humanitarian law and human rights law, as well as the inconsistent positions of the US. She concludes that neither state is a persistent objector to the concurrent application rule. Ibid. at 8.

[77] *ICJ Reports 1996*, 226, para. 25.

[78] Report of the Office of the High Commissioner on the outcome of the expert consultation on the issue of protecting the human rights of civilians in armed conflict, 2 June 2010, UN Doc. A/HRC/14/40, §§ 1–2.

MARY ELLEN O'CONNELL

is the legality of an initial resort to armed force, as discussed in the commentary to Section 101.[79] Humanitarian law sets limits to the way in which force may be used by prohibiting certain weapons (such as poison gas) and methods of warfare (such as indiscriminate attacks), by insisting that attacks be directed only at military objectives, and even then that they should not cause disproportionate civilian casualties. It also regulates the treatment of persons who are *hors de combat*: the wounded, sick, shipwrecked, persons parachuting from a disabled aircraft, prisoners of war, and civilian internees, as well as the enemy's civilian population. Although primarily concerned with the relationship between the parties to a conflict, a distinct branch of the laws of armed conflict, the law of neutrality, regulates the relationship between the belligerents and states not involved in the conflict. Unlike the rules dealing with the relationship between the parties to a conflict, the law of neutrality has not been the subject of much codification and still consists largely of customary international law. It is considered in Chapter 11 of this Handbook.

2. Most rules of humanitarian law concern the way in which a party to a conflict treats the persons loyal to or under the control of its adversary. For the most part, humanitarian law does not attempt to regulate a state's treatment of its own citizens. Thus, it has been held, for example, that a national of one party to a conflict who serves in the armed forces of an adversary against his own state is not entitled to be treated as a prisoner of war if captured,[80] although this decision has been criticized[81] and is probably untenable today for a variety of reasons. For example, many persons have multiple nationalities; nationality is sometimes forced upon people (e.g. as a result of the annexation of the territory in which they reside); and there have been instances where large numbers of people have taken up arms against the state of their nationality.[82] Some provisions of humanitarian law, however, do apply expressly to the relationship between a state and its own citizens. Article 3 common to the four Geneva Conventions and AP II each lay down a legal regime for non-international armed conflicts. In addition, some provisions of the Geneva Conventions and AP I require a state to take positive steps in relation to its own citizens by, for example, ensuring that members of its armed forces receive instruction in international humanitarian law, or encouraging the dissemination of the principles of that law among the civilian population.[83] A state is also required to take steps to prevent its citizens from violating provisions of humanitarian law and must, for example, take action to prevent or prosecute grave breaches of that law by its nationals.[84]

---

[79] Nevertheless, it would be unrealistic to think that the legality of the resort to armed force has no influence on perceptions and assessments of the conduct of armed conflict or vice versa. For a general discussion of the interrelationship of the three sets of rules discussed in this chapter, see William Schabas, 'Lex Specialis? Belt and Suspenders? The Parallel Operation of Human Rights and the Law of Armed Conflict, and the Conundrum of Jus Ad Bellum' (2007) 40 *Israel Law Review* 592.

[80] See the decision of the Privy Council in *Public Prosecutor v Oie Hee Koi*, 42 *ILR*, 441.

[81] Howard S. Levie, 'Prisoners of War in International Armed Conflict' (Naval War College, 1978) 59 *International Law Studies* 74–6; R. R. Baxter, 'The Privy Council on the Qualifications of Belligerents' (1969) 63 *AJIL* 290.

[82] H. Lauterpacht (ed.), 'Vol. II: Disputes, War and Neutrality', *Oppenheim's International Law*, 7th edn (David McKay, 1952), 252–3.

[83] See Section 137 below.

[84] See Section 1410–5.

MARY ELLEN O'CONNELL

While general rules apply to all types of warfare, special rules apply to the law of   104
land warfare, the law of air and missile warfare, the law of naval warfare, and the
law of neutrality.[85]

The general rules of humanitarian law and their application in land and aerial warfare are considered in Chapters 2–9 and Chapter 12 of this Handbook. The law of naval warfare is the subject of Chapter 10. Although many of the rules of humanitarian law (e.g., those related to the treatment of prisoners of war) are common to all forms of warfare, naval warfare is in other respects subject to a distinct legal regime. The environment in which naval warfare takes place is very different from that of land warfare, its scope for affecting the rights of neutrals is far greater, and the rules which govern naval warfare have not, for the most part, been the subject of as much attention in recent years as the rules applicable to land warfare. Apart from the GC II, which deals with the wounded, sick, and shipwrecked at sea, none of the post-1945 treaties have been specifically concerned with naval warfare and some of the most important provisions of AP I are not applicable to warfare at sea, except in so far as it may affect the civilian population on land or is directed against targets on land.[86] The result is that much of the law of naval warfare still consists of rules of customary international law. The International Institute of Humanitarian Law has conducted a study on international law applicable to armed conflict at sea.[87] The law of air and missile warfare focuses particularly on targeting and has been the subject of a study by Harvard's Program on Humanitarian Policy and Conflict Research.[88] The law of neutrality is, like the law of naval warfare, also largely a matter of customary law. The entire institution of neutrality has been questioned in recent times, on the ground that the UN Charter has effectively rendered it obsolete.[89] Nevertheless, the events of the Iran–Iraq War show that the law of neutrality may still have relevance, even if there are doubts about its exact content.

II. Historical Development

The following historical references may promote appreciation of the development   105
and value of international humanitarian law.

Throughout its history, the development of international humanitarian law has   106
been influenced by religious concepts and philosophical ideas. Customary rules of
warfare are part of the very first rules of international law. The development from
the first rules of customary law to the first written humanitarian principles for the
conduct of war, however, encountered some setbacks.

---

[85] A few rules exist respecting military uses of outer space and new rules may be emerging to govern military uses of cyberspace. See GA Res. 66/24, UN Doc. A/RES/66/24 (13 December 2011) on keeping cyberspace free of military uses. But see also M. N. Schmitt (ed.), *Tallinn Manual on the International Law Applicable to Cyber Warfare* (CUP, 2013); D. Fleck, 'Searching for International Rules Applicable to Cyber Warfare—A Critical First Assessment of the New Tallinn Manual' (2013) 18–2 *JCSL*.

[86] See Art. 49, para. 3, AP I.

[87] San Remo Manual, 1994.

[88] See *HPCR Manual* 2009.

[89] See E. Lauterpacht, 'The Legal "Irrelevance" of the State of War' (1968) 62 *Proceedings of the American Society of International Law* 58; P. M. Norton 'Between the Ideology and the Reality: The Shadow of the Law of Neutrality' (1976) 17 *Harvard Journal of International Law* 249.

MARY ELLEN O'CONNELL

The laws of war have a long history,[90] as the following paragraphs show, although it has been suggested that military practice in early times fell far short of existing theory, and that such rules of warfare as can be identified in early times have little similarity to modern international humanitarian law.[91] From the Middle Ages until well into the seventeenth century, discussion of the rules of war in Europe was dominated by theological considerations, although some elements of classical philosophy remained influential.[92] The codification and written development of the law did not begin until the nineteenth century.

107   Some rules which imposed restrictions on the conduct of war, the means of warfare, and their application can be traced back to ancient times.

— The Sumerians regarded war as a state governed by the law, which was started by a declaration of war and terminated by a peace treaty. War was subject to specific rules which, *inter alia* guaranteed immunity to enemy negotiators.
— Hammurabi King of Babylon, (1728–1686 BC), wrote the 'Code of Hammurabi' for the protection of the weak against oppression by the strong and ordered that hostages be released on payment of a ransom.
— The law of the Hittites also provided for a declaration of war and for peace to be concluded by treaty, as well as for respect for the inhabitants of an enemy city which has capitulated. The war between Egypt and the Hittites in 1269 BC, for instance, was terminated by a peace treaty.
— In the seventh century BC, Cyrus I, King of the Persians, ordered the wounded Chaldeans to be treated like his own wounded soldiers.
— The Indian epic *Mahabharata* (*c.* 400 BC) and the Laws of Manu (*c.* 200 BC – 200 AD) contained provisions which prohibited the killing of a surrendering adversary who was no longer capable of fighting; forbade the use of certain means of combat, such as poisoned or burning arrows; and provided for the protection of enemy property and prisoners of war.
— The Greeks, in the wars between the Greek city-states, considered each other as having equal rights and in the war led by Alexander the Great against the Persians, respected the life and personal dignity of war victims as a prime principle. They spared the temples, embassies, priests, and envoys of the opposite side and exchanged prisoners of war. For example, the poisoning of wells was proscribed in warfare. The Romans also accorded the right to life to their prisoners of war. However, the Greeks and Romans both distinguished between those peoples whom they regarded as their cultural equals and those whom they considered to be barbarians.

1. These examples show that the laws regulating the conduct of hostilities were recognized in many early cultures. The theory that humanitarian law is essentially 'Eurocentric' is in reality more a criticism of most literature on the subject than a reflection of historical fact. Thus, several of the principles of modern humanitarian law have precursors in

[90] J. H. W. Verzijl, *International Law in Historical Perspective*, Vols. IX and X: The Laws of War (Leiden: Sijthoff, 1978); L. Friedman (ed.), *The Law of War: A Documentary History*, two vols (Random House, 1972).
[91] F. Münch, 'War, Laws of History' IV *Encyclopedia of Public International Law* (Amsterdam: Elsevier, 2000), 1386–8.
[92] T. E. Holland, *Studies in International Law* (Oxford: Clarendon Press, 1898), 40.

MARY ELLEN O'CONNELL

ancient India.[93] Humanitarian law principles have been identified in African customary traditions.[94] As may be expected, the wide range of cultural traditions to which this paragraph refers displays a diversity of practice. Nevertheless, certain common themes can be identified, several of which continue to enjoy a prominent place in modern international humanitarian law.

a) In many cultural traditions, there was an emphasis upon the formalities for opening and closing hostilities. The Sumerian and Hittite traditions are in this respect similar to the later Roman *jus fetiale* which required a formal declaration of war at the commencement of hostilities. In part, this tradition reflects the perception of war as a formal legal condition, as opposed to a factual condition, a perception which has only declined in importance in the twentieth century.[95] The attachment to formalities was also important, however, in serving to distinguish between hostilities entered into by a state and violence which had no official sanction.

b) The protection accorded to ambassadors and the respect for truces and for negotiations held during a war was the precursor of modern principles regarding ceasefires and parlementaires.[96]

c) The prohibition on certain types of weapon, particularly poison, is found in many different traditions and is now embodied in a number of important modern agreements.[97]

2. However, while some cultures respected the lives of prisoners and the wounded, the majority of prisoners faced death or enslavement. A similar fate usually befell the civilian population of a city which resisted attack, although in some traditions the population was spared if there was a timely surrender and the city did not have to be taken by storm.

> **Islam also acknowledged the essential requirements of humanity. In his orders to** **108**
> **his commanders, the first caliph, Abu Bakr (about 632), stipulated for instance**
> **the following: 'The blood of women, children and old people shall not stain your**
> **victory. Do not destroy a palm tree, nor burn houses and cornfields with fire, and**
> **do not cut any fruitful tree. You must not slay any flock or herds, save for your**
> **subsistence.' While in many cases Islamic warfare was no less cruel than warfare**
> **by Christians, under the reign of leaders like Sultan Saladin in the twelfth cen-**
> **tury, the laws of war were observed in an exemplary manner. Saladin ordered the**
> **wounded of both sides to be treated outside Jerusalem and allowed the members of**
> **the Order of St John to discharge their hospital duties.**

Several studies have now shown that many of the central principles of humanitarian law were deeply rooted in Islamic tradition.[98] Although Saladin was unusual among both Muslims and Christians during the Crusades in his humane treatment of prisoners and the wounded, he was by no means alone in regarding warfare as subject to principles of law. Three centuries after Saladin, the Turkish Sultan Mehmet extended to the population of Constantinople a greater degree of mercy than might have been expected given that the city had been taken by storm.[99]

---

[93] N. Singh, 'Armed Conflicts and Humanitarian Law of Ancient India' in C. Swinarski (ed.) (n. 75), 531; see also, Hugo Grotius, *De Jure Belli ac Pacis* (first published in 1625, translated by A. Campbell, London: Hyperion, 1990), Book III, Chapter XI, § XI.

[94] E. Bello, *African Customary Humanitarian Law* (Geneva: ICRC, 1980).

[95] See Sections 203 and 246–55 below.

[96] See Chapter 2 below.

[97] Art. 23, lit. a, HagueReg and GasProt.

[98] M. Khadduri, *War and Peace in the Law of Islam* (Baltimore: John Hopkins University Press, 1955).

[99] S. Runciman, *The Fall of Constantinople* (CUP, 1969), 152.

MARY ELLEN O'CONNELL

109   In the Middle Ages, feud and war were governed by strict principles. The principle
         of protecting women, children, and the aged from hostilities was espoused by St
         Augustine. The enforcement of respect for holy places (Truce of God) created a right
         of refuge, or asylum, in churches, the observance of which was carefully monitored
         by the Church. Knights fought according to certain (unwritten) rules which were
         enforced by tribunals of knights. These particular rules applied only to knights,
         not to ordinary people. Among the knights' rules was the requirement to regard
         an enemy knight as an equal combatant who had to be defeated in an honourable
         fight, and it was forbidden to start a war without prior notification.

         St Augustine's influence on the laws of war during the Middle Ages derived in part from
         his development of the theory of the 'just war'. Whereas the earliest Christian writers had
         generally been pacifists, St Augustine reasoned that a Christian could justify fighting for
         certain limited causes: self-defence, punishment of wrongs, and recovery of property.[100]
         Augustine's views were later adopted by influential writers such as St Thomas Aquinas,
         who maintained that a just war required lawful authority, just cause, and rightful inten-
         tion.[101] The first requirement was important in distinguishing between hostilities entered
         into on the authority of a prince, on the one hand, from the lawless activities of brigands
         and war lords on the other. Once the idea that warfare might have a legal and theological
         basis was accepted, it followed naturally (at least in conflicts between Christian princes)
         that considerations of law and humanity should also influence the conduct of war. The
         rules which developed for the regulation of warfare between knights reflected these
         considerations as well as a general code of chivalry.[102] These rules undoubtedly had a
         civilizing effect and were a valuable humanitarian development.[103] It should, however,
         be borne in mind that this code was largely devised for the benefit of the knights and
         that the purpose of some of the rules was not so much humanitarian as an attempt to
         prevent the development of weapons and methods of warfare which would threaten
         their position. Thus, the attempt by the Lateran Council in 1137 to ban the crossbow
         was motivated as much by a desire to get rid of a weapon which allowed a foot soldier
         to threaten an armoured knight as by humanitarian concern at the injuries which cross-
         bow bolts could cause. Moreover, the code was intended to apply only to hostilities
         between Christian princes and was seldom applied outside that context, for example, in
         the Crusades.

110   The 'Bushi-Do', the medieval code of honour of Zen Buddhism in Japan, included the
         rule that humanity must be exercised even in battle and towards prisoners of war.

111   In the seventeenth century, the Confucian philosopher Butsu Sorai wrote that
         whoever kills a prisoner of war shall be guilty of manslaughter, whether that pris-
         oner had surrendered or fought 'to the last arrow'.

112   As a result of the decline of the chivalric orders, the invention of firearms, and above
         all the creation of armies consisting of mercenaries, the morals of war regressed

---

[100] Joachim von Elbe, 'The Evolution of the Concept of the Just War in International Law' (1939) 33 *AJIL*
665; F. H. Russell, *The Just War in the Middle Ages* (CUP, 1975).
[101] Von Elbe (n. 100), 669.
[102] M. H. Keen, *The Laws of War in the Late Middle Ages* (Routledge, 1965); G. I. A. D. Draper, 'The
Interaction of Christianity and Chivalry in the Historical Development of Law of War' (1965) 7 *IRRC* 3.
[103] See Geoffrey Parker, 'Early Modern Europe' in M. Howard et al. (eds), *The Laws of War* (Yale
University Press, 1994), 40, 51–5.

MARY ELLEN O'CONNELL

towards the end of the Middle Ages. Considerations of chivalry were unknown to these armies. Equally, they made no distinction between combatants and the civilian population. Mercenaries regarded war as a trade which they followed for the purpose of private gain.

For the modern law regarding mercenaries, see Article 47, para. 1, AP I and Section 303 below.

> At the beginning of modern times the wars of religion, and particularly the   **113**
> Thirty Years War, once again employed the most inhuman methods of warfare.
> The cruelties of this war particularly led to the jurisprudential consideration of
> the *jus in bello* and established a number of principles to be observed by com-
> batants. In his work '*De iure belli ac pacis*', published in 1625, Hugo Grotius,
> the father of modern international law, emphasized the existing bounds to the
> conduct of war.

The savagery of warfare in the late sixteenth and early seventeenth centuries is summed up by Grotius in a passage in which he explained why he wrote about the laws of war: 'I saw prevailing throughout the Christian world a licence in making war of which even barbarous nations should be ashamed; men resorting to arms for trivial or for no reasons at all, and when arms were once taken up no reverence left for divine or human law, exactly as if a single edict had released a madness driving men to all kinds of crime.'[104] In effect, what Grotius described was the breakdown of both the *jus ad bellum* of the Middle Ages (the 'just war' doctrine) and the *jus in bello*. His '*De iure belli ac pacis*' was to have considerable influence on the rebuilding of the latter body of law, although it was not until the twentieth century that any real progress was made in developing a new *jus ad bellum*. Nevertheless, Grotius was not the only writer of this period to focus on the laws of war. Gentili, who like Grotius was an exile from his own country, published his seminal work '*De iure belli*' in England in 1598,[105] while the Spanish writer Vitoria was also influential in reviving interest in this area of the law, particularly by suggesting that rules of international law might apply to warfare between Christian states and the Indians of the New World.[106]

> A fundamental change in the attitude of states to the conduct of war came only   **114**
> with the advent of the Age of Enlightenment in the eighteenth century. In 1762,
> Jean-Jacques Rousseau made the following statement in his work '*Du Contrat
> Social*': 'War then is a relation, not between man and man, but between State
> and State, and individuals are enemies only accidentally, not as men, nor even as
> citizens, but as soldiers; not as members of their country, but as its defenders...
> The object of the war being the destruction of the hostile State, the other side has
> a right to kill its defenders while they are bearing arms; but as soon as they lay
> them down and surrender they become once more merely men, whose life no one
> has any right to take.'[107] From this doctrine, which was soon generally acknowl-
> edged, it follows that acts of hostility may only be directed against the armed
> forces of the adversary, not against the civilian population which takes no part

---

[104] Hugo Grotius, *De Jure Belli ac Pacis* (n. 93).
[105] Holland, (n. 92), 40.
[106] Francisco de Vitoria, *De Indis De Jure Belli* (originally published 1532, reprinted E. Nys (ed.), Oceana, 1964), <http://en.wikisource.org/wiki/De_Indis_De_Jure_Belli>.
[107] J.-J. Rousseau, *Du Contrat Social ou Principes du Droit Politique* (1762), Livre I, Chapitre IV.

MARY ELLEN O'CONNELL

in the hostilities. These ideas also found expression in several international treaties concluded at that time.

The acceptance during the late eighteenth century of the ideas to which Rousseau gave voice in the passage quoted was a landmark in the development of humanitarian law; it was the first recognition of the principle that the purpose of using force is to overcome an enemy state, and that to do this it is sufficient to disable enemy combatants. The distinction between combatants and civilians, the requirement that wounded and captured enemy combatants must be treated humanely, and that quarter must be given, some of the pillars of modern humanitarian law, all follow from this principle. While the French revolutionary wars were in many respects cruel by modern standards, they are important for the development of humanitarian law in that they demonstrated in military practice many of the ideas enunciated by Rousseau and other writers of the Enlightenment.[108] The treaty of friendship and commerce between Prussia and the US in 1785, whose most important authors are deemed to be King Frederick the Great and Benjamin Franklin, contained some exemplary and pioneering provisions for the treatment of prisoners of war. It was also one of the first attempts to record new principles of humanitarian law in written form, although it was to be another seventy years before the conclusion of the first multilateral treaty on the subject.

115   **In the nineteenth century, after a few interim setbacks, humanitarian ideas continued to gain ground. They led to remarkable initiatives by individuals as well as to numerous international treaties. These treaties imposed restrictions on both the instruments of warfare and the methods of their use.**

The nineteenth century saw the ideas which had gained acceptance in the late eighteenth century given practical effect. A number of major international treaties, some of which are still in force, were adopted, codifying several of the customary rules of warfare and developing those rules in various ways. In addition, the initiative of a number of private individuals led to the creation of what became the International Committee of the Red Cross, which has played a central role in the development and implementation of the rules of humanitarian law.[109]

116   **Florence Nightingale soothed the sufferings of the sick and wounded through her efforts as an English nurse in the Crimean War (1853–1856). She later made an essential contribution towards the renovation of both the civil and military nursing systems of her country.**

Although Nightingale cannot be said to have had a direct effect upon the development of humanitarian law, her work in developing a military medical and nursing service to care for the wounded and sick on the battlefield (which was also a feature of the American Civil War) was an essential prerequisite to the development of that body of humanitarian law which deals with the wounded and sick and which was the subject of the first Geneva Convention.[110]

---

[108] Geoffrey Best, *Humanity in Warfare: The Modern History of the International Law of Armed Conflicts* (Methuen, 1983), 31–127.
[109] See Section 1424 below.
[110] See Sections 118 and 119 below.

MARY ELLEN O'CONNELL

In 1861, Francis Lieber (1800–1872), a German-American professor of political   117
science and law at Columbia College, which later became Columbia University,
prepared on the behalf of President Lincoln a manual based on international law
(the Lieber Code) which was put into effect for the first time in 1863 for the Union
Army of the US in the American Civil War (1861–1865).

The Lieber Code[111] is the origin of what has come to be known as 'Hague Law', so called
because the principal treaties which dealt with the subject were concluded at The Hague.
Hague Law is the law of armed conflict written from the standpoint of the soldier, in
the sense that it takes the form of a statement of the rights and duties of the military in
a conflict. Lieber's Code was the first attempt to set down, in a single set of instructions
for forces in the field, the laws and customs of war. Its 157 Articles are based on the
philosophy of the Enlightenment described in the preceding paragraph, stressing, for
example, that only armed enemies should be attacked,[112] that unarmed civilians and
their property should be respected,[113] and that prisoners and the wounded should be
humanely treated.[114] The Code is, however, far more than a statement of broad general
principles. The treatment of prisoners of war is the subject of detailed regulation,[115] as
are the arrangements for exchange of prisoners, truce, and armistice.[116] The Code is the
more remarkable for having been issued during a civil war when the Union government
had been at pains to insist that no state should recognize the Confederacy. In that sense
it was many years ahead of its time; even today, the treaty rules on humanitarian law
applicable in internal armed conflicts are more limited in their scope than the provisions
of the Lieber Code.

The Genevese merchant Henry Dunant who, in the Italian War of Unification, had   118
witnessed the plight of 40,000 Austrian, French, and Italian soldiers wounded on
the battlefield of Solferino (1859), published his impressions in his book *A Memory
of Solferino*, which became known all over the world. In 1863, the International
Committee of the Red Cross (ICRC) was founded in Geneva on his initiative.

What shocked Dunant after the Battle of Solferino was the lack of any systematic effort
by the armies concerned to care for the wounded, who were left to die on the battlefield,
and often robbed and murdered by local inhabitants. In so far as medical services were
available, their providers appeared unprotected from attack or capture. Dunant organized teams of volunteers to collect and care for the wounded at Solferino. The ICRC,
founded largely thanks to Dunant, was and remains predominantly a Swiss organization
that has promoted the creation of better medical services in wartime, and the adoption
of international agreements dealing first with the wounded and subsequently with the
whole field of humanitarian law.[117]

---

[111] D. Schindler and J. Toman, *The Laws of Armed Conflicts: A Collection of Conventions, Resolutions and Other Documents*, 4th edn (Nijhoff, 2004), 3. See also, Richard Shelly Hartigan, *Lieber's Code of the Law of War* (Chicago: Precedent Publishing, 1983).

[112] Art. 15.

[113] Arts. 22–3 and 34–8.

[114] Art. 49.

[115] Arts. 49–59.

[116] Arts. 105–47.

[117] See G. Willemin, R. Heacock, and J. Freymond, *The International Committee of the Red Cross* (Nijhoff, 1984); P. Boissier, *From Solferino to Tsushima* (Henry Dunant Institute, 1985); A. Durand, *Histoire du*

MARY ELLEN O'CONNELL

119   The 1864 Geneva Convention for the Amelioration of the Condition of the
Wounded in Armies in the Field defined the legal status of medical personnel. It
stipulated that wounded enemy soldiers were to be collected and cared for in the
same way as members of friendly armed forces. These rules were extended and
improved by the Geneva Convention for the Amelioration of the Condition of the
Wounded and Sick in Armies in the Field of 1906.

The 1864 Geneva Convention marks the beginning of the development of what has
become known as 'Geneva Law'. In contrast to Hague Law (see commentary to Sections
121, 127), Geneva Law is written from the standpoint of the 'victims' of armed conflict:
the wounded, sick, shipwrecked, prisoners of war, and civilians. It does not purport to
define the rights and duties of the military but rather to lay down certain basic obligations designed to protect those victims, while leaving to customary law and Hague Law
questions which do not fall within its provisions. The borderline between Hague and
Geneva Law has now largely been eroded and AP I contains elements of both these legal
traditions. The 1864 and 1906 Conventions have been superseded by the more detailed
provisions of GC I and GC II, 1949.[118] Certain principles are, however, common to
all these treaties. All provide that the parties to a conflict must not only abstain from
attacking the wounded and medical personnel attending them, but must also collect and
provide care for them. The use of the Red Cross emblem (and later the Red Crescent and
Red Diamond) as a protected sign also stems from these conventions.[119]

120   The 1868 Declaration of St Petersburg was the first to introduce limitations on the
use of weapons of war. It codified the customary principle, still valid today, prohibiting the use of weapons to cause unnecessary suffering. It also confirmed that 'the
only legitimate object which States should endeavour to accomplish during war is
to weaken the military forces of the enemy'.

1. The Declaration of St Petersburg was the result of an initiative by the Russian government to obtain the agreement of the major powers to outlaw the use in war between
themselves of 'rifle shells', small projectiles which exploded or caught fire on impact.[120]
These exploding or inflammable bullets caused far worse injuries than the ordinary
bullets of the time (the effects of which were almost invariably disabling and frequently
fatal). The Preamble to the Declaration states that: 'the only legitimate object which
States should endeavour to accomplish during war is to weaken the military forces of
the enemy; for this purpose it is sufficient to disable the greatest possible number of men;
this object would be exceeded by the employment of arms which uselessly aggravate the
sufferings of disabled men or render their death inevitable'. It concludes that 'the employment of such arms would, therefore, be contrary to the laws of humanity'. The parties
therefore agreed to renounce the use, in conflicts between themselves, of 'any projectile
of a weight below 400 grammes, which is either explosive or charged with fulminating
or inflammable substances'. This provision remains in force and has now acquired the

Comité international de la Croix-Rouge, two vols (Henry Dunant Institute, 1978). See also Frits Kalshoven
and Lisbeth Zegveld, *Constraints on the Waging of War: An Introduction to International Humanitarian Law*,
4th edn (ICRC, 2011).

[118] See Chapter 6 below.
[119] The Red Diamond was added in AP III of 2005, which entered into force in 2007.
[120] F. Kalshoven, 'Arms, Armaments and International Law' [1985 II] 191 RdC 183, 205. See also,
R. L. O'Connell, *Of Arms and Men: A History of War, Weapons, and Aggression* (OUP, 1989).

MARY ELLEN O'CONNELL

status of customary international law, although the evolution of aerial warfare led to it being interpreted as permitting the use of such projectiles against aircraft.[121]

2. The importance of the 1868 Declaration lies not so much in the specific ban which it introduced as in its statement of the principles on which that ban was based. The Preamble to the Declaration reflects the theories developed by Rousseau nearly a century earlier[122] and is the classic statement of the principle that it is prohibited to employ weapons or methods of warfare which are likely to cause unnecessary suffering.[123] Humanitarian law accepts that one of the legitimate objects of warfare is to disable enemy combatants (and in many cases this necessarily involves killing) but it rejects the use of weapons which cause additional suffering for no military gain.[124] That principle continues today as one of the general principles of humanitarian law by which the legality of all weapons and means of warfare fall to be measured. It also inspired a number of other international agreements banning specific weapons, such as poison gas and soft-headed or 'Dum-Dum' bullets.[125]

> **The 1874 Brussels Declaration provided the first comprehensive code of the   121
> laws and customs of war. That Declaration was further developed at the Hague
> Peace Conferences of 1899 and 1907. The most important result was the Hague
> Regulations Concerning the Laws and Customs of War on Land (HagueReg).**

The conference which drew up the Brussels Declaration was also the result of a Russian initiative, although some of the inspiration for the project lay in the earlier Lieber Code. The Declaration[126] itself was never ratified but many of its provisions were incorporated into the Manual of the Laws and Customs of War adopted by the Institut de Droit International at its Oxford session in 1880 ('the Oxford Manual').[127] The Brussels Declaration and the Oxford Manual, although not legally binding, were highly influential and many of the provisions of the Hague Regulations can be traced back to them. Although parts of the Regulations have been superseded by the Geneva Conventions and AP I, many remain in force and are now regarded as declaratory of customary international law.[128] Thus, the section of the Regulations dealing with the government of occupied territory is still of considerable importance and is generally regarded as applicable to current occupations.[129]

> **World War I, with its new munitions and unprecedented extension of combat   122
> actions, demonstrated the limits of the existing law.**

The most important development of World War I, in so far as it affected humanitarian law, was the evolution of aerial warfare and other forms of long-range bombardment.

---

[121] See, e.g., Art. 18, para. 1, HRAW 1923. The closest relevant provision in the *HPCR Manual* is Section C, Weapons, 6: 'Specific weapons are prohibited in air or missile combat operations, these include (e) small arms projectiles calculated, or of a nature, to cause explosion on impact with or within the human body.'

[122] See Section 120 above.

[123] See now Art. 35, para. 1, AP I and Art. 23, lit. e, HagueReg. See also Section 131 below.

[124] See Chapter 4.

[125] See Section 129 below.

[126] D. Schindler and J. Toman (n. 113), 25.

[127] D. Schindler and J. Toman (n. 113), 35.

[128] Decision of the International Military Tribunal in Nuremberg.

[129] See Eyal Benvenisti, *The International Law of Occupation*, 2nd edn (OUP, 2011). See also, Tristan Ferraro (ed.), *Occupation, and Other Forms of Administration of Foreign Territory* (ICRC, 2012) available at <http://www.icrc.org/eng/assets/files/publications/icrc-002-4094.pdf>.

MARY ELLEN O'CONNELL

These took place in spite of the requirement of Article 25 HagueReg, that attacks on undefended towns and villages were prohibited. An undefended town was defined as one which could be captured without the use of force (a legacy of early customary rules which distinguished between the treatment of a city taken by storm and one which surrendered). Aerial warfare opened up the possibility of bombarding towns hundreds of miles behind enemy lines. These towns might be undefended in the sense that no forces were stationed near them, but they did not fall within the terms of Article 25 because they could not be captured without force. Aerial warfare thus posed an unprecedented threat to civilians for which the existing laws made no provision. World War I also revealed deficiencies in the legal protection of the wounded and prisoners of war, which led to the adoption of new Geneva Conventions in 1929 (see Section 124). The widespread use of poison gas during World War I also resulted in the adoption in 1925 of the Geneva Gas Protocol.[130]

123   In 1923, the Hague Rules of Aerial Warfare (HRAW 1923) were formulated, together with rules concerning the control of radio communications in times of war. Although they were never legally adopted, they were influential in the development of legal opinion. Harvard University's Program on Humanitarian Policy and Conflict Research developed a manual in 2010 elaborating on the rules of air and missile warfare (*HPCR Manual*).[131]

1. World War I had highlighted the danger to the civilian population from aerial warfare, and in the aftermath of that war numerous proposals were made to subject aerial warfare to new legal constraints. The obvious military advantages of aerial warfare, however, prevented agreement on a new legal regime at the Washington Conference on the Limitation of Armaments, 1921–1922. Nevertheless, some of the states represented at that conference appointed a Commission of Jurists, chaired by the US lawyer John Bassett Moore, with representatives from France, Italy, Japan, the Netherlands, and the UK, to investigate the subject and to make proposals. That Commission drew up the HRAW 1923 in an attempt to achieve a balance between military interests and the protection of the civilian population. The rules[132] prohibited attacks on civilians and aerial bombardment 'for the purpose of terrorizing the civilian population'.[133] Attacks had to be confined to military objectives, and in Article 24 the Commission attempted to draw up a list of these. Certain objectives were given special protection and the Rules also included a duty to minimize incidental civilian casualties.

2. The HRAW 1923 were never legally adopted and their principles were widely disregarded during World War II.[134] The attempt to devise a list of military objectives was probably doomed to failure, since objectives which have military value will vary over time and from one conflict to another. Nevertheless, although they never entered into force, the Rules were widely regarded at the time as an important statement of the legal principles which should govern aerial warfare. The basic principles which they laid down, though not the list of targets, were embodied in a resolution of the Assembly of the League of

---

[130] See Section 129 below.
[131] See Section 104 below.
[132] For more detailed consideration, see Sections 326–31 and 449–52.
[133] Art. 22.
[134] See J. M. Spaight, *Air Power and War Rights*, 3rd edn (London: Longmans, 1947).

MARY ELLEN O'CONNELL

Nations in 1938. That resolution (modelled on a statement by the Prime Minister of the UK to the House of Commons) recognized the urgent need for the adoption of regulations dealing with aerial warfare and stipulated that the Assembly: 'Recognizes the following principles as a necessary basis for any subsequent regulations: (1) The intentional bombing of civilian populations is illegal; (2) Objectives aimed at from the air must be legitimate military objectives and must be identifiable; (3) Any attack on legitimate military objectives must be carried out in such a way that civilian populations in the neighbourhood are not bombed through negligence.'[135]

3. After World War II, the ICRC drew up in 1956 the Delhi Draft Rules for the Limitation of the Dangers Incurred by the Civilian Population in Time of War.[136] These Draft Rules and the *ICRC Commentary* upon them show the influence of the HRAW 1923. More importantly, many of the principles laid down in the 1923 Rules have been adopted, albeit in a modified form, in AP I of 1977, and have thus become binding treaty law. In 2010, many of the rules were included in the *HPCR Manual*.

> **In 1929, the Convention for the Amelioration of the Condition of the Wounded** 124
> **and Sick in Armies in the Field and the Convention relative to the Treatment of**
> **Prisoners of War were signed in Geneva. They developed the terms of the Geneva**
> **Convention of 1906 and part of the Hague Regulations of 1907.**

The 1929 Geneva Conventions[137] were influenced by the experience of World War I and contained more detailed regulations for the treatment of the wounded and prisoners of war than their predecessors. Although the Conventions were in force during World War II, some of the major protagonists, including the USSR and Japan, were not parties to them. Nevertheless, at the end of the war, tribunals in a number of war crimes trials ruled that the main provisions of the Prisoners of War Convention had become part of customary international law and were thus binding on all states by 1939.[138] The 1929 Conventions have now been superseded[139] by the 1949 Geneva Conventions.

> **The first regulations on naval warfare were already developed by the Middle** 125
> **Ages. These regulations, which primarily embodied the right to search vessels**
> **and their cargo and the right of seizure, were subsequently changed several**
> **times. The treatment of ships belonging to neutral states lacked uniform regula-**
> **tion and was disputed. In the Baltic Sea, the Hanseatic League used its almost**
> **unrestricted naval supremacy to enforce embargoes in times of war, which were**
> **not only detrimental to its adversary, but also made it impossible for neutral**
> **states to trade with that adversary. The ability of neutral states to pursue their**
> **maritime trade activities in times of war could only override the attempts by**
> **belligerents to cut their adversaries off from ship-to-shore supplies if the position**
> **of these powerful neutral states was secured. In the eighteenth century, this led**
> **to the formation of alliances between neutral states, and to the deployment of**

---

[135] D. Schindler and J. Toman, (n. 111), 221.
[136] D. Schindler and J. Toman, (n. 111), 251.
[137] D, Schindler and J. Toman, (n. 111), 325 and 339.
[138] *US v von Leeb*, 15 *Annual Digest* 376; R. R. Baxter, 'Multilateral Treaties as Evidence of Customary International Law' (1965–6) 41 *BYIL* 286.
[139] While it took some time for states parties to the 1929 Conventions to become parties to the 1949 Conventions, the latter are today universally binding. See below, Section 126, para. 1.

MARY ELLEN O'CONNELL

their naval forces to protect their right to free maritime trade. The 1856 Paris Declaration Concerning Maritime Law was the first agreement to address the protection of neutral maritime trade. A major restatement of current international principles and rules at sea was achieved by an international group of legal and naval experts with the 1995 San Remo Manual on International Law Applicable to Armed Conflicts at Sea.

1. Although the law of naval warfare has never been subjected to such detailed regulation by treaty as the law of land warfare, the customary law on the subject developed at an earlier date. This development was largely due to the fact that naval warfare involved a far greater degree of contact between combatants and neutrals and so brought into conflict the right of a combatant to conduct war effectively and the right of a neutral state's shipping to enjoy the freedom of the seas. Moreover, the law of naval warfare was unusual in that each warring nation established a tribunal (or series of tribunals) to rule on the legality of interference with neutral shipping. The British Prize Court played a particularly important part in the development of the laws of naval warfare, since throughout the eighteenth and nineteenth centuries Great Britain was the dominant maritime power. Nevertheless, belligerent treatment of neutral shipping remained a source of controversy and the US, which remained neutral throughout the French Revolutionary and Napoleonic wars, engaged in hostilities with France (1797–1801) and Britain (1812–1815) partly on account of what it regarded as the infringement of neutral rights.

2. The influence of neutral states generally declined after the late eighteenth century and the balance tipped in favour of belligerent rights, although the Paris Declaration went some way to arrest this process. The US, which had been a champion of neutral rights in the period 1789–1815, took a broad view of the rights of a belligerent during the Civil War (1861–1865), greatly extending for example the doctrine of continuous voyage. This process was taken even further during the World Wars of the twentieth century, although some rights of belligerents narrowed. For example, the practice of capturing prizes came to an end, and the extension of the Geneva Conventions to protections of victims of armed conflict at sea introduced new constraints in the waging of war at sea.

3. The Paris Declaration of 1856 was important not only for its provisions on neutrality but also for its abolition of privateering, in which a belligerent authorized private shipping to prey upon the enemy's merchant ships.

III. Legal Sources

126   The four Geneva Conventions have come to be internationally binding upon all states:

— Geneva Convention I for the Amelioration of the Condition of the Wounded and Sick in Armed Forces in the Field (GC I);
— Geneva Convention II for the Amelioration of the Condition of the Wounded, Sick and Shipwrecked Members of Armed Forces at Sea (GC II);
— Geneva Convention III Concerning the Treatment of Prisoners of War (GC III);
— Geneva Convention IV Concerning the Protection of Civilian Persons in Time of War (GC IV).

MARY ELLEN O'CONNELL

The Geneva Conventions of 1949 have now achieved universal participation with 194 parties (there are 193 members of the UN). Since the Conventions will therefore apply as treaties in almost any international armed conflict, the question of whether their provisions have achieved the status of customary international law might be thought irrelevant. It may, however, still be significant in two respects. First, the decision of the International Court of Justice in *Nicaragua v US*[140] shows that an international tribunal may sometimes be able to apply rules of customary international law even though it lacks the competence to apply the provisions of a multilateral treaty. Second, in some states (noticeably the UK and many Commonwealth countries, as well as Israel) treaties do not form part of national legislation and cannot be applied by national courts, whereas national courts can and do apply rules of customary international law.[141] It seems likely that most, if not all, of the provisions of the Conventions would now be regarded as declaratory of customary international law.[142]

> The 1907 Hague Conventions are binding not only upon the contracting parties, but have also been largely recognized as customary law. The documents relevant to international humanitarian law are:
> — Hague Convention IV Concerning the Laws and Customs of War on Land (HC IV), and Annex to the Convention: Regulations Concerning the Laws and Customs of War on Land (HagueReg);
> — Hague Convention V Concerning the Rights and Duties of Neutral Powers and Persons in Case of War on Land (HC V);
> — Hague Convention VI Concerning the Status of Enemy Merchant Ships at the Outbreak of Hostilities (HC VI);
> — Hague Convention VII Concerning the Conversion of Merchant Ships into Warships (HC VII);
> — Hague Convention VIII Concerning the Laying of Automatic Submarine Contact Mines (HC VIII);
> — Hague Convention IX Concerning Bombardment by Naval Forces in Times of War (HC IX);
> — Hague Convention XI Concerning Certain Restrictions with Regard to the Exercise of the Right of Capture in Naval War (HC XI);
> — Hague Convention XIII Concerning the Rights and Duties of Neutral Powers in Naval War (HC XIII).

127

1. The current importance of some Hague Conventions is greater than others. HC IV and the annexed Regulations remain of the utmost importance. Articles 42–56 HagueReg still constitute the principal text on the government of occupied territory and the treatment of property in occupied territory.[143] In addition, the provisions on methods and

---

[140] *ICJ Reports 1986*, 14; R. Abi-Saab, 'The General Principles of Humanitarian Law According to the International Court of Justice' (1987) 29 *IRRC* 367.

[141] See F. Jacobs and S. Roberts, *The Effects of Treaties in Domestic Law* (Sweet & Maxwell, 1987); Theodor Meron, *Human Rights and Humanitarian Norms as Customary International Law* (OUP, 1989), 3–78; M. Bothe, P. Macalister-Smith, and T. Kurzidem (eds), *National Implementation of International Humanitarian Law*. Proceedings of a Colloquium held at Bad Homburg, 17–19 June 1988 (Dordrecht: Nijhoff, 1990), 1–71.

[142] See generally on the subject of rules of international humanitarian law as customary international law, *CIHL*. See also T. Meron (n. 141), 61–2 and the Kammergericht, Berlin, of 13 July 1967, 60 *ILR*, 208, *Fontes Iuris Gentium, Series A, Section II, I Tomus 6* 234. See also Section 134 below.

[143] See Sections 526–587.

MARY ELLEN O'CONNELL

means of warfare,[144] on spies,[145] on flags of truce, and on armistices[146] retain importance even though for parties to AP I the sections on spies and methods and means of warfare have now been largely superseded. The International Military Tribunal at Nuremberg held that the provisions of the Regulations had become part of customary international law by 1939 and accordingly they are binding on all states. Their application as customary law has recently been confirmed by the ICJ.[147]

2. By contrast, the provisions of HC III, which require that hostilities should not 'commence without prior and explicit warning, in the form either of a declaration of war, giving reasons, or of an ultimatum with conditional declaration of war' has been completely disregarded. Since 1945, declarations of war have become virtually unknown[148] and it is difficult to regard HC III as a rule of contemporary customary international law.

3. In some respects, the most important of the Hague Conventions are those dealing with the law of naval warfare, although the status of many of their provisions is uncertain today. Their provisions and current legal status are considered in Chapters 10 and 11.

128   The three Protocols Additional to the Geneva Conventions are designed to reaffirm and develop the rules embodied in the laws of Geneva of 1949 and part of the laws of The Hague of 1907:
— Protocol of 8 June 1977 Additional to the Geneva Conventions of 12 August 1949, and Concerning the Protection of Victims of International Armed Conflicts (AP I);
— Protocol of 8 June 1977 Additional to the Geneva Conventions of 12 August 1949, and Concerning the Protection of Victims of Non-International Armed Conflicts (AP II); and
— Protocol of 8 December 2005 Additional to the Geneva Conventions of 12 August 1949, Relating to the Adoption of an Additional Distinctive Emblem (AP III).

1. The Additional Protocols of 1977 have not yet achieved the near-universal acceptance achieved by the 1949 Geneva Conventions. By 2014, there were 173 parties to AP I and 167 to AP II. However, the US and a number of other significant military powers (such as Iran, Israel, and India) have so far decided not to become parties to AP I.[149] Protocol III, which is far more restricted in its scope, has 67 parties.

2. *The legal effects of Additional Protocol I.* AP I was first applicable in the Kosovo conflict in 1999. It was technically only applicable between the Federal Republic of Yugoslavia and those NATO states that had become party to AP I.[150] However, NATO inter-operability requirements meant AP I was generally applied by NATO member states. Moreover, many of AP I's provisions are declaratory of customary international law or reflect general

---

[144] Arts. 22–8.
[145] Arts. 29–31.
[146] Arts. 32–41.
[147] ICJ, *Case Concerning Armed Activities on the Territory of the Congo (DRC v Uganda), ICJ Reports 2005.*
[148] See Section 203.
[149] For a statement on the extent to which the US regards AP I reflective of customary international law, see Michael Matheson, 'The United States' Position on the Relation of Customary International Law to the 1977 Protocols Additional to the 1949 Geneva Conventions' (1987) 2 *American University International Law Review* 419.
[150] See C. Greenwood, *Essays* (n. 3), 631.

principles of law and are thus applicable in all international armed conflicts.[151] The influence of the declaratory provisions of AP I is illustrated by the 1990–1991 Kuwait conflict. Although the Protocol was not generally applicable to that conflict, since several of the main protagonists including Iraq were not parties, the targeting policy announced by the coalition states reflected Articles 48–57, most of which are widely regarded as declaratory of custom, or as representing developments of customary law which are generally acceptable to the international community.[152] Thus, the coalition made clear that it would attack only military objectives and its announcement of this policy was in terms very similar to those of Article 52 AP I. Coalition announcements that every effort would be made to avoid excessive collateral damage and civilian casualties were also couched in language very similar to that of Articles 51, para. 5, lit. b, and 57.[153] The ICRC's appeals to the parties during the conflict also reflected the language of the Protocol.[154] Even those provisions of AP I that may not yet have achieved the status of rules of customary international law (e.g. the rules on protection of the natural environment in Articles 35, para. 3, and 55) have influenced public opinion and the perceptions of states as to what is permissible in conflict. Thus, reference was made to the environmental provisions of AP I in a number of governmental and ICRC pronouncements during the Kuwait conflict.[155]

3. *Additional Protocol II.* AP II lays down rules for certain non-international conflicts (NIAC), developing them beyond the more general provisions of common Article 3 of the 1949 Geneva Conventions. AP II was applicable in the civil war in El Salvador[156] and in 2012 was being applied in Afghanistan by the United Nations Assistance Mission to Afghanistan (UNAMA), NATO, the International Security Assistance Force (ISAF), and Afghan forces.[157] It is also now accepted that many of the rules reflected in AP II are part of customary international law.[158] Certain conceptual controversies remain,

---

[151] C. Greenwood, 'Customary Law Status of the 1977 Geneva Protocols' in A. J. M. Delissen and G. J. Tanja (eds), *Humanitarian Law of Armed Conflict—Challenges Ahead: Essays in Honour of Frits Kalshoven* (Nijhoff, 1991), 93; T. Meron (n. 141), 62; D. Fleck, 'The Protocols Additional to the Geneva Conventions and Customary International Law' (1990) XXIX *RDMilG* 497; Cassese, 'The Geneva Protocols of 1977 on the Humanitarian Law of Armed Conflict and Customary International Law' (1984) 3 *UCLA Pacific Basin Law Journal* 55.

[152] C. Greenwood, 'Customary International Law and the First Geneva Protocol of 1977 in the Gulf Conflict' in P. Rowe (ed.), *The Gulf War 1990–91 in International and English Law* (London: Sweet & Maxwell, 1993).

[153] See the US Department of Defense, Conduct of the Persian Gulf War: An Interim Report to Congress (1991); C. Greenwood, (n. 152).

[154] ICRC, 'Action by the International Committee of the Red Cross in the event of violations of international humanitarian law or of other fundamental rules protecting persons in situations of violence' (2005) 858 *ICRC* 393.

[155] See the US Department of Defense (n. 149); ICRC statement at *IRRC* (1991), 25 and 27; but cf. the US Department of Defense *Final Report to Congress: Conduct of the Persian Gulf War* Appendix O, 0–26.

[156] See, e.g., ICRC, *Annual Report* 1989.

[157] See UNAMA, *Afghanistan, Midyear Report 2011, Protection of Civilians in Afghanistan*, <http://unama.unmissions.org/Portals/UNAMA/Documents/2011%20Midyear%20POC.pdf> (accessed 23 July 2012). It is expected that after 2014, AP II will continue to be applied, see, Memorandum of Understanding between the Islamic Republic of Afghanistan and the United States of America on Afghanization of Special Operations on Afghanistan Soil, 8 April 2012, <http://www.afghanistan-un.org/2012/04/memorandum-of-understanding-between-the-islamic-republic-of-afghanistan-and-the-united-states-of-america-on-afghanization-of-special-operations-on-afghan-soil/> (accessed 23 July 2012). See also Rule of Law in Armed Conflicts Project, www.geneva-academy.ch.

[158] See *CIHL*.

MARY ELLEN O'CONNELL

however.[159] Article 1 AP II stipulates that the rules apply in non-international armed conflicts wherein an organized armed group controls territory within a state party to the Protocol. This raises the issue respecting what rules of international humanitarian law apply in other armed conflicts besides international armed conflicts to which the customary law rules of AP I apply as just described. Would AP II rules that are part of customary international law apply beyond the restrictive scope provision of AP II to all non-international armed conflicts? Another serious controversy concerns the implications of AP II targeting and detention rules. Some scholars contend that only the regular armed forces of a state have the so-called 'combatant's privilege' to kill during armed conflict without facing prosecution, so long as international humanitarian law is followed. This position means that regardless of how carefully members of a non-state actor organized armed group comply with the targeting rules of AP II or other customary international law targeting rules, the members will be subject to prosecution at the conclusion of the fighting. Similarly, despite detailed detention rules in AP II, some contend that regardless of how carefully the non-state actor complies with the rules, the non-state group has no right to detain enemy combatants during a non-international armed conflict. Yet, there is little or no state practice demanding that non-state actors that defeat their opponents are subject to enforcement of laws against unlawful killing or arbitrary detention. The better view may be that within an armed conflict, as defined by international law,[160] members of non-state organized armed groups must obey, at the least, the customary law of non-international armed conflict and may claim the belligerent's privilege to kill without warning and detain without trial.

129   Other agreements refer to specific issues of warfare and the protection of certain legal assets. The most important documents are:
— St Petersburg Declaration of 11 December 1868 Renouncing the Use, in Times of War, of Explosive Projectiles under 400 grammes Weight (PetersburgDecl 1868);
— Hague Declaration of 29 July 1899 Concerning Expanding Bullets, so-called 'dum-dum bullets' (Dum-Dum Bullets HagueDecl 1899);
— Geneva Protocol of 17 June 1925 for the Prohibition of the Use in War of Asphyxiating, Poisonous or Other Gases and of Bacteriological Methods of Warfare—Geneva Protocol on Gas Warfare (GasProt);
— London Procès-Verbal on 6 November 1936 Concerning the Rules of Submarine Warfare (LondonProt 1936);
— Hague Convention of 14 May 1954 for the Protection of Cultural Property in the Event of Armed Conflict—Cultural Property Convention (CultPropConv) with Protocols adopted on 14 May 1954 and 26 May 1999;
— Convention of 10 April 1972 on the Prohibition of the Development, Production and Stockpiling of Bacteriological (Biological) and Toxin Weapons and on their Destruction—Biological Weapons Convention (BWC);
— Convention of 18 May 1977 on the Prohibition of Military or any Other Hostile Use of Environmental Modification Techniques—ENMOD Convention (ENMOD);

---

[159] See below, Section 1201, and commentary para. 5. See also 11th Bruges Colloquium Proceedings, *Technological Challenges for the Humanitarian Legal Framework*, (ICRC, 2010); M. E. O'Connell, 'Saving Lives through a Definition of International Armed Conflict', 10th Bruges Colloquium Proceedings (ICRC, 2009), 19.
[160] ILA Use of Force Committee, *Final Report on the Meaning of Armed Conflict in International Law* (The Hague Conference 2010).

MARY ELLEN O'CONNELL

— Convention of 10 October 1980 on Prohibitions or Restrictions on the Use of Certain Conventional Weapons which May be Deemed to be Excessively Injurious or to Have Indiscriminate Effects (CCCW, amended on 20 December 2001) with Protocols adopted on 10 October 1980, 13 October 1995, 3 May 1996, and 28 November 2003;

— International Convention of 4 December 1989 Against the Recruitment, Use, Financing and Training of Mercenaries (MercenaryConv);

— Convention of 13 January 1993 on the Prohibition of the Development, Production, Stockpiling and Use of Chemical Weapons and on their Destruction (Chemical WeaponsConv);

— Ottawa Convention of 3 December 1997 on the Prohibition of the Use, Stockpiling, Production, and Transfer of Anti-personnel Mines and on their Destruction (LandMinesConv);

— Rome Statute of the International Criminal Court of 17 July 1998 (ICC Statute, amended on 10 and 11 June 2010);

— Dublin Convention of 30 May 2008 on Cluster Munitions;

— Arms Trade Treaty of 2 April 2013.[161]

1. Most of the agreements listed in this section concern weapons and means of warfare and are dealt with in greater detail in Chapter 4. The PetersburgDecl 1868 and the HagueDecl 1899 have already been the subject of comment.[162] Both remain in force and are widely regarded as declaratory of customary law.

2. The GasProt 1925 is also still in force and now has more than one hundred signatories. The ban on chemical and biological weapons which it imposed has generally been observed, although Iraq employed poisonous gas in breach of the Protocol on several occasions during the Iran–Iraq War[163] and threatened to do so during the Kuwait conflict. Following the use of gas in the Iran–Iraq War, the ban on chemical and biological weapons was expressly reaffirmed in a resolution adopted by the Paris Conference on the Prohibition of Chemical Weapons in 1989.[164] Although the GasProt has attracted a large number of parties, many states have made their acceptance of the Protocol subject to a reservation to the effect that they retain the right to use chemical weapons in the event that such weapons are first used against them or their allies.[165] These reservations are based on reciprocity, that is a state engaged in a conflict against one of the reserving states would also be entitled to rely upon the reservation to justify a retaliatory use of chemical weapons. The Protocol is therefore at present effective only as a ban on the first use of the weapons to which it applies. The Protocol bans only the use, not the possession of these weapons. Both the possession and use (including retaliatory use) of chemical weapons are, however, unlawful under the Convention on the Prohibition of the Development, Production, Stockpiling and Use of Chemical Weapons and on their Destruction, 1993, which is framed in absolute terms.[166]

---

[161] See below, p 33. For details, see the website of the UN Office for Disarmament Affairs, <http://www.un.org/disarmament/ convarms/ArmsTrade/>.

[162] See commentary to Section 120.

[163] See UN Docs. S/20060 and 20063 (1988).

[164] (1989) *ILM* 28, 1020. (1989) *Europa-Archiv* 111.

[165] See, e.g., the reservations by France and the US, in A. Roberts and R. Guelff (eds), Documents on the Law of War, 3rd edn (OUP, 2000), 144–6.

[166] See Sections 437–39.

MARY ELLEN O'CONNELL

3. The possession of biological weapons was outlawed by the Biological Weapons Convention of 10 April 1972.

4. The Certain Conventional Weapons Convention of 1980 is an umbrella agreement and provisions banning or restricting the use of specific weapons or means of warfare are contained in a series of Protocols annexed to it. As of 2012, there were five Protocols, dealing with weapons which injure with fragments which cannot be detected by X-rays (Protocol I), mines, booby traps, and other devices (Protocol II),[167] certain uses of incendiary weapons (Protocol III), blinding laser weapons (Protocol IV), and explosive remnants of war (Protocol V). A state must accept at least two of the Protocols if it becomes party to the Convention. The Convention provides for the adoption of additional protocols.[168]

5. The ENMOD Convention is designed to prevent the deliberate manipulation of the environment for military purposes (and is thus distinct from the provisions of API which concern incidental damage to the environment).

6. The Cultural Property Convention was adopted in 1954 in order to prevent attacks on and the looting of buildings and works of cultural, historical, and religious significance which had been a feature of World War II. In 2014, the Convention had 126 state parties; most major military powers have joined, with the notable exception of the UK.[169] The principles underlying the Convention are incorporated in Article 53 AP I. The protection of cultural property is dealt with in Chapter 9.

7. The London Procès-Verbal of 1936 is discussed in Chapter 10. Its requirement that submarines should conform to the rules applicable to surface vessels in their dealings with merchant ships was widely disregarded in World War II, and the status of the Procès-Verbal today has therefore been the subject of some controversy. Nevertheless, it seems that the agreement remains valid, although some of the assumptions on which it was based may have changed.[170]

8. The Mercenaries Convention develops the provisions of Article 47 AP I, which is discussed in Section 303, below.

9. The Landmines Convention is an absolute ban on the possession or use of anti-personnel landmines to which 161 states were party in June 2014. Unlike most of the other treaties considered here, it binds the states party to it irrespective of whether they are engaged in conflict or not and irrespective of whether their adversary is party to the Convention.

10. The Cluster Munitions Convention is also an absolute ban on the possession or use of cluster munitions. Cluster munitions are bombs containing numerous bomblets or submunitions. Their purpose is to deny access of a wider area than may occur with

---

[167] Many states are parties to an amended and more extensive version of Protocol II adopted in 1996.
[168] Art. 8.
[169] After many years as a signatory only, the US ratified the Hague Convention in 2009. See <http://portal.unesco.org/en/ev.php-URL_ID=13637&URL_DO=DO_TOPIC&URL_SECTION=201.html>.
[170] R. Tucker, *The Law of War and Neutrality at Sea* (US Govt. Print Office, 1957), 67; E. I. Nwogogu, 'Commentary on Submarine Warfare' in N. Ronzitti (ed.), *The Law of Naval Warfare: A Collection of Agreements and Documents with Commentaries* (Nijhoff, 1988), 359–60.

MARY ELLEN O'CONNELL

the use of a unitary munition, but inevitably a certain number of submunitions do not explode when the bomb is dropped. These explosive remnants of war have led to deaths even long after a conflict has ended. In June 2014, the Cluster Munitions Convention had 84 states party.

11. The unregulated trade in conventional weapons, especially small arms, has long been linked to the prolongation and exacerbation of armed conflicts. In April 2013, after many years of effort and several failures, the Arms Trade Treaty (ATT) was adopted, leaving many issues still unsolved. It remains the case, as of time of writing, the trade in bananas is more highly regulated than trade in weapons.[171] In June 2014, it had 40 parties.

> **Many rules of international humanitarian law are binding as rules of customary**   130
> **international law or general principles of law.**

The extent to which provisions of humanitarian law treaties have become declaratory of custom is considered above.[172]

> **If an act of war is not expressly prohibited by international agreements or**   131
> **customary law, this does not necessarily mean that it is actually permissible.**
> **The Martens Clause, developed by the Livonian Professor Friedrich von Martens**
> **(1845–1909), delegate of Tsar Nicholas II at the Hague Peace Conferences, which**
> **was included in the Preamble to the 1907 Hague Convention IV and reaf-**
> **firmed in the 1977 Additional Protocol I and other international treaties, provides**
> **as follows:**
>
> > 'In cases not covered by international agreements, civilians and combatants remain
> > under the protection and authority of the principles of international law derived
> > from established custom, from the principles of humanity and from the dictates of
> > public conscience.'

1. The Martens Clause[173] was originally devised to cope with a disagreement between the parties to The Hague Peace Conferences regarding the status of resistance movements in occupied territory.[174] Those states which had argued that inhabitants of occupied territory who took up arms against the occupying forces should be treated as lawful combatants had been unable to obtain a majority for their proposal and the provisions on combatant status in Articles 1 and 2 HagueReg did not include resistance fighters in the list of those entitled to combatant status. The Martens Clause was seen by many states as a reminder that Articles 1 and 2 should not be seen as the last word on the subject of

---

[171] See The Arms Trade Treaty, available at <http://www.un.org/disarmament/ATT/>; see also 'UN Arms Trade Conference Fails', DW (Deutsche Welle) 29 July 2012, available at <http://www.dw.de/dw/article/0,, 16129663,00.html>; M. M. Mutschler, 'Regeln für den internationalen Waffenhandel. Wie es nach dem vorläufigen Scheitern mit den Verhandlungen über einen Waffenhandelsvertrag weitergehen sollte' (Stiftung Wissenschaft und Politik, 49 *SWP-Aktuell* August 2012) <http://www.swp-berlin.org/de/publikationen/ swp-studien-de/swp-studien-detail/article/regeln_fuer_den_internationalen_waffenhandel.html>.

[172] See R. R. Baxter (n. 134), *CIHL*, and Greenwood, *Essays* (n. 3), 179.

[173] J. von Bernstorff, 'Martens Clause' in *MPEPIL*; A. Cassese, 'The Martens Clause: Half a Loaf or Simply Pie in the Sky?' (2000) 11 *EJIL* 187. See also T. Meron, 'The Martens Clause, Principles of Humanity and Dictates of Public Conscience' (2000) 94/1 *AJIL* 78–89.

[174] See Sections 309–10 and commentary thereon.

MARY ELLEN O'CONNELL

combatant status and that the question of whether resistance fighters were entitled to that status should not be decided simply by pointing to their omission from Articles 1 and 2 but should be resolved by reference to '*des principes du droit des gens, tels qu'ils resultent des usages établis entre nations civilisées, des lois d'humanité et des exigences de la conscience publique*'.[175] Today, however, the Martens Clause is applicable to the whole of humanitarian law and it appears, in one form or another, in most of the modern treaties on humanitarian law.[176]

2. The exact significance of the Clause is more difficult to assess. It certainly means that the mere omission of a matter in a treaty does not mean that international law should necessarily be regarded as silent on that subject, and serves as a reminder that the adoption of the treaty in question does not preclude protection by customary international law. What is not clear is whether the Martens Clause goes further and introduces into humanitarian law a rule that all weapons and means of warfare are to be judged against the standard of 'the public conscience' even if their use does not contravene the specific rules of customary international law such as the unnecessary suffering principle.[177] Although this suggestion has been made from time to time,[178] it is impracticable since 'the public conscience' is too vague a concept to be used as the basis for a separate rule of law and has attracted little support. The Martens Clause should be treated as a reminder that customary international law continues to apply even after the adoption of a treaty on humanitarian law and as a statement of the factors which are likely to lead states to adopt a ban on a particular weapon or means of warfare. Moreover, as new weapons and launch systems continue to be developed, incorporating ever more sophisticated robotic and computer technology, the venerable Martens Clause will ensure that that technology will not outpace the law.

IV. Humanitarian Requirements and Military Necessity

132   **In armed conflict, a belligerent may apply only that amount and kind of force necessary to defeat the enemy. Acts of war are only permissible if they are directed against military objectives, if they are not likely to cause unnecessary suffering, and if they are not perfidious.**

1. *Necessity and proportionality in humanitarian law.* The principle that a belligerent may apply only that amount and kind of force necessary to defeat the enemy prohibits unnecessary or wanton application of force and is a long-established principle of humanitarian law. Thus, Articles 14–16 of the Lieber Code[179] make clear that only the necessary use of force against persons and property is permissible. Similarly, the *US Naval Manual* (1997)

---

[175] The original form of the clause.
[176] Art. 63, para. 4, GC I; Art. 62, para. 4, GC II; Art. 142, para. 4, GC III; Art. 158, para. 4, GC IV and Preamble, para. 5, WeaponsConv.
[177] See commentary to Section 120.
[178] See, e.g., *ICRC, Conference of Government Experts on the Use of Certain Conventional Weapons* (Lucerne, 24 September–18 October), Report, 35–6; *ICRC, Second Working Group of Experts on Battlefield Laser Weapons* (Geneva, 5–7 November 1990), Report, 35–6; reproduced in ICRC, *Blinding Weapons* (ICRC, 1994).
[179] D. Schindler and J. Toman, (n. 111), 3.

MARY ELLEN O'CONNELL

states, as general principles of law, that: '(1) Only that degree and kind of force, not otherwise prohibited by the law of armed conflict, required for the partial or complete submission of the enemy with a minimum expenditure of time, life and physical resources may be applied. (2) The employment of any kind or degree of force not required for the partial or complete submission of the enemy with a minimum expenditure of time, life and physical resources is prohibited.'[180] These general principles are the basis for numerous specific rules of humanitarian law, such as the prohibition of the use of weapons and means of warfare likely to cause unnecessary suffering (Article 23, lit. e, HagueReg), the prohibition of the unnecessary destruction of property (Article 23, lit. g, HagueReg), and the principle that even military objectives should not be attacked if this would cause excessive civilian casualties or damage to civilian objects (Article 51, para. 5, lit. b, AP I).[181]

2. *The effects of the* jus ad bellum. The changes in the *jus ad bellum* brought about by the UN Charter[182] have added a new dimension to this principle of military necessity.[183] Prior to 1945, once a state was justified in going to war it was invariably entitled to seek the complete submission of its adversary and to employ all force, subject only to the constraints of humanitarian law, to achieve that goal.[184] That is no longer permissible. Under the UN Charter, a state which is entitled to exercise the right of self-defence is justified only in seeking to achieve the goals of defending itself immediately and taking reasonable measures to provide for its future security in light of the nature of the violation of Article 2(4). The defending state may therefore use whatever force is necessary (within the limits of humanitarian law) to recover any part of its territory which has been occupied as the result of its adversary's attack, to put an end to that attack, and to remove the threat which the attack poses. In an extreme case, the achievement of these defensive goals might be possible only by securing the complete submission of the adversary, but that will not generally be the case. Thus, the right of the UK to use force in response to Argentina's invasion of the Falkland Islands could not have justified the UK seeking the complete submission of Argentina. The only legitimate goal permitted by the inherent right of self-defence was the recovery of the Islands and their protection from further attack.

3. *Necessity*. The humanitarian law principle of necessity and the limitations which form part of the right of self-defence, taken together, produce the following result: (1) the humanitarian law principle of necessity forbids a state to employ force in an armed conflict beyond what is necessary for the achievement of the goals of that state; and (2) the modern *jus ad bellum* contained in the UN Charter limits those lawful goals to the defence of the state (including its territory, citizens, and shipping).

   a) In other words, a state may use only such force (not otherwise prohibited by humanitarian law) as is necessary to achieve the goals permitted by the right of self-defence.[185]

---

[180] *US Naval Manual*, para. 5.2; see also the decision in *US v List*, 15 *Annual Digest* 632 at 646.

[181] See generally, M. E. O'Connell, 'Self-Defense' (n. 32) and J. Gardam, (n. 24).

[182] See commentary to Section 101.

[183] C. Greenwood, 'Self-Defence and the Conduct of International Armed Conflict' in Y. Dinstein and M. Tabory (eds), *International Law at a Time of Perplexity: Essays in Honour of Shabtai Rosenne* (Nijhoff, 1989), 273.

[184] See *US v List*, (n. 66).

[185] Other justifications for the unilateral use of force by states, in so far as they are well founded, also permit the use of force only in order to achieve limited objectives.

MARY ELLEN O'CONNELL

In that sense, the *jus ad bellum* has an effect upon the conduct of hostilities as well as upon the initial right to resort to force.[186] That does not mean that a state which is the victim of an armed attack and exercises its right of self-defence must always fight on its adversary's terms. A state acting in self-defence may take the fighting to its adversary's territory if that is necessary to recover territory of its own or to ensure its defence. What it does mean is that such action will be lawful only if, in the circumstances, it is necessary for the defence of that state.

b) It follows that, even if the legal basis for the coalition's use of force against Iraq in 1991 had been the right of collective self-defence with Kuwait,[187] that would not have prevented the coalition states from sending forces into Iraq itself rather than launching a frontal attack upon the Iraqi forces in Kuwait, since outflanking the Iraqi forces offered the possibility of achieving the liberation of Kuwait with far fewer coalition and civilian casualties than would otherwise have been sustained. In fact, however, the legal basis for the coalition operations against Iraq was the mandate granted to the coalition states by the Security Council in Resolution 678 (1991). The permitted goals of the coalition states were laid down by the Council in that resolution: the expulsion of Iraqi forces from Kuwait, ensuring Iraqi compliance with all relevant Security Council resolutions, and the restoration of peace and security in the region. Where a state uses force under a mandate from the Security Council, it may use only such force (not otherwise prohibited by humanitarian law) as is necessary to achieve the objectives set out (expressly or impliedly) in that mandate.

The objective in the case of the liberation of Kuwait was to push Iraqi armed forces out of Kuwait and to ensure that they would not immediately retake the country. This second consideration permitted the establishment of a defensive perimeter on Iraqi territory. Holding more Iraqi territory or advancing all the way to Baghdad to topple the government there would have constituted excessive force, well beyond what was militarily necessary in defending Kuwait.[188]

4. Distinction and perfidy. Section 132 also refers to two other general principles of great importance. The principle of distinction requires states to distinguish between combatants and military objectives on one hand, and non-combatants and civilian objects on the other, and to direct their attacks only against the former.[189] The principle of perfidy forbids the use of treacherous methods and means of warfare.[190]

133 International humanitarian law in armed conflicts is a compromise between military and humanitarian requirements. Its rules comply with both military necessity

---

[186] C. Greenwood (n. 152); Gardam (n. 22); Lagoni, in W. Heintschel v. Heinegg (ed.), *The Military Objective and the Principle of Distinction in the Law of Naval Warfare* (Bochum: Brockmeyer, 1992), 56; Langdon, ibid. 86; D. P. O'Connell, 'Limited War at Sea since 1945' in M. Howard (ed.) *Restraints on War* (OUP, 1979), 123; N. Ronzitti, in N. Ronzitti (ed.), *The Law of Naval Warfare: A Collection of Agreements and Documents with Commentaries* (Nijhoff, 1989), 2–10. For a contrary view, see W. Fenrick, 'The Merchant Vessel as Legitimate Target in the Law of Naval Warfare' in A. J. M. Delissen and G. J. Tanja (n. 151), 439, and G. J. F. van Hegelsom, 'Comments' in I. Dekker and H. Post (n. 34), 127.

[187] See commentary to Section 101 for the view that this was an enforcement action.

[188] M. E. O'Connell, 'Enforcing the Prohibition on the Use of Force: The U.N.'s Response to Iraq's Invasion of Kuwait' (1991) 15 *South Illinois University Law Journal* 453, 479–80. But see Dinstein, *War, Aggression and Self-Defence*, 5th edn (CUP, 2012), 231–2.

[189] Arts. 51–2 AP I; see Sections 480–2 and 442–66.

[190] See Sections 471–3.

MARY ELLEN O'CONNELL

and the dictates of humanity. Considerations of military necessity cannot, therefore, justify departing from the rules of humanitarian law in armed conflicts to seek a military advantage using forbidden means.

Any exception to the prescribed behaviour for reasons of military necessity shall be permissible only if a rule of international humanitarian law expressly provides for such a possibility. The Hague Regulations Concerning the Laws and Customs of War on Land, for instance, prohibit the destruction or seizure of enemy property, 'unless such destruction or seizure be imperatively demanded by the necessities of war' (Article 23, lit. g, HagueReg). **134**

1. Although it was at one time contended by some writers that the necessities of war prevailed over legal considerations,[191] this argument has now been decisively rejected.[192] Thus, the US Military Tribunal in *US v List* ruled that 'military necessity or expediency do not justify a violation of positive rules'[193] and a similar approach was adopted in many other war crime trials after World War II.[194] AP I also makes clear that military necessity can never justify the killing of prisoners of war, even when these prisoners have been captured by special forces units who cannot evacuate them in the manner required by GC III. Article 41, para. 3, AP I provides that in such circumstances the prisoners must be released and 'all feasible precautions shall be taken to ensure their safety'. The reference to 'all feasible precautions' illustrates that many of the rules of humanitarian law already make allowance for considerations of military necessity. In such cases, military necessity does not override the law; it is an integral part of it. The existence of these rules shows that considerations of military necessity have already been taken into account in framing the rules of humanitarian law, which are intended to achieve a balance between military necessity and the requirements of humanity. A state cannot, therefore, be allowed to invoke military necessity as a justification for upsetting that balance by departing from those rules.

2. Indeed, as Section 132 makes clear, far from justifying a state in acting contrary to humanitarian law, the principle of necessity operates as an additional level of restraint by prohibiting acts which are not otherwise illegal, as long as they are not necessary for the achievement of legitimate goals. Similarly, considerations derived from the Charter cannot justify a departure from the rules of humanitarian law.[195]

3. It should not be assumed, however, that humanitarian law and military requirements will necessarily be opposed to one another. On the contrary, most rules of humanitarian

[191] For discussion, see H. Lauterpacht (ed.), *Oppenheim's International Law*, Vol. II, 231.
[192] Y. Dinstein, 'Military Necessity', *MPEPIL*.
[193] 15 *Annual Digest* 632, 647.
[194] For example, Manstein, 16 *Annual Digest* 509, 511–3; *Thiele/Steinert*, in *Law Reports Trials of War Criminals*, Vol. III, 56; *The Peleus*, ibid. Vol. I, 1.
[195] This point raises the question, what if the UN Security Council authorizes a violation of IHL rules in a particular case? Article 103 of the UN Charter does state: 'In the event of a conflict between the obligations of the Members of the United Nations under the present Charter and their obligations under any other international agreement, their obligations under the present Charter shall prevail.' In the *Lockerbie* case, the ICJ found that states were obligated to violate certain aviation treaties to comply with a sanctions regime imposed on Libya. Such a conflict of obligations would not, however, arise in the case of fundamental rules of international humanitarian law because the Security Council is bound by such rules equally to individual states. See Section 136 below. See M. E. O'Connell, 'Debating the Law of Sanctions' (2002) 13 *EJIL* 63. See also Section 101 and the view that international humanitarian law applies to UN forces and forces fighting with UN Security Council authorization.

MARY ELLEN O'CONNELL

law reflect good military practice, and adherence by armed forces to those rules is likely to reinforce discipline and good order within the forces concerned.[196]

V. Binding Effect of International Law for the Soldier

135   The obligations of a state under international humanitarian law are binding not only upon its government and its supreme military command but also upon every individual.

One of the unusual features of humanitarian law is that, unlike most rules of international law, it binds not only the state and its organs of government but also the individual. Thus, the individual soldier or civilian who performs acts contrary to humanitarian law is criminally responsible for those acts and liable to trial for a war crime.[197] This criminal responsibility for violations of humanitarian law applies to members of the armed forces of all ranks. By contrast, the trials held after World War II established that only those individuals at the highest levels of government and the supreme military command could be convicted of crimes against the peace, that is the deliberate violation of the *jus ad bellum*.[198]

136   Basic rules of international humanitarian law are classic examples for peremptory norms (*jus cogens*), so that any other rule which conflicts with such basic rules is void.

It can easily be argued that the fundamental principles of the *jus in bello* have become norms of *jus cogens*, that is norms from which no derogation is permitted.[199] However, many of the more detailed rules of humanitarian law do not have that status. Moreover, while ordinary norms of international law yield if they conflict with norms of *jus cogens*, on closer examination very few norms do in fact so conflict. For example the rules of international law on state immunity do not conflict with the prohibition of torture[200] or other prohibitory rules since they do not purport to legitimize such conduct only to determine the forum in which attempts to enforce such norms can be made.

137   Apart from these basic rules, all members of the armed forces are obliged to comply and ensure compliance with all rules of international humanitarian law binding upon their state.

---

[196] See A. J. P. Rogers, *Law on the Battlefield*, 3rd edn (Manchester: Manchester University Press, 2012) and W. Hays Parks, 'Teaching the Law of War' [1987] *The Army Lawyer* 4.

[197] See Sections 1410–8.

[198] *Von Leeb* (n. 134); C. Greenwood, (n. 35), 221.

[199] See Art. 53 Vienna Convention on the Law of Treaties of 1969. It is, however, the case that authoritative lists of *jus cogens* norms tend not to include even the fundamental specialized principles of IHL such as those governing targeting: distinction, necessity, proportionality, and humanity. For an argument supporting the inclusion of such fundamental IHL rules in the list of *jus cogens* norms, see M. E. O'Connell, 'Jus Cogens: International Law's Higher Ethical Norms' in D. E. Childress III (ed.), *The Role of Ethics in International Law* (CUP, 2011).

[200] See the judgment of the ICJ in *Jurisdictional Immunities of the State* (*Germany v Italy*) Judgment of 3 February 2012; see also the judgment of the ECtHR in *Al-Adsani v UK* (application no. 35763/97) of 21 November 2001 and the decision of the House of Lords in *Jones v Saudi Arabia* ([2006] UKHL 26) of 14 June 2006.

MARY ELLEN O'CONNELL

The duty not merely to comply but to ensure compliance by others is stated in common Article 1 GC I–IV and Article 1 AP I.

> The four Geneva Conventions and the Protocols Additional to them oblige all   138
> contracting parties to disseminate the text of the Conventions as widely as pos-
> sible (Article 47 GC I; Article 48 GC II; Article 127 GC III; Article 144 GC IV;
> Article 83, para. 1 AP I; Article 19 AP II; Article 7 AP III). This shall particularly
> be accomplished through programmes of instruction for the armed forces and by
> encouraging the civilian population to study these Conventions (Article 83, para.
> 1, AP I). Considering their responsibility in times of armed conflict, military and
> civilian authorities shall be fully acquainted with the text of the Conventions and
> the Protocols Additional to them (Article 83, para. 2, AP I). Members of the armed
> forces shall be instructed in their rights and duties under international law in
> peacetime and in times of armed conflict.

> Instruction of soldiers in international law should be conducted in the military units   139
> by senior officers and legal advisers and at the armed forces schools by teachers of
> law. The emphasis must be made on teaching what is related to practice. Soldiers
> should be instructed, using examples, in how to deal with the problems of and the
> issues involved in international law. The purpose of this instruction is not only to
> disseminate knowledge, but also and primarily to develop an awareness of what is
> right and what is wrong. The soldier must be taught to bring his conduct into line
> with this awareness in every situation.

> The commanding officer must ensure that all subordinates are aware of their duties   140
> and rights under international law. Commanders are obliged to prevent, and where
> necessary to suppress or to report to competent authorities, breaches of interna-
> tional law (Article 87 AP I). They are supported in these tasks by a legal adviser
> (Article 82 AP I).

A commanding officer has a duty to ensure that the forces under his command conduct themselves in accordance with the rules of international humanitarian law. In the case of *Yamashita*,[201] the US Supreme Court held that General Yamashita was guilty of a war crime for failing to control the troops under his command and to prevent the atrocities which they committed in areas occupied by the Japanese army. This principle has now been incorporated into the leading texts on international criminal law such as the Statute of the International Criminal Court (Articles 25 and 28) and the International Criminal Tribunal for the Former Yugoslavia (Article 7).

> It shall be the duty of a member of the armed forces to follow the rules of inter-   141
> national humanitarian law. With whatever means wars are being conducted, the
> soldier will always be obliged to respect and observe the rules of international law
> and to base all actions upon them. If, in a particular situation, there is doubt as to
> what international law prescribes, the issue shall be referred to the superior officer to
> decide. If this is not possible, the soldier will always be right to let himself or herself
> be guided by the principles of humanity and to follow their conscience.

The statement that the rules of humanitarian law must be obeyed 'whatever means' are used to prosecute a war is of the utmost importance. The fact that a conflict is labelled

---

[201] Re Yamashita 327 US 1 (1946) reprinted in *Law Reports of Trials of War Criminals*, Vol. IV, 1–96. See also L. C. Green, *Essays on the Modern Law of War*, 2nd edn (Transnational Publishers, 2000), 215.

MARY ELLEN O'CONNELL

'total war', 'guerrilla warfare', 'asymmetrical war', or 'war of national liberation' does not alter the duty to comply with the rules of humanitarian law. The use of nuclear weapons is also subject to the rules of humanitarian law, suggesting to many that the use of such weapons could never be lawful.[202]

142   The soldier shall avoid inhumanity even in combat and refrain from using force against defenceless persons and persons needing protection, and from committing any acts of perfidy and brutality. Soldiers shall look upon wounded opponents as fellow persons in need. They shall respect prisoners of war as opponents fighting for their country. They shall treat the civilian population as they would wish civilians, civilian property, and cultural property of their own people to be treated by the adversary. Similar respect shall be shown to foreign property and cultural assets.

This section states some of the basic principles of humanitarian law, the details of which are elaborated in later chapters. The duty to avoid inhumanity even in combat is particularly significant. Although many of the provisions of the Geneva Conventions deal with events outside the immediate combat zone, even in the heat of combat humanitarian law requires that certain standards be observed, for example that quarter be given to anyone who clearly evinces an intention to surrender (Article 40 AP I) and that enemy combatants who are incapacitated by wounds should not be made the object of attack (Article 12, para. 1, GC I; Article 12, para. 1, GC II). The final sentence of the section should not be read as implying a principle of reciprocity: the soldier is required to treat enemy civilians as he or she would want their own people to be treated by the enemy, not as the enemy actually treats them. Apart from the law of reprisals,[203] failure by the forces of a state to comply with humanitarian law does not release their adversaries from their obligations.

143   Superiors shall only issue orders which are in conformity with international law. Superiors who issue an order contrary to international law expose not only themselves but also their subordinates obeying these orders to the risk of being prosecuted (Article 86 AP I).

An officer, of whatever rank, who orders the commission of an unlawful act is guilty of a war crime, as is the soldier who carries out that order. The 'grave breaches' provisions of the Geneva Conventions and AP I stipulate that ordering the commission of an act amounting to a grave breach is itself a grave breach.[204]

144   An order is not binding if:
             — it violates the human dignity of the third party concerned or the recipient of
                 the order;
             — it is not of any use for service; or
             — in the particular situation, the soldier cannot reasonably be expected to
                 execute it.
             Orders which are not binding need not be executed by the soldier. Moreover, it is
             expressly prohibited to obey orders whose execution would be a crime.

---

[202] Sections 431–6. See ICJ, Advisory opinion on *Nuclear Weapons, ICJ Reports 1996*, 226.
[203] Sections 485–88 and 1408.
[204] Arts. 49–50 GC I; Arts. 51–51 GC II; Arts. 129–30 GC III; Arts. 146–7 GC IV; and Arts. 85–6 AP I. On war crimes, see Sections 1410–8.

MARY ELLEN O'CONNELL

Grave breaches of international humanitarian law (Article 50 GC I; Article 51 GC   145
II; Article 130 GC III; Article 147 GC IV; Article 85 AP I) shall be penal offences
under national law.

A plea of superior orders shall not be a good defence if the subordinate realized or   146
should have realized that the action ordered was a crime.

Punishment for disobedience or refusal to obey is proscribed if the order is   147
not binding.

These sections state two principles of particular importance:

a) A member of the armed forces who commits an unlawful act is not relieved of criminal responsibility merely because he or she was carrying out an order. Superior orders do not provide a general defence to liability for war crimes, a point established in the Nuremberg and Tokyo trials and applied in numerous other war crimes trials after World War II.[205] A soldier who carries out an order by action which is illegal under international humanitarian law is guilty of a war crime, provided that he was aware of the circumstances which made that order criminal or could reasonably have been expected to be aware of them. Superior orders may, however, amount to a factor mitigating the level of punishment.

b) A member of the armed forces has no legal obligation to obey an order which would result in a grave breach of international humanitarian law. On the contrary, he or she is legally obliged not to carry out such an order (see below, commentary to Section 1436).

VI. Tasks of the Legal Adviser

States must ensure that legal advisers are available, when necessary: 148
— to advise military commanders in all matters pertinent to military law and
  international law;
— to examine military orders and instructions on the basis of legal criteria;
— to participate in military exercises as legal officers whose duties include giving
  advice on matters pertinent to international law; and
— to give legal instruction to soldiers of all ranks, particularly including the further education in the rules of international humanitarian law.

Legal advisers should have direct access to the commander to whom they are   149
assigned. The commander may give directives to a legal adviser only with respect
to general aspects of duty.

The legal advisers receive directives and instructions pertinent to legal matters only   150
from their supervising legal adviser, via the legal specialist chain of command.

A legal adviser may additionally exercise the functions of a Disciplinary Attorney   151
for the Armed Forces. In the case of a severe disciplinary offence the legal adviser
may then conduct the investigation and bring the charge before the military
disciplinary court. Such a disciplinary offence may include a grave breach of

---

[205] G. Mettraux, *The Law of Command Responsibility* (OUP, 2009); L. C. Green, *Superior Orders in National and International Law* (Sijthoff, 1976); Y. Dinstein, *The Defence of Obedience to Superior Orders in International Law* (Sijthoff, 1965).

MARY ELLEN O'CONNELL

international law which in addition to its criminal quality also has a disciplinary significance.

Article 82 AP I requires the parties to the Protocol to ensure that legal advisers are available at all necessary times 'to advise military commanders at the appropriate level on the application of the Conventions and this Protocol and on the appropriate instruction to be given to the armed forces on this subject'.[206]

[206] A. P. V. Rogers and D. Stewart, 'The Role of the Military Legal Advisor' in T. D. Gill and D. Fleck, *The Handbook of the International Law of Military Operations* (OUP, 2010), 537–64; for the development of the use of legal advisers in the armed forces, see W. K. Lietzau and J. A. Rutigliano Jr, 'History and Development of the International Law of Military Operations', in Gill and Fleck, *op. cit.*, 11–31. See also G. I. A. D. Draper, 'Role of Legal Advisers in Armed Forces' [1978] *IRRC* 6–17; M. Denny, 'The Impact of Article 82 of Protocol I on the Organization of a Division SJA Office' (1980) 14 *The Army Lawyer*. On the role of legal adviser during the Kuwait conflict, see M. Keeva, 'Lawyers in the War Room' [December 1991] *American Bar Association Journal* 52.

MARY ELLEN O'CONNELL

2

SCOPE OF APPLICATION
OF INTERNATIONAL
HUMANITARIAN LAW

I. Material Scope

International humanitarian law regulates, and as a rule applies in times of, armed   201
conflict.

1. International humanitarian law regulates, and as a rule[1] applies in times of, armed conflicts. Accordingly, it is also referred to as the law of armed conflict or *jus in bello.* The three interchangeable terms denote the only branch of public international law that is specifically intended to preserve humanitarian values during armed conflicts by protecting those who do not or no longer directly participate in hostilities and by limiting the right of parties to the conflict to use armed force only to the amount necessary to achieve the aim of the conflict, which is to weaken the military potential of the enemy. International humanitarian law is not concerned with the legality *of* the armed conflict (see also below Section 206). Instead, it reflects the reality of organized armed violence, unleashed by states or by organized armed groups, and regulates what parties to an armed conflict may or may not do in the course of an armed conflict. International humanitarian law rests upon a balance between humanitarian concerns and considerations of military necessity. Each and every rule of this branch of law reflects that balance. As a branch of public international law, it is primarily states that determine how the balance between humanitarian concerns and considerations of military necessity is struck. That determination is articulated in the course of the lawmaking process. Thus, when negotiating international conventional humanitarian law, in the course of customary law formation through state practice and *opinio juris*, through the development of general principles of international humanitarian, and by virtue of other legally binding sources (such as unilateral declarations and binding resolutions of international organizations), states identify what they consider to be the acceptable balance between humanitarian concerns and considerations of military necessity. Naturally, such a state-centric lawmaking process does not take place in isolation, but is informed by non-state constituents, such as humanitarian and civil society organizations, not the least the International Committee of the Red

---

[1] As an exception to the rule that international humanitarian law applies in times of armed conflicts, some rules, such as those relating to dissemination, are applicable in peacetime as well. For these exceptions, see e.g. Arts. 23, 44, 47 GC I; Art. 127 GC III; Art. 144 GC IV; Arts. 6, para. 1, and 83, para. 1 AP I; Art. 7 AP III.

Cross (ICRC) with its express mandate to promote and act as guardian of international humanitarian law.

2. While international humanitarian law is the only branch of public international law that *specifically* regulates situations of armed conflicts, it does not automatically supersede all other areas of public international law in the event of an armed conflict. The move from the formal notion of 'war' in the legal sense—predicated by a declaration of war—to the objective, fact-driven notion of 'armed conflict' has brought with it the gradual abandonment of the traditional rigid distinction in international law between the state of peace and the state of war.[2] Today, the outbreak of an armed conflict will not necessarily mean that all other rules of international law cease to apply. See below, Sections 246–256.

3. International humanitarian law distinguishes between two generic types of armed conflicts: armed conflicts of an international character, including belligerent occupations, and armed conflicts not of an international character (see below, Sections 202, 204, 208–209). The distinction between international and non-international armed conflicts rests upon the parties to the armed conflict. International armed conflicts occur between two or more states, whereas non-international armed conflicts occur between states and organized non-state armed groups or between such groups. International and non-international armed conflicts are subject to distinct sets of rules of international humanitarian law: the law of international armed conflicts,[3] including the law of belligerent occupation,[4] and the law of non-international armed conflicts.[5]

202   **An international armed conflict exists if one state uses armed force against another state. It is irrelevant whether the parties to the conflict consider themselves to be at war with each other and how they describe this conflict.**

1. In the words of the Geneva Conventions, the law of *international armed conflict* applies to 'all cases of declared war or of any other armed conflict which may arise between two or more of the High Contracting Parties, even if the state of war is not recognized by one of them'.[6] The *ICRC Commentary* further explains that 'any difference arising between two states and leading to the intervention of members of the armed forces is an armed conflict'.[7] Similarly, the ICTY has held that an international armed conflict exists whenever there is 'resort to armed force between States'.[8] These views adhere to the so-called 'first-shot' theory, according to which the law of international armed conflict applies from the first moment that force is used by one state against another state. It is irrelevant,

[2] On the state of war doctrine, see Brownlie, *International Law and the Use of Force by States* (OUP, 1963), 26–8.
[3] Chiefly comprising the 1907 Hague Regulations on Land Warfare, the four 1949 Geneva Conventions (except Common Article 3), the 1977 Additional Protocol I, and a significant number of treaties pertaining to more specific issues, as well as customary international law.
[4] In the main comprising Arts. 42–56 HagueReg 1907; Arts. 47–78 GC IV; and customary international law.
[5] The most important treaty rules are Common Art. 3 and AP II. Furthermore, rules of customary international humanitarian law apply.
[6] Common Article 2 Geneva Conventions of 1949.
[7] J. Pictet (ed.), Commentary to the First Geneva Convention for the Amelioration of the Condition of the Wounded and the Sick in Armed Forces in the Field (ICRC 1952), 32.
[8] Cf. *Prosecutor v Tadić*, Decision on the Defence Motion for Interlocutory Appeal on Jurisdiction, IT-94-1, Appeals Chamber (2 October 1995) 70.

JANN K. KLEFFNER

according to that view, what form that force takes or what its intensity or duration is.[9] An alternative view to the 'first-shot' theory holds that any armed conflict, including those that occur between two or more states, requires the parties to it to be 'engaged in fighting of some intensity'.[10] According to the latter view, not any resort to armed force between states would suffice. 'Border clashes', for instance, would not amount to an international armed conflict,[11] nor would, presumably, the singular abduction and subsequent detention of a member of the armed forces of one state by (members of the armed forces of) another state. It is submitted, however, that this latter view requiring a certain level of intensity for the resort to armed force between states to amount to an international armed conflict bears the risk of creating an international legal vacuum or of depriving certain categories of persons of the protections that international humanitarian law provides. One fails to see, for instance, what international legal parameters would govern the conduct of hostilities during a border clash between two states. And a member of the armed forces of a state captured by another state would be deprived of the rights and privileges granted to prisoners of war under conventional and customary international humanitarian law.[12] While the better view thus is to adhere to the 'first-shot' theory and consider an international armed conflict to exist to which international humanitarian law applies as soon as there is resort to armed force between states, it is ultimately the facts on the ground that determine the extent to which international humanitarian law becomes operable. A minor incursion by the armed forces of one state into another state, for instance, will not bring into operation the whole plethora of rules of international humanitarian law. Rather, the factual circumstances of a military operation amounting to an international armed conflict will determine which of the rules are practically relevant and, as a consequence, the extent to which the law becomes operable. If, during such an operation, no member of the opposing armed forces is captured the law pertaining to prisoners of war will not become operable. Pivotal in that regard is, however, that the reason for the inapplicability is purely *factual* rather than *legal*, namely that the facts are such that the preconditions for the operation of the law pertaining to prisoners of war are absent. As soon as a member of the opposing armed forces falls into the power of the enemy, s/he becomes a prisoner of war entitled to the full protection that international humanitarian law grants to that category of persons.

2. The existence of an international armed conflict is a question of fact and is independent of the subjective views of the parties to the armed conflict. As a matter of law, it is irrelevant whether the warring states consider themselves to be engaged in an armed conflict, even less so whether they formally acknowledge the existence of a state of armed conflict or war. The adoption of the Four Geneva Conventions of 1949 marked a significant shift away from formal preconditions for the applicability of international humanitarian law to a fact-based approach (see further Section 203).

---

[9] Pictet, Commentary GC I, 32.

[10] ILA Committee on the Use of Force, Final Report on the Meaning of Armed Conflict in International Law (2010), 2.

[11] Ibid. 28, and supportive state practice at 16–7.

[12] For the pertinent case of a US pilot shot down and captured by Syrian forces over Lebanon in the 1980s, when the US maintained that this incident amounted to an armed conflict and that the pilot was thus entitled to be treated as a prisoner of war under GC III, see (1988) 82 *Proceedings of the American Society of International Law* 602–3 and 609–11.

JANN K. KLEFFNER

3. According to Article 1(4) of AP I (1977), armed conflicts 'in which peoples are fighting against colonial domination and alien occupation and against racist régimes in the exercise of their right to self-determination' trigger the applicability of the law of international armed conflict. The contemporary relevance of this provision is uncertain. It has been argued that its field of application was intended to be quite restricted.[13] Furthermore, the fact that 'wars against colonial domination' in the traditional sense are largely a thing of the past may be seen to further indicate a decline in contemporary relevance. The reference to alien occupation, in turn, adds little to Article 2 of the Geneva Conventions, except perhaps where the territory occupied was not part of the territory of a state at the time of the occupation, and the *ICRC Commentary* regards the reference to racist regimes as applying only to 'regimes founded on racist criteria'.[14] Article 1, para. 4, AP I was undoubtedly not intended to apply to any conflict in which an ethnic group or the inhabitants of a territory attempted to secede from a parent state. At the same time, the concept of self-determination has evolved, although its exact contemporary contours are subject to considerable debate.[15] Whether that evolution involves also a wider application for Article 1, para. 4 remains to be seen. Where Article 1, para. 4, does apply, Article 96, para. 3, AP I provides that an authority representing the people engaged in such a conflict may make a declaration addressed to the depositary of the Protocol (the Government of Switzerland), undertaking to apply the Conventions and the Protocol, in which case the Conventions and the Protocol shall become binding on both parties to the conflict. Article 7, para. 4, of the Weapons Convention 1981 contains a similar provision. Opinions differ as to whether Article 1, para. 4, AP I can be regarded as stating a rule of customary international law.[16] The controversy which Article 1, para. 4, has aroused ever since it was first proposed suggests that states do not regard it as declaratory of customary international law, although there is some evidence that it has had an influence on practice.[17]

203   The application of international humanitarian law is not dependent on a formal declaration of war. Formal declarations of war (Article 1 HC III) nowadays occur only very rarely.

1. In contradistinction to the period preceding the adoption of the Four Geneva Conventions of 1949, the applicability of the law of international armed conflict is not conditioned by a formal declaration of war. This is notwithstanding the possibility that international humanitarian law may also be rendered applicable through a formal declaration of war in the absence of any resort to armed force between the state declaring war, on the

---

[13] H. A. Wilson, *International Law and the Use of Force by National Liberation Movements* (Clarendon, 1988), 168. See also the declarations made by the UK on ratifying the Protocol, Roberts/Guelff (eds), *Documents on the Laws of War*, 3rd edn (OUP, 2000), 510–2.

[14] *ICRC Commentary*, para. 112.

[15] Cf. ICJ, *Kosovo* Advisory Opinion (2010) para. 82.

[16] Compare G. Abi-Saab, 'Wars of National Liberation in the Geneva Conventions and Protocols' (1979-IV) 165 *RdC* 353, 371–2 and Cassese, 'The Geneva Protocols of 1977 on the Humanitarian Law of Armed Conflict and Customary International Law' (1984) 3 *UCLA Pacific Basin Law Journal* 55, 68–71, with Aldrich, 'Progressive Development of the Laws of War: A Reply to Criticisms of the 1977 Geneva Protocol I' (1986) 26 *Va/Int* 703; Draper, 'Wars of National Liberation and War Criminality' in Howard (ed.), *Restraints on War* (OUP, 1979); Greenwood, 'Customary Law Status of the 1977 Geneva Protocols' in Delissen/Tanja (eds), *Humanitarian Law of Armed Conflict: Challenges Ahead. Essays in Honour of F. Kalshoven* (Nijhoff, 1991), 93–114, at 111–12.

[17] See C. Murray, 'The 1977 Protocols and the Conflict in Southern Africa' (1984) 33 *ICLQ* 462.

JANN K. KLEFFNER

one hand, and the state against whom war is being declared, on the other hand.[18] Such a declaration would trigger those parts of the law of international humanitarian law that are not directly concerned with, or dependent on, the conduct of hostilities. Examples of these parts are the rules on the treatment of aliens in the territory of a party to the conflict[19] and those governing the treatment of internees.[20] Be that as it may, the possibility of a formal declaration of war without the occurrence of actual hostilities today seems remote, not the least because states today generally abstain from making formal declarations of war.

> International humanitarian law also applies to all cases of total or partial military occupation, even if this occupation meets with no armed resistance (Article 2, para. 2 common to the Geneva Conventions).
204

1. As part of the law of international armed conflict, the law of *belligerent occupation* applies to situations in which territory of one state is placed under the authority of a hostile army.[21] The occupation extends only to the territory where such authority has been established and can be exercised.[22] Once the aforementioned conditions are fulfilled, the law of belligerent occupation applies, whether or not the occupation meets with resistance.[23] As in the case of determining whether an international armed conflict exists by virtue of the fact that there is 'resort to armed force between States', the determination of a given situation as amounting to belligerent occupation is exclusively governed by the facts on the ground. The evidence must be sufficient to demonstrate that the said authority was in fact established and exercised by the intervening state in the areas in question.[24] Relevant indicative factors in making that determination include the ability of the occupying power to substitute its own authority for that of the occupied authorities, which must have been rendered incapable of functioning publicly; the surrender, defeat, or withdrawal of enemy forces; the presence of a sufficient force, or the capacity to send troops within a reasonable time to make the authority of the occupying power felt; the establishment of a temporary administration over the territory; and the issuance and enforcement of directions to the civilian population.[25] It follows from the foregoing that battle areas may not be considered as occupied territory.[26]

> The application of international humanitarian law pertaining to international armed conflicts is not affected by whether or not the parties to an armed conflict recognize one another as states (Article 13, para. 3, GC I; Article 13, para. 3, GC II; Article 4 A, para. 3, GC III; Article 43, para. 1, AP I).
205

1. The applicability of the rules of international humanitarian law regulating international armed conflicts is not dependent upon whether the parties to a conflict recognize one another as states. As a consequence of the fact-driven notion of an armed conflict—as

---

[18] For historical examples, see Dinstein, *War, Aggression and Self-Defence*, 5th edn (CUP, 2011), 9.
[19] Cf. Arts. 35–46 GC IV.
[20] Cf. Arts. 79–135 GC IV.
[21] Cf. Art. 42 HagueReg (1907). As to the customary status of Art. 42, see ICJ *Legal Consequences of the Construction of a Wall in the Occupied Palestinian Territory*, Advisory Opinion, *ICJ Reports* 2004, 167, paras. 78 and 172, para. 89; ICJ *DR Congo v Uganda*, para. 172.
[22] Id.
[23] Cf. Common Art. 2, para. 2 GCs.
[24] ICJ, *DR Congo v Uganda*, para. 173.
[25] Cf. ICTY *Prosecutor v Naletilić and Martinović*, Trial Chamber Judgment, 31 March 2003, para. 217.
[26] Id.

JANN K. KLEFFNER

opposed to a subjective approach to the existence of it—several rules expressly stipulate, for example, that the protection granted to the wounded, sick, and shipwrecked, as well as the protection of prisoners of war, equally extends to those 'who profess allegiance to a Government or an authority not recognized by the Detaining Power'.[27] Similarly, AP I includes into the notion of 'armed forces of a Party to a conflict' those organized armed forces, groups, and units which are under a command responsible to a party for the conduct of its subordinates, even if that party is represented by a government or an authority not recognized by an adverse party.[28] The underlying principle is also borne out by the practice of states that participated in international armed conflicts in which AP I was inapplicable. Thus, throughout the Arab–Israel conflict, the Arab states did not recognize Israel as a state,[29] yet both sides in that international armed conflict have accepted the applicability of international humanitarian law.

2. The question of whether the parties to an armed conflict are states is objective and not a matter to be determined by the subjective recognition policies of each party. Where, however, there is real doubt about whether one side in a conflict is a state, rather than a secessionist movement within the rival party, recognition by other states may have an important evidential effect.

206   **The application of international humanitarian law does not depend on whether an armed conflict has been started in violation of a provision of international law regulating the use of force (*jus ad bellum*). International humanitarian law applies equally to all the parties to an armed conflict irrespective of the legality or illegality of their resort to force.**

1. The legality or otherwise of an armed conflict under the law regulating the recourse to the use of armed force is irrelevant for the applicability and interpretation of international humanitarian law. International humanitarian law applies equally to all parties to an armed conflict, irrespective of whether an armed conflict is waged in compliance or in violation of the general prohibition of the use of force embodied in the UN Charter[30] or any of the recognized exceptions to that prohibition, that is the right to use force in self-defence against an armed attack[31] and the right to use force with authorization of the Security Council acting under Chapter VII of the Charter.[32] Acts of members of the armed forces participating in an illegal use of armed force are subject to the same constraints under international humanitarian law as those of their opponents. Although international law is agnostic as regards the legality of the use of force *within*—as opposed to *between*—states, the separation between the cause for initiating a non-international armed conflict and the applicable rules of international humanitarian law applies *mutatis mutandis*.[33]

---

[27] Art. 13, para. 3, GC I; Art. 13, para. 3, GC II; Art. 4 A, para. 3, GC III.
[28] Art. 43 AP I.
[29] Egypt, however, recognized Israel in 1979 when the two states concluded a peace treaty, as did Jordan in 1994. See Section 243.
[30] Cf. Art. 2(4) UN Charter.
[31] Cf. Art. 51 UN Charter.
[32] Cf. Art. 42 UN Charter.
[33] M. Sassòli, 'Ius ad Bellum and Ius in Bello—The Separation between the Legality of the Use of Force and Humanitarian Rules to be Respected in Warfare: Crucial or Outdated?' in Schmitt/Pejic, *International Law and Armed Conflict: Exploring the Faultlines—Essays in Honour of Yoram Dinstein* (Brill, 2007), 241–64, 254–7.

JANN K. KLEFFNER

2. While conventional humanitarian law is, as a rule, only binding between those states which are parties to the respective treaties, it remains applicable between those parties in their mutual relations even if another party to the conflict has not become a party to the respective treaty.[34] However, once the applicability of international humanitarian law has been determined, the obligation to respect and ensure respect for international humanitarian law does not depend on reciprocity.[35]

> **During an international armed conflict, the law of neutrality shall be applied to the relations between the belligerent parties and states not participating in the conflict (Article 2 HC III; see below, Chapter 11).**   **207**

1. Prior to the shift from formal preconditions for the applicability of international humanitarian law to a fact-based approach, the law of neutrality was only triggered between neutral powers and belligerent states in case of a formal declaration of war made by the belligerent states. Some support persists in academic writings for the view that the law of neutrality applies only if there is a formal state of war.[36] There is also evidence that a number of states take the same view.[37]

2. Yet, an alternative view has emerged over the years, which holds that the law of neutrality governs the relation between neutral and belligerent states in the event of an international armed conflict, also in the absence of a formal state of war.[38] This second approach more adequately reflects the current, fact-based approach to the applicability of international humanitarian law. This question is examined in more detail in Chapter 11.

> **A non-international armed conflict is a situation of protracted armed violence between governmental authorities and organized armed groups or between such groups within a state.**   **208**

> **In a non-international armed conflict, each party shall be bound by the applicable conventional and customary international humanitarian law. Regular armed forces should comply with the rules of international humanitarian law in the conduct of military operations in all armed conflicts, however such conflicts are characterized (see below, Chapter 12).**   **209**

1. Two basic requirements condition the existence of a non-international armed conflict: the armed violence must be of sufficient intensity and the parties must be sufficiently organized. The following are indicative factors in assessing whether the requirement of intensity is satisfied: the number, duration, and intensity of individual confrontations;

---

[34] Cf. Common Art. 2 (3) GCs.

[35] Rule 140 *CIHL*. See below, commentary para. 4(b) to Section 1201.

[36] R. Tucker, *The Law of War and Neutrality at Sea* (US Government Printing Office, 1957), 199–200. See also D. Schindler, 'State of War, Belligerency, Armed Conflict' in Cassese (ed.), *The New Humanitarian Law of Armed Conflict* (Editoriate Scientifica, 1979), 3, 5; E. Castren, *The Present Law of War and Neutrality* (Helsinki: Suomalaisen Kirjallisuuden Seuran Kirjapainon Oy, 1954), 34–5; H. Lauterpacht (ed.), *Oppenheim's International Law*, Vol. II, 7th edn (David McKay, 1952), 655.

[37] Greenwood, 'The Concept of War in Modern International Law' (1987) 36 *ICLQ* 283, 297–301; statements by India quoted in S. P. Sharma, *The Indo-Pakistan Maritime Conflict 1965* (Bombay: Academic Books, 1970), 87 and by Canada (1983) XXI *CYIL* 326.

[38] See, e.g., *US Naval Manual* (2007) at para. 7(i); *US Operational Law Handbook* (2012), 41; *UK Manual* (2004), 19 at 1.42; *Australian Manual* (2006) at 11.1–11.3; *France Manuel* (2012), 66; Bothe, 'Neutrality in Naval Warfare: What is Left of Traditional International Law?' in Delissen/Tanja (eds), *Humanitarian Law of Armed Conflict—Challenges Ahead: Essays in Honour of Frits Kalshoven* (Nijhoff, 1991), 387–405.

JANN K. KLEFFNER

the type of weapons and other military equipment used; the number and calibre of munitions fired; the number of persons and type of forces partaking in the fighting; the number of casualties; the extent of material destruction; and the number of civilians fleeing combat zones. The involvement of the UN Security Council may also be a reflection of the intensity of a conflict.[39] As far as the requirement of organization is concerned, the following factors are relevant: the existence of a command structure and disciplinary rules and mechanisms within the group; the existence of a headquarters; the fact that the group controls a certain territory; the ability of the group to gain access to weapons, other military equipment, recruits, and military training; its ability to plan, coordinate, and carry out military operations, including troop movements and logistics; its ability to define a unified military strategy and use military tactics; and its ability to speak with one voice and negotiate and conclude agreements such as ceasefire or peace accords.[40] The aforementioned factors for determining the intensity of the armed violence and the organization of the parties to it must not be understood as a conclusive checklist, however. Rather, they are guidelines in distinguishing non-international armed conflicts from situations in which violence occurs that does not rise beyond internal disturbances and tensions, such as riots, isolated and sporadic acts of violence, and other acts of a similar nature.[41] Such instances of lesser violence are not considered armed conflicts. While there is thus a need to distinguish non-international armed conflicts from internal disturbances and tensions on the lower end of the spectrum, non-international armed conflicts on the higher end of the spectrum may reach the threshold for the applicability of AP II. This is the case when the armed conflict 'take[s] place in the territory of a High Contracting Party between its armed forces and dissident armed forces or other organized armed groups which, under responsible command, exercise such control over a part of its territory as to enable them to carry out sustained and concerted military operations and to implement this Protocol'.[42] This latter requirement of territorial control distinguishes non-international armed conflicts under AP II from other non-international armed conflicts. Furthermore, AP II does not apply to non-international armed conflicts in which organized armed groups are pitted against each other, without the state being a party to the armed conflict.

2. As already alluded to (see above, Section 201, para. 3), the distinction between international and non-international armed conflicts rests on the question who the parties to the armed conflict are. The fact that an armed conflict is not limited to the territory of a single state does not mean, without more, that a non-international armed conflict changes its character and is to be considered international.[43] In that sense, 'non-international' is not to be equated with 'internal'. This is not to suggest, however, that *prima facie* non-international armed conflicts may in certain cases be rendered international in character, for instance when the control exerted by a state over an organized armed group fighting another state is such that the conflict is to be considered as occurring between the two states. For further discussion, see Section 1201.

---

[39] ICTY *Prosecutor v Ramush Haradinaj, Idriz Balaj and Lahi Brahimaj*, Judgment, 3 April 2008, Case No. IT-04–84-T, para. 49.
[40] Ibid. para. 60.
[41] Cf. Art. 1(2) AP II, Art. 8(2)(d) and (f) ICC Statute.
[42] Cf. Art. 1(1) AP II.
[43] *Hamdan v Rumsfeld*, 548 US 557, 628–31.

JANN K. KLEFFNER

3. The attacks on the US in September 2001 led the then US Administration to refer to a 'war against terrorism'. That concept is controversial.[44] Other states, including those which are close allies of the US, have not generally employed the term 'war against terrorism'. Indeed, subsequent US administrations have taken a different position and instead refer to an armed conflict of the US with al-Qaeda and its associated forces.[45] Whether and to what extent that assertion is correct as a matter of international humanitarian law depends on the fulfilment of the same criteria as those for any armed conflict—whether international or non-international in character—referred to above. In other words, it is possible that violent acts that are being described as 'terrorist' by the victim state can bring international humanitarian law into operation. This can happen, for instance, when those acts are attributable to a state and give rise to an international armed conflict between that state and the state that is the target of the violent acts. It can also occur if the violent acts are not attributable to a state, when they reach the required degree of intensity and the group that engages in such acts is sufficiently organized so that the situation amounts to a non-international armed conflict. Thus, the fighting between the US and allied forces on the one side and Afghan forces on the other in 2001–2002 was an international armed conflict irrespective of whether Afghanistan was responsible for the al-Qaeda attacks in New York and Washington on 11 September 2001 which prompted the military operations in Afghanistan.[46] Furthermore, the organized armed violence that ensued after the ousting of the Taliban government between the newly installed Afghan government and coalition forces, on the one hand, and various organized armed groups (remnants of the Taliban, al-Qaeda, etc.), on the other hand, amounted to a non-international armed conflict.

4. Although non-international armed conflicts are, in principle, subject to a different and more limited legal regime than that which applies in an international armed conflict, the evolution of conventional and customary international humanitarian law has brought about a tangible approximation between the law of international and non-international armed conflicts. A considerable body of treaty rules and customary international humanitarian law has evolved which applies in both types of armed conflicts.[47] However, important differences remain. One pivotal example of these differences is the absence of combatant status in non-international armed conflicts, which entails the right to participate directly in hostilities[48] and is the precondition for the status of prisoner of war.[49] Another example is the law of occupation, which exclusively applies in international armed conflicts. Moreover, the applicability in non-international armed conflicts of a number of rules regulating methods and means of combat, that is tactics and weapons, is uncertain according to the ICRC Customary Law Study.[50] Some other

---

[44] See Greenwood, *Essays on War in International Law* (Cameron May, 2006), 409.

[45] See, e.g., H. H. Koh, Legal Adviser, US Department of State, Address to the Annual Meeting of the American Society of International Law: The Obama Administration and International Law (25 March 2010), <http://www.state.gov/s/l/releases/remarks/139119.htm>.

[46] See commentary to Section 101 on the quite different question of whether the events of 11 September 2001 constituted an armed attack for the purposes of the law of self-defence.

[47] As for treaty law, see Sections 1207–11. For customary international humanitarian law, see *CIHL*, concluding that of the 161 Rules that were found, 159 apply in international armed conflicts and 148 apply in non-international armed conflicts.

[48] Cf. Art. 43(2) AP I.

[49] Cf. Art. 44(1) AP I.

[50] See the findings of the Study on the prohibition of the improper use of the flags or military emblems, insignia, or uniforms of the adversary, applicable in international armed conflicts, but only 'arguably' so in non-international armed conflicts. Cf. *CIHL* Rules 62 and 63.

JANN K. KLEFFNER

findings of the ICRC Customary Law Study on methods and means of warfare in non-international armed conflicts have also given rise to a critical response from the US government and academics.[51]

5. Despite these differences between the law regulating international armed conflicts and the law of non-international armed conflicts, it is possible that some or all of the law of international armed conflicts may become applicable, either through a mutual agreement between the parties to such an armed conflict, or by a unilateral declaration of one of the parties to that effect. Indeed, Common Article 3 encourages the parties to a non-international armed conflict to conclude special agreements to bring 'all or part' of the other provisions of the Geneva Conventions into force between them.

6. The final sentence of Section 209 adds an important policy rule, namely that regular armed forces should comply with all rules of international humanitarian law in the conduct of any armed conflict, irrespective of whether that conflict is characterized as non-international or international. Compliance with the full body of rules of international humanitarian law in non-international conflicts undoubtedly presents practical problems, but it serves not only humanitarian interests but also operational requirements. This policy has received support from a number of other sources (see below, Section 1216).[52]

7. An application of international humanitarian law beyond the legally required minimum needs to be distinguished from an application of it in situations that may involve a certain degree of (armed) violence without amounting to an armed conflict, such as internal disturbances or violent demonstrations. In such situations, a 'choice' to apply international humanitarian law is not available to the extent that the situation is governed by more stringent rules of international law. For instance, international humanitarian law allows certain actions, such as the rendering *hors de combat* of combatants, fighters, and civilians directly participating in hostilities, and the destruction or damage of military objectives, while the wounding and killing of persons and the destruction or damage of property is subject to more rigid rules during peacetime under human rights law. States and international organizations do not have the choice to replace the legal obligations under the more stringent legal framework applicable during peacetime for the more permissive rules of international humanitarian law. In short, parties to an armed conflict have the possibility to go beyond the minimum legally required under international humanitarian law, but those conducting military operations are not allowed to apply the permissive aspects of international humanitarian law in the absence of an armed conflict.

II. Personal Scope

210   **International humanitarian law binds parties to an armed conflict and individuals.**

---

[51] See, e.g., John B. Bellinger III and William J. Haynes II, 'A US government response to the International Committee of the Red Cross study Customary International Humanitarian Law' (2007) 866 *IRRC* 443–71 at 460, 465; D. Turns, 'Weapons in the ICRC Study on Customary International Humanitarian Law' (2006) 11 *JCSL* 201–37. For a response to the US criticisms, see J. M. Henckaerts, 'Customary International Humanitarian Law: a response to US comments' (2007) 866 *IRRC* 473–88.

[52] International Institute for Humanitarian Law, 'Declaration on the Rules of International Humanitarian Law Governing the Conduct of Hostilities in Non-International Armed Conflicts' (1990) *IRRC* 404–8; see also

1. International humanitarian law first and foremost binds parties to an armed conflict. These parties may be states, international organizations or organized armed groups.

2. States are bound by those treaties of international humanitarian law to which they have consented, as well as the rules of customary international humanitarian law to which they have not persistently objected. Likewise, states are equally bound by those principles of international humanitarian law that amount to general principles of law in the sense of Article 38(1)(c) of the ICJ Statute. Furthermore, applicable binding resolutions of intergovernmental organizations may be the source for obligations of states under international humanitarian law, regardless of whether or not the rule in question applies to the respective state by virtue of its being embodied in a treaty binding upon that state, in the corpus of customary international humanitarian law or in the body of general principles of law in the sense of Article 38(1)(c).[53]

3. While international humanitarian law treaties do not provide for the possibility of international organizations to become parties, such organizations are bound by customary international humanitarian law by virtue of their international legal personality,[54] when they are a party to an armed conflict.[55] The binding force of international humanitarian law on UN forces under that condition is also confirmed by a number of other instruments.[56] The determination whether or not, and for what time, international organizations are to be considered 'a party to an armed conflict' may involve complex issues of fact and law. As a general rule, this will be the case once, and for such time as, military personnel

the discussion in the *US Naval Manual* (2007) 5–3 and Department of Defense (DoD) Directive 5100.77 of 10 July 1979, restated in DoD Directive 2311.01E of 9 May 2006, DoD Law of War Program, Section 4.1.

[53] Although the Security Council has not acted, through the exercise of its Chapter VII powers, as legislator in the field of international humanitarian law thus far, that possibility cannot be excluded. See G. Nolte, 'The Different Functions of the Security Council with Respect to Humanitarian Law' in Lowe/Roberts/ Welsh/Zaum (eds), *The United Nations Security Council and War—The Evolution of Thought and Practice since 1945* (OUP, 2008), 532.

[54] For the UN, see ICJ *Reparations*, Advisory Opinion (1949) 179. Whether all international organizations possess international legal personality is largely a definitional question. However, in the following, use will be made of the definition of an international organization as expounded in the Draft Articles on Responsibility of International Organizations. Draft Article 2 defines an international organization as 'an organization established by a treaty or other instrument governed by international law and possessing its own international legal personality'. Cf. ILC Report on the work of its 59th Session (7 May to 5 June and 9 July to 10 August 2007), GAOR 62nd Session, Supplement No. 10 (A/62/10), p. 185. For the commentary to this article, see Official Records of the General Assembly, 58th Session, Supplement No. 10 (A/58/10), pp. 38–45.

[55] See among many others, C. Greenwood, 'International Humanitarian Law and United Nations Military Operations' (1998) 1 *YIHL* 3–34 at 16; D. Shraga, 'The United Nations as an Actor Bound by International Humanitarian Law' (1998) 5 *International Peacekeeping* 64–81 at 65. For parallel arguments vis-à-vis the EU, see M. Zwanenburg, 'Toward a More Mature ESDP: Responsibility for Violations of International Humanitarian Law by EU Crisis Management Operations' in: S. Blockmans (ed.), *The European Union and Crisis Management* (Asser Press, 2008), 395–415 at 400–1. See also ECJ, *Racke* (Case C-162/96) [1998], para. 45; Poulsen and Diva Navigation Case C-286/90 [1992] ECR I-6019, para. 9, confirming that the EC is required to comply with the rules of (customary) international law in the exercise of its powers.

[56] See, e.g., Articles 2(2) and 20 of the 1994 Convention on the Safety of United Nations and Associated Personnel ['Convention shall not apply to a United Nations operation authorized by the Security Council as an enforcement action under Chapter VII of the Charter of the United Nations in which any of the personnel are engaged as combatants against organized armed forces and to which the law of international armed conflict applies.' 'Nothing in this Convention shall affect: (a) The applicability of international humanitarian law and universally recognized standards of human rights as contained in international instruments in relation to the protection of United Nations operations and United Nations and associated personnel or the responsibility of such personnel to respect such law and standards']; UN Secretary General,

JANN K. KLEFFNER

of an international organization take direct part in hostilities. Such direct participation needs to be distinguished, however, from the situation in which military personnel of an international organization exercise their right to individual self-defence. It has also been suggested that the threshold of direct participation is equally not reached by the fact alone that such personnel use force in self-defence in the discharge of their mandate, provided that it is limited to such use.[57] Similarly complex issues of fact and law evolve around the question whether and to what extent an international organization is to be considered subject to the law of belligerent occupation.[58] Although international humanitarian law thus applies to international organizations in the aforementioned situations, two qualifications must be made. The first is that the application of the law of neutrality may be affected in a conflict in which the UN is involved, whether directly through forces under its command or indirectly because it has authorized military action. All states are, today, members of the UN and, as such, are under a legal obligation to carry out Security Council decisions relating to the maintenance of international peace and security.[59] In addition, Article 2, para. 5 of the UN Charter provides that: 'All Members shall give the United Nations every assistance in any action it takes in accordance with the present Charter, and shall refrain from giving assistance to any State against which the United Nations is taking preventive or enforcement action.' This obligation will prevail over the laws of neutrality by virtue of Article 103 of the UN Charter. A member state may not, therefore, rely upon the law of neutrality in order to evade the obligation to carry out binding Security Council resolutions. In addition, any state, whether or not a member of the UN, may assist a UN force or a force acting under the authorization of the Security Council even if such assistance would normally be a violation of the law of neutrality.[60] The second qualification is that the application of international humanitarian law may be affected by binding decisions of the Security Council. This is particularly likely to be the case with respect to the law of belligerent occupation (see below, Chapter 5). That law places a high priority on the maintenance of the status quo in occupied territory pending a definitive settlement but the Council may well adopt decisions requiring structural change within the occupied territory (as it did in Iraq in 2003–2004).[61] See further Chapter 13.

4. It is generally accepted that international humanitarian law, and in particular the law of non-international armed conflicts, binds organized armed groups. This is not only evident from the wording of Common Article 3, which is addressed to 'each Party to the conflict', and some other instruments applicable in non-international armed conflicts,[62]

Secretary-General's Bulletin: Observance by United Nations Forces of International Humanitarian Law, 6 August 1999. ST/SGB/1999/13; UN DPKO Department of Field Support, 'United Nations Peacekeeping Operations—Principles and Guidelines' [Capstone Doctrine] 15 January 2008.

[57] Cf. Special Court for Sierra Leone, *Prosecutor v Sesay, Kallon and Gbao*, Trial Chamber Judgment, 2 March 2009, para. 233.

[58] For a summary of the debate surrounding the issue vis-à-vis UN operations, see ICRC, Occupation and other Forms of Administration of Foreign Territory, Report of Expert Meeting, Geneva (2012) <http://www.icrc.org/eng/assets/files/publications/icrc-002–4094.pdf>, 33–4.

[59] Article 25 UN Charter.

[60] See the 1975 Wiesbaden resolution of the *Institut de droit international, Annuaire de l'Institut*, 56 Vol. II (1975), 541, Schindler/Toman (eds), *The Laws of Armed Conflict*, 4th edn (Nijhoff, 2004), 907 and Dinstein, above (n. 18), 154–5.

[61] See, e.g., SC Res. 1483 (2003), 1511 (2003), and 1546 (2004).

[62] Cf. e.g. Articles 7 and 8 of the 1999 Second Hague Protocol, both equally addressed to 'each Party' or 'Parties to the conflict'; Articles 8(2)(e)(vii) ['conscripting or enlisting children ... into armed forces or

but also confirmed by various resolutions and decisions of international bodies[63] as well as the ICRC. Beyond this general acceptance, however, the conceptual basis for the binding force of international humanitarian law on organized armed groups is far from settled.[64] For further discussion, see Chapter 12, Section 1201, para. 5.

5. The binding force of international humanitarian law on individuals has been recognized for a long time. Ever since individuals have been punished for transgressions of the law, it is clear that individuals bear duties under international humanitarian law.[65] Such duties do not only extend to the individual combatant but to members of organized armed groups as much as to civilians.[66] International humanitarian law imposes such duties upon individuals directly on the international plane, that is without requiring the interposition of a rule of domestic law for establishing individual criminal responsibility.

International humanitarian law protects persons who do not or no longer directly participate in hostilities.	211

1. In international armed conflicts, international humanitarian law formally recognizes and defines distinct categories of persons who do not or no longer directly participate in hostilities as 'protected persons'. These are the wounded, sick and shipwrecked,[67] prisoners of war,[68] and civilians.[69] While no formal categories of 'protected persons' exist in non-international armed conflict, the applicable international humanitarian law nevertheless grants material protection to those who do not or no longer actively participate in hostilities.

2. Among the aforementioned persons that enjoy general protection, international humanitarian law grants special protection to certain groups of persons, namely women,[70] children,[71] refugees and displaced persons,[72] missing persons,[73] medical and religious

groups... '] and (2)(e)(xi) ['subjecting persons who are in the power of another party to the conflict to physical mutilation... '] ICC Statute.

[63] See for recent examples. e.g. SC Res. 1868 (2009), Preamble (Afghanistan); 1863 (2009) para. 15 (Somalia); 1856 (2008) para. 23 (DR Congo); all calling upon, or demanding that all parties to the respective armed conflicts comply with international humanitarian law; UN Commission on Human Rights... See also Special Court for Sierra Leone, *Prosecutor v Kallon and Kamara*, Appeals Chamber Decision on Challenge to Jurisdiction: Lomé Accord Amnesty (13 March 2004) para. 45.

[64] Kleffner, 'The Applicability of International Humanitarian Law to Organized Armed Groups' (2011) 93 *IRRC* 443–61.

[65] For an early example, see e.g. the Henfield's case, 11 F. Cas. 1099 (C. C. D. Pa. 1793)(No. 6,360), reproduced in J. Paust, M. C. Bassiouni, M. Scharf et. al. (eds), *International Criminal Law, Cases and Materials*, 2nd edn (Carolina Academic Press, Durham, 2000), 232–8.

[66] For the criminal responsibility of civilians for war crimes, see among many others, Trial of Alfried Felix Alwyn Krupp and Eleven Others, US Military Tribunal, Nuremberg 17 November 1947–30 June 1948. *Law Reports of Trials of War Criminals*, Vol. X, p. 150. For a useful summary of other case-law, including criminal trials of civilians for war crimes, see Provost, *International Human Rights Law and Humanitarian Law* (CUP, 2002), 75–102. For a recent restatement, see *Prosecutor v Akayesu*, ICTR-96-4-T, Judgment, Appeals Chamber, 1 June 2001, paras. 443–4.

[67] Cf. Arts. 13 of GC I and II respectively, and Art. 8(a) and (b) AP I.

[68] Cf. Art. 4 GC III and Arts. 43 and 44(1) AP I.

[69] Cf. Art. 4 GC IV and Art. 50 AP I.

[70] GC I, Art. 12(4); GC II, Art. 12(4); GC IV, Art. 27; AP I, Art. 76; GC III, Arts. 25, 97; GC IV, Arts. 76, 85, 124; AP I, Art. 75(5); AP II, Art. 5(2)(a); GC III, Art. 14; GC IV, Art. 97; GC III, Art. 29; GC IV, Art. 85(4); GC III, Art. 88; AP I, Art. 76(2), (3); AP II, Art. 6.

[71] See, e.g., GC IV Arts. 23–4, 38, 50, 76, 89; AP I, Arts. 70(1), 77; AP II Art. 4(3); Convention on the Rights of the Child, Article 38.

[72] See, e.g., GC IV, Arts. 44, 45, 49, 70; AP I, Arts. 73, 85; AP II, Art. 17.

[73] See, e.g., AP I, Arts. 32–4.

JANN K. KLEFFNER

personnel,[74] humanitarian relief personnel,[75] journalists,[76] and personnel involved in a peacekeeping mission who are entitled to the protection given to civilians under international humanitarian law.[77]

3. While international humanitarian law provides a great number of—at times very detailed—rules that stipulate the treatment that parties to an armed conflict are obliged to grant to persons who do not or no longer directly participate in hostilities, the underlying principle is that they must be respected and protected in all circumstances, and must be treated humanely, without any adverse distinction founded on sex, race, nationality, religion, political opinions, or any other similar criteria.[78] The obligation to respect them means that parties to an armed conflict must refrain from harming them, from exposing them to suffering and from killing them. The active notion of the obligation to protect such persons means that parties to an armed conflict are obliged to ward off dangers and to prevent harm. The obligation to afford humane treatment entails that parties to an armed conflict ensure to persons who do not or no longer directly participate in hostilities an existence worthy of human beings. The treatment must be afforded without discrimination on any ground. On the prohibition of reprisals against persons who do not or no longer directly participate in hostilities, see Section 488.

212   **Although members of the armed forces of a party to an armed conflict and civilians directly participating in hostilities may be subject to direct attack, they enjoy the protection of international humanitarian law against certain methods and means of warfare.**

1. Combatants in international armed conflicts, fighters in non-international armed conflicts, and civilians directly participating in hostilities are legitimate targets, that is they may be subjected to direct attack. They nevertheless enjoy a certain degree of protection through some rules on methods and means of warfare, first and foremost the prohibition of certain methods and weapons deemed to inflict superfluous injury and/or unnecessary suffering, and of those that actually do.

III. Geographical Scope

213   **In international armed conflicts, military operations may only be carried out in:**
         — the territories of the parties to the conflict as defined by the national boundaries;
         — the high seas (including the airspace above and the sea floor); and
         — exclusive economic zones.

1. In international armed conflicts, military operations may not be carried out beyond what is at times referred to as 'the area of war'.[79] That area includes all the territory of the parties to the conflict,[80] and the high seas, and exclusive economic zones (EEZs),

---

[74] See, e.g., GC I, Arts. 24–6; GC II, Art. 36; GC IV, Art. 20; AP I, Art. 15; AP II, Art. 9.
[75] See, e.g., AP I, Art. 71(2); AP II, Art. 18(2).
[76] See, e.g., AP I, Art. 79.
[77] Cf. Rule 33 *CIHL*.
[78] Arts. 12 GC I and II; 16 GC III; 27 GC IV; 75 AP I; 2 and 4 AP II.
[79] H. Lauterpacht (ed.), *Oppenheim's International Law*, Vol. II, 236–44; C. Greenwood in the 2nd edn of this Handbook, 59.
[80] Unless somehow excluded, e.g. by neutralization; see Sections 216–217.

JANN K. KLEFFNER

including the EEZs of neutral states[81] (although military operations in the EEZ of a neutral state must show due regard for the rights and interests of that state).[82] International humanitarian law applicable in international armed conflicts as a whole thus has an extensive geographical scope. However, the geographical scope of individual rules may very well be more limited. Thus, the nature of the rules pertaining to the protection of prisoners of war and civilians have been mentioned as examples of rules that apply to the entire territory of the parties to the conflict, not just to the vicinity of actual hostilities, whereas other provisions have been held to be so clearly bound up with the hostilities that their geographical scope is limited to the territory in which hostilities occur.[83]

2. The territory (including internal and territorial waters) of neutral states and the airspace above them may not be made part of the area of war, unless the neutral state has allowed one of the belligerents to conduct military operations on its territory, in which case the rival belligerent has a right to take measures in that territory to terminate those operations.[84]

3. Besides the aforementioned geographical confines emanating from international humanitarian law and the law of neutrality, the *jus ad bellum* may impose further restrictions. See below Section 218.

> The national territory includes: 214
> — land territory;
> — rivers and landlocked lakes;
> — national maritime waters and territorial waters; and
> — the airspace above these territories.

> The dividing line between the airspace of the national territory of a state and outer   215
> space shall be drawn where, due to existing physical conditions, the density of the
> air is small enough to permit the employment of satellites. According to the present
> state of the art, the minimum flight altitude of satellites ranges between 80 and 110
> km above ground level.

> Subject to the agreement of the parties to the armed conflict, it is prohibited to   216
> extend military operations to demilitarized zones (Article 60 AP I), in particular
> hospital and safety zones (Article 23 GC I; Article 14 GC IV) and neutralized zones
> (Article 15 GC IV). Non-defended localities (Article 25 HagueReg; Article 59 AP
> I) may not be attacked (see Section 461 below).

1. Zones within the territory of the parties to a conflict may be excluded from the area in which military operations may be conducted by agreement between the parties. Thus Article 23 GC I and Article 14 GC IV provide for the establishment of hospital zones for the treatment of the wounded and sick. Article 15 GC IV provides for the establishment of safety zones intended to shelter the wounded, sick, and civilians 'who take no part in hostilities'. Such zones are to be established by agreement between the parties and a Draft Agreement is attached to the Geneva Conventions as a precedent. The parties can also, if they so wish, establish zones on the high seas in which no hostile operations

---

[81] See Chapter 10.
[82] Article 58, Law of the Sea Convention 1982.
[83] ICTY, *Tadić* Interloc. App., para. 68.
[84] See Chapter 11.

JANN K. KLEFFNER

are to take place. The provision in Article 60 AP I for the creation, again by agreement between the parties, of demilitarized zones builds upon the concept of the safety zones in the Fourth Convention. It should be noted that the establishment of all these zones requires agreement between the parties; a unilateral announcement by one party to the conflict is not sufficient. See further, Sections 461–3, 624–7.

2. Undefended localities are those which can be occupied at will by a belligerent. They are therefore confined to 'places in or near a zone where armed forces are in contact' (Article 59 AP I) and do not extend to places far behind a state's 'lines' since such a place, although it may have no forces anywhere near it, is not open for occupation. Undefended localities may be established without agreement between the parties. Undefended localities declared by a state remain part of the area of war but the adverse party may not bombard or otherwise attack them, although it may send forces to occupy them.

217   **Military operations shall not be carried out in the national territories of neutral or other states not parties to the conflict and in neutralized areas in which, according to contractual agreements, no military operations shall take place, even if the state to whose area of jurisdiction they belong is a party to the conflict. There are, for instance, binding agreements not to execute any military operations in Spitsbergen, in the area of the Åland Islands, in the Suez Canal, the Panama Canal, and in the Antarctic regions.**

The duty of the belligerents not to conduct military operations in the territory of neutral states and states not parties to the conflict applies to all such states and not just to those states, such as Switzerland, with a permanent regime of neutrality. In addition, a number of treaties provide for the neutralization of areas of territory, even if those areas form part of the territory of a belligerent.[85] The Spitsbergen Treaty, 1920,[86] by which eleven states recognized the 'full and absolute sovereignty of Norway over the Archipelago of Spitsbergen', required Norway not to construct any naval base or fortification on the archipelago, 'which may never be used for warlike purposes'. Spitsbergen was, however, used for military operations during World War II. When Norway placed Spitsbergen under NATO command after World War II, the USSR protested. Norway replied that no bases or fortifications were to be built upon the archipelago.[87] The Åland Islands were made a 'neutral zone' by a multilateral agreement of 1921,[88] following the recommendation of the Council of the League of Nations. This status was reaffirmed in Article 5 of the Peace Treaty with Finland, 1947. Article 1 of the Antarctic Treaty 1959[89] reserves the Antarctic for peaceful purposes and forbids the establishment of military bases and fortifications within Antarctica.[90] The Suez Canal is subject to a detailed regime regarding its use and protection in time of war, contained in the Constantinople Convention 1888.[91] However, the measures taken to close the Canal to German shipping during World Wars I and II and to Israeli shipping during the Egypt–Israel War called into question aspects of this regime. The Hay-Pauncefote Treaty 1901[92] between the UK and the US

[85] H. Lauterpacht, *Oppenheim's International Law*, Vol. II, 244–7; Afsah, 'Neutralization', *MPEPIL*.
[86] LNTS 2, 7; Ulfstein, 'Spitsbergen/Svalbard', *MPEPIL*.
[87] Afsah, above (n. 85).
[88] LNTS 9, 212; Hark, Åland Islands, *MPEPIL*.
[89] UNTS 402, 71; Vöneky/Addison-Agyei, 'Antarctica', *MPEPIL*.
[90] Jennings and Watts, *Oppenheim's International Law*, Vol. I, 693.
[91] Jennings and Watts, *Oppenheim's International Law*, Vol. I, 592; Arcari, 'Suez Canal', *MPEPIL*.
[92] 190 CTS 215.

JANN K. KLEFFNER

prohibits acts of hostility within the Panama Canal Zone.[93] The Treaty Concerning the Permanent Neutrality and Operation of the Panama Canal Zone 1977[94] between the US and Panama, and the annexed Protocol on neutrality, open to accession by all states, provides for the permanent neutrality of the Panama Canal.[95]

> **The zones in which military operations actually take place shall be designated as   218
> the area of operations.**

Military operations will not normally be conducted throughout the area of war. The area in which operations are actually taking place at any given time is known as the 'area of operations' or 'theatre of war',[96] although these are not legal terms of art. The extent to which a belligerent today is justified in expanding the area of operations will depend upon whether it is necessary for him to do so in order to exercise his right of self-defence. While a state cannot be expected always to defend itself solely on ground of the aggressor's choosing, any expansion of the area of operations may not go beyond what constitutes a necessary and proportionate measure of self-defence. In particular, it cannot be assumed—as in the past—that a state engaged in armed conflict is free to attack its adversary anywhere in the area of war.[97]

> **The law of belligerent occupation applies in territory that has actually come under   219
> the authority of hostile armed forces (see further Section 527).**

> **In non-international armed conflicts the applicability of international humanitarian   220
> law extends to the entire territory of the state concerned (see below, Section 1201).**

1. The territorial applicability of the law of non-international armed conflict extends to the entire territory of the state concerned.[98] The geographical scope of international humanitarian law applicable in this type of armed conflict is thus not limited to areas of actual combat or their vicinity. While some rules, for instance those governing the conduct of hostilities, are practically relevant first and foremost in those areas where such hostilities actually occur, other rules apply throughout the territory irrespective of whether or not combat takes place.[99]

2. Complex questions relating to the geographical scope of international humanitarian law are raised by non-international armed conflicts that are not limited to the territory of one single state; non-international armed conflicts that are not internal in nature, in other words. See Section 1201.

---

[93] Jennings and Watts, *Oppenheim's International Law*, Vol. I, 595; Arcari, 'Panama Canal', *MPEPIL*.

[94] (1977) 16 *ILM* 1021–98; Jennings and Watts, *Oppenheim's International Law*, Vol. I, 597–8.

[95] A number of other cases in which territory is said to have been neutralized are discussed in H. Lauterpacht, *Oppenheim's International Law*, Vol. II, 244–7 and Afsah, above (n. 85).

[96] H. Lauterpacht, *Oppenheim's International Law*, Vol. II, 237.

[97] This question is discussed further by Greenwood, 'Self-Defence and the Conduct of International Armed Conflict' in Dinstein/Tabory (eds), *International Law at a Time of Perplexity* (Nijhoff, 1989), 273, 276–8.

[98] ICTR *Akayesu*, paras. 635–6.

[99] ICTY *Tadić*, Interloc. App., para. 69.

JANN K. KLEFFNER

IV. Temporal Scope

221   International humanitarian law begins to apply from the beginning of the international armed conflict, the situation of belligerent occupation, or the non-international armed conflict.

1. Subject to the limited exceptions of those rules that apply also in peacetime,[100] international humanitarian law begins to apply as soon as an armed conflict has come into existence. As soon as the factual requirements for that existence are met, the situation begins to be governed by international humanitarian law.

2. To the extent that one subscribes to the first-shot theory,[101] that means that the law of international armed conflict begins to apply with the resort to armed force between states.

3. In a similar vein, the law of belligerent occupation begins to apply as soon as the factual conditions for the existence of a belligerent occupation are fulfilled. The precise determination when that is the case raises a number of complicated and contested questions. Thus, there is no unanimous agreement on the questions at what point in time the invasion by one state of the territory of another state turns into a situation of belligerent occupation; whether an intermediate period between the invasion phase and a situation of belligerent occupation may exist; whether occupation implies some degree of stability in the area subject to the foreign forces' intervention; and to what extent the law of belligerent occupation can be applied gradually.[102]

4. The law of non-international armed conflicts begins to apply as soon as the armed violence is sufficiently intense and the armed group(s) sufficiently organized so as to meet the legally required threshold. This is notwithstanding the fact that non-international armed conflicts are often preceded by a period of internal disturbances and tensions that is not governed by international humanitarian law. It will then be necessary to determine at what point in time such disturbances and tensions reach the threshold of intensity, and the parties to it the required degree of organization, for the situation to be governed also by international humanitarian law rather than exclusively by human rights law and national law.

222   In international armed conflicts, international humanitarian law ceases to apply on the general close of military operations. The law of belligerent occupation ceases to apply at the termination of the occupation. In non-international armed conflict, international humanitarian law ceases to apply at the end of the armed conflict. However, persons deprived of their liberty or whose liberty has been restricted for reasons related to an armed conflict continue to benefit from the protections of international humanitarian law until the end of such deprivation or restriction of liberty (Article 6, paras. 2 and 3, GC IV; Article 3, lit. b, AP I; Art. 5 GC I; Art. 5, para. 1, GC III; Art. 6, para. 4, GC IV; Article 3, lit. b, AP I; Article 2, para. 2, AP II).

---

[100] See above n. 1.
[101] See above Section 202, at 1.
[102] For a summary of the opinions of experts, see ICRC, *Occupation and other Forms of Administration of Foreign Territory* (n. 113), 24.

JANN K. KLEFFNER

1. As much as the beginning of the applicability of international humanitarian law, the end of that applicability is essentially a matter of fact. As far as international armed conflicts are concerned, the law ceases to apply 'on the general close of military operations'.[103] This is different in situations of belligerent occupation. Article 6(3) GC IV stipulates that in such a case, the Convention ceases to apply 'one year after the general close of military operations' except for certain rules which apply for the duration of the occupation and 'to the extent that [an Occupying Power] exercises the functions of government in [occupied] territory'. AP I differs to some extent from GC IV in as much as it extends the applicability of the entire law of belligerent occupation until the 'termination of the occupation'.[104] Regardless of whether or not there is a general close of military operations or a termination of the occupation, persons for whom the final release, repatriation, or re-establishment is pending continue to benefit from the relevant rules of international humanitarian law.[105] In the case of a non-international armed conflict, international humanitarian law ceases to apply with the 'end of the armed conflict', with a similar exception as regards those deprived of their liberty or whose liberty is restricted for reasons related to that conflict. They continue to benefit from a limited number of protections, regardless of whether they are so deprived or restricted during or after the conflict.[106]

2. It may at times be difficult to ascertain the point at which there is a 'general close of military operations', an occupation is 'terminated', and a non-international armed conflict has ended. However, the determination whether or not the conditions for an end of the applicability of international humanitarian law are fulfilled has to be made on the basis of the facts on the ground. The subjective views of the parties to the armed conflict or of the occupying power are immaterial if contradicted by the facts. It is also neither necessary nor determinative that a peace agreement has been reached by the parties to an armed conflict. Such an agreement may be indicative of the intentions of the parties to an armed conflict to end hostilities and move from a time of armed conflict to peace. However, if and when these intentions are not followed by actual conduct, it is that actual conduct which is determinative.

> In international armed conflicts, hostilities may be terminated temporarily or permanently. Even a definite cessation of hostilities does not alter the fact that there is a state of war. A state of war will be ended only by a conclusion of peace unless it has already been expressly terminated. The following sections on activities relating to the termination of hostilities and on the conclusion of peace are based on treaty law and custom applicable in international armed conflicts. However, they partly affect activities to terminate hostilities and conclude peace agreements in non-international armed conflicts (see also below, Section 1221).

223

1. The termination of the applicability of international humanitarian law discussed in the previous section needs to be distinguished from the termination of hostilities. The latter term is not identical with the notion of 'armed conflict' as a factual determinant of the beginning and end of the temporal scope of applicability of international humanitarian law. The term 'hostilities' in turn, refers to the resort by the parties to the conflict to

---

[103] Cf. Arts. 6(2) GC IV and 3(b) AP I.
[104] Cf. Art. 3(b) AP I. For discussion, see ICRC, *Occupation and other Forms of Administration of Foreign Territory*, 26–33.
[105] Cf. Arts. 5 GC I, 5(1) GC III, Art. 6(4) GC IV, Art. 3(b) AP I.
[106] Cf. Art. 2(2) AP II.

JANN K. KLEFFNER

means and methods of injuring the enemy.[107] In other words, 'hostilities' are a narrower concept than, and form only one part of, an 'armed conflict'. Hostilities can be terminated temporarily or permanently by means of an armistice or ceasefire (see below).

2. Where a state of war has come into being through a formal declaration of war, the fact that hostilities have been terminated is not in itself sufficient to terminate the state of war. Historically, it has generally been accepted that as a corollary to the formal requirement of a declaration of war to bring about the state of war, it is also only through the formal instrument of a peace treaty which terminates the state of war.[108] Today, some other clear indication on the part of the belligerents that they intend to terminate the state of war can fulfil the same function as a peace treaty (on the role of armistices in that respect, see below, Section 245). Although active hostilities during World War II ceased in Europe in May 1945, it was not until 31 December 1946 that the US formally announced that hostilities had terminated.[109] Even then, the state of war was regarded as continuing, pending the adoption of a peace treaty between Germany and her former adversaries. In the end, no peace treaty was concluded.[110] The state of war was, however, formally declared terminated by France (9 July 1951), the UK (9 July 1951), the US (24 October 1951), and the USSR (25 January 1955). Similar declarations were made by Germany's other former adversaries.[111] Until those declarations were made, national courts continued to hold that the state of war obtained for most purposes.[112]

1. Parlementaires and Protecting Powers

224   **A cessation of hostilities is regularly preceded by negotiations with the adversary. The parties to the conflict frequently use parlementaires for this purpose.**

Parlementaires[113] are used not only for negotiations about a cessation or temporary suspension of hostilities but also for negotiations on such matters as the recovery of wounded persons or exchange of prisoners, and for communicating messages to an adversary's forces. Today, negotiations for a general cessation of hostilities are more likely to be conducted at the political level,[114] frequently through an intermediary such as the UN. The use of parlementaires as the means of communication between opposing forces nevertheless remains important, especially when forces are deployed in remote areas, as in the Falklands conflict. The parlementaire must be authorized by the commander of the forces which sent him. Traditionally, this authorization should be in writing and signed by the commander concerned, although there is no express provision in the Hague Regulations to that effect.

225   **Parlementaires are persons authorized by one party to the conflict to enter into negotiations with the adversary. Parlementaires and persons accompanying**

---

[107] ICRC, *Interpretive Guidance on the Notion of Direct Participation in Hostilities under International Humanitarian Law*, 43.

[108] Kleffner, 'Peace Treaties', *MPEPIL*.

[109] M. Whiteman, *Digest of International Law*, Vol. X (Washington, 1968), 89.

[110] See, however, the Treaty on the Final Settlement with respect to Germany, (1990) 29 *ILM* 1186.

[111] Whiteman, Vol. X, 89–95; J. L. Kunz, 'The Chaotic Status of the Laws of War and the Urgent Necessity for their Revision' (1951) 45 *AJIL* 37–61; 'Ending the War with Germany' (1952) 46 *AJIL* 114.

[112] See the cases discussed at Whiteman, Vol. X, 93–4.

[113] *UK Manual* (2004), para. 10.4; M. Greenspan, *The Modern Law of Land Warfare* (University of California Press, 1959), 380–5.

[114] *UK Manual* (2004), para. 10.3.1.

JANN K. KLEFFNER

them, for example drivers and interpreters, have a right to inviolability (Article 32 HagueReg). They make themselves known by a white flag.

1. The parlementaire is usually, but not necessarily, an officer. He may be of any nationality. Defectors or persons taken prisoner by the adversary cannot have the status neither of parlementaires nor of persons accompanying parlementaires, and hence have no right of inviolability. They can be detained if the tactical situation so requires.

2. A parlementaire has a duty to make himself and the purpose of his mission known to the adversary; his own protection may depend upon this. For that reason, the law has traditionally required that a parlementaire display a white flag (Article 32 HagueReg). A white flag is, however, no more than a signal that an armed force wishes to open negotiations. By hoisting a white flag a force is asking its adversary whether it is willing to receive a communication. It does not necessarily indicate an intention to surrender, although it has come to indicate such an intention when raised by an individual soldier or a small group of soldiers during an exchange of fire. Although it is unlawful for a force displaying a white flag to carry on firing, great caution is necessary, for the flag may have been hoisted by some members of a unit without the knowledge or consent of the commander.[115] During the Battle for Goose Green in the Falklands conflict, some Argentine soldiers displayed a white flag without authorization from their commander and unknown to the rest of the Argentine forces engaged in the battle. A British party who went into the open to investigate were fired on and killed by other Argentine soldiers who were apparently unaware of the white flag raised by their colleagues.

3. Traditionally, a parlementaire may approach the enemy alone, carrying the white flag himself. It is, however, more usual for him to be accompanied. According to Article 32 HagueReg, he may be accompanied by a trumpeter, bugler, or drummer, a flag-bearer, and an interpreter. In modern warfare, however, the parlementaire is more likely to be accompanied by a driver, wireless or loudhailer operator, and an interpreter.[116] The interpreter need not be a member of the armed forces to which the parlementaire belongs.

> When entering the territory of the adversary, parlementaires and the persons   226
> accompanying them shall not be taken prisoner or detained. The principle of
> inviolability shall apply until they have returned safely to friendly territory.
> The adverse party is not required to cease firing in the entire sector in which a
> parlementaire arrives.

1. The parlementaire and those accompanying him or her are accorded inviolability. This means that they may not be fired upon or otherwise attacked, nor may they be detained. Except by prior agreement, however, the approach of a parlementaire does not require opposing forces to cease firing throughout a whole sector of the battlefield. Nevertheless, the entitlement of parlementaires and those accompanying them to be accorded inviolability is not absolute. First, they may be temporarily detained if they have (accidentally) acquired information the disclosure of which to the adversary would jeopardize the success of a current or impending operation of the friendly armed forces.[117] In this case, the parlementaire

---

[115] *UK Manual* (2004), para. 10.5.2.
[116] *UK Manual* (2004), para. 10.7.
[117] *UK Manual* (2004), para. 10.9.

JANN K. KLEFFNER

may be detained until the operation has been completed. In the meantime, he shall be treated with the respect appropriate to his position and at least like a prisoner of war. For a second exception, see the following section.

2. Distinct from the question of inviolability and loss of it is the question whether the commander to whom a parlementaire is sent is in all cases obliged to receive him or her. According to Article 33, para. 1 of the Hague Regulations of 1907, that question is to be answered in the negative. The commander may refuse to receive a parlementaire, for instance because reception would bear the risk of revealing operationally or tactically sensitive information. However, it is not considered lawful for a commander to announce in advance that parlementaires will not be received.[118]

3. In contrast, it is permissible to take all necessary steps (e.g. blindfolding) to prevent the parlementaire from taking advantage of his mission to obtain information.[119] Likewise, the commander who receives a parlementaire is entitled to direct the time and route by which he and his party should approach and the point at which they should enter the area controlled by his forces. Once the parlementaire is in territory controlled by the opposing forces, those forces are entitled to direct his movements in whatever way is necessary, commensurate with the safety of the parlementaire, to protect their security.

227   **Parlementaires lose their right of inviolability if it is proved in an incontestable manner that they have taken advantage of their privileged position for provoking or committing an act of treason (Article 34 HagueReg).**

A parlementaire is entitled to observe and report on anything he sees which the adversary has not hidden. It is an abuse of the parlementaire's position, however, for the parlementaire or those accompanying him or her to commit acts contrary to international law and to the detriment of the adversary during their mission. Such acts include the taking of photographs, making sketch maps of defensive positions, engaging in secret intelligence gathering, committing acts of sabotage, organizing acts of espionage in the territory of the adverse party, inducing soldiers of the adverse party to collaborate in collecting intelligence, instigating soldiers of the adverse party to refuse to do their duty; or encouraging them to desert. Should the parlementaire or those accompanying him or her do so, they may be detained temporarily (Article 33, para. 3, HagueReg) and, if it is proved 'in a clear and incontestable manner' that any of them have abused their position to provoke or commit an act of treason, the person concerned forfeits his or her inviolability and may be tried. Any measures taken against a parlementaire or members of his party should be communicated to the enemy at once.[120]

228   **Misusing the flag of truce constitutes perfidy and is thus a violation of international law (Article 23 lit. f, HagueReg; Article 37, para. 1 lit. a, Article 38, para. 1, AP I). The flag of truce is misused, for instance, if soldiers approach an enemy position under the protection of the flag of truce in order to attack.**

Misuse of the flag of truce has long been a war crime under customary international law. Under Articles 37 and 38 of AP I, such acts are treated as perfidy.

---

[118] H. Lauterpacht (ed.), *Oppenheim's International Law*, Vol. II, 539; Greenspan, id. 382.
[119] Article 33, para. 2, HagueReg.
[120] *UK Manual* (2004), para. 10.10.

JANN K. KLEFFNER

> Apart from dispatching parlementaires, the parties to a conflict may also com-   229
> municate with each other through the intermediary of Protecting Powers.
> Protecting Powers are neutral or other states not parties to the conflict which
> safeguard the rights and interests of a party to the conflict and those of its nation-
> als vis-à-vis an adverse party to the conflict (Article 2 lit. c, AP I). Particularly,
> the International Committee of the Red Cross may act as a 'substitute' (Article
> 5, para. 4, AP I) if the parties to the conflict cannot agree upon the designation
> of a Protecting Power.

For discussion of the now little-used institution of the Protecting Power, see Sections 1420–
1421. The ICRC is now used more frequently as an intermediary.

2. Ceasefire and Armistice

> An armistice agreement is characterized by the intention to provide an opportu-   230
> nity for making preparations for the termination of an armed conflict. Its aim
> is to terminate hostilities permanently. That is what distinguishes an armistice
> from a ceasefire. An armistice may be local (Article 37 HagueReg). As a matter
> of principle, however, an armistice agreement shall be designed to suspend mili-
> tary operations between the parties to the conflict and to pave the way for peace
> negotiations.

1. The distinction between a general armistice and a ceasefire has traditionally been that
the armistice was considered a step on the road to a permanent end to hostilities and the
conclusion of a treaty of peace. Thus the armistice of Rethondes in 1918 was a prerequisite
for the commencement of negotiations which led in 1919 to the Treaty of Versailles and
the termination of World War I. Since World War II, however, there have been a number
of cases in which hostilities were brought to a close by the conclusion of an armistice
agreement and no peace treaty was subsequently agreed. The hostilities in Korea were
brought to an end by the conclusion of the Panmunjom Armistice Agreement in 1953,
and the first Arab–Israeli hostilities ceased with the conclusion of the 1949 armistice
agreements between Israel, Egypt, Jordan, Lebanon, and Syria.

2. Historically, it has always been considered that the conclusion of a ceasefire or an
armistice did not terminate the state of war.[121] It has been questioned whether this
principle is still part of the law, especially where, as in the case of the 1949 armistice
agreements between Israel and four Arab states, an armistice is concluded under UN
auspices.[122] The correct view is probably that stated by Judge Baxter, namely that such an
instrument *can* terminate the state of war, if the parties intend that it should have that
effect,[123] for just as the creation of a state of war is brought about by a clear expression of
the intentions of a country, that state of war can also be terminated by an indication of
the intention to do so.

3. On the question of whether an armistice agreement or ceasefire can terminate
an armed conflict, which has not amounted to war in the legal sense, see below,
Section 245.

---

[121] H. S. Levie, 'The Nature and Scope of the Armistice Agreement' (1956) 50 *AJIL* 880.
[122] See, e.g., the statement by the representative of Israel, SCOR 549th Meeting, 26 July 1951, paras.
40–1; S. Rosenne, *Israel's Armistice Agreements with the Arab States* (Tel-Aviv: Blumstein, 1951), 45.
[123] R. Baxter, 'Armistices and other Forms of Suspension of Hostilities' (1976) 149 *RdC* 353.

JANN K. KLEFFNER

231   A ceasefire is defined as a temporary interruption of military operations which
        is limited to a specific area and will normally be agreed upon between the local
        commanders. It shall generally serve humanitarian purposes, in particular search-
        ing for and collecting the wounded and the shipwrecked, rendering first aid to
        these persons, and removing civilians (Article 15 GC I; Article 18 GC II; Article 17
        GC IV). The regulations governing armistices (Articles 36–41 HagueReg) shall be
        applied *mutatis mutandis.*

Now that so few conflicts are treated, either by the parties or by other nations, as giving
rise to a formal state of war, the dividing line between ceasefires, armistices, and other
forms of suspension of hostilities has become increasingly blurred.[124] In many cases, a
ceasefire is of indefinite duration. That was the case with the ceasefire concluded in the
Iran–Iraq War in 1988, although that was concluded under UN auspices and followed
the adoption of a binding resolution of the Security Council.[125]

232   If the parties to the conflict have not defined the duration of an armistice, it
        shall, as a matter of principle, be considered a valid assumption that the armi-
        stice is designed to be the transition to a definite cessation of hostilities. The ban
        on the use of force embodied in the UN Charter shall also be observed during
        this period of transition. In contrast to the provisions of the Hague Regulations
        Concerning the Laws and Customs of War on Land (Article 36 HagueReg), the
        parties to a conflict may not, at any time, resume operations after the conclusion
        of an armistice except in the exercise of the right to self-defence in accordance
        with the UN Charter.

1. The changes in the law regarding resort to force brought about by the adoption of the
UN Charter have had a particular effect on the right of the parties to resume hostilities
after the conclusion of an armistice. Whereas the law once admitted there was a general
right to resume hostilities (Article 36 HagueReg), today it would be a violation of Article 2(4)
for a state to resume hostilities unless the behaviour of the other party to the armistice
amounted to an armed attack or an imminent threat of an armed attack. Similarly,
although under the traditional law the conclusion of an armistice did not prejudice the
right of a party to exercise belligerent rights against shipping, such action would now be
lawful only if it constituted a necessary and proportionate measure of self-defence.

2. That the law relating to the resumption of hostilities and the exercise of belligerent
rights has changed in this way since the Hague Regulations were adopted was made
clear by the Security Council in 1951, when it ruled that Egypt's continued exercise of
belligerent rights against shipping was incompatible with the Egypt–Israel Armistice
Agreement 1949. The Council ruled that: '. . . since the armistice regime, which has been
in existence for nearly two and a half years, is of a permanent character, neither party
can reasonably assert that it is actively a belligerent or requires to exercise the right of
visit, search and seizure for any legitimate purpose of self-defence . . . '.[126]

3. It stands to reason that there is no difference between a general, indefinite ceasefire
and an armistice in this respect. Whether a resumption of hostilities is justified after

[124] Azarov/Blum, 'Suspension of Hostilities', *MPEPIL.*
[125] SC Res. 598 (1987); see M. Weller, 'The Use of Force in Collective Security' in Dekker/Post (eds), *The Gulf War of 1980–1988* (Nijhoff, 1992), 77–90.
[126] SC Res. 95 (1951).

JANN K. KLEFFNER

a general, indefinite ceasefire must be assessed by reference to the same criteria in the Charter in each case.[127]

> **Any serious violation of a ceasefire or an armistice may give the other party the**   233
> **right of denouncing it and, provided that the conditions for an exercise of the right**
> **to self-defence in accordance with the UN Charter are fulfilled, to recommence**
> **hostilities. A denunciation of the armistice will be necessary only if the military**
> **situation so permits (Article 40 HagueReg; Articles 2, no. 4, and 51 UN Charter).**

> **A violation of the terms of the armistice by individuals acting on their own ini-**   234
> **tiative does not entitle the injured party to denounce the agreement but only to**
> **demand the punishment of the offenders and reparation for the losses sustained**
> **(Article 41 HagueReg).**

A serious violation of an armistice or ceasefire will give rise to a right to resume hostilities. Again, however this right exists as an aspect of the right of self-defence, rather than as a right to punish the state responsible for the violation. Hostilities may be resumed if, and to the extent that, to do so is a necessary and proportionate measure of self-defence. Violations of armistice and ceasefire conditions committed by individuals acting without the authorization of their state will not normally give rise to such a right, although the true facts may be very difficult to ascertain in a particular case. Partly for that reason, many ceasefires are now monitored by UN peacekeeping forces to deter violations and to provide an authoritative machinery for determining the truth where violations have been alleged.

> **The terms of the armistice treaty shall be strictly observed by the parties to a conflict.**   235
> **It is not permissible to carry out any military operations giving an advantage over**
> **the adversary. To what extent this shall also apply to other actions taken during the**
> **armistice depends on the terms of the agreements made.**

Where an armistice regime becomes permanent, in the sense that all hostilities cease but normal relations are not resumed between the parties, the extent to which a party to the armistice agreement is prevented from moving its forces within the territory which it holds will depend upon the specific terms of the armistice, rather than upon any general rule. In the absence of any provision to the contrary, activities such as entrenching, ammunition resupply, and prepositioning of reinforcements shall be permissible. During an armistice it is, however, forbidden to move forward forces who are close to the enemy, or to employ reconnaissance patrols.[128]

> **The area of application of a limited armistice shall be defined as precisely as pos-**   236
> **sible. If, for instance, wounded persons are to be recovered it must be clear if and**
> **up to what line bombardments further to the rear remain permissible. Sometimes**
> **it will also be necessary to coordinate the utilization of the airspace and the pas-**
> **sage of ships.**

> **An armistice must be notified in an unmistakeable form and in good time.**   237
> **Hostilities are to be suspended immediately after the notification, or on the date**
> **fixed (Article 38 HagueReg).**

---

[127] S. Bailey, 'Cease-fires, Truces and Armistices in the Practice of the UN Security Council' (1977) 71 *AJIL* 461.

[128] Greenwood, in the 2nd edn of this Handbook, at 69.

JANN K. KLEFFNER

238   The terms of an armistice shall not deviate from the provisions of the Geneva
          Conventions to the detriment of protected persons (Article 6 common to GC I–III;
          Article 7 GC IV).

International humanitarian law exists primarily to protect individuals rather than to
establish rights for states.[129] The states party to a conflict may not, therefore, waive by
agreement between them any of the rights conferred upon individuals by international
humanitarian law. However, they may of course agree to accord greater protection than
is required by international humanitarian law.

3. Capitulation

239   A capitulation is the unilateral or mutually agreed termination of hostilities. It must
          take into account the rules of military honour (Article 35, para. 1, HagueReg).

240   It may be a total capitulation applying to all armed forces of a state, or a partial
          capitulation limited to specific units.

241   Every commander may declare or accept a capitulation only for his particular
          area of command. The capitulation and its acceptance are binding upon the states
          involved in the conflict. Every state may, however, call a capitulating commander
          to account if he has violated his duties, for example acted against orders.

242   A capitulation must be faithfully observed by the parties to the conflict (Article 35,
          para. 2, HagueReg). Persons who infringe the terms of the capitulation may be
          called to account by the adversary.

While the capitulation of the forces in a particular part of the area of operations will not
affect the existence of the state of armed conflict elsewhere, when the surrender effectively applies to all the forces of one party in the area of operations and when there is
every indication that the state on which those forces depend will not resume operations
elsewhere, then the surrender may mean that active hostilities between the parties have
ceased, with consequences for such matters as the duty to repatriate prisoners of war.[130]
The surrender of Argentine forces in the Falkland Islands in June 1982 led to the end of
active hostilities and the repatriation of prisoners of war within a very short period once
the British forces had taken the surrender of outlying Argentine garrisons not covered
by the principal instrument of surrender and once it became clear that Argentina had no
intention of carrying on hostilities from the mainland.[131]

4. Conclusion of Peace

243   While a ceasefire, an armistice, or a capitulation only lead to a suspension or tem-
          porary cessation of hostilities, a conclusion of peace results in the termination of the
          state of war or armed conflict.

The conclusion of a ceasefire, armistice, or capitulation will not necessarily terminate a
state of war or armed conflict. See, however, the commentary to Sections 224 and 245

---

[129] See commentary to Section 102.
[130] Article 118 GC III.
[131] For the text of the instrument of surrender, see (1982) 53 BYIL 526–7; see also the statements at 537–8.

JANN K. KLEFFNER

for the suggestion that any of these acts may have the effect of terminating a state of armed conflict and possibly a state of war if the parties so intend.

A frequently used instrument to conclude peace is a peace treaty.   244

1. Parties to an armed conflict frequently use peace treaties to conclude peace. One can broadly distinguish between two types of peace treaties. First, *peace treaties strictu senso* are agreements concluded between belligerent states in written form and governed by international law that bring to an end the formal or material state of war and to restore amicable relations between them. These peace treaties may only be concluded by heads of states or explicitly authorized representatives of the government of a state. Secondly, agreements that are concluded between a non-state party to an armed conflict, on the one hand, and either one or more states or one or more non-state parties, on the other hand, with a view to bring to an end a non-international armed conflict are commonly referred to as *peace agreements*.[132]

2. Peace treaties regularly address the following broad categories of issues:

— the consequences of the conflict, including matters such as prisoners of war and other conflict-related detainees and displaced persons;
— measures that are taken to avoid a relapse into armed conflict, such as the peaceful settlement of territorial disputes, disarmament, demobilization, rehabilitation and reintegration of members of the armed forces of organized armed groups, restructuring and training of governmental armed forces, democratization and power-sharing, and human rights issues, and the granting of amnesty;
— the procedural and institutional dimensions of the implementation of, and monitoring over the compliance with, the terms of the peace treaty, such as the setting up of, and the procedures applicable to, Joint Commissions, bodies entrusted with investigating the causes of the conflict and boundary commissions in the case of territorial disputes, and the role of third parties, such as intergovernmental and regional organizations and third states in implementation and monitoring, and, in case of peace agreements, the establishment of transitional bodies, including transitional governments and transitional justice mechanisms, such as Truth and Reconciliation Commissions.[133]

The aforementioned issues only partially overlap with those that featured in classical peace treaties.[134]

Armed conflicts may also be terminated by a ceasefire without any peace treaty, or   245
other modes that reflect the mutual consent of the parties to an armed conflict to
terminate the armed conflict.

Armed conflicts are oftentimes terminated by less formalized modes than by peace treaties. These modes include implied mutual consent that can be inferred from the mere termination of hostilities; the complete defeat of one of the belligerents (*debellatio*)

---

[132] Kleffner, above (n. 108).
[133] For references, see Kleffner id.
[134] On these, see R. Lesaffer (ed.), *Peace Treaties and International Law in European History—From the Late Middle Ages to World War One* (CUP, 2004), 36, 404; S. Neff, *War and the Law of Nations—A General History* (CUP, 2005), 117–8. See also Greenwood in the 2nd edn of this Handbook at 71.

JANN K. KLEFFNER

and unilateral declarations.[135] It has also been suggested that certain instruments which are traditionally regarded to merely suspend hostilities but which do not terminate the state of war or the armed conflict, such as armistices, have nowadays at times effectively assumed roles comparable to those of peace treaties.[136] It must be stressed, however, that these modes to terminate an armed conflict—whether formalized or not—do not automatically bring to an end the applicability of international humanitarian law. That question is dependent on the purely factual equation of the existence of an international armed conflict, belligerent occupation, or a non-international armed conflict. In other words, a unilateral declaration to the effect that one of the parties to an armed conflict considers the armed conflict to have ended has no bearing on the question whether the situation after such a declaration is governed by international humanitarian law. If the situation continues to be one of resort to armed force between states, of belligerent occupation of protracted armed violence between governmental forces and organized armed groups or between such groups, international humanitarian law continues to apply (see above Section 222).

V. Relevance of Other Fields of International Law

246   International humanitarian law must be applied in context with other principles and provisions of international law.

The most obvious manifestation of this principle is that the rules of general international law relating to such matters as treaty interpretation and application[137] and state responsibility[138] are as applicable in times of armed conflict as they are in times of peace. International humanitarian law is not a self-contained body of law but part and parcel of international law as a whole. The 2005 decision of the ICJ in *DRC v Uganda*[139] is a good example of international humanitarian law being applied within the framework of international law as a whole. Moreover, the outbreak of armed conflict no longer suspends the operation of that part of international law known as the law of peace, so that it remains applicable between the belligerents and neutrals and, subject to the effect of international humanitarian law, between the belligerents themselves.

1. Peacetime Rules

247   The continued applicability of peacetime rules of international law during situations of armed conflicts must not be neglected.

Whereas it was at one time widely assumed that the creation of a state of war between states automatically terminated, or at least suspended, all treaty relations between them (except, of course, for treaties which were specifically intended to apply during wartime),[140]

---

[135] For international armed conflicts, cf. Dinstein, *War, Aggression and Self-Defence* above (n. 18), 47–50.
[136] Id. at 42.
[137] See the provisions of the Vienna Convention on the Law of Treaties, 1969, which are generally taken as declaratory of customary international law and thus applicable to all treaties.
[138] See the ILC Articles on State Responsibility 2001, Crawford, *The ILC Articles on State Responsibility.*
[139] ICJ, *Case Concerning Armed Activities on the Territory of the Congo (DRC v Uganda)*, *ICJ Reports 2005.*
[140] A. McNair, *The Effect of War upon Treaties* (CUP, 1943).

JANN K. KLEFFNER

today neither an international armed conflict, nor even a formal state of war, has such an effect. Rather, the effects of an outbreak of war or international armed conflict on treaty relations between the parties will depend upon whether it may be inferred from the treaties concerned that it was intended that they should cease to be effective in such circumstances.[141]

> **In armed conflicts, the international law of peace will continue to be of practical**   248
> **relevance, particularly for the relationship between the parties to a conflict and**
> **neutral states.**

As a general rule, the law of peace continues to apply between each belligerent state and the non-belligerent or neutral countries, subject only to the effects of the law of neutrality. The law of neutrality qualifies the law of peace by conferring certain additional rights and obligations upon both belligerents and neutrals. Nevertheless, in many modern conflicts, there has been a reluctance to apply the law of neutrality and belligerents have frequently dealt with states not party to the conflict solely on the basis of the law of peace. As explained above, the law of peace will also continue to apply between the belligerents themselves. It is, however, subject to two qualifications. First, some rules of the law of peace contain within themselves limitations which become applicable in time of armed conflict or permit parties to derogate in time of armed conflict. Second, the law of armed conflict operates as a *lex specialis* which—in certain circumstances at least—will override conflicting obligations under the law of peace. This issue is discussed further below in connection with the operation of human rights law in time of armed conflict.

2. Human Rights

> The main sources of human rights law are conventional and customary international   249
> law. The major universal human rights treaties include:
> — the International Covenant on Civil and Political Rights of 19 December 1966
>   with its Optional Protocols;
> — the International Covenant on Economic, Social and Cultural Rights of 19
>   December 1966;
> — the Convention against Torture and Other Cruel, Inhuman or Degrading
>   Treatment or Punishment of 10 December 1984 with its Optional Protocol;
> — the Convention on the Rights of the Child of 20 November 1989 with its
>   Optional Protocols;
> — the International Convention for the Protection of all Persons from Enforced
>   Disappearance of 23 September 2005.

> Other human rights treaties have developed at regional level: 250
>
> — the European Convention for the Protection of Human Rights and Fundamental
>   Freedoms of 4 November 1950;
> — the American Convention on Human Rights of 22 November 1969;
> — the African Charter on Human and Peoples' Rights of 27 June 1981;
> — the Arab Charter on Human Rights of 15 September 1994.

---

[141] 61 *Annuaire de l'Institut* (1985) Vol. II, 278. For the special case of human rights treaties, see the commentary on Sections 251–4, below. See also UN International Law Commission (ILC), Draft Articles on the effect of armed conflicts on treaties and commentaries thereto (2011) *Official Records of the General Assembly, 66th Session, Supplement No. 10* (A/66/10), paras. 100 and 101.

JANN K. KLEFFNER

251   The application of international humanitarian law does not exclude that interna-
           tional human rights law may also be applicable to a particular situation. The rela-
           tionship between international humanitarian law and the law of human rights has
           been shaped as part of a development, which started after the Second World War and
           is expressed in the adoption of major human rights principles in Article 75 AP I.

1. International humanitarian law obviously has much in common with the law of human
rights, since both bodies of rules are concerned with the protection of the individual.[142]
Nevertheless, there are important differences between them. Human rights law is designed
to operate primarily in normal peacetime conditions, and within the framework of the
legal relationship between a state and its citizens. Human rights law applies primarily—
albeit not exclusively (see below, Section 254)—within the territory of the state that is
subject to the human rights obligation in question. Human rights law binds primarily
states, whereas its binding nature vis-à-vis non-state actors, especially organized armed
groups, is a matter of dispute (see below, Section 255). International humanitarian law,
by contrast, is chiefly concerned with the abnormal conditions of armed conflict and
the relationship between armed actors and victims of armed conflicts or between such
armed actors themselves, a relationship otherwise based upon power rather than law.
The extraterritorial applicability of international humanitarian law is a given in international armed conflicts and situations of belligerent occupation. The binding nature
of international humanitarian law vis-à-vis non-state actors, such as organized armed
groups and individuals, is generally accepted. These differences between human rights
law and international humanitarian law have led some to argue that human rights law is
only intended to be applicable in time of peace. This view is not generally accepted and
the better view is that human rights continues to apply during armed conflict.[143]

2. Nevertheless, this does not mean that human rights law displaces or supersedes international humanitarian law. Indeed, both areas of law can apply simultaneously in a number
of situations. That is the case, for instance, when a non-international armed conflict occurs
on a state's territory. Another situation of simultaneous application is belligerent occupation, where the occupying power is bound by the law of belligerent occupation as well as
by human rights law. Furthermore, international humanitarian law and human rights law
apply simultaneously when, in times of armed conflict, persons are being detained.

252   When applicable simultaneously, this relationship between human rights law and
           international humanitarian law is characterized by mutual complementarity[144] and
           the *lex specialis* principle.

---

[142] A. H. Robertson, 'Humanitarian law and human rights' in Swinarski (ed.), *Studies and Essays in Honour of Jean Pictet* (Nijhoff, 1984), 793–802.

[143] See ICJ, *Legality of the Threat or Use of Nuclear Weapons*, Advisory Opinion of 8 July 1996, para. 25, and ICJ, *Legal Consequences of the Construction of a Wall in the Occupied Palestinian Territory*, Advisory Opinion of 9 July 2004, paras. 102–42, at 106. See also 'Resolution XXIII Human Rights in Armed Conflict' in Schindler/Toman (eds), *The Laws of Armed Conflict*, 4th edn (Nijhoff, 2004), 347 and M. Bothe, 'The Historical Evolution of International Humanitarian Law, International Human Rights Law, Refugee Law and International Criminal Law' in H. Fischer/U. Froissart/W. Heintschel v. Heinegg/C. Raap (eds), *Krisensicherung und Humanitärer Schutz—Crisis Management and Humanitarian Protection, Festschrift für Dieter Fleck* (Berliner Wissenschafts-Verlag, 2004), 37–45.

[144] General Comment No. 31 'The Nature of the General Legal Obligation Imposed on States Parties to the Covenant', UN Doc. CCPR/C/21/Rev.1/Add. 13 (4 September 2006), paras. 2, 10, 11; see also General Comments Nos. 15, 18, and 28. All General Comments are available at <http://www.unhchr.ch/tbs/doc.nsf>.

JANN K. KLEFFNER

The *lex specialis* principle, however, should not be misunderstood as applying to
the general relationship between the two branches of international law as such, but
rather relating to specific rules in specific circumstances.

1. In cases of simultaneous application, the relationship between international humanitarian law and human rights law is often referred to as 'complementary'.[145] The two fields are thus regarded to be mutually reinforcing in as much as they complete and perfect each other. That mutual reinforcement can manifest itself in a number of ways, which depend on whether (a) a given question is regulated exclusively by humanitarian law; (b) a given question is regulated exclusively by human rights law; and (c) a given question is regulated by both humanitarian law and human rights law.[146]

In the first situation, the mutual reinforcement takes the form of international humanitarian law filling the gaps left by human rights law. The use of the red cross, red crescent, and red crystal emblem may serve as an illustration of such an area unregulated by human rights law. The pertinent rules of international humanitarian law then apply exclusively.[147] In the second situation, the reverse is true: for instance, since only human rights law regulates rights such as freedom of expression and freedom of assembly, international humanitarian law is irrelevant to the issue. Answers to questions pertaining to such rights thus fall into the exclusive province of human rights law.[148] In the third situation, where a matter is regulated by international humanitarian law and human rights law, however, the applicable law will have to be determined by recourse to the general rule that priority should be given to the norm that is more specific (*lex specialis derogat legi generali*).

2. The maxim of *lex specialis derogat legi generali* is a technique of interpreting legal rules and a means to resolve conflicts between legal norms. The maxim can be conceived in two ways. Either the specific rule is to be read and understood within the confines or against the background of the general rule, as an elaboration, updating or specification of the latter.[149] Or the specific rule is applied instead of, and as an exception to, the general rule.[150] Whether a rule is seen as an 'application', 'modification', or 'exception' to another rule, depends on how those rules are viewed in the environment in which they are applied, including their object and purpose.[151] The maxim of *lex specialis derogat legi*

[145] See, e.g., Human Rights Committee, *General Comment No 31* (n. 9483) at 11; ICRC, 'IHL in brief—What is the difference between humanitarian law and human rights law?' (2002) <http://www.icrc.org/Web/Eng/siteeng0.nsf/html/5KZMUY>. Note that far less frequently, the relationship between international humanitarian law and human rights law is described as mutual exclusion so that human rights law ceases to apply in times of armed conflict. This is the position taken by the US in certain instances, for which see P. Alston, J. Morgan-Foster, W. Abresch, *The Competence of the UN Human Rights Council and its Special Procedures in relation to Armed Conflicts: Extrajudicial Executions in the 'War on Terror'*, (2008) Vol. 19, No. 1 *EJIL* 185–90, and discussion of that position at 191–7.
[146] On these three possible situations, see also ICJ *The Wall* Advisory Opinion, para. 106; Armed Activities on the Territory of the Congo (*Democratic Republic of the Congo v Uganda*), para. 216.
[147] For this and other pertinent examples, see M. Sassòli, 'Le droit internationale humanitaire, une lex specialis par rapport aux droits humains?' in Aue/Flückiger/Hottelies (eds), *Les droits de l'homme et la constitution: Études en l'honneur du Professeur Giorgio Malinverni* (Schulthess, 2007), 375–95, 386.
[148] Id. 393–5.
[149] International Law Commission, 58th Session (1 May–9 June and 3 July–11 August 2006), Fragmentation of International Law: Difficulties arising from the Diversification and Expansion of International Law, Report of the Study Group of the International Law Commission, Finalized by Martti Koskenniemi, UN Doc. A/CN.4/L.682, para. 56.
[150] Id. para. 57.
[151] Id. para. 97.

generali functions in the aforementioned ways also in the relationship between international humanitarian law and human rights law.

3. As a *technique of interpretation*, international humanitarian law informs the interpretation of human rights law if and when the former is more specific. This is the approach adopted by the ICJ in its *Nuclear Weapons* Advisory Opinion when discussing the right not arbitrarily to be deprived of one's life in times of armed conflict. In the words of the Court, '[t]he test of what is an arbitrary deprivation of life [...] falls to be determined by the applicable *lex specialis,* namely, the law applicable in armed conflict which is designed to regulate the conduct of hostilities'.[152] However, when applying the maxim of *lex specialis derogat legi generali* as a technique of interpretation, the more specific norm may also derive from human rights law, which then informs a more general rule of international humanitarian law. When Common Article 3 prohibits, for instance, 'the passing of sentences and the carrying out of executions without previous judgment pronounced by a regularly constituted court, affording all the judicial guarantees which are recognized as indispensable by civilized peoples', the notions of 'regularly constituted court' and 'judicial guarantees' will have to be determined by reference to human rights law, which is more specific on these matters.[153]

4. As a *means to resolve conflicts between legal norms,* the maxim of *lex specialis derogat legi generali* suggests that, in times of armed conflicts, a rule of international humanitarian law, will often prevail over an incompatible norm of human rights law. This is so because international humanitarian law is specifically devised to regulate situations of armed conflicts. For example, when international humanitarian law stipulates that prisoners of war may, as a rule, be detained until the cessation of active hostilities[154] without having the right to legally challenge that detention, while human rights law provides for a right of everyone to make such challenges,[155] the latter right is set aside as far as prisoners of war are concerned. Similarly, when human rights law prohibits imposing the death penalty on persons under the age of eighteen when committing the crime, and carrying out the death penalty on pregnant women,[156] while several rules of international humanitarian law are more restrictive in several respects[157] or fall short of them in some limited respects,[158] the applicable international humanitarian law prevails over the incompatible human rights norms. However, the rule that international humanitarian law functions in the aforementioned way as *lex specialis* to human rights law in times of armed conflicts is not absolute. In certain areas, human rights law supplies the more specific standards even in times of armed conflict. This is notably the case in situations that, while occurring during an armed conflict, closely resemble those for which

---

[152] ICJ, *Nuclear Weapons*, para. 25.

[153] See *CIHL*, Vol. I, at xxxi.

[154] Cf. Arts. 21, 118 GC III.

[155] Art. 9(4) ICCPR; 5(4) ECHR; 7(6) IACHR.

[156] Art. 6(5) ICCPR; 4(5) IACHR [also prohibiting to impose the death penalty on persons over 70 years of age].

[157] Cf., Arts. 100–1 of the Third Geneva Convention, Arts. 68 and 75 of the Fourth Geneva Convention, Arts. 76(3), 1st sentence; Art. 6(4) of Additional Protocol II [extending prohibition to carry out death penalty to 'mothers of young children'].

[158] Art. 77(5) of Additional Protocol I [only prohibiting the execution of, but not to impose, the death penalty for an offence related to the armed conflict on persons under the age of eighteen at the time the offence was committed].

JANN K. KLEFFNER

human rights standards have been developed. Examples include the use of force in relatively calm situations of occupation for the purpose of maintaining public order and safety[159] or in areas under the firm control of state authorities in times of non-international armed conflicts.[160]

> **Whether human rights obligations of a sending state apply extraterritorially** **254** **depends upon the terms of the human rights treaty in question. In many cases, a decisive factor will be whether the individuals concerned come within the jurisdiction of the state with whose armed forces they come into contact.**

1. In the words of the ICCPR, states parties have to respect and ensure civil and political rights 'to all individuals within [their] territory and subject to [their] jurisdiction'.[161] This wording differs in some respects from regional instruments,[162] while an indication as to the territorial reach is absent from the ICESCR. These divergences have led to deviating jurisprudence and a considerable debate about the extraterritorial applicability of human rights.

2. The Human Rights Committee has interpreted Article 2(1) of the ICCPR to mean that a state party 'must respect and ensure the rights laid down in the Covenant to anyone within the power or effective control of that State Party, even if not situated within the territory of the State Party... This principle also applies to those within the power or effective control of the forces of a State Party acting outside its territory, regardless of the circumstances in which such power or effective control was obtained, such as forces constituting a national contingent of a State Party assigned to an international peace-keeping or peace-enforcement operation.'[163] That interpretation, although contested by a limited number of states,[164] finds further support in other findings of the Human Rights Committee,[165] endorsed by the International Court of Justice's jurisprudence,[166] and in some judgments of domestic courts.[167] Examples of situations in which persons have been found to find themselves 'within the power or effective control' of a state

---

[159] Cf. University Centre for International Humanitarian Law, Expert Meeting on the Right to Life in Armed Conflicts and Situations of Occupation (2005), <http://www.adh-geneve.ch/pdfs/3rapport_droit_vie.pdf>, 23. Whether and to what extent human rights law also governs the use of force in calm situations of occupation for other purposes remains subject to divergent opinions among experts, see id.

[160] M. Sassòli and L. Olson, 'The relationship between international humanitarian and human rights law where it matters: admissible killing and internment of fighters in non-international armed conflicts' (2008) 90 No. 871 *IRRC* 599–627, at 613–4.

[161] Cf. Art. 2(1) ICCPR.

[162] Art. 1 ECHR ['to everyone within their jurisdiction']; Art. 1(1) IACHR ['to all persons subject to their jurisdiction'].

[163] HRC General Comment no. 31: Nature of the General Legal Obligation on States Parties to the Covenant, UN Doc. CCPR/C/21/Rev.1/Add.13 (2004) at 10.

[164] See, e.g., the positions taken by the Netherlands, Israel, the UK, and the US before the Human Rights Committee, referred to in C. Droege, 'The Interplay between International Humanitarian Law and International Human Rights Law in Situations of Armed Conflict' (2007) 40 *Israel Law Review* 310–55, 326 (n. 64). For a critique of the position taken by the Human Rights Committee, see M. J. Dennis, 'Application of Human Rights Treaties Extraterritorially in Times of Armed Conflict and Military Occupation' (2005) 99 *AJIL* 119–41.

[165] See in particular for observations on military occupation or control by a state party, D. McGoldrick, 'Extraterritorial Application of the International Covenant on Civil and Political Rights' in F. Coomans/M. T. Kamminga (eds), *Extraterritorial Application of Human Rights Treaties* (Intersentia, 2004), 63–6.

[166] ICJ, *The Wall*, paras. 108–111; Armed Activities (*DRC Congo v Uganda*), para. 216.

[167] For an overview, see C. Droege, above (n. 164), 325–7.

party include extraterritorial detention by a state party to the ICCPR,[168] and belligerent occupation.[169]

3. In its case law, the ECtHR has held on various occasions that the *European Convention* applies extraterritorially if and when a state party acts abroad so as to bring the person concerned into its 'jurisdiction' in the sense of Article 1 of the ECHR. This is the case, for instance, 'when as a consequence of military action—whether lawful or unlawful—it exercises effective control of an area outside its national territory. The obligation to secure, in such an area, the rights and freedoms set out in the Convention derives from the fact of such control whether it be exercised directly, through its armed forces, or through a subordinate local administration.'[170] As to the level of 'effective control' required to satisfy the threshold for the applicability *ratione loci* of the European Convention, the Court further specified that '[i]t is not necessary to determine whether [the state concerned] actually exercises detailed control over the policies and actions' of the authorities in question. Rather, 'effective overall control' is sufficient.[171] The Court has further clarified the extraterritorial reach of obligations under the European Convention by determining that aerial bombardment is, without more, insufficient to bring persons affected by such bombardments into the 'jurisdiction' of states parties to the Convention that carry out the bombardments.[172] In contrast, a person that finds itself in the hands of state organs abroad, for instance by virtue of being detained, finds itself in the 'jurisdiction' of that state.[173] The Court has once restricted the reach of the extraterritorial application of the Convention to contracting states, holding that it operated in 'an essentially regional context and notably in the legal space (*espace juridique*) of the Contracting States'.[174] The Court suggested that the 'Convention was not designed to be applied throughout the world, even in respect of the conduct of Contracting States' and only applied extraterritorially 'when the territory in question was one that, but for the specific circumstances, would normally be covered by the Convention'.[175] However, that restriction seems to have been abandoned in subsequent case law of the ECtHR,[176] although it has been followed by the UK House of Lords.[177] In contrast to its earlier jurisprudence,[178] the

---

[168] See, e.g., Human Rights Committee, *Lopez Burgos v Uruguay*, para. 12.1.

[169] HRC Concluding Observations on Israel, UN Doc. CCPR/C/79/Add.93, para. 10 (1998); Concluding Observations on Israel, UN Doc. CCPR/CO/78/ISR (2003) para. 11.

[170] ECtHR, *Loizidou*, preliminary objections, para. 62; Merits, para. 52.

[171] ECtHR, *Loizidou*, Merits, para. 56. Confirmed in *Cyprus v Turkey*, para. 77; *Ilasc v Moldova and Russia*.

[172] ECtHR, *Banković and others v Belgium, the Czech Republic, Denmark, France, Germany, Greece, Hungary, Iceland, Italy, Luxembourg, the Netherlands, Norway, Poland, Portugal, Spain, Turkey and the UK* (Application no. 52207/99), Grand Chamber, admissibility decision of 12 December 2001, 41 *ILM* 517 (2002), paras. 75–80.

[173] ECtHR, *Ocalan v Turkey*, Application no. 46221/99, judgment of 12 May 2005, *Ocalan*, para. 91; *Issa and others v Turkey*, Application no. 31821/96, judgment of 16 November 2004, *Issa v Turkey*, para. 71 ['under the former State's authority and control through its agents operating—whether lawfully or unlawfully—in the latter State'].

[174] ECtHR, *Banković*, para. 80.

[175] Id.

[176] See, e.g., ECtHR, *Ocalan v Turkey*, Application no. 46221/99, judgment of 12 May 2005, para. 91 (Grand Chamber) [concerning actions of Turkish officials in Kenya]; *Issa and others v Turkey*, Application no. 31821/96, judgment of 16 November 2004, para. 71 [concerning military operations of Turkish armed forces in Iraq].

[177] See notably UK House of Lords, *R (on the application of Al-Skeini) v Secretary of State for Defence*, Application for judicial review, (2007) UKHL 26; ILDC 702 (UK 2007), paras. 76–80 per Lord Rodger of Earlsferry, para. 127 per Lord Brown of Eaton-Under-Heywood

[178] See in particular, *Banković*, para. 75.

JANN K. KLEFFNER

ECtHR now also seems to accept the possibility that a contracting state's extraterritorial obligations under the European Convention can be divided and tailored in as much as its obligation under Article 1 to secure to an individual the rights and freedoms enshrined in the Convention that are relevant to the situation of that individual.[179]

4. The Inter-American Court and Commission on Human Rights have also held the human rights instruments of the Inter-American system to be applicable outside the territory of the states parties. Thus, in the words of the Commission, the obligation to uphold the protected rights of any person subject to the jurisdiction of a state 'may, under given circumstances, refer to conduct with an extraterritorial locus where the person concerned is present in the territory of one state, but subject to the control of another state—usually through the acts of the latter's agents abroad. In principle, the inquiry turns not on the presumed victim's nationality or presence within a particular geographic area, but on whether, under the specific circumstances, the State observed the rights of a person subject to its authority and control.'[180] Cases of 'authority and control', according to the Commission's findings, do not only comprise extraterritorial detention,[181] but also military operations conducted by a state outside its territory,[182] including—and in contrast to the findings of the ECtHR in *Bankovic*[183]—military air operations in international airspace.[184]

5. The International Court of Justice has held the *International Covenant on Economic, Social and Cultural Rights* to also apply extraterritorially. It endorsed the views of the Committee on Economic, Social and Cultural Rights that the obligations of states under the Covenant extend to all territories and populations under their effective control.[185]

**Human rights obligations are binding upon states and international organizations.   255
Their binding effect on organized armed groups is controversial.**

1. The primary addressees of international human rights law, whether emanating from treaty, custom, or general principles of law, are *states*. In addition, international organizations are bound by customary international human rights law by virtue of their international legal personality, to the extent that they exercise functions in a way that can be equated with the exercise of jurisdiction by a state (on the notion of 'jurisdiction', see the previous section). In addition, the binding force of international human rights law upon international organizations can at times be construed on the basis of, or further strengthened by, their constituent treaties, internal rules, and practice.[186]

---

[179] *Al Skeini and Others v UK*, App. No. 55721/07 (ECtHR, 7 July 2011) para. 137.

[180] IACHR, *Coard et al. v US*, Case 10.951, Report No. 109/99 (29 September 1999), para. 37.

[181] Request for Precautionary Measures Concerning the Detainees at Guantanamo Bay, IACHR 12 March 2002, (2002) 41 *ILM* 532.

[182] *Salas v US*, Case 10.573 (1994), para. 6 ['use of military force [that] has resulted in non-combatant deaths, personal injury, and property loss' as falling within the territorial reach of a state's human rights obligations].

[183] Above (n. 172) and text.

[184] *Armando Alejandre Jr et al. v Cuba* ('Brothers to the Rescue'), IACHR Report No. 86/99, Case No. 11.589, 29 September 1999, para. 23.

[185] *The Wall*, paras. 111–112.

[186] For the UN, see in particular the reference to the promotion and encouragement of respect for human rights as one of its purposes (Art. 1(3) UN Charter), but also Decision No. 2005/24 of the Secretary-General's Policy Committee on Human Rights in Integrated Missions, which directs that human rights be fully integrated into peace operations and all human rights functions coordinated by one component. See also UN Department of Peacekeeping Operations & United Nations Department of Field Support, *United Nations Peacekeeping Operations: Principles and Guidelines*—Capstone Doctrine (United Nations, 2008), 14, 27.

2. The applicability of international human rights law to *organized armed groups* is hotly contested. While some evidence suggests that organized armed groups are gradually brought into the reach of international human rights law by virtue of a process of international customary law formation,[187] the better view is that such evidence currently is insufficient to conclude that such a customary process has already reached the point of crystallizing into a firm rule.[188]

3. International Criminal Law

256   Important principles and rules of international humanitarian law have been reaffirmed in the progressive development of international criminal law which applies in peacetime and in times of armed conflict.

See below, Chapter 14.

VI. Relevance of International Humanitarian Law in Peacetime and Post-Conflict Military Operations

257   Principles and rules of international humanitarian law are also relevant in peacetime and post-conflict military operations.

See above, Section 208, and below, Chapter 13.

---

[187] That customary process consists, among others, of instances in which UN organs and other bodies have addressed organized armed groups in monitoring human rights and/or condemning human rights violations. See, e.g. ,Commission on Human Rights, UN Doc. E/CN.4/2005/3 (7 May 2004) CHR, 61st Session, Item 4, Situation of Human Rights in the Darfur Region of the Sudan; UN Doc. E/CN.4/2006/53/ Add.5 (27 March 2006) Report of the Special Rapporteur, Philip Alston, Addendum, 'Mission to Sri Lanka' (28 November to 6 December 2005) especially paras. 24–7 and accompanying footnotes. For the Security Council, see e.g. SC Res.1814 (2008) on the situation in Somalia, para. 16; SC Res. 1778 (2007) on the situation in Chad, the Central African Republic and the subregion, Preamble. For further relevant resolutions of the Security Council and the General Assembly pertaining to violations of human rights (as well as humanitarian law) committed in the Former Yugoslavia, Afghanistan, the Sudan, Sierra Leone, Ivory Coast, the Congo, Angola, Liberia, and Somalia, and further discussion, see C. Tomuschat, 'The Applicability of Human Rights Law to Insurgent Movements' in H. Fischer et al., above (n. 143) 577–85.

[188] For contrary practice that supports that conclusion, see L. Zegveld, *Accountability of Armed Opposition Groups in International Law* (CUP, 2002), 39–46.

JANN K. KLEFFNER

3

COMBATANTS AND
NON-COMBATANTS

Introductory Remarks

1. International law regarding persons taking part in or affected by an international armed conflict makes a fundamental distinction between combatants and civilians, a distinction being the leading principle and the unchangeable core of international humanitarian law applicable in international armed conflicts.[1] This distinction determines the international legal status of these two categories. They indicate the *primary status* of persons in the event of an international armed conflict. The acquisition of a new, *secondary status* is linked to this primary status when there is an actual change in circumstances (the combatant who falls into the power of the enemy becomes a prisoner of war). The primary status determines the protection afforded to a person by international law (e.g. the general protection of civilians against dangers arising from military operations; the special protection of a combatant *hors de combat*). Finally, an individual's primary status determines the *legal consequences* of his or her conduct (e.g. the consequences of a violation of international law by a combatant, or of the direct participation in hostilities by a civilian).

2. International law applicable in international armed conflicts determines which persons are entitled to the status of combatant or of civilian. Regardless of this basic classification, persons can be in closer proximity to one or the other primary status—either due to national law or administrative measures, or because of actual circumstances. As a rule, for example, members of the armed forces of a state (or another party to the conflict which is a recognized subject of international law) are combatants; thus they are authorized, within the limits imposed by international law applicable in international armed conflicts, to participate directly in hostilities. Members of the medical and religious personnel are exceptions to this rule. In addition, other members of the armed forces may, in accordance with decisions made at national level, be excluded from a direct participation in hostilities, thus being 'non-combatants' in the literal sense. Finally, persons can be attached to the armed forces without actually being members. They are generally known as 'persons who accompany the armed forces', which is an indication that their primary status is that of civilians. The authorization to fight as a combatant is

---

[1] The ICJ in its *Advisory Opinion on the Legality of the Threat or Use of Nuclear Weapons* qualifies this distinction as the 'cardinal principle' (*ICJ Reports* 1996, 257). Y. Dinstein denotes it as the 'very bedrock' of IHL. See 'The System of Status Groups in International Humanitarian Law' in W. H. v. Heinegg/V. Epping (eds), *International Humanitarian Law Facing New Challenges* (Berlin: Heidelberg/New York: Springer, 2007), 145–56, at 146.

KNUT IPSEN

denied, on one hand to 'non-combatants' *despite* their membership of the armed forces, and on the other hand to 'persons who accompany the armed forces' *because* of their primary status. However, persons who do *not* belong to the armed forces can, under exceptional circumstances, attain combatant status by virtue of an act of their state or through their own decision, as is illustrated by the inclusion of police forces in the 'armed forces' or the armed resistance of the civilian population against an invasion (the '*levée en masse*').

3. It follows from the above that the heading of this chapter should not be taken to indicate that combatants and non-combatants are categories on the same level of legal quality. The primary status under international law of persons in an international armed conflict will be one of two categories of persons: '*combatants and civilians*'. Combatants may fight within the limits imposed by international law applicable in international armed conflict, that is they may participate directly in hostilities, which members of medical or religious personnel and 'non-combatants' may not do because they are excluded—the former by international law and the latter by a legal act of their party to the conflict—from the authorization to take a direct part in hostilities.

I. General Rules

301   The armed forces of a party to a conflict consist of combatants and non-combatants. Combatants are persons who may take a direct part in the hostilities (Article 3 HagueReg; Article 43, para. 2, AP I), that is participate in the operation or control of a weapon or a weapon-system in an indispensable function. The other members of the armed forces are regarded as non-combatants. The status of the various groups of service personnel will be determined by national decision in accordance with the aforementioned international legal principles.

1. To the extent that the armed forces are described as consisting of 'combatants', this corresponds to the fundamental tenet of international law that a party to an international armed conflict, being a subject of international law, exercises the force of arms against another party to the conflict through an organ expressly denoted as its 'armed forces' and that, in accordance with the armed forces' capacity and its tasks, its members as a rule have combatant status. This means that only a party to a conflict which is a subject of international law can have armed forces whose members are combatants. This reflects the basic relation in international law between the state (as a subject of international law), its armed forces (as its organ), and the members of the armed forces (as combatants). The armed forces are described as consisting also of 'non-combatants'; this refers to the exception that, in addition to the medical and religious personnel, there may be other members of the armed forces which are not authorized to participate directly in hostilities. The description of the armed forces as comprising combatants and non-combatants should not, however, detract from the fact that for members of the armed forces combatant status is the rule, while the classification as non-combatant is an exception. This follows both from the ordinary meaning and additionally from the historical origin of the relevant norms of international law. Article 3 HagueReg provides that the armed forces of the parties to a conflict 'may' consist of combatants and non-combatants. This reflects the basic fact, already generally recognized at the time when the HagueReg came into being, that according to a national decision, armed forces may consist of persons both with

and without combat tasks.[2] Both the ordinary meaning and the drafting history of Article 3 HagueReg prove that it was intended to afford to all captured members of the armed forces the status of prisoner of war, regardless of whether or not they were directly involved in the hostilities. That the combatant status of members of armed forces has always been and is still today the deciding factor is made particularly clear by the wording of Article 43, para. 2, AP I, which in brackets expressly identifies medical personnel and chaplains as an exceptional group not possessing combatant status. In the light of this state of international law it should be underlined that members of armed forces as a rule are combatants and that a non-combatant status of members of the armed forces only applies in exceptional cases.

2. In the description of combatants in the second sentence of this section as 'persons who may take a direct part in the hostilities', the legal definition of combatants contained in Article 43, para. 2, AP I is repeated almost word for word. The additional explanation that combatants 'participate in the operation or control of a weapon or a weapon-system in an indispensable function' in no way restricts the ambit of the definition: members of the armed forces whose function in the operation or control of a weapon or a weapon-system is not 'indispensable' do not, for this reason, lose their combatant status. The formula of the 'indispensable function' can only serve to differentiate between combatant and non-combatant members of the armed forces in national organizational decisions. Persons, however, who participate in the operation or control of a weapon or a weapon-system in an indispensable function may not under any circumstances be designated as non-combatants by national decision.

Hence on the basis of the ordinary meaning, a combatant is a person who fights. This is also the generic meaning of the term. If the generic meaning of the term 'combatant' is supposed to be understood as 'indicating persons who do not enjoy the protection against attack accorded to civilians',[3] only a mere consequence for the adverse party to the conflict is defined, but not the generic meaning of the term. As an international legal term, 'combatant' means a person who is authorized by international law to fight in accordance with international law applicable in armed conflicts. This authorization is not an individual right afforded to the combatant by international law, but results from the affiliation of the combatant to an organ (i.e. the armed forces) of a party to the conflict, which is itself a subject of international law.[4]

3. The statement that '[t]he other members of the armed forces are regarded as non-combatants' could be taken to mean that the combatant is defined narrowly as a specific

---

[2] See for this already the Russian Draft *'Projet d'une Convention Internationale concernant les lois et Coutumes de la Guerre'*, Actes de la Conférence de Bruxelles 1874, Bruxelles 1899, and, taken from this Draft, Article XI of the Declaration of Brussels 1874: 'The armed forces of the belligerents may be composed of combatants and non-combatants.'

[3] *CIHL*, Vol. I, 3.

[4] A party to a conflict to which under IHL rights and duties are attributed has consequently to be qualified as an at least partial subject of international law. The *ICRC Commentary*, Art. 43, para. 1661, does not sufficiently clarify this logical legal consequence. The fundamental and, therefore, indispensable structure both of customary and treaty law with regard to combatant status, that is the legitimizing chain between a state or at least a partial subject of international law, the armed forces as an organ of this legal entity, and the combatant as the constituent part of this organ is diametrically opposed to a universal combatant status for international and non-international armed conflicts as proposed by some groups and authors, see recently Emily Crawford, *The Treatment of Combatants and Insurgents Under the Law of Armed Conflict* (OUP, 2010), 153 *et seq.*

member of the armed forces and that all other members of the armed forces are non-combatants. Such a false conclusion would be diametrically opposed to the principle of international law: that members of the armed forces are as a rule combatants, and are non-combatants only in exceptional cases.

4. Finally, the observation that the 'status of the various groups of service personnel will be determined by national decision in accordance with the aforementioned international legal principles' does not mean that, regardless of the definition of a combatant in Article 43, para. 2, AP I, a state or other party to the conflict which is recognized as a subject of international law has a broad discretion in classifying the members of its armed forces as combatants or as non-combatants. In fact, the opposite is true.

If a state, or a party to a conflict bound in accordance with Article 1, para. 4, Article 96, para. 3, AP I, maintains armed forces, then the members of these armed forces (with the exception of medical and religious personnel) *are* combatants by international legal definition, that is they are entitled to participate directly in hostilities without any further legal act beyond the act of establishing armed forces.

If, however, the subject of international law maintaining the armed forces wishes to exclude members of the armed forces beyond the medical and religious personnel from direct participation in hostilities, then for *this reason alone* an internal legal act is required. Reduced to a concise formula: a member of the armed forces is a combatant by nature; the status of non-combatant can only be granted to a member of the armed forces by an internal constitutive legal act.

302   Whereas combatants may not be punished for the mere fact of fighting, persons who take a direct part in the hostilities without being entitled to do so (unprivileged belligerents or unlawful combatants) face penal consequences. They do not have the right to prisoner-of-war status. Yet they have a legitimate claim to certain fundamental guarantees (Article 75 AP I) including the right to humane treatment and a proper judicial procedure.

1. The 'mere fact of fighting', for which combatants are not punishable, means participating directly in hostilities within the limits imposed by international humanitarian law, provided that all of the relevant norms of this body of law with respect to military activities are observed (see below, Section 519). Thus the combatant must particularly abide by the rules on methods and means of combat (Chapter 4 below) as well as by the regulations concerning persons receiving special protection (Chapters 5–7 below).

If combatants breach rules of international law applicable in international armed conflict and relevant for their military acts, they shall be called to account in accordance with the military or military penal law of their party to the conflict. If, following the violation of international law, they come into the power of the adversary, then the punishment under criminal law is determined by Articles 99 *et seq.* GC III (see Chapter 7 III below).

If, on the other hand, persons who do not have combatant status participate directly in hostilities then they are treated as unprivileged belligerents or unlawful combatants if they fall into the hands of the enemy.[5] Such fighters cannot be classified as belonging

---

[5] See R. R. Baxter, 'So-Called "Unprivileged Belligerency": Spies, Guerillas and Saboteurs' (1951) XXVIII *BYIL* 325–45; K. Dörmann, 'The Legal Situation of "Unlawful/Unprivileged Combatants" ' (2003) 85 No. 849 *IRRC* 45–74; Dörmann, 'Combatants, Unlawful', *MPEPIL*; J. Callen, 'Unlawful Combatants and the

to a state or a party to the conflict recognized as a subject of international law, and are therefore not authorized to undertake armed acts against the adversary. Such irregular fighters, that is fighters not belonging to a subject of international law involved in the conflict, if taken by the adversary, are prosecuted as criminals and sentenced for their direct participation in hostilities, in compliance with Article 45 AP I.

If it becomes clear that neither the assumption of prisoner-of-war status (Article 45, para. 1, AP I) can be invoked for the captured person, nor that the preliminary judicial decision about prisoner-of-war status (Article 45, para. 2, AP I) has been successful, then the person shall at least be treated in accordance with the fundamental guarantees of Article 75 AP I, provided that GC IV—to the extent that it is applicable—does not grant a more favourable treatment.

2. The term 'unlawful enemy combatant' was particularly used after 11 September 2001, to introduce a third category of persons which under existing law may be either combatants or civilians, but are denied such status as not fulfilling essential conditions. The US Military Commissions Act of 2006[6] defined an unlawful enemy combatant as '(i) a person who has engaged in hostilities or who has purposefully and materially supported hostilities against the United States or its co-belligerents who is not a lawful enemy combatant (including a person who is part of the Taliban, al-Qaida, or associated forces); or (ii) a person who, before, on, or after the date of the enactment of the Military Commissions Act of 2006 has been determined to be an unlawful enemy combatant by a Combatant Status Review Tribunal or another competent tribunal established under the authority of the President or the Secretary of Defense'. Although 'lawful enemy combatants' are correctly defined by this Act, the strict avoidance of the distinctive legal term 'civilian' combined with the provision that no alien unlawful enemy combatant under the jurisdiction of military commissions is permitted to invoke the Geneva Conventions as a source of rights is hardly compatible with the spirit, object, and purpose of these Conventions. The US Supreme Court ruling on the Military Commissions Act in re *Boumediene v Bush*[7] has held the Guantànamo prisoners as authorized by reason of *habeas corpus* to appeal to the US judicial system; the Combatant Status Review Tribunals were estimated to be inadequate. The Supreme Court, however, has not adequately criticized the third category in addition to combatants and civilians which, due to another proponent of this category,[8] means that 'any so-called civilian who takes a "direct" (or "active") part in hostilities, becomes *eo ipso* an unlawful combatant, that is to say, not only does he lose the status of civilian but he fails to gain the status of an ordinary (lawful) combatant'.

Hence the treatment of 'unlawful enemy combatants' as a third category is and will remain controversial and, indeed, questionable. If a person is not a combatant, he or she may be targeted only if he or she takes a direct part in hostilities. Neither does such third category exactly define the crime committed by the person in question, nor does

---

Geneva Conventions' (2004) 44 *VaJIntL* 1025 *et seq.*; K. W. Watkin, 'Combatants, Unprivileged Belligerents and Conflicts in the 21st Century', Harvard International Humanitarian Law Research Initiative Working Paper (June 2003), <http://www.ihlresearch.org>. For a discussion of the notion 'direct participation in hostilities' see below, Section 517.

[6] 10 USC § 948a–949u.
[7] *Lakhdar Boumediene et al. v George W. Bush, President of the US et al.*, decision of 12 June 2008, 553 US 723; 128 S. Ct. 2229.
[8] See Y. Dinstein (above n. 1), 151.

KNUT IPSEN

it indicate the amount of humanitarian protection even criminals are entitled to.[9] To use this third category in order to reduce the individual protection below the minimum standard of human rights is under no circumstances legally acceptable.

303   **In particular, mercenaries shall be regarded as unlawful combatants. A mercenary is any person who is motivated to take a direct part in the hostilities by the desire for private gain without being a national or a member of the armed forces of a party to the conflict (Article 47 AP I). The provisions of the 1989 MercenaryConv then also apply.**

Under Article 47, para. 1, AP I, mercenaries are not entitled to the status either of combatant or of prisoner of war. To regard them as 'unprivileged belligerents' or 'irregular fighters' does not accord with the meaning of these terms, as mercenaries can certainly take part in hostilities on the side of a recognized subject of international law which is a party to the conflict.

The denial of the status of combatant and prisoner of war to mercenaries can be explained by the crucial and fatal role which mercenaries—especially of European and North American origin—have played in armed conflicts on the African continent. In 1967, the UN Security Council had already called upon states to prohibit the recruitment of mercenaries on their territory for the purpose of removing foreign governments; the Security Council repeated this request specifically in the final phase of the negotiations in Geneva on AP I.[10] Article 47, para. 2, AP I defines a mercenary as fulfilling six criteria: recruitment (locally or abroad) in order to fight in an armed conflict; actual and direct participation in hostilities; participation motivated by desire for private gain with payment which substantially exceeds that of normal combatants; lack of legal ties to the party to the conflict based on nationality or residency in a territory controlled by that party; lack of membership in the armed forces of the party to the conflict; and not being on official duty in the armed forces of a state not party to the conflict.[11]

The 1977 OAU Convention for the Elimination of Mercenarism in Africa and the 1989 MercenaryConv have adopted this definition, which is so narrow that even members of armed forces who are not nationals of the party to the conflict are not considered to be 'mercenaries' if they serve in special units consisting only of foreigners (e.g. the French Foreign Legion).

This particular point illustrates that the exclusion of mercenaries from combatant and prisoner-of-war status is essentially justified by the failure of such a person to be a member of the armed forces of a party to the conflict. First and foremost it is the person belonging to the armed forces of a party to the conflict who has the primary status of combatant. It is this assignment to an organ which constitutes authorization to carry out armed acts causing damage. A simple contract between an individual and a party to the conflict—fighting in exchange for payment—is not sufficient. Thus the rule regarding mercenaries does not amount to an exception but represents a logical consequence of the law: a person who is not a member of the armed forces is not (with the exception of participants in a *levée en masse*) a combatant either.

---

[9] D. Fleck, 'International Humanitarian Law After September 11: Challenges and the Need to Respond' (2006) 6–2003 *YIHL* 41–77, at 56–9.

[10] SC Res. 239 of 10 July 1967; SC Res. 405 of 16 April 1977.

[11] For a detailed assessment of these criteria see *ICRC Commentary*, Article 47, paras. 1801 *et seq.*

KNUT IPSEN

II. Combatants

The key rule for determining a person's status as combatant is contained in Article 43 AP I, which defines armed forces and provides that members of the armed forces (not including the medical and religious personnel) are combatants.

> The armed forces of a party to a conflict consist of all its organized armed forces, groups, and units. They also include militias and volunteer corps integrated in the armed forces. The armed forces shall be:
> — under a command responsible to that party for the conduct of its subordinates; and
> — subject to an internal disciplinary system which, *inter alia*, shall enforce compliance with the rules of international law applicable in armed conflict (Article 43, para. 1, AP I).

304

1. The definition of armed forces contained in the first sentence of this section is identical with the definition laid down by Article 43 AP I. The wording of this provision is clear and therefore requires no further interpretation; it provides that all armed forces of a party to the conflict have the legal status of an organ of that party. According to the broad legal definition of armed forces, these 'consist of all organized armed forces, groups, and units which are under a command responsible to that Party for the conduct of its subordinates'.

2. The definition is comprehensive: it refers expressly to 'all' organized armed forces of a party to a conflict. This comprehensivity puts an end to the long-standing controversy regarding the definition of 'armed forces' in international legal instruments pertaining to Geneva and Hague Law. The second sentence of this section should not be misconstrued to mean that only those militias and voluntary corps forming a component of the armed forces according to the relevant national law are part of the armed forces. Such an interpretation could lead to a false conclusion that the differentiation made in Article 1 HagueReg is being stressed. In this article, a distinction is made between states in which militias or volunteer corps constitute the army or a part of it, and those states which have militias or voluntary corps in addition to their army. This division is also reflected in Article 4 A, Nos. 1 and 2, GC III. Section 304 is based only on the category of No. 1 (militias and volunteer corps forming part of the armed forces of a party to the conflict), thus neglecting No. 2 (other militias and volunteer corps). However, both organizational forms of militias and volunteer corps now fall within the term 'armed forces' of Article 43, para. 1, 1st sentence, AP I.

3. The construction of this key regulation is based on the following indispensable legal elements. Only states or other parties which are recognized as subjects of international law can be parties to an international armed conflict. However, a subject of international law can act only through its own organs. If it uses armed force, the subject can thus act only through the instruments organized for this purpose, that is through the armed forces. Militias or voluntary corps of which a party to an international armed conflict makes use are therefore part of its armed forces within the meaning of Article 43, para. 1, 1st sentence, AP I, regardless of whether they are incorporated into the regular armed forces, for example the army, or are separate.

The two express requirements—of a responsible command and an internal disciplinary system—contained in Article 43, para. 1, follow from the aforesaid construction of the term 'armed forces' contained in AP I. Each party to a conflict must in all circumstances observe the international law applicable in international armed conflict, as is stipulated for example with respect to AP I in its Article 1, para. 1.

A party to an international armed conflict acts through its armed forces as its organs. Given its fundamental duty to comply with the law, such a party is also bound to ensure that its organs' behaviour is lawful. Article 3, 2nd sentence, HC IV expressly lays down this duty with the same words as Article 91, 2nd sentence, AP I. To secure that this duty is performed, a command of the armed forces which is responsible to the party to the conflict for the conduct of its subordinates is required. However, a breach of international law leads to responsibility in international law of the party to the conflict recognized as a subject of international law. It is in the general interest of the party to the conflict to prevent contraventions of international law, in order to avoid responsibility. Hence it is necessary to implement a system of sanctions, together with the internal disciplinary system, both of which are required by Article 43, para. 1, 2nd sentence, AP I (see below, Sections 1410–1418).

4. According to Article 43, para. 2, AP I, only members of the armed forces as defined above (with the exception of the medical and religious personnel specially protected by Article 33 GC III) are combatants, 'that is to say, they have the right to participate directly in hostilities'. Thus membership of the armed forces is an indispensable prerequisite to combatant status; 'armed forces' in the meaning of international law, however, have the legal status of an organ of a party to the conflict. If persons participating directly in hostilities lack either of these two prerequisite elements of combatant status, then they cannot have combatant status. Thus, if they fall into the hands of the enemy, they cannot acquire the secondary status of prisoner of war.

5. To sum up, it has to be established that Article 43, para. 1, AP I has created a standard international legal term of 'armed forces' covering all combatant forces (except participants in a *levée en masse*) which are listed in addition to the regular 'armed forces' in the older relevant conventions (HagueReg, GC); they are now included within the term 'armed forces'.

It was the natural and legally logical consequence of this broad definition of armed forces to define the combatant as a member of the armed forces who is entitled to participate directly in hostilities. The fundamental structure of the term 'combatant' in international law which was established prior to AP I, however, has not been changed: it describes a person who is a member of the armed forces, being an organ of a party to a conflict which is a subject of international law.

The party to the conflict determines the type and size of its armed forces in accordance with its national laws. On the level of international law, the members of these armed forces are entitled to take part directly in hostilities (for the interpretation of the term 'direct participation' see below, Section 517). This point deserves emphasis. With regard to the direct participation in hostilities, combatants are privileged solely by that entitlement, the lack of which makes them criminals liable to prosecution. On the other hand, the duties of the combatant impose limits on that entitlement (see Sections 308, 309, 311 below).

305   It shall be left to the discretion of the individual states to choose whether to admit women to their armed forces. Their combatant or non-combatant status is determined by the same principles as that of male members of armed forces.

KNUT IPSEN

1. Since the primary status of combatant is derived from membership in the armed forces of a party to the conflict, women and children also have this status if they are members of the armed forces. A party to the conflict may, however, be bound by international conventions prohibiting the recruitment of children below a certain age into their armed forces or may, by national law, exclude women from direct participation in hostilities or from military service altogether.

2. In so far as women are members of the armed forces they have the same authorization under Article 43, para. 2, AP I as male members. They are entitled—as long as they do not belong to medical or religious personnel—to participate directly in hostilities. It is left to the discretion of the states or other parties to a conflict recognized as subjects of international law whether or not to admit women to the armed forces.

> **The parties to the conflict shall take all feasible measures to ensure that children**   306
> **who have not attained the age of eighteen years do not take part in hostilities**
> **and, in particular, they shall refrain from recruiting them into their armed forces**
> **(Article 77, para. 2, AP I; Article 38 ChildConv, and ProtChildConv; see below**
> **Section 505).**

1. This provision reproduces exactly the same duties as imposed upon the parties to AP I by Article 77, para. 2 and by Article 38, paras. 2 and 3, 1st sentence, of the Convention on the Rights of the Child. The two provisions of AP I and of the Convention on the Rights of the Child cited above have identical contents. In addition, Article 38, para. 1, of the Convention on the Rights of the Child commits states parties to respect and to ensure respect for the rules of international humanitarian law applicable in armed conflicts which are relevant to children. At the same time, this is a reference to the fundamental rule of Article 77, para. 1, AP I, according to which children in international armed conflicts have to be treated with special care.

2. Article 77, para. 3, AP I takes into account the circumstances arising from a breach of the duties laid down in para. 2. If a child who has not reached the age of eighteen and has participated directly in hostilities falls into the hands of the adversary, that child is nevertheless entitled to the special protection provided under Article 77 regardless of whether or not he or she is a prisoner of war. However, children protected under Article 77 can only be prisoners of war if they had previously attained the primary status of combatant by being unlawfully recruited into the armed forces of one of the parties to the conflict. This is particularly significant because the combatant status protects the child against being prosecuted upon capture for its direct participation in hostilities.

3. In conclusion: every party to a conflict bound by AP I and/or the Convention on the Rights of the Child is subject to the clear duty to keep children out of the armed forces and away from direct participation in hostilities. If a party to a conflict fails to carry out this duty then it breaches international law, but the children affected are nonetheless entitled to the maximum protection provided by Article 77 AP I and Article 38 of the Convention on the Rights of the Child.

> **Whenever a party to a conflict incorporates a paramilitary or armed law enforce-**   307
> **ment agency into its armed forces it shall notify the other parties to the conflict**
> **(Article 43, para. 3, AP I).**

KNUT IPSEN

1. The task of armed law enforcement agencies of a state (e.g. the police), even if they are of a paramilitary nature, is as a rule only to protect and maintain the internal order of the state. The legal status of such armed, possibly paramilitary, law enforcement agencies in relation to the armed forces is regulated differently by different states: some states incorporate their police, or police units, into their armed forces in the event of an international armed conflict. Some states have police units permanently incorporated into their armed forces, even in peacetime. In other states there is a strict division between the armed forces and the police. The purpose of the following regulation is to establish a common denominator in international law for these different categories of national organization.

2. Section 307 confirms the finding described in connection with the definition of armed forces (Section 304 above) that the state or party to the conflict which is a subject of international law determines the type and size of its own armed forces through a national legal act. This also holds true in principle for the decision of whether or not to incorporate paramilitary or armed law enforcement agencies into the armed forces. The first half of the first sentence of Article 43, para. 3, AP I is based on the assumption that the question of whether or not paramilitary or armed law enforcement agencies will be incorporated into the armed forces and thus employed as fighting forces in the armed conflict is to be determined by the sovereign decision of each state or other party to the conflict. From the point of view of international law, this decision—just like any similar internal act with international legal relevance—only becomes effective through the international legal act of notification, that is either an ad hoc notification vis-à-vis the opposing party in a conflict, or vis-à-vis the depositary of the AP I. If such notification has been given then the combatant status under international law of the affected paramilitary or armed law enforcement agencies in the event of a conflict is clearly secured. The effectiveness of combatant status in international law is established—and this is crucial—solely by the act of notification.

3. Furthermore, international law does not take national constitutions into consideration. Any doubts regarding the conformity of the notification with the constitution or other laws of the respective state are therefore irrelevant. This situation in international law is both clear and practical: it simply cannot be expected that the recipient of the notification regarding the combatant status of paramilitary or armed law enforcement agencies should become involved in a jurisprudential dispute about a foreign legal order.

Along with the combatant status attained through the incorporation into the armed forces, these (police) forces also become a military target (as defined by Article 52, para. 2, AP I) and are therefore subject to armed attacks by the opposing party to the conflict just like any other unit of the armed forces. This is also the inevitable consequence of notifying to the Swiss depositary: after this notification has been made, the forces so notified become part of the armed forces and thus also military objectives, regardless of whether or not they are restricted by a national order only to carry out police functions and defend themselves against a combatant enemy.

4. Armed law enforcement agencies, especially police forces without the aforementioned notified combatant status, are protected by international law as civilians—in particular by Part IV of AP I and by GC IV. International law applicable in international armed conflict does not provide for a special primary status of the police. The fact that members

of the police receive the primary status of protected civilians creates a large number of practical and legal problems both in the theatre of operations of an armed conflict and in occupied territories (e.g. police intervention against persons whose primary status either as combatants or as civilians is not recognizable; intervention against commandos who conceal their combatant status; intervention against other armed units whose primary status is doubtful).

5. While membership of the armed forces of a party to a conflict is the basic and indispensable factor which determines the primary status as combatant, the distinction from civilians represents a duty deriving from the combatant status, the breach of which at worst leads to the forfeiture of the secondary status of prisoner of war. This is a further proof that it would be illogical to describe the generic meaning of the term 'combatant' as the absence of protection against attack (see para. 2 to Section 301 above). The following applies with respect to the duty of distinction.

> **Combatants are obliged to distinguish themselves from the civilian population**   308
> **while they are engaged in an attack or in a military operation preparatory to an**
> **attack (Article 44, para. 3, AP I). In accordance with the generally agreed prac-**
> **tice of states, members of regular armed forces shall wear their uniform (Article**
> **44, para. 7, AP I). Combatants who are not members of uniformed armed forces**
> **shall wear a permanent distinctive sign visible from a distance and carry their**
> **arms openly.**

1. The first sentence of this regulation has the same content as Article 44, para. 3, 1st sentence AP I. In addition, this norm, which lays down the fundamental obligation of combatants to distinguish themselves from the civilian population during attacks or military activities in preparation for an attack, is expressly intended to promote the protection of the civilian population against the effects of hostilities. Interpreting this provision in the systematic context of AP I leads to the following observations. Part IV of AP I, which is dedicated to the protection of the civilian population, begins with the basic rule of Article 48 which obligates the parties to a conflict 'at all times [to] distinguish between the civilian population and combatants . . . [i]n order to ensure respect for and protection of the civilian population'. Since the explicit reason, according to Article 44, para. 3, 1st sentence, AP I, for the fundamental obligation of the combatants to distinguish themselves from the civilian population is to increase the protection of the civilian population against the effects of hostilities, the compelling result is that this duty of the combatants to distinguish themselves is the basic rule.

2. Following this basic rule it would be systematically appropriate subsequently to stress next the generally agreed practice by states of the wearing of uniforms by regular armed forces, as is done in Section 308. Article 44 dedicates a later paragraph, para. 7, to this principle. This is acceptable because it expressly applies to the entire article and makes clear that none of the regulations of this article are intended 'to change the generally accepted practice of States with respect to the wearing of the uniform by combatants assigned to the regular, uniformed armed units of a Party to the conflict'. Article 44, para. 7, AP I refers to a rule of international customary law according to which regular armed forces shall wear the uniform of their party to the conflict when directly involved in hostilities.

   This rule of international customary law had by the nineteenth century already become so well established that it was held to be generally accepted at the Conference in Brussels in 1874. The armed forces listed in Article 4, No. 1, GC III are undoubtedly regarded as 'regular' armed forces within the meaning of this rule. This is the meaning of 'armed forces' upon which the identical Articles 1 of the Hague Regulations of 1899 and 1907 were based. Both these conventions retained Article IX of the Brussels Declaration of 1874 without alteration.

Hence Article 4 A, No. 1, GA III is based on this historically evolved meaning of regular armed forces, which No. 3 of the said provision also relies on: it specifically mentions 'regular armed forces', which unequivocally means those described in No. 1.

3. The obligation to wear a uniform does not apply to the armed units listed in Article 4 A, No. 2, GC III. These do fall under the broad category of 'armed forces' covered by Article 43, para. 1, AP I, but they are not obliged to wear a uniform, although they must wear a permanent and distinctive sign which is visible from a distance, and carry their arms openly. It confirms, though, that the basic rules regarding the distinction of forces from the civilian population apply to them as well.

This category is dealt with in Section 308, which refers to '[c]ombatants who are not members of uniformed armed forces'. Thus, members of 'militias and . . . other volunteer corps, including those of organized resistance movements, belonging to a Party to the conflict' (not incorporated into the armed forces) are mentioned. From Article 4 A, No. 2, lit. b and c, it follows that these armed groups must wear 'a fixed distinctive sign recognizable at a distance' and carry 'arms openly'. It should be noted that this category is also included in the definition of armed forces contained in Article 43, para. 1, AP I. The category is exempted from the obligation to wear a uniform, but the fundamental duty to distinguish themselves in the manner described still applies.

309   Recognizing that there are situations in occupied territories and in wars of national liberation where, owing to the nature of the hostilities, a combatant (especially a guerilla) cannot so distinguish himself from the civilian population, he shall retain his status as a combatant, provided that, in such situations, he carries his arms openly:
— during each military engagement; and
— during such time as he is visible to the adversary while he is engaged in a military deployment preceding the launching of an attack in which he is to participate (Article 44, para. 3, sentence 2, AP I).

The term 'military deployment' refers to any movement towards the point from which an attack is to be launched.

1. Article 44, para. 3, 2nd sentence, AP I which is identical to this provision was one of the most controversial provisions at the 1977 Geneva Diplomatic Conference on the Reaffirmation and Development of International Humanitarian Law Applicable in Armed Conflicts. It is formulated as an unambiguous exception from the basic rule providing that combatants must distinguish themselves from the civilian population. States which acquired their independence by successful guerilla warfare or which supported guerilla liberation movements strongly advocated the elimination of criteria distinguishing such combatants from civilians. Other states were resolutely opposed to an exception for guerillas to the rule requiring distinction from the civilian population. Article 44, para. 3, 2nd sentence, AP I represents the compromise achieved after a long argument.

KNUT IPSEN

2. The delegation of the Federal Republic of Germany played an active role in the establishment of this compromise and even formulated some of the drafts. For this reason the Federal Republic of Germany's interpretation, as contained in a declaration of interpretation submitted with the document of ratification, carries significant weight. According to this declaration, the criteria used to distinguish between combatants and civilians contained in the exceptional rule apply only in occupied territories and in armed conflicts of the kind described in Article 1, para. 4, of AP I. This is an interpretation which, in the light of the general rule of interpretation of Article 31 of the Vienna Convention on the Law of Treaties, is undoubtedly correct. According to the wording of Article 44, para. 3, 2nd sentence, the reason for the exceptional rule lies in the fact that 'there are situations in armed conflicts where, owing to the nature of the hostilities, an armed combatant cannot so distinguish himself' from the civilian population. However, such situations can in fact only arise if a people within the meaning of Article 1, para. 4 AP I is engaged in a 'war of liberation' as described therein, for this is one of two typical situations of guerilla warfare. The other is the situation in occupied territories which is repeatedly marked by guerilla fighting through organized resistance movements. This interpretation based on the object and purpose of the provision is supported by the historical development which has led to this exception.[12] The protagonists of guerilla warfare were mainly concerned to include all wars of liberation as defined by Article 1, para. 4, whereas some Western states in particular sought to restrict such exceptional circumstances to occupied territories. By its restrictive interpretation, which has been made *lege artis*, Germany has taken into account both of these positions.

In addition, according to the declaration of interpretation submitted upon ratification, the Federal Republic of Germany understands 'military deployment [as] any movement towards the point from which an attack is to be launched'. This interpretation is also contained in a number of declarations submitted by other member states of AP I, but it carries a special weight as the term 'military deployment/*militärischer Aufmarsch*' has been introduced into AP I by the Federal Republic of Germany. The German delegation had already given this explanation of the term at the Geneva Conference which had met with general approval. To date, no reasons have emerged for abandoning this object- and purpose-oriented interpretation aimed at a minimal distinction.

3. Thus, the exceptional rule consists of a narrowing of the scope of application and of a reduction of the distinctive criteria. It only applies in occupied territories and when a people fights for national liberation according to Article 1, para. 4, AP I; the requirement of distinction from the civilian population is already fulfilled if the combatants carry their arms openly from the time of the initial deployment to the place of attack (at the latest), and of course during every military engagement.[13]

---

[12] See Bothe/Ipsen/Partsch, 'Die Konferenz über humanitäres Völkerrecht—Verlauf und Ergebnisse' (1978) 38 *ZaöRV* 34 *et seq.*

[13] The ICRC's *Interpretive Guidance on the Notion of Direct Participation in Hostilities* (Geneva: ICRC, 2009) which restates the principle of distinction also in modern armed conflicts holds it as lawful to regard 'fighters' in a non-international armed conflict having a continuous combat function as military objectives. These persons may be attacked if clearly identified, even if they are not carrying arms openly or at all. For further details see below, Section 1203, and R. Geiß, 'The Conduct of Hostilities in Asymmetric Conflicts—Reciprocity, Distinction, Proportionality, Precautions' (2010–2013) *HuV-I* 122–32, at 124–6. The same applies for, fighters of a non-state party to a conflict in the meaning of Article 1, para. 4, AP I, having a continuous combat function.

KNUT IPSEN

4. Paragraph 7 expressly indicates that Article 44 is not intended to change the generally accepted practice of states concerning the wearing of uniforms by combatants who are members of the regular armed forces. This might lead to the conclusion that the exceptional rule of para. 3, 2nd sentence, does not apply to members of the regular armed forces. This would, however, directly contradict the principle of equal participation which governs international humanitarian law and which is expressed for example in the Preamble to AP I.[14] Despite this legal equality the exceptional rule will in practice only be applied to guerilla fighters.

5. If combatants within the scope of the exceptional rule do not meet the minimal requirements of the rule, then, according to Article 44, para. 4, 1st sentence, they forfeit their secondary status as prisoners of war in the event of capture by the enemy. Nevertheless, they shall be afforded protection equivalent to that of GC III and AP I, which includes protection in the case of criminal prosecution. This is expressly mentioned in the second sentence of Article 44, para. 4; the first sentence only takes into account the equivalence of protective provisions, not of criminal provisions (in particular Articles 82–88 GC III). Those combatants who have forfeited their prisoner-of-war status under Article 44, para. 3, 2nd sentence, in conjunction with para. 4 may thus be prosecuted and punished under the national criminal law of the detaining power. However, treatment equivalent to that of Articles 99–108 GC III shall be ensured.

6. If a combatant who is a member of the regular armed forces and is captured while participating directly in hostilities is not wearing the appropriate uniform, or if such a captured combatant who is a member of a militia, voluntary corps, or an organized resistance movement does not wear a permanent distinctive sign visible from a distance, then generally a breach of the duty of distinction and additionally a charge of perfidy according to Article 37, para. 1, AP I must be considered, unless an exception under Article 44, para. 3, 2nd sentence, AP I is applicable.

310 The inhabitants of a territory which has not yet been occupied who, on the approach of the enemy, spontaneously take up arms to resist the invading troops without having had time to form themselves into armed units (so-called *levée en masse*) shall be combatants. They shall carry arms openly and respect the laws and customs of war in their military operations (Article 2, HagueReg; Article 4 A, No. 6, GC III).

1. The combatant status generally depends—as has been clearly shown in the comments to Section 304 above—upon the authorization by the state or party to the conflict recognized as a subject in international law, because the armed forces are, within the meaning of Article 43, para. 1, AP I, assigned to these entities as organs of the parties. Only in one situation does international law applicable in international armed conflict permit persons to participate directly in hostilities solely on the basis of their autonomous decision: this is the *levée en masse* defined by Article 2 HagueReg and Article 4 A, No. 6, GC III.

2. Such spontaneous resistance must therefore meet four requirements in order for the persons taking part to obtain the primary status of combatants:
   a) Spontaneous armed resistance is permitted by international law only in 'territory which is not occupied'. A territory is considered to be 'not occupied' if it is not (yet)

---

[14] Likewise, although based on different reasoning, J. de Preux, *ICRC Commentary*, Art. 44 AP I, para. 1723.

under the factual control of the enemy as arises by *argumentum e contrario* from Article 42 HagueReg. It follows that resistance movements which are organized autonomously by the population of an already occupied territory do not fall into the category of *levée en masse*.

b) The population of this unoccupied territory must take up arms 'spontaneously' on the approach of the enemy. This requires two conditions to be met: first, only a resistance initiated by the population itself, not one directed or organized in advance by organs of the state, fulfils this condition. Secondly, armed resistance is only permitted against 'invading troops' and therefore not in territory which is already occupied. These two conditions are obviously not met by organized resistance movements.

c) Furthermore, the civilians involved in armed resistance may not have had the time to organize themselves (within the meaning of Article 1 HagueReg) as militia or volunteer corps. This requirement clearly emphasizes the principle of authorization: only a state or another party to the conflict recognized as a subject of international law has the authority to decide on the use of armed force within the framework of international law. In every developed legal order, self-help is the exception.

International law, as a legal order, also in principle prohibits private individuals from deciding on the use of armed force, even if their motivation in a concrete case can be recognized as stemming from patriotism or other ethical reasons. The rule in Article 2 HagueReg is unambiguous: persons wanting to resist an attack must secure the authorization of their state by joining the armed forces, a militia, or a volunteer corps. Only if it is in fact impossible to join these armed units, and provided that the conditions of Article 2 are met, are civilians exceptionally permitted to take up arms by their own decision.

d) Finally, the participants in such a *levée en masse* must respect 'the laws and customs of war' and are thus bound by the basic duty which applies to all combatants.

3. If spontaneous resistance fighters fulfil these four conditions then they have the primary status of combatants. In the event of capture by the adverse party to the conflict they are granted the secondary status of prisoners of war. It should be noted, however, that in modern-day armed conflicts the *levée en masse* has become less significant because, as a rule, the regular armed forces of an attacking party are armed to a degree that simply cannot be countered with the weapons available to a spontaneous resistance (such as hunting weapons).

> **While all combatants are obliged to comply with the rules of international law**   **311**
> **applicable in armed conflict, violations of these rules shall not deprive a combatant**
> **of his right to be a combatant (Article 44, para. 2, AP I).**

1. Although the duty of all combatants to comply with the rules of international law applicable in armed conflict is only briefly mentioned in Article 44, para. 2, AP I, this constitutes a codification of a general principle of international humanitarian law which applies as customary law in addition to the respective international conventions. Article 1 HagueReg already binds the armed forces as well as (independent) militias and volunteer corps to '[t]he laws, rights, and duties of war', thereby reiterating the wording of Article IX of the Brussels Declaration of 1874. It is a basic rule already considered to be a customary norm of international law at that time. Thus, the first half of the sentence in Article 44, para. 2, AP I is a reaffirmation of a rule which has long been codified (and which was effective even before that).

KNUT IPSEN

In addition, the combatant's duty to comply with the law is the expression of another fundamental principle of international law: the principle of reciprocity. General practice can only arise through reciprocity; sanctions such as reprisals are a negative aspect of reciprocity. Consequently, privileges granted under international law, such as that of combatant status which, after all, privileges those persons who use force, can only be realized on the basis of reciprocity. This means, however, that combatants are also compelled by the principle of reciprocity to act within the restrictions and limitations imposed on them by international law applicable in international armed conflict.

Sporadic attempts have been made among legal scholars to develop a concept of international law of war which discriminates against the aggressor and whose restrictions apply only to the combatants of the aggressor, thus ruling out legal equality of treatment. This concept, however, has not found its way either into treaty law or into customary law. The same has to be stated with regard to terrorist means and methods of the use of force, which by their very nature cannot be included into the framework of permitted means and methods of warfare. Therefore the duty of combatants to abide by the rules of international law applicable in armed conflicts is all-encompassing and incumbent equally upon the combatants of all parties to the conflict.

2. If combatants breach the rules of international law applicable in armed conflicts then it is the responsibility of the party to the conflict to which they belong to punish this behaviour through disciplinary measures or prosecution. This is an obligation attached to the party to the conflict concerned under Articles 85, 86 AP I.

If combatants fall into the hands of the adverse party after having breached international law then, according to Articles 82–88 GC III, they shall be called to account under the applicable legal regulations of the detaining power. In principle the breach of rules of international law applicable in armed conflicts does not result in the offenders forfeiting their primary status as combatants. Thus, if they fall into the hands of the adverse party to the conflict they do not forfeit the secondary status of prisoners of war. A breach of the obligation of minimal distinction according to Article 44, para. 3, 2nd sentence AP I (see Section 309 above) is an exception. Article 44, para. 4, AP I lays down that a breach of this duty results in forfeiture of prisoner of-war-status.

312   **Combatants who fall into the hands of the adversary shall be prisoners of war (Article 3, sentence 2, HagueReg; Article 44, para. 1, AP I). They shall not be called to account for their participation in lawful military operations. Violations of international law committed by them may be prosecuted under the laws of the detaining power and international law (Articles 82 *et seq.* GC III).**

The status of prisoner of war is attached to the primary status of combatant as a secondary status (see above, Section 301). Article 44, para. 1, AP I simply confirms existing international law when it lays down that a combatant (as defined by Article 43, para. 2, AP I) 'who falls into the power of an adverse party shall be a prisoner of war'. This basic rule was already established in Article 3 HagueReg and Article 4 A, Nos. 1–3 and 6, GC III. It has not been altered by AP I (for details regarding the status of prisoners of war and their protection, see below, Chapter 7).

313   **Should any doubt arise as to whether a person who have taken part in hostilities and fallen into the hands of the adversary shall be deemed a combatant or civilian, that person shall continue to be treated as a prisoner of war until such time as his**

or her status has been determined by a competent tribunal (Article 5, para. 2, GC III; Article 45, para. 1, AP I).

Article 5, para. 2, GC III and Article 45, para. 1, AP I are intended to apply when persons directly involved in the hostilities are captured and there are doubts as to whether they are combatants or civilians (see below, Section 703). In particular, deserters and persons accompanying the armed forces who are unable to present their identity cards, but also the aforementioned cases of minimal distinction (cf. Section 309) could raise such doubts. Article 5, para. 2, GC III clearly indicates that the fundamental distinction between combatants and civilians does logically not tolerate a third category (i.e. unlawful enemy combatants) on the same legal level. Such legally equal category may neither be based on well-established customary law nor on treaty law.

III. Non-combatants

1. *The historical development of the division of members of the armed forces into combatants and non-combatants.* The autonomy to organize the internal structure of their armed forces is granted to states by Article 3 HagueReg, according to which the 'armed forces ... may' consist of combatants and non-combatants. It has its origin in a factual situation which had already been taken into account by the Brussels Declaration of 1874. In 1874, the Brussels Conference based the negotiations on a draft presented by the Russian delegation, which stated in section 10, 1st sentence: 'The armed forces of the belligerents may be composed of combatants and non-combatants.'[15] In a further provision (section 38) the Russian draft provided for the 'neutralization' of medical personnel, just as Articles I–III of the Geneva Red Cross Convention of 1864 had already stated. Consequently, the Russian draft included all persons who—being members of the armed forces—belonged to various branches of the military administration. They were categorized as 'non-combatants'. Apart from medical and religious personnel they included quartermasters, members of the legal services, and other non-fighting personnel. Obviously, the actual composition of the armed forces at that time had been taken into account, with the explicit purpose of granting to all members of the armed forces the secondary status of prisoners of war in the event of capture. From this general category of 'non-combatants' the members of the medical and religious personnel were singled out again—in accordance with the Geneva Red Cross Convention signed ten years earlier—in order to grant them the 'right of neutrality' guaranteed by that Convention. Section 23 of the draft expressly repeated that combatants and non-combatants, with the exception of the neutralized medical and religious personnel, acquired prisoner-of-war status in the event of their capture.

As prisoner-of-war status was thus guaranteed twice, namely in sections 10 and 23 of the Russian draft, there was inevitably some criticism in the negotiations.[16] It was suggested that section 10 (the division into combatants and non-combatants) be entirely omitted as this rule did not establish a new principle and could lead to misunderstandings in practice. It was argued that medical and religious personnel were already protected

---

[15] See in this connection, *Projet d'une déclaration internationale conçernant les lois et coutumes de la guerre adoptés par la Conférence de Bruxelles, Actes de la Conférence, Bruxelles* 1874 (*juillet-août* 1874)—translated by the author.

[16] See *Actes de la Conférence de Bruxelles, Prot. XIII*, session of 17 August 1874, 183 *et seq.*

KNUT IPSEN

by the Geneva Convention of 1864. Combatants and non-combatants received prisoner-of-war status anyway upon being captured; yet this was also guaranteed by section 23 which said that all combatants and non-combatants are entitled to prisoner-of-war status. To the extent that it was desired to maintain section 10 (laying down that the armed forces may be composed of combatants and non-combatants), it was said that a clause should be inserted stipulating that non-combatants are exposed to the misfortunes and dangers of war in the same way as the units to which they belong. The conference, however, was of the opinion that such a provision was already tacitly included in the rule.[17]

The documents cited lead to the following observation. It was obviously not the intention of the Brussels Conference to create a non-combatant status in international law determined by the fact that persons with this status are not entitled under international law to participate directly in hostilities. Nor was it intended to treat non-combatants belonging to the armed forces in the same way as civilians. Instead, the point of departure was the actual and widespread awareness that armed forces are composed both of persons who fight and of persons who (because of their function) do not take a direct part in the fighting.

The approach of the Brussels Conference was based on this finding, as illustrated by its discussion of the duty of non-combatants to wear uniform. The delegate of the German Reich raised the question of whether it would not be appropriate to require that the non-combatants mentioned in the draft should wear uniform during wartime. Without such a duty it would be difficult to distinguish between non-combatant members of the armed forces and civilians accompanying the armed forces (mentioned in section 24 of the Russian draft). Other delegates objected to this proposal, saying that the wearing of a uniform was anyway common practice for non-combatants. It would therefore be superfluous to lay down a special duty for them to wear uniforms.[18] Immediately after this discussion, section 10 was put into the version which was then adopted as section 11 of the Brussels Declaration, and several decades later without further controversy as Article 3 of the Hague Regulations of 1899 and 1907: 'The armed forces of the belligerent parties may consist of combatants and non-combatants. In the case of capture by the enemy, both have a right to be treated as prisoners of war.'

Since then the non-combatant, within the meaning of Article 3 HagueReg, has not acquired a special status in international law entailing special rights or duties on this level. This explains why the comprehensive definition of armed forces given in Article 43, para. 1, AP I, and the related definition of members of the armed forces as combatants in para. 2, no longer refer to non-combatants. During the negotiations on the definition of armed forces at the Geneva Conference, only one delegation pointed out that the members of armed forces could comprise both combatants and non-combatants. Nobody objected. Therefore this comment was incorporated into the report of the Third Commission: 'It should, however, be noted that the term "members of armed forces" is all-inclusive and includes both combatants and non-combatants'.[19]

In view of the wording and the historic origin of Article 43 AP I, one should agree with the opinions of legal scholars that international law does not afford the non-combatant

[17] Ibid. 184.
[18] Ibid. 185.
[19] Official records of the Diplomatic Conference on the Reaffirmation and Development of International Humanitarian Law Applicable in Armed Conflicts, Geneva (1974–77), Vol. XV, 390.

KNUT IPSEN

any better protection than the combatant.[20] Thus the non-combatant, as a member of the armed forces, is not protected from being the object of an attack. Furthermore, as non-combatants are not mentioned in Article 43 AP I, it was argued that the differentiation in Article 3 HagueReg between combatants and non-combatants in the armed forces is no longer useful.[21]

2. No better protection under international law for non-combatants than for combatants. Even though the view stated above goes beyond that what can clearly be derived from the historical origin of the norm, one result remains certain: the non-combatant has never enjoyed a special status under international law, either before or after the entry into force of AP I. Before AP I, non-combatants belonged to the armed forces (according to Article 3 HagueReg or Article 4 A, No. 1, GC III) without this membership being linked to special protection under international law. Even the classification as an enemy *hors de combat* under Article 23 lit. c HagueReg did not provide any other protection than that afforded to combatants in the same situation. Since AP I entered into force, non-combatants are no longer even expressly included in the members of the armed forces, although the historic origin of Article 43, para. 1, AP I would justify their inclusion in that provision's definition of armed forces. In any event, on the level of international law the only consequence of classifying members of the armed forces as non-combatants is that they acquire prisoner-of-war status if they fall into the hands of the adverse party.

3. Non-legal use of the term 'non-combatant'. The use of the term 'non-combatant' is sporadically to be found in state practice denoting an all-inclusive category comprising all persons not taking a direct part in hostilities.[22] This use corresponds to the Lieber Code of 1863 which included in this category without giving a precise definition all unarmed and inoffensive citizens of the hostile country (e.g. Articles 18 *et seq.*). Such an understanding, however, is incompatible either with the development or the content of treaty law. There is no criterion in treaty law that permits to define civilians whose protection is the basic object and purpose of international humanitarian law as a mere sub-category of non-combatants. Besides that the unification of civilians and non-combating members of the armed forces in one sub-category on an equal footing with combatants would be counterproductive with regard to the fundamental principle of distinction between civilians and combatants. Finally, the sporadic practice just mentioned is not appropriate to derogate existing treaty law which confines the term 'non-combatant' to non-combating members of the armed forces.

> Persons who are members of the armed forces but who, by virtue of national regulations, have no combat mission, such as judges, government officials, and blue-collar workers, are non-combatants. If they fall into the power of the adversary, they will be prisoners of war as will combatants (Article 4 A, No. 1, GC III).   314

[20] As stated correctly by Solf in M. Bothe/K. J. Partsch/W. Solf, *New Rules for Victims of Armed Conflicts* (Nijhoff, 1982), 240.
[21] See *ICRC Commentary*, para. 1676. This position, however, is not compatible with the *travaux préparatoires* of the Diplomatic Conference, for the Conference accepted the Report of the III. Commission expressly stating that the term members of the armed forces is all-inclusive and includes both combatants and non-combatants (CDDH/236/Rev. 1).
[22] *CIHL*, Vol. I, 6 and n. 27.

1. As a rule, persons who are members of the armed forces are combatants—as laid down in Article 43, para. 2, AP I—and are entitled, as such, to participate directly in hostilities. It remains in the discretion of the states and other parties to the conflict recognized as subjects of international law to restrict this entitlement of international law with respect to certain categories of the members of their armed forces and to prohibit them by legal act from direct participation in hostilities. Any such national legal act has no effect whatsoever in international law, since prisoner-of-war status is already attained by virtue of the fact that the non-combatant is a member of the armed forces and thus falls under Article 4 A, No. 1, GC III.

It follows from this that non-combatants are not nor could they under any circumstances be protected as civilians, for Article 50, para. 1, 1st sentence, AP I determines with a negative legal definition: 'A civilian is any person who does not belong to one of the categories of persons referred to in Article 4 A (1), (2), (3), and (6) of the Third Convention and in Article 43 of this Protocol.' However, non-combatant members of the armed forces clearly belong to the armed forces within the meaning of Article 4 A, No. 1, GC III or Article 43, para. 1, AP I, if these provisions are interpreted in the light of their object and purpose. This interpretation will have to take into account the stipulation's all-encompassing scope as well as its drafting history.

From the negative legal definition of civilians it also follows that members of the armed forces do *not* enjoy the 'general protection against dangers arising from military operations' which Article 51, para. 1, 1st sentence, affords to the civilian population and to individual civilians. The non-combatant members of the armed forces are not protected by the prohibition of attacks according to Article 51, para. 2, 1st sentence, AP I, since they do not enjoy the protection of Article 51. Therefore the non-combatant members of the armed forces are not merely subjected to the risk of collateral damage in the sense of Article 51, para. 5 lit. b. This Article concerns exclusively the 'protection of the civilian population', to which the non-combatant members of the armed forces do not belong. AP I and international humanitarian law protect the civilian population but not the armed forces against dangers arising from military operations.

2. According to Article 52, para. 2, 1st sentence, AP I, 'attacks shall be limited strictly to military objectives'. The armed forces of the enemy are a military objective. This is a general principle of customary international law. The Russian draft convention negotiated at the Brussels Conference of 1874 had already taken this legal finding as a starting point. Furthermore, it is clarified by the regulations of the Brussels Declaration and by the prohibition of bombardment of undefended places included in the Hague Regulations.[23] Article 2 HC IX likewise makes clear that facilities of the armed forces also represent military objectives. Article 24, para. 1, of the HRAW 1923 (which did not enter into force as a treaty) contains a definition of military objectives as targets 'of which the destruction or injury would constitute a distinct military advantage to the belligerent'. Finally, Article 52, para. 2, 2nd sentence, AP I defines military objectives, in so far as they are objects, as 'those objects which by their nature, location, purpose or use make an effective contribution to military action and whose total or partial destruction, capture or neutralization, in the circumstances ruling at the time, offers a definite military advantage'. With

---

[23] See K. Ipsen, in D. Fleck (ed.), *Beiträge zur Weiterentwicklung des humanitären Völkerrechts für bewaffnete Konflikte,* 71 Veröffentlichungen des Instituts für Internationales Recht an der Universität Kiel (Hamburg: Hansischer Gildenverlag, 1973), 153 *et seq.*

KNUT IPSEN

the exception of the term of 'definite military advantage', this legal definition essentially contains those characteristics which are required by customary law for the determination of a military objective. Members of the armed forces (with the exception of the specially protected medical and religious personnel) are, however, military objectives as they clearly have these features of military objectives under customary law. As the organization of armed forces—including and especially with regard to their non-combatant members—is concentrated on efficiency, it must be assumed that the main purpose of armed forces is effective participation in hostilities. This participation includes their non-combatant members which, therefore, effectively contribute to military operations.

3. The presence of non-combatant members of the armed forces in a mobile or immobile facility representing a military objective, therefore, does not even require the attacking forces of the adversary to take special precautionary measures. They do not have to differentiate during their attack between combatant and non-combatant members of the adverse armed forces, provided that no medical or religious personnel are present.

As an object of such attack, the—possibly unarmed—non combatant member of the armed forces can at best be entitled to protection as an enemy *hors de combat* within the meaning of Article 41 AP I. Of the variations of the legal definition provided in Article 41, para. 2, only lit. b or c come into consideration. In this respect, too, the position of the non-combatant member of the armed forces is not better than that of the combatant, to whom Article 41 AP I applies equally.[24]

4. As members of the regular armed forces, which non-combatants undoubtedly are, they are required to wear a uniform by Article 44, para. 7, AP I. As mentioned above, this rule had already been accepted at the Brussels Conference of 1874 as also applying to non-combatants in customary law; it has not subsequently been changed through any contrary, generally recognized practice.

5. International law does not determine which state organ must decide upon the classification of persons as combatant or non-combatant members of the armed forces. International law accepts the national decision as a factual precondition, just as it accepts an organizational decision by state organs as to which of its armed agencies are to be qualified as 'armed forces' within the meaning of Article 4 A, No. 1, GC III or Article 43, para. 1, AP I in the event of an international armed conflict. The definition of armed forces in international law, therefore, follows the definition of, respectively, national armed forces as laid down by acts of state and the definition of armed forces of non-state parties to a conflict being recognized as subjects of international law.

> Members of the medical service and religious personnel (chaplains) attached to the   315
> armed forces enjoy special protection. Medical personnel and chaplains who have
> fallen into the hands of the adversary shall be detained only in so far as it is neces-
> sary for assisting prisoners of war. Although they shall not be deemed prisoners of
> war, they shall be granted the same legal protection (Articles 24, 28 and 30 GC I;
> Articles 36 and 37 GC II; Article 33 GC III).

1. The evolution over the last 140 years of the special position of medical and religious personnel in international law precludes their simply being listed, without any further

---

[24] M. N. Schmitt, ' "Direct Participation in Hostilities" and 21st Century Armed Conflicts' in Fischer/Froissart/Heintschel von Heinegg/Raap (eds), *Krisensicherung und Humanitärer Schutz—Crisis Management and Humanitarian Protection* (Berliner Wissenschafts-Verlag, 2004), 505–29, at 512–19.

KNUT IPSEN

qualification in the category of 'non-combatants'. It is true that the Russian draft convention, which formed the basis of the Brussels Conference of 1874, classified members of the religious and medical service (in addition to quartermasters, the military judiciary, and other branches of the military administration) as non-combatants. However, persons employed in hospitals and ambulances and chaplains were immediately differentiated in that they were acknowledged to be neutral when they fell into the hands of the adversary. The draft expressly reiterated in another context that chaplains and members of the medical service could not be made prisoners of war but instead would, in accordance with Articles I–III of the Geneva Red Cross Convention of 1864, enjoy the right of neutrality. As negotiations progressed, references to combatants and non-combatants were directed solely to the fact that both have prisoner-of-war status in the event of capture. Thus the wording of the later Article 3 HagueReg was laid down. It was, therefore, recognized by 1874 at the latest that the legal status of medical and religious personnel was determined by Geneva Law, that is by the Geneva Red Cross Convention of 1864. These regulations became more concrete through subsequent Red Cross Conventions. However, at the Brussels Conference, medical and religious personnel had already been excluded from the category of non-combatants defined by the later Article 3 HagueReg.

2. It would be against the historical development of medical and religious personnel in international law as described above, to classify these persons simply as one of several categories of non-combatants. To avoid any erroneous impression medical and religious personnel should not simply be treated as a secondary group of non-combatants. The fact that medical and religious personnel have been expressly removed from the scope of regulation of Hague Law and left within the scope of Geneva law since 1874 and even earlier requires to differentiate between the personnel mentioned in Section 314 and 315.

3. The chain of provisions protecting medical and religious personnel laid down within the Red Cross Conventions since 1864 shows how inappropriate it is to include these personnel in the category of non-combatants. Article II of the Red Cross Convention of 1864 granted medical personnel and chaplains 'the benefit of . . . neutrality'. Article IX of the subsequent Convention of 1906 determines that medical personnel and religious personnel assigned to the armed forces 'shall be respected and protected under all circumstances'; they were not to be considered as prisoners of war. Article IX of the Convention of 1929 included a similar regulation. Finally, the currently applicable Articles 24 and 28 GC I, 36 GC II, and 33 GC III all contain regulations with identical contents.

From this it can be concluded that medical personnel belonging to the armed forces enjoy an international legal status under Geneva Law which has been developed with rare consistency and continuity. This status has not been fundamentally altered since 1864. It has, decisively, never constituted a subcategory of 'non-combatants'. Religious personnel are often not even members of the armed forces, which is an indispensable requirement for non-combatants. All of the aforementioned Geneva Conventions assume that protected religious personnel are 'attached' to the armed forces, but not necessarily members thereof.

While the first sentence of Section 314 classifies those persons who are members of the armed forces but do not have a combat mission as non-combatants, in the first sentence of Section 315 there is already a divergence from this basic definition, as medical and religious personnel are not necessarily members of but may be merely *attached to*

KNUT IPSEN

the armed forces. Consequently, it should be emphasized that medical and religious personnel have a special primary status under Geneva Law which has been developed since 1864 through all of the Geneva Conventions to the status which is now set out in GC I–III.

4. The second sentence of Section 315, according to which medical personnel and chaplains who have fallen into the hands of the adversary may only be detained to assist prisoners of war of their own party to the conflict, is a rule of international law which was already contained in the Red Cross Convention of 1864. This Convention ensured that the medical and religious personnel who had fallen into the hands of the adversary could either continue their duties or return to the units to which they belonged (Article III).

According to the Geneva Convention of 1906 these personnel were permitted to continue carrying out their functions under the direction of the detaining power, but were to be returned to their own country or army when their assistance was no longer required (Article 12). The Convention of 1929 contained a regulation to the same effect (Article 12). Thus the regulations applicable today (Articles 28–30 GC I; Article 37 GC II; Article 33 GC III) are an uninterrupted continuation of the protection of the Geneva Law, although according to Article 33 GC III, the return of the protected persons to their state or army of origin does require an agreement between the parties to the conflict, an agreement which the parties are obliged to negotiate. The legal finding that members of the medical and religious personnel are not prisoners of war can also be found in all the Red Cross Conventions since 1864. As shown above (Section 314), this has led to the exclusion of medical and religious personnel from the provisions of Hague Law, which is logically correct.

It is consistent that Article 21 HagueReg in connection with this protection refers to the Geneva Law. This state of the law has remained unchanged. With regard to the protection of medical and religious personnel who have fallen into the hands of the adversary, the antecedents of the four Geneva Conventions of 1949 maintained the obligation upon the detaining power under all circumstances to respect and protect those personnel, even those who fell into their power.

Article 33 GC III specifies this obligation to protect by guaranteeing to the members of medical and religious personnel all the benefits and protections of this Convention as well as 'all facilities necessary' to provide for the medical care of, and religious ministration to, prisoners of war. In this respect the legal position of medical and religious personnel exceeds the best possible treatment available under GC III.

> **Non-combatants, too, have the right to defend themselves or others against any**   316
> **attacks. Medical personnel and chaplains are allowed to bear and use small arms**
> **(pistols, rifles, or sub-machine-guns) for this purpose (Article 22 No. 1 GC I;**
> **Article 35 No. 1 GC II; Article 13, para. 2 lit. a, AP I). This presupposes a national**
> **authorization for the handling of firearms and ammunition.**

Members of these categories are in different situations, from the point of view of international law, when they themselves are the object of an attack by combatants of the adverse party.

a) The first sentence of this section should not be misunderstood to mean that non-combatants as defined in Section 314 are as widely protected by international law against attacks by combatants of the adverse party as medical and religious personnel defined in Section 315; that such attacks are therefore contrary to international law; and that non-combatants must therefore only protect themselves against attacks contravening international law. However, as non-combatants are members of the armed forces, which represent a military objective against which international law permits armed acts, they can certainly be the object of attacks consistent with international law applicable in international armed conflict. In such a case, non-combatants, as members of the armed forces, are naturally authorized to defend themselves. Thus the non-combatants' right of self-defence is not restricted to those attacks which involve prohibited methods and means of warfare, such as a violation of the prohibition of perfidy (Article 37 AP I) or of the obligation to protect an enemy *hors de combat* (Article 41).

In contrast to the applicable rules of Geneva Law regarding self-defence of medical personnel, Hague Law contains no express regulation about the right of self-defence of non-combatants. However, since membership in the armed forces according to Article 43, para. 2, AP I generally leads to the authorization of combatants to take part in hostilities, the denial of this authorization to participate, which in any event is mere domestic law, should be regarded as obsolete if non-combatants created by a national legal act (and not by international law) themselves become the object of an attack. If they defend themselves against such an attack, they take a direct part in hostilities, which, by virtue of Article 43, para. 2, AP I, they are permitted to do as members of the armed forces.

In summary, this means: an attack against a member of the armed forces who is classified by a national legal act as a non-combatant activates the entitlement of every member of the armed forces (except medical and religious personnel) to take a direct part in hostilities. The attack activates their latent combatant status. The first sentence of Section 316 underlines therefore that non-combatants are authorized to defend themselves and others against any attack, irrespective of whether such attack is contravening international law or not.

b) The situation regarding medical personnel is different. They are protected by the absolute rule—continuously repeated by the Geneva Conventions—of respect and protection 'under all circumstances' against *every* attack. An attack against medical personnel is, therefore, always contrary to international law. Beginning with the Geneva Convention of 1906 (in Article 8 No. 1), it is expressly laid down that medical personnel may be armed and may use their weapons for their own defence or for the defence of the wounded and sick entrusted to them. Article 13, para. 2, lit. a, AP I, therefore, merely confirms the law which has already long been in force when it stipulates that medical personnel 'are to be equipped with small-arms for their own defence or for that of the wounded and sick in their charge'. The firearms listed in Section 316 (pistols, rifles, or sub-machine-guns) are clearly small-arms. At national level an authorization which puts the law into concrete terms will be required to implement the prerequisites of international law.

c) The legal situation concerning religious personnel is more complex. As far as their protection is concerned, the position is the same as for medical personnel; both must be respected and protected under all circumstances, which also means that every attack against religious personnel is contrary to international law. The reference in Section 316 to both medical and religious personnel and to the rules of Geneva Law applicable to the arming and authorization of self-defence for *medical* personnel should not be taken to mean that the treaty rules referred to here also authorize the arming and self-defence of *religious* personnel. Since the Convention of 1906 provisions for arming and for self-defence apply exclusively to medical personnel, not to religious personnel. This is systematically confirmed by all relevant Conventions since 1906, all of which regulate the arming and the right of self-defence of medical personnel under the rubric of 'Medical Units and Establishments' and the protection of religious personnel under the rubric 'Personnel'. Finally, it must be noted that these Conventions generally classify medical personnel as *members* of the armed forces, but religious personnel as chaplains '*attached to* the armed forces'. According to the legal definition in Article 8, lit. d, AP I, religious personnel may include military and civilian persons. They must, however, be exclusively engaged in the work of their ministry and at least attached to the armed forces. Thus treaty provisions concerning arming and the right of self-defence applicable for medical personnel do not automatically apply to religious personnel (see below, commentary to Section 825, para. 2).

A detainee shall not be prosecuted for his participation in hostilities unless he or   317
she has been positively identified as an unlawful combatant.

1. If during direct participation in hostilities, members of the armed forces (combatants or non-combatants) abide by the international law applicable in international armed conflicts then they cannot be punished, either by their own party to the conflict or by the competent tribunals of the adversary, in the event of their capture.

a) The context of the first phrase shows that this section refers solely to those prisoners of war who are either members of the armed forces (whether combatant or non-combatant) under Article 4 A, No. 1, or combatants under Article 4 A, Nos. 2, 3, or 6, GC III, thereby falling under the new comprehensive notion of armed forces of Article 43, para. 1, AP I. The other two categories mentioned in Article 4 A as being entitled to prisoner-of-war status in the hands of the adversary (civilians accompanying the armed forces without actually being members thereof, and members of crews of the merchant navy and of civil aircraft) are *not* entitled to take a direct part in hostilities. In the event of such participation as unprivileged belligerents (see above, Section 302) they must expect to be prosecuted in the same manner as all other civilians who are prohibited from taking a direct part in hostilities.

b) Persons whose prisoner-of-war status is unquestionable because they belong to the categories listed in Article 4 A, Nos. 1, 2, 3, or 6, GC III and who have engaged in any activity contrary to international law must also expect to be prosecuted while in the hands of the adversary. This follows from Article 85 GC III. That provision guarantees convicted prisoners of war the benefits listed in GC III, that is the right of appeal, notification of the judgment to the protecting power in accordance with Article 107, a (humane) enforcement procedure in accordance with Article 108, and—in the event of a death penalty—suspension of the execution for a period of six months following notification of the protecting power according to Article 101. If, however, it is clearly established by the courts that the person in question is not entitled to prisoner-of-war status according to Article 4 A, Nos. 1, 2, 3, or 6, or Article 43 in conjunction with Article 44, para. 1, AP I, then his or her direct participation in the hostilities was also unauthorized. He or she is thus an unprivileged belligerent and responsible under criminal law for all acts committed against the adversary. The detaining power is obliged under international law to afford to every prosecuted person of the adverse party to a conflict the treatment which is more favourable either under GC III or under Article 75 AP I.

KNUT IPSEN

2. The punishment of criminal acts within the meaning of substantive criminal law is subject to special conditions imposed by international law (as for the punishment of disciplinary offences, see Sections 727–729 and 1410–1418 below).

318   No sentence may be passed and no penalty may be executed except pursuant to a conviction pronounced by an impartial and regularly constituted court respecting the generally recognized principles of regular judicial procedure (Article 84 GC III; Article 75, para. 4, AP I).

This section repeats word for word the main contents of Article 75, para. 4, 1st sentence, AP I, which in turn corresponds to the special regulation for prisoners of war contained in Article 84 GC III. Thus the principle of more favourable treatment laid down in Article 75, para. 1, AP I applies here as well. Article 75, para. 4, only applies—to fill in the gaps, as it were—in so far as it provides for more favourable treatment of prisoners of war than the applicable provisions of Chapter III of GC III in respect of the sentencing and execution of punishments.

In particular, in Articles 86 and 99 to 108, Chapter III of GC III sets down a standard of treatment not less favourable than that in Article 75, para. 4, AP I. Thus, according to the general rule of interpretation of Article 31, para. 3, lit. c, Vienna Convention on the Law of Treaties, this regulation, which to a large extent was modelled on the judicial guarantees in Articles 14 and 15 ICCPR, must be referred to in interpreting Chapter III of GC III. Therefore the principle *'nulla poena sine lege'* contained in Article 99 GC III is specified by Article 75, para. 4, lit. c, just as the procedural guarantees of Article 105 GC III are put into concrete terms through lit. d (presumption of innocence until proven guilty according to the law), lit. e (the right of persons charged to be present at trial), and lit. f (no compulsion to confess guilt). With regard to the execution of a punishment, Article 108 GC III contains detailed rules which are not found in Article 75 AP I.

IV. Persons Accompanying the Armed Forces

319   Persons who accompany the armed forces without being members thereof, such as war correspondents, members of labour units, or of services responsible for the welfare of the soldiers, shall not be deemed combatants. If they fall into the power of the adversary, they shall become prisoners of war (Article 4 A, No. 4, GC III).

1. Civilians accompanying the armed forces are formally protected by the obligation of the armed forces which they accompany to provide them with identity cards, an example of which is contained in Annex IV A of GC III. Substantially, the members of this category are protected as civilians. The function for which they (as civilians) accompany the armed forces must be recorded on the identity card. Their function should be stated in such a manner that they cannot be suspected of having taken a direct part in the hostilities. Article 50, para. 1, 2nd sentence, AP I states clearly that 'in any case of doubt as to whether a person is a civilian, that person shall be considered to be a civilian'. However, if a person accompanying the armed forces is suspected of combatant behaviour, and if this suspicion is confirmed, then this regulation, which was intended as a protective provision, has adverse repercussions on the person in question. If persons accompanying the armed forces conduct themselves according to their status as civilians

then they run the risk of collateral injury. Conversely, the responsible military leader who attacks a military objective containing civilians accompanying armed forces must carry out the precautionary measures stipulated by Article 57 (especially in para. 2, lit. a) in order to keep collateral injuries to the civilians accompanying the armed forces to a minimum.

2. If civilians accompanying the armed forces fall into the hands of the adversary then they attain prisoner-of-war status in accordance with Article 4 A, No. 4, GC III (see below Section 707). Apart from merchant navy or civil aircraft crews, civilians accompanying the armed forces are therefore the only category of civilians without combatant status who attain the status of prisoner of war.

V. Civilian Contractors

**Private contractors and civilian employees of the armed forces may not assume   320
combatant functions. Their geographical and organizational closeness to the armed
forces may increase the risk of incidental death or injury among such personnel (see
below Section 446). If they directly participate in hostilities they will lose protection for the duration of each specific act amounting to direct participation (see
below, Section 517).**

Various factors led to a 'civilianization' of tasks which traditionally belonged to the military domain: shrunken defence budgets and the downsizing of military forces have required the outsourcing of certain tasks to cheaper and often more effective civilian enterprise; at the same time, technological demands have increased reliance on civilian expertise. While such developments have been perceived as a change of paradigms in international humanitarian law,[25] it is important to maintain that contractor personnel do not share the 'combatant privilege' in armed conflicts[26] and any manpower management must observe that certain activities are inherently governmental and remain military in nature.[27] 'Civilian contractors', as the clear-cut meaning of this term already denotes, are not and cannot be members of the armed forces of a party to the conflict, thus lacking the indispensable precondition for combatant status. Contractor personnel taking a direct part in hostilities are, therefore, running the risk of being treated as mercenaries, if they fall into the hands of the adversary and if Article 47 AP I or one of the mercenary conventions is applicable (see Section 303 above). In any case, the adverse party may qualify and treat them as unprivileged belligerents.

VI. Special Forces

**It shall be lawful for combatants recognizable as such (by their uniform, insignia,   321
etc.) to participate in raids, acts of sabotage, and other attacks carried out by special**

---

[25] M. N. Schmitt (above, n. 24).

[26] See US Department of Defense Instruction 3020.41 USD (AT&L) of 3 October 2005 'Contractor Personnel Authorized to Accompany the US Armed Forces'; US Department of Defense Instruction 1100.22 USC (P&R) of 7 September 2006 'Guidance for Determining Workforce Mix'.

[27] See Montreux Document on Private Military and Security Companies (17 September 2008), <http://www.eda.admin.ch/eda/en/home/topics/intla/humlaw/pse/parsta.html>; International Code of Conduct for Private Security Service Providers—ICoC—(9 November 2010), <http://www.icoc-psp.org>.

forces in the enemy's hinterland or in forward areas. Combatants who commit such acts wearing plain clothes or the uniform of the adversary are liable to be punished. They shall nevertheless have the right to a regular judicial procedure (Articles 82 *et seq.* GC III; Article 75, para. 4, API).

1. In past international armed conflicts, long-distance reconnaissance patrols (with or without combat tasks) and task forces on remote missions against military objectives located to the rear of the adversary have repeatedly raised the problem of whether members of armed forces involved in such actions could permissibly be camouflaged in plain clothes or in the uniform of the enemy, at least during the phase preceding military engagement.

2. Section 321 adopts a clear position towards a question which remains controversial even today. During the Second World War, the camouflaging of long-distance reconnaissance patrols or of task forces wearing plain clothes or the uniform of the adversary was regarded as perfidious and was universally accepted as being prohibited (the prohibition against the misuse of the adversary's uniform was already expressly contained in Article 23, lit. f, HagueReg).[28] After the Second World War, the acquittal in the *Skorzeny* case led to some legislation adopting a partial rather than a total prohibition against using the adversary's uniform as camouflage. The case concerned the deployment of commando forces of the German *Wehrmacht* in connection with the Ardennes offensive in December 1944 against military objectives to the rear of Western Allied forces, during which the advance was carried out in the enemy's uniform, the actual fighting being carried out in the uniform of the *Wehrmacht*.[29] The conclusion drawn from the case that such camouflaging is permitted under international law was, appropriately, countered with the argument that such generalization is incompatible with both the ordinary meaning and the historical origins of Article 23, lit. f, HagueReg.[30] However, the same controversy arose again during the Geneva Conference on the Reaffirmation and Development of International Humanitarian Law Applicable in Armed Conflicts. Several states supported a clear and universal prohibition, allowing no exceptions, while other states were of the opinion that only the use of the enemy's uniform or other insignia for camouflage and to make operations easier should be prohibited. The compromise now contained in Article 39, para. 2, is—as can be seen—closer to this second position.

3. The meaning of this section, which should be interpreted in connection with Section 308, 2nd sentence, is unequivocal: participation in armed acts causing harm by special forces in the forward area or to the rear of the adversary is a permitted act provided that the members of the armed forces involved can be identified by their uniform (in so far as they are members of the regular armed forces) or by other clearly recognizable distinctive emblems. If this requirement, which derives from the basic rule of distinction contained in Article 44, para. 3, 1st sentence, AP I, is not fulfilled, then the following alternative legal consequences apply, depending on the type of camouflage used. If the members of special command units wear plain clothes and if the other conditions are fulfilled, then

---

[28] In this connection see the detailed remarks in D. Fleck, 'Ruses of War and Prohibition of Perfidy' (1974) XIII *RDMilG* 269–314.

[29] *Trial of Otto Skorzeny and Others*, General Military Government Court of the US Zone of Germany, 18 August–9 September 1947, in *Law Reports of Trials of War Criminals*, Vol. IX, 90–4.

[30] As D. Fleck (above, n. 28) has stated correctly.

KNUT IPSEN

there is a violation of the prohibition of perfidy under Article 37, para. 1, lit. c, AP I, unless all the conditions of the special situation envisaged in Article 44, para. 3, 2nd sentence, AP I, that is the ordered minimum degree of distinction (see the comments to Section 309 above), are met. It is, therefore, possible that the legal result will be the forfeiture of the combatant status provided by Article 44, para. 4, 1st sentence, AP I.

If, on the other hand, members of armed forces involved in special units wear the uniform of the adverse party to the conflict, then they violate the prohibition under Article 39, para. 2, AP I. The alternative contained in this norm (as a result of the compromise described above) will normally be present cumulatively: members of commando forces wear the uniform of the enemy above all in order to 'shield, favour, [and] protect . . . military operations'. If they fall into the hands of the adversary prior to their attack against the chosen military objective, then as a rule the wearing of the enemy's uniform provides the intended prohibited purpose.

This result is supported by a further consideration: Article 44, para. 3, 2nd sentence, lit. b, AP I describes the special situation wherein arms are required to be carried openly during 'a military deployment preceding the launching of an attack' and thus clearly equates this phase with an act of military operations. As many states have formally declared upon ratification, such acts include any movement towards a place from which an attack is to be launched. This legal position clearly falls within the scope of interpretation of the applicable provision of the Protocol. Consequently, a military deployment preceding an attack or an advance of commando forces *as a whole* is deemed to be an act of military operations within the meaning of Article 39, para. 2, AP I, and thus invariably the wearing of the enemy's uniform will be deemed to be for the prohibited purpose of shielding, favouring, or protecting that military operation. If members of the armed forces involved in special units are caught wearing the uniform of the adverse party to the conflict 'while engaging in attacks', then the violation of the prohibition contained in Article 39, para. 2, AP I is evident.

Undoubtedly, therefore, camouflage in plain clothes or the enemy's uniform by members of special units of armed forces is a violation of the applicable norms of international law, for which legally permissible sanctions may be imposed. The framework set out in international law for such sanctions has been dealt with in detail above (see Section 318).

VII. Spies

Spies are persons who clandestinely, or under false pretences, for example not wearing the uniform of their armed forces, gather information in the territory controlled by the adversary. Even if they are members of armed forces, they do not have the right to prisoner-of-war status. Persons who fall into the hands of the adversary while engaged in espionage shall be liable to punishment (Articles 29–31 HagueReg).   322

1. In the light of the sophistication of modern-day reconnaissance with electronic instruments, especially satellite-supported reconnaissance, it may come as a surprise that 'spies' are dealt with under a rubric comparable to that dedicated to combatants. Apart from the fact that most states do not (as yet) have at their disposal the highest standard of reconnaissance technology, international law applicable in international armed conflict must take a position on the issues of who is a spy, and how spies may be treated.

KNUT IPSEN

2. The definition of spies in the first sentence of this regulation stems from Article 29, para. 1, HagueReg and Article 46, para. 2, AP I. For this reason the individual elements of this definition must be determined according to the HagueReg or AP I. In so far as the definition speaks of 'persons', these can have the primary status of either civilians or combatants.

Article 46 AP I, contained in the section 'Combatant and Prisoner-of-War Status', only applies to persons who are members of the armed forces; it says nothing about spies whose primary status is that of civilians. In contrast the definition contained in Article 29, para. 1, HagueReg applies to both civilians and members of the armed forces who do not wear the uniform of their party to the conflict.

The first sentence of Section 322 makes use of the definition of the HagueReg. However, it would be an unacceptably narrow interpretation of this sentence to define spies simply as members of the armed forces who clandestinely or under false pretences gather information in the territory controlled by the adversary. For one thing, spies can—as stated above—also have the primary status of civilians, which means that, as a rule, they are in any event not entitled to prisoner-of-war status if they fall into the hands of the adversary. On the other hand, persons within the meaning of Article 29 HagueReg could have the primary status of civilians and, at the same time, of persons accompanying the armed forces (see Section 319 above). As such they are certainly entitled to prisoner-of-war status.

Properly understood, therefore, three groups of persons are involved: persons who have the primary status of civilians and who do not become prisoners of war even if they fall into the hands of the adversary; civilians who have the primary status of civilians but who, in the event of their capture by the enemy, attain prisoner-of-war status in accordance with Article 4 A GC III; and finally, persons who are members of armed forces but who engage in espionage without wearing the uniform of their party to the conflict.

3. As for the requirement regarding location, the section's phrase 'in the territory controlled by the adversary' makes use of the further requirement of Article 46, para. 2, AP I (Article 29, para. 1, HagueReg: zone of operations of a belligerent). This location requirement, therefore, refers to the entire territory held by the party being spied upon, either under sovereign power as state territory or under occupational force as occupied territory.

4. As for espionage activity, this relates to information gathering which occurs 'clandestinely or under false pretences'. This is the literal formulation used in Article 29, para. 1, HagueReg, which incidentally is also contained in the Lieber Code (Article 88) and in the Brussels Declaration of 1874 (Article 19).

The fact that Article 46, para. 2, AP I does not specify the gathering of information in the same way should not obscure the fact that AP I has left the old law unaltered in this respect. Instead, it follows from the connection between para. 2 (definition) and para. 3 (information gathering on territory occupied by the adversary), where espionage is understood to be an activity carried out under false pretences or deliberately in a clandestine manner, that in this respect the Hague Law has not been altered.

Following these comments it can be stated that espionage activity, that is the gathering of information clandestinely or under false pretences, has been construed in the same way from the time of the Lieber Code until the date of AP I.

KNUT IPSEN

5. Spies are not entitled to prisoner-of-war status even if they are members of the armed forces, persons accompanying the armed forces, or members of merchant navy or civil aircraft crews, and notwithstanding that these categories of persons do without exception acquire prisoner-of-war status in the hands of the enemy (according to Article 43, para. 1, AP I in conjunction with Article 4 A, Nos. 1–5, GC III) when they are not involved in espionage. As far as members of the armed forces are concerned, this follows explicitly from Article 46, para. 1, AP I. With regard to the aforementioned civilians who are entitled to prisoner-of-war status, this derives from Article 29, para. 1, in connection with the *argumentum e contrario* drawn from Article 31 HagueReg.

The fundamental permissibility of punishing spies who have fallen into the hands of the adversary arises from Article 46, para. 1, AP I and Article 29, para. 1, HagueReg in conjunction with Article 30 HagueReg.

> **Even if captured while engaged in espionage, a spy shall not be punished without**   323
> **prior conviction pursuant to regular judicial proceedings (Article 30 HagueReg;**
> **Article 75, para. 4, AP I).**

The Brussels Declaration of 1874 already contained the rule that a spy who is caught in the act of spying is treated and prosecuted in accordance with the detaining power's applicable laws (Article 20). The HagueReg has put this into more concrete terms by prohibiting the punishment of spies caught in the act of spying without prior conviction (Article 30). This judicial guarantee is again made concrete by Article 75, para. 4, AP I as set out above (Section 318).

> **A spy who, after rejoining his own or allied armed forces upon completion of his**   324
> **mission, is subsequently captured by the adversary, shall be treated as a prisoner**
> **of war and incur no responsibility for his previous acts of espionage (Article 31**
> **HagueReg; Article 46, para. 4, AP I).**

This regulation represents a rule already contained in the Brussels Declaration of 1874 (Article 21) which was adopted almost literally by the two Hague Regulations (HagueReg 1907: Article 31). This traditional rule has been specified in relation to members of the armed forces who have been engaged in espionage on the territory of the adversary, although not residing there, and who have then returned to a unit or a formation of their own armed forces. This could be the case, for example, if a member of the armed forces who has been active as a spy in an occupied territory joins a long-distance reconnaissance patrol or a commando unit of his own party to the conflict. If he is captured, he shall be deemed to have returned to his armed forces and is entitled to prisoner-of-war status.

> **Combatants, such as reconnaissance patrols, who, marked as such, reconnoitre**   325
> **the adversary's area of operations shall not be deemed engaged in espionage**
> **(Article 29, para. 2, HagueReg; Article 46, para. 2 AP I). The same applies**
> **to military aircraft on overt missions of information gathering (Rule 123**
> ***HPCR Manual*).**

1. The substance of this regulation corresponds to Article 29, para. 2, HagueReg and, furthermore, is a logical legal consequence of the rule contained in the first sentence of Section 321. This section repeats the broad territorial criteria of AP I (territory controlled by an adverse party) while Section 325 uses the narrower formulation of the HagueReg

(area of operations of the hostile army). This does not mean that long-distance recon-naissance is only permitted within the zone of operation of the hostile army. Rather, Section 325 must be understood as also permitting members of the armed forces (within the meaning of Article 43, para. 1, AP I) who can be identified as such (as members of the regular armed forces: by their uniform), to gather information in the entire territory controlled by an adverse party to the extent that this is efficient and feasible from a military and tactical point of view. This is expressly confirmed by Article 46, para. 2, AP I. A similar provision for air warfare is contained in Rule 123 *HPCR Manual* stating that 'military aircraft on mission to gather, intercept or otherwise gain information are not to be regarded as carrying out acts of espionage'.[31]

2. A special rule worth noting in this context results from Article 46, para. 3, AP I, which recognizes the loyalty of a member of armed forces to his own party to the conflict. If a member of armed forces who is a resident of territory occupied by an adverse party gath-ers information of military value in that territory, then this is not regarded as espionage, unless he gathers information clandestinely or through an act of false pretences. If those characteristics of espionage are met by a member of armed forces who is caught in the act, he may be treated as a spy, as has been the case since the Brussels Declaration.

VIII. Special Aspects of Aerial and Naval Warfare

Since the Second Geneva Convention of 1949 there have been no universal international treaties on the law of naval warfare. The same applies to air warfare. However, as shown by the 1954 CultPropConv, and by Article 49, para. 3, AP I—which makes Section I, Part IV of AP I applicable to any land, air, or sea warfare—these dimensions of armed conflicts have not been disregarded.

Sections 326–331 deal only with a limited aspect of air and sea warfare, namely that which concerns combatant and prisoner-of-war status.

326   **Unlike military ground vehicles, manned military aircraft and ships are required to bear external marks indicating their nationality and military character. Non-uniformed members of armed forces who take part in hostilities using correctly marked military aircraft or ships shall remain combatants. When captured by the adversary they shall prove their military status by an identity card.**

1. A warship is a ship belonging to the naval forces of a state and bearing external marks which distinguish the warship and its nationality (see below, Section 1002). Likewise, a military aircraft is defined as an aircraft belonging to the air forces of a state and bear-ing external military marks distinguishing its nationality. Apart from the controversial issue of warships displaying false flags and emblems during their approach and the obligation to display their own flag before opening fire (see below, Section 1018),[32] war-ships and military aircraft shall be clearly and unambiguously recognizable as military objec-tives by their external marks. This accords with the requirement of distinction which in

---

[31] Harvard Program on Humanitarian Policy and Conflict Research/*HPCR Manual on International Law Applicable to Air and Missile Warfare* (intended to be a restatement of existing law) <http://www.ihlresearch.org/amw/manual>.

[32] Cf. D. Fleck (above, n. 28); W. Fenrick, 'Military Objectives, in the Law of Naval Warfare' in Heintschel v. Heinegg (ed.), *The Military Objective and the Principle of Distinction in the Law of Naval Warfare*, 7 Bochumer Schriften zur Friedenssicherung und zum humanitären Völkerrecht (Bochum: Universitätsverlag

the case of ground forces is met by the obligation of the individual combatant to wear uniform or other distinguishing emblems in order to protect the civilian population. Consequently, members of armed forces not wearing uniforms on board a properly marked warship or military aircraft and taking part in hostilities are and remain combatants regardless of this circumstance. Naturally, the same applies to armed forces members on board of such warships or military aircraft who are, according to national decision, non-combatants. As proved and explained in detail above (Sections 301 and 314), both combatants and non-combatants are members of armed forces. If combatants and non-combatants find themselves on board a military aircraft or warship, then the aircraft or ship in question becomes a military objective which the adversary is allowed to attack with the permitted methods and means of warfare. The adversary cannot—and is not required to—take into consideration the fact that there are non-combatants on board in addition to the combatant crew (with the exception, of course, of the specially protected medical and religious personnel). Combatants and non-combatants (excluding medical and religious personnel) as armed forces members are military objectives who according to international law may be attacked. There is clearly *no* duty to distinguish between combatants and non-combatants, for instance during a use of arms against a military aircraft or warship.

2. If crew members of a military aircraft or warship not in uniform fall into the hands of the adversary, they must prove their membership of the armed forces by displaying an identity card (if necessary with an identification tag).

> **No aircraft other than military aircraft of the parties to an international armed conflict shall engage in any form of hostilities (Article 16, para. 1, HRAW 1923; Rule 17 *HPCR Manual*).**   327

The prohibition contained in Article 16, para. 1, HRAW 1923, that no aircraft other than belligerent military aircraft shall engage in hostilities in any form, never entered into force as a provision of international treaty law, but is regarded as a rule of customary international law (see Section 1016 below). This principle corresponds with Article 44, para. 3, 1st sentence, AP I: 'In order to promote the protection of the civilian population from the effects of hostilities, combatants are obliged to distinguish themselves from the civilian population while they are engaged in an attack or in a military operation preparatory to an attack.' The civilian aircraft is a civilian object which is fully protected in international law by Article 52, para. 1, AP I. The military aircraft, on the other hand, is a military objective according to Article 52, para. 2, AP I, must be identifiable, and is permitted to take part directly in military operations, but may also be the object of armed attacks by the adversary. As stated in Rule 17 *HPCR Manual*, only military aircraft are entitled to engage in attacks and in the exercise of other belligerent rights, such as interception.

> **A military aircraft shall be under the command of a duly commissioned soldier. The crew must be subject to military discipline (Article 14 HRAW 1923; Rule 1, lit. x, *HPCR Manual*).**   328

N. Brockmeyer, 1991), 1–44 [38]; G. J. F. van Hegelsom, 'Methods and Means of Combat in Naval Warfare' in W. Heintschel v. Heinegg (ed.), *Methods and Means of Combat in Naval Warfare, 8 Bochumer Schriften zur Friedenssicherung und zum humanitären Völkerrecht* (Bochum: Brockmeyer, 1992), 1–59, at 16 *et seq.*

This provision reiterates the contents of Article 14 HRAW 1923. This requirement of international law, which must be met by the internal organization of the party to the conflict, has been applied to ground forces in various respects (Article 1, No. 1, HagueReg, Article 13, No. 2, lit. a, GC II; Article 4 A, No. 2, lit. a, GC III; Article 43, para. 1, AP I). It is based upon a principle of customary law and takes into account the principle of authorization, which is an essential prerequisite for classification as a combatant (see above, Section 304). If a party to a conflict acts in accordance with international law applicable in international armed conflict through its armed forces as the organ provided for this purpose, then the connection between the armed forces and the state party to the conflict must be guaranteed. This requirement is fulfilled by the chain of command and by a system of military discipline. Thus, Rule 1(x) *HPCR Manual* requires military aircraft being commanded by a member of the armed forces and manned (or preprogrammed) by a crew subject to regular armed forces discipline.

329   No civilian aircraft shall be armed (Article 16, para. 3, HRAW 1923).

The definition of civilian aircraft as an object which is neither a military nor a public aircraft and 'exclusively' serves the civilian transport of passengers or cargo (see below, Section 1009) excludes any arming of such aircraft during an international armed conflict even within its own state. The arming of a civilian aircraft for the purpose of direct participation in military operations (for purposes of attack) can therefore be ruled out from the outset. If one wishes to arm a civilian aircraft within the jurisdiction of its own country for the purpose of countering an attack (i.e. in self-defence) then under the present state of technological development this purpose would be better served by equipping the aircraft with electronic defence systems against radar target detection, missile attacks, and so on, than by arming it.

330   Public non-military aircraft shall be treated as civilian objects (Articles 5 and 6 HRAW 1923; Rules 17, 22 *HPCR Manual*). Public aircraft employed for jurisdictional purposes (customs, police) shall also carry papers and bear marks evidencing their non-military character (Article 4 HRAW 1923; Rule 17 *HPCR Manual*). Public aircraft are subject to confiscation, unless specially protected (Article 32 HRAW 1923; Rule 136(a) *HPCR Manual*). Enemy private aircraft are liable to capture and adjudication by a prize court in order that any neutral claim may be duly heard and determined (Articles 52, 55 HRAW 1923; Rule 134 *HPCR Manual*).

1. This provision deals with the same problem in international law as has occurred in connection with paramilitary or armed law enforcement agencies of a party to a conflict; a problem which has been regulated by Article 43, para. 3, AP I (see Section 307 above). It follows particularly from Article 43, para. 3, AP I that members of armed law enforcement agencies of a party to a conflict always have the primary status of civilians unless the party incorporates them into its armed forces and properly notifies the adversary thereof. The logical legal result is that the aircraft of armed law enforcement agencies which are not incorporated into the armed forces are civilian objects, just as their members are civilians. Furthermore, it follows that a public non-military aircraft must be marked in order to distinguish it from military aircraft belonging to armed forces.

2. HRAW 1923, which is not treaty law, lays down in Article 32 that public non-military aircraft are subject to confiscation 'without prize proceedings', which actually means they may be captured. It would be incorrect to conclude *a contrario*, that prize proceedings

are required in the case of civilian aircraft. HRAW 1923, Chapter VII, clearly differentiates between enemy and neutral private aircraft. Enemy private aircraft 'are liable to capture in all circumstances' (Article 52 HRAW 1923). As far as the legal act and legal consequences of capturing are concerned, Rule 136(a) *HPCR Manual* puts military aircraft and all other public aircraft on the same footing by the statement that 'enemy military, law enforcement and customs aircraft are booty of war. Prize procedures do not apply to captured enemy military aircraft and other State aircraft, inasmuch as their ownership immediately passes to the captor government by virtue of capture.'

A neutral private aircraft, by contrast, is only liable to capture under certain preconditions (Article 53). The capture of an aircraft or of the goods on board shall only be brought before a prize court in so far as neutral claims must be heard and determined (Article 55). If a private aircraft is proven to belong to the adverse party to the conflict, it may even be destroyed after any persons on board have been placed in safety. However, the rules of HRAW 1923 may be put aside, for the nine decades following its formulation have not evolved a corresponding state practice and *opinio iuris*.

For the most part in international armed conflicts, in particular during the Second World War, public non-military aircraft and private aircraft that had fallen into the power of the adversary have been treated by the adversary power as booty and have been confiscated, without prize proceedings regularly being carried out for civilian aircraft. Rule 136(a) *HPCR Manual* apparently has formulated the restatement of customary law on the basis of these historical facts.

3. With regard to the law of AP I, public non-military aircraft are usually, and civilian aircraft always, civilian objects in the sense of Article 52, para. 1, 1st sentence, AP I and therefore they may neither be attacked nor made the object of reprisals. It could prove difficult to differentiate in cases where public non-military aircraft are used for military purposes, especially as airborne headquarters of the state leaders; in such a case it would be impossible to exclude such an aircraft from the definition of military objectives in Article 52, para. 2, AP I, or in Rule 22 *HPCR Manual*.

Special provisions relating to naval warfare are contained in Chapter 10.   331

For more detailed provisions concerning military, public non-military, and civilian aircraft, see the 'Definitions' in Chapter 10.

4

METHODS AND MEANS
OF COMBAT

Introductory Remarks

1. *Historical development of the rules on warfare and weapons.* The concern to protect the civilian population, as well as combatants, against excessive and exceptionally cruel violence might have been the beginning of all moral and philosophical attempts to mitigate the horrors of war (Sections 107–123). The ancient civilizations experienced—as did the cultures of the Far East, India, and Islam[1]—religiously motivated efforts to set bounds to the spread of belligerent violence (*supra*, Section 107). These attempts to control war, however, succeeded only to a limited degree.

Like all 'modern international law', the contemporary law of war has its roots primarily in European history since the Middle Ages.[2] Christian moral theology and the natural law theories of early modern times made intense efforts to alleviate the sufferings of war but they failed to find real resonance in the belligerent practice of medieval feuds or the religious wars of the sixteenth and seventeenth centuries.[3] The code of honour of European chivalry had imposed certain ritual limits on the permitted forms of combat towards 'equal' enemies, but did little to protect the hostile 'civilian population'.[4] Combat to the prejudice of the peasant and urban population reached a sad climax in the Thirty Years War of 1618–1648, when a third of Central Europe's population fell victim to the excesses of unlimited warfare.

This background must be kept in mind when dealing with the desperate endeavours of the classical authors of international law to achieve a legal limitation of belligerent practice. The famous work of Hugo Grotius, *De Jure Belli ac Pacis Libri Tres*, was primarily a treatise on laws of war founded on natural law theory. '*Necessaria ad finem belli*' for Grotius was the ultimate limit of admissible use of force in war.[5] The rise of disciplined professional armies, the monopolization of the means of force in the hands of the developing state bureaucracy, and the 'nationalization of war' by the absolutist regimes of

---

[1] Concerning Japanese and Islamic traditions cf. S. Adachi, 'La conception asiatique', UNESCO/Institut Henri Dunant (eds), *Les dimensions internationales du droit humanitaire* (Pedone, 1986), 31–6, and H. Sultan, 'La conception islamique', ibid. 47–60.

[2] See Hans-Ulrich Scupin, 'History of International Law, 1815 to World War I' *MPEPIL*, paras. 7–19; Hans-Peter Gasser and Daniel Thürer, 'Humanitarian Law, International' *MPEPIL*, paras. 7–29.

[3] See J. H. W. Verzijl, *International Law in Historical Perspective*, Vol. IX-A: *The Laws of War* (Sijthoff, 1978), 131–5.

[4] See W. G. Grewe, *Epochen der Völkerrechtsgeschichte* (Nomos, 1984), 141–3.

[5] Cf. Kunz, *loc. cit.*, 354; G. I. A. D. Draper, 'Le développement du droit international humanitaire' in UNESCO/Institut Henri Dunant (eds), *Les dimensions internationales du droit humanitaire* (Pedone, 1986), 89–114, at 90.

STEFAN OETER

Europe were the basic conditions of the ongoing process of 'delimitation' of permissible means of use of force, as well as of the connected concept that war constitutes a struggle between states but does not create a relation of enmity between its citizens.[6]

The fundamental idea underlying all humanitarian rules on methods and means of warfare has, since that time, always been the concept of military necessity. According to the traditional approach, only the use of those weapons and means of combat which is necessary to attain the military purposes of war, purposes based on the ultimate goal of overpowering the enemy armed forces,[7] are permitted. Accordingly, the civilian population and civilian objects do not constitute legitimate military targets, as was recognized by the Lieber Code of 1863;[8] equally prohibited is the deliberately cruel killing of enemy combatants by weapons which uselessly aggravate suffering, a principle codified at around the same time in the St Petersburg Declaration of 1868.[9] Because these principles of 'limited warfare' which were formed during the nineteenth century became the nucleus of the (originally customary) laws of war, *opinio juris* and the practice of the nineteenth century have had a decisive impact on the shaping of modern humanitarian law.[10]

Nevertheless, the attempt at codification of these humanitarian rules by the two Hague Peace Conferences of 1899 and 1907,[11] proved unsuccessful. The Hague Regulations were scarcely ever applicable as treaty law, due to the extreme form of the general participation clause.[12] Moreover, the substantive provisions of the Hague Regulations proved to be too cautious, and in a sense also fragmentary, since to a large degree they were oriented towards the problems of the past. Article 22 HagueReg had, of course, explicitly settled the basic principle that: 'The right of belligerents to adopt means of injuring the enemy is not unlimited', and Article 23 HagueReg had prohibited the use of poison and poisoned weapons as a means of warfare, as well as the employment of 'arms, projectiles, or material calculated to cause unnecessary suffering'. The same article also stated that it was prohibited 'to destroy or seize the enemy's property, unless such destruction or seizure be imperatively demanded by the necessities of war'. The proper prohibition of indiscriminate warfare, however, had only found a rather imperfect echo in the treaty provisions on the laws of war; Article 25 HagueReg merely prohibited the 'attack or bombardment, by whatever means, of towns, villages, dwellings, or buildings which are undefended'. The most important achievement of the Hague Conferences was probably the so-called 'Martens clause' which was included in the Preamble of the Fourth Hague Convention, a dynamic reference to customary law not affected by the Conventions and

---

[6] Cf. Grewe, *op, cit*, (n. 4), 247–54, 428–9, and Geoffrey Best, *Humanity in Warfare: The Modern History of the International Law of Armed Conflicts* (London: Methuen, 1983), 53–9.

[7] See above, n. 2.

[8] See above, Section 117; W. Hays Parks, 'Air War and the Law of War' (1990) 32 *Air Force Law Review* 1–225, at 7–8.

[9] See Yves Sandoz, *Des armes interdites en droit de la guerre* (Geneva: Grounauer, 1975), 16–22; Dietrich Schindler, 'L'évolution du droit de la guerre des Conventions de la Haye aux Protocoles Additionnels aux Conventions de Genève' (1982) XXI *RDMilG* 23–33, at 24, and in particular detail Frits Kalshoven, 'Arms, Armaments and International Law' (1985 II) 191 *RdC* 183–341, at 205–13.

[10] See, in particular, Best, above (n. 6) 128–215.

[11] Draper, above (n. 5) 92–3; Parks, above (n. 8) 8–20, esp. 19; Marco Sassòli, *Bedeutung einer Kodifikation für das allgemeine Völkerrecht mit besonderer Betrachtung der Regeln zum Schutze der Zivilbevölkerung vor den Auswirkungen von Feindseligkeiten* (Basel/Frankfurt: Helbing & Lichtenhahn, 1990), 247–50; David D. Caron, 'War and International Adjudication: Reflections on the 1899 Peace Conference' (2000) 94 *AJIL* 4–30.

[12] See Kalshoven, above (n. 9) 292–3.

STEFAN OETER

to the 'principles of the law of nations, as they result from the usages established among civilized peoples, from the laws of humanity, and the dictates of public conscience'.[13]

The most serious problem of rapidly developing modern warfare soon proved to be the use of the air force. In less than three decades the air weapon became an important military instrument. An early attempt to regulate the ensuing problems of air warfare were the HRAW 1923.[14] They failed, however, because the consent of the states concerned was lacking; this abortive attempt never found a successor, and the (draft) Hague Air Rules unfortunately remained without a parallel. In addition to the frustration of attempts to codify the rules of air warfare, technical developments in warfare on land (the emergence of gas warfare is an example) brought increased risks for the civilian population in its wake.

World War II finally demonstrated the immense discrepancy between the noble but lofty principles of customary law and a practice which had been barbarized by technological changes and ideological polarization.[15] The killing of civilians and widespread destruction of civilian objects (in particular at the Eastern, Russian, front and in the territories occupied by Nazi Germany) took place on a massive scale, while air warfare was taken to horrifying excesses, consigning almost to oblivion the basic principle that the civilian population should be protected as far as possible.[16] In World War I civilian casualties amounted to some 5 per cent of those killed, whereas in World War II they rose to nearly 50 per cent.[17]

The indiscriminate use of the air force, which made terrorizing the civilian population the dominant purpose of air warfare, threatened to bury all restrictions on the use of force which were derived from the guiding principle of military necessity.[18] Unleashed by the German side, the practice of total disdain for all the traditional customary principles quickly became a widespread practice of all parties.[19] At the instigation of the Allied Powers, the violation of the principle of discrimination was excluded from the charges brought at the Nuremberg trials.[20]

The main question concerning the regulation of weapons and means of warfare, an adjustment of warfare to the principles of military necessity and humanity, was subsequently also excluded from the work of the Red Cross meetings which preceded the Geneva Conventions, although the Geneva Red Cross Conventions of 1949 made an effort to regulate most of the problems that had arisen in the wake of World War II (and to fill the gaps which had become obvious in earlier treaties).[21] The Fourth Geneva Convention developed a

---

[13] Theodor Meron, 'The Humanization of Humanitarian Law' (2000) 94 *AJIL* 78–89; on the Martens clause, see above, Section 131.

[14] Concerning the HAWR 1923, cf. Eberhard Spetzler, *Luftkrieg und Menschlichkeit* (Göttingen: Musterschmidt, 1956), 156–7; Verzijl, above (n. 3) 328–31; Parks, above (n. 8) 25–36.

[15] Concerning this problem see in detail Parks, above (n. 8) 50–4.

[16] See esp. Sassòli, above (n. 11) 257–66.

[17] Schindler, above (n. 9) 28.

[18] Best, above (n. 6) 262–85.

[19] See esp. Henri Meyrowitz, 'Le bombardement stratégique d'après le Protocole additionnel I aux Conventions de Genève' (1981) 41 *ZaöRV* 1–68, at 12–18.

[20] *ICRC Commentary*, 587 (para. 1828); cf. also Louise Doswald-Beck, *The Value of the Geneva Protocols for the Protection of Civilians*, in Michael Meyer (ed.), *Armed Conflict and the New Law: Aspects of the 1977 Geneva Protocols and the 1981 Weapons Convention* (British Institute of International and Comparative Law, 1989), 137–72, at 145–6.

[21] For the reasons underlying that approach cf. J. L. Kunz, 'The Chaotic Status of the Laws of War and the Urgent Necessity for their Revision' (1951) 45 *AJIL* 37–61, at 58–61; Georg Schwarzenberger, 'The Law of Armed Conflict: A Civilized Interlude?' (1974) 28 *Yearbook of World Affairs* 293–309, at 302; Parks, *supra* (n. 8) 55–9.

STEFAN OETER

rather detailed legal regime for the problems of military occupation, but the questions of possible limits on air warfare and on arms that cause unnecessary suffering (which were at least as delicate as the problem of occupied territories) were left to customary law with all its inherent lacunae and vagueness.

Eventually, during the decades after 1945 there appeared on the scene the third (and most recent) complex of problems of humanitarian law, namely the question of weapons and means of warfare affecting the environment. Not only did lawyers pay attention to the (rather dated) problem of collateral effects of warfare damaging the environment, but also to the possibility of deliberate destruction of the environment as a means of weakening the enemy. The large-scale deforestation carried out by the US Army in the course of the war in Vietnam[22] and then by the Soviet campaign in Afghanistan which, at least in part, deliberately destroyed the environment of peasant regions which resisted,[23] demonstrated that the question of environmental modification is not merely a question of pure theory, but now constitutes a part of military reality. The deliberate employment of burning oil-wells as an environmental weapon in the Kuwait War in 1991 thus represents only a sad climax of a practice which has developed over many decades.[24]

The concern that these hitherto neglected problems needed to be addressed on a solid basis in treaty law dominated the Diplomatic Conference on the Reaffirmation and Development of International Humanitarian Law Applicable in Armed Conflicts, held in Geneva from 1974 until 1977.[25] At the conference it soon became clear how difficult a practicable codification of the traditional principles of customary law would be, if one wanted to give the principles some concrete contours. With the provisions of Article 51 AP I on the protection of the civilian population and of Articles 52–56 AP I on the protection of civilian objects, an attempt was nevertheless made to achieve such a concretization and specification of customary rules, although it remains open to debate to what extent these provisions constitute a pure codification of (pre-) existing customary law and to what extent they constitute further development or even creation of new rules. The provisions accordingly were heavily attacked by some military experts, and—in connection with the absolute prohibition against reprisals against the civilian population contained in AP I—they are probably the main reason why important military powers still refuse to ratify the First Additional Protocol. In particular, on the hotly disputed question of the legal status of nuclear weapons, which has repeatedly provoked doubts about the compatibility of the traditional doctrines of nuclear deterrence with the new regime of AP I,

[22] Frits Kalshoven/Lisbeth Zegveld, *Constraints on the Waging of War: An Introduction to International Humanitarian Law*, 3rd edn (ICRC, 2001), 93.

[23] See the report of the special rapporteur appointed by the UN Human Rights Commission in order to investigate human rights violations in Afghanistan, Felix Ermacora, UN Doc. E/CN.4/1985/21 of 19 February 1985, 33 (paras. 122–3).

[24] Concerning the use of environmental damage as a means of war in the Kuwait War 1991, see C. York, 'International Law and the Collateral Effects of War on the Environment: The Persian Gulf' (1991) 7 *South African Journal on Human Rights* 269–90; Djamchid Momtaz, 'Les règles relatives à la protection de l'environnement au cours des conflits armés à l'épreuve du conflit entre l'Iraq et le Koweit' (1991) 37 *Annuaire Français de Droit International* (1991), 203–19, at 203–19; Adam Roberts, 'La destruction de l'environnement pendant la guerre du Golfe de 1991' (1990) 72 *RIC* 559–77; L. Lijnzaad/G. J. Tanja, 'Protection of the Environment in Times of Armed Conflict: The Iraq–Kuwait War' (1993) 40 *Netherlands International Law Review* 169–99, at 169–71.

[25] For the course of the Conference, cf. M. Bothe/K. Ipsen/K. J. Partsch, 'Die Konferenz über humanitäres Völkerrecht—Verlauf und Ergebnisse' (1978) 38 *ZaöRV* 1–85; Parks, above (n. 8) 76–94.

STEFAN OETER

the treaty's provisions have often been perceived as constituting too radical a shift, to the detriment of the requirement of military necessity (see Section 433).

With regard to the prohibition against excessive damage to the environment, however, Additional Protocol I regulates only a part of the question, namely the issue of collateral damage. The international community (at the same time as the Geneva Diplomatic Conference) concluded a special treaty, the 1977 Convention on the Prohibition of Military or Any Other Hostile Use of Environmental Modification Techniques (ENMOD) to deal with the problem of environmental damage as a deliberate means of warfare. The prohibition against arms calculated to cause excessive suffering also received only marginal attention in the course of the negotiations on the Additional Protocols and has been touched on only in a minor provision. In its Article 35, para. 2, AP I reaffirmed the old (and imprecise) prohibition against excessive sufferings by a formula nearly identical to Article 23, lit. e, HagueReg. Concrete shape was given to this prohibition by the UN Weapons Convention negotiated in the wake of the Geneva Diplomatic Conference, a treaty supplemented by specific protocols on non-detectable fragments, mines and booby traps, incendiary and blinding laser weapons.[26]

2. *The relationship between treaty law and customary law.* Customary law might still be said to have a decisive role in the international regulation of warfare, bearing in mind that until recently the treaty provisions on weapons and means of warfare were somewhat rudimentary, and also due to the fact that the new provisions of the Additional Protocols, the ENMOD Convention, and the UN Weapons Convention are not of universal application.[27] A majority of Third World states, some of the NATO states, and the overwhelming majority of former Warsaw Pact members (including the Soviet Union/Russia) have ratified the Additional Protocols; not bound by the Protocols are, however, the US as well as many Third World states actually involved in armed conflicts. The UK ratified both AP I and AP II only in 1998, whereas France ratified AP I not earlier than in 2001. Accordingly, the most severe international armed conflicts of the last decades, namely the First and the Second Gulf Wars as well as the ongoing conflicts in Afghanistan and Iraq, were mainly fought by armed forces of states not subject to the rules of the First Additional Protocol,[28] which renders serious comment on the practical effects of the provisions of AP I almost impossible.

To a large degree, however, the combat operations of the armed forces involved were adjusted to comply with the legal guidelines of AP I, which is probably due to the fact that the provisions of Articles 51–60 AP I are mostly considered to represent established rules of traditional customary law. Also, it may be that there is a certain effect of 'radiation' of the provisions of AP I concerning the protection of the civilian population, because

---

[26] Nicholas Sitaropoulos, 'Weapons and Superfluous Injury or Unnecessary Suffering in International Humanitarian Law' (2001) 54 *Revue hellénique de droit international* 71–108, at 92; concerning the UN Weapons Conference and its results, see William Fenrick, 'New Development in the Law Concerning the Use of Conventional Weapons in Armed Conflict' (1981) XIX *CYIL* 229–56, at 239–40; Kalshoven, above (9) 251–65.

[27] Cf. the general studies of L. R. Penna, 'Customary International Law and Protocol I: An Analysis of Some Provisions' in C. Swinarski (ed.), *Essays in honour of Jean Pictet* (Nijhoff, 1984), 201–25; Antonio Cassese, 'The Geneva Protocols of 1977 on the Humanitarian Law of Armed Conflict and Customary International Law' (1984) 3 *UCLA Pacific Basin Law Journal,* 55–118; Meron, 'The Continuing Role of Custom in the Formation of International Humanitarian Law' (1996) 90 *AJIL* 238–49.

[28] See Gasser, 'Humanitäres Völkerrecht in Aktion: Einige erste Folgerungen aus der Operation "Desert Storm" ' (1991/4) *HuV-I* 30–3, at 30–1.

STEFAN OETER

these relatively specific rules are much easier to apply than the vaguer principles of customary law.[29] Even more, recent conflicts such as 'Operation Desert Storm', the NATO Kosovo Air Campaign and the US Air Campaign in Afghanistan demonstrated that the advance of modern weapons technology[30] facilitates respect for the guarantees of AP I, so far as the protection of the civilian population is concerned, since discrimination between military and civilian objectives can be implemented much more easily with the new generations of 'precision-guided munitions'[31] than was possible with traditional weapons.

So far as conventional warfare is concerned, therefore, there is every reason to believe that customary law standards will come into line with the provisions of Articles 51–56 AP I (even if only *de lege ferenda*), with a resulting merger of relevant conventional and customary norms. With regard to nuclear operational planning (as well as the use of chemical weapons for reprisals), however, the question of what actually constitutes the customary standard of feasible protection for the civilian population remains a matter of contention. Even if the provisions of Articles 51–56 AP I, which are intended to specify and develop customary law, have any effect upon these problems, (cf. Sections 431–434), the US nuclear power still remains subject to the traditional regime of discriminate warfare, which imposes in principle an obligation to distinguish between military and civilian objectives, but not to all the other specific provisions of Part III of Additional Protocol I.

Comparable questions arise as to the regulation of non-international armed conflicts, a problem which is of enormous importance in practice. It is generally recognized now that common Article 3 of the four Geneva Conventions, which requires that the utmost care should be taken of the civilian population even in internal armed conflicts, constitutes a reflection of fundamental principles of customary law, if not an expression of the 'elementary considerations of humanity' referred to in the Martens Clause.[32] Since these principles have been expressed in a formula of considerable vagueness—even in its reflection in common Article 3—whereas the more specific provisions of Additional Protocol II are subject to certain conditions which must be fulfilled before Protocol II becomes applicable (not to mention the absence of ratifications by the states most concerned) the question arises: to what degree does a parallel customary law exist which could fill the gaps left by treaty law?[33]

[29] Ibid.

[30] Cf. the observations by Parks, above (n. 8) 113, n. 353; Matthew Lippmann, 'Aerial Attacks on Civilians and the Humanitarian Law of War: Technology and Terror from World War I to Afghanistan' (2002) 33 *California Western International Law Journal* 1–67, at 55–7.

[31] Gasser, above (n. 28) 31; regarding this advantage as well as contrary effects, see Michael N. Schmitt, 'The Impact of High and Low-Tech Warfare on the Principle of Distinction' in Roberta Arnold and Pierre-Antoine Hildbrand (eds), *International Humanitarian Law and the 21st Century's Conflicts: Changes and Challenges* (Geneva: Editions interuniversitaires Suisse, 2005), 169–89, 6–7.

[32] See the Judgment of the ICJ in the *Nicaragua* case, *Case Concerning Military and Paramilitary Activities in and against Nicaragua (Nicaragua v US)*, Judgment of 27 June 1986, *ICJ Reports 1986*, 114 (para. 218); cf. also the report of the special rapporteur W. Kälin to the UN Human Rights Commission concerning human rights violations of Iraq in occupied Kuwait, UN Doc. E/CN.4/1992/26 of 16 January 1992, 10–11 (paras. 35–8).

[33] See Kalshoven, 'Applicability of Customary International Law in Non-International Armed Conflicts' in Cassese (ed.), *Current Problems of International Law* (Milan: Giuffrè, 1975), 267–85; Kalshoven, above (n. 9) 295–6; Judith G. Gardam, 'Women and Armed Conflict: The Response of International Humanitarian Law' in *Listening to the Silences: Women and War* (Nijhoff, International Humanitarian Law Series, 2005), 164–80.

STEFAN OETER

Even with respect to the provisions of the UN Weapons Convention it would be interesting to clarify how far the treaty provisions are paralleled by any analogous customary law. One could argue in that direction, since (at least in theory) the provisions of the Convention constitute only a specification and development of the general prohibition against unnecessary suffering which dates back to the St Petersburg Declaration of 1868, later codified in Article 23, lit. e, HagueReg. It is, however, to say the least, open to doubt how far it is really possible to deduce from the general customary prohibition of *maux superflus* the concrete prohibitions of specific weapons stated by the five Weapons Protocols to the 1980 Convention;[34] comparable problems are raised by the question of whether there exist further prohibitions of weapons besides the specific prohibitions of the UN Weapons Convention, that is additional prohibitions deduced directly from the general principle of prohibition of unnecessary suffering codified in Article 23, lit. e, HagueReg.[35]

Concerning the prohibition of methods of warfare that cause widespread, long-term, and severe damage to the natural environment,[36] the question remains seriously in dispute whether there exists any possibility at all of a parallel customary law. The entire problem has only recently arisen in military practice so that it is still difficult to find substantial state practice in that respect. Thus, it remains challenging to prove the formation of a specific rule of customary international law from state practice (see Section 403). One could point to the fact, however, that even this complex of rather novel provisions constitutes only an implementation and materialization of the old maxim of customary law that the ultimate barrier of any legally permitted warfare is to be found in the principle of military necessity (understood in the sense that the damaging action must be imperatively required by operational necessities).[37] The traditional formula, which has found expression in Article 22 HagueReg and in Article 35, para. 1, AP I, provides that: 'the right of belligerents to choose methods or means of warfare is not unlimited' ('to adopt means of injuring the enemy' in the language of the Hague Regulations). One might deduce from this principle a requirement that the weapons or means employed to achieve a military goal should be in an adequate proportion to the destruction and suffering inflicted by the operation, which accordingly would mean that one could construct under existing traditional customary law a far-reaching prohibition against excessive damage applicable also to environmental warfare.[38]

I. General Rules

The right of the parties to an armed conflict to choose means (Article 22   **401**
HagueReg) and methods (Article 35, para. 1, AP I) of warfare is not unlimited. It

---

[34] The problem is raised by Kalshoven, 'Les principes juridiques qui sous-tendent la Convention sur les armes classiques' (1990) 72 *RIC* 556–67, at 563–6.

[35] See Kalshoven, above (n. 9) 295–6; cf. Rules 70–86 *CIHL*.

[36] As to the established principles concerning environmental warfare, see Alexandre Kiss, 'Les Protocoles additionels aux Conventions de Genève de 1977 et la protection de biens de l'environnement' in C. Swinarski (ed.), *Essays in honour of Jean Pictet* (Nijhoff, 1984), 181–92; Jozef Goldblat, 'Legal Protection of the Environment Against the Effects of Military Activities' (1991) 22 *Bulletin of Peace Proposals* 399–406; Kalshoven/Zegveld, above (n. 22) 92–3; Bothe, 'The Protection of the Environment in Times of Armed Conflict' (1991) 34 *GYIL* 54–62, at 55–8; Lijnzaad/Tanja, above (n. 24) 178–89.

[37] See Lijnzaad/Tanja, above (n. 24) 183–4.

[38] Bothe, above (n. 36) 55–6; Lijnzaad/Tanja, *loc. cit.*,; cf. Rules 43–45 *CIHL*.

STEFAN OETER

is particularly prohibited to employ means or methods which are intended or of a nature:

— to cause superfluous injury or unnecessary suffering (Article 23, lit. e, HagueReg; Article 35, para. 2, AP I);

— to injure military objectives, civilians, or civilian objects without distinction (Article 51, paras. 4 and 5, AP I; see below, sub-Chapter III 2); or

— to cause widespread, long-term, and/or severe damage to the natural environment (Articles 35, para. 3, and 55, para. 1, AP I; ENMOD; see below, sub-Chapter III 3).

1. The fundamental maxim of humanitarian rules on warfare which is reproduced in the first sentence constitutes the basis of any regulation of the methods and means of warfare employed.[39] The formula puts in a nutshell the customary principle that any act of warfare should be guided by the requirements of military necessity. The formula expressed in the version cited had already been adopted in Article 22 of the Hague Regulations; now it is repeated almost verbatim in Article 35, para. 1, AP I and in the Preamble of the UN Weapons Convention. The principle forms one of the core 'principles of international law derived from established custom, from the principles of humanity, and from the dictates of public conscience' in the sense of the Martens Clause. As Jean de Preux has written in the *ICRC Commentary* on the Additional Protocols,[40] all of Part III of AP I is implicitly (but clearly) based on the assumption of a final rejection of the idea of 'total war'. The opposing principle, the principle of 'limited warfare', which is intimately connected to the condition of 'military necessity', thus has a key function in relation to the other provisions of Part III (and implicitly probably also Part IV) of Additional Protocol I.[41] The basic approach of 'limited warfare', which dominates the modern laws of war, requires every belligerent to strike a balance between the conflicting concerns of humanity and military necessity.[42] To curtail the objective of humanization of warfare is justified only in so far as military necessity inevitably requires a certain military operation, not to mention the further condition that the damage inflicted must be proportionate to the military advantage sought.[43] What should be perceived as an adequate equilibrium between the damage likely to result from the operation and the military advantage aspired to is a question further elaborated, and regulated in detail, by the specific provisions of humanitarian law which will be explained in the following sections. All customary as well as conventional regulation of means and methods of warfare could be understood in one sense as a comprehensive attempt to give the principle of 'limited warfare', that is the limitation of belligerent use of force by the condition of military necessity, some specific and practical shape.

---

[39] See Kalshoven, above (n. 34) 556–63; Kalshoven/Zegveld, above (n. 22) 35; *UK Manual* (2004), Section 2.1.

[40] de Preux, *ICRC Commentary*, para. 1367.

[41] Cf. in the same sense Waldemar Solf, in Bothe/Partsch/Solf, *New Rules for Victims of Armed Conflicts* (Nijhoff, 1982), 193–8; Sassòli, *op. cit.*, (n. 11), 344–7.

[42] Cf. Sassòli, *op. cit.*, 344.

[43] Cf. Yoram Dinstein, *The Conduct of Hostilities under the Law of International Armed Conflict*, 2nd edn (CUP, 2010), 4–8; Gabriella Venturini, *Necessità e proporzionalità nell'uso della forza militare in diritto internazionale* (Milan: Giuffrè, 1988), 145–50; regarding the role of the two principles 'necessity' and 'proportionality' in contemporary international humanitarian law, see also Judith G. Gardam, *Necessity, Proportionality and the Use of Force by States* (CUP, 2004).

STEFAN OETER

2. Flowing from the general principle of 'limited warfare' (limited to what is militarily absolutely necessary in order to achieve the military objectives[44]) several sub-principles have developed historically, giving the rule of military necessity its specific contours. These specific expressions of the principle of military necessity have different purposes and reflect very different historical stages of the evolution of humanitarian law.

3. The concept of the utmost protection of the civilian population constitutes the oldest stage, or layer of that evolution, a layer now reflected in the binding rules of Article 48 AP I (basic rule) and Article 51 AP I (specific provisions on the protection of the civilian population). The humanitarian principles of Islamic legal culture and the moral theological postulates of medieval scholars already contemplated a principle of distinction between combatants and civilians and called for extensive protection of the civilian population.[45] More recently, the legal practice of the nineteenth century established the prohibition against indiscriminate warfare as a customary rule.[46] In the Hague Regulations, however, this customary rule was only incompletely reflected (see Articles 23, para. 1, lit. g, and 25 HagueReg). The requirement of discrimination did not find expression in a general formula nor was the question of collateral damages in the course of attacks on military objectives regulated by any of the provisions. The Hague Rules on Air Warfare, which some decades later attempted to codify the prohibition of indiscriminate attacks by air, did not find acceptance. Nevertheless, the customary validity of the prohibition of indiscriminate warfare was never seriously disputed.[47] Even the excesses of World War II did not change the basic validity of the customary protection of the civilian population.[48] In Part IV of Additional Protocol I these firmly established principles of customary law were explicitly laid down in a treaty for the first time. Article 48 AP I formulates the basic principle of discrimination: 'In order to ensure respect for and protection of the civilian population and civilian objects, the Parties to the conflict shall at all times distinguish between the civilian population and combatants and between civilian objects and military objectives and accordingly shall direct their operations only against military objectives.' The overall validity of this principle today is beyond any doubt. However, even bearing in mind that the principle of distinction, as enshrined in Article 48 AP I, constitutes an ancient and established rule of customary law, and not a new principle created recently by conventional law,[49] one must admit that concrete shape is given to the fundamental maxim mainly by the detailed treaty provisions of Articles 50–56 AP I (cf. Sections 442–466).

---

[44] For the dazzling relationship between the political objective pursued by war and the 'military objective' in the sense of AP I, cf. Henri Meyrowitz, 'Buts de guerre et objectifs militaires' (1983) XXII *RDMilG* 93–115, at 95 *et seq.*

[45] Cf. Pictet, *Development and Principles of International Humanitarian Law* (Institut Henry-Dunant, 1985), 5–25; esp. concerning the Islamic concepts cf. Sultan, above (n. 1) 56–9.

[46] Cf. Pilloud/Pictet, *ICRC Commentary*, paras. 1823–7; Rules 1, 11 *CIHL*.

[47] See J. Kunz, *Kriegsrecht und Neutralitätsrecht* (Springer, 1935), 75–6 with extensive references to the literature of that time; but cf. also Erik Castrén, *The Present Law of War and Neutrality* (Suomalaisen Kirjallisuuden Seuran Kirjapainon Oy, 1954), 174–8; Schwarzenberger, above (n. 21) 109–17, 293–309; Charles Rousseau, *Le droit des Conflits Armés* (Pedone, 1983), 67–9.

[48] Bothe, 'Moderner Luftkrieg und Schutz der Zivilbevölkerung' (2002/1) 15 *HuV-I* 31; the intense discussion about this question is reflected in detail in the article by Meyrowitz, above (n. 19) 24–5.

[49] See in extensive detail Sassòli, *op. cit.*, (n. 11), 342–59. Cf. also Venturini, *op. cit.*, (n. 43), 149; Michael N. Schmitt, 'Fault Lines in the Law of Attack' in Susan Breau/Agnieszka Jachec-Neale (eds), *Testing the Boundaries of International Humanitarian Law* (British Institute of International and Comparative Law, 2006), 277–307 at 278–9.

STEFAN OETER

4. The prohibition against *maux superflus*, that is against weapons and materials causing excessive suffering, is also an old normative principle.[50] The prohibition of poisoned weapons and of the use of poison as a means of warfare, which had been so deeply rooted in medieval custom, could be seen as a precursor. The objective of banning super-fluous injury/unnecessary suffering was formulated for the first time *expressis verbis* in the St Petersburg Declaration of 1868 which outlawed explosive projectiles under 400 g weight.[51] This regulatory approach was continued in the Hague Declaration of 1899 concerning dum-dum bullets.[52] As a general prohibition of arms or material 'of a nature to cause superfluous injury' (HagueReg 1899) or 'calculated to cause unnecessary suffer-ing' (HagueReg 1907) it was included in Article 23, lit. e, HagueReg. The bans on the use of poisonous gases as a means of warfare provided for by the Geneva Gas Protocol of 1925[53] and the Biological Weapons Convention of 1972 were further steps on the way to a total ban on the use of certain particularly barbaric weapons. Additional Protocol I now contents itself with repeating the abstract prohibition of weapons causing unnecessary suffering, in Article 35, para. 2. The UN Weapons Convention of 1980 and its Protocols gave a much more precise content to the prohibition of specific weapons, origi-nally intended for inclusion in Additional Protocol I.[54] This body of rules was enlarged by Protocols IV (1995) and V (2003) on Blinding Laser Weapons and on Explosive Remnants of War (see Sections 419–421, 428) as well as by the 1997 LandMinesConv introducing a complete ban of anti-personnel mines[55] (see Section 409). An attempt to weaken the comprehensive ban of cluster bombs in the UN Weapons Convention failed in 2011 when the adoption of Protocol VI, which intended to ban all cluster munition produced before 1980 but authorizing in particular circumstances others, was rejected by a majority of the contracting states. Thus, the prohibition of *maux superflus* is charac-terized by a particularly complex mixture of very definite prohibitions of certain specific categories of arms on one hand, and a rather abstract prohibition of means of warfare which cause unnecessary sufferings on the other; the relationship between these two sets of rules is far from clear. How far the definite prohibitions are only specific expressions or materializations of the general prohibitory provision, and to what extent they are, to the contrary, constitutive developments of a merely political programme envisaged in Article 23(e) Hague Regulations, is a question which still needs careful consideration.[56]

5. Similar questions can be asked about the most recent exposition of the principle of 'limited warfare', namely the prohibition against methods of warfare which cause widespread, long-term, and severe damage to the natural environment (cf. Section 403). This sub-principle might also be deduced logically from the requirements of military necessity, and from its supplement, the principle of proportionality of the damages inflicted in relation to the

---

[50] Rule 70 *CIHL*.

[51] See esp. Kalshoven, above (n. 9) 205–13; Sandoz, above (n. 9) 16–22; Dinstein, above (n. 43) 63–7; William H. Boothby, *Weapons and the Law of Armed Conflict* (OUP, 2009), 10–1, 73.

[52] Boothby, *op. cit.*, 12–13.

[53] Boothby, *op. cit.*, 16–17.

[54] For the attempts to include prohibitions of specific categories of arms in Additional Protocol I see Solf, in Bothe/Partsch/Solf, above (n. 41) 197–8; Boothby, *op. cit.*, 18–20.

[55] For the LandMinesConv, see ICRC, *Banning Anti-Personnel Mines: The Ottawa Treaty Explained* (ICRC, 1998).

[56] The question is elaborated by Kalshoven, above (n. 34) 556–67, at 563–6; Eric David, *Principes de droit des conflits armés*, 3rd edn (Bruyland, 2002), 316–25.

STEFAN OETER

military objective.[57] However, the military practice of the last decades demonstrates considerable carelessness on the part of belligerent forces as to the preservation of the natural environment. Thus, it seemed sensible to embody provisions which explicitly include the environment as an object entitled to the protection granted by the rules of humanitarian law.[58] The Convention on the Prohibition of Military or Any Other Hostile Use of Environmental Modification Techniques (ENMOD Convention) of 1977 and Articles 35, para. 3, and 55, para. 1, AP I accordingly addressed that problem. The relationship between these treaties, however, as well as their relationship to the rules of customary law is problematic and needs further analysis (cf. Section 403).[59]

> **'Superfluous injury' and 'unnecessary suffering' are caused by the use of weapons and methods of combat whose foreseeable harm would be clearly excessive in relation to the lawful military advantage intended.**   402

1. The provision of Article 35, para. 2, AP I, which was taken as a precedent when formulating the rule above, clarifies the principle of 'limited warfare'. It is a reaffirmation of the prohibition of *maux superflus* laid down in the St Petersburg Declaration of 1868 and later codified in the Hague Regulations.[60] The attempt to link the use of force to the requirement of 'military necessity' is thus given a much more precise shape: to inflict physical or psychological harm is justified only in so far as it is really necessary to attain the military advantage intended.[61] Necessity and proportionality of the means employed thus become conditions of the lawfulness of the use of specific weapons.[62]

2. Article 23, lit. e, HagueReg and Article 35, para. 2, AP I prohibit in a nearly identical formula the use of weapons, projectiles, and materials of war calculated to cause superfluous injury or unnecessary sufferings.[63] The category of 'superfluous injury', which was newly integrated in the provision of Article 35, para. 2, AP I, implicitly clarifies what should properly constitute the decisive criterion of proportionality. Injuries can only be 'superfluous' either if they are not justified by any requirement of military necessity or if the injuries normally caused by the weapon or projectile are manifestly disproportionate to the military advantage reasonably expected from the use of the weapon. The first will only rarely be the case, since the intended injuring effect generally serves a military goal,

---

[57] In its *Advisory Opinion on Nuclear Weapons*, the ICJ underlined the impact of the environment when assessing whether an action is in conformity with the principles of necessity and proportionality, cf. *ICJ Reports 1996*, 241–3 (paras. 27–33).

[58] Kalshoven/Zegveld, above (n. 22) 92–3; concerning more recent efforts to ameliorate the protection of the environment in times of armed conflict, see Dinstein, 'Protection of the Environment in International Armed Conflict' (2001) 5 *Max Planck Yearbook of United Nations Law* 523–49; regarding the applicability of peacetime environmental law in armed conflict, see Boothby, above (n. 51) 104–5.

[59] See, e.g., Boothby, *op. cit.*, 94–6 and 100–3.

[60] For the historical development of the prohibition of *maux superflus* see Roger S. Clark, 'Methods of Warfare that Cause Unnecessary Suffering or are Inherently Indiscriminate: A Memorial Tribute to Howard Berman' (1998) 28 *California Western International Law Journal* 379–89, at 384; Kalshoven, above (n. 9) 205–24; Kalshoven, above (n. 34) 557–63; Boothby, *op. cit.*, 55–68.

[61] In that sense already provided in the Preamble to the St Petersburg Declaration of 1868—see Kalshoven, above (n. 9) 206, 212.

[62] Sitaropoulos, above (n. 26) 81; concerning that problem see the comments on Article 35, para. 2, AP I by de Preux, in *ICRC Commentary*, 399–410 (paras. 1410–39) and by Solf, in Bothe/Partsch/Solf, above (n. 41) 195–8; see also Gardam, above (n. 43) 15–16.

[63] Concerning the textual differences between the two provisions see Solf, in Bothe/Partsch/Solf, *op. cit.*, 195.

STEFAN OETER

namely the neutralization of enemy combatants or military material. The second condition will only be fulfilled if the weapon is at least relatively superfluous—which requires a comparative judgment as to how much suffering various weapons cause and whether alternative military means could achieve the same results with less suffering.[64]

3. Concerning the classical formula of 'unnecessary suffering' (*maux superflus*) it is much more difficult to find an adequate description of the effects of weaponry which are intended to be outlawed by the choice of that wording. The notion of 'suffering' is not quantifiable under a medical perspective, for it is defined according to psychological criteria.[65] Accordingly, attempts have been made to find alternative formulae, which are more accessible to technical operationalization, and recent terminology favours the (more objective) term of 'injury'.[66] The traditional notion of 'unnecessary suffering' means essentially the same, namely a physical or emotional impairment which cannot be justified by military necessity.[67] To this extent it is a concept which enables the effects of various methods of warfare to be compared, and also opens to question the military usefulness of a weapon in relation to its adverse consequences on those affected by it.[68] In the words of the ICJ in its Advisory Opinion on Nuclear Weapons, 'unnecessary suffering' stands for 'a harm greater than that unavoidable to achieve legitimate military objectives'.[69]

4. 'Relevant military advantage' in this sense is judged only by reference to direct attacks upon military objectives, irrespective of the fear and terror caused among enemy personnel and the civilian population. The notion of 'lawful military advantage intended', which is used in Section 402, refers to this type of direct advantage. The precise definition of a military advantage justifying the use of arms is provided elsewhere in the law on methods and means of warfare (see Section 445).

403   **'Widespread', 'long-term', and/or 'severe' damage to the natural environment is a major interference with human life or natural resources which considerably exceeds the battlefield damage to be regularly expected in a war. Such damage to the natural environment by means of warfare (Articles 35, para. 3, and 55, para. 1, AP I) and severe manipulation of the environment as a weapon (ENMOD) are likewise prohibited (see below, Section 469).**

1. Against the background of US warfare in Vietnam[70] the UN Committee on Disarmament drew up a specific treaty concluded in 1977, the Convention on the Prohibition of Military or Any Other Hostile Use of Environmental Modification Techniques (the ENMOD Convention).[71] Article I of the Convention prohibits 'to

---

[64] Solf, in Bothe/Partsch/Solf, above (n. 41) 196.
[65] See P. Bretton, *Principes humanitaires et impératifs militaires* dans le domaine des armes classiques à travers le droit international actuel', in *Société Française pour le Droit International, Colloque de Montpellier—le droit international et les armes* (Pedone, 1983) 35–50, at 39.
[66] Ibid.
[67] Sitaropoulos, above (n. 26) 91.
[68] Solf, in Bothe/Partsch/Solf, above (n. 41) 196; see also Kalshoven, above (n. 9) 234–6.
[69] ICJ, *Nuclear Weapons, ICJ Reports 1996,* 257 (para. 78).
[70] See the contribution by Richard Falk in G. Plant (ed.), *Environmental Protection and the Law of War: A 'Fifth Geneva' Convention on the Protection of the Environment in Time of Armed Conflict* (Belhaven Press, 1992), 90.
[71] Concerning ENMOD see Goldblat, above (n. 36) 401; Falk, in Plant (ed.), *op. cit.,* 90; Lijnzaad/ Tanja, above (n. 24) 185–9; Adam Roberts, 'The law of war and environmental damage', in Jay E. Austin/ Carl E. Bruch (eds), *The Environmental Consequences of War: Legal, Economic, and Scientific Perspectives* (CUP, 2000), 47–86, at 57–9; for a critical assessment, see Rosario Domínguez-Matés, 'New Weaponry

engage in military or any other hostile use of environmental modification techniques having widespread, long-lasting, or severe effects' for the purpose of destroying, damaging, or injuring the enemy. The subject matter of the treaty is thus the use of so-called 'environmental modification techniques' as military instruments, that is the calculated abuse of the environmental damage for offensive purposes.[72]

2. Definitions of 'widespread', 'long-lasting', and 'severe' were provided by the UN Committee on Disarmament in a series of so-called 'Understandings'.[73] Damage is 'widespread' if it affects an area which encompasses several hundred square kilometres; 'long-lasting' (or 'long-term') means damage lasting for a period of several months, or approximately a season, while 'severe' was defined as involving serious or significant disruption or harm to human life, natural or economic resources, or other assets. If any one of these thresholds is passed then the ENMOD prohibition is breached. This link between the prohibition against environmental modification techniques and the crossing of a certain threshold of application was (and is) often heavily criticized.[74] It seems, however, that such a formula is sensible, because it pursues the objective of distinguishing warfare by environmental modification techniques, which is generally condemned, from the common practice of intervening in the environment on an operative level. ENMOD was not intended to affect the established practice of tactical intervention in the environment in the framework of specific combat operations, like the flooding of restricted sectors of ground or the burning of isolated woods.[75] The definition of both categories, nevertheless, remains a difficult undertaking, which is not altogether achieved in 'Understandings' annexed to the ENMOD Convention.

3. An even more delicate question is the delimitation of the various fields of application of the relevant provisions of the First Additional Protocol. By Article 35, para. 3, AP I and the complementary provision of Article 55 AP I, the Diplomatic Conference in Geneva has introduced—going beyond the traditional requirement of 'military necessity'—an absolute prohibition against severe environmental damage.[76] In the case of 'widespread, long-lasting or severe damages to the natural environment', even the referral to military necessity may not justify the use of weapons or means of warfare which are intended or may be expected to cause such damage; calculated imposition (and reckless disregard) of long-lasting and severe damage to the environment was accordingly banned absolutely.[77]

Technologies and International Humanitarian Law: Their Consequences on the Human Being and the Environment' in Pablo Antonio Fernández-Sánchez (ed.), *The New Challenges of Humanitarian Law in Armed Conflicts* (Nijhoff, 2005), 91–119, at 100–3; Boothby, above (n. 51) 92–4.

[72] See Goldblat, above (n. 36) 401; Domínguez-Matés, 'New Weaponry Technologies, Environment and Hostile Purposes: the Revival of the Convention on Environmental Modification Techniques of 1976 up to Day' (2006) 19 *HuV-I* 93–102, at 95.

[73] For the text of the 'Understandings' see UN Doc. CCD/520 of 1976 Sep. 3, Annex A.

[74] See, e.g., Goldblat, above (n. 36) 403; Domínguez-Matés, above (n. 72) 93–102, calling for a substantial amendment of the ENMOD in view of the use of geophysical environmental modification technology for warfare purposes in the near future.

[75] See York, above (n. 24) 287–8.

[76] For the history of Articles 35, para. 3, and 55 AP I see de Preux, in *ICRC Commentary*, 411–14 (paras. 1444–9); Solf, in Bothe/Partsch/Solf, above (n. 41) 344–5; Kiss, above (n. 36) 182–4; Lijnzaad/Tanja, above (n. 24) 178–81.

[77] See de Preux, in *ICRC Commentary*, paras. 1440–3; Kiss, *loc. cit.*, 184–6; A. P. V. Rogers, *Law on the Battlefield*, 3rd edn (Manchester University Press, 2012), 218.

STEFAN OETER

The provisions in AP I therefore go much further than the prohibition in ENMOD, covering not only the intentional infliction of damage to the environment in the course of warfare (as in the ENMOD Convention), but also purely unintentional and incidental damage.[78]

4. Since every method of warfare causes collateral damage to the environment, the question arises as to the exact thresholds of application of Articles 35, para. 3, and 55 AP I. The Diplomatic Conference made use of the threshold notions (analogous to the ENMOD Convention[79]) of 'widespread', 'long-lasting', and 'severe', although it used them not alternatively (as in ENMOD) but cumulatively.[80] Collateral damage is covered by the prohibitions of Articles 35, para. 3, and 55 AP I only if it affects large areas *and* lasts for a long period (and not only for a few months as in the ENMOD Convention) *and also* causes severe damage to the natural environment.[81] The usual collateral damage caused by large military operations in the course of conventional warfare (which can be quite considerable) are thus excluded from the scope of the prohibitions against environmental damage of AP I[82] and accordingly continue to fall under the basic requirement of military necessity.

5. The fundamental principle of military necessity also forms the basic long-stop provision of humanitarian law when the conventional provisions of AP I and ENMOD are not applicable, as for example in the Kuwait conflict ('Operation Desert Storm') of 1991.[83] For the time being, it remains hotly disputed whether the specific prohibitions against environmental warfare in ENMOD and the prohibitions against environmental damage in AP I have customary equivalents. While this is denied by many authors,[84] others hold that at least the provisions in this regard in AP I have been accepted as part of customary international law.[85] The ICJ in its Nuclear Weapons Advisory Opinion considered implicitly the provisions not to be customary.[86] However, the Committee Established to Review the NATO Bombing Campaign Against the Federal Republic of Yugoslavia stated in its Final Report that Article 55 AP I 'may . . . reflect current customary law'.[87] In addition, the military manuals of numerous states, even if not being party to AP I, include prohibitions equivalent to the ones of Articles 35, para. 3, and 55,

---

[78] Concerning the difficult relationship between Article 35, para. 3, AP I and the ENMOD Convention see de Preux, in *ICRC Commentary*, paras. 1450–6, and Solf, in Bothe/Partsch/Solf, above (n. 41) 347; see also Kiss, *loc. cit.*, 187; Lijnzaad/Tanja, *loc. cit.*, 197–8, and Dinstein, above (n. 43) 204–5; Schmitt, 'War and the Environment: Faultlines in the Prescriptive Landscape' in Austin/Bruch (eds), above (n. 71) 104–13; Boothby, above (n. 51) 94–6.

[79] For the parallels of wording in Articles 35, para. 3, and 55 AP I and the ENMOD Convention, negotiated simultaneously, see de Preux, in *ICRC Commentary*, paras. 1452–4; Rogers, above (n. 77) 212–20. The analogous wording does not automatically mean that the notions have to be interpreted identically in both Conventions, although textual logic seems to point in that direction.

[80] Solf, in Bothe/Partsch/Solf, above (n. 41) 347; Roberts, in Austin/Bruch (eds), above (n. 71) 59.

[81] Where the threshold of application of Articles 35, para. 3, and 55 AP I really lies, remains in dispute—see Solf, in Bothe/Partsch/Solf, above (n. 41) 347–8; de Preux, *ICRC Commentary*, 416–8 (paras. 1454–1456); Kiss, above (n. 71) 189–90.

[82] See de Preux, in *ICRC Commentary*, para. 1454; Lijnzaad/Tanja, above (n. 24) 180–5.

[83] Concerning the legal problems of environmental warfare in the Gulf in the course of 'Operation Desert Storm' against Iraq, see York, above (n. 24) 269–90; Roberts, above (n. 24); Rogers, above (n. 77) *226–31*; Dinstein, above (n. 43) 212–16.

[84] Dinstein, above (n. 58) 534–5; Boothby, above (n. 51) 99–103.

[85] David, above (n. 56) 299; Rule 45 *CIHL*.

[86] ICJ, *Nuclear Weapons, ICJ Reports 1996*, 242 (para. 31).

[87] 'Final Report to the Prosecutor by the Committee Established to Review the NATO Bombing Campaign Against the Federal Republic of Yugoslavia' (2000) *ILM* 39, 1262 para. 15.

STEFAN OETER

para. 1, AP I. In general, one might state that evidence of a widespread *opinio juris* as well as of a pertinent state practice has increased.[88] As far as objections against these rules have been raised explicitly and persistently, they were predominantly related to the use of nuclear weapons on the one hand and to the phrase 'may be expected to cause' on the other.[89] The distinction between 'intended' and 'expected' damages is also reflected in Article 8, para. 2, lit. b(iv) of the ICC Statute that defines as a war crime only deliberately caused damages.[90] Following this distinction, it seems worth considering that customary equivalents to the provisions of AP I at least have emerged in so far as intended damages to the environment are concerned with the possible exception of those caused by nuclear weapons. In general, customary law only prohibits those impairments of the environment which are manifestly superfluous under the principle of military necessity, since they are in no way militarily required.[91]

> The prohibition of indiscriminate warfare means that both the civilian popu- **404**
> lation as a whole and individual civilians shall be spared as far as possible from
> attack.

1. The prohibition of indiscriminate warfare probably constitutes the most important expression of the principle of 'limited warfare'. It is both the greatest consequence of and a modification of the fundamental orientation of warfare towards the requirements of 'military necessity'.[92]

2. The requirement to distinguish between the civilian population and the combatants, as well as between military objectives and civilian objects (Article 48 AP I) is a classical result of the attempt to restrict warfare to acts of violence against the enemy which are strictly 'necessary' from a military perspective. Use of force is permitted only in so far as it is directed against a specific military objective, be it a military installation, an object used for military purposes, or an individual combatant or group of combatants.[93] A 'specific military objective' accordingly is the fundamental precondition for an act of force to be justifiable under humanitarian law.[94] The use of force must not only be directed against this specific (and separable) target, but it must also employ specific weapons and methods of warfare that are limited (or at least limitable) in their results. In its effects the military instrument may not exceed what is warranted by the military objective of the operation.[95]

---

[88] *CIHL* Vol. II/1, 876–903.

[89] Wolfrum, 'Der Schutz der Umwelt im bewaffneten Konflikt' in Klaus Grupp/Ulrich Hufeld (eds), *Recht—Kultur—Finanzen: Festschrift für Reinhard Mußgnug* (C. F. Müller, 2005), 295–304, at 304.

[90] Article 8, para. 2, lit. b(iv), ICC Statute; in addition, the provision requires a breach of the principle of proportionality; see also Henckaerts, 'Towards Better Protection for the Environment in Armed Conflict' (2000) 9 *Review of European Community & International Environmental Law* 13, 16 ff.; Peterson, 'The Natural Environment in Times of Armed Conflict: A Concern for International War Crimes Law?' (2009) 22 *Leiden Journal of International Law* 325 ff.; Julian Wyatt, 'Law-making at the intersection of international environmental, humanitarian and criminal law: the issue of damage to the environment in international armed conflict' (2010) 92 *IRRC* 593, 633 ff.

[91] See Falk, in Plant (ed.), above (n. 70) 84 *et seq.*, Bothe, ibid. 117–18, and Wolfgang Lohbeck, *Umwelt und bewaffneter Konflikt: Dilemma oder Ausweg?* (Hamburg: Institut für Friedensforschung und Sicherheitspolitik, 2004), 76.

[92] See Pilloud/Pictet, in *ICRC Commentary*, paras. 1822–37 and Sassòli, above (n. 11) 342–50.

[93] Concerning the classical principle of distinction see Kunz, *op. cit.*, (n. 47) 75–7; Castrén, *op. cit.*, (n. 47) 174–83; Pilloud/Pictet, in *ICRC Commentary*, paras. 1863–71.

[94] See below Section 442.

[95] See Cassese, 'The Prohibition of Indiscriminate Means of Warfare' in Robert J. Akkerman (ed.), *Declarations on Principles, Festschrift für B.V.A. Röling* (Sijthoff, 1977), 171–94, at 171–82.

STEFAN OETER

The following conclusion can be drawn: the use of means of force must, in its intention, be limitable to combat against purely military objectives, and in its results it must be limited to damaging only military targets (Article 51, paras. 2 and 4, AP I).[96]

3. Civilians taking direct part in hostilities, however, can also be a target of a military operation. Mainly due to the privatization of war, more and more civilians are engaged in and around armed conflicts. Before, civilians traditionally were employed distant from the combating fields (equipment, food, administrative support, etc.). Nowadays, civilians are in a very close proximity to combat actions and have even taken over formerly official functions.[97] As a consequence, the situation on battlefields is extremely blurred and the implementation of the principle of distinction causes difficulties. According to Article 51, para. 3, AP I and Article 13, para. 3, AP II, civilians shall benefit from protection against the effects of hostilities 'unless and for such time as they take a direct part in hostilities'. During their active participation in hostilities, they lose their protection as civilians and the rules concerning combatants apply to them. To further guarantee the protection of civilians, the ICRC in 2009 adopted a Guidance on the Direct Participation in Hostilities, which include ten recommendations and a commentary reflecting the ICRC's position in this regard.[98] The ICRC came to the conclusion that there exist three constitutive elements to qualify a civilian act as direct participation: a threshold of harm has to be reached, a direct causation between the act and the harm, as well as a belligerent nexus have to be established.[99] According to the so-called 'revolving door'-effect, civilians lose their protection for the duration of each act of direct participation.[100] In case of doubt, all possible precautions have to be undertaken to determine whether a civilian participates directly in hostilities. Civilian losses during a direct participation have to be evaluated in terms of military necessity.

4. The prohibition against indiscriminate warfare, however, potentially exceeds even that limitation to the requirements of 'military necessity' by laying down the fundamental principle of proportionality.[101] The use of means and methods of warfare may be illegal, even if collateral damage to the civilian population and civilian goods could be justified in principle by reference to 'military necessity', on the grounds that such damage is unavoidable in mounting an effective attack on a military objective in the centre of the operation. Manifestly disproportionate collateral damage inflicted in order to achieve operational objectives will result in the action being deemed an (illicit) form of indiscriminate warfare (Article 51, para. 5, lit. b, AP I).

5. Accordingly, all methods and means of warfare which primarily damage the civilian population, such as the practice of indiscriminate area bombing[102]—a strategy used

---

[96] See the comments of Solf on Art. 51 AP I, in Bothe/Partsch/Solf, above (n. 41) 299–311; Baxter, in UNESCO/Institut Henry Dunant (eds), *op. cit.*, (n. 1) 117–62, at 146–58; Blix, ibid. 174–8.

[97] Melzer, 'Civilian Participation in Armed Conflict', *MPEPIL*, para. 2.

[98] ICRC, *Interpretive Guidance on the Notion of Direct Participation in Hostilities under International Humanitarian Law* (2008) 80 *IRRC* (2008), 991–1047.

[99] Ibid. 995–6.

[100] Ibid. 1033.

[101] Concerning the principle of proportionality generally regarded as already embodied in customary law, see Cassese, above (n. 27) 85–6; Bretton, *op. cit.*, (n. 65) 47–8; Venturini, *op. cit.*, (n. 43) 145–50; Dinstein, above (n. 43) 128–30; Rogers, above (n. 77) 21–7.

[102] See Art. 51, para. 5, lit. a, AP I.

STEFAN OETER

excessively by both sides during World War II[103]—are prohibited. Likewise, 'scorched earth' strategies on enemy territory, the indiscriminate dispersal of mines and booby traps on enemy territory (see Sections 412–418), and several other forms of warfare which primarily damage the civilian population, such as the use of incendiary weapons against civilian settlements (see Section 426), starving the population of besieged areas, artillery bombardment of 'enemy' settlements, or the use of snipers to terrorize the 'enemy' civilian population are also forbidden.[104]

6. One specific achievement of the Additional Protocols was the prohibition against starvation as a method of warfare, as provided by Article 54, para. 1, AP I. Methods of warfare that attempt to destroy the logistical basis of the enemy were traditionally popular in military tactics.[105] Sieges of encircled settlements deliberately tried to force the enemy to lay down their weapons by starving out the civilian population; strategies of 'scorched earth' employed during a retreat from enemy territory or in the abandonment of one's own territory were an instrument frequently used by belligerents in order to prevent the enemy from achieving its strategic goals.[106] Since these ways of conducting war are primarily damaging to the civilian population, the international community has outlawed such methods and means of warfare; narrow bounds have been set by Articles 54 AP I and 14 AP II to traditional tactics of siege, laying waste of areas, and so on.[107] (For further details, see Section 466.)

7. The general prohibition against indiscriminate warfare applies independently of Articles 48 and 51 AP I. The relevant provisions of the Additional Protocols merely codify pre-existing customary law, because the principle of distinction belongs to the oldest fundamental maxims of established customary rules of humanitarian law.[108] It is also virtually impossible to distinguish between international and non-international armed conflict in this respect, since common Article 3 of the Geneva Conventions already provides for extensive protection of the civilian population even in internal armed conflicts. Although the law of 'non-international armed conflict' has no specific notion of 'the combatant', it is undisputed that attacks on the life and health of civilians, in particular intentional killing and cruel treatment such as torture and mutilation, are absolutely prohibited under the customary minimum standards set out in common Article 3.[109] As was already expressed in the *Nicaragua* judgment,[110] the ICJ reaffirmed in its Advisory Opinion on Nuclear Weapons the particular dignity of the distinction

---

[103] See Parks, above (n. 9) 1–2; Rogers, above (n. 77) 17–20.

[104] See Art. 54, para. 1, AP I.

[105] See Dinstein, 'Siege Warfare and the Starvation of Civilians' in A. J. M. Delissen/G. J. Tanja (eds), *Humanitarian Law of Armed Conflict: Challenges Ahead—Essays in Honour of F. Kalshoven* (Nijhoff, 1991), 145–52, at 145–7.

[106] See Solf, in Bothe/Partsch/Solf, above (n. 41) 337 and Dinstein, *loc. cit.*, 146–7.

[107] Concerning Art. 54, para. 1, AP I see Pilloud/Pictet, in *ICRC Commentary*, paras. 2083–91; Solf, in Bothe/Partsch/Solf, ibid. 336–42; Dinstein, *loc. cit.*, 148–52; David, above (n. 56) 290–4; Dinstein, above (n. 43) 218–25.

[108] See Cassese, above (n. 27) 82 *et seq.*; Fleck, 'The Protocols Additional to the Geneva Conventions and Customary International Law' (1990) XXIX *RDMilG* 495–517, at 500–1; Rogers, above (n. 77) 11; Rules 1, 7, 11 *CIHL*.

[109] See Kalshoven, above (n. 9) 296.

[110] ICJ, *Case Concerning Military and Paramilitary Activities in and against Nicaragua (Nicaragua v US)*, Judgment of 27 June 1986, *ICJ Reports 1986*, 114 (para. 218); see also the report of special rapporteur W. Kälin to the UN Human Rights Commission concerning the human rights violations of Iraq in occupied Kuwait, UN Doc. E/CN.4/1992/26 of 16 January 1992, 10–1 (paras. 35–8).

STEFAN OETER

between combatants and non-combatants, qualifying it as one of the 'cardinal principles contained in the texts constituting the fabric of humanitarian law'.[111]

405   In the study, development, acquisition, or adoption of new means or methods of
           combat it shall be determined whether these means and methods are compatible
           with the rules of international law (Article 36 AP I).

In order to guarantee effective implementation of the prohibition of certain means and methods of warfare emanating from the principles described above it is necessary to provide for an efficient procedure to ensure the legality of new weapons.[112] Some states had already created such procedures prior to the elaboration of the Additional Protocols (the Federal Republic of Germany, the US, Sweden),[113] but for most states such a form of preventive control will be a novel institution. Originally, an internationalized procedure of control had even been considered.[114] In view of the legitimate requirements of secrecy that surround the development of new weapons, however, the concept of the internationalization of controls proved to be impracticable and refuge was taken in the already established procedures of national control of legality, although these control procedures were made obligatory.[115]

II. Means of Combat

1. Certain Conventional Weapons

406   In the 1868 St Petersburg Declaration the use of explosive and incendiary projectiles
           weighing under 400 g was prohibited, since these projectiles were deemed to cause
           disproportionately severe injury to soldiers, which is not necessary to put them out
           of action. This prohibition is now only of limited importance, since it is reduced by
           customary law to the use of explosive and incendiary projectiles of a weight signifi-
           cantly lower than 400 g which can disable only the individual directly concerned
           but not any other persons. 20 mm high-explosive grenades and projectiles of a
           similar calibre are not prohibited.

1. The St Petersburg Declaration of 1868 was the first instrument to outlaw specific weapons.[116] One of its most interesting parts is the Preamble, where the motivation (and dilemma) of all humanitarian prohibitions of weapons has found a convincing expression. In the Preamble the states parties declared their acceptance of an obligation to restrict the use of certain projectiles considering that 'the progress of civilization should have the effect of alleviating as much as possible the calamities of war' and that 'the only legitimate object

---

[111] *ICJ Reports 1996*, 257.

[112] See Solf, in Bothe/Partsch/Solf, above (n. 41) 199 and de Preux, in *ICRC Commentary*, 421–5 (paras. 1463–71).

[113] See Solf, in Bothe/Partsch/Solf, ibid. 199 n. 1 and de Preux, in *ICRC Commentary*, 423 (para. 1467), 426–7 (n. 19).

[114] Solf, in Bothe/Partsch/Solf, ibid. 200.

[115] Dinstein, above (n. 43) 86–8; Domínguez-Matés in Fernández-Sánchez, above (n. 71) 116–7; for the standards of control see also Isabelle Daoust/Robin Coupland/Rikke Ishoey, 'New wars, new weapons? The obligation of States to assess the legality of means and methods of warfare' (2002) 84 *IRRC* 345–63; de Preux, in *ICRC Commentary*, paras. 1472–7; Justin McClelland, 'The review of weapons in accordance with Article 36 of Additional Protocol I' (2003) 85 *IRRC* 397–415.

[116] For the historical background see Kalshoven, above (n. 9) 205–13; Boothby, above (n. 51) 55–6, 141.

STEFAN OETER

which States should endeavour to accomplish during war is to weaken the military forces of the enemy'. For this purpose it is sufficient 'to disable the greatest possible number of men'; this object would be exceeded 'by the employment of arms which uselessly aggravate the sufferings of disabled men, or render their death inevitable', not to mention that 'the employment of such arms would be contrary to the laws of humanity'. The only legitimate purpose of any use of weapons is the disabling of enemy combatants.[117]

2. According to the judgment of the International Military Commission which assembled at St Petersburg at the instigation of the Imperial Cabinet of Russia,[118] the use of explosive projectiles against infantry failed to meet this standard. The laws of war, as the principles 'at which the necessities of war ought to yield to the requirements of humanity', should not prohibit the use of explosive projectiles per se. The use of such projectiles as artillery munition had already been long established and was perceived to be militarily necessary. However, the use against individual combatants of explosive projectiles was seen to be avoidable in military terms, and therefore superfluous.[119] The weight limit used to distinguish between infantry and artillery munitions (400 g) was set rather arbitrarily; artillery projectiles of the time were considerably heavier, whereas infantry munitions were much lighter than 400 g. The absolute weight limit set in 1868 should therefore not be taken too strictly.[120] The basic principle of the declaration has, therefore, been transformed not into customary law as a prohibition of explosive projectiles weighing under 400 g, but into a prohibition against infantry munitions with explosive or inflammable effects.[121] According to the UK Manual, this rule has become obsolete, since modern munition does not reach the 400 g limit due to the combined effects of 20 mm and 25 mm munitions.[122] Modern artillery munitions under the weight limit of the St Petersburg Declaration are therefore legally permissible under international customary law (as a Convention provision, the St Petersburg Declaration is scarcely ever applicable, due to its general participation clause).

> It is prohibited to use bullets which expand or flatten easily in the human body 407
> (Dum-Dum Bullets HagueDecl 1899). This applies also to the use of shotguns,
> since its shot causes similar suffering unjustified from the military point of view. It
> is also prohibited to use projectiles of a nature:
> — to burst or deform while penetrating the human body;
> — to tumble early in the human body; or
> — to cause shock waves leading to extensive tissue damage or even lethal shock
>   (Articles 35, para. 2, and 51, para. 4, lit. c, AP I; Article 23, lit. e, HagueReg).

1. The attempt to outlaw excessively cruel weapons, which was the basis of the St Petersburg Declaration of 1868, was continued in the Declaration Concerning Expanding Bullets adopted at the Hague Peace Conference in 1899.[123] The intended object of the prohibition was the projectile developed by the British Army for use against tribesmen in India,

[117] For an analysis of the Preamble to the St Petersburg Declaration 1868 see Kalshoven, in *loc. cit.*, 206–7, 212.
[118] Kalshoven, *loc. cit.*, 205–8, 212–13.
[119] Ibid.
[120] Kalshoven, *loc. cit.*, 207; Sitaropoulos, above (n. 26) 86–7.
[121] See, e.g., Kalshoven, *loc. cit.*, 222–3; cf. Sandoz, above (n. 9) 18–19; Rule 78 *CIHL*.
[122] See Boothby, above (n. 51) 142.
[123] As to its historical background, see Kalshoven, *loc. cit.*, 213–17 and Boothby, above (n. 51) 144–6.

STEFAN OETER

which had become known as the 'Dum-Dum bullet'.[124] The declaration must be seen as an undertaking parallel to the prohibition against the use of poison or poisonous weapons included by the Hague Peace Conference in Article 23, lit. a, HagueReg and to the (admittedly rather general) prohibition of 'arms, projectiles, or material calculated to cause unnecessary suffering' in Article 23, lit. e, HagueReg (see above, Section 402).

2. What exactly is covered by the firmly established prohibition against (in the original French version) *'maux superflus'* remains, however, in doubt, although the Geneva Diplomatic Conference 1974–1977 reaffirmed the basic prohibition in Articles 35, para. 2, and 51, para. 4, lit. c, AP I in a formula nearly identical to Article 23, lit. e, HagueReg. One could reasonably argue, as the German administration, for example, does, that the use of shotguns has essentially to be regarded as prohibited under these provisions, since its shot inflicts extremely painful wounds which cause grave difficulties in medical treatment, but is not much more efficient in its effects than normal infantry munition. Nevertheless, no real consensus has developed on this issue. The same could be said of other variants of recently developed infantry weapons and munitions which cause excessive injuries without achieving particularly impressive military advantages: projectiles which burst or deform while penetrating the human body; projectiles which tumble early in the human body (causing particularly severe internal injuries); and weapons and munitions which cause shock waves leading to extensive tissue damage or even lethal shock. The analogy with the dum-dum bullets outlawed in 1899 is obvious, and a prohibition on the general ground of 'excessive suffering' suggests itself;[125] an explicit prohibition anchored in treaty law, however, has not yet been agreed by the international community. Also, far from easy to evaluate is the question of precisely which new weapons are covered by the prohibitions in Article 23, lit.e, HagueReg and Article 35, para. 2, AP I. That discussions on modern small-calibre high-velocity weapons systems over the last decades has produced no agreement is telling in that respect.[126]

408   It is also prohibited to use any weapon the primary effect of which is to injure by fragments which in the human body escape detection by X-rays (Non DetectableFragmentsProt).

1. The prohibition laid down in the Protocol on Non-detectable Fragments is the only specific prohibition of a weapon in the tradition of the St Petersburg Declaration and Article 23, lit. e, HagueReg which met with unanimous approval by state representatives at the meetings of experts in Lucerne and Lugano in the 1970s, and then at the concluding UN Weapons Conference of Geneva in 1980.[127] As Protocol No. I, it was annexed to the Inhumane WeaponsConv.[128]

---

[124] In Article 8, para. 2, lit. b(xix), ICC Statute the use of bullets 'which expand or flatten easily in the body, such as bullets with a hard envelope which does not entirely cover the core or is pierced with incisions' is listed as a 'war crime' in respect of international armed conflicts. As to the application of this prohibition in non-international armed conflicts, see *CIHL* Vol. I, 270, and Watkin, above (n. 5) 51–2.

[125] See Boothby, above (n. 51) 142.

[126] See Kalshoven, *loc. cit.*, 259–61; Boothby, *op. cit.*, 150, 152–3 as for applying weapons law rules by analogy.

[127] See Kalshoven, *loc. cit.*, 241–4, 251–3.

[128] As to the framework agreement of the UN Weapons Convention system, see the detailed comments by J. Ashley Roach, 'Certain Conventional Weapons Convention: Arms Control or Humanitarian Law' (1984) 105 *Military Law Review* 3–72, at 16–68 and William J. Fenrick, 'La Convention sur les armes classiques: un traité modeste mais utile' (1990) 72 *RIC* 542–55.

STEFAN OETER

2. The prohibition in this Protocol is formulated restrictively, being deemed to cover only weapons the primary effects of which lie in the spread of non-detectable fragments ('weapons which were *designed* to injure by such fragments', according to the report of the working group),[129] and also it covers only the extreme cases of fragments not readily detectable, namely those not detectable even by X-rays. This means, in particular, fragments of plastic, wood, or glass which cause unnecessarily severe suffering because medical care is impeded and long periods of rehabilitation become unavoidable if such weapons are used.[130] However, weapons which contain plastic or other non-metallic parts for purposes other than those aimed at by Protocol No. I, such as grenades or mines with plastic detonators, are not covered.[131]

> Recently adopted treaty law prohibits to use anti-personnel mines, to develop, **409** produce, acquire, stockpile, retain, or transfer them. All existing anti-personnel mines shall be destroyed (Article 1 LandMinesConv). 'Anti-personnel mine' means a mine designed to be exploded by the presence, proximity, or contact of a person and that will incapacitate, injure, or kill one or more persons (Article 2, para. 1, LandMinesConv).

1. In 1997, the Ottawa Convention on the Prohibition of the Use, Stockpiling, Production, and Transfer of Anti-personnel Mines and on their Destruction was adopted and entered into force on 1 March 1999. The global campaign for the adoption of the Convention thus bore fruit; the International Campaign to Ban Landmines (ICBL), the ICRC, and numerous states supporting the initiative had considered the 1996 amendments of the Protocol II to the Weapons Convention (Mines Protocol, see the following sections) as insufficient.[132] In their view, only a complete ban of anti-personnel mines would effectively counter the indiscriminate effects of these mines and their long-lasting impairments of civil life. The Convention has been ratified by 159 states as of 17 March 2012, not including Russia, China, and the US. The US refused to sign the treaty primarily because its request for a geographical exception for the use of mines in South Korea had not been granted.[133]

2. The Convention establishes a comprehensive ban on anti-personnel mines. According to Article 1, their use, development, production, acquisition, stockpiling, retention, and transfer is prohibited; the parties also undertake never to assist, encourage or induce anyone to engage in any of these activities. Moreover, they are obligated to destroy or ensure the destruction of all stockpiled and cleared anti-personnel mines.

3. An anti-personnel mine is defined by the treaty as a mine 'designed to be exploded by the presence, proximity or contact of a person and that will incapacitate, injure or kill one or more persons. Mines designed to be detonated by the presence, proximity or contact of a vehicle as opposed to a person, that are equipped with anti-handling devices, are not considered anti-personnel mines as a result of being so equipped' (Article 2, para. 1). Thus, the prohibition covers all dual-purpose mines as long as one of its functions is

---

[129] Roach, *loc. cit.*, 69–70.

[130] See the memorandum of the German Government annexed to the draft of an approving statute to the Weapons Convention, BR-Drs. 117/92, 25.

[131] Ibid.

[132] ICRC, above (n. 55) 3; Kalshoven/Zegveld, above (n. 22) 187; Stuart Maslen, *Commentaries on Arms control Treaties, Vol. I, The Convention on the Prohibition of the Use, Stockpiling, Production, and Transfer of Anti-personnel Mines and on their Destruction* (OUP, 2004), 21–44.

[133] Maslen, *op. cit.*, 39–43.

STEFAN OETER

to be detonated by a person; in contrast, the relevant definition of anti-personnel mines in the Mines Protocol confines its scope of application to mines '*primarily* designed . . .', provoking thereby one of its criticized weaknesses (see Section 416).[134] The sole exception to the prohibition of dual-purpose mines admitted by the Ottawa Convention applies to anti-vehicle mines equipped with an anti-handling device.

4. Whereas in the recent past there has been no evidence of use of anti-personnel mines by Landmines Convention states parties, several non-party states continued to use (especially Myanmar, Israel, and Libya) or to produce these mines.[135] Therefore, the specific prohibitions in the Landmines Convention are not likely to have customary equivalents so far.[136] As anti-tank and other anti-vehicle mines are out of the scope of application of the Convention, the Mines Protocol also maintains importance for states parties to both of the treaties.

410   **Under the Convention on Cluster Munitions, states parties undertake never under any circumstances to use or develop, produce, otherwise acquire, stockpile, retain, or transfer to anyone, directly or indirectly, cluster munitions, and to co-operate in munition clearance and destruction, victim assistance and risk education programmes.**

1. The Convention on Cluster Munitions, adopted in Dublin on 30 May 2008 and initially signed in Oslo on 3 and 4 December 2008 by 94 states, entered into force on 1 August 2010. It is the result of another open and time-bound diplomatic process that included states, civil society, the ICRC and the UN (the Oslo Process, see <http://www.clusterconvention.org/>). At the same time, some states initiated an attempt to weaken the Convention on Cluster Munitions under the auspices of the UN Convention on Conventional Weapons by allowing in its Protocol VI the usage of some cluster munitions produced after 1980. However, during the 2011 review conference of the UN Convention on Conventional Weapons in Geneva, the adoption of Protocol VI failed due to a lack of consensus among the member states. Thus, the outcome of the Oslo Process is still the only valid and broad regulation of cluster munition.

Cluster munition means a conventional munition that is designed to disperse or release explosive submunitions each weighing less than 20 kg, and includes those explosive submunitions. Nuclear, chemical, or biological weapons included in submunitions are not addressed.[137] It does not mean munition or submunition designed to dispense flares, smoke, pyrotechnics, or chaff; or a munition designed exclusively for an air defence role; munition or submunition designed to produce electrical or electronic effects; or munition that, in order to avoid indiscriminate area effects and the risks posed by unexploded submunitions, has all of the following characteristics: (a) each munition contains fewer than ten explosive submunitions; (b) each explosive submunition weighs more than 4 kg; (c) each explosive submunition is designed to detect and engage a single target object; (d) each explosive submunition is equipped with an electronic self-destruction

[134] Dinstein, above (n. 43) 74; ICRC, above (n. 55) 5; Maslen/Herby, 'Interdiction internationale des mines antipersonnel: Genèse et négociation du traité d'Ottawa' (1998) 80 *RIC* 751–74, at 759–60.
[135] International Campaign to Ban Landmines (ICBL), 'Landmine Monitor 2011', 1.
[136] *CIHL* Vol. I, 282; Dinstein, above (n. 43) 74–5.
[137] Gro Nystuen/Stuart Casey-Maslen, *The Convention on Cluster Munitition—A Commentary* (OUP, 2010), 2.109.

STEFAN OETER

mechanism; and (e) each explosive submunition is equipped with an electronic self-deactivating feature.

> The use of other mines and other devices on land is, in principle, permissible   **411**
> (Article 1 MinesProt). The following definitions apply:
> — 'mine' means any device placed—or remotely delivered—under, on, or near the
>   ground or other surface area and designed to be detonated or exploded by the pres-
>   ence, proximity, or contact of a person or vehicle (Article 2, No. 1, MinesProt);
> — 'other devices' means manually emplaced munitions or devices designed to kill,
>   injure, or damage and which are actuated by remote control or automatically
>   after a lapse of time (Article 2, No. 5, MinesProt).

1. The most important result of the negotiations on conventional weapons that cul-minated in the UN Weapons Convention of 1980 was the 'Protocol on prohibitions or restrictions on the use of mines, booby-traps, and other devices'. Contrary to Protocol I (on non-detectable fragments), it did not use the prohibition against unnecessary suffer-ing as its starting point, but the prohibition against indiscriminate warfare and against weapons with indiscriminate results. This does not prohibit the possession or even the use of mines and booby traps as such; the purpose of the Protocol was only to pro-hibit the use of mines and booby traps in certain situations, where the danger of indis-criminate effects is particularly grave.[138] Therefore, the Protocol in principle recognized the legality of the use of mines in common practice. When the Protocol was amended in 1996, despite the widespread support for a total ban on anti-personnel landmines, the negotiating states parties were not able to agree upon a general prohibition against these mines in the framework of the Protocol.[139] Instead, they adopted a highly compli-cated instrument, introducing further restrictions on the use of mines and booby traps, including several specific prohibitions in respect of anti-personnel mines.[140] However, the amended Protocol does not proscribe the use of detectable anti-personnel mines equipped with a self-deactivation device or placed in an area marked, fenced, and moni-tored by military personnel.[141] Beside some relative, situational prohibitions against the use of mines, the Protocol also contains absolute prohibitions against the use of mines equipped with an anti-detection mechanism and of certain perfidiously hidden explo-sive devices (booby traps) which are often, in practice, deployed not against combatants, but for the sake of terrorizing the civilian population in order to break its will to resist (as demonstrated especially in, e.g., the war in Afghanistan during the 1980s).[142] A par-ticular problem is posed by modern mines that can be remotely delivered deep into the enemy hinterland by the use of mortars, rockets, or air vehicles. The Protocol here has obliged states to undertake certain safeguarding measures, by which the dangers of such uncontrolled minefields shall be reduced as far as possible.[143]

---

[138] For technical details of the Mines Protocol, see in particular Burrus M. Carnahan, 'The Law of Land Mine Warfare: Protocol II to the United Nations Convention on Certain Conventional Weapons' (1984) 105 *Military Law Review* 73–95.

[139] David, above (n. 56) 365; Maslen, *op. cit.*, (n. 132) 17–22.

[140] David, ibid. 365–7; Kalshoven/Zegveld, above (n. 22) 181–3; Boothby, above (n. 51) 168–76.

[141] David, above (n. 56) 367; Dinstein, above (n. 43) 72–3; Herby, 'Troisième session de la Conférence d'examen des États parties à la Convention des Nations Unies de 1980 sur certaines armes classiques: Genève, 22 avril–3 mai 1996' (1996) 78 *RIC* 389–98, at 393.

[142] See Memorandum of the German Government on the UN Weapons Convention, *BR-Drs.* 117/92, 25.

[143] David, above (n. 56) 366–7; for the fierce debate on remotely delivered mines that had developed at the conferences of Lucerne and Lugano and at the UN Weapons Conference in 1980, see Elmar Rauch, 'The

STEFAN OETER

2. Article 2 MinesProt defines exactly what constitutes mines and booby traps. According to that definition, a 'mine' is any 'munition placed under, on, or near the ground or other surface area and designed to be exploded by the presence, proximity, or contact of a person or vehicle'. The essential point in the definition is the explosion of the device by an action of a third person or vehicle. Such third-party intervention is the characteristic which distinguishes between 'mines' and 'other devices', which are detonated by remote control or delayed-action cap.

412   **It is prohibited to direct the above-mentioned munitions—even by way of repris-als—against the civilian population as such or against individual civilians (Article 3, para. 7, MinesProt). Any indiscriminate use of these weapons is prohibited (Article 3, para. 8, MinesProt).**

1. Paragraphs 7 and 8 of Article 3 MinesProt lay down the fundamental principle of the entire regulation. It is forbidden to use any of the weapons covered by the Protocol (mines, booby traps, and other devices) against the civilian population or against individual civilians[144] in any circumstances, whether offensive, defensive, or by way of reprisal. All forms of indiscriminate use are likewise prohibited, that is any use which is not specifically directed against a military objective, which employs a weapon or means of delivery which cannot be limited in its effects to military objectives, or which is likely to cause disproportionate collateral damage.[145]

2. Careful analysis of these elementary safeguards of Article 3 reveals that they merely reaffirm the principle of distinction and the prohibition against indiscriminate warfare, codified in the provisions of Articles 48 and 51 AP I (see Sections 442, 454, 457, and 459). Both fundamental rules are expressly repeated here with regard to mine warfare. This is made explicit, in particular, by paragraph 8 of Article 3 MinesProt (prohibition of indiscriminate use) which adopts almost verbatim the wording of Article 51, para. 4, AP I[146] and includes in the amended version of the Protocol the presumption of the civilian purpose of an object laid down in Article 52, para. 3, AP I (see Section 447). Thus, these provisions of Article 3 could be seen as merely affirming a truism, namely that the general provisions on weapons and means of warfare in Article 51 AP I are applicable also to mine warfare.[147] It is therefore stressed that the specific regulation of the Mines Protocol constitutes nothing more than a concretization of the basic principles of distinction and the prohibition against 'indiscriminate warfare' which were in any event applicable to mine warfare.[148] Therefore, even when parties to a conflict are not bound by the UN Weapons Convention, they will be bound by most of the specific provisions of the Mines Protocol to the extent that these represent the general principles embodied in Article 51 AP I for the special case of mine warfare.[149]

Protection of the Civilian Population in International Armed Conflicts and the Use of Landmines' (1981) 24 *GYIL* 262–87, at 269–80; Carnahan, *loc. cit.*, 79–80.

[144] Cf. also Kalshoven/Zegveld, above (n. 22) 175–6.

[145] For the parallel legal consequences resulting from Art. 51, para. 4, AP I, see Kalshoven/Zegveld, ibid. 175–6.

[146] Kalshoven/Zegveld, above (n. 22) 175.

[147] See Rauch, *loc. cit.*, 265–6, 279; cf. however, Fenrick, 'New Development in the Law Concerning the Use of Conventional Weapons in Armed Conflict' (1981) XIX *CYIL* 229–56, at 243–4.

[148] See Kalshoven/Zegveld, above (n. 22) 175–6.

[149] See Kalshoven/Zegveld, ibid. 176.

STEFAN OETER

3. These principles also apply to non-international armed conflicts as is stated by Article 1, para. 2, of the amended MinesProt and Article 1, para. 2, Inhumane WeaponsConv as of 21 December 2001 with the same extension for the whole of the Convention and its then four additional Protocols.[150] Admittedly, however, there exist serious difficulties concerning the implementation of the fundamental rules for the protection of the civilian population against the dangers of mines in civil wars.[151] The present problem of the millions of mines scattered throughout areas of conflict undoubtedly constitutes one of the main scourges for the civilian population of regions plagued by civil wars.

All feasible precautions shall be taken to protect civilians also from unintended   413
effects of these munitions (Article 3, para. 10, MinesProt).

Article 3, para. 10, MinesProt repeats once again the fundamental rule of Article 57 AP I, although with a specific orientation towards problems of mine warfare (see Section 460), but even here in a formula nearly identical to the wording of Article 57 AP I.[152] The general explanations given above under Section 412 as to Article 3 MinesProt are valid also concerning this provision: the 'active' precautions required in general by Article 57 AP I ('every precaution practically feasible') must in principle always be taken by the responsible military leaders, including cases of mining operations. The employment of mines and booby traps is of particular importance, since the dangers for the civilian population arising from such means of combat are particularly high. Accordingly, the location of a minefield must be chosen with due regard to civilian protection; the location and pattern of the minefield should be recorded, in order that the mines may be removed as soon as they are no longer needed, and the mines should be guarded and marked, as far as is feasible, in order to prevent unnecessary civilian casualties. The amended Mines Protocol now lists in Article 3, para. 10 as examples of circumstances to be taken into account: the short- and long-term effect of mines upon the local civilian population for the duration of the minefield, possible measures to protect civilians (e.g., fencing, signs, warning, and monitoring), the availability and feasibility of using alternatives, and the short- and long-term military requirements for a minefield.

Booby traps and other devices shall not be used in any built-up area, or other area   414
predominantly inhabited by civilians, in which there is no actual or imminent
combat between ground forces (Article 7, para. 3, MinesProt). Exceptions are per-
missible if:
— **these munitions are placed on or in the close vicinity of a military objective; or**
— **measures are taken to protect civilians from their effects, for example, the post-**
  ing of warning sentries, the provision of fences, or the issue of warnings (Article
  7, paras. 3, lit. a and b, MinesProt).

1. The above rule repeats Article 7, para. 3, MinesProt. That provision contains special guidelines for the use of manually emplaced booby traps and explosive devices in towns, villages, or other areas with a similar population density of civilians, to the extent that such use is not a compelling military necessity arising immediately out of situations of

---

[150] In force since 18 May 2004.
[151] Kalshoven/Zegveld, above (n. 22) 181.
[152] Concerning the parallelism of Art. 57, para. 2, AP I and Art. 3, para. 4, of the original Mines Protocol, see G. Würkner-Theis, *Fernverlegte Minen und humanitäres Völkerrecht* (Frankfurt a. M.: Lang, 1990), 181–97, at 191–5.

STEFAN OETER

combat (which can only be the case when combat between ground forces takes place or appears to be imminent directly in the zone of a settlement).[153] Inside such zones or settlements the use of booby traps has in practice been shown to pose particularly serious dangers.[154] Article 7, para. 3, therefore provides for a general prohibition on the use of booby traps in such areas—as long as they are not inside the combat zone.

2. The use of booby traps in densely populated areas, however, is exceptionally admissible according to the provision of Article 7, para. 3 if booby traps are employed directly to protect a military installation, or for combat against an enemy military objective (placement directly 'on or in the close vicinity of a military objective'[155]), or when precautionary measures have been taken which reduce the risk for the civilian population to a tolerable degree.[156] Article 7, para. 3, lit. b, enumerates some examples of these precautionary measures: the posting of warning sentries, the issue of warnings, and the provision of fences. The following conclusion may be drawn. The preventive placement of booby traps and other devices is permitted even in conurbations and settlements,[157] if they are guarded and secured against intrusion by civilians—a modification which seems sensible, since under those conditions the dangers for the civilian population are kept in reasonable bounds.[158]

3. In contrast to the original 1980 Mines Protocol, the amended provision in Article 7, para. 3, does not cover the emplacement of mines.[159] Thus, it could be argued that this fundamental prohibition against the use of weapons in densely populated areas and settlements does no longer apply to mines. Nevertheless, it must be doubted whether this is a sensible conclusion. The general prohibition against 'indiscriminate warfare' which was reaffirmed in respect of the use of all mines, booby traps and other devices by Article 3, para. 8 of the amended Mines Protocol leads to the same conclusions as were explicitly drawn by Article 4 of the original Protocol. The employment of mines in densely populated areas poses extremely high risks to the civilian population if the minefields are not marked or controlled or guarded. How the use of mines in densely populated areas could ever be justifiable, given the prohibition against indiscriminate warfare, remains difficult to conceive, unless the civilian population has fled the combat area or been evacuated. However, an explicit insertion of this restriction would have clarified the scope of the prohibition, thus preventing a possible abusive interpretation of the amended Article 7 MinesProt.

415   **It is prohibited to use mines, booby traps, or other devices equipped with a mechanism designed to detonate the munition by the presence of commonly available mine detectors during normal use in detection operations (Article 3, para. 5, MinesProt). The use of a self-deactivating mine equipped with an anti-handling device capable of functioning after the mine has ceased to be capable of functioning is prohibited (Article 3, para. 6, MinesProt).**

---

[153] For a criticism of the distinction between combat zone and hinterland see Rauch, above (n. 143) 280–1.

[154] See the Memorandum of the German Government on the UN Weapons Convention, BR-Drs. 117/92, 26.

[155] As to that formula see Rauch, *loc. cit.*, 278–9.

[156] For the debate on that formula, see Carnahan *loc. cit.*, (n. 138) 81–2.

[157] For a different opinion, however, see Rauch, *loc. cit.*, 281–2.

[158] See the Memorandum of the German Government on the UN Weapons Convention, BR-Drs. 117/92, 26; moreover, see Fenrick, *loc. cit.*, (n. 147), 245.

[159] Kalshoven/Zegveld, above (n. 22) 182.

STEFAN OETER

1. Paragraphs 5 and 6 of Article 3 MinesProt constitute two additional prohibitions introduced by the 1996 amendment. They are destined to facilitate detection operations and to reduce the risks to mine-clearance personnel.[160] Article 3, para. 5, proscribes the use of mines and other devices designed to explode just as a result of a normal detection operation.[161]

2. The other prohibition concerns the use of self-deactivating mines equipped with an anti-handling device which is designed to be actuated by a handling attempt even after the mine has self-deactivated. Such a device with a lifetime greater than that of the self-deactivation mechanism endangers for an extended period both mine-clearance personnel and the civilian population.[162] Therefore, the ban of such mines constitutes a sensible amendment of the Mines Protocol.

> **The use of anti-personnel mines which are not detectable is prohibited (Article 4**   416
> **MinesProt). Anti-personnel mines other than remotely delivered mines must either**
> **be equipped with a self-destruction mechanism and a self-deactivation device or be**
> **placed in an area marked, fenced, and monitored by military personnel (Article 5**
> **MinesProt).**

1. Although the advocates for a complete ban of anti-personnel mines had failed, the 1996 amendment of the Mines Protocol introduced several specific restrictions with respect to anti-personnel mines. Accordingly, Article 2, para. 3, of the amended Protocol defines what constitutes such a mine: ' "Anti-personnel mine" means a mine primarily designed to be exploded by the presence, proximity or contact of a person and that will incapacitate, injure or kill one or more persons.' The insertion of the notion 'primarily' has been heavily criticized as it allows an interpretation excluding all 'dual use' mines from the scope of application; in response to such an ambiguous definition, the ICRC published a list of mine technologies which could be said to have another 'primary' purpose, even though they are in fact designed to explode upon contact with a person and are designed to kill or injure persons. The list includes mines designed with both anti-personnel and anti-vehicle or anti-helicopter capabilities, anti-handling mechanisms on anti-tank mines, and 'runway denial' submunitions.[163] Owing to the criticism, Germany delivered on behalf of several other states an official interpretation, asserting that the term 'primarily' was solely inserted to ensure that 'mines designed to be detonated by the presence, proximity or contact of a vehicle as opposed to a person, that are equipped with anti-handling devices, are not considered anti-personnel mines as a result of being so equipped',[164] anticipating thus in identical wording the exception made in Article 2, para. 1, LandMinesConv (see Section 409).

2. Article 4 of the amended MinesProt prohibits the use of anti-personnel mines which are not detectable, as specified in para. 2 of the Technical Annex. The provision aims to ban the employment of plastic mines that can escape detection by standard mine-detection equipment and thus present a severe risk to mine-clearance personnel, as well

---

[160] Michael J. Matheson, 'The revision of the Mines Protocol' (1997) 91 *AJIL* 158–67, at 164.

[161] Mario Bettati, 'L'interdiction ou la limitation d'emploi des mines (Le Protocole de Genève du 3 mai 1996)' (1996) 42 *Annuaire français de droit international* 187–205, at 193.

[162] Ibid.; Matheson, above (n. 160) 164.

[163] ICRC, Official statement: Expert Meeting on the Convention for the Prohibition of Anti-personnel Mines, 12 February 1997, <http://www.cicr.org/web/eng/siteeng0.nsf/htmlall/57jnf9?opendocument>; Bettati, *loc. cit.*, 199.

[164] Herby, *loc. cit.*, (n. 141) 391; Maslen, *op. cit.*, (n. 132) 108.

STEFAN OETER

as to civilians.[165] According to the detailed regulation in the Technical Annex, all anti-personnel mines shall incorporate (as regards mines produced after 1 January 1997) or have at least attached (as regards mines produced before) a material rendering the mine detectable by commonly available mine-detection equipment and providing a response signal equivalent to a signal from 8 g or more of iron. With respect to the anti-personnel mines produced before 1 January 1997, the Protocol offers a deferral period of nine years from its entry into force.[166] If one takes seriously the concept of the best feasible protection of civilians after the end of hostilities, one can argue that—irrespectively of this prohibition laid down in the amended Mines Protocol—the use of non-metallic anti-personnel mines outside recorded minefields should be regarded as illegal according to the customary standards of responsible warfare which require respect for the prohibition against indiscriminate warfare.

3. In order to reduce the risks especially for the civilian population, Article 5 imposes further restrictions on the use of anti-personnel mines, except for the remotely delivered anti-personnel mines which fall under the particular provisions of Article 6 (see Section 417). According to Article 5, para. 2, the use of such weapons is prohibited unless they are equipped with a self-destruction and self-deactivation device as specified in the Technical Annex or they are placed in an area marked and fenced and monitored by military personnel to ensure the effective exclusion of civilians from the area. The Technical Annex requires a self-destruction within 30 days of emplacement with a reliability of 90 per cent and a self-deactivation within 120 days with a combined reliability of 99.9 per cent.[167] Regarding the placement in marked and protected areas, Article 5, para. 3, provides an exception for certain situations, including where direct enemy military action made it impossible to comply.[168]

4. It is particularly due to the complicated restrictions imposed on anti-personnel mines that the amendment of the Mines Protocol was subject to severe criticism leading to the adoption of the Landmines Convention. However, as the latter instrument still has not been ratified by a considerable number of states involved in the production, transfer, or use of mines (e.g., China, the Russian Federation, the Republic of Korea, the US), the Mines Protocol remains of importance, confining to a certain degree the use of anti-personnel mines.

417   **The use of remotely delivered mines is prohibited unless such mines are equipped with an effective self-deactivation device (Article 6, paras. 2 and 3, MinesProt). After emplacement, their location shall be accurately recorded (Article 6, para. 1, MinesProt). Effective advance warning shall be given of any delivery or dropping of remotely delivered mines which may affect the civilian population, unless circumstances do not permit this (Article 6, para. 4, MinesProt).**

1. The particular problem of remotely delivered mines led to fierce debates during the Weapons Conference of 1980, debates which had already arisen at the preparatory

---

[165] Matheson, *loc. cit.*, (n. 160) 163; concerning the problems of non-metallic anti-personnel mines see the observations based on the experience of the Falklands War made by Rogers, (1990) 72 *RIC* 580–1 and the technical remarks by G. C. Cauderay, 'Les mines antipersonnel' (1993) 75 *RIC* 293–309.

[166] Bettati, *loc. cit.*, (n. 161) 193; Matheson, *loc. cit.*, (n. 160) 163–4.

[167] As to the technical distinction between self-destruction and self-deactivation, see Bettati, *loc. cit.*, 193–4; Matheson, *loc. cit.*, 162.

[168] Maslen, *op. cit.*, (n. 132) 22.

STEFAN OETER

meetings of Lucerne and Lugano.[169] While many states (particularly those from the Third World) had demanded that a total prohibition against the use of remotely delivered mines should be included in Protocol II, most of the industrialized states argued that a complete prohibition against such devices would be in total contradiction with requirements of military necessity. In particular, the member states of NATO claimed that the possibility of employing mines in enemy territory in order to hamper the enemy's operations in its hinterland and to block deployment areas was militarily absolutely necessary. The reasons are obvious: NATO states thought it necessary to retain the option of disturbing and delaying the advance of the second and third attack formation of Warsaw Pact armies.[170] The compromise finally agreed upon has been supplemented by further restrictions introduced by the 1996 amendment. Article 6 does not completely ban the use of remotely delivered mines, but it requires the parties to the treaty to take far-reaching precautionary measures and technical safeguards against the risks to the civilian population resulting from such devices,[171] imposing particular limits regarding anti-personnel mines.

2. Thus, the use of remotely delivered mines is prohibited unless they are recorded with the utmost possible precision, specifying the estimated location and area by coordinates of reference points and ascertaining and marking it on the ground at the earliest opportunity.[172] Whereas the legitimacy of the use of remotely delivered anti-personnel mines depends invariably on their compliance with the provisions of self-destruction and self-deactivation laid down in the Technical Annex (see in detail Section 416),[173] other remotely delivered mines are only required, 'to the extent feasible', to be equipped with an effective self-destruction or self-neutralization mechanism and to have a back-up self-deactivation feature.[174]

3. The amended Protocol has not adopted the original rule of Article 5, para. 1, requiring that remotely delivered mines may only be employed within an area which itself constitutes a military objective or which contains military objectives.[175] Although the general prohibition against 'indiscriminate warfare', reaffirmed by Article 3, para. 8, lit. b, leads to the same conclusion, a maintenance of the original provision would have clarified that a purely preventive placement of minefields with a view to potential future operations remains prohibited under the amended Protocol.

4. In order to protect the civilian population against the dangers of remotely delivered mines the party responsible for their use is obliged to give an effective advance warning if the civilian population actually risks damage by such mines.[176] This warning may only be omitted if the specific circumstances of the operation make it impossible (as to the warning prior to an attack in general, see Section 456). It is open to debate, however, in what situations circumstances do not permit a warning. Some authors argue that tactical

[169] See Carnahan, *loc. cit.*, (n. 138) 79–80; Rauch, *loc. cit.*, (n. 143) 269–80.
[170] Such is the reasoning of the German Government's Memorandum, submitted to Parliament before ratification, see BR-Drs. 117/92, 26.
[171] For the compromise character of Article 5, see Roberts, above (n. 24) 576–7.
[172] Article 1, lit. b of the Technical Annex; cf. Bettati, *loc. cit.*, (n. 161) 194.
[173] Article 6, para. 2, MinesProt; see Matheson, *loc. cit.*, (n. 160) 161–2.
[174] Article 6, para. 3, MinesProt; whether this requirement is really mandatory has been disputed with respect to its precedent provision in 1980 MinesProt, see Roberts, above (n. 24) 576–7.
[175] As to the problem what constitutes a military objective in the use of remotely delivered mines, see Würkner-Theis, *op. cit.*, (n. 152) 121–40.
[176] See Rogers, above (n. 77) 138–9.

STEFAN OETER

necessities, such as ensuring surprise or the necessity to protect the delivering aeroplane, may justify a deviation from the basic rule of Article 6, para. 4 Mines Protocol.[177] Whether this is true, or whether Article 6, para. 4 Mines Protocol should not be read more restrictively, remains in dispute.

418   It is prohibited in all circumstances to use:
   a) any booby trap in the form of an apparently harmless portable object (Articles 2, para. 4, and 7, para. 2, MinesProt);
   b) booby traps which are in any way attached to or associated with:
      — internationally recognized protective emblems, signs, or signals;
      — sick, wounded, or dead persons;
      — burial or cremation sites or graves;
      — medical facilities, transportation, equipment, or supplies;
      — food or drink;
      — objects of a religious nature;
      — cultural objects;
      — children's toys and all other objects related to children;
      — animals or their carcasses (Article 7, para. 1, MinesProt); or
   c) any mine, booby trap or other device which is designed or of a nature to cause superfluous injury or unnecessary suffering (Article 3, para. 3, MinesProt).

Article 7 Mines Protocol lays down an absolute prohibition against the use of certain types of booby traps. The humanitarian necessity of such a prohibition was and is undisputed. The so-called 'booby traps', that is devices which are constructed to kill or injure by an explosion initiated unexpectedly 'when a person disturbs or approaches an apparently harmless object or performs an apparently safe act' (the definition in Article 2, para. 4, MinesProt),[178] have gained tragic prominence in recent practice. During the Soviet campaign in Afghanistan, in particular, they were frequently used, despite the pre-existing prohibition in the UN Weapons Convention.[179] Due to their apparent harmlessness, booby traps are extremely dangerous for the civilian population, and their primary effect is to terrorize the civilian population, a purpose strictly prohibited under humanitarian law. Article 7, para. 1, MinesProt enumerates some of the most repellent variants of booby traps, the express prohibition of which should be a matter of common sense.[180] The same is true for the general principle embodied in Article 3, para. 3, which repeats the fundamental prohibition of *maux superflus* in respect of the employment of all weapons covered by the Mines Protocol; already the 1980 version of the Protocol laid down this principle expressly for booby traps.[181] These provisions, and probably all of Article 7 seem to be merely declaratory, since such means and methods of combat are already prohibited under the general rules.

419   This prohibition does not apply to fixed demolition appliances or to portable demolition devices lacking any harmless appearance.

[177] Rogers, above (n. 77) 139.
[178] As to the definition of Article 2, para. 4, MinesProt see Carnahan, *loc. cit.*, (n. 138) 89–90; Boothby, above (n. 51) 166–8.
[179] See the findings of the special rapporteur appointed by the UN Human Rights Commission to investigate human rights violations in Afghanistan, Felix Ermacora, in his report presented in 1988, UN Doc. A/43/742 of 24 October 1988, 23 (paras. 103–4).
[180] See Carnahan, *loc. cit.*, 91–2; Kalshoven, above (n. 9) 255.
[181] See Carnahan, *loc. cit.*, 90; Fenrick, *loc. cit.*, (n. 147) 245; and Sitaropoulos, above (n. 26) 95.

STEFAN OETER

The admissibility of the use of other explosive devices results from the basic approach of Article 7, paras. 1 and 2, MinesProt by way of an *argumentum e contrario*. All fixed demolition appliances, and portable demolition devices not disguised as harmless objects, are permitted, provided that they are immediately recognizable as dangerous devices and have not been heavily camouflaged.[182] Even these demolition devices, however, fall under the general rules of Articles 3 and 7, para. 3, and are therefore covered by the prohibition against indiscriminate warfare as well as that against weapons and munitions which have indiscriminate effects, not to mention the strict limitations on the use of explosive devices in populated areas. In particular, with camouflaged demolition devices which function by an actuating mechanism such as a trip wire, the belligerent parties must take strict precautionary measures, in most cases probably by guarding the appliances in order to prevent triggering of the device by civilian persons not involved in combat.

> **The location of minefields, mines, booby traps, and explosive remnants of war shall be recorded. The parties to the conflict shall retain these records and, whenever possible, by mutual agreement, provide for their publication (Article 9 MinesProt, Article 4 ERWProt).**   420

1. The obligation to record the existence of minefields and booby traps has been significantly strengthened by the 1996 amendment. In contrast to its predecessor, Article 9, para. 1, MinesProt requires the parties to the conflict to record the location of all mines, booby traps, and other devices in all circumstances, and not only in the case of pre-planned minefields and of large-scale pre-planned booby traps.[183] Furthermore, the minimum standards of recording are now laid down in a binding 'Technical Annex' to the Protocol,[184] limiting the required information no longer to the geographic location of minefields, booby traps, and demolition appliances,[185] but including specifications such as to the type, number, and lifetime of the weapons laid.[186]

2. The creation of records not only about location, but also nature, quantity, and patterns of delivery will normally be in the military interest of the parties to the conflict, since systematic mining documentation enables the parties to protect their own armed forces against the dangers arising from uncontrolled minefields.[187] Particularly in the case of complex and rapidly moving combat operations, the armed forces of a belligerent can only be protected against the dangers of minefields placed by allied units if the minefields and booby traps are carefully documented and the mining documentation is systematically collected and administered. An equally strong argument can also be made for extensive documentation concerning the removal of mixed fields which combine anti-tank mines and anti-personnel mines with fragmentation mines; rapid and

---

[182] Dinstein, above (n. 43) 70–2; L. C. Green, *The Contemporary Law of Armed Conflict*, 2nd edn (Manchester University Press, 2000), 139–40.

[183] Dinstein, above (n. 43) 72–3; Peter Herby, 'Troisième session de la Conférence d'examen des États parties à la Convention des Nations Unies de 1980 sur certaines armes classiques: Genève, 22 avril–3 mai 1996' (1996) 78 *RIC* 392; concerning the problematic notion of 'pre-planned minefields', see Carnahan, *loc. cit.*, (n. 138) 84; Fenrick, *loc. cit.*, 245–6.

[184] Concerning the preceding non-binding Technical Annex, see Carnahan, *loc. cit.*, 84–5.

[185] See Carnahan, *loc. cit.*, 84.

[186] Article 1, lit. a(iii) Technical Annex of the MinesProt; Bettati, *loc. cit.*, (n. 161) 195; as to the recording of remotely delivered mines, see Section 416.

[187] See Fenrick, *loc. cit.*, 242–3.

STEFAN OETER

secure removal of such minefields by a different unit from that which planted the field becomes possible only if exact documentation is available on the location and pattern of delivery. Without solid documentation, removal of one's own minefields would endanger engineer units. Thus in the German armed forces it is required that every unit placing a minefield records the necessary information in a standardized document; these documents are continually collected and combined into all-embracing mining documents for the respective territories by territorially competent regional command authorities.[188]

3. After the end of hostilities, the parties are required to take protective measures specified in Article 9, para. 2, MinesProt. In areas under their control, the parties to a conflict must take all feasible measures, including the use of records, to protect the civilian population against danger from minefields and other explosive devices; the military authorities of the occupying powers must mark the minefields, warn the civilian population, and in some cases guard minefields. On the other hand, concerning the areas no longer under their control, the parties shall make available to each other and to the Secretary-General of the UN all information in their possession concerning the location of minefields, mines, and booby traps laid by them in these territories. By imposing this obligation even if parties to the conflict are still in occupation of enemy territory, the amendment has improved the required exchange of information. In these cases, however, the Protocol still allows the parties to withhold such information, subject to reciprocity, as far and as long as security interests require such withholding, at the most until complete withdrawal. In the meantime, they shall seek, 'by mutual agreement, to provide for the release of such information at the earliest possible time in a manner consistent with the security interests of each party'.

4. Apart from the obligation of recording under the Mines Protocol, comparable requirements have recently been laid down in the ERWProt, adopted on 28 November 2003, for the so-called 'explosive remnants of war'.[189] This instrument aims to reduce the civilian casualties and to minimize the socio-economic consequences caused by explosive munitions that remain after the end of an armed conflict.[190] It refers to both international and non-international conflicts and applies to explosive munitions that have been fired, dropped, or otherwise delivered during fighting but have failed to explode, as well as to explosive ordnance that has not been used during fighting and has been left behind, abandoning the control by the party (Article 2, paras. 2–3, ERWProt).[191] Artillery shells, hand grenades, and cluster-bomb submunitions are only some examples of these weapons often found in war-affected countries such as, in the recent past, Iraq after Operation Iraqi Freedom, and Kosovo.[192] By establishing post-war responsibilities for parties who have used such weapons, the Protocol complements pre-existing instruments, designed to reduce the serious dangers faced by the civilian population in post-conflict countries,

---

[188] See, e.g., the Memorandum of the German Government on ratification of the UN Weapons Convention, BR-Drs. 117/92, 27.

[189] Entry into force on 12 November 2006; 78 ratifications in February 2012. Regarding the history, see Boothby, above (n. 51) 299–302.

[190] Louis Maresca, 'A new Protocol on explosive remnants of war: The history and negotiation of Protocol V to the 1980 Convention on Certain Conventional Weapons' (2004) 86 *IRRC* 815.

[191] Maresca, *loc. cit.*, 815–6, 823–5.

[192] Peter Herby/Anna R. Nuiten, 'Explosive remnants of war: Protecting civilians through an additional protocol to the 1980 Convention on Certain Conventional Weapons' (2001) 83 *IRRC* 195–205, at 198–201; Maresca, *loc. cit.*, 816–18.

STEFAN OETER

such as the Amended Mines Protocol and the Landmines Convention.[193] However, the new instrument reveals some potential weaknesses by specifying a considerable number of obligations in a non-binding 'Technical Annex'[194] and employing in many of its key provisions qualifying phrases such as 'as far as feasible' and 'where feasible'. Although these phrases are only intended to provide a certain flexibility, the possible abuse of these clauses risks to affect the effective implementation of the provisions.[195]

5. Article 4, para. 1, ERWProt requires the parties to the conflict to record and retain information on the use or abandonment of explosive ordnance to the maximum extent possible and as far as practicable. The Protocol contains in the aforementioned 'Technical Annex' the minimum standards of recording, including location, types, and number of the explosive ordnance used or abandoned. Paragraph 2 of the provision imposes on the parties to make available such information to the parties in control of the affected area 'without delay after the cessation of active hostilities and as far as practicable, subject to these parties' legitimate security interests'. With respect to the territory under their own control, the parties have to take, according to Article 5, all feasible precautions to protect the civilian population from the risks and effects of explosive remnants of war, including warnings, risk education to the civilian population, marking, fencing, and monitoring of the affected territory.[196]

> When a UN force or mission performs peacekeeping, observation, or similar functions, each party to the conflict shall, if requested:
> — render harmless all mines or booby traps (Article 12, para. 2, lit. b(ii), MinesProt);
> — take such measures as may be necessary to protect the force or mission from the effect of mines, booby traps, and explosive remnants of war while carrying out its duties (Article 12, para. 2, lit. b(i) MinesProt, Article 6, para. 1, lit. a, ERWProt); and
> — make available to the head of the force or mission all pertinent information in the party's possession (Article 12, para. 2, lit. b(iii), MinesProt; Article 6, para. 1, lit. B, ERWProt).
> Likewise, humanitarian and fact-finding missions of the UN System as well as missions of impartial humanitarian organizations shall be protected from the effect of mines, booby traps, and other devices and shall be provided with safe passage (Article 12, paras. 3–5, MinesProt).

421

Besides the general safeguards provided by the prohibitions against indiscriminate warfare, excessive suffering, and perfidious methods of warfare, the Mines Protocol also includes provisions concerning the duty of parties to co-operate with UN forces and missions in respect of mines. The Protocol undoubtedly created new obligations in requiring parties to an armed conflict to protect UN forces and missions against dangers resulting from mines and to assist and co-operate with such forces or missions;[197] the 1996 amendment extended this protection to missions of the ICRC, of national Red Cross and Red Crescent Societies as well as of other impartial humanitarian organizations.[198]

---

[193] However, the Protocol does not contain a prohibition of the use of cluster bombs, which has been adopted later in 2008 (see below Section 458).
[194] Maresca, *loc. cit.*, 823, 828.
[195] Maresca, *loc. cit.*, 834.
[196] Maresca, *loc. cit.*, 827–9.
[197] See Carnahan, *loc. cit.*, (n. 138) 94–5.
[198] Herby, *loc. cit.*, (n. 183) 392.

STEFAN OETER

In a much simpler format, Article 6 ERWProt equally requires the parties to safeguard, 'as far as feasible', humanitarian missions and organizations from the effects of explosive remnants of war.[199] Practical experience has shown that peacekeeping forces and observer missions[200] of the UN, as well as personnel of humanitarian organizations, are particularly endangered by minefields and booby traps, since these units and missions must often move between the lines of the adverse armed forces. Extensive safeguards and protective measures for UN forces and observer missions as well as humanitarian organizations are thus undoubtedly necessary. Of particular relevance is the general duty of the parties to provide to the head of the UN force or mission all available information on the location of minefields, mines, and booby traps in the area concerned.

422   **After the cessation of an international armed conflict, the parties to the conflict shall, both among themselves and, where appropriate, with other states or international organizations, exchange information and technical assistance necessary to remove or otherwise render ineffective minefields, mines, booby traps, and explosive remnants of war (Article 10 MinesProt, Article 3 ERWProt).**

Article 10 of the amended MinesProt underlines the responsibility of the parties to a conflict for the clearance, removal, destruction, or maintenance of all mines, booby traps, and other devices in areas under their control (para. 2) and provides for international co-operation in the removal of minefields after the cessation of active hostilities.[201] The amended provision identifies an explicit responsibility of the users of mines and other devices laid in areas over which they no longer exercise control to provide to the party in control of the area technical and material assistance in the clearance and removal of such weapons (para. 3). For the rest, the parties shall endeavour, according to para. 4, to agree (both among themselves and, where appropriate, with other states and with international organizations) on co-operation in the neutralization and removal of minefields, mines, and booby traps. That agreement should cover the provision of information on the location and nature of minefields and booby traps, and provision of technical and material assistance in the clearance of minefields and the removal of mines and booby traps, including in appropriate circumstances joint operations for removal.[202] Similar requirements are laid down in Article 3 ERWProt with respect to explosive remnants of war.[203] In most cases, the realization of these objectives would constitute a great step forward, particularly in view of the fact that it is normally the civilian population which suffers as a result of lack of co-operation in the neutralization and removal of mines after the cessation of hostilities. The experience of the last decades proves, however, that non-international armed conflicts in practice cause the main problem in this respect; thus, securing implementation and compliance among non-state actors will be a major challenge.[204] Another question remains open to debate, namely how far general standards of customary law prohibiting indiscriminate warfare do also entail responsibilities

[199] Maresca, *loc. cit.*, 829–30.
[200] The provision does not refer to fighting troops of the UN in enforcement operations under Chapter VII; they are probably not protected under this provision—see Carnahan, *loc. cit.*, (n. 138) 95; the explicit reference to missions established under Chapter VIII in Article 12, para. 2, lit. a(ii), of the amended Mines Protocol also indicates this interpretation.
[201] See Würkner-Theis, *op. cit.*, (n. 152) 229–32.
[202] For examples of such agreements see Carnahan, *loc. cit.*, (n. 138) 82–3.
[203] Maresca, *loc. cit.*, 825–7; Boothby, above (n. 51) 305–7.
[204] Maresca, *loc. cit.*, 835.

STEFAN OETER

for the clearance of mines and explosive remnants of war, as long as the explicit treaty provisions do not apply.[205]

> **Incendiary weapons are weapons or munitions primarily designed to set fire to**   **423**
> **materials or objects or to cause burn injury to persons through the action of flame,**
> **heat, or a combination thereof. Examples are: flame-throwers, fougasses (hand-**
> **held weapons containing liquid incendiaries), shells, rockets, grenades, mines,**
> **bombs, and other containers of incendiary substances (Article 1, para. 1, lit. a,**
> **IncendiariesProt).**

One of the main topics of the 1980 UN Weapons Conference was the issue of incendiary weapons (the US Air Force use of napalm bombs in Vietnam were still fresh in the memory).[206] Some of the states participating at the conference (including Sweden, Mexico, and the majority of the non-aligned states) demanded a complete ban on incendiary weapons, for these weapons—such was the argument—always cause unnecessary suffering and generally have also indiscriminate effects;[207] but the superpowers, led by the US and the USSR, openly declared that—due to the military importance of incendiary weapons—they would accept, at the maximum, a few (and limited) restrictions on the use of such weapons.[208] The traditional military powers thought these weapons to be militarily absolutely necessary to attack certain objectives, and particularly specific operations such as 'close air support' in the combat zone against immediately adjacent enemy positions.[209] A compromise only became possible when the delegation of the US began to request a prohibition of all air-launched attacks by incendiary weapons (including napalm) in settlements and populated areas, thus providing an opening for the resumption of the stalled negotiations.[210] The resulting definition of the incendiary weapons covered by Protocol III of the WeaponsConv is extremely broad, since it includes not only incendiary materials based on hydrocarbon (like napalm) but also all means of combat designed to set fire to objects or to cause burn injury to persons through the action of flame, heat, or a combination thereof.[211] The only important factor in the definition is the causation of burns through chemical reaction of a substance brought on the target.

> **Incendiary weapons do not include:**   **424**
> — munitions which may have incidental incendiary effects (e.g. illuminants, trac-
>   ers, smoke, or signalling systems, Article 1, para. 1, lit. b(i), IncendiariesProt);
>   or
> — munitions designed to combine penetration, blast, or fragmentation effects
>   with an additional incendiary effect (e.g. armour-piercing projectiles, fragmen-
>   tation shells, explosive bombs). The incendiary effect shall only be used against
>   military objectives (Article 1, para. 1, lit. b (ii), IncendiariesProt).

---

[205] See Rule 83 *CIHL*; Maresca, *loc. cit.*, 826–33.

[206] Concerning the military background to the use of incendiary weapons, see Fenrick, *loc. cit.*, 247.

[207] See, e.g., the Memorandum of the German Government on ratification of the UN Weapons Convention, BR-Drs. 117/92, 27; see also Fenrick, *loc. cit.*, 248; Kalshoven, above (n. 9) 256–7; W. Hays Parks, 'Le protocole sur les armes incendiaires' (1990) 72 *RIC* 588–94.

[208] Ibid.

[209] See, in particular, Fenrick, *loc. cit.*, 247–8; Sitaropoulos, above (n. 26) 96; cf. also the Memorandum of the German Government on ratification of the UN Weapons Convention, BR-Drs. 117/92, 27.

[210] See, e.g., the Memorandum of the German Government *loc. cit.*, 27 and Fenrick, *loc. cit.*, 248.

[211] On the definition of Article 1, para. 1, see Kalshoven, *loc. cit.*, (n. 9); Fenrick, *loc. cit.*, 248; Parks, *loc. cit.*, 594–5; Boothby, above (n. 51) 200–5.

STEFAN OETER

Article 1, para. 1, of the Protocol excludes from its definition of 'incendiary weapons' all means of combat which produce burns only as a side effect of a different primary objective (like illuminants, smoke, or signalling systems).[212] It also excludes weapons which cause burns only as part of an integrated mode of action mainly involving other mechanisms, that is munitions not specifically designed to cause burn injury to persons (like anti-tank munitions with an armour-piercing projectile working by extremely high temperature, or fragmentation shells and explosive bombs which combine penetration, blast, or fragmentation effects with an additional incendiary effect).[213] The exclusion of such munitions makes sense in the light of the overall objective of the Protocol, since such munitions with a combined effect are normally used for operation against 'hard' military targets, and not against persons.[214]

425   **When incendiary weapons are used, all precautions shall be taken which are practicable or practically possible, taking into account all the current circumstances, including humanitarian and military considerations (Article 1, para. 5, IncendiariesProt).**

The parties to an armed conflict are already obliged, under the general rules on weapons and means of combat, to take all precautions which are practically possible in order to protect civilians or civilian objects from unnecessary damage (Article 57 AP I; see Section 457). Article 1, para. 5, defines exactly what are 'practically possible precautions' for the purpose of Weapons Protocol III: namely, those precautions which are 'practicable or practically possible, taking into account all circumstances ruling at the time, including humanitarian and military considerations'. Responsible military leaders must with all due diligence take such precautions before an attack, because the risks of indiscriminate effects are extremely high in the case of attack with incendiary weapons. This is particularly the case in attacks on settlements and other concentrations of civilian population; Article 2, para. 3, IncendiariesProt requires explicitly that parties take 'all feasible precautions'. That formula requires particular precautions to limit the incendiary effects on the military objective. However, attacks with incendiary weapons *outside* any concentration of civilians also requires a considerable degree of diligence, even if the Protocol on Incendiary Weapons is not intended to protect combatants.

426   **The civilian population, individual civilians, and civilian objects shall be granted special protection. They shall not be made the object of attack by incendiary weapons (Article 2, para. 1, IncendiariesProt).**

Article 2, para. 1 of the Protocol repeats the prohibition of deliberate attacks on civilians and civilian objects (particularly, the prohibition of terrorizing attacks) and directs this general prohibition explicitly to the use of incendiary weapons. Thus, the provision merely repeats the self-evident, elementary minimum standards of modern humanitarian law which can be deduced directly from Article 51, para. 2, AP I[215] (see Section 454).

---

[212] Fenrick, *loc. cit.*, 248; Parks, *loc. cit.*, 596; Dinstein, above (n. 43) 78.

[213] See Fenrick, *loc. cit.*, 249; Kalshoven/Zegveld, above (n. 22) 179; Parks, *loc. cit.*, 597–8; Green, *op. cit.*, (n. 182) 141.

[214] See, e.g., the Memorandum of the German Government on ratification of the UN Weapons Convention, BR-Drs. 117/92, 27.

[215] Dinstein, above (n. 43) 77, claims that the provision is, strictly speaking, a redundant reaffirmation.

STEFAN OETER

It is prohibited under any circumstances to make any military objective located   427
within a concentration of civilians the object of attack by incendiary weapons
(Article 2, paras. 2 and 3, IncendiariesProt).

1. Strictly speaking the Protocol on Incendiary Weapons distinguishes in its substantial provisions between incendiary weapons delivered by the air (e.g. the notorious
napalm bombs) and other incendiary weapons used on land. Concerning attacks with
air-delivered incendiary weapons, Article 2, para. 2 of the Protocol sets up an absolute
prohibition against attacks on any objective located within a concentration of civilian
population.[216] Attacks with other incendiary weapons are, in principle, also prohibited
inside settlements and other concentrations of civilian population; however, under certain conditions specified in Article 2, para. 3 they remain admissible, namely insofar
as the attack is directed against a military objective which is clearly separate from the
concentration of civilians and provided that all feasible precautions are taken to limit the
incendiary effects so that they damage only the military objective, and to avoid, or to
minimize, incidental loss of life and incidental damage to civilian objects.[217]

2. These restrictions on the use of incendiary weapons undoubtedly constitute the core
of the Protocol. The civilian population is protected against attacks by incendiary weapons (and, in particular, by incendiary bombs) within its cities, villages, and comparable
settlements. At the same time, military necessity is respected by delimiting the object
of protection not in purely spatial terms, but in qualitative aspects. Not every area of a
settlement is protected, only the concentration of civilians within that settlement. This
means that attacks on important military objectives remain legally possible under certain conditions, even if they are located within inhabited areas, as long as these military
objectives are not inseparably linked to real concentrations of civilian population (as
would be probably: harbour facilities, airports, fuel and munition depots, anti-aircraft
gun positions inside large parks, etc.).[218]

It is further prohibited to use incendiary weapons against forests or other kinds of   428
plant cover except when such natural elements are used by the adversary to cover,
conceal, or camouflage a military objective, or are themselves military objectives
(Article 2, para. 4, IncendiariesProt).

In this rule Protocol III clearly exceeds its original objective of protection, that is the
prohibitions against unnecessary suffering and indiscriminate warfare. The provision
was included in the Protocol following a proposal by the USSR (supported by numerous
Third World states). It extends the scope of protection to certain kinds of natural plant
cover, in particular forests.[219] The provision is not problematic in military terms, since it
explicitly excludes protection in all cases in which flora is used to conceal military objectives, or in which natural cover itself constitutes a military objective.[220] The provision
exceeds even the scope of Articles 35, para. 3, and 55, para. 1, AP I and the ENMOD

[216] Concerning the complicated drafting history of that provision, see Kalshoven, above (n. 9) 258–9;
Fenrick, *loc. cit.*, 248; Parks, *loc. cit.*, 591–4, 600–1.
[217] See, e.g., the Memorandum of the German Government on ratification of the UN Weapons
Convention, BR-Drs. 117/92, 28; see also Parks, *loc. cit.*, 602.
[218] See Fenrick, *loc. cit.*, 249; Green, *op. cit.*, (n. 182) 141; cf. also the Memorandum of the German
Government on ratification of the UN Weapons Convention, BR-Drs. 117/92, 27.
[219] See Fenrick, *loc. cit.*, 250; cf. also the Memorandum of the German Government, *loc. cit.*, 28.
[220] See the Memorandum of the German Government, *loc. cit.*, 28.

STEFAN OETER

Convention, in that it is designed to cover isolated attacks on the natural environment even if these are spatially limited, in contrast to the general prohibitions of environmentally damaging warfare, see below, Sections 467–469.

429 **It is prohibited to employ laser weapons specifically designed, as their sole combat function or as one of their combat functions, to cause permanent blindness to unenhanced vision (Article 1 LasersProt).**

1. The Protocol on Blinding Laser Weapons adopted on 13 October 1995 as Protocol IV to the 1980 Weapons Convention[221] presents the first instrument after the 1868 St Petersburg Declaration banning a weapon of military interest before being used on the battlefield.[222] Laser Systems have become prevalently used for functions such as target marking or projectile guidance; however, when the laser beam hits a human eye, this can have a temporary or permanent blinding effect.[223] As permanent blinding cannot be military necessary, but inflicts superfluous injury or unnecessary suffering, the prohibition laid down in the Lasers Protocol is fully justified.[224] Due to the amendment of Article 1, para. 2, Inhumane WeaponsConv as of 21 December 2001, the Protocol also applies to non-international conflicts.

2. According to Article 1, the employment and transfer of laser weapons specifically designed, as their sole combat function or as one of their combat functions, to cause permanent blindness to unenhanced vision, that is to the naked eye or to the eye with corrective eyesight devices, is prohibited.[225] 'Permanent blindness' is defined in Article 4 as 'irreversible and uncorrectable loss of vision which is seriously disabling with no prospect of recovery'. Article 3 states that blinding as an incidental or collateral effect of the employment of laser systems, including systems used against optical equipment,[226] is not covered by the prohibition. However, Article 2 requires the contracting parties to take all feasible precautions, including training of their armed forces, to avoid the incidence of permanent blindness to unenhanced vision.

430 **It is prohibited to employ poison and poisoned weapons (Article 23, lit. a, HagueReg).**

The prohibition against poison referred to above is probably the most ancient prohibition of a means of combat in international law.[227] Since the late Middle Ages, the use of poison has always been strictly prohibited. With Article 23, lit. a of the Hague Regulations that firmly established prohibition was codified in an international treaty.[228] Beyond any doubt, the ancient prohibition of poison is still valid today.

---

[221] Entry into force: 30 July 1998; in detail, see Markus C. Zöckler, 'Laserwaffen und humanitäres Völkerrecht' in Bruno Simma/Constanze Schulte (eds), *Völker- und Europarecht in der aktuellen Diskussion: Akten des 23. Österreichischen Völkerrechtstages* (Wien: Linde Verlag. 1999). 191–212.

[222] Boothby, above (n. 51) 209.

[223] Kalshoven/Zegveld above (n. 22) 180; Zöckler *loc. cit.*, 194–7.

[224] Dinstein, above (n. 43) 79.

[225] Concerning the debated interpretation of the notion 'specifically designed', see Zöckler in Simma/Schulte (eds), *loc. cit.*, 205–6; Boothby, above (n. 51) 210.

[226] The scope of this exception remains disputed: Doswald-Beck, 'Le nouveau Protocole sur les armes à laser aveuglantes', 78 *RIC* (1996), 314; Zöckler in Simma/Schulte (eds), 208.

[227] See Sandoz, above (n. 9) 11–14; Green, *op. cit.*, (n. 182) 142; Boothby, above (n. 51) 117.

[228] Concerning Article 23, lit. a, HagueReg and the problem of defining exactly what constitutes 'poison', see Sandoz, above (n. 9) 27–8.

STEFAN OETER

2. Weapons of Mass Destruction

a. *Nuclear weapons*

Numerous multilateral and bilateral treaties already exist which are designed to   431
prohibit the proliferation of nuclear weapons, to restrict the testing of nuclear
weapons, to prohibit the stationing of nuclear weapons, to provide for nuclear
weapon-free zones, to limit the scope of nuclear armament, and to prevent the
outbreak of nuclear war. These include:

— Treaty on the Non-Proliferation of Nuclear Weapons (NPT) of 1 July 1968;
— Treaty Banning Nuclear Weapon Tests in the Atmosphere, in Outer Space, and
  under Water (Partial Nuclear Test Ban Treaty) of 5 August 1963;
— Treaty on Principles Governing the Activities of States in the Exploration and
  Use of Outer Space, including the Moon and Other Celestial Bodies (Outer
  Space Treaty) of 27 January 1967;
— Treaty on the Prohibition of the Emplacement of Nuclear Weapons and Other
  Weapons of Mass Destruction on the Seabed and the Ocean Floor and the
  Subsoil Thereof (Seabed Treaty) of 11 February 1971;
— Treaty for the Prohibition of Nuclear Weapons in Latin America (Treaty of
  Tlatelolco) of 14 February 1967;
— South Pacific Nuclear-Free Zone Treaty (Treaty of Rarotonga) of 6 August
  1985;
— Treaty on the Elimination of American and Soviet Intermediate-Range and
  Shorter-Range Missiles of 8 December 1987;
— Treaty on the Southeast Asia Nuclear Weapon-Free Zone (Treaty of Bangkok)
  of 15 December 1995;
— African Nuclear-Weapon-Free Zone Treaty (Treaty of Pelindaba) of 11 April
  1996;
— Comprehensive Nuclear-Test-Ban Treaty of 24 September 1996; and
— Treaty on a Nuclear-Weapon-Free Zone in Central Asia (Treaty of Semipalatinsk)
  of 8 September 2006.

1. Nuclear weapons belong to the category of weapons of mass destruction (WMD).
In 1948, the Commission for Conventional Armaments determined that weapons of
mass destruction should be defined as 'atomic explosive weapons, radio-active material
weapons, lethal chemical and biological weapons, and any weapons developed in the
future which have characteristics comparable in destructive effect to those of the atomic
bomb or other weapons mentioned above.'[229] Today, they are simply defined as nuclear,
chemical, and biological weapons.[230]

2. When dealing with weapons of mass destruction, and in particular with nuclear
weapons, one should bear in mind that production and possession of nuclear weapons
are primarily issues of arms control, and not questions of humanitarian law. However,
the possibility of the future use of nuclear weapons obviously has an important humanitarian aspect which makes it impossible to relegate the subject matter to be dealt with
according to the usual political calculations of arms control treaties. Nuclear weapons
are also of extreme importance for modern security policy, a policy that is embedded
in a system of deterrence backed by the threat of mutual destruction. Accordingly, the
question of the military-technical balance of powers is so weighty that it must be seen as

---

[229] Cf. UN Doc. A/RES/32/84B of 12 December 1977.
[230] Hendrik A. Strydom, 'Weapons of Mass Destruction', *MPEPIL*, para. 2,

legitimate for the superpowers (as well as for the international community) to evaluate, primarily as a matter of security policy, whether and to what degree production and possession of nuclear weapons should be limited.[231] The regulatory instruments of bans and limitations of nuclear armaments are therefore arms control treaties, and not primarily the humanitarian rules of the Geneva Conventions and the Additional Protocols. Over the last decades, states have concluded a whole network of treaties concerning nuclear arms control and disarmament on the global as well as the regional level; the most important of these treaties are listed above.[232]

3. As a first step, a definition and differentiation of the different kinds of weapons of mass destruction has to be evaluated.

432   **The international law in force, however, does not contain any explicit prohibition against the use of nuclear weapons, nor can any such prohibition be derived from current contractual or customary law.**

1. The principle formulated above deals with what is probably the most delicate question of current humanitarian law. For decades, the question of whether the use of nuclear weapons is permissible has placed state practice and international doctrine in a kind of religious war, leaving unresolved the problem of whether humanitarian law implicitly answers the question of legality of possession, and especially of use of nuclear weapons.[233] It is indisputable that customary law imposes limitations on the use of nuclear weapons in specific situations. It is not clear, however, whether one can deduce from these traditional restrictions on methods and means of warfare a comprehensive prohibition of nuclear weapons as such. Under merely quantitative criteria the above formulated (official) position of the Federal Republic of Germany (and of the other NATO states) probably now constitutes a minority position, since the number of doctrinal studies attempting to prove an absolute prohibition on the use of nuclear weapons is overwhelming.[234] Whether the arguments of these studies are really convincing in the perspective of current state practice, however, remains open to doubt. Neither the claim that there exists a customary prohibition, founded mainly upon the principle of 'limited warfare' and the resulting prohibition of indiscriminate warfare,[235] nor the attempt to derive a general conventional prohibition

---

[231] As to the eminently political character of these treaties, see Wolfgang Graf Vitzthum, 'Rechtsfragen der Rüstungskontrolle im Vertragsvölkerrecht der Gegenwart', *Berichte der Deutschen Gesellschaft für Völkerrecht Heft* 30 (C. F. Müller, 1990), 95–149, at 110–14.

[232] For a comprehensive study on the current system of arms control treaties, see Bothe, ibid. 36–79; Guido Dekker, *The Law of Arms Control: International Supervision and Enforcement* (Nijhoff, 2001); International Law Association, *Final Report of the Committee on Arms Control and Disarmament Law*, Report of the 71st Conference, Berlin, 2004.

[233] Concerning the course of debates in the relevant international forums, see the instructive presentation by Kalshoven, above (n. 9) 271–83.

[234] See Georg Schwarzenberger, *The Legality of Nuclear Weapons* (London: Stevens, 1958), 35–49; Ian Brownlie, 'Some Legal Aspects of the Use of Nuclear Weapons' (1965) 14 *ICLQ* 437–51; Erik Castrén, 'The Illegality of Nuclear Weapons' (1971) 3 *University of Toledo Law Review* 89–98; Sandoz, above (n. 9) 62–74; R. Falk/H. Meyrowitz/J. Sanderson, 'Nuclear Weapons and International Law' (1980) 20 *Indian Journal of International Law* 561–95; Eric David, 'A propos de certaines justifications théoriques à l'emploi de David', above (n. 56) 339–44; Robert Kolb, *Ius in Bello*, 2nd edn (Helbing Lichtenhahn/Bruylant, 2009), 302–5; Charles J. Moxley, *Nuclear Weapons and International Law in the Post Cold War World* (Austin & Winfield, 2000), 651–727.

[235] See, in particular, N. Singh/E. McWhinney, *Nuclear Weapons and Contemporary International Law*, 2nd edn (Nijhoff, 1989), 313–9, for further references; Moxley, *loc. cit.*, 699.

STEFAN OETER

from the ban on the use of poisonous gases in the Hague Regulations (Article 23a) and the Geneva Gas Protocol of 1925[236] is really convincing. This position has been confirmed by the ICJ in its Advisory Opinion on Nuclear Weapons, as the Court—particularly by referring to 'the fundamental right of every State to survival, and thus its right to resort to self-defence, in accordance with Article 51 of the Charter, when its survival is at stake'—did not consider itself as enabled 'to conclude with certainty that the use of nuclear weapons would necessarily be at variance with the principles and rules of law applicable in armed conflict in any circumstance'.[237]

2. The argument that a customary prohibition on the use of nuclear weapons exists has two important weaknesses. First, the principle of distinction between combatants and civilians and the corresponding prohibition of indiscriminate warfare, which were rooted solely in customary law until their codification in AP I, present rather blurred contours in practice (see Sections 442, 454, and 457–460). It is certainly possible to find a consensus that there exists such a principle; the ICJ in its Advisory Opinion even regarded the use of nuclear weapons as 'scarcely reconcilable' with respect for the requirement of distinction and for the prohibition against unnecessary suffering.[238] It is hopelessly disputed, however, how far the normative effects of the principle of distinction reach and to what extent it effectively prohibits belligerents from using certain weapons. Even the general prohibition on indiscriminate target-area bombardment, affirmed in principle by so many authors, has always remained in dispute in that a real consensus has never been reached on the extent of permissible collateral damages.[239]

3. At the same time, the argument that the use of nuclear weapons per se constitutes prohibited indiscriminate warfare is founded on an image of nuclear war which perhaps had some justification in the era of the doctrine of 'massive retaliation', but which fails to appreciate the current options of use, which include militarily targeted employment of precision-guided warheads with limited destruction capability. The option most likely

---

[236] See also Singh/McWhinney, 307–12, for further references.

[237] *ICJ Reports 1996*, 262–3 (paras. 95–6); for general discussions of the Advisory Opinion, see Dapo Akande, 'Nuclear Weapons, Unclear Law? Deciphering the Nuclear Weapons Advisory Opinion of the International Court' (1997) 68 *BYIL* 165–217; Bothe, 'Nuklearstrategie nach dem IGH-Gutachten?' (1996) 71 *Friedens-Warte* 249–59; John Burroughs, *The Legality of Threat of Use of Nuclear Weapons: A Guide to the Historic Opinion of the International Court of Justice* (Münster: Lit-Verlag, 1997); Luigi Condorelli, 'La Cour internationale de Justice sous le poids des armes nucléaires: Jura non novit curia?' (1997) *RIC* 79 9–21; Yoram Dinstein, *War, Aggression and Self-Defence*, 4th edn (CUP, 2005), 161–2; Richard Falk, 'Nuclear Weapons, International Law, and the World Court: An Historic Encounter' (1996) 71 *Friedens-Warte* 235–48; Terry D. Gill, 'The Nuclear Weapons Advisory Opinion of the International Court of Justice and the Fundamental Distinction Between the Jus ad Bellum and the Jus in Bello' (1999) 12 *Leiden Journal of International Law* 613–24; Christopher Greenwood, 'Jus ad bellum and jus in bello in the Nuclear Weapons Advisory Opinion' in Laurence Boisson de Chazournes/Philippe Sands (eds), *International Law, the International Court of Justice and Nuclear Weapons* (CUP, 1999), 259–66; Michael J. Matheson, 'The Opinions of the International Court of Justice on the Threat or Use of Nuclear Weapons' (1997) 91 *AJIL* 417–35; Rein Müllerson, in Boisson de Chazournes/Sands, *op. cit.*, 267–74; Ved P. Nanda/David Krieger, 'Nuclear Weapons and the World Court' (Transnational Publishers, 1998), 105–47; Michael N. Schmitt, 'The International Court of Justice and the Use of Nuclear Weapons' (1998) 51 *Naval War College Review* 91–116.

[238] *ICJ Reports 1996*, 262 (para. 95); see Burroughs, *op. cit.*, 32–7; Manfred Mohr, 'Avis consultatif de la Cour internationale de Justice sur la licéité de l'emploi d'armes nucléaires: Quelques réflexions sur ses points forts et ses points faibles' (1998) *RIC* 79 107–8.

[239] See James M. Spaight, *Air Power and War Rights*, 3rd edn (Longmans, 1947), 270–8, 280–1; Julius Stone, *Legal Controls of International Conflict* (Stevens, 1954), 627–31; Morris Greenspan, *The Modern Law of Land Warfare* (University of California Press, 1959), 336; Hans Blix, 'Area Bombardment: Rules and Reasons' (1978) IXL *BYIL* 54–61; Sassòli, above (n. 11) 409–11.

STEFAN OETER

to be adopted under the current operational doctrine, use of precision-guided tactical nuclear warheads in limited operations against purely military objectives, would result in consequences which cannot be adequately dealt with by a broad reference to principles such as the prohibition of indiscriminate warfare and the protection of the civilian population. The collateral damage likely to be caused by such attacks is not necessarily much higher than the damage to be expected from modern conventional weapons, which are now designed to create comparable explosive force.[240] This question was also raised by the ICJ in its Advisory Opinion, but the Court finally refrained from assessing on the legality of the 'clean' use of smaller, low-yield, tactical nuclear weapons.[241]

4. As a consequence, only one conclusion seems possible: even taking into consideration the implications of the Nuclear Weapons Advisory Opinion, the claimed customary prohibition on the use of nuclear weapons is more an aspiration *de lege ferenda* founded in natural law theory and moral philosophy than a definite provision of positive customary international law derived from state practice and *opinio juris*.[242] This does not mean, however, that no legal limitations to the use of nuclear weapons follow from the prohibition of 'indiscriminate attack': on the contrary it must be stressed that legal limits *in concreto* may be deduced from the general rules on means and methods of warfare, notwithstanding that these limits are only relevant as to the concrete fashion in which the weapons are employed, and do not constitute an absolute prohibition on any one category of weapons.[243]

5. Comparable objections should be raised against broad generalizations which assume that nuclear weapons always qualify as 'poisonous weapons' in the sense of Article 23, lit. a, HagueReg, or as 'poisonous gases' in the sense of the Geneva Protocol of 1925.[244] Admittedly, both notions were deliberately expressed in an 'open' fashion, in order to cover future advances in weapons technology. At the same time, however, it is beyond doubt that

---

[240] As to the compatibility of certain uses of nuclear weapons with the general humanitarian requirement to distinguish between combatants and civilians, see Martin C. Ney, *Der Einsatz von Atomwaffen im Lichte des Völkerrechts* (Frankfurt a. M.: Lang, 1985), 276–81, 285, 292–8; Henri Meyrowitz, 'Quel droit de la guerre pour l'OTAN?' (1986) 17 *Etudes Internationales* 549–69, at 560–2; Fleck, 'NATO-Strategie und Völkerrecht' (1987) 29 *NZWehrr* 221–9.

[241] *ICJ Reports 1996*, 262 (para. 94); see Bothe, 'Nuklearstrategie nach dem IGH-Gutachten?' (1996) 71 *Friedens-Warte* 254–5; Simon Chesterman, 'The International Court of Justice, Nuclear Weapons and the Law' (1997) 44 *Netherlands International Law Review* 158–9; John H. McNeill, 'L'avis consultatif de la Cour internationale de Justice en l'affaire des armes nucléaires: Première évaluation' (1997) 79 *RIC* 110–26, at 123; as to the implications of the Court's Advisory Opinion on the controlled use of precision-guided nuclear weapons in limited operations, see Gill, above (n. 237) 622–3.

[242] To the same conclusion come H. Lauterpacht (ed.), *Oppenheim's International Law*, Vol. II: *Disputes, War and Neutrality*, 7th edn (David McKay, 1952), 351; Stone, above (n. 239) 343–8; R. Tucker, *The Law of War and Neutrality at Sea* (US Government Printing Office, 1957), 50–5; M. S. McDougal/J. P. Feliciano, 'International Coercion and World Public Order: The General Principles of the Law of War' (1958) 67 *Yale Law Journal* 771–845, at 830–1; Ney, above (n. 240) 292–3; Kalshoven, above (n. 9) 286–8; Pilloud/ Pictet, in *ICRC Commentary*, para. 1857; O. E. Bring/H. B. Reimann, 'Redressing a Wrong Question: The 1977 Protocols Additional to the 1949 Geneva Conventions and the Issue of Nuclear Weapons' (1986) 33 *Netherlands International Law Review* 99; L. C. Green, 'Nuclear Weapons and the Law of Armed Conflict' (1988) 17 *Denver Journal of International Law and Policy* 1–27; C. Greenwood, 'Jus ad bellum and jus in bello in the Nuclear Weapons Advisory Opinion' in Boisson de Chazournes, above (n. 237) 264–6.

[243] See esp. Bring/Reimann, 99–105; cf. Kalshoven, above (n. 9) 286–7 and the *US Naval Manual*, para 10.2.1; Green, *Essays on the Modern Law of War*, 2nd edn (Transnational Publishers, 1999), 161; Greenwood, 'L'avis consultatif sur les armes nucléaires et la contribution de la Cour internationale de Justice au droit international humanitaire' (1997) 79 *RIC*; McNeill, above (n. 241) 124; Matheson, above (n. 237) 428.

[244] So argue, e.g., Schwarzenberger, above (n. 234) 48; Sandoz, above (n. 9) 62–5; Falk/Meyrowitz/ Sanderson, above (n. 234) 561 *et seq.*; Singh/McWhinney, above (n. 235) 307–12.

STEFAN OETER

new means of combat were intended to be covered by these 'open' provisions only to the extent that the physical effects of such weapons are subject to the same principles as the means of warfare originally covered by the ban. However, it is precisely this comparability of operating principles which may be doubted with plausible arguments concerning nuclear weapons. The physical destruction of enemy objectives by nuclear weapons relies on the same effects as the operation of conventional explosive warheads, namely the results of the explosion (i.e. the pressure wave and subsequent burn effects), whereas the release of poison is an unintended side effect. In this respect, the use of nuclear weapons is different from the use of 'poison' or 'poisonous gases' which are by definition intentionally designed to cause poisoning.[245] Only in so far as nuclear weapons are also designed intentionally to cause poisoning (or radiation) as the primary instrument to weaken the enemy, as with the so-called 'neutron bomb', can one argue plausibly for a 'progressive' and 'dynamic' interpretation which extends the scope of these provisions to cover recent weapons.[246]

> International humanitarian law imposes the same general limits on the use of   433
> nuclear weapons as on the use of conventional weapons: it is prohibited to make
> the civilian population the object of attack. A distinction shall at all times be made
> between persons who take part in hostilities and members of the civilian popula-
> tion, who are to be granted maximum protection.

To conclude that the general rules of customary and convention law impose no absolute prohibition on the use of nuclear weapons is not to say that the use of nuclear weapons is free of all legal limitation. On the contrary: nobody has ever claimed seriously that the traditional principles concerning warfare and weapons have been derogated as regards nuclear weapons; such a claim could not be argued plausibly.[247] This leads to the conclusion that the above-mentioned general rules of customary law are applicable also to the use of nuclear weapons. The most important consequence of this is that the general prohibition of indiscriminate warfare must cover the use of nuclear weapons. Nuclear weapons may be employed only under strictly specified conditions and only after taking restrictive precautions to restrict their effect on civilians (except in reprisal, so far as reprisals are permissible,[248] see Sections 485–488). First use, or use beyond the law of reprisals, is only permissible for modern, precision-guided munitions furnished with nuclear warheads which are employed against military objects and concentrations of armed forces in uninhabited or sparsely populated areas. Care must always be taken to ensure that the pressure wave, the consequent burn effects, and the radioactive fallout cause the minimum possible damage or injury to the civilian population as well as to the environment (as to the principle of proportionality, see Section 459).[249]

---

[245] For the same conclusions, see Kalshoven, above (n. 9) 283–4; Ney, above (n. 240) 186–91, 290–1; Matheson, above (n. 237) 424–5; ICJ, Advisory Opinion on Nuclear Weapons, *ICJ Reports 1996*, 248 (paras. 54–6).

[246] See the detailed analysis by Ney, 188–9, 291; see also US Department of the Army Pamphlet FM 27-161-2, *International Law*, Vol. II (1962), 43.

[247] See Meyrowitz, above (n. 240) 553–5; Hisakazu Fujita, 'Au sujet de l'avis consultatif de la Cour internationale de Justice rendu sur la licéité des armes nucléaires' (1997) 79 *RIC* 60–9, at 61–2; Greenwood, above (n. 242) 259; McNeill, above (n. 241) 121–2; ICJ, Advisory Opinion on Nuclear Weapons, *ICJ Reports 1996*, 259 (paras. 85–6).

[248] See esp. Kalshoven, above (n. 9) 286 and Kalshoven, *Belligerent Reprisals*, 2nd edn (Nijhoff, 2005), 353–61.

[249] For comparable conclusions, see Dinstein, above (n. 43) 86; Schmitt, above (n. 237) 108; for the significance of the environment, see *ICJ Reports 1996*, 242–3 (paras. 30–3); Akande, above (n. 237) 182–9; Djamchid Momtaz, 'The use of nuclear weapons and the protection of the environment: the contribution

434   The new rules introduced by Additional Protocol I were intended to apply to con-
       ventional weapons, irrespective of other rules of international law applicable to
       other types of weapons. They do not influence, regulate, or prohibit the use of
       nuclear weapons.

1. When the original draft of the Additional Protocols was presented, and during the later negotiations at the Diplomatic Conference in Geneva 1974–1977, there was intense controversy over whether the new Convention should also cover the use of nuclear weapons. The position of the ICRC and of the most important military powers was, from the beginning, that the Additional Protocol should not affect nuclear weaponry.[250] Accordingly, at the opening of the negotiations in 1974 the mandate of the Diplomatic Conference had been restricted to conventional weapons.

2. Most of the NATO allies have stressed this precondition of consent by submitting a corresponding declaration upon its ratification of AP I. The German declaration says: 'It is the understanding of the Federal Republic of Germany that the rules relating to the use of weapons introduced by Additional Protocol I were intended to apply exclusively to conventional weapons without prejudice to any other rules of international law applicable to other types of weapons.'[251] The German government thus implicitly refers to the declarations filed by the US and the UK when signing the Additional Protocols.[252] In these 1977 declarations the nuclear powers explicitly referred to the general 'nuclear consensus' which existed at the outset of the negotiations,[253] a general understanding which purported to exclude discussion on nuclear weapons from the negotiations.

3. This limitation of the negotiations may be explained by the original negotiating proposal of the ICRC. In its introduction is the following formula concerning the question of nuclear weapons: 'Problems relating to atomic, bacteriological and chemical warfare are subjects of international agreements or negotiations by governments, and in submitting these draft Protocols the ICRC does not intend to broach these problems.'[254]

4. In the course of the Diplomatic Conference of 1974–1977, the US, Great Britain, and France repeatedly stressed the limitation of the negotiations, while other states openly attempted to extend the scope of Additional Protocol I to include express regulation concerning nuclear weapons. However, those attempts to take up the question of nuclear warfare finally failed. Nevertheless, no formal agreement on the scope of application could be reached until the end of the conference, which was why the US and Great Britain annexed their declarations to the Treaty on the occasion of its signature.[255]

---

of the International Court of Justice' in Boisson de Chazournes/Sands, above (n. 237) 354–74; Schmitt, 'Future War and the Principle of Discrimination' (1998) 28 *IsrYHR* 59–60.

[250] For a description of the historical background, see Kalshoven, above (n. 9) 278–83 and Pilloud/Pictet, *ICRC Commentary*, paras. 1842–6.

[251] Published in *BGBl* 1991 II, 968.

[252] Printed in Bothe/Partsch/Solf, above (n. 41) 190, 721–2.

[253] See Meyrowitz, 'Le statut des armes nucléaires en droit international' (1982) 25 *GYIL* 229–37, and Kalshoven, above (n. 9) 282–3.

[254] Printed in Bothe/Partsch/Solf, above (n. 41) 188–9; as to the background of the exclusion of NBC weapons from the negotiations, see Kalshoven, *loc. cit.*, 271–82.

[255] As to the history of the negotiations see Solf, in Bothe/Partsch/Solf, above (n. 41) 188–92; Ney, above (n. 240) 193–209; Pilloud/Pictet, in *ICRC Commentary*, paras. 1839–51.

STEFAN OETER

5. By these declarations the so-called 'nuclear consensus' has become directly relevant to the interpretation of the Treaty, because all treaties shall be, according to Article 31, para. 1 of the Vienna Convention on the Law of Treaties of 1969, 'interpreted in good faith in accordance with the ordinary meaning to be given to the terms of the treaty in their context'. Pursuant to Paragraph 2 of Article 31 of that Convention the context there is included *in the list of matters* relevant to the interpretation of a treaty provision, in addition to the text (including any preamble and annexes), and 'any instrument which was made by one or more parties in connexion with the conclusion of the treaty and accepted by the other parties as an instrument related to the treaty'. The declarations which were deposited by the US and the UK are such instruments, and are directly connected to the text of the Treaty.[256] It is undisputed that they were made on the occasion of the conclusion of the Treaty. It should also be indisputable—although this is questioned by some authors[257]—that the declarations were 'accepted by the other parties as an instrument related to the treaty'. Acceptance by the other parties, referred to in Article 31, para. 2(b) of the Vienna Convention, requires only a consensus on the connection with the treaty, not a consensus on the substantial content of the declaration.[258] Those authors who argue to the contrary misunderstand that basic principle if they contend that the so-called 'nuclear consensus' is irrelevant in the light of the 'unequivocal' wording of the Additional Protocol, and that the preparatory work of the Treaty and the circumstances of its conclusion are relevant only as a supplementary means of interpretation, pursuant to Article 32 Vienna Convention, if on the textual interpretation the meaning is ambiguous or obscure.[259] An interpretation based on these assumptions is plausible only if the declarations do not belong to the 'general means of interpretation' in the sense of Article 31 Vienna Convention. Yet, the exclusion of Article 31, para. 2, lit. b, can be argued only if it is mistakenly assumed that instruments according to Article 31, para. 2, lit. b, require a consensus on the correctness of the substance of the declaration.[260] The correct construction of the declarations of the Western nuclear powers is that they are complementary instruments in accordance with Article 31, para. 2, lit. b, Vienna Convention, and it therefore follows from the context of AP I that there was no consensus among the parties concerning the scope of the new rules. Accordingly, to clarify the question of whether AP I covers the use of nuclear weapons, one must rely upon the preparatory work and the circumstances of conclusion of AP I, which sources in turn prove that the (politically delicate) question of use of nuclear weapons was excluded from the scope of the Treaty.[261]

---

[256] The same is argued by Solf, in Bothe/Partsch/Solf, above (n. 41) 191 (n. 12).

[257] See Horst Fischer, *Der Einsatz von Nuklearwaffen nach Art.51 des I. Zusatzprotokolls zu den Genfer Konventionen von 1949* (Duncker & Humblot, 1985), 155–60.

[258] See R. Kühner, *Vorbehalte zu multilateralen völkerrechtlichen Verträgen* (Springer, 1986), 37 (with further references) and M. Pechstein, 'Die Ratifizierung der Zusatzprotokolle zu den Genfer Konventionen durch die Bundesrepublik Deutschland' (1992) 30 *AVR* 292.

[259] See Fischer, above (n. 257) 167–72; Rauch, 'L'emploi d'armes nucléaires et la réaffirmation et le développement du droit international humanitaire applicables dans les conflits armés' (1980) 33 *Revue Hellénique du droit international* 1–60, at 53–60.

[260] Fischer, *op. cit.*, 156–8.

[261] With the same result, see Meyrowitz, 'La stratégie nucléaire et le Protocole additionnel I aux Concentions de Genève de 1949' (1979) 83 *RGDIP* 904–61, at 933–8; George Aldrich, 'New Life for the Laws of War' (1981) 75 *AJIL* 764–83, at 781–2; Meyrowitz, above (n. 253) 238–42; Solf, in Bothe/Partsch/Solf, above (n. 41) 188–92; Ney, 193–209; Kalshoven, above (n. 9) 283; Pilloud/Pictet, in *ICRC Commentary*, paras. 1852, 1858; Fleck, above (n. 240) 227; Pechstein, above (n. 258) 290–4.

STEFAN OETER

6. It follows that the rules of the Additional Protocol are not applicable as treaty law on the use of nuclear weapons. The customary rules, reaffirmed by the provisions of AP I, are, however, applicable to nuclear warfare.[262] Accordingly, the 'nuclear clause' is of importance primarily regarding Article 51, para. 6, AP I (prohibition of reprisals towards the civilian population and civilian goods) and regarding Article 49, para. 2, AP I (inclusion into the scope of AP I of the territory of a party which is under the control of the enemy). These two provisions undoubtedly constitute new rules introduced into humanitarian law by Additional Protocol I.[263] In addition to these two obviously new rules, the provisions of Article 51, paras. 2–5, and Article 52 AP I could be considered as exceeding traditional customary law. Although they intended only to give more concrete shape to the customary prohibition of indiscriminate warfare, they in fact contain a decisive element of new law. Although these provisions primarily reaffirm and develop customary law, it must also be admitted that it is extremely difficult to distinguish the expression of pre-existing rules from the more innovative elements inherent in any codification, particularly concerning convention codification of pre-existing customary rules, that is of rules previously not fixed with sufficient precision in written form.[264] Such attempts at codification always involve both the definition of pre-existing customary law and the creation of new law by treaty, and are inevitably, as Henri Meyrowitz has expressed it: 'a mixture . . . of elements of the *lex lata* and of the *lex ferenda*'.[265] Particular difficulties are created in that regard by the basic rules of paragraphs 4 and 5 of Article 51, in particular by the codification of the principle of proportionality in Article 51, para. 5, lit. b, AP I, parts of which are seen as new rules created by the Protocol, but other parts as mere reaffirmation of customary law already in existence at the time of codification.[266] That the principle of proportionality as such existed in previous customary law is beyond doubt. Its specific expression in Articles 51, para. 5, lit. b, and 57, para. 2, lit. a(ii), AP I, however, should only be applied to the use of nuclear weapons with some caution.

435   **As weapons of last resort, nuclear weapons continue to fulfil an essential role to prevent war by ensuring that there are no circumstances in which the possibility of nuclear retaliation in response to military action might be discounted.**

1. It is difficult to evaluate the repercussions of customary law rules on the strategic planning of nuclear weapons states and alliances such as the North Atlantic Alliance. This is mainly due to the fact that such repercussions can be discussed in practical terms only concerning the concrete details of operational planning. On an abstract level, one can only state that a strategy of 'massive retaliation'—at least in the form of a threat of first strike or of escalation—is not compatible with the general principles of distinction and the prohibition of indiscriminate warfare.[267]

2. However, the operational planning for the use of nuclear weapons for self-defence purposes, including deterrence of attack, cannot be considered as an unlawful threat

---

[262] In that regard, see Meyrowitz, above (n. 253) 243–51; cf. also Pilloud/Pictet, in *ICRC Commentary*, para. 1852; Green, above (n. 243) 157.

[263] See Meyrowitz, above (n. 240) 555 and Kalshoven, above (n. 9) 283.

[264] As to that problem, see Meyrowitz, above (n. 240) 554.

[265] Ibid.

[266] See Meyrowitz, above (n. 240 and 253).

[267] As to the repercussions of the general rules on methods of war on the legality of strategies of massive retaliation, see Ney, above (n. 240) 275; Meyrowitz, above (n. 240) 560.

STEFAN OETER

in every case. The ICJ itself refers to the policy of deterrence as an established practice of major countries.[268] Attacks with tactical nuclear weapons (and perhaps also with precision-guided strategic weapons) could be legally permissible if they are specifically aimed at military objectives and they are also proportionate, with collateral damage to civilian objects being commensurate with the military purpose intended.[269] It is, however, absolutely necessary in these cases that the requirements of distinction and of proportionality are strictly observed.[270]

3. An assessment of nuclear strategy remains essential even after the profound political changes occurring in the 1990s in Central and Eastern Europe. Although NATO commits itself to a world without nuclear weapons, it reconfirmed in its 'Strategic Concept' in 2010 to remain a nuclear alliance, as long as the nuclear disarmament is not completed.[271] Nuclear and conventional weapons will both remain an essential part in the future strategy of the Alliance.[272] 'The supreme guarantee of the security of the Allies is provided by the strategic nuclear forces of the Alliance.'[273] It is true that in the light of the drastically changed security situation, the Alliance has taken a series of steps. It has 'dramatically reduced the number of nuclear weapons stationed in Europe'.[274] Additionally, the Alliance has reduced the reliance on nuclear weapons in its strategy. To conclude: the threat to use nuclear weapons continues to be regarded by the NATO Allies as an essential instrument for the prevention of war; this is true all the more with respect to the alarming fact that a growing number of states are recently seeking the ability to produce nuclear weapons.[275]

> **The threat and use of nuclear weapons are subject to political control, which shall observe the principles of proportionality, limiting damage on the territory of the enemy as well as the risk of damage on friendly territory.**

436

Decisions on whether to use nuclear weapons are not purely military. On the contrary, nuclear forces have a primarily political character. Their purpose is primarily to keep a balance of mutual deterrence, not intervention in combat operation. Accordingly, decisions on the use of such weapons cannot be left to the military alone. Nuclear strikes have such far-reaching political implications that they must be authorized by the highest political authorities. This is true not only for all states which possess nuclear weapons, but also for states on whose territory nuclear weapons are deployed. The political decision to use such weapons should be taken with due regard to the question of legal justification of the operation, and its concrete modalities, and in strict observance of the relevant legal rules. These legal considerations are of the utmost importance since the boundary between legally permissible combat and prohibited indiscriminate attack can easily be overstepped in nuclear warfare. The criteria of proportionality, of limiting damage on the territory of the enemy as well as limiting the risk of damage on friendly territory, are of paramount importance.

[268] ICJ, Advisory Opinion on Nuclear Weapons, *ICJ Reports 1996*, 254, 263 (paras. 67, 96); see Chesterman, above (n. 241) 162–3; Fujita, above (n. 247); Matheson, above (n. 237) 431.

[269] See Kalshoven, above (n. 9) 287.

[270] As to the problems resulting from such principles, see Meyrowitz, above (n. 240) 560–3.

[271] NATO 2010 Strategic Concept 'Active Engagement, Modern Defence' <http://www.nato.int/cps/en/natolive/topics_56626.htm>.

[272] NATO 2010 Strategic Concept, para. 17.

[273] NATO 2010 Strategic Concept, para. 18.

[274] NATO 2010 Strategic Concept, para. 26.

[275] See Shannon N. Kile et al., 'World nuclear forces', in *SIPRI Yearbook 2012* (OUP, 2012), 307–50.

STEFAN OETER

b. Chemical weapons

437   The use in war of asphyxiating, poisonous, or other gases, and of all analogous liquids, materials, or similar devices is prohibited (GasProt; Article 23, lit. a, HagueReg). This prohibition also applies to toxic contamination of water-supply installations and foodstuffs (Article 54, para. 2, AP I; Article 14 AP II) and the use of irritant agents for military purposes. This prohibition does not apply to unintentional and insignificant poisonous secondary effects of otherwise permissible munitions.

1. There is no dispute as to the basic rule: the use of chemical weapons is prohibited.[276] A prohibition on wartime use of potentially lethal substances which cause asphyxiation or poisoning effects had already been codified in Article 23, lit. a, HagueReg (prohibition against using poison or poisoned weapons, see *supra*, Section 430). Despite that regulatory safeguard, massive military use was made of poisonous gases in World War I. After the war it was therefore felt that the prohibition should be reaffirmed. The Geneva Protocol of 17 June 1925 for the Prohibition of the Use of Asphyxiating, Poisonous or Other Gases, and of Bacteriological Methods of Warfare thus consolidated the general prohibition of poisonous weapons in 1925 and explicitly outlawed all use of the gas weapon which had been so common during World War I.[277]

2. The general prohibition against the use of poisonous gases—which now constitutes a rule of customary law[278]—applies not only to their direct use against enemy combatants, but extends also to the toxic contamination of water-supply installations and foodstuffs. This could in theory be deduced from the pre-existing general prohibition of poison and poisoned weapons in Article 23, lit. a, HagueReg; nowadays it is expressly provided for in Article 54, para. 2, AP I and Article 14 AP II on the protection of objects and installations indispensable to the survival of the civilian population (see Section 466). As the analogous regulation in Additional Protocols I and II already indicates, the prohibition on the use of chemical weapons is applicable irrespective of whether the conflict is international or non-international. Even in internal conflicts it is prohibited to use chemical agents to place members of armed forces *hors de combat* or to terrorize the civilian population;[279] contaminating water supplies and foodstuffs is only one example of such illicit chemical warfare the primary goal of which is to spread terror among the 'enemy population' (as demonstrated most strikingly by Iraq's 'Operation Anfal' against its Kurdish population[280]).

3. Concerning the category of 'irritant agents', which is included in the scope of the prohibition by sentence 2 of the above-cited Section 437 of the Manual, it should be

---

[276] Concerning the legality of depleted uranium projectiles, see David, above (n. 56) 356; Rogers, above (n. 77) 225.

[277] Concerning the legal regime of the two treaty prohibitions see Bothe, *Das völkerrechtliche Verbot des Einsatzes chemischer und bakteriologischer Waffen* (Heymann, 1973), 4–18, 21–9; Frailé, 31–6; Dinstein, above (n. 43) 80–2.

[278] Rule 74 *CIHL*; see Bothe, *op. cit.*, 39–47; Watkin, above (n. 5) 47.

[279] Watkin, *loc. cit.*, 47; ICTY, *Prosecutor v Tadić* (Case IT-94-1, Appeals Chamber), 2 October 1995, *ILM* 105 (1997), 519, para. 124.

[280] See the reports on human rights in Iraq, prepared by the Special Rapporteur of the UN Commission on Human Rights, Max van der Stoel, UN Doc.A/46/647, paras. 22, 23, 74, and 75; UN Doc. E/CN.4/1993/45 of 18 February 1992, paras. 49, 50, 102; UN Doc. E/CN.4/1993/45 of 19 February 1993, paras. 89–97.

STEFAN OETER

noted that a serious dispute continues as to whether these substances were covered by the traditional prohibition of chemical weapons. State practice was not unequivocal in that regard; one thinks of the US operations in Vietnam.[281] Article 1, para. 5, of the Chemical Weapons Convention of 1993 now settles the controversy by explicitly prohibiting the use of 'irritant agents' in warfare (under the notion 'riot control agents').[282] In addition, the Preamble of the new Convention also refers to herbicides,[283] although the reference is not as clear as the explicit prohibition of 'irritant agents'. The most important point concerning all these disputes about the definition of 'poisonous gases' (clarified to a large extent by the new Chemical Weapons Convention) is the intentional design of a weapon in order to inflict poisoning as a means of combat. Only in so far as the poisoning effect is the intended result of the use of the substances concerned does the use of such munitions qualify as a use of 'poisonous gases'. If the asphyxiating or poisoning effect is merely a side effect of a physical mechanism intended principally to cause totally different results (as, e.g., the use of nuclear weapons), then the relevant munition does not constitute a 'poisonous gas'. Nuclear weapons, for example, are not prohibited as 'poisonous weapons' although they cause asphyxiation and poisoning as secondary effects.

The scope of this prohibition is restricted by the fact that, when signing the Geneva Gas   438
Protocol, numerous states declared that this Protocol should cease to be binding in regard to
any enemy state whose armed forces fail to respect the prohibition embodied in the Protocol.
According to the principle of reciprocity, states which did not record such a reservation will
also not be legally bound by the Protocol with respect to a follow-on use of chemical weapons
against states which launch, support, or assist in planning an attack by chemical weapons
contrary to international law.

1. Nearly all the important military powers have lodged reservations to the Geneva Gas Protocol which limit the Protocol to a prohibition only against first use and/or restrict the effects of the prohibition as between the contracting parties.[284] The results of such reservations must be judged according to the general rules on legal effects of reservations in Article 21 of the Vienna Convention on the Law of Treaties. Accordingly, a reservation modifies the provisions of the treaty to which it relates also for the other contracting parties as far as their convention relations with the reserving state are concerned. This means in effect that in the treaty relations with the major military powers the prohibition of chemical weapons is generally reduced to a prohibition against first use.[285] Even beyond the technical effects of reservations, the general principle of reciprocity applies in

---

[281] Concerning the problem of 'irritant agents' see Bothe, above (n. 278) 49–61; Kalshoven, above (n. 9) 268 and *US Naval Manual*, para 10.3.2.

[282] Convention on the Prohibition of the Development, Production, Stockpiling and Use of Chemical Weapons and on their Destruction, Paris, 13 January 1993, (1993) 32 *ILM* 800; for a brief description of the Convention's approach see also T. Taylor, 'The Chemical Weapons Convention and Prospects for Implementation' (1993) 42 *ICLQ* 913–4; see also Rule 75 *CIHL*; Boothby, above (n. 51) 135, and for a critical comment of this rule Watkin, above (n. 5) 48–9.

[283] On the dispute concerning herbicides, see Andrea Gioia, 'The Chemical Weapons Convention and its application in time of armed conflict' in M. Bothe/N. Ronzitti/A. Rosas (eds), *The New Chemical Weapons Convention—Implementation and Prospects* (Kluwer, 1998), 387–90.

[284] As to the reciprocity of reservations, see Bothe, above (n. 278) 66–78; Kalshoven, 'Belligerent Reprisals Revisited' (1990) 21 *NYIL* 43–80, at 73–4.

[285] David, above (n. 56) 331–2; on the legal effects of reservations see Kalshoven, *loc. cit.*, 74.

STEFAN OETER

that (prohibited) first use by one contracting party would entitle the adversary to make subsequent use of chemical weapons by way of military reprisal, as long as the subsequent use is not proscribed by specific prohibitions against reprisals.

2. Apart from the above, chemical weapons are covered by the same fundamental principles which apply to nuclear weapons. The use of chemical weapons is also subject to the general customary rules on weapons and warfare, and particularly the basic principle of military necessity and the prohibition of indiscriminate warfare.[286] Retaliatory use is justifiable only under the aspect of reprisal, and the legal limits of the law of reprisals must also be observed, in particular the requirement that reprisals be restricted to measures absolutely necessary in order to put an end to the infringement of law by the state who first violated the law (making first use of chemical weapons). The specific prohibition of reprisals in Article 51, para. 6, AP I, however, does not in principle apply to the use of chemical weapons (as in the case of nuclear weapons), since the so-called 'nuclear consensus'—which was an agreement to leave out of consideration the whole complex of ABC weapons—leads to the non-applicability of the new rules of Additional Protocol I, *inter alia* Article 51, para. 6, AP I.[287]

439   The Convention on Chemical Weapons of 13 January 1993 includes comprehensive prohibitions of any development, production, stockpiling, transfer, and use of chemical weapons, as well as provisions on international control of compliance with these provisions.

1. For decades the member states of the UN have negotiated within the framework of the UN Conference on Disarmament in order to reach agreement on a treaty prohibiting not only the use, but also the production and stockpiling of chemical weapons.[288] In 1992, they finally succeeded, after the decisive participation of German diplomacy, in concluding the new Chemical Weapons Convention.[289] The Convention comprehensively bans all development, production, stockpiling, and transfer of chemical weapons and provides for a detailed regulatory framework on the destruction of stockpiled resources.[290] It thus goes far beyond what had been provided for in the old 1925 Geneva Gas Protocol which had prohibited only the *use* of chemical weapons. Since the Biological Weapons Convention of 1972 the new treaty was only the second to outlaw completely a specific category of weapons.

2. One characteristic decisively distinguishes the new Chemical Weapons Convention from the Biological Weapons Convention of 1972, however, and that is its comprehensive verification regime,[291] the preparation of which was the major impediment during decades of negotiations.[292] Under the new verification regime there has been established

---

[286] Thilo Marauhn, 'Chemical Weapons and Warfare', *MPEPIL*.

[287] See Solf, in Bothe/Partsch/Solf, above (n. 41) 188–91.

[288] Concerning the course of negotiations see the detailed analysis in M. Bothe/N. Ronzitti/A. Rosas (eds), above (n. 284).

[289] In force since 29 April 1997.

[290] On the final phase of the negotiations, see T. Bernauer, *The Chemistry of Regime Formation: Explaining International Co-operation for a Comprehensive Ban on Chemical Weapons* (Dartmouth, 1993), 27–30; concerning the Convention's legal regime, see T. Taylor, above (n. 283) 912–4.

[291] See Bernauer, *The Projected Chemical Weapons Convention: A Guide to the Negotiations in the Conference on Disarmament* (UN Doc. UNIDIR/90/7, 1990), 119 *et seq.*, 164 *et seq.*, 173 *et seq.*; Winfried Lang, 'Compliance with Disarmament Obligations' (1995) 55 *ZaöRV* 69–88, at 84–6; Boothby, above (n. 51) 138–9.

[292] As to the course of negotiations see Bernauer, above (n. 291), 18–59.

STEFAN OETER

for the first time in history a far-reaching system not only of routine inspections, but also of 'challenge inspections' at the request of a state party, to investigate allegations of non-compliance. Even the private chemical industry is included in the system of on-site inspections.[293]

c. *Bacteriological (biological) and toxin weapons*

The use of bacteriological weapons is prohibited (GasProt).   440

The prohibition of use laid down in the Geneva Gas Protocol is not limited to 'poisonous gases' in a strict sense; the wording of the Treaty covers also bacteriological weapons.[294] Even according to customary law one must assume an absolute prohibition of any use of bacteriological weapons,[295] be it in international or internal conflicts.

> **The development, manufacture, acquisition, and stockpiling of bacteriological**   441
> **(biological) and toxin weapons is prohibited (BiologicalWeaponsConv). These pro-**
> **hibitions apply both to biotechnological and synthetic procedures serving other**
> **than peaceful purposes. They also include genetic engineering procedures and the**
> **alteration of micro-organisms through genetic engineering.**

The Biological Weapons Convention of 1972 was the first universal treaty to codify the prohibition of an entire category of weapons.[296] According to the Convention, the development, manufacture, acquisition, or stockpiling of bacteriological weapons, as well as their use in any military conflict, are prohibited. The Convention requires the complete destruction of all such weapons—without, however, providing for a specific regime of verification. In 1994, member states had created an 'Ad Hoc Group' in an effort to establish a compliance system laid down in a binding protocol to the Convention; however, the negotiations were brought to a halt in 2001 by the US who rejected the draft protocol.[297] The Convention also refrains from defining exactly what constitutes bacteriological (biological) weapons.[298] Nevertheless, there seems to exist general agreement that all living organisms fall under the Treaty which could be used to cause or spread diseases, or which are intended to cause the death of humans, animals, or plants, in so far as these organisms are designed to be used for hostile purposes in armed conflicts. Such organisms may be bacteria, microbes, viruses, fungi, or rickettsiae, or other living organisms damaging to other organisms. The notion 'biological weapons' covers also so-called 'toxins', that is all substances extracted from living organisms designed to be used for hostile purposes.[299]

---

[293] See Taylor, above (n. 283) 915–6; Bernauer, above (n. 291) 38–9; Walter Krutzsch/Ralf Trapp, *Verification Practice under the Chemical Weapons Convention: A Commentary* (Kluwer, 1999); Eric Myjer, A Reporting System: An Arms Control Law Experience, in Bothe, *Towards a Better Implementation of International Humanitarian Law* (Berlin: Verlag, 2001), 39–54, at 41–52.

[294] See Bothe, above (n. 278) 25.

[295] Bothe, *op. cit.*, 48–9; Rule 73 *CIHL*.

[296] Concerning the substance of the Convention see the brief description by Bothe, *op. cit.*, 36–8, and the detailed analysis of the Convention's legal regime by E. Stein, 'Impacts of New Weapons Technology on International Law' (1971 II) 133 *RdC* 223–388, at 337 *et seq.*, 358 *et seq.*; Boothby, above (n. 51) 125–8.

[297] Alexander Kelle/Kathryn Nixdorff/Malcolm Dando, *Controlling Biochemical Weapons: Adapting Multilateral Arms Control for the 21st Century* (Palgrave Macmillan, 2006), 48–59.

[298] See Bothe, *op. cit.*, 37.

[299] See Dominika Švarc, 'Biological Weapons and Warfare', *MPEPIL*, para. 1.

STEFAN OETER

III. Methods of Combat

1. Military Objectives

442   **Attacks, that is any acts of violence against the adversary, whether in offence or in defence (Article 49, para. 1, AP I), shall be limited exclusively to military objectives.**

1. The basic principle laid down in Section 442 is an attempt to codify the customary requirement of distinction and to transform it into a specific rule of combat. Military use of force is only permissible—such is the basic requirement of customary law—against an objective which constitutes a military objective by virtue of its being part of the military endeavours of the adversary. Only for the purpose of combat against such objectives does the regulation of customary international law recognize military necessity.[300] Whether the conflict is international in character or non-international makes no difference, because even in internal conflicts states are obliged under customary law to spare the civilian population and civilian objects.[301]

2. Article 48 AP I, which explicitly lays down such a maxim of 'limited warfare', makes use of the rather untechnical term 'operations' ('. . . shall direct their operations only against military objectives'). Article 49, para. 1, AP I goes on to give an express definition of what constitutes an 'attack' in the technical sense of the Protocol: 'attacks' are all 'acts of violence against the adversary, whether in offence or in defence'. This definition raises another question, however: namely whether the term 'attacks'—which must be understood as identical with 'acts of violence against the adversary'—has a narrower meaning than the rather wide term 'military operations'. The answer must be 'yes', since many types of military operations are carried out without any direct violence against the adversary. Such military operations performed without the direct use of violence do not need any limitation concerning legitimate objectives of attack, that is 'military objectives', since they entail no risk of direct violence for the civilian population.[302]

3. The Protocol's use of the term 'attacks' to include all acts of violence against the adversary has been severely criticized by some military writers. The main point of criticism has been that such an interpretation removes the terminology of the Protocol too far from daily language (W. Hays Parks has claimed it to be 'etymologically inconsistent with its customary use' and even 'contrary to its ordinary meaning').[303] To label even a purely defensive operation an 'attack' on the basis that violence is employed—so claim the critics of AP I—is incomprehensible for the non-lawyer and places a pejorative value-judgement on any use of armed force.[304] This critique is certainly exaggerated; but

---

[300] As to the basic set of rules, see the comments of Solf on Article 48 AP I, in Bothe/Partsch/Solf, above (n. 41) 282–6; see also M. Arrassen, *Conduite des hostilités, droit des conflits armés et désarmement* (Bruylant, 1986), 260–4; Baxter, in UNESCO/Institut Henry Dunant (eds), above (n. 1) 117–62, at 146–55; Blix, ibid. 163–81, at 174–8.

[301] See Kalshoven, above (n. 9) 296; Rules 1, 7 *CIHL*.

[302] See also Solf, in Bothe/Partsch/Solf, above (n. 41) 289 and Kalshoven/Zegveld, above (n. 22) 99–100.

[303] Parks, *supra* (n. 8) 114 and 115.

[304] See esp. Parks, ibid. 113–16; cf. Pilloud/Pictet, in *ICRC Commentary*, para. 1879.

STEFAN OETER

it must be admitted that the all-embracing use of the term 'attack' as including all acts of violence can be quite confusing and does not always assist the understanding of the provisions of Additional Protocol I.[305] On the other hand, the definition of the notion 'attack' is primarily intended to clarify that the point of departure of the provisions of the Protocol is the individual military operation of a specific unit,[306] and not the entire network of all coordinated military operations of a party to the conflict (as to the problems resulting from such an approach, see Section 445). If the term 'attack' is understood as a short formula for any kind of 'combat action', the semantic combination of offensive and defensive operations in a single unitary concept has a striking advantage: it unmistakeably brings home to commanders and soldiers in combat that the 'defensive character' of a specific act of violence does not exempt it from the provisions for the protection of the civilian population.[307] This applies under certain conditions even for a party's preventive operations in its own 'hinterland', as for example in the case of laying mines in anticipation of a future offensive by the adversary.[308]

4. The same basic lesson is also given by para. 2 of Article 49 AP I which expressly provides that the provisions of the Protocol, particularly the provisions on protection of the civilian population, apply not only to operations on the territory of the adversary but also to combat operations on the national territory of a party, even if this is occupied by the adversary.[309] Thus the pretence is excluded that the safeguard provisions of humanitarian law should be seen to protect only the enemy civilian population and not a party's own population. Even the civilian population of a state which comes under the control of the adversary in the course of the armed conflict enjoys the protection of the Protocol against actions by its national armed forces[310] (see also Section 466). Thus, a party to the conflict may not mount attacks on objects which are indispensible to the survival of the population in its own territory being occupied by the adversary, but it may destroy, in case of imperative military necessity, such objects in territory still under its own control in order to counter the invasion. Such destructive acts by a belligerent on his own territory will often not even constitute an 'attack', for they may be acts of violence which are not mounted 'against the adversary'.[311]

5. Paragraph 3 of Article 49 regulates the scope of the Protocol's provisions on the protection of the civilian population. Included are attacks by sea or air against objectives on land, and also any air or sea warfare which may affect the civilian population or civilian objects on land. By contrast, armed conflict at sea or in the air with no consequences for the area protected under Part IV of the Protocol (which refers uniquely to land territory) is not covered by Article 49, para. 3, AP I.[312] However, these operations are covered by the relevant general rules of customary law. As paragraph 4 of Article 49 expressly states, the provisions of the Protocol are *additional to* the other rules concerning humanitarian

---

[305] See Pilloud/Pictet, ibid.

[306] Solf, in Bothe/Partsch/Solf, above (n. 41) 288.

[307] Pilloud/Pictet, in *ICRC Commentary*, para. 1880; Kalshoven/Zegveld, above (n. 22) 100.

[308] Pilloud/Pictet, ibid. para. 1881; cf. also Rauch, above (n. 143) 270–8; Kalshoven/Zegveld, above (n. 22) 175.

[309] Sassòli, above (n. 11) 337–41, proves that such an understanding corresponds to the basic approach of the relevant rules of customary law.

[310] Pilloud/Pictet, in *ICRC Commentary*, paras. 1883–91; Solf, in Bothe/Partsch/Solf, above (n. 41) 289–90; Kalshoven/Zegveld, above (n. 22) 100.

[311] Pilloud/Pictet, in *ICRC Commentary*, paras. 1888, 1890.

[312] See Sassòli, above (n. 11) 334–7.

STEFAN OETER

protection contained in the Fourth Geneva Convention and in other international agreements as well as to the customary rules relating to the protection of civilians; those rules are not replaced by the provisions of the new Protocol.[313]

443   **Military objectives are armed forces—with paratroops in descent (Article 42, para. 3, AP I) but not crew members parachuting from an aircraft in distress (Article 42, para. 1, AP I)—and also objects which by their nature, location, purpose, or use make an effective contribution to military action and whose total or partial destruction, capture, or neutralization, in the circumstances ruling at the time, offer a definite military advantage (Article 52, para. 2, AP I).**

1. The attempt to define exactly what constitutes a military objective is an essential step in making the principle of distinction operative. For a long time, belligerent practice tended to leave uncertain the precise contours of the notion. Accordingly, belligerents were often tempted to manipulate the rules by choosing—according to the situation—either a restrictive or an extensive definition of the term 'military objective'.[314]

2. Since time immemorial, enemy combatants have constituted the principle 'military objective'.[315] The category of 'combatants' includes units of land armies, navies, and air forces, also under certain conditions guerilla fighters as well as the civilian population of an invaded territory taking part in hostilities in the wake of a *levée en masse*. (As to lawful combatants, see above, Sections 304 to 310.)

3. The specific problem of air force crews parachuting in distress merits attention. It has been disputed under what circumstances crew members of a military aircraft may be fired upon. Concerning parachute troops and airborne combat units it is beyond doubt that they constitute a lawful military objective, because in parachuting from aircraft they perform an offensive operation (an 'attack'). Thus, even while parachuting they may be perceived and attacked as legitimate military objectives (Article 42, para. 3, AP I).[316] One exception, however, was stated by the rapporteur of the Diplomatic Conference in that regard: when a plane has been shot down, that is in cases of emergency descent outside the target area of the intended attack, even airborne troops should not be counted as military objectives.[317] Nevertheless, this exception probably will be of no relevance in practice. The land troops of the adversary will not normally know when parachuting results from an emergency, and will have to assume that enemy parachute troops are carrying out an attack operation. Accordingly, they will treat airborne troops as a military objective unless it is obvious that they are *enemies hors de combat*, either from signs that they have no hostile intent or from surrender (which would bring them under the protection of Article 41 AP I).

4. The contrary applies to crew members of an aircraft in distress, according to Article 42, paras. 1 and 2, AP I. For some time it was not clear whether crew members parachuting in distress should still be treated as military objectives—as during a flight which constitutes

---

[313] See the observations on Article 49 in the Memorandum of the German Government annexed to the statute transforming the Additional Protocols, BR-Drs. 64/90 of 2 February 1990, 111.

[314] See Sassòli, 'Military Objectives', *MPEPIL*.

[315] See the Preamble to the St Petersburg Declaration of 1868 which is worded: 'Considering . . . that the only legitimate object which States should endeavour to accomplish during war is to weaken the military forces of the enemy . . .'

[316] See de Preux, in *ICRC Commentary*, para. 1652; cf. also the *US Naval Manual*, paras. 8.10.2.1, 8.2.3.1.

[317] See de Preux, in *ICRC Commentary*, para. 1652.

STEFAN OETER

an attack—or whether during their descent they qualify as persons *hors de combat*.[318] Article 42, para. 1, AP I now settles the question by providing that with the descent from an aircraft in distress the 'combat action' of its crew is terminated and they may no longer be attacked.[319] Having landed, it is presumed that they constitute persons *hors de combat* who have no hostile intent. The adversary must give them an opportunity to surrender and may continue to attack them as a military objective only if it becomes obvious by their commission of a hostile action that they intend to continue combat.[320]

5. The definition of the boundary between military objectives and civilian objects remains a critical problem. By Article 52, para. 2, AP I the international community has attempted to clarify the question of how to distinguish between these categories.[321] The general definition of 'military objectives' in Article 52, para. 2, AP I, however, constitutes one of the most heavily debated provisions of the Additional Protocol and, in particular, military circles in Western countries have been extremely hostile to it.[322] The background to this condemnation is the restrictive nature of the definition, which purports radically to limit the category of legitimate objectives of military operations.[323] For that purpose the provision uses two basic elements which are combined with one another.[324] First, Article 52, para. 2, AP I requires that military objectives should be objects 'which by their nature, location, purpose, or use make an effective contribution to military action'. The formula used constitutes a general criterion the existence of which can be judged *in abstracto*. Under the category of 'military objectives' therefore are installations, buildings, or ground sectors which are directly involved in the military endeavour of the enemy, that is which make an effective contribution to the military operations due to their inclusion in the military dispositions of the adversary. In essence, this is a return to the restrictive definitional approach of the Hague Rules of Air Warfare, with the corresponding purpose of repressing the subsequent (and extremely broad) construction of 'military objectives' favoured by the proponents of 'strategic air warfare'.[325] Almost boundless interpretations of 'military objective' have been adopted in doctrines of 'total warfare', such as that advanced by Air Marshall Trenchard in 1928, which included as military objectives 'any objectives which will contribute effectively towards the destruction of the enemy's means of resistance and the lowering of his determination to fight'.[326] These are now replaced by the more recent doctrine of 'limited warfare'. It must be admitted that such an approach considerably limits the military opportunities for a belligerent and is therefore not without problems, since successful modern warfare requires great strategic and tactical flexibility.[327] The purpose of any military action must

---

[318] See de Preux, in *ICRC Commentary*, paras. 1634–51.

[319] See in detail de Preux, in *ICRC Commentary*, paras. 1639–43; Green, above (n. 182) 151–2; cf. Rule 48 *CIHL*.

[320] See in detail de Preux, in *ICRC Commentary*, paras. 1644–51; cf. also *US Naval Manual*, paras. 8.10.2.1, 8.2.3.1.

[321] As to the drafting history of Article 52, para. 2, AP I see Sassòli, above (n. 11) 370–2; see also Rule 8 *CIHL*.

[322] For the massive criticism from the US military, see, e.g., Parks, *supra* (n. 8) 137–44.

[323] Parks, *loc. cit.*, 138–41.

[324] As to the systematic structure of Article 52, para. 2, AP I see Pilloud/Pictet, in *ICRC Commentary*, para. 2018.

[325] See Parks, *loc. cit.*, 138–41.

[326] See Parks, *loc. cit.*, 139 (n. 412).

[327] Concerning this problem, see Parks, *loc. cit.*, 139–44.

STEFAN OETER

always be to influence the political will of the adversary,[328] especially in defence where the enemy's determination to pursue its goals by violence must be broken; the destruction of the enemy's military apparatus is thus never an end in itself. Therefore, the US has substituted the words 'military action' by the phrase 'war-sustaining capability'.[329] Though, such an interpretation would allow to declare nearly every civilian activity as indirectly sustaining the war effort and thus goes too far.[330] For the protection of civilian populations requires a basic limitation of violence, a restriction on the use of force against the enemy's military organization. If the intention directly to influence the enemy population's determination to fight were recognized as a legitimate objective for military force, then no limit to warfare would remain. This is what happened in World War II. The limitation of admissible military objectives is accordingly a step of the utmost importance for the implementation of the principle of non-combatant immunity. The legitimate interest of states to preserve strategic and tactical manoeuvring space can be taken into account only by interpreting and applying the inherent definition of 'military objectives', not by abandoning any limitation of lawful military objectives. As to the precise construction of the notion 'military objectives', see Section 444.

6. Article 52, para. 2, AP I combines this 'objective' element (concerning the capacity to contribute effectively to military operations) with a second 'subjective' criterion which refers to the military purposes of the acting state. It is not sufficient that the objective contributes to the military arrangements of the adversary; the destruction, capture, or neutralization of the objective must also offer the belligerent, in the specific circumstances obtaining at the time of the attack, a 'definite military advantage'.[331] This is both a 'situative' element, since Article 52, para. 2, refers expressly to the 'circumstances ruling at the time',[332] and also a 'relative' criterion since the 'military advantage' can only be realistically evaluated in the light of the tactical and strategic goals of the belligerent.[333] The attack must profit the armed forces using violence; to put it in extremely simple terms: it must be militarily necessary in order to reach a permissible operative goal. For details, see Section 445. Attacks launched for the purpose of terrorizing the enemy civilian population, to break its determination to fight, are accordingly prohibited, as are attacks of a purely political purpose, whether to demonstrate military strength, or to intimidate the political leadership of the adversary.[334]

7. The abstract definition laid down in Article 52, para. 2, AP I has a distinct advantage over the lists of admissible military objectives proposed earlier, namely the flexibility of its practical implementation, preserved by the abstraction of the formula. However, the same abstraction can be a disadvantage, in that it leaves a wide margin of interpretation which

[328] Ibid. 141.

[329] *US Naval Manual*, para. 8.2; Schmitt, above (n. 31), 3; C. J. Dunlap, 'The End of Innocence: Rethinking Noncombatancy in the Post-Kosovo Era' (2000) 9 *Strategic Review* 9, at 17. Cf. also in detail as a critical assessment of such position, J. Holland, 'Military Objective and Collateral Damage: Their Relationship and Dynamics' (2004) 7 *YIHL* 35–78, at 57–64; Dinstein, above (n. 43) 95; K. Watkin, Assessing Proportionality: Moral Complexity and Legal Rules (2005) 8 *YIHL* 3–53, at 16–7.

[330] Rogers, above (n. 77) 122–4; see also Section 444.

[331] On the background and problematic of the formula, see Pilloud/Pictet, in *ICRC Commentary*, paras. 2019 and 2027; Parks, *supra* (n. 8) 141–4; Solf, in Bothe/Partsch/Solf, above (n. 41) 324–6; Gardam, above (n. 43) 100–2; Watkin, above (n. 329) 17–23.

[332] See Solf, ibid. 324.

[333] See Solf, ibid.; Watkin, above (n. 329) 19–21.

[334] Bothe, 'Moderner Luftkrieg und Schutz der Zivilbevölkerung' (2002) 15 *HuV-I* 31–2.

STEFAN OETER

allows belligerents to construe it with completely different results according to their particular interest.[335] It also means that an officer, in determining whether a specific target is a lawful military objective, requires precise information as to the exact nature, purpose, and use of the objective concerned.[336] AP I appears to presuppose 'a greater certainty in the mind of an attacker as to the connection between a segment of a target system and military operations than an attacker normally would possess'.[337] Exact reconnaissance and the procurement of precise information by military intelligence services become key factors of lawful warfare. The technologically and institutionally highly developed military organizations of the industrial states could probably manage these requirements;[338] military actors without efficient means of reconnaissance and intelligence, however, will encounter serious difficulties in meeting the requirements of Article 52, para. 2, AP I.[339] However, these problems seem to be unavoidable if one wants to improve the protection of the civilian population by imposing legal restrictions on permissible means and methods of combat. The problems described result from the enormous complexity of the questions which need to be regulated, and not from a misguided politico-legal approach or a malicious conspiracy against specific military powers.

> **Military objectives include particularly:**   **444**
> — armed forces;
> — military aircraft and warships;
> — buildings and objects for combat service support; and
> — commercial objectives which make an effective contribution to military action (transport facilities, industrial plants, etc.).

1. As explained above, the ICRC and the Diplomatic Conference employ an abstract definition in order to limit the scope of the term 'military objective'. Such an approach has been criticized repeatedly, for it leaves a large margin of interpretation.[340] Ultimately, however, the Conference had no real choice but to take such an approach, since it would have been impossible for the delegations participating at the Conference to reach agreement on a detailed and exhaustive list of permissible military objectives.[341] There is, however, a precedent which could be used as an interpretative aid: the list of 'military objectives' drafted by the ICRC as an annex to the 'Draft Rules for the Limitation of Dangers incurred by the Civilian Population in Time of War' adopted in 1956 by the Red Cross Conference in New Delhi.[342]

2. At the heart of the category of military objectives are the armed forces of the adversary, including all military auxiliary organizations and paramilitary units fighting side by side with the regular armed forces. As well as the regular units of army, navy, and air

---

[335] See Dinstein, above (n. 43) 90.

[336] Ibid. 36; see also Parks, *supra* (n. 8) 141 (n. 416).

[337] Ibid. 140–1.

[338] As an example, the experience of the Allied armies (in particular the US Armed Forces) in the course of 'Operation Desert Storm'; see T. P. Keenan, 'Die Operation "Wüstensturm" aus der Sicht des aktiven Rechtsberaters' (1991/4) *HuV-I* 36.

[339] Regarding the different requirements dependent on the technological state of the belligerent, see Oeter, 'Comment: Is the Principle of Distinction Outdated?' in: Wolff Heintschel von Heinegg/Volker Epping (eds), *International Humanitarian Law Facing New Challenges* (Springer, 2007), 53–62; Schmitt, above (n. 31) 11; see also Section 448.

[340] See, e.g., Dinstein, above (n. 43) 90.

[341] See Kalshoven/Zegveld, above (n. 22) 105–6.

[342] Reprinted in Pilloud/Pictet, in *ICRC Commentary*, 632 (n. 3) and Parks, *supra* (n. 8) 138–9; see also Sassòli, 'Military Objectives', *MPEPIL*, para. 3; Fleck, 'Strategic Bombing and the Definition of Military Objectives' (1997) 27 *IsrYHR* 41–64, at 45 (n. 15).

STEFAN OETER

force, and all militia and volunteer corps incorporated in the armed forces, that group also includes all other persons who, together with (or instead of) the armed forces fight against the adversary (see Section 304). This also includes any part of the population of a non-occupied territory who, on the approach of the enemy, spontaneously takes up arms to resist the invading forces (the so-called '*levée en masse*'; see Section 310), and also guerilla forces in occupied territories (see Section 309).[343] The group of 'lawful combatants' also includes paramilitary or armed law enforcement agencies which are incorporated to the armed forces in accordance with Article 43, para. 3 AP I (see Section 307). Most police forces, which in general serve to enforce law and order and in principle do not take part in hostilities, however, are not included in the category of legitimate 'military objectives'; normally they do not possess arms suitable for military combat, being armed at most with small-arms and light equipment.[344] The only exception is needed for regular police in the enemy hinterland in the case of commando operations; police officers pursuing an enemy detachment become an admissible military objective.[345]

3. Also valid as a military objective is equipment serving a navy or air force for combat purposes, namely military aircraft (see Sections 327–328) and warships (see Sections 1001–1006, 1021).

4. The installations and objects for immediate combat service support, which are usually regarded as having a military nature, such as barracks, fortifications, staff buildings, military command and control centres, military airfields, port facilities of the navy (also ministries of a military nature, e.g. of the army, navy, air force, national defence, supply) also constitute traditional military objectives.[346] Also included in that category are logistical bases of the armed forces, namely stores of arms or military supplies, munition dumps, fuel stores, military vehicle parks, and so on.

5. The term 'buildings and objects for combat service support' has an additional layer of meaning which creates many more problems of delimitation than the case of buildings with an obvious military function. What is meant here is the category which is covered by the notion (in the terminology of the Red Cross list of 1956) of 'positions, installations or constructions occupied by the forces' and of 'combat objectives'.[347] The term 'positions, installations or constructions occupied by the forces' prompts thoughts of civilian objects and ground positions temporarily used for military purposes by an armed force in the course of its operations. These might be schools, hospitals, or residential premises used to lodge troops or to serve staff purposes; but they can also be buildings or installations where troops have entrenched themselves, where observation posts have been installed, or which serve military purposes in another way. The notion 'combat objectives' (or better: 'combatted objects') indicates objects or topographically exposed ground positions which in the course of a specific military operation suddenly become important for both sides, and the

---

[343] See Oeter, in Heintschel v. Heinegg/Epping (eds), above (n. 340) 59; Schmitt, ibid. 27–8.

[344] See de Preux, in *ICRC Commentary*, paras. 1682–3; Solf, in Bothe/Partsch/Solf, above (n. 41) 240.

[345] See Solf, ibid.; the question whether Yugoslavian police forces were legitimate targets during the Kosovo conflict is dealt with by Peter Rowe, 'Kosovo 1999: The air campaign: Have the provisions of Additional Protocol I withstood the test?' (2000) 82 *IRRC* 147–64, at 151–2.

[346] See no. 3 of the Red Cross list annexed to the New Delhi 'Draft Rules'of 1956: 'installations, constructions and other works of a military nature, such as barracks, fortifications, War Ministries (. . .) and other organs for the direction and administration of military operations'; see also nos. 4 and 5 of the list.

[347] See no. 2 of the Red Cross list.

STEFAN OETER

possession or destruction of which accordingly becomes decisive in achieving operative goals (e.g. church or other towers, hills, steep slopes, exposed farms, etc., the control of which both sides try to achieve). The German government, for instance, on ratification of the Additional Protocols, filed an interpreting declaration, according to which Germany construes Article 52 to mean 'that a specific area of land may also be a military objective if it meets all the requirements of Article 52, paragraph 2'.[348]

6. The most delicate distinction between permissible military objectives and civilian objects concerns the 'commercial objectives which make an effective contribution to military action'. It has long been hotly disputed as to what exactly is covered by this category. Even the different attempts to draw up specific lists of recognized 'military objectives' did not bring about a real clarification. The ICRC's 1956 list, for example, includes under this heading lines and means of communication, broadcasting and television stations, as well as telephone and telegraph installations, in so far as all these are of fundamental military importance, and also the 'industries of fundamental importance for the conduct of war'.[349] *In abstracto*, these categories seem to be capable of finding consensus. The difficulties begin when one attempts to delimit the permissible objectives of attack in detail. In April 1999, for example, NATO bombed the Serbian state television and radio station in Belgrade. A committee of experts appointed by the Prosecutor of the ICTY assessed the attack as legally acceptable insofar as it actually was aimed at disrupting the command, control, and communications network; in contrast, had the attack been made because the station was part of the propaganda machinery, the legal basis was considered more debatable.[350] During the Operation 'Iraqi Freedom', the US forces attacked in March 2003 the main television station in Baghdad, asserting that the building was part of Iraq's military command and control system;[351] if these allegations were correct, the television station would have presented a legitimate military objective. Equally, certain lines of communication such as railway lines, roads, bridges, or tunnels may undoubtedly be of fundamental military importance, and as such would be legitimate objectives for attack. The adversary belligerent, however, will be able to compensate for the destruction of such 'strategically important' lines of communication by switching to railway lines or roads which had previously been totally unimportant.[352] But does this not lead to the conclusion that such objects or lines which for the present seem 'unimportant' may be

---

[348] See BR-Drs. 64/90 of 2 February 1990, 132; see also the explanations given to Article 52 in the Memorandum of the German Government submitted with the draft of a statute transforming the Additional Protocols, BR-Drs. 64/90 of 2 February 1990, 112.

[349] See nos. 6, 7, and 8 of the Red Cross list—cf. *ICRC Commentary*, 632 n. 3.

[350] Final Report to the Prosecutor by the Committee Established to Review the NATO Bombing Campaign Against the Federal Republic of Yugoslavia, 39 *ILM* (2000), 1278 paras. 75–6; see Rogers, above (n. 77) 122–122; Matthew Lippmann, 'Aerial Attacks on Civilians and the Humanitarian Law of War: Technology and Terror from World War I to Afghanistan' (2002) 33 *California Western International Law Journal* 1–67, at 50–3; Gary D. Solis, *The Law of Armed Conflict* (CUP, 2010), 535–6; for a critical review of the Report, see Bothe, 'The Protection of the Civilian Population and NATO Bombing on Yugoslavia: Comments on a Report to the Prosecutor of the ICTY' (2001) 12 *EJIL* 531–5; in contrast, Charles J. Dunlap 'Targeting Hearts and Minds: National Will and Other Legitimate Military Objectives of Modern War', in Wolff Heintschel von Heinegg/Volker Epping (eds), International Humanitarian Law Facing New Challenges (Berlin: Springer, 2007), 117–25 in Heintschel v. Heinegg/Epping (eds), above (n. 340) 117–25, at 123–4; Christine Byron, 'International Humanitarian Law and Bombing Campaigns: Legitimate Military Objectives and Excessive Collateral Damage' (2010) 13 *YIHL* 175–211, at 184–6.

[351] Rogers, above (n. 77) 121.

[352] As to that problem, see Parks, above (n. 8) 139–40 n. 413.

STEFAN OETER

perceived as militarily important from the beginning, and may accordingly constitute relevant military objectives *ab initio*?[353] Concerning the attacks on bridges during the Kosovo air campaign in 1999, it remains disputed whether they constituted objects which made an effective contribution to military action.[354] Comparable questions may be asked of networks of telecommunication. In the case of modern densely interlinked infrastructures of telecommunication, it may be doubted whether any 'unimportant' installation still exists (with the exception of the periphery of the network). The practice of the Kuwait 'Desert Storm' operation in 1991 demonstrated that an attacker nowadays must probably destroy a network of telecommunication *in toto* (or at least its central connection points) in order to paralyse the command and control structures of the enemy armed force, which in themselves clearly constitute a legitimate military objective.

7. Considerable problems are created also by the exact delimitation of what constitute 'industries of fundamental importance for the conduct of war'. It is indisputable that industries for the production of armaments fall within this category, as also the heavy industries delivering the metallurgical, engineering, and chemical products upon which that industry relies, as well as storage and transport installations serving the armament industries and the heavy industries assimilated to it.[355] Also generally counted as undisputed 'military objectives' are the numerous installations for the production of electric energy for mainly military purposes (here again arises the above-mentioned problems of internetting and delimitation between military power supplies and 'purely civilian' energy installations[356]), and finally the research and development facilities of the armaments sector.[357] There remain large uncertainties, however, concerning the supply industry of armaments production and subcontractors of the defence industry. If those enterprises were also brought within the notion of 'industries of fundamental importance for the conduct of war', then nearly all areas in a highly developed industrial society with an elaborate division of labour in production would comprise lawful military objectives, thus undermining the overall attempt to limit warfare. Yet, if such industries are excluded, there is created an enormous (and extremely dangerous) opportunity to 'immunize' armaments production by subcontracting, and decentralizing production into 'civilian' firms,[358] which would ultimately erode the basis of the entire system, tempting states to ignore the whole regulatory framework and to return to strategies of 'total war', aiming directly at the economic capacity of the adversary. This dilemma probably cannot be solved in the abstract. However, a careful implementation of the relevant rules by *bona fide* interpretation of the requirements of Article 52, para. 2, AP I should be capable of producing satisfactory results in individual cases.

---

[353] In the affirmative: Dinstein, above (n. 43) 98; more deprecative Rowe, above (n. 345) 151–2.

[354] Bothe, above (n. 351) 534; James A. Burger, 'International humanitarian law and the Kosovo crisis: Lessons learned or to be learned' (2000) 82 *IRRC* 129–45, at 131–2; Dinstein, *loc. cit.*, 101–2; Rogers, above (n. 77) 116.

[355] See nos. 8(a), (b), (c), and (d) of the ICRC list of 1956.

[356] See Parks, *supra* (n. 8) 141 n. 415; Byron, *supra* (n. 351) 183; in detail see Daniel T. Kuehl, 'Airpower vs. Electricity: Electric Power as a Target for Strategic Air Operations' (1995) 18/1 *Journal of Strategic Studies* 237–66, who gives an overview of the targeting of enemy electric power systems in the 20th century, including US-Operation 'Desert Storm' in Iraq; as to the impact of these attacks on the water supply, 254–6.

[357] See Oeter, in Heintschel v. Heinegg/Epping (eds), above (n. 340) 58.

[358] Ibid. 140 n. 414.

STEFAN OETER

8. The current asymmetries in military technology and resources and its repercussions on military strategies[359] have led to a fierce debate on the definition of 'military objectives'. An issue of particular concern is the tendency of the US military, in the context of the doctrine of 'effects based-operations', to extend the ambit of 'military objectives' to so-called 'war-sustaining' objects (primarily economic and political-administrative in nature).[360] Target of military operations here is not the military effort of the enemy any more, but the political command and control system and its resource basis. The requirement of a close nexus between the target and ongoing military operations is given up in this approach.[361] In this context, the legitimacy of Israel's attacks against power plants and water supply devices during the offensive in Lebanon in summer 2006 is disputed. While from one side, the attacks are justified with reference to the peculiarities of the asymmetric confrontation between the technologically advanced state Israel on the one hand and the non-state actor Hezbollah operating from Lebanon on the other hand,[362] other authors argue rightly that such a broad interpretation of the notion 'military objective' is going to put into question the entire differentiation between military objectives and civilian objects.[363]

> **The term 'military advantage' refers to the advantage which can be expected from   445**
> **an attack as a whole and not only from isolated or specific parts of the attack.**

AP I relies on a relatively specific concept of 'attack' (provided for in Article 49, para. 1, AP I) as an isolated ground operation by a specific unit. This notion is linked to that of the 'military objective', and both are relevant to the determination of the 'definite military advantage' which is to be expected from the attack concerned. Such a conceptual foundation seems to suggest a very narrow idea of what constitutes a 'definite military advantage' under Article 52, para. 2. One could be tempted to conclude that a 'military advantage' which justifies classifying an object as a 'military objective' must result from the specific military operation which constitutes the 'attack'. Such a construction, however, would ignore the problems resulting from modern strategies of warfare, which are invariably based on an integrated series of separate actions forming one ultimate compound operation. The separate action within an operation, that could be described as a specific 'attack', is hardly ever an end in itself. Normally, such an action is directed towards a goal which lies outside the single action, as part of the complex mosaic of a bigger integrated operation conceived in a kind of division of labour, and thus depends in its purpose on the aggregate strategy of the party to the conflict. The aggregate military operation of the belligerent may not be divided up into too many individual actions, otherwise the operative purpose for which the overall operation was designed slips out of sight. It is this elementary condition of any sensible interpretation of the concept of 'military advantage' which the German government—in accordance with important

---

[359] Schmitt, 'Asymmetrical Warfare and International Humanitarian Law' in Heintschel v. Heinegg/Epping (eds), above (n. 340) 11–48.

[360] Burger, above (n. 355) 132; Dunlap, in Heintschel v. Heinegg/Epping (eds), above (n. 352) 123–5.

[361] Schmitt, above (n. 31) 2; in detail, see Oeter in Heintschel v. Heinegg/Epping (eds), above (n. 340) 56–7; Dinstein, above (n. 43) 95–6; Watkin, above (n. 329) 16–7.

[362] Herfried Münkler, 'Asymmetrie und Kriegsvölkerrecht. Die Lehren des Sommerkrieges 2006' (2006) 81 *Friedens-Warte* 59–65.

[363] Martin Beck, 'Zur Kritik am Sommerkrieg 2006 im Nahen Osten' (2006) 81 *Friedens-Warte* 91–5, at 92; Tomuschat, 'Der Sommerkrieg des Jahres 2006: Eine Skizze' ibid. 187–8; Tomuschat, 'Der Sommerkrieg des Jahres 2006: Ein Schlusswort' (2007) 82 *Friedens-Warte* 107–16, at 109.

STEFAN OETER

voices in international legal literature[364]—took into account when it annexed like several other states[365] to its ratification an interpreting declaration concerning the construction of what constitutes a 'definite military advantage'. The declaration is worded: 'In applying the rule of proportionality in Article 51 and Article 57, "military advantage" is understood to refer to the advantage anticipated from the attack as a whole and not only from isolated or particular parts of the attack.'[366] Although the declaration expressly refers only to the rule of proportionality in Articles 51 and 57 AP I, it seems also to apply the same interpretation to the construction of what constitutes a 'definite military advantage' in the sense of Article 52, para. 2, AP I.

446   Civilians present in military objectives are not protected against attacks directed at those objectives; the presence of civilian workers in an arms production plant, for instance, will not prevent opposing armed forces from attacking this military objective.

1. Persons who are not combatants according to Article 4 GC III and Article 43 AP I must be seen as 'civilians'. Both the civilian population and individual civilians according to Article 51, para. 1, AP I enjoy 'general protection against dangers arising from military operations'; they shall not be made the object of an attack (Article 51, para. 2, AP I; see Sections 404 and 451). Even the presence within the civilian population of individual combatants does not deprive the population of its civilian character, and thus it retains the protection accorded to it under Additional Protocol I.[367]

2. Only if civilians fight side by side with the regular armed forces is the position different, and then only as long as they directly take part in hostilities (Article 51, para. 3).[368] These civilians, by taking up arms against the enemy, become lawful military objectives (e.g. the case of police officers in a commando operation—see Section 444, para. 2). The same is true for civilians present in military objectives, that is civilian persons who are integrated into the military endeavours and logistics of a belligerent. The classic example of such integration is that of civilian workers in arms production plants (or, more extremely, the civilian personnel of armed forces who maintain military installations). These workers do not become combatants by working in arms factories or military installations; however, their workplace is a permissible military objective. The qualification of such an installation as a military objective is not changed by the presence of civilians who work in it, even if there are hundreds or thousands of them.[369] Even the deliberate use of parts of a civilian population as a 'human shield'[370] does not change the status of an installation (as a military objective), as long as it delivers an effective contribution

[364] See particularly Solf, in Bothe/Partsch/Solf, above (n. 41) 325, who uses the example of preparations of the invasion in Normandy in 1944; Dinstein, above (n. 43) 92–5.

[365] For instance Belgium, declaration of 20 May 1986; Italy, Declaration of 27 February 1986; and Spain, Declaration of 21 April 1986.

[366] See BR-Drs. 64/90 of 2 February 1990,132; Gardam, above (n. 43) 102.

[367] Concerning this operating practice used by Hizbullah during the Israeli offensive in Lebanon in summer 2006, see Münkler, above (n. 362) 64; Tomuschat (2007), above (n. 363) 112.

[368] See Pilloud/Pictet, in *ICRC Commentary*, paras. 1942–1945; Solf, in Bothe/Partsch/Solf, above (n. 41) 301–4; and Kalshoven/Zegveld, above (n. 22) 106.

[369] See Kalshoven/Zegveld, ibid. 106, and Sassòli, above (n. 11) 393–4; cf. (as an extremely critical voice towards AP I) Parks, above (n. 8) 120–35, 134–5.

[370] Solis, above (n. 350) 319–21; for examples of the practice to use 'human shields', see Parks, 'The Protection of Civilians from Air Warfare' (1997) 27 *IsrYHR* 65–113 at 98–104.

STEFAN OETER

to the military activity of the belligerent. The actions of Iraqi forces during 'Operation Iraqi Freedom' are a relevant example. Iraq deliberately used civilians to physically shield their operations.[371] Attacks against such installations remain lawful in principle; only the principle of proportionality may cause the attacker difficulties when trying to justify such an attack (see Section 459). It is, however, debatable whether human shields that have been placed voluntarily may be taking direct part in hostilities during their employment as such.[372] Consequently, the shielded installation would remain a lawful target, without even having to consider aspects of proportionality.

3. One point remains unclear in respect of the prohibition of disproportionate attacks. It must be asked whether the deliberate taking of the risk by any civilian who stays in a military installation should influence the balance which must be struck between the intended military advantage and the collateral damage to be taken into account. What has been clarified is only the basic premise that collaboration in the military endeavours of the belligerent does not make the civilian a 'quasi-combatant', the civilian is therefore not a military objective himself.[373] Direct bombardment of civilian living quarters of arms production plant workers (such as occurred in World War II) can no longer be justified by the argument that these workers are military objectives by virtue of their essential contribution to warfare.[374] Whether collateral damage to civilians working in military objectives (and thus contributing to the military endeavour of its state) is of lesser weight in striking a balance with the military advantage than potential damage to 'innocent' civilians is a question not yet answered, but which needs careful study.[375] Although an affirmative answer might create serious ethical difficulties, reasons of military practicability (and of soldiers' common sense) might point in that direction.

> **An objective which is normally dedicated to civil purposes shall, in case of doubt, be assumed not to be used in a way which makes an effective contribution to military action (Article 52, para. 3, AP I), and shall therefore be treated as a civilian object.**

447

1. The presumption laid down in Article 52, para. 3, AP I is complementary to the complex provision of Article 52, para. 2 (definition of 'military objectives'). The presumption expressly refers to objects which are normally dedicated to civilian purposes, 'such as a place of worship, a house or other dwelling or a school', but which may, if used to make an effective contribution to military action, become a military objective.[376] Only with respect to those objects which originally had a purely civil purpose can there be any serious doubt as to the military nature of the objective. Means of transport and of communication (which it was proposed, at the beginning of the Diplomatic Conference, should also be covered by the presumption) fall into a different category. They were excluded

---

[371] Schmitt, in Heintschel v. Heinegg/Epping (eds), 26–7; concerning the practice to use 'human shields' especially in the asymmetrical warfare, see also Oeter, above (n. 339) 57–8.

[372] In favour Schmitt, 'Computer Network Attack and the Use of Force in International Law: Thoughts on a Normative Framework' (1998–9) 47 *Columbian Journal of Transnational Law* 336; dismissive Jean-Francois Quéguiner, 'Precautions under the law governing the conduct of hostilities' 88 *IRRC* (2006), 815–7.

[373] Doswald-Beck, above (n. 20) 154.

[374] Ibid.

[375] Parks, above (n. 370) 109–10.

[376] Critical towards this regulation Parks, *supra* (n. 8) 136–7.

STEFAN OETER

from the presumption because, if they are of military utility at all, there can be no doubt as to their 'contribution to military action'.[377]

2. Ultimately, when applying Article 52, para. 3, AP I, one should bear in mind that, according to the external circumstances and the information available to the attacker, before the presumption comes into play there must be a serious doubt as to whether the object in question contributes to military action. In most situations such doubt will not exist; in the combat zone, for example, there will normally be no question and the combatants will generally assume that an object constitutes a military objective the possession or destruction of which is essential for both sides. 'Combatants are not likely to entertain any doubt about the military use of buildings located in an area on land where the forward elements of opposing forces are in contact with each other, especially where they are exposed to direct fire from the ground.'[378] The decisive factor in that respect should be the perspective of the soldier acting on the ground, or of the military commander deciding on the attack: serious doubts must be obvious from his perspective before there is any reason to invoke the presumption contained in Article 52, para. 3. Several NATO states filed declarations confirming such an understanding when ratifying the Additional Protocols; the German declaration says that 'the decision taken by the person responsible has to be judged on the basis of the information available to him at the relevant time, and not on the basis of hindsight'.[379]

448   Attacks against military objectives shall be conducted with maximum precautions to protect the civilian population (Article 51, para. 1, AP I; Article 13 AP II). Attacks which may affect the civilian population shall be preceded by an effective warning, unless circumstances do not permit this (Article 26 HagueReg; Article 57, para. 2, lit. c, AP I). These rules shall also apply to attacks by missiles and remotely controlled weapons.

1. The corollary of the principle of distinction and the subsequent limitation of legally permissible military objectives is the fundamental maxim that the civilian population must be spared as far as possible.[380] As a customary rule this maxim has long been recognized;[381] indeed it is arguable that the principle of distinction and of non-combatant immunity today constitutes one of the few peremptory norms of humanitarian law, and accordingly also a part of '*ius cogens*'[382] which is applicable regardless of whether the conflict is international or internal in character.[383] In Article 51 AP I and Article 13 AP II the maxim is now reaffirmed and codified. The rule prohibits not only attacks against the general civilian population

---

[377] Solf, in Bothe/Partsch/Solf, above (n. 41) 326.

[378] Ibid. 327.

[379] See BR-Drs. 64/90 of 2 February 1990, 132 (Germany), 125 (Belgium), 127 (Italy), 129 (the Netherlands), 130 (Spain); see also Schindler/Toman, *The Laws of Armed Conflicts*, 4th edn (Sijthoff, 2004), 707, 712, 714, and 717.

[380] As to the codification of that maxim in Article 51 AP I see Solf, in Bothe/Partsch/Solf, above (n. 41) 299; Pilloud/Pictet, in *ICRC Commentary*, paras. 1923–33, 1935; Gardam, above (n. 43) 114–8; concerning the growing risk of collateral damages arising from modern warfare, see Oeter, in Heintschel v. Heinegg/Epping (eds), above (n. 339) 58; Schmitt, above (n. 249) 70–1.

[381] See Venturini, above (n. 43) 127–50; Sassòli, above (n. 11) 344–50; Gardam, above (n. 43) 132–62; Fleck, above (n. 343) 52.

[382] In that sense argue, e.g., S. Miyazaki, 'The Martens Clause and International Humanitarian Law', in Swinarski (ed), *Essays in Honour of Jean Pictet*, 433–44 in Swinarski (ed.), *Essays in Honour of Jean Pictet* (Nijhoff, 1984), 436–9 and Fleck, above (n. 108) 501.

[383] See, e.g., Gardam, above (n. 43) 176–9.

STEFAN OETER

but also attacks likely to cause incidental loss of civilian life, injury to civilians, or damage to civilian objects which are excessive in relation to the expected advantage. This formula covers all kinds of attacks which, under the perspective of military necessity, could cause unnecessary violence and which accordingly would unduly endanger the civilian population (measured according to the strict requirements of military necessity).[384] Thus, there must be inherent in the principle of utmost protection of the civilian population a rule requiring that the military use of force be both necessary and appropriate, whenever damage to the civilian population is to be expected.[385] Collateral injury to the civilian population must be minimized by the operational arrangements under which the attacks are performed, either by an exact delimitation of the targets of the attack, by the use of precisely targetable weapons in the 'weapons mix' used for the attack, or by other precautionary measures in planning or implementing the military operations.[386] It will be difficult, however, to deduce from such general principles a specific rule that any particular type of weapons (in particular 'precision-guided munitions') must be used in a specific case; precision-guided munitions are still too expensive and too rare for even military superpowers to be required to use them in all cases where civilian losses might thereby be minimized.[387] However, these states can in fact meet higher requirements concerning the precautionary measures than lower developed belligerents.[388] The armed forces of belligerents therefore retain considerable discretion, which will be exercised primarily according to military considerations, in the framework of operational priorities, and not mainly according to humanitarian aspects.

2. The rule of utmost protection of the civilian population includes the requirement of a previous warning, if possible. This requirement was already recognized by customary law.[389] In so far as the planned attack is likely to cause serious losses to the civilian population, the competent authorities of the adversary shall be given an effective warning prior to the attack, allowing an opportunity to evacuate the civilian population, or at least to place the population in specifically protected locations (see Section 456). Article 26 of the Hague Regulations provided that the 'commander of an attacking force, before commencing a bombardment, except in the case of an assault, should do all he can to warn the authorities'. Only in the case of an assault attack, namely an attack primarily based on the element of surprise, is such a warning logically excluded by considerations of military necessity.[390] Article 57, para. 2, lit. c, AP I, which addressed the question again, in essence goes no further than the traditional rule codified as early as 1907,[391] since it requires nothing more than an effective advance warning—unless the specific circumstances of the planned operation do not permit such a warning, as especially before an assault.[392]

[384] As to the practical difficulties of implementing the general rule see Parks, *supra* (n. 8) 152–63.

[385] In this sense see para. 3 of *US Army Manual* FM 27–10: 'The law of war ... requires that belligerents refrain from employing any kind or degree of violence which is not actually necessary for military purposes'; US Army Civilian Casualties Mitigation of July 2012, ATTP 3–37.31 <http://www.lawfareblog.com/wp-content/uploads/2012/07/attp3_37x31.pdf-approved.pdf>; see Sassòli, above (n. 11) 346.

[386] On the relevant experiences of the Kuwait War, see Keenan, above (n. 338) 34–7, at 36; concerning a critical assessment of the Afghanistan Air Campaign in 2001–2, see Lippmann, above (n. 350) 56–64.

[387] Bothe, above (n. 334) 31, 33.

[388] Bothe, *loc. cit.*, 33; Oeter, in Heintschel v. Heinegg/Epping (eds), above (n. 339) 59.

[389] Rule 20 *CIHL*.

[390] Concerning Article 26 HagueReg, see Parks, above (n. 8) 157.

[391] Of a different opinion is Parks, ibid. 158; to the point, however, Solf, in Bothe/Partsch/Solf, 368.

[392] See Pilloud/Pictet, in *ICRC Commentary*, paras. 2223–5 and Solf, in Bothe/Partsch/Solf, above (n. 41) 367–8.

STEFAN OETER

3. The same principles apply to attacks by missiles and remotely controlled weapons. The danger of militarily excessive collateral damage in these cases is particularly high (unless the attack uses the new generation of remotely controlled 'precision-guided munitions'), since the targeting capabilities of remotely controlled weapons are traditionally extremely bad even if recent technological innovations have significantly improved their accuracy.[393] Accordingly, it is unlawful not only to use such weapons against the civilian population as such in order to terrorize it (as was done by the Iraqi 'Scud' attacks on Israel in the course of the Kuwait War 1991), but also to use these weapons indiscriminately against military pin-point targets in urban settlements or other concentrations of civilian population. Such supposedly 'military' use of remotely controlled weapons against military installations in urban areas makes little sense from a military perspective, since the low targeting capability of such weapons leads to minimal success in combating a specific military objective; the collateral damage from such attacks, on the other hand, is usually extremely high. Traditional remotely controlled weapons and missiles may thus be used only with extreme precaution, for example against concentrations of enemy forces in scarcely populated areas of deployment, or (if precisely targeted) against lines of communication in the enemy hinterland.

4. It is not only the attacker who is subject to specific obligations to minimize civilian casualties and collateral damage. The state responsible for a certain territory is also obliged to avoid collateral damage therein.[394] Article 58 AP I requires that parties to a conflict shall endeavour to remove the civilian population and civilian objects under their control away from the vicinity of military objectives (the traditional practice of evacuating the population of important cities),[395] and that the responsible state shall avoid locating military objectives within or near densely populated areas,[396] and obliges the belligerents to 'take other necessary precautions to protect the civilian population, individual civilians and civilian objects under their control against the dangers resulting from military operations'.[397] The last covers preparations for civil defence, such as the provision of adequate shelters, the training and build-up of civil defence organizations, and the maintenance of adequate fire-fighting brigades.

449   **Unmanned aerial vehicles (UAVs) may be used for target control and other purposes. They may be equipped with arms—unmanned combat aerial vehicles (UCAVs). UAVs and UCAVs must be remotely controlled and piloted.**

1. Over the past decades, the employment of UAVs has become more and more popular. Starting in 2002, the first UCAV was used in the targeting of a high-ranked Taliban by the CIA.[398] Since then, UAVs and UCAVs have mostly been employed in Somalia, Yemen, and Pakistan, either for different purposes of surveillance and intelligence or for

---

[393] Concerning the innovative weapon technology used during the US attack in Afghanistan in 2001–2, see Lippmann, above (n. 350) 56.

[394] See Pilloud/Pictet, in *ICRC Commentary*, paras. 2239–44; Solf, in Bothe/Partsch/Solf, above (n. 41) 371–3; Sassòli, above (n. 11) 490–3; Fleck, above (n. 342) 52.

[395] Details can be found in the studies of Sassòli, *op. cit.*, 493–5, in the comments by Pilloud/Pictet, *op. cit.*, paras. 2247–50; Dinstein, above (n. 43) 145; Quéguiner, above (n. 372) 817–20.

[396] Concerning details see Pilloud/Pictet, *op. cit.*, paras. 2251–6; Sassòli, *op. cit.*, 496–8.

[397] See Sassòli, *op. cit.*, 498–9 and Pilloud/Pictet, *op. cit.*, paras. 2257–8.

[398] Cf. Miller/Schmitt, 'Ugly Duckling Turns Out to be Formidable in the Air', *New York Times* of 23 November 2011, available at <http://www.nytimes.com/2001/11/23/international/23PRED.html?pagewanted=print>.

STEFAN OETER

support of ground troops. IHL does not only cover and regulate traditional weapons, according to Article 36 AP I, new technologies and methods of warfare have to be evaluated in the light of the IHL.[399]

2. In 2009, the Program on Humanitarian Policy and Conflict Research at Harvard University published the 'Manual on International Law Applicable to Air and Missile Warfare' (*HPCR Manual*) in which it codified the existing rules governing air warfare.[400] According to Rule 1, lit. dd, *HPCR Manual*, a UAV is an 'unmanned aircraft of any size which does not carry a weapon and which cannot control a weapon'. UAVs are used solely to gather intelligence and for purposes of surveillance and reconnaissance (ISR functions). Unmanned vehicles only used for ISR function do not raise questions with regard to *ius in bello*; their deployment may only contravene over flight rights and so on.[401]

3. A UCAV, on the other hand, is 'an unmanned military aircraft of any size which carries and launches a weapon, or which can use on-board technology to direct such a weapon to a target' and is used to support of ground troops and for ISR functions.[402] A missile is distinct to UCAVs, according to Rule 1, lit. z, *HPCR Manual*. It is a 'self-propelled unmanned weapon—launched from aircraft, warships or land-based launchers—that are either guided or ballistic'. It itself is a weapon, while UCAVs only carry one and don't constitute a weapon themselves.[403] The most popular UCAV is the Predator drone, which can stay in the air up to forty hours and can carry—apart from different possible kinds of missiles—surveillance technology.[404]

4. Both types of unmanned vehicles are either remote-controlled by pilots, which are mostly located in the sending state, or include an autonomous attack system which is always considered by a weapons reviewer.[405] So far, all decisions of the deployment, including flight routes, choice of weapons and choice of target, are made by human beings and not standardized and automated. As long as these decisions are made by military personnel, the unmanned vehicle is a military aircraft.[406]

5. The questions whether the situations in which UAVs and UCAVs are employed, for example in Yemen, Pakistan, and Somalia, actually pass the threshold of an armed

[399] Whether this article reflects custom is disputed: in favour ICRC, 'A Guide to the Legal Review of New Weapons, Means and Methods of Warfare: Measure to Implement Article 36 of Additional Protocol I of 1977' in (2009) *IRRC* 88 933; critical Dinstein, above (n. 43) 214.

[400] Available at <http://ihlresearch.org/amw/HPCR%20Manual.pdf>; additionally, in 2012, the International Human Rights Clinic together with Human Rights Watch published 'Losing Humanity: The Case Against Killer Robots', a legal evaluation on drones, calling for an international treaty, available at <http://www.hrw.org/reports/2012/11/19/losing-humanity>; furthermore, the International Human Rights and Conflict Resolution Clinic (Stanford Law School) and the Global Justice Clinic (NYU School of Law) published another legal analysis in September 2012 'Living under Drones', available at <http://livingunderdrones.org/wp-content/uploads/2012/09/Stanford_NYU_LIVING_UNDER_DRONES.pdf>.

[401] See Schmitt, 'Drone Attacks Under the Jus ad Bellum and the Jus in Bello: Clearing the "Fog of Law" ' (2010) 13 *YIHL* 311–26, at 313 ff.

[402] *HPCR Manual*, rule 1, lit. ee.

[403] Commentary on the *HPCR Manual*, available at <http://ihlresearch.org/amw/Commentary%20on%20the%20HPCR%20Manual.pdf> (last accessed 20 December 2012), rule 1, lit. x, no. 1; Robert Frau, 'Unbemannte Luftfahrzeuge im international bewaffneten Konflikt' (2011) 24 *HuV-I* 63.

[404] For further information about the Predator performance, see <http://www.ga-asi.com/products/aircraft/predator.php>.

[405] See Boothby, above (n. 51) 230 ff; regarding autonomous weapons systems, see, e.g., DoD Directive on Autonomy in Weapon Systems of 21 November 2012, No. 3000.09.

[406] Cf. Commentary on *HPCR Manual*, rule 1, lit. x, no. 15.

conflict, and whether it is international in nature will be left aside, since these very controversial issues raise questions of *ius ad bellum* which are not the subject of this chapter.[407]

6. As stated by Special Rapporteur Philip Alston in his report on extrajudicial, summary, or arbitrary executions in 2010, 'a missile fired from a drone is no different from any other commonly used weapon, including a gun fired by a soldier or a helicopter or gunship that fires missiles'.[408] He stressed that the legal evaluation of the employment of any weapon depends on its specific use.[409] Outside an armed conflict, the use of lethal force must comply with human rights limitations.[410] The fact that UAVs/UCAVs have no on-board pilot does not change the applicability of the principles of armed conflict to UAVs/UCAVs.[411] The deployment of unmanned vehicles in armed conflicts raises questions about its legality with regard to the principles of distinction and of precaution as well as the principle to prevent superfluous injury or unnecessary suffering. The particularities of unmanned vehicles have to be considered while analysing their conduct and deployment.

7. According to the customary principle of distinction, codified in Art. 48 AP I, the intended purpose and the circumstances of the employment have to be considered when legally analysing the attack on a specific military target as well as the effects of the attack.[412] The employment of UCAVs in general does not contravene the principle of distinction. UCAVs are equipped with precision guided munition. Due to this technology, the distinction between civilian and lawful military objectives can be made even more precisely than with other weapons.[413] Still, mistakes may derive from unreliable intelligence, a basic problem in warfare.[414] The lawfulness under IHL differentiates depending on the actual facts and the concrete employment on the field.[415] UCAVs with an automated system have to be legally reviewed by a military, taking into account the sensors of the system, guidance technology on board, and their ability to direct attacks solely at military objectives.[416]

8. The US approach to target individuals on basis of certain categories (so-called 'signature strikes') raises questions with regard to the principle of distinction.[417] For instance, attacks based on the category 'military-age male' are unlawful and contravene the

---

[407] For further information, see Chris Jenks, 'Law from Above: Unmanned Aerial Systems, Use of Force, and the Law of Armed Conflict' (2009) 85 *North Dakota Law Review* 649, 656 ff.; regarding the situation in Pakistan, see Andrew C. Orr, 'Unmanned, Unprecedented, and Unresolved: The Status of American Drone Strikes in Pakistan Under International Law' (2011) 44 *Cornell International Law Journal* 729 ff.

[408] Report of the Special Rapporteur on extrajudicial, summary, or arbitrary executions, Philip Alston, from 28 May 2010, UN Doc. A/HRC/14/24/Add.6, para. 79.

[409] Ibid.

[410] Ibid. para. 85.

[411] Cf. Boothby, 'The Law Relating to Unmanned Aerial Vehicles, Unmanned Combat Air Vehicles and Intelligence Gathering from the Air' (2011/2) 24 *HuV-I* 81, 82.

[412] See Boothby, above (n. 51) 231.

[413] See P. W. Singer, *Wired for War: The Robotics Revolution and Conflict in the Twenty-First Century* (Penguin, 2009), 33.

[414] See Dinstein, above (n. 43) 140.

[415] See Michael N. Schmitt, 'Drone Attacks under the Jus Ad Bellum And Jus in Bello: Clearing the "Fog of Law" ' (2010) 13 *Yearbook of International Humanitarian Law* 311–26, at 321.

[416] Cf. Boothby, above (n. 51) 231.

[417] See Heller, ' "One Hell of a Killing Machine": Signature Strikes and International Law' (2013) *Journal of International Criminal Justice* (forthcoming).

STEFAN OETER

concept of direct participation in hostilities, since status-based attacks are only permissible in non-international armed conflict and against members of an organized armed group.[418] According to the ICRC, such an abstract affiliation is prone to error, since direct participation requires actual and continuous participation.[419] Furthermore, the mere 'consorting with known militants', for example sympathizing or collaborating, does not amount to a direct participation in hostilities and is therefore not an adequate criterion when determining a lawful target.[420] On the other hand, the signature 'transporting weapons' is lawful under IHL, since the attack would offer a military advantage and thus qualifies as a military objective, as long as the attacker differentiates between the transport of weapons and the mere fact that the object is armed.[421]

The disputed practice of targeted killings raises the question whether the situation it is used in actually qualifies as an armed conflict. Once this is established, such a killing is only lawful when targeting soldiers, members of an armed group or civilians directly participating in hostilities.

9. The principle of precaution requires the attacking state to take all feasible[422] steps to ensure to minimize the risk of civilian casualties, to cancel an operation when disproportionate consequences are expected or intelligence reveals that the targeted object is not military and to warn possibly affected civilians, if this does not contravene the purpose of the attack.[423] This may lead to the conclusion that in cases of availability of UAVs/UCAVs in a certain region and by a specific party to a conflict, they might be the only legal choice of weapon.[424]

10. With regard to automated systems, the legal reviewer has to evaluate whether the equipment and intended method of deployment meet the criteria of Article 57 AP I or, if the attacking party has not joined AP I, criteria set forth in customary law codified partly in Article 57 AP I, in Article 27 of the 1907 Hague Regulations and in rules 15 to 21 of the ICRC Customary Law Study.[425] Since Article 57, para. 2, lit. a, AP I addresses 'those who plan and decide upon an attack', problems derive regarding autonomous systems. Nobody decides or plans a specific attack using automated systems. The application of the principle of precaution may be guaranteed by so-called persons 'in the loop' who overview the attack and are fed with information on the targeted area and object and in the consequence can stop the automated attack, even if there is an interruption of communication with the automated UCAV.[426] However, even without a person 'in the loop', other human decisions taken in advance, depending on their algorithms, sophistication, and reliability,[427] may result in a positive legal evaluation. So far though, the

[418] Kevin J. Heller, *Journal of International Criminal Justice* (forthcoming), at 11.
[419] Cf. ICRC, 'Interpretive Guidance on the Notion of Direct Participation in Hostilities Under International Humanitarian Law' (2008) 90 *IRRC* 991, 1007.
[420] Cf. Heller, ibid. at 12.
[421] Cf. Heller, ibid. at 9.
[422] See Michael N. Schmitt, 'Unmanned Combat Aircraft Systems and International Humanitarian Law: Simplifying the oft Benighted Debate' (2012) 30 *Boston University International Law Journal* 595, 614 ff.
[423] Boothby, *loc. cit.*, (n. 412) 81, 84.
[424] Boothby, ibid. 81, 84.
[425] See Boothby, above (n. 51) 232.
[426] Cf. Frau, above (n. 404) 60, 65; Sebastian Wuschka, 'The Use of Combat Drones in Current Conflicts—A Legal Issue or a Political Problem?' (2011) 3 *Goettingen Journal of International Law* 891, 896.
[427] See Boothby, above (n. 51) 233.

requirements of customary law and Article 57 AP I can only be met by human decision-making; technology has not advanced far enough yet to address, for example, risks to civilians (autonomous systems).[428, 429]

11. The deployment of unmanned vehicles in non-international armed conflicts, according to common Article 3 of the Geneva Conventions and AP II, has been adapted over the past decades to the rules governing international armed conflicts.[430] Although members of organized armed groups in a non-international armed conflict are not referred to as combatants,[431] their involvement with unmanned vehicles may amount to a direct participation in hostilities.[432] It is questionable, however, whether the pilot of an unmanned vehicle, that may be situated far away from the actual combat action (or even in a third state[433]), is a lawful object under IHL, in particular if he is not a member of the regular armed forces, but an intelligence official or contractor.[434] Common Article 3 of the Geneva Conventions restricts the scope of application of IHL in an non-international armed conflict to the territory of a contracting party where the conflict takes place. AP II even states more precisely that only to the territory under the control of an involved organized armed group IHL applies. However, the ICTY in Tadić stated that the provisions at least partly apply to the entire territory.[435] In the case of the control of unmanned vehicles from a pilot situated in the territory of a contracting party, but not in the 'vicinity of actual hostilities', it appears reasonable to broaden the geographical frame.

450   In the aerial war zone, enemy military aircraft may be attacked without warning in order to make them crash or land. Downed aircraft shall become spoils of war. The members of the crew and the passengers—save unlawful combatants and mercenaries—shall become prisoners of war (Article 36, para. 1, HRAW 1923; Article 4 A, paras. 2 and 4 GC III).

In aerial warfare, the military aircraft of all parties to a conflict are entitled to take part in hostilities and to attack military objectives (see Section 327). At the same time, military aircraft constitute a lawful military objective, against which violence may be used. The attack against such objects is permitted at any time and requires no specific safeguards.[436] Even if there are persons on board such aircraft who are civilians according to the general rules, this does not prevent these aircraft from qualifying as military objectives, since those passengers voluntarily run the risk of being shot down. The attacking enemy has the choice of shooting down the aircraft or of forcing it to land. Any planes

---

[428] See ICRC, Report on International Humanitarian Law and the challenges of contemporary armed conflicts, 31st International Conference, 1 December 2011, p. 39 ff.

[429] See Boothby, above (n. 51) 233.

[430] Cf. Zimmermann, 'Die Wirksamkeit rechtlicher Hegung militärischer Gewalt' in Hobe et al. (ed.), *Moderne Konfliktformen—Humanitäres Völkerrecht und privatrechtliche Folgen*. Berichte der Deutschen Gesellschaft für Völkerrecht (C. F. Müller, 2010) 44, 9 ff.

[431] Rule 3 *CIHL*.

[432] Cf. Frau, above (n. 404) 60, 67 ff.

[433] For an in depth evaluation, see Jann Kleffner, in Gill/Fleck (ed.), *The Handbook of the International Law of Military Operations* (OUP, 2010) para. 4.01, no. 29.

[434] Cf. Ian Henderson, 'Civilian Intelligence Agencies and the Use of Armed Drones' (2010) 13 *YIHL* 133–73.

[435] Cf. ICTY, *Prosecutor v Tadić* (Decision on the Defence Motion for Interlocutory Appeal on Jurisdiction), IT 94–1-AR72, Appeals Chamber (2 October 1995), para. 68 ff.

[436] See Dinstein, 'Air Warfare', *MPEPIL*, para. 18.

STEFAN OETER

shot down or forced to land are legitimate booty of war pursuant to established practice, and may be used by the adversary for its own military purposes.[437] Crew members and passengers become prisoners of war, because they are deemed to be combatants due to integration in the military structure of the enemy (only *franc tireurs* and mercenaries, who are covered by particular rules of international law, are excluded; see Sections 302 and 303). Captivity begins, however, only when those persons are taken into custody by state organs of the adversary. Accordingly, those who have parachuted or made an emergency landing do not acquire prisoner-of-war status immediately upon leaving their aircraft; for as long as they remain uncaptured, they are still regular combatants and must conform to the general rules governing troops who have advanced behind the enemy's lines (such as patrols or commandos). They must therefore wear uniform and carry their weapons openly.

> Other enemy public aircraft shall not be attacked without warning. They may, however, by force of arms, be intercepted and compelled to land (Article 34 HRAW 1923; Rule 136(a) *HPCR Manual*). Such aircraft may be attacked if they:
> — escort enemy military aircraft;
> — fly through an aerial zone interdicted by the adversary; or
> — take part in hostilities.

451

Other public aircraft, that is planes and helicopters which are used by state organs but which are not designed for military purposes and do not take part in the hostilities, are not a legitimate military objective. The neutralization of such aircraft will not normally be militarily necessary, because they make no contribution to the military activities of the adversary. On the contrary, they should usually be considered as civilian objects. Therefore, like aircraft that enter foreign territory without authorization in peacetime, they may be forced to land, but they may not be shot down without previous warning. The only exception applies if such aircraft escort enemy military aircraft, enter into an interdiction zone, or participate directly in hostilities. In those cases, aircraft become military objectives. Even a non-military aircraft, by its integration in the operative framework of the enemy's warfare, then renders itself liable to attack, like in the case of UCAVs operated by civilian intelligence services.

> Should a belligerent party establish an 'exclusion zone' in international airspace, the same rules of international humanitarian law will apply inside and outside the 'exclusion zone' (Rule 107 *HPCR Manual*). Even where a 'no-fly zone' is established in belligerent airspace to warn aircraft entering that zone without special admission (Rule 108 *HPCR Manual*), the principles of target discrimination still apply.

452

1. Exclusion zones and no-fly zones belong to the concept of war zones.[438] An exclusion zone, according to Rule 107 *HPCR Manual*, is defined as a 'three dimensional space beyond the territorial sovereignty of any State in which a Belligerent Party claims to be relieved from certain provisions of the law of international armed conflict, or where that Belligerent Party purports to be entitled to restrict the freedom of aviation (or navigation) of other States'.[439] On the other hand, the belligerent party restricts or prohibits in a no-fly zone its aviation in its own or in enemy national territory, it

---

[437] Ibid.
[438] See Heintschel von Heinegg, 'War Zones', in *MPEPIL*, para. 1.
[439] Cf. Commentary on *HPCR Manual*, Section P, p. 235.

STEFAN OETER

cannot be established in international airspace.[440] In consequence, in a no-fly zone only aircrafts of the enforcement air forces are permitted.[441] The general legality of no-fly zones has not been disputed, while the lawfulness of exclusion zones has been questioned. Most war zones established during the past decades have been in contradiction to international humanitarian law, because they resulted in unrestricted warfare.[442] However recently, they have been recognized as a legal method of warfare as long as certain parameters are met. According to Rule 107 *HPCR Manual*, obligations under IHL apply to exclusion zones and no-fly zones, in particular concerning neutrality and targeting.[443] Thus, civilian aircraft may not be attacked and the principle of distinction and the rules to take all feasible precautions have to be applied. The mere presence in such a zone does not amount to the assumption that the entering aircraft is a lawful target. Zones established in the 'vicinity of hostilities' may prevent collateral damages to civilian aviation by prohibiting to enter the area or setting up special restrictions.[444] The establishment of these zones has to be published, in particular via diplomatic ones.[445] In case an aircraft enters an established zone, the belligerent party shall warn the aircraft. If the aircraft, however, continues its course, it may be a lawful target when military necessity demands so.[446]

2. No-fly zones were established after the 1991 Gulf War to protect the Kurdish population, although their legal foundation in SC Resolution 688 (1991)[447] is questionable, in 1992 in the Bosnia conflict[448] by SC Resolution 816 (1993)[449] and in 2011 in Libya,[450] the most robust no-fly zone was established by SC Resolution 1973 (2011).[451]

453   It is prohibited to order that there shall be no survivors. It is also prohibited to threaten an adversary with such an order or to conduct military operations on that basis (Article 40 AP I; Article 23, lit. d, HagueReg).

1. There is an ancient customary principle prohibiting orders 'to give no quarter' to captured enemies.[452] This well-established rule has now been reaffirmed by Article 40 AP I; it constitutes in essence a logical expression of the principle that the legal use of military violence is strictly limited to what is required by military necessity; clearly there is no necessity to kill persons *hors de combat*. Only for so long as the enemy combatant

---

[440] Cf. Commentary *HPCR Manual*, Section P, p. 235.

[441] See Schmitt, 'Clipped Wings: Effective and Legal No-Fly Zone Rules of Engagement' (1998) 20 *Loyola of Los Angeles International and Comparative Law Review* 727, 729 ff.

[442] Cf. Commentary on *HPCR Manual*, Section P, p. 235 ff.

[443] Cf. Commentary on *HPCR Manual*, Section P, p. 237.

[444] Cf. Commentary on *HPCR Manual*, Section P, p. 239

[445] Cf. Commentary on *HPCR Manual*, Section P, p. 240.

[446] Cf. Commentary on *HPCR Manual*, Section P, p. 239.

[447] UN Doc. S/RES/0688 (1991) of 5 April 1991.

[448] See Timothy P. McIlmail, 'No-Fly Zones: The Imposition and Enforcement of Air Exclusion Regimes over Bosnia and Iraq' (1994) 17 *Loyola of Los Angeles International and Comparative Law Review* 35.

[449] UN Doc. S/RES/816 (1993) of 31 March 1999.

[450] See Schmitt, 'Wings over Libya: The No-Fly Zone in Legal Perspective' (Spring 2011) 36 *The Yale Journal of International Law Online* 45.

[451] UN Doc. S/RES/1973 (2011) of 17 March 2011.

[452] Rule 46 *CIHL*; concerning the historic background of this customary rule, see de Preux, in *ICRC Commentary*, paras. 1589–90.

STEFAN OETER

participates in hostilities is he to be considered as a legitimate military objective.[453] As soon as he lays down his arms or drops out of combat because of wounds, to kill him becomes a useless act from the perspective of strict military necessity,[454] since it does not contribute to the military objectives of the belligerents (see also Article 41 AP I; see Sections 601 and 707). The mere intimidation or terrorization of the adversary with no other purpose, however, is not permitted under international law.

2. The principle codified in Article 40 AP I has been seriously violated even in our century, particularly in the practice of World War II (Hitler's order to kill all Soviet commissars, liquidation of so-called 'irregulars', martial law executions of 'saboteurs' and parachute commandos),[455] but also in numerous civil wars since 1945, when the minimum standard of common Article 3 would have prohibited such an action. The Diplomatic Conference therefore thought it necessary explicitly to codify such a maxim in AP I (Article 40) as well as in AP II (Article 4, para. 1, last sentence), although there is a considerable overlap with the fundamental rules of Articles 41 and 51, para. 4, AP I, for combatants *hors de combat* do not constitute lawful military objectives. Even without the specific provision of Article 40 AP I attacks on those *hors de combat* would thus have been regarded as unlawful indiscriminate attacks.[456]

2. Protection of Civilian Objects

> It is prohibited to fire at or bombard—whether to terrorize them or for any other   454
> purpose—members of the civilian population, unless and for such time as they
> take a direct part in hostilities (Article 51, paras. 2–3, AP I), and to make civilian
> objects the object of attack. Such attacks in reprisal are also prohibited (Articles 51,
> para. 6, 53 lit. c, 54, para. 4, 55, para. 2, and 56, para. 4, AP I).

1. The prohibition against attacks on civilian persons and on the civilian population as such (the principle of non-combatant immunity) is the logical consequence of the fundamental principle of limited warfare and of the rule ensuing from this basic foundation, namely the principle of distinction between military objectives and the civilian population.[457] Since only attacks on military objectives are admissible under the rule of military necessity (see Sections 442–444), it is clear that neither the civilian population nor individual civilians can ever be permissible objects of attack. As a fundamental maxim of customary international law, this rule has been undisputed for decades;[458] Article 51, para. 2, AP I is therefore a reaffirmation of established principles of customary law.[459]

2. The same is true of the prohibition against terror attacks stated in Article 51, para. 2, 2nd sentence AP I. An attack solely designed to spread terror among the civilian

---

[453] See Solf, in Bothe/Partsch/Solf, above (n. 41) 219–23; Nils Melzer, *Targeted Killing in International Law* (OUP, 2008), 367–71.

[454] Solf, ibid. 217.

[455] See de Preux, in *ICRC Commentary*, para. 1595; Solf, in Bothe/Partsch/Solf, above (n. 41) 217; Solis, above (n. 350) 260–1, 44.

[456] See de Preux, in *ICRC Commentary*, para. 1598.

[457] Fleck, above (n. 342) 43.

[458] See Sassòli, above (n. 11) 387–8, with further references; see also H. Lauterpacht, (ed.), above (n. 242) Vol. II, 524–30; Castrén, above (n. 47) 174–5; Kalshoven, *The Law of Warfare* (Sijthoff, 1973), 59–70; Green, above (n. 243) 586; MacDonald/Bruha, 'Bombardment', *MPEPIL*, para. 8.

[459] That was the position argued by the ICRC and the negotiating delegations when drafting the Additional Protocols, as well as the position of subsequent state practice (cf. Sassòli, *op. cit.*, 388–9).

STEFAN OETER

population constitutes a special case of unlawful attack on the civilian population. The bombardment of the civilian population or of civilian objects in such cases is deliberately intended to intimidate the adversary and the enemy civilian population.[460] Although it constitutes a blatant violation of fundamental humanitarian law,[461] which undoubtedly falls within the category of 'grave breaches' which should be sanctioned as war crimes, this particularly barbarian variant of 'total' warfare is unfortunately used regularly by military actors in practice. The 'Yugoslav', or rather Serbian Army, for example, has repeatedly launched terror attacks on the civilian population and threatened attacks on purely civilian objects in the course of the wars in Croatia in 1991 and in Bosnia since 1992, in order to intimidate the 'secessionist' republics and to expel the indigenous population from the territories claimed as 'historically Serbian'.[462] Soviet warfare in Afghanistan during the 1980s[463] and the Iraqi attacks with 'Scud' missiles on Saudi and Israeli cities during the Kuwait War in 1991[464] also provide recent examples of such blatantly illegal belligerent practices, to which the international community has not yet found an adequate mode of reaction.

3. The lack of any adequate response to such barbaric excesses is connected with a dilemma besetting the international community, which has found only a rather one-sided solution (in favour of direct humanitarian concerns) in the First Additional Protocol. For a long time it was disputed whether cases of blatant violation of the rules safeguarding the civilian population justify reprisals which injure the enemy's civilian population.[465] Additional Protocol I now unequivocally states that reprisals against the civilian population and against civilian objects are absolutely prohibited. The strictly reciprocal character inherent in traditional rules of humanitarian law has thus been superseded by an 'objective regime' which marginalizes the interests of individual member states in favour of 'community interests' of a purely humanitarian nature.[466] The fundamental provisions of Part IV of AP I cannot therefore be brushed aside under the system of the Protocol even for reprisal, that is by a reaction in deliberate disregard of international law to a prior violation of the law by another state.[467] The prohibition of attacks on the civilian population and on purely civilian objects (Articles 51, para. 6, and 52, para. 1, AP I), on important cultural objects (Article 53, lit. c, AP I), on objects indispensable to the survival of the civilian population (Article 54, para. 4, AP I), on works and installations containing dangerous forces (Article 56, para. 4, AP I), and

[460] See, in particular, Sassòli, *op. cit.*, 396–402; Solf, in Bothe/Partsch/Solf, above (n. 41) 300–1; Dinstein, above (n. 43) 125–6.

[461] Already concerning the traditional customary law, to the same conclusion come Greenspan, above (n. 239) 337; Castrén, above (n. 47) 200–1; Spetzler, above (n. 14) 191–2; Ney, above (n. 240) 224–5; Sassòli, *op. cit.*, 398–9.

[462] As to Bosnia, see the detailed materials on the practices of so-called 'ethnic cleansing' contained in the reports of the Special Rapporteur on Bosnia of the UN Commission of Human Rights, Mazowiecki, esp. UN Doc.A/47/418 of 3 September 1992, 4–9, and UN Doc. A/47/666 of 17 November 1992, 6–12; see also the appeal to the parties of the conflict by the ICRC on 13 August 1992, 74 *RIC* (1992), 511–2.

[463] See F. Ermacora, 'Der Afghanistankonflikt im Lichte des humanitären Völkerrechts' in Haller, Kölz, Müller, Thürer (eds), *Im Dienst an der Gemeinschaft: Festschrift für Dietrich Schindler* (Helbing & Lichtenhahn, 1989), 201–14, at 206.

[464] Cf. H. McCoubrey/N. D. White, *The Blue Helmets: Legal Regulation of United Nations Military Operations* (Aldershot, 1996), 366.

[465] As to that debate, see Kalshoven, above (n. 248) 353–61.

[466] As to the problems of that approach, see Kalshoven, above (n. 285) 54–67.

[467] As to 'reprisal', see Sassòli, *op. cit.*, 428–32, and esp. Kalshoven, above (n. 248) 11–33.

STEFAN OETER

on the natural environment (Article 55, para. 2, AP I) is now absolute and may not be waived even in reprisal, according to a whole series of provisions scattered throughout Chapters II and III of Part IV AP I. The peremptory character of these fundamental safeguards for the benefit of the civilian population is thus most clearly emphasized. In cases of direct participation of civilians in hostilities, they are, however, a lawful target (see Section 404).

> **Defended localities or buildings may be fired at or bombarded in order to:**   455
> — **break down active resistance (conquering fire, bombardment);**
> — **eliminate military objectives located therein (destructive fire, bombardment).**
>
> **In both cases, the fire or bombardment shall be locally limited to the actual resistance and the military objectives.**

Unlike 'undefended localities' (see Sections 461–463), which the prohibition of attacks on the civilian population covers, 'defended localities' constitute legitimate military objectives.[468] Whole cities or villages, however, do not become military objectives merely because some combatants resisting enemy forces remain there. Contemporary humanitarian law in that regard deviates from the approach traditional before World War II, which qualified defended (and in particular besieged) localities as legitimate military objectives *in toto*, thus permitting wholesale destruction of such settlements.[469] Even against such localities, military force is permissible only if and in so far as the violence is justified by military necessity, in order to neutralize enemy resistance and to destroy specific military objects located in it. Only if bombardment of such a locality could achieve military purposes in a strict sense is the use of force justifiable under Article 52, para. 2, AP I. Accordingly, those sections of such a locality the bombardment of which does not offer a definite military advantage must be spared the bombardment—although it must be admitted that the defence of a locality will normally lead to practically all the important objects becoming military objectives.[470]

> **Effective advance warning shall be given of any bombardment, unless circumstances**   456
> **do not permit this (Article 57, para. 2 lit. c, AP I; Article 26 HagueReg).**

Customary law already included an obligation, deduced from the principle of utmost minimization of collateral civilian casualties, that the opposing side should be given advance warning. The enemy authorities should be given the opportunity to evacuate the civilian population (or at least to lodge them in specifically protected localities, such as prepared shelters). Accordingly, Article 26 HagueReg required that the commander of an attacking force should inform the competent authorities of the target location of the fact that a bombardment is planned. Only in a case of assault, that is when the success of an attack depends on surprise, was such a warning deemed to be superfluous (or rather: militarily counterproductive), and therefore a warning of assault is logically excluded by considerations of military necessity.[471] Article 57, para. 2 lit. c, AP I addressed again the question of warning. In essence the new provision in AP I does not go much beyond

---

[468] See Sassòli, *op. cit.*, 355–8; Doswald-Beck, above (n. 20) 158; Dinstein, above (n. 43) 108–11.

[469] See Lauterpacht (ed.), Vol. II, above (n. 242) 421; Castrén, above (n. 47) 201; Meyrowitz, *loc. cit.*, 28; Sassòli, *op. cit.*, 356–7.

[470] In that regard, see Sassòli, *op. cit.*, 357–8.

[471] As to Article 26 Hague Regulations, see Parks, *supra* (n. 8) 157, and Sassòli, 478–81.

STEFAN OETER

what was contained already in Article 26 Hague Regulations,[472] since Article 57, para. 2 lit. c, does not require anything other than an effective advance warning in cases where the attack is likely to cause severe civilian casualties and collateral damage to civilian goods. The attacker may dispense with a warning if 'circumstances do not permit', namely when the specific circumstances of the planned operation do not make it possible to inform the defender because the purpose of the operation could not then be achieved (which in essence is no more than an abstract description of the 'assault' problem).[473] The formulation of the exception in Article 57 AP I is even more vague than the old one contained in Article 26 HagueReg; but again the formula must be interpreted in the light of the overarching principle of military necessity. That means *in concreto* that the advance warning really must be excluded under a military perspective, because for example the element of surprise is crucial for the success of the whole operation. Two problems therefore become decisive, namely the repercussions of the warning on the chances of success of the operation on one hand, and the casualties which the attacking forces are likely to sustain if a warning is issued on the other hand.[474] A general preference for leaving the adversary in doubt about one's operations is obviously not sufficient to fulfil the criteria of the 'exception formula'; the relevant yardstick, however, must not be exaggerated, since it would undermine the plausibility of the system if too high a level were imposed on the extent of casualties which attackers should risk in order to provide an opportunity for evacuation.

457   **It is prohibited in any circumstances to fire at or bombard civilian and military objects without distinction (Article 51, paras. 4–5, AP I).**

1. Article 51, paras. 4 and 5, AP I states the most important consequence of the principle of limited warfare. Essentially, the prohibition against indiscriminate attacks is no more than a logical conclusion from the principle of distinction. The fundamental maxim of distinction and non-combatant immunity not only prohibits attacks on the civilian population but also requires that belligerents must always distinguish between military objectives on one hand and the civilian population and objects on the other.[475] The prohibition of indiscriminate attacks laid down in Article 51, para. 4, AP I is thus a more or less self-evident inference from the fundamental rules of humanitarian law, if not from 'elementary considerations of humanity'. The ICRC and government delegates who were decisive in negotiating, and the Diplomatic Conference as a whole, accordingly considered it—in its abstract version—to be a fundamental rule of humanitarian law firmly established in custom.[476]

2. At the same time, however, the prohibition of indiscriminate attack as enshrined in Article 51 AP I, in its detailed version with many specific rules on combat, is also a development of convention law which far exceeds the customary core of traditional practice.[477] For example, it is way beyond a mere logical deduction from military necessity to state

---

[472] Of a different opinion seems to be Parks, *loc. cit.*, 158; to the point Solf, in Bothe/Partsch/Solf, above (n. 41) 368; Sassòli, 481–4; Quéguiner, above (n. 372) 806–9.

[473] See Pilloud/Pictet, in *ICRC Commentary*, paras. 2223–5 and Solf, ibid. 367–8.

[474] See Burrus Carnahan, ' "Linebacker II" and Protocol I: The Convergence of Law and Professionalism' (1982) 31 *American University Law Review* (1982), 861–70, at 866, with an illustration of the practical problems in the case of the US bombardment of Northern Vietnam in December 1972; as to the NATO Kosovo Air Campaign, see Rowe above (n. 345) 154.

[475] See Kalshoven, above (n. 458) 64; Blix, above (n. 239) 47; Sassòli, *op. cit.*, 403.

[476] See Sassòli, *op. cit.*, 405–8.

[477] Sassòli, *op. cit.*, 407.

STEFAN OETER

that losses among the civilian population, even if resulting from an attack on a military objective and being necessary in a military perspective, may not always be legally permissible. Such a proposition cannot, in pure logic, be derived from the principle of military necessity. The restrictive approach which outlaws collateral damage even if 'militarily necessary' in the traditional sense, therefore needs a further value-judgement and a second fundamental principle, namely the essential principle of proportionality.[478] Only if the concept of military necessity is combined with the principle of proportionality, can one come to the conclusion that collateral damage which is unavoidable in achieving certain military objectives may nevertheless be prohibited by law.[479] The traditional approach, according to which all collateral damage that is unavoidable in attacking a certain military objective must be accepted, is no longer valid.[480] Extreme cases demonstrate the point: the accidental presence of a civilian in a military objective does not render it immune under the rule of distinction; equally, an attack upon a military objective inside a city but which is in itself totally unimportant does not justify an attack on the city as a whole which causes enormous damage to the civilian population. The prohibition of excessive damage, inherent in the prohibition of indiscriminate attack, requires belligerents to relate the military advantage which is expected from an attack to the possible civilian losses.[481] Only if the expected military advantage is of such tactical or strategic importance as to outweigh the collateral damage is the attack justifiable under Article 51 AP I. The criteria of such a balancing act necessarily remain indefinite, and inevitably leave considerable latitude in the assessment of probable consequences and the balancing of the various concerns.[482] However, there is no alternative. The intellectual process of balancing the various elements is so complicated, needs to take into account such a huge amount of data and so many factors, that any attempt to design a formula which is both comprehensive and precise would be ridiculous. In short: common sense is irreplaceable.

3. Though, in the context of modern warfare, if led by high-tech military forces, this balancing act takes a particular risk to blur decisively proportionality. The more professionalized and technologically advanced military forces become, the more military commanders will perceive the life of their soldiers as a precious asset that should be sacrificed only when it becomes unavoidable. They will consider it a decisive military advantage if they can spare the life of their own soldiers, an advantage that justifies a certain amount of collateral damages.[483] With such a reasoning, however, there would not be much left of the principle of distinction.[484]

> **Indiscriminate firing and bombardment means attacks:**   **458**
> — which are not directed at a specific military objective (Article 51, para. 4, lit. a, AP I);
> — which cannot be directed at a specific military objective (Article 51, para. 4, lit. b, AP I); or

[478] On the rule of proportionality in the context of humanitarian law, see Parks, *supra* (n. 8) 168–85; Venturini, above (n. 43) 127–50; Gardam, above (n. 43); R. Geiß/M. Siegrist, 'Has the armed conflict in Afghanistan affected the rules on the conduct of hostilities?' (2011) 93 no 881 *IRRC* 29–34.

[479] Solf, in Bothe/Partsch/Solf, above (n. 41) 304–5.

[480] See Solf, *Protection of Civilians*, 119; Pilloud/Pictet, in *ICRC Commentary*, para. 1946.

[481] See Sassòli, *op. cit.*, 404.

[482] See Bothe, above (n. 350) 535.

[483] See Schmitt, above (n. 31) 10–11.

[484] Oeter, in Heintschel v. Heinegg/Epping (eds), above (n. 339) 58; Geiß/Siegrist, above (n. 478) 34–6.

STEFAN OETER

— whose intended effects cannot be limited to the military objective (Article 51, para. 4 lit. c, AP I).

1. Article 51, para. 4, lit. a–c, AP I undertakes to give concrete meaning to the notion of 'indiscriminate attack'. Whether such a definition is helpful, and whether it does not risk confusing soldiers involved more than it enlightens them (which was the initial purpose of the provision) was a question hotly debated in the course of its drafting.[485] Ultimately, the opinion prevailed that the laconic sentence 'indiscriminate attacks are prohibited' would be too imprecise and would fail to provide practical guidance to the field commanders and staff officers who have to plan and implement military operations.[486] The 'official' explanation of the term 'indiscriminate attack' which, despite its use of a rather abstract formula, already goes into more detail than the earlier definitions, thus tries to elaborate the definitional approach. It carves out three different types of specific attacks which must be considered as violations of the rule of distinction.[487]

2. Article 51, para. 4, lit. a, AP I prohibits attacks which are not directed at a specific military objective; in essence a self-evident consequence of the rule of distinction. The attacker must be sure that the target against which the use of force is directed constitutes a military objective in accordance with humanitarian law, and he must restrict his action as far as possible to that specific objective alone, not objects and persons around it.[488] This raises two particular concerns. The attacking force must—using all available means of intelligence—make sure of directing its operation against a genuine military objective, that is it must clarify whether the object or ground position against which firing or bombardment is directed actually constitutes a military objective the neutralization of which is essential.[489] Blind fire into territory controlled by the adversary is clearly forbidden, which means that firing without reliable information about the objective, and therefore without a clear idea of the nature of the objective, is now strictly outlawed.[490] Also forbidden is the practice of releasing bombs over enemy territory, particularly over settlements, after missing the original objective, which was common in World War II. Such an attack constitutes a paradigm case of indiscriminate warfare. Modern rules of engagement usually exclude this method of disposal of bomb loads; in 'Operation Desert Storm' the rules of engagement of the Allied forces expressly ordered air crews to bring home the entire bomb load when target identification had failed. In addition, the attacker must direct fire specifically at the identified military objectives. In combating a certain objective (or a compound of objectives) he may spread his fire power over a certain area, either as 'harassing fire' against the enemy's lines and deployment areas,[491] or as 'interdiction fire' against certain strategic points, bridgeheads, or ground positions the use of which is intended to be denied to the adversary.[492] Even such kinds of 'barrage fire' covering a certain area, however, must fulfil the basic condition of being directed against

---

[485] Sassòli, *op. cit.*, 405.

[486] Pilloud/Pictet, in *ICRC Commentary*, para. 1950.

[487] That it is not a mere list of examples but a genuine definition 'by law', is demonstrated convincingly by Fischer, above (n. 257) 1831–90; see Rule 12 *CIHL*.

[488] As a general explanation of Article 51, para. 4, lit. a, AP I see Sassòli, *op. cit.*, 420–2; Pilloud/Pictet, in *ICRC Commentary*, paras. 1951–5 and in much detail Fischer, above (n. 257) 185–90.

[489] Pilloud/Pictet, in *ICRC Commentary*, para. 1952; Fischer, *op. cit.*, 189–90.

[490] Sassòli, *op. cit.*, 421.

[491] Cf. Solf, in Bothe/Partsch/Solf, above (n. 41) 307.

[492] Solf, ibid. 308; Pilloud/Pictet, in *ICRC Commentary*, para. 1955.

STEFAN OETER

a specific objective. Accordingly, in these cases the ground area serving as a target must be definable as a military objective in its entirety, that is the whole ground sector must in itself be militarily relevant. It is prohibited to combine clearly separate objectives in one single target area covered by an overall 'area bombardment', since such untargeted fire exposes the civilian population and civilian goods in the intermediate zones to risk.[493] The basic requirement of Article 51, para. 4, lit. a, AP I that the attack should be directed against a 'specific' military objective, draws a boundary which the belligerent may not overstep.[494] The same applies to the use of mines (cf. Sections 411–417). Although it is impossible to deduce a general prohibition on the laying of mines from Article 51, para. 4, AP I, even the ground sector blocked by mines must always constitute a military objective in itself. The neutralization (or closing) of the target area of a mine attack must be militarily necessary, and the surveillance and timely removal of the minefield must ensure that the civilian population will not be injured by the mining operation.[495]

3. Article 51, para. 4, lit. b, AP I prohibits attacks which cannot be directed against a specific military objective. This also concerns methods of warfare which are obviously prohibited by customary law as indiscriminate. The drafters of the provision had primarily in mind traditional remotely controlled weapons with extremely low target accuracy, such as long-range missiles with only a rudimentary guidance system. In these cases, the construction of the weapon itself (in combination with the specific operative modalities under which these weapons are used) leaves no doubt as to the nature of the attack. The mode of operation of such an attack usually makes it impossible to distinguish between military objectives and civilian objects.[496] Thus, the attack is inherently unable to fulfil the requirements of distinction. The prime example of such an operation which *per definitionem* leads to an indiscriminate attack is the German use of V2 missiles against British cities in World War II.[497] More recent practice also provides examples of such indiscriminate missile attacks, such as the series of missiles launched on Iraqi and Iranian cities during the Gulf War and the Iraqi attacks with 'Scud' missiles on Israel in the Kuwait War of 1991.[498] Aside from these self-evident cases, it remains in dispute how far (beyond the core just described) the prohibition in Article 51, para. 4, lit. b really reaches. For example, there are many arguments in favour of including in the prohibition certain kinds of conventional bombing raids, at least those where the bombardment cannot in practice be limited to specific military objectives. Night attacks without adequate targeting equipment fall into this category, or bombing raids from extremely high altitudes where the target accuracy becomes unacceptably low.[499] The prohibition seems, however, not to cover specific categories of weapons as such. Some states insisted on this during the drafting of the provision.[500] Certain operational uses of dangerous weapons were thought to be outlawed under Article 51, para. 4, lit. b: operations where the distinction between military objectives and civilian objects is by

[493] See Sassòli, *op. cit.*, 421–2; Fleck, above (n. 342) 52–3; Dinstein, above (n. 43) 118–20.

[494] See Sassòli, *op. cit.*, 421–2; Fischer, *op. cit.*, 186, 188–9.

[495] See Solf, in Bothe/Partsch/Solf, above (n. 41) 308 (he mainly refers to Article 51, para. 4, lit. b, AP I).

[496] Sassòli, *op. cit.*, 422–5.

[497] See Spaight *op. cit.*, (n. 239) 214–7; Castrén, above (n. 47) 204; Greenspan, above (n. 239) 365–7.

[498] See Schmitt, above (n. 249) 55.

[499] See Ney, above (n. 240) 226; Sassòli, *op. cit.*, 424; Byron, *supra* (n. 350) 1893.

[500] Solf, in Bothe/Partsch/Solf, above (n. 41) 306; Sassòli, *op. cit.*, 424; Domínguez-Matés in Fernández-Sánchez, above (n. 71) 109.

STEFAN OETER

definition impossible because the weapons cannot be directed specifically at individual military objectives. In principle, this sounds convincing. However, there remains an inherent tendency which extends the provision's application beyond a mere prohibition of certain operational designs; 'blind' weapons such as long-range missiles without adequate guidance systems, or traditional minefields laid without customary precautions (i.e. unrecorded, unmarked, and not designed to destroy themselves within a reasonable time) are difficult to imagine as compatible with Article 51, para. 4, lit. b.[501]

4. Article 51, para. 4, lit. c, API, outlaws attacks whose intended effects cannot be limited to the military objective, and is the most controversial part of the definition of indiscriminate attacks. Lit. c of Article 51, para. 4, reads as follows: 'Indiscriminate attacks are . . . (c) those which employ a method or means of combat the effects of which cannot be limited as required by this Protocol.' This refers to a whole series of limitations on the use of force: the rules on the protection of the environment (Articles 35, para. 3, and 55, para. 1), the prohibition of attacks on works and installations containing dangerous forces (Article 56), and the principle of proportionality.[502] Proportionality, in particular, has been a point of a fierce controversy. It was debated to what extent a prohibition of excessive damage really constitutes an established part of previously existing customary law, or to put it in another way, to what extent Article 51, para. 4, lit. c, AP I refers to an established principle of proportionality.[503] The starting point is the fact that the version of the rule which was finally adopted by the Diplomatic Conference deliberately included the problem of disproportionate attacks. The formulation of this, however, was rather cryptic, since it implicitly focused on methods of warfare which necessarily cause excessive losses to the civilian population.[504] Thus, the weapons primarily concerned are those whose effects are spread over a wide area, such as phosphorous incendiary bombs or other variants of incendiary weapons, or so-called 'cluster bombs'.[505] If these undirected weapons are used in densely populated regions their effects will necessarily be disproportionate[506] and accordingly they are prohibited under Article 51, para. 4, lit. c, AP I. During Operation Desert Storm, more than 61,000 cluster bombs were dropped by coalition forces on Iraq and Kuwait;[507] the NATO forces, during the Kosovo Air Campaign, dropped an estimated 1,400 cluster bombs, each containing between 147 and 202 submunitions, on targets in Serbia and Kosovo.[508] Recently, cluster bombs were being extensively used during the Israeli offensive in Lebanon in summer 2006.[509] Some authors argue that military planners are capable of directing cluster munitions at lawful military objectives; according to them, it rather depends on the specific employment of the weapon whether it entails indiscriminate attacks.[510] In contrast, the ICRC

---

[501] Convincingly argued by Solf, ibid. 305.
[502] Solf, in Bothe/Partsch/Solf, above (n. 41) 305–6.
[503] See Sassòli, *op. cit.*, 427.
[504] Fischer, above (n. 257) 195.
[505] Herby/Nuiten, above (n. 192) 198; as to the cluster bomb technology, see Thomas J. Herthel, 'On the Chopping Block: Cluster Munitions and the Law of War' (2001) 51 *Air Force Law Review* 234–5; as to the use of white phosphorous and its problematic results, see I. J. MacLeod and A. P. V. Rogers, 'The Use of White Phosphorous and the Law of War' (2007) 10 *YIHL* 75–97.
[506] See Sassòli, *op. cit.*, 426–7.
[507] Herthel, above (n. 505) 239.
[508] Herby/Nuiten, above (n. 505) 199; Herthel, *loc. cit.*, 231.
[509] ICRC, *Annual Report 2006*, 335–9.
[510] Herthel, above (n. 505) 264–9.

STEFAN OETER

calls upon the states to end the use of inaccurate and unreliable cluster munitions and to prohibit the targeting of cluster munitions against any military objective located in a populated area.[511] This proposal is being supported by the 'Cluster Munition Coalition', a network founded in 2003 by civil society organizations; equally, a growing number of states pleads for the adoption of a binding instrument containing such a prohibition.[512] Although the international community has concluded special agreements on most of the armament items inherently covered by the provision (UN Weapons Convention of 1980; see Sections 402, 411–429) it remains to be resolved under a general perspective whether the particular convention rules which refer only to specific categories of weapons (excluding, e.g., cluster bombs) are really exhaustive, or whether the general rule of Article 51, para. 4, lit. c, AP I should not be seen as providing an overriding legal framework which imposes a final limit. Most considerations speak in favour of such a proposition, so that weapons not regulated by the 1980 Convention are subject to the more general principle codified in Article 51, para. 4, lit. c, AP I.[513]

5. Particular problems arise from the definition of legally permissible uses of nuclear weapons (see Sections 432 to 434). If one assumes, as did the ICRC in its original draft, and which the nuclear powers later confirmed in their declarations, that the Additional Protocol did not intend to broach the question of legality of nuclear weapons, a further question arises immediately. Must Article 51, para. 4, lit. c, AP I be considered as an expression of established customary law, which continues to exist alongside the convention regulation in Additional Protocol I?[514] As long as Article 51, para. 4, lit. c is seen to rely only on an established principle of proportionality, that question must be answered in the affirmative. Therefore, the use of weapons of mass destruction, which inevitably causes disproportionate collateral damage if used in densely populated areas, would in principle have to be considered as prohibited by public international law, independent of Article 51, para. 4, lit. c, AP I as a convention norm. At least first use of such nuclear munitions against urban settlements is accordingly already prohibited under customary principles. Only modern precision-guided nuclear warheads for combat against purely military objectives, and retaliatory use of nuclear weapons by way of reprisal, remain permissible, and not subject to the legal obstacles imposed by the customary standards here analysed.

> **Attacks and bombardments are also to be considered as indiscriminate if:**   **459**
> — **a number of clearly separate and distinct military objectives located in a built-up area are attacked as if they were one single military objective (Article 51, para. 5, lit. a, AP I);**
> — **they are likely to cause loss of civilian life, injury to civilians or damage to civilian objects which would be excessive in relation to the concrete and direct military advantage anticipated (Article 51, para. 5, lit. b, AP I);**
> — **they also cause excessive injury and damage to civilians or civilian objects located outside the actual target area and its immediate vicinity.**

---

[511] ICRC, *Official Statement* of 6 November 2006 <http://www.icrc.org/web/eng/siteeng0.nsf/htmlall/cluster-munition-statement-061106?opendocument>.

[512] See <http://www.stopclustermunitions.org/>.

[513] So argues Sassòli, *op. cit.*, 427–8.

[514] Ibid. 426–8.

STEFAN OETER

1. The still abstract definition of what constitutes an 'indiscriminate attack' contained in Article 51, para. 4, AP I is supplemented in para. 5 of Article 51 by two examples of situations which had long been debated. Article 51, para. 5, now states expressly that they are covered by the prohibition of indiscriminate attack.[515] The clarification concerns on one hand the practice of 'area bombardment' which had become common in World War II and which was claimed to be legal by the Allied Powers at the time.[516] It is true that discussion has continued for decades as to whether area bombardments are not already outlawed under the customary prohibition of indiscriminate attacks,[517] 'area bombardments' being defined as bombardments which combine a number of clearly separate and distinct military objectives located in a built-up area and treating them as one single military objective. State practice hitherto had not demonstrated its willingness to accept such a prohibition,[518] although it is not difficult to argue that a prohibitory rule follows from the general prohibition of indiscriminate attacks. Thus, Article 51, para. 5, lit. a, AP I constitutes an important innovation, since it makes clear that such practices of area bombardment are generally inadmissible.[519] Only where a genuine target area is attacked (i.e. a passage or ground sector the whole of which constitutes a military objective, or where several military objectives are so intermingled that they are practically inseparable and thus can only be attacked together) does bombardment of a wide area remain permissible.[520]

2. The second important point of debate clarified by Article 51, para. 5, AP I is the validity and scope of the principle of proportionality. Admittedly, it had already been widely accepted before the adoption of AP I that attacks on military objectives are subject to elementary restrictions. If collateral damage is likely to affect the civilian population and civilian goods as a consequence of the attack, the anticipated damage must not be excessive in relation to the intended military advantage.[521] Beyond that minimum requirement, Article 51, para. 5, lit. b, now ultimately settles that all damaging effects of military operations must be measured on the yardstick of proportionality.[522] The collateral damage which inevitably occurs on the occasion of nearly every attack is justifiable only in so far as losses to the 'innocent' civilian population are commensurate with the military advantage which the operation sought to achieve.[523] As a general rule

---

[515] On Article 51, para. 5, AP I see Solf, in Bothe/Partsch/Solf, above (n. 41) 309–11; Pilloud/Pictet, in *ICRC Commentary*, paras. 1967–81.

[516] See Spaight, *op. cit.*, (n. 239) 270–81; Greenspan, above (n. 239) 336; Rousseau, above (n. 47); Blix, above (n. 239) 36–7; Dinstein, above (n. 43) 118–20.

[517] See Spaight, *op. cit.*, (n. 239) 270–3, 280–1; Stone, above (n. 239) 627–31; MacDonald/Bruha, Bombardment, *MPEPIL*, para. 8; Baxter, in UNESCO/Institut Henry Dunant (eds), above (n. 1) 148; Blix, above (n. 239); Rule 13 *CIHL*.

[518] See Sassòli, *op. cit.*, 409–11, with a detailed presentation of the relevant state practice.

[519] See Aldrich, above (n. 261) 780; Sassòli, *op. cit.*, 411; Blix, above (n. 239) 61–9.

[520] See Solf, in Bothe/Partsch/Solf, above (n. 41) 309; see also the US persistence during the negotiations on the condition of a 'significant distance' between the different military objectives; cf. Parks, *supra* (n. 8) 161.

[521] On the customary rule of proportionality see Venturini, above (n. 43) 127–32; Parks, *loc. cit.*, 168–75; Solf, ibid. 309; Greenspan, above (n. 239) 335; Aldrich, above (n. 261) 778; Doswald-Beck, above (n. 20) 156; Sassòli, *op. cit.*, 412–5; Holland, above (n. 329) 51–2; Rule 14 *CIHL*.

[522] Concerning the rather controversial debate on including criteria of proportionality in AP I, see Fenrick, 'The Rule of Proportionality and Protocol I in Conventional Warfare' (1982) 98 *Military Law Review* 91–112; Pilloud/Pictet, in *ICRC Commentary*, paras. 2204–18; Solf, ibid. 309–10, 361; Sassòli, *op. cit.*, 415–8; as to the combination of indiscriminate and disproportionate attacks in Article 51, para. 5, AP I, see Gardam, above (n. 43) 93–6.

[523] See Solf, ibid. 310.

STEFAN OETER

this sounds reasonable. However, the principle of proportionality creates serious difficulties in practice, since it necessarily remains loosely defined and is subject to subjective assessment and balancing. In the framework of the required evaluation, the actors enjoy a considerable margin of appreciation.[524] This is particularly true in view of the strongly prognostic character of any such assessment, which must always be an assessment of the future effects of the operation. Objective standards for the appraisal and balancing of expected collateral damage and intended military advantage are virtually non-existent. Proportionality requires that two very unlike values be weighed and balanced against each other, without any objective method to compare two such disparate categories.[525] In the final result, therefore, it is for the competent military commander and the staff planning the operation—who should know best the possible results and repercussions—to assess the consequences of the operation and to ensure its proportionality.[526] Final responsibility is thus laid in the hands of the military, which can act only on the basis of the information available at the time of the decision. Germany, like most other NATO members ratifying AP I, therefore filed a declaration that 'the decision taken by the person responsible has to be judged on the basis of all information available to him at the relevant time, and not on the basis of hindsight'.[527] In a second interpretative declaration Germany stated that by 'definite military advantage' in Article 51, para. 5, lit. b, AP I it understands 'the advantage anticipated from the attack considered as a whole and not only from isolated or particular parts of the attack'.[528] This means that the point of reference of the required balancing is not the gain of territory or other advantage expected from the isolated action of a single unit, but the wider military campaign of which that action forms part. Only in the framework of the more complex overall campaign plan of a belligerent can one assess the relative military value of the specific purpose of an individual attack.[529] In essence, this should be self-evident: actions of individual units are not ends in themselves in modern integrated warfare. To the contrary, they must be placed in their operational context.

3. A further problem makes the handling of the proportionality requirement of Article 51, para. 5, lit. b, AP I extremely difficult. In practice, the circumstances usually involve combatants and civilians, military objects or installations and civilian settlements; industrial plants, and infrastructure installations of dual use. Such a complicated mixture of categories, however, not only makes it difficult to meet the requirements of distinction, but also makes collateral damage inevitable, and often considerable. To prevent

[524] As to these problems see esp. Fenrick, *loc. cit.*, 126, and Solf, ibid. 310.
[525] See Holland, above (n. 329) 46–7.
[526] Doswald-Beck, in Meyer (ed.), above (n. 20) 156; see also Kalshoven/Zegveld, above (n. 22) 115; for the subsequent difficulties with respect to the criminal responsibility according to Article 8, para. 2, lit. b(iv), ICC Statute, see Torsten Stein, 'Collateral Damage, Proportionality and Individual International Criminal Responsibility' in Heintschel v. Heinegg/Epping, above (n. 339) 158–61.
[527] See BR-Drs. 64/90 of 2 February 1990, 132 (Germany), 125 (Belgium), 127 (Italy), 129 (the Netherlands), 130 (Spain); see also Schindler/Toman, above (n. 380) 707, 712, 714, 717; as to the underlying problem see B. J. Bill, 'The Rendulic "Rule": Military Necessity, Commander's Knowledge, and Methods of Warfare' (2009) 12 *YIHL* 119–55, at 133–42.
[528] See BR-Drs. 64/90 of 2 February 1990, 132; as to the background of the declaration see also Fenrick, in (1982) 98 *Military Law Review* 107; Parks, *supra* (n. 8) 172; Solf, in Bothe/Partsch/Solf, above (n. 41) 311, 325; Sassòli, *op. cit.*, 417; Doswald-Beck, in Meyer (ed.), above (n. 20) 156–7; Dinstein, above (n. 43) 92–5.
[529] See Sassòli, *op. cit.*, 414, with further references, as well as N. Neuman, 'Applying the Rule of Proportionality: Force Protection and Cumulative Assessment in International Law and Morality' (2004) 7 *YIHL* 79–112, at 96–100; see also Watkin, above (n. 329) 19–21.

STEFAN OETER

excessive losses and damage to the civilian population proves extremely difficult in such situations, unless the adversary takes it upon himself to ensure a certain minimum separation between military objectives and civilian population.[530] For example, the NATO bombing of the Serbian state television in 1999 (which has been classified as a military objective, see Section 444) caused the death of up to seventeen civilians; these casualties were assessed by the Committee Established to Review the NATO Bombing Campaign Against the Federal Republic of Yugoslavia as not 'clearly disproportionate'.[531] A particularly difficult problem is caused for the attacker if the opposing side illegally uses the civilian population to shield military activities, whether by transferring parts of the civilian population deliberately to military installations, or by calculatedly establishing military objectives among the civilian population and civilian objects, a common example of which is sub-contracting in the armaments industry.[532] Article 51, para. 8, AP I now expressly confirms that the violation of international legal obligations by the adversary does not exempt the attacker from his legal obligations with regard to the civilian population.[533] The problem is obviously not solved by that new provision—quite the contrary. The attacker will face extreme difficulties of justification, without having the alternative of accepting a higher level of collateral damage, if he wants effectively to counter the moves of the other side.[534] Also, the role of civilians deliberately incorporated into the military organization of the belligerent, such as workers in arms factories or civilian drivers of munitions transports, has remained unclear in that regard.[535] Does the loss of thousands of workers in an attack on a munitions factory have the same relative value, in terms of the proportionality of collateral damage, as the predictable deaths of women and children caused by an attack on a military command centre located in the midst of a densely populated civilian quarter? Does the rule of proportionality allow measures avoiding risks of casualties among one's own soldiers to the detriment of the civilian population?[536] Many would argue no, but it must be admitted that many questions are left open.[537] The role of the commander responsible for the operation is not made easier by these uncertainties, although one should not exaggerate demands for exact detail in such a rule. What is required is no more than a sincere effort to cope with the problem of collateral damage, and a proper application of common sense. Humanitarian law in that regard is dependent on an inherent sense of humanity, whose impulse is to avoid attacks causing catastrophic collateral damage when the objective is of only marginal importance; in other words, which shuns blatant disproportionality. Judging proportionality thus is, in essence, a decision that appeals to individual morality and relies on moral judgement of deciding commanders.[538]

4. Comparable elementary considerations underlie the third sub-category, the case of excessive injury and damage to civilians or civilian objects located outside the actual target area and

---

[530] See the critical observations by Parks, *loc. cit.*, 152–6.

[531] Final Report to the Prosecutor by the Committee Established to Review the NATO Bombing Campaign Against the Federal Republic of Yugoslavia, (2000) 39 *ILM* 1279 para. 77.

[532] See Parks, *supra* (n. 8) 159–68; Oeter, in Heintschel v. Heinegg/Epping (eds), above (n. 339) 59–60.

[533] See Parks, *loc. cit.*, 163–4; Sassòli, *op. cit.*, 447–53; and Pilloud/Pictet, in *ICRC Commentary*, paras. 1989–93.

[534] See the critical remarks of Parks, *loc. cit.*, 164–5, on that point.

[535] Ibid. 174–9.

[536] See Neuman, above (n. 529) 90–6.

[537] See, e.g., Dinstein, above (n. 43) 131, 136, and Byron, above (n. 350) 195.

[538] See Holland, above (n. 329) 73–4.

STEFAN OETER

its immediate vicinity. The pre-existing customary prohibition of such attacks results from the rule of distinction and the prohibition of attacks which are not directed against a specific objective, or the effects of which cannot be directed against a military objective (see Section 455). The damaging effects must not only be specifically directed (or directable) against the military objective; the planning and implementation of the attack must also ensure that the effects of the force employed are restricted to the military objective and do not result in the civilian population living nearby being damaged more than the military objective which was targeted.[539] At the same time proportionality must be observed, with the dictate that collateral damage may not exceed the direct military advantage achieved by the operation.

> **Before engaging an objective, every responsible military leader shall:**   **460**
> — **verify the military nature of the objective to be attacked (Article 57, para. 2, lit. a(i), AP I);**
> — **choose means and methods minimizing incidental injury and damage to civilian life and objects (Article 57, para. 2, lit. a(ii), AP I);**
> — **refrain from launching any attack which may be expected to cause incidental injury and damage to civilian life and objects which would be excessive in relation to the concrete and direct military advantage anticipated (Article 57, para. 2, lit. a (iii), AP I);**
> — **give the civilian population advance warning of attacks which may affect it, unless circumstances do not permit this (Article 57, para. 2, lit. c, AP I);**
> — **when a choice is possible between several military objectives of equal importance, engage that objective the attack on which is likely to cause the least incidental injury or damage (Article 57, para. 3, AP I).**
>
> **The obligation to take feasible precautions in attack applies equally to the operation of unmanned combat aerial vehicles—UCAVs—(Rule 39 *HPCR Manual*).**
>
> **An attack shall be suspended if it becomes apparent that the objective is not military or is subject to special protection or that the attack may be expected to cause excessive incidental loss of civilian life (Article 57, para. 2 lit. b, AP I).**

1. The rule repeats almost verbatim the content of Article 57 AP I. By that article the international community drew its conclusions from the above explained rules on methods of warfare as to the precautions required by the attacking party in order to avoid or minimize civilian loss and damage. The military authorities responsible for preparing and implementing an attack are required by Article 57 AP I to implement certain elementary safeguards and are subject to stringent standards in their attempts to protect the civilian population from collateral damage.[540] Paragraph 1 of the provision begins by stating the general principle underlying the whole provision, namely that the attacker shall take 'constant care' to spare the civilian population and civilian objects in the conduct of military operations, or—as formulated in the 1967 ICRC Memorandum—to reduce the damage inflicted upon non-combatants to a minimum.[541] This rule may be deduced from the general principle of military necessity provided by customary law.[542] With regard to non-international armed conflicts the same result is achieved by

---

[539] As to the practical problems of such a rule, see Doswald-Beck, above (n. 20) 157.
[540] As to the history and substance of Article 57 AP I, see Sassòli, *op. cit.*, 459–89; Solf, in Bothe/Partsch/Solf, above (n. 41) 361–9; Pilloud/Pictet, in *ICRC Commentary*, paras. 2184–8.
[541] See Sassòli, *op. cit.*, 458.
[542] See Castrén, above (n. 47) 202; Spetzler, above (n. 14) 193; Sassòli, *op. cit.*, 456–64; Rule 16 *CIHL*.

STEFAN OETER

the humanitarian minimum standard laid down in common Article 3 of the Geneva Conventions.

2. Although the general rule requiring precautions is undisputed, one essential problem remains, namely as to which individuals are addressed by Article 57. The obligations should be understood to address primarily commanders and staff officers who are directly responsible for specific operations, and only to a lesser degree the individual soldiers participating directly in the attack.[543] Due to the lack of sufficient information, even non-commissioned officers and unit commanders up to the level of company commanders will not normally have the overview of the military situation which is required for an adequate evaluation of the legality of operations under Articles 48–57 AP I, in particular for the assessment of proportionality. Without an adequate idea of the operational framework and of the nature and importance of the target, however, the safeguard measures provided for in Article 57 AP I cannot be implemented satisfactorily. Junior officers and soldiers in the field will thus have to rely on the assessment given by their superiors,[544] with the exception of obvious war crimes such as deliberate indiscriminate attacks. Only in so far as these officers and soldiers independently plan and carry out operations will comparable precautions be required of them. Some states have expressly recorded their understanding as to this point by filing corresponding declarations or reservations. Switzerland, for example, declared on the occasion of ratification: 'The provisions of Article 57, para. 2, are binding only on battalion or group commanders and higher echelons. The determining factor shall be the information available to such commanders at the time of reaching a decision.'[545]

3. The point of reference of this declaration is the introductory formula of Article 57, para. 2, lit. a, AP I, which reads: 'Those who plan or decide upon an attack . . .' Such a restrictive clause is necessary since the specific precautions required by lit. a apply only to the planning staff and commanders who decide upon an attack. These persons bearing responsibility for operational decisions are required by point (i) of lit. a to 'do everything feasible to verify that the objectives to be attacked are neither civilians nor civilian objects and are not subject to special protection but are military objectives within the meaning of para. 2 of Article 52, and that it is not prohibited by the provisions of this Protocol to attack them'. This is clearly intended primarily to impose a duty of verification, a duty to collect sufficient information to clarify the nature of the objective.[546] The command authorities responsible for planning and deciding upon an attack must employ all means of reconnaissance and intelligence available to them unless and until there is sufficient certainty of the military nature of the objective of an attack.[547] Since there is an inherent danger of cognitive bias in that regard, all feasible precautions must be taken to avoid and counter such biases. What is required is a subjective certainty: the standard of Article 57 in that regard is relative, for there is no absolute obligation to employ all means until the ultimate attack. As soon as there are no longer any serious doubts concerning the military character of the objective (and the other requirements of lawfulness, such as proportionality have been

[543] As to the question of who is primarily affected by Article 57 see Sassòli, *op. cit.*, 461, 463; Pilloud/Pictet, in *ICRC Commentary*, para. 2197; Kalshoven/Zegveld, above (n. 22) 115; Byron, above (n. 350) 200.
[544] Solf, in Bothe/Partsch/Solf, above (n. 41) 366–7.
[545] Printed in Schindler/Toman, above (n. 379) 716. See also Sassòli, *op. cit.*, 463; Solf, ibid. 362–3.
[546] Sassòli, *op. cit.*, 464–70; Pilloud/Pictet, in *ICRC Commentary*, paras. 2194–6.
[547] See Solf, in Bothe/Partsch/Solf, above (n. 41) 363, and Byron, above (n. 350), 196.

STEFAN OETER

observed), the duty of Article 57, lit. a(i) is satisfied.[548] Where doubt remains, however, the situation is more problematic. For a military actor lacking elaborate means of gathering the necessary intelligence (a case not far from reality in most Third World conflicts), there is a simple alternative: refraining from attack or attacking without sufficient certainty as to the military character of the objective. Under Article 57 AP I (and the corresponding customary rule in non-international conflicts) only the first option is legal; the second risks violating the principle of distinction. Although most military actors in internal conflict tend to an attack on the basis of mere suspicion in such cases,[549] they should be aware that this may constitute a war crime (or a crime against humanity in internal conflict), to which lack of information is no defence.

4. Sub-paragraph a(ii) calls upon commanders and planning staff officers to 'take all feasible precautions in the choice of means and methods of attack with a view to avoiding, and in any event to minimizing, incidental loss of civilian life, injury to civilians and damage to civilian objects'.[550] The required measures relate in particular to the problems of so-called 'targeting', including target development and battle damage assessment, and to the choice of weapons and ammunition used in the attack.[551] How to select and locate the objective, and the linked question of selecting the weapons best suited for the attack, is probably the essential question in the practical implementation of the principles of distinction and proportionality.[552] Only if the target becomes, as far as possible, precisely demarcated and if, in selecting the means of attack and establishing the mission parameters, it is ensured that the effects of the use of force are as far as possible limited to the military objective, can the 'rule of proportionality' be realized in military practice.[553] Yet, the logistics of such mission parameters are so complex and depend on so many factors that it is impossible to express the consequences of distinction and proportionality in a precise formula. The flexibility of the clauses contained in AP I reflect the recognition by the international community that it is not possible to regulate all the infinite variables affecting military operations in a stringent provision. The location and physical character of the objective, the configuration of the surrounding terrain, the presence of civilians in the vicinity of the objective and the adjacency of military and civilian objects, the degree to which the target is defended and the resulting risks for the attacker's personnel and equipment, the quality of the weaponry used by attacker and defender (in particular the relative accuracy of artillery, bombs, and missiles), the standards of technical training of combatants and their physical and psychological condition, meteorological conditions—all these may be factors decisive to the final result.[554] The list could easily be extended. Also the 'rules of engagement' governing the operating forces might play a key role in conforming with Article 57, para. 2, lit. a(ii); to give

---

[548] See Pilloud/Pictet, in *ICRC Commentary*, para. 2195; see also as to corresponding problems in the course of the Kuwait War 1991, McCoubrey/White, above (n. 464) 366.

[549] See R. K. Goldman, 'International Humanitarian Law: Americas Watch's Experience in Monitoring Internal Armed Conflicts' (1993) 9 *American University Journal of International Law and Policy* 67–8.

[550] Rule 17 *CIHL*; cf. also the US Army Guidelines on 'Civilian Casualty Mitigation', Headquarters, Department of the Army, Doc. ATTP 3-37.31 of July 2012, available at <https://armypubs.us.army.mil/doctrine/index.html>.

[551] Pilloud/Pictet, in ICRC *Commentary*, para. 2200, but see also. Watkin, above (n. 329) 23–5.

[552] See Sassòli, *op. cit.*, 470; Castrén, above (n. 47) 202; Kalshoven/Zegveld, above (n. 22) 113–4; Bothe, above (n. 334) 33; Byron, above (n. 350), 197.

[553] Pilloud/Pictet, in *ICRC Commentary*, para. 2200.

[554] Solf, in Bothe/Partsch/Solf, above (n. 41) 364.

STEFAN OETER

one example, the principle included in the rules of engagement of the US Air Force in Vietnam and in the Kuwait War of 1991, according to which bomber aircraft must return home with the entire bomb load unless they are 100 per cent certain of their target,[555] may have decisive importance in minimizing unnecessary collateral damage in aerial operations. In general, the weapon with most accurate delivery parameters should be employed to attack a military objective with civilian objects in its vicinity.[556] In some cases there may also be a requirement to use infantry operations in circumstances where firepower (air support or artillery) would traditionally have been employed. However, it is not to be expected that one could ever structure the whole question in a short and precise formula; the individual responsibility of the competent commander will therefore be sanctioned only in extreme cases, such as deliberate attacks on obviously civilian objects, because the above-mentioned uncertainties must be taken into account when assessing *ex post facto* the legality of an operation. What is required is a decision taken in good faith according to the standard of a 'reasonable military commander', and nothing more.[557] However, some general safeguards will also apply in nearly every case at the level of high command. In order to avoid precipitate decisions being made without sufficient information, also certain procedural safeguards must be taken in order to counter the inherent cognitive biases that accompany that type of decision. It is advisable to follow the example of the US forces during 'Operation Desert Storm' (Kuwait/ Iraq 1991) and a number of other recent operations, which provided for the control of targeting decisions and operations plans by legal advisers to the armed forces who were specially trained for that task.[558] Admittedly, such an additional precaution is not required by Article 57, para. 2, lit. a(ii), but the mechanism is effective in assisting the competent commander in the exercise of his responsibilities, as long as the legal advice is properly taken into account.

5. Article 57, para. 2, lit. a(iii) also reiterates the rule of proportionality. Command authorities and planning staff must ensure that operations remain within the bounds of proportionality, that is that they do not cause collateral damage which is excessive in relation to the expected military advantage.[559] Excessive attacks may result in criminal responsibility for the competent commander and staff officers responsible for their operation, since indiscriminate attacks in violation of the requirement of proportionality constitute 'grave breaches' as provided by Article 85, para. 3, lit. b, AP I, which must be sanctioned as war crimes by the criminal justice system.[560] Some military authors, particularly in the US, have argued that an offence based on the principle of proportionality is too vague and uncertain to form the basis of a prosecution according to the rule

---

[555] Concerning the US practice in Vietnam, see Carnahan, above (n. 474) 866 and Parks, *supra* (n. 8) 154 n. 459.

[556] See also Byron, above (n. 350) 197.

[557] See Holland, above (n. 329) 48–9.

[558] See Keenan, above (n. 338) 36.

[559] As to background and legal effects of Article 57, para. 2, lit. a(iii), AP I, see Sassòli, *op. cit.*, 473–4; Solf, in Bothe/Partsch/Solf, 364–5; Pilloud/Pictet, in *ICRC Commentary*, paras. 2204–19; see also Rule 18 *CIHL* and US Army Guidelines on 'Civilian Casualty Mitigation', above (n. 550), paras. 1–10.

[560] See Pilloud/Pictet, in *ICRC Commentary*, para. 2216; Zimmermann, ibid. 995–6 (paras. 3477–81); Partsch, in Bothe/Partsch/Solf, above (n. 41) 511–22, at 516; in this context, the Committee Established to Review the NATO Bombing Campaign Against the Federal Republic of Yugoslavia undertook an examination as to a possible criminal responsibility of military leaders concerning the NATO attacks during the Kosovo Air Campaign: 'Final Report to the Prosecutor', (2000) 39 *ILM* 1257–83; see also Bothe, above (n. 334) 34.

STEFAN OETER

of law.[561] It must be admitted that there is a debatable point here; war crime definitions in general, however, may not be equated with ordinary provisions in internal criminal codes, since war crimes are always dependent on imprecise rules of public international law, the violation of which is defined as a crime under international law. Since blatant violations of the principle of proportionality are traditionally considered to be unlawful indiscriminate attacks resulting in international responsibility, the objection is ultimately not convincing.

6. Article 57, para. 2, lit. c, also repeats the requirement of an effective advance warning prior to attacks which may cause damage to the civilian population, a rule which in principle was already binding on belligerents by virtue of Article 26 HagueReg (for details, see Section 456).

7. Article 57, para. 3, AP I stresses the self-evident consequence of the principle of proportionality and the corresponding general principle of optimal minimization of collateral civilian damage:[562] the need to choose, when several military objectives would provide equal military advantage, the objective 'the attack on which is likely to cause the least danger to civilian lives and objects'.[563] An example often cited is the option to attack, instead of a railway station inside a city, an equally important railway junction or line at a strategically important point outside a densely populated area, on the basis that the destruction of such a crucial point causes as much disruption to the enemy lines of communication as the destruction of an urban station.[564]

8. The duties of military leaders to take precautions in favour of the civilian population relates not only to the planning and preparation prior to an attack, but also to its implementation.[565] The officers responsible for carrying out each operation must minimize collateral damage to the civilian population even during the course of combat operations (Article 57, para. 2, lit. b, AP I). They must call off the attack immediately if it becomes clear that the attacked objective does not have the supposed military character, but constitutes a purely civilian object.[566] They must halt fire if it becomes apparent that the incidental danger to the civilian population is more serious than had been expected.[567] The commanders responsible for the attack must also call off the attack if the military advantage which can still be obtained from the operation becomes too small in relation to the probable collateral damage to the civilian population.[568] Military leaders, therefore, must ensure for the entire course of the operation that the attack remains inside the limits drawn by the rules of humanitarian law. All this relates primarily to military leaders, as was made clear by the wording of the preceding phrases. Whether a corresponding duty also affects the lower levels of hierarchy actually engaged in combat remains

---

[561] See G. S. Prugh, 'American Issues and Friendly Reservations Regarding Protocol I, Additional to the Geneva Conventions' (1992) XXXI *RDMilG* 272–3.

[562] See Sassòli, *op. cit.*, 485; Solf, in Bothe/Partsch/Solf, above (n. 41) 368; Kalshoven, above (n. 458) 66.

[563] As to the interpretation of Article 57, para. 3, AP I see Sassòli, *op. cit.*, 485–9, and Solf, ibid. 368–9; Gardam, above (n. 43) 96–8; Rule 21 *CIHL*.

[564] See Pilloud/Pictet, in *ICRC Commentary*, para. 2227; Sassòli, *op. cit.*, 487.

[565] Pilloud/Pictet, in *ICRC Commentary*, para. 2220.

[566] See Solf, in Bothe/Partsch/Solf, above (n. 41) 366; Sassòli, *op. cit.*, 474–7; Pilloud/Pictet, in *ICRC Commentary*, para. 2221; Kalshoven/Zegveld, above (n. 22) 113–14.

[567] See Sassòli, *op. cit.*, 474–6, and Byron, above (n. 350), 198.

[568] Solf, in Bothe/Partsch/Solf, above (n. 41) 366–7; Gardam, above (n. 43) 98.

STEFAN OETER

in doubt, however. On one hand, if there is a duty on ordinary soldiers to halt fire or break off an attack in the case of flagrant indiscriminate attack, this can relate only to the decisive phase of immediate combat.[569] Yet, ordinary soldiers and junior officers have no authority to resist their superiors' orders and to break off an operation; they would risk sanction under domestic martial law if in following their personal judgement they refused to obey orders. Accordingly, the obligation in Article 57, para. 2, lit. b, AP I for ordinary cases cannot extend below the level of commanders with authority to stop or modify an operation.[570] Only in extraordinary cases does there exist a counterbalance: an order to commit a war crime (which in this respect means the order to attack an obviously purely civilian object or to attack despite blatantly excessive collateral damage) must not be obeyed (see Section 1436); just to the contrary, in such cases a superior order is no defence to a combatant in criminal proceedings, who bears individual criminal responsibility.[571]

9. In particular, with regard to unmanned combat aerial vehicles (see Section 449), the obligation to take all feasible precautions has to be applied to their deployment. To minimize the risks for civilians, human decision-making is essential. Evaluating the situation based on the provided intelligence, the equipment, and the intended method of deployment is only possible by a human being so far.

461   **The attack or bombardment of non-defended localities is prohibited (Article 59, para. 1, AP I; Article 25 HagueReg).**

Traditional customary law recognized a distinction between defended localities, which by the fact of being defended become military objectives in their entirety,[572] and non-defended localities which may not be made the object of attack.[573] The Hague Peace Conferences had already codified this customary rule in Article 25 of the Hague Regulations.[574] By declaring a city or village a non-defended locality, and thus ceding it to the adversary without resistance, the belligerent can exclude certain settlements from combat activity, in the interest of the civilian population, and to preserve important buildings or works of art; the adverse effects of warfare may be thus limited to the proper area of combat.[575] Non-defended localities *qua definitionem* cannot be military objectives, for the adversary has deliberately excluded them from his military activities, so that the intended military advantage could be achieved by mere occupation without combat activity, whereas a bombardment would be evidently unnecessary. Article 59, para. 1, AP I restates this rule explicitly, although it follows logically from the general

---

[569] See Roberts, *loc. cit.*, 160; Solf, ibid. 366.

[570] See Fleck, 'Military Manuals on the Law of Armed Conflicts' in Bothe/Kurzidem/Macalister (eds), *National Implementation of International Humanitarian Law* (Nijhoff, 1990), 185–92, at 192.

[571] For 'Obedience to Orders' in general, see Solis, above (n. 350) 341–64.

[572] As to the debate on the concept of 'defended locality', see H. Lauterpacht (ed.), above (n. 242) Vol. II, 421; Castrén, above (n. 47) 201; Doswald-Beck, above (n. 20) 158; Sassòli, *op. cit.*, 355–9; Fleck, above (n. 342) 54; Henckaerts, 'Non-defended Towns', *MPEPIL*.

[573] See Ipsen, 'Die "offene Stadt" und die Schutzzonen des Genfer Rechts' in Fleck (ed.), *Beiträge zur Weiterentwicklung des humanitären Völkerrechts für bewaffnete Konflikte* (Hamburg: Hanseatischer Gildenverlag, 1973), 149–210, at 152–80; the *US Field Manual* FM 27–10, para. 39 b and the *US Naval Manual*, para. 8.9.1.3; Rule 37 *CIHL*; Dinstein, above (n. 43) 108–11.

[574] As to the history and legal effects of Article 25 HagueReg, see Ipsen, ibid. 153–60.

[575] Concerning the declaration of an undefended locality, see Ipsen, ibid. 160–6; Pilloud/Pictet, in *ICRC Commentary*, paras. 2282–6.

STEFAN OETER

principles of distinction and necessity.[576] The same rules must apply also to non-international armed conflicts, since the fundamental principle of distinction between fighting
troops and military objectives on one hand and the civilian population on the other is
valid also for internal conflicts. The civilian population must be spared as far as possible
even in domestic conflicts (Article 13, para. 2, AP II), which leads to the conclusion
that even for internal conflicts a prohibition against attacks on non-defended localities
applies.[577]

A locality shall be considered non-defended if it has been so declared by its competent authorities, is open for occupation, and fulfils the following conditions:
— all combatants, mobile weapons, and mobile military equipment must have
been evacuated;
— no hostile use will be made of fixed military installations and establishments;
— no acts of hostility shall be committed by the authorities or the population;
and
— no activities in support of military operations will be undertaken (Article 59,
para. 2, AP I).

462

1. The protection afforded by Article 59, para. 1, AP I applies only if certain conditions are fulfilled.[578] In general: the locality must be totally excluded from the military
activities of the belligerent hitherto exercising control, that is it must play no role in its
operations; the locality must be open for occupation by the opposing side, and this fact
must be declared to the adversary.

2. The declaration by the power responsible for the locality is intended to remove uncertainties, and binds the adversary to protect the 'open city' by formally announcing abandonment without resistance. The protection of Article 59, para. 1, AP I then enters into
force—unlike the provisions for demilitarized zones in Article 60 AP I—*ipso iure*, as
soon as the preconditions of Article 59 are fulfilled. The declaration must define and
describe the exact limits of the undefended locality.[579] The adverse party must acknowledge
receipt of the declaration, and must protest immediately if it considers that the conditions laid down in Article 59, para. 2, are not fulfilled.[580] Otherwise, it is bound by the
protective provisions of Article 59 AP I. The non-defended locality must subsequently
be marked by special signs, in order to enable the fighting troops of both sides to respect
the protection of the locality at all times.[581]

3. For the purposes of Article 59 AP I, a non-defended locality must be situated in the
immediate zone of combat or in its vicinity. The locality must be open to immediate
entry by the adversary armed forces, and open to occupation without a fight, following
its evacuation.[582] A city or town behind enemy lines, or even far in its hinterland, may
not be a lawful target of military attack if there are no combatants or other military
objectives in it; such a town, however, is not a 'non-defended locality', because the armed

[576] As to background, history, and relevance of Article 59 AP I see Solf, in Bothe/Partsch/Solf, above
(n. 41) 380–5.
[577] See Junod, in *ICRC Commentary*, paras. 4766–72.
[578] See Pilloud/Pictet, in *ICRC Commentary*, paras. 2267–74; Solf, in Bothe/Partsch/Solf, above
(n. 41) 383.
[579] See Pilloud/Pictet, in *ICRC Commentary*, para. 2284.
[580] Ibid. paras. 2285–6.
[581] Ibid. paras. 2289–94.
[582] Solf, in Bothe/Partsch/Solf, above (n. 41) 382; Pilloud/Pictet, in *ICRC Commentary*, para. 2268.

STEFAN OETER

forces of the adverse party are prevented from entering it by the troops in between, at the line of combat.[583]

4. In order to enjoy the protection of Article 59 AP I, the town or city must be free from all military activities. All combatants, mobile weapons, and mobile military equipment must be evacuated from the locality (Article 59, para. 2, lit. a, AP I). No hostile use may be made of fixed military installations and establishments (although it is not necessary that they be made unfit for use or destroyed). Neither the authorities nor the population of the town or city shall participate in acts of hostility, nor may the town or specific installations or establishments in it be in any way involved in the military activities of any party to the conflict, whether by production of armaments or by provision of transport or telecommunications services with a military purpose.[584]

463   **A locality shall not on suspicion be deemed defended unless the behaviour of the adversary substantiates such a supposition.**

If by formal declaration a town or city has become an undefended locality, and if the adverse party has not transmitted a counterdeclaration in accordance with Article 59, para. 4, sentence 2, AP I, the advancing belligerent is bound by the declaration.[585] Even in other cases the attacker must, according to Article 57, para. 2, lit. a(i), AP I (see Section 460), make sure that the town or city to be attacked constitutes a military objective. If there is no indication that combatants, military installations, or other military objectives are present in the town which serve to assist the combat activities of the adverse party, then such a town or city is by definition not a legitimate military objective, and thus may not be made an object of attack.

464   **It is prohibited to extend military operations to demilitarized zones. The prerequisites for establishing such a zone are the same as those applying to non-defended localities (Articles 59, para. 2, and 60, para. 3, AP I). Demilitarized zones are created by agreement between the parties to the conflict either in peacetime or in the course of conflict. It is prohibited for any party to the conflict to attack or occupy such zones (Article 60, para. 1, AP I).**

1. Unlike non-defended localities, the specific protection for demilitarized zones does not apply *ipso iure*, even when the conditions in Article 60, para. 3, AP I are fulfilled.[586] A separate agreement between the parties to the conflict is required which establishes the specific modalities of demilitarization. The agreement may be concluded in peacetime, and may facilitate both disarmament and confidence building;[587] it can also be concluded ad hoc after the outbreak of a conflict in order to preserve certain areas from the effects of combat.[588] The requirement of an express agreement is sensible in this respect, since demilitarization of larger areas needs a whole series of complex and detailed provisions which cannot be deduced *in abstracto* from the general rules of humanitarian

---

[583] Solf, ibid. 382.

[584] See Pilloud/Pictet, in *ICRC Commentary*, paras. 2271–2.

[585] Solf, in Bothe/Partsch/Solf, above (n. 41) 383–4.

[586] Pilloud/Pictet, in *ICRC Commentary*, para. 2304.

[587] As to the difference between demilitarized areas in peacetime international law and protected zones under Article 60 AP I, see ibid. paras. 2302–3.

[588] Ibid. paras. 2308–9.

STEFAN OETER

law.[589] Both the specific limits of the zone and the mechanisms of verification require a detailed legal framework, and these are only two examples of the many questions which require legal clarification in such cases. Also, the question of any militarily relevant activities which may exceptionally be allowed should be regulated before it becomes a point of dispute.

2. The preconditions for establishing a demilitarized zone are nearly the same as those required for declaring a non-defended locality, that is the area must be entirely free from all military activities, and in principle also from all activities assisting the efforts of warfare.[590] Demilitarized zones, however, need not necessarily be situated in the combat zone. Even areas behind the enemy lines may be brought under the protection of Article 60 in anticipation. By agreement, the zone becomes legally closed to military activities of both sides. No party to the conflict shall attack a demilitarized zone, or occupy it, or use it for military purposes in any other way.[591]

> **If a party to the conflict breaches these provisions, the non-defended localities,**   465
> **open towns or cities, or demilitarized zones will lose their special protection. The**
> **general provisions for the protection of the civilian population and civilian objects**
> **shall, however, continue to apply (Articles 59, para. 7, and 60, para. 7, AP I).**

Paragraph 7 of both Article 59 and Article 60 Additional Protocol I contains one of the few express convention provisions concerning the consequences of violation of the treaty. If any party violates Article 59 or 60 or an agreement concluded on the basis of these provisions, the non-defended locality or demilitarized zone automatically loses the protection accorded to it under these provisions.[592] This results from the basic logic behind these institutions, because by extending military operations to the respective localities or areas, the conditions required for protection are removed. The adverse party may then lawfully use force against the newly created military objective. As a matter of good policy, however, it should warn the party violating the demilitarization provisions that such practice endangers the protected status of the town or zone, to provide an opportunity to redress the grievance and to give the population time for precautions.[593] In the case of an attack, the attacker must still limit combat operations to the adverse armed forces and other military objectives. The civilian population continues to enjoy the protection afforded by the general principles of distinction and proportionality, with all the specific rules resulting from that body of law.[594]

> **It is further prohibited to attack:**   466
> — **safety zones and neutralized zones, that is zones designed to give shelter to**
>   **wounded and sick soldiers and to civilians who take no part in hostilities**
>   **(Article 23 GC I; Articles 14, 15 GC IV);**
> — **medical and religious personnel (Articles 12, 15 AP I);**

---

[589] See Solf, in Bothe/Partsch/Solf, above (n. 41) 388.

[590] Concerning such activities there are possible (or even required) specific agreements: Article 60, para. 2, last sentence; see Pilloud/Pictet, in *ICRC Commentary*, para. 2311; Solf, in Bothe/Partsch/Solf, above (n. 41) 389.

[591] See Pilloud/Pictet, ibid. paras. 2305–6; Rule 36 *CIHL*.

[592] Solf, in Bothe/Partsch/Solf, above (n. 41) 384–5; Pilloud/Pictet, ibid. paras. 2295–7 and 2315–18.

[593] Pilloud/Pictet, in *ICRC Commentary*, para. 2316.

[594] Ibid. para. 2317.

STEFAN OETER

— hospital ships (Article 22 GC II);
— hospitals and associated personnel (Article 19 GC I; Articles 18, 20 GC IV);
— objects indispensable to the survival of the civilian population (e.g. production of foodstuffs, clothing, drinking water installations) with intent to deprive the civilian population of their supply (Article 54, para. 2, AP I; Article 14 AP II); any deviations from this prohibition shall be permissible only on friendly territory if required by cogent military necessity (Article 54, paras. 3 and 5, AP I; Article 14 AP II);
— coastal lifeboats and associated fixed coastal installations (Article 27 GC II);
— cultural objects (Article 53 AP I);
— aircraft protected by international law:
employed for the purpose of exchanging prisoners;
on the assurance of safe-conduct;
medical aircraft (Articles 36, para. 1, and 37, para. 1, GC I; Article 39 GC II; Articles 24 *et seq.* AP I;
Article 17 AP II); and civilian aircraft.

1. The system of the Geneva Conventions and Additional Protocols, supplemented by customary law, recognizes a whole series of specifically protected objects, against which the use of any form of force is prohibited. Such objects shall not be made the object of attack, and conversely they may not be used by belligerents for hostile purposes in the framework of military operations.

2. Comparable to demilitarized zones are the safety zones and neutralized zones provided for in Article 23 Geneva Convention I and in Articles 14 and 15 GC IV (see also Sections 512–513 and 634). Specified localities may be declared safety zones to provide safe shelters for the wounded and sick, as well as for children, mothers, and the aged.[595] These zones shall serve only as lodging for protected persons (including the personnel taking care of them and the local population); they shall not contain any military objects and must be situated in areas which in all probability are not relevant for the conduct of hostilities. The agreement on a neutralized zone around the Anglican Cathedral in Port Stanley on the Falkland Islands, concluded between the Argentine and British authorities on 13 June 1982, is an example of such an arrangement in contemporary practice.[596]

3. Under the system of the First, Second, and Fourth Geneva Conventions and the Additional Protocols, absolute protection is accorded to medical and religious personnel, to hospital ships, and to hospitals and personnel associated with them. The comprehensive standard of protection created by Articles 19 and 24 of the First Geneva Convention in regard to military hospitals, military medical personnel, and chaplains attached to the armed forces (and also that of Articles 18 and 20 GC IV in regard to civilian hospitals and their personnel) was extended by Articles 12 and 15 AP I to civilian medical and religious personnel (see Sections 623–633, 818–826). Even in non-international armed conflicts, Articles 9 and 11 AP II provide analogous protection for medical and religious personnel, as well as for medical units and their means of transport.[597] Hospital ships (as a special case) already enjoyed a certain protection from the Hague Convention on

---

[595] As to the system of safety zones according to Articles 23 GC I, 14 and 15 GC IV, see Pictet, *Commentaire* I, 227 *et seq.*; ibid. Vol. IV, 129–37, 138–43; Rule 35 *CIHL*.
[596] The case is mentioned in the *US Naval Manual* (1997), para. 8.5.1.5, n. 121.
[597] See Junod, in *ICRC Commentary*, 1417–36.

Hospital Ships of 21 December 1904.[598] Articles 22–35 Geneva Convention II consolidated the protected status of hospital ships (as to which, see Sections 1054–1064). In the course of the new codification in Article 27 GC II a specific regime of protection was accorded also to coastal lifeboats and associated fixed coastal installations (see Section 1054).

4. A new creation, in contrast, is the special category of protected objects, now codified in Article 54 AP I and Article 14 AP II, namely 'objects indispensable for the survival of the civilian population'.[599] In traditional customary law such a category was not recognized, even if the principle of proportionality had always set bounds on attacks on such objects, whose damage or destruction logically leads to particularly grave suffering for the civilian population.[600] As an expression of the general prohibition against the starvation of civilians as a method of warfare, laid down in Article 54, para. 1, AP I, para. 2 of Article 54 now prohibits any form of violence against 'objects indispensable for the survival of the civilian population'.[601] The most common examples of such protected objects are specifically listed as objects 'such as foodstuffs, agricultural areas for the production of foodstuffs, crops, livestock, drinking water installations and supplies, and irrigation works'. These examples clarify the core of the protection, but the list is not exhaustive. It is beyond doubt that the objects primarily protected under the provision are the food and water supply of the civilian population, being the basic means of subsistence;[602] this does not mean, however, that objects not directly linked to food and water supply are necessarily excluded from the category of 'objects indispensable for the survival of the civilian population'. It depends on the particular situation, and under certain circumstances (e.g. in climatically rough mountainous regions) other goods, such as the supply of clothing or the basic shelter of the civilian population, will undoubtedly be protected under Article 54, para. 2, AP I.[603] It is prohibited 'to attack, destroy, remove, or render useless' such objects. 'Rendering useless' may include acts such as deliberate pollution, by chemical or other agents, of water reservoirs or the contamination of crops by defoliants.[604] The destruction, removal, or rendering useless of foodstuffs, water, or other 'indispensable' objects is only prohibited, however, in so far as it is committed deliberately for the purpose of depriving the civilian population of such objects 'because of their sustenance value'. By contrast, it is legitimate to damage the protected objects and installations by military operations if the impairment is only an incidental effect of the attack.[605] An irrigation channel, for example, shall not be destroyed deliberately in order to interrupt agricultural production; the same is true for the destruction of crops or gardens because of their importance to the sustenance of the civilian population. Nevertheless, the destruction of an irrigation channel may be permissible if the channel is used as a defensive position by the military forces in occupation and a field of crops

---

[598] Printed in Schindler/Toman, above (n. 379) 295–7.

[599] See Pilloud/Pictet, in *ICRC Commentary*, paras. 2083, 2088, 2091; Solf, in Bothe/Partsch/Solf, above (n. 41) 336–7.

[600] See Cassese, above (n. 27) 91; but see Rule 54 *CIHL*.

[601] As to the history of Article 54 AP I see Pilloud/Pictet, in *ICRC Commentary*, paras. 2083–2085; Solf, in Bothe/Partsch/Solf, above (n. 41) 336–40.

[602] Pilloud/Pictet, ibid. 6, paras. 2102–3; Solf, in Bothe/Partsch/Solf, above (n. 41) 339–40.

[603] Pilloud/Pictet, ibid. para. 2103; Solf, ibid. 340.

[604] See Pilloud/Pictet, ibid. para. 2101.

[605] Solf, ibid. 339.

STEFAN OETER

may be burnt down in order to clear the field for artillery.[606] Installations for electric power supply have proved particularly problematic. To the extent that the power supply serves military purposes, in maintaining military installations, it undoubtedly constitutes a military objective (see Section 444). At the same time, however, electric power supply installations will often constitute an 'object indispensable for the survival of the civilian population'. The elimination of the power supply network will also cause considerable disruption to other elements of the civilian infrastructure, for example the drinking water supply system (as happened e.g. in the course of 'Operation Desert Storm' in 1991 in Iraq). Especially in arid regions, the breakdown of such vital sustenance systems may, albeit indirectly, expose the civilian population to the very risk that Article 54 AP I was intended to prevent.

5. The protection of 'objects indispensable for the survival of the civilian population' is—as stated above—part of a far-reaching new approach underlying the provisions of Articles 54 AP I and 14 AP II. Article 54, para. 1, AP I contains a new general prohibition against the starvation of civilians as a method of warfare.[607] This rule completely outlaws traditional warfare methods, such as sieges of defended towns, or 'scorched earth' strategies.[608] Even in the course of the war crime trials after World War II, the deliberate devastation of occupied territories during operations of retreat, as well as the starvation of populations in besieged enemy towns, were still considered permissible.[609] In the wake of the reorientation effected by the general rules of Articles 54, para. 1, AP I and Article 14 AP II, however, such practices must be reassessed.[610] The Fourth Geneva Convention already provided, in Article 17, for evacuation of certain groups of persons from besieged territories, and in Article 23 it called for the admission of humanitarian assistance deliveries into besieged localities for the assistance of specific groups of the population.[611] The general prohibition of starvation of the civilian population now implies that deliveries of foodstuffs, medicines, drinking water, and other goods indispensable for the survival of the civilian population must not be hindered by the adverse party, provided that they are delivered solely to the civilian population of the town under siege, and not to the military persons defending the town.[612] Article 70 AP I now expressly requires the admission of humanitarian relief operations for the civilian population,[613] which completely outlaws siege strategies such as those still being used by the Serbian troops in Bosnia.

6. As a specific exception to Article 54, para. 2, AP I, para. 5 of Article 54 AP I provides that derogations from the prohibition of attacks on 'objects indispensable for the survival of the civilian population' may be made 'in recognition of the vital requirements of any Party to the conflict in the defence of its national territory against invasion', where

---

[606] These examples are contained in the report of Committee III of the Diplomatic Conference—see Solf ibid.; Pilloud/Pictet, in *ICRC Commentary*, para. 2110.

[607] See Rule 53 *CIHL*.

[608] On the background of Article 54, para. 1, see Pilloud/Pictet, in *ICRC Commentary*, paras. 2087–91; Solf, in Bothe/Partsch/Solf, 336–8; see also Dinstein, above (n. 43) 218–23 and Bill, above (n. 527) 148–54.

[609] See Solf, ibid. 337; Dinstein, 'Siege Warfare and the Starvation of Civilians' in Delissen/Tanja (eds), *Humanitarian Law of Armed Conflict: Challenges Ahead—Essays in Honour of F. Kalshoven* (Nijhoff, 1991), 145–52, at 146–7.

[610] Solf, ibid. 338; Dinstein, *loc. cit.*, 152.

[611] See Dinstein, *loc. cit.*, 147–8; Pictet, *Commentaire I*, 148–51, 192–8.

[612] Dinstein, *loc. cit.*, 150.

[613] Cf. Sandoz, in *ICRC Commentary*, pp. 816–29; Rule 55 *CIHL*.

STEFAN OETER

'required by imperative military necessity'; such derogations are allowed, however, only within territory under a party's own control. The defender fulfilling this precondition may impede the advance of the enemy by deliberately devastating the areas from which he is retreating. In view of the fundamental interest of any defender in minimizing his own damage it was considered that in these exceptional circumstances the defender should be permitted to employ 'scorched earth' strategies.

7. Particular protection is granted to cultural objects. The Hague Convention of 14 May 1954 for the Protection of Cultural Property in the Event of Armed Conflict, and the supplementary provisions of Articles 53 AP I and Article 16 AP II, have developed an elaborate protective regime for historical monuments, works of art, and places of worship 'which constitute the cultural or spiritual heritage of peoples'. These specific safeguards are dealt with below; see Chapter 9.

8. Aircraft are covered by specific regulation of mostly customary character. Civilian aircraft may not be attacked in peacetime and may not be shot down. For ordinary public international law this follows already from the fundamental rule of prohibition of the use of force and from the general rules of air law, now codified in the Chicago Convention on International Civil Aviation (Article 3 bis); in an armed conflict such a prohibition can be inferred from the principle of distinction, since a civilian aircraft rarely constitutes a military objective in the sense of Article 52, para. 2, AP I. In this respect, problems arise mainly in respect of the practical implementation of the rule of distinction, for in situations of limited armed conflict the air space is normally used at the same time for both hostile military operations and civil aviation. The accidental downing of the Iranian civil aircraft (Airbus A300) over the Persian Gulf by the US Navy warship USS *Vincennes* on 3 July 1988 was a telling example of the dangers inherent in such situations of confusion.[614] In addition to these general rules, particular protection is granted by customary law to: military aircraft employed for the purpose of exchanging prisoners; aircraft, whether civilian or military, which have been assured safe conduct,[615] and medical aircraft, the status of which has recently been exhaustively regulated by Articles 24–31 AP I (see Sections 620–623).

3. Protection of the Natural Environment

The general principles on the conduct of hostilities apply to the natural environment (Rule 43 *CIHL*):   467

A. No part of the natural environment may be attacked, unless it is a military objective.
B. Destruction of any part of the natural environment is prohibited, unless required by imperative military necessity.
C. Launching an attack against a military objective which may be expected to cause incidental damage to the environment which would be excessive in relation to the concrete and direct military advantage anticipated is prohibited.

---

[614] See the report on the investigation undertaken by the International Civil Aviation Organization of November 1988, printed in (1989) 28 *ILM* 900–43, and the Iranian statement of claim filed in the ICJ of 17 May 1989, printed in (1989) 28 *ILM* 842–6.

[615] See H. Lauterpacht (ed.), above (n. 242) Vol. II, 542; Castrén, above (n. 47) 126–7; Greenspan, above (n. 239) 397–9.

STEFAN OETER

1. The protection of the environment has become more and more important over the past decades. Armed conflicts often have consequences on the environment, even a long time after a conflict has ended.[616] However, international law was very slow in granting the environment a specific protection in times of armed conflict.[617] In 1996, the ICJ in its Advisory Opinion on Nuclear Weapons stated that 'the environment is under daily threat' and recognized that 'the environment is not an abstraction but represents the living space, the quality of life and the very health of human beings'.[618] However, there has been no international legal regime dealing with the protection of the environment during armed conflict conclusively.[619] Neither the 1907 Hague Convention nor the 1949 Geneva Conventions deal with the natural environment as such.

2. Starting in the 1970s, the matter of the protection of the environment during times of armed conflict was firstly politicized. Mostly due to the Vietnam War, the effects of defoliation due to the usage of herbicides by the US administration became apparent. Even more recently, strikes against oil refineries have been an often chosen military target, whose destruction led to a serious pollution of the air, for example the Iraqi–Kuwait War in 1990–1991,[620] the NATO bombing at Pančevo in 1999,[621] and the bombing of the Jiyeh petroleum storage[622] during the Lebanon conflict[623] in 2006. Due to the public awareness, some of the international conferences convened to further develop the law of armed conflict dealt also with issues of environmental warfare. The 1977 Additional Protocol I to the Geneva Conventions deals with environmental matters in two articles, namely in its Articles 35 para. 3 and 55. Furthermore, the 1976 Convention on the Prohibition of Military or Any Other Hostile Use of Environmental Modification Techniques (ENMOD) and the 1980 Convention on Prohibition or Restriction on the Use of Certain Conventional Weapons (InhumaneWeaponsConv) were adopted, among other conventions prohibiting or restricting biological, chemical or nuclear weapons.

3. In 2011, the International Law Commission (ILC) decided to include the topic 'Protection of the Environment in relation to Armed Conflict' to its work programme.[624] Additionally, the ILC treated the subject of 'Effects of Armed Conflict on Treaties', by analysing *inter alia* the coexistence of environmental treaties and the law of armed conflict,[625]

---

[616] See M. Bothe/C. Bruch/J. Diamond/D. Jensen, 'International law protecting the environment during armed conflict: gaps and opportunities' (2010) 92 *IRRC* 569–92, at 570.

[617] See P. J. Richards/M. N. Schmitt, 'Mars Meets Mother Nature: Protecting the Environment during Armed Conflict' (1999) 28 *Stetson Law Review* 1047–92, 1051 ff.; Henckaerts, 'General Developments—Armed conflict and the environment' (2002) 13 *Yearbook of International Environmental Law* 241, 243 ff.

[618] ICJ, Advisory Opinion on Nuclear Weapons, *ICJ Reports 1996*, 241 (para. 29).

[619] See D. Fleck, 'The Protection of the Environment in Armed Conflict: Legal Obligations in the Absence of Specific Rules' (2013) 82 *Nordic Journal of International Law* 7–20, at 7–8.

[620] See US Department of Defense, 'Conduct of the Person Gulf War: Final Report to Congress' 624 (1992) at <http://www.ndu.edu/library/epubs/cpgw.pdf>.

[621] See United Nations Environment Programme (UNEP), 'The Kosovo Conflict: Consequences for the Environment & Human Settlements', 1999, p. 32 ff. (<http://www.grid.unep.ch/btf/final/finalreport.pdf>).

[622] See UNEP, 'Lebanon—Post Conflict Environmental Assessment', 2007, p. 42 ff. (<http://postconflict.unep.ch/publications/UNEP_Lebanon.pdf>).

[623] See for a legal analysis of the 2006 Israeli–Lebanon Conflict, Ling-Yee Huang, 'The 2006 Israeli–Lebanese Conflict: A Case Study for Protection of the Environment in Times of Armed Conflict' (2008) 20 *Florida Journal of International Law* 103 ff.

[624] Ch. XIII, A.1., UN Doc. A/RES/66/10.

[625] See not only with regard to nuclear weapons Erik Koppe, *The Use of Nuclear Weapons and the Protection of the Environment during International Armed Conflict* (Oxford: Hart, 2007); see on the

which resulted in the adoption of the Draft Articles on Effects of Armed Conflict on Treaties in 2011.[626] The ICRC in its study on customary IHL in 2005 analysed, among other topics, the law of armed conflict and its relation to the natural environment. According to this study, the general principles on the conduct of hostility apply to the natural environment, in international armed conflicts as well as in non-international armed conflicts.[627] Another project of the ICRC with regard to the protection of the environment, the *Guidelines for Military Manuals and Instructions on the Protection of the Environment in Times of Armed Conflict*, published in 1994, was only referred to in GA Resolution 49/50[628] and had no further measurable success.[629]

4. The principle of distinction prohibits attacks against the natural environment,[630] as long as there is no military objective that justifies an attack. In this context, it is debatable whether the protection of the environment derives from the protection of civilian objects according to Article 52, para. 1 AP I.[631] However, the prevailing view is that the environment is civilian in nature and thus in principle immune from attacks.[632] Just in exceptional cases, parts of the environment may turn into lawful targets, for example when a military objective such as soldiers cross agricultural fields. This is also codified in Article 2, para. 4 of the Protocol III to the Convention on Certain Conventional Weapons, which states only when natural elements cover, conceal or camouflage military objectives, they are themselves a lawful target. Nevertheless, the principles of proportionality and necessity also apply and might render an attack unlawful.

5. The principle of proportionality protects the environment as an illicit target as long as the collateral civilian casualties are disproportionate to the specific military advantage.[633] Excessive damages to the environment that are disproportionate to the military advantage are thus unlawful. The anticipated military advantage has to be balanced against the foreseeable collateral damages. In the case of the destruction of the environment, this might be damage to facilities resulting in air and soil pollution, leaks of sewage and wastewater, and so on.

6. An evaluation of the past conflicts shows that states have taken environmental matters into account when assessing questions of proportionality.[634] The US Army has just recently published in its *Civilian Casualty Mitigation Manual* that considerations of proportionality also have to take into account 'long-term effects such as contaminating the environment'.[635] With regard to the bombing campaign against the Former Federal

---

coexistence of environmental treaties and the laws of war the substantial work of Vöneky, *Die Fortgeltung des Umweltvölkerrechts im internationalen bewaffneten Konflikt* (Springer, 2001).

[626] See UN Doc. A/RES/66/99 of 9 December 2011.

[627] See Rules 43–5 *CIHL*; Boothby, above (n. 51) 103.

[628] See UN Doc. A/RES/49/50 of 29 January 1996.

[629] See Bothe/Bruch/Diamond/Jensen, above (n. 616) 573.

[630] See Dinstein, above (n. 43) 198, and Fleck, above (n. 619), 9–15.

[631] See in favour Dinstein, *op. cit.*, 204; opposing Karen Hulme, 'Armed Conflict, Wanton Ecological Devastation and Scorched Earth Policies' (1997) 2 *Journal of Conflict and Security Law* 45–81, at 59; Fleck, above (n.619), 13.

[632] See Dinstein, *loc. cit.*, 204–5.

[633] On the complexity of environmental considerations with regard to proportionality, see Richards/Schmitt, above (n. 617) 1082 ff.

[634] ICJ, Advisory Opinion on Nuclear Weapons, *ICJ Reports 1996*, 241 (para. 30).

[635] See US Army Civilian Casualties Mitigation of July 2012, ATTP 3–37.31 (<http://www.lawfareblog.com/wp-content/uploads/2012/07/attp3_37x31.pdf-approved.pdf>).

STEFAN OETER

Republic of Yugoslavia, for instance, the Committee Established to Review the NATO Bombing Campaign Against the Federal Republic of Yugoslavia came to the conclusion that the requirements of proportionality are only met when a grave environmental harm is justified by a very substantial military objective.[636] The ICJ in its Advisory Opinion on Nuclear Weapons in 1996 also stressed: 'States must take environment considerations into account when assessing what is necessary and proportionate in the pursuit of a legitimate military objective.'[637] However, the uncertainty with regard to the possible long-term damage renders it difficult to decide on the proportionality in these cases.[638]

7. In the Nuclear Weapons Advisory Opinion, the ICJ furthermore stated that 'respect for the environment is one of the elements that go to assessing whether an action is in conformity with the principles of necessity and proportionality'.[639] Additionally, environmental matters have to be taken into account when assessing whether an attack fulfils the requirements of military necessity.[640] Also, the Fourth Geneva Convention stresses in Article 147 that the extensive destruction of property is only lawful when it is justified by military necessity. The ICRC study, however, refers to Rule 50, which requires a justification by imperative military necessity. Among scholars, it is highly disputed whether custom requires *imperative* military necessity and not only military necessity as such.[641]

468   Methods and means of warfare must be employed with due regard to the protection and preservation of the natural environment. In the conduct of military operations, all feasible precautions must be taken to avoid, and in any event to minimize, incidental damage to the environment. Lack of scientific certainty as to the effects on the environment of certain military operations does not absolve a party to the conflict from taking such precautions (Rule 44 *CIHL*).

1. The ICJ recognized in 1997 in the Gabčíkovo-Nagymaros Project case that the natural environment may be of 'essential interest' to a state and in consequence justify an abrogation from existing obligations.[642] According to customary law, states must pay due regard to the environment.[643] As stated in Principle 2 of the non-binding Rio Declaration and Principle 21 of the Stockholm Declaration on the Human Environment, states committed themselves to ensure that activities within their jurisdiction and control respect the environment of other states and areas beyond national control.

2. Rule 44 *HPCR Manual* includes the obligation of the belligerent to take all feasible precautions to avoid or minimize damage to the environment. Due to the scientific progress, long-term risks and the consequences of certain substances on the ecological system are better known each day.[644] The belligerent has to choose the target carefully

[636] 'Final Report to the Prosecutor by the Committee Established to Review the NATO Bombing Campaign Against the Federal Republic of Yugoslavia' (2009) 39 *ILM* 22.

[637] ICJ, Advisory Opinion on Nuclear Weapons, *ICJ Reports 1996*, 241 (para. 30).

[638] Cf. Bothe/Bruch/Diamond/Jensen, above (n. 616) 577 ff.

[639] ICJ, Advisory Opinion on Nuclear Weapons, *ICJ Reports 1996*, 241 (para. 30).

[640] ICJ, Advisory Opinion on Nuclear Weapons, *ICJ Reports 1996*, 241 (para. 30).

[641] See Boothby, above (n. 51) 100.

[642] See ICJ, Gabčíkovo-Nagymaros Project case, *ICJ Reports 1997*, 41 (para. 53).

[643] For further elaboration on the principle of due regard, see Bothe's keynote speech 'Protection of the environment in and after armed conflict: overview and trends' at the workshop on 'Exploring the legal framework for Toxic Remnants of War', TRW Project, 22 June 2012 (<http://www.toxicremnantsofwar.info/wp-content/uploads/2012/09/Michale-Bothe-_-Protection-of-the-environment-in-and-after-armed-conflict-overview-and-trends1.pdf>).

[644] See Dinstein, above (n. 43) 198.

STEFAN OETER

and determine the particular circumstances of the targeting to ensure the protection of the environment. The wording in Rule 44 *HPCR Manual* is more flexible than the provisions in AP I, thus more favourable for the protection of the environment.[645]

3. The principle of precaution is also included in Rule 44 *CIHL*. It derives from international environmental law and is also applied in the laws of armed conflict. According to it, the lack of scientific certainty may not be invoked to abstain from preventive measures to protect the environment during an attack. At the 1992 Rio Conference, states addressed this issue and declared in its Principle 15 that 'where there are threats of serious or irreversible damage, lack of full scientific certainty shall not be used as a reason for postponing cost-effective measures to prevent environmental degradation'.[646] Thus, taking adequate measures is not at the discretion of a State in cases of scientific uncertainty, only questions regarding the choice of measures are at the discretion of the state concerned.[647] However, it is not clear whether this rule is actually part of custom.[648]

> The use of methods of means of warfare that are intended, or may be expected,   **469**
> to cause widespread, long-term and severe damage to the natural environment is
> prohibited. Destruction of the natural environment may not be used as a weapon
> (Articles 35, para. 3, and 55, para. 1, AP I; ENMOD; Rule 45 *CIHL*; see above,
> Section 403).

1. The use of methods and means of warfare is not only regulated by custom, but also by certain treaties. First of all, the 1976 Convention on the Prohibition of Military or Any Other Hostile Use of Environmental Modification Techniques (ENMOD) needs to be mentioned, which entered into force in 1978. It prohibits environmental modification techniques that are used in a military or hostile capacity, thus prohibiting using the environment itself as a weapon.[649] According to Article II ENMOD, the modification techniques must consist of a manipulation of a natural process and be deliberate; mere collateral damages of such a process are not included. The only states protected by the ENMOD provisions are those party to the Convention. The ENMOD Convention does not codify existing customary law, rather it includes innovative and progressive regulations.[650] Most of its provisions prohibiting certain techniques are future-oriented[651] and do not reflect existing capabilities.

2. Additionally, AP I in its Articles 35(3) and 55(1) regulate the protection of the environment during armed conflict. AP I, in contrast to ENMOD, protects the natural environment as such and does not prohibit the usage of the environment as a weapon.[652] While Article 55(1) AP I includes a reference to the health and survival of the population, this reference is lacking in Article 35(3) AP I. The reasoning and consequences of this difference are disputed. However, according to the prevailing view, Article 55(1) AP I does not imply that the

---

[645] Cf. Bother/Bruch/Diamond/Jensen, above (n. 616) 575.

[646] See Rio Declaration on Environment and Development, UN Doc. A/CONF.151/26, Vol. I of 13 June 1992.

[647] See Beyerlin/Grote Stoutenburg, Environment, International Protection, *MPEPIL*.

[648] See Boothby, above (n. 51) 101.

[649] See Boothby, above (n. 51) 93.

[650] See Dinstein, above (n. 43) 202.

[651] See Dinstein, 'Protection of the Environment in International Armed Conflict' (2001) 5 *Max Planck United Nations Year Book* 523, at 532.

[652] See Vöneky/Wolfrum, 'Environment, Protection in Armed Conflict', *MPEPIL*, para. 36; Henckaerts, above (n. 617) 244.

STEFAN OETER

environment itself is not protected by the provisions.[653] Rather, Article 55(1) AP I reinforces Article 35(3) AP I. Both articles include an absolute limitation to environmental
damages which cannot be overcome by considerations of military necessity.[654] However,
the protection of the environment derived from AP I is of no practical relevance: the
threshold of 'widespread, long-term and severe' damage is set very high.[655] As explained
above (see Section 403), the threshold of damage to the environment set in Articles
35(3) and 55(1) AP I is higher than the one established by ENMOD. While ENMOD
only requires widespread, long-lasting, or severe effects, AP I asks for widespread, long-
term, and severe damages. All three conditions must be fulfilled cumulatively to invoke
the protection of AP I. This discrepancy between the two international treaties was
not only an oversight, but intentional.[656] Furthermore, ENMOD only requires 'long-
lasting effects' which are counted in months; AP I requires 'long-term' damages which
are measured in decades. To calculate the implications and consequences decades in
advance is almost impossible, even when examining nuclear weapons.[657] Thus, since
Articles 35 and 55 AP I do not cover many cases of the protection of the environment
during armed conflict, other conventional and customary rules continue to be of great
importance with relation to the environment.[658] Whether Articles 35(3) and 55(1) AP
I are understood as customary international law is still disputed. In 1977, they did not
reflect custom and even after some decades it is still questionable whether these provisions have become customary in nature (see Section 403).[659]

3. Additionally, there is an indirect protection of the environment deriving from AP I.
Article 56 AP I prohibits the release of dangerous forces from dams, dykes, and nuclear
electricity-generating stations and thus protects the environment indirectly. Article 54(2)
AP I deals with the protection of objects indispensable to the survival of the civilian populations and names agricultural areas or irrigation works among other objects. Furthermore,
Article 52 dealing with the protection of civilian objects and Article 57 codifying the rule
of precaution play a role in the protection of the environment during armed conflict.

4. The current regulations with regard to the natural environment are not satisfactory.[660]
Neither AP I nor ENMOD would apply to the 1991 Gulf War. Iraq was not party to
the protocols or convention. And even if Iraq was, according to the US Department
of Defense's review, the threshold of AP I, consisting of the mentioned three cumulative conditions, would not have been met.[661] And at the same time, ENMOD was not
breached either, since the man-made explosion of oil wells was not a 'manipulation of
natural processes'. Protection is only granted on the basis of the principles of military
necessity, proportionality, and distinction. Consequently, it is necessary to identify a
more practical threshold of environmental damages that amounts to a breach of international law.

[653] See Vöneky/Wolfrum, 'Environment, Protection in Armed Conflict', *MPEPIL*, para. 25.
[654] See *US Army Handbook*, Ch. 19, Section VII, A.7.a.
[655] See Boothby, above (n. 51) 96.
[656] Cf. Bothe/Bruch/Diamond/Jensen, above (n. 616) 572.
[657] See Dinstein, above (n. 43) 211.
[658] Cf. Henckaerts, above (n. 617) 244 ff.
[659] See Dinstein, above (n. 43) 205.
[660] See Fleck, above (n. 619), 8.
[661] US Department of Defense Report to Congress on the Conduct of the Persian Gulf War (1992) 31
ILM 612, 636–7.

STEFAN OETER

4. Protection of Works and Installations Containing Dangerous Forces

Works and installations containing dangerous forces, namely dams, dykes, and   **470**
nuclear electricity-generating stations (Article 56, para. 1, AP I) shall not be made
the object of attack, even where these objects are military objectives, if such attack
could cause the release of dangerous forces and consequent severe damage to the
civilian population (Article 56, para. 1, AP I).

1. Article 56 AP I (and the analogous Article 15 AP II concerning non-international armed conflicts) introduced a new category hitherto totally unknown, namely 'works and installations containing dangerous forces'.[662] According to the official definition of Article 56, this category comprises three types of installation: dams, dykes, and nuclear power plants.[663] All three types of installation are potentially extremely dangerous, since in the event of their destruction uncontrollable forces are released that may cause immense damage to the civilian population.[664] The regulation of their status in warfare by a separate provision is undoubtedly justified by virtue of these risks. Although a considerable degree of caution was required under traditional customary law (because there was always a risk of excessive collateral damage in case of attacks on such objects),[665] there was no absolute prohibition of attack upon them in humanitarian law prior to the adoption of the Additional Protocols. In belligerent practice, attacks had always occurred on such objects,[666] even if only under extreme precautions in recent times.[667]

2. The new rule of Article 56 AP I must be understood in an overall perspective as an essential part of the general attempt to restrict the extent of permissible collateral damage. The evaluation of what constitutes admissible collateral damage has undergone a great change since World War II, a fact demonstrated with utmost clarity by US practice in the course of the last decades. An attack on a specifically dangerous installation in the sense of Article 56 AP I would only be allowed—even without the special rule of Article 56—under exceptional circumstances, given the strict precaution currently required to minimize loss of civilian lives and damage to civilian objects. The collateral damage likely to be caused by such an attack is so high that the deliberate acceptance of such a risk would in any event qualify as a blatant violation of the prohibition against indiscriminate attack. Thus, even the undeniably novel rule of Article 56 is arguably only an illustration of the standard of protection which is already provided for by customary law.

3. The installations referred to in Article 56 will normally constitute military objectives, and accordingly would be admissible objects of attack under normal circumstances. The regulation of AP I, like that of AP II, has adopted a different yardstick, however, by providing a special degree of protection for these installations, in order to protect the civilian population against the catastrophic effects of damaging or destroying such objects.[668]

---

[662] Concerning the character of Article 56 AP I as a completely novel creation, see Cassese, above (n. 27) 94. On the drafting history of the rule see Solf, in Bothe/Partsch/Solf, above (n. 41) 350–3; Pilloud/Pictet, in *ICRC Commentary*, para. 2145.

[663] Solf, ibid. 350; Pilloud/Pictet, ibid. paras. 2146–50.

[664] Solf, ibid. 350.

[665] See Parks, *supra* (n. 8) 168–9; Rule 42 *CIHL*.

[666] Parks, ibid. 206–9.

[667] See esp. Parks, *supra* (n. 8), who gives the example of the attack by the US Air Force on the Lang Chi dam in Northern Vietnam in 1972.

[668] See Solf, in Bothe/Partsch/Solf, above (n. 41) 350–7; Pilloud/Pictet, in *ICRC Commentary*, pp. 666–70.

STEFAN OETER

Attacks are prohibited even if the installation obviously constitutes a military objective 'if such attack may cause the release of dangerous forces from the works or installations and consequent severe losses among the civilian population'.[669] The same considerations led to an expansion (by Article 56, para. 1, second sentence) of the protection of 'other military objectives located at or in the vicinity of these works or installations', since comparably severe effects are likely to be caused by an attack on such objectives as from a direct attack on the dams, dykes, or nuclear plants.[670] Hydroelectric facilities at the foot of dams, for example, fall into that category, since such electricity-generating plants usually constitute a military objective, the destruction of which would necessarily risk the damage or destruction of the dam itself.[671]

4. Underlying the prohibition of Article 56 AP I is a sort of 'worst case' analysis, an assessment which deems the serious risk of releasing dangerous forces to constitute an unacceptably high risk of collateral damage. In view of the risk potential inherent in the respective installations, that assessment is doubtless correct. It is nearly inconceivable that massive risks for the civilian population could ever be outweighed by military considerations so as to justify an attack on such installations used for purely civilian purposes. The attack is accordingly strictly prohibited and cannot be justified by any claim of military necessity, except under the exception of para. 2 of Article 56.

471   **This protection shall cease if these plants are used in regular, significant, and direct support of military operations and such attack is the only feasible way to terminate such use (Article 56, para. 2, lit. a–b, AP I). This shall also apply to other military objectives located at or in the vicinity of these plants or installations (Article 56, para. 2, lit. c, AP I).**

1. The mere fact that an installation which is protected under Article 56 AP I constitutes, according to general criteria, a 'military objective' does not justify an attack on such an object. There exist, however, certain situations in which such an installation abandons its original purposes in favour of military concerns, when its use exceeds its common contribution to military activities ('for other than its normal function') in order directly to support military operations.[672] This must be a form of use alien to its normal function, which does not result from its ordinary use, but which is given to it ad hoc in the framework of military activities. Dykes, for example, are often integrated in defence positions as a part of the system of fortifications. Roads on the top of a dam offer a strategic advantage for military transport, either for the movement of armed forces or logistical support for the combat troops. In such cases of immediate use for 'regular, significant and direct support of military operations' even dangerous installations in the sense of Article 56 may be attacked and destroyed, 'if such attack is the only feasible way to terminate such support'.[673] There must, however, be no other objective which is not protected under Article 56 but the destruction of which would achieve an equal military advantage to that gained by destroying the installation. For example, if a strategically important transport route includes a dyke and also another weak point, the destruction

---

[669] As to the background of this rule, see Solf, ibid. 351–2; Pilloud/Pictet, ibid. para. 2153.
[670] See Pilloud/Pictet, ibid. paras. 2155–7.
[671] See the example given by Parks, *supra* (n. 8) 169.
[672] See Pilloud/Pictet, in *ICRC Commentary*, para. 2162.
[673] As to the interpretation of this clause, see ibid. (para. 2162); Solf, in Bothe/Partsch/Solf, above (n. 41) 354–5.

STEFAN OETER

of which would prevent the use of the whole route for military transport, the other target must be chosen in preference to the dyke.

2. Article 56, para. 2, AP I differentiates between dams and dykes (lit. a), in the case of which acts of regular, significant and direct support of military operations distinct from their normal function may lead to exclusion of the protection afforded by Article 56, para. 1, and nuclear power plants (lit. b), in the case of which a different problem arises.[674] Nuclear electricity-generating stations often constitute the central source of energy for modern electricity supply networks, and thus constitute—in contrast to dams and dykes—in their normal function a military objective of the first order.[675] Their contribution to military operations—that is the delivery of electric energy in 'regular, significant, and direct support of military operations'—can sometimes only be neutralized by destroying the power plant. In order to justify the extremely high risks of collateral damage resulting from such an attack, however, it is essential that the attack is absolutely necessary, which means that there must not exist any other 'feasible way' to terminate the support flowing from the nuclear plant. Accordingly, the exception of Article 56, para. 2, lit. b requires that there must be no other way of neutralizing the power supply, for example by destroying the essential installations of the distribution network (transformer stations, or main circuit lines).[676]

3. Other military objectives located at or in the vicinity of these 'dangerous installations' (such as strategically important bridges or works of the defence industry) may also be destroyed only for compelling reasons of military necessity, and only if the objectives are used for 'regular, significant, and direct support of military operations', and then only if their contribution to military operations cannot be neutralized in another way.[677] After all, even for the cases excluded under Article 56, para. 2 from the specific protection of Article 56, para. 1, the rule still applies that, notwithstanding the special protection of Article 56, the civilian population always enjoys the protection afforded by the general principles of distinction and proportionality.[678] Even in cases of exclusion from specific protection, due to direct contribution to warfare, all feasible precautions must be taken to prevent the release of dangerous forces (Article 56, para. 3, AP I).

> **Regular, significant, and direct support of military operations (Article 56, para. 2, lit. a–c, AP I) includes, for instance, the manufacture of weapons, ammunition, and defence material. The mere possibility of use by armed forces is not subject to these provisions.**

472

The definition of what constitutes 'regular, significant, and direct support of military operations' is extremely difficult. Problems of delimitation exist in particular concerning lit. b and c of Article 56, para. 2, AP I. In the case of direct military appropriation of dams and dykes, the identification of such support does not constitute a real problem. This is less clear-cut, however, as regards the directness of contributions from nuclear power plants and industrial works at or near installations containing dangerous

---

[674] Solf, ibid. 354; Pilloud/Pictet, ibid. paras. 2161, 2164.
[675] See Pilloud/Pictet, in *ICRC Commentary*, para. 2165; Solf, in Bothe/Partsch/Solf, above (n. 41) 355.
[676] See Pilloud/Pictet, ibid. para. 2166.
[677] Christian Zeileissen, *Der völkerrechtliche Schutz vor militärischen Angriffen auf Kernkraftwerke: Protection under International Law against Military Attacks on Nuclear Power Stations* (Duncker & Humblot, 1997), 193–9.
[678] Pilloud/Pictet, in *ICRC Commentary*, paras. 2168–9; Fleck, above (n. 342) 55–66.

STEFAN OETER

forces.[679] A power-generating station which supplies electrical energy mainly for military installations undoubtedly delivers a direct contribution to warfare. As for a nuclear power plant delivering energy mainly for industrial works of the defence industry, the point is already debatable.[680] What directly supports warfare in such a case is the industry supplied with power, not the power station in itself. However, even such a primarily defence industry-related function should probably be regarded as a 'regular, significant, and direct contribution'. Only in cases where defence industry and genuinely civilian industry are intimately compounded will one have to conclude that immediacy is interrupted, even if the 'civilian' industrial installations produce goods with both civilian and military uses (so-called 'dual-use items').[681] Clearly excluded from the category of 'regular, significant, and direct support' is the case of normal power stations feeding electric energy into the normal electricity power grid, despite the fact that military installations may also be supplied by the same grid.

473   **The decision to launch an attack shall be taken on the basis of all information available at the time of action. The parties to a conflict shall be bound by the principle of proportionality to refrain from launching an attack if the risk of releasing dangerous forces is such that it is excessive to any military advantage.**

Article 56 AP I contains in paragraphs 1 and 2 a whole series of vague notions evidently needing some clarification. They preserve a considerable degree of discretion for the military actors who are bound to apply the provision, but they also place on the military command authorities an enormous responsibility to assess the factual situation and apply the ill-defined notions of Article 56. In particular, the prognostic requirements of the provision are extremely difficult to fulfil. Whether an attack on a protected installation will release dangerous forces, and thus risk severe damage to the civilian population; and whether the planned attack is the only feasible means of ending the military use; these are complex factual questions which require considerable technical expertise for their evaluation. However, all military actions involve an extremely high degree of factual uncertainty, which necessarily means that the decision of the responsible commander can only be judged on the basis of the information available to him at the time of the decision, and not on the basis of hindsight (see Section 447).

474   **Military objectives shall not be located in the vicinity of works and installations containing dangerous forces unless they are necessary for the defence of those works (Article 56, para. 5, AP I).**

In para. 5 of Article 56 AP I the Diplomatic Conference has included a concrete expression of the principle of 'passive precautions' as it applies to 'dangerous installations'. Military objects and other installations which qualify as military objectives (such as armaments and munitions factories) should be geographically clearly separate from installations containing dangerous forces, such as dams, dykes, and nuclear power stations; the state responsible for them should locate all potential military objectives at a considerable distance from such protected installations, in order to minimize the risks of

---

[679] See in detail Zeileissen, *op. cit.*, 168–87.
[680] See on the one hand Solf, in Bothe/Partsch/Solf, above (n. 41) 355; on the other hand Pilloud/Pictet, in *ICRC Commentary*, para. 2165.
[681] Solf, ibid. 355; Pilloud/Pictet, ibid. para. 2165.

STEFAN OETER

attack on its 'dangerous installations'.[682] Only military installations erected for the sole purpose of defending the protected installations from attack are excluded from this rule. Since a military or police guard—even if of limited size—is always necessary to protect such installations against terrorists and saboteurs (at least in the case of nuclear power stations), one must accept as normal a certain minimum degree of military defence located at the installation itself. The character of the installation is not changed by such small-scale defence arrangements, and in particular such military defence does not render it an admissible target according to Article 56, para. 2, as long as the military guard and their facilities (such as guarded enclosures, anti-aircraft guns, etc.) serve the sole purpose of defending the installation against sabotage.[683]

> The parties to the conflict shall remain obliged to take all precautions to protect   475
> dangerous works from the effects of attack (e.g. by shutting down nuclear electricity-
> generating stations).

Besides the specific rule of Article 56, para. 5, AP I, there apply also the general rules of Article 58 AP I on 'passive precautions' (see Section 447, para. 4) concerning the protection of dams, dykes, and nuclear power stations. According to Article 58, lit. c, AP I the parties to the conflict shall take the 'necessary precautions to protect the civilian population, individual civilians, and civilian objects under their control against the dangers resulting from military operations'. In the case of 'dangerous installations', this could mean also that the party on whose territory, for example, an endangered dam lies, must drain the lake in order to minimize the risk of collateral damage if the combat zone approaches the dam; a similar requirement is applicable to nuclear power stations, where the party responsible for the plant might even be obliged to switch off the reactor if imminent danger of combat in the vicinity of the nuclear installation arises.

> Works and installations containing dangerous forces may be marked with a special   476
> protective sign consisting of three bright orange circles on a horizontal axis (Article
> 56, para. 7, AP I).

The First Additional Protocol introduced in Article 56, para. 7, lit. a, a protective sign (analogous to the system of the Hague Convention for the Protection of Cultural Property; see Sections 931–935), to be attached to protected objects. The lack of a protective sign, however, does not mean that the parties are exempted from the protective provisions of Article 56; to the contrary, the obligations resulting from Article 56 bind the parties irrespective of marking of the installations in accordance with Article 56, para. 7.[684]

5. Aerial Blockade

> An aerial blockade is a means to prevent aircraft and unmanned aerial vehicles   477
> from entering or leaving a certain airspace of the adversary. The blockade must be
> declared and notified to all states. It must be enforced impartially. In order to be
> binding, it must be effective.

---

[682] See Solf, in Bothe/Partsch/Solf, above (n. 41) 356; Zeileissen, *op. cit.*, 203–6.

[683] See Solf, *op. cit.*, 356; Pilloud/Pictet, in *ICRC Commentary*, paras. 2173–6; a critical position towards this provision is taken by Kalshoven/Zegveld, above (n. 22) 117.

[684] Zeileissen, *op. cit.*, 212–13.

STEFAN OETER

1. An aerial blockade is an operation by which the belligerent party prevents any air-craft to enter or exit airports of the enemy state.[685] It is meant to deny the enemy the use of aircraft to transport personnel or goods inside or outside its territory. Historically, the law of blockade developed in the naval domain.[686] The enforcement of an aerial block-ade, which can be done by military aircraft or even naval vessels, may involve actual use of force to prohibit the landing or take-off of aircraft. Accordingly, the law of armed conflicts applies to its execution. Blockades in general are the only legal method of war-fare that entitles the belligerent to prevent enemy exports.[687] It is a method of warfare exclusively applicable in international armed conflicts.

2. As stated in the 1909 London Declaration,[688] which codified the law at that time, a blockade must be declared by the belligerent in order to be binding, also upon neu-trals.[689] The notification must include specific information on the date of beginning, duration, location, extent, and period of time it is supposed to last.[690] Blockades that have been declared, but never been executed or only partly executed,[691] are not effec-tive.[692] Whether a blockade is effective has to be determined on a case-by-case basis and the actual facts. It also depends on the technological instruments available to the belligerent. According to the commentary on Rule 151 *HPCR Manual*, it is considered to be effective 'if any attempt to leave or enter the blockaded area proves to be a hazardous undertaking'.[693]

478   The party declaring the blockade must consider its consequences. The suffering of the civilian population must not be excessive to the concrete and direct military advantage anticipated. Starvation of the civilian population as a method of warfare is prohibited. The right to receive humanitarian assistance must be respected (see below, Sections 503, 524–525).

The principle of humanity does not prohibit aerial blockades per se.[694] However, an aer-ial blockade will always affect the civilian population. Therefore, its anticipated concrete and military advantage has to be balanced against the suffering of the population; exces-sive suffering leads to an unlawful blockade. According to Article 54, para. 1, AP I and customary international law, starvation of the civilian population as a method of warfare is prohibited. Rule 157, lit. a, *HPCR Manual* also prohibits a blockade at the expense of the civilian population with regard to starvation.[695] In the case that the provision of food and so on is not ensured, the blockading state has to give free passage of food and other supplies, Rule 158 *HPCR Manual*, although this right to free passage is easily misused.

---

[685] See Heintschel von Heinegg, 'Blockade', *MPEPIL* para. 6 ff.
[686] Cf. Commentary on *HPCR Manual*, Section V, p. 287.
[687] See Heintschel von Heinegg, 'Blockade', *MPEPIL*, para. 2
[688] Although the 1909 London Declaration never entered into force.
[689] Cf. Commentary on *HPCR Manual*, Section V, p. 288.
[690] Heintschel von Heinegg, 'Blockade', *MPEPIL*, para. 28.
[691] See M. N. Schmitt, 'The Confluence of Law and Morality: Thoughts on Just War' (1992) 3 *US Air Force Academy Journal of Legal Studies* 21, 44 ff.
[692] Cf. Principle 4 of the 1856 Paris Declaration and Arts. 2 and 3 of the 1909 London Declaration.
[693] Cf. Commentary on *HPCR Manual*, Section V, p. 291.
[694] Cf. Schmitt, above (n. 691) 51.
[695] The same applies to naval blockades according to paras. 102 and 103 of the *San Remo Manual on International Law Applicable to Armed Conflicts at Sea* of 12 June 1994.

STEFAN OETER

As a consequence, an impartial humanitarian organization (ICRC etc.) or the protecting power may supervise the passage, Rule 158, lit. a and b, *HPCR Manual*.

> The principles and rules of naval blockades apply *mutatis mutandis* to aerial block-   479
> ades (see below, Sections 1051–1053; see Rules 147–159 *HPCR Manual*).

Traditionally, blockades were declared with regard to the sea. Most of the rules governing the law of blockades derive therefore from naval blockades. In 1908–1909, the law applicable to naval blockades was codified during the London Naval Conference.[696] The contemporary law of naval warfare, including naval blockades, is summarized in the 1994 *San Remo Manual on International Law Applicable to Armed Conflict at Sea*.[697] Due to the industrialization and the progress regarding aircraft, states declared also aerial blockades. The principles codified with regard to naval blockade apply *mutatis mutandis* to aerial blockade. They have the same purpose and their execution relies on the same military means.

6. Ruses of War and the Prohibition against Perfidy

> Ruses of war and the employment of measures necessary for obtaining information   480
> about the adverse party and the country are permissible (Article 37, para. 2, AP I;
> Article 24 HagueReg) (e.g. the use of enemy signals, passwords, signs, decoys, etc.;
> to be distinguished from espionage, see Sections 322–325).

Deceiving the enemy about the military situation, in particular about the strength of one's own forces, their location, and one's own intentions and plans, has belonged to the common arsenal of warfare since time immemorial.[698] Since warfare has always been at least as much a psychological attempt to bring one's influence to bear on the adversary as it has necessarily comprised the use of physical violence against the enemy, deception is often better suited to achieve results than the blatant use of violence.[699] Camouflaging one's own defence positions and using them for ambushes, setting up surprise attacks from such camouflaged positions, simulating operations of retreat, as well as simulating operations of attack, using dummy weapons, transmitting misleading messages, *inter alia* by using the adversary's radio wavelengths, passwords, and codes, infiltrating the enemy's command chain in order to channel wrong orders, moving landmarks and route markers, giving members of one military unit the signs of other units to persuade the enemy that one's force is larger than it really is—all these are established elements of traditional tactics.[700] The laws of war have never prohibited such measures of deception, or 'ruses of war'.[701] Article 24 of the Hague Regulations states only the simple rule: 'Ruses of war and the employment of measures necessary for obtaining information about the enemy and the country are permissible.'[702] Article 37, para. 2, AP I has added nothing

---

[696] See Heintschel von Heinegg, 'Blockade', *MPEPIL*, para. 8.

[697] Available at <http://www.icrc.org/ihl.nsf/full/560?opendocument>.

[698] See Ipsen, 'Ruses of War', *MPEPIL*.

[699] See Fleck 'Ruses of War and Prohibition of Perfidy' (1974) XIII *RDMilG* 269–314, at 298.

[700] See de Preux, in *ICRC Commentary*, para. 1521; Solf, in Bothe/Partsch/Solf, above (n. 41) 207; Ipsen, ibid.

[701] Solf, ibid. 202–3; Green, *op. cit.*, (n. 182) 171–3; Rule 57 *CIHL*.

[702] Concerning Articles 24 and 23 HagueReg, see Ipsen, *loc. cit.*, 1390; de Preux, in *ICRC Commentary*, para. 1513; Fleck, above (n. 699) 276–85.

STEFAN OETER

new to this old rule, and is worded in terms reminiscent of Article 24 HagueReg: 'Ruses of war are not prohibited. Such ruses are acts intended to mislead an adversary or to induce him to act recklessly but which infringe no rule of international law applicable in armed conflict and which are not perfidious because they do not invite the confidence of an adversary with respect to protection under that law. The following are examples of such ruses: the use of camouflage, decoys, mock operations, and misinformation.'

481   **Perfidy is prohibited. The term 'perfidy' refers to acts misleading the adverse party into the belief that there is a situation affording protection under international law (e.g. humanitarian agreement to suspend combat with the intention of attacking by surprise the adversary relying on the agreement, Article 37 AP I).**

1. The real problem underlying Article 37 AP I—already apparent from the wording of Article 37, para. 2, AP I—is the threshold between a lawful ruse of war and an unlawful act of perfidy. What primarily distinguishes perfidy from ordinary ruses of war is, according to the definitional approach of Article 37 AP I, the exploitation of deliberately induced trust on the part of the adversary in order to injure, kill, or capture him. There must be a deliberate attempt to instil confidence with an 'intent to betray'.[703] As it is expressed in Article 37, para. 1: 'Acts inviting the confidence of an adversary to lead him to believe that he is entitled to, or is obliged to accord, protection under the rules of international law applicable in armed conflict, with intent to betray that confidence, shall constitute perfidy.'[704] Deception is not limited here to questions of general military interest, such as the disposition of forces, or potential strategic planning, but concerns the existence of a right to protection provided by international law.[705] Moral and legal duty requires the combatant in such situations to protect the adversary and the innocent civilian. Elementary rules of international law, the observance of which should be a matter of honour (and a product of a genuine sense of justice) are grossly abused by perfidy.[706] Accordingly, the old notion of breach of honour is still present in the notion of perfidy: the (dishonourable) violation of the rules of 'chivalry', which in medieval customs constituted the core of perfidy.[707]

2. Article 37, para. 1, AP I illustrates the abstract definition of perfidy by examples—which, however, are not meant to be exhaustive, since the Diplomatic Conference in its drafting of Article 37 limited itself to uncomplicated examples, avoiding debatable situations.[708] Prohibited as perfidy is *inter alia* (a) the abuse of a flag of truce by feigning an intent to negotiate or surrender, (b) the feigning of incapacity to fight due to wounds or

[703] See the classical explanation given in H. Lauterpacht (ed.), above (n. 242) Vol. II, 430: 'Stratagems must be carefully distinguished from perfidy, since the former are allowed, whereas the latter is prohibited. Halleck correctly formulates the distinction by laying down the principle that, whenever a belligerent has expressly or tacitly engaged, and is therefore bound by a moral obligation, to speak the truth to an enemy, it is perfidy to betray his confidence, because it constitutes a breach of good faith.'
[704] As to the drafting history of the prohibition of perfidy in Article 37, para. 1, AP I, see in particular H. P. Furrer, *Perfidie in der Geschichte und im heutigen Kriegsvölkerrecht* (Zurich: Juris Druck & Verlag, 1988), 62–80.
[705] Furrer, ibid. 81–2; Kalshoven/Zegveld, above (n. 22) 94–5; Rusinova, 'Perfidy', *MPEPIL*; Solf, in Bothe/Partsch/Solf, above (n. 41) 204–5; de Preux, in *ICRC Commentary*, para. 1500.
[706] Fleck, above (n. 699) 285.
[707] See de Preux, in *ICRC Commentary*, para. 1498; Solf, in Bothe/Partsch/Solf, 202.
[708] Solf, ibid. 205; V. Rusinova, 'Perfidy', *MPEPIL*; Furrer, 85–6; de Preux, in *ICRC Commentary*, paras. 1502–3.

STEFAN OETER

sickness, (c) the feigning of civilian, non-combatant status, and (d) 'the feigning of protected status by the use of signs, emblems, or uniforms of the United Nations or of neutral or other States not Parties to the conflict'.[709] Of most importance in that respect is example (c), because the feigning of civilian, non-combatant status in order to attack the enemy by surprise constitutes the classic case of 'treacherous killing of an enemy combatant' which was already prohibited by Article 23, lit. b, HagueReg; it is the obvious case of disgraceful behaviour which can (and should) be sanctioned under criminal law as a killing not justified by the laws of war, making it a common crime of murder.[710] Obscuring the distinction between combatants and civilians is extremely prejudicial to the chances of serious implementation of the rules of humanitarian law; any tendency to blur the distinction must be sanctioned heavily by the international community; otherwise the whole system based on the concept of distinction will break down.[711] Article 37, para. 1, lit. c, AP I, has a parallel provision in Article 44, para. 3, AP I, which signals (although only indirectly) attacks in violation of the conditions set out in Article 44, para. 3, AP I as being perfidious (see Sections 309, 312). A problematic question has been how to distinguish permitted cases of operating in civilian clothes (guerilla fighters in occupied territories and in wars of national liberation) from cases of legally forbidden perfidy,[712] such as in the case of command units operating and attacking in civilian clothes, as was, for example, the concept of the former Soviet Spetsnaz troops (see Section 321).

3. The phrase 'perfidy is prohibited' does not reproduce the entire current rule of international law. According to Article 37 AP I, perfidy is prohibited only in so far as it intentionally wounds, kills, or captures the enemy.[713] Perfidy as such, beyond this restrictive definition based on hostile intent, is not banned under international law; if it is used solely for combat against military objects, for example, without affecting any enemy combatant, it is permissible.[714] 'Perfidious' acts are also allowed in order to evade capture or to escape from a prisoner-of-war camp, as long as no attack is committed under cover of the disguise;[715] the same is true for all *attempts* to commit acts covered by Article 37, para. 1.[716] To reiterate: only the commission of a treacherous attack on enemy personnel which wounds, kills, or captures them is prohibited. That limitation of the prohibition on hostile attacks under cover of disguise has been heavily criticized,[717] but it corresponds to the general attitude of most states which were involved in drafting the provision. Accordingly, it was impossible to avoid such a limitation to the prohibition of perfidy, and one must accept that most acts committed under camouflage and feigning still constitute legitimate ruses of war, and not perfidy.

It is prohibited to make improper use of flags of truce, enemy or neutral national 482
flags, military insignia and uniforms, and internationally acknowledged protective
emblems, for example the red cross or the red crescent (Article 39 AP I; Article 23,

[709] As to the interpretation of these examples, see de Preux, in *ICRC Commentary*, 439 (paras. 1508–11); Solf, ibid. 206; Rusinova, 'Perfidy', *MPEPIL*.
[710] See de Preux, in *ICRC Commentary*, 438 (paras. 1506–7); see also Fleck, *loc. cit.*, 278.
[711] So argues convincingly de Preux, in *ICRC Commentary*, 438 (para. 1506).
[712] See Solf, in Bothe/Partsch/Solf, above (n. 41) 205–6.
[713] See Vera Rusinova, 'Perfidy', *MPEPIL*; Solf, ibid. 203–4; Rule 65 *CIHL*.
[714] See Rusinova, ibid.; Furrer, 82–3; Solf, ibid.
[715] See Kalshoven/Zegveld, above (n. 22) 95.
[716] See Kalshoven/Zegveld, ibid. 95.
[717] See Rusinova, op. cit.

STEFAN OETER

para. 1, lit. f, HagueReg; Article 17, para. 2, CultPropConv), distress codes, signals or frequencies (Rule 115 *HPCR Manual*). For specific rules of naval warfare, see below Chapter 10.

Apart from the basic rule of Article 37, para. 1, AP I, the system of the Additional Protocols, Hague Regulations, and customary law contains a whole series of other prohibitions of various kinds of deception, that is prohibitions on specific ruses or stratagems.[718] The prohibition of abuse of flags of truce (now expressly defined as perfidy by Article 37, para. 1, lit. a, AP I) was mentioned above; in Article 38 AP I it is further enlarged to an all-embracing prohibition against any abuse of such signs.[719] In a parallel provision, Article 38 AP I prohibits the abuse of 'recognized emblems' such as the emblems of the red cross, of civil defence, the protective emblem of cultural property, or of 'other internationally recognized protective emblems, signs, or signals'.[720] Article 39 AP I prohibits also the improper use of false flags, military insignia, emblems, or uniforms. Whereas according to Article 39, para. 1, the use of the flags, military emblems, insignia, or uniforms of 'neutral or other States not Parties to the conflict' is generally prohibited,[721] para. 2 of the same Article imposes a different rule on the use of the flags, military emblems, insignia, or uniforms of adverse parties to the conflict. The use of such symbols of the opposing belligerent is prohibited only during attacks or if it serves 'to shield, favour, protect, or impede military operations'.[722] Although the use of enemy flags, insignia, or uniforms does not constitute perfidy in the strict sense, since those items do not create a specific confidence (i.e. the confidence of protection demanded by the moral code of chivalry) state practice has nonetheless for centuries considered such deception to be dishonourable, and accordingly not permissible.[723] Article 23, lit. f, HagueReg puts the abuse of national flags, military emblems, insignia, and uniforms of the enemy on the same footing as abuses of flags of truce or the red cross emblem, and expressly prohibits such abuses as means of warfare;[724] military operations using false insignia or uniforms are not lawful under international law and may be prosecuted under criminal law as illegitimate acts of violence.[725] Apart from that, the mere fact of operating behind enemy lines in civilian clothes or false uniforms may be considered to be espionage and may be punished as such (see Sections 322–325) although such acts (if not accompanied by the use of force against the adversary) are not prohibited per se by Article 39, para. 2, AP I.[726]

---

[718] See Rules 58–62 *CIHL*.

[719] See de Preux, in *ICRC Commentary*, para. 1504, paras. 1551–6.

[720] See the detailed description of the rule by de Preux, in *ICRC Commentary*, pp 446–60; also Solf, in Bothe/Partsch/Solf, above (n. 41) 208–11; Rusinova, Perfidy, *MPEPIL*; as to the misuse of protective emblems by Iraqi forces during the Operation 'Iraqi Freedom', see Schmitt, above (n. 371) 31.

[721] See Solf, in Bothe/Partsch/Solf, above (n. 41) 213; and in great detail de Preux, in *ICRC Commentary*, pp. 462–5; see also the *US Naval Manual*, para. 12.3.3.

[722] As to Article 39, para. 2, AP I, see de Preux, in *ICRC Commentary*, paras. 1572–9; Solf, in Bothe/Partsch/Solf, above (n. 41) 214.

[723] Fleck, above (n. 699) 276–85; de Preux, *loc. cit.*, para. 1573; the contrary position is taken, however, by the *US Naval Manual*, para. 12.5.3.

[724] Concerning the much-debated interpretation of Article 23, lit. f, HagueReg see Fleck, above (n. 699) 279 *et seq.*; Solf, in Bothe/Partsch/Solf, above (n. 41) 212–3.

[725] See Solf, *op. cit.*, 206 n. 23 and de Preux in *ICRC Commentary*, p 467 n. 26. A US occupation tribunal came to the opposite conclusion in 1947 in the *Skorzeny* case: see Fleck, above (n. 699) 279 (with critical comments on that judgment ibid. 280 *et seq.*); the position taken in the *Skorzeny* judgment still seems to be the official US position today; see *US Naval Manual*, para. 12.5.3.

[726] As to the discussion of this provision, see Solf, above (n. 41) 214–5 and de Preux, *op. cit.*, paras. 1580–1, 1583.

STEFAN OETER

7. Psychological Warfare

> It is permissible to engage in political and military propaganda by spreading false   483
> information to undermine the adversary's will to resist and to influence the mili-
> tary discipline of the adversary (e.g. instigation to defect).

Propaganda with intent to influence the adversary's civilian population and to work on the members of the opposing armed forces has been an important means of warfare throughout this century.[727] During World War I, the issue arose for the first time and had led to a fierce debate on the legality of psychological warfare.[728] By the 1920s, how-ever, the use of propaganda was generally considered to be legally permissible (see Article 21 HRAW 1923). In the course of World War II, all sides made active use of the new weapon, as have the parties of all wars since 1945.[729] Classic forms of propaganda, often listed under the heading of (permissible) ruses of war, are the spreading of false rumours; the erosion of adverse armed forces' fighting morale by the dissemination of misleading information; the incitement of enemy combatants to rebel, mutiny, or desert; and the incitement of the entire enemy population to revolt against its government.[730]

> Incitement to commit crimes and breaches of international law is prohibited.   484

The expression of the rule in this Section is not totally correct, since it gives the impres-sion that incitement to commit any crime is illegal. In fact, not all acts classified by the adversary as crimes are taboo for the power engaging in psychological warfare.[731] Many generally accepted forms of hostile propaganda are in essence incitement to commit crimes, for example to desert to the enemy, which is a crime sanctioned with severe penalties according to all legal systems, as are all acts of mutiny and treason.[732] Also, the common incitement to overthrow a 'war-mongering' regime clearly constitutes (from the perspective of the affected nation) incitement to commit high treason.[733] However, all these subversive activities may undoubtedly be lawfully encouraged (and assisted) by the opposing belligerent. What is generally recognized to be prohibited as disgrace-ful is incitement to commit common crimes such as murder, robbery, or rape,[734] and particularly incitement to commit war crimes or crimes against humanity, which would evidently constitute an illegal act leading to state responsibility.[735] The same would apply to elementary violations of rules of international law, although this seems to be a rather hypothetical question (the only case yet discussed is the dissemination of falsified banknotes in order to wreck the monetary order of the adverse power).[736]

---

[727] Michael G. Kearney, 'Propaganda for War, Prohibition of', *MPEPIL*; Greenspan, above (n. 239) 322–3.

[728] Kearney, ibid.

[729] Ibid.

[730] See Kunz, *Kriegsrecht, op. cit.*, (n. 47) 82; Castrén, above (n. 47) 208–10; Greenspan, above (n. 239) 323; Solf, in Bothe/Partsch/Solf, above (n. 41) 206–7; Kearney, 'Propaganda of War', *MPEPIL*; de Preux, in *ICRC Commentary*, 443–4 (para. 1521).

[731] See Kalliopi Chainoglou, 'Psychological Warfare', *MPEPIL*.

[732] See also Kunz, *op. cit.*, (n. 47) 82.

[733] The question of the legality of incitement to rebel against one's government was still disputed at the turn of the twentieth century, see Kunz, ibid. 82; in the literature published after 1945, however, the ques-tion is generally considered to be solved; see H. Lauterpacht (ed.), above (n. 242) Vol. II, 426–8; Castrén, above (n. 47) 209–10; de Preux, in *ICRC Commentary*, para. 1521.

[734] See Chainoglou, above (n. 731).

[735] Kearney, above (n. 727); Greenspan, above (n. 239) 324.

[736] Kearny, ibid.

STEFAN OETER

8. Reprisals

485   **Reprisals are coercive measures which would normally be contrary to international law but which are taken in retaliation by one party to a conflict in order to stop the adversary from violating international law.**

1. The law of reprisals is one of the classic instruments to implement the rules of public international law (see also Section 1408). It must be seen as closely connected with the principle of reciprocity, since it allows one state illegally injured by another to react to the violation of the law by an action which itself would normally breach international legal obligations.[737] The underlying purpose of the law of reprisals is to induce a law-breaking state to abide by the law in future, and to respect the demands of law in its further conduct.[738]

2. The instrument of reprisal, however, involves serious difficulties. On one hand, experience shows that reprisals are not necessarily effective in forcing the adverse party to respect the law, since reprisals often produce the contrary effect, tending to prompt a harsher reaction to every new reprisal of the adverse side, thus setting up a process of escalation.[739] Also, on the other hand, the institution is prone to all kinds of abuse, because it offers an excuse serving merely to palliate breaches of law which would have been committed in any event—and this, in cases of reprisals concerning humanitarian law, to the detriment of innocent civilians or prisoners.[740] Accordingly, there has long existed a tendency which sought to bind the use of reprisals in a compelling legal framework, in order to make the use of reprisals dependent on strict observance of certain formalities.[741] At last, humanitarian law since the Geneva Conventions of 1949 has progressively developed a system with protective rules for specific groups of persons or objects who become immune from reprisals, in order to prevent any erosion of humanitarian rights under the guise of reprisal.[742]

486   **Because of their political and military significance, reprisals shall be authorized by the highest political level. No individual soldier is authorized to order reprisals on his own accord.**

Because of the extremely complex legal and political assessment which must precede any reprisal, it is necessary that the political leadership of a belligerent state decide on any possible use of reprisals. The exact legal nature of the adverse belligerent's actions may be extremely difficult to determine; even more importantly, a decision to use reprisals requires a genuine assessment of the political risks as well as the immediate dangers connected with use of a reprisal. It is not only uncertain whether the enemy will be forced to abide by the law, but under certain circumstances reprisals may even—particularly if at or near the limits of proportionality—set in motion an uncontrollable process of escalation which could expose one's own civilian population to considerable

---

[737] As to the institution of reprisals in general, see Kalshoven, above (n. 248) 11–33, and R. Bierzanek, 'Reprisals as a Means of Enforcing the Laws of Warfare: The Old and the New Law', in Cassese (ed.), *The New Humanitarian Law of Armed Conflict* (Napoli: Ed. Scientifica, 1979), 232–57, at 232–40.

[738] Kalshoven, above (n. 248) 33.

[739] Kalshoven, *loc. cit.*, 42.

[740] See Bierzanek, above (n. 737) 237–40 and Kalshoven, above (n. 248) 367–70.

[741] Bierzanek, *loc. cit.*, 241–3; Kalshoven, *op. cit.*, 5–10.

[742] Kalshoven, *op. cit.*, 263–77; Kalshoven, above (n. 284) 45–52.

STEFAN OETER

danger. Accordingly, it is not appropriate for individual military commanders to undertake reprisals on their own accord; this is the sole responsibility of the highest political authority, in the case of Germany: the Federal government.

> **Reprisals shall not be excessive in relation to the offence committed by the adversary and shall be preceded by a warning. They must be the last resort, when all other means to stop the illegal behaviour have failed and the warning has not been heeded.**

487

There are two basic preconditions of customary law for legal reprisals: the requirement of proportionality concerning the original breach of law and the reaction, and the duty to warn in advance that such a reaction is imminent.[743] These two limitations on the use of reprisals have proven to be the most efficient safeguards in preventing fundamental abuses of reprisals, or at least to reveal improper reliance on the law of reprisals.

> **It is expressly prohibited by international agreement to take reprisals against:**
> — **the wounded, sick, and shipwrecked; medical and religious personnel; medical facilities and supplies (Article 46 GC I; Article 47 GC II; Article 33, para. 2, lit. b, GC III; Article 20 AP I);**
> — **prisoners of war (Article 13, para. 3, GC III);**
> — **the civilian population or civilians (Article 33, para. 3, GC IV; Article 51, para. 6, AP I);**
> — **civilian objects (Article 52, para. 1, AP I);**
> — **private property of civilians on occupied territory or of enemy foreigners on friendly territory (Article 33, para. 3, GC IV);**
> — **objects indispensable to the survival of the civilian population (Article 55, para. 2, AP I);**
> — **the natural environment (Article 55, para. 2, AP I);**
> — **works and installations containing dangerous forces (Article 56, para. 4, AP I); or**
> — **cultural objects and places of worship (Article 53, lit. c, AP I; Article 4, para. 4, CultPropConv).**

488

1. In the course of the last decades, humanitarian law was developed by a process which gradually excluded more and more groups of persons and protected objects from the scope of reprisals. The process was begun, after the Geneva Convention on Prisoners of War of 1929 which included a prohibition of reprisals,[744] by the provisions of Articles 46 GC I, 47 GC II, 13, para. 3 GC III, and 33 GC IV, in which all reprisals were prohibited that prejudice the protection of the specific groups covered by the four Conventions (wounded, sick, and shipwrecked; medical and religious personnel; prisoners of war; civilians in occupied territories) and to the protection of certain objects (medical facilities and supplies, private property of civilians in occupied territories).[745] The Hague Convention on the Protection of Cultural Property of 1954 contains an analogous prohibition of reprisals in favour of objects protected under that Convention.[746]

---

[743] See Bierzanek, above (n. 737) 241–3; Rule 145 *CIHL*.
[744] See Kalshoven, above (n. 284) 45–6.
[745] See the detailed explanations given by Kalshoven, above (n. 248) 263–71.
[746] Kalshoven, above (n. 284) 272–7.

STEFAN OETER

2. The First Additional Protocol now enlarges the traditional prohibitions of reprisals considerably.[747] True, the comprehensively formulated proposal which sought to exclude all groups of persons and objects protected under the Convention from reprisals was rejected.[748] The final text of the Protocol, however, represented agreement on a whole catalogue of additional and specific prohibitions of reprisals. Reprisals in disregard of the protection of the natural environment (provided for in Article 55) as well as reprisals to the detriment of objects indispensable for the survival of the civilian population (Article 54, para. 4, AP I) and to the detriment of works and installations containing dangerous forces are now absolutely prohibited.

3. The most important of these safeguards, however, is the prohibition in the Additional Protocol, Article 51, para. 6, namely the prohibition against attacks on a civilian population based on a justification of reprisal. Such reprisals had been permitted under traditional customary law,[749] and they constituted the bulk of all measures declared to be reprisals. The prohibition set out in Article 51, para. 6, AP I has been fiercely criticized in legal literature as well as in practice, since it almost completely prevents the taking of reprisals as a response to breaches of humanitarian law by the adverse side.[750] It also creates considerable difficulties in the legal justification of the dominant doctrines of nuclear deterrence, since even the planned inclusion of large-scale use of strategic nuclear weapons as a military option might be justified only in the framework of belligerent reprisals;[751] from this follows the immense importance of the nuclear declarations and of the resulting exclusion of the nuclear question from the applicability of all the new rules in AP I (and implicitly from the prohibition against reprisals contained in Article 51, para. 6, AP I; see Section 434). Only by recourse to reprisal can current nuclear strategies be legitimated under international law. For a long time, the predominantly adopted position accepted reprisals against civilians as permissible under customary law; though, the assertion of the ICTY in two decisions that customary law contains an absolute ban on such reprisals evoked a lively discussion of this question.[752] Apart from that, one must consider the prohibitions of reprisals included in Additional Protocol I to be one of the great achievements brought about by the development of humanitarian law, although it makes the entire system more dependent on an international system of implementation if decentralized reaction to breaches of law is to be excluded.

---

[747] Kalshoven, above (n. 284) 49–52; Bierzanek, above (n. 737) 251–5.

[748] See Bierzanek, ibid. 249–50; Kalshoven, above (n. 248) 474–9.

[749] Kalshoven, above (n. 9) 286; Kalshoven, above (n. 248) 353–61.

[750] As critical voices, see in particular Greenwood, 'The Twilight of the Law of Belligerent Reprisals' (1989) 20 *NYIL* 35–69; F. J. Hampson, 'Belligerent Reprisals and the 1977 Protocols to the Geneva Conventions of 1949' (1988) 37 *ICLQ* 818–43; as a (convincing) response, see Kalshoven, above (n. 284) 53–63; the US expressly rejects the bans imposed by Articles 51, para. 6, and 52, para. 1, AP I, cf. *US Naval Manual*, para. 6.2.4.

[751] See Kalshoven, above (n. 248) 348–53.

[752] ICTY, *Prosecutor v Martić* (Case IT-95-11-R61), 8 March 1996, *ILR* 108, 46–7, paras. 15–17; ICTY, *Prosecutor v Kupreskić et al.* (Case IT-95-16-T), 14 January 2000, 207–9, paras. 527–531; *CIHL* Vol. I, 520–3.

STEFAN OETER

5

PROTECTION OF THE CIVILIAN POPULATION

I. General Rules

Introductory Remarks

1. For the purpose of discussion it is useful to divide the international rules on the protection of the civilian population and of individual civilians during armed conflict into two groups, which are the response to two distinct situations: (a) the rules providing protection to the civilian population or individual persons under the control of the adversary against violence or arbitrary acts; and (b) the rules providing protection of the civilian population against direct effects of military operations and other acts of hostility. The first group relates to the legal protection of human beings against violence and abuse of power. These rules are often called the Law of Geneva or Red Cross Law as they were essentially codified in the Geneva Conventions. The second group of rules sets limits to the conduct of military operations itself. This law is called the Law of The Hague, as the 1907 Hague Regulations annexed to HC IV was the first comprehensive codification in this area. This distinction based on where the rules were negotiated is nowadays rather historical. The two 1977 Additional Protocols to the Geneva Conventions in fact contain both types of rules.

2. The affinity of the rules protecting the human beings against violence and against abuse of power in armed conflict to the international regime of protecting human rights is particularly striking (see Sections 249–255, Introductory Remarks, para. 2, and Section 518).

3. This chapter discusses the provisions of international law concerning the protection of civilians in armed conflict. The rules applicable in international armed conflict are highly developed and extensively codified. Of course, their scope of application is limited to conflicts of an international character, in particular armed clashes between states. Situations of foreign occupation are also international armed conflicts. The four Geneva Conventions, supplemented by their first 1977 Additional Protocol constitutes the heart of protections granted to civilians in international armed conflicts. The law protecting civilians in non-international armed conflicts has been codified by Article 3 common to the four Geneva Conventions and developed in 1977 by AP II. Although these provisions are more summary in nature than the law on international armed conflicts, they contain important rules on the protection of civilians in an internal conflict. In both cases the written law is supplemented by rules of international customary law. As shown by the Customary Law Study, the ICRC was mandated to conduct, there is an important

HANS-PETER GASSER AND KNUT DÖRMANN

set of rules protecting the civilian population that applies in any type of armed conflict, independent of its character as international or non-international.[1]

4. In particular, as recognized by the ICJ in its *Nicaragua* judgment,[2] the fundamental provisions of international humanitarian law as codified by Article 3 common to the Geneva Conventions (see Section 209), apply to all types of armed conflicts. Accordingly, the obligation to treat humanely all persons once they are in the power of the adverse party, including those persons who have actively participated in hostilities must be respected in all circumstances. After the adoption of the 1977 Protocols there is hardly a significant difference between the two legal regimes as far as the fundamental guarantees are concerned, since AP II designed for non-international armed conflict protects individuals against the misuse of power just as clearly as the law of international armed conflicts (see in particular Articles 4–6 AP II and Article 75 AP I, which reflect customary international law).[3] In addition, no distinction should be made between international and non-international armed conflicts as far as rules governing the conduct of military operations are concerned, in particular the rules derived from the principle of distinction. Remaining differences between the two legal systems should, however, not be neglected: important parts of the 'Geneva Law', such as the legal status of combatants or the law applying to belligerent occupation, are relevant for international conflict situations only.[4]

501   In order to ensure respect for and protection of the civilian population and civil-
        ian objects, the parties to an armed conflict shall at all times distinguish between
        the civilian population and combatants and between civilian objects and military
        objectives. Accordingly, they shall direct their operations only against military
        objectives (Article 48 AP I).

1. Members of the armed forces (and persons participating in a *levée en masse*) are combatants in the sense of international humanitarian law applicable to international armed conflicts.[5] They alone have the right to take a direct part in military operations and thereby to kill, injure, or destroy without being personally held responsible for the consequences of their acts, provided, of course, they respect the constraints of international humanitarian law. On the other hand, combatants may be targeted by the armed forces of the adverse party. Civilians have no such right to take a direct part in hostilities. The non-involvement of civilians in hostilities is the precondition of the functioning of the principle according to which the civilian population shall be protected from military operations in all circumstances. Indeed, combatants are only willing to distinguish between members of the enemy armed forces and civilians, and thus spare the adversary's civilian population, if they do not have to fear to be attacked by these same civilians (see below, Section 519). If civilians nevertheless take a direct part in hostilities, they lose their protection against direct attacks (see below).

---

[1] Cf. *CIHL* Rules 1–6, 87–138. See also, with respect to the law on non-international armed conflict, below, Chapter 12.

[2] ICJ, *Military and Paramilitary Activities in and against Nicaragua* (*Nicaragua v US*), Merits, Judgment, *ICJ Reports 1986*, para. 218.

[3] *CIHL* Rules 87–105.

[4] See below, Section 1213 ff.

[5] See above, Sections 301 *et seq.*, especially Section 304.

HANS-PETER GASSER AND KNUT DÖRMANN

2. For the purpose of international humanitarian law, as far as the rules on the conduct of hostilities are concerned, a civilian is a person who is not a member of the armed forces or of a *levée en masse* (Article 50, para. 1, AP I).[6] This (negative) definition, linked to that of members of the armed forces, has the advantage of being conclusive. In traditional warfare it has usually been clear who is a member of the opposing armed forces or who is not and thus is entitled to protection. This is particularly true for international armed conflicts. In internal armed conflicts also, it has generally been evident who is in fact involved in acts of violence and who is not. In present forms of armed conflict it may be more and more difficult to distinguish between fighters and non-fighters, particularly in non-international armed conflicts. Yet, the obligation to distinguish remains a fundamental principle of the law applicable in armed conflict. The Customary Law Study mentions this obligation as Rule 1 in its Chapter 1.[7]

3. Civilians do not have to identify themselves as such, in order to claim the protection to which they are entitled (such as by carrying an identity card). Rather, it is the duty of combatants to distinguish themselves from the civilian population, by wearing a uniform or at least a permanent distinctive sign visible from a distance, and by carrying their arms openly (see above, Section 308). In case of doubt, a person shall be treated as a civilian (Article 50, para. 1, 2nd sentence, AP I).

4. Persons accompanying the armed forces, or who are in the service of armed forces, without being members thereof are considered to be civilians. They may not take a direct part in military operations nor commit otherwise any act of violence. Yet, in case of capture they are to be treated as if they were prisoners of war. That category of civilians who are only indirectly involved in the war effort includes war correspondents, members of labour units or of services responsible for the soldiers' welfare, and civilian members of military aircraft crews or crews of merchant ships (Article 4 A, paras. 4 and 5, GC III; Section 319). The same holds true for persons who—although undoubtedly civilians—are involved in the war effort in some other form, for example as workers in armaments factories. Their activities are not considered to be a direct participation in hostilities in the sense of international law. Finally, civilians serving as advisors to the armed forces and employees of private (civilian) contractors in the service of armed forces, but not being part thereof, are also not supposed to take part in hostilities. This holds true, in particular, for employees of civilian contractors.[8]

5. On the consequences of civilians taking a direct part in hostilities, see below, Section 517.

6. There is only one situation where it is legitimate for civilians to engage in acts of hostility under the same conditions as members of armed forces: the *levée en masse*, that is taking up arms against advancing armed forces occupying their country; in such a

---

[6] The law of non-international armed conflicts does not contain such an explicit definition. It is submitted that all persons who are not members of state armed forces or organized armed groups of a party to the conflict are civilians. Organized armed groups constitute the armed forces of a non-state party to the conflict and consist only of individuals whose continuous function it is to take a direct part in hostilities ('continuous combat function'). See Nils Melzer, *Interpretive Guidance on the Notion of Direct Participation in Hostilities under International Humanitarian Law* (ICRC 2009), 27–36.

[7] See *CIHL* Rule 1.

[8] See Section 320 and *Montreux Document on Pertinent International Legal Obligations and Good Practices for States related to Operations of Private Military and Security Companies during Armed Conflict* (ICRC and the Federal Department of Foreign Affairs of the Swiss Confederation 2009).

HANS-PETER GASSER AND KNUT DÖRMANN

situation they enjoy combatant status (see above, Section 310). Of course, they may also be targeted by the advancing forces. If captured, they shall be treated as prisoners of war (Article 4 A, para. 6, GC III).

7. In the law relating to non-international armed conflict, the non-participation of civilians in hostilities is an implicit prerequisite for their protection. According to Article 13, para. 3, AP II civilians shall enjoy the protection afforded by the provisions on the civilian population, 'unless and for such time they take a direct part in hostilities'. However, a civilian disregarding this prohibition remains protected by international humanitarian law, in particular by the fundamental guarantees for humane treatment (Article 3 GC I–IV; Articles 4–6 AP II). Such protection does not exclude prosecution under national law of persons who have engaged in hostilities. The legal guarantees of due process and a fair trial, embodied in common Article 3 of the Geneva Conventions and Article 6 AP II, must be observed under all circumstances.

502   Civilians shall be respected and protected. They are entitled to respect for their persons, their honour, their family rights, their religious convictions, and their manners and customs (Article 27, para. 1, GC IV; Article 46, para. 1, HagueReg). Their property is also protected (Article 46, para. 2, HagueReg). Neither the civilian population as such, nor individual civilians not taking a direct part in hostilities, shall be the object of attacks (Article 51, para. 2, AP I; Article 13, para. 2, AP II). Civilians shall not be killed, wounded, or detained without sufficient reason. While in detention, civilians must be treated humanely (Article 27, 76, and 79–134 GC IV; Articles 11, 75 AP I; Article 5 AP II).

1. Persons who are not members of the armed forces and who do not or have ceased to take a direct part in hostilities shall under all circumstances be respected and protected: war shall not be waged against civilians uninvolved in the hostilities, and they shall at all times be treated humanely. The duty to protect, to respect, and to treat civilians humanely is no doubt part of customary international law.[9] In treaty law, it is Article 27, para. 1, GC IV, which gives forceful expression to this general obligation. Article 27 covers all situations in which a party to an armed conflict comes into contact with civilians of the opposing side, especially with aliens on its own territory and with inhabitants of occupied territories. This protection is supplemented by Article 75 AP I, which clarifies that all persons in the power of a party to an international armed conflict are entitled to such protection, including those who due to the nationality criterion of Article 4 of the Fourth Geneva Convention would not be protected by that Convention. Common Article 3 of the Geneva Conventions, as developed by AP II, obliges the parties to a non-international armed conflict in the same way to treat humanely all those not or no more directly involved in hostilities.

2. The first sentence of Article 27 says that civilians be 'respected' and 'protected'. The 'duty to respect' civilians requires a conduct defined in the negative: all acts that might unjustifiably cause harm to a civilian must be avoided. The 'duty to protect' civilians goes an important step further and calls for affirmative action. Accordingly, everything necessary must be done to ward off or reduce suffering. This means taking all measures required to ensure the safety of civilians, for example evacuation from dangerous places

[9] *CIHL* Rules 87–105.

HANS-PETER GASSER AND KNUT DÖRMANN

or the establishment of safety zones (see below, Sections 512–513). It also means guaranteeing the protection of the inhabitants of occupied territories against the effects not only of military operations, but also of belligerent occupation as such (see in particular Section 533). To leave the civilian population to its fate when danger arises from fighting would be a breach of this general 'duty to protect'. It must be borne in mind that under the conditions of modern warfare such danger exists not only in the immediate vicinity of combat areas, but also in areas far removed from the fighting.

3. The second sentence specifies the interests and rights that must be respected and protected: the persons themselves, their honour, their family rights, their religious convictions and practices, and their manners and customs. The list is not exhaustive. It does, however, clearly show that, even in the exceptional circumstances of war, human beings are entitled to protection and respect, in conformity with the basic principles of international law on the protection of human rights. The ICJ has underlined the close links between the two domains of international law.[10]

4. In particular, the obligation of respect for persons includes the duty to protect and respect both their physical and mental or intellectual integrity. All physical or moral coercion, for example to obtain information, is prohibited from the outset (Article 31 GC IV). Torture of any kind is not only prohibited under all circumstances (Article 32 GC IV), but also must be prosecuted as a grave breach of the Geneva Conventions. Committing torture is a war crime (see Article 147 GC IV and ICC Statute, Article 8, para. 2, lit. a(ii)). Likewise, it is prohibited to undertake medical and scientific experiments or organ transplants that are not therapeutically justified (see below, Section 606). Other types of ill treatment, such as mutilation or corporal punishment, are prohibited (Article 32 GC IV, Article 75, para. 2, lit. a(iv), AP I). International humanitarian law comprehensively prohibits outrages upon personal dignity, in particular humiliating and degrading treatment, enforced prostitution, and any form of indecent assault (Article 75, para. 2, lit. b, AP I). The mentioned acts constitute war crimes (see ICC Statute, Article 8, para. 2, lit. a(iii), lit. b(x), (xxi), (xxii)). Death sentences against a civilian person are allowed only in cases permitted by GC IV (see below, Section 573).

5. Respect and protection of mental and intellectual integrity, which includes regard for personal honour, means that the person's uniqueness as an individual and as a member of a social group must be respected. In practical terms this means, for example, that his or her image may not be exposed to the curiosity of the public (e.g. in photographs or on television). Article 27 GC IV explicitly states this as a consequence of the obligation of humane treatment. The family's rights to protection include the right to continue to live within the family unit. The separation and dispersion of families are prohibited. Respect for family rights implies not only that family ties must be maintained, but also further that they must be restored should they have been broken as a result of armed conflict. Article 26 GC IV intends to safeguard the family unit, to re-establish contact between members of a dispersed family. The parties to an armed conflict must not only

---

[10] ICJ, *Legal Consequences of the Construction of a Wall in the Occupied Palestinian Territory*, Advisory Opinion of 9 July 2004, para. 104, with reference to ICJ, *Legality of the Threat or Use of Nuclear Weapons*, Advisory Opinion of 8 July 1996, para. 25; ICJ, *Case Concerning Armed Activities on the Territory of the Congo (Democratic Republic of the Congo v Uganda)*, Judgment of 19 December 2005, para. 216. See Sections 254 ff.

HANS-PETER GASSER AND KNUT DÖRMANN

allow members of dispersed families to make enquiries, but also they must facilitate such enquiries.

6. The religious convictions of civilians in the power of the adversary shall be respected. This obligation covers any system of philosophical or religious beliefs. It encompasses the freedom to practise religion through religious observances, services, and rites. Protected persons in the territory of a party to the conflict or in occupied territory must be able to practise their religion freely, without any restrictions other than those necessary for the maintenance of public law and morals. They shall not be forced to profess any specific religion or belief. This prohibition protects first and foremost the persons concerned, especially against possible persecution.

7. The reference to the manners and customs to be respected is a reminder that the individual is also part of the social fabric. Accordingly, the adversary has no right to tear a civilian out of his or her social surroundings or to destroy that context through fundamental alteration. International humanitarian law also expressly prohibits forced removal of protected persons from their place of residence in order to settle them else-where (see Sections 541–542). The entire law governing belligerent occupation is based on the principle that, in general, the social order of the occupied territory shall not be altered by the occupying power (see below, Sections 526 ff.).

8. The third sentence stipulates that the personal property of civilians shall also be pro-tected. The legal basis for the guarantee of property rights in time of armed conflict is to be found not so much in the Geneva Conventions as in the HagueReg (Article 46, para. 2). The obligation to protect property rights is part of customary law.[11] The law governing belligerent occupation establishes in detail under what circumstances the occupying power may seize private property (see below, Sections 555 ff.). GC IV also prohibits the occupying power from unjustifiedly destroying movable or immovable property of inhabitants of the occupied territories (Article 53). Unlawful and wanton destruction or appropriation of property on a large scale, which cannot be justified by military necessity, is a grave breach within the meaning of Article 147 GC IV (see also ICC Statute, Article 8, para. 2, lit. a(iv)).

9. The fourth sentence recalls that neither the civilian population as such nor individual civilians are legitimate targets of attacks (see in detail Sections 442 ff.). Attacks against the civilian population or individual civilians resulting in death or serious injuries are punishable as grave breaches of AP I, that is as war crimes (Article 85, para. 3, lit. a, AP I, and ICC Statute, Article 8 para. 2, lit. b(i) even if they do not result in death or injury). Wilful killing of civilians in the power of the enemy is also a grave breach of GC IV (Article 147—ICC Statute, Article 8, para. 2, lit. a(i)).

10. The prohibition of the use of force against civilians is not absolute. For example, if a civilian is reasonably suspected of an offence for which an arrest would be a com-mensurate measure, then such arrest is permissible under international humanitarian law. It may involve the use of force, if necessary, in accordance with the standards of law enforcement. As has been shown above (Section 501, para. 5), force may be used against civilians taking a direct part in hostilities as they lose protection against direct attacks

---

[11] *CIHL* Rules 50–2.

HANS-PETER GASSER AND KNUT DÖRMANN

for the time of their direct participation (see below, Section 517). Yet, considerations of military necessity and humanity set limits to the amount of force to be used in such situations. Moreover, force against civilians is permitted as an act of self-defence, again, taking into account the limits imposed by the rule of proportionality. Finally, death or injury of civilians is lawful if it is an unavoidable and proportionate side effect of a lawful attack directed at a military objective ('collateral damage'—see below, Section 509 and Sections 442 ff.).

11. Not only acts of violence but also threatening with such acts is prohibited if their primary purpose is to spread terror among the civilian population (Article 51, para. 2, 2nd sentence, AP I). Threats may be expressed in the form of proclamations, verbal intimidation, media campaigns, and so on. International humanitarian law prohibits terrorism in all its aspects and under all circumstances: Article 33 GC IV ensures this for civilians in the hands of an adverse party; the rules on the conduct of hostilities prohibit all acts that would be deemed terrorist when committed outside armed conflict.[12]

12. In non-international armed conflicts, 'persons taking no active part in the hostilities...shall in all circumstances be treated humanely' (Article 3, para. 1, GC I–IV). This includes the right of civilians to be treated humanely and consequently prohibits violence to life and person. AP II confirms common Article 3 and extends the legal protection of civilians (Article 4, para. 2, AP II). Article 13, para. 2, AP II prohibits not only attacks as such against civilians but also acts or threats of violence the primary purpose of which is to spread terror.

13. The protection of persons in detention is one of the core purposes of international humanitarian law. The different situations in which civilian persons may be detained will be discussed at the appropriate place in this commentary.

14. Certain particularly reprehensible attacks on a person's physical or mental integrity are treated as grave breaches of international humanitarian law or are other serious violations of international humanitarian law (Article 147 GC IV; Article 11, para. 4 AP I; Article 85, paras. 3 and 4, AP I, and ICC Statute, Article 8, para. 2, lit. a and b—for international armed conflict—and Article 8, para. 2, lit. c and e for non-international armed conflicts. See before in this section and also below, Sections 1408 ff.).

15. The discussion of the legal provisions on the protection of the civilian population not only underlines the close links between international humanitarian law and human rights law, but also shows the manifold interaction between these two domains of international law.[13]

> **If the civilian population of a party to the conflict is inadequately supplied with indispensable goods, relief actions, which are humanitarian and impartial in character and conducted without any adverse distinction, shall be permitted. Every state, and in particular the adversary, is obliged to grant such relief actions free transit, subject to its right of control (Articles 23, 38 GC IV; Article 70 AP I).**   503

---

[12] ICRC, *International Humanitarian Law and the challenges of contemporary armed conflicts* (ICRC 2011) 47–53 (<http://www.icrc.org/eng/assets/files/red-cross-crescent-movement/31st-international-conference/31-int-conference-ihl-challenges-report-11-5-1-2-en.pdf>).

[13] See above, 'Introductory Remarks', para. 2, and Sections 255 ff.

HANS-PETER GASSER AND KNUT DÖRMANN

1. 'Starvation of civilians as a method of warfare is prohibited' (Article 54, para. 1, AP I). Thus, to starve civilians deliberately is unlawful. While the law of armed conflict permits the blockade of enemy territory intended to prevent the shipment of goods of any sort (see below, Sections 1051 *et seq.*) and while the siege of an enemy position may result in the supply of goods for the civilian population being cut off, Section 503 reminds that starving the civilian population may never be the purpose of sieges and blockades. Furthermore, hunger among the civilian population may not simply be accepted. Therefore, if the civilian population is inadequately supplied with indispensable goods as a result of the war, then relief actions intended for the needy population must be allowed (Article 23 GC IV; Article 70 AP I). Using starvation as a method of warfare is a war crime (ICC Statute, Article 8, para. 2, lit. b (xxv)).

2. GC IV also contains detailed regulations about supplying the population of an occupied territory (see below, Sections 561–564). At this point, only the situation of civilians in the territory of each belligerent will be examined.

3. According to Article 70 AP I, relief actions intended for the civilian population shall be undertaken if persons are not adequately provided with supplies essential to their survival (Article 69 AP I). Article 70 refers to civilians, which happen to be on a territory under the control of an adverse party. Such relief actions can be undertaken only with the agreement of that party. While such actions are subject to consent, parties concerned may only withhold for valid reasons and not for arbitrary ones. Other parties to the conflict may also be concerned, in particular if relief actions must pass through their territory or through a blockaded territory. As Article 54 AP I expressly prohibits starvation of the civilian population under the control of the enemy, passage of relief convoys must be allowed if its refusal would result in the starvation of those affected. Third states not involved in the conflict are bound by Article 23 GC IV, as developed by Article 70, para. 2, AP I, to allow the free passage through their territory of relief convoys intended for the civilian population of a party to the conflict.

4. States which allow a relief action must not only permit the transfer of the actual relief supplies, but also the passage of relief personnel and of the necessary equipment, such as means of transport. On the other hand, they are entitled to determine the technical arrangements for the transfer through their own territory, including search of the consignment for control purposes, and to require that distribution of the relief supplies be made under the supervision of the protecting power or of the ICRC. The relevant party to the conflict shall protect the relief action and facilitate distribution of the supplies. Such supplies may include, in particular, essential foodstuffs and medical supplies, but also other items essential for survival (clothing, bedding, etc.). The distribution of supplies shall respect priorities established in particular by Article 70, para. 1, third sentence. The list includes children, expectant mothers, maternity cases, and nursing mothers.

5. The question arises of who should carry out relief operations for the civilian population of a party to the conflict. Article 70 AP I is addressed to all states parties to Protocol I, without expressly saying so. That means that the world community at large is called upon to undertake or contribute to relief actions in an armed conflict when the civilian population of any party to that conflict is exposed to excessive suffering as a result of war. Article 70 also lays down expressly that proposing relief to a party to an armed conflict

shall neither be seen as interference in the conflict nor as an unfriendly act. In today's armed conflicts, international organizations usually take the initiative for carrying out relief operations and, traditionally, the ICRC plays an important role. Its mandate, and in particular its 'right of humanitarian initiative' as laid down in Articles 9/9/9/10 GC I–IV, and Article 81 AP I, allow the ICRC to pursue negotiations proactively, even if the concerned party has a negative attitude.

6. The law applicable in non-international armed conflicts also prohibits the use of starvation as a method of warfare, including acts committed against objects indispensable for the survival of the civilian population (in slightly different terms than in international armed conflicts, Article 14 AP II). It also states similarly that relief actions are to be undertaken if the civilian population 'is suffering undue hardship owing to a lack of the supplies essential for its survival, such as foodstuffs and medical supplies' (Article 18, para. 2, AP II). Impartial humanitarian organizations, especially the ICRC, are called upon where necessary to provide help to the population not taking part in the hostilities.

7. For further rules on the right to receive humanitarian assistance see below, Sections 524 ff.

**Any attack on the honour of women, in particular rape, enforced prostitution, or   504
any form of indecent assault, is prohibited (Article 27, para. 2, GC IV; Article 76,
para. 1, AP I).**

1. The Geneva Conventions contain different provisions intended to protect women affected by armed conflict.[14] Article 27, para. 2, GC IV and Article 76 AP I, which combine these rules and at the same time extend the protection, provide for general protection to be observed under all circumstances. Accordingly, women must be the object of special respect. They must be protected, in particular, against rape and enforced prostitution. It should be emphasized that this rule applies to all situations to which GC IV and AP I are applicable, in particular in occupied territories and in the case of aliens in the territory of a belligerent. Serious contravention of this rule is punishable as a grave breach, a war crime, if the material and mental elements of, for example, torture, inhuman treatment, or outrages upon personal dignity are met (Article 147 GC IV). The ICC Statute in Article 8, para. 2, lit. b(xxii), and Article 8, para. 2, lit. e(vi) contains for the first time a specific list of sex crimes constituting serious violations of international law, that is war crimes.

2. If a pregnant woman or a mother with small children is detained on suspicion of an offence, her case is to be treated with priority and particular dispatch (Article 76, para. 2). In the case of an offence related to the armed conflict, pregnant women and mothers having small children a death sentence shall be avoided. Under no circumstances shall the death penalty be carried out (Article 76, para. 3).

---

[14] Helen Durham, 'International Humanitarian Law and the Protection of Women' in Helen Durham and Tracey Gurd (eds), *Listening to the Silences: Women and War* (Koninklijke Brill, 2005), 95–107, and Judith Gardam, 'Women and Armed Conflict: The Response of International Humanitarian Law' in Durham and Gurd (eds) 111–23.

HANS-PETER GASSER AND KNUT DÖRMANN

505 Children shall be the object of special respect and protection. They shall be provided with the care and aid they require, whether because of their youth or for
any other reason (Art. 24 GC IV; Article 77, para. 1, AP I). Children who have
not attained the age of eighteen shall not take part in hostilities. They shall not be
enlisted into the armed forces. If they fall into the power of an adverse party they
shall be granted special protection (Article 77, para. 3, AP I; see also Article 38
ChildConv; ProtChildConv; see above Section 306).

1. Children deserve respect and special protection during an armed conflict.[15] They are
entitled under all circumstances to be treated in accordance with their age. In particular,
they must be protected against any form of indecent assault (Article 77, para. 1, AP I).
Children under fifteen who are orphaned and children separated from their families as
a result of the war or for other reasons shall not be left to their own resources (Article
24, para. 1, GC IV). With the consent of the protecting power, such children may be
taken to a neutral country for the duration of the conflict (Article 24, para. 2). In order
to avoid permanent transfer to a foreign country not in the child's interest, AP I only
permits evacuation as a temporary measure, if necessary for reason of the child's health,
for medical treatment, or to ensure the child's safety (Article 78 AP I). Return to their
country of origin must always be possible as soon as circumstances allow. Adoption of
children is generally inadmissible. Adoption might be possible in the case of orphans
provided all applicable legal conditions are met.

2. AP I does not give a definition of the notion 'child' and, in particular, does not, in
most cases, fix an age limit, a deliberate omission. In this way, varying views of different
cultures may be taken into consideration.[16]

3. A particularly tragic aspect of modern warfare is the role which children sometimes
have to play in hostilities: the child soldiers. While it would have been helpful to say in
an unambiguous way that children under fifteen years of age are not permitted to take
a part in hostilities, the law is not so affirmative. Article 77, para. 2, AP I reads in its
first sentence that all parties to the conflict shall take 'all feasible measures' to ensure
that children below the age of fifteen years take no direct part in hostilities and, in particular, that they refrain from recruiting them into their armed forces. Article 38 of the
1989 ChildConv confirms this rule, while Articles 1 and 2 of the 2000 ProtChildConv
puts the age limit at eighteen years for state armed forces, both for participating in
combat and for being compulsorily recruited in armed forces. Voluntary recruitment
below the age of eighteen remains under certain conditions possible (Article 3 of the
2000 ProtChildConv). Article 4 of the 2000 ProtChildConv provides '(a)rmed groups
that are distinct from the armed forces of a State should not, under any circumstances,
recruit or use in hostilities persons under the age of 18 years'. AP I further adds that in
the age group of 15–18-year-olds, the oldest shall be recruited first, if at all (Article 77,
para. 2, second sentence, AP I). It is hoped, however, that the 'straight 18' approach of
the 2000 ProtChildConv for direct participation in hostilities becomes the universal
standard. The Rome Statute has declared conscripting or enlisting children below the

---

[15] Rachel Harvey, *Children and Armed Conflict: A Guide to International Humanitarian and Human
Rights Law* (International Bureau for Children's Rights, 2003).
[16] Article 1 Optional Protocol to the Convention on the Rights of the Child on the involvement of children in armed conflict; *ICRC Commentary*, para. 3179.

HANS-PETER GASSER AND KNUT DÖRMANN

age of fifteen years to be a war crime (ICC Statute, Article 8, para. 2, lit. b(xxvi) and Article 8, para. 2, lit. (e)(vii)). The same holds true for 'using them to participate actively in hostilities' (ibid.).

4. If children under the age of fifteen years nonetheless take part in military operations, they shall, if captured, be detained under conditions which take their age into consideration. Such special conditions shall be afforded whether or not they are recognized as prisoners of war. In particular, such 'child soldiers' shall be detained separately from adults (Article 77, paras. 3 and 4 AP I).

5. If a person sentenced to death for an offence related to the armed conflict was below eighteen years of age at the time the offence was committed, the sentence shall not be carried out (Article 77, para. 5 AP I).

6. The provisions on the protection of children in non-international armed conflict are essentially identical to those applicable in international conflicts (Article 4, para. 3, AP II).

7. The obligation to grant special respect to women and children is anchored in customary law, in particular also the prohibition to recruit children into the armed forces or armed groups.[17]

> **None of the parties to the conflict shall use civilians as a shield to render certain   506
> points or areas immune from military operations (Article 28 GC IV; Article 51,
> para. 7, AP I).**

1. This prohibition follows directly from the rule that neither the civilian population as such nor individual civilians shall be involved in hostilities. The immunity granted to the civilian population may not be abused for military purposes and, therefore, civilians shall not be used in order to gain a military advantage or to deny the adversary such an advantage. The adversary would otherwise be in a position where he would have to choose between attacking (protected) civilians in an otherwise lawful military operation and relinquishing a possible military advantage.

2. AP I distinguishes between two situations. First, objects which may be military objectives must not be installed in a civilian area in order to benefit from the prohibition of attacks against the civilian population. This applies especially when the same military purpose can be achieved by putting the military object at another location where there are no problems in terms of protecting the civilian population. Second, civilians may not be deliberately 'used' as a shield for cover a potential military objective. In the same way, civilians may not be misused to protect a military operation. The following examples illustrate the prohibition: the deployment of a military unit with protection by a column of refugees; the transfer of protected persons (prisoners of war, civilian internees) to strategically significant locations (weapon positions, communication centres, etc.); the closing of a militarily important road by assembling a crowd of women and children.

3. Violation of the prohibition to use civilians as a shield does not exempt the other side from observing the constraints on military attacks in general (Article 51, para. 8, AP I).

---

[17] *CIHL* Rules 134 and 135/136 respectively.

HANS-PETER GASSER AND KNUT DÖRMANN

Thus, for example, the military commander must take into account the column of refugees used by the adversary to shield the target.

4. The prohibition of (mis)using civilians as a shield against the military operations must not be misunderstood as meaning that international humanitarian law provides the civilian population absolute immunity against attacks. Section 506 only prohibits the deployment of civilians as a shield against the adversary's military activities. The extent to which casualties among the civilian population as a side effect of military attacks may be tolerated is discussed in detail in Sections 509 ff.

5. Using civilians as a shield 'to render certain points, areas or military forces immune from military operations' is a war crime (ICC Statute, Article 8, para. 2, lit. b(xxiii)).

507   **Collective penalties (Article 33, para. 1, GC IV), measures of intimidation or terrorism (Article 33, para. 1, GC IV, Article 51, para. 2, AP I; Article 13, para. 2, AP II), reprisals against the civilian population and its property (Article 33, para. 3, GC IV; Articles 20, 51, para. 6, and 52, para. 1, AP I), and pillage (Article 33, para. 2, GC IV; Article 47 HagueReg) are all prohibited.**

1. Collective penalties, acts of terrorism, reprisals, and pillage are examples for the use of force against the civilian population or individual civilians. Article 27 GC IV prohibits all these acts, without exception. According to that provision, civilians shall 'at all times be humanely treated, and shall be protected especially against all acts of violence or threats thereof and against insults and public curiosity'. Article 27 GC IV, together with Article 33 GC IV, and Article 51, para. 2, AP I outlaw in clear terms any resort to acts of terrorism in the course of an international armed conflict. Common Article 3 GC I–IV and Article 13, para.2, AP II do the same for non-international armed conflicts. International humanitarian law forbids terrorism under all circumstances, at all times and without exception.

2. Collective penalties no doubt contradict the principle of individual penal responsibility, according to which no one may be convicted of or punished for an act which he or she did not personally commit. They are prohibited (Article 33, para. 1, GC IV). This prohibition is an aspect of the universally accepted principle of fair trial. The right to a fair trial is guaranteed by all international human rights conventions and by the four Geneva Conventions (for civilians: Article 38 GC IV—with reference to the rules of general international law applicable in times of peace—and Articles 67 and 71 ff., GC IV; Article 75, para. 4, AP I).

3. For non-international armed conflicts, Article 6, para. 2, lit. b, AP II also expressly lays down the principle of individual penal responsibility in addition to other fair trial rights in para. 2. It gives concrete form to common Article 3 of the Geneva Conventions, which requires a fair trial by a regularly constituted court.

4. According to Article 33, para. 1, second sentence, GC IV, every measure aimed at 'intimidating or terrorizing' civilians is prohibited.[18]

5. Over and above the general prohibition which is codified in Article 33 GC IV, Article 51, para. 2, second sentence, AP I contains a rule drawn up specifically for military operations: 'Acts or threats of violence the primary purpose of which is to spread terror

---

[18] See above, Section 502.

HANS-PETER GASSER AND KNUT DÖRMANN

among the civilian population are prohibited.' This prohibits acts of terrorism as a weapon against the civilian population. It should be pointed out that not every causing of terror among the civilian population can be prevented by international law. Military operations against (lawful) military objectives in proximity to a concentration of civilians will always arouse fear and terror, without making the attack necessarily an illegal operation. In such situations, the rule of proportionality, that is whether the incidental civilian harm or damage is not excessive to the expected military advantage, is the determining factor (see Section 509). In other words, it is not causing terror among the civilian population as such that is prohibited, but the use of such measures with the primary intention of spreading terror. The same holds true for non-international armed conflicts (Article 13, para. 2, second sentence, AP II).

6. Reprisals against the civilian population, individual civilians, or their property are prohibited (Article 33, para. 3, GC IV). AP I has extended the prohibition of reprisals to the law on the conduct of military operations (e.g. Article 51, para. 6; Article 52, para. 1). Civilians and the civilian population as a whole are now comprehensively protected against reprisals, at least in an international armed conflict. On the problem of reprisals in general, see above, Sections 473–476.

7. Finally, Article 33, para. 2, GC IV also prohibits pillage. A comprehensive prohibition of pillage is likewise to be found in Article 47 HagueReg. Pillaging is a war crime under the Rome Statute (ICC Article 8, para. 2, lit. b(xvi)).

The taking of hostages is prohibited (Article 34 GC IV).   508

1. The term 'hostages' applies to persons who are held in the power of the adversary, with the aim of obtaining a specific action (such as release of prisoners, cancellation of a military operation, etc.) from the other party to the conflict or from particular individuals as a condition for the safe release of the person held.

2. While in the past the taking of hostages to gain military advantage was considered lawful, since the GCs came into force the parties to a conflict are prohibited from taking hostages of protected persons in any circumstances (Article 34 GC IV). AP I reinforces this prohibition, so that there are no conceivable gaps in the legal protection (Article 75, para. 2(c)). The taking of hostages is also prohibited in non-international armed conflicts (common Article 3 GC, Article 4, para. 2, lit. c, AP II). It is to be punished as a grave breach of the Geneva Conventions or a war crime (Article 147 GC IV, ICC Statute, Article 8, para. 2, lit. a(viii) and Article 8, para. 2, lit. c(iii)). The prohibition of taking civilians as hostages is considered to be part of customary law.[19]

Attacks on military objects must not cause incidental loss of civilian life, injury to civilians, or damage to civilian objects excessive in relation to the concrete and direct military advantage anticipated (Article 51, para. 5, lit. b, AP I; Article 23, para. 1, lit. g, HagueReg).   509

1. Attacks on the civilian population as such or on individual civilians are prohibited (see above, Sections 442 ff. and 502). The same applies to civilian objects. This does not mean, however, that in a war all casualties among civilians and any destruction of

---

[19] *CIHL* Rule 96.

civilian objects must be considered to be violations of international humanitarian law. With pragmatic acceptance of reality the law takes into account such losses and damage as unavoidable, incidental consequences of (lawful) military operations. Section 509 states the conditions in which such 'collateral damage' may be acceptable. The relevant criterion is the principle of proportionality, one of the fundamental principles of international humanitarian law.

2. The requirement that the damage caused in the area surrounding a military operation shall not exceed a 'reasonable' proportion in relation to the military success strived for is probably as old as warfare itself. In the year 1907, the HagueReg introduced this principle into international treaty law in the following form ' . . . it is especially forbidden: . . . to destroy or seize the enemy's property, unless such destruction or seizure be imperatively demanded by the necessities of war' (Article 23, para. 1, lit. g). Expanding on this, AP I conferred its present form on the principle of proportionality as applied to the assessment of expected collateral damage: incidental losses among the civilian population and damage to civilian objects.

3. Accordingly, an attack is prohibited 'which may be expected to cause incidental loss of civilian life, injury to civilians, damage to civilian objects, or a combination thereof, which would be excessive in relation to the concrete and direct military advantage anticipated' (Article 51, para. 5, lit. b, AP I). This is an explicit expression of the underlying idea of international humanitarian law to find a balance between military considerations on one hand and the principle of humanity on the other.

4. This approach requires military officers in charge of planning, deciding, and carrying out a military operation to reflect on the possible damaging effects of the action on the civilian population and civilian objects. The same idea can be found in Article 57 AP I, under the heading 'Precautions in attack', which urges persons in charge of a military operation to take all feasible precautions to ensure that the civilian population and civilian objects are spared from the effects of hostilities as far as possible and that losses or destruction in the civilian domain is kept to a minimum (see Section 510). This obligation of military commanders to judge the situation also from the point of view of international humanitarian law must be established and enforced within the armed forces through generally applicable instructions.

5. A reasoned decision on the incidental losses to be anticipated among the civilian population or civilian objects as the result of a military attack can be reached only if information is available concerning not only the military value of the target but also on any civilian environment that may be involved. The military commander is therefore obliged within the bounds of what is 'feasible' (Article 57, para. 2, lit. a(i), AP I), to obtain information necessary to decide on the admissibility of the planned military operation.

6. Concerning the scale of the information-gathering required, several states expressed their understanding in a declaration submitted upon ratification of AP I that 'feasible' is to be understood as 'that which is practicable or practically possible, taking into account all circumstances ruling at the time including humanitarian and military considerations'.[20] Any decision taken by a military commander must be based on information

---

[20] Such declarations were submitted upon ratification *inter alia* by: Australia, Belgium, Canada, Egypt, Germany, Italy, the Netherlands, New Zealand, Spain, and the UK. No state party to AP I has raised any objection to these declarations.

HANS-PETER GASSER AND KNUT DÖRMANN

obtained according to accepted, common standards (by reconnaissance, etc.). The decision should only be assessed on the amount of information available or reasonably available at the moment the decision is taken and not on the basis of subsequent knowledge nor, of course, on the actual course of the military operation. States have also made formal statements on this point.[21]

7. However, if in the course of a military operation it appears that the attack will cause incidental casualties among civilians and/or destruction of civilian objects that can no longer be considered proportional, the action must be cancelled or at least suspended (Article 57, para. 2, lit. b, AP I).

8. The anticipated incidental loss of civilian life and destruction must be measured against the 'concrete and direct military advantage' (Article 51, para. 5, lit. b, AP I). 'Military advantage' is to be understood as any advantage 'anticipated from the attack considered as a whole and not only from isolated or particular parts of the attack', as expressly stated in some declarations of interpretation.[22]

9. Civilians must be warned in advance of military actions that may affect them, 'unless circumstances do not permit' (Article 57, para. 2, lit. c, AP I).

10. Military decisions must be based on sound information, on military experience, and on the realization that respect for the civilian population is an absolute obligation in international law concerning the conduct of military operations. 'Anticipated military advantage' and 'possible losses of civilian life, which shall be avoided' are concepts tinged with subjectivity, giving those in charge of military operations quite a margin of discretion. Military considerations require this kind of latitude. Those making decisions, however, may not escape responsibility by claiming that they were not authorized or able to reach such decisions. Solf rightly stresses that most important decisions in all areas of life ultimately involve balancing factors which are not quantifiable.[23] International humanitarian law makes great demands on the judgement of military commanders, but it does not require them to do the impossible.

11. The rule discussed here sets no absolute limits to the acceptable level of damage; it expresses a ratio between two quantities. Under Article 51, para. 5, lit. b, AP I, the greatest potential incidental losses among the civilian population during a military action are to be measured in proportion to the extent of the anticipated military advantage. The greater this advantage, the greater the acceptable level of civilian casualties and destruction. Although the rule is silent on this point, it must be assumed that there is an upper limit to the extent of acceptable damage to the civilian sector. It would be absurd if the rule governing collateral damage could completely nullify the fundamental prohibition of waging total war against the civilian population (Article 48 AP I).[24]

---

[21] Corresponding declarations were submitted *inter alia* by Australia, Belgium, Canada, Germany, Italy, the Netherlands, New Zealand, Spain, Switzerland, and the UK, with no objections raised.

[22] Such declarations were submitted upon ratification by Australia, Belgium, Canada, Germany, Italy, the Netherlands, New Zealand, Spain, and the UK, with no objections raised.

[23] Michael Bothe, Karl Josef Partsch, and Waldemar A. Solf, *New Rules for Victims of Armed Conflicts: Commentary of the Two 1977 Protocols Additional to the Geneva Conventions of 1949* (Nijhoff, 1982), 310.

[24] Similarly, *ICRC Commentary*, paras. 1979 *et seq.*

HANS-PETER GASSER AND KNUT DÖRMANN

510   When launching an attack on a military objective, all feasible precautions shall be taken to avoid, and in any event to minimize, incidental loss of civilian life, injury to civilians, and damage to civilian objects (Article 57, para. 2, lit. a(ii), AP I).

1. This rule stresses the obligation of all those responsible for planning, deciding, or carrying out a military operations to take all measures for the greatest possible protection of civilians and civilian objects, as well as other groups of persons entitled to respect and protection, for example wounded and sick military personnel, or protected objects such as military medical units, military hospitals, and so on. Furthermore, an attacking party must respect any existing safety zones, undefended localities, and demilitarized or neutralized zones. This precautionary measure goes beyond the obligation to refrain from deciding to launch an attack which may be expected to cause excessive incidental civilian casualties or damages (Article 57, para. 2, lit. a(iii), AP I). Even if an attack against a legitimate target would comply with the rule of proportionality contained in the said Article, additional precautions must be taken, if feasible, to further minimize or avoid incidental civilian harm or damage.

2. The other precautionary measures to be taken when preparing and carrying out a military action are dealt with in detail in Sections 448, 460, and 509. At this point it should be pointed out that the party to a conflict whose civilian population or civilian objects might suffer incidental losses or damage in an (as such lawful) attack by the enemy forces also has specific obligations. In particular, the said party must make it possible that the adversary forces may attack military objectives without excessive collateral damage to civilians. This is the counterpart to the obligation according to which a distinction must always be made between combatants or military objectives on the one hand and civilian persons or civilian objects on the other. Each party to a conflict therefore has the duty to remove the civilian population, individual civilians, and civilian objects under its control from the vicinity of military objectives 'to the maximum extent feasible' (Article 58, lit. a, AP I). Moreover, military objectives must, to the maximum extent feasible, not be located within or near densely populated areas (Article 58, lit. b). Finally, the said party to the conflict must, to the maximum extent feasible, take other precautions to protect the civilian population, individual civilians, and civilian objects against the dangers associated with military operations (Article 58, lit. c). Among these measures are civil defence activities (see below, Sections 519–522). Moreover, the duty to take precautions against the effects of military actions applies not only with regard to a party to the conflict's own population but also to other civilians temporarily under its control, for example aliens, refugees, and others. It also applies to occupied territories (see below, Sections 526 ff.).

3. In the course of the deliberations it was argued that in modern wars it would no longer be possible to make a distinction between potential military objectives on one hand and the civilian infrastructure on the other. It was reasoned that the prohibition of retaining or locating military objectives in civilian areas could make military defence measures impossible, and this would amount to an unacceptable breach of the right of self-defence.[25] Article 58 responds to this objection by expressing very pragmatically the duty to take precautions 'to the maximum extent feasible'. The precise meaning of 'feasible'

[25] Bothe, Partsch, and Solf (n. 23) 373. Austria and Switzerland submitted similarly worded declarations upon ratification, according to which Article 58 can be applied only subject to the requirements of national defence.

HANS-PETER GASSER AND KNUT DÖRMANN

was set down in some declarations of interpretation of AP I in the following manner: 'that which is practicable or practically possible, taking into account all circumstances ruling at the time including humanitarian and military considerations'.[26] According to this interpretation, it is also possible in a defensive war to find an acceptable compromise between military arguments and humanitarian considerations, especially since in this case it is a question of protecting the civilian population of the defending party.

> If soldiers are employed for the protection of civilian objects, they may be attacked,   **511**
> on account of their status as combatants. Their presence is therefore a factor endan-
> gering the object to be protected. Whenever soldiers are employed for the protec-
> tion of civilian objects, the situation must be assessed by weighing the expected
> military advantage (see above, Section 509).

The presence of members of armed forces on or at a civilian object does not *ipso facto* turn the object into a military objective which may legitimately be attacked. Only the soldiers employed for the protection of the object and the military equipment are lawful targets of an attack. Such an attack against them is then subject to the usual obligation which requires to weigh the expected military advantage against the expected incidental loss of civilian life or the probable damage to civilian objects (see above, Section 509). If the anticipated damage is excessive in relation to the desired military success, then the attack must not be carried out; other ways to achieve the same aim must be found.

> Hospital and safety zones and localities may be established by agreement so as to   **512**
> protect wounded, sick, and aged persons, children, expectant mothers, and mothers
> of children under seven from any attack (Article 14 GC IV). Military objects shall
> not be located within or in the vicinity of hospital and safety zones. These zones
> shall be neither used for military purposes nor defended.

1. Hospital zones and localities are zones and localities intended for the accommoda-tion and care of wounded and sick persons of military or civilian origin. They may be established for members of the armed forces (Article 23 GC I) or for civilians (Article 14 GC IV; see below, Sections 624 ff.). The provisions relating to hospital and safety zones in the First and Fourth Geneva Conventions are sufficiently flexible to make vari-ous combinations possible. There is, for instance, no reason why a hospital zone should not combine the two types and provide shelter for both soldiers and civilians in need of treatment, since once a soldier is wounded or sick, he may be said to be a suffering, inoffensive human being. Safety zones or localities, reserved solely for the categories of civilians enumerated in the Convention, may be set up independently of hospital zones. Or zones which are at the same time hospital and safety zones might be set up, to shelter both civilian and military wounded and sick, as well as certain categories of the civilian population.[27]

2. Hospital and safety zones and localities provide safe accommodation for certain cat-egories of especially vulnerable civilians, such as the wounded and sick, elderly persons,

---

[26] Such declarations were submitted by Belgium, Canada, Germany, Italy, the Netherlands, New Zealand, Spain, and the UK, with no objections raised against them.
[27] Jean Pictet, *Commentary to the IV Geneva Convention Relative to the Protection of Civilian Persons in Time of War* (ICRC 1958), 125.

HANS-PETER GASSER AND KNUT DÖRMANN

children under fifteen, expectant mothers, and mothers of children under seven (Article 14 GC IV).

3. Neutralized zones are specified areas within operational zones where military operations are excluded, by mutual agreement of the belligerents, so that wounded and sick combatants as well as civilians not taking part in the hostilities may be brought to safety (Article 15 GC IV). There are also 'non-defended localities' and 'open cities', which likewise serve to protect the civilian population (Article 59 AP I), as well as demilitarized zones (Article 60 AP I; see Section 513).

4. In order that such zones and localities can fulfil their purpose, they must be secured as fully as possible against the effects of military operations. Such refuges are usually required most urgently within or in the vicinity of a zone where fighting is either taking place or likely to occur. On the question of safety, therefore, a difficult compromise must be reached between the need for a protected zone, on one hand, and military considerations, on the other.

5. Only hospital and safety zones and localities serving humanitarian purposes are entitled to protection by the Conventions.

6. Hospital and safety zones or localities may be established in time of peace already. After the outbreak of hostilities, the parties to the armed conflict are called upon to declare such zones through mutual agreement. This may mean the establishment of new zones or localities or the recognition of existing zones or localities established unilaterally by a party to the conflict before or during the hostilities. Hospital or safety zones can be set up in a party's own territory or in occupied territory. A draft agreement relating to hospital and safety zones and localities is provided in Annex I to GC IV.

7. In addition to the exact determination of the geographical position of the hospital and safety zones and localities in the agreement, such areas, in particular their limits, must be clearly and recognizably marked. Only in this way can their protection be ensured in practice.

8. The following categories of persons may find refuge in hospital zones or localities or in safety zones or localities:

— the wounded and sick of military or civilian origin;
— the frail and aged;
— children under fifteen; and
— expectant mothers and mothers of children under seven.

In practice it is not always possible to differentiate between hospital zones or localities and safety zones or localities, for example because wounded persons have been admitted to a safety zone or children to a hospital locality. This is not a problem provided that the concerned persons are not or no longer involved in hostilities, or that anyway they do not present a danger to the enemy, in which case they are entitled unconditionally to respect and protection. AP I makes no distinction between the legal status of wounded or sick civilians and that of wounded and sick combatants (Article 8, lit. a).

9. It is self evident that no adverse discrimination founded on irrelevant criteria may be made when admitting persons seeking protection (Article 9 and Article 75, para. 1, AP I). Only the need for protection counts.

HANS-PETER GASSER AND KNUT DÖRMANN

10. In addition to the listed categories of persons, administrative personnel and persons who provide care are permitted to stay inside the zones. The original inhabitants of the territory or the locality where a protected zone is located may also remain. The latter must abide by the rules applicable to the zone or the locality.

11. Hospital and safety zones or localities shall not be attacked and they shall be protected against attacks. This means that measures shall be taken to provide protection for all, in the sense of ensuring personal security against acts of violence. However, defence of the zone or locality as a whole, with the aim of preventing enemy forces from taking it over, is prohibited. It must be handed over to the approaching forces of the adverse party without fighting, if possible in accordance with an arrangement, in order to avoid any danger to the persons accommodated in the zone or locality. If the zone or locality is defended militarily against the advancing enemy it loses its special protection, after a preliminary warning. The persons within the zones or localities, however, remain entitled to protection as wounded or sick members of the armed forces, or as civilians.

12. Objects which may be military objectives may not be brought into these zones or localities, nor into the vicinity thereof. Particular care shall be taken that the special protection of the place of refuge is not endangered by the effects of possible (lawful) attacks on nearby military objectives (collateral damage). Those who attack a military objective in such circumstances must take into consideration the presence of a protected zone in the vicinity of a chosen target (see Section 510).

13. It is the task of protecting powers and/or the ICRC to offer their good offices to the parties to the conflict for the establishment of hospital and safety zones or localities or for the recognition of existing ones (Article 23, para. 3, GC I; Article 14, para. 3, GC IV). The ICRC's comprehensive right of initiative in humanitarian matters gives it the right to make suggestions to the parties to a conflict at any time and to provide assistance in establishing protection zones or localities (Article 9 GC I–III; Article 10 GC IV; see below, Section 1424).

14. The law of non-international armed conflict does not include provisions on protective zones. However, nothing prevents parties to such an internal conflict from establishing zones or localities through special agreements. Common Article 3, para. 3, GC I–IV, is the legal basis for such an ad hoc agreement.

> **The parties to the conflict may agree to establish demilitarized (neutralized) zones**   513
> **(Article 15 GC IV; Article 60 AP I). No military activities shall be carried out in**
> **these zones. Their sole purpose is to provide shelter for wounded, sick, and other**
> **persons not involved in the conflict.**

1. Demilitarized zones are tracts of land which, according to an express arrangement between two states, shall not be drawn into hostilities (Article 60 AP I). In contrast, other rules apply to agreements concluded during a conflict and which concern hospital and safety zones in regions where fighting is taking place (see Section 512) or 'open cities' (Sections 461 ff.).

2. The specifically humanitarian justification for demilitarized zones, that is the protection of civilians and civilian objects against the effects of hostilities, distinguishes them from similar institutions such as regions that have been permanently neutralized

or demilitarized by international treaty, for example the Antarctic[28] or the Åland Islands.[29]

3. The establishment of a demilitarized zone requires an explicit agreement between two or more parties to an armed conflict. To avoid misunderstanding, a tacit understanding is not sufficient. An agreement may be concluded either in time of peace or during a conflict. It is self-evident that the location and extent of the zone to be demilitarized must be precisely described. The zone must also be clearly marked, so that its boundaries can be recognized in all circumstances and at all times.

4. A region may be made into a demilitarized zone by agreement if the following conditions are met:

a) Combatants, mobile weapons, and mobile military equipment must be removed from the zone. Military members of the medical service are not affected by this requirement.

b) No hostile use shall be made of fixed military installations or establishments.

c) No acts of hostility shall be committed by the authorities or the population.

d) No activities in support of military operations shall be undertaken. This point must be dealt with in detail in the agreement, providing expressly for any exceptions, such as, for example, the ongoing activities of industrial installations which could be used for arms production. Misunderstandings must be avoided through clear agreements.

5. A demilitarized zone is first and foremost open to the population already living there. In addition, other persons may be granted access, in particular civilian and military wounded and sick persons and civilians in need of special protection. The local authorities may usually continue their activities. In particular, (civilian) police forces shall continue to maintain public order.

6. If enemy armed forces approach the demilitarized zone, control must be handed over without resistance. The zone retains its status after passing to the other party to the conflict, if this was so determined in the agreement or if the occupying power unilaterally so decides. As before, it must not be used for military purposes, otherwise the zone loses its special status.

7. A breach by one of the parties to the conflict (usually the party controlling the zone) of the rules applying to a demilitarized zone does not release the other party from its obligation to respect the zone unless it was a 'material breach' (Article 60, para. 7, AP I). Such a 'material breach' carries with it the serious consequence of loss of immunity for the zone. What constitutes such a 'material breach'? The moving of heavy weapons into the zone would undoubtedly fall into this category, while the presence of a few scattered soldiers, even if armed, could not be regarded as a material breach. As a matter of principle, the removal of protected status must be preceded by a warning.

8. If a zone has lost its special status, military operations must comply with the limits imposed by other rules of international law applicable in armed conflict. Accordingly,

---

[28] See Article 1 of the Antarctic Treaty of 1 December 1959.
[29] See Alfred Verdross and Bruno Simma, *Universelles Völkerrecht: Theorie und Praxis* (Duncker & Humblot, 1984), 991.

HANS-PETER GASSER AND KNUT DÖRMANN

for example, the civilian population of the area in question or the displaced persons and refugees located there must be spared and respected according to the general rules.

9. An attack against a demilitarized zone is a grave breach of AP I if it causes death or serious injury (Article 85, para. 3, lit. d, AP I). The Rome Statute does not contain this war crime, it only contains the crime of 'attacking or bombarding, by whatever means, towns, villages, dwellings or buildings which are undefended and which are not military objectives' is a war crime (ICC Statute, Article 8, para. 2, lit. b(v), which is based on Article 25 HagueReg and Article 59 AP I).

> **Journalists engaged in dangerous professional missions in areas of armed conflict are considered as civilians. They are protected, provided that they take no action adversely affecting their status as civilians (Article 79 AP I). War correspondents are journalists accredited by the armed forces, yet they remain civilians. As persons accompanying the armed forces without being members thereof, in case of capture they benefit of the status of prisoners of war (Article 4 A, para. 4, GC III). Journalists may obtain an identity card which attests to their status (Article 4 A, para. 4, and Annex IV, GC III; 79, para. 3 and Annex II, AP I).**   514

1. The term 'journalist' encompasses all occupations associated with the media, including reporters, cameramen, sound technicians, and photographers. International humanitarian law differentiates between 'war correspondents' on one hand and 'journalists engaged in dangerous professional missions' on the other. Both categories are treated as civilians by international humanitarian law.

2. War correspondents are representatives of the media who, in the case of an armed conflict, are formally accredited to the armed forces of a party to the conflict, without being members thereof (Article 4 A, para. 4, GC III). They accompany the forces in the area of operations, or work in locations to which the armed forces permit them to go. The armed forces shall provide them with a special identity card which confirms their status (see Annex IV A to GC III). War correspondents are and remain civilians. They work on their own responsibility or the responsibility of editors or an agency. They must therefore not be confused with persons working in the information services of the armed forces, which are members of the armed forces and have combatant status. Whether or not war correspondents are subject to censorship is not a question for international humanitarian law.

3. War correspondents are permitted to carry out all those activities in the area of operations which normally form part of their occupation, including 'looking around', taking notes, making visual and audio recordings, etc. Such activity may not be considered hostile acts justifying military action against the person. On the other hand, as civilians who are not members of the armed forces, war correspondents must not under any circumstances take a direct part in hostilities. If they do so, they have to accept the consequences (see below, Section 517). In military operations, practically speaking, war correspondents can only be spared if they are clearly recognizable as civilians. This is hardly possible if journalists wear uniform-like clothing or ride on a military vehicle or are together with members of the armed forces ('embedded journalists'). If they are close to a military target or if they accompany a military unit on patrol, they accept the risk of becoming victims of (lawful) military operations (on such 'collateral' damage, see Section 509).

HANS-PETER GASSER AND KNUT DÖRMANN

4. Injured or shipwrecked war correspondents shall be treated in accordance with the provisions of GC I or GC II. If captured, they are entitled to the same treatment as a prisoner of war, under the provisions of GC III (see Section 319), without however losing their civilian status.

5. AP I knows a special provision on journalists engaged in a dangerous professional mission (Article 79).[30] Those journalists are dealt with distinctly from war correspondents. Originally, the UN had the intention to draft a special convention relating to the protection of journalists in war. When the above-mentioned Article 79 was included in AP I, however, work on the planned convention was abandoned, and the General Assembly of the UN explicitly stated its satisfaction with the adoption of Article 79, AP I.[31]

6. Without creating new law and without changing the legal situation of war correspondents (see above, para. 2), Article 79 confirms that journalists are civilians. A special legal category was deliberately not created. Journalists enjoy the same rights and must abide by the same rules of conduct as all civilians. They may not be made the target of a military attack. They must, however, behave in such a way as to make themselves recognizable as civilians in an area of military operations, a condition under which their immunity may become effective. Naturally, journalists may not take a direct part in hostilities, yet their professional activity may never be considered to be a hostile act. In an operational zone they accept the risks which are always associated with operations against military objectives. If captured, they shall be treated as civilians who have fallen into the hands of a party to the conflict (see below, Sections 581 and 585 ff.).

7. Journalists who engage in dangerous professional missions in war zones may receive an identity card confirming their status. This identity card must resemble the model in Annex II of AP I. The authorities of the state in which journalists reside or of which they are nationals or in which the news agency employing them is located are responsible for issuing such an identity card (Article 79, para. 3).

8. On a different level it should be recalled that, according to a judgment of the ICTY, a journalist who has witnessed atrocities on his professional assignment may not be compelled to testify in criminal proceedings against a person accused of an international crime.[32] According to Article 73 of the ICC Rules of Procedure and Evidence, communications made and information gained in the course of a confidential relationship may be considered as privileged and consequently not subject to disclosure. This exception to the obligation to testify may also be invoked by a journalist in a case related to an armed conflict.

515   **Civilians may at any time seek assistance from a protecting power, the International Committee of the Red Cross (ICRC), or any relief organization (Article 30, para. 1, GC IV). Representatives of protecting powers and of the ICRC shall be entitled to visit protected persons at any place and at any time they choose (Article 143 GC IV).**

---

[30] See Hans-Peter Gasser, 'The journalist's right to information in time of war and on dangerous missions' (2006) 9 *YIHL* 366.

[31] See *ICRC Commentary*, paras. 3250 *et seq.*

[32] ICTY, *The Prosecutor v Radoslav Brdjanin and Momir Talić*, Case No. IT-99–36-AR73.9, Decision on Interlocutory Appeal, 11 December 2002, paras. 34 *et seq.*

HANS-PETER GASSER AND KNUT DÖRMANN

1. This provision must be read in connection with Chapter 14, which gives more detail on the procedures and institutions for monitoring the implementation of international humanitarian law. In particular, for the status and tasks of the protecting power see Sections 1420 ff. and for the role of the ICRC, Section 1424. In the present chapter on the protection of the civilian population it may be useful to briefly consider the respective roles of the protecting power, the ICRC, and private relief organizations.

2. Under Article 30 GC IV, the civilian population is entitled to contact at any time these institutions and organizations with personal requests. The authorities must not only make such contacts possible but must facilitate them. Indeed, the protecting power and the ICRC can only carry out their duties if they have direct contact with the population. Only in this way can they obtain unimpeded access to information enabling them to form as true a picture as possible of the effects of possible breaches of international humanitarian law.

3. Of the relief societies also mentioned in Section 516, the most prominent are the national Red Cross and Red Crescent societies.[33] As national societies 'duly recognized and authorized' by their government (Article 26 GC I), they undertake wartime duties in favour of the victims of armed conflicts. Those duties are embodied in part in the four GCs and otherwise are rooted in the free initiative of these oldest of all relief societies. The national Red Cross and Red Crescent societies are bound by the Statutes of the International Red Cross and Red Crescent Movement to carry out their activities on the basis of the seven Fundamental Principles of the Movement, among which the principles of Humanity, Neutrality, Impartiality, and Independence should be specially noted in this context. The ICRC recognizes a national society if it fulfils the conditions laid down in the Movement's Statutes. The ICRC also has the mandate of verifying that the Fundamental Principles are observed by the components of the Movement, while at the same time respecting the independence of individual national societies.[34]

4. The tasks of national Red Cross and Red Crescent societies during armed conflict are laid down in numerous provisions of the Geneva Conventions. In summary, Article 81, para. 2, AP I requires the parties to a conflict to grant to their national societies facilities necessary for their humanitarian activities. These facilities undoubtedly include the ability of inhabitants to approach a society freely and without hindrance. On the role of Red Cross and Red Crescent societies in occupied territories, see Section 566 and Article 63 GC IV. In addition to the Red Cross and Red Crescent societies, other relief organizations may work for the benefit of the population.

5. The population not only has the right to approach these institutions but the authorities must grant the facilities and freedom of movement so that this right may be exercised. Only military reasons or security requirements can justify temporary restrictions (Article 30, para. 2, and Article 63, para. 1, GC IV). It is self-evident that no disadvantage to a person may result from having approached one of these institutions with a request for assistance or for any other reason.

---

[33] A society may also choose a third name and emblem: the red crystal on a white ground (see AP III).
[34] Statutes of the International Red Cross and Red Crescent Movement (1986, amended in 1995 and 2006), particularly Articles 3, 4, and 5, reprinted in *Handbook of the International Red Cross and Red Crescent Movement* (14th edn, 2008) <http://www.icrc.org/eng/resources/documents/publication/p0962.htm>.

HANS-PETER GASSER AND KNUT DÖRMANN

6. GC IV contains a number of provisions which oblige parties to an armed conflict to transmit to the protecting power or, in its absence, to the ICRC information on persons on the other side of the front line. This is especially the case with respect to restrictions on personal freedom by court order or administrative decision (see Sections 572, 582, and 585). The ICRC has a Central Tracing Agency which processes and stores information and which permanently carries out the tasks set out in Article 140, GC IV for the Central Information Agency.

7. Representatives of a protecting power and delegates of the ICRC are entitled to go to all places where protected persons may be, including places of detention or internment (Article 143 GC IV). These visits serve in particular to clarify whether and to what extent the rules of international humanitarian law are being observed. In this regard, see Sections 575, 586, 1420, and 1424.

8. The law of non-international conflicts contains no corresponding provision with a clear-cut obligation of parties to an armed conflict to accept the activities of humanitarian organizations. According to common Article 3 of the Geneva Conventions, an impartial humanitarian organization, such as the ICRC, may offer its services to the parties to the conflict. Such an offer by the ICRC must not be seen as interference in internal affairs. It must be examined in good faith and may not be arbitrarily refused. Any person must be allowed to approach delegates of the ICRC, without fear of negative effects. If such right were not guaranteed, the ICRC would be unable to carry out its mandate and it would no doubt withdraw its delegates from that country.

516

> **Persons who are reasonably suspected of activities hostile to the security of the state are not entitled to claim the respect of all rights accorded to civilians, in particular not those which, if exercised in favour of that person, would be prejudicial to the security of the State (Article 5, paras. 1 and 2, GC IV). Yet these persons shall always be treated humanely. In particular, they shall have the right to a regular and fair judicial procedure (Article 5, para. 3, GC IV; Articles 45, para. 3, and 75 AP I).**

1. A protected person, in this case a civilian belonging to the adverse party who is reasonably suspected of being engaged in activities hostile to the security of that state, remains under the protection of international humanitarian law. Yet he is not entitled to claim all the rights usually granted to protected persons (Article 5, para. 1, GC IV). Although GC IV does not further specify, it can be assumed that this rule refers primarily to acts of espionage or sabotage. Article 5, para. 2 elaborates that in occupied territory a person detained as a spy or saboteur, or 'under definite suspicion of activity hostile to the security of the Occupying Power', may forfeit his or her right of communication as guaranteed by the Convention.

2. In both situations the detaining power is temporarily released from the obligation to respect the totality of rights granted by GC IV, although only to the extent that these rights would, 'if exercised in favour of such individual person, be prejudicial to the security of such State' (Article 5, para. 1, GC IV). In practice, this means that the right to have contact with the outside world may be suspended.[35] In contrast, the obligation to respect the fundamental guarantees of international humanitarian law may never be derogated from. The respect for the detained person's fundamental rights is in no

---

[35] See Pictet, *Commentary*, Vol. IV (n. 27) 56.

HANS-PETER GASSER AND KNUT DÖRMANN

circumstances 'prejudicial to the security of such State'. In close alliance with international law on human rights,[36] Article 75 AP I has codified the fundamental guarantees making up the minimum standard to which everyone, without exception, is entitled. Even spies and saboteurs are protected by this 'humanitarian safety net'. In particular, the detaining power is bound to report the identity of captured civilians to their state of origin no later than two weeks after their capture (Article 136, para. 2, GC IV). The same applies for persons detained according to Article 5 GC IV. The restrictions must be lifted as soon as they are no longer justified and *incommunicado* detention is no longer necessary for security reasons (Article 5, para. 3, second sentence).

3. As mentioned above, certain rights of civilians who are detained for activities hostile to the security of the state may be suspended (Article 5, para. 1, GC IV), but the detainees shall always be treated with humanity. In particular, they have the right to a regular and fair trial (Article 5, para. 3, GC IV; Article 75 AP I).

> **Civilians taking a direct part in hostilities lose their right to protection against the** **517** **effects of hostilities for the duration of each specific act amounting to direct participation (Article 51, para. 3, AP I; Article 13, para. 3, AP II). In case of doubt a person shall be protected against direct attack. When civilians cease to take a direct part in hostilities, they may no longer be attacked, but remain subject to criminal prosecution for violations of international or domestic law they may have committed during such participation (see below, Sections 1409–1414).**

1. Only members of the armed forces have the right to take a direct part in hostilities (Article 43, para. 2, AP I), civilians have not (see above, Sections 301 *et seq.* and 501). Yet, practice shows that under certain circumstances civilians do take up arms. There are different types of civilian involvement in military activities, such as individual civilians taking spontaneously and individually an active part in hostilities, civilians resorting to violence as members of an organized armed group, or armed forces hiring individual civilians or entire companies, usually called military/security companies, to carry out tasks which normally belong to the armed forces, such as logistical support, maintenance of weapon systems, protection of persons or premises, training assignments, or even interrogation and custody of detainees.

2. International humanitarian law is built upon the assumption that civilians do not take a direct part in hostilities. It therefore provides for protection of civilians against the effects of hostilities, but only for such time as they do not take a direct part in the hostilities themselves (Article 51, para. 1, AP I, Article 13, para. 3, AP II). Yet, such participation is not prohibited by international humanitarian law, nor is it an international crime.

3. What does 'taking a direct part in hostilities' mean? While neither the Geneva Conventions nor the 1977 Protocols give much guidance for the interpretation of that notion, an analysis of practice has to step in. After intensive consultation of academic and military experts the ICRC made the following interpretive recommendation: in order to qualify as direct participation in hostilities three cumulative criteria must be met:

1. the act must be likely to adversely affect the military operations or military capacity of a party to an armed conflict or, alternatively, to inflict death, injury, or destruction on persons or objects protected against direct attack (threshold of harm);

---

[36] In particular, Articles 10 and 14 ICCPR.

HANS-PETER GASSER AND KNUT DÖRMANN

2. there must be a direct causal link between the act and the harm likely to result either from that act, or from a coordinated military operation of which that act constitutes an integral part (direct causation); and
3. the act must be specifically designed to directly cause the required threshold of harm in support of a party to the conflict and to the detriment of another (belligerent nexus).[37]

If these conditions are met, civilians[38] performing such acts lose their protection against direct attacks. Moreover, if they were killed or injured incidentally in an attack on a military objective, their loss of lives or injury would not count as relevant civilian incidental casualty when assessing the proportionality of an attack (see above, Section 509).

4. The notion of direct participation in hostilities should, however, not be understood too broadly. Not every activity carried out in the course of an armed conflict is a hostile act incompatible with the protection afforded to civilians against direct attack. Employment in the (civilian) armament industry, for example, does not mean that its employees are necessarily taking a direct part in hostilities. Since, on the other hand, buildings and infrastructure of the armament industry usually are lawful targets for military operations and may be destroyed, the rules governing the assessment of possible collateral damage to civilians must be observed (see above, Section 509).

5. Civilians taking a direct part in hostilities against the adversary may be resisted or attacked. That means that force may be used against civilians who capture or attack enemy personnel, destroy military equipment, or gather information for the direct use in military operations. The same applies to civilians who operate a weapons system, supervise such operation, or service such equipment. The transmission of information concerning targets directly intended for an attack of this target may also be considered as taking a direct part in hostilities.

6. Once civilians taking a direct part in hostilities are captured, or are otherwise *hors de combat*, they must be treated according to the rules applying to civilians—if they fulfil the nationality criteria in accordance with the rules of GC IV, if not in accordance with Article 75 AP I as reflective of customary international law. No doubt, they may be detained if presumed to have committed a crime or interned for security reasons as long as such detention is justified (see Article 5 GC IV). Although as civilians they are not entitled to a prisoner-of-war status (Article 4 GC III), the detaining power may grant persons having directly participated in hostilities an equivalent treatment. Experience from several conflicts in the past, especially in civil wars with foreign military intervention, has shown that such a measure may not only be justified for humanitarian reasons

---

[37] See ICRC, *Interpretative Guidance* (n. 6) 16. It should be noted that, while the experts consulted in the process did not manage to reach agreement on all aspects dealt with in the guidance, the vast majority of experts supported the three cumulative conditions. An overview of issues that led to debate can be found in ICRC, *International Humanitarian Law and the Challenges of Contemporary Armed Conflicts* (n. 12), 44.

[38] The ICRC Interpretive Guidance distinguishes for the purpose of the conduct of hostilities members of organized armed forces or groups (whose continuous function is to conduct hostilities on behalf of a party to an armed conflict) from civilians (who do not directly participate in hostilities, or who do so on a merely spontaneous, sporadic, or unorganized basis). The notion of direct participation with the temporal suspension of protection against direct attacks only applies to the latter. For former protection against attack is suspended for as long as they are members of the armed forces or assume a continuous combat function. For more details see online: <http://www.icrc.org/eng/assets/files/other/icrc-002-0990.pdf>.

HANS-PETER GASSER AND KNUT DÖRMANN

but also for military considerations. This must, however, not deprive them of procedural guarantees applicable to internment as contained in Articles 42, 43, or 78 GC IV.

7. Such civilians may be held to account for their acts, in conformity with applicable (international and domestic) law, in particular criminal law. They enjoy the benefit of judicial guarantees, in particular the right to a fair trial, in the same way as any other civilian (see below, Section 572).

8. Article 13, para. 3, AP II stipulates in identical terms that in a non-international armed conflict civilians are entitled to protection of their person 'unless and for such time as they take a direct part in hostilities'. They may likewise be held accountable for their acts. When detained or interned they enjoy the protections as contained in Article 3 common to the GCs, Articles 4–6 AP II and customary international law, which apply to all persons not or no longer taking a direct part in hostilities.

9. In conclusion, the fact of having taken a direct part in hostilities does not confer the status of a combatant to a civilian. International law does not know anything like 'unlawful combatants' or 'illegal combatants', supposed to be an intermediate status between civilians and combatants.[39]

> **Basic rules protecting the civilian population and individual civilians which bind**   518
> **parties to an international armed conflicts also apply to non-international armed**
> **conflicts. Customary law has gone beyond treaty law and binds all parties to a non-**
> **international armed conflict, the government and insurgent groups, likewise (see**
> **below Section 1212).**

This is to recall and to underline what has been mentioned several times in Part I of Chapter 5: first, that the general rules protecting the civilian population or civilians individually are part of international customary law. And second that these rules bind parties to an international and a non-international armed conflict alike.[40]

II. Civil Defence

Introductory Remarks

1. The purpose of civil defence is to protect the civilian population as far as possible from the effects of hostilities and to help it to survive during the war despite death, injuries, and destruction. The function of civil defence is to protect and to assist exclusively the civilian population. Civil defence is not part of a country's war effort; civil defence organizations belong to the civilian sphere, even if military units are assigned to support them. This is the meaning of 'civil defence' as codified by AP I and recognized by international law.[41]

2. During negotiation of the new provisions, difficult questions had to be answered, since numerous countries had already found different solutions for the organized protection of

---

[39] Knut Dörmann, 'The Legal Situation of "Unlawful/unprivileged Combatants" ' (2003) 879 *IRRC* 45–74.
[40] See above, n. 1.
[41] See, however, Article 63, para. 2 GC IV (occupied territories).

their civilian population in the event of war. They differed, for example, as to whether and to what extent such an organization should also have defence responsibilities.

3. The solution chosen in 1977 is based on the concept of non-military protection of the civilian population. The organizations undertaking civil defence functions are civilian organizations. This does not mean that members of the armed forces or even entire military units cannot be assigned to a civil defence organization if the need arises (Article 67). It is quite possible for military units to bring aid to the civilian population, in coordination with the civil defence organization, while retaining their status as a part of the country's armed forces, that is being permitted to engage in military operations. Civil defence units, in contrast, may under no circumstances perform military tasks. They must be permanently assigned and exclusively devoted to civil defence tasks as defined in Article 61 AP I.

4. Each state is free to decide whether and how it will guarantee the protection of the civilian population by a civil defence organization. AP I simply lays down the conditions under which a civil defence organization is entitled to protection by international law and to privileged status. Similarly, it is for the state to determine whether it wishes to use its civil defence organization in disasters and emergencies other than those arising in armed conflict, for example in natural disasters. Such activities are not covered by international humanitarian law. The provisions of AP I do however apply if a natural disaster occurs in a country involved in an armed conflict.

519   Civil defence organizations are protected in like manner as the medical service (Articles 61–67 AP I). Civil defence tasks are particularly warning, rescue and maintenance, fire protection, medical service, protection against the effects of nuclear, biological and chemical weapons (NBC defence), construction of shelters, and other measures to restore and maintain order (Article 61 AP I). Civil defence organizations, their personnel, buildings, and vehicles as well as shelters provided for the civilian population shall be especially respected and protected (Articles 62–64 AP I).

1. Like medical services, civil defence organizations and their personnel and equipment must not be involved in military operations. They may not be attacked. Personnel and equipment must be kept safe so that civil defence is able to step in and carry out its duties when war has brought death, destruction, and despair to the civilian population. The rule prohibiting interference with the activities of the civil defence organization of the opposing side is an imperative duty of all parties to a conflict. Article 62, para. 1, second sentence, does, however, permit restriction of their tasks 'in case of imperative military necessity'. This exception must be interpreted restrictively and in any case may endure only for a limited period.

2. Civil defence personnel must not take part in hostilities, nor shall hostile acts be carried out under the protection of a civil defence organization. Here again, civil defence organizations and medical units are dealt with in the same way.

3. The possible tasks of a civil defence organization are listed in Article 61, lit. a, AP I. They are exclusively humanitarian tasks 'intended to protect the civilian population against the dangers, and to help it to recover from the immediate effects, of hostilities or disasters and also to provide the conditions necessary for its survival'. A civil defence

HANS-PETER GASSER AND KNUT DÖRMANN

organization may, according to this provision, carry out all or some of the following tasks:

'(i)   warning;
(ii)   evacuation;
(iii)   management of shelters;
(iv)   management of black-out measures;
(v)   rescue;
(vi)   medical services including first aid, and religious assistance;
(vii)   fire-fighting;
(viii)   detection and marking of danger areas;
(ix)   decontamination and similar protective measures;
(x)   provision of emergency accommodation and supplies;
(xi)   emergency assistance in the restoration and maintenance of order in distressed areas;
(xii)   emergency repair of indispensable public utilities;
(xiii)   emergency disposal of the dead;
(xiv)   assistance in the preservation of objects essential for survival;
(xv)   complementary activities necessary to carry out any of these tasks, including, but not limited to, planning and organization'.

4. These tasks are exclusively allowed for the protection of the civilian population, for fulfilling a humanitarian purpose. Some of the tasks listed may not be exclusively humanitarian. It is therefore crucial to clearly define what aspect of a task will be assigned to civil defence, thus clearly distinguishing it from what might be considered a contribution to the war effort. Task (viii), 'detection and marking of danger areas', for example, may not be abused in order to seek information that can be used for military purposes, but must be performed solely to prevent the civilian population from entering dangerous areas (e.g. mined zones) and sustaining harm. Moreover, the question arises whether the list in Article 61, lit. a is an exhaustive description of the tasks of civil defence in wartime, or whether other tasks could be added, for example measures to protect the environment. The history of this provision in fact indicates that the list is final.[42] On the other hand, it seems reasonable to interpret the provision as meaning that a task not expressly included may also be allocated to civil defence, as long as it directly serves the well-being of the civilian population in a situation of armed conflict. Measures to limit environmental disasters resulting from armed conflict could, for example, be included, since it is almost inevitable that such disasters would cause loss or damage to the civilian population.

5. Civil defence organizations are establishments or other units organized or authorized to perform the tasks enumerated *supra* 3 and 'which are assigned and devoted exclusively to such tasks' (Article 61, lit. b). Therefore there may be more than one organization in a state. Private institutions, performing perhaps only some of the tasks assigned to civil defence, may be employed in addition to a state-run service, provided that they are devoted exclusively to civil defence work. This does not mean that such institutions may not occasionally serve other purposes. However, while they are employed in connection with civil defence they may only carry out civil defence duties. Private organizations wishing to undertake civil defence duties must be authorized by the appropriate

---

[42]   See Bothe, Partsch, and Solf (n. 23) 394–5.

HANS-PETER GASSER AND KNUT DÖRMANN

national authorities, in order to avoid abuse of the—protected—status of civil defence organizations.

6. The personnel of civil defence organizations must be respected and protected, and enabled to perform their tasks without hindrance except in case of imperative military necessity (Article 62). The personnel comprise all those persons who, as a part of an organization, perform civil defence work, including administrative activities, and not only permanent staff but also persons actually carrying out civil defence work under the supervision of such a recognized organization. Article 62, para. 2 also provides for the protection of all those who respond to an appeal from the competent authorities and perform civil defence work under their control.

7. Medical personnel working in civil defence have special status: they are protected as members of civilian medical services. They must be respected and protected and may not be hindered from carrying out their tasks (see below, Section 623). Their integration in a civil defence organization does not change this. Medical personnel may make themselves recognizable by means of the red cross, red crescent, or red crystal emblem, or with the distinctive sign of civil defence (see below, Section 522), or both (see Article 66, para. 9, AP I).[43] Civil defence organizations may also employ, for medical duties, persons who either additionally or primarily also perform other tasks, which Article 8, lit. c, AP I prohibits for medical personnel. This may for instance include first aid workers. They may wear the distinctive sign of civil defence but not the red cross emblem.

8. Members of the armed forces permanently assigned to a civil defence organization in order to perform civil defence work have a position different from that of civilian personnel (Article 67). Such military personnel must be employed exclusively for civil defence and in particular may not have a combat task or perform any other military duties. Although they retain their position as members of the armed forces, they must be respected and protected. If they should fall into the power of the adversary, they are prisoners of war.

9. It is self-evident that civil defence organizations require equipment, vehicles, buildings, and so on in order to carry out their tasks. These objects must not be attacked. They may not be diverted from their proper use except by the party to which they belong (Article 62, para. 3).

10. Of particular interest is the legal status of shelters provided for the civilian population. To the extent that such a structure serves solely to accommodate civilians, it is considered to be a civilian object within the meaning of Article 52 AP I. Attacks against civilian objects are prohibited (see above, Sections 448 ff). This holds true whether the shelter formally belongs to a civil defence organization or not. If it does, then the actual protection can be increased by marking it with the distinctive sign of civil defence (Section 523). The integration of shelters into the sphere of responsibility of civil defence increases the degree of protection.

11. With the consent and under the control of the relevant party to the conflict, civil defence organizations of neutral or other states not parties to the conflict may be employed on its territory (Article 64). They are subject to the same provisions and enjoy

---

[43] See *ICRC Commentary*, paras. 2696 ff.

HANS-PETER GASSER AND KNUT DÖRMANN

the same protection as the national organization. It should be noted that such assistance by a civil defence organization of a state not involved in the conflict shall not be considered as interference in the conflict.

12. The relevant party to the conflict must, when appropriate, facilitate the international coordination of civil defence measures through the relevant international organization (Article 64, para. 2), namely the International Civil Defence Organization (ICDO), an intergovernmental organization for civil defence matters.

> The protection accorded to (civilian) civil defence organizations, their personnel, and facilities under international law shall cease if, in spite of a warning, such an organization commits acts harmful to the enemy (Article 65, para. 1, AP I). Co-operation with military authorities and the employment of members of the armed forces shall not be considered as acts harmful to the enemy. The performance of civil defence tasks may also benefit military victims (Article 65, para. 2, lit. c, AP I). Civil defence organizations may be formed along military lines (Article 65, para. 4, AP I). Their personnel may be enlisted for compulsory service (Article 65, para. 4, AP I) and bear individual weapons for the purpose of maintaining internal order and for self-defence (Article 65, para. 3, AP I).

520

1. Under the heading 'Cessation of protection', Article 65 AP I lays down the following principle: the special protection of civil defence ends only if acts harmful to the enemy are committed and if a warning with a reasonable time limit has remained unheeded. This applies to the organizations as such and also to their personnel, buildings, vehicles, and equipment. This statement of principle is followed by a description of acts not to be considered 'harmful to the enemy' and require no further comment, merely the observation that civil defence personnel are permitted to carry light personal handguns (Article 65, para. 3). Such weapons may be used only to maintain order and in self-defence against attacks. This rule is modelled on the provisions governing medical personnel (see below, Section 627).

2. The significance of cessation of the legal protection of civil defence requires clarification. It is true that civil defence organizations on the one hand and personnel and equipment on the other under certain circumstances can no longer claim the protection of Articles 61 to 67 AP I. Since members of civil defence are necessarily civilians, however, they remain entitled to the general protection owed to all civilians (see Sections 502 *et seq.*). Only if such persons take a direct part in hostilities may they lose temporarily the protection afforded to civilians (Article 51, para. 3). The same holds true, *mutatis mutandis*, for their equipment, which is considered to be a (protected) civilian object (Article 52).

> Civilian civil defence organizations may be permitted to continue their humanitarian activities in occupied territories (Article 63 GC IV; Article 63 AP I).

521

1. Article 63, para. 2, GC IV allows local civil defence organizations to continue their activities when their territory is occupied. Article 63 AP I has enhanced their status in case of belligerent occupation and thus increased their protection.

2. Article 63 AP I is to be understood in the context of the Protocol's Chapter VI (Articles 61–67 AP I), on civil defence. These provisions are also relevant for status,

duties, entitlement to protection, and cessation of this protection of civil defence in occupied territories. The occupying power must not only allow civil defence organizations of the occupied territories to continue their work but must also guarantee 'the facilities necessary for the performance of their tasks' (Article 63, para. 1). For this reason, the occupying power may not, for example, requisition buildings or equipment belonging to civil defence, if it is harmful for the population of the occupied territory (Article 63, para. 4).

3. As already noted, military personnel serving with civil defence organizations become prisoners of war when captured. Under specific conditions they may be employed for civil defence tasks in the interest of the civilian population of the occupied territories by the occupying power (Article 67, para. 2, AP I).

4. The occupying power must allow civil defence organizations of neutral or other states not parties to the conflict to perform civil defence duties in occupied territories, unless it can adequately carry out such work with its own resources (Article 64, para. 3, AP I). The use in occupied territories of civil defence organizations from states not involved in the conflict requires the consent of the occupying power.

522   **The international distinctive sign of civil defence is an equilateral blue triangle on an orange ground (Article 66, para. 4, AP I). It is shown in the Annex on Distinctive Emblems, No. 5. Civil defence personnel shall be recognizable by this distinctive sign and by an identity card (Article 66, para. 3, AP I). Aid organizations may also use their own traditional signs.**

1. AP I establishes the equilateral blue triangle on an orange ground as the distinctive sign of civil defence (see Annex, No. 5; Article 66, para. 4, and Annex I, Article 16, AP I). A special identity card for civil defence personnel was also introduced. The distinctive sign serves to make civil defence organizations as such, their personnel, buildings, vehicles, and other equipment recognizable. Shelters for the civilian population which are not under the control of a civil defence organization may also be marked with this sign. For the distinctive sign to serve its purpose, it must be sufficiently large to be recognizable from a distance.

2. The provisions relating to the civil defence sign have been modelled on the rules applicable to the distinctive sign of medical personnel and medical units and transports (see below, Sections 612–618). These may be consulted for guidance concerning display.

3. Abuse of the civil defence sign is forbidden and should be punished by the relevant party to the conflict. Perfidious use of the sign is a grave breach of AP I (in other words, a war crime) when committed wilfully and causing death or serious injury (Article 85, para. 3, lit. f, AP I; see Section 1410).

4. The marking of all establishments, personnel, and equipment serving civil defence purposes is intended to enable the civilian population to survive during a war. The blue triangle on an orange ground alone can fulfil this task only to a very limited extent. What is decisive is that the civil defence establishments are kept as far as possible out of the firing line. In particular, shelters for the civilian population must be constructed in such a way that they have the greatest possible chance of being spared in the event of war. Effective civil defence helps to create the conditions necessary for international

humanitarian law to be observed and for the civilian population to be respected and protected.

III. Humanitarian Assistance

Persons not or no longer taking a direct part in hostilities and who are in need have the right to receive humanitarian assistance. Humanitarian assistance includes the right to receive essential goods such as food, water, medicine, medical help, and shelter. It also covers the right to basic education.   **523**

1. The right to humane treatment is at the very core of international humanitarian law protecting persons in war. With respect to civilians it is Article 27 GC IV which codifies this basic obligation of parties to an international armed conflict. Common Article 3 GC I–IV expresses the same idea for non-international armed conflicts. The obligation to treat civilians in a humane way not only means the prohibition of certain behaviour, but expresses also an obligation to act. Providing assistance in time of armed conflict to those who are in need is such an obligation to act—it may be the most important one. Articles 70, 71 AP I, and 18, para. 2, AP II have adapted the law to the exigencies of modern conflict situations. See Section 503.

2. Civilian persons who find themselves during an international armed conflict on the territory of the other party to that conflict, as aliens on enemy territory, must be enabled to receive individual or collective relief (Articles 23, 38 GC IV; see Section 503). They shall receive medical treatment in the same way as the nationals of the state. A person in need has the right to receive the necessary assistance from the authorities of his country of residence. The most urgent case for assistance for civilians in an international armed conflict may well be occupied territories and their population (see Section 525).

3. AP II clearly states that the needs of civilians must be satisfied by the parties to a non-international armed conflict as well. Its Article 18, para. 2, says in a concise way: 'If the civilian population is suffering undue hardship owing to a lack of the supplies essential for its survival, such as food-stuffs and medical supplies, relief actions for the civilian population which are of an exclusively humanitarian and impartial nature and which are conducted without any adverse distinction shall be undertaken . . .' Article 18 adds, however, a condition: 'subject to the consent of the High Contracting Party concerned'. That means, in practice, that the consent has to be given by the government for assistance to the insurgent side. In view of the overwhelming value of the principle of humanity, which includes the right to assistance, the government is under an obligation to give its consent to a proposed relief operation once the conditions are met.

4. Education must be ensured namely in accordance with Articles 24 and 50 GC IV, 78 AP I and 4 AP II.

Whenever circumstances permit, belligerent parties ought to suspend air or missile attacks in order to permit the distribution of humanitarian assistance (Rule 103 *HPCR Manual 524*).   **524**

HANS-PETER GASSER AND KNUT DÖRMANN

This is an application of the general rule which obliges parties to the conflict to respect the adversary's civilian population under all conditions, including allowing distribution of relief to civilians in need.

525   **The party in control of territory, including occupied territories, is under an obliga-tion to provide humanitarian assistance to civilians who are in need. If it is unable to do so, it has to accept offers of assistance from impartial humanitarian bodies such as the International Committee of the Red Cross. Measures of protection must be extended to humanitarian assistance personnel, their installations and vehicles.**

1. GC IV deals extensively with the material needs of the residents of occupied territories (Articles 55, 56, 59, and 60). According to Article 55, para. 1, GC IV the occupying power has the duty to ensure that food and medical supplies are available in an occupied territory. In case of inadequate resources, the occupying power has to supply 'the neces-sary foodstuffs, medical stores and other articles'. Under the heading 'Collective Relief', Article 59 GC IV adds: 'If the whole or part of the population of an occupied territory is inadequately supplied, the Occupying Power shall agree to relief schemes on behalf of the said population, and shall facilitate them by all the means at its disposal.'

2. Thus, the occupying power either has to provide the necessary assistance itself or it has to accept relief by third parties, in particular by states or by impartial international relief agencies. If the occupying power is not in a position to provide the necessary goods, it is under an obligation to accept foreign aid. Such aid may come from (usually friendly) states, but today much more from international bodies, in particular the UN and the ICRC.

3. The occupying power is under an obligation to ensure orderly distribution of the relief goods to the persons in need, without any discrimination. Diverting assistance or impeding its prompt delivery to those who are in need is, of course, forbidden. For security purposes, the occupying power is entitled to check the relief goods, in order to be sure that no unacceptable goods, such as weapons, are brought into the country. On the other side, it is under an obligation to protect the personnel accompanying the relief consignments. Third states have to authorize the transfer of the relief goods through their territory, if necessary.

IV. Belligerent Occupation

Introductory Remarks

1. International law on belligerent occupation determines the rights and obligations of a party to an armed conflict which occupies territory of the adverse party.[44] It also codifies the rights and duties of the residents of such occupied territory. The international rules on occupation have undergone major development over the past two centuries. While

---

[44] On the law on belligerent occupation in general, see Eyal Benvenisti, *The International Law of Occupation*, 2nd edn (OUP, 2011); Yoram Dinstein, *The International Law of Belligerent Occupation* (CUP, 2009); Robert Kolb and Sylvain Vité, *Le droit de l'occupation militaire: Perspectives historiques et enjeux jurid-iques actuels* (Collection de l'Académie de droit international humanitaire et de droits humains à Genève Bruylant, 2009); *Expert meeting, Occupation and other Forms of Administration of Foreign Territory, Report prepared and edited by Tristan Ferraro* (ICRC, 2012).

HANS-PETER GASSER AND KNUT DÖRMANN

the population of such territories originally had virtually no rights at all, the status and rights of their residents have been greatly developed and are now securely anchored in international law. The first codified international rules relating to belligerent occupation can be found in the HagueReg, which themselves are built on customary international law. As the Nuremberg Military Tribunal determined, the content of the HagueReg was binding as customary law during the Second World War already.[45] That statement also covers the provisions relating to occupied territories which are undoubtedly part of customary law. The ICJ has confirmed this finding in its Advisory Opinion of 2004 on the Wall in the Occupied Palestinian Territory.[46] Many lessons drawn from crimes committed in the occupied territories of Europe and the Far East found their expression in GC IV, which codifies modern international law applicable to belligerent occupation, amended by a few provisions of AP I.

2. The redrafting of the international law of belligerent occupation by GC IV in 1949 has been followed by a strong upswing of the international protection of human rights (see Sections 255–262 and 517). In its Advisory Opinion of 2004 on the Legal Consequences of the Construction of a Wall in Occupied Palestinian Territory, the ICJ has reached the following conclusion:

'. . . the Court considers that the protection offered by human rights conventions does not cease in case of armed conflict, save through the effect of provisions for derogation of the kind to be found in Article 4 ICCPR. As regards the relationship between international humanitarian law and human rights law, there are thus three possible situations: some rights may be exclusively matters of international humanitarian law; others may be exclusively matters of human rights law; yet others may be matters of both these branches of international law. In order to answer the question put to it, the Court will have to take into consideration both these branches of international law, namely human rights law and, as *lex specialis*, international humanitarian law.'[47]

International practice has followed up.[48] The treatment of the population of an occupied territory is increasingly measured against standards set by international humanitarian law and human rights law concurrently (e.g. by UN resolutions or other statements). However, the ICJ left no doubt that as a rule the specific provisions of GC IV and relevant rules of customary law relating to belligerent occupation take precedence over human rights law, as law specifically drawn up for issues arising out of belligerent occupation (*lex specialis*). In an exceptional case, however, it may be determined that a human rights rule offers greater protection to the inhabitants of an occupied territory. Moreover, human rights law may help to find an answer in cases where international humanitarian law may not be clear or contains a *lacuna*. When assessing the interplay between international humanitarian law and human rights law, this must be done on a right-by-right

---

[45] Trials of the Major War Criminals before the International Military Tribunal, Nuremberg, Vol. XXII, 497.

[46] See above, n. 10, para. 89.

[47] Ibid. para. 106. See as well ICJ, *Armed Activities on the Territory of the Congo (Democratic Republic of the Congo v Uganda)*, Judgment, 19 December 2005, *ICJ Reports 2005*, para. 216.

[48] Noam Lubell, 'Human Rights Obligations in Occupied Territory' (2012) 94 *IRRC* 318 with further references.

HANS-PETER GASSER AND KNUT DÖRMANN

or case-by-case basis, respecting the special situation of occupation, rather than in a wholesale manner.[49]

3. The sources of the law of belligerent occupation are Articles 42–56 HagueReg, GC IV (especially Articles 27–34 and 47–78), customary law,[50] and general principles of international law. A situation of belligerent occupation is characterized by a trilateral relationship: between the occupying power, the displaced sovereign, and inhabitants of the occupied territory. The law of belligerent occupation, therefore, regulates the relationship between the occupying power on the one hand and the—wholly or partially—occupied state and its inhabitants (including refugees and stateless persons)[51] on the other. Not included in the category of protected persons are nationals of the occupying power (excluding refugees), nationals of states not bound by GC IV, and nationals of a co-belligerent state, to the extent that their interests are safeguarded by diplomatic representatives accredited to the occupying power. Nationals of a neutral state are protected persons when they are in occupied territory (however, in the territory of a belligerent state they are only protected if their state has normal diplomatic relations with the state on whose territory they are). In occupied territory they have thus a dual status: their status as nationals of a neutral state, resulting from the relations maintained by their government with the government of the occupying power, and their status as protected persons.[52]

4. For foreign citizens not protected by GC IV and residing in occupied territories, the ordinary law of the territory occupied (i.e. pre-existing domestic law and legislation established by the occupying power under Article 43 HagueReg and Article 64 GC VI) applicable to foreign residents remains applicable. Their state of origin may, if necessary, take steps to protect its nationals. Moreover, under the heading 'General protection of populations against certain consequences of war', GC IV has a number of provisions relating to the protection of all inhabitants (Articles 13–26). They apply, in particular, also to foreigners who are not nationals of the occupied state and are present in the occupied territory. Finally, Article 75 AP I enjoins an occupying power to respect certain minimum standards dictated by human rights law which must be respected under all circumstances, that is also with respect to those categories of persons not directly covered by the protection of GC IV. Thus all residents of an occupied territory are entitled to fundamental guarantees meant to ensure humane treatment: these include prohibition of violence to life and health, of humiliating and degrading treatment, and the entitlement to fair-trial guarantees.

5. Belligerent occupation of a foreign territory is a form of foreign domination. Its effects on the population are mitigated by the provisions of international law drafted especially for that situation. Hence, GC IV (together with relevant customary law) appears as a kind of bill of rights with its catalogue of fundamental human rights which, upon occupation by foreign forces and without any further action on the part of those affected

---

[49] Yoram Dinstein (n. 44), 88; *Expert Meeting, Occupation and other Forms of Administration of Foreign Territory* (n. 44) 12 and 61 ff.

[50] See *CIHL* 299 ff.

[51] See Article 73 AP I.

[52] Pictet, *Commentary*, Vol. IV (n. 27) 48.

HANS-PETER GASSER AND KNUT DÖRMANN

by it, becomes immediately applicable to the occupied territories and its population, limiting thereby the power of the occupying state.

6. The distinction between *ius ad bellum* and *ius in bello* does also apply in situations of belligerent occupation. The legality of belligerent occupation is governed by the rules of *ius ad bellum*. The law of occupation (*ius in bello*) applies irrespective of the legality of the occupation. As pointed out in the *Hostages* trial after the Second World War:

'International Law makes no distinction between a lawful and an unlawful occupant in dealing with the respective duties of occupant and population in occupied territory. There is no reciprocal connection between the manner of the military occupation of the territory and the rights and duties of the occupant and population to each other after the relationship has in fact been established. Whether the invasion was lawful or criminal is not an important factor in the consideration of this subject.'[53]

7. The law of belligerent occupation has been developed for armed conflicts between states. There is debate as to whether the law of belligerent occupation applies to UN administered territory, and, if yes, under which circumstances.[54] While some commentators exclude a *de iure* applicability, others, more appropriately, assess the situation based on the criteria of Article 42 HagueReg (see Section 527) and if they are met the multinational forces would be occupying powers. The criterion of consent will preclude the *de iure* applicability of occupation law to UN administration of territory, when the multinational forces are present with the consent of the host state, a situation the UN normally seeks to ensure. In such a situation the forces would not appear to be the 'hostile' entity required by Article 42. Yet, it may well be appropriate to conclude that, in the absence of a specific international legislation on this situation, the UN administration and its forces be guided by appropriate standards established by the law on belligerent occupation, a situation with which UN control of a territory has much in common.

8. In a non-international armed conflict, the retaking by government forces of national territory previously held by the insurgents is not 'occupation' but the re-establishment of control over a lost part of its own national territory. The government's forces are bound to respect their own domestic law, taking into consideration international commitments, especially those concerning human rights. The insurgents, on the other hand, do not 'occupy' part of the national territory. Yet, when exercising control over national territory, they must always abide by the provisions of common Article 3 of the Geneva Conventions and of AP II, in particular the provisions protecting the civilian population.

9. International law on belligerent occupation has recently been moved to the centre of interest of the international legal debate by the occupation of Iraq (see below Section 527, para. 7) and, in particular, the Advisory Opinion of the ICJ on the Wall in Occupied Palestinian Territory (9 July 2004).[55] At the request of the UN General Assembly the ICJ had to give its opinion on whether the construction by Israel of a wall (also

---

[53] *Hostages* trial (US Military Tribunals at Nuremberg, *US v Wilhem List et al.*), *Trials of War Criminals before the Nuremberg Military Tribunals Under Control Council Law No. 10*, Vol. 11 (1950), 1247.
[54] *Expert Meeting, Occupation and other Forms of Administration of Foreign Territory* (n. 44) 78 ff.
[55] See above, n. 10.

called: a fence) on the territory of occupied Palestine is compatible with international law, in particular the law of belligerent occupation, or not (see above, 'Introductory Remarks', paras. 1 and 2).[56]

1. General Provisions

526   **The occupying power shall assume the administration of the occupied territory and the responsibility for the welfare of the occupied territory's inhabitants (Articles 29 and 47–135 GC IV; Article 43 HagueReg).**

1. The first step towards an understanding of the international legal consequences of occupation of foreign territory is to recognize the general ban on acquiring foreign territory by force, derived from the prohibition of the use of force in international relations by the UN Charter, in particular its Article 2, paras. 3 and 4.[57] The annexation of foreign territory is no doubt prohibited by international law. This means that if one state gains control over (parts of) another state's territory, by use of force or by threatening such use of force, that situation may only have a temporary character. International law of belligerent occupation is therefore built upon the assumption that the occupying power does not acquire sovereign rights over the territory, but exercises provisional and temporary control. The legal status of the territory can be altered only through a peace treaty or *debellatio*. It follows from this that the occupying authorities can only administer the territory, without changing the existing order, except when authorized by the relevant provisions of occupation law, in particular Article 43 HagueReg and Article 64 GC IV (see also Section 530). It is in this sense that the occupying power assumes 'the administration of the occupied territory and the responsibility for the welfare of the occupied territory's inhabitants'.

527   **Territory shall be considered occupied if it has actually come under the authority of armed forces of a foreign power and if those forces are in a position to exercise their authority over the territory (Article 42 HagueReg).**

1. The definition of belligerent occupation is contained in Article 42 HagueReg, which is quoted here in its entirety:

'(1) Territory is considered occupied when it is actually placed under the authority of the hostile army.

(2) The occupation extends only to the territory where such authority has been established and can be exercised.'

This standard is generally accepted in case law, state practice and literature.[58] The GCs have not altered the definition. Article 2, para. 2 common to the GCs has just expanded

---

[56] In the view of the Court, the construction of the wall on the occupied territory is not compatible with international law. It held that Israel is under an obligation to dismantle the structure insofar as it is built on occupied territory. The wall and its associated regime as create a fait accompli would be tantamount to annexation. The ICJ thereby confirms the illegality of annexation of occupied territories. The Advisory Opinion also discusses other issues of interest for the understanding of the law on belligerent occupation, thereby reaffirming the importance of that part of international law.

[57] See also *Declaration on Principles of International Law concerning Friendly Relations and Co-operation among States in accordance with the Charter of the United Nations*, Resolution of the UN General Assembly No. 2625 (XXV) of 24 October 1970.

[58] ICJ, *Legal Consequences of the Construction of a Wall in the Occupied Palestinian Territory* (n. 10) para. 78; ICJ, *DRC v Uganda* (n. 10) paras. 172–7; ICTY, *Prosecutor v M. Naletilić and V. Martinović*, Judgment,

HANS-PETER GASSER AND KNUT DÖRMANN

the notion. In accordance with that provision the law of belligerent occupation also applies when the occupation does not meet armed resistance. This clarification indicates that occupation is not limited to situations where a belligerent gains control over the adversary's territory as a consequence of armed hostilities in the course of an armed conflict. The identification of a territory or part of it as 'occupied' is a factual matter.[59] Thus, recognition of an occupation by the invading state or states is not constitutive, but merely declaratory. Based on Article 42 HagueReg, the central question is whether the armed forces of one state have brought territory belonging to a third state under their effective control, to the extent that they are in a position to exert authority over that territory and thereby assume the responsibility of administering it. The notion of effective control has been developed in legal doctrine, military manuals, and case law to describe the circumstances and conditions for determining the existence of a situation of belligerent occupation.

2. The *UK Manual* (2004) suggests the following criteria for assessing effective control in a given situation: (a) due to the presence of hostile armed forces, the former government has been rendered incapable of publicly exercising its authority in the territory concerned; and (b) the occupying power, by contrast, is in a position to substitute its own authority for that of the former government.[60] This test essentially requires three elements: the unconsented-to presence of foreign armed forces (otherwise one could not speak of a 'hostile army' in the sense of Article 42 HagueReg), the foreign forces ability to exercise authority, namely to exercise governmental functions, over the areas in lieu of the territorial sovereign, and the related inability of the latter to exert its authority. While the notion of control is obviously a matter of degree, this test should suffice in practice.

3. The law of occupation applies only to those parts of a foreign territory actually controlled by the occupying power and not to parts not controlled. The ability to exercise authority is a prerequisite for the applicability of the international law of occupation, establishing hereby international responsibility of the occupying power for the occupied territory. However, 'exercising authority' does not necessarily require physical presence of the occupying power's forces in every part of the said territory.[61] The possibility to intervene and enforce a decision suffices, for example by positioning its troops in strategic positions. And land within the territory whose access by residents of the territories is forbidden by the occupying power (e.g. a 'no-go zone' along the border) is to be considered occupied. In other words, the capacity to exercise its power in the territory suffices to engage the responsibility of the occupying power.[62] Supremacy in the air alone does not meet the requirement of effective control.

4. It necessarily follows as a corollary that any control by one state over territory of another state brings with it the obligation to respect the international law of belligerent

Case No. IT-98–34-T, Trial Chamber, 31 March 2003, paras. 215–16; Tristan Ferraro, 'Determining the Beginning and End of an Occupation under International Humanitarian Law' (2012) 94 *IRRC* 139 ff.

[59] Knut Dörmann and Laurent Collassis, 'International Humanitarian Law in the Iraq Conflict' (2004) 47 *GYIL* 298 with further references.

[60] *UK Manual* (2004), para. 11.3.

[61] For example ICTY, *Prosecutor v Naletilić and Martinović*, Case No. IT-98–34-T, Trial Chamber Judgment, 31 March 2003, para. 217.

[62] See *Report of the Independent International Fact-Finding Mission [on Palestine]*, A/64/490, 29 October 2009, 275–9. See also Section 537.

HANS-PETER GASSER AND KNUT DÖRMANN

occupation. In other words, if the armed forces of a state actually control foreign territory, that state cannot evade the obligations established by international law towards this territory and its inhabitants. The reasons given for the occupation of foreign territory are irrelevant. Even if the stated strategic goal is not to gain control of foreign territory or of its inhabitants, but for example 'merely' to secure its own territory close to the border against attacks from that territory, the invading power bears responsibility for the land actually under its control. Similarly, neither the (pretended) short duration of the occupation nor the absence of an established military administration releases the occupying power of its responsibilities.

5. The occupation of part of the Western part of the Kingdom of Jordan (West Bank), of the Sinai Peninsula, of the Gaza Strip, and of the Golan Heights by Israel's armed forces in 1967 raised particular questions concerning the applicability of the law of belligerent occupation to the disputed territories. Having initially left the question unanswered, the Israeli government later took the view that GC IV was not applicable to these territories.[63] Israel's government considered their international status as ambiguous, in particular that of the West Bank and of the Gaza Strip, as in its view neither Jordan nor Egypt could claim territorial sovereignty over the West Bank or the Gaza Strip respectively. Therefore, Israel did not (and still does not) consider itself to be occupying *foreign* territory.[64] The Israeli authorities stated, however, their determination to respect the humanitarian provisions of GC IV on a *de facto* basis.[65] Israel's reasoning is not tenable under international law, as the denial of the applicability of GC IV is based upon Israel's pretended doubts regarding the legal status of the occupied territories. It is sufficient that the territory in question was not under the sovereignty of the party occupying it, when the armed conflict broke out. The Eritrea/Ethiopia Claims Commission, for example, also held that the language of the GC and AP I does not support the view that 'only territory the title to which is clear and uncontested can be occupied territory'.[66] The purpose of the law of belligerent occupation, however, is to ensure protection for persons and objects which are no longer under the control of their own authorities but of a foreign power, and this as a result of armed conflict. There is no doubt that, from the viewpoint of the inhabitants of the West Bank and the Gaza Strip, Israel is a foreign power. Moreover, GC IV deals anyway with humanitarian issues only, resulting from the presence of foreign forces and its effects for the inhabitants of the territory. Israel's declaration that the humanitarian provisions will be respected despite the denial of the law's applicability is welcome but does not alter the occupying power's commitments.

6. In conclusion, the issue of the legal status of occupied land is a question which must be kept distinct from the humanitarian purposes of Geneva Law. Israel's position on the (non-)applicability of the GC IV to the territories occupied in 1967 has been rejected by states parties to the Geneva Conventions, acting individually and through international organizations, in particular various UN bodies including the General Assembly, by the

---

[63] See Supreme Court of Israel, Judgment of 13 December 2006, para. 20.
[64] For the position of the Israeli government, see Shamgar, (1971) 1 *IsrYHR* 262–77. Shamgar was Israel's Attorney General during the Six Days War and later judge at the Supreme Court of Israel.
[65] Shamgar, ibid. 266.
[66] Eritrea Ethiopia Claims Commission, Partial Award (Central Front), Ethiopia's claim 2, 28 April 2004, para. 29 (<http://www.pca-cpa.org/showpage.asp?pag_id=1151>).

HANS-PETER GASSER AND KNUT DÖRMANN

ICRC and by academic writing.[67] Finally, in its Advisory Opinion of 9 July 2004 on the Legality of the Wall, the ICJ has confirmed the applicability of occupation law to the Palestinian Territories without further comment.[68]

7. The armed conflict against Iraq (2003–2004) also led to a situation of belligerent occupation. While there was some debate as to the moment when occupation law started to apply, the US and the UK were at some point during the conflict occupying powers.[69] These two states had established the Coalition Provisional Authority (CPA) which exercised powers of government temporarily in order to provide for the effective administration of Iraq.[70] With the deployment of their ground forces, the US and the UK had established and were exercising authority over the territory of Iraq—even before the CPA was created. The question arose which other states, that had troops on the ground, could be considered occupying powers in Iraq.

In the preamble to Security Council Resolution 1483 of 22 May 2003, the Security Council expressly recognized

'the specific authorities, responsibilities and obligations under applicable international law of these States [the UK and the US] as occupying powers under unified command (the "Authority").'

The position of other members of the coalition that had provided troops was more complicated. To the authors' knowledge, none of the states claimed publicly that they were occupying powers. The preamble of the same Security Council Resolution notes that

'other States that are not occupying powers are working now or in the future may work under the Authority.'

While this could be interpreted as excluding other states as occupying powers, operative paragraph 5 of the resolution

'[c]alls upon all concerned to comply fully with their obligations under international law including in particular the Geneva Conventions of 1949 and the Hague Regulations of 1907.'

This reference to 'all concerned' is wider than the language of other provisions in the resolution, which are addressed only to the Authority. This could indicate that in the Security Council's view, not just the US and the UK could be occupying powers. In such situations a functional approach with regard to the law of occupation should be applied to states that had actually provided combat personnel, to the exclusion of those that had provided experts such as engineers or medical staff. The fact that certain states had only

---

[67] For example, UN SC Resolutions S/RES/242 (22 November 1967); S/RES/252 (21 May 1968); S/RES/259 (27 September 1968); S/RES/271 (15 September 1969); S/RES/446 (22 March 1979); S/RES/465 (1 March 1980); S/RES/478 (20 August 1980).

[68] See ICJ, *Legal Consequences of the Construction of a Wall in the Occupied Palestinian Territory* (n. 10) paras. 78, 101.

[69] Dörmann and Collassis (n. 59) 302.

[70] CPA, Regulation 1 of 16 May 2003, Section 1, para. 1. The letter from the Permanent Representatives of the UK and the US to the UN, addressed to the President of the Security Council, 8 May 2003, UN Doc. S/2003/538, contains similar terms. This letter is referred to in SC Res. 1483 of 22 May 2003. Although it is implicit from the responsibilities of the CPA outlined in the letter that the US and UK are occupying powers, the words 'occupation', 'occupiers', or 'occupying power' do not appear therein.

HANS-PETER GASSER AND KNUT DÖRMANN

been assigned very small sections of territory and had very few troops on the ground should not make a difference. Within this assigned territory, troops may be carrying out functions for which respect for the law of occupation could be relevant. Examples would include carrying out patrols, mobile checkpoints, or arrests and detention of persons protected by the law of occupation. While strictly speaking, the armed forces of some of these states were probably not exercising authority over territory within the meaning of Article 42 HagueReg, they could find themselves in a situation where they exercised control over protected persons and, in interacting with these persons, would have to respect the laws of occupation.[71]

Following a specific timetable agreed upon between the CPA and the Iraqi Governing Council in November 2003, later on accompanied by UN Security Council Resolution 1546 of 8 June 2004 on the political transition of Iraq,[72] steps were taken for the establishment of a sovereign Iraqi government. On 28 June 2004—two days earlier than foreseen in the UN Security Council Resolution—authority was formally transferred from the CPA to the newly established Iraqi Interim Government. As of then—in the words of Security Council Resolution 1546—the assumption of full responsibility and authority for Iraq lay in the hands of the Interim Government of Iraq. The CPA ceased to exist. Arguably, the belligerent occupation ended then. The continued fighting between the coalition forces operating with the consent of the Interim Government of Iraq (and later the Government of Iraq) and armed opposition groups was as of then governed by the rules of non-international armed conflicts.[73]

8. To recognize the applicability of the law of belligerent occupation to a given situation implies, politically speaking, two things: (1) the recognition that the territory is foreign land, and (2) the determination to respect the commitments of relevant international law. Such a decision may not be easy (since being labelled occupying power has often politically negative connotations),[74] yet it has to be taken, for the sake of the territory's population. Beyond the territories occupied in the Middle East the situation in other cases of foreign military presence also remained (or still remains) unrecognized or unanswered, such as the presence of Soviet Forces in Afghanistan (1979–1989), the invasion of Grenada (1983) and Panama (1989) by US Forces, the invasion of Southern Lebanon by Israeli Forces (1982), the occupation of Kuwait by Iraq (1990–1991), or the different conflicts in the Eastern Congo region (since 1996—the ICJ held in the Armed Activities case in 2005 that Uganda had been an occupying power in the Ituri region of the DRC between 1998 and 2003)[75] and in Somalia (UNITAF).

528   **Occupied territory does not include areas still embattled and in which the occupying power cannot make its authority felt within reasonable time. Therefore, these areas are not subject to the authority of a foreign power.**

---

[71] Dörmann and Collassis (n. 59) 304.; see also Robert Kolb, 'Occupation in Iraq since 2003 and the Powers of the UN Security Council' (2008) 90 *IRRC* 41 ff. There should be a—rebuttable—presumption of status of occupying power for states participating in a coalition enforcing effective control, see Ferraro (n. 58) 162.

[72] SC Res. 1546 (2004) of 8 June 2004. See A. Roberts, (2005) 54 *ICLQ* 27–48.

[73] Dörmann and Collassis (n. 59) 327. Kolb indicates that at that time the situation on the ground did not militate in favour of a clear break, highlighting the continued US influence, Kolb (n. 71) 43 ff with further references. Dinstein argues that the Security Council Resolution had the effect of terminating the belligerent occupation, see Dinstein (n. 44) 273.

[74] Adam Roberts, 'The End of Occupation: Iraq 2004' (2005) 54 *ICLQ* 32.

[75] ICJ, *DRC v Uganda* (n. 10) para. 179.

HANS-PETER GASSER AND KNUT DÖRMANN

1. The law of occupation is not applicable until the armed forces invading a foreign country have established effective control over a certain territory, that is has the power to exercise its authority. Local resistance does not preclude the applicability of the law of occupation. Even a temporarily successful rebellion is not sufficient to interrupt or terminate occupation, provided that the authority of the legitimate government is not effectively re-established.[76]

However, if foreign armed forces need to engage in significant combat operations to (re)capture the area in question from forces of the local armed resistance, that part of the territory cannot be considered to be occupied until the foreign forces have managed to (re-)establish effective control over it.

2. The law of occupation ceases to apply when the foreign armed forces no longer have effective control (generally after their withdrawal).[77]) The test to determine the beginning and end of an occupation is essentially the same.

3. There is international debate as to whether some provisions of the law of occupation apply in the invasion phase, prior to the moment the foreign armed forces have established effective control.[78] *Jean Pictet* in the *ICRC Commentary* to the Fourth Geneva Convention takes the view that the law of occupation would apply:

'So far as individuals are concerned, the application of the Fourth Geneva Convention does not depend upon the existence of a state of occupation within the meaning of the Article 42 [of the 1907 Hague Regulations]. The relations between the civilian population of a territory and troops advancing into that territory, whether fighting or not, are governed by the [Fourth Geneva] Convention. *There is no intermediate period between what might be termed the invasion phase and the inauguration of a stable regime of occupation.* Even a patrol which penetrates into enemy territory without any intention of staying there must respect the Conventions in its dealings with the civilians it meets.'[79]

An alternative and more restrictive approach would be to say that a situation of occupation only exists once a party to a conflict is in a position to exercise the level of authority over enemy territory necessary to enable it to discharge the obligations imposed by the law of occupation, that is by substituting its own authority for that of the government of the territory.[80] Thus, the invasion phase would be excluded. On the basis of this approach, the rules on occupation would not cover the invasion phase and battle areas. This does not, however, create a legally unprotected period; all other provisions of international humanitarian law must be respected by the armed forces, especially those dealing with the conduct of military operations (see para. 4).

---

[76] See also *UK Manual,* para. 11.7.1.

[77] See also Section 537. For a situation in which foreign forces withdraw from occupied territory (or parts thereof) while retaining key elements of authority or other important governmental functions therein, thus continue to exercise control from outside the territory, see Ferraro (n. 58) 157.

[78] See most recently *Expert Meeting, Occupation and other Forms of Administration of Foreign Territory* (n. 44) 24 ff; Marten Zwanenburg, Michael Bothe, and Marco Sassòli, 'Is the Law of Occupation Applicable to the Invasion Phase?' (2012) 94 *IRRC* 29 ff.

[79] Pictet, *Commentary,* Vol. IV (n. 27) 60.

[80] For example, Lassa F. L. Oppenheim/Hersch Lauterpacht (ed.), *International Law—A Treatise,* Vol. II (War), 7th edn, 1952, 434.

HANS-PETER GASSER AND KNUT DÖRMANN

Interestingly, the *US Field Manual* 27-10[81] and the old *British Manual—The Law of War on Land* [82]—adopted in the 1950s stated that as a matter of policy the entire range of obligations attached to occupied territory should, as far as possible, apply during invasion phases. This may be an indicator that both identified a situation in which civilians may be affected by parties to a conflict or hostilities and where their consequent protection needs were not adequately addressed by law.

Based on these protection needs, it seems to be a sensible approach to apply those provisions of the law of occupation which factually can be applied, and do not require a longer term, stable presence, also in an invasion phase to persons falling in the hands of a hostile party at that moment.[83]

4. In the invasion phase and in situations where foreign armed forces lose effective control over territory, all other provisions of international humanitarian law must be respected by the armed forces, including Articles 27–34 in the chapter on 'Provisions Common to the Territories of the Parties to the Conflict and to Occupied Territories' of GC IV and the fundamental guarantees of Article 75 AP I, reflective of customary international law, but especially also those dealing with the conduct of military operations. Therefore, the armed forces must under all circumstances observe the provisions relating to methods and means of warfare (see above, Sections 401 ff. and 501 ff.). Accordingly, and in particular, attacks against civilians and civilian objects are always prohibited.

5. Under the heading 'General protection of populations against certain consequences of war', Part II of GC IV (Articles 13–26) lays down a number of provisions that also apply in the situation described above. Of particular importance are:

— the establishment of hospital and safety zones (Article 14) and neutralized zones (Article 15);
— the protection of the wounded and sick, the infirm, and pregnant women (Article 16);
— the conclusion of agreements for the evacuation of especially vulnerable categories of persons (Article 17);
— the protection of civilian hospitals (Article 18);
— the protection of medical personnel (Article 20);
— the protection of transport of sick and wounded civilians and other especially vulnerable categories of persons on land, on sea, or by air (Articles 21 and 22);
— allowing the free passage of aid consignments (Article 23), especially the delivery of medical and hospital stores for the civilian population and essential foodstuffs for especially vulnerable categories of persons;
— the special protection of children (Article 24);
— the right to exchange family news (Article 25); and
— facilitation of enquiries relating to missing family members (Article 26).

529   **In occupied territory the sovereignty of the occupied state is temporarily suspended and superseded by the *de facto* authority of the occupying power. The occupying**

---

[81] US, Department of the Army, *The Law of Land Warfare—Field Manual* FM 27-10, 1956, 138, para. 132, lit. b.
[82] UK, The War Office, *The Law of War on Land Being Part III of Manual of Military Law*, 1958, 141, para. 501.
[83] Dörmann and Collassis (n. 59) 301. See also *Expert Meeting, Occupation and other Forms of Administration of Foreign Territory* (n. 44) 24 ff.

HANS-PETER GASSER AND KNUT DÖRMANN

power is not a successor in the rights of the state whose territories are (in part) occupied.

Belligerent occupation as such does not lead to a transfer of sovereignty to the occupying power. Sovereignty—or the totality of sovereign rights—may be seen suspended during belligerent occupation, or rather considerably weakened since the displaced sovereign retains *de iure* title. Decisions not related to physical control over the occupied territory may still be taken by the government in exile or by authorities responsible for the unoccupied part of the state.[84]

On the other hand, the occupying power does not assume sovereign rights over the territory and its population. Article 4 AP I also clearly states '(n)either the occupation or a territory nor the application of the Conventions and this Protocol shall affect the legal status of the territory in question.'

> **The occupying power is not entitled to bring about changes in the status and intrinsic characteristics of the occupied territory. In particular, the existing legal order shall be respected as far as possible (Article 43 HagueReg).**   530

1. This provision is derived from the principle that the appropriation by force of foreign territory is prohibited by general international law and cannot result in a transfer of sovereignty to the conqueror. Through its acts, the occupying power may not create commitments, for example signing international agreements, for the state whose territory it occupies. Unilateral annexation by the occupying power does not confer sovereign rights over the occupied territory. The occupying power enjoys only the rights granted by international law relating to belligerent occupation.

2. International law on belligerent occupation imposes on the occupying power the obligation, among others, not to change the *status quo* in the occupied territory (conservationist principle) or, if adapting elements of it is indispensable, to change as little as possible. The occupying power certainly cannot impose its own constitutional system on the occupied territory. However, while the occupying power is bound to respect and to apply the domestic law of the territory it also remains bound by international law, in particular by international rules protecting human rights. Therefore, the occupying power must not implement local law incompatible with human rights commitments. It may introduce changes to bring the legal order in the occupied territory in line with human rights law and international humanitarian law obligations.[85] On the other hand, not only the legal order of the territory but also the sociological structure of the territory's population may not be changed by the occupying power. In this connection, mention should be made of Article 49, para. 6, GC IV, which provides that the occupying power 'shall not deport or transfer parts of its own civilian population into the territory it occupies'. In particular, Article 49, para. 6, prohibits the settlement of nationals of the occupying power in the occupied territory. Under Article 8, para. 2, lit. b(viii), ICC Statute the transfer, indirectly or directly, by the occupying power of parts of its civilian is a war crime (see also Article 85, para. 4, lit. a, AP I).

---

[84] With regard to vertical sharing of authority with local authorities see *Expert Meeting, Occupation and other Forms of Administration of Foreign Territory* (n. 44) 20 and Ferraro (n. 58) 148 ff.

[85] For a discussion of what changes may be permissible in light of the conservationist principle, see *Expert Meeting, Occupation and other Forms of Administration of Foreign Territory* (n. 44) 67 ff.

HANS-PETER GASSER AND KNUT DÖRMANN

3. The fact that the occupying power does not take over the rights and duties of the (suspended) national authority is made manifest, for example, in the fact that it is a mere administrator and beneficiary of the public buildings and other property of the state (Article 55 HagueReg; see below, Section 558).

4. Not only must the legal status of the territory remain unaltered by the occupying power, but also its political institutions and public life in general have to continue with as little disturbance as possible. However, the provisional and temporary character of the occupation does not mean that the occupying authorities need not make arrangements to secure public order and safety, if necessary (see Sections 544–545). Should belligerent occupation persist over a long time, certain measures which have a permanent effect on matters internal to the territory may prove to be necessary. The well-being of the inhabitants of an occupied territory must be the guiding principle. Examples are the introduction of new taxation (see Section 555) or the construction of a road, even if such undertaking means requisitioning of private property.[86]

531   Protected persons in occupied territories are entitled to respect for their persons, their honour, family rights, religious convictions, and manners and customs (Article 4, 27, para. 1, GC IV; Articles 48–67, and 75 AP I). Their private property is protected (Article 46 HagueReg).

1. The protection to which the inhabitants of an occupied territory are entitled is laid down in general terms in Article 27 GC IV. This is a typical example of a rule with human rights content which has a central position in international humanitarian law on belligerent occupation. It must, therefore, be interpreted in the light of provisions for the protection of human rights. In addition to Article 27, numerous provisions in GC IV deal with individual aspects of the protection of the human person.

2. The general rule of humane treatment is intended to guarantee that the inhabitants of occupied territory may benefit from the protection of those individual human rights to which all persons are entitled at all time. These fundamental rights include, in particular, the entitlement to respect for the person, also for honour, religious or other convictions, and so on. The occupying power must respect these rights under all circumstances and without exception, to the extent permitted by the special conditions of belligerent occupation. Over and above individual rights, the occupying power must also respect and leave unchanged the social context in which the inhabitants of the occupied territories live. This results from the rule that manners and customs must be respected. See also Section 530.

3. Under special circumstances, injury to physical or mental health may amount to a grave breach of GC IV, punishable as a war crime (Article 147—see also ICC Statute, Article 8, para. 2, lit. a(i)–(iii), lit. b(x), (xxi), and (xxii)).

4. GC IV does not provide a universal guarantee of property rights. However, the provisions of the HagueReg dealing with occupied territories give extensive protection to private property. According to Article 46, para. 2, HagueReg private property cannot be confiscated. The protection of private property in the event of occupation is part

[86] *Expert Meeting, Occupation and other Forms of Administration of Foreign Territory* (n. 44) 72 ff. On the question of long-term occupation in general, see Roberts, (1990) 84 *AJIL* 44.

HANS-PETER GASSER AND KNUT DÖRMANN

of international customary law (see 'Introductory Remarks' to Sections 526 ff.). The permanent confiscation of private property by the occupying power during belligerent occupation is prohibited by international law (see below, Section 558). The legal situation is the same, for example, if the occupying authorities wish to confiscate land for their own use or to the benefit of a third party.

5. According to Article 147 GC IV, 'extensive destruction and appropriation of property, not justified by military necessity and carried out unlawfully and wantonly' must be punished as a grave breach (see also ICC Statute, Article 8, para. 2, lit. a(iv)).

> **Any discrimination for reasons of race, nationality, language, religious convictions   532
> and practices, political opinion, social origin or position, or similar consideration
> is unlawful (Articles 13, 27 GC IV; Article 75 AP I).**

1. This provision makes the general prohibition of discrimination, as guaranteed by all human rights codifications, applicable to the special situation of occupied territories.[87] In addition to Article 27 GC IV, Article 75 AP I has restated the ban on discrimination in a comprehensive manner. Due to its supplementary character, Article 75 applies to international humanitarian law as a whole and to all persons in the power of a party to an international armed conflict. Accordingly, residents of an occupied territory enjoy protection by international humanitarian law 'without any adverse distinction based upon race, colour, sex, language, religion or belief, political or other opinion, national or social origin, wealth, birth or other status, or on any other similar criteria' (Article 75, para. 1).

2. According to Article 85, para. 4, lit. c, AP I 'practices of apartheid and other inhuman and degrading practices involving outrages upon personal dignity, based on racial discrimination' shall be prosecuted as grave breaches of AP I. This provision as well is fully applicable to occupied territories.

> **Protected persons in occupied territories shall be humanely treated at all times and   533
> protected from any acts of violence or threats thereof (Article 27 GC IV; Article 46
> HagueReg).**

1. The duty to protect the inhabitants of occupied territories against acts of violence acquires particular significance because of the tense circumstances which characterize any belligerent occupation. Article 27 GC IV is complemented by other rules such as Article 32 GC IV and Article 75 AP I. The occupying power must ensure that members of its own armed and police forces refrain from use of force towards the inhabitants of the territory, unless the situation make such use necessary. Outside the conduct of hostilities against organized armed resistance, the obligation to ensure public order and civil life in the occupied territory might necessitate that the occupying power resorts to force against the local inhabitants. Such use of force must always be made in accordance with well-accepted law enforcement standards (necessity, proportionality).[88]

2. The occupying power must also take all measures to protect the inhabitants of occupied territories from violence by third parties, as required by Article 43 HagueReg ('to

---

[87] See, for example, Article 2 of the Universal Declaration of Human Rights.
[88] For a discussion on the rules on the use of force in occupied territories see *Expert Meeting, Occupation and other Forms of Administration of Foreign Territory* (n. 44) 109 ff.; also Kenneth Watkin, 'Use of Force during Occupation: Law Enforcement and Conduct of Hostilities' (2012) 94 *IRRC* 295 ff.

HANS-PETER GASSER AND KNUT DÖRMANN

restore, and ensure, as far as possible, public order and safety'). This might be violence by private groups or individuals. The occupying authorities may under no circumstances tolerate the activities of such groups, much less support or even use them to promote their own purposes. Moreover, in exceptional cases the inhabitants of occupied territories may have to be protected from their own authorities. Under all circumstances, the occupying power bears ultimate responsibility for the personal security of the inhabitants of the occupied territories.

534   **Reprisals against civilians and their property are prohibited (Article 33, para. 3, GC IV; Articles 20 and 51, para. 6, AP I). The same applies to collective penalties and to measures of intimidation and terrorism (Article 33, para. 1, GC IV). Pillage is prohibited (Article 33, para. 2, GC IV; Article 47 HagueReg).**

1. Reprisal is a form of self-help in response to a breach of international law. Reprisals should be understood as acts which are normally prohibited, but which may be legal if certain conditions are met.[89] In particular, such acts must be aimed at causing the adversary to desist from his unlawful behaviour (see Sections 485 ff.). If all the conditions are met, reprisal actions are permitted—unless they are specifically prohibited by the relevant provision, in the case of so-called 'reprisal-proof rules'. Reprisal actions, or threats with it, are exclusively intended to secure the enforcement of obligations under international law. Experience during wartime has shown, however, that their value as a means of implementing humanitarian protection is not great, as reprisals usually call for counter-reprisals, which means violence spiralling upwards. The Geneva Conventions and Additional Protocol now contain extensive prohibitions of reprisals against protected persons and objects.

2. Reprisals against inhabitants of occupied territories and their property are prohibited without exception. This comprehensive prohibition can be found in Article 33, para. 3, GC IV, which is among the common provisions relating to the protection of the civilian population. Threats with reprisals are also prohibited and considered to be an attempt to intimidate individuals. The absolute prohibition of reprisals against civilians is an achievement of the codification of 1949, which outlawed the sort of terrible reprisal actions taken against civilians during the Second World War and replaced them by clear and specific prohibitions.

3. Collective penalties, to be understood in a broad sense, and all measures of intimidation and terrorism carried out by the occupying power have only one purpose: to force the population of the occupied territory to submit to their authority. Such measures may take different forms, such as a curfew, not responding to security exigencies, but preventing the inhabitants from fulfilling their daily duties, punishment or detention of several members of a group or family for an alleged offence by one of their members, or the destruction of the house belonging to the family of an alleged offender. Such acts are prohibited, without exception, by Article 33, para. 1, GC IV.

4. While in earlier times pillage was considered a legitimate reward for the efforts of soldiering, it is now universally prohibited (Article 33, para. 2, GC IV; see also ICC Statute, Article 8, para. 2, lit. b(xvi)). This applies not only to occupied territories but

---

[89] *CIHL* Rule 145.

HANS-PETER GASSER AND KNUT DÖRMANN

also for the period immediately preceding occupation, that is during the military operations at the time of invasion. This is clearly shown by the inclusion of the prohibition of pillage among the common provisions of GC IV dealing with the status and treatment of civilians applicable to all territories of the parties to the conflict.

> **No one may be punished for an offence he or she has not personally committed. The taking of hostages is prohibited (Articles 33, para. 1, and 34 GC IV).**   **535**

1. The principle that only personal responsibility for an alleged breach of the law can lead to conviction and punishment is now undisputed. Article 33, para. 1, GC IV has codified this principle in the law of belligerent occupation. Article 75, para. 4, lit. b, AP I has placed the rule in the context of the generally recognized principles guaranteeing a regular judicial procedure to which all protected persons are entitled.

2. Article 34 GC IV states: 'The taking of hostages is prohibited.' In earlier times, hostages were taken (or given) in order to achieve a certain conduct from the inhabitants or from individual persons under enemy occupation (e.g. members of resistance movements). Hostages answered with their lives for the behaviour of other people. As recently as the Second World War, serious crimes were committed in this respect. Under present law, not only the execution but even the taking of hostages is prohibited. As held by the ICTY, 'hostage-taking exists when a person seizes or detains and threatens to kill, injure or continue to detain another person in order to compel a third party to do or to abstain from doing something as a condition for the release of that person'.[90] According to Article 147, any taking of hostages is to be punished as a grave breach of GC IV (see also ICC Statute, Article 8, para. 2, lit. a(viii)).

3. The use of human beings as a shield to ward off attacks by the enemy against important positions may amount to hostage-taking. This is expressly prohibited (see above, Section 506).

> **The occupying power shall forward information regarding the fate of protected**   **536**
> **civilians who are in its power (Article 136 GC IV), as well as of prisoners of war (Article 122 GC III), the wounded, sick, shipwrecked, and dead (Article 16 GC I; Article 19 GC II; see below Sections 611, 708). For this purpose a National Information Bureau shall be established after the outbreak of a conflict and in all cases of belligerent occupation (Articles 136–141 GC IV). The Bureau shall cooperate with the Central Tracing Agency of the International Committee of the Red Cross (Article 140 GC IV).**

1. The search for missing persons in wartime is a task whose humanitarian significance needs no explanation. Article 15, para. 1, GC I obliges the parties to a conflict to search for the wounded, sick, and dead 'at all times, and particularly after an engagement'. This refers to the situation existing directly after a military engagement. Article 26 GC IV requires that parties to the conflict facilitate enquiries by persons looking for family members dispersed by the conflict. Articles 32–34 AP I go significantly further. On the basis of 'the right of families to know the fate of their relatives', Article 33 lays down a number of obligations intended to find missing persons, or at least to get information

---

[90] ICTY, *The Prosecutor v Tihomir Blaškić*, Case No. IT-95-14-A Appeals Chamber Judgment, 29 July 2004, para. 639.

about their whereabouts. Each party to the conflict must search 'as soon as circumstances permit, and at the latest from the end of active hostilities . . . for the persons who have been reported missing by an adverse Party' (Article 33, para. 1).

2. The obligation to search for missing persons applies equally to both members of the armed forces and civilians.[91] In the present context, only the fate of missing civilians is dealt with. Two situations must be mentioned: first, on taking control of enemy territory an occupying power is obliged to search for persons reported missing and, second, a party to the conflict is obliged to search its own territory for members of an adverse party who may have been reported missing. The obligation to account for missing persons is an obligation of means. Each party to the conflict must use its best efforts in this respect. This includes searching for, but also facilitating the search for, persons reported missing as a result of the conflict.[92]

3. The establishment of a National Information Bureau is an international obligation on every party to an armed conflict (Articles 136–139 GC IV). Although such a bureau must not be ready to operate until the outbreak of an armed conflict, for practical reasons preparatory work must be undertaken in peacetime already. The Information Bureau, operating at national level, collects information regarding the fate of protected persons, registers this information, undertakes searches, and transmits all information through the protecting power, the ICRC, or the National Red Cross or Red Crescent Society to the state concerned.

4. In practice it is the Central Tracing Agency of the ICRC, a permanent institution, which collects, registers, processes, and transmits incoming data at international level (Article 140 GC IV, Article 33, para. 3, AP I).

537 **Belligerent occupation of foreign territory (or parts thereof) ends when the occupying forces cease to exert effective control over it.**

1. Belligerent occupation means effective control by a state of territory not its own (for details see Section 527). Such occupation ends when that state no longer *de facto* exercises its control over the territory. That may happen for a number of reasons, for example if control is regained by the party to which that territory belongs; if the occupying power withdraws voluntarily from the territory (e.g., in response to a decision by the Security Council or a peace treaty);[93] or if there is *debellatio*. Annexation does not end the status of belligerent occupation, since international law does not recognize annexation as a lawful means to acquire foreign territory (see commentary to Section 526). Nor does a declaration of the occupying power to end occupation without actually relinquishing *de facto* its control over that territory. Such 'ongoing occupation' may mean that the occupying power limits its control to certain aspects of life in the occupied territory, such as its own security or its own economic gains, without assuming its obligations in favour of the territories' population.

---

[91] *CIHL* Rule 117.

[92] Ibid.

[93] For a situation in which foreign forces withdraw from occupied territory (or parts thereof) while retaining key elements of authority or other important governmental functions therein, thus continue to exercise control from outside the territory, see Ferraro (n. 58) 157.

HANS-PETER GASSER AND KNUT DÖRMANN

2. As long as the occupying power exercises effective control over an occupied territory (or part of it), that state remains bound by the whole body of international law applicable to belligerent occupation even in the absence of permanent presence in the territories. The relevant obligations have to be respected until the (real) end of the occupation. That means, for example, that the occupying power is responsible for ensuring that the basic needs of the territory's population are satisfied, particularly also in the medical field (see Sections 563 and 565).

3. Article 6, para. 3, GC IV states that 'the application of the present Convention shall cease one year after the general close of military operations', that is after the beginning of the occupation. Should occupation continue beyond this period, the occupying power is bound to respect the more limited number of provisions of GC IV enumerated by its Article 6. Such a division of the (codified) law of occupation into one set of rules for the first year of occupation and a 'hard core' of provisions applicable during the remaining time is artificial and hardly satisfactory. There is no reason why the protection of the inhabitants of such territories should be reduced after a period of twelve months. Problems remain—or may become more serious with time going on. Moreover, the concurrent applicability of international human rights law may make this rule redundant. Article 3, lit. b, AP I, developed Article 6, para. 3, GC IV, and states 'the application of the Conventions and of this Protocol shall cease,... in the case of occupied territories, on the termination of the occupation, except, in either circumstance, for those persons whose final release, repatriation or re-establishment takes place thereafter'. It might also be argued that customary law has modified the legal situation.[94] Indeed, it seems neither Israel nor the US (in the case of occupation of Iraq), both not parties to AP I, have ever referred to this clause.

2. Legal Status of the Population

The legal status of the population shall not be infringed by any agreement concluded between the authorities of the occupied territories and the occupying power, nor by annexation of the whole or part of the territory (Article 47 GC IV).   538

1. According to Article 47 GC IV, the rights of the inhabitants of occupied territories shall not be curtailed by any agreement or other arrangement between the occupying power on one hand and the authorities of the occupied territory on the other. This provision is intended to prevent local authorities, under pressure from the occupying power, from making concessions, to the detriment of the inhabitants of the territory and which may impair their legal status. Any such agreement is void.

2. In particular, the annexation of foreign territory by the occupying power is not recognized by international law (see above, commentary to Section 526). Such annexation would be invalid even if 'concessions' in this respect were offered to the local authorities.

---

[94] Vaios Koutroulis, 'The application of international humanitarian law and international human rights law in situation of prolonged occupation: only a matter of time?' (2012) 94 *IRRC* 173 ff. The ICJ in its Advisory Opinion may have 'resurrected' Article 6, para. 3, GC IV, *Legal Consequences of the Construction of a Wall in the Occupied Palestinian Territory* (n. 10) para. 125 ff.

HANS-PETER GASSER AND KNUT DÖRMANN

539   Protected persons cannot renounce their rights under the Fourth Geneva
           Convention (Article 8 GC IV).

This principle applies to the entirety of international humanitarian law. In no circumstances can inhabitants of an occupied territory renounce their rights under GC IV.
Whether on their own initiative or as a result of coercion, such a renunciation would
be null and void. This is to prevent the occupying power, acting from a position of
strength, from exploiting the weakened position territory's inhabitants and thus to abro-
gate, apparently legally, their protection guaranteed by international law.

540   The occupying power shall not detain protected persons in an area particularly
           exposed to the dangers of war (Article 49, para. 5, GC IV).

1. The occupying power must permit the inhabitants of an occupied territory to seek
safety from the effects of military operations. Their freedom of movement may be curtailed as permitted by Article 27, para. 4, GC IV, and the affected persons detained in
an area particularly exposed to the dangers of hostilities, but for two reasons only: for
the safety of the population itself, or for compelling military considerations of the occupying power. This may be necessary to prevent panic-stricken and uncontrolled flight,
which could not only endanger those fleeing but also make movements by the armed
forces impossible.

2. In certain circumstances, however, the occupying power may be required to evacuate
the inhabitants of occupied territories from dangerous zones (see below, Section 541).

541   Deportation of protected persons from occupied territories is absolutely prohibited,
           whether outside the territories nor inside. A temporary evacuation of specific areas
           is permissible if the security of the population or compelling military reasons so
           demand. An evacuation of persons to areas outside the bounds of the occupied ter-
           ritory shall be permitted only in case of emergency (Article 49, para. 2, GC IV).
           Persons must be allowed to return to their homes as soon as the security situation
           so permits.

1. Article 49 GC IV prohibits individuals or entire groups of an occupied territory being
forcibly removed from this territory to that of the occupying power, to the unoccupied
part of the country of origin, or to a third state. Forced resettlement (or forcible transfer in the words of the Convention) within the occupied territory is also prohibited.[95]
These prohibitions are among the significant achievements of the codification of international humanitarian law in 1949. As grave infringements of the rights of inhabitants
of occupied territories forced removal is now unlawful, regardless of the political motives
behind it. The alleged consent of those affected is immaterial (Article 8 GC I–III; Article
9 GC IV; see Section 539). Legitimate requests for resettlement—for example, by members of a minority—must be verified and confirmed by a neutral authority.

2. According to Article 147, the 'unlawful deportation or transfer' of inhabitants of an
occupied territory to the territory of the occupying power, or to the unoccupied territory

---

[95] With regard to the difference between deportation and forcible transfers (essentially in the context
of crimes against humanity) see ICTY, *The Prosecutor v Milorad Krnojelac*, Case No. IT-97–25-A Trial
Chamber Judgment, 15 March 2002, para. 474.

HANS-PETER GASSER AND KNUT DÖRMANN

of the same state, or to a third state, or within occupied territory (in the case of forced transfer) is a grave breach of GC IV (see also ICC Statute, Article 8, para. 2, lit. a(vii)).

3. If the safety of the population or imperative military reasons so demand, the occupying power may nevertheless undertake temporary evacuation of a specific area (Article 49, para. 2, GC IV). The evacuated population may be provisionally accommodated in another part of the occupied territory, unless evacuation outside the occupied territory—to the territory of the occupying power or to a third state—is the only way to guarantee the safety of the evacuees. Persons must be allowed to return to their homes as soon as the security situation so permits. The authorities of the occupying power are responsible for the repatriation.

4. On the other hand, the parties to a conflict have a general obligation, under Article 58 AP I, to take precautionary measures to protect the civilian population against the effects of hostilities. This also applies to the population of occupied territories and means that the occupying power is not only authorized (under Article 49, para. 2, GC IV; see above, para. 3) but also required to take measures to protect endangered civilians against direct effects of military operations. However, the restrictions of Article 49, para. 2, GC IV discussed above, which specifically prohibit permanent evacuation of parts of the occupied territory, remains the general rule.

> **If evacuation is necessary, the occupying power shall provide sufficient accommo-**   542
> **dation and supply. Members of the same family shall not be separated (Article 49,**
> **para. 3, GC IV).**

Moreover, representatives of a protecting power or delegates of the ICRC must be informed that evacuations have taken place (Article 49, para. 4, GC IV) and be given the opportunity to visit protected persons at the new place of accommodation (Article 143 GC IV). For this reason, the protecting power and/or the ICRC have to be informed in advance of such evacuation.

> **For imperative reasons of security, the occupying power may subject individual**   543
> **civilians to assigned residence or internment (Article 78, para. 1, GC IV, see below,**
> **Sections 590–598).**

1. Under Article 27, para. 4, GC IV the parties to a conflict are entitled to 'take such measures of control and security in regard to protected persons as may be necessary as a result of the war'. This also applies in the case of occupation. Further developing this rule the Convention's Article 78 states that occupying authorities may subject protected persons 'at the most' to assigned residence or to internment, but only if 'imperative reasons of security' so require. Such measures must not have a penal character. They may be justified only by security considerations.

2. Persons may be subjected to assigned residence in their place of residence or elsewhere. The restrictions imposed by Article 49 GC IV on any such decision must be observed (see above, Section 541); in particular, a person may not be transferred outside the occupied territory.

3. For questions arising in connection with the internment of inhabitants of an occupied territory, see below, Sections 590 ff.

HANS-PETER GASSER AND KNUT DÖRMANN

3. Rights and Duties of the Occupying Power

544   The national laws applicable in the occupied territory shall, in principle, remain in force. Laws which constitute a threat to security of the occupying forces or an obstacle to the application of humanitarian law may be repealed or suspended by the occupying power (Article 64 GC IV; Article 43 HagueReg).

1. The occupying power does not assume the rights of a sovereign state upon occupation of foreign territory (see above, Sections 529 ff.). Sovereign power rests with the lawful authorities of the state, even if they are temporarily unable to exercise control over the territory. The authority to enact laws is unquestionably an attribute of sovereignty. Thus the lawful authorities alone—even if absent from the country and in exile—can make laws for the occupied territory. The occupying power must administer the occupied territory within the framework of its existing law. Exceptions to this principle, that is the right of the occupying power to repeal or suspend, are listed in the second sentence of Section 544 (see below, para. 3). That the occupying power is generally bound by the existing national system is clearly laid down in Article 43 HagueReg. Based on experiences in the Second World War, Article 64 GC IV has developed this principle.

2. Although Article 64 mentions only criminal law which remains in force, the entire legal system of the occupied territories is actually meant by this rule.[96] Incidentally, Article 43 HagueReg speaks unambiguously and without restriction of 'the laws in force in the country'. The express reference to criminal law in GC IV can be explained by the fact that, during the Second World War, occupying powers interfered in a particularly scandalous manner with the criminal laws of occupied territories. Other areas of law, however, are not thereby excluded.

3. Of the two exceptions to the binding character of national law mentioned in Section 544, the first should be understood as reservation justified by considerations of military necessity. This exception is of great practical importance. Accordingly, occupying authorities do not have to observe national law if its application would directly prejudice their security. This exception must be understood in a narrow sense. It is not permissible to suspend all national legislation in the occupied territory by resorting to a broad interpretation of this rule.

4. Second, the occupying authorities should not observe provisions of the national law of the occupied territory which 'constitute . . . an obstacle to the application of humanitarian law' (see the similar wording of Article 64, para. 1, GC IV). This refers to national regulations not compatible with the provisions of international humanitarian law and applicable to the occupying power during occupation, for example openly discriminatory measures (e.g. 'race laws'). Moreover, in administering an occupied territory the occupying power shall not apply domestic law which is incompatible with international law, whether customary or treaty-based (the latter as far as accepted by the occupied state), in particular with provisions concerning the protection of human rights[97] (see 'Introductory Remarks', para. 2, and Sections 255 ff.).

---

[96] See Pictet, *Commentary*, Vol. IV (n. 27) 335.
[97] See also *Expert Meeting, Occupation and other Forms of Administration of Foreign Territory* (n. 44) 58 ff.; Marco Sassòli, 'Legislation and maintenance of public order and civil life by occupying powers' (2005) 16 *EJIL* 661 ff.

HANS-PETER GASSER AND KNUT DÖRMANN

The occupying power may enact legal provisions of its own if military neces-   545
sity, obligations under international humanitarian law, or the obligation to
maintain orderly government so demand (Article 64, para. 2, GC IV; Article 43
HagueReg).

1. This rule is directly linked with the status and obligations of the occupying power,
which must be in a position to exercise its role as administrator of the occupied territory.
Consequently, it must be authorized to enact those provisions and adopt those organizational measures that appear necessary to maintain public order in the occupied territory.
This includes all precautions necessary to ensure its own security. Obviously, such enact-
ments may not derogate from its responsibilities under international law.

2. On the other hand, the occupying authorities may not enact provisions other than
those directly justified by considerations of military security or orderly government
(this fairly open-ended justification may be particularly relevant to ensure the welfare
of the inhabitants in situations of prolonged occupation to avoid freezing life and allow
for normal development of the occupied territory),[98] as well as those to implement the
Geneva Conventions (and other binding norms of international law, whether customary
or treaty-based—for the occupied state).

The administration of the occupied territory shall be given the opportunity to   546
carry on its activities. The jurisdiction of the occupied territory shall remain in
force.

1. The administration and judicial organization of the occupied territory may not be
replaced by institutions established by the occupying power. This follows directly from
Article 43 HagueReg which states that the public order of the occupied territory shall
remain in place and that public life shall continue 'while respecting, unless absolutely
prevented, the laws in force in the country' (see Sections 526 and 530). It is not the occupying authorities but the administration and the courts of the occupied country that
must ensure the maintenance of public order, applying its own domestic law. This rule
does not contradict the obligation to adapt the administrative system to new requirements, particularly if the occupation is long-lasting.

2. If there are no administrative bodies or courts at the moment the territory is occupied
or if they are unable or unwilling to perform their duties, the occupying authorities
have the right to remedy this situation. In such a case, they are entitled to set up their
own civilian administration and/or new courts for the occupied territories, and to bring
in judges of their own choosing to fill vacant posts. There is usually no objection to
such measures if they are taken to fill a vacuum, for example because local authorities,
administrative officials, and judges have left the occupied territory. In no circumstances,
however, may those newly in power simply sweep away the existing order and replace it
with a new one, without compelling reasons. According to the principle of subsidiarity,
they may intervene and take their own decisions only to the extent that this is absolutely
necessary and is in the interest of the population of the occupied territory. National

---

[98] Vaios Koutroulis, 'The application of international humanitarian law and international human rights
law in situation of prolonged occupation: only a matter of time?' (2012) 94 *IRRC* 173 ff. with further
references.

HANS-PETER GASSER AND KNUT DÖRMANN

administrative bodies or courts which are still functioning may not be altered, unless their activities are detrimental to the occupying rights and duties under IHL.

547　　　**The occupying power may set up administrative bodies of its own if military necessity or the obligation to maintain public order so demand (Article 64, para. 2, GC IV).**

In contrast to Section 546, the occupying authorities may under certain conditions set up administrative bodies and courts of their own in the occupied territories. These bodies will then exist alongside the national institutions and perform tasks of the occupying power, as the organization temporarily responsible for the occupied territory. These duties relate chiefly to maintaining security and public order (for instance, matters arising from the stationing of occupying troops and civilian members of the occupying authorities). The legal basis for this authority of the occupying power is Article 64, para. 2, GC IV. Section 547, which deals with enforcement, must be read together with Section 545, which establishes the power of the occupying authorities to make laws.

548　　　**The status of judges and public officials shall not be altered. It is prohibited to compel them to carry on their functions against their conscience (Article 54, para. 1, GC IV). Public officials may be removed from their posts (Article 54, para. 2, GC IV).**

1. Under Article 54, para. 1, GC IV it is prohibited for the occupying power to 'alter the status of public officials or judges in the occupied territories'. This provision also stems directly from the general principle of the law of occupation according to which the administration in the occupied territory shall remain in place during belligerent occupation. Judges and officials must be retained by the occupying authorities.

2. The independent status of members of the administration and the judiciary is guaranteed in international law but (as explained below) in a limited measure. That status can be justified on three grounds. First, it should ensure the uninterrupted functioning of the administration in the interests of the population of the occupied territory. Second, the population will be as undisturbed as possible by foreign control if day-to-day matters continue to be dealt with by local and therefore familiar administrative bodies. Finally, officials and judges should not suffer disadvantages or lose their posts because they have performed official duties in the past (guarantee of status).

3. This means specifically that judges and public officials may continue to carry out their activities in accordance with their obligations and without hindrance. In so doing, public officials have to accept instructions from the occupying authorities which, even if only for a limited time, exercise control over the territory. No doubt, under the circumstances of occupation officials will be confronted with difficult and contentious situations. However, it should be possible to find satisfactory solutions if the occupying authorities strictly observe international law and if the government in exile takes into account the delicate situation of its municipal authorities who must carry out their tasks under the control of a foreign power.

4. The term 'public official' must be interpreted broadly. Elected officials, such as mayors or elected members of a municipal council, are included. It should be noted particularly that the civilian police must also be enabled to continue performing their duties of upholding law and order.

HANS-PETER GASSER AND KNUT DÖRMANN

5. To guarantee essential public services, the occupying power may compel the inhabitants of occupied territories to work (see Sections 563–565). Such compulsory assignments may be required particularly from members of public services. Beyond this, however, the occupying power may not, in principle, force public officials or judges to remain in their positions. Officials may resign if they do not wish to serve under the occupying authorities, without suffering disadvantage as a result.

6. On the other hand—and herein lies the important reservation to the guarantee of their status—public officials may be removed from their posts by the authorities (Article 54, para. 2, GC IV). Such a measure is possible if a public official refuses to fulfil his or her tasks under the control of the occupying authorities. In this case, the public interest in the performance of administrative functions has priority over the interests of the individual official. Once dismissed, however, such an official may not be sanctioned for his attitude. The occupying authorities may replace an official who resigns or is dismissed, to the extent required for the proper functioning of the administration.

7. Under Article 54, para. 2, GC IV the occupying power may remove public officials (including judges) from their posts. The principle of independence of the judiciary applies absolutely, even in the law of belligerent occupation. This can lead to difficult situations if judges collectively refuse to fulfil their tasks. Since paralysing the judicial system cannot be in the interest of the population of an occupied territory, the occupying power is entitled in such a case to appoint new judges. On the question of jurisdiction in occupied territories, see Sections 565 ff.

8. Finally, it should be recalled that public officials and judges working in occupied territory are always civilians and thus protected persons. As such, they are entitled to all the rights specifically granted by international humanitarian law to civilians under the control of the enemy. This also applies to public officials and judges dismissed for whatever reason.

> The occupying power may not compel members of the population to serve in its   **549**
> armed forces (Article 51, para. 1, GC IV) or otherwise to take part in military
> operations against their own country (Article 52, para. 1, HagueReg). Any pressure
> or propaganda by the occupying power which aims at securing enlistment in its
> armed forces is prohibited (Article 51, para. 1, GC IV).

1. The prohibition of compelling members of the population of occupied territories to serve in the armed forces of the occupying power is absolute and knows no exception (Article 51, para. 1, GC IV). The recruitment of such persons for auxiliary forces of the occupying power is likewise prohibited. This rule indirectly strengthens the customary law prohibition against compelling persons to participate in military operations against their own country (Article 23, para. 2, HagueReg). The prohibition in GC IV is expressed more broadly, however, than that of the HagueReg, since it prohibits not only participation in military operations but also the mere recruitment into the forces of the occupying power, whether in armed or auxiliary forces. Thus it is prohibited to use members of the population of occupied territories, for example, to fight against members of the resistance.

2. This prohibition does not cover the situation of the occupied territory's civilian police force whose duty is to maintain public order. On the issue of recruiting civilian members of local authorities, see Section 565.

HANS-PETER GASSER AND KNUT DÖRMANN

3. Pressure or propaganda aimed at encouraging inhabitants of the occupied territories to serve in the armed forces is also prohibited. In practice, it is hardly possible to distinguish pressure from propaganda; there is no clear line separating one from the other, and both are in any case covered by this prohibition.

4. To compel members of the population of an occupied territory to serve in the armed forces of the occupying power is a grave breach of GC IV, punishable as such (Article 147 GC IV; see below, Sections 1411 ff. See also ICC Statute, Article 8, para. 2, lit. a(v)).

550   **It is prohibited to exercise physical or moral coercion against members of the civilian population in order to obtain general (Article 31 GC IV) or military (Article 44 HagueReg) information.**

The HagueReg forbid the occupying power to coerce the population of occupied territories 'to furnish information about the army of the other belligerent, or about its means of defence' (Article 44). Article 31 GC IV goes one step further by prohibiting any kind of coercion to obtain any type of information.

551   **For the benefit of the occupational forces or for ensuring public utility services and the feeding, sheltering, clothing, transportation, and health of the inhabitants of the occupied territories, the occupying power may compel civilians over eighteen years to work. Work which would oblige them to take part in military operations (Article 51, para. 2, GC IV; Article 52 HagueReg) or lead to the mobilization of workers in military or paramilitary organizations is not allowed (Article 51, para. 4, GC IV).**

1. Section 558 deals specifically with assignments of inhabitants of occupied territories. It permits compulsory labour only in two situations: to serve the immediate needs of the occupation forces, or for the benefit of the population of the occupied territory. It is emphasized that civilians compelled to work by the occupying authorities always retain their status as civilians.

2. Work for the benefit of the occupation forces is permitted only in very limited conditions. It is evident that inhabitants of the occupied territory may not be ordered to carry out work to contribute to military operations of the occupational forces and their preparation. According to Pictet's *Commentary*, work connected with, for example, public transportation, the reconstruction of roads, bridges, or harbours, or laying telephone lines, however, could under certain circumstances be permitted.[99] It is difficult, however, not to see this type of work as a contribution to military preparation of the armed forces. It would probably be better to prohibit all work for the benefit to the occupational forces that may be perceived as being part of military preparation of the armed forces.

3. Clearly, the construction of trenches, fortifications, or airstrips must be considered as work that inhabitants of occupied territories may not be compelled to carry out. Work in the armaments industry is also prohibited. Moreover, Article 51, para. 2, GC IV states explicitly that the inhabitants of occupied territories may not be compelled to do work 'which would involve them in the obligation of taking part in military operations'. This applies to military operations against their own country or against another state, also to

[99] Pictet, *Commentary*, Vol. IV (n. 27) 294.

HANS-PETER GASSER AND KNUT DÖRMANN

actions against members of the resistance and partisans in the occupied territory (but not to be part of civilian police force whose duty is to maintain public order, see Section 549).

4. The assignment to projects which are in the immediate interest of the inhabitants of the occupied territory raises fewer questions. An example that springs to mind is work to re-establish public utility services following their destruction in the war, for example water supplies, electricity supply, transportation lines, and so on. Certain branches of industry, for example for the production of foodstuffs, fertilizers, or cement, must be set into motion again. Inhabitants of the occupied territory may be compelled to perform this kind of work. However, the work must always be in the occupied territory itself (Article 51, para. 3, GC IV) and in the interests of its population. Persons under eighteen years of age may not be compelled to work in any circumstances (Article 51, para. 2, GC IV).

5. Workers from occupied territories may not be grouped into 'an organization of a military or paramilitary character' (Article 51, para. 4, GC IV). This provision is aimed at barring practices which were common during the Second World War.

6. The narrow wording of the types of work to which persons may be compelled should protect individuals against abuse and injury. It prohibits modern slavery for the benefit of the occupying power. It is also intended to prevent the assignment of inhabitants of occupied territories to locations that might be military objectives, since they would then be exposed to the dangers associated with attacks against military targets. Moreover, it should be recalled that it is absolutely forbidden to use civilians as shields (see above, Section 506).

> **Civilians liable to work shall, as far as possible, be kept in their usual place of**   552
> **employment, if they are required by the occupying power to perform work.**
> **Existing working conditions (e.g. wages, working hours, labour protection) shall**
> **not be altered by the occupying power (Article 51, para. 3, GC IV).**

1. Persons compelled to work shall, if possible, be employed where they already live and work. This again emphasizes the requirement to permit the inhabitants of occupied territories to continue their normal way of life as far as possible.

2. Article 51, para. 3, GC IV refers to the provisions on working conditions in force at the moment of occupation and confirms that they shall remain in effect. This detailed and very useful regulation, which forms part of international labour law and of the laws of war, was formulated jointly with the International Labour Organization (ILO). The relevant ILO agreements on the protection of workers remain in force in the occupied territories.[100]

> **It is prohibited to employ protected persons for work outside the occupied territory**   553
> **(Articles 51, para. 3, and 49, para. 1, GC IV).**

Persons may be ordered to carry out work only within the limits of the occupied territory. Work assignments in the country of origin of the occupying authorities are prohibited

---

[100] See John Dugard, 'Enforcement of Human Rights in the West Bank and the Gaza Strip' in Emma Playfair (ed.), *International Law and the Administration of Occupied Territories* (OUP, 1992), 484.

HANS-PETER GASSER AND KNUT DÖRMANN

without exception. This prohibition, like others, is a response to a practice common during the Second World War.

554   **The occupying power shall not deport or transfer parts of its own civilian population in the territory it occupies (Article 49, para. 6, GC IV).**

According to Article 49, para. 6, GC IV the occupying power 'shall not deport or transfer parts of its own civilian population into the territory it occupies' (see above, Section 530, para. 2). In particular, the policy of settlement of nationals of the occupying power in the occupied territory is contrary to international humanitarian law. By way of example, the settlement of civilians in the territories occupied by Israel contravenes Article 49, para. 6, GC IV. In its Advisory Opinion on the Construction of the Wall in Palestine, the ICJ leaves no doubt that the settlements 'have been established in breach of international law'.[101]

4. Requisition of Civilian Resources by the Occupying Power

555   **In accordance with legislation in force in the occupied territories, the occupying power may collect taxes, tariffs, and dues, for the purpose of defraying expenses of the administration of the occupied territory (Article 48 HagueReg). Any additional contribution shall only be levied to meet the requirements of the occupational forces or to cover its administrative costs (Article 49 HagueReg). No extra charges (contributions) shall be collected except under a written order issued by a commander-in-chief. For every contribution a receipt shall be given to the contributors (Article 51 HagueReg).**

1. The reference to 'legislation in force' means that taxes, tariffs, and tolls shall be imposed, as far as possible, according to the existing national provisions (namely the rules of assessment and incidence) in effect in the occupied territory enacted by the displaced sovereign. The occupying power is required to use the money to cover the expenses of the administration of the occupied territory to the same extent as the displaced sovereign. New taxes, that is additional contributions, may be levied in compliance with Article 49 HagueReg, thus for two purposes, for the administration of the territory, if the needs are not met by existing taxation, and for the needs of the army. Money collected may not be used for the enrichment of the occupying power or its personnel, or to alleviate the costs of the general war effort.[102]

2. The Supreme Court of Israel has had occasion to pronounce on the question of whether new taxes may be introduced in occupied territories (in this case, the West Bank). In 1976, the military government enacted orders introducing value added tax to 'serve as an equalizing device, so as to augment the free flow of goods and services between the occupied territories and Israel'.[103] The legality of the measure was challenged. The Court answered the question of legality affirmatively, invoking the ground of necessity

---

[101] See above, n. 10, para. 120. The justification of settlements as a security measure in 1979 by the Supreme Court of Israel in *Ayub v Minister of Defence*, Judgment of 15 March 1979, Case H.C. 606/78, (1979) 9 *IsrYHR* 337–342, is incompatible with the present-day systematic policy of establishing civilian settlements all over the West Bank. See also Section 558.

[102] *UK Manual* para. 11.31; Dinstein (n. 44) 126.

[103] Dinstein (n. 44) 128.

HANS-PETER GASSER AND KNUT DÖRMANN

as foreseen in Article 43 HagueReg. The Court held that the clause contained in that Article could be grafted on Articles 48 and 49 HagueReg, thus modifying their restrictions.[104] That decision is difficult to reconcile with the law of belligerent occupation, and not or hardly supported by state practice or legal literature.

3. Extra charges shall be collected according to the domestic laws of the occupied territories.

> A local commander may demand contributions in kind and services (requisitions) from   556
> the population and the authorities of the occupied territory to satisfy the needs of the
> occupational forces (Article 52, paras. 1 and 2 HagueReg). Contributions in kind shall,
> on principle, be paid for in cash, if not a receipt shall be given and payment shall be
> effected as soon as possible (Article 52, para. 3, HagueReg).

1. The traditional right of the occupying power to demand contributions in kind and services from the population or from the local authorities has been codified by Article 52 HagueReg. Such services may be required only 'for the needs of the army of occupation' or 'for the public utility services, or for the feeding, sheltering, clothing, transportation, or health of the population of the occupied country', and then only in so far as they are indispensable for these purposes (Article 51, para. 2, GC IV). Contributions in kind and services may never be demanded to benefit the occupying power's own population.[105]

2. The right to demand contributions in kind and services for the needs of occupational forces is laid down in Article 52 HagueReg and in customary law. Under GC IV the occupying power may also introduce compulsory labour if it is required to meet essential needs of the population of the occupied territories (Article 51, para. 2).

3. Requisitions in kind or services benefiting the occupying power must 'be in proportion to the resources of the country' (Article 52, para. 1, HagueReg), that is they may not exceed the capabilities of the occupied territory or its population. The occupied territory may not be bled dry by the occupying authorities. Similarly, covering the needs of the population of the occupied territory generally has priority over the requirements of the occupying authorities and its military forces. As Article 55, para. 2, GC IV explicitly states, foodstuffs, articles, and medical supplies, in particular, may be requisitioned 'only if the requirements of the civilian population have been taken into account'. This is understandable since, after all, the occupying power is obliged to guarantee the provision of foodstuffs and medical supplies for the occupied territories (Article 55, para. 1, GC IV; Article 69, para. 1, AP I; see Sections 563 ff.).

4. 'Such requisitions and services shall only be demanded on the authority of the commander in the locality occupied' (Article 52, para. 2, HagueReg). The seizure of goods without the authority of the commanding officer or the occupying authority is pillage, which is prohibited in all circumstances (see Section 507). Contributions in kind shall be compensated (Article 52, para. 3, HagueReg); Article 55, para. 2, GC IV stipulates that 'fair value' shall be paid. Work performed shall be remunerated by a fair wage (Article 51, para. 3, GC IV). Section 549 deals with the circumstances under which persons can be compelled to work.

---

[104] *Abu Aita et al. v Commander of the Judea and Samaria Region et al.*, H.C. 69/81, Judgment of 4 April 1983, reprinted in (1983) 13 *IsrYHR* 348–359.
[105] Dinstein (n. 44) 229, with reference to Second World War case law.

557 Movable government property which may be used for military purposes shall become spoils of war (Article 53, para. 1, HagueReg). Upon seizure it shall, without compensation, become the property of the occupying power. Such property includes, for instance, means of transport, weapons, and food supplies (Article 53, para. 1, HagueReg). The latter shall not be requisitioned unless the requirements of the civilian population have been taken into account (Article 55, para. 2, GC IV). The requirements of the civilian population shall be satisfied first (Article 55, para. 1, GC IV).

1. These provisions deal with the fate of movable government property. Movable government property 'which may be used for military operations' (Article 53, para. 1, HagueReg) is spoils of war, that is it can be freely requisitioned by the occupying power and becomes its property without compensation. According to the HagueReg this may include, for example, cash, other funds, realizable securities, military equipment (weapons, ammunition, etc.), and means of transport.

2. Foodstuffs and other supplies, and particularly medical supplies, may be requisitioned only if the needs of the inhabitants of the occupied territory have been met (Article 55, para. 2, GC IV). This drastic restriction on the right of seizure follows directly from the obligation of the occupying power to ensure 'to the fullest extent of the means available to it . . . the food and medical supplies of the population' (Article 55, para. 1, GC IV).

558 Movable private property which may be used for military purposes and immovable government property may only be requisitioned and not confiscated (Article 53, para. 2, and 55, HagueReg). Title to such property shall not pass to the occupying state. At the end of occupation, seized items and real estate shall be restored. All private property shall be protected from permanent seizure (Article 46, para. 2, HagueReg), except for commodities designed for consumption.

1. As is clearly laid down by Article 46, para. 2, HagueReg, movable private property is protected in the event of belligerent occupation. This rule has the character of customary law (see 'Introductory Remarks', Pt IV, 'Belligerent Occupation', para. 1). Therefore, as a rule, movable property of private persons may not be confiscated.

2. By contrast, Article 53, para. 2, HagueReg permits the occupying power to requisition the following objects, even if they belong to private persons: means of transport for persons or things by land, sea, or air; appliances for the transmission of news; and, in general, war material and ammunition. After the war has ended, seized property must be returned and, if appropriate, compensation must be paid.

3. In recent past, the relationship between the requirements of military security, on the one hand, and the guarantee of private property, on the other, has become a burning issue. The Israeli occupying authorities have repeatedly seized privately owned land in the Occupied Palestinian Territories and permitted its acquisition by private persons, for the purpose of establishing settlements for Israeli civilian residents. The Supreme Court of Israel has approved these 'requisitions' with the explanation that such settlements increased the security of the occupying power and could thus be justified on the basis of military interests.[106] Such an overstretched concept of a security-based exception to

---

[106] For a description of the jurisprudence, see David Kretzmer, 'The law of belligerent occupation in the Supreme Court of Israel' (2012) 94 *IRRC* 216 ff.

HANS-PETER GASSER AND KNUT DÖRMANN

the protection of private property rights contradicts international law. It undermines the guarantee of individual property rights in occupied territories. Under existing law, seizure of land may be only temporary, which is incompatible with the construction of a residential settlement for aliens.[107]

4. The occupying power does not acquire ownership (in private law) of 'public buildings, real estate, forests, and agricultural estates' located in the occupied territory and belonging to the state whose territory is occupied (Article 55 HagueReg). It is only the administrator and usufructuary. The list of state assets is not exhaustive. It should also include, for example, land which is not private or community property. For the situation regarding the property of the community or public institutions, see Section 559.

5. The occupying authorities shall, however, manage the assets of the state unless they transfer management to institutions of the occupied territory. As beneficiary owner of the assets the occupying power is under the obligation to maintain them, to preserve the property, and ensure its continued existence. The products or proceeds arising out of the capital of immovable properties administered by the occupying power cannot be used at its discretion. In particular, such proceeds cannot be utilized for the purposes of furthering or enriching the occupying power's own economy. However, the occupying power is entitled to use the products coming from the exploitation of immovable properties in order to defray the expenses involved in the occupation, to meet the occupying forces' needs or to ensure the welfare of the occupied population.[108] It is also worth noting that at the occasion of the occupation of Iraq in 2003–2004, the occupying powers and the Security Council decided to act in a way to ensure that Iraq's oil would be used only for one specific objective: the benefit of Iraqi people.[109] These positions appear to be in line with the traditional interpretation of Article 55 HagueReg but also inform the discussions on the purposes for which state-owned immovable can be exploited by the occupying power under IHL.

6. If the occupying power requires a piece of public land for military reasons (e.g. as a defence position or to construct accommodation for its forces), then it may requisition this land, for the duration of the occupation.

> **The property of municipalities, of institutions dedicated to religion, charity, educa-**   559
> **tion, and arts and sciences shall be treated as private property (Article 56, para. 1,**
> **HagueReg).**

Article 56 HagueReg, which protects the property of municipalities and certain public institutions, refers to the provisions of the HagueReg for the protection of private property (see Sections 557 ff.). The duty to protect institutions dedicated to religion also arises from Article 58 GC IV. Regarding the protection of 'institutions dedicated to . . . the arts and sciences', see also Section 562.

---

[107] As seen in practice, settlements in the occupied territory have increased tensions and created themselves security risks.

[108] Antonio Cassese, 'Powers and duties of an occupant in relation to land and natural resources' in Emma Playfair (ed.), *International Law and the Administration of Occupied Territories* (OUP, 1992), 419–42. For a contrary view, see Dinstein (n. 44) 215, with reference to Glahn.

[109] Letter addressed to the Security Council dated May 2003 from the permanent representatives to the UN of the United Kingdom of Great Britain and Northern Ireland and the USA, UN Doc. S/2003/538; SC Resolution 1483, 22 May 2003, S/RES/1483, para. 20.

HANS-PETER GASSER AND KNUT DÖRMANN

560   **Under the above-mentioned provisions of the law of occupation relating to taxes, requisitions, seizures and management of public and private properties in occupied territory, the occupying forces are constrained by the obligation to ensure that the economy of the occupied territory can only be required to bear the expenses of the occupation to the extent of the capabilities of the occupied country.**

This section reminds and reaffirms what has been mentioned before under a different perspective (see Sections 555 ff.): the occupying power may not make an economic or financial profit out of its administration of an occupied territory. The local economy is first of all in the service of the occupied territory and its population or, in different words, its resources benefit the territory's own population. This is a fundamental aspect of the legal regime governing belligerent occupation. Therefore, the occupying power may only withdraw resources from the occupied territory, be it to cover its expenses or for other purposes, if the needs of the territory's population are covered.

561   **Civilian hospitals may be requisitioned only temporarily and in cases of urgent necessity. The care and treatment of patients must be ensured (Article 57, para. 1, GC IV). The material and stores of civilian hospitals cannot be requisitioned as long as they are needed for the civilian population of the occupied territories (Article 57, para. 2, GC IV; Article 14, para. 2, AP I).**

1. Under Article 57, para. 1, GC IV, the occupying authorities may requisition hospitals in the occupied territory for their own use only if, and for as long as, these are urgently needed for the care of injured and sick of their own military personnel. The care of the inhabitants of the territories must, however, be guaranteed otherwise. AP I limits therefore the right of the occupying power to use hospitals in occupied territories for its own purposes by giving absolute priority to the needs of the inhabitants of the territory (Article 14, para. 2). The same applies to the equipment, material, and personnel of such units. Thus it is made clear that the civilian hospitals of an occupied territory should primarily serve the same purpose as before the invasion: the care of the local population. When requisition is admissible, it is subject to three conditions as set out in Article 14, para. 3, in particular the necessity for immediate treatment of injured and sick of the occupying power's military personnel and prisoners of war and for as long as the necessity exists.

2. The provision regarding hospitals comes within the wider context of the occupying power's obligation to guarantee medical care for the civilian population in occupied territories (Article 56 GC IV; Article 14 AP I; see below, Section 565).

562   **It is prohibited to requisition, destroy or damage cultural property (Article 56 HagueReg; Articles 4, para. 3, and 5 CultPropConv).**

1. As to the protection of cultural property in armed conflict, see Chapter 9.

2. The ban on requisitioning, destroying, or damaging cultural property, publicly or privately owned, must be placed in a broader context. The occupying power is bound, under Article 5 CultPropConv, to 'support the competent national authorities of the occupied country in safeguarding and preserving its cultural property', although only to the extent possible. The occupying power should take measures to preserve cultural property, and in particular cultural property damaged as a result of the war. In accordance

with both the First and Second Protocols to the CultPropConv (Articles 1 and 9, para. 1 respectively), exports of cultural property from occupied territory are prohibited and must be prevented. If exported, nevertheless, it must be returned at the close of hostilities and holders in good faith will receive an indemnity from the occupying power.

5. Supply Activities in Occupied Territory

> The occupying power is obliged to ensure that the basic needs of the occupied population are met. The provision of supplies to the civilian population shall be ensured to the fullest extent of the means available to it. The resources of the occupied territory shall be used in the first place. If necessary, supplies shall be brought in by the occupying power (Article 55, para. 1, GC IV; Article 69, para. 1, AP I).

563

1. The HagueReg only require the occupying power to maintain public order and life in the occupied territories and, at the same time, limit its right to use its resources for its own purposes (Article 43; Articles 52 *et seq.*). GC IV goes a significant step further and imposes on the occupying power the duty to ensure that the population of an occupied territory has all essential supplies to meet its basic needs (Articles 55–63). AP I makes this obligation even more specific and enlarges the list of indispensable supplies (Article 69). Just as human rights law has developed from the mere obligation to ensure the individual's freedom—traditional human rights law—to the obligation to implement its economic and social rights, so international humanitarian law today includes a whole series of rules obliging the occupying power to undertake specific actions in favour of the inhabitants of an occupied territory. At this place we examine the obligation to ensure the survival of the population in a situation which requires urgent supply of goods.

2. Under Article 55 GC IV the occupying power must ensure that the population is provided with supplies 'to the fullest extent of the means available to it'. It is therefore not obliged to ensure the provision of all supplies to the occupied territories. First of all, the population of the occupied territories has to look after itself, as well as it can. Nevertheless, it is the obligation of the occupying power to make such self-help possible. Therefore, for example the occupying authorities may make use of the economic infrastructure of an occupied territory for its own purposes only to the extent permitted by the needs of the local population (see Sections 556 ff.).

3. If the supplies available in the occupied territories are not sufficient, the occupying power must undertake to provide such supplies. The representatives of a protecting power, where applicable, and/or the delegates of the ICRC have the right to verify, on the spot and at any time, subject to temporary restrictions for imperative military requirements, the state of supplies available to the population (Article 55, para. 3, GC IV). They are in a position to give an objective picture of the actual conditions.

4. If supplies are inadequate, the occupying power has a number of options. First, it shall permit authorities or private persons to import the goods that are lacking from a third state or from the unoccupied part of their own country. If this is not enough, the occupying power must itself provide the required supplies. However, nothing impossible should be expected: the occupying power must only act 'to the fullest extent of the means available to it' (Article 55, para. 1, GC IV; Article 69, para. 1, AP I). Finally, if

certain conditions are met, it must permit relief actions by other, third states (see Section 564).

5. What categories of goods are meant? Article 55 GC IV speaks of foodstuffs and medical supplies. Under the heading 'Basic needs in occupied territories', AP I adds clothing, bedding, means of shelter, and 'other supplies essential to the survival of the civilian population of the occupied territory', as well as objects necessary for religious worship (Article 69). In this way, the range of goods to be supplied to the population of the occupied territories was extended by AP I. The occupying power not only has to supply basic food and medical supplies, but also other items indispensable for survival, such as clothing and shelter. How far this obligation goes in a particular case depends on the specific circumstances. In cold regions, for example, the delivery of fuel for heating purposes would be necessary. With regard to medical supplies, see Section 565.

6. It is self-evident that, in allocating and providing relief supplies, the occupying power is bound by the general prohibition of discrimination (Article 27, para. 3, GC IV in association with Article 75, para. 1, AP I). Special treatment may be justified if the medical condition, age, or sex of the concerned persons so require.

564   Stocks available in the occupied territory may be requisitioned for use by the occupying power only if the needs of the civilian population have been taken into account and a fair price is paid for the requisitioned goods (Article 55, para. 2, GC IV). See also Sections 554 and 567. If the whole or part of the population of an occupied territory is inadequately supplied, the occupying power shall agree to relief actions by other states or by humanitarian organizations (Article 59 GC IV; Articles 69–71 AP I).

1. This provision, which is very important in practice, states that the occupying power is obliged, when preliminary conditions are met, to permit relief actions for the benefit of the population of the territory that it occupies. A population suffering hunger is no longer an 'internal matter' for the occupying power. The processes of international solidarity must then be set in motion, and the occupying power may not block their efforts.

2. This provision applies only when the supplies to part or all of the population of the occupied territory are inadequate. It is a question of judgement whether or not supplies are inadequate in a specific situation. The occupying authorities are obliged to assess the situation to the best of their knowledge, taking into account the interests of the population only and neglecting considerations of prestige. The representatives of a protecting power and delegates of the ICRC are bound to inform the occupying authorities of the true situation and to advise them on the measures to be taken (Article 55, para. 3, GC IV).

3. If the population is adequately supplied, the occupying power is not obliged to accept any offer for relief made by another state or by a humanitarian organization. This also applies to offers from the unoccupied part of the country. However, the occupying power is well advised to accept such gestures from the unoccupied part, for the benefit of the population of the occupied territory. The population of an occupied territory, on the other hand, is always permitted to receive private relief consignments, subject to compelling security considerations (Article 62 GC IV).

HANS-PETER GASSER AND KNUT DÖRMANN

4. If the population is inadequately supplied and cannot remedy this situation itself, then the occupying power is obliged under international law to allow aid by other states. This refers to relief for the population as a whole, not for individuals. The occupying power must not only allow such relief actions but must also facilitate these 'by all the means at its disposal' (Article 59, para. 1, GC IV). This includes granting the necessary protection for relief actions. On the other hand, the occupying authorities may impose measures of control necessary for their own safety and that of the population. The contents of relief consignments are foodstuffs, medication, articles of clothing, bedding, means of shelter, and 'other supplies essential to the survival of the civilian population of the occupied territory', as well as objects necessary for religious worship. Recipients are residents of the occupied territory which need help, in particular also inmates of prisons. Internees have a specially detailed right to relief supplies (Articles 108 ff. GC IV). 'Wilfully impeding relief supplies as provided for under the Geneva Conventions' may be a war crime under Article 8, para. 2, lit. b(xxv), ICC Statute.

5. States not involved in the armed conflict are under an obligation to allow free passage of relief consignments through their territory (Article 59, para. 3) and must guarantee the safety of the relief convoys. This applies also to states which may be in conflict with the occupying power. In the event of a blockade, the passage of relief consignments for the benefit of occupied territories must be authorized. In other words, supplies necessary to meet the basic needs of the population in occupied territories may not be affected by a blockade. Third states always have the right to make sure that relief actions are carried out properly. They may check the contents of consignments in order to prevent, for example, the delivery of weapons. Such controls must not interfere with or delay excessively the relief action, as expressly laid down by AP I (Article 69, para. 2).

6. Under Article 59 GC IV, relief actions can be carried out either by a state or by 'impartial humanitarian organizations such as the International Committee of the Red Cross'. In the practice of armed conflict, neutrality is an important element for the success of a relief operation, since only a neutral state or organization can convince the occupying power and the population of the occupied territory that a relief action is impartial and free of political considerations. GC IV specifically names the ICRC among the 'impartial humanitarian organizations'. Because of its neutral stance, recognized by all sides, and its extensive experience it is most often the ICRC which carries out relief actions for the benefit of the civilian population in need. Its delegates stationed in the occupied territory are best placed to distribute or supervise the distribution of relief supplies according to need and without discrimination based on irrelevant criteria.

7. The personnel involved in a relief action shall be respected and protected (Article 71 AP I). The co-operation of technical and administrative personnel is indispensable, especially for the transport and distribution of goods. The participation of such personnel in a relief action in occupied territory requires the permission of the occupying power. Obviously, such workers must keep strictly to their tasks and observe the security requirements of the occupying power. If a relief action is carried out or accompanied by representatives of the protecting power or by delegates of the ICRC, these persons enjoy the rights and immunities due to the protecting power or the ICRC respectively. Attacks against relief personnel may be war crimes under Article 8, para. 2, lit. b(i) or (iii), ICC Statute.

HANS-PETER GASSER AND KNUT DÖRMANN

8. Relief actions by a third party do not release the occupying power from its obligation under international law to meet the needs of the population of the territory it occupies (Article 60 GC IV).

565

The occupying power has the obligation to provide medical care for the civilian population as well as to ensure and maintain public health and hygiene, in co-operation with the appropriate authorities of the occupied territory. Adequate prophylactic measures shall be taken to prevent contagious diseases and epidemics (Article 56, para. 1, GC IV; Article 14, para. 1, AP I).

1. Regarding the obligation to ensure and maintain medical care for the population of the occupied territory, the comments made in Sections 563 and 564 on the duty of the occupying power to provide for the basic needs of the population give a first answer. As Article 56 explicitly states, the occupying power must provide medical care for the inhabitants of the occupied territory, to the fullest extent of the means available to it (see also Article 14 AP I, which does not contain the limitation). The authorities have to rely, of course, on available personnel and on the existing infrastructure. If medical supplies are lacking then the occupying power must either itself import them or accept relief consignments by third states or by relief organizations (see Section 564).

2. The medical infrastructure of an occupied territory must be allowed to continue to serve the local population. According to Article 57 GC IV, the occupying authorities are only permitted to requisition temporarily civilian hospitals if this is urgently and exclusively necessary for the treatment of injured and sick military personnel. Article 14, para. 2, AP I, however, says that in the case of belligerent occupation the civilian medical infrastructure in the territories must remain at the disposal of the local population. If the occupying authorities make use of such hospitals for the immediate treatment of members of their own armed forces or of prisoners of war, and only for the time such necessity exists, they must guarantee otherwise medical care for the population of the occupied territory. Under no circumstances are they permitted to use medical facilities of the occupied territory for their own population.

3. Medical equipment and supplies may not be requisitioned as long as and to the extent that they are required for the population of the occupied territory (Article 57, para. 2, GC IV; Article 14, para. 2, AP I).

4. In accordance with Article 15, para. 3, AP I, the 'Occupying Power shall afford civilian medical personnel in occupied territories every assistance to enable them to perform, to the best of their ability, their humanitarian functions. The Occupying Power may not require that, in the performance of those functions, such personnel shall give priority to the treatment of any person except on medical grounds. They shall not be compelled to carry out tasks which are not compatible with their humanitarian mission.'

566

The national Red Cross or Red Crescent society shall be authorized to pursue its activities, in accordance with Red Cross Principles. Other relief societies may continue their humanitarian activities under similar conditions (Article 63 GC IV).

1. This provision confirms the special status of the national Red Cross or Red Crescent society among the social organizations of a given country (see above, Section 515). In the event of belligerent occupation, the Red Cross or Red Crescent society of that country

must be allowed to remain active on the spot and to continue its traditional activities, with its volunteers, its specialized personnel, and appropriate equipment. Article 63 GC IV, therefore, places an explicit obligation on the occupying power to permit the local branches of the Red Cross or Red Crescent society to continue their activities 'in accordance with Red Cross Principles'. Article 81, para. 3, AP I confirms the role of these societies and expressly stipulates that all parties to the conflict must facilitate the assistance provided by them to the victims of armed conflicts. The right of national societies to continue their activities for the benefit of the population of an occupied territory, in accordance with the Fundamental Principles of the Red Cross, is a legally anchored right, in conformity with international law, and does not depend on the goodwill of the occupying power.

2. Only Red Cross or Red Crescent societies recognized by the ICRC may rely on Article 63 GC IV. The ICRC grants recognition to a national society once it fulfils the conditions established by the Statutes of the International Red Cross and Red Crescent Movement.[110] These include the obligation to respect the principles of the Red Cross, among them the principles of impartiality, that is the principle of non-discrimination, and neutrality. Once recognized, a society not only becomes a full partner in the worldwide Red Cross and Red Crescent Movement, but is also under an obligation to abide by the Statutes of the Movement. It is the task of the ICRC to check the observance of the principles by the national societies, while fully respecting their independence.[111] One of the conditions for recognition by the ICRC is that a national society has been formally recognized as a voluntary humanitarian aid society by the government of its country.[112] On the situation of Red Cross organizations that are not recognized, see below, para. 4.

3. If the entire territory of a state is occupied, its national society falls fully under the control of the occupying power. In such circumstances it is entitled to continue its activities, within the scope of its humanitarian objectives. Article 63 GC IV provides one exception: for urgent reasons of security, the occupying power may impose temporarily certain restrictive measures. These reasons may, in particular, concern the safety of the national society's staff. Yet, it should also be borne in mind that the Red Cross was founded precisely in order to assist people in need in conflict situations, a task which always involves danger. The traditional activities of the Red Cross may under no circumstances be seen as a security risk for the occupying authorities or occupation forces. Restrictions imposed by the occupying power upon the national society are justified only if, for example, by acting against the interests of the occupying authorities the society disregards its obligation to remain neutral.

4. If only parts of a state's territory falls under the control of the adversary, chapters of the national society which are active in that part of the territory may continue their activities. With its general reference to 'organizations' of the Red Cross, Article 81 AP I leaves the door open to unrecognized societies, provided that they are guided in their activities by the Fundamental Principles of the Red Cross. Such groups are entitled to the same privileges as other relief societies (see below, para. 6).

---

[110] See Article 4, Statutes of the International Red Cross and Red Crescent Movement.
[111] Article 5, para. 2, lit. a, Statutes of the Movement.
[112] Article 4, Statutes of the Movement, pursuant to Article 26 GC I.

HANS-PETER GASSER AND KNUT DÖRMANN

5. The occupying authorities shall not interfere with the internal affairs of a Red Cross society. They may not change the organization of the society nor replace its leadership or personnel in a way that would prejudice their work (Article 63, para. 1, lit. b, GC IV). In the event of partial occupation of a state, the occupying power must take into account the legitimate desire of those parts of the national society which are under its control to maintain contact with the society's central bodies in the (unoccupied) capital.

6. Under Article 63 GC IV, the occupying power shall also allow other relief societies to carry out their activities for the benefit of the population of the occupied territory. The article refers in addition to existing or newly established, non-military organizations performing the following activities: maintenance of essential public utility services, distribution of relief, and rescue.

7. Finally, mention should be made of the activities which the ICRC must undertake to implement international law relating to belligerent occupation. In this regard see below, Chapter 14: 'Enforcement of International Humanitarian Law', especially Section 1422. Under Article 143 GC IV, ICRC delegates have in particular the right, while carrying out their activities, to go to all places where inhabitants of the occupied territory may be living. This includes especially all establishments where detained persons may be found (prisons, detention camps, etc.—see below, Sections 575 and 586).

6. Penal Responsibility in Case of Violation of International Humanitarian Law

567   Domestic laws relating to prosecution of criminal offences shall, in principle, remain in force. Penal laws of the occupied territory may be repealed by the occupying power only when they constitute a threat to its security or an obstacle to the application of international humanitarian law (Article 64, para. 1, GC IV).

1. Belligerent occupation of a country by the armed forces of another state does not invalidate its domestic legal system (see above, Section 544). This is of special significance for penal law, a set of rules which encroach markedly upon the life of individuals. During the period of foreign occupation, inhabitants of occupied territories remain subject to the pre-existing provisions of domestic penal law with which they are familiar. Not only does the domestic legal order remain in force in occupied territories, but also the jurisdiction of the national courts remains untouched (Section 546).

2. The occupying power may repeal the penal laws of the occupied territory or suspend their effect 'in cases where they constitute a threat to its security or an obstacle to the application of the . . . Convention' (Article 64, para. 1, GC IV). The latter covers by extension as well other binding international humanitarian law. For the Conventions and AP I this may be derived from common Article 1 GC and Article 1 AP I, the undertaking to respect and ensure respect in all circumstances. Moreover, the occupying power shall not apply domestic law which is incompatible with international law, whether customary or treaty-based (the latter as far as accepted by the occupied state), in particular with provisions concerning the protection of human rights. (See also Section 544, paras. 3–4.)

HANS-PETER GASSER AND KNUT DÖRMANN

For these reasons, and particularly to maintain an orderly administration, the   568
occupying power may enact penal provisions of its own (Article 64, para. 2, GC
IV). These provisions shall not come into force unless they have been published in
the language of the occupied territory (Article 65 GC IV).

1. As a general comment, see Sections 544–545 and commentary.

2. Newly enacted penal law provisions may not be retroactive (Article 65 GC IV).
Occupying authorities are bound to respect this principle, without which there is no
legal system deserving that name. The principle is now part of the generally recognized
guarantees of a fair criminal trial as codified by human rights law and customary international law applicable in all armed conflicts.[113] Therefore, an inhabitant of an occupied
territory may not be prosecuted for an offence allegedly committed before the occupation and made punishable by the occupying power only after the event.

3. The requirement that new penal provisions must be made known to the population
of an occupied territory in its own language is more than a mere administrative regulation. Publication in the national language is a necessary condition for the effectiveness of
such rules as inhabitants of occupied territories must be able to understand the law that
directly affects them. Publication shall be accomplished in such a way that everyone is
in fact enabled to become aware of it (notices, publication in the press, announcement
in other media, etc.).

The occupying power may not prosecute criminal offences committed by protected   569
persons before the occupation, unless they constitute a breach of international
humanitarian law (Article 70, para. 1, GC IV).

1. International humanitarian law does not confer on the occupying power the authority
to arrest, prosecute, or convict inhabitants of the occupied territory for offences committed prior to the occupation. For such offences, the normal rules governing the states'
jurisdiction apply. The same is true for offences allegedly committed during an interruption in the occupation.

2. According to Article 70, para. 1, GC IV, breaches of 'the laws and customs of war'
are the only exception to this principle. These are breaches of the conventions applicable
in armed conflicts, such as the GCs and AP I, and of general principles of law and rules
of customary law. Such breaches may be prosecuted by the occupying authorities, that
is any breach of the Conventions, not only those expressly defined as a grave breach. In
the case of a grave breach the occupying power is under an obligation to prosecute (see
below, Sections 1411 ff.).

3. Further exceptions to the prohibition against prosecution are 'crimes against the
peace and security of mankind' and other breaches of international criminal law (e.g.
genocide, crimes against humanity, torture, etc.). For both categories the jurisdiction
is unrelated to the belligerent occupation of foreign territory. According to the Rome
Statute the ICC may have jurisdiction over the crime of genocide, over crimes against
humanity, and over war crimes, as well as the crime of aggression once the amendment
to the Statute enters into force (see Chapter 14, Sections 1408 ff.).

---

[113] See, in particular, Article 15 ICCPR, and Article 75, para. 4, lit. c, AP I.

HANS-PETER GASSER AND KNUT DÖRMANN

4. In a non-international armed conflict, the legal situation is different. As a rule, offences are prosecuted by the state in whose territory the civil war is being waged, according to its domestic legislation. Conventional international humanitarian law on non-international armed conflict merely knows some provisions aimed at ensuring a fair trial (Article 3, para. 1, No. 1, lit. d, GCs I–IV; Article 6 AP II). In accordance with customary international law, a third state may also have jurisdiction to prosecute.[114] Moreover, the Rome Statute attributes jurisdiction to the ICC over some crimes committed in the course of a non-international armed conflict (ICC Statute, Article 8, para. 2, lit. c and e).

570   **Breaches of the penal laws of the occupied territory by residents of the occupied territory shall continue to be prosecuted by local courts (Article 64, para. 1, GC IV). Jurisdiction shall pass to a military court of the occupying power only if local courts are not able to work.**

This rule is also of great importance for inhabitants of occupied territories. It says that the ordinary courts of the country, which are familiar to them, remain competent to judge all 'ordinary' criminal cases, that is offences not having an immediate effect on the security of the occupying power (Article 64, para. 1, second sentence, GC IV). The local courts must apply domestic law and act in accordance with the rules of procedure in force prior to the occupation. Only if the national authorities or courts do not function and with the sole purpose of ensuring the administration of justice may the occupying power itself assume responsibility for penal jurisdiction. This could be the case, for example, if the judges left the country at the time of the invasion or resigning for reasons of conscience as foreseen by Article 56 GC IV. The occupying power may then call upon inhabitants of the occupied territory, or on former judges, or it may set up courts composed of judges of its own nationality. They must not be commingled with the military courts as set up in accordance with Article 66 HagueReg (see next section). However, in any case the laws which must be applied are the penal laws in force in the territory. See also Sections 547 and 548.

571   **Any breaches of penal provisions enacted by the occupying power may be prosecuted by properly constituted military courts established by the occupying power (Article 66 GC IV).**

1. For the right of the occupying power to enact its own provisions for the occupied territory, see Section 545.

2. The occupying authorities are competent to punish breaches of the laws which they have enacted (i.e. those to enable the occupying power to fulfil its obligations under the present Convention, to maintain the orderly government of the territory, and to ensure the security of the occupying power). Jurisdiction to prosecute may be assigned either to their own military tribunals or to military courts established for the occupied territories. In either case, it must be a military court, that is the judges must be members of the armed forces of the occupying power. In this way, the responsibility of the armed forces for the administration of the occupied territory and for enforcing the law of occupation is emphasized. The court, however, must be 'non-political' and regularly constituted. Special courts set up on an ad hoc basis are therefore not permitted. As

---

[114] *CIHL* Rule 157.

Article 66 expressly states, military courts must sit within the occupied territories: the accused should be tried in his own surroundings. If the military courts are sitting, for any special reason, outside the occupied territory, they must move into it in order to try the cases mentioned here. This obligation is in accordance with the principle of the territoriality of penal jurisdiction. It prevents protected persons who are accused of an offence from being brought before a court in a country other than that in which the offence was committed.[115]

3. With respect to the procedure of the courts of the occupying power, see below, Section 572.

4. The occupying authorities may establish an appeal court, but they have no obligation to do so (Article 73, para. 2, GC IV). If a court of appeal already exists, it should preferably sit in the occupied territory (Article 66, second sentence, GC IV).

> **Legal proceedings by military courts of the occupying power shall be conducted in**   572
> **accordance with the rule of law (Articles 67 and 69–75, GC IV; Article 75 AP I).**

1. The courts of the occupying power must in all circumstances respect the provisions and procedural guarantees codified in Articles 67 and 69–75 GC IV and generally recognized in international law. As mentioned by Article 71, para. 1, GC IV, no court of the occupying power may pass judgment without prior regular proceedings. The provisions of GC IV are supplemented by Article 75 AP I, which lists the minimum requirements of a regular and fair-trial procedure to be respected in a case against protected persons. Article 75 AP I reflects in this respect customary international law and is non-derogable (see also Article 5, para. 3, GC IV). Article 75 AP I builds the bridge to the provisions of international human rights law. In general, the courts of the occupying power must take into consideration that the accused person is not a national of the occupying power (Article 67 GC IV) and therefore does not owe allegiance to it.

2. The rules governing criminal proceedings before a military court of the occupying power include:

— the prohibition of retroactive effects of criminal provisions and of a heavier penalty than was permissible at the time of the commission of the offence (*nullum crimen sine lege*, Article 67 GC IV, Article 75, para. 4, lit. c, AP I),
— the right to be afforded all rights and means of defence (Article 75, para. 4, lit. a); written notice of the charges in a language that the accused understands (Article 71, para. 2, GC IV; Article 75, para. 4, lit. a, AP I),
— the right to be represented by an advocate or counsel of the accused's choice (Article 72, para. 1, GC IV); in serious cases, the right to defence counsel provided by the protecting power or, if necessary, by the court (Article 72, para. 2, GC IV),
— the right to present the necessary evidence for the defence, in particular to call witnesses (Article 72, para. 1, GC IV; Article 75, para. 4, lit. g, AP I),
— the right to an interpreter (Article 72, para. 3, GC IV),
— presumption of innocence (Article 75, para. 4, lit. d, AP I),

---

[115] Pictet, *Commentary*, Vol. IV (n. 27) 340.

HANS-PETER GASSER AND KNUT DÖRMANN

— the right not to be compelled to testify against him/herself or to confess guilt (Article 75, para. 4, lit. f, AP I),
— proportionality between the offence and any penalty imposed (Article 67 GC IV),
— deduction of the period spent awaiting trial (Article 69 GC IV),
— the provision of information concerning any right of appeal or petition (Article 73, para. 1, GC IV; Article 75, para. 4, lit. j, AP I),
— rapid conclusion of the case (Article 71, para. 2),
— public pronouncement of the judgment (Article 75, para. 4, lit. i), and
— notification to the protecting power regarding the proceedings (Article 71, paras. 2 and 3), representatives of which may attend the proceedings at any time and obtain information on their progress (Article 74 GC IV).

3. As pointed out in para. 4 of Section 579, GC IV does not require that a judgment be subject to review by an appeal court. If there is no possibility of appeal, then the person convicted must always be able to petition the authorities of the occupying power (Article 73, para. 2, GC IV), who are obliged to review the findings and the sentence of the judgment.

4. Denying a protected person of a fair trial has long been accepted as constituting a war crime. Precedents go back to the post-Second World War case law, namely the *Justice* trial.[116] In accordance with Article 147 GC IV, wilfully depriving a protected person of the rights of fair and regular trial as prescribed by GC IV constitutes a grave breach. It is also a war crime under the ICC Statute, Article 8, para. 2, lit. a(vi).

5. The protecting power has an important role to play in surveying criminal proceedings against inhabitants of occupied territories. Where such a protecting power exists, it shall be informed of every criminal proceeding 'in respect of charges involving the death penalty or imprisonment for two years or more' (Article 71, para. 2, GC IV). Article 71, para. 3, GC IV gives details of the contents of the required notification and stipulates that the protecting power must receive this information at least three weeks before the trial begins. The trial may start only after verification that these provisions have been respected. Representatives of the protecting power have the right to attend the trial in person. Consequently, they must be informed in good time of the location and date of the trial. If any part of the proceedings is held *in camera* for security reasons, the court must so inform the representatives of the protecting power (Article 74, para. 1).

6. The protecting power may at any time request information concerning criminal proceedings against inhabitants of the occupied territory (Article 71, para. 2). The occupying authorities are obliged, in particular, to notify the protecting power of all judgments involving the death penalty or imprisonment for more than two years and to state the reasons for the sentence. The period allowed for appeal does not begin until after this notification. The records of all other judgments shall be open to inspection by representatives of the protecting power (Article 74, para. 2).

7. Under Article 136 the National Information Bureau must also be informed of every judgment. The Bureau passes this information on to the Central Tracing Agency of the

---

[116] Military Tribunal III, *US v Alstötter et al.* ('*The Justice Case*') 3 T.W.C. 1 (1948), 6 L.R.T.W.C. 1 (1948), 14 Ann. Dig. 278 (1948).

HANS-PETER GASSER AND KNUT DÖRMANN

ICRC (Article 140 GC IV), which collects, transmits, and stores all information regarding protected persons. In this way, the country of origin and, if applicable, the relatives of the person accused or convicted can also be informed. In addition, every change in the relevant details must be reported. For general remarks on the National Information Bureau and the Central Tracing Agency, see Section 536.

> **Minor offences shall only be punishable by internment or simple imprisonment (Article 68, para. 1, GC IV). Serious offences (such as espionage, serious acts of sabotage, or homicide) may only be punishable by death if such offences were liable to death penalty under the law of the occupied territory before the occupation (Article 68, para. 2, GC IV; Articles 76, para. 3, and 77, para. 5, AP I).**   573

1. A principle generally applicable in penal law also applies to occupying powers: the sentence must in all circumstances be proportionate to the gravity of the offence. Moreover, the court must always bear in mind that inhabitants of the occupied territory accused of criminal offences do not owe allegiance to the occupying power (Articles 67 and 68, para. 3, GC IV).

2. Under Article 68, para. 1, GC IV, a minor offence is a criminal act 'solely intended to harm the occupying power' and which does not cause bodily harm or serious damage to property. Such offences should be punished at most with imprisonment or 'internment'. If the criminal judge orders 'internment' in place of imprisonment for less serious cases, that is to be understood as an alleviation of the penalty. In contrast to 'real' internment (within the meaning of Article 78 GC IV—see Sections 585–587), the length of punishment must be determined by the judge. In other words, the duration of 'internment' as penalty must be established at the outset.

3. GC IV permits the death penalty in particularly serious cases. By doing so, international humanitarian law in no way expresses an opinion as to the controversial question of whether the death penalty is compatible with fundamental human rights guarantees. Provisions of GC IV regarding the death penalty place restrictions on those states which apply this penalty. According to Article 68, para. 2, GC IV, the occupying power may impose the death penalty for the following cases only:

— espionage,
— serious acts of sabotage against military installations of the occupying power, or
— intentional offences causing the death of one or more persons,

and under the condition that domestic law in effect prior to the occupation allows the death penalty for such acts.

4. The death penalty may be pronounced only if the court's attention has been expressly called to the fact that, as an inhabitant of the occupied territory, the accused does not have a duty of allegiance to the occupying power (Article 68, para. 3, GC IV). In addition to a right of appeal, where applicable, persons sentenced to death always have the right to petition the authorities of the occupying power for pardon or reprieve (Article 75, para. 1, GC IV), and they must be given the opportunity to do so. A death penalty may in no circumstances be executed earlier than six months after the sentence (Article 75, para. 2, GC IV). This period does not begin until the protecting power has received notification of the final judgment or of the denial of pardon or reprieve. Exceptions are only possible under strictly limited conditions (Article 75, para. 3, GC IV).

HANS-PETER GASSER AND KNUT DÖRMANN

5. The death penalty may in no circumstances be pronounced on a person who was under eighteen years of age at the time of the offence (Article 68, para. 4, GC IV). Article 76, para. 3, AP I calls upon the occupying power not to pronounce the death penalty on pregnant women and mothers with infants. If the death penalty is pronounced on such women, it may not be carried out under any circumstances.

6. If the occupying power is party to human rights treaties prohibiting the death penalty, its military—no less than the civil—courts would be barred from sentencing a person to death. The question is to what extent an occupying power would be entitled or even obligated to interfere with local courts, which do apply the death penalty.[117]

574   Nationals of the occupying power who, before the occupation, sought refuge in the territory of the occupied state shall not be prosecuted on that account. Only crimes and other punishable offences committed after the outbreak of hostilities which would have justified extradition in times of peace shall be liable to prosecution (Article 70, para. 2, GC IV).

1. This rule addresses the special situation of nationals of the occupying power who left their country before the outbreak of hostilities and sought refuge in the territory subsequently occupied, possibly as refugees within the meaning of international refugee law.[118] While as nationals of the occupying power, in accordance with Article 4 GC IV they are excluded from the scope of protected persons, this rule recognizes that the right to asylum, enjoyed by refugees before the outbreak of hostilities 'must continue to be respected by their home country when it takes over control as Occupying Power in the territory of asylum'.[119] With the occupation of the territory by the armed forces of their state of origin, they fall into the hands of their own authorities. Article 70, para. 2, GC IV stipulates that such persons may not be prejudiced and, in particular, may not be transferred from the occupied territory to another place. They may be prosecuted only for an offence punishable under domestic penal law and committed prior to the occupation, if the law of the occupied state would have allowed extradition for this offence. For offences committed after occupation, the general provisions relating to prosecution of inhabitants of the occupied territory apply.

2. According to Article 44 GC IV and (particularly) Article 73 AP I refugees and stateless persons are entitled to the same legal protection as nationals of the adverse party, thus these articles expand the scope of protected persons of Article 4 GC IV (namely pre-war refugees nationals of the occupying power) and grant more protections than just those of Article 70 GC IV. For the general position of refugees in international humanitarian law, see below, Section 582.

575   Persons accused or convicted of offences shall be detained under humane conditions. All sentences passed must be executed in the occupied territory (Article 76, para. 1, GC IV). Detainees have the right to be visited by delegates of the protecting power and of the International Committee of the Red Cross in accordance with Article 143 GC IV (Article 76, para. 6, GC IV).

---

[117] Dinstein (n. 44) 145.
[118] See in particular the 1951 Convention Relating to the Status of Refugees and the 1967 Protocol Relating to the Status of Refugees.
[119] Pictet, *Commentary*, Vol. IV (n. 27) 351.

HANS-PETER GASSER AND KNUT DÖRMANN

1. In contrast to Sections 585–587, which deal with internment as an administrative measure ordered for security reasons, this section applies to the treatment of persons accused or lawfully convicted of having committed a criminal offence. With regard to the treatment of detained persons, it is irrelevant whether the punishable act is a common law offence or a violation of an order for the protection of public security or of the security of the occupying power.

2. The term 'persons accused of offences' as used here must be understood in a broad sense. It includes all persons deprived of their liberty because they are suspected of having committed a punishable offence. This means that a person is under the special protection of humanitarian law provisions regarding the treatment of prisoners from the moment that he or she is detained. This observation is particularly significant for the initial period of the investigation, which often takes place in complete isolation from the outside world. Article 5, para. 2, GC IV, which permits for a limited period *incommunicado* detention of persons suspected of having committed espionage, sabotage, or other offence directed against the security of the occupying power, expressly states that any prisoners held *incommunicado* must always and without exception be treated humanely. Article 45, para. 3, AP I limits the possibility of *incommunicado* detention to spies.

3. Article 76 GC IV states the following conditions for the treatment for prisoners accused or convicted of an offence:

— food and hygiene must enable good health, and at least be equal to those subject to normal imprisonment in the occupied territory;
— detainees shall receive the medical attention required by their state of health;
— women shall be confined in separate quarters and under the direct supervision of women;
— minors are entitled to special treatment;
— detainees have the right to maintain contact with the outside world (family, lawyer, etc.);
— they have the right to receive spiritual sustenance of their own choice;
— they have the right to receive at least one relief parcel monthly.

As a matter of course, the relevant international rules regarding detention established by human rights documents must be respected.[120]

4. Under Article 76, para. 1, GC IV convicted persons must be able to serve the sentence in a prison located in the occupied territory. The same applies for persons detained pending trial. This provision is a specific application of the general prohibition against displacement of persons from the occupied territories into the territory of the occupying power (Article 49 GC IV; see above, Section 541). In addition, it is intended to facilitate contact between detainees and their families.

5. Under Article 143 GC IV, representatives of the protecting power and delegates of the ICRC have the right 'to go to all places where protected persons are found, particularly places of internment, detention, and work'. Regarding the role of protecting

[120] See especially the *Standard Minimum Rules for the Treatment of Offenders*, adopted by ECOSOC on 31 July 1957 and 13 May 1977, and the *Body of Principles for the Protection of All Persons under any Form of Detention or Imprisonment*, Res. 43/173 (9 December 1988) of the UN General Assembly.

HANS-PETER GASSER AND KNUT DÖRMANN

powers see Sections 1420 ff., and on the tasks of the ICRC see Section 1424. Prisons in which persons from the occupied territories accused or convicted of offences are held are indisputably such places. ICRC delegates in fact spend a great deal of their time visiting prisoners in their places of detention. The reason for detention is of no importance. The protecting power and the ICRC are interested to see all persons detained by the occupying authorities for reasons connected with the conflict, because these individuals are exposed to the greatest risks to their life and well-being. Nevertheless, prisoners convicted under domestic law who are under the control of the occupying power are also visited.

6. Representatives of the protecting power and delegates of the ICRC primarily examine the conditions of detention and, if necessary, require to have them improved. Moreover, they show an interest for the personal problems of the detainees, who ask for assistance by an outside and neutral institution. Any visit to a prison by representatives of the protecting power or by delegates of the ICRC includes inspection of all rooms and places where detainees may be held, possibility to have access to all detainees, followed by private conversation with the detainees of their choice or who wish to meet a delegate (Article 143, para. 2). The conclusions are forwarded to the responsible authorities of the occupying power. Visits are repeated at irregular intervals until all detainees have been released.

7. The occupying authorities may suspend visits to a prison only for imperative military reasons, and only for a limited period (Article 143, para. 3, GC IV).

576   **At the close of occupation all detainees and relevant records shall be handed over by the occupying power to the authorities of the liberated territory (Article 77 GC IV).**

This rule covers all persons who have been accused of offences or convicted by the courts in occupied territory and the obligation is absolute. The handover procedure must be orderly and requires suitable preparation and organization. The protecting power and/or the ICRC may be involved in the process. GC IV does not deal with the question of whether prisoners must remain in detention following their transfer to their own authorities or whether they may be released.

V. Aliens in the Territory of a Party to the Conflict

Introductory Remarks

1. The fate of civilians which happen to be in the territory of the enemy at the outset of hostilities, as residents, as persons in transit or as asylum seekers/refugees, has changed greatly, from enslavement to the securing of their rights by modern international humanitarian law.

2. Under the heading 'Aliens in the Territory of a Party to the Conflict', Section II of Part III of GC IV regulates a number of situations that arise when nationals of one party to a conflict, for whatever reasons, fall into the power of an adverse party. In contrast to the law on belligerent occupation (Articles 47–78), this part of GC IV is not intended to be a comprehensive codification of all the rights of such persons. That would be unnecessary, since the state of residence is already obliged to treat these persons in accordance with international law governing the treatment of nationals of other states. As such, in normal

times aliens are entitled to all their rights under international customary law and, more and more, under the various human rights conventions.

3. The provisions of general international law for the protection of aliens in the power of the adverse party are applicable also in times of armed conflict, in accordance with Article 38 GC IV (on this point, see Section 578). These rights have found expression in international conventions and in international customary law. Most human rights conventions permit a state party, at the outbreak of an armed conflict and under certain conditions, to suspend the guarantee of a number of human rights.[121] Such restriction must be publicly announced and apply to citizens and resident aliens alike. GC IV goes one step further and expressly regulates a number of intricate questions that can arise during a war concerning the relationship between a party to the conflict and nationals of the opposing side. These provisions are the subject of this section.

4. Articles 13–26 GC IV formulate a number of obligations on the protection of the civilian population as such. Thus, all civilians, including the belligerent's own population, must be protected against the effects of the war; they are protected persons. On the other hand, Articles 27–34 and 35–46 deal in particular with the position of alien civilians who find themselves in the hands of a party to the conflict. 'Aliens in the territory of a party to the conflict' are, first and foremost, nationals of the state with which their state of residence is in armed conflict. They also include nationals of a neutral state not involved in the conflict, who do not enjoy actual protection due to the absence of diplomatic representation in their state of residence (Article 4, para. 2, GC IV). In practice, these persons would be nationals of a state which, although not taking part directly in the conflict, supports the cause of the 'other side', or is perceived as doing so by the state of residence. Finally, asylum seekers, refugees, and stateless persons are also aliens entitled to protection under the provisions of GC IV (and Article 73 AP I). These categories of persons are hereafter referred to as 'aliens'.

5. The citizens of states with which their country of residence has normal diplomatic relations, who find themselves on the territory of a party to a conflict, are not 'protected persons' since they enjoy the usual diplomatic protection. They come under the provisions of international law effective in peacetime and have, for example, the unconditional right to leave the country. The consular representatives of their state of origin must be in a position to look after them. It should be noted, however, that this category of persons does not fall entirely outside the protection of international humanitarian law. For example, Articles 13–26 GC IV, under the heading 'General Protection of Populations against Certain Consequences of War', apply to these persons as well. Also, Article 75 AP I acts as a 'legal safety net' guaranteeing a minimum standard of human rights for all persons who in fact do not have protection on other grounds. Finally, it should be recalled that such aliens are always protected by the provisions of international humanitarian law prohibiting military operations directed against civilians (see Sections 502 ff.).

---

[121] ICCPR (Article 4: 'In time of public emergency which threatens the life of the nation . . .'); ECHR (Article 15: 'In time of war or other public emergency threatening the life of the nation . . .'); ACHR (Article 27: 'In time of war, public danger, or other emergency that threatens the independence or security of a State Party . . .'). The African Charter of Human and People's Rights does not know such a rule for conflict situations.

HANS-PETER GASSER AND KNUT DÖRMANN

6. This section deals only with international armed conflict and the law applicable in such situations. In a non-international conflict, the members of the insurgent party who fall into the hands of the opposing side, that is of the government, are usually nationals of that same state. They are in any case entitled to the rights and guarantees owed to all nationals, including protection by human rights conventions. Nationals of third states must be dealt with according to the rules applicable to aliens and, in particular, common Article 3 of the Geneva Conventions and AP II. Persons belonging to the government side which are in the hands of the insurgents are also protected by these provisions.

577   **Protected persons may leave the territory of the state of residence, unless their departure is contrary to the national interest (Article 35, para. 1, GC IV). The departure shall be carried out in humane conditions (Article 36 GC IV). If any such person is refused permission to leave, such a decision must be reviewed by a court or an administrative board (Article 35, para. 2, GC IV).**

1. Aliens have the right to leave the territory of their state of residence, but they are not under an obligation to do so. Aliens who have spent many years in this country may be forced to leave the country only in exceptional circumstances, as stipulated in GC IV (see Section 583).

2. Yet the right to leave a state involved in an armed conflict is significantly restricted by GC IV. Under Article 35, para. 1 persons are not entitled to leave the territory if their departure is contrary to the national interest. This reference to the national interest of the state of residence allows this state to prohibit residents suitable for military service from leaving. Likewise, economic considerations may be adduced in order to prohibit persons from leaving on the grounds of 'national interest'.[122] The wide discretionary power granted to the authorities by Article 35 may well be restricted today by Article 12 ICCPR, according to which departure from a country may be refused only on specific grounds. This provision may however be suspended in a state of emergency.

3. Under Article 35 the request for departure must be dealt with by 'regularly established procedures'. This means, among others, that persons applying for departure must be heard and enabled to present evidence. As expressly laid down in Article 35, para. 1, the decision shall be made, and the grounds given, 'as rapidly as possible'. If the request is refused, then the applicant must be entitled to have the decision reconsidered by an ordinary court or by a specially created administrative board (para. 2). The protecting power must be notified of the names of all persons whose application for departure has been rejected (para. 3). In addition, information concerning the reasons for rejection shall be provided.

4. Persons leaving the territory of a party to a conflict, with or without an explicit decision by the authorities, must be allowed to depart in an orderly manner. Article 35, para. 1, states in particular that they must be allowed to take with them the money necessary for the journey and 'a reasonable amount of their effects and articles of personal use'. The departure itself must take place 'in satisfactory conditions as regards safety, hygiene, sanitation, and food' (Article 36). The costs are chargeable to the country of destination or, in the case of departure for a third country, to the state of origin. Collective

---

[122] Pictet, *Commentary*, Vol. IV (n. 27) 236.

HANS-PETER GASSER AND KNUT DÖRMANN

repatriation, based on a special agreement between the states concerned, is also possible. The departure arrangements may be entrusted to the protecting power or the ICRC (see also Section 583).

Aliens remaining in the territory of a party to the armed conflict shall, in principle,   **578**
be treated in the same way as in peacetime (Article 38, para. 1, GC IV).

1. Even a national of an adverse power is entitled to humane treatment by the authorities of the country of residence. In principle, such an alien may claim the protection of international human rights law also during an armed conflict, in the same way as in peacetime. As expressly laid down in Article 38 GC IV: 'the situation of [civilians belonging to the enemy state] shall continue to be regulated, in principle, by the provisions concerning aliens in time of peace', subject to the special provisions of GC IV. See in particular Section 579.

2. In wartime, the authorities of the state of residence may apply to aliens such measures of control and security as they deem necessary in the prevailing circumstances as a result of armed conflict (Article 27, para. 4, GC IV). If it is absolutely necessary for security reasons, assigned residence or internment may be ordered (see Section 581).

3. As any other protected person aliens on the territory of a party to a conflict have the right to approach the protecting power, if any, or the ICRC. They may also contact the National Red Cross or Red Crescent Society, or any other organization that may be able to assist them (Article 30 GC IV). Conversely, representatives of the protecting power and delegates of the ICRC have unrestricted access to all places where protected persons might be found, especially places of detention and internment camps (Articles 30 and 143 GC IV; see Section 586).

Aliens must be ensured, in particular: **579**
— **freedom of religion,**
— **medical care, and**
— **the right to leave areas exposed to the dangers of the conflict.**

They are entitled to these rights to the same extent as the nationals of the state in which they are living (Article 38 GC IV).

1. Article 27 GC IV, insofar as it applies to aliens on the territory of a party to a conflict, requires the authorities to 'respect . . . their persons, their honour, their family rights, their religious convictions and practices, and their manners and customs'. In the event of armed conflict, the nationals of an enemy state must be protected particularly from violence, intimidation, insults, and from public curiosity. If necessary, the authorities must order special measures for the protection of persons particularly at risk. Article 37 specifically reminds that aliens who are confined pending proceedings or serving a sentence involving loss of liberty, shall during their confinement be humanely treated. Moreover, unjustified discrimination is prohibited under all circumstances (Article 27, para. 3, GC IV; Article 75, para. 1, AP I).

2. The taking of hostages is prohibited (Article 34 GC IV; Article 75, para. 2, lit. b, AP I). Furthermore, aliens who have stayed in the country may not be moved to places of military importance in order to prevent the adversary from attacking these objects (Article 28 GC IV). On the contrary, the authorities must protect aliens from harm

caused by military operations in the same way as they protect their own citizens, that is as far as circumstances permit (see above, Sections 506 and 510).

3. In addition to the fundamental rights codified by Article 27, Article 38, GC IV guarantees to aliens a few additional rights:

— to receive individual and collective relief consignments;
— to receive medical attention if their state of health requires;
— to practise their religion and to receive spiritual sustenance;
— to be protected from the dangers of war, especially the right to leave a dangerous area;
— to receive preferential treatment for children (see also Article 77 AP I—special care, and Article 78 AP I—evacuation), pregnant women, and mothers of small children (see also Article 76—special care).

4. The general prohibition against discrimination, which is given particular weight by Article 38, is intended to ensure that aliens remaining in the territory of a party to a conflict do not have to suffer more from immediate effects of war than nationals of the state in question. On the other hand, aliens may not claim any preferential treatment.

5. The rights listed under paras. 1 and 3 of Article 38 are examples only. The reference to 'the provisions concerning aliens in time of peace' makes it clear that the list is not exhaustive. A right not explicitly listed which no doubt deserves special mentioning is the right to a fair trial. Aliens accused of having committed a criminal offence in connection with the conflict are entitled to a trial in accordance with the international obligations of the state, in particular the human rights conventions. The prohibition of discrimination must be respected under all circumstances. In addition, the minimum standard codified by Article 75, para. 4, AP I, must be heeded in all judicial proceedings (see Section 516).

6. Detained persons accused or convicted of a criminal offence shall be treated in accordance with the provisions applicable to detainees in peacetime, and without discrimination. See also Section 573, paras. 3 and 4.

7. By way of exception, Article 5, para. 1, GC IV restricts the rights of detained persons suspected of being engaged in activities detrimental to the security of the state (see above, Sections 516 ff.).

580   **Aliens shall be given the opportunity to find a job. That opportunity shall be equal to that enjoyed by the nationals of the state in which they are living (Article 39 GC IV). Aliens may be compelled to work only under the same conditions as nationals of the state in which they are living (Article 40, para. 1, GC IV).**

1. Persons remaining in the territory of the opposing party to the conflict must be given the opportunity to earn their own living, irrespective of whether they are in the hands of the adversary on their own free will or not. When looking for work, aliens may not be put in a worse situation than nationals of the state. The state retains, however, the right to prevent aliens from being employed for certain types of work, for security reasons (Article 27, para. 4, GC IV; see Section 578).

2. If persons are prevented from earning their own living because of security measures applied to them, for example an order placing them in assigned residence, the authorities must support them (Article 39, para. 2, GC IV).

HANS-PETER GASSER AND KNUT DÖRMANN

3. Like nationals of the state, aliens may be compelled to work. Aliens of enemy nationality may be assigned only to work 'which is normally necessary to ensure the feeding, sheltering, clothing, transport, and health of human beings and which is not directly related to the conduct of military operations' (Article 40, para. 2, GC IV). Activities connected with the armed forces or work in weapons factories, for example, are prohibited. The obligation of equal treatment of aliens and nationals is applicable particularly with regard to safety at the workplace, measures of protection, salary, and compensation payments in case of industrial accidents or occupational diseases.

4. Article 40, para. 4, GC IV, expressly provides that aliens may submit complaints to the protecting power (if any), to the ICRC, or to the National Red Cross or Red Crescent Society.

> **The placing in assigned residence or internment of aliens may be ordered only if** **581**
> **security considerations make it absolutely necessary (Article 42, para. 1, GC IV)**
> **or if other measures of control prove to be insufficient (Article 41, para. 1, GC IV).**
> **Such decisions are subject to review by a court or an administrative board (Article**
> **43, para. 1, GC IV).**

1. Assigned residence and internment are the severest security measures that authorities of the state of residence may decide against protected persons, in particular nationals of the opposing side (Article 41, para. 1, GC IV). Regarding the legal questions associated with deportation of aliens to their own country or to a third state, see Section 583. Assigned residence restricts personal freedom of movement. Internment involves sending a person to a place of detention or a camp established for the purpose. Both measures may be ordered only if national security makes this 'absolutely necessary' (Article 42, para. 1, GC IV—see also Section 585). Only considerations related to the security of the state can justify internment. An order for internment or for the less restrictive measure of assigned residence must be determined in accordance with the specific circumstances and the principle of proportionality. Finally, the provisions in force in peacetime shall be applied (see Section 578).

2. GC IV says little about which institution should make decisions concerning assigned residence or internment, or about the procedure to be followed. It may be assumed that this will probably be an administrative body. In practice, proceedings must be rapid, so there is little alternative. By contrast, Article 43 expressly stipulates that such decisions may be reviewed by a court or a special administrative board, either at the request of the concerned person or on its own initiative. In particular, this authority must review, at least twice yearly, the legality of every decision ordering assigned residence or internment. This control procedure is intended to safeguard the rights of persons affected.[123]

3. Regarding assigned residence, with its less far-reaching restrictions, Article 41, para. 2, GC IV implies that the authorities must always take action if, as a result of the assigned residence, the concerned persons can no longer support themselves or their dependants.

4. Finally, it should be noted that a person may request his/her own internment 'if his situation renders this step necessary' (Article 42, para. 2, GC IV), that is if he/she no longer feels safe. The state of residence must comply with this request.

---

[123] See also Jelena Pejic, 'Procedural principles and safeguards for internment/administrative detention in armed conflict and other situations of violence' (2005) 87 *IRRC* 375–91.

HANS-PETER GASSER AND KNUT DÖRMANN

582   **Refugees and stateless persons shall in all circumstances be treated as protected persons (Article 44 GC IV; Article 73 AP I).**

1. Article 73 AP I says unequivocally that refugees and stateless persons who find themselves in the territory of a party to an armed conflict have the same right to protection as nationals of the adversary state. This applies particularly to refugees who are nationals of the other party to the conflict, who have left their country because they felt threatened. The term 'refugee' must be understood in a broad sense. A refugee in this connection is any person who does not in fact enjoy the protection of a government.[124]

2. Refugees and stateless persons shall be regarded as protected persons in every respect. As expressly laid down by Article 44 GC IV, refugees may not be regarded as enemy aliens on the mere basis of their nationality. Thus they may not automatically be subject to the same measures of control. This applies, for instance, to assigned residence or internment. The state of residence must always grant equal treatment to nationals of the adversary, taking into consideration the special circumstances resulting from their status as refugees or stateless persons.

583   **Enemy aliens may be transferred to a state party to the Fourth Geneva Convention if this does not cause any disadvantage for these persons (Article 45 GC IV).**

1. This provision relates to the handing over of civilians in the power of a party to an armed conflict to a third state, which may or may not be involved in the conflict. Such a transfer may well be in the interest of the concerned person, especially if living conditions in the accepting state are less difficult than those in the territory of the party to the conflict.

2. The legal position of the person may not be worsened by such a transfer. Under Article 45 GC IV, certain conditions must be met to ensure that the transfer is in the interests of the persons concerned and therefore permissible. A person may only be transferred to a state party to GC IV, which safeguards their legal protection. Moreover, the transferring state must ascertain that the accepting state is actually willing and able to treat the persons concerned according to the provisions of international humanitarian law. If these conditions are met, civilian nationals of the opposing party to the conflict, including refugees, stateless persons, and nationals of third states with which there are no normal diplomatic relations, may be transferred to a third state, even against their own will. Thereupon, that state becomes responsible for fulfilling its obligations under GC IV, including the obligation to permit such persons to leave the country at any time (see Section 577).

3. In no circumstances may civilians be transferred to a country where they reasonably have to fear persecution on account of their political opinions or religious convictions (Article 45, para. 4, GC IV—an expression of the principle of non-refoulement specific to a situation of armed conflict), or where they will not be afforded the protection guaranteed by Articles 27–141 GC IV. If the transferring state realizes that the accepting state does not respect the obligations under international humanitarian law

---

[124] See *ICRC Commentary*, para. 2942 (conc. Article 73 AP I).

HANS-PETER GASSER AND KNUT DÖRMANN

on important matters,[125] that state must find an effective remedy and, if necessary, take the already transferred person back (Article 45, para. 3, GC IV). Extradition treaties concluded before the outbreak of the conflict continue to apply to persons accused of criminal offences under the domestic law (Article 45, para. 5, GC IV).

4. If, at the outbreak of an armed conflict, aliens find themselves in the territory of a party to the conflict, is it permissible for the authorities simply to put them against their will on an aircraft or to have them cross the border with a neighbouring state? GC IV does not expressly regulate the conditions in which individual or collective deportation is permissible in such a situation. No doubt, the general rules made for peacetime apply, namely the principle of non-refoulement. In particular, persons may not be deported to a country where they can expect to be persecuted for their political opinions or religious conviction. Article 45, para. 4, GC IV has established a universally applicable principle of international law. In this connection, attention is also drawn to Article 13 ICCPR, which requires an orderly procedure for expulsion of aliens and, in particular, a procedure enabling the persons concerned to present their own case. This rule should be applied generally. If these conditions are met, then nothing stands in the way of deportation, also from the point of view of international humanitarian law. Of course, it must be carried out in a humane way. See also Section 575.

5. GC IV does not say whether members of one party to the conflict may be handed over or deported against their will to their state of origin, if that state is the other party to the conflict. Here again, the rule undoubtedly applies that persons may not be transferred to a country where they have reasons to fear, in particular, persecution for their political opinions or religious convictions (Article 45, para. 4, GC IV) or torture, other forms of ill-treatment or arbitrary deprivation of life. Apart from these special circumstances, repatriation must be considered as permissible. Special attention should be paid to the circumstances of such individual or collective deportation. In particular, the persons concerned may not be exposed to danger. An orderly, previously arranged transfer is essential.

> **All restrictions imposed on aliens shall be cancelled as soon as possible after the** 584
> **close of hostilities (Article 46 GC IV).**

The term 'close' means a permanent termination of hostilities. For interpretation of this term, see Section 222. If necessary, the return of assets or the procedure for the transfer of compensation payments, for example for the benefit of interned persons, shall be regulated by special agreement.

VI. Internment of Civilians

Introductory Remarks

1. Section 590 reminds that a person may be interned only if such a measure is absolutely necessary, that is 'if the security of the Detaining Power makes it absolutely necessary'

---

[125] See Pictet, *Commentary*, Vol. IV (n. 27) 269: 'As examples Articles 27, 28 and 30 to 34 may be quoted; if the persons transferred are interned, which will most often be the case, a great many of the provisions in the chapter on internment will also have to be borne in mind, in particular those dealing with civil capacity, maintenance, food, clothing, hygiene and medical attention, religious and intellectual activities, correspondence and relief. In the treatment accorded to protected persons, the application of all these provisions is essential.'

HANS-PETER GASSER AND KNUT DÖRMANN

(Article 42, para. 1, GC IV; see also Article 78 GC IV). Section 543 recalls the conditions under which an inhabitant of an occupied territory may be interned, while Section 581 states the circumstances in which the internment of aliens present in the territory of a party to the conflict is permissible.

2. Sections 586 ff. deal with the treatment of interned civilians. They apply both to internment in occupied territories and to internment of aliens in the territory of a party to a conflict.

3. The internment of a belligerent's own nationals during wartime is not covered by international humanitarian law (except through Article 75 AP I). The international provisions concerning the protection of human rights are applicable.

585   Internment of civilians shall be permissible only in exceptional cases:
— if such a measure is absolutely necessary for imperative reasons of security (Articles 41–43, and 78, para. 1, GC IV); or
— as a penalty to be imposed on civilians (Article 68 GC IV).

Decisions regarding such internment shall be made according to regular procedures and subject to review by an independent institution (Articles 43 and 78, para. 2, GC IV).

1. Internment is a drastic restriction of personal freedom. It is permitted only as *ultima ratio*, that is only if security requirements cannot be satisfied by less severe measures, such as, for example, the obligation to register with the police or assigned residence. Internment is permissible solely as a measure to ensure public order in the state of residence. It is not a form of punishment. GC IV lists in a conclusive way the reasons allowing internment of a civilian who is a national of the adverse party.

2. Civilians present in the territory of the other party may be interned 'if the security of the detaining power makes it absolutely necessary' (Article 42, para. 1, GC IV). In the event of belligerent occupation, the occupying power may intern a person if it regards it as necessary 'for imperative reasons of security' (Article 78, para. 1, GC IV). In both situations the person in question must be a threat to public security in the state of residence. GC IV gives the authorities a great latitude.[126] In exercising their discretion they must take into account the personal situation of the person concerned. Internment may be ordered only as a last resort, if other measures are not sufficient. The ICTY held

'the mere fact that a person is a national of, or aligned with, an enemy party cannot be considered as threatening the security of the opposing party where he is living and is not, therefore a valid reason for interning him... To justify recourse to such measures, the party must have good reason to think that the person concerned, by his activities, knowledge or qualifications, represents a real threat to its present or future security.'[127]

It further held that internment is an 'exceptional measure to be taken only after careful consideration of each individual case. Such measure must never be taken on a collective

[126] ICTY, *The Prosecutor v Zejnil Delalić et al.*, Trial Chamber, Judgment of 16 November 1998, para. 574.
[127] ICTY, *The Prosecutor v Zejnil Delalić et al.*, Trial Chamber Judgment (n. 126) para. 577, Appeals Chamber, Judgment of 20 February 2001, para. 327.

HANS-PETER GASSER AND KNUT DÖRMANN

basis.'[128] The internee must be informed promptly, in a language he or she understands, of the reasons why these measures have been taken. He or she must be released with the minimum delay possible and in any event as soon as the circumstances justifying the internment have ceased to exist (Article 75, para. 3, AP I).

3. GC IV regulates the procedure by which a decision to intern a person shall be taken, both in the case of belligerent occupation and in the case of aliens present in the territory of the adverse party to the conflict (Articles 42 ff. and Article 78, para. 2). In particular, in the event of occupation Article 78, para. 2, GC IV requires a 'regular procedure'. This includes the right of the person to be heard. The same must unquestionably also apply to internment of aliens in the hands of the opposing side, although Articles 42 ff. GC IV remain silent on this point. This idea is supported by Article 38 GC IV, with its reference to 'provisions . . . in time of peace' (see Section 583). Moreover, any 'regular procedure' must take into account international humanitarian law, in particular GC IV.[129] It is clear, however, that according to the provisions of GC IV decisions concerning internment may be taken by an administrative body and must not necessarily be submitted to a court.

4. In both situations, also in light of the latitude for the detaining power in its initial decision to detain, the competent authorities must establish review procedures which allow the examination of internment orders (Article 43; Article 78, para. 2 GC IV). On the one hand, the person concerned by the internment order must be able to have the decision reconsidered by a court or an administrative board which must reach a decision within the shortest possible time.[130] On the other hand, this authority, whether a court or an administrative board, must on its own initiative periodically, and at least every six months, review all decisions regarding internment and decide whether the conditions for internment are still met. As pointed out by the ICTY, the court or board must have the 'necessary power to decide finally on the release of prisoners whose detention could not be considered as justified for any serious reason' and as to the onus of justifying detention of civilians, it 'is upon the detaining power to establish that the particular civilian does pose such a risk to its security that he must be detained, and the obligation lies on it to release the civilian if there is inadequate foundation for such a view'.[131] There must be an 'objective foundation' for a 'definite suspicion'.[132] This supervision by a special, independent body is extremely important and should be suitable of ending abusive internment. In the context of the war crime/grave breach of unlawful confinement (Articles 147 GC IV and 8, para. 2, lit. a(vii), ICC Statute), the ICTY found that '(a)n initially lawful internment clearly becomes unlawful if the detaining party does not respect the basic procedural rights of the detained persons and does not establish an appropriate court or board'.[133] The process should be such that the person interned is in a position to meaningfully challenge the (continued) legality of detention.[134]

---

[128] ICTY, *The Prosecutor v Zejnil Delalić et al.*, Trial Chamber paras. 578 and 583; ICTY, *The Prosecutor v Dario Kordić and Mario Cerkez*, Trial Chamber, Judgment of 26 February 2001, paras. 285 and 289.

[129] See also Pejic (n. 123).

[130] ICTY, *The Prosecutor v Zejnil Delalić et al.*, Trial Chamber, para. 580

[131] ICTY, *The Prosecutor v Zejnil Delalić et al.*, Appeals Chamber, para. 329.

[132] ICTY, *The Prosecutor v Zejnil Delalić et al.*, Appeals Chamber, para. 328.

[133] ICTY, *The Prosecutor v Zejnil Delalić et al.*, Appeals Chamber, para. 322.

[134] Pejic lists the following safeguards: the right to information about the reasons for internment, the right to be registered and held in a recognized place of internment, the national authorities of a foreign person

HANS-PETER GASSER AND KNUT DÖRMANN

586   The treatment of internees basically corresponds to the treatment of prisoners of war, yet always taking into account the civilian character of the persons concerned (Articles 79–141 GC IV).

— Representatives of the protecting power and delegates of the ICRC may visit the internees at any time in their place of detention and talk to them individually and without witnesses (Article 143 GC IV).

— The place of internment shall be placed under the authority of a responsible officer or a public official chosen from the civil administration of the detaining power (Article 99, para. 1, GC IV). The internees shall, as far as possible, be accommodated according to their nationality, language, and customs (Article 82, para. 1, GC IV). Members of the same family shall be lodged together. Separation of a temporary nature may be decided only for reasons of employment or health or for the purpose of implementing penal or disciplinary measures (Article 82, para. 2, GC IV).

— Internees shall always be accommodated separately from prisoners of war and from persons detained for any other reason, in particular convicted prisoners (Article 84 GC IV).

— Internees shall be treated humanely. In particular, any victimization, punishment drill, military drill, or reduction of food rations is prohibited (Article 100 GC IV). Contact with the exterior shall be permitted (Articles 105–16 GC IV).

— In principle, internees are not obliged to work (Article 95, para. 1, GC IV). Internees may, however, be employed for work within places of internment or for activities serving their own interests, but not in relation with the conduct of military operations (Article 95, para. 3, GC IV).

— Internees who commit offences shall be subject to the laws in force in the territory in which they are detained (Article 117, para. 1, GC IV).

— Internees have the right to have personal and confidential contact with representatives of protecting powers and with delegates of the International Committee of the Red Cross.

1. Section IV of Part III of GC IV, entitled 'Regulations for the Treatment of Internees', includes detailed provisions on the organization of places of internment and on the treatment of internees. They closely follow the rules applicable to the detention of prisoners of war (Articles 21–108 GC III; see Chapter 7, in particular Sections 716–728).

2. Articles 79–135 GC IV regulate the following matters (according to the headings of the individual chapter of Section IV):

— General provisions (Articles 79–82)
— Places of internment (Articles 83–88)
— Food and clothing (Articles 89 *et seq.*)
— Hygiene and medical attention (Articles 91 *et seq.*)
— Religious, intellectual, and physical activities (Articles 93–96)
— Personal property and financial resources (Articles 97 *et seq.*)
— Administration and discipline (Articles 99–104)

interned must be informed, right of a person interned to challenge, with the least possible delay, the lawfulness of his or her detention, the review of the lawfulness of internment must be carried out by an independent and impartial body, the internee should be allowed to have legal assistance, the right to periodical review of the lawfulness of continued detention, the possibility for the internee's legal representative to attend the proceedings in person, the right to have contacts with—to correspond with and be visited by—members of his or her family, the right to the medical care and attention required by his or her condition, the right to make submissions relating to his or her treatment and conditions of detention, and (ICRC) access to persons interned. See Pejic (n. 123) 384–91.

HANS-PETER GASSER AND KNUT DÖRMANN

— Contacts with the exterior, including provisions dealing with relief consignments (Articles 105–116)
— Penal and disciplinary sanctions (Articles 117–126)
— Transfer of internees (Articles 127 *et seq.*)
— Deaths (Articles 129–131)
— Release, repatriation, and accommodation in neutral countries (Articles 132–135).

3. Certain provisions of this well-elaborated code for the protection of civilian internees deserve closer attention:

a) The party to the conflict that interns civilians must inform immediately the internees themselves, the authorities of their state of origin and the protecting power (if any) of the measures taken in connection with the internment and any subsequent modifications (Article 105 GC IV). In practice, this means particularly that the Central Tracing Agency of the ICRC is to be informed of every decision regarding internment and of any change in the condition of an internee, through the National Information Bureau.

b) Directly following their internment, in the event of transfer to another place of internment, or in the case of illness, internees must be given the opportunity to personally inform their families and the Central Tracing Agency of the ICRC with an internment card (Article 106 GC IV).

c) Internees must be given detailed information about their rights and obligations through notices posted in the place of internment. The full text of GC IV shall also be available in the place of internment, in a language that the internees can understand (Article 99 GC IV).

d) Representatives of protecting powers and delegates of the ICRC have the right to visit interned civilians in their place of internment (Article 143 GC IV). The purpose of these visits is to check that the provisions of GC IV are observed by the detaining power and to deal with any personal requests by the internees which may require action by a neutral institution. During such visits, relief supplies may also be distributed to the internees. For the right to contact the protecting power or the ICRC, see Sections 516 and 575.

> Upon the close of hostilities or occupation, the belligerent parties shall ensure the   587
> return of all internees to their last place of residence or facilitate their repatriation
> (Article 134 GC IV).

1. As civilians can be interned only for so long as security considerations so require (see Sections 543, 581, and 585), the detention must be ended and the internees released as soon as the motive for internment ceases to exist. This clearly follows from Article 132, para. 1, GC IV, and Article 75, para. 3, AP I. The periodical review of decisions regarding internment by the responsible court or the administrative body (see Section 581 and commentary) serves to ensure that the release is ordered when necessary, even without being requested by the concerned person.

2. Article 132, para. 2, GC IV, calls upon the parties to the conflict to attempt, while the conflict is in progress, through agreement to find alternative solutions for internment of certain categories of detained persons. We thereby mean children, pregnant women, mothers with infants or small children, the injured and sick, and in general any person interned for a long time. Other categories are not excluded from such agreements; Article 132, para. 2, GC IV, merely states an order of priority.

HANS-PETER GASSER AND KNUT DÖRMANN

3. The following alternative measures are possible: release, repatriation, return to the place of residence, or accommodation in a neutral country (Article 132, para. 2, GC IV). Every release or return must be carried out in orderly conditions. The protecting power and/or the ICRC should be asked to assist the release of internees and, in particular, to facilitate the transfer to a third state.

4. When repatriation or transfer to a third state is ordered during the conflict, to what extent should the wishes of the concerned person be taken into consideration? Any refusal to be transferred to a specific country must at all times be respected if a person fears and there is a real risk for persecution, arbitrary deprivation of life, torture, other forms of ill-treatment or enforced disappearance; this principle is rooted in the general rules of international humanitarian law and of human rights law (principle of non-refoulement, see also Section 578). In the case of occupied territories, any transfer against their will of inhabitants of an occupied territory from such territory to the territory of the occupying power, to the unoccupied part of their state of origin, or to a third state is prohibited (see Section 541), even with the consent of the concerned person. The general rule codified by Article 49, para. 2, GC IV undoubtedly applies also to internees.

5. At the close of hostilities, which is a situation of fact and not a legal situation for example fixed by decrees,[135] all internment decisions shall be suspended and the internees released as quickly as possible. Article 133, para. 1, GC IV makes clear that this is an absolute obligation. The release must be carried out in an orderly way and must take into account the state of health of the internees. The states involved must guarantee and facilitate the return of the internees to their last place of residence or facilitate their repatriation (Article 134 GC IV). They are also required to search for dispersed internees through setting up committees by agreement (Article 133, para. 3, GC IV). Aliens repatriated from the territory of a party to the conflict must have their wishes taken into consideration, in that they shall not be transferred to a country in which they may fear persecution, arbitrary deprivation of life, torture, other forms of ill-treatment or enforced disappearance (see above, para. 4). Upon the return of occupied territory to the original country, a solution must be found, justified by human rights considerations, for those persons who would face persecution, arbitrary deprivation of life, torture, other forms of ill-treatment or enforced disappearance if transferred to the authorities of that country.

6. With the close of hostilities the detaining power may detain those internees against whom criminal proceedings have been initiated or who have a sentence to serve (Article 133, para. 2, GC IV). They shall be released at latest once the sentence has been served or, unless circumstances require continued detention, the trial has ended.

---

[135] Pictet, *Commentary*, Vol. IV (n. 27) 514.

HANS-PETER GASSER AND KNUT DÖRMANN

6

PROTECTION OF THE WOUNDED, SICK, AND SHIPWRECKED

Introductory Remarks

1. The protection of the wounded, sick, and shipwrecked during armed conflicts has a long history in various cultures and traditions[1] and retains its universal relevance to the present day.[2] However, much as in other areas of international humanitarian law in particular, and public international law more generally, the root of the codification in international legal instruments of this universal idea lies in Europe. It was there where a vast number of special agreements, which contained *inter alia* provisions on the protection of each other's wounded and the exemption of army surgeons from captivity, were concluded between states since the seventeenth century.[3] It was also in Europe, where the first general multilateral convention, the 1864 Geneva Convention for the Amelioration of the Condition of the Wounded in Armies in the Field, took shape. The 1864 Convention was the result of an initiative by the Swiss businessman, Henry Dunant. After having eyewitnessed the fate of those wounded during the battle of Solferino in 1859, and having attended to them together with a number of other volunteers, he wrote *Un Souvernir de Solferino* (1862) in which he recorded the lack of arrangements made for those who had been wounded in battle (see above, Sections 118–119). In this book, he made two suggestions as to the measures, which should be taken to ameliorate the situation: the establishment of 'relief societies for the purpose of having care given to the wounded in wartime by zealous, devoted and thoroughly qualified volunteers'[4] and 'to formulate some international principle, sanctioned by a Convention inviolate in character, which, once agreed upon and ratified, might constitute the basis for societies for the relief of the wounded in the different European countries'.[5] His book had a profound impact on the political elites and the general public in Europe and both of Dunant's suggestions came to fruition shortly afterwards. In 1863, an 'International Committee for Relief of to the Wounded' was established, which later became the 'International Committee of the Red Cross' in 1876. And in 1864, the aforementioned Geneva Convention for the

---

[1] Henry Dunant Institute (ed.), *International Dimensions of Humanitarian Law*, with early examples from Africa (7), Asia (13), Islam (37–8), Latin America (42), Western States (60); Wahbeh M. Sheikh al-Zuhili, 'Islam and international law' (2005) 87 No. 858 *IRRC* 269–83, at 283. See also M. H. Coursier, 'L'Évolution du Droit International Humanitaire', (1960) 99-I *RdC* I 361–465, at 364–9.
[2] ICRC, *Health Care in Danger: Making the Case* (2011) 24 pp.
[3] H. Lauterpacht (ed.), *Oppenheim's International Law*, Vol. II: *Disputes, War and Neutrality*, 7th edn (Longman, 1952), 353.
[4] Henri Dunant, *The Battle of Solferino* (ICRC, 1986), at 25.
[5] Ibid. at 30.

Amelioration of the Condition of the Wounded in Armies in the Field was adopted.[6] The 1864 Convention rested on three broad principles. First, it stipulated the fundamental obligation of states parties to collect and care for wounded or sick combatants, regardless of their nationality (Article 6). Second, Articles 1–5 regulated the neutrality and inviolability of medical personnel and inhabitants of the country who bring help to the wounded, as well as of medical establishments, units, and equipment. Third, the 1864 Convention introduced the distinctive sign of the red cross on a white ground for the purpose of identifying hospitals, ambulances, evacuation parties, and medical personnel.

2. The 1864 Geneva Convention is the root of what has since become known as 'Geneva Law', that is the law of protected persons. With the sick and wounded military personnel as the first object of humanitarian care, preceding prisoners of war and later civilians, it is the precursor of a number of subsequent treaties, which build on and develop the three underlying principles of the 1864 Convention. The first attempt to do so failed, however: although 'Additional Articles relating to the Condition of the Wounded in War' were adopted in 1868 to clarify some provisions and to adapt the principles of the 1864 Convention to sea warfare, these Articles were never ratified. The latter aim was realized during the First Hague Peace Conference, with the adoption of the 1899 Convention (III) for the Adaptation to Maritime Warfare of the Principles of the Geneva Convention of 22 August 1864, which was subsequently revised by the 1907 Hague Convention (X) for the Adaptation to Maritime Warfare of the Principles of the Geneva Convention. One year prior to the adoption of the latter 1907 Hague Convention (X), states were able to agree on how to improve and supplement the provisions of the 1864 Convention, and adopted the 1906 Geneva Convention for the Amelioration of the Condition of the Wounded and Sick in Armies in the Field. That agreement was subsequently replaced by the 1929 Geneva Convention with the same title. Following the Second World War, GC I superseded the 1929 Convention and GC II extended the latter's protective regime to wounded, sick, and shipwrecked members of armed forces at sea. Furthermore, GC IV introduced a number of provisions with a view to ameliorate the condition of wounded and sick civilians, although these rules lacked behind the detailed regulation in GC I and II. The First Additional Protocol, which supplements the 1949 Geneva Conventions, has overcome that division between members of armed forces and civilians and applies to all wounded, sick, and shipwrecked regardless of their status.

3. Many of the aforementioned treaty rules applicable in international armed conflicts are today generally accepted to reflect customary international law.[7] Since the adoption of Common Article 3 and AP II,[8] the law of non-international armed conflict also incorporates a number of treaty rules, which protect the wounded, sick, and shipwrecked, albeit with lesser detail than the treaty rules of international armed conflicts. However, almost all customary rules on the protection of the wounded, sick, and shipwrecked are purported to apply in both international and non-international armed conflicts.[9]

[6] C. Moorehead, *Dunant's Dream—War, Switzerland and the History of the Red Cross* (Harper Collins, 1998), 1–22.

[7] Cf. in particular Rules 25–6, 28–30, 35, 109–17 *CIHL*.

[8] Cf. Part III, Articles 7–12 AP II.

[9] See below, Chapter 12. According to the *CIHL*, most of the Rules cited therein are applicable in both types of armed conflicts, with few exceptions. For a critical examination of that assertion, see J. P. Benoit,

JANN K. KLEFFNER

I. Wounded, Sick, and Shipwrecked Persons

'Wounded' and 'sick' mean persons, whether military or civilian, who, because of
trauma, disease, or other physical or mental disorder or disability, are in need of
medical assistance or care and who refrain from any act of hostility. These terms
also cover maternity cases, newborn babies, and other persons who may be in need
of immediate medical assistance or care, such as the infirm or expectant mothers,
and who refrain from any act of hostility (Article 8, lit. a, AP I).

601

'Shipwrecked' persons are those, whether military or civilian, who are in peril at
sea or in other waters as a result of misfortune and who refrain from all acts of
hostility (Article 8, lit. b, AP I).

602

1. The definition of persons protected under the various treaties for the protection of
the wounded, sick, and shipwrecked evolved constantly from the adoption of the 1864
Geneva Convention, which only applied to 'combatants'. The 1906 Geneva Convention
subsequently broadened the scope of application to add 'other persons officially attached
to the armed forces', and the 1929 Geneva Convention similarly referred to 'officers and
soldiers and other persons officially attached to the armed forces'. As far as warfare at
sea was concerned, the Hague Convention (III) of 1899 applied to 'sailors and soldiers
who are taken on board', while the 1907 Hague Convention (X) added to this definition
'other persons officially attached to fleets or armies' in analogy to the 1906 Geneva
Convention. GC I and II are again broader in their scope *ratione personae*. Article 13 of
GC I and II stipulates that the two conventions apply to all those wounded, sick, and
shipwrecked, who are also entitled to prisoner-of-war status in accordance with Article
4 (A) of GC III (see below, Chapter 7). Accordingly, if these persons fall into the hands
of the enemy, they enjoy the protection of GC I, II, and III, although the applicability
of the latter Convention, will, as a matter of fact rather than law, only materialize in
full once wounded and sick military personnel are brought back behind the lines and
are on the way to convalescence and cure.[10] Besides the difference that GC I applies to
wounded and sick on land and GC II applies to wounded, sick, and shipwrecked at sea,
the protective regimes under the two conventions are virtually identical. Article 4, para.
2, GC II also clarifies that forces put ashore become subject to GC I.

2. The first treaty, which regulates certain aspects of the protection of wounded and sick
civilians, is GC IV. Its rules include those, which apply in general to all wounded and
sick civilians as well as other civilians in need of medical attention, such as the infirm

---

'Mistreatment of the Wounded, Sick and Shipwrecked by the ICRC Study on Customary International
Humanitarian Law' (2008) 11 *YIHL* 175–219.

[10] J. S. Pictet, *The Geneva Conventions of 12 August 1949, Commentary*, Vol. I (ICRC, 1952), 159 (referring to 'latent' prisoner-of-war status and further describing the position in the following terms: 'The gradual
improvement in [the condition of the wounded and sick under GC I and II] implies a corresponding change
in their claim to protection. From the moment when the wounded are picked up by the enemy's medical
personnel they are under the protection of the two Conventions, the First and the Third. But certain provisions of the latter Convention will remain (so to speak) in the background until such time as the individual
who has been picked up is no longer a wounded man in need of special protection and care. Gradually, as
he ceases to be a wounded man, the Third Convention as a whole will become applicable, until finally, when
he has recovered, it is the only instrument governing his status.') See also *mutatis mutandis* Pictet, *Commentary*,
Vol. II (1960) 137.

JANN K. KLEFFNER

and expectant mothers.[11] GC IV further stipulates other rules on the treatment of more specific categories of civilians, namely wounded and sick in occupied territory and those who are interned.[12] Prior to the adoption of AP I, international humanitarian law thus knew a twofold system of protection: a virtually identical regime under GC I and II for both wounded and sick on land and wounded, sick, and shipwrecked at sea on the one hand, and a more rudimentary system of protection for civilians under GC IV. The deficiencies of that approach under the GCs were remedied by AP I. Article 8, lit. a and b, AP I, which reflect customary international law,[13] do not distinguish between military or civilian persons and establish a uniform protective regime.

3. The generic categories of sick, wounded, and shipwrecked in GC I and II and AP I also extend to air forces.[14] Thus, a wounded member of the air force enjoys the protection of GC I and AP I if found on land, and the protection of GC II and AP I if found at sea. Article 12 GC II also expressly clarifies that members of the armed forces who are forced to land at sea by or from aircraft are to be considered shipwrecked. Besides the aforementioned provision, the only special regulation with regard to occupants of aircraft concerns persons parachuting from an aircraft in distress. In accordance with Article 42 AP I, such persons are protected from being attacked during their descent and upon reaching the ground in territory controlled by an adverse party must be given an opportunity to surrender before being made the object of attack, unless it is apparent that they are engaging in a hostile act. Article 42 does not protect airborne troops, however.

4. In order to qualify as 'wounded' or 'sick', a person must be in need of medical assistance or care for the mentioned reasons of trauma, disease, or other physical or mental disorder or disability.[15] This definition in AP I also extends to persons, who are neither 'sick' nor 'wounded' in the ordinary meaning of these words, which is clear from the express inclusion of newborn babies and expectant mothers into the definition.[16] 'Shipwrecked', in turn, is defined equally broadly in AP I in as much as it applies not only to those in peril at sea, as did GC II, but also to those in peril in other waters. Article 8, lit. b, AP I further clarifies the temporal scope of being protected because of the status as a shipwrecked person: the protection continues until the shipwrecked person acquires another status under the GCs or AP I, such as combatant, sick, or wounded if rescued by his or her own armed forces, prisoner of war if rescued by enemy armed forces, or civilian if rescued by the adverse party.[17]

5. Persons who commit any act of hostility are not considered 'wounded, sick, or shipwrecked', even if they are in need of medical attention, or are in peril at sea, or in other waters. They are not protected from being made the object of attack within the parameters of international humanitarian law. The law does not answer clearly the question when an act is to be considered 'hostile'. However, the term must be interpreted in analogy to the term 'hostile act' in Articles 41, para. 1, lit. c, on enemies *hors de combat*

[11] Articles 14–22 GC IV.
[12] See, e.g., Articles 57, 76, 81, 91, 106, 127, 132 GC IV.
[13] Rule 109 *CIHL*, and commentary, Vol. I, 399.
[14] Pictet, *Commentary*, Vol. II, 86.
[15] Article 8, lit. a, AP I.
[16] *ICRC Commentary*, 117, paras. 300–1.
[17] Ibid. 120–4.

JANN K. KLEFFNER

and 42, para. 2, AP I on occupants of aircraft parachuting in distress. Further guidance can be drawn from Article 51, para. 3, AP I on civilians who directly participate in hostilities.[18] Accordingly, 'hostile acts' are those which by their nature and purpose are intended to cause actual harm to the personnel and equipment of the opposing armed forces.[19] Such acts thus clearly include the firing of shots, but also the destruction of installations and military equipment, an attempt to escape or to communicate with the party to the conflict to which the wounded, sick, or shipwrecked person belongs, unless this communication concerns the wounded and sick who require assistance from the party's medical service.[20] The rule of thumb is, in short, that persons commit 'hostile acts' when they (continue to) perform functions inherent to being combatants. Beyond performing such functions, it has also been argued that to act as a voluntary human shield may equally trigger the loss of protection.[21] Conversely, as soon as a person in need of medical attention, or in peril at sea, or in other waters ceases to commit 'hostile acts', that person is entitled to protection as a wounded, sick, or shipwrecked. This is without prejudice to any possible prosecution for a war crime of perfidy, provided the conditions of Article 37 AP I are fulfilled (on perfidy see above, Sections 480–482).

> The wounded, sick, and shipwrecked, to whichever party they belong, shall be respected and protected in all circumstances (Articles 12, para. 1, and 35, para. 1, GC I; Article 12, para. 1, GC II; Article 3, para. 1 No. 2, GC III; Article 16 GC IV; Article 10, para. 1, AP I; Article 7, para. 1, AP II). Any attempts upon their lives, or violence to their persons, are prohibited. They shall be treated humanely and cared for without any adverse distinction founded on any grounds other than medical ones (Article 12, para. 2, GC I; Article 12, para. 2, GC II; Article 10, para. 2, AP I; Article 7, para. 2, AP II).

603

1. The wounded, sick, and shipwrecked must be 'respected' and 'protected'. To 'respect' alludes to sparing the wounded, sick, or shipwrecked persons and to not attacking them. The obligation to respect requires parties to an armed conflict and their individual members to abstain from acts, which would endanger a wounded, sick, or shipwrecked person or inflict (further) injury on him or her. That obligation also extends to civilians and the civilian population. While this is so with international humanitarian law in general (see above, Sections 133–134), the rules regulating the protection of the wounded, sick, and shipwrecked are explicit in that regard.[22] To 'protect', on the other hand, denotes that parties to an armed conflict must take active measures to ensure that the rights of a protected person are safeguarded.[23] The obligation to respect and protect is the foundation

[18] F. Kalshoven/L. Zegveld, *Constraints on the Waging of War: An Introduction to International Humanitarian Law*, 4th edn (ICRC, 2011), 117.

[19] *ICRC Commentary*, 618 (para. 1942).

[20] Ibid. 118–19 (paras. 306–7, 315), 488–9 (paras. 1621–4).

[21] M. N. Schmitt, ' "Direct Participation in Hostilities" and 21st Century Armed Conflict' in Fischer et al. (eds), *Crisis Management and Humanitarian Protection* (Berliner Wissenschafts-Verlag, 2004), 505–29, at 521; *The Public Committee against Torture in Israel and Palestinian Society for the Protection of Human Rights and the Environment v The Government of Israel*, Israeli Supreme Court, HCJ 769/02, Judgment of 11 December 2005, para. 36. But see Human Rights Watch, International Humanitarian Law Issues in a Potential War with Iraq (20 February 2003); N. Melzer, *Interpretive Guidance on the Notion of Direct Participation in Hostilities Under International Humanitarian Law* (ICRC, 2009), 57 (stating that voluntary and deliberate shielding of military objectives by some civilians 'does not, without more, entail the loss of their protection and their liability to direct attack independently of the shielded objective').

[22] Cf. Article 18, para. 2, GC I; Article 17 AP I.

[23] Pictet, *Commentary*, Vol. I, 134–5.

JANN K. KLEFFNER

of the protective regime established by the GCs, AP I and II, as well as customary international humanitarian law. All other rules, including the duty to treat humanely the wounded, sick, and shipwrecked and care for them, and the prohibition of attempts upon their lives or violence to their persons, are concrete manifestations of that general obligation.

2. What is to be considered 'humane treatment' very much depends on the concrete circumstances. In general terms, however, acts or omissions, which cause mental or physical suffering, represent attacks on bodily or mental integrity or on human dignity clearly fall short of that standard.[24] Humane treatment requires in general terms that the individual concerned is treated so as to lead an acceptable existence in as normal a manner as possible.[25] As such, humane treatment goes beyond medical treatment and encompasses all aspects of a person's existence.[26]

3. The requirement that wounded, sick, and shipwrecked are also to be cared for is a derivative of the obligation to protect: it requires belligerent parties and individual soldiers to ensure the medical care and attention, which the condition of the person concerned requires. Nevertheless, the concrete instance of complying with the obligation to provide such care is subject to the material possibility to do so. In the words of Article 10, para. 2, AP I, such care is to be provided 'to the fullest extent practicable and with the least possible delay'.

4. The categorical prohibition of attempts upon the lives of, or violence to wounded, sick, and shipwrecked covers a wide range of acts. Article 12, para. 2, GC I and GC II contain non-exhaustive lists of concrete examples, such as murder, extermination, torture, or biological experiments. The prohibition of biological experiments mentioned in GC I and II is a precursor of the more detailed prohibition to subject persons who are in the power of the adverse party or who are deprived of liberty to any medical procedure which is not consistent with generally accepted medical standards (see below, Section 606). The aforementioned instances of attempts upon the lives of, or violence to wounded, sick, and shipwrecked amount to grave breaches of the GCs, which states are obliged to punish.[27]

5. The obligation to respect and protect the wounded, sick, and shipwrecked is applicable 'in all circumstances'. The formulation epitomizes that parties to an armed conflict cannot invoke military necessity as a ground precluding the wrongfulness of non-compliance, unless the relevant rule is expressly subject to exceptions on grounds of military necessity.[28] Much as elsewhere in international humanitarian law, considerations of military necessity are incorporated into the law on the protection of the wounded,

---

[24] For the qualification of these acts as the war crime of inhuman treatment, provided that the mental harm, physical suffering, injury or attack on human dignity is 'serious', see, e.g., ICTY, *Prosecutor v Kordić and Cerkez*, (Appeals Chamber), 17 December 2004, para. 39. Also, cf. ICC Elements of Crimes, Article 8, para. 2, lit. a(ii) and para. 2, lit. c(i).

[25] Pictet, *The Fundamental Principles of the Red Cross Proclaimed by the Twentieth International Conference of the Red Cross, Vienna, 1965. Commentary* (Henry Dunant Institute, 1979), I (Principle of Humanity).

[26] Pictet, *Commentary*, Vol. I, 137.

[27] Article 50 GC I; Article 51 GC II. See below, Chapter 14, 'Introductory Remarks', para. 4, and Sections 1410–18.

[28] Kalshoven/Zegveld, above (n. 18), 37, 84.

JANN K. KLEFFNER

sick, and shipwrecked, but do not have a generally suspensory effect.[29] Openings for considerations of military necessity in the area of the protection of the wounded, sick, and shipwrecked can be found for example in the wording in Article 10, para. 2, AP I referred to previously, which obliges states to provide care 'to the fullest extent practicable and with the least possible delay', or in Article 12 of GC I, which sets forth the obligation that, if compelled to abandon wounded or sick to the enemy, a party to an armed conflict must, 'as far as military considerations permit', leave with them a part of its medical personnel and material to assist in their care.

6. Any adverse distinction between wounded, sick, and shipwrecked on grounds other than medical ones is prohibited. The *rationale* of that prohibition is to ensure that the wounded, sick, and shipwrecked, whether friend or foe, military personnel or civilian, are entitled to the same protection, respect and care, if and to the extent that they are in the same need of it. As such, the aforementioned rules in GC I and II and in AP I and II are a further manifestation of the general principle of non-discrimination, which underlies international humanitarian law as a whole.[30] It needs to be emphasized, however, that that principle only prohibits *adverse* distinctions, but does not preclude preferential treatment and care for those in more urgent need of medical attention than others.[31] Such preferential treatment and care may be warranted by the nature of the wounds of a protected person, but also by other (physical) attributes.[32] Indeed, common Article 12, para. 4, GC I and II makes the preferential treatment of women compulsory in as much as it provides that they 'shall be treated with all consideration due to their sex'. Article 12, para. 3, GC I and II also allow a prioritization of treatment when urgent medical reasons so require, so that doctors are allowed to treat those in more urgent need of treatment first, and those who do not require immediate treatment and care later.[33] Nevertheless, international humanitarian law does not set forth a concrete set of 'medical grounds' or 'reasons', which provide criteria for the justification of treating one protected person differently from another person. Such criteria instead derive from standards of medical ethics (see below, Section 614).

> Reprisals against the wounded, sick, and shipwrecked persons and against persons   604
> or objects protected by GC I and GC II and AP I are prohibited (Article 46 GC I;
> Article 47 GC II; Article 20 AP I; see above, Section 488).

In contrast to the express prohibition of reprisals against prisoners of war in Article 2 of the 1929 Convention relative to the Treatment of Prisoners of War, all conventions on the wounded, sick, and shipwrecked, which preceded the 1949 GCs, were silent on the issue of reprisals. However, such silence was not attributable to the belief that reprisals against the wounded, sick, and shipwrecked and other persons and objects necessary

---

[29] See generally, H. McCoubrey, 'The Nature of the Modern Doctrine of Military Necessity' (1991) XXX *RDMilG* 215–52, at 229.

[30] Cf. Rule 88 *CIHL*. For other examples of the prohibition of adverse distinction in the law on the protection of the wounded, sick, and shipwrecked, see, e.g., Article 9, para. 1, AP I, and Article 9, para. 2, AP II.

[31] Rule 110 *CIHL*, Vol. I, 309, 402–3.

[32] Pictet, *Commentary*, Vol. I, 138 (mentioning as examples special consideration for women and special treatment in the matter of lodging, heating, and clothing in the case of wounded or sick accustomed to a tropical climate).

[33] Pictet, 'The medical profession and international humanitarian law' (1985) 247 *IRRC* 191–209, at 198.

JANN K. KLEFFNER

for their care were permissible prior to the entry into force of the 1949 GCs. Rather, a prohibition of reprisals was clearly already on the minds of the Commission of Experts, which was convened by the International Committee of the Red Cross in 1937 to study the revision of the 1929 Geneva Convention for the Amelioration of the Condition of the Wounded and Sick in Armies in the Field.[34] However, since that attempt to revise the 1929 Convention failed, express treaty prohibitions of reprisals against the wounded, sick, and shipwrecked persons and against protected personnel, buildings, or equipment were only introduced into GC I and II, albeit on the understanding that these prohibitions confirmed a generally accepted rule.[35] The prohibition of reprisals is comprehensive in as much as it does not only encompass reprisals against the wounded, sick, and shipwrecked themselves, but also against personnel, buildings, vessels, or equipment protected by GC I and GC II. Article 20 AP I extends that prohibition to the persons and objects protected by Part II of the Protocol.

605   All possible measures shall be taken at all times to search for, collect, and evacuate the wounded, sick, and shipwrecked and to ensure their adequate medical assistance (Article 15 GC I; Article 18, para. 1, GC II; Article 19 GC III; Article 16 GC IV; Article 8 AP II). They shall be protected against pillage and ill-treatment (Article 15 GC I; Article 18, para. 1, GC II; Article 16 GC IV; Article 8 AP II).

1. Parties to an armed conflict are under an obligation to actively search for, collect, and evacuate the wounded, sick, and shipwrecked, provided circumstances permit them to do so. That obligation is incumbent upon them especially after an engagement. GC I also stipulates that parties to an armed conflict must arrange for an armistice, ceasefire, or local arrangement with a view to remove, exchange, and transport the wounded left on the battlefield.[36] Parties to an armed conflict thus are obliged to create circumstances, which make the search for and collection of the wounded, sick, and shipwrecked possible. GCs I, II, and IV further contain virtually identical provisions, which enjoin parties to an armed conflict to endeavour to conclude local agreements for the removal from besieged or encircled areas, of wounded, sick, and shipwrecked, and for the passage of ministers of all religions, medical personnel, and medical equipment on their way to such areas.[37] The obligation to take 'all possible measures' to search for, collect, and evacuate and to ensure the adequate medical assistance of the wounded, sick, and shipwrecked further entails that parties to an armed conflict, which prove unable to do so themselves, must permit humanitarian organizations to fulfil that role or assist in that endeavour.[38] In addition, in international armed conflicts, the military authorities may appeal to the civilian population to collect and care for the wounded, sick, and shipwrecked, and the civilian population may also do so on its own initiative.[39] No one may be harmed, prosecuted, convicted, or punished for performing such humanitarian acts.[40] The law of non-international armed conflicts is less far-reaching as regards the

---

[34] Pictet, *Commentary*, Vol. I, 344.
[35] Kalshoven, *Belligerent Reprisals*, 2nd edn (Nijhoff, 2005), 263.
[36] Article 15, para. 2, GC I.
[37] Article 15, para. 3, GC I; Article 18, para. 2, GC II; Article 17 GC IV.
[38] *CIHL*, Vol. I, 398, 402.
[39] Article 18 GC I; Article 21 GC II; 17 AP I.
[40] Article 18, para. 3, GC I; Article 17, para. 1, AP I.

right of initiative of humanitarian organizations and the civilian population. Article 18, para. 1, AP II only allows relief societies to 'offer their services for the performance of their traditional functions' and the civilian population 'may, even on its own initiative, offer to collect and care for the wounded, sick, and shipwrecked'. However, while the provision clarifies that the competent authorities may decline such offers, they may not do so arbitrarily in the face of urgent needs.[41]

2. As far as the evacuation of prisoners of war is concerned, GC III provides for the general obligation in Article 19, para. 1, GC III to evacuate them away from the combat zone, whether they are in good health or wounded, sick, or shipwrecked (see below, Section 711). However, as an exception to that rule, Article 19, para. 2, allows wounded and sick prisoners of war to be kept back in a danger zone if an evacuation would be of greater risk to their health than to remain where they are. Article 47 GC III contains a similar provision for situations in which prisoners of war are transferred after their arrival in a camp. Sick or wounded prisoners of war may not be transferred as long as their recovery may be endangered by the journey, unless their safety imperatively demands it. They are also not to be transferred if the combat zone draws closer to a camp, unless their transfer can be carried out in adequate conditions of safety, or unless they are exposed to greater risks by remaining where they are than by being transferred.

3. The obligation to protect the wounded, sick, and shipwrecked against pillage and ill-treatment entails that parties to an armed conflict must take active measures and ensure that protected persons be guarded and, if necessary, defended against pillage and ill-treatment.[42] A prohibition of pillage in occupied territory had earlier been included in the Hague Regulations of 1899 and 1907 (both Articles 47) and, with regard to the wounded, sick, and shipwrecked, in Hague Convention (X) of 1907 (Article 16). The latter provision also included a prohibition of ill-treatment. The prohibition in Article 16 of the Hague Convention (X) was echoed in the 1929 Geneva Convention (Article 3), subsequently included into GCs I, II, and IV and extended to non-international armed conflicts under AP II. 'Pillage', sometimes also referred to as 'looting' or 'plunder', means the appropriation of property by individuals for private or personal use, to which the rightful owner has not consented.[43] Although it is sometimes suggested that such appropriation is required to be systematic and violent in order to amount to pillage,[44] neither element is a prerequisite. Even an individual soldier, who appropriates property from a wounded person and does not use any force to do so commits pillage. As regards the second prohibition of 'ill-treatment', no actual meaning of the terms is spelled out in international humanitarian law. However, the categorical wording of the relevant provisions ('at all times') and the absence of any degree of severity that such treatment must attain in order to fall foul of the prohibition suggests to interpret the terms as widely as possible. As such, the prohibition covers a range of acts, including torture, inhuman, humiliating and degrading treatment prohibited under international humanitarian and human rights law,[45] but goes beyond them in as much as it covers any form of treatment, which causes physical pain or mental suffering to the victim.

---

[41] *ICRC Commentary*, 1478 (para. 4876).
[42] Pictet, *Commentary GC*, Vol. I, 152.
[43] Cf. Article 8, para. 2, lit. b(xvi), ICC Statute.
[44] P. Verri, *Dictionary of the International Law of Armed Conflict* (ICRC, 1992), 85.
[45] For the definition of these terms, see Rule 90 *CIHL*, Vol. I, Summary, 317–9.

JANN K. KLEFFNER

606   It is prohibited to subject wounded, sick, and shipwrecked persons who are deprived
            of their liberty as a result of an armed conflict or occupation to any medical pro-
            cedure not consistent with generally accepted medical standards (Article 11 AP I;
            Article 5, para. 2, lit. e, AP II).

1. Article 11 AP I and Article 5, para. 2, lit. e, AP II build on and develop the protection
of wounded, sick, and shipwrecked persons against abusive medical procedures in the
Geneva Conventions, which prohibit biological experiments and the creation of conditions through which such persons are exposed to contagion or infection[46] and medical
and scientific experiments not justified by the state of health of the person concerned.[47]
In order to comply with the obligation not to endanger the physical and mental health
and integrity of persons who are deprived of their liberty as a result of an armed conflict
or occupation, parties to an armed conflict must take all hygienic measures to prevent wounds to become infected, for example, and medication must be provided and so
on. Medical experiments, which affect the mental equilibrium of protected persons are
equally prohibited.[48] Furthermore, Article 11, para. 1, AP I and Article 5, para. 2, lit. e,
AP II prohibit any medical procedure, which is not indicated by the state of health of the
person concerned and which is not consistent with generally accepted medical standards
which would be applied under similar medical circumstances to persons who are in
no way deprived of their liberty. This rule is the corollary to the protection of persons
against punishment for carrying out medical activities compatible with medical ethics
(see below, Section 614). The obligations under Article 11, para. 1, AP I and Article 5,
para. 2, lit. e, AP II are quite similar. However, a significant difference is that the former
contains categorical rules, which have to be complied with under any circumstance,
while AP II subjects those who are responsible for the internment or detention to the
obligations under Article 5, para. 2, lit. e, only 'within the limits of their capabilities'.[49]

2. Article 11 AP I applies to all persons 'who are in the power of the adverse Party or
who are interned, detained or otherwise deprived of liberty as a result of [an international armed conflict or occupation]'. The category of persons 'who are in the power of
the adverse party' include prisoners of war, civilian internees, persons who have been
refused authorization to leave the territory of the adverse party, inhabitants of territory
occupied by the adverse party or who are otherwise in the power of the adverse party.[50]
'Persons deprived of their liberty as a result of an armed conflict or occupation', on the
other hand, include nationals of neutral states or other states not parties to the conflict
which have normal diplomatic relations with the party to the conflict responsible for
the deprivation of liberty, nationals of a co-belligerent state, those who have become
refugees after the outbreak of hostilities, nationals of states not parties to AP I and even
the nationals of the party to the conflict, which is responsible for the deprivation of
liberty, provided that the deprivation of their liberty is a result of the armed conflict or
occupation.[51] It is worth of note, however, that a breach of Article 11 AP I in the form

[46] Common Article 12, para. 2, GC I and II.
[47] Article 13, para. 1, GC III, Article 32 GC IV.
[48] *ICRC Commentary*, 152 (paras. 462–3).
[49] On this point, see W. Solf, 'Development of the protection of the wounded, sick and shipwrecked
under the Protocols Additional to the 1949 Geneva Conventions' in C. Swinarski (ed.), *Studies in Honour of
Jean Pictet* (Nijhoff, 1984), 237–48, at 243.
[50] *ICRC Commentary*, 152 (paras. 462–3), 1391–1393 (paras. 4588–94), 153 (para. 468).
[51] Ibid. 153–4 (para. 470).

JANN K. KLEFFNER

of a 'wilful act or omission which seriously endangers the physical or mental health or integrity of any person' only amounts to a grave breach of AP I if the victim is a person 'who is in the power of a Party other than the one on which he depends'.[52] In other words, violations of Article 11 committed against a party's own nationals do not amount to grave breaches.[53] In contrast to its twin provision in Article 11, para. 1, AP I, Article 5, para. 2, lit. e, AP II, applies to all persons deprived of their liberty for reasons related to a non-international armed conflict by internment or detention.

3. Article 5, para. 2, lit. e, AP II is limited to the aforementioned generic obligations. The law of international armed conflict, however, translates the obligations in Article 11, para. 1, AP I into a number of more specific rules on the protection of these persons in the context of their medical treatment. First, to physically mutilate, carry out medical or scientific experiments, and remove tissue organs for transplantation is impermissible, even if the person who is subjected to such treatment consents to it, except when these acts are justified in conformity with the conditions mentioned in Article 11, para. 1, AP I.[54] This prohibition is subject to one important, but narrowly circumscribed exception: if given voluntarily, without any coercion or inducement, and only for therapeutic purposes, under conditions consistent with generally accepted medical standards and controls designed for the benefit of both the donor and the recipient, persons may donate blood for transfusion or skin for grafting.[55] Each party to the armed conflict must keep a medical record for every such donation.[56] Second, wounded, sick, and shipwrecked persons have the right to refuse any surgical operation, even if such refusal is clearly detrimental to their health or even means certain death. In such cases, medical personnel must endeavour to obtain a written statement to that effect, signed or acknowledged by the patient.[57] Third, each party to the conflict must endeavour to keep medical records with respect to persons deprived of their liberty as a result of an international armed conflict or occupation, and must make them available at all times for inspection by the protecting power.[58]

> **Parties to the conflict shall record in respect of each wounded, sick, shipwrecked, or dead person of the adverse party falling into their hands, any particulars which may assist in his identification. All pertinent information shall be forwarded to the appropriate information bureau (Article 16 GC I; Article 19 GC II; see below, Section 711).**   607

The particulars in respect of each wounded, sick, or dead person, which parties to the conflict are obliged to record, if possible, include the designation of the power on which he depends; army, regimental, personal, or serial number; surname; first name or names; date of birth; any other particulars shown on his identity card or disc; date and place of capture or death; and particulars concerning wounds or illness, or cause of death.[59] That list is flexible and non-limitative. Other information may be added or supplied in the place of the particulars mentioned, if the latter are unavailable.[60] By and large,

---

[52] Article 11, para. 4.
[53] Solf, above (n. 49), 242.
[54] Article 11, para. 2, AP I.
[55] Article 11, para. 3, AP I.
[56] Article 11 para. 6, 1st sentence, AP I.
[57] Article 11, para. 5, AP I.
[58] Article 11, para. 6, AP I.
[59] Article 16, para. 1, lit. a–h, GC I.
[60] Pictet, *Commentary*, Vol. I, 162.

JANN K. KLEFFNER

the system of recording particulars of wounded, sick, and shipwrecked persons and the dead, and communicating these particulars through information bureaux, correspond to the system under Articles 122 and 123 of GC III (see below Section 711). Article 16, para. 4, sets forth further rules on the recording of and forwarding information on dead persons.

II. The Dead and Missing

Introductory Remarks

The central consideration of the rules of international humanitarian law on the dead and missing persons is that families have the right to know the fate of their relatives.[61] Although it has been suggested that such a right is not to be understood to create a subjective right of families to gain information,[62] the opposite conclusion flows from human rights jurisprudence.[63] The main difference between the rules relating to the dead on the one hand, and those relating to missing persons, on the other hand, stem from the fact that the fate of a missing person remains uncertain, although a point may be reached at which missing persons can be equated with dead persons if they can be presumed to have deceased.[64] The following rules apply to dead and missing persons without any adverse distinction. It therefore is of no relevance whether they are combatants or civilians or whether and on whose behalf they participated in hostilities.[65]

608   The dead are to be searched for, collected, identified, and prevented from being despoiled (Articles 15, para. 1, and 16 GC I; Article 18 and 19 GC II; Article 16, para. 2, GC IV; Article 33, para. 4, AP I; Article 8 AP II). Burial or cremation of the dead shall be preceded by a documented examination of the bodies (Article 17, para. 1, GC I; Article 20, para. 1, GC II). The dead must be disposed of in a respectful manner and their graves respected and properly maintained (Article 17, para. 3, GC I; Article 120, para. 4, GC III; Article 130, para. 1, GC IV; Article 34 AP I; Article 8 AP II).

1. Parties to an armed conflict, whether international or non-international, are under an obligation to take all possible measures to search for the dead whenever circumstances permit, and particularly after an engagement.[66] That obligation corresponds to the obligation to search for the wounded, sick, and shipwrecked (see above, Section 605). However, in contrast to the rules in relation to the wounded and sick, GCs I and II are silent on arrangements between the belligerent parties with a view to remove the dead. AP I and customary international humanitarian law have closed this gap by establishing the duty to endeavour to agree on arrangements for teams to search for, identify, and

---

[61] Cf. Article 32 AP I.

[62] See, e.g., the German Explanatory memorandum on the Additional Protocols to the Geneva Conventions, reproduced in *CIHL*, Vol. II, Chapter 36, § 169; *ICRC Commentary*, 345 (para. 1212).

[63] See references to this jurisprudence in *CIHL*, Vol. I, 425. See also the recount of the controversy surrounding the question during the negotiations of AP I in *ICRC Commentary*, paras. 1211–12.

[64] This approach was adopted by the UN Claims Commission, Recommendations Made by the Panel of Commissioners Concerning Individual Claims for Serious Personal Injury or Death (Category 'B' Claims), UN Doc. S/AC.26/1994/1 (26 May 1994), 17.

[65] Cf. Rule 88 *CIHL* and summary of Rule 112 *CIHL*, Vol. I, 408.

[66] Article 15, para. 1,GC I; Article 18 GC II; Article 8 AP II.

recover the dead from the battlefield.[67] These teams, whose members are to be respected and protected, may be accompanied by the personnel of the adverse party while carrying out these missions in areas controlled by the adverse party.[68] After the search for and collection of the dead, they must be identified (see above, Section 607). While the law of international armed conflicts is explicit in that regard, it is less clear whether the law of non-international armed conflict imposes such a duty of identification. However, supplementary obligations, at least of states, flow from human rights norms.[69] Furthermore, parties to an armed conflict must prevent the despoliation of the dead. That prohibition of despoiling the dead has long been recognized[70] and, the obligation of parties to an armed conflict to prevent such acts requires them to thwart acts of pillage (see above, Section 605).

2. The dead are generally to be interred in graves, unless religious reasons or the demands of hygiene require that they be cremated. In any case, funerals must take place in an honourable manner and in accordance with the religious rites of the deceased and only after careful examination with a view to confirming death, establishing identity, and enabling a report to be made. Graves must be properly maintained and marked, and, if possible arranged according to the nationality of the deceased. At the commencement of hostilities, the parties to the conflict must establish an Official Graves Registration Service whose main task it is to allow subsequent exhumations and identification of bodies or ashes and their transportation to the home country. As soon as practically possible, the parties to an armed conflict must also inform the Information Bureau about the location and markings of the graves and the particulars of the dead interred therein. AP I supplements the aforementioned rules and establishes further obligations of parties to an armed conflict to endeavour to conclude agreements on the protection and maintenance of and access by relatives to gravesites as well as on the return of the remains of the deceased and his or her personal effects.[71] Exhumations by the state on whose territory the gravesites are situated are, in principle, prohibited unless the aforementioned agreements provide for it or, absent such agreement, where that state has offered to facilitate the return of the remains of the deceased to the home country, but such an offer has been rejected. In the latter case, a number of further safeguards apply.[72] An additional exception to the rule that exhumations are prohibited is for reasons of overriding public necessity.[73]

3. The treatment of persons killed in naval warfare as described in Article 20 GC II, corresponds for the most part with GC I. As long as no funeral at sea takes place the regulations of the GC I apply once dead persons are landed. Warships sunk with their crews are considered to be war graves.[74] Examples from World War I are the British warships HMS *Royal Oak*, *Edinburgh*, and *Repulse*, and also the *Hampshire* which sank with Lord Kitchener aboard.[75]

---

[67] As to the customary status, see Rule 112 *CIHL*, especially Summary of the Rule, Vol. I, 407–8.
[68] Article 33, para. 4, AP I.
[69] Cf. the reference on applicable human rights norms *supra*, n. 63.
[70] See, e.g., *US v Pohl et al.*, US Military Tribunal at Nuremberg (1947).
[71] Article 34, para. 2, AP I.
[72] Article 34, para. 3, 2nd sentence.
[73] Article 34, para. 4, lit. b.
[74] D. P. O'Connell, *The International Law of the Sea*, 2 vols edited by I. A. Shearer (Clarendon Press, 1984), Vol. II, 912.
[75] H. McCoubrey, *International Humanitarian Law*, 2nd edn (Aldershot: Dartmouth, 1998), 48 (n. 16).

JANN K. KLEFFNER

609   Each party to the conflict must search for missing persons as soon as circumstances permit and shall transmit all relevant information concerning such persons (Article 33, para. 1, AP I).

1. Article 33 AP I builds on a number of rules in the GCs, including those relating to providing information to families and authorities under the GCs and the exchange of information through the Information Bureau.[76] In order to facilitate the search for missing persons, parties to an armed conflict must record particulars of persons held in captivity for more than two weeks,[77] and facilitate and carry out the search for and the recording of information concerning persons who have died in other circumstances as a result of hostilities or occupation.[78] These obligations of parties to an armed conflict are, however, without prejudice to further reaching obligations vis-à-vis persons who enjoy more favourable considerations under international humanitarian law.[79] The gathered information and requests for such information are transmitted through the protecting power, the Central Tracing Agency of the ICRC, or national Red Cross societies (cf. Sections 538, 708).[80]

III. Medical Units and Transport

610   Medical units and medical transports must be respected and protected at all times and shall not be made the object of attack (Article 27, para. 1, HagueReg; Article 19, para. 1, GC I; Article 18, para. 1, GC IV; Article 12, para. 1, and Article 21 AP I; Article 11, para. 1, AP II). As far as possible, medical units shall be so sited that attacks against military objectives do not imperil their safety (Article 19, para. 2, GC I; Article 18, para. 5, GC IV; Article 12, para. 4, AP I).

1. Similar to the extension of the definition of 'wounded', 'sick', and 'shipwrecked' to also cover civilians (see above Sections 601–602), the definition of 'medical units' in Article 8, lit. e, AP I expands the coverage in comparison with Article 19 GC I. While the latter provision only refers to 'fixed establishments and mobile units of the Medical Services', Article 8, lit. e, AP I defines as 'medical units' all 'establishments and other units, whether military or civilian, organized for medical purposes, namely the search for, collection, transportation, diagnosis, or treatment—including first-aid treatment—of the wounded, sick, and shipwrecked, or for the prevention of disease'. These medical units can be fixed or mobile, permanent or temporary.[81] The provision further contains a non-exhaustive list of examples, such as hospitals and other similar units, blood transfusion centres, preventive medicine centres and institutes, medical depots and the medical and pharmaceutical

---

[76] Articles 16–17 GC I; 19 GC II; 70, 71, and 122 GC III; 26, 106, 136, and 140 GC IV.

[77] Cf. Article 33, para. 2, lit. a. The following particulars are mentioned in Article 138 GC IV: name(s), place and date of birth, nationality, last residence and distinguishing characteristics, name of the father and maiden name of the mother, the date, place and nature of the action taken with regard to the individual in question, the address at which correspondence may be sent, and the name and address of the person to be informed.

[78] Article 33, para. 2, lit. b.

[79] For an overview over these categories of persons and the applicable rules, see *ICRC Commentary*, 356–9 (paras. 1253–62).

[80] Article 33, para. 3, AP I. See generally on the role of the ICRC as regards missing persons, Sassòli/ Tougas, 'The ICRC and the missing' (2002) 84 No. 848 *IRRC* 727–49.

[81] Cf. Article 8, lit. e, 3rd sentence, AP I.

JANN K. KLEFFNER

stores of such units. This enlarged definition also moves beyond the protection provided under Articles 1, 8, para. 1, GC IV in as much as that latter provision only covered civilian hospitals. The central criterion deriving from the definition in Article 8, lit. e, AP I, which is generally considered to reflect customary international humanitarian law and equally applicable in non-international armed conflicts,[82] is that establishments or other units be 'organized for medical purposes' and exclusively assigned to these purposes,[83] while it is the use at the relevant moment which is decisive in that respect.[84] As far as their entitlement to, and meaning of 'respect' and 'protection' is concerned, the observations above (Section 603) apply *mutatis mutandis*. In order for civilian medical units to be considered 'medical units' entitled to that respect and protection, however, Article 12 requires them to either belong to one of the parties to the conflict, be recognized and authorized by the competent authority of one of the parties to the conflict, or be authorized in conformity with Article 9, para. 2, AP I or Article 27 GC I.[85]

2. With a view to strengthen the safety of medical units, parties to an armed conflict are recommended to notify each other of the location of their fixed medical units.[86] However, not to so notify the adverse party does not deprive medical units of their entitlement to respect and protection.[87] As a further measure to decrease the likelihood of medical units being caught in the midst of fighting and collaterally damaged, the warring parties are under an obligation to locate medical units away from military objectives whenever possible.[88] Indeed, the deliberate use of medical units in an attempt to shield military objectives from attack is expressly prohibited.[89] In the latter case, the attacking party is nevertheless not released from the obligation to take all possible precautionary measures with a view to limit incidental damage to medical units, in analogy to Article 51, para. 8, AP I.[90] With regard to the marking of medical units and transports with the distinctive emblem of the Red Cross, Red Crescent, and Red Crystal, reference is made to the discussion below (Sections 624 *et seq*).

3. According to Article 21 AP I, the rules on medical means of transportation by land (medical vehicles), as defined in Article 8, lit. h, AP I[91] correspond to those on mobile medical units. In contrast, the regime for medical ships, craft, and aircraft differs in important respects (see below, Sections 1054 *et seq*).

> **The requisition of medical units and medical vehicles is permissible only if the medical needs of the civilian population, as well as those of any wounded and sick under treatment are satisfied (Articles 19, paras. 1, 33, 35, para. 2, GC I; Article 57 GC IV; Articles 14, 21 AP I).** **611**

---

[82] Rule 28 *CIHL*, Summary, Vol. 1, 95.

[83] While the requirement of exclusivity is not spelled out in Article 8, lit. e, AP I, Article 8, lit. k, AP I defines 'permanent medical units' and 'temporary medical units' (alongside permanent and temporary medical transports and personnel) as those 'assigned' or 'devoted exclusively to medical purposes'.

[84] *ICRC Commentary*, 128 (paras. 371–2).

[85] Article 12, para. 2, AP I.

[86] Article 12, para. 3, 1st sentence, AP I.

[87] Article 12, para. 3, 2nd sentence, AP I.

[88] Article 12, para. 4, 2nd sentence, AP I.

[89] Article 12, para. 4, 1st sentence, AP I.

[90] In this vein, *ICRC Commentary*, 170–1 (paras. 539–40).

[91] Cf. Article 21 in conjunction with Article 8, lit. g and h, AP I. See also Article 35 GC I.

The respect and protection of medical units and medical vehicles does not prevent them from ever being requisitioned. However, in such cases, a number of important limitations apply. The *rationale* of these limitations is that the medical needs of wounded and sick persons remain satisfied. First, the personnel of requisitioned medical units must be allowed to freely pursue their duties, as long as the capturing power has not itself ensured the necessary care of the wounded and sick found in such units.[92] In other words, such personnel are protected as part of the medical unit, notwithstanding additional rules, which apply to them specifically as medical personnel (see below, Sections 613 *et seq.*). Second, the material, buildings and stores of medical units of the armed forces of the adversary may not be diverted from their purpose as long as they are required for the care of the wounded and sick. This is subject to the exception that commanders in the field may make use of them, in case of urgent military necessity, although they may only do so if previous arrangements are made for the welfare of the wounded and sick who are nursed in them.[93] Third, property of aid societies may not be requisitioned except in case of urgent necessity, and only after the welfare of the wounded and sick has been ensured.[94] Fourth, the law of occupation subjects the power of an occupying power to requisition medical units to stringent conditions. Underlying this regulatory framework is the general responsibility of an occupying power for ensuring and maintaining the medical and hospital establishments and services, public health, and hygiene in territory occupied by it.[95] Accordingly, when an occupying power requisitions civilian hospitals in occupied territory, such seizure may only be temporary and must be urgently necessary for the care of military wounded and sick. Furthermore, requisitioning civilian hospitals under the aforementioned conditions is only permissible if and when suitable arrangements are made in due time for the care and treatment of the patients and for the needs of the civilian population for hospital accommodation. In any case, the material and stores of civilian hospitals cannot be requisitioned so long as they are necessary for the needs of the civilian population.[96] Article 14 AP I imposes further obligations on an occupying power vis-à-vis the requisitioning of civilian medical units. It is unlawful to requisition any resources, which are indispensable to the proper functioning of medical units, including their equipment, materiel, or the services of their personnel, as long as the seizing of such resources would render it impossible to provide adequate medical services and care. Requisition is nevertheless rendered unlawful if the resources are used for purposes other than the adequate and immediate medical treatment of the wounded and sick members of the armed forces of the occupying power or of prisoners of war. In addition, the requisition of these resources must cease as soon as the necessity of their use disappears. However, even if the aforementioned conditions are met, requisitioning civilian medical units and their resources is lawful only if immediate arrangements are made to ensure that the medical needs of the civilian population, as well as those of any wounded and sick under treatment who are affected by the requisition, continue to be satisfied.

---

[92] Article 19, para. 1, 2nd sentence, GC I.
[93] Article 33, paras. 1 and 2, GC I.
[94] Article 34 GC I.
[95] Cf. Article 56 GC IV, and also Article 55 GC IV. This responsibility is reiterated in Article 14, para. 1, AP I. For an analysis of the differences in wording between the provisions in GC IV and Article 14, para. 1, AP I, see *ICRC Commentary*, 182–3 (paras. 580–4).
[96] Article 57 GC IV.

JANN K. KLEFFNER

Medical units and transports lose their protection if they are used to commit, outside their humanitarian function, acts harmful to the enemy, but only after a due warning has been given and such warning has remained unheeded (Article 21 GC I; Article 19, para. 1, GC IV; Articles 13, paras. 1, 21 AP I; Article 11, para. 2, AP II).

1. The conditions under which medical units and transports lose their protection differ in some important respects from the condition for the status of wounded, sick, and shipwrecked persons to abstain from any act of hostility (above Sections 601–602). The first such difference is that the notion of 'acts of hostilities' is narrower than 'acts harmful to the enemy'. The latter include all acts, the purpose or effect of which is to harm the adversary by facilitating or impeding military operations,[97] so that the use of medical units and transports for acts, which do not amount to acts of hostilities may nevertheless entail that the unit or transport loses its protection, provided that due warning has been given.[98] Often-cited examples of acts harmful to the enemy are the installation of an observation post on a hospital roof or a firing position in a medical post, sheltering able-bodied combatants in a medical unit or transport, using medical units as a weapons or ammunitions dump or an ambulance to transport weapons or ammunitions, or the siting of a medical unit or transport so as to impede the military operations of enemy armed forces.[99] Indeed, these and other acts harmful to the enemy do not only entail the loss of protection, but also amount to violations of international humanitarian law, which may be punishable as the war crimes of making improper use of the distinctive emblems of the Geneva Conventions if its results in death or serious personal injury[100] or of perfidy if it results in the death, injury, or capture of an adversary.[101]

At the same time, international humanitarian law expressly excludes certain acts from being considered 'harmful to the enemy', namely:

— that the personnel of the unit are equipped with, or use, light individual weapons for their own defence or for that of the wounded and sick in their charge;
— that medical units or transports are protected by sentries or by an escort;
— that small arms taken from the wounded and sick, and not yet handed to the proper service, are found in the units or transports; and
— that members of the armed forces or other combatants are in the unit or transport for medical reasons.[102]

2. However, the fact alone that medical units or transports are used for harmful acts is not enough for them to be deprived of their protection. A first additional condition that must be met is that such a harmful act is committed 'outside their humanitarian function'. This condition conversely implies that certain acts, which may be considered harmful to the enemy, may nevertheless not entail a loss of protection because they are committed in fulfilment of the humanitarian function of the medical unit or transport in question. Thus, an ambulance which is unable to move because it has run out of petrol

---

[97] Pictet, *Commentary*, Vol. I, 200.
[98] *ICRC Commentary*, 175 (para. 551).
[99] Cf. id. See also the examples provided in the military manuals of Argentina, the Netherlands, South Africa, Switzerland, and the US, *CIHL*, Vol. II/1, 537–43 (paras. 595, 609, 612, 614, and 619).
[100] Cf. Article 8, para. 2, lit. b (vii), ICC Statute.
[101] Article 85, para. 3, lit. f, AP I.
[102] Cf. Article 22, para. 2, GC I; Article 35, para. 3, GC II; Articles 13, para. 2, and 19, para. 2, AP I.

JANN K. KLEFFNER

and thereby impedes the military operation of the enemy does not lose its protection, for example, nor does a medical unit whose electronic medical equipment happens to interfere with the military communications of the enemy armed forces.[103]

3. As a second condition before an attack on a medical unit or transport, which is used to commit acts harmful to the enemy outside its humanitarian function, becomes lawful is that due warning be given and that warning has remained unheeded. The aim of this warning is to reconcile the military necessity to attack medical units and transport, which are abused for military purposes, with the humanitarian concern for those who are in need of medical assistance or care and others who use the unit or transport for legitimate, that is medical, purposes. There is no requirement as to the form in which such a warning has to be given, but the warning must, in all appropriate cases, name a reasonable time limit. When cases are to be considered 'appropriate' and what is to be considered a 'reasonable' time limit is context-specific. An obvious case in which it would not be appropriate to issue a warning is that of a medical transport, which approaches a military checkpoint while firing upon those manning the checkpoint. Needless to say, even in such a case, where those manning the checkpoint can return fire without issuing a warning, they must comply with the principle of proportionality and thus seek to avoid and minimize incidental loss of life of and injury to any wounded or sick person within such a transport. If a warning is appropriate, on the other hand, the requirement that a 'reasonable time limit' be set entails that the period of respite must be long enough either to allow the harmful acts to be stopped or for the wounded and sick inside the medical unit or transport to be evacuated.[104]

IV. Medical Personnel

613   'Medical personnel' means those persons assigned, by a party to the conflict, exclusively to medical purposes or to the administration of medical units or to the operation or administration of medical transports. Such assignments may be either permanent or temporary. The term includes:

  i) medical personnel of a party to the conflict, whether military or civilian, including those described in the First and Second Conventions, and those assigned to civil defence organizations;
  ii) medical personnel of national Red Cross (Red Crescent) societies and other national voluntary aid societies duly recognized and authorized by a party to the conflict;
  iii) medical personnel made available to a party to the conflict for humanitarian purposes by a neutral or other state which is not a party to that conflict; by a recognized and authorized aid society of such a state; and by an impartial international humanitarian organization (Articles 24–26 GC I; Articles 36 GC II; Articles 8, lit. c, and 9, para. 2. AP I).

1. The definition of 'medical personnel' in the present section flows from AP I and the identical definition under customary international humanitarian law.[105] It consolidates and expands the definitions in GCs I and II and earlier instruments, which only apply to

---

[103] *ICRC Commentary*, 175 (para. 552).
[104] Pictet, *Commentary*, Vol. I, 202.
[105] Cf. Rule 25 *CIHL*, Summary, Vol. I, 81–2.

medical personnel serving the armed forces.[106] It further goes beyond the protection provided in accordance with Article 20 GC IV, which only applied to the medical personnel of civilian hospitals. In order to qualify as 'medical personnel' under Article 8, lit. c, AP I, persons must be assigned to those medical purposes, which are mentioned in connection to the definition of 'medical units' in Article 8, lit. e, that is the search for, collection, transportation, diagnosis or treatment of the wounded, sick, and shipwrecked, or for the prevention of disease. However, with a view to avoid abuse of the distinctive emblem for military or other purposes, these categories of persons must be assigned to the aforementioned tasks 'exclusively', that is they must be their sole tasks.[107] In addition, those who are engaged in the administration of medical units or to the operation or administration of medical transports also qualify as 'medical personnel'. The formal status of medical personnel—and the entitlement to the protection that this status entails—is nevertheless contingent on the assignment of a party to the armed conflict. This is especially relevant for civilian medical personnel. Persons engaged in the medical care of others, while not being members of the armed forces, may not automatically be assumed to also fulfil that task vis-à-vis the wounded and sick during armed conflicts.[108] Although the civilian population and aid societies have the right to collect and care for the wounded and sick on their own initiative,[109] they will not enjoy the protection of 'medical personnel' absent the official assignment of medical tasks by the competent authority. While no corresponding definition of 'medical personnel' exists in treaty law applicable to non-international armed conflict, the drafting history of AP II suggests that the aforementioned definition equally applies.[110]

2. The following observations are warranted in relation to the three categories of 'medical personnel' mentioned in Article 8, lit. c(i)–(iii). The first category consists of medical personnel of a party to the conflict. This category includes permanent medical personnel of the armed forces and auxiliary medical personnel of the armed forces mentioned in GC I.[111] Further included are medical and hospital personnel of hospital ships and their crews to whom GC II applies.[112] The first category also comprises civilian medical personnel and medical personnel assigned to civil defence organizations. The latter organizations are subject to detailed regulation in Part IV, Chapter VI (Articles 61–67) AP I. Their personnel, which can be civilian or military,[113] may fulfil a variety of tasks, but enjoy the protection of medical personnel only if they are assigned by the party to the conflict to the performance of medical services.[114]

The second category of protection personnel of national Red Cross societies and other recognized relief societies had already been recognized in accordance with Article 26 GC I and Article 24 GC II. The question arises as to the requirements that these societies must fulfil in order for their medical personnel to come within the notion of 'medical personnel' as defined in Article 8, lit. c(ii), AP I. The provision requires such

---

[106] Cf. Articles 24, 25, 26, para. 1 GC I, Article 36 GC II.
[107] *ICRC Commentary*, 125 (para. 353).
[108] Ibid. para. 354.
[109] Cf. Article 17, para. 1, 2nd sentence, AP I; see also above, Section 605.
[110] Cf. Rule 25 *CIHL*, Summary, Vol. I, 82–3.
[111] Articles 24–5.
[112] Article 36.
[113] As to the latter, cf. Article 67 AP I.
[114] For an enumeration of other tasks of civil defence organizations, see Article 61, lit. a, AP I.

organizations to be *national* societies (i.e. they must be established in the territory of the party to the conflict concerned); they must be *recognized* by that party (i.e. they must have been regularly constituted in accordance with national legislation); and they must be *authorized* (i.e. the party to the conflict must agree that personnel of these societies are employed as medical personnel).[115] Article 26 GC I further requires staff of these national aid societies to be subject to military laws and regulations of their government. States must notify each other about the societies which they have thus authorized.

The third category comprises three sub-categories of permanent medical personnel made available to a party to the conflict by third states or impartial international humanitarian organizations with the previous consent of both their own government and the party to the conflict concerned.[116] The first two of these sub-categories broadly correspond to the first two aforementioned categories (medical personnel of a state and of a national aid society). The third sub-category then extends the definition to medical personnel of an impartial international humanitarian organization. The requirement that such an organization be 'impartial' denotes that it makes no adverse distinction founded on any ground, including nationality, race, religious beliefs, class or political opinions, and that the only ground for discriminating between different persons is the urgency and degree of need of medical care of them.[117] As such the impartiality requirement is a further encapsulation of the general principle of non-discrimination (see above Section 603). In order to be considered 'humanitarian', such an organization also 'must be concerned with the condition of man, considered solely as a human being without regard to the value which he represents as a military, political, professional or other unit'.[118]

614   **Medical personnel shall be respected and protected in all circumstances (Articles 24 and 25 GC I; Articles 36 and 37 GC II; Article 15 AP I; Article 9 AP II). It is prohibited to punish persons for carrying out medical activities compatible with medical ethics or to compel persons engaged in medical activities to perform acts or to carry out work contrary to the rules of medical ethics (Article 16 AP I; Article 10 AP II).**

1. As regards the content of the general obligation to respect and protect medical personnel, reference is made to Section 603 above, which apply *mutatis mutandis*. In addition, the applicable rules provide further detail as to how such respect for and protection of medical personnel is to be implemented. AP I sets forth the obligation to grant all available help needed to civilian medical personnel in an area where civilian medical services are disrupted by reason of combat activity.[119] In a similar vein, an occupying power must also render assistance to civilian medical personnel in occupied territory.[120] A comparable obligation applies in non-international armed conflict, where parties to an armed conflict are obliged to grant all available help for the performance of the duties of medical personnel.[121] In contrast to AP I, however, AP II does not provide for the right of civilian medical personnel to be granted access to any place where their services are

[115] *ICRC Commentary*, 126–7 (para. 358).
[116] Cf. Article 9, para. 2, AP I in conjunction with Article 27, para. 1, GC I.
[117] Cf. also Pictet, *The Fundamental Principles of the Red Cross* (above n. 25) II. Impartiality.
[118] Pictet, *Commentary*, Vol. I, 108.
[119] Article 15, para. 2, AP I.
[120] Article 15, para. 3, AP I.
[121] Article 9, para. 1, 1st sentence, AP II.

JANN K. KLEFFNER

essential, albeit subject to such supervisory and safety measures as the relevant party to the conflict may be necessary.[122]

2. Further, rules protect medical duties. In addition to those provisions, which stipulate that priority in the treatment of the wounded and sick must be based on no grounds other than medical ones, and the general interdiction to compel medical personnel to carry out tasks which are incompatible with their humanitarian mission,[123] Article 16 AP I and Article 10 AP II establish a detailed protective framework for medical personnel to be able to act in accordance with medical ethics. This framework consists of three distinct prohibitions: the prohibition of punishing medical personnel for fulfilling their medical duties, the prohibition of coercing them to act contrary to theses duties, and the prohibition to compel them to disclose information concerning the wounded and sick if they deem that information to be harmful to the patients concerned or their families. The first two of these prohibitions also entail that medical personnel have the right to refuse to obey an illegal order.[124] The precise content of the third prohibition applicable in international armed conflict differs from that applicable in non-international armed conflict. In the former case, the prohibition is subject to two exceptions, namely that medical personnel must disclose information on wounded and sick in their care to their own party to the conflict, if such a duty is imposed on them by virtue of that party's national law, and that medical personnel must comply with regulations that oblige them to notify communicable diseases. In contrast, medical confidentiality is subject more generally to any national law during a non-international armed conflict. Consequently, medical personnel may be compelled to disclose information on their patients if domestic law so provides, with all potential negative consequences for the patients that such a disclosure might entail.

3. The references in Article 16 AP I and Article 10 AP II to 'medical ethics' raise the question as to the content of these ethical standards, as they derive from relevant instruments, including the Hippocratic Oath and its modern version, the Declaration of Geneva (also referred to as 'Geneva Oath') adopted by the World Medical Association[125] and its supplementary Code of Medical Ethics.[126] In addition, a number of documents have specifically been drafted with a view to identify medical ethics in times of armed conflicts, most importantly the Regulations in Time of Armed Conflict of the World Medical Association[127] and the Rules Governing the Care of Sick and Wounded, Particularly in

[122] Article 15, para. 4, AP I.
[123] Article 12, para. 3, GC I and II; Article 33 GC III; Article 56 GC IV; Articles 10, para. 2, and 15, para. 3, AP I; Article 9, para. 2, AP II.
[124] Solf, above (n. 49) 237–48, at 244.
[125] Adopted by the 2nd General Assembly of the World Medical Association, Geneva, Switzerland, September 1948, amended by the 22nd World Medical Assembly, Sydney, Australia, August 1968 and the 35th World Medical Assembly, Venice, Italy, October 1983 and the 46th WMA General Assembly, Stockholm, Sweden, September 1994, and editorially revised at the 170th Council Session, Divonne-les-Bains, France, May 2005 and the 173rd Council Session, Divonne-les-Bains, France, May 2006.
[126] Adopted by the 3rd General Assembly of the World Medical Association, London, England, October 1949, and amended by the 22nd World Medical Assembly Sydney, Australia, August 1968 and the 35th World Medical Assembly Venice, Italy, October 1983 and the WMA General Assembly, Pilanesberg, South Africa, October 2006.
[127] Adopted by the 10th World Medical Assembly, Havana, Cuba, October 1956, *edited* by the 11th World Medical Assembly, Istanbul, Turkey, October 1957, and *amended* by the 35th World Medical Assembly,

Time of Conflict.[128] Accordingly, medical personnel's primary obligations are to their patients and they are *inter alia* obliged to always exercise their independent professional judgement and maintain the highest standards of professional conduct; respect a competent patient's right to accept or refuse treatment; not allow their judgement to be influenced by personal profit or unfair discrimination; be dedicated to providing competent medical service in full professional and moral independence, with compassion and respect for human dignity; and act in the patient's best interest when providing medical care. Furthermore, it is, among others, deemed unethical for medical personnel to give advice or perform prophylactic, diagnostic, or therapeutic procedures that are not justifiable for the patient's health care; weaken the physical or mental strength of a human being without therapeutic justification; employ scientific knowledge to imperil health or destroy life; employ personal health information to facilitate interrogation; and condone, facilitate, or participate in the practice of torture or any form of cruel, inhuman, or degrading treatment.[129]

615   **Medical personnel lose their protection if they commit, outside their humanitarian function, acts harmful to the enemy.**

The notion of 'committing, outside their humanitarian function, acts harmful to the enemy' corresponds to the condition under which medical units and transports lose their protection. Reference is therefore made to Section 612 above.[130]

616   **Military medical personnel are medical personnel who are members of the armed forces. Military medical personnel are military non-combatants (Article 43, para. 2, AP I).**

617   **If military medical personnel and protection personnel of recognized national relief societies fulfilling the same duties fall into the hands of the adversary, they may be retained as long as the state of health and the number of prisoners of war so require. They will not themselves be regarded as prisoners of war. They will nevertheless benefit at least from all the provisions of GC III (Article 28 GC I; Article 37 GC II; Article 33 GC III).**

618   **Medical personnel whose retention is not indispensable for the care of prisoners of war shall be repatriated (Article 30 GC I; Article 37 GC II).**

1. Although military medical personnel mentioned in Articles 24 and 25 GC I are members of the armed forces, they do not have the right to participate directly in hostilities. Together with army chaplains, they thus constitute the exception to the rule that members of the armed forces are combatants entitled to prisoner-of-war status *and* treatment

---

Venice, Italy, October 1983 and the World Medical General Assembly, Tokyo 2004, and *editorially revised* at the 173rd Council Session, Divonne-les-Bains, France, May 2006.

[128] Adopted by the 10th World Medical Assembly, Havana, Cuba, October 1956, edited by the 11th World Medical Assembly, Istanbul, Turkey, October 1957, and amended by the 35th World Medical Assembly, Venice, Italy, October 1983.

[129] See generally on medical ethics in the context of armed conflicts, A. Baccino-Astrada, *Handbook on the Rights and Duties of Medical Personnel in Armed Conflicts* (ICRC/League, 1989), 36 *et seq*; Torelli, 'La protection du médecin dans les conflits armés' in Swinarski (ed.), above (n. 49) 581–601, at 585–92.

[130] Also cf. Rule 25, 2nd sentence *CIHL*, Vol. I, 85 (suggesting a separate rule on the loss of protection of medical personnel, whose content is analogous to the Rule on the loss of protection of medical units and transports).

JANN K. KLEFFNER

when they fall into the power of an adverse party. Their non-combatant status does not mean, however, that they must be repatriated immediately if they fall into the hands of the enemy, as used to be the case prior to the 1949 GCs.[131] Rather, they and protection personnel of recognized national relief societies fulfilling the same duties, may be retained if and for such time as the state of health and the number of prisoners of war require. In that case, permanent medical personnel of the armed forces and protection personnel of recognized national relief societies are not deemed prisoners of war, but entitled to treatment at least as beneficial as that granted in accordance with the provisions of GC III; they are, in other words, entitled to prisoner-of-war treatment as long as treatment under GC III is to their advantage.[132] During their retention, they must continue to carry out their medical duties on behalf of prisoners of war, preferably those of the armed forces to which they themselves belong, while being subject to the military laws and regulations of the detaining power.[133] In the context of fulfilling these duties, the detaining power is obliged to grant them certain facilities and privileges. These include the authorization to periodic visits of prisoners of war in labour units and hospitals outside the prisoners-of-war camp, and the privilege not to be made to work outside their medical duties.[134] In each camp, the senior officer is answerable to the camp authorities for the work of medical personnel. In order to avoid uncertainty about the rank of medical personnel the parties shall reach agreement at the beginning of the conflict.[135] Importantly, Article 28, para. 4, GC I and Article 33, para. 4, GC III remind the detaining power that retention of medical personnel is no substitute for the fulfilment of its own duties with regard to the medical welfare of prisoners of war.

2. In contrast to permanent medical personnel of the armed forces and protection personnel of recognized national relief societies fulfilling the same duties, auxiliary medical personnel of the armed forces mentioned in Article 25 GC I do become prisoners of war if they fall into the hands of the enemy. They too must be employed on their medical duties in so far as the need arises.[136]

3. Article 32 GC I provides that the personnel of aid societies of neutral states shall not be retained if they fall into the hands of the adverse party. Unless otherwise agreed, they must be permitted to return to their country, or if this is impossible, to the territory of the party to the conflict in whose service they were. The same applies to other permanent medical personnel made available to a party to the conflict by third states or by impartial international humanitarian organizations, referred to in Article 9, para. 2, AP I.[137]

4. As to the personnel of hospital ships, see below, Section 1063.

5. As soon as the retention of medical personnel for the treatment of prisoners of war is no longer required they shall be repatriated. The selection of personnel to be repatriated

---

[131] Cf. Article 3 of the 1864 Geneva Convention and Article 12 of the 1906 Geneva Convention. On the evolution of the current regulation in GC I to III, see Pictet, above (n. 33) at 199.
[132] Pictet, *Commentary*, Vol. I, 243, 252–7.
[133] Article 28, para. 2, GC I; Article 33, para. 2, GC III.
[134] Article 28, para. 2, lit. b and c, GC I; Article 33, para. 2, lit. b and c, GC III.
[135] Article 28, para. 2 lit. a, GC I; Article 33, para. 2 lit. a, GC III.
[136] Article 29 GC I.
[137] Cf. Article 9, para. 2, AP I in conjunction with Article 32 GC I.

JANN K. KLEFFNER

must not be discriminatory. Preferably, those who were retained first and those whose state of health so requires should be given priority.[138]

619   Medical personnel must identify themselves

See below, Sections 628–631.

V. Medical Aircraft

620   Medical aircraft are military or civilian aircraft, designed exclusively for medical transport on a permanent or temporary basis and subordinate to a competent authority of a party to the conflict. As well as the national emblem they must carry the distinctive emblem on their wings and hull and may not be attacked (Article 39 GC II; Articles 26, para. 1, and 29 AP I).

1. *Definition* (Article 39, para. 1, GC II and Article 8, lit. j and g, AP I). Any aircraft, independent of ownership or prior design and function may become a medical aircraft if assigned exclusively to the aerial transportation of wounded, sick, and shipwrecked and/or the aerial transport of medical personnel, medical equipment, or medical supplies. Hence, medical aircraft may either be owned by the armed forces, leased, requisitioned, or belong to a relief organization.[139] Although this section as well as the relevant provisions of AP I are limited to medical transport, there are convincing reasons to include into the category of medical aircraft those aircraft that are also designed for the medical treatment of sick and wounded (MedEvac).[140] It is important to note, however, that search-and-rescue aircraft, especially aircraft assigned to combat search-and-rescue operations do not qualify as medical aircraft. In order to qualify, an aircraft must be exclusively assigned to one of the humanitarian tasks just mentioned. The performance of other tasks, for example the transport of troops, would deprive the aircraft of its protected status. Moreover, the assignment to the protected function must be given by a competent authority and the aircraft must, for the duration of the assignment, remain under the control of a party to the conflict. The rationale of that requirement is to ensure that medical aircraft are operated for the said humanitarian purposes only and that there is a subject of international law bearing responsibility in case the aircraft is abused. The assignment may be permanent or temporary. It is permanent if the aircraft is to serve the said purposes 'for an indeterminate period'; it is temporary, if limited to a given period of time.

2. *Protection*. Article 24 AP I provides: 'Medical aircraft shall be respected and protected, subject to the Rules of this Part.' The obligation to respect is not limited to a prohibition of attacks against medical aircraft. Rather, it implies a prohibition of impeding or preventing the medical aircraft from performing its humanitarian functions. The obligation to protect is positive in character insofar as the parties to the conflict must take all feasible measures to ensure others, especially non-state actors, do respect the protected status and the genuinely humanitarian function. However, in view of the characteristics of aircraft the obligation is not absolute in character, as medical aircraft are accorded

[138] Articles 30–1 GC I.
[139] See J. S. Pictet, *Commentary*, Vol. II (ICRC, 1960), 216.
[140] See *HPCR Manual*, commentary accompanying Rule 1(u), para. 3.

protected status only if they are flying at the altitude and time and on the route specifically agreed upon between the parties to the conflict.[141] In the absence of such agreement they may not fly over enemy or enemy-occupied territories.[142] The respect and protection of medical aircraft is not dependent upon any agreement in and over land areas physically controlled by friendly forces, or in and over sea areas not physically controlled by an adverse party (Article 25 AP I). Still, for greater safety in these areas, according to the second sentence of Article 25 AP I, a party to the conflict is advised to notify the adverse party, particularly when such aircraft will come within range of surface-to-air weapons systems of the adverse party. In and over those parts of the contact zone (i.e. any area on land where the forward elements of opposing forces are in contact with each other)[143] which are physically controlled by friendly forces and in and over those areas where control is not clearly established, protection for medical aircraft can be fully effective only by prior agreement between the competent military authorities of the parties to the conflict.[144] Although, in the absence of such an agreement, medical aircraft operate at their own risk, they shall nevertheless be respected after they have been recognized as such.

A medical aircraft which flies over an area physically controlled by the enemy without, or in breach of the terms of, an agreement, either through navigational error or because of an emergency affecting the safety of the flight, shall make every effort to identify itself and to inform the enemy of the circumstances. As soon as such medical aircraft has been recognized, the enemy is obliged to undertake all reasonable efforts which enable it to land or alight on water, or to take other measures to safeguard its own interests, and, in either case, to allow the aircraft time for compliance before resorting to attack.[145]

Upon alighting involuntarily on land or water in enemy or enemy occupied territory, the wounded, sick, and shipwrecked, as well as the crew of the aircraft, shall be prisoners of war. The medical personnel continue to be protected.[146]

3. *Markings.* According to Article 39, para. 2, GC II, medical aircraft shall be clearly marked with the distinctive emblem, together with their national colours, on their lower, upper, and lateral surfaces. They shall also be provided with any other markings or means of identification which may be agreed upon between the parties to the conflict. Such technical means of identification, according to the regulations of Annex I to AP I, may include the flashing blue light,[147] the radio signal,[148] and the Secondary Surveillance Radar (SSR) system.[149,150] As in the case of hospital ships and other medical vessels, markings are merely intended to facilitate identification and do not themselves confer protected status.[151]

---

[141] Article 39, para. 1, GC II.
[142] Article 39, para. 3, GC II; Article 27 AP I.
[143] Article 26, para. 2, AP I.
[144] Article 26, para. 1, AP I. See also *HPCR Manual*, Rule 78(a); Bothe, in Bothe/Partsch/Solf, *New Rules for Victims of Armed Conflicts* (Nijhoff, 1982), 149 *et seq.*
[145] Article 27, para. 2, AP I. See also *HPCR Manual*, Rule 78.
[146] Article 39, para. 5, GC II.
[147] Article 6, Annex I, to AP I.
[148] Article 7, Annex I, to AP I.
[149] Article 8, Annex I, to AP I.
[150] See also the recommendations in *ICRC Manual for the use of technical means of identification* by hospital ships, coastal rescue craft, other protected craft and medical aircraft (ICRC, 1995).
[151] See also *San Remo Manual*, para. 176; *HPCR Manual*, Rule 76(d).

WOLFF HEINTSCHEL VON HEINEGG

621   The parties to a conflict are prohibited from using their medical aircraft to gain any military advantage over an adversary. The presence of medical aircraft shall not be used in an attempt to render military objectives immune from attack (Article 28 AP I).

Medical aircraft, like hospital ships and other protected vessels, must not be used to commit acts harmful to the enemy. This customary principle has now been codified in Article 28 AP I.[152] They lose their protected status if they carry any equipment intended to collect or transmit intelligence data.[153] However, they may 'be equipped with encrypted communications equipment intended solely for navigation, identification and communication consistent with the execution of [their] humanitarian mission'.[154] Medical aircraft shall not be armed, except for small arms for self-defence.[155] They may, however, be 'equipped with deflective means of defence (such as chaff or flares)'.[156]

A medical aircraft that loses its exemption as described above is liable to capture. It may be attacked only if:[157] (a) diversion for landing, inspection and search, and possible capture, is not feasible; (b) no other method is available for exercising military control; (c) the non-compliance is sufficiently grave that the aircraft has become, or may reasonably be assumed to be, a military objective; and (d) the collateral casualties or damage will not be disproportionate to the military advantage gained or anticipated.

In cases of doubt as to whether a medical aircraft is being used to make an effective contribution to military action, it shall be presumed not to be so used.[158]

622   Medical aircraft may be ordered to land, whether on land or on water, to permit inspection. The inspection shall be commenced without delay and shall be conducted expeditiously. The inspecting party shall not require the wounded and sick to be taken off the aircraft unless this is essential for inspection. In any event, the inspecting party shall ensure that the condition of the wounded and sick is not adversely affected (Article 30, para. 2, AP I).

The right to order a medical aircraft to alight on land or water is expressed in Article 39, para. 4, GC II and Article 30, paras. 1 and 2, AP I.[159] Its purpose is to enable belligerents to verify whether such aircraft are in fact innocently employed in their normal role. In any event, the condition of the wounded and sick on board shall not be adversely affected.

623   If inspection discloses that the aircraft does not meet the requirements for special protection or has acted in breach of its obligations, it may be seized. An aircraft which has been assigned as a permanent medical aircraft and is seized may be used thereafter only as a medical aircraft (Article 30, para. 4, AP I).

---

[152] See also Bothe, in Bothe/Partsch/Solf (above, n. 144), 157 *et seq*; *San Remo Manual*, para. 178.

[153] *HPCR Manual*, Rule 81.

[154] Ibid. See also the statement made by the UK upon ratification of AP I in respect of Article 28, para. 2 AP I: 'Given the practical need to make use of non-dedicated aircraft for medical evacuation purposes, the UK does not interpret this paragraph as precluding the presence on board of communications equipment and encryption materials or the use thereof solely to facilitate navigation, identification or communication in support of medical transportation as defined in Article 8(f).'

[155] Article 28, para. 3, AP I; *San Remo Manual*, para. 178.

[156] *HPCR Manual*, Rule 82.

[157] Ibid. para. 57.

[158] *San Remo Manual*, para. 58.

[159] See also *HPCR Manual*, Rule 80(a).

WOLFF HEINTSCHEL VON HEINEGG

As in the case of protected vessels, any breach of the requirements for protection set out in the preceding paragraphs leads to loss of exemption of medical aircraft. They may then be captured and used for the captor's own purposes.[160] However, any aircraft captured which had been assigned as a permanent medical aircraft may be used thereafter only as a medical aircraft.[161]

VI. Hospital and Safety Zones and Localities; Neutralized Zones

Preliminary Remarks

1. International humanitarian law applicable in international armed conflicts provides for the establishment of different types of zones and localities, intended to provide protection to the wounded and sick from the effects of war. The first type of these zones and localities, namely hospital zones and localities established in accordance with Article 23 GC I, are *specifically* designed to provide such protection to the wounded and sick as well as medical personnel. By and large, the regulation of hospital *and safety* zones and localities under Article 14 GC IV closely resemble that for hospital zones and localities. One difference is, however, that hospital and safety zones and localities are also established for other categories of persons, who are not strictly speaking 'wounded' or 'sick', namely aged persons, children under fifteen, expectant mothers, and mothers of children under seven (hence the addition 'safety'). In the light of the broad definition of 'sick' and 'wounded' under AP I, which extends to all persons who may be in need of immediate medical assistance (see above, Section 601), the distinction between hospital zones and localities, on the one hand, and hospital and safety zones and localities, on the other, has become largely obsolete.[162]

2. The categories of potential beneficiaries of the second type of protected zones, neutralized zones established under Article 15 GC IV, are even broader than those of hospital and safety zones and localities. Neutralized zones can be established to shelter, in addition to wounded and sick combatants or non-combatants, all civilians who do not take part in hostilities and who perform no work of a military character while residing in such a neutralized zone.[163] Besides this difference in coverage, hospital and safety zones and localities are distinguishable from neutralized zones by a number of other features, which reflect the fact that neutralized zones are established in the regions where fighting is taking place and are more temporary in nature.[164]

3. Despite the possibility to establish hospital and safety zones and localities and neutralized zones in the Geneva Conventions, their relevance in actual practice has thus far been limited, notwithstanding the fact that various other types of protected zones

---

[160] *HPCR Manual*, Rule 80(c). As regards attacks on medical aircraft which have lost their protected status, see the commentary on Section 621.

[161] Article 40, para. 4, AP I. See also *HPCR Manual*, Rule 80(d).

[162] Y. Sandoz, in Institut Henri Dunant (ed.), 'Localités et Zones Sous Protection Spéciale', in *Quatre études du droit international humanitaire, Etudes présentées à la Dixième Table Ronde de l'Institut international de droit humanitaire*, San Remo, septembre 1984 (Institut Henri Dunant, 1985) 35–47, at 40.

[163] On the terminology and the distinction between the different types of zones and localities, see Pictet, *Commentary*, Vol. I, 206–7.

[164] Pictet, *Commentary*, Vol. IV (1958) 129.

JANN K. KLEFFNER

have been established in some armed conflicts, especially by, or on the initiative of, the ICRC.[165]

4. AP I adds two further types of protected zones, 'demilitarized zones' (Article 60 AP I) and non-defended localities (Article 59 AP I). Demilitarized zones and non-defended localities are primarily designed to enhance the general protection of the civilian population against the effects of hostilities. They are discussed above in Sections 512–513.

5. While treaty provisions on the institution of protected zones are not available in the law applicable during non-international armed conflicts, nothing prevents parties to such an armed conflict to agree to establish such zones.

624   **The parties to an armed conflict may agree to establish hospital and safety zones and localities to protect from the effects of the conflict the wounded and sick as well as personnel entrusted with the organization and administration of these zones and localities and with the care of the persons assembled therein (Article 23 and Annex I GC I; Article 14 and Annex I GC IV).**

1. Hospital and safety zones and localities can be established in time of peace or upon the outbreak and during the course of hostilities. However, their special protection during times of armed conflict are contingent on the agreement between the parties to the armed conflict. A blueprint for such an agreement, which states may, but are not obliged to use,[166] is annexed to both GC I and IV (Annex I). The absence of such an agreement is, of course, without prejudice to the general protection of a hospital and safety zone established in time of peace as a civilian object.

2. According to the Draft Agreement under both GC I and IV, all persons residing in a hospital and safety zone must refrain from any work directly connected with military operations or the production of war material.[167] Furthermore, the power establishing such a zone must do everything possible to prevent persons who have no right of residence therein from gaining entry.[168] Importantly, the Draft Agreement also sets forth four conditions, which a hospital and safety zone must fulfil. First, it must comprise only a small part of the territory governed by the power which has established it.[169] This rule is designed to forestall parties to an armed conflict immunizing large parts of territory under their control from military operations by establishing a hospital and safety zone. Second, hospital and safety zones must be thinly populated in relation to the possibilities of accommodation in them. However, in the case of a sudden increase in the number of persons, parties to an armed conflict are nevertheless left with the alternative

---

[165] For a discussion of various zones established during the armed conflicts in the Former Yugoslavia, see Lavoyer, in W. Biermann and M. Vadset (eds), *UN Peacekeeping in Trouble: Lessons Learned from the Former Yugoslavia—Peacekeepers' Views on the Limits and Possibilities of the United Nations in a Civil War-like Conflict* (Ashgate, 1998), 262–79, at 265–74. See also for a brief overview over ICRC practice in other conflicts, Sandoz, above (n. 162), 42–5.

[166] In the words of Article 23, para. 2, 2nd sentence, and Article 14, para. 2, 2nd sentence, parties to an armed conflict 'may for this purpose implement the provisions of the Draft Agreement [...], with such amendments as they may consider necessary'.

[167] Article 2 Draft Agreement, Annex I, GC I and IV.

[168] Ibid. Article 3.

[169] Ibid. Article 4, lit. a.

JANN K. KLEFFNER

to agree to the establishment of a neutralized zone in accordance with Article 15 GC IV.[170] Third, and hardly surprisingly, hospital and safety zones must be removed and free from all military objectives, or large industrial or administrative establishments.[171] If their purpose to enhance the protection of the wounded and sick is to be achieved, the need of removal from and absence of anything which is, or might be considered, a military objective is evident. Fourth, hospital and safety zones may not be situated in areas which, according to every probability, may become important for the conduct of the war.[172] The determination whether a given area qualifies as one which may become important will be difficult to be made, and may turn out to be wrong in hindsight. Much will depend on the strategy and tactics employed by the adversary and the geographical configuration of a state.[173]

3. In addition to the aforementioned conditions, hospital and safety zones must also comply with two obligations.[174] First, the lines of communication and means of transport that they possess must not be used for the transport of military personnel or material, even in transit. Second, hospital and safety zones may never be defended by military means.

4. The Draft Agreement further provides for the possibility of a system of control for the purpose of ascertaining if the zones fulfil the conditions and obligations by means of Special Commissions.[175] Their members, who are nominated by either the parties to the armed conflict or by the protecting powers, must have free access to the zones and be given the facilities for their duties of inspection.

5. The protecting powers and the International Committee of the Red Cross are invited to lend their good offices in order to facilitate the institution and recognition of hospital and safety zones and localities.[176] This includes the possibility for them to take the initiative and approach the parties to an armed conflict with a view to suggest the establishment of such zones and localities.[177]

Parties to an armed conflict may propose to establish, in the regions where fighting is taking place, neutralized zones (Article 15 GC IV).   625

As alluded to previously, a number of differences exist between neutralized zones, on the one hand, and hospital and safety zones and localities, on the other. In addition to their broader protective scope *ratione personae*, neutralized zones are established in the area where actual fighting is taking place, whereas hospital and safety zones and localities are to be far removed from such fighting. Neutralized zones can be proposed to an adverse party either directly (i.e. the adverse party makes such a proposal), or indirectly (i.e. the proposal comes from a neutral state or by a humanitarian organization).

---

[170] Pictet, *Commentary*, Vol. I, 419.
[171] Article 4, lit. c, Draft Agreement, Annex I, GC I and IV.
[172] Article 4, lit. d.
[173] Pictet, *Commentary*, Vol. I, 420.
[174] Article 5, Draft Agreement, Annex I, GC I and IV.
[175] Articles 8–10.
[176] Article 23, para. 3, GC I; Article 14, para. 3, GC IV.
[177] For the ICRC's role in that regard during the conflicts in the Former Yugoslavia, see J. P. Lavoyer, 'International Humanitarian Law, Protected Zones and the Use of Force' in Biermann and Vadset, above (n. 165), 262–79, at 267–72.

JANN K. KLEFFNER

What is more, Article 15, para. 2, GC IV specifies further procedural and formal steps towards an agreement on the institution of a neutralized zone. The agreement has to be in written form and must be signed by the representatives of the parties to the conflict. It must further specify the beginning and end of the neutralization of the zone, thus underlining the temporary nature of it. It has, however, been suggested that these steps should be regarded as mere recommendations rather than being mandatory, given the possibility that the neutralization of a zone may become of such urgency that compliance with the procedural and formal requirements should not be to the detriment of those who benefit from neutralized zones.[178] Practice seems to have borne out such a more flexible approach.[179] Again, as in the case of hospital and safety zones and localities, neutralized zones which do not satisfy the procedural and formal requirements under Article 15 GC IV are nevertheless entitled to the general protection granted to civilian objects, provided, of course, that they qualify as such.

626   **Hospital and safety zones and localities and neutralized zones shall not be the object of attack. They must be protected and respected at all times (Annex I, Article 11, GC I and Annex I, Article 11, GC IV).**

In contrast to the rules on wounded, sick, and shipwrecked, medical units and transports and medical personnel, Article 23 GC I and Articles 14 and 15 GC IV do not contain any express language, which prohibits attacks on hospital and safety zones and localities and neutralized zones. Nevertheless, such a prohibition is a logical consequence of the special protection that they enjoy under international humanitarian law and the general protection afforded to civilian objects. The same holds true for the obligation to respect and protect these zones. The wounded and sick and (certain categories of) civilians are the ultimate beneficiaries of the establishment of hospital and safety zones and localities and neutralized zones. As much as they themselves and persons and objects which are necessary to ensure their medical care must be respected and protected under all circumstances (see above Sections 603, 610, and 614), so must the zones in which they are assembled with a view to protect and shelter them from the effects of war. It should be recalled in that regard that the only express provisions to that effect in Article 11 of the Draft Agreement annexed to GC I and GC IV, is a recommendation as to the possible content of an agreement to establish a hospital or safety zone or locality. It is not mandatory for the parties to an armed conflict to include this provision into an agreement with a view to establish hospital and safety zones or localities, let alone neutralized zones.[180] Article 11 of the Draft Agreement can, therefore, not be assumed to be constitutive of the prohibition of attacking these zones and the obligation to respect and protect them. Should parties to an armed conflict for whatever reason decide not to include the model provision in Article 11 of the Draft Agreement into an agreement on the establishment of such zones, they would remain prohibited from attacking such a zone and obliged to respect and protect it. The obligation to respect and thus not to attack hospital and safety zones and localities and neutralized zones is further confirmed in military manuals,[181]

[178] Pictet, *Commentary*, Vol. IV, 132.
[179] Cf. above (n. 177).
[180] Id.
[181] Cf. *CIHL*, Vol. II, 673–8, §§ 9–17, 19, 24–26, 31–33 (Cameroon, Canada, Ecuador, France, Germany, Hungary, Italy, Madagascar, Spain, Sweden, Switzerland, and the US).

JANN K. KLEFFNER

and by the criminalization of such attacks in national legislation[182] and as a war crime under the ICC Statute.[183]

> **Hospital and safety zones and localities and neutralized zones shall be clearly marked (Annex I, Article 6, GC I and Annex I, Article 6, GC IV).**   627

See below, Sections 628 *et seq.*

VII. The Distinctive Emblem

The distinctive emblems of the Geneva Conventions and Additional Protocols are   628 the red cross, the red crescent, or the red crystal (a red frame in the shape of a square on edge) on a white ground(Article 38 GC I; Article 41 GC II; Article 8, para. 1, AP I; Article 12 AP II; Article 2, para. 2, AP III, see below Annex 'Distinctive Emblems', No. 1).

1. Until the adoption of the 1864 Geneva Convention, a great variety of symbols were used by the medical services of armed forces during armed conflicts. However, because these symbols were often unknown to the adverse party and did not enjoy any legal protection, disrespect of such symbols was common. In order to improve that situation, the 1864 Geneva Convention recognized for the first time a red cross on a white ground as a distinctive and uniform sign, to be adopted for hospitals, ambulances and evacuation parties, as well as for armlets issued by the military authorities and worn by military medical personnel.[184] Since then, the character and function of what is being referred to as 'distinctive emblem', as well as the persons it is meant to protect, and the regulation of its use, has evolved.[185] The underlying idea has nevertheless remained unchanged: the distinctive emblem is a visible sign of the neutral status and the protection granted by international humanitarian law to medical personnel and objects.

2. As a response to the practice of the Ottoman Empire to use the red crescent on a white background rather than the red cross during its war with Russia (1876–1878), the red crescent and the red lion and sun were recognized as distinctive emblems in addition to the red cross. The use of the new distinctive signs was restricted, however, to states that already used them, namely Turkey, Persia, and Egypt.[186] In the course of drafting the 1949 Geneva Conventions, attempts proved unsuccessful to introduce a new single symbol, to revert to using the single symbol of the red cross, and to recognize a new emblem in addition to the already existing ones (the red shield of David, which was used as the distinctive symbol of the Israeli armed forces' medical services). The three distinctive emblems already recognized thus became those of the 1949 Geneva Conventions,[187] and

---

[182] Ibid. 678–9, §§ 35–41 (Argentina, Colombia, Italy, El Salvador, Nicaragua, Poland, and Spain). See also the other national practice referred to ibid. 679.

[183] Cf. Article 8, para. 2, lit. b(ix) ICC Statute; D. Pfirter, in R. S. Lee (ed.), *The International Criminal Court—Elements of Crimes and Rules of Procedure and Evidence* (Transnational Publishers, 2001), 162 (referring *inter alia* to Article 23 GC I and Article 14 GC IV).

[184] Article 7 of the 1864 Geneva Convention.

[185] See generally, Bugnion, *The Emblem of the Red Cross: a Brief History* (ICRC, 1977).

[186] Cf. Article 19 of the 1929 Geneva Convention.

[187] Cf. Article 38 GC I, Article 41 GC II, Articles 18, 20–3 GC IV.

JANN K. KLEFFNER

later AP I and II.[188] The red lion and sun subsequently became obsolete for all practical purposes because the only state that ever used it, Iran, replaced it by the red crescent in 1980. The remaining two distinctive emblems continued to give rise to considerable controversy. Central to that controversy was the wish of some states and their relief societies to use both or neither of the recognized two distinctive emblems. In addition, in some armed conflicts, the emblems were wrongly perceived as having national, political, or religious connotations, thereby undermining respect for their neutrality. These problems led to the call, in 1992, by the ICRC for the creation of an additional emblem. That appeal was endorsed by the 1999 International Conference of the Red Cross and Red Crescent, which also called for the setting up of a working group to find 'a comprehensive and lasting solution acceptable to all parties in terms of substance and procedure'.[189] The ensuing process led to the adoption, in December 2005, of the Protocol Additional to the Geneva Conventions of 12 August 1949, and relating to the Adoption of an Additional Distinctive Emblem (AP III). AP III entered into force on 14 January 2007. In accordance with Article 2 of AP III, an additional emblem is created alongside the red cross and red crescent. The new emblem—known as the red crystal—consists of a red frame in the shape of a square on edge on a white ground. It may be used for the same purposes and under the same conditions as the other two distinctive emblems of the Geneva Conventions. All distinctive emblems enjoy equal status and are entitled to identical respect.[190]

3. One broadly distinguishes between two forms of using the distinctive emblems.[191] The first one, protective use, relates to their being used during armed conflicts as the visible sign of the protection granted to medical personnel and objects by the Conventions and Protocols. The second form of use is when the distinctive emblems symbolize, mainly during peacetime, persons, equipment, and activities affiliated with a Red Cross or the Red Crescent Society, without implying that they are placed under the protection of the Conventions or Protocols. This use is referred to as 'indicative use'.

629   **The distinctive emblem shall be used to identify medical and religious personnel, medical units and transports and medical equipment (Articles 39–43 GC I; Articles 41–43 GC II; Articles 18, paras. 3 and 4, 20, paras. 2 and 3, 21, and 22 para. 2 GC IV; Article 18 AP I; Article 12 AP II; Article 2 AP III).**

1. Medical and religious personnel mentioned in GC I and II must wear an armlet or brassard bearing the distinctive emblem. That armlet is to be issued and stamped by the military authority. Medical personnel referred to in Articles 24, 26, and 27 GC I and Articles 36 and 37 GC II, must also carry with them, and may not be deprived of,[192] a special identify card bearing the distinctive emblem. Similar rules require armlets and identity cards to be worn by permanent and temporary medical personnel of civilian hospitals in occupied territory and zones of military operations.[193] Instead of identity cards, auxiliary medical personnel of the armed forces mentioned in Article 25 GC I

---

[188] Cf. Article 8, para. l, AP I; Article 12 AP II.
[189] Resolution 3, adopted by the 27th International Conference of the Red Cross and Red Crescent, Geneva, 31 October to 6 November 1999, Annex, para. 1, lit. a.
[190] Cf. Article 2, paras. 1 and 3, AP III.
[191] Cf. Article 44 GC I.
[192] Cf. Article 40, para. 4, GC I.
[193] Article 20, paras. 2 and 3, GC IV.

JANN K. KLEFFNER

must carry with them military identity documents, which specify what special training they have received, the temporary character of the duties they are engaged in, and their authority for wearing the armlet.[194] The purpose of such identity cards and documents is that medical personnel are provided with a piece of evidence, which proves that they are entitled to the respect and protection that the distinctive emblem signifies, in case they fall into enemy hands.

2. The provisions in AP I on the identification of civilian medical and religious personnel are less categorical as regards the use of the same armlets and identity cards than the aforementioned rules. Although states are under the obligation to 'endeavour to ensure that medical and religious personnel and medical units and transports are identifiable',[195] Article 18, para. 3, AP I merely provides that '[i]n occupied territory and in areas where fighting is taking place or is likely to take place, civilian medical personnel and civilian religious personnel *should* be recognizable by the distinctive emblem and an identity card certifying their status.'[196] While this wording implies that the use of the distinctive emblem and identity card are not mandatory, it does not mean that civilian medical and religious personnel lose their protection in case such emblems and cards are not used.[197] Nevertheless, not to use them obviously increases the risks for civilian medical and religious personnel. In any case, Article 18, para. 3, AP I does not allow for the use of a different emblem other than the distinctive emblem if and when one is used.[198] Article 18, para. 3, also applies to the identification of medical personnel assigned to civil defence organizations.[199]

3. Article 40, paras. 2 and 3, GC I and Articles 1 and 2 of the 'Regulations concerning Identification' as amended on 30 November 1993, contained in Annex 1 to AP I, set forth a number of requirements, which identity cards issued to medical personnel must satisfy. These requirements relate, *inter alia*, to the information that they must contain (such as the name, date of birth, in what capacity the holder is entitled to the protection of the Conventions and of the Protocol, date of issuance) and to the way in which they have to be authenticated, namely by the stamp and signature of the competent authority. Identity cards must be uniform throughout the territory of each high-contracting party and, as far as possible, of the same type for all parties to the conflict. Both Annex II to GC I and the 'Regulations Concerning Identification' in AP I contain a model identity card, which parties to an armed conflict may use. Irrespective of whether they decide to adopt the model, they must inform each other about the identity card they use at the outbreak of hostilities. With respect to the issuance of identity cards to temporary medical civilian personnel, the formal requirements are less stringent. Such personnel may be called upon at short notice, leaving insufficient time for the issuance of identity cards which satisfy the same formal requirements as those issued to permanent medical personnel. In case it proves impossible to issue the same identity cards to them as to permanent

---

[194] Article 41 GC I.

[195] Article 18, para. 1, AP I.

[196] Emphasis added.

[197] *ICRC Commentary*, 228, para. 763.

[198] Ibid. Cf. also Article 5, para. 4, of the 'Regulations concerning Identification', Annex 1 to AP I (as amended on 30 November 1993), providing that medical and religious personnel carrying out their duties in the battle area shall, as far as possible, also wear headgear and clothing bearing the distinctive emblem.

[199] Article 66, para. 9, AP I. See also Article 15 of the 'Regulations concerning Identification', Annex 1 to AP I.

JANN K. KLEFFNER

medical personnel, temporary medical civilian personnel may instead be provided with a certificate signed by the competent authority certifying that the person to whom it is issued is assigned to duty as temporary personnel.[200]

4. Duly authorized personnel of the international Red Cross organizations are also permitted to make protective use of the distinctive emblems.[201] The same right is granted under AP III to the medical services and religious personnel participating in operations under the auspices of the UN, provided the participating states agree to do so.[202]

5. Medical units and transports must be marked with the distinctive sign with the consent of the competent authority.[203] With a view to enable parties to an armed conflict to make out medical objects from a distance and in good time, Articles 4 and 5 of the 'Regulations concerning Identification' in AP I further specify how such identification has to be implemented. The distinctive emblem shall be as large as appropriate under the circumstances. What is 'appropriate under the circumstances' depends on a variety of factors, including the weather, daytime, and the type of weapons used.[204] Whenever possible, the distinctive emblem must be displayed on a flat surface or on flags visible from as many directions and from as far away as possible. At night or when visibility is reduced, the distinctive emblem may be lighted or illuminated and it may also be made of materials rendering it recognizable by technical means of detection. Note, however, that there is no obligation to do so, in order not to compel a party to an armed conflict to provide enemy aircraft with landmarks which will assist them in attacking military objectives.[205] On the other hand, while the lack of illumination of medical units or transports may increase the risk of their being mistakenly targeted or incidentally damaged, it does not deprive medical establishments of the protection accorded to them by international law. Furthermore, Article 5 of the 'Regulations concerning Identification' contains a suggestion to the effect that the red part of the distinctive emblem should be painted on top of black primer paint in order to facilitate its identification, in particular by infrared instruments.[206]

6. Parties to an armed conflict may also use distinctive signals to identify medical units and transports.[207] These additional means of identification can consist of light and radio signals and electronic systems, such as the Secondary Surveillance Radar (SSR) system, as specified in Annex 10 to the Chicago Convention on International Civil Aviation of 7 December 1944.

7. Hospital zones and localities established under GC I must be marked by means of the distinctive emblem placed on the outer precincts and on the buildings.[208] Their marking at night by means of appropriate illumination is optional,[209] for the same reasons

---

[200] Cf. Article 3 of the 'Regulations concerning Identification', Annex 1 to AP.
[201] Cf. Article 44, para. 3, GC I; Article 4 AP III.
[202] Article 5 AP III.
[203] Article 42, para. 1, GC I; Article 18, para. 3, GC IV; Article 18, para. 4, AP I.
[204] For the summary of a number of tests on the visibility of the distinctive emblem under varying conditions and using modern technical means of observation, see G. C. Cauderay, 'Visibility of the distinctive emblem on medical establishments, units, and transports' (1990) 277 *IRRC* 295–321.
[205] Pictet, *Commentary*, Vol. I, 321–2.
[206] Article 5, para. 3, of the 'Regulations concerning Identification', Annex 1 to AP I.
[207] Cf. Article 18, para. 5, and Chapter III of Annex I to AP I.
[208] Article 6, 1st sentence, of the Draft Agreement, Annex I GC.
[209] Ibid. 2nd sentence.

JANN K. KLEFFNER

as in the case of medical units. The marking of hospital and safety zones established in accordance with GC IV is slightly different. Article 6 of the Draft Agreement in Annex I GC IV only foresees an obligation of parties to an armed conflict to mark them by means of oblique red bands on a white ground, placed on the buildings and outer precincts. When such zones are reserved exclusively for the wounded and sick, their marking by the distinctive emblem is optional. Since the GCs are silent on the marking of neutralized zones, everything is left to the solution found in the agreement establishing such a zone. States are nevertheless not precluded from agreeing on a solution similar to the one foreseen for hospital and safety zones and localities.[210]

8. On the identification of hospital ships, see above, Sections 620–623.

> In times of peace, the distinctive emblem may also be used by national Red Cross   630
> or Red Crescent societies, the international Red Cross organizations and their duly
> authorized personnel and, in exceptional circumstances, to identify ambulances
> and aid stations providing free treatment to the wounded and sick (Article 44,
> paras. 2–4, GC I, Article 3 AP III).

Article 44, paras. 2–4, regulates three forms of 'indicative use' of the distinctive emblem. First, national Red Cross, Red Crescent or (in the future possible) Red Crystal societies may make use of the distinctive emblems in times of peace only in accordance with national legislation, but only for such activities which are in conformity with the fundamental principles laid down by the International Red Cross Conferences.[211] The distinctive emblem may under these conditions be used, for example, to show that persons or objects belong to a Red Cross or Red Crescent society, or for decorative purposes. Importantly, Article 44, para. 2, also allows such indicative use to continue in time of war, provided that it is done in a way so that it cannot be considered as conferring the protection of the GCs and APs. One compulsory measure to avoid confusion is that the emblem, if used for indicative purposes in times of armed conflict, must be smaller in size than the distinctive emblem used for protective purposes. However, the indicative use of the distinctive emblem on armlets or the roof of buildings is prohibited in times of armed conflicts.[212] Second, the international Red Cross organizations and their duly authorized personnel may also make indicative use of the distinctive emblem at all times.[213] Third, indicative use is permissible for the identification of ambulances and to mark aid stations providing free treatment. This indicative use is subject to rigorous conditions. National legislation must allow for it and it must be expressly authorized by the national Red Cross or Red Crescent society. Furthermore, a prerequisite for the indicative use of the distinctive emblem for aid stations is that they are exclusively assigned to the purpose of giving free treatment to the wounded and sick. Indicative use in relation to ambulances and aid stations is restricted to peacetime and must cease as soon as hostilities break out.[214]

> States are obliged to supervise the use of the distinctive emblems and signals and   631
> shall prevent and repress any misuse thereof (Articles 53, 54 GC I; Article 45 GC

---

[210] Pictet, *Commentary*, Vol. IV, 133–4.
[211] Article 44, para. 2, 1st sentence, GC I.
[212] Ibid. 2nd sentence.
[213] Article 44, para. 3.
[214] Article 44, para. 4.

JANN K. KLEFFNER

II; Articles 18, para. 8, 37–8, 85, para. 3, lit. f, AP I; Article 6 AP III; Article 23, lit. f, HagueReg).

1. Any improper use of the distinctive emblem is prohibited.[215] In order to enforce this prohibition, states must take all the necessary measures, including those of a legislative nature,[216] for the prevention and repression of abuses of the distinctive signs. These obligations rest upon states irrespective of whether the abuse concerns the protective or indicative purpose served by the distinctive emblem, although the former type of misuse generally entails more serious consequences, including the mandatory criminalization as a grave breach of AP I, if such misuse amounts to an act of perfidy[217] (for further detail on the prohibition of perfidy, and its distinction from ruses of war, see above, Sections 480–482). The obligation to take the appropriate legislative measures to make (certain types of) the misuse of the distinctive emblem punishable is amongst the earliest examples of such an obligation, having already been included in the 1906[218] and 1929[219] Geneva Conventions.[220] In more recent times, the ICRC has developed a model law concerning the use and protection of the distinctive emblem, intended to assist states in fulfilling their obligations in relation to the prevention and repression of the misuse of the distinctive sign under the GCs and APs.[221]

2. Article 53 GC I details a number of specific prohibitions, which concern the misuse of the distinctive emblem and the arms of Switzerland (the white cross on a red ground) as the sign most closely resembling it. Accordingly, no individual, society, firm or company, which is not entitled to do so in accordance with the GCs or the APs, may use the distinctive emblem. The same prohibition concerns the designation 'Red Cross' or 'Geneva Cross' and their alternatives 'Red Crescent' and 'Red Crystal'.[222] Furthermore, imitations of both the distinctive emblem and the designations just referred to are equally prohibited. These prohibitions apply regardless of the motive of the use of the (imitation of) the emblem or designation. They thus concern the misuse for commercial purposes, for example, as much as a well-intended misuse, for instance by a doctor who is not authorized to use the distinctive emblem in accordance with international humanitarian law. These prohibitions apply 'at all times', that is in peacetime and during armed conflicts; retrospectively in relation to past practices of misuse, and in relation to present and future misuses.[223]

3. In order to avoid confusion, misuse of the arms of Switzerland by private individuals, societies, or firms, or an imitation of those arms is also prohibited. However, in

---

[215] Article 53, para. 1; Articles 18, para. 8, 38, para. 1, AP I; Article 12, 3rd sentence, AP II.
[216] Cf. Article 54 GC I.
[217] Cf. Article 37 AP I.
[218] Articles 27–8, 1906 Geneva Convention.
[219] Article 28, 1929 Geneva Convention.
[220] An instructive early case, which demonstrates the adverse consequences of the absence of adequate legislation in the context of the indicative use of the distinctive sign relates to a laundry plant in the Netherlands, which used the emblem of the Red Cross for its commercial purposes. Since the Dutch government had failed to enact a law according to Article 28 of the Convention for Wounded of 1929, years passed before this violation was prosecuted; see *Annual Digest* 1933–4, Case No. 220; *Annual Digest* 1952, Case No. 128 (19 ILR, 598).
[221] 'Model law concerning the use and protection of the emblem of the Red Cross or Red Crescent', (1996) 313 *IRRC* 486–95. See also the more recent 'Model law concerning the use and the protection of the emblem of the red cross, the red crescent and the red crystal', developed for civil law states.
[222] Cf. Article 53, para. 4, GC I; Article 6 AP III.
[223] Pictet, *Commentary*, Vol. I, 387.

JANN K. KLEFFNER

contrast to the misuse of the distinctive emblem, the prohibition only relates to the use of the arms of Switzerland as (parts of) trademarks or commercial marks, or 'for a purpose contrary to commercial honesty, or in circumstances capable of wounding Swiss national sentiment'.[224]

> Camouflage of medical units in order to protect them against discovery by the enemy may exceptionally be permitted when compelling military reasons so require. It may only be ordered by brigade commanders and comparable and superior officers. The senior medical officer in charge and the legal adviser shall be consulted in advance.

632

> The camouflage should be limited in space and time. During an attack it should be suspended.

633

> Camouflage does not deprive medical units of the protection accorded to them by international law. They are, however, exposed to the risk that the adversary might consider them to be military objectives and attack them.

634

The basic requirement of Article 42, para. 4, GC I is distinct marking of medical units and establishments by day and night. In exceptional situations, compelling military reasons may, however, require camouflage to conceal landmarks from the adversary, and particularly from its army and air force. In such a situation, camouflage may exceptionally be extended to medical units, provided that all limitations provided in Sections 632–634 are strictly observed.[225] While such camouflage increases the risk of medical units being mistaken for military objectives or of becoming collaterally damaged during an attack, the fact itself does not alter the protected status of the medical unit in question.

[224] Article 53, para. 2.
[225] Pictet, *Commentary*, Vol. I, 321–2.

JANN K. KLEFFNER

PROTECTION OF PRISONERS IN ARMED CONFLICT

I. General

Introductory Remarks

1. *The legal framework.* The protection of prisoners in armed conflict is based on ethical, military, and political elements. The humane treatment derives from fundamental legal obligations and the conviction that captured enemies no longer pose any threat to the lives of persons nor to the detaining power. While specific forms and procedures of treatment may be influenced by the former conduct of the prisoner during the combat, for example the use of prohibited weapons, attacks against protected persons, or perfidious conduct, standard rules of protection apply. These are deeply rooted in international humanitarian law and human rights.

Military considerations also play an important role in the treatment of prisoners in armed conflict. In principle, prisoners are of military value to the adversary. They can be used as sources of information or to influence their comrades who are still fighting. On the other hand, taking and detaining prisoners can impede the detaining power's military operations. Prisoners must be taken care of and guarded, and they may even have to be protected from the angry population of the detaining power. In order to remove prisoners from forward positions, transport facilities must be available. These few examples show that the humane treatment of prisoners in armed conflict is embedded in a moral, military, and political framework that is likely to influence the interpretation and further development of relevant legal provisions. This must be taken into account to ensure that applicable law can fulfil its purpose and remains practicable.

International humanitarian law provides a detailed framework for the protection of prisoners of war, a legal term of art (GC III Article 4) with GC III and AP I as well as civilian internees (GC IV, see above, Chapter 5, Section VI) during international armed conflicts. Prisoners in international armed conflict who are denied protected-person status under this binary civilian–combatant framework remain protected by AP I Article 75 (see below Section 704) and Common Article 3 (see below Section 706) applicable as well during international armed conflicts as a reflection of 'elementary considerations of humanity'.[1] In contrast, detainees during non-international armed conflicts (see below, Sections 1215 and 1217), including multinational military operations abroad, enjoy only

---

[1] *Military and Paramilitary Activities in and against Nicaragua (Nicaragua v US)*, Merits, *ICJ Reports 1986*, 14, §218. See also ICTY, *Prosecutor v Delalić*, Case No. IT-96–21-A, Judgment of 20 February 2001, para. 143.

SANDRA KRÄHENMANN

rudimentary protection in the form of Common Article 3 as well as AP II Article 5, if the latter is applicable (see below Chapter 12).

While GC III and AP I are *lex specialis* for prisoners of war,[2] the applicability of fundamental human rights standards is of specific practical relevance for detainees in international armed conflicts who are denied protected status under the Geneva Conventions as well as for detainees in non-international armed conflicts (see below Sections 706, 708, and 737). Fundamental human rights of people in detention are enshrined in the 1957 Standard Minimum Rules for the Treatment of Prisoners,[3] the 1988 Body of Principles for the Protection of all Persons under any Form of Detention or Imprisonment,[4] Part III of the ICCPR, the CAT, the International Convention for the Protection of All Persons from Enforced Disappearances, and in regional human rights treaties.[5] International and national courts have ruled on the human rights protection of prisoners during armed conflicts.[6]

To be effective, the relevant provisions and any attempts for developing new rules must resolve five questions:

— Who can be detained and on what basis?
— How should prisoners be treated?
— What are the fundamental rights both of the prisoner and the detaining power?
— For how long and under what circumstances shall protection of the prisoner be guaranteed?
— Which institutions or organizations supervise this treatment and thereby contribute to the enforcement of the protective provisions?

2. The treatment of prisoners of war until the end of the nineteenth century. Until the end of the nineteenth century the treatment of prisoners of war varied depending on the conflict, its geographical area, and the parties involved.[7] Prisoners were usually either killed or enslaved. This treatment mainly resulted from the lack of distinction between combatants and civilians. It was not until Jean-Jacques Rousseau had established the basis for this distinction in *Du Contrat Social* in 1762,[8] that attempts were made to draft

---

[2] Arguably, the refusal of the European Commission on Human Rights to analyse the lawfulness of the detention of the detention of prisoners of war under the European Convention on Human Rights can be read in this sense, see EComHR, *Cyprus v Turkey* (Nos. 6780/74 and 6950/75), Report of 10 July 1976, (1982) 4 *EHRR* 482, para. 313.

[3] 1957 Standard Minimum Rules for the Treatment of Prisoners, UN Doc. A/CONF/611, Annex I, ESC Res. 663C (XXIV), 31 July 1957, 24 UN ESCOR Supp. (No. 1) at 11, UN Doc. E/3048 (1957), amended ESC Res. 2076, 13 May 1977, 62 UN ESCOR Supp. (No. 1) at 35, UN Doc. E/5988 (1977).

[4] 1988 Body of Principles for the Protection of All Persons under any Form of Detention or Imprisonment, annexed to UN GA Res. 43/173, 9 December 1988, UN Doc. A/RES/43/173.

[5] For a detailed overview, see N. S. Rodley, *The Treatment of Prisoners Under International Law*, 3rd edn (OUP, 2009).

[6] See, for example, HRC, *Carranza Alegre v Peru* (No. 1126/2002), Views of 28 October 2005, UN Doc. CCPR/C/85/D/1126/2002; IAComHR, *Coard et al. v the US*, Case 10.951, Report No. 109/99, 29 September 1999; IACtHR, *Blake v Guatemala,* Judgment (Merits), Series C No. 36, 24 January 1998; ECHR, *Bazorkina v Russia* (No. 69481/01), Judgment, 27 July 2006.

[7] On the development of the law in this area before the twentieth century see J. C. Bluntschli, *Das moderne Völkerrecht der zivilisirten Staaten* (1872) 339–51; G. F. von Martens, *Völkerrecht* (Vol. 2 1886) 499–505; Werner, 'Les prisonniers de guerre' (1928) *RdC* I 5; F. J. Scheidl, *Die Kriegsgefangenschaft von den ältesten Zeiten bis zur Gegenwart* (Berlin: Ebering, 1943); S. C. Neff, 'Prisoners of War in International Law: The Nineteenth Century' in S. Scheipers (ed.) *Prisoners in War* (OUP, 2010), 57.

[8] See above, Section 114.

SANDRA KRÄHENMANN

protective provisions for prisoners of war. The 1785 Treaty of Amity and Commerce between the King of Prussia and the US[9] contains the obligation of the contracting parties to protect prisoners of war. The 1863 Lieber Code[10] embodies detailed provisions to secure protection for prisoners of war. The Code, which expressly prohibits any inhumane treatment of prisoners of war, had an important impact on the European policy and practice in the nineteenth century. Following its establishment in 1863, the ICRC played an important role in this development. A report dealing with general questions concerning the treatment of prisoners of war was presented at the first International Red Cross Conference in Paris in 1867. Henry Dunant finally initiated international negotiations with a speech held in London in 1872 on 'A proposal for introducing uniformity into the condition of prisoners of war'. The Brussels Conference of 27 August 1874 resulted in the first twelve articles on the protection of prisoners of war during armed conflict.[11] Although the Final Act of the Brussels Conference never became a treaty, it was of considerable influence and formed the basis for the protective provisions contained in the Hague Conventions of 1899 and 1907.

3. *The Hague Rules.* The HagueReg annexed to HC IV provided a first set of multilateral treaty rules on the treatment of prisoners of war. Covering the first four of the five key questions identified above, these rules identified the groups of persons to be considered as prisoners of war and specified the principle of 'humane treatment'. Article 20 HagueReg stipulated that following the conclusion of peace, prisoners of war were to be repatriated as quickly as possible. During the First World War, when some of the provisions of the HagueReg were felt to be insufficient, Germany concluded bilateral treaties relating to prisoners of war with Great Britain (2 July 1917) and France (26 April 1918).

4. *The Geneva Conventions of 1929.* In 1921 a conference organized by the ICRC adopted a draft convention on the treatment of prisoners of war. This draft separated the protection of prisoners of war from the Hague Law, which deals with methods and means of warfare. The new draft served as the basis for the discussions between the ICRC and the states parties in the 1920s. These resulted in the 1929 Geneva Convention concerning the Treatment of Prisoners of War, which was negotiated by forty-seven states. Although the Geneva Convention was based on the relevant rules of the HagueReg, it may be regarded as the beginning of a new era of protection for prisoners of war.[12] The 1929 Convention lays down that prisoners must at all times be treated humanely and be protected, particularly against acts of violence, insults, and public curiosity. Necessary additions to the existing rules were also made, for example the prohibition of reprisals against prisoners of war. One of the most widely known Articles of the Convention introduced the right of prisoners of war to give only certain information when questioned. Obvious deficiencies of the HagueReg, like the repatriation provision required on the conclusion of peace, were removed. The 1929 Convention was the first to provide for a control mechanism.

---

[9] See above, Section 114, commentary. Text in G. F. de Martens, *Nouveau Recueil Général de Traités et autres Actes Relatifs aux Rapports des Droit International* (Leipzig: Theodor Weicher, 1917).

[10] See above, Section 117.

[11] Text in D. Schindler and J. Toman, *The Laws of Armed Conflicts*, 4th edn (Nijhoff, 2004), No 2.

[12] For a detailed analysis of the 1929 Convention, see N. Wylie, 'The 1929 Prisoner of War Convention and the Building of the Inter-war Prisoner of War Regime', in Scheipers, above (n. 7), 91.

SANDRA KRÄHENMANN

5. *The Second World War.* Forty-six states had signed the 1929 Geneva Convention. Most of them, including Germany, Great Britain, France, and the US, had ratified it prior to the outbreak of World War II. The Soviet Union, however, did not. As a result, during the Second World War there were different legal requirements concerning the protection of prisoners of war among the main parties to the conflict. The Convention of 1929 was the basis of the legal relationship between Germany and its Western adversaries, whereas between Germany and the Soviet Union the applicable provisions were those of the Hague Conventions of 1907 and the rules of customary law.

a) During the Second World War, there were violations of the existing rules in all the areas identified above. Individual violations, as well as complete disregard for the humanitarian foundations of the provisions of the Geneva Convention of 1929, had to be ascertained. Hitler's so-called Commissar Order (*Kommissar-Befehl*) of 1941, for instance, was incompatible with the HagueReg: the denial of prisoner-of-war status for the political commissars of the Red Army and the order to execute them had no basis in international law.[13] A further gross violation of international law by Germany in its treatment of prisoners of war was the so-called Commando Order (*Kommando-Befehl*) of 1942, which ordered the execution of commando units operating behind German lines without wearing uniforms who were taken captive.[14] There were also problems on the side of the Allies concerning the recognition of prisoner-of-war status of persons engaged in combat. For instance, members of the *Wehrmacht* who surrendered to Allied armed forces following the capitulation of 8 May 1945 were denied prisoner-of-war status and given a so-called 'Surrendered Enemy Personnel (SEP) Status' instead.[15] 'SEP' prisoners were denied the guarantees for prisoners of war of the Geneva Convention of 1929, for example supervisory control by the ICRC in camp visits. Similarly, the Soviet Army refused to grant prisoner-of-war status to Germans whom they considered to be war criminals.

b) In addition to the status problem, there were many violations of fundamental guarantees for the treatment of prisoners of war, especially on the German and Soviet sides. For example, Soviet prisoners of war in German camps were not provided with necessary food rations nor, in some cases, with any food at all. Many of them were transferred to concentration camps or forced to do dangerous work in industries important for the war effort. It is assumed that of the 5.7 million Soviet prisoners of war in German captivity, 3.3 million died. Of the 3 million German prisoners of war in Soviet camps, approximately 1 million died during captivity.[16] The large number of deaths among German prisoners of war in Soviet camps was especially due to lack of care, the so-called death marches from the battle fields to the final place of internment, and forced labour under life-threatening conditions. Besides the insufficient care given to prisoners of war during the Second World War, medical experiments had been carried out on captured Allied soldiers in German and Japanese camps. While in camps of the Western Allies the treatment of German and Japanese prisoners of war was far more positive, the 'SEP' prisoners were subjected to hard conditions for weeks or even months after 8 May 1945.

---

[13] R. Overmans, 'The Treatment of Prisoners of War in the Eastern European Theater of Operations, 1941–56', in Scheipers, above (n. 7), 127.

[14] XXVII *IMT*, doc. 1266-PS, cf. F. Kalshoven, *Belligerent Reprisals*, 2nd edn (Nijhoff, 2005), 184–93.

[15] B. Moore, 'The Treatment of Prisoners of War in the Western European Theatre of War, 1939–45', in Scheipers, above (n. 7), 111.

[16] Cf. Rousseau, *Le Droit des Conflits Armés* (Pedone, 1983), 100, bases his observations on similar figures.

SANDRA KRÄHENMANN

c) In addition to the insufficient care provided during the Second World War, prisoners were often executed for violations of the laws of war or of laws of the detaining power. While the 1929 Convention permitted the death penalty for certain crimes committed by the prisoner of war, a fair trial for accused prisoners was rare. In many cases, prisoners were not permitted to defend themselves or to present evidence in their defence.

d) A further threat to prisoners of war during the Second World War was that the parties to the conflict exercised reprisals against them. Although the 1929 Convention expressly prohibited reprisals against prisoners of war, even between parties to the Convention violations of protective rules were claimed to be justified as reprisals. Thus, for example, eighty German prisoners of war were executed by French authorities as a reprisal after the occupying German authority had executed eighty French hostages near Lyon in 1944.[17]

e) From 1945 to 1955, the unresolved question concerning the repatriation of prisoners of war proved to be a major stumbling block in the restoration of a peaceful relationship between Germany and the Soviet Union. In 1950, the Soviet Union stated that 12,000 German prisoners of war were held in captivity. Of these, 9,000 were regarded as war criminals. In contrast to the US repatriation policy, which led to the termination of prisoner-of-war exchange in July 1946, it took until 1955 to resolve the German–Soviet prisoner-of-war problem. Among the numerous reasons why the Soviet Union held prisoners of war for so long, the labour provided by them for post-war reconstruction played a crucial role. Other wartime adversaries of Germany also used German prisoners of war for reconstruction work. For example, in 1947 there were still 630,000 German prisoners of war being held in France, many of whom were so employed.

6. *Development of the law after the Second World War.* The numerous violations of the rules of the 1929 Geneva Conventions had revealed the necessity for extension and clarification of the protection of war victims. As after the First World War, the ICRC again took the initiative. Between 1946 and 1948 a number of drafts were discussed with the representatives of national Red Cross societies and representatives of states. After the Red Cross Conference in Stockholm in 1948, at which also the ICRC's draft for an improved convention for the protection of prisoners of war was discussed, Switzerland convened the Diplomatic Conference of Geneva in 1949, in which sixty-two states participated. This diplomatic conference adopted the Four Geneva Conventions of 12 August 1949. The Third Convention (GC III) expands and improves the provisions of the Convention on Treatment of Prisoners of War of 1929. GC III is one of the most extensive codifications of international humanitarian law. Based on experiences of violations of the humanitarian rules of the 1929 Convention, important fundamental rules for the protection of prisoners of war were clarified, expanded, or completely revised. New provisions were added and existing ones were set in a different order to increase their significance.

In virtually all armed conflicts since 1949, violations, and sometimes grave breaches, of the provisions of GC III of 1949 were ascertainable. As in the Second World War, violations of fundamental provisions for the protection of prisoners of war were at the forefront. The community of states did not respond to these violations by attempting

---

[17] ICRC, *Report on Activities during the Second World War*, Vol. I, 522–3; J. Hinz, *Das Kriegsgefangenenrecht unter besonderer Berücksichtigung seiner Entwicklung durch das Genfer Abkommen vom 12 August 1949* (Vahlen, 1955), 58–9; A. Rosas, *The Legal Status of Prisoners of War* (Suomalainen Tiedeakatemia, 1976).

SANDRA KRÄHENMANN

further codification. GC III had established such a detailed regime that further attempts to improve the protection of prisoners of war would merely clarify individual rules. Such clarifying additions were negotiated during 1974–1977 and included in Articles 43–45 AP I. These provisions reflect the efforts of the community of states to deal with problems relating to the treatment of guerrillas as combatants and prisoners of war which arose particularly during the Vietnam War. They are supplementary to GC III without altering its character as the most important basis of the protection of prisoners of war. Only parts of Articles 43 to 45 are regarded to be customary law today.[18]

7. *The 'Global War on Terror' and the Geneva Conventions.* The terrorist attacks of 11 September 2001 led to a political and scholarly debate about the appropriateness of international humanitarian law[19] in the 'Global War on Terror'. Specifically, the decision of the US administration to deny prisoner-of-war status to captured Taliban and al-Qaeda fighters[20] fostered an ongoing discussion on whether the protection provided by GC III and AP I is adequate with regard to persons allegedly involved in a terrorist acts.[21] The US had detained some 50,000 persons between 2001 and 2004 in the conflicts in Afghanistan, Iraq, and other areas. European states had been very explicit on the fundamental protection to be applied to all detained persons. Public debates are still ongoing.[22]

8. *Operational detentions[23] outside international armed conflicts.* The international military operations in Afghanistan and Iraq highlight the legal uncertainties surrounding the detention regime during military operations abroad with a broad range of objectives, ranging from peace enforcement to ensuring law and order, outside an international armed conflict. Ongoing debates[24] centre around the respective role of international

---

[18] Cf. Rule 106 *CIHL*.

[19] For a detailed overview of the various issues raised by terrorism from the perspective of international humanitarian law, see A. Bianchi and Y. Naqvi, *International Humanitarian Law and Terrorism* (Oxford: Hart Publishing, 2011).

[20] Memorandum of President George W. Bush to Secretary of State et al., 7 February 2002. This memorandum as well as other documents discussing the status and treatment of captured fighters in the 'Global War on Terror' are available on the website of the George Washington University: <http://www.gwu.edu/~nsarchiv/torturingdemocracy/documents/theme.html>. For a detailed analysis of the US administration's decision and its consequences for the treatment of detainees, see D. E. Graham, 'The Dual US Standard for the Treatment and Interrogation of Detainees: Unlawful and Unworkable' (2008–9) 48 *Washburn Law Journal* 325.

[21] See, for example, E. Crawford, *The Treatment of Combatants and Insurgents under the Law of Armed Conflict* (OUP, 2010), 53–61; D. Jinks, 'The Applicability of the Geneva Conventions to the "Global War on Terrorism" ' (2005) 46 *Virginia Journal of International Law* 165; and S. Murphy, 'Evolving Geneva Convention Paradigms in the "War on Terror": Applying the Core Rules to the Release of Persons Deemed "Unprivileged Combatants" ' (2007) 75 *George Washington Law Review* 1105, at 1119–40.

[22] For the position of the ICRC, see the 'Report on International Humanitarian Law and the Challenges of Contemporary Armed Conflict', submitted to the 30th International Conference of the Red Cross and Red Crescent, available on the ICRC website: <http://www.icrc.org/eng/assets/files/other/ihl-challenges-30th-international-conference-eng.pdf>.

[23] See J. Kleffner, 'Operational Detention and the Treatment of Detainees', in T. D. Gill and D. Fleck, *The Handbook of the International Law in Military Operations* (OUP, 2010) 465–79.

[24] See, for example, J. B. Bellinger III and V. M. Padmanabhan, 'Detention Operations in Contemporary Armed Conflicts: Four Challenges for the Geneva Conventions and Other Existing Law' (2011) 105-2 *AJIL* 201–43; B. Oswald, 'Detention of Civilians on Military Operations: Reasons for and Challenges to Developing a Special Law of Detention' (2008) 32-2 *Melbourne University Law Review* 524; J. Pejic, 'Conflict Classification and the Law Applicable to Detention and the Use of Force' in E. Wilmshurst (ed.), *International Law and the Classification of Conflicts* (OUP, 2012), 80; and M. Sassòli and M. L. Olson, 'The relationship between international humanitarian law and human rights law where it matters: admissible killings and internment of fighters in non-international armed conflicts' (2011) 871 *IRRC* 599.

SANDRA KRÄHENMANN

humanitarian law, human rights law and relevant Security Council resolutions to determine the legal basis for detention,[25] the standard of treatment, the procedural safeguards of detainees and the detaining authority's responsibility in cases of transfers of detainees, including in-country transfers. In order to provide minimum standards, the ICRC issued in 2007 its institutional guidelines on 'Procedural Principles and Safeguards for Internment/Administrative Detention in Armed Conflicts and Other Situations of Violence'.[26] Furthermore, a 2011 ICRC report recognized the need to strengthen the legal protection provided to detainees during non-international armed conflicts,[27] a conclusion endorsed by the 31st International Conference of the Red Cross and the Red Crescent.[28] A first step in this direction was launched by Denmark in 2007 with the Copenhagen Process on the Handling of Detainees in International Military Operations,[29] which resulted in the adoption of the 'Copenhagen Process: Principles and Guidelines'[30] in October 2012 by a group of states, including the five permanent members of the Security Council.[31]

9. *Protection of prisoners of war and customary law.* It is generally agreed by the community of states and most international lawyers that the fundamental provisions of GC III are valid as customary law. In addition, some provisions are accepted as *ius cogens.* Due to their universal applicability today, the qualification of the fundamental provisions of GC III as rules of customary law is only of minor significance for their application by states.

10. *Penal sanctions for violations.* The question as to which violations of GC III should constitute war crimes and should thus be internationally punishable is increasingly important. Article 130 GC III lists those acts which are regarded as grave breaches of the Convention while Article 85 AP I lists grave breaches of the Protocol. These include

---

[25] Recently, the Grand Chamber of the European Court of Human Rights held in *Al-Jedda v the UK* (No. 27021/08), Judgment of 7 July 2011, that administrative detentions in Iraq by the UK violated the right to liberty of the ECHR in the absence of a derogation. For a critical discussion of the Court's judgment and its failure to apply IHL, see V. Gowlland-Debbas and G. Gaggioli, 'The Relationship between International Humanitarian Law and Human Rights: An Overview' in R. Kolb and G. Gaggioli (eds), *Research Handbook on Human Rights and Humanitarian Law* (Edward Elgar Publishing, 2013), 77, at 93.

[26] The Guidelines are annexed to the 2007 ICRC report on 'International Humanitarian Law and Challenges of Contemporary Armed Conflicts', submitted to the 30th Conference of the Red Cross and the Red Crescent (available on <http://www.icrc.org/eng/assets/files/other/ihl-challenges-30th-international-conference-eng.pdf>). See also J. Pejic, 'Procedural Principles and Safeguards for Internment/Administrative Detention in Armed Conflicts and Other Situations of Violence' (2005) 858 *IRRC* 375.

[27] ICRC report 'Strengthening Legal Protection For Victims of Armed Conflicts', submitted to the 31st International Conference of the Red Cross and Red Crescent (available at <http://www.rcrcconference.org/docs_upl/en/31IC_5.1.1_Report_Strength_IHL_en.pdf>). Similarly, during the public discussion held by the Human Rights Committee in October 2012 to prepare a new General Comment on Article 9 ICCPR (Prohibition of Arbitrary Detention), several participants suggested to include the thematic issue of detention during armed conflicts.

[28] Resolution 1 adopted at the 31st Conference on 1 December 2011, available at: <http://www.rcrcconference.org/docs_upl/en/R1_Strengthening_IHL_EN.pdf>.

[29] T. Winkler, 'The Copenhagen Process: A Necessity' (2009) 78 *Nordic Journal of International Law* 489.

[30] The Principles with Commentary, and the minutes of the 2012 meeting are available at: <http://um.dk/en/politics-and-diplomacy/copenhagen-process-on-the-handling-of-detainees-in-international-military-operations/>.

[31] Both the process and its outcome were severely criticized by human rights organizations, see for example Amnesty International, *Outcome of Copenhagen Process on Detainees in International Military Operations Undermines Respect for Human Rights*, 23 October 2012, available at: <http://www.amnesty.org/en/library/info/IOR50/003/2012/en>.

SANDRA KRÄHENMANN

wilful killing and torture or inhumane treatment of, including biological experiments on, prisoners of war, unjustifiable delay in the repatriation as well as depriving prisoners of war of the rights of fair and regular trial. During the Second Gulf War and the war in the Former Yugoslavia, both the member states of the European Community and the Security Council of the UN confirmed the content of Article 130 GC III.[32] The ICTY Statute expressly refers to grave breaches of the Geneva Conventions. Such breaches are now incorporated in the ICC Statute (see below, Chapter 14, 'Introductory Remarks', para. 5, and Sections 1410–1411).

701   **Detention of persons is a wide-spread phenomenon in armed conflict to respond to serious threats to the security of the detaining authority. While civilians may be interned only in exceptional cases (see above, Section 581), captured enemy soldiers may be deprived of their liberty as a general rule. The purpose of captivity is to exclude them from further military operations. As long as they have not committed crimes detainees must be treated as persons captured for reasons of security, not as criminals.**

1. The purpose of captivity is not defined in GC III. It is in the interest of the detaining power to prevent enemy combatants from taking part in further military operations. The group of persons liable to being taken prisoner goes beyond the narrow term of 'soldiers'. All persons falling into the hands of the detaining power and considered to be prisoners of war under Article 4 GC III and Article 43 AP I belong to this group. War correspondents or supply contractors, for example, in so far as they are authorized to carry out their activities by the armed forces which they accompany, shall also be considered prisoners of war if they possess the identity card required for their activities. A new practice regarding journalists has emerged during the Iraq War in 2003. TV and other journalists had been permitted to observe and report about the fighting between Allied and Iraqi forces while embedded in units of the US forces. Iraq also permitted journalists to report on the hostilities from Baghdad. Several of those reporting were killed as a result of US attacks. Embedded journalists who do not qualify as war correspondents, however, are not prisoners of war when captured and cannot be attacked due to their civilian status.[33]

2. Leaving aside the question of responsibility for waging aggressive war, lawful military operations in armed conflict are not contrary to international law. Thus, attacks against military objectives of the adversary are permitted if carried out by lawful methods of warfare. International law does not provide sanctions for such conduct. Taking an enemy combatant prisoner can therefore never serve as a punishment but only to prevent further participation in military operations against the detaining power. Because of this fundamental perception of lawful operations during an armed conflict, the internment conditions of prisoners of war must differ from those of convicts. It is only in exceptional cases that GC III permits prisoners of war to be interned in prisons. If prisoners of war are, for example, sentenced to imprisonment for acts committed prior to their capture, they may be held in prisons if members of the armed forces of the detaining power would also be treated in this manner. However, their right of complaints under Article

---

[32] Cf. the statement of the EC of 22 January 1991, reprinted in (1993) 4 *EJIL* 146–7.
[33] See O. Bring and P. Broström, 'The Iraq War and International Law' in J. Hallenberg and H. Karlsson (eds), *The Iraq War: European Perspectives on Politics, Strategy and Operations* (Routledge, 2005), 118–40, at 127.

SANDRA KRÄHENMANN

78 GC III and the supervision rights of protecting powers under Article 126 GC III still apply in the case of such punishment.

> In international armed conflicts, captured enemy combatants and other groups of persons defined in Article 4 of the Third Geneva Convention and Article 43 of Additional Protocol I enjoy prisoner-of-war status. They may not be prosecuted for lawful acts of violence committed in the course of hostilities ('combatant privilege'), but only for violations of international humanitarian law, in particular war crimes, genocide, or crimes against humanity. The state to whose armed forces the capturing unit belongs (detaining power) is responsible for the treatment of prisoners of war (Article 12, para. 1, GC III).

702

That prisoners of war are to be regarded as prisoners of a state, the detaining power, is linked to the fact that armed conflicts have since the eighteenth century no longer been considered as a struggle of man against man, but rather as a conflict between one state and another. In practice, the effect of this principle is twofold: first, it serves to protect prisoners of war, who must not be subjected to arbitrary acts by the adversary's soldiers who take them captive. Even if their lives were in danger only a few minutes prior to the capture, the captors may not view the captives as their personal prisoners, nor may they subject them to arbitrary acts. The principle that prisoners of war are considered to be prisoners of the state also constitutes the basis of the responsibility for their treatment: it is the detaining power's obligation to require its organs to abide by the rules of international law on the treatment of prisoners of war, and to ensure the application of these rules. Irrespective of any improper conduct by individual soldiers when capturing or dealing with prisoners of war, the detaining power is responsible under international law for the treatment of prisoners of war. Claims relating to the improper conduct of its organs can therefore be directed against the detaining power under the principles of international responsibility.

> In any case of doubt as to whether persons having committed a belligerent act and having fallen into the hands of the enemy are to be protected as prisoners of war, such persons shall enjoy that protection until such time as their status has been determined by a competent tribunal (Article 5, para. 2, GC III; Article 45, paras. 1 and 2, AP I).

703

1. The presumption of prisoner-of-war status in any case of doubt is important both for the maintenance of the rule of law of the detaining power and the humanitarian protection of individual detainees. It would lead to an erosion of legal principles and might soon prove counterproductive for any attempt to establish post-conflict order, if prisoner-of-war protection would be denied at will. Categorizing individuals as so called 'unlawful combatants' is contrary to the Convention and to international humanitarian law in general.[34] An individual detainee denied of an objective status decision would be deprived important protections under GC III he or she might be entitled to.

2. The requirement of a competent status determination and full interim protection in any case of doubt was included in GC III at the request of the ICRC. While the original ICRC proposal had aimed at a status decision 'by some responsible authority', delegates preferred to have the decision taken by a court, and after some discussion whether a

---

[34] See above, Section 302. See also Israel Supreme Court, Judgment 769/02 of 14 December 2006.

SANDRA KRÄHENMANN

military tribunal would in any case be available and competent to make a convincing determination, the requirement of a decision taken by a 'competent tribunal' was accepted.[35] Three decades later, further specifications were introduced with Article 45, para. 1, AP I: the interim protection as prisoner of war and the requirement of a status determination by a competent tribunal applies (a) if the person claims prisoner-of-war status; (b) if the detaining power has doubts whether the person may be entitled to such status; and (c) if the party on which the person concerned depends claims the status of prisoner of war on his or her behalf.[36] Article 45, para. 2, AP I established a new procedural right for prisoners tried for an offence arising out of the hostilities, to assert entitlement to prisoner-of-war status before a 'judicial tribunal' and to have that question adjudicated, whenever possible under the applicable procedure, before the trial for the offence.

3. No mention is made in either GC III or AP I, which tribunal may be competent to make such determination. From the difference made in Article 45 AP I between 'judicial tribunal' for persons tried for an offence and 'competent tribunal' in normal cases, it may be concluded that in the latter case there exist no requirement for a court decision. But even if states prefer to establish government commissions for making such decision, the rule of law requires to follow firm principles of procedure with a possibility to appeal. Any possibility of interference in individual cases must convincingly be excluded.[37] Thus, independence in decision-making must be guaranteed.

704   **Persons who are in the power of a party to the conflict and who do not benefit from more favourable treatment shall be treated humanely under all circumstances and shall enjoy, as a minimum, fundamental human rights protections (Article 75 AP I).**

1. The fundamental guarantees of Article 75 AP I are of significant importance for detainees who do not enjoy prisoner-of-war status (see above, Section 302) or whose status is in doubt. These guarantees have customary law status[38] and they may be enforced under relevant human rights conventions, for example the ICCPR, and regional human rights systems.

2. The field of application of Article 75 AP I includes internment in other situations of violence, and any administrative detention which is found absolutely necessary for imperative security reasons (see below Section 708). Internment or detention for the sole purpose of intelligence gathering without the person involved presenting a real threat to security can never be justified.[39]

---

[35] J. de Preux, *Geneva Convention Relative to the Treatment of Prisoners of War* (ICRC, 1960), 77.

[36] *ICRC Commentary* to Article 45 AP I, paras. 1730–49.

[37] The US Supreme Court confirmed that both US citizens held in the US and foreign nationals held in Guantanamo Bay as enemy combatants are to be given a meaningful opportunity to contest the factual basis for that detention before a neutral decision-maker, see *Hamdi et al. v Rumsfeld, Secretary of Defense et al.* (28 June 2004) and *Rasul et al. v Bush* (28 June 2004). These rulings led to the establishment of the Combatant Status Review Tribunals, see for example J. Blocher, 'Combatant Status Review Tribunals: Flawed Answers to the Wrong Questions',(2006) 116-3 *Yale Law Journal* 667 and G. S. Corn, E. Talbot Jensen, and S. Watts, 'Understanding the Distinct Function of the Combatant Status Review Tribunals: A Response to Blocher' (2007) 116 *The Yale Law Journal Pocket Part* 327. A comprehensive database with the publicly released proceedings of the Combatant Status Review Tribunals is available at <http://human-rights.ucdavis.edu/projects/the-guantanamo-testimonials-project/testimonies/testimonies-of-the-defense-department/CSRT_new>.

[38] See Rules 87–105 *CIHL*.

[39] Pejic, 'Procedural Principles', above (n. 26) at 380.

SANDRA KRÄHENMANN

3. The right of persons in custody to be assisted by legal counsel must be respected and periodical review of the detention must be guaranteed.

4. Where foreigners are detained, their national authorities must be promptly and duly informed, and be given the opportunity to personal visits, unless the detainee has expressed a wish to the contrary.[40]

> A detaining power may transfer prisoners of war to another power only if it has   705
> satisfied itself of the willingness and ability of the latter to apply the rules of inter-
> national law as to the protection of prisoners of war (Article 12, para. 2, GC III).
> In no circumstances shall a detainee be transferred to a country where he or she
> would be under the risk of violation of fundamental rights including torture or
> cruel, inhuman or degrading treatment or punishment; arbitrary deprivation of
> life or have reason to fear persecution for his or her political opinions or religious
> beliefs (Article 12, para. 2, GC III; Article 45 GC IV; Articles 6–7 ICCPR; Article
> 3 CAT).

1. *Transfer.* In international armed conflicts of previous decades the transfer of prisoners of war was common practice. The reasons for transfer differed. In most cases the feasibility of interning and taking care of a large number of prisoners of war played the decisive role in the transfer. However, transfers have also been decided on the basis of considerations of alliance policy. After the Second World War, for example, the US has transferred a large number of the aforementioned German 'SEP' to France and Great Britain.[41] During the Second Gulf War, the US has transferred Iraqi prisoners of war to Saudi Arabia.[42] More recently, the so-called flights of rendition have been discussed by the public and scholars. After the Afghanistan War and in the context of the war on terror the US had been flying via European airports detained persons to prisons in countries both outside as well as inside Europe.[43] That practice included persons who could have been regarded as prisoners of war.

Before a transfer may take place, three requirements must be met. First, the detaining power may only transfer prisoners of war to a state party to GC III. In addition, the other power's willingness to apply GC III must have been ascertained, and the preconditions for the application of the provisions must be objectively fulfilled. Therefore, a transfer may not take place if the receiving power, for instance, has indicated that it will refrain—wholly or in part—from applying GC III. Unavailability of shelter, in adequate camps, or predictably inadequate supplies for the prisoners of war prevent the transfer of prisoners of war. The transfer of prisoners of war to other states not party to the armed conflict for the purpose of interrogation is unlawful independently of whether the interrogation entails prohibited practices including torture.[44]

---

[40] Article 36 of the 1963 Vienna Convention on Consular Relations which is mandatory even in wartime.

[41] See above, 'Introductory Remarks', para. 5(a).

[42] Department of Defense, 'Conduct of the Persian Gulf War: final report to Congress' (1992) Appendix L-3, <http://www.ndu.edu/library/epubs/cpgw.pdf>.

[43] See Council of Europe doc. AS/Jur (2006) 16 Committee on Legal Affairs and Human Rights, Alleged secret detentions and unlawful inter-state transfers involving Council of Europe member states,—Part II (Explanatory memorandum) Rapporteur: Mr Dick Marty, Switzerland.

[44] See the report by Mr Claudio Fava to the European Parliament A6–0020/2007 and the decision of the European Parliament of 14 February 2007.

SANDRA KRÄHENMANN

The conditions for open transfers are usually determined in treaties concluded by the states involved. In the Second Gulf War, the US concluded transfer agreements with Saudi Arabia, Great Britain, and France.[45] These treaties dealt with every aspect of the transfer procedure, starting with the capture of Iraqi soldiers, through their questioning and medical treatment, and up to their transfer to prison camps of the receiving state.

2. *Eligible receiving powers.* The aforementioned preconditions apply to the transfer of prisoners of war from the detaining power to another power. There are no further requirements. GC III does not, for example, specify whether the receiving power must be a party to the conflict. In the absence of a contrary provision, it can be assumed that any party to GC III can be a receiving state if the conditions described are met. During the Afghanistan conflict 1978–1989, for example, Switzerland agreed to receive Soviet soldiers who had been captured by Afghan rebels.[46]

3. *Permanent responsibility.* By transferring prisoners of war to another power, the transferring power does not entirely shed its responsibility for the prisoners. The transfer is only effective as long as the receiving state applies GC III in all its important respects. In the event of violation of these rules, the transferring power has not only a right but, as the wording of Article 12, para. 3, suggests, but also an obligation to take effective measures in order to provide a remedy. For instance, the US changed its practice of transferring prisoners of war to South Vietnam during the Vietnam War when violations of the provisions of GC III by South Vietnam during the phase following the transfer were made public.[47] The detaining power cannot avoid responsibility by placing the prisoner-of-war camp outside its territory or by keeping the detained persons for a longer period on ships or planes. The transferring state may also request the return of prisoners of war and such request may not be refused. Moreover, by labelling prisoners 'unlawful combatants', states cannot deviate from the general obligations vis-à-vis the prisoner to guarantee the application of GC III by the third state.[48]

The ICTY Statute as well as the ICC Statute raise problems as to the obligations of states under GC III. According to the Statutes, states with suspected war criminals under their control are obliged to transfer these persons to the tribunal[49] or decide about the request to surrender.[50] As the UN is not a party to the Geneva Conventions, this statutory obligation contradicts Article 12, para. 2, GC III. Further problems arise as to imprisonment: the Statute lays down that imprisonment shall be served according to the law of the state which has agreed to accept the convicted war criminal.[51] While it is to be criticized that no reference is made here to the guarantees of GC III, in practice the provisions of GC III on the treatment of prisoners have been respected.

---

[45] See above (n. 42).

[46] UN Doc. 47/428 of 16 December 1992, 'Prisoners of war and persons missing as a result of war in Afghanistan'.

[47] H. Levie, *Procedures for the Protection of Prisoners of War in Vietnam: A Four-way Problem* (Washington: ASIL Proceedings, 1971) 209–14, at 212.

[48] For the relationship between the concept and the transfer of prisoners, see R. Chesney, 'Leaving Guantanamo: The Law of International Detainee Transfers' (2006) *University of Richmond Law Review* 259–368, at 281–99.

[49] UN Doc. S/25704 of 23 May 1993, 32.

[50] Article 89 ICC Statute.

[51] Above (n. 49), 31.

SANDRA KRÄHENMANN

4. *Non-refoulement.* The prohibition of non-refoulement[52] forbids the transfer of all detainees to another detaining power if he or she risks a violation of fundamental human rights, namely torture, inhuman and degrading treatment, arbitrary deprivation of life, a 'flagrant breach'[53] of the prohibition of arbitrary detention or 'a flagrant denial of justice.'[54] The absolute, non-derogable prohibition of torture and other prohibited ill-treatment does not allow for any balancing of interests[55] between the security threat represented by the individual to be removed and the probability of a violation in case of a transfer.[56] The Grand Chamber of the European Court of Human Rights recently confirmed that the prohibition applies as well to in-country transfers of individuals detained abroad during international military operations.[57] The use of so-called 'diplomatic assurances' to prevent the risk of ill-treatment remains highly controversial,[58] in particular due to their unreliability and the difficulty to establish effective post-transfer monitoring mechanisms.[59]

> Fundamental rules for the treatment of prisoners are: 706
> — It is prohibited to treat prisoners inhumanely or dishonourably (Common Article 3 GC; Articles 13 and 14 GC III; Article 75 AP I; Article 4 AP II, Article 10 ICCPR).
> — Any discrimination on the grounds of race, nationality, religious belief or political opinions, or similar criteria is unlawful (Article 16 GC III; Article 26 ICCPR).
> — Reprisals against prisoners are prohibited (Article 13, para. 3, GC III; Article 51, para. 6, AP I; see above, Section 488).

---

[52] For an analysis of the applicability of the prohibition of non-refoulement during armed conflict as well as its legal basis in refugee law, human rights law and international humanitarian law, see E. Gillard, 'There's No Place Like Home: States' Obligations in Relation to Transfers of Persons' (2008) 871 *IRRC* 703; C. Droege, 'Transfers of Detainees: Legal Framework, *Non-Refoulement* and Contemporary Challenges' (2008) 871 *IRRC* 669. For a detailed analysis, see K. Wouters, *International Legal Standards for the Protection from Refoulement* (Intersentia, 2009).

[53] ECtHR, *Othman (Abu Qatada) v UK* (No. 8139109), Judgment, 17 January 2012, para. 232.

[54] Ibid. para. 285. See also ECtHR, *Babar Ahmad and Others v the UK* (No. 24027/07), Decision of 6 July 2010 and ECtHR, *Al-Moayad v Germany* (No. 35965/03), Decision of 20 February 2007.

[55] ECtHR, *Saadi v Italy* (No. 37201/06), Judgment (Grand Chamber), 28 February 2008, for a forceful rejection of such a balancing test, advocated in particular by the UK as a third-party intervener.

[56] In this respect, the prohibition of refoulement under human rights law is broader than under the 1951 Refugee Convention which allows for exclusion if a person is suspected of crimes against peace, a war crime, a crime against humanity or acts contrary to the purposes and principles of the UN (Article 1 F 1951 Refugee Convention).

[57] ECtHR, *Al-Saadoon and Mufdhi v the UK* (No. 61498/08), Judgment (Grand Chamber), 2 March 2010. In its review of the reports of the US and the UK, the Committee against Torture adopted the same position, see Committee against Torture, Conclusions and Recommendations: United Kingdom, 10 December 2004, UN Doc. CAT/C/CR/33/3, para. 4(b) and para. 5(e); Committee against Torture, Conclusions and Recommendations: United States, 26 July 2004, UN Doc. CAT/C/USA/CO/2, para.15. Both governments had denied the applicability of the non-refoulement provision in CAT to in-country transfers abroad.

[58] Human rights organizations reject the use of diplomatic assurances, see Amnesty International, *Dangerous Deals, Europe's Reliance on Diplomatic Assurances Against Torture*, 10 April 2010, available at <http://www.amnesty.org/en/library/info/EUR01/012/2010>; Human Rights Watch, *Still At Risk: Diplomatic Assurances No Safeguard Against Torture*, 10 April 2005, available at <http://www.hrw.org/reports/2005/04/14/still-risk>. In favour, see, for example, Bellinger and Padmanabhan, above (n. 24), at 239. Human rights bodies have not categorically rejected the use of diplomatic assurances, but remain highly sceptical, see the analysis in Gillard, above (n. 52), at 742 and Droege, above (n. 52), at 694.

[59] HRC, *Alzery v Sweden* (No. 1416/2005), Views, 10 November 2006, UN Doc. CCPR/C/88/D/1416/2005, para. 11.5; Committee Against Torture, *Agiza v Sweden* (No. 233/2003), Views, 24 May 2005, UN Doc. CAT/C/34/D/233/2003, para.13.4.

SANDRA KRÄHENMANN

> Representatives of the protecting power and delegates of the ICRC may visit
> prisoners in their camps at any time and talk to them individually and without
> witnesses.

1. *Humane treatment.* Section 706 summarizes the fundamental provisions on the treatment of prisoners of war. Prisoners of war must be treated humanely *at all times.* The most important parts of the basic provision are already contained in Articles 4–20 HagueReg.

It is not specified in the HagueReg nor in the Geneva Conventions of 1929 what constitutes inhumane treatment of prisoners of war. In view of certain problems of interpretation which had emerged during the Second World War, the wording of Article 13 GC III has introduced examples of inhumane treatment. Acts or omissions causing death or seriously endangering the health of the prisoners of war are clear violations of the principle of humane treatment. The same is true for physical mutilation or medical or scientific experiments, unless these acts are justified by the medical treatment of the prisoners of war and carried out in their interest. The jurisprudence of the ICTY and ICTR provide examples of inhumane treatment of detained persons. While the judgments deal with the crimes provisions of the respective statutes they permit conclusions concerning the content of the humanitarian law rules entailing obligations. With regard to the identical rules of GCs III and IV, it is also justified to refer to the said jurisprudence, although in most of the cases the detained persons were civilians.[60]

The principle of humane treatment is not limited to prisoners of war. Common Article 3 confirms the requirement of human treatment for all detainees in an armed conflict, regardless of their status or the nature of the conflict. In addition, the principle of humane treatment is enshrined in human rights law, providing an additional layer of protection for all detainees (Article 10 ICCPR).[61] Since detainees are unable to provide on their own for their basic needs, the principle of humane treatment requires states to provide adequate detention conditions.[62] Mirroring the specific provisions in GC III for prisoners of war (see below Section 720), states have to provide to all detainees adequate space, food and drinking water, medical treatment, clothing and sanitary conditions.[63]

Non-state actors are bound by the principle of humane treatment enshrined in Common Article 3 and, if applicable, Article 5 AP II. As the reports of widespread abuses of detainees by armed militia during the conflict in Libya[64] and Syria[65] illustrate, this provision is often violated.

[60] For a definition of inhumane treatment see ICTY, *Kordić and Cerkez*, case No. IT-95–14/2-T, Judgment of 26 February 2001, para. 256.
[61] HRC, General Comment No. 21: Humane Treatment of Persons Deprived of their Liberty (Article 10), 6 April 1992, UN Doc. HRI/GEN1/Rev. 9 (Vol. 1) 202.
[62] IACtHR, *Juvenile Reeductation Institute v Paragua*, Judgment (Preliminary Objections, Merits, Reparations and Costs), Series C No. 112, 2 September 2004, para. 152.
[63] For a detailed overview of the practice of human rights bodies, see N. S. Rodley, *Treatment of Prisoners*, above (n. 5), at 377–426.
[64] Amnesty International, *Militias Threaten Hopes for New Libya*, Report of 16 February 2012, available at <http://www.amnesty.org/en/news/libya-out-control-militias-commit-widespread-abuses-year-uprising-2012-02-15>.
[65] Human Rights Watch, *Syria: End Opposition Use of Torture, Executions: Abuses Show Need for Accountability*, Report of 17 September 2012, available at <http://www.hrw.org/news/2012/09/17/syria-end-opposition-use-torture-executions>.

SANDRA KRÄHENMANN

2. *'At all times'*. It must be emphasized that the principle of humane treatment applies 'at all times'. In contrast to the Convention of 1929, this term was expressly included in GC III. The experiences of the wars of the first half of the twentieth century, especially the Second World War, were the reason for introducing this terminology. Thus, it is no longer possible for the detaining power to justify inhumane treatment by reference to the circumstances of the hostilities, causes of the conflict, or similar grounds in particular the security of the detaining power and the perceived duration of the conflict. The Human Rights Committee confirmed that the principle of humane treatment is non-derogable and applies at all times.[66]

3. *Obligation to protect*. Humane treatment requires not only that the detaining power desist from inhumane acts, but also—as expressly emphasized in Article 13, para. 2—that the detaining power prevent such acts by any other party. In particular, prisoners of war shall be protected against violence and intimidation, insults and public curiosity (see Section 713). Following incidents during the Second World War, documented for example in the so-called *Essen lynching* case,[67] express reference was made to this in 1949. Thus, prisoners of war may not, for example, be transported through the streets of a town in order to subject them to acts of violence or intimidation. Incidents of this type have occurred in many conflicts. During the Second World War, for instance, French prisoners of war were paraded through German towns. During the Vietnam War, Allied pilots were put on display in Hanoi. Also, during the Second Gulf War, captured Allied pilots were publicly displayed in the streets of Baghdad in 1991.[68] Soldiers can incur criminal responsibility for aiding and abetting the ill-treatment and executions of prisoners of war if they fail to discharge their legal duty to protect them.[69]

Even if there are no acts of violence or intimidation, it must be asked whether there is a violation of the prohibition of exposing the prisoners of war to public curiosity. Pictures of prisoners of war[70] can be broadcasted worldwide almost instantaneously due to modern technology, as happened now on a number of occasions following the Second Gulf War since 1991. Broadcasts by Iraqi television, in which Allied pilots were coerced to denounce their own countries, and also television broadcasts of interviews with Iraqi prisoners of war directly following their capture were correctly deemed to be violations of Article 13 GC III.[71] In the Kosovo War in 1999, US soldiers serving in UNPREDEP

---

[66] HRC, General Comment No. 29: States of Emergency (Article 4), 31 August 2001, UN Doc. CCPR/C/21/Rev.1/Add.11, para. 13(a).

[67] *The Essen Lynching Case, Trial of Erich Heyer and Six Others Before British Military Court*, reprinted in Friedman, Vol. II, 1482–6.

[68] On this problem, see Fischer/Wallenfels, 'Bildberichterstattung und der Schutz der Kriegsgefangenen im Zeitalter des Satellitenfernsehens', in Institut für Friedenssicherungsrecht und Humanitäres Völkerrecht (ed.), *Beiträge zum humanitären Völkerrecht, zur völkerrechtlichen Friedenssicherung und zum völkerrechtlichen Individualschutz, Festgabe für Georg Bock* (Bochum: Brockmeyer, 1993), 17–47, 28–46 with further references.

[69] ICTY, *Mrkšić et al.* (IT-95-13/1-A), Judgment of the Appeals Chamber, 5 May 2009.

[70] The admissibility of pictures was also recognized as a problem by the American side, T. P. Keenan, 'Die Operation "Wüstensturm" aus der Sicht des aktiven Rechtsberaters' (1991/4) *HUV-I* 34–7, at 37.

[71] Ipsen, 'Auswirkungen des Golfkriegs auf das humanitäre Völkerrecht', in Voit (ed.), *Das humanitäre Völkerrecht im Golfkrieg und andere Rotkreuzfragen* (Bochum: Brockmeyer, Schriften zur Friedenssicherung und zum Humanitären Völkerrecht, 1992), 29–48, at 44. The report of the US Department of Defense on the Gulf War mentions the problem of reporting and refers to measures adopted to avoid placing the prisoners of war in danger, without listing in detail the actions of the Allies: Department of Defense, *Conduct of the Persian Gulf War*, above (n. 42) Appendix O-18.

SANDRA KRÄHENMANN

forces in Macedonia allegedly detained on Serbian territory were shown on Serbian television,[72] and in the Iraq War of 2003 individual Iraqi soldiers were broadcasted live when surrendering to Allied forces. Photos of detained persons from Guantanamo kneeling shackled and blindfolded, wearing surgical masks and earmuffs were condemned as a violation of the prohibition to expose prisoners of war to public curiosity.[73]

Even if such cases were not anticipated during the negotiations for GC III in 1949, the underlying purpose of rules on humane treatment prohibits the transmission of pictures of prisoners of war by the detaining power. Only two types of cases may be considered permissible.[74] First, photographic reports about prisoners of war do not violate the principle of humane treatment if the photographs do not enable the identification of individual prisoners. The other permitted case applies to reporting on prisoners and their conditions of captivity by the protecting power, the ICRC, or other internationally recognized organizations. Although in such cases the prisoners are exposed to public curiosity, reporting about them contributes to enforcing international humanitarian law and to improving the conditions in captivity. The examples of reports on prisoner-of-war camps in the Former Yugoslavia illustrate the requirement to weigh the protection of prisoners against the rule prohibiting their exposure to public curiosity. In the case of reporting by international observers, the protection of prisoners must prevail.

4. *Prohibition of discrimination.* GC III takes a clear stance on equality of treatment of prisoners of war. Equal treatment must be guaranteed by the detaining power, in particular where there are differences of race, nationality, religious belief, and the other aforementioned characteristics. However, Article 22, para. 3, GC III contains a rule on positive discrimination: it might be advantageous for prisoners of war to be grouped together in camps on the basis of their nationality, language, and customs. Such grouping is only possible if the prisoners are not thereby separated from the armed forces in which they were serving at the time of their capture, unless with their consent.

Article 14, para. 2, GC III contains further positive obligations for the treatment of women, who must be afforded special protection during their internment.[75] With this exception, international humanitarian law does not adequately address the needs of specific categories of detainees, such as women, children, the elderly and detainees with disabilities, in particular during non-international armed conflicts,[76] and needs to be supplemented by the relevant provisions of human rights law.[77]

5. *Prohibition of reprisals.* Article 13, para. 3, GC III lays down an absolute prohibition of reprisals against prisoners of war. There is no exception whatsoever to this principle. Even the most severe violations of GC III by the opposing side do not entitle the detaining power to resort to reprisals against prisoners. Unlike other branches of international law, humanitarian law is not governed by the principle of reciprocity (see above, Sections 141, 206, and below, Sections 1219 and 1402–1404). This is made clear in common Article

---

[72] See <http://www.un.org/Depts/DPKO/Missions/unpred_r.htm>.

[73] *The Independent*, 22 January 2002, 1.

[74] Fischer/Wallenfels, above (n. 68), 28–46.

[75] During the Second Gulf War, two female US soldiers were taken prisoner by Iraqi armed forces: Department of Defense, *Conduct of the Persian Gulf War*, above (n. 42) Appendix R-2.

[76] ICRC report 'Strengthening Legal Protection For Victims of Armed Conflicts' above (n. 27), at 8.

[77] For example, children are protected under the almost universally ratified 1989 Convention on the Rights of the Child (Article 37).

SANDRA KRÄHENMANN

1, in which the high contracting parties commit themselves to respect the Conventions in all circumstances. Violations of the provisions of GC III, therefore, cannot be justified with violations committed by the adversary. The clear and express prohibition of reprisals has repeatedly been disregarded in conflicts since 1949. For example, in the war between Iran and Iraq both states sought to justify certain operations by reference to violations by the adversary. Obviously, the conduct of the parties to the conflict was based on notions of reciprocity and reprisals.[78] On the other hand, the Second Gulf War also proved that the provisions of GC III can be respected even in the face of the most severe violations. Following the obvious maltreatment of allied pilots and their presentation in Iraqi television, the allied powers expressly confirmed that their troops would abide by GC III. During the course of the war on land the Iraqi prisoners were treated in accordance with GC III.[79]

6. *Prisoner's consent.* During the Second World War, it was often pretended that violations of the provisions of the law on prisoners of war were justified because the relevant prisoner consented. Article 7 GC III prevents the detaining power from relying on consent by the prisoner. Prisoners cannot, even partially, renounce their rights under GC III. Thus it is impossible for a detaining power to justify violations of GC III by claiming that a prisoner of war consented. Where the rights of prisoners are limited in their effect or tailored to certain groups, for example the rules on work by prisoners of war, GC III contains express stipulations for these cases. The highly detailed character of GC III is therefore an additional safeguard against a claim that prisoners of war had renounced certain rights.

7. *Implementing responsibility of the detaining power.* The detaining power is responsible for respecting the provisions of GC III. In order to fulfil this responsibility, GC III contains obligations, applicable in peace as well as in wartime. According to Article 127, the text of GC III is to be disseminated as widely as possible and its study is to be included in military training programmes, if possible, also in civil instruction. All armed forces and the civilian populations are thereby to be made familiar with the principles of GC III.

8. *Protecting powers.* The institution of the 'protecting power' was introduced to ensure compliance with the provisions of GC III (see below, Sections 1418–1419). As protection of prisoners of war is one of the most important mandates of a protecting powers, the main issues shall be discussed here.[80]

A protecting power is any state instructed by one of the parties to a conflict to safeguard its interests. The protecting power appoints delegates to carry out its tasks. These can be chosen from among its diplomatic or consular representatives, its nationals, or the nationals of other neutral powers. The party to the conflict must approve the delegates appointed. GC III enables an organization to act as a protecting power if it is clearly impartial and effective. The organization can be either international or non-international. It is a precondition, however, that the parties agree to confer the duties of a protecting power on that organization.

---

[78] P. Tavernier, 'Combatants and Non-Combatants' in I. Dekker/H Post (eds), *The Gulf War of 1980–1988* (Nijhoff, 1992), 129–44, at 132.

[79] Department of Defense, *Conduct of the Persian Gulf War*, above (n. 42) Appendix L-12.

[80] For a detailed analysis, see H. S. Levie, ' Prisoners of War and the Protecting Power' (1961) 55-2 *AJIL* 374–97.

SANDRA KRÄHENMANN

It is a fundamental weakness of the system under GC III that approval is necessary from the detaining party before the delegates appointed by the protecting power can carry out their activities. There is no general obligation to accept the appointed delegates, and furthermore no procedures for the selection of protecting powers by the parties to a conflict are generally available. Thus detaining powers can paralyse the system of protecting powers completely by refusing to approve the delegates. With the adoption of AP I in 1977 this situation changed considerably. Under Article 5 AP I the parties to a conflict are obliged to ensure the implementation of GC III and AP I by applying the system of protecting powers from the beginning of the conflict. Each party to the conflict shall without delay designate a protecting power at the outbreak of an armed conflict. The commencement of activities by this protecting power, however, depends on its acceptance by the adverse party. In contrast to Article 9 GC III, Article 5 AP I provides a procedure intended to facilitate the selection of a substitute protecting power in the event of non-acceptance of the appointed protecting powers. Yet, according to Article 5, para. 4, the substitute protecting power must also be accepted by the parties to the conflict before it may commence its services.

The main task of the delegates of the protecting powers is to visit prisoners of war and to question them without witnesses. To ensure that delegates can obtain a comprehensive and clear idea of the extent to which the provisions of GC III are being met, they may, as a rule, visit any place where prisoners of war are being held. This applies first to prisoner-of-war camps, but also to other places of detention and work as well as to points of departure, transit, and arrival of transferred prisoners of war. The right to visit is not subject to temporal restrictions. The length and frequency of visits is left for the delegates of the protecting powers to determine. The planning of visits by the delegates in terms of their location and timing may only be restricted by the detaining power for imperative military reasons, and then only temporarily. Such imperative military reasons may not be claimed on a regular basis. Visits shall be permitted even in transit camps as long as the delegates do not interfere with military operations of the detaining power and are not endangered by their visit.

A further function of the protecting powers is their participation in the settlement of disputes. According to Article 11 GC III, the protecting powers may offer their good offices particularly in cases of disagreement between the parties to the conflict regarding the application or interpretation of GC III, if they consider it necessary in the interest of the protected persons. The protecting powers' mediation services are not confined to these cases.

The system of protecting powers has only rarely been used since the Second World War. During the Suez crisis in 1956, protecting powers were designated by Israel, but Egypt did not authorize them to perform any duties. In the Falklands/Malvinas War, Switzerland assumed the function of protecting power for Great Britain and Brazil did likewise for Argentina. This is one of the few cases in which protecting power functions were utilized. Protecting powers were appointed neither in the conflicts in Korea and Vietnam nor in the war between Iraq and Iran. The consent of the detaining power which is a prerequisite to the protecting power's delegates commencing their activities continues to be a considerable restriction on the functioning of the system of protecting powers in international humanitarian law.

9. *The role of the ICRC.* The role of the ICRC is well defined in treaty law and custom (see below, Section 1424). It can assume the duties assigned to protecting powers under

two scenarios. First, the detaining power can request the ICRC or another humanitarian organization to carry out protecting power duties. A second possibility is for the ICRC, for instance, to offer its services under the system of protecting powers; yet it is not before the detaining power has accepted such offer the services can be performed. Thus in both cases, ICRC activities within the system of protecting powers depend on invitation or acceptance by the detaining power. That acceptance can be facilitated, and even replaced in exceptional situations, by the international community. In the conflict in Bosnia-Herzegovina, the Security Council had called on all parties to grant international humanitarian organizations, and particularly the ICRC, access to camps, prisons, and detention centres on the territory of the Former Yugoslavia.[81] In this case of gross violations of international humanitarian law, the Council obviously did not consider the approval of the ICRC's activities by the detaining power as necessary.

10. *The role of the UN and regional organizations.* Following the response of the international community to the conflicts in the Former Yugoslavia, one may even expect a further development in the understanding of the function of protecting powers. Such functions may be carried out by international organizations and special organs. For instance, delegations of the Conference for Security and co-operation in Europe visited prisoner-of-war camps in the Former Yugoslavia.[82] The former Polish Prime Minister Mazowiecki, appointed by the Human Rights Commission of the UN, also visited camps in the Former Yugoslavia on several occasions and reported violations against international humanitarian law.[83] These activities, and particularly the international debate on the findings of the investigations and its influence on the parties to the conflict, seem to indicate that international organizations and organs created especially for this purpose might be put in a position to carry out the functions of protecting powers (see below, Sections 1420–1421).

II. Beginning of Captivity

The status of prisoner of war begins as soon as a combatant (Articles 4 A, Nos. 1–3   707
and 6, GC III; Article 44 AP I) or other person with equal status (Article 4 A, Nos.
4 and 5; Article 4 B, No. 1; and Article 5, para. 2, GC III; Article 45, para. 1, AP
I) and *hors de combat* (Article 41, para. 2, AP I) falls into the hands of the adversary. An adversary who, having laid down his arms, or no longer having means
of defence, surrenders or is otherwise unable to fight or defend himself shall no
longer be made the object of attack (Article 41, para. 1, AP I; Article 23, para. 1,
HagueReg). He shall be taken prisoner of war.

1. *The connection between combatant and prisoner-of-war status.* The definite linkage between combatant and prisoner-of-war status is one of the fundamental principles of international humanitarian law. Article 44 AP I has confirmed this by categorically linking the status of prisoner of war with that of combatant. Only one precondition is

---

[81] SC Res. 771 (1992) of 13 August 1992.

[82] The suggestion of the Committee of Senior Officials of the CSCE of 9 February 1993 concerning an international criminal court refers to the various CSCE missions; *Proposal for an International War Crimes Tribunal for the Former Yugoslavia*, 30–3.

[83] See *Report on the situation of human rights in the territory of the former Yugoslavia*, UN Doc. E/CN.4/1993/50.

SANDRA KRÄHENMANN

laid down for the applicability of prisoner-of-war protection: the combatant must be captured by the adverse party to the conflict. The definitions of combatants in AP I, GC III, and the HagueReg therefore determine which group of persons is entitled to claim protection as prisoner of war (see above, Chapter 3). The relations established through treaties and by customary law between the parties to the conflict are the foundation for granting combatant status. If Article 43 AP I is seen as a further development of humanitarian law (see Sections 304–313) which also changed the constitutive preconditions for the classification as a combatant, then problems may arise in the uniform application of international humanitarian law in an armed conflict where several states are involved but only some of them are bound by AP I. If one party to the conflict is bound by AP I, members of its armed forces shall be treated as prisoners of war even if they only carry their weapons openly prior to an attack. For parties to the conflict only bound by GC III, the situation is different so that prisoner-of-war status cannot be claimed.[84]

Since the Second Gulf War, a new problem has emerged as to the point in time and the act by which persons become members of the armed forces. The UK had interned Iraqi students studying in London and kept them as prisoners of war. The reason stated was that the students were registered on a list of Iraqi reserve forces. The British position was criticized because the mere inclusion on a reserve list does not prove membership of the armed forces. Instead, passive and active reservists have to be distinguished.[85] As every state determines autonomously the composition of its armed forces, the commencement and termination of service in the armed forces must be ascertained according to the national law of the state involved.

Non-combatants also enjoy prisoner-of-war status. In contrast to what the term suggests, they do not belong to the civilian population, but are members of the armed forces who have been assigned special non-combatant functions (see above, Section 301). Accordingly, they shall be treated as prisoners of war on capture.

2. *Capture.* As the prisoner-of-war status begins at the moment of their capture, it has to be clarified when and by which act a person 'falls into the hands' of the adversary. The definition of *hors de combat* in Article 41, para. 2, AP I presumes that the detaining power has established its power over the person. On the battlefield this usually means that soldiers either surrender to the enemy or fall under the enemy's power after becoming unable to fight through injury.

As Article 12, para. 2, GC III lays down that the detaining power is responsible for prisoners of war, 'falling into the hands' can only occur if the combatants are captured or taken into custody by the competent state organs. During the Second Gulf War, for example, Iraqi soldiers have surrendered to journalists in the desert.[86] They did not attain prisoner-of-war status until they were handed over to the allied armed forces. Being on the adversary's territory does not fulfil the condition of 'falling into the hands'. Custody of a prisoner of war only commences with an act by a competent state organ. It is immaterial whether the prisoners of war surrender to the enemy following the cessation of their state's military operations. Persons captured after the surrender of their

---

[84] A. Rosas, above (n. 17), 342–3.
[85] F. Hampson, 'The Geneva Conventions and the Detention of Civilians and Alleged Prisoners of War' (1991) *Public Law* 507–22, at 515.
[86] *Süddeutsche Zeitung*, 28 February 1991.

SANDRA KRÄHENMANN

power are also considered to be in the hands of the enemy. They shall also be treated as prisoners of war.[87]

3. *Captured war criminals.* The Convention of 1929 contained no clear provisions about the status of captured war criminals. After the Second World War, allied courts denied of prisoner-of-war status to German and Japanese soldiers who were involved in unlawful war activities.[88] GC III determines in Article 85 that prisoners of war do not lose the benefits of the Convention because of acts committed prior to their capture. A detaining power is therefore not permitted to deny prisoner-of-war status to enemy combatants with the justification that they had allegedly committed war crimes. Nonetheless, in numerous conflicts since the Second World War persons have been denied prisoner-of-war protection for this reason.[89] After ratification of GC III, the Soviet Union and a number of other states made a reservation with regard to Article 85 aimed at changing the legal effect of that Article. Properly construed, this reservation[90] meant that persons convicted of war crimes or crimes against humanity should not receive the protection of GC III.[91] The reservation is considered today to be impermissible.[92] The majority of authors argue that even combatants who have obviously committed a war crime before being taken prisoner are entitled to the benefits of GC III, notwithstanding penal and disciplinary sanctions in accordance with Articles 82–108 GC III. Article 44 AP I strengthens this rule by stipulating that, in principle, uncertainties about the status of prisoners must be interpreted in their favour.

Furthermore, combatants may not be denied prisoner-of-war status on the grounds that the state for which they were fighting no longer exists or that its territory belongs to the state which is taking the soldiers prisoner. This latter was claimed by Iraq following the invasion of Kuwait in 1990.[93]

> **Detention of other persons in relation to an armed conflict must be restricted and procedures must be introduced to ensure periodical independent review. Arbitrary deprivation of liberty is prohibited (Rule 99 *CIHL*).**   708

1. *The legal framework.* With recent conflicts between states and non-state actors, a new issue came to the forefront: the question whether and how international law protects prisoners who are denied protected status under the Geneva Conventions or who are detained in a non-international armed conflict,[94] including international military

---

[87] H. Levie, *Prisoners of War in International Armed Conflict* (59 International Law Studies Newport RI: Naval War College, 1978), 35.

[88] Cf. in this respect Levie, above (n. 87), 384, 385.

[89] On the cases in North Vietnam cf. Levie, 'The Maltreatment of Prisoners of War in Vietnam', in R. Falk (ed.), *The Vietnam War and International Law*, Vol. 2 (Princeton, 1969), 361–937, at 383.

[90] The text of the reservation is reprinted in Levie, ibid. 386.

[91] On the assessment of the North Vietnamese reservation and the debate thereon during the Vietnam War, see H. Meyrowitz, 'The Law of War in the Vietnamese Conflict', in Falk (ed.), *The Vietnam War and International Law*, Vol. 2 (Princeton, 1969), 516–71, at 565–6.

[92] H. McCoubrey, *International Humanitarian Law: Modern Developments in the Limitation of Warfare*, 2nd edn (Aldershot: Dartmouth, 1998), 105.

[93] T. Meron, 'Prisoners of War, Civilians and Diplomats in the Gulf Crisis' (1991) 85 *AJIL* 104–16.

[94] For the applicability of international law in non-international armed conflicts, see below, Section 1201, para. 5. For an argument in favour of a universal combatant and prisoner-of-war status including during non-international armed conflicts, see E. Crawford, above (n. 21), at 153. Similarly, S. Scheipers concludes that 'the boundaries and cleavage lines that exclude captives from POW status are man-made and neither "objective" nor "natural"... the way in which these boundaries are drawn largely reflects the distribution of social and political power at a particular point in time', see S. Scheipers, 'The Status and Protection of

SANDRA KRÄHENMANN

operations abroad. The ongoing debates on who may be detained, on what grounds, for how long, and with what procedural guarantees[95] are often overshadowed by an assessment of the US policy of administrative detention of 'unlawful combatants' in the 'Global War against Terror',[96] although such questions arise as well outside this particular context.[97] Unlike prisoners of war and civilian internees (on the internment of civilians see above, Sections 585–587) in international armed conflict, international humanitarian law does not provide a straightforward answer to these questions.[98] Common Article 3, Article 75 AP I and Article 5 AP II foresee that individuals are detained in relation to an armed conflict, but these provisions fail to define the permissible grounds of detention, neither do they specify due process guarantees, presumably because such issues were to be addressed by domestic law, informed by international human rights law.[99] Although, in general, the applicability of human rights law during times of armed conflicts is well accepted,[100] the exact modalities of the interplay between human rights law and international humanitarian law remain controversial,[101] including the question of detention as such. In the absence of specific rules in international humanitarian law, some advocate the use of human rights law as the default, *lex specialis* regime to be applied. Others acknowledge that the difference between war and peace requires an adaptation of the general human rights law regime to detention during times of armed conflicts. Finally, on account of the difficulties to apply human rights law to such issues, a third position consists in stressing that treaty and customary international humanitarian law provide an adequate legal basis for detention with procedural safeguards to be developed.[102] Even if accepted, resorting to human rights law to fill the gap in international humanitarian law is fraught with difficulties. First, detention for security reasons in human rights law is generally linked to criminal prosecution,[103] in particular in the European Convention

Prisoners of War and Detainees', in H. Strachan and S. Scheipers (eds), *The Changing Character of War* (OUP, 2011), 394–409, at 406.

[95] E. Crawford, ibid. 100 ff.; Pejic, 'Conflict Classification', above (n. 24), at 80 and Sassòli and Olson, above (n. 24), 599.

[96] M. Hakimi, 'International Standard for Detaining Terrorism Suspects: Moving Beyond the Armed Conflict–Criminal Divide' (2008) 33 *Yale Journal of International Law* 369; Bellinger and Padmanabhan, above (n. 24); Jinks, above (n. 21), and Murphy, above (n. 21).

[97] For an account of the historic evolution of international humanitarian law leading to the exclusion of irregulars, see Scheipers, above (n. 94) and Crawford, above (n. 94), at 68.

[98] ICRC report 'Strengthening Legal Protection For Victims of Armed Conflicts' above (n. 27), at 6.

[99] Pejic, 'Conflict Classification', above (n. 24), at 90.

[100] G. Gaggioli and R. Kolb, 'A Right to Life in Armed Conflicts? The Contribution of the European Court of Human Rights' (2007) 37 *Israel Yearbook of Human Rights* 115–17. However, some states continue to contest the application of human rights law during times of armed conflict, see for example the Response of the United States to Specific Recommendations Identified by the Committee Against Torture, UN Doc. CAT/C/USA/CO, 25 July 2006; see also P. Alson, J. Morgan-Foster, and W. Abresch, 'The Competence of the UN Human Rights Council and its Special Procedures in Relation to Armed Conflicts: Extrajudicial Executions in the "War on Terror" ' (2008) 19-1 *EJIL* 183.

[101] For an overview, see, for example, Gaggioli and Kolb, above (n. 100), at 118–23; W. Abresch 'A Human Rights Law of Internal Armed Conflict: The European Court of Human Rights in Chechnya' (2005) 16-4 *EJIL* 741; F. Hampson, 'The Relationship between International Humanitarian Law and Human Rights Law from the Perspective of a Human Rights Treaty Body' (2008) 871 *IRRC* 558–62; H. J. Heintze, 'On the Relationship Between Human Rights Law Protection and International Humanitarian Law' (2004) 856 *IRRC* 789–98; C. Droege, 'Elective Affinities? Human Rights and Humanitarian Law' (2008) 871 *IRRC* 501.

[102] For an overview of these positions, see Hakimi, above (n. 96), at 370–5 and Pejic, 'Conflict Classification', above (n. 24), at 93–4.

[103] Hakimi, ibid. 383; Bellinger and Padmanabhan, above (n. 24), at 211.

SANDRA KRÄHENMANN

of Human Rights with its exhaustive list of grounds of detention.[104] However, provided that adequate procedural safeguards are in place, administrative detention for security reasons has been accepted,[105] including by the European Court of Human Rights if a valid derogation was made.[106] Second, the application of human rights law to military operations abroad is further complicated by the contested extraterritorial reach of human rights treaties.[107] Linked to this, it remains uncertain whether an armed conflict abroad might amount to a 'state of emergency' under human rights law and thus allow for a valid derogation.[108] Third, in cases of multinational operations abroad, the participating states might have differing human rights obligations. Finally, resorting to human rights law does not adequately deal with the question of detention by non-state actors[109] on account of the traditional perception that human rights law does not per se bind non-state actors, a perception that has, however, never been supported by UN practice.[110]

2. *The prohibition of arbitrary deprivation of liberty.* Despite these ongoing debates, it is accepted that the arbitrary deprivation of liberty is prohibited during an armed conflict.[111] Deprivation of liberty may be arbitrary on account of the legal ground of detention. Drawing on the regime for the internment of civilians, the 2005 ICRC guidelines suggest that 'imperative reasons of security' must be applied as a minimum standard.[112] Although not in the context of armed conflicts, human rights bodies condemned detention as arbitrary on account of the vague reasons for detention, often combined with executive discretionary powers.[113] In other words, the prohibition of arbitrary detention conveys the idea that even in the absence of clear guidelines freedom is the rule and detention the exception. Hence, detention must be restricted to instances where

---

[104] Article 5 ECHR.

[105] For an overview of the practice of human rights bodies, see, for example, L. Doswald-Beck, *Human Rights in Times of Conflict and Terrorism* (OUP, 2011), 263 and Hakimi, above (n. 96), at 386.

[106] ECtHR, *Lawless v Ireland* (No. 5310/71), Judgment, 1 July 1961, paras. 31–8; ECtHR, *Ireland v the UK* (No. 5310/71), Judgment, 18 January 1978, paras. 202–24.

[107] For a detailed analysis, see M. Milanovic, *Extraterritorial Application of Human Rights Treaties. Law, Principles and Policy* (OUP, 2011). The European Court of Human Rights confirmed the application of the ECHR to detainees in Iraq, see *Al-Jedda*, above (n. 25) and *Al-Saadoon and Mufdhi*, above (n. 57).

[108] See General Comment 29, above (n. 66), para. 3; ECtHR *A. and others v UK* (No. 3455/05), Judgment (Grand Chamber), 19 February 2009, paras. 82–6 and paras. 173–81.

[109] On this question, see D. Casalin, 'Taking Prisoners: Reviewing the International Humanitarian Law Grounds for Deprivation of Liberty by Armed Opposition Groups' (2011) 883 *IRRC* 743.

[110] See C. Tomuschat, 'The Applicability of Human Rights Law to Insurgent Movements', in H. Fischer, U. Froissart, W. Heintschel von Heinegg, C. Raap (eds), *Krisensicherung und Humanitärer Schutz—Crisis Management and Humanitarian Protection* (Berliner Wissenschafts-Verlag, 2004), 573–91, drawing on a coherent practice of the General Assembly and the Security Council to make insurgent movements responsible for respecting human rights. See also UNAMA, 'Afghanistan, Mid-Year Report 2012, Protection of Civilians in Armed Conflict' (Kabul, July 2012), at iii, and 'Afghanistan, Annual Report 2011, Protection of Civilians in Armed Conflict' (Kabul, February 2012), at iv, citing the 'Report of the Secretary-General's Panel of Experts on Accountability in Sri Lanka' (31 March 2011), 188; and the 'Report of the International Commission of Inquiry to investigate all Alleged Violations of International Human Rights Law in the Libyan Arab Jamahiriya', UN Doc. A/HRC/17/44 (1 June 2011) for the opinion that where non-state actors, such as the Taliban, exercise *de facto* control over territory, they are bound by international human rights obligations.

[111] See Rule 99 *CIHL* and the supporting practice.

[112] See Pejic, 'Procedural Principles', above (n. 26), at 380; see also Report of the Expert Meeting on Procedural Safeguards for Security Detention in Non-International Armed Conflict, (2009) 876 *IRRC* 859, 864–6.

[113] Doswald-Beck, above (n. 105), at 387.

SANDRA KRÄHENMANN

it is absolutely necessary and requires compelling reasons to be determined in each individual case.[114]

3. *Procedural safeguards.* A lack of procedural safeguards may render detention arbitrary. In addition to being informed of the grounds of detention, any detainee must be provided with the opportunity to periodically challenge the lawfulness of detention (habeas corpus) before an independent and impartial body, an obligation that may never be completely suspended.[115]

709   Prisoners of war shall be disarmed and searched. Their military equipment and military documents shall be taken away from them (Article 18, para. 1, GC III).

1. *Disarming and search.* The wording of Section 708 takes into account the security requirements of the detaining power. The detaining power's right to search is not restricted: the detaining power is entitled to find out what objects the prisoners of war are carrying with them. However, the authority to take away items is limited to arms, military equipment, and objects other than those listed in Section 709 below.

2. *Tying up prisoners of war.* It is not expressly laid down in GC III whether or not prisoners of war may be tied up following their capture. In 1942, German soldiers were captured and bound by British and Canadian task forces near Dieppe at the French Channel coast.[116] They were shackled in order to prevent them from destroying military documents. By way of reprisal for this incident allied prisoners of war in German camps and again German prisoners of war in Allied camps were bound. Tying of prisoners of war as a security measure also occurred during the Second Gulf War. Pictures of Iraqi soldiers in the Saudi desert with their hands tied behind their backs and waiting to be transported were seen worldwide.

There is no doubt that, as a general rule, binding prisoners of war in camps is prohibited.[117] Other standards might be applicable to tying on the battlefield, because the first goal of the detaining soldiers must be to prevent the prisoners of war from escaping or—as in Dieppe in 1942—to prevent the destruction of information. If it is permissible to shoot at prisoners of war in order to prevent them from escaping, then it is argued that the less drastic measure of tying them also complies with GC III.

The decisive argument against the permissibility of tying prisoners of war under battlefield conditions can be found in the detaining power's obligation to provide care for prisoners of war. As prisoners of war generally require freedom of movement on the battlefield in order to escape from danger, for example to seek cover from the use of weapons, tying them can be seen as a violation of the rule that prisoners of war shall not be subjected to unnecessary dangers prior to being moved from the battlefield.[118] Practices

---

[114] For a discussion of the potential pitfalls of a regime based on individualized determinations, see Bellinger and Padmanabhan, above (n. 24), at 220 and 227.

[115] Pejic, 'Procedural Principles', above (n. 26), at 385. The main controversy relates to whether or not judicial review is required, see Bellinger and Padmanabhan, above (n. 24), at 227.

[116] Cf. the description of the incident, ICRC, *Report on its Activities during the Second World War*, Vol. I (1948), 368–70.

[117] On the shackling of US prisoners of war in Vietnamese camps, see R. I. Miller, *The Law of War* (Lexington, MA, 1975), 172.

[118] Kalshoven, above (n. 14), 182.

SANDRA KRÄHENMANN

such as those seen occasionally during the Second Gulf War must therefore be regarded as violations of GC III.[119]

> Prisoners of war shall keep all effects and articles of personal use, their metal hel-   710
> mets, and NBC protective equipment as well as all effects and articles used for
> their clothing and feeding (Article 18, para. 1, GC III). They shall also keep their
> badges of rank and nationality, their decorations, and articles of mainly personal
> or sentimental value, for example pictures of family members (Article 18, paras. 3,
> 40 GC III).

1. For centuries, an important part of the law of war was the right to booty. Article 18 GC III restricts this right with regard to the effects of prisoners of war. This takes into account the security interests of the prisoners of war and of the detaining power as well as the special circumstances of captivity. Article 18 is based not on ownership of items carried by prisoners but on the use of the objects to the prisoner. Articles of personal use, regardless of whether they are owned by the prisoners of war or were provided by the home state, may not be confiscated. Also, clothing and items of food which are part of the prisoner's military equipment may not be taken away. It is essential for the safety of prisoners of war that helmets, gas masks, and similar items used for personal protection are left to them.

2. Article 18, para. 3, lists items of personal or sentimental value separately. Their signifi-cance to the well-being of the prisoner of war is obvious. Wedding rings or keep-sakes shall therefore not be confiscated. Not all articles of value are exempt from seizure by the detaining power. In this respect, the GC III is less restrictive than the Convention of 1929 which did not permit any objects of value to be taken away. Because during the Second World War prisoners of war used articles of value which they had been permit-ted to keep for their escape, GC III contains a special rule applicable to articles of value and money in Article 18, paras. 4 and 5 (see below, Section 712). Confiscation of arms, military equipment, horses, and military documents is permitted, even if these items are the personal property of the prisoner of war.

For answering the question whether prisoners of war must be permitted to keep objects which could be used for escape, the security interest of the detaining power and the interest of protecting the prisoner of war, both of which find expression in Article 18 GC III, must be taken into consideration. Confiscation is only permitted if two condi-tions are met: the objects must be essential for an escape and they must be replaceable by other objects provided by the detaining power. For instance, if the prisoners' clothing resembles that of the civilian population, the detaining power may replace it with other clothing.

> The detaining power is obliged to forward information regarding the fate of prison-   711
> ers of war (Article 122 GC III) as well as of wounded, sick, shipwrecked, and dead
> (Article 16 GC I; Article 19 GC II), and of protected civilians (Articles 136–141
> GC IV). For this purpose, each of the parties to the conflict shall institute an offi-
> cial Information Bureau on the outbreak of a conflict and in all cases of occupa-
> tion (Article 122, para. 1, GC III). The Bureau shall co-operate with the Central

---

[119] Ipsen, *Auswirkungen*, above (n. 71) 43. The report of the US Department of Defense on the Gulf War does not refer to these practices, Department of Defense, *Conduct of the Persian Gulf War*, above (n. 42) Appendix L.

SANDRA KRÄHENMANN

Prisoners of War Information Agency of the ICRC (Articles 122, para. 3, and 123
GC III).

1. *Obligation and organizational consequences.* Informing the relatives of prisoners of war
would be impossible without imposing an obligation on the detaining power to provide
information about the fate of prisoners of war. Article 122 GC III lists the details concerning prisoners of war and their well-being which the detaining power shall pass on.
It covers personal data such as name, first name, rank, and so on; information about
the medical condition of seriously ill prisoners; and notification of release, repatriation,
escape, and so on. The degree of fulfilment by the detaining power of the obligation
regarding personal data depends on the conduct of the prisoners of war. The detaining
power can pass this information on only if they give details beyond those required by
Article 17, for example their place of birth. If the prisoners of war fail to give such details,
the context of the GC III rules implies that the non-fulfilment of the obligation under
Article 122 cannot be held against the detaining power.[120]

The obligation of the detaining power to provide information is not limited to the
establishment of an official Information Bureau. Its organizational structure has to
ensure effective functioning. The detaining power may employ prisoners of war to work
in the bureau, taking into account the rules of GC III. The main task of the bureau is
to forward the information gathered to the home state of the prisoner of war. This shall
be done as quickly as possible. In former conflicts the question of the burden of costs for
forwarding such communications by international mail and telegraph service has played
a crucial role.[121] This problem may be diminishing under today's technological conditions. The wording of Article 124 GC III indicates a general exemption from charges for
communications by the national Information Bureaux and the Central Prisoners of War
Information Agency. However, state practice since the Second World War has shown a
need for separate regulations to cover the question of costs, for example in connection
with the International Telecommunications Union.[122]

The information is forwarded to the home state either by the protecting power or
by the Central Prisoners of War Information Agency. This agency, set up by the ICRC
under Article 123 GC III, not only deals with forwarding information received from
the national Information Bureaux, it also collects all available information and often
assumes the role of a mediator. In the conflict in the Former Yugoslavia, for example, the
ICRC dealt with about 3,000 prisoners during the first months of 1993.[123] The Central
Prisoners of War Information Agency played an important part in this. States cannot
avoid providing the relevant information by referring to a war on terror and the need to
keep information on the persons detained secret. GC III as well as international human
rights instruments provide protection against the disappearance of prisoners.[124]

The issue of persons missing in connection with armed conflict and other situations
of armed violence has lead to ever increasing problems, despite the rapid development
of modern information technologies. Hence it forms a priority task in the Agenda for

---

[120] Cf. also Levie, *Prisoners of War*, above (n. 87), 155.
[121] By 30 June 1947 the Central Tracing Agency of the ICRC had received 347,892 telegrams, J. de Preux,
above (n. 35), 592.
[122] Cf. de Preux, 591.
[123] *Süddeutsche Zeitung*, 4 June 1993.
[124] See Human Rights Council, A/HRC/1/L.2, International Convention for the Protection of All
Persons from Enforced Disappearance

SANDRA KRÄHENMANN

Humanitarian Actions, adopted at the 28th International Conference of the Red Cross and Red Crescent (Geneva, 2003). States are challenged to make specific contributions to solving current concerns and implementing existing obligations.

2. *Registration and special agreements.* In many conflicts since the Second World War parties have violated their obligations under Article 122 GC III to collect and forward information. Severe violations occurred, for example, during the Korean War, the border conflict between India and China in 1962, and the Vietnam War.[125] In order to rectify violations of the obligation to report states often conclude agreements, once conflicts are settled, to arrange for the joint search for missing war victims and prisoners of war. The US–Vietnamese Agreement of October 1992 on the opening of Vietnamese military archives has facilitated some access to government archives, but has not yet led to large numbers of Americans being removed from the rolls of missing people.[126] In some conflicts the parties did not even meet the basic precondition for gathering information, namely the registration of prisoners of war. The Iraq–Iran war is a typical example.[127]

3. *The duty to account for the fate of missing war victims and prisoners in war.* Human rights law further reinforces the obligations of states to provide information on the fate of missing war victims and prisoners.[128] Relying on the well-established principle that states have to account for the fate of individuals in custody,[129] human rights bodies routinely hold states responsible for the disappearances of individuals in times of armed conflicts if they were last seen in the power of state authorities[130] or in an area under the control of the state's armed forces.[131] The obligation to investigate the fate of the missing is a continuing obligation.[132] The suffering caused to family members by not knowing the fate of their relatives can in itself constitute prohibited ill-treatment, in particular if the state refuses to open an investigation or to provide information.[133] In order to enable states to do so and to prevent enforced disappearances, Article 17 of the 2006 Convention for the Protection of All Persons from Enforced Disappearances requires states to register all persons deprived of liberty and to make this information available if necessary.

---

[125] See Levie, *Prisoners of War*, above (87), 156, 157, n. 221; on the development in Vietnam, Miller, above (n. 117), 182–5.

[126] Cf. C. A. Henning, CRS- 'POWs and MIAs [Servicemen Missing in Action], Status and Accounting Issues', CRS Report for Congress (Library of Congress, 1 June 2006), CRS-5 <http://www.fas.org/sgp/crs/natsec/RL33452.pdf>.

[127] Cf. P. Tavernier, 'Combatants and Non-Combatants', in Dekker/Post (eds), *The Gulf War of 1980–1988* (Nijhoff, 1992), 129–44, at 132.

[128] M. Sassòli, 'La Cour européenne des droits de l'homme et les conflits armés,' in S. Breitenmoser et al. (eds), *Human Rights, Democracy and the Rule of Law* (Dike, 2007), 709, at 718–19.

[129] See, for example, HRC, *Zheikov v Russia* (No. 889/1999), Views, 31 March 2006, UN Doc. CCPR/C/86/D/889/1999, para. 7.2; ECtHR, *Salman v Turkey* (No. 21986/93), Judgment, 26 June 2000, paras. 99–100; IACtHR, *Baldéon-García v Peru*, Judgment, Series C No. 147, 6 April 2006, para. 120.

[130] HRC, *Mojica v Dominican Republic* (No. 449/1991), Views, 10 August 1994, UN Doc. CCPR/C/51/D/449/91; ECtHR, *Timurtaş v Turkey* (No. 23531/94), Judgment, 13 June 2000; ECtHR, *Bazorkina v Russia* (No. 69481/01), Judgment, 27 July 2006.

[131] See, for example, ECtHR *Luluyev and others v Russia* (No. 6948/01), Judgment, 9 November 2006, paras. 80–5; ECtHR, *Varnava and others v Turkey* (Nos. 16064/90 et al.), Judgment (Grand Chamber), 18 September 2009, paras. 181–6: disappearance of nine men during the armed conflict in Cyprus in an area under the control of the Turkish forces.

[132] ECtHR, *Varnava and others v Turkey*, paras. 147–9.

[133] Rodley, *Treatment of Prisoners*, above (n. 5), at 351–3.

SANDRA KRÄHENMANN

712   **Sums of money and articles of value carried by prisoners of war may not be taken away from them except by order of an officer of the detaining power and after a receipt has been given. Such money and objects shall be returned to prisoners of war at the end of their captivity (Article 18, paras. 4–6, GC III).**

1. The specific regulation concerning money and articles of value constitutes an exception to the prohibition of Article 18, para. 1, GC III. It provides only for temporary removal of money and articles of value. Thus the security of the prisoner of war's personal articles of value under the 1929 Convention remains intact in GC III, although it is now permitted to take away money from prisoners of war in the prescribed manner at all times. Articles of value may only be taken away from the prisoners of war for security reasons. The detaining power must decide whether or not articles of value, such as jewellery, could be used for an escape. In this case the same procedure must be followed as for taking away money.

2. The application of Article 18, para. 4, GC III involves two main problems which have not been dealt with satisfactorily to date. The first is connected with the actual securing of the money and articles of value, the issuing of a receipt, the registration, and the return at the end of captivity. Although the prescribed procedure is appropriate in principle for enabling the return of money and articles of value after the end of the conflict, the actual observation of the rule in practice, particularly when larger sums are involved, depends on the honesty of the officers and lower ranks. Furthermore, the detaining power must be able to administer and allocate the money to accounts. This is doubtful during the first phase of a conflict as well as in cases of great financial need of the parties to the conflict.

3. If the prisoners of war have in their possession money in the currency of the detaining power or of a neutral state, it may be questioned whether this money is subject to Article 18 GC III. Article 18 GC III does not differentiate between currencies. This is criticized by legal scholars, because prisoners of war could have acquired money through pillage, or receiving it from their home state in order to facilitate an escape. By applying Article 18 GC III in these cases and crediting their account with money attained in these ways, the prisoners of war might be rewarded for an illegal act.[134] In wartime, it will be nearly impossible to determine the origin of money and it will be difficult for all prisoners of war to prove the origin if special information is not available. For example, the involvement of prisoners of war in capturing soldiers of the detaining power could indicate illegal acquisition. The burden of proof in respect of the origin of money cannot, however, be imposed on the prisoners of war,[135] as this would mean that the prisoners of war would also have to provide proof of ownership of their articles of value. Only if there are clear indications that the money has been obtained illegally is the detaining power permitted to deviate from its obligations under Article 18 GC III.

713   **Prisoners of war shall be evacuated as soon as possible to camps situated in an area far enough from the area of operations for them to be out of danger. Prisoners of war shall not be unnecessarily exposed to danger while awaiting evacuation (Article 19 GC III).**

---

[134] Levie, *Prisoners of War*, above (87), 114, 115.
[135] Taking the point too far, Levie, ibid.

SANDRA KRÄHENMANN

1. *Aim of the evacuation*. From the beginning of their captivity the detaining power is responsible for the lives of the prisoners of war. This not only implies obligations to refrain from certain acts, as in the cases described in Sections 706 and 717–729, but it also imposes a positive duty to act in order to protect the lives of prisoners of war. The obligation to evacuate is one element of this duty to act. The geographical location of the camps to which prisoners may be taken (see Section 717) shall ensure that prisoners of war are not exposed to the effects of action on the battlefield. The basic duty to evacuate is complemented by the obligation to provide care intended to protect the lives of the prisoners of war, from the time of their capture until they are evacuated. This does not mean, however, that the detaining power has to plan and execute its hostilities solely with the protection of the prisoners of war in mind. It is merely expected that the dangers which already exist for the prisoners of war are minimized following their capture.

2. *Distance from the area of operations*. Section 713 refers to 'distance from the area of operations'. This is a term not used in GC III. In specifying the obligation to evacuate and to provide assistance prior to evacuation, Article 19 GC III uses the three terms 'combat zone', 'danger zone', and 'fighting zone'. The area of operations should be construed as referring to that part of the area of war which is required for offensive or defensive military operations under a task assigned and for administrative measures in connection with these military operations. Hence, the area of operations includes, first, the combat or fighting zone and the danger zone, as offensive or defensive military operations undoubtedly occur there. Second, the obligation under Article 19 GC III is extended to those areas necessary for administrative measures. Hence, the term 'area of operations' is consistent with international law even though the feasibility of fulfilling the obligation in a conflict may be doubtful.

The evacuation of prisoners of war from the combat zone does not guarantee complete and absolute safety from the effects of hostilities. During the Second Gulf War, Allied air raids as well as the use of long-range missiles turned the entire territory of the opposing state into a combat zone. In view of this, it is questionable whether the term 'combat zone' in Article 19 GC III reflects the standards of modern warfare. For example, was the accommodation of Allied pilots in hotels in Baghdad during the Second Gulf War equivalent to an internment in camps as required by Article 19 GC III? Baghdad could at any time be attacked, for instance, by sea-launched cruise missiles from Allied ships. De Preux defined the combat zone by reference to the range of land- and sea-launched weapons. Prisoner-of-war camps would have to be situated beyond their range to comply with Article 19.[136] Obviously, this interpretation requires critical review, as no party to a modern conflict can fulfil its obligations.

It may be considered that warfare employing modern long-range weapons is already taken into account on three levels by GC III: first, Article 23 provides prisoners of war with the same protection against air bombardment and other hazards of war as the civilian population. Second, through the protecting powers, the detaining powers can exchange information about the geographical location of prisoner-of-war camps. Third, camps shall be marked with the letters PG or PW (see Section 718 and Annex, Distinctive Emblems). In addition, a detaining power is not permitted to use prisoner-of-war camps in order to shield certain points from military operations.

---

[136] Cf. de Preux, above (n. 35), 172.

SANDRA KRÄHENMANN

The terms combat and fighting zone used in Article 19 GC III must therefore today be construed as being confined to the area of military ground operations and tactical measures supporting them from air or sea. This interpretation is also in line with the object of Article 47, para. 2, GC III concerning the transfer of prisoners of war when the front line draws closer, which may only occur under certain conditions.

3. *Timing.* The detaining power does not have an unlimited discretion regarding the evacuation, which must be carried out as soon as possible. This temporal requirement is not defined any more specifically in GC III. Its interpretation depends on the circumstances of the individual capture and the tactical and strategic battle situation. GC III undoubtedly permits a waiting period for prisoners of war following their capture, as expressed by Article 19, para. 3, GC III which imposes a duty on the detaining power to prevent unnecessary dangers prior to evacuation. It should also be kept in mind that the detaining power has an interest in questioning the prisoners of war on the battlefield in order to obtain information which can be of military use (see Section 716).

4. *Transport facilities.* What transport facilities have to be maintained in an armed conflict by the detaining power in order to fulfil the obligation under Article 19 GC III? During the Second Gulf War, the unpredictably large number of Iraqi soldiers who surrendered sometimes caused unavoidable delays in their evacuation from the front line and from temporary camps. The shortfalls in transport capacities were classified as a shortcoming in the report of the US Department of Defense on the Gulf War.[137] This cannot be called a violation of GC III, as the number of Iraqi prisoners of war was unforeseeable. The detaining power violates the obligation to evacuate if it makes available no, or obviously insufficient, transportation for prisoners of war. What constitutes as insufficient capacity depends on the circumstances of the conflict. No detaining power can avoid its obligation under Article 19 GC III by claiming that available transport vehicles were required for its military operations. If no transport is available or if the detaining power cannot ensure a timely evacuation, it has a duty under Article 41 AP I to release the prisoners of war (cf. Section 715).

714   **The evacuation of prisoners of war shall be effected in humane conditions, similar to those for the forces of the detaining power in their changes of station. Prisoners of war shall be supplied with sufficient food, clothing, and medical care. The civilian population shall be prevented from attacking prisoners of war (Article 20 GC III).**

1. *Transport conditions.* During the Second World War, transport conditions were one of the greatest difficulties in the treatment of prisoners of war. Prisoners of war died on their way from their place of capture to the camps because of insufficient care. As a result of such experience, Section 714 underlines the requirement of humane treatment, setting express and absolute restrictions on the treatment of prisoners of war during transportation. In this sense, Article 20 GC III is a specific instance of the general principle of humane treatment laid down by Article 13 GC III. The reference to sufficient food, clothing, and medical care exemplifies three areas essential to humane treatment. The connection between Articles 13 and 20 shows that treatment generally prohibited by Article 13 is also prohibited during transportation.

[137] Department of Defense, *Conduct of the Persian Gulf War*, above (n. 42) Appendix L-18.

SANDRA KRÄHENMANN

In an armed conflict, it cannot realistically be expected that the transport of prisoners of war will be carried out in a way similar to the transfer of forces of the detaining power,[138] although this standard is required by the wording of Article 20 GC III. The conditions for the transport of own troops are inevitably different from those for the transport of prisoners of war. Transferring units might have a decisive impact on the hostilities, whereas these considerations are immaterial in the case of transporting prisoners of war. The reference to the conditions of transport of the detaining power's troops can therefore only be understood as strengthening the requirement of humane treatment. On the other hand, such reference can by no means justify a violation of the principle of humane treatment. Even if the detaining power transports its own troops with insufficient care, this cannot be used as a justification for inhumane treatment of prisoners of war.

2. *Daily marches*. Both in the Second World War and the Korean War, excessively long daily marches have also caused the death of many prisoners of war on their way from the place of capture to their camps, apart from insufficient care. Although Article 7 of the Convention of 1929 prohibited marches longer than 20 km per day, prisoners of war were forced to march much greater distances.[139] Those responsible for these so-called 'death marches' in the Pacific theatre of war were found guilty of war crimes.[140] Despite the means of transportation available to every army, marches still play an important role in the evacuation and transfer of prisoners of war. In contrast to the 1929 Convention, Article 20 GC III does not specify a maximum number of kilometres the prisoners of war can be made to march per day. This obvious gap has been criticized,[141] and today a limit for prisoners of war of about 20 km or 12 miles per day is suggested for marches,[142] which was the figure stated in the 1929 Convention.

The reference to a specific distance in kilometres should not detract from the fact that, in practice, it is the physical condition of the prisoners of war, their clothing, mental state, the climate, and geographical conditions which have to determine the required marching distance. For soldiers fallen into the hands of the detaining power in a weakened state of health, marches of 20 km per day can mean certain death. On the other hand, troops in good physical condition with sufficient supplies and favourable climatic conditions can cover considerably greater distances. The commander responsible must, in the light of all of the circumstances, determine the distance which can be expected from the prisoners of war within the bounds of humane treatment. Hence, any suggested distances can only serve as guideline for the decision-makers of the detaining power.

3. *Transit camps*. The detaining power is also obliged to treat prisoners of war humanely in transit camps. Two types of transit camps are dealt with in GC III. First, there are those which the detaining power is permitted to establish under Article 20, para. 3, GC III for the temporary accommodation of prisoners of war transferred to their permanent camps. Second, there are the permanent transit camps mentioned in Article 24. These camps are

---

[138] Levie, *Prisoners of War*, above (n. 87), 101.

[139] On 'death marches' of the Second World War and in the Korean War: Levie, *Prisoners of War*, above (n. 87), 102; on the observations of the US Military Tribunal in Nuremberg of 14 April 1949: J. H. W. Verzijl, *International Law in Historical Perspective*, Vol. IX-A: *The Laws of War* (Sijthoff, 1978), 115.

[140] R. C. Hingorani, *Prisoners of War* (Oceana, 1982), 117.

[141] Levie, *Prisoners of War*, above (n. 87), 104.

[142] Hingorani, 132, n. 42.

SANDRA KRÄHENMANN

permanent establishments, accommodating prisoners of war before they are relocated to other camps. The permanent transit camps shall meet the standards set out in Articles 17–108 GC III for all camps (see Section 717). Due to the conditions of transport and the temporary nature of the transit camps regulated by Article 20, para. 3, GC III, more detailed rules do not apply there.[143] However, it must be guaranteed that transit installations are not used as permanent camps, as was the case in the Second World War.

4. *Protection against attacks on prisoners.* The duty to protect prisoners of war from attacks by the civilian population is a general principle of the treatment of prisoners of war. Therefore, it also applies to the transport phase, during which the prisoners may come into contact with the civilian population. This holds true for cases in which the transport of prisoners involves driving through localities as well as situations in which they are deliberately paraded before the civilian population. Attacks on prisoners include any actual attacks, insults, and defamations. The parading of prisoners of war shall also be regarded as a prohibited infringement, as it is not permitted to expose prisoners of war to public curiosity (see Section 706).

715   **Prisoners of war who, under unusual conditions of combat, cannot be evacuated shall be released; in this case, too, all feasible precautions shall be taken to ensure their safety (Article 41, para. 3, AP I).**

1. *Duty to release.* A significant addition to GC III concerning the treatment of prisoners of war is stipulated in Article 41 AP I. Under Article 19 GC III the obligation to release or repatriate prisoners of war during an armed conflict is limited to cases of injury and sickness and it thus depends on the physical condition of the prisoner of war. In contrast, Article 41 AP I applies irrespective of the physical condition of the prisoners of war. If the lives of prisoners cannot be protected because evacuation is impossible, they must be released. Article 41 AP I thus adds a further responsibility to the duty to evacuate and care for prisoners under Article 19 GC III. During the 1994–1977 Diplomatic Conference the capture of soldiers by commandos operating behind enemy lines was mentioned as a typical example of situations with unusual conditions of combat to which Article 41 AP I might apply.[144] Yet, neither the wording nor the object and purpose of Article 41 AP I indicate that its scope is limited to this type of situation. It is true that Article 41 AP I must be regarded as an exceptional rule. However, whenever an evacuation is impossible because of the circumstances of combat, the prisoners must be released. The term 'unusual conditions of combat' includes situations resulting from a normal battle situation, where climatic circumstances would render it impossible to care for or to evacuate the prisoners of war over a longer period of time.

2. *Safety measures.* The duty arising out of Article 41 AP I is not fulfilled simply through the act of release. The safety of the prisoners of war following their release shall also be taken into consideration. This requires positive action on the part of the releasing party. It is not clear which particular acts can be expected. Rowe points out that international customary law requires that the prisoners of war are provided with sufficient amounts of food and water to ensure their survival.[145] However, if all food supplies of a

---

[143] Cf. de Preux, above (n. 35), 176.
[144] Cf. de Preux, 489.
[145] P. J. Rowe (ed.), *The Gulf War 1990–91 in International and English Law* (Routledge, 1993), 164.

SANDRA KRÄHENMANN

commando unit are necessary for a long operation, Article 41, para. 3, AP I should not be construed as requiring that some of these supplies be given to the prisoners of war being released.[146]

> Every prisoner of war, when questioned on the subject, is entitled to give only   716
> his surname, first names, rank, date of birth, and army, regimental, personal,
> or service number. The exercise of this right shall not cause him any disadvan-
> tage (Article 17, para. 4, GC III). The questioning of prisoners of war shall be
> carried out in a language which they understand (Article 17, para. 6, GC III).
> No physical or mental torture, nor any other form of coercion, may be inflicted
> on prisoners of war to secure from them information of any kind whatsoever.
> Prisoners of war who refuse to answer may not be threatened, insulted, or exposed
> to unpleasant or disadvantageous treatment of any kind (Article 17, para. 4,
> GC III).

1. *The right to question and its limits.* The provisions on the right to question and the limits imposed on this right are among the best-known rules of GC III. The detaining power has a substantial interest in obtaining information about military planning of the enemy. Prisoners of war, on the other hand, cannot usually estimate how the interrogating officer would react if refused information. If they give information about military actions of their units and armed forces, they infringe the obligation of loyalty owed to their state. Hence, it is of great practical importance to refer to Article 17 GC III as an objective parameter. The information on name, army, regiment, personal or serial number, and so on permits the detaining power to identify the prisoner of war and to pass on information to the official Information Bureau in accordance with Article 122 GC III.

While the prisoner of war's obligation to provide information is limited under Article 17, the detaining power is not prohibited to ask further questions. But the questioning procedure is regulated particularly as to the mode of questioning, the duties of the prisoner of war to co-operate, and possible reactions of the detaining power. The questioning must be carried out in such a manner that the prisoner of war is able to respond to the questions posed. Therefore, a language which the prisoner understands must be chosen for the questioning. Hence, the native tongue of the prisoner of war must be used if he does not speak and understand any other language. All types of coercion on the part of those questioning in order to secure information from prisoners of war are prohibited. Article 17 expressly forbids the use of physical and mental torture as coercive measures. Physical coercion falling short of torture is also generally prohibited. The beating of allied pilots held as prisoners of war by Iraq in the Gulf War in 1991 was therefore correctly referred to as a violation of Article 17 GC III.[147]

Article 17 does not mention any other kinds of influence apart from coercing prisoners of war in order to obtain information. The promise of privileges or the use of psychological tricks would not be in breach of Article 17 GC III.[148] This interpretation reflects the reality of armed conflicts, in which parties continue to try to obtain information from prisoners of war. As was demonstrated by the preparation and operation of the Allied forces' land warfare in the Gulf War against Iraq in 1991, information about

---

[146] Cf. Solf, in Bothe/Partsch/Solf, *New Rules for Victims of Armed Conflicts* (Nijhoff, 1982), 224.
[147] Department of Defense, *Conduct of the Persian Gulf War*, above (n. 42) Appendix 0–19.
[148] Levie, *Prisoners of War*, above (87) 108 with further references.

SANDRA KRÄHENMANN

the morale of enemy troops, for instance, plays an important part in the conduct of hostilities. However, psychological interrogations techniques which result in inhumane treatment are prohibited.[149]

The general permissibility of questioning should not obscure the fact that the questioning procedure must be strictly observed in order to fulfil the object and purpose of Article 17. Prisoners of war are in danger of being punished by their home state for giving information to the detaining power, even if this information was obtained by adopting skilful methods of questioning, rewards, or privileges. In addition, other prisoners in the same camps may punish them for the information disclosed, if they find out about it. Questioning on crimes committed by the prisoners during or before the conflict has to follow the same rules and limitations even if the national criminal law would permit physical or psychological force to get information. States cannot deviate from their international treaty obligations by referring to necessities of national security.[150]

2. Sanctions for denial of information. The prohibition against coercing prisoners of war does not restrict the detaining power's ability to prosecute them for acts committed prior to their capture. The wording of Article 85 is clear in this respect (see below, Section 728).

III. Conditions of Captivity

717   The detaining power may subject prisoners of war to internment, that is put them into camps and guard them (Article 21, para. 1, GC III). These camps shall not be situated in danger zones (Articles 19, para. 1, and 23, para. 1, GC III). They shall not be used to render certain areas immune from military operations (Article 23, para. 1, GC III).

1. The right of internment. Article 23 GC III confirms the traditional right of the detaining power to intern prisoners of war in order to preclude them from participating further in hostilities. The detaining power may restrict the movement of the prisoners, depending on the organization of individual prisoner-of-war camps. This can, but need not necessarily, coincide with the boundaries of the camp. Prisoners of war may be granted greater freedom of movement. They may only be locked up in a cell as a disciplinary or penal measure under Chapter VI GC III. Tying up prisoners of war in the camps is prohibited.

2. The use of weapons. The right of internment implies that the detaining power also has a right, as a last resort, to use weapons against prisoners of war. This is expressly laid down in Article 42 GC III, listing escape and attempted escape as examples. With the purpose of internment and the detaining power's general obligations towards the prisoners of war in mind, it can be concluded that the use of weapons against rioting prisoners of war is also permitted. Weapons may only be used if actually *necessary*. This means that the use of force by a single prisoner of war against guards does not necessarily entitle them

---

[149] For an evaluation of such techniques see the Church report, <http://www.defenselink.mil/news/detainee_investigations.html>.

[150] The statements in J. R. Schlesinger, H. Brown, et al., *Final Report of the Independent Panel to Review DoD Detention Operations*, 2004, <http://www.isn.ethz.ch/pubs/ph/details.cfm?lng=en&id=10157>, 85–9, are a deviation from existing international law.

SANDRA KRÄHENMANN

to use weapons. Only if the guards are in serious danger may prisoners of war be shot at.[151] What precautions have to be taken into account by the guards is not regulated. However, the obvious excessive use of force has to be avoided even if the prisoners are rioting.[152] A prisoner of war who surrenders while fleeing may not be fired at, as the reason for using arms has ceased to exist.

The use of weapons must always be preceded by an appropriate warning. A warning shot qualifies as reasonable warning. Other forms of acoustic or visual signals might also meet the requirement. The crucial point is that the prisoner of war can recognize the warning for what it is. The establishment of so-called death lines, the crossing of which leads to the immediate shooting of the prisoner of war without warning, is therefore not permitted.[153]

3. *Prisoners of war as shields.* The obligation to carefully choose the location for camps entails two consequences for the detaining power. The distance from the combat zone is the first factor in determining the position of prisoner-of-war camps (see Section 713). Additionally, the detaining power shall not use camps in order to secure a military advantage. Article 23, para. 1, does not define the meaning of 'certain points or areas' which can be rendered immune from military operations by the presence of prisoner-of-war camps. A reference to the definition of military objectives in Article 52 AP I undoubtedly indicates that only military objectives of the detaining power are included, as attacks against other, civilian, objects are already prohibited by international humanitarian law. The use of prisoner-of-war camps as a shield for civilian objects can be eliminated by definition. As the headquarters of the Iraqi secret service in Baghdad was a military objective, the internment of US prisoners of war in that building was a violation of Article 23 GC III.[154] Also, individual prisoners of war may never be used as human shields.

> The camps shall meet certain minimum requirements of hygiene and health (Article 22, para. 1, GC III). They shall be provided with shelters against air raids and other hazards of war (Article 23, para. 2, GC III). Whenever the military situation permits, prisoner-of-war camps shall be marked by the letters PG (*prisonniers de guerre*) or PW (prisoners of war), clearly visible from the air (Article 23, para. 4, GC III).

718

1. *Minimum requirements.* It stems from the general requirement of protecting prisoners of war that appropriate conditions of hygiene for prisoner-of-war camps must be met. Article 22, para. 1, GC III refers to localities affording every guarantee of hygiene and health rather than to the hygiene conditions within the camps. This follows both from the wording and from the relation between Articles 22, para. 1, 22, para. 2, and 29 GC III. The reference to the climatic conditions in Article 22, para. 2, GC III elucidates the connection between the minimum requirements and the geographical location of the camp. In addition, the requirements for camps concerning cleanliness and health are

---

[151] Taking the point too far: M. Greenspan, *The Modern Law of Land Warfare* (University of California Press, 1959), 104; see also Levie, *Prisoners of War*, above (87), 403.

[152] For the events in Mazar-I-Sharif in Afghanistan in 2001, see the critical view of M. Byers, *War Law* (Douglas & McIntyre, 2005), 131.

[153] A. H. Harvey, 'The Maintenance of Control over Prisoners of War' (1963) II *RDMilG* 127–51, at 137.

[154] Department of Defense, *Conduct of the Persian Gulf War*, above (n. 42) Appendix O–19.

SANDRA KRÄHENMANN

dealt with explicitly in Article 29 GC III.[155] The following situations are practical examples of violations of Article 22, para. 1, GC III:

— the construction of a camp in a region in which water is not available and to which sufficient amounts of water cannot be brought;
— the construction of a camp in an area which is chemically contaminated.

Furthermore, the obligation from Article 29 GC III is not met in cases where the detaining power, for example, does not provide any or enough facilities for personal hygiene within prisoner-of-war camps. Article 29, para. 2, GC III also provides that separate conveniences shall be provided for female prisoners of war.

2. *Protection against air raids.* In all conflicts since air warfare began, the protection of prisoners of war against air raids has caused great difficulties. The 1929 Convention contained neither a rule about the protection of prisoners of war against air raids nor about the marking of prisoner-of-war camps. Article 23, para. 2, GC III does not impose an absolute duty on the detaining power to provide the camps with air raid shelters. The detaining power's duty to provide protection for prisoners of war is linked to the protection provided to the civilian population. Shelters shall be provided for prisoners of war only 'to the same extent' as that afforded to the civilian population. Thus, there are two possible scenarios for prisoners of war in camps which are located near towns. Either the same shelters must be built for prisoners of war as for the civilian population or the existing shelters for the civilian population must also be made available to the prisoners of war.[156] The second alternative is expressed in Article 23, para. 2, second sentence, GC III.

In respect of camps located close to inhabited areas, Section 718 exceeds the obligations imposed by GC III. GC III does not require the construction of any shelters in prisoner of war camps separate from residential areas of the civilian population. The protection of prisoners of war against attacks in these cases can be achieved through the marking of the camps. The detaining power has, however, no choice as to other protective measures, as these are for the benefit of the prisoners of war as much as for the civilian population. The distribution of gas masks, for example, may not be limited only to the civilian population.

3. *Obligation to mark prisoner-of-war camps.* In the Second World War, approximately 1,000 prisoners of war died as a result of air raids. In view of the dangers of air warfare, Article 23, para. 4, GC III introduced the duty to mark prisoner-of-war camps with the letters PG or PW (see Annex, Distinctive Emblems). However, this obligation is qualified by the words 'when the military situation permits'. The question arises as to whether marking is therefore left to the unrestricted discretion of the detaining power. De Preux has correctly stated that marking does not depend on criteria to be determined by the detaining power alone.[157] In the age of satellite reconnaissance, concerns that enemy air forces could use the marks as a navigation aid[158] are no longer a convincing argument.

---

[155] On the conditions in Iraqi and Iranian prisoner-of-war camps during the war between Iraq and Iran, cf. S. Lamar, 'The Treatment of Prisoners of War: The Role of the International Committee of the Red Cross in the War Between Iran and Iraq' (1991) 5 *Emory International Law Review* 243–83, at 270–3.

[156] Cf. de Preux, above (n. 35), 188.

[157] Cf. de Preux, above (n. 35), 190.

[158] This concern was expressed by some states at the diplomatic conference of 1949, *Final Record of the Diplomatic Conference of Geneva*, Vol. II, Section A, *Report of Committee* II, 564.

SANDRA KRÄHENMANN

As a rule, the detaining power will not be able to avoid marking the camps. In practice, since the Second World War, however, the marking of prisoner-of-war camps has caused difficulties despite the rule in GC III. In the Korean War, US aircraft bombarded Korean prisoner-of-war camps, thus causing the death of US soldiers.[159] North Vietnam did not mark any of its prisoner-of-war camps during the Vietnam War, and US soldiers who had attempted to mark the camps themselves were punished.[160]

> **As far as possible, prisoners of war shall be assembled according to their national-   719
> ity, language, and customs (Article 22, para. 3, GC III).**

The obligations binding the detaining power as to the treatment of and supplies for prisoners of war in camps includes their accommodation according to nationality, language and customs. Article 22 GC III is of practical importance particularly in cases in which several allied parties fight in an armed conflict. Under Article 22, para. 3, GC III, there is no discretion for the detaining power as to the internment, but rather an absolute obligation which the detaining power must fulfil.

The assembling of prisoners of war according to language serves primarily to improve their conditions of captivity. It also helps the detaining power to meet its obligations in respect of the dietary needs of prisoners from different cultures and with different customs and to meet their religious requirements. To alleviate the special psychological problems of prisoners of war, grouping under Article 22 GC III also serves to maintain personal ties between the individual prisoners and facilitate their mutual assistance.

The grouping together of prisoners of war is irrelevant to maintaining discipline.[161] GC III presupposes the separate internment of officers; this practice is generally accepted.

> **Prisoners of war shall receive sufficient food (Article 26 GC III) and cloth-   720
> ing (Article 27 GC III), as well as necessary medical attention (Articles 29–31
> GC III).**

1. *Sufficient food.* This section specifies the general obligation of the detaining power to protect the lives of the prisoners of war in terms of providing food, clothing, and medical care. In contrast to Article 11 of the 1929 Convention, Article 26 GC III does not link the amount and quality of food required to the supplies of the troops of the detaining power. During the Second World War, some parties to the conflict had limited or altogether denied the provision of food to prisoners of war and referred to the poor food supplies of their own troops in order to justify their actions by referring to the wording of the Convention of 1929.

GC III has not left the decision of what is considered to be sufficient up to the detaining power. According to Article 26, the food must be sufficient to keep prisoners of war in good health and to avoid weight loss and deficiency symptoms. This rule sets out an objective standard which must be applied to each individual prisoner of war. GC III does not allow exceptions to the obligation to provide care. Prisoners of war may not receive insufficient care because of their religion or association with an aggressor state. The insufficient care for the prisoners in the so-called starvation camps, such as

---

[159] P. Spinnler, *Das Kriegsgefangenenrecht im Koreakonflikt: Eine Untersuchung über die Konfrontation des traditionellen Kriegsgefangenenrechts mit Erscheinungsformen moderner bewaffneter Konflikte* (Rüegger, 1976), 51.
[160] Miller, above (n. 117), 287.
[161] Spinnler, 70–3.

SANDRA KRÄHENMANN

Omarska near Banja Luka in 1992,[162] was a flagrant violation of Article 26 GC III. This is also true of the insufficient nutrition given to some US prisoners of war held captive in Iraq during the Second Gulf War in 1991.[163]

The wording of Article 26 GC III raises two problems. First, it is possible that weight loss occurs not as a result of insufficient food but due to the psychological condition of prisoners of war. In this case, the detaining power would have to prove that the weight loss could not be due to poor nutrition. More important in practice is the situation where prisoners of war receive insufficient food because the detaining power is also unable to provide its own troops with sufficient food. Levie refers to this problem.[164] GC III states a strict obligation to provide the prisoners of war with sufficient food, with no exceptions.[165]

The significance which GC III gives to the nutrition of the prisoners of war is also illustrated by Article 26, para. 6. According to this provision, the detaining power is not permitted to impose collective disciplinary measures by withholding food from prisoners of war. Prisoners are thus protected against reductions of food rations for disciplinary reasons, which are a reaction to the misconduct of some prisoners but affect other members of the group. Furthermore, the link between Article 26 GC III and 89 GC III clearly shows that disciplinary punishments must not, as a rule, affect the provision of food as required under Article 26 to the extent that the health of the prisoners of war is endangered.[166] Only special privileges going beyond the scope of Article 26, for example special rations, may be affected by disciplinary punishments.

It is disputed whether food may be used to enforce order in the camp. Is it permitted, for instance, to provide rioting prisoners of war with food only in certain areas of a camp in order to induce them to return to those areas? This measure may be less detrimental to the health of prisoners of war than, for example, the lawful use of weapons by guards under Article 42 to maintain order in the camps in the event of revolt (see Section 717). However, danger of abuse of such measures should not be underestimated. If a detaining power permits visits to the camps by ICRC delegates under Article 122, the reasons for such measures are still relatively easy to ascertain. Harvey is therefore correct in arguing for the lawfulness of such actions.[167]

2. *Sufficient clothing.* In contrast to the provision of food, the obligation to provide clothing is not expressly linked to the medical condition of the prisoners of war. Qualifications, such as preventing the prisoners from freezing to death, burning, and so on are not included in the wording of Article 27 GC III. The purpose behind the provisions for the treatment of prisoners of war in captivity is to keep them alive and respect their dignity. Clothing must correspond to this purpose. This holds true generally, and particularly in areas with harsh climatic conditions. The greater the dangers of the climate to the health of prisoners of war, the stricter the requirements are for the detaining power to provide prisoners of war with adequate clothing.

---

[162] The Canadian report to the Secretary General of 10 March 1992 contains a comprehensive overview of the conditions in the camps in the Former Yugoslavia, UN Doc. S/25392, 10 *et seq.*

[163] Department of Defense, *Conduct of the Persian Gulf War*, above (n. 42) Appendix 0–19.

[164] Levie, *Prisoners of War*, above (n. 87), 127.

[165] Cf. de Preux, above (n. 35), 196.

[166] Cf. de Preux, 200.

[167] Harvey, above (n. 153), 143, also citing the different position of the ICRC.

SANDRA KRÄHENMANN

3. *Medical attention.* The fundamental duty to provide prisoners of war with medical attention is stipulated in Article 15 GC III and complemented by the special duties for preventing and treating illness in Articles 29–31 GC III. The provisions of Chapter III GC III concern both the prevention of sickness and its treatment. The required medical attention stated in Section 720 applies to the treatment of sick prisoners of war. They should primarily be treated by doctors of their own state. The treatment by doctors of the detaining power is secondary to this.

Article 31 GC III is directly connected with Article 13 GC III, which specifies the obligation of humane treatment in terms of providing medical treatment. Generally, the treatment of sick prisoners of war required by Article 31 GC III prohibits medical or scientific experiments. Such experimentation is permitted only if justified by the medical treatment of the prisoners of war and is in their interest. In practice, this leads to the complicated clause that, as a rule, medical experiments of any kind are prohibited unless they are required to keep a certain prisoner of war alive. This formula prevents any type of experimentation on prisoners of war being carried out, as was the case during the Second World War in German and Japanese prisoner-of-war camps. On the other hand, there is enough latitude to enable doctors to use all possible treatments for prisoners of war without running the risk of being found guilty of a war crime.

Latitude in the exercise of religious duties shall be ensured (Article 34 GC III).   721

1. *Religious practice.* The obligation to ensure freedom of worship touches on one of the most important preconditions for the mental well-being of prisoners of war. It is of particular importance during conflicts in which soldiers of different religions fight against one another. The practice of religion is subject only to the disciplinary routine prescribed by the military authorities. The interpretation of the term disciplinary routine and its contents may cause problems in individual cases. Under no circumstances may the disciplinary routine render the practice of religion impossible or substantially impede it. On the other hand, the practice of religion must not interfere with the maintenance of discipline in the camps. It is in the interest of both the prisoners of war and the detaining power that the camp commander arranges the disciplinary order of the camp so as to enable prisoners of war to carry out their religious customs. This is particularly important because under Article 34, para. 2, GC III, the detaining power must provide adequate premises for religious services.

2. *Chaplains.* In addition to the freedom of worship of prisoners of war, Article 35 GC III contains special provisions regarding the work of chaplains (see below, Chapter 8). They are permitted to minister to the prisoners of war and the detaining power shall permit them to have access to the necessary facilities. If chaplains care for prisoners of war located outside the camps, the detaining power must provide them with the means of transportation required for these visits. Chaplains also have a special privilege in respect of communication. Subject to permitted censorship by the detaining power they are allowed to correspond with the ecclesiastical authorities of the detaining power and with international religious organizations and to send letters and cards in addition to the usual quota laid down in Article 71 GC III.

The detaining power may utilize the labour of able-bodied enlisted men for cer-   722
tain non-military works (Articles 49, para. 1, and 50 GC III). Non-commissioned

SANDRA KRÄHENMANN

officers shall only be required to do supervisory work. Officers are exempted from compulsory work (Article 49, paras. 2 and 3, GC III).

1. *Obligation and right to work.* The Hague Regulations already permitted prisoners of war to be employed for work. Both the Convention of 1929 and GC III have maintained this right of the detaining power. As is made clear by Article 49, para. 3, GC III, the detaining power is entitled to compel prisoners of war to work. The disciplinary measures under Article 89 GC III may be used as a means of enforcement of the work.

Originally, work was regarded from the point of view of its importance to the health of prisoners of war. In both World Wars, the value of the labour of prisoners of war to the detaining power's economy also became apparent. The wording of Article 49 GC III is based on the entitlement of the detaining power.[168] There is, however, no express duty for the detaining power to provide work. According to Article 49, para. 1, GC III, a special purpose of work can be to maintain the prisoners of war in a good state of physical and mental health. From this addition to the general right to employ prisoners, a right of prisoners of war to be given work can be derived.[169] Section III of GC III, concerning the labour of prisoners of war, contains no further definition of any such a right of prisoners of war to work. The general obligations of the detaining power under Articles 29 and 38 GC III do not refer to a right of prisoners of war to work either. This right is merely hinted at by the general purpose of GC III, that is to guarantee the protection of prisoners of war as far as possible. In practice, this can only be relevant if the health of prisoners of war is likely to suffer if they do not work.

2. *Conditions and limitations.* The detaining power's right to utilize the labour of prisoners of war is not unlimited. The obligation to work only applies to healthy prisoners of war. Their age, sex, rank, and physical aptitude must all be taken into consideration. The employment of sick prisoners of war for labour is prohibited, as is the use of physically weak prisoners of war for hard physical work. In this respect, special protection is provided to women.

The categories of work permitted and the working conditions of prisoners of war are laid down in much greater detail than in the 1929 Convention. Work in agriculture, domestic service, and in commercial arts and crafts areas are permitted without restriction. Employment in metallurgical, chemical, and machinery industries is absolutely excluded because these industries play an important role in the production of weapons in wartime.[170] The employment of prisoners of war in industries of military importance, which was required of prisoners during the Second World War in Germany, is thus prohibited.[171]

Work involving the transport and handling of stores, public works, and building operations is permissible if this work has a civilian character and purpose. The detaining power shall ensure working conditions equal to those for nationals of the detaining power.

3. *Exceptions to the duty to work.* Article 49 GC III sets down exemptions from the duty to work for officers, thereby preserving the differential treatment which has been

---

[168] This aspect is neglected by de Preux, above (n. 35), 260, when he sees the purpose of Article 49 only in maintaining the health of prisoners of war.

[169] Hinz, above (n. 17), 98, acknowledges this duty to a certain extent.

[170] Cf. de Preux, above (n. 35), 266.

[171] C. Rousseau, above (n. 16), 92, 93; on the employment of Vietcong in South Vietnamese military projects, see Meyrowitz, above (n. 91), 560.

SANDRA KRÄHENMANN

accepted since the nineteenth century. GC III does not define what is meant by 'supervisory work', which non-commissioned officers may be required to do. It is generally agreed that manual labour does not qualify in this context. Both groups may, however, ask for suitable work and may also give it up without restriction. The special rules concerning officers were for the most part complied with during the Second World War.[172]

Prisoners of war carrying out certain special functions are also exempt from the duty to work. Enlisted men fall under this category if they are assigned to officers' camps under Article 44, para. 2, GC III. If among prisoners of war there are doctors and nurses who do not belong to the medical service of their armed forces, they may be assigned by the detaining power to care for other prisoners. In that case they are also exempt from the duty to work.

> No prisoner of war shall be employed against his will on labour which is of an unhealthy or otherwise dangerous nature (e.g. mine-clearing), or which is humiliating; nevertheless, he may volunteer to do dangerous or unhealthy work (Article 52 GC III).

723

1. Article 52 GC III contains a special qualification to the detaining power's general right to employ prisoners in labour. The general right is limited in three cases. First, the prisoner of war may not be used for unhealthy or dangerous work; GC III repeats the words of the 1929 Convention. The conference of 1949, however, was unable to agree on which types of work should be regarded as unhealthy or dangerous. Article 52, para. 3, GC III mentions only the removal of mines or similar devices as dangerous work. This express reference to mine-clearing combined with the possibility of voluntarily carrying out such work is the result of intense debates at the diplomatic conference of 1949. There were considerable differences of opinion as to the employment of prisoners of war in mine-clearing operations. On the one hand, there was the opinion that prisoners of war should not be used for mine-clearing on the basis of humanitarian considerations. On the other hand, the fact that some of the mines were likely to have been laid by the prisoners themselves was put forward. Furthermore, it was suggested that prisoners of war were better trained for mine-clearing than the civilian population who would be adversely affected by clearing operations. The conference eventually agreed on the provision on mine-clearing, having in mind that in the final phase of the Second World War German prisoners of war were employed in France on such work which resulted in numerous deaths.[173]

2. Types of work classified as unhealthy or dangerous are limited to the permitted types expressly identified by Article 50. Work in agriculture, if it is connected with unhealthy conditions, can be prohibited work within the meaning of Article 50.[174] This also applies to work in industries that could endanger the lives of the prisoners of war. There is an exception to the prohibition of dangerous labour. If prisoners of war volunteer to do unhealthy or dangerous work the detaining power may employ them in this way. Positive action by the prisoners of war is required to ensure that the preconditions of Article 52 GC III are fulfilled. The act of volunteering meets these requirements. Thus,

[172] Levie, *Prisoners of War*, above (n. 87), 224, n. 39, however, mentions violations of this rule by Japan.
[173] ICRC *Report on its Activities during the Second World War*, Vol. I (1948) 333–4.
[174] The ICRC, for instance, protested during the Second World War against the work of German prisoners of war in sugar plantations in the US because the prisoners were subjected to the sun in the tropical climate all day long without protection, ibid.

SANDRA KRÄHENMANN

the detaining power may not impute consent to employment in unhealthy or dangerous work. On acceptance the prisoner of war must be aware of the danger or health risks involved; the detaining power must inform the prisoner of war about the risks involved in the work. As far as unhealthy and dangerous labour is concerned, the quality of the work has to be weighed against the physical condition of the prisoner of war. Arduous unpaid work from morning to night with very little food and water over a longer period and under hot weather conditions had been regarded by the ICTY as war crime.[175]

This does not apply to humiliating work. In the latter case, the application of the prohibition depends on how the work is classified by the detaining power if it is to be done by the members of its own armed forces. If in such cases the work is considered to be humiliating, then prisoners of war may not be employed to do it either. In contrast to unhealthy or dangerous work, prisoners of war cannot validly consent to do humiliating work. In combination with Article 14 GC III, Article 52, para. 2, GC III secures the principle of the inalienability of rights also contained in Article 7 GC III. Under no circumstances may the detaining power circumvent the limits imposed by GC III by giving the prisoners of war a partially civilian status. The French practice of giving prisoners of war the status of 'travailleur civil' violated the 1929 Convention.[176]

724   **Not more than one week after arrival at a camp, every prisoner of war shall be enabled to write direct to his family and the Central Prisoners of War Agency, informing them of his captivity (Articles 70 and 123 GC III), and to correspond regularly with his relatives thereafter.**

1. Contact with the outside world is very important for the well-being of prisoners of war. Such contact also allows the protecting power or the ICRC to ensure that GC III is enforced. As a rule, therefore, prisoners of war are permitted to send and receive correspondence. Although the detaining power is entitled to limit the number of letters and postcards sent, at least two letters and four postcards per month must be permitted.

2. The notification to the family and the Central Prisoners of War Agency about the capture as expressly provided in Article 70 GC III does not count as part of the permitted quota of letters and postcards. With this card the prisoners of war are given the opportunity to communicate with their relatives and also with the central information agency established by the ICRC. The detaining power cannot prevent or delay this communication. This message must be permitted to be sent after one week and, as laid down in Article 71, para. 1, fifth sentence, GC III, shall be forwarded by the fastest method available. Neither the initial message to families and the information agency nor normal correspondence may be prevented for disciplinary reasons. This applies to both incoming and outgoing post. Restrictions imposed by North Korea and China during the Korean War were a clear violation of this obligation.[177] Since correspondence provides contact between prisoners of war and their relatives, the protecting power, and so forth, it is unlawful for the detaining power to misuse the post for propaganda purposes.

725   **Regarding inadequate conditions of captivity, prisoners of war may apply to the authorities of the detaining power or to a protecting power (Article 78, paras. 1 and**

---

[175] ICTY, *The Prosecutor v Naletilić and Martinović*, Case No. IT-98–34-T, Trial Chamber Judgment of 31 March 2003, para. 323.
[176] Cf. Rousseau, above (n. 16), 93.
[177] Spinnler, above (n. 158), 74.

SANDRA KRÄHENMANN

2, GC III). The exercise of the right to make complaints shall not give rise to any punishment (Article 78, para. 3, GC III).

1. One of the prerequisites for observing the provisions of GC III is the detaining power's awareness of the conditions in the prisoner of war camps. Article 78, para. 1, GC III gives prisoners of war the right to appeal to the detaining power in respect of all matters relating to the conditions of captivity. As pointed out in Section 725, it especially includes those cases concerning poor camp conditions. GC III is based on the idea that prisoners of war apply in writing to the military authorities detaining them. Article 78, para. 3, GC III expressly sets out that requests and complaints may not be limited and must be transmitted immediately. In particular, inspection visits by representatives of the protecting power serve to check compliance with GC III. Under Article 78, para. 2, GC III the right of prisoners of war to present requests and complaints also exists vis-à-vis representatives of the protecting power. Prisoners of war can apply to the representative of the protecting power with their complaints either directly of through their representative. Article 78, para. 2, GC III names the representative of the protecting power as the contact person. The International Committee of the Red Cross and its delegates are not separately mentioned. An analogous application of Article 78 GC III to the representatives of the ICRC follows from Article 126, para. 4, GC III, which gives the delegates of the International Committee the same privileges as representatives of the protecting powers. This is especially important for prisoners of war, as the system of protecting powers has not functioned to date.

2. The detaining power is not permitted to punish requests and complaints by prisoners of war. Even if their assertions prove unfounded, the requests and complaints may not give rise to any punishment. Thus both disciplinary punishments and penal measures of the detaining power against prisoners of war for exercising their right under Article 78 are prohibited.

> **The prisoners of war shall elect representatives to represent their interests; where officers are among the prisoners of war, the senior officer shall be recognized as the camp prisoners' representative (Articles 79–81 GC III).**   726

Communication by prisoners of war with the organs of the detaining power and with the delegates of the protecting power or of the ICRC can be difficult due to the large number of prisoners of war in camps. In addition, it might sometimes be difficult for prisoners of war to make their needs clear. GC III provides for the election of prisoners' representatives whose task it is to promote the physical, moral, and mental well-being of the prisoners of war. Representatives are elected every six months by free and secret ballot. Article 79 GC III lays down two conditions for the election of prisoners' representatives. First, Article 79, para. 2, GC III stipulates that in officers' camps and mixed camps the most senior officer who is a prisoner of war is automatically the prisoners' representative. In mixed camps the representative's assistant shall be elected from among the prisoners of war who are not officers. This preference for officers serves to improve communication between the detaining power and the protecting power since officers have more experience in negotiating than other prisoners of war. Both elected and recognized representatives must be approved by the detaining power. The detaining power therefore has the right to decide on the commencement of duties of the prisoners' representatives. If they do not approve they must inform the protecting power of the reason. If prisoners

SANDRA KRÄHENMANN

of war of different nationalities, languages, and customs live in the same camp a separate representative shall be elected for each of these groups.

727   **A prisoner of war shall be subject to the laws, regulations, and orders effective in the armed forces of the detaining power. The detaining power shall be justified in taking judicial or disciplinary measures in respect of any offence committed by a prisoner of war against these provisions (Article 82, para. 1, GC III).**

1. *Applicability of the detaining power's legal order.* The special situation of prisoners of war in camps becomes especially clear in Chapter III of GC III. During captivity prisoners of war, who are normally subject to the national law of their home state, are subject to those legal rules of the detaining power which also apply to its armed forces. This subjection lasts until captivity ends, either by escape or release. This rule also applies if a prisoner of war is transferred from one detaining power to another under Article 12, para. 2, GC III. On transfer, the law applicable to the armed forces of the new detaining power automatically applies to the prisoners of war. GC III reiterates the rule already laid down in the HagueReg and the Convention of 1929, although following the Second World War intensive debates took place about other rules which would more appropriately take into account the interests of prisoners of war.[178]

The application to prisoners of war of the law governing the armed forces of the detaining power requires that the prisoners be aware of the applicable rules. The detaining power has an obligation under Article 41, para. 2, GC III to inform prisoners of war of the rules governing their conduct. Two conditions must be met in this respect: the information must be given in a language understood by the prisoners of war, and displayed in locations in the camp where all prisoners of war can read them.

2. *Restrictions on the choice of procedure.* As with its own troops, the detaining power can choose between two types of punishment for violations of the aforesaid provisions. Due to the special situation of prisoners of war, Article 83 GC III directs the authorities of the detaining power to choose disciplinary rather than judicial measures whenever possible. For two types of offences judicial measures are expressly prohibited and disciplinary measures prescribed. Certain offences committed by prisoners of war while attempting to escape are subject exclusively to disciplinary measures (see Section 731). Violations of national laws, regulations, and so on of the detaining power which are only punishable if committed by prisoners of war, under Article 82 GC III, entail only disciplinary punishment. An act violating administrative rules of a prisoner-of-war camp, for example, which of course do not apply to the detaining power's own troops, may only result in disciplinary punishment by the camp commanders.

3. *Prosecution of war crimes and criminal offences.* Article 85 GC III provides a special ground for prosecution. The detaining power is permitted to prosecute prisoners of war for acts committed prior to capture. Thus prisoners of war can be held responsible by the detaining power for both war crimes and for criminal offences.[179] The status as prisoner of war cannot be used as argument challenging jurisdiction of the court of the detaining power in a trial where the defendant is charged with ordinary crimes.[180] Any criminal

---

[178] Hinz, above (n. 17), 144, 145.
[179] See below, Chapter 14, 'Introductory Remarks', para. 4, and Sections 1410–18.
[180] *US v Noriega*, Case No. 88–79-CR, US District Court for the Southern District of Florida, Judgment of 8 June 1990.

SANDRA KRÄHENMANN

offence committed prior to capture including terrorist crimes can be prosecuted. The provisions of GC III entailing the judicial rights of prisoners of war have to be applied.

> **Penal and disciplinary sanctions are governed by the following rules:**   728
> — **No prisoner of war may be punished or disciplined more than once for the same act (Article 86 GC III).**
> — **Prisoners of war may not be sentenced to any penalties except those provided for in respect of members of the armed forces of the detaining power for the same acts (Article 87, para. 1, GC III).**
> — **Prisoners of war shall be given an opportunity to present their defence (Articles 96, para. 4, and 99, para. 3, GC III).**
> — **Collective punishment for individual acts and cruel punishment are forbidden (Article 87, para. 3, GC III).**

1. Without procedural guarantees, the detaining power would be in a position to endanger the life and health of prisoners of war on the basis of judicial decisions. As a result of the experiences of the Second World War, during which numerous violations of the 1929 Convention occurred in respect of the punishment of prisoners of war, GC III established procedural rules for both disciplinary and juridical procedures. This is of particular importance with regard to disciplinary procedures, because in 1949 the rights of the defendant in disciplinary procedures varied greatly in the different national legal orders. With the often limited possibilities for camp commanders to determine who is responsible for violations of camp rules, the prohibition of collective penalties is an important restatement of the rule in the Convention of 1929. It protects the innocent and prevents arbitrary punishment by the camp authorities.

2. In addition to the fundamental guarantees of criminal law, Article 84 GC III determines the composition of the trial court. As a rule, this shall be a military court. Civil courts may only try prisoners of war in exceptional cases where they would also have jurisdiction had the alleged offence been committed by a member of the detaining power's armed forces. Under no circumstances shall a prisoner of war be tried by a court which does not guarantee independence and impartiality.

> **Acts which constitute offences against discipline shall be investigated immediately**   729
> **(Article 96, para. 1, GC III). Disciplinary punishment may be ordered only by appropriate courts of law, military commanders, camp commanders, and their representatives who have been assigned disciplinary powers (Article 96, para. 2, GC III). In no case may prisoners of war themselves exercise disciplinary powers (Article 96, para. 3, GC III).**

1. *Responsible organs.* Usually, prisoner-of-war violations of disciplinary rules occur more frequently than offences against criminal law. This is why GC III sets out not only general procedural rules for disciplinary punishment, but also who may order such punishment, what form the punishment may take, and how it shall be implemented. In view of the special circumstances particularly of large prisoner-of-war camps, GC III requires an immediate examination of offences against discipline. This rule promotes the safety of prisoners of war from arbitrary treatment by camp commanders or fellow prisoners. Despite the possibility of punishment being ordered by subordinates of the camp commander, it is always the commander's responsibility to ensure compliance with GC III. The practice during the Second World War of permitting prisoners of war to punish

SANDRA KRÄHENMANN

violations of the rules of the camp, for example theft from fellow prisoners, is clearly prohibited by the wording of Article 96, para. 3, GC III.

2. *Disciplinary punishments.* The organs of the detaining power are not free to choose any disciplinary punishment. Article 89 GC III contains an exhaustive list of permissible disciplinary punishments. By stating that disciplinary punishments shall not be inhumane, Article 89 GC III does not open the door to punishments not mentioned in GC III, but instead imposes a further restriction on the execution of the prescribed disciplinary punishments.[181] The punishment of a prisoner of war by sentencing him to a permitted form of work can be inhumane if the prisoner is in no physical condition for it. An execution of a disciplinary punishment in penal establishments is also not permitted. As a rule, food and correspondence by mail may not be withheld as a disciplinary punishment from prisoners of war. The restriction in GC III on the types of permissible disciplinary punishment could make it difficult to maintain order in a prisoner-of-war camp if the prisoners break the rules of the camp frequently and severely. The camp commander can take all measures necessary to prevent such violations, provided that none of the guarantees for prisoners of war in GC III are infringed. Usually, severe violations of camp rules are also included in the criminal law of the detaining power. Criminal prosecution is therefore possible in these cases.[182]

IV. Escape of Prisoners of War

730   Prisoners of war who have made good their escape and who are recaptured shall not be liable to any punishment in respect of their escape (Article 91, para. 2, GC III). The escape of a prisoner of war shall be deemed to have succeeded when the person (Article 91, para. 1, GC III):
— has joined friendly or allied armed forces;
— has entered neutral territory or otherwise left the territory under control of the adversary; or
— has joined a ship in the territorial waters but not under the control of the detaining power.

The regime governing prisoners of war is based on the detaining powers exercise of control over them. If this is no longer possible, captivity in the sense of international law ceases. The Brussels Declaration as early as 1874 contained a rule about the termination of captivity by escape. Since 1874, this general principle has not been the subject of any serious discussion. Only defining a successful escape proved to be difficult. The rules of GC III for the most part do not raise any problems from a legal point of view. The definition of a successful escape is based on the possibility of the actual exercise of control, either on land or at sea. An escape can therefore not be considered successful simply because the prisoner of war has reached the high seas with a rowing boat. On the other hand, captivity ends if the detaining power cannot exercise its territorial sovereignty on its own territory, as is the case when foreign ships are in its territorial waters or when part of its territory is occupied. If several escaped prisoners of war continue their escape jointly or if they join a unit of their own armed forces which is about to be captured,

---

[181] Cf. de Preux, above (n. 35), 440.
[182] Harvey, above (n. 153) at 147.

SANDRA KRÄHENMANN

the conditions of Article 91, para. 1, GC III are not fulfilled as there is no actual interruption, not even a brief moment of being beyond the detaining power's reach.[183] The question of whether the preconditions of Article 91 GC III are in fact fulfilled will only be relevant if prisoners of war are recaptured by troops of the detaining power and penal or disciplinary punishment is considered for acts committed during the escape.

> **A prisoner of war who has been captured in his attempt to escape shall be liable**   731
> **only to disciplinary punishment in respect of his act (Article 92, para. 1, GC III);**
> **this shall also apply to a repeated offence.**

Article 92 GC III imposes an absolute prohibition on the punishment of prisoners of war in cases of attempted escape. One of the reasons why penal and other non-disciplinary punishments are categorically prohibited is that, particularly during the Second World War, prisoners of war who attempted to escape were subjected to draconian punishment and even killed. Article 92 GC III does not exclude the use of weapons under the circumstances described above (see Section 717) in order to prevent escape. In order to avoid the use of weapons once the escape has been discovered, and in order to qualify for the privilege of Article 92 GC III, prisoners of war should indicate unequivocally that they will not continue with their attempt to escape.

> **A prisoner of war shall not be liable to judicial prosecution even when committing**   732
> **offences to facilitate his or her escape, for example theft of food or clothing, or**
> **the drawing up and use of false papers. This shall not apply to cases in which the**
> **escapee has used violence against life or limb during his escape (Article 93, para.**
> **2, GC III).**

1. Article 92, para. 2, GC III singles out a special case of disciplinary punishment of prisoners of war following an attempted escape. Judicial prosecution is not permitted in these cases. Punishable acts shall merely lead to the disciplinary punishment of prisoners of war, unless they do not involve criminal intent, for example in the case of violent acts against life or limb. However, the privilege concerning punishment only applies if the acts were committed in order to facilitate an escape. Facilitating the escape must have been the primary and only reason for committing the offence.

2. In the case of theft, the prisoner of war loses the privilege if he also has the intent to enrich himself. For example, if prisoners of war steal an automobile in order to help them to escape with the intention of selling it after escaping, then Article 93 GC III does not prohibit their criminal prosecution.[184] It is difficult to ascertain their intention if prisoners of war destroy public property possibly impeding their escape. The demolition of a bridge or the destruction of a telephone switchboard can make it more difficult to trace the escapee and thus facilitate the escape.[185] Such acts could also be seen as unnecessary acts of destruction. In the second case, punishment according to the criminal law of the detaining power is possible. The fact that as combatants they are permitted to carry out legal acts of war cannot be used by prisoners of war as a defence. Until the termination of

---

[183] Inferring from de Preux, 446.

[184] Examples of the punishment of prisoners of war for theft of automobiles and other articles during the Second World War are given by H. Frey, *Die disziplinarische und gerichtliche Bestrafung von Kriegsgefangenen* (Springer, 1948), 95–7.

[185] Harvey, ibid. 146, considers such acts or destruction to be permitted.

SANDRA KRÄHENMANN

captivity either by release or escape, prisoners are subject to the legal order of the detaining power to the same extent as the detaining power's own troops. The detaining power may try prisoners for sabotage in connection with acts of destruction.

3. There is no such privilege if the acts carried out involved violence against life or limb. This is particularly important if escaped prisoners of war are recaptured. It is true that the detaining power's right of disciplinary punishment for acts connected to the escape is not revived following recapture.[186] For all other offences, however, the detaining power's right to punish persists. A murder which was committed during an escape, for instance, can be prosecuted following recapture.

V. Termination of Captivity

733　　Save by a successful escape, captivity shall cease with the release of the prisoner from the custody of the detaining power.

1. GC III provides two possibilities for the termination of captivity. The successful escape mentioned in Section 732 terminates captivity. In this case, the detaining power is released from all obligations under GC III concerning the captivity. The term release includes both the repatriation of seriously sick and seriously wounded prisoners of war during the conflict and the release and repatriation of prisoners of war after the conflict has ended. In both cases, the duties of the detaining power are not fulfilled by merely releasing the prisoners, but the release is linked with the repatriation of the prisoners of war.

2. Captivity is formally terminated by the death of a prisoner of war. In view of the detaining power's fundamental duty to care for prisoners of war, Article 121 GC III requires an enquiry and report, for example that the cause of death is unknown or the death was caused by a sentry. In fulfilment of the duty to carry out an official enquiry into deaths of prisoners of war and in order to inform the protecting power, the US forwarded enquiry reports about three deaths in Saudi Arabian prisoner-of-war camps to the ICRC following the Gulf War.[187] Human rights law requires states to carry out an investigation into the death of every prisoner, including during military operations abroad.[188]

734　　Seriously wounded and seriously sick prisoners of war who are fit to travel and whose mental or physical fitness has been incurably or permanently diminished or whose recovery may not be expected within one year shall be repatriated during the armed conflict. No prisoner of war, however, may be repatriated against his will during hostilities (Articles 109, 110 GC III).

1. *Duty to repatriate during the conflict.* Article 109 GC III is an exception to the detaining power's right to intern prisoners of war for the duration of the conflict. Article 110, para. 1, GC III lays down an obligation to repatriate for the three categories of wounded and sick prisoners of war named in Section 733. The reason for imposing this duty on the detaining power can be found in the state of health of the prisoner of war. The detaining power has to send these prisoners of war back to their own country without

---

[186] Apparently de Preux, above (n. 35), 454, concurs.
[187] Department of Defense, *Conduct of the Persian Gulf War*, above (n. 42) Appendix 0–18.
[188] *Al-Skeini and Others v the UK* (No. 55721/07), Judgment (Grand Chamber), 7 July 2011.

SANDRA KRÄHENMANN

delay. For other wounded and sick prisoners of war whose physical condition is less critical, the detaining power has a discretion to transfer them to neutral states for hospitalization.[189] The precondition for such transfer is the expectation that through internment in a neutral country the prisoners of war will recover, or recover more quickly, or that a threat to health from continued captivity can be avoided.

2. *Renewed involvement in hostilities.* One aim of captivity is to prevent the prisoners from taking further part in hostilities against the detaining power. The repatriation prescribed in Article 109 GC III for prisoners of war during a conflict increases the risk that, after recovering, the prisoners will once again take part in hostilities on the side of their own country. For this reason, Article 117 GC III prohibits the employment of repatriated persons in active military service. The US respected this obligation following the repatriation of three pilots by North Vietnam during the Vietnam War in 1972.[190]

Since this obligation is addressed to the home state, it is generally assumed that the prisoners of war cannot be held responsible for violations of Article 117 if recaptured by the detaining power.[191] Prisoners of war may not be charged with a war crime for their renewed involvement in hostilities.[192] The list of grave breaches in Article 130 GC III does not refer to Article 117 GC III. Neither has a recognition that breaches of Article 117 GC III constitute war crimes emerged in customary law.

> **All prisoners of war shall be released and repatriated without delay after the cessa   735
> tion of active hostilities (Article 118 GC III). This requires neither a formal armi
> stice agreement nor the conclusion of a peace treaty. What matters is the actual
> cessation of hostilities, provided that, according to a reasonable estimate, they are
> unlikely to resume. Repatriation is carried out in an orderly manner, in accordance
> with a plan agreed by all parties, working with and under the control of the pro
> tecting powers and the International Committee of the Red Cross (Articles 8–10
> GC III).**

1. *Duty to release.* Article 118 GC III stipulates the general duty of the detaining power to release prisoners of war. This duty is qualified in a number of respects. First, in terms of timing, the prisoners shall be released after the cessation of active hostilities. Furthermore, this Article prohibits every detaining power from determining a time for the release. The phrase 'without delay' clarifies that the obligation to release is in force directly after the cessation of active hostilities. The duty to repatriate is not affected by peace negotiations.[193] Under international law the obligation to release is not dependent on corresponding conduct of the enemy.[194] Practice has shown, however, that states do base their conduct on such reciprocity. Parties may also not retain prisoners of war for

---

[189] During the First World War, many prisoners of war were interned in Switzerland under an agreement between the parties to the conflict, J. W. Garner, *International Law and the World War*, Vol. 1 (Longmans, 1920), 55, 56.

[190] R. Falk, 'International Law Aspects of Repatriation of Prisoners of War During Hostilities' (1973) 67 *AJIL* 465–78, at 470.

[191] Cf. de Preux, above (n. 35), 539.

[192] Cf. in this respect the comments of Y. Dinstein, 'The Release of Prisoners of War', in Swinarski (ed.), *Essays in Honour of Jean Pictet*, 38–45, at 39.

[193] H. Fischer, 'Die Rückführung von marrokanischen Kriegsgefangenen in der Hand der Polisario', (1990/1) *HuV-I* 14–16; 'Neue Studien über "Der geplante Tod" von James Bacque' (1991/3) *HuV-I* 117–18.

[194] J. Quigley, 'Iran and Iraq and the Obligations to Release and Repatriate Prisoners of War After the Close of Hostilities' (1989) 5 *The American Journal of International Law and Policy* 73–86, at 80.

SANDRA KRÄHENMANN

using them to overcome labour shortage as a result of the armed conflict[195] or to facilitate negotiations on ending the hostilities.[196]

The duty to release is interwoven with the duty to repatriate. These terms are linked by the wording of Article 118, para. 1, GC III so that the mere release of prisoners of war after the cessation of active hostilities does not fulfil the obligation. Repatriation requires a plan which may either be concluded by agreement among the parties to the conflict or, failing such agreement, may be set up by the detaining power.[197] Article 118 GC III does not allow for repatriation without a plan. The release of Kuwaiti prisoners of war following the Second Gulf War, when Iraq sent prisoners of war on their way home through the desert, constituted a breach of Article 118 GC III.[198]

A repatriation plan must stipulate the type of repatriation, the time schedule, and the persons involved. In practice after long conflicts such a plan is developed by the parties when the UN is involved.[199] Furthermore the requirements laid down in Article 119 GC III shall be taken into consideration. Thus articles of value must be returned to the prisoners before repatriation. They are permitted to take with them their personal effects, their money, and parcels they received during detention.

The possibility of exchanging prisoners of war during a conflict is not expressly mentioned in GC III. In modern wars, such exchanges have almost never occurred. In the conflict between Croatia and Serbia in 1991, however, the parties concluded an agreement on the release of 1,600 prisoners through the mediation of the ICRC.[200]

2. *Cessation.* Unlike the Hague Regulations and the Geneva Convention of 1929, the obligation to release does not arise only by agreement between the parties to the conflict. While the Hague Regulations considered a peace treaty to be such an agreement, the first Convention on Treatment of Prisoners of War of 1929 stipulated that an armistice agreement effected the obligation to release. The practice of wars after 1907, particularly the two World Wars, demonstrated that linking the duty to release to an international treaty on final settlement provided the detaining powers with a means of keeping prisoners of war under their power for as long as possible. This is now precluded under Article 118 GC III. The actual cessation of hostilities automatically effects the obligation to release prisoners of war.

What is meant by cessation of hostilities and who decides when this actually occurs? A formulation coined by Schwarzenberger is frequently adopted, according to which hostilities have ceased if 'neither side expects a resumption of hostilities'.[201] This definition permits parties to a conflict to estimate subjectively the intention of the adversary.

---

[195] See *New York Times*, 'Red Cross Officials to Discuss P.O.W.'s Still Alive in North Korea', 23 August 2005

[196] *New York Times*, 'U.S. to Press Hanoi to Explain '72 P.O.W. Report', 13 April 1993.

[197] On the repatriation of prisoners in conflicts in Chechnya, see <http://www.hrw.org/reports/1997/russia2/Russia-03.htm>. On the role of NGOs, see Weissbrodt.

[198] See Gasser, 'Die Aktivitäten des Internationalen Komitees vom Roten Kreuz im Golfkrieg', in Voit (ed.), *Das humanitäre Völkerrecht im Golfkrieg und andere Rotkreuz-Fragen* (*Bochumer Schriften zur Friedenssicherung und zum Humanitären Völkerrecht* 1992), 5–28, at 15.

[199] See as an example UN Doc. S/2004/645 of August 2004 on the repatriation of prisoners of war after the conflict between Ethiopia and Eritrea.

[200] On the assessment of these agreements in the Former Yugoslavia from the point of view of international law, see B. Jakovljević, 'Armed Conflict in Yugoslavia, Agreements in the Field of International Humanitarian Law and Practice' (1992/3) *HUV-I* 108–11.

[201] G. Schwarzenberger, *International Law as Applied by International Courts and Tribunals Vol. II: The Law of Armed Conflict* (Stevens and Sons, 1968), 134.

SANDRA KRÄHENMANN

In particular, states which are ideologically on hostile terms may always claim that a resumption of hostilities forms a part of the other party's politics. The term 'active' makes clear that the mere expectation of parties to the conflict that hostilities *could* be resumed does not justify retaining prisoners of war.

In order to protect prisoners of war it is more appropriate to refer to the military circumstances accompanying the cessation of hostilities and to choose an objective approach. An armistice agreement is not necessarily a cessation within the meaning of Article 118 GC III. The circumstances of the individual case indicate whether an armistice appears to be a return to lasting peace or merely an interruption of the hostilities.[202] If the armistice is monitored by peacekeeping forces, for instance, this is a good indication of a lasting cessation of hostilities if it involves the demobilization of the parties to the conflict. General demobilization of the enemy parties, withdrawal of troops from the front line, compliance with demands, and resolution of disputed questions can also be indications of the cessation of active hostilities. If the fighting has stopped, then despite the continued occupation of territory a cessation of hostilities might still have been achieved.[203] All attempts to define the term of cessation of hostilities more clearly[204] depend on the geographic and military circumstances of the conflict and its historic-political causes. In future, regional organizations of the UN Security Council might assist in determining a cessation under Article 118 GC III.

3. *The duty to repatriate.* After almost every conflict since 1945, especially the Korean, Vietnam, Iran–Iraq, and Second Gulf Wars, some prisoners of war have refused repatriation. For political, economic, or humanitarian reasons large numbers of prisoners of war have requested to stay in the territory of the detaining power or in another state not involved in the conflict. Approximately 15,000 Iraqi prisoners of war declined to return to Iraq following the Second Gulf War,[205] about one-eighth of the total number of Iraqi prisoners of war. Thus, the question arises whether Article 118 GC III imposes a duty on the detaining power to repatriate in these circumstances.[206] The wording indicates this duty through the formulation that prisoners of war shall be released *and* repatriated. The option of leaving prisoners of war with the detaining power after the conflict cannot be derived from the wording. International lawyers have repeatedly claimed that any discretion for the detaining power in whether or not to repatriate would considerably increase the risks to prisoners of war. Such an option would give the detaining power the opportunity to breach the duty to repatriate under Article 188 GC III by referring to the will of the prisoner of war.

On the other hand, the humanitarian problems resulting from forced repatriation of prisoners of war are also relevant. Article 109, para. 3, GC III, which prohibits the repatriation of sick or wounded prisoners of war against their will during a conflict, has been

---

[202] Too critical: Dinstein, above (n. 192), at 45.

[203] H. Schneider, 'Zur Auslegung des Art. 118 Abs. 1 der Genfer Konvention über die Behandlung von Kriegsgefangenen von 1949' (1989/2), *HUV-I* 13–21, at 14.

[204] C. Shields-Delessert, *Release and Repatriation of Prisoners of War at the End of Active Hostilities: A Study of Article 118, Paragraph 1, of the Third Geneva Convention Relative to the Treatment of Prisoners of War* (Schulthess, 1977), 111 *et seq.*, suggests a differentiation which takes into account the various categories of prisoners of war.

[205] Gasser, above (n. 198), at 15.

[206] On the organization of the mass flight of North Korean prisoners of war by the Allies in order to avoid the problem of repatriation, see J. Kunz, 'Die koreanische Kriegsgefangenenfrage' (1954) 4 *Archiv des Völkerrechts* 408–42, at 416–19.

SANDRA KRÄHENMANN

referred to in this respect. The problem of fulfilling the requests of the prisoners of war and at the same time preventing abuse by the detaining power has not been solved in a satisfactory manner to date.[207] State practice in this respect is inconsistent.[208] The report of the Pentagon to Congress on the Second Gulf War presumes a right of the prisoners to decide about being repatriated. It is expressly stated that since the entry into force of GC III 'this principle has become conditional: each POW must consent to repatriation rather than being forced to return'.[209]

Gasser convincingly refers to the importance of the role of ICRC delegates.[210] They alone are in a position to determine whether prisoners of war in fact prefer to remain in the state of the detaining power, or in another state, rather than returning to their home country. In this respect the detaining power's duty to repatriate under Article 118 GC III cannot be limited. The duty is absolute. In individual cases, exceptions can be made for humanitarian reasons if the life of the prisoner of war might be endangered by the repatriation (see also above Section 705). However, this goal can only be achieved on a case-by-case basis taking into account the supervision by the ICRC. After the Second Gulf War the US provided the ICRC with the names of prisoners of war who were not willing to be repatriated. Prior to repatriation, the ICRC delegates asked all Iraqi prisoners of war about their willingness to return. Those prisoners of war who refused to return to Iraq were transferred back to the detaining power.[211]

736   **Detainees who have committed an indictable offence and against whom criminal proceedings are pending or who have yet to complete a punishment may be detained beyond the cessation of active hostilities (Article 119, para. 5, GC III).**

Article 119, para. 5, GC III provides an exception to the duty to release. Those prisoners of war against whom criminal proceedings for an indictable offence are pending may be detained until the end of such proceedings, and if necessary until the completion of the punishment. As is expressly laid down, the same applies to prisoners of war already convicted of an indictable offence. The first alternative requires that proceedings are already afoot. Prisoners of war cannot be retained on mere suspicion until evidence can be found which allows proceedings to be initiated. As a rule, the detaining power has a power to delay the release until the completion of the punishment imposed if proceedings have been issued or if prisoners of war are already serving a sentence. In this case the requirements for their internment are set out in Article 88 GC III.

737   **Other detainees in armed conflict must be released upon decision of a competent court or review board.**

The end of active hostilities is even more difficult to ascertain outside the context of a traditional international armed conflict. In particular the open-ended nature of conflicts

---

[207] Kunz, 'The Laws of War' (1956) *AJIL* 313–37, at 336, proposed a revision of Article 118 as early as 1956 on the basis of experiences of the Korean War.

[208] Sassòli, 'The Status, Treatment and Repatriation of Deserters under International Humanitarian Law', in International Institute of Humanitarian Law (ed.), *Yearbook 1985* (1986), 9–36, at 32.

[209] Department of Defense, *Conduct of the Persian Gulf War*, above (n. 42) Appendix 0–20.

[210] Gasser, 'Das humanitäre Völkerrecht', in H. Haug, *Menschlichkeit für alle, Die Weltbewegung des Roten Kreuzes und des Roten Halbmonds* (Institut Henry Dunant/Haupt, 1993), 517–618, at 538.

[211] Department of Defense, *Conduct of the Persian Gulf War*, above (n. 42) Appendix 0–20.

SANDRA KRÄHENMANN

with non-state actors, including the 'Global War on Terror'[212] raises the possibility of the potentially indefinite detention without trial of 'unlawful combatants', which further highlights the need for adequate procedural guarantees, in particular the possibility to periodically challenge the lawfulness of the detention (see above, Section 708).[213] Following the decision of a competent court or review board, such detainees must be released, otherwise their continued detention would become arbitrary, as there is no longer any legal basis for their detention.[214] In combination with the prohibition of refoulement (see above, Section 705), the obligation to release detainees following the decision of an impartial and independent body raises new difficult questions. First, it has proven to be difficult to find states willing to resettle them since they potentially represent a security threat. Second, their continued detention pending deportation may be unlawful.[215]

---

[212] Murphy, above (n. 21), 1148 ff., and J. B. Bellinger III and V. M. Padmanabhan, above (n. 24), 228.
[213] For an analysis of the US policy in this respect, see S. Murphy, ibid. 1149 ff.
[214] *CIHL* Rule 99.
[215] Bellinger and Padmanabhan, above (n. 24), 238 ff.

SANDRA KRÄHENMANN

8

PROTECTION OF RELIGIOUS PERSONNEL

Introductory Remarks

1. The presence of religious personnel in armed conflict is a reflection of the most basic sentiments of humanity and respect for the individual. In Europe, as early as in the Middle Ages, the norms of the Catholic Church established two related prohibitions: clergy were not to be targeted in military campaigns, and they were not allowed to actively engage in warfare. Almost every state takes a different approach in the way it integrates religious personnel into its military, whether they wear a uniform, are part of the chain of command, or teach ethical precepts. These representatives of various religions often belong to a priestly class having regard to their background, training, or experience. They provide spiritual assistance to military personnel or protected persons. These military or civilian persons are exclusively engaged in religious duties.

2. Military 'chaplains assigned to the armed forces' are, in accordance with Article 24 GC I, protected in the same way as medical personnel. In contrast to GC I, Article 8, lit. d, AP I uses the term 'religious personnel' as more neutral than the Christian term of 'chaplain'. This is in conformity with Article 36 GC II where the same term has been used already. The said personnel is assigned to the armed forces of a party to the conflict either permanently or temporarily (Article 8, lit. d(i–iii), AP I). In case of temporary assignment, protection is also limited in time (Article 8, lit. k, AP I). These provisions imply that religious personnel shall not be the object of discrimination by the adversary with regard to their particular religion. Moreover, religious personnel must not be hindered in pursuing their religious duties among their own citizens, even if the national regulations of the state in which they are working prohibit it. These protections are applicable to all religious personnel irrespective of their age or length of experience.

3. An occupying power is under an obligation to provide moral care to the wounded and sick (Article 18, para. 4, GC I). Such care may be provided by religious personal of the occupying power even if they are members of enemy armed forces.

4. The content of the Geneva Conventions and AP I indicate that the term 'religious' is to be interpreted in a restricted sense.[1] 'Political commissaries', for example, are excluded from this definition.

5. Modern armed conflicts often have religious motives. But under international humanitarian law, religious personnel must refrain from preaching hatred against other religions

---

[1] S. Lunze, 'Serving God and Caesar: Religious Personnel and their Protection in Armed Conflict' (2004) 86 *IRRC* 69–91; M. Bothe/K. J. Partsch/W. A. Solf, *New Rules for Victims of Armed Conflicts* (The Hague/Boston/London: Nijhoff, 1982), 99.

NILENDRA KUMAR

and against the adversary (see below, Section 806). Otherwise, it would be questionable whether in practice religious personnel and medical personnel can be treated equally.[2]

6. The dissemination of knowledge of international humanitarian law must be extended to religious personnel (Article 47 GC I; Article 48 GC II; Article 127 GC III; Article 144 GC IV). This responsibility would devolve upon the commanders and legal advisors.

I. General Rules

801

Religious personnel are chaplains, ministers of religion, or religious teachers assigned to the armed forces of a state to provide spiritual care to the persons in their charge including the dead (Article 24 GC I; Article 37 GC II; Articles 8, lit. d, and 23, para. 5, AP I).

1. 'Religious personnel' means military or civilian persons, such as chaplains, who are exclusively engaged in the work of their ministry and attached: (i) to the armed forces of a party to the conflict; (ii) to medical units or medical transports of a party to the conflict; (iii) to medical units or medical transports (Article 9, para. 2, AP I); or (iv) to civil defence organizations of a party to the conflict. The attachment of religious personnel may be either permanent or temporary (Article 8, lit. d, AP I). This definition clearly includes the two criteria that are constitutive of protection for religious personnel: attachment and exclusivity.

2. The Geneva Conventions and Protocols at various places use a number of words connected to religion. Some of them appear to be synonymous. Examples for words used are religious personnel (Article 15, para. 3, GC I, Articles 18, para. 2, and 36 GC II), religious belief (Article 16 GC III), religious beliefs (Article 45 GC IV), religious convictions (Article 27 GC IV), religious ministration (Article 33, para. 1, GC III), religious duties (Article 28, para. 2, lit. c, GC I and Article 93, para. 1, GC IV), rites of the religion (Article 120 GC III and Article 130 GC IV), religious organizations (Article 125 GC III and Article 93 GC IV), religious authorities (Article 93 GC IV), religious purposes (Article 142 GC IV), and religious communities (Article 58 GC IV). The term 'religious personnel' is used to denote the protected category of non-combatants within the armed forces who are ministers of religion. It includes any priest, deacon, father, pastor, preacher, bishop, elder, padre, minister, guru, pandit, pujari, granthi, imam, maulavi, mufti, rabbi, and religious teacher. Responsibility of this personnel includes the religious needs of members of the armed forces, people in hospitals, and inmates of prisons, and so on. The term 'religious' is not in the context of any particular religion. 'Religion' means the belief in the existence of a god or gods, and the activities that are connected with the worship of them.

3. The meaning of the term 'spiritual care' is connected with the human spirit, rather than the body or physical assistance. A number of words connected to 'spiritual' have been used at different places in the Geneva Conventions and Protocols. Examples are spiritual needs (Article 28 GC I and Article 37 GC II), spiritual duties (Article 28 GC

---

[2] H. McCoubrey, *International Humanitarian Law: Modern Developments in the Limitation of Warfare*, 2nd edn (Dartmouth, 1998), 53 n. 37.

NILENDRA KUMAR

I), spiritual welfare (Article 28 GC I), spiritual care (Article 37 GC II), spiritual functions (Article 33 GC III), spiritual assistance (Article 38 GC IV), and spiritual well-being (Article 80 GC III). Care is the process of giving attention or thought to something that one is doing so or that one will do to do it well and avoid mistakes or damage. It should be noted that religious personnel may also offer material assistance within their responsibility (see below, Section 805).

> The same status is accorded to religious personnel who: 802
> — belong to a militia not forming part of the regular armed forces, a volunteer corps, or an organized resistance movement whose members are combatants (Article 13, para. 2, GC I);
> — have been charged by the appropriate military authority to care for the personnel accompanying the armed forces (Article 13, para. 4, GC I);
> — are assigned to hospital ships (Article 36 GC II); or
> — are serving on board of merchant ships (Articles 37 GC II).

Religious personnel serving in armed opposition groups during non-international armed conflicts are not listed here, as relevant treaty law applies to international armed conflicts only. However, under general principles of law and custom such personnel deserve similar protection.[3]

> Other persons serving as non-permanent religious personnel are not accorded the   803
> same status having regard to their duties. They are, however, protected as civilians under Geneva Convention IV, AP I and customary law.

There may be situations when other persons undertake the role of religious personnel. Such persons must also be protected.

> The auxiliaries of religious personnel (assistants and drivers) assigned to the armed   804
> forces should be accorded the status of soldiers or persons accompanying the armed forces (see below, Section 805). It is, however, in keeping with the principles of international humanitarian law to respect and protect these persons, too, as far as possible.

Respect and protection is owed also to religious personnel in view of their specific tasks (Article 24 GC I).

> Religious personnel may include personnel of services responsible for the welfare of   805
> the armed forces (Article 13, para. 4, GC I).

The role of religious personnel may also be undertaken by authorized members of welfare units accompanying the armed forces or the instructors of education corps assigned the duties to provide motivation to the personnel assigned under their care.

> Religious personnel perform their role under the rules and regulations of their   806
> church or religious congregation. They should refrain from preaching hatred against other religions and against the adversary.

1. Religious personnel have a particular responsibility to act with sensitivity and tolerance for other religions and denominations. The development of conscience in order

---

[3] Rules 25–30 *CIHL*.

NILENDRA KUMAR

to foster an authentic desire for peace is an important part of their duties. Like the international Red Cross and Red Crescent movement, they must encounter different perceptions,[4] in order to win hearts and minds for accepting humanitarian law as an essential legal framework for their own mission, even if compliance with its rules is endangered.[5]

2. A full understanding of other religious perceptions remains essential in this respect. Any assertion to the contrary, for example that Sharia law would 'override the laws of war and human rights', ignore authoritative and traditional Islamic rules of war which emphasize that non-combatants are not permitted legitimate targets and religious belief alone does not make anyone the object of attack.[6]

807   Religious personnel shall treat all protected persons humanely in all circumstances, irrespective of their religion or faith (Article 3, para. 1, sub-para. 1, GC I–IV).

The word 'faith' refers to any particular belief.

808   The groups of persons to be attended by religious personnel of the armed forces include:
— members of the armed forces to which they themselves belong;
— for religious personnel who fall into the hands of the adversary, also prisoners of war of the same religion belonging to allied armed forces (Articles 33, para. 2 and 35, first sentence GC III);
— in exceptional cases, members of the opposing armed forces who have been taken prisoner (Article 37 GC III);
— in case of need, wounded, sick, and shipwrecked members of opposing armed forces of their faith or a similar denomination; and
— for the duration of an occupation, the civilian population in particular children (Articles 13, 24, 27, para. 1, 38, para. 3, 50, para. 3 and 58, para. 1, GC IV), protected persons accused of offences (Article 6, para. 3, GC IV), and internees (Articles 86, 93, and 94 GC IV).

1. This list is indicative and not enumerative.

2. The word 'denomination' is not limited to Christian churches. It comprises all different religious traditions and developments (Article 86 GC IV).

3. Information to assist the identification of protected persons shall also, if possible, include particulars of their religion or faith, so as to facilitate arrangement for the services of religious personnel and also burial or cremation if needed (Articles 16 and 17 GC I, Article 122 GC II).

809   Religious personnel of the armed forces shall exercise their functions within the scope of the laws and regulations and in accordance with their professional etiquette and religious conscience. They shall, however, not be confined to their religious duties and may particularly:

---

[4] See A. Wigger, 'Encountering perceptions in parts of the Muslim world and their impact on the ICRC's ability to be effective' (2005) 858 *IRRC* 343–65.

[5] G. Filibeck, 'The Church and Humanitarian Law', Pontifical Council for Justice and Peace (ed.), *Humanitarian Law and Military Chaplains* (Libreria Editrice Vaticana, 2004), 41–6 (45).

[6] *Open Letter to His Holiness Pope Benedict XVI*, published in October 2006 by thirty-eight Muslim leaders, <http://www.islamicamagazine.com/letter/>, 2.

NILENDRA KUMAR

—perform the functions of a personal adviser;
—receive and forward the last wishes of dying soldiers; and
— provide material assistance to those in need.

1. These responsibilities and duties described in Articles 28 GC I; 37 GC II; and 33 GC III as rights and privileges of religious personnel retained by a detaining power (see below, Sections 827–846), must also be respected internally (i.e. in the relationship between religious personnel and the armed forces they are assigned to).

2. Religious personnel may engage in activities that do not derive exclusively from their spiritual mission as long as they are not harmful to the enemy. They may undertake social work to assist combatants and their families and could also be engaged in organizing recreational activities.

3. The tasks of religious personnel may include functions of a personal (i.e. not official) adviser; receiving and forwarding the last wishes of dying soldiers;[7] and material assistance like religious books, photographs, compact discs, rosary, idol, and so on to those in need, to meet spiritual needs and spiritual welfare.

> Wherever possible, the dead shall be interred by religious personnel of the same   810
> denomination. The states concerned have the duty to assist such personnel, within
> the means available, in fulfilling this task (Article 17, para. 3 GC I).

> Religious personnel shall wear, affixed to the left arm, a water-resistant armlet dis-   811
> playing the red cross or red crescent or red crystal on a white ground (Article 40,
> para. 1, GC I; Article 42, para. 1, GCII; Article 18, paras. 1 and 3, AP I; Article
> 12 AP II; Article 2 AP III; see below Annex, No. 1). The armlet shall be issued and
> stamped by the appropriate authority (Article 40, para. 1, GC I; Article 42, para.
> 1, GC II).

1. Religious personnel and objects are protected because of their role and functions. The display of the emblems is the visible manifestation of that function but does not confer protection as such. These signs are meant to caution belligerents to the entitlement to protection and are designed to avoid religious personnel, especially those in uniform, being mistaken for combatants. They do not constitute any protection in themselves.

2. Transport or any means of conveyance used by religious personnel to undertake their duties shall carry a distinctive emblem.

3. Civilian persons performing the religious functions may not display the distinctive emblem.

> In addition to the armlet and identity disk to be worn by all members of the armed   812
> forces, religious personnel shall also carry a special identity card, certifying their
> status (Article 40, para. 2, GC I; Article 42, para. 2, GC II).

This card shall be of such size that it can be carried in the pocket. It shall be worded at least in the national language, shall mention at least the surname and first names, the date of birth, the rank and the service number of the bearer, and shall state in what capacity he is entitled to protection. The card shall bear the photograph of the owner and

---

[7] The scope of the term 'last wish' is broader than 'last will' or 'will' as used in Art. 129 GC IV.

NILENDRA KUMAR

also either his signature or his finger prints or both. It shall be embossed with the stamps of the military authority. The identity card shall be uniform throughout the same armed forces and, as far as possible, of a similar type in all armed forces.

813   Religious personnel may not be deprived of their special insignia, armlets, or identity cards. In case of loss or destruction, they have the right to replacements (Article 40, para. 4, GC I; Article 42, para. 4, GC II). Should they fall into the hands of the adversary, the latter shall be obliged to allow new identity cards or armlets to be forwarded to retained religious personnel (Article 40, para. 4, GC I; Article 42, para. 4, GC II). They may be allowed to retain articles of personal use.

This provision ensures that religious personnel retained to assist prisoners of war will not loose their special status under Article 28, para. 2, GC I; Article 36 GC II; Article 33, para. 1, GC III (see below, Sections 827–846).

814   Local arrangements may be concluded between parties to the conflict for the passage of religious personnel or equipment on their way to a besieged or encircled area (Article 15 GC I).

815   Any special agreement drawn by the parties to an armed conflict which adversely affects the situation or rights conferred upon religious personnel is contrary to international humanitarian law (Article 6 GC I).

816   The ICRC or other humanitarian organizations may, subject to the consent of the parties to the conflict, arrange for humanitarian activities for the protection and relief of religious personnel (Article 9 GC I).

1. For the role of the ICRC see below, Section 1422. For the notion of other humanitarian organizations see below, Section 1431.

2. The term 'humanitarian' is used in the Geneva Conventions and Protocols in various contexts; see, for example, humanitarian activities (Article 9 GC II and Article 10 GC IV), humanitarian functions (Article 9 GC I, Article 11, para. 3, GC IV, and Article 15, para. 2, AP I), humanitarian duties (Article 19 GC IV), and humanitarian principles (Article 100 GC IV). While there is no exact definition, the intent and purport is the same in each case and no undue restriction should be used in its interpretation. The humanitarian functions of churches and religious organizations are widely recognized.

3. Arrangements between the parties to an armed conflict may be facilitated by the ICRC or other humanitarian organizations.

817   A meeting of the religious personnel can take place on a neutral territory suitably chosen, when a need arises to settle the disagreement between the parties to the conflict on the application or interpretation of the provisions of the First Geneva Convention (Article 11 GC I).

II. Protection of Religious Personnel

818   Religious personnel shall be respected and protected in all circumstances (Article 24 GC I; Articles 36 and 37 GC II; Article 15, para. 5, AP I). This shall apply:

NILENDRA KUMAR

— at any time throughout the duration of an armed conflict;
— at any place; and
— in any case in which religious personnel are retained by the adversary, whether temporarily or for a prolonged period of time.

1. Free exercise of religion forms a crucial aspect of human dignity. Religious personnel exclusively assigned to religious duties must be respected and protected in all circumstances. They lose their protection if they commit, outside their humanitarian function, acts harmful to the enemy.[8]

2. Attacks directed against religious personnel and objects displaying the distinctive emblem of the Geneva Conventions in conformity with international law are prohibited.[9]

3. Religious personnel must not be compelled to carry out tasks that are not compatible with their humanitarian mission (Article 9, para. 1, AP II).

4. The protection of religious personnel is not merely for their personal safety but would extend to their personal belongings, place of worship, and freedom to perform their role. In order to make this clause meaningful, it also provides for their suitable relief. For the procedure of such relief, see Articles 9 and 28 GC I.

> **Religious personnel are entitled to the protection provided by international law.**   819
> **Direct participation in rendering assistance to the victims of war (wounded, sick, shipwrecked, prisoners of war, protected civilians) is not required.**

1. Religious personnel are entitled to the protection provided by international law. They may not be subjected to military attack. This protection applies at any place and at any time throughout the duration of an armed conflict, both on the battlefield and behind the lines.

2. Protection is not limited to acts of rendering assistance to the victims of war (wounded, sick, shipwrecked, prisoners of war, protected civilians).

> **Unlike medical supplies, the articles used for religious purposes are not explicitly**   820
> **protected by international law. It is, however, in keeping with the spirit of the Geneva Conventions to respect the material required for religious purposes and not to use it for alien ends.**

Places of worship forming part of a people's cultural or spiritual heritage are protected under international humanitarian law. 'Ordinary' religious buildings are protected by their civilian nature and, in case of doubt, are presumed not to be used for military purposes (Articles 52 and 53 API; Article 16 AP II).

> **Reprisals against religious personnel are prohibited (Article 46 GC I; Article 47**   821
> **GC II). This prohibition shall protect religious personnel from any restriction of the rights assigned to them.**

See above, Section 485–488, and below, Section 1408.

> **Religious personnel may in no circumstances renounce the rights secured to them**   822
> **by international humanitarian law (Article 7 GC I; Article 7 GC II).**

[8] Rule 28 *CIHL*.
[9] Rule 30 *CIHL*.

NILENDRA KUMAR

The protection of religious personnel is absolute, as in the case of medical personnel. See above, Sections 613–619.

823   Any attack directed against religious personnel and any infringement of their rights constitutes a grave breach of international law, which shall be liable to criminal prosecution (Article 49 GC I; Article 50 GC II).

Article 8, para. lit. b(xxiv), ICC Statute criminalizes intentionally directing attacks against personnel using the distinctive emblem. An attack on them would constitute a war crime in international armed conflicts. This would be so because religious personnel are entitled to use the distinctive emblem. The specific mention made of them in various elements of crimes adds to the protection of religious personnel from being murdered, mutilated, treated cruelly, tortured, degraded, taken hostage, and sentenced without due process.

824   The fact that religious personnel may be armed, and that they may use the weapons in their own defence or in that of the wounded, sick, and shipwrecked shall not deprive them of the protection accorded to them by international law (Article 22 GC I; Article 35 GC II).

825   The only arms which may be used by religious personnel are weapons suited for self-defence and emergency aid (individual weapons).

1. Religious personnel do not lose their protection under international law, if they are equipped with light individual weapons and they may use these weapons in their own defence against acts of violence, for example, against marauders or in defence of persons under their care.

2. The use of weapons by religious personnel even for self-defence and emergency aid may be excluded under national law and ethical principles (see above, commentary to Section 316, sub-para. c).

826   The protection accorded to religious personnel shall cease if they use weapons for any other purpose than that of self-defence and defence of protected persons.

1. A clear determination of acts that violate the non-combatant status of religious personnel is difficult. As they are supposed to render religious service, such personnel must not take a direct part in the war effort. Thus, they must not operate any weapons systems in combat. Furthermore, they are not allowed to engage in backup military efforts, such as carrying or conveying military intelligence, planning military actions, transporting weapons or ammunition, translation and interrogation or the assessment of data for military purposes.

2. Religious personnel must abstain from all hostile acts. Participation in combat or engagement in conduct incompatible with their status will entail in loss of their protection. Religious personnel attacking enemy forces become lawful targets themselves.

III. Legal Status of Religious Personnel Retained by a Foreign Power

827   Religious personnel who are retained by an adverse party shall not be considered as prisoners of war (Article 28, para. 2, GC I; Article 36 GC II; Article 33, para. 1, GC III).

NILENDRA KUMAR

1. Prisoners of war are entitled to complete latitude in the exercise of their religious duties; including observance of attendance at the service of their faith (Article 34 GC III). This right is conditional upon compliance with the disciplinary routine prescribed by the military authorities. Special challenges in reconciling the two sometimes opposing standards of latitude and disciplinary routine may arise with regard to religious practices of a physical character, methods of preparing food, periods of fasting or prayer, or the wearing of ritual adornments. In addition, specific stipulations apply for the receipt of articles of a religious character, activities of representatives of religious organizations in prisoner-of-war camps, spiritual assistance to prisoners of war serving a penal sentence, and religious burial of deceased (Articles 12, para. 4; 72; 108, para. 3; and 125 GC III).

2. Deprivation of liberty to adhere to religious beliefs in certain situations may be an unjustified act or omission affecting mental health and integrity of interned or detained persons (Article 11 AP I). The right of prisoners of war to make a complaint or request regarding the conditions of captivity to which they are subjected may relate to a grievance concerning religious or spiritual matters (Article 78 GC III).

3. Because of their status as non-combatants, religious personnel who are retained by an adverse party shall not be considered as prisoners of war (Article 28, para. 2, GC I; Article 36 GC II and Article 33, para. 1, GC III). Religious personnel are not prisoners of war, but retained personnel.

4. With the consent of the detaining power a treatment similar to that of detained religious personnel may be granted to prisoners of war who are ministers of religion even though they may not have officiated as religious personnel to their own forces (Article 36 GC III).

> **Religious personnel may be retained to assist prisoners of war of the armed forces**   **828**
> **to which they themselves belong in so far as the state of health, spiritual needs, and**
> **number of prisoners require (Article 28 GC I; Articles 36 and 37 GC II; Article 33**
> **GC III).**

1. Captured religious personnel may be retained to assist prisoners of war of the armed forces to which they themselves belong in so far as the state of health, spiritual needs, and in proportion to the number of prisoners and the distribution of the said personnel in the camps (Article 28 GC I; Articles 36 and 37 GC II; Article 33 GC III).

2. Religious personnel may be retained only to meet the spiritual needs of prisoners of war and only in numbers appropriate for that purpose. They shall exercise their functions within the scope of the laws and regulations of the detaining power and in accordance with their professional etiquette and religious conscience (Articles 33, para. 2; and 35, first sentence, GC III).

3. An attempt to flee can be considered a breach of camp discipline and punished by disciplinary measures of the detaining power.

> **The provisions of Geneva Conventions I and III apply to the treatment of the**   **829**
> **retained religious personnel as minimum requirements for protection. As a conse-**
> **quence, they shall receive at least the benefits accorded to prisoners of war by these**
> **conventions (Article 30 GC I; Article 33 GC III). In particular, the detaining power**
> **shall ensure the representatives of religious organizations a proper reception.**

NILENDRA KUMAR

The detaining power shall provide the duly accredited agents of these organizations with all necessary facilities for visiting prisoners of war and religious personnel in their camps; distributing relief supplies and material intended for religious, educational, or recreative purposes; and assisting prisoners of war and religious personnel in organizing their leisure time (Article 125 GC III).

830   Like prisoners of war, religious personnel shall be released and repatriated without delay after the cessation of active hostilities (Article 118, para. 1 GC III).

1. Selection for their repatriation shall take place irrespective of any consideration of race, religion, or political opinion, but preferably according to the chronological order of their capture and their state of health.

2. Repatriate means to restore or return to one's country of origin, allegiance, or citizenship.

831   The provisions of the Geneva Conventions apply by analogy to religious personnel received or interned in neutral territory (Article 4 GC I; Article 5 GC II).

832   Religious personnel who are not retained shall be returned (Articles 28 and 30 GC I; Article 37 GC II).

833   Religious personnel shall be returned to the party to the conflict to which they belong. A detaining power which merely releases a person into the territory of his home state which the said power still occupies does not fulfil its duty to return this person.

834   The repatriation of religious personnel depends on the condition that a means is open for their return and that military requirements permit (Article 30, para. 3, GC I; Article 37 GC II).

835   Religious personnel who are repatriated may take with them the effects, personal belongings, valuables, and ritual objects belonging to them (Article 30, para. 3, GC I; Article 37 GC II).

836   Retained religious personnel shall continue to exercise their spiritual functions for the benefit of prisoners of war, preferably those belonging to the armed forces upon which they depend. They shall perform their duties within the scope of the military laws and regulations of the detaining power and in accordance with their professional etiquette and their religious conscience. Their work shall be subject to the control of the competent services (Article 28, para. 2, GC I; Article 37 GC II; Articles 33, para. 2; and 35 GC III).

837   The spiritual functions to be exercised for the benefit of prisoners of war particularly include:
— holding religious services (Article 34 GC III);
— ministering to prisoners of war of the same religion (Article 35 GC III); and
— burying prisoners of war who have died according to the rites of the religion to which they belong (Article 120, para. 4, GC III).

Bodies shall not be accorded last rites by way of cremation except for imperative reasons of hygiene or for motives based on the religion of the deceased (Article 17 GC I). Wherever possible, the dead shall be interred by religious personnel of the same denomination. The states concerned have the duty to assist such personnel, within the means available, in fulfilling this task (Article 17, para. 3, GC I).

In order to ensure a uniform level of assistance for prisoners of war, religious personnel will be allocated to camps and labour detachments containing prisoners of war belonging to the same forces, speaking the same language, or practising the same religion (Article 35, second sentence, GC III).   838

The detaining power shall provide religious personnel with facilities necessary for the exercise of their spiritual functions (Article 35 GC III).   839

In particular, they shall be accorded the following facilities: 840
— They shall be provided with adequate premises where religious services may be held (Article 34, para. 2, GC III).
— They shall be authorized to visit periodically prisoners of war situated outside the camp (e.g. in working detachments or hospitals, Article 35 GC I). For this purpose, the detaining power shall place at their disposal the necessary means of transport (Articles 33, para. 2 lit. a; and 35, third sentence, GC III).
— They shall have the right to deal with the competent authorities of the camp on all questions relating to their duties (Article 33, para. 2 lit. b, third sentence, GC III).
— They shall enjoy all facilities for correspondence on matters concerning their duties. They shall be free to correspond, subject to censorship, with the ecclesiastical authorities in the country of detention and with international religious organizations. Letters and cards which they send for this purpose shall be in addition to the quota provided for prisoners of war (Articles 35, fourth and fifth sentences, and 71 GC III).
— They shall be allowed to receive by any means whatsoever individual parcels or collective shipments containing devotional articles (e.g. the Bible, the Koran, prayer and service books, hymnals, ritual articles, sacramental wine, crucifixes, and rosaries) (Articles 33 and 72, para. 1, GC III).

This includes means of transport for visiting prisoners of war who are outside their camp (Articles 33, para. 2, lit. a, 35 GC III), and the right to receive relief shipments with articles of a religious character (Article 72 GC III).[10]

Retained religious personnel shall be subject to the disciplinary authority of the detaining power (Article 28, para. 2 GC I; Article 33, para. 2 GC III). They shall therefore be subordinate to the general orders of the camp commander. This shall not apply to the exercise of their religious duties.   841

Religious personnel may not be compelled to carry out any work other than that concerned with their religious duties (Article 28, para. 2, GC I; Article 33, para. 2 lit. c, GC III).   842

Prisoners of war who are chaplains, ministers of religion or religious teachers, but serve in the armed forces as soldiers only, shall be at liberty to minister freely to the members of their community (Article 36, first sentence GC III). The detaining power has the duty to give them an appropriate authority if prisoners of war of the same faith are to be ministered. Those who have been accorded this authority shall   843

---

[10] This right applies to prisoners of war as well. It should be interpreted similar to the right of internees in relation to objects of a 'devotional' character (Art. 108 GC IV).

NILENDRA KUMAR

enjoy the same privileges and facilities as retained religious personnel. They shall also not be compelled to carry out any work (Article 36 GC III). Nevertheless, they shall remain prisoners of war, although endowed with special rights.

844   When prisoners of war do not have the assistance of a chaplain, ministers of religion or religious teachers, another qualified person belonging to the prisoners or another religious denomination may act in their place at the request of the prisoner concerned. These persons will normally be selected from among the prisoners of war, but they may also be members of the civilian population of the detaining power.

The term 'qualified layman' used in the Conventions has not been defined (Article 37 GC III and Article 93 GC IV).

845   Such persons shall regularly be appointed with the agreement of the community of prisoners concerned and subject to the approval of the detaining power and, whenever necessary, the approval of the local religious authorities of the respective faith (Article 37 GC III).

846   The persons thus appointed shall enjoy the same privileges and facilities as religious personnel. They are subject to the discipline of the camp as well as to all regulations established by the detaining power in the interests of discipline and military security (Article 37, third sentence, GC III). If these persons are selected from the prisoner of war community their status will not change.

9

PROTECTION OF CULTURAL PROPERTY

Introductory Remarks

1. The protection of cultural property in armed conflict, by which is meant its protection from damage and destruction and from all forms of misappropriation, has been a matter of legal concern since the rise of modern international law in the sixteenth and seventeenth centuries. When the laws of war were codified over the second half of the nineteenth and at the beginning of the twentieth centuries, cultural property was treated for certain purposes as a species of enemy property generally, so that it was protected by the classical rule as to military necessity which governed destruction and seizure of such property (Article 23, lit. g, HagueRegs) and by the prohibition on pillage (Articles 28 and 47 HagueRegs; Article 7 HC IX). For other purposes, it was treated specifically as cultural property, with special rules requiring its sparing as far as possible in the course of bombardment by land and air (Article 27 HagueRegs)[1] and by sea (Article 5 HC IX) and prohibiting its destruction, wilful damage, and seizure during belligerent occupation (Article 56 HagueRegs).

2. After the First World War, various efforts were made to establish a further, specialized treaty regime for the wartime protection of cultural property, starting with a 1919 proposal by the Netherlands Archaeological Society,[2] which was partly reflected in Article 26 of the 1923 draft Hague Rules on Aerial Warfare (HRAW). A draft text dedicated to the question, instigated by Nikolai Roerich, was picked up and adopted by a number of states of the Pan-American Union as the 1935 Treaty on the Protection of Artistic and Scientific Institutions and Historic Monuments, known as the Roerich Pact.[3] In 1938, the International Museums Office of the League of Nations finalized a Preliminary Draft International Convention for the Protection of Historic Buildings and Works of Art in Times of War, with annexed Regulations for its execution,[4] but the Second World War broke out before a diplomatic conference for its adoption could be held. In the immediate aftermath of the War, the relevant Hague Regulations, which were treated as declaratory of customary international law, provided the basis on which several defendants at Nuremberg, chief among them Alfred Rosenberg, were convicted of war crimes for their roles in organizing the seizure and destruction of cultural property in occupied territory.[5] The same acts were also held to constitute crimes against humanity.

---

[1] The rule on aerial bombardment was subsequently reiterated in Article 25 HRAW 1923.

[2] (1919) 26 *RGDIP* 329, at 331.

[3] 167 LNTS 290. The Pact, still in force among eleven US states, applies during both war, as such, and peace. It has never been invoked, and will not be considered in detail.

[4] LNOJ, 19th Year, No. 11 (November 1938), 937.

[5] See Misc. No. 12 (1946), Cmd 6964, 56, 64–5, 95–6, 129. At the other end of the scale of gravity, see *Trial of Karl Lingenfelder*, 9 LRTWC 67 (1947).

ROGER O'KEEFE

3. The Second World War spurred the eventual adoption of the 1954 Hague Convention on the Protection of Cultural Property in the Event of Armed Conflict and the Regulations for its execution,[6] along with a separate optional Protocol, now known as the First Protocol.[7] The preamble to the former declares that 'damage to cultural property belonging to any people whatsoever means damage to the cultural heritage of all mankind, since each people makes its contribution to the culture of the world'. CultPropConv applies during international armed conflict whether or not a legal state of war exists between the belligerents (Article 18, para. 1, CultPropConv), as well as to all cases of partial or total occupation of the territory of a party (Article 18, para. 2, CultPropConv). The provisions relating to respect for cultural property, by which is meant the various paragraphs of Article 4 (headed 'Respect for cultural property'), also apply to non-international armed conflict occurring within the territory of one of the parties (Article 19, para. 1, CultPropConv). CultPropConv offers two levels of protection for cultural property. So-called 'general protection'[8] (Chapter I CultPropConv) extends to all immovables and movables satisfying the definition of cultural property. 'Special protection' (Chapter II CultPropConv; Chapter II RegExCultPropConv) imposes a supplementary and nominally stricter standard of respect in relation to a narrower range of property. CultPropConv also lays down rules on the transport of cultural property during armed conflict (Chapter III CultPropConv; Chapter III RegExCultPropConv), the treatment of personnel engaged in its protection (Chapter IV CultPropConv), the creation and use of a 'distinctive emblem' for cultural property (Chapter V CultPropConv; Chapter IV RegExCultPropConv), the establishment and functioning of an elaborate international regime of control (RegExCultPropConv, Chapter I), the imposition of penal or disciplinary sanctions for breach (Article 28 CultPropConv) and the submission by the parties of periodic implementation reports (Article 26, para. 2, CultPropConv). UNESCO is granted a right of initiative in both international (Article 23, para. 2) and non-international (Article 19, para. 3, CultPropConv) armed conflict. For its part, Prot1CultPropConv deals with questions regarding the exportation and importation of cultural property from occupied territory, and with the return of cultural property deposited abroad for the duration of hostilities. By 1 June 2012, CultPropConv had 125 states parties and Prot1CultPropConv 101. CultPropConv remains the centrepiece of the international legal protection of cultural property in armed conflict, although some of its provisions now need to be read in the light of subsequent customary international law and, for parties to it, the Second Protocol to CultPropConv.

4. Although not itself an international humanitarian law treaty, the UNESCO-sponsored Convention on the Means of Prohibiting and Preventing the Illicit Import, Export and Transfer of Ownership of Cultural Property,[9] adopted in 1970, contains provisions for the protection of movable cultural property in occupied territory.

5. The 1977 Additional Protocols to the Geneva Conventions both embody brief provisions specifically relating to respect for cultural property. The motivation behind Article 53 AP I and Article 16 AP II was to affirm in a single article in each instrument the

---

[6] CultPropConv, 249 UNTS 240.
[7] Prot1CultPropConv, 249 UNTS 358.
[8] The label is not in fact used in CultPropConv. Ch. I lays down what it calls 'general provisions regarding protection'.
[9] IllicitImpExpTransConv, 823 UNTS 231.

essential obligations of respect for cultural property embodied more exhaustively in CultPropConv.[10] The derivative or secondary nature of these provisions is highlighted by the 'without prejudice' clause in the chapeau to each, which makes it clear that the provisions are not intended to modify the existing legal obligations of those parties to AP I and AP II which are also parties to CultPropConv,[11] a point underscored in Resolution 20(IV) of the Diplomatic Conference of Geneva.[12] The desire was to avoid the 'parallel application of two divergent systems for the protection of cultural property, which could only be a source of confusion',[13] with several delegates placing the primary emphasis on CultPropConv.[14] In certain cases, an attack against cultural property can constitute a grave breach (Article 85, para. 4, lit. d, AP I). In addition, the improper use of the emblem of cultural property is prohibited (Article 38, para. 1, AP I). Outside the scope of the *lex specialis* represented by Article 53 AP I and Article 16 AP II, cultural property is considered a civilian object, so that in international armed conflict it benefits from the prohibition on indiscriminate attacks (Article 51, paras. 4 and 5, lit. b, AP I) and from mandatory precautions to be taken in attack (Article 57 AP I).

For their part, 1980 Protocol II and 1996 Amended Protocol II to the 1980 Conventional Weapons Convention each contain two provisions relevant to cultural property.[15]

6. A process of review undertaken throughout the 1990s with a view to updating and improving aspects of CultPropConv's regime culminated in 1999 with the adoption of the Second Protocol to CultPropConv.[16] Prot2CultPropConv applies to international and non-international armed conflict without distinction. As made clear in the preamble, the instrument is designed to supplement, not supplant, the provisions of CultPropConv. It leaves intact the basic architecture of CultPropConv and operates, on a technical level, by reference back to it, elaborating on, refining and in places adding to CultPropConv's various obligations as between parties to Prot2CultPropConv, which, as a precondition to participation, must be parties to CultPropConv (Articles 40–42 Prot2CultPropConv). Prot2CultPropConv maintains the distinction between general and special protection of cultural property, albeit effectively replacing CultPropConv's scheme of the latter with a regime of 'enhanced' protection (Chapter 3 Prot2CultPropConv). General protection is updated and added to (Chapter 2 Prot2CultPropConv). A comprehensive regime of penal sanctions is provided for (Chapter 4 Prot2CultPropConv), as is a formalized institutional framework to facilitate and supervise the protection of cultural property in the event of armed conflict, comprising, *inter alia*, an intergovernmental Committee for

---

[10] *ICRC Commentary*, paras. 2039–40, 4826–7.
[11] *ICRC Commentary*, paras. 2046, 4832.
[12] Records 1974–7, I, Part I, 213.
[13] CDDH/SR.53, para. 4, Records 1974–7, VII, 142 (FRG).
[14] As regards AP I, see CDDH/SR.42, para. 12, Records 1974–7, VI, 207 (Belgium); CDDH/SR.42, Annex, Records 1974–7, VI, 224 (Canada), 234 (Poland); CDDH/III/SR.15, para. 22, Records 1974–7, XIV, 121 (USSR); CDDH/III/SR.16, para. 15, Records 1974–7, XIV, 129 (Poland); CDDH/III/SR.24, paras. 28–30, Records 1974–7, XIV, 221–2 (the Netherlands). As regards AP II, see CDDH/SR.52, paras. 2, 7, Records 1974–7, VII, 125, 126 (Belgium).
[15] See Article 6, para. 1, lit. b(ix), Prot2WeaponsConv and Article 7, para. 1, lit. i, AmendedProt2WeaponsConv, prohibiting the use of booby traps which are in any way attached to or associated with cultural property, as well as Article 6, para. 1, lit. b(i), Prot2WeaponsConv and Article 7, para. 1, lit. a, AmendedProt2WeaponsConv, prohibiting the same as regards internationally protected signs and signals, which include the emblem of cultural property.
[16] Prot2CultPropConv, 2253 UNTS 212.

ROGER O'KEEFE

the Protection of Cultural Property in the Event of Armed Conflict and a centralized Fund for the Protection of Cultural Property in the Event of Armed Conflict (Chapter 6 Prot2CultPropConv). The instrument also incorporates obligations relating to the dissemination of information and to international assistance, and UNESCO is granted a right of initiative (Chapter 7 Prot2CultPropConv). In 2009, the third Meeting of the Parties endorsed both the Guidelines for the Implementation of the Second Protocol and the Guidelines concerning the Use of the Fund, each prepared by the Committee (Articles 23, para. 3, lits. b and c, 27, para. 1 lit. a, and 29, para. 3, Prot2CultPropConv).[17] As of 1 June 2012, Prot2CultPropConv had sixty-two states parties.

7. In parallel with these treaty regimes, a body of customary international law has developed over the years to protect cultural property in armed conflict. Many of the provisions cited above, where not declaratory of custom when adopted, have come to reflect it in the period since.[18]

The relationships among these various bodies of law are considered in the following sections, which give a synthetic account of the basic rules governing the protection of cultural property in armed conflict.[19]

I. Definition of 'Cultural Property'

901   The term 'cultural property' means movable or immovable property of great importance to the cultural heritage of peoples (e.g. buildings and other monuments of historic, artistic or architectural significance; archaeological sites; artworks, antiquities, manuscripts, books, and collections thereof; archives; etc.), whether of a secular or religious nature and irrespective of origin or ownership (Article 53, lit. a, AP I; Article 16 AP II; Article 1, lit. a, CultPropConv). The term extends to buildings for preserving or exhibiting, and refuges intended to shelter, movable cultural property (Article 1, lit. b, CultPropConv) and to centres containing a large amount of movable or immovable cultural property, known as 'centres containing monuments' (Article 1, lit. c, CultPropConv).

1. CultPropConv and its two Protocols are the only conventions in the field of international humanitarian law actually to use the term 'cultural property', the formal legal definition of which for the purposes of all three instruments is found in Article 1 CultPropConv. This provision forms the basis of the definition given here. The term 'cultural property' refers in essence to 'movable or immovable property of great importance to the cultural heritage of every people' (Article 1, lit. a, CultPropConv). While the property protected by Articles 27 and 56 HagueRegs and Article 5 HC IX, by RoerichPact and by Article 53 AP I and Article 16 AP II can be referred to generically and in a strictly informal sense as cultural property, the provisions themselves use different terminology.

---

[17] See Guidelines for the Implementation of the 1999 Second Protocol to the Hague Convention of 1954 for the Protection of Cultural Property in the Event of Armed Conflict, CLT-09/CONF/219/3 REV.3 (24 November 2009) and Guidelines concerning the use of the Fund for the Protection of Cultural Property in the Event of Armed Conflict, CLT-09/CONF/219/4 REV (24 November 2009).

[18] A full account justifying this chapter's conclusions on points of customary international law can be found in R. O'Keefe, *The Protection of Cultural Property in Armed Conflict* (CUP, 2006), 316–59. See also *CIHL*, Ch. 12.

[19] Purely procedural rules, institutional arrangements and sanctions are not examined. Reference throughout to numbered/lettered documents is to UNESCO documents unless otherwise specified.

ROGER O'KEEFE

2. Whereas the relevant provisions of HagueRegs and HC IX apply *mutatis mutandis* to all buildings dedicated to religion, charitable purposes, and the arts and sciences and to every historic monument and work of art, the drafters of CultPropConv opted for a more selective approach.[20] CultPropConv seeks to protect only those immovable and movable objects 'of great importance to the cultural heritage of every people' (Article 1, lit. a, CultPropConv). On its face, the phrase 'of every people' is capable of two meanings, *viz* 'of all peoples jointly' or 'of each respective people'. Recourse to the French and Spanish texts, which are also authoritative, fails to establish which of these meanings is to be preferred, since both refer instead to the cultural heritage 'of peoples' ('le patrimoine culturel des peuples' and 'el patrimonio cultural de los pueblos'). But the second alternative is the correct one: the term 'cultural property' in Article 1 CultPropConv refers to movable or immovable property of great importance to the cultural heritage of each respective people—in other words, of great importance to the national cultural heritage of each respective party.[21] This follows from the preambular recital which declares 'that damage to cultural property belonging to any people whatsoever means damage to the cultural heritage of all mankind, since each people makes its contribution to the culture of the world', especially the words 'any people' and 'each people' and their use in contradistinction to 'all mankind' (as opposed to 'every people'). It is also borne out in the practice of many parties, as evidenced in their implementation reports.[22] The definition of cultural property thus reflects the conviction, in the words of a former president of the International Court of Justice, that 'cultural objects and properties which make up a national heritage [are], consequently, the world's heritage'.[23]

3. It is left to each party to determine the property in its territory to which CultPropConv applies, in accordance with its own criteria of 'great importance' to its cultural heritage,[24] a discretion circumscribed only by the ordinary meaning of the words and the requirement

[20] Cultural objects not qualifying for CultPropConv's protection remain protected by the 1907 rules themselves and as civilian objects.
[21] See also M. Frigo, *La protezione dei beni culturali nel diritto internazionale* (Milan: Giuffrè, 1986), 98, 100, 272; J. H. Merryman, 'Two Ways of Thinking About Cultural Property' (1986) 80 *AJIL* 831 at 837 n. 2; A. Przyborowska-Klimczak, 'Les notions des "biens culturels" et du "patrimoine culturel mondial" dans le droit international' (1989–90) 18 *Polish Yearbook of International Law* 47 at 53; J. Toman, *The Protection of Cultural Property in the Event of Armed Conflict: Commentary on the Convention for the Protection of Cultural Property in the Event of Armed Conflict and its Protocol, signed on 14 May 1954 in The Hague, and on other instruments of international law concerning such protection* (Paris/Aldershot: UNESCO/Dartmouth, 1996), 50; D. Sabelli, 'La Convenzione sul patrimonio mondiale: limiti giuridico-politici', in M. C. Ciciriello (ed.), *La protezione del patrimonio mondiale culturale e naturale a venticinque anni dalla Convenzione dell'UNESCO* (Naples: Editoriale Scientifica, 1997), 143 at 149; Y. Dinstein, *The Conduct of Hostilities under the Law of International Armed Conflict*, 2nd edn (CUP, 2010), para. 435; K. Chamberlain, *War and Cultural Heritage: An Analysis of the 1954 Convention for the Protection of Cultural Property in the Event of Armed Conflict and its Two Protocols* (Leicester: Institute of Art and Law, 2004), 29; R. Wolfrum, 'Cultural Property, Protection in Armed Conflict', in *MPEPIL*, at para. 8.
[22] See, most explicitly, CLT-95/WS/13, 19 (Bulgaria), 31, 34 (Iran), 35 (Liechtenstein), 36 (Madagascar), 42 (Slovenia), 43–4 (Switzerland), 48 (Ukraine); CC/MD/11, 16 (India), 27 (the Netherlands), 38 (USSR); CLT/MD/3, 21 (Austria), 24 (Byelorussian SSR); CC/MD/41, 19 (Hungary), 20 (Jordan), 25 (Niger); SHC/MD/6, 16 (Luxembourg); SHC/MD/1, 32–3 (San Marino).
[23] CLT/MD/3, 15 (Nagendra Singh). See also CLT/MD/3, 13 (Manfred Lachs). This idea was expressed during the drafting of CultPropConv: see Records 1954, paras. 136 (USSR), 146 (FRG). It is also echoed in some parties' implementation reports: see CC/MD/41, 15 (Byelorussian SSR), 20 (Jordan), 27 (USSR); CLT-95/WS/13, 31, 34 (Iran), 48 (Ukraine).
[24] See, e.g., 7 C/PRG/7, Annex I, 7; CBC/4, 7 (Israel); Records 1954, paras. 163 (Israel), 164 (France), 869 (Denmark), 1201 (Italy). See also H. Niecówna, 'Sovereign Rights to Cultural Property' (1971) 4 *Polish Yearbook of International Law* 239 at 250; S. Nahlik, 'Convention for the Protection of Cultural Property in

of good faith. In practice, the overwhelming majority of parties which have submitted implementation reports appear, in the case of immovable cultural property, to consider CultPropConv to apply either to the full complement of their national cultural heritage, as defined and formally identified by domestic law and procedure, or to a not insubstantial proportion of the same. While few parties have cited figures, those given are of an order of magnitude of tens of thousands.[25] As for movable cultural property, only two states have cited figures, and they refer to the contents of between 100 and 250 museums, art galleries, libraries, and archives.[26] In the final analysis, however, numbers are less important than the principle reiterated by the twenty-seventh General Conference of UNESCO—comprising representatives of every member state of the organization, most of them parties to CultPropConv—that CultPropConv 'offers protection to cultural property that is of national and local importance as well as to sites of outstanding universal importance'.[27]

4. Since the object and purpose of Article 53 AP I and Article 16 AP II was to restate the fundamental obligations of respect laid down in CultPropConv, it stands to reason that the property protected by the provision, *viz* 'historic monuments, works of art or places of worship which constitute the cultural or spiritual heritage of peoples',[28] should equate, as far as the ordinary meaning of the words permit, to cultural property within the meaning of its predecessor. In short, the wording of Article 53 AP I and Article 16 AP II was intended as an abbreviation or simplification of the formula used in Article 1 CultPropConv, the relevant working group speaking of 'the cultural heritage of peoples, in the words of the Hague Convention of 1954'.[29] Indeed, in the equally authentic French and Spanish texts of both instruments, the language is identical (except for the insertion of the words 'or spiritual'): the French and Spanish texts of

---

the Event of Armed Conflict, The Hague 1954: General and Special Protection', in Istituto Internazionale di Diritto Umanitario (ed.), *The International Protection of Cultural Property: Acts of the Symposium organized on the Occasion of the 30th Anniversary of the Hague Convention on the Protection of Cultural Property in the Event of Armed Conflicts* (Rome: Fondazione Europea Dragan, 1986), 87 at 89, 95; A. Przyborowska-Klimczak (above, n. 21), at 53; M. Cornu, *Le droit culturel des biens. L'intérêt culturel juridiquement protégé* (Brussels: Bruylant, 1996), 159; Toman (above, n. 21), 50; M. Seršić, 'Protection of Cultural Property in Time of Armed Conflict' (1996) 27 *NethYIL* 3 at 9.

[25] See CLT/MD/3, 21 (Austria, 76,890); CC/MD/11, 27 (the Netherlands, 43,000); CLT-95/WS/13, 19 (Bulgaria, 39,412), 24 (Germany, 10,000 in former FRG alone, plus 2,000 museums, archives, libraries and archaeological sites); CC/MD/11, 20 (Iraq, 10,000 archaeological sites alone); CC/MD/11, 35 and CLT-95/WS/13, 43 (Switzerland, 8,000); CC/MD/41, 15 (Byelorussian SSR, more than 6,000); CLT-95/WS/13, 66 (Slovenia, 5,550). Because of its enormous size, the former USSR cited a figure of 254,000: CC/MD/11, 38. The UK, which in 2004 announced its intention to ratify CultPropConv and both of its Protocols, currently proposes to extend general protection to around 10,800 immovables: Department for Culture, Media and Sport Cultural Property Unit, *Consultation Paper on The 1954 Hague Convention on the Protection of Cultural Property in the Event of Armed Conflict and its two Protocols of 1954 and 1999* (September 1995), 13.

[26] See CLT-95/WS/13, 20 (Bulgaria, 222 museums and art galleries). The UK currently proposes to extend general protection to the contents of 102 museums, galleries and collections, and to the contents of the National Record Offices and the country's five legal deposit libraries: Department for Culture, Media and Sport (above, n. 25), 13. Germany has cited a figure of 2,000 museums, archives, libraries and archaeological sites in the former FRG alone, although this is confounded for present purposes by the inclusion of archaeological sites: see CLT-95/WS/13, 24.

[27] 27 C/Resolution 3.5, para. 3. See also 142 EX/Decision 5.5.2, para. 7 lit. c; 142 EX/15, para. 8.

[28] The relevant provisions of Prot2WeaponsConv and AmendedProt2WeaponsConv also use this terminology.

[29] CDDH/III/224, Records 1974–7, XV, 333. See also CDDH/215/Rev.1, para. 69, Records 1974–7, XV, 278.

ROGER O'KEEFE

Article 1 CultPropConv make no use of the word 'every' found in the English version, referring simply to 'le patrimoine culturel des peuples' and 'el patrimonio cultural de los pueblos' respectively, while the French and Spanish texts of Article 53 AP I and Article 16 AP II speak of 'le patrimoine culturel ou spirituel des peuples' and 'el patrimonio cultural o espiritual de los pueblos'. The *ICRC Commentary* on the Additional Protocols, referring to the superficial divergence between the relative clause 'which constitute the cultural and spiritual heritage of peoples' in Article 53 AP I and Article 16 AP II and the clause 'which are of great importance to the cultural heritage of every people' in Article 1 CultPropConv, states that it 'does not seem that these expressions have a different meaning',[30] and makes it clear that 'there was no question of creating a new category of cultural objects'.[31] This view was endorsed by the Appeals Chamber of the ICTY in *Kordić*, where, drawing attention to the variation in wording between Article 53 AP I and Article 1 CultPropConv, it cited the *ICRC Commentary* to hold that, 'despite this difference in terminology, the basic idea is the same'.[32]

5. In this light, the terms 'historic monuments' and 'works of art' in Article 53 AP I and Article 16 AP II should be seen as shorthand for the full range of immovable and movable cultural property referred to Article 1 CultPropConv.[33] Additionally, the former's reference to the cultural or spiritual heritage 'of peoples' is to be construed as meaning the cultural or spiritual heritage of each respective people—that is, of each party, as determined by it according to its own criteria. In fact, the initial draft of Article 53 AP I spoke of 'the cultural heritage of a country',[34] and the earliest draft of the Article 16 AP II used the expression 'the national heritage of a country'.[35] Moreover, in its discussion of the differences of opinion which arose in relation to an intermediate draft over the application to places of worship of the clause 'which constitute the cultural heritage of peoples', Committee III of the Diplomatic Conference (in a statement applicable *mutatis mutandis* to historic monuments and works of art) suggested that 'cultural heterogeneity may be the key, for among some peoples any place of worship may be part of the cultural heritage, while among others only some places of worship may be so described'.[36] Similarly, the *ICRC Commentary*'s gloss on the notion of the spiritual heritage of peoples

[30] *ICRC Commentary*, para. 4844. See also J. Toman, 'La protection des biens culturels en cas de conflit armé non international', in W. Haller et al. (eds), *Im Dienst an der Gemeinschaft. Festschrift für Dietrich Schindler zum 65. Geburtstag* (Basel: Helbing & Lichtenhahn, 1989), 311 at 333–4.

[31] *ICRC Commentary*, para. 2064 n. 23.

[32] *Prosecutor v Kordić and Čerkez*, IT-95-14/2-A, Appeals Chamber Judgment, 17 December 2004, para. 91, citing *ICRC Commentary*, para. 2064. This was followed in *Prosecutor v Strugar*, IT-01-42-T, Trial Chamber Judgment, 31 January 2005, para. 307, which left open '[w]hether there may be precise differences'. See also para. 3 of the Russian Federation's declaration of 2 March 2005, 2308 *UNTS* 134, on becoming party to AmendedMinesProt, Article 7, para. 1, lit. i of which uses the expression 'historic monuments, works of art or places of worship which constitute the cultural or spiritual heritage of peoples' as found in Article 53 AP I and Article 16 AP II. The paragraph states: 'For the purposes of interpreting subparagraph 1(i) of article 7, of Protocol II, the Russian Federation understands the cultural or spiritual heritage of peoples as cultural property in the terms of article 1 of the Convention for the Protection of Cultural Property in the Event of Armed Conflict of 1954.'

[33] See also *ICRC Commentary*, paras. 2068, 4838; K. J. Partsch, 'Protection of Cultural Property', in D. Fleck (ed.), *The Handbook of Humanitarian Law in Armed Conflicts*, 1st edn (OUP, 1995), 377 at 382.

[34] CDDH/III/17 and Rev.1, Records 1974–7, III, 213.

[35] CDDH/III/GT/95, Records 1974–7, IV, 65. See also CDDH/III/SR.49, paras 13, 14, Records 1974–7, XV, 110 (Greece); CDDH/III/SR.24, para. 29, Records 1974–7, XIV, 222 (the Netherlands).

[36] CDDH/236/Rev.1, para. 62, Records 1974–7, XV, 395. See also CDDH/III/353, Records 1974–7, XV, 437.

ROGER O'KEEFE

(applicable *mutatis mutandis* to the idea of the cultural heritage of peoples) is instructive: acknowledging that 'the expression remains rather subjective', it suggests that, in case of doubt, 'reference should be made in the first place to the value or veneration ascribed to the object by the people whose heritage it is'.[37]

6. The obvious textual divergence between Article 1 CultPropConv, on the one hand, and Article 53 AP I and Article 16 AP II, on the other, is the insertion in the latter of places of worship and of the concept of the spiritual heritage of peoples. The *ICRC Commentary* elaborates that in general 'the adjective "cultural" applies to historic monuments and works of art, while the adjective "spiritual" applies to places of worship', yet emphasizes that a religious building may qualify for protection on account of its cultural value, just as under CultPropConv.[38] Putting it more simply, the majority of delegates, who adopted Article 53 AP I and Article 16 AP II by consensus, took the unequivocal view that not all places of worship are protected by these provisions but only those which constitute the cultural or spiritual heritage of peoples.[39] In practice, the addition of places of worship which constitute part of the cultural or spiritual heritage of peoples does not make a real difference to the relative scope of application of Article 53 AP I and Article 16 AP II vis-à-vis Article 1 CultPropConv. Those places of worship important enough to constitute part of the spiritual heritage of a people will, in practice, also be historic monuments forming part of the cultural heritage of that people for the purposes of both Article 53 AP I and Article 16 AP II, on the one hand, and Article 1 CultPropConv, on the other.[40] Indeed, the drafting records make it clear that the insertion of places of worship and of the concept of the spiritual heritage of peoples had a purely rhetorical significance.[41]

7. The conclusion that Article 53 AP I and Article 16 AP II serve to protect the national cultural and spiritual heritage of each party as determined by that party is not undermined by the *ICRC Commentary*'s additional assertion that 'the Conference intended to protect in particular the most important objects, a category akin to property granted special protection as provided in Article 8 of the Hague Convention'.[42] The apparent attribution to the drafters of explicit reference to Article 8 CultPropConv is editorial licence.[43] The *travaux* reveal no such reference or, indeed, specificity. Committee III spoke only of 'objects of considerable historical, cultural, and artistic importance'.[44] Furthermore, the suggestion that Article 53 AP I and Article 16 AP II apply to a category of cultural property akin to that covered by Article 8 CultPropConv fails to account for

---

[37] *ICRC Commentary*, para. 2065.

[38] *ICRC Commentary*, paras. 2065, 4843.

[39] *ICRC Commentary*, para. 2067. Places of worship not constituting the cultural or spiritual heritage of peoples are protected as civilian objects by Article 52 AP I, as made clear by the reference to them in Article 52, para. 3.

[40] See, e.g., CDDH/III/SR.59, para. 61, Records 1974–7, XV, 219 (Ireland).

[41] See CDDH/SR.42, Annex, Records 1974–7, VI, 227. See also CDDH/SR.41, para. 167, Records 1974–7, VI, 171 (Holy See). The relevant amendment was proposed by Saudi Arabia, the Holy See, Italy, and a coalition of Islamic states.

[42] *ICRC Commentary*, para. 4844.

[43] So too the statements in *ICRC Commentary*, paras. 2064 and 4840, based solely on an intervention by the Greek delegate at the diplomatic conference (CDDH/III/SR.59, para. 69, Records 1974–7, XV, 220), subsequently cited in *Kordić*, Appeals Chamber Judgment, para. 91.

[44] CDDH/215/Rev.1, para. 69, Records 1974–7, XV, 278. See also CDDH/III/224, Records 1974–7, XV, 333.

ROGER O'KEEFE

the fact that the latter encompasses only immovable cultural property, with movables enjoying only *de facto* protection insofar as they are placed in specially protected refuges or situated in specially protected centres containing monuments. Article 53 AP I and Article 16 AP II, on the contrary, expressly apply to 'works of art' in their own right. It is also hard to imagine that the Geneva diplomatic conference would have troubled itself to debate and adopt Article 53 AP I and Article 16 AP II for the benefit of what were at the time eight examples of immovable cultural property, as inscribed in the International Register of Cultural Property under Special Protection.

8. Nonetheless, the ICRC Study on Customary International Humanitarian Law draws a distinction between cultural property 'which forms part of the cultural or spiritual heritage of "peoples" (i.e., mankind)', as protected by Article 53 AP I and Article 16 AP II, and the 'broader' scope of CultPropConv, 'which covers property which forms part of the cultural heritage of "every people" ',[45] concluding that the property covered by the Additional Protocols 'must be of such importance that it will be recognised by everyone'.[46] But this statement reflects only the English-language texts. As seen above, leaving aside Article 53 AP I and Article 16 AP II's reference to the spiritual heritage, the equally authentic French and Spanish texts of the respective wordings are identical: both translate as 'the cultural heritage . . . of peoples'. Additionally, even restricting one's attention to the English text, the ICRC's construction of the word 'mankind' overlooks the key statement in the preamble to CultPropConv that 'damage to cultural property belonging to any people whatsoever means damage to the cultural heritage of all mankind, since each people makes its contribution to the culture of the world'. The ICRC Study claims support for its view in the interpretative declarations entered by several states at the time of Article 53 AP I's adoption.[47] But, as reproduced in the Study itself, the distinction drawn by these states is between the scope of application of Article 53 of AP I and the scope of application of Article 27 HagueRegs, not of Article 1 CultPropConv.[48]

9. In principle it is up to each party in whose territory the relevant property is situated to determine whether or not that property is of great importance to its cultural heritage and is therefore protected as cultural property. In practice, however, things are not so straightforward. Unless a party has taken measures to notify other parties of the identity and location of all such property by means of inventories and/or maps, or has marked all such property with CultPropConv's distinctive emblem, there will be no definitive way for an opposing party to know what movables and immovables are protected. In such a situation, which is likely to be the rule rather than the exception, it will ultimately fall by default to the opposing party to determine, for the purposes of compliance with its own obligations of respect, which movables and immovables situated in the territory of the first party satisfy the definition of 'cultural property' by being of great importance to the cultural heritage of that first party. In such an event, the safest course is to err on the side of caution.

---

[45] Vol. I *CIHL*, 130, 132.
[46] Vol. I *CIHL*, 130.
[47] Vol. I *CIHL*, 130, especially n. 19.
[48] See Vol. II/1 *CIHL*, chap. 12, paras. 180 (Canada), 193 (FRG), 220 (UK), 227 (the US). The statement by the Netherlands cited, as reproduced and in the original, makes no reference either to Article 1 CultPropConv or to Article 27 HagueRegs, and the Australian statement cited deals with a different question altogether.

ROGER O'KEEFE

II. Respect for Cultural Property

1. General Rules

902   It is prohibited to attack cultural property unless it becomes a military objective and there is no feasible alternative for obtaining a similar military advantage (Articles 53, lit. a, and 52 AP I; Article 16 AP II; Article 4, paras. 1 and 2, CultPropConv and Article 6, lit. a, Prot2CultPropConv). The parties to the conflict shall do everything feasible to verify that objectives to be attacked are not cultural property (Article 57, para. 2, lit. a(i), AP I; Article 7, lit. a, Prot2CultPropConv). They shall cancel or suspend an attack if it becomes apparent that the objective is cultural property (Article 57, para. 2, lit. b, AP I; Article 7, lit. d(i), Prot2CultPropConv).

1. The three rules stated here are applicable during both international and non-international armed conflict, and apply to all attacks, whether by land, sea, or air. In the context of international armed conflict, all three accord with customary international law. In the context of non-international armed conflict, the first is customary, but evidence in support of the second and third is not yet conclusive.

2. The second limb of Article 4, para. 1, CultPropConv obliges parties to respect cultural property by refraining from any act of hostility against such property, an obligation encompassing *inter alia* attacks against such property. This must be read subject to Article 4, para. 2, CultPropConv, which provides that the obligations laid down in the preceding paragraph may be waived where military necessity imperatively requires such a waiver. On the face of it, the phrase 'where military necessity imperatively requires' is an open-textured one. But the waiver in Article 4, para. 2, CultPropConv must today be read through the lens of the customary rules on targeting, applicable to both international and non-international armed conflict, which emerged after the adoption of CultPropConv, specifically the subsequent definition of a military objective, as per Article 52, para. 2, AP I.[49] This is in line with the approach taken to the phrase 'not justified by military necessity' by the ICTY.[50] As a consequence, a party may invoke the waiver in Article 4, para. 2, CultPropConv to justify attacking cultural property only in cases where the cultural property in question, by its nature, location, purpose or use, makes an effective contribution to military action and where its total or partial destruction, capture or neutralization, in the circumstances ruling at the time, offers a definite military advantage.

3. In accordance with Article 53, lit. a, AP I and Article 16 AP II, it is prohibited to direct acts of hostility against cultural property. But whereas Article 4, para. 1, CultPropConv is subject to Article 4, para. 2, Article 53, lit. a, AP I and Article 16 AP II contain no exception in respect of military necessity. Military necessity as such provides no justification under these articles for attacking cultural property. Nor is the prohibition on acts

---

[49] See also *ICRC Commentary*, para. 2079, n. 30; Toman (above, n. 21), 389; *UK Manual*, para. 5.26.8.
[50] *Prosecutor v Brđanin*, IT-99-36-A, Appeals Chamber Judgment, 3 April 2007, para. 337. See also Article 8, para. 2 lit. b(ix) and Article 8, para. 2, lit. e(iv), ICC Statute, providing for the war crime of directing attacks against historic monuments 'provided they are not military objectives'.

of hostility against cultural property reciprocal with the prohibition on the use of such property in support of the military effort.[51] That said, if and for as long as an object covered by Article 53, lit. a, AP I is used in support of the military effort contrary to Article 53, lit. b, the legality of any attack against that object (and only that object) falls to be determined by reference to Article 52, para. 2, AP I,[52] and will be lawful provided such use makes an effective contribution to military action and the object's total or partial destruction, capture, or neutralization, in the circumstances ruling at the time, offers a definite military advantage. The practical effect, therefore, of the additional protection afforded by Article 53 AP I is that whereas other civilian objects may be targeted pursuant to Article 52, para. 2, AP I on account of their nature, location, purpose or use, cultural property may be attacked only on account of its use. For its part, AP II contains no provision equivalent to the definition of a military objective in Article 52, para. 2, AP I, since nowhere does AP II embody a prohibition on attacking civilian objects as such or the concomitant obligation to limit attacks strictly to military objectives. The use of cultural property contrary to Article 16 AP II results, therefore, in the lawfulness of any attack against it falling to be determined by reference to the customary international law of targeting in non-international armed conflict. In the end, however, there is no practical difference between the situation under AP I and that under AP II, since it is now sufficiently clear that customary international law prohibits attacks against cultural property in the course of non-international armed conflict unless such property becomes a military objective within the meaning of the definition encapsulated in Article 52, para. 2, AP I. In short, under both AP I and AP II, cultural property may be attacked only on account of its use.

4. But Article 53, lit. a, AP I and Article 16 AP II are stated to be without prejudice to CultPropConv. As a consequence, where the parties to an armed conflict are parties both to AP I and AP II, on the one hand, and to CultPropConv, on the other, conduct covered by both regimes is governed by the provisions of CultPropConv.[53] The result is that parties to both regimes are entitled to invoke the waiver as to military necessity embodied in Article 4, para. 2, CultPropConv, as elaborated on by customary international law, to justify attacking cultural property.[54] But the difference is slight: whereas parties to AP I and AP II alone may attack cultural property only on account of its use, parties to AP I and AP II which are also parties to CultPropConv may additionally invoke its nature, location, and purpose—which, in the context of cultural property, is scarcely a difference at all (see below).

5. Article 6, lit. a, Prot2CultPropConv refines the application of Article 4, para. 2, CultPropConv among parties to Prot2CultPropConv. It states that a waiver on the basis of imperative military necessity pursuant to Article 4, para. 2, CultPropConv may be invoked to direct an act of hostility against cultural property only when, and for as long as, two cumulative conditions are met: first, when and for as long as the cultural property

---

[51] See also *ICRC Commentary*, para. 2079.
[52] See also *ICRC Commentary*, para. 2079; Toman (above, n. 21), 390; Wolfrum (above, n. 21), para. 17.
[53] See Article 30, para. 2, Vienna Convention on the Law of Treaties.
[54] See also *Strugar*, Trial Chamber Judgment, para. 309; *ICRC Commentary*, para. 2072 n. 28; Toman (above, n. 21), 389; E. David, *Principes de droit des conflits armés*, 4th edn (Brussels: Bruylant, 2008), para. 2.82; R. Kolb, *Ius in bello. Le droit international des conflits armés*, 2nd edn (Basel/Brussels: Helbing & Lichtenhahn/Bruylant, 2009), 282.

ROGER O'KEEFE

in question has, by its function, been made into a military objective (Article 6, lit. a(i), Prot2CultPropConv); and, second, when and for as long as there is no feasible alternative available for obtaining a similar military advantage to that offered by directing an act of hostility against that objective (Article 6, lit. a(ii)). 'Military objective' is defined in Article 1, lit. f, Prot2CultPropConv in accordance with the now-customary definition found in Article 52, para. 2, AP I. But a terminological disjuncture is immediately apparent: Article 6, lit. a(i), Prot2CultPropConv refers to cultural property being made into a military objective by its 'function', whereas Article 1, lit. f, speaks of its 'nature, location, purpose, or use'. The daily précis of the 1999 Hague diplomatic conference[55] reveal the explanation. Opinion was sharply divided between those states which supported reference to cultural property which 'has, by its use, become a military objective',[56] 'feeling that "nature", "purpose" and/or "location" were not on their own sufficient to define a military objective',[57] and those which sought a full restatement of the definition of a military objective found in Article 1, lit. f, Prot2CultPropConv. In other words, some delegates favoured the higher standard of protection afforded cultural property by Article 53, lit. a, AP I and Article 16 AP II, whereas others wished simply to put on an explicit treaty footing the customary gloss on Article 4, para. 2, CultPropConv. Faced with this impasse, the chair of the conference invited the informal working group on Chapter 2 of the draft Prot2CultPropConv to reconvene 'in order to try to find a balance between the need to protect cultural property, and the actions that have to be taken in certain military situations'.[58] The upshot was the compromise word 'function', a term open-textured enough to accommodate both positions—indeed, deliberately designed to permit a degree of discretion in its interpretation and application. Those states favouring the lower standard are free to hold that cultural property can become a military objective under Article 6, lit. a(i), by virtue of its nature, location or purpose, in addition to its use.[59] At the same time, states supporting the higher standard are not precluded from maintaining that only its use can make cultural property a military objective. Room is also left for the possibility that the higher standard may emerge in future as customary international law, in which case Article 6, lit. a(i), will have to be read consistently with it. It should be emphasized, however, that the practical difference between the two levels of protection is unlikely to be great (see below).

6. The requirement in Article 6, lit. a(ii), Prot2CultPropConv that there be no feasible alternative available for obtaining a similar military advantage to that offered by attacking

---

[55] Diplomatic Conference on a Draft Second Protocol to the 1954 Hague Convention for the Protection of Cultural Property in the Event of Armed Conflict, 15–26 March 1999, Daily précis of the Diplomatic Conference, <http://www.unesco.org/new/fileadmin/MULTIMEDIA/HQ/CLT/pdf/hague_1999_diplo-conf_precis_en_20120523.pdf>. The full *travaux préparatoires* of Prot2CultPropConv remain publicly unavailable. But see the excerpts reproduced in J. Toman, *Cultural Property in War: Improvement in Protection. Commentary on the 1999 Second Protocol to the Hague Convention of 1954 for the Protection of Cultural Property in the Event of Armed Conflict* (Paris: UNESCO Publishing, 2009), 105–10.

[56] HC/1999/5/Add.5, draft Article 4 (eventual Article 6 Prot2CultPropConv).

[57] Précis, Wednesday 24 March 1999, in Diplomatic Conference on a Draft Second Protocol, Daily précis (above, n. 55), sixteenth unnumbered page.

[58] Ibid. seventeenth unnumbered page.

[59] Canada, for example, annexed to its instrument of accession to Prot2CultPropConv a statement declaring its understanding 'that the definition of a military objective in Article 2(f) is to be interpreted the same way as Article 52(2) of Additional Protocol I to the Geneva Conventions of 1949' and 'that under Article 6(a)(i), cultural property can be made into a military objective because of its nature, location, purpose or use' (<http://portal.unesco.org/en/ev.php-URL_ID=15207&URL_DO=DO_TOPIC&URL_SECTION=201.html#RESERVES>).

ROGER O'KEEFE

the cultural property is really no more than an explicit elaboration of the limits imposed by imperative military necessity, as embodied in Article 4, para. 2, CultPropConv and reflected in Article 57, para. 3, AP I.[60]

7. The reference in Article 53 AP I's 'without prejudice' clause to 'other relevant international instruments' would appear to be to RoerichPact, in force when the provision was adopted, but the ordinary meaning of the phrase would also encompass any similar specialist international agreement for the protection of cultural property in the event of armed conflict as may be concluded in the future. In this light, where parties to AP I are also parties to Prot2CultPropConv, conduct covered by both instruments is governed by the provisions of Prot2CultPropConv. Article 16 AP II's 'without prejudice' clause makes no mention of 'other relevant international instruments', seemingly reflecting the fact that, insofar as it applies during wartime, RoerichPact applies only to wars between states, and not to civil wars. Given the relationship between Article 53 AP I and Prot2CultPropConv, however, and in the light of the drafters' intention that Article 16 AP II should not affect the application of the specialist regime represented at the time by CultPropConv, it is reasonable to treat Prot2CultPropConv as a *de facto* integral part of CultPropConv for the specific purposes of Article 16 AP II, with the result that Article 16 AP II is without prejudice to the provisions of Prot2CultPropConv. As such, where a state is party to both AP II and Prot2CultPropConv, conduct by that state which is covered by both instruments is governed by the provisions of Prot2CultPropConv. At present, however, in neither international nor non-international armed conflict does any of this make a practical difference.

8. When it comes to applying the rule on attacks against cultural property, such property may be considered a military objective in certain circumstances, although these circumstances will be rare. It is not absurd to suggest that very specific cultural property— historic fortresses, barracks, arsenals, and the like—can, by its nature, make an effective contribution to military action. That said, if it is decommissioned, an eighteenth-century fortress, to take an example, is better characterized by its nature as a historic monument, rather than a fortress; and if it is still in service, any effective contribution it may make to military action will be through its use, rather than its nature. Similarly, while the vast majority of cultural property cannot make an effective contribution to military action through its purpose (defined as 'the future intended use of an object'[61]), a historic bridge, railway station, or dock could conceivably, by its purpose, make such a contribution, although whether this contribution is genuinely effective will depend on the circumstances. Generally speaking, one would not expect infrastructure built in and for another age to play a significant military role today. As for location, it is not unimaginable that the position of cultural property during a battle could serve to block a party's line of fire. At the same time, any contribution this may make to the military action of the opposing party is arguably better seen as a function of the property's passive or

---

[60] Article 57, para. 3, AP I provides that when a choice is possible between several military objectives for obtaining a similar military advantage, the objective to be selected must be the one which, if attacked, may be expected to cause the least danger to civilian lives and to civilian objects. Cultural property is a species of civilian object.

[61] *Western Front, Aerial Bombardment and Related Claims, Eritrea's Claims 1, 3, 5, 9–13, 14, 21, 25 & 26* (Eritrea/Ethiopia), Partial Award, 135 ILR 565 at para. 120, endorsing *UK Manual*, para. 5.4.4, in turn endorsing *ICRC Commentary*, para. 2022.

ROGER O'KEEFE

de facto use.[62] In the final analysis, then, it is principally through its use, if it all, that cultural property could be expected to make an effective contribution to military action.[63] In other words, use in support of military action is the principal reason which a party to the conflict could be expected to invoke to justify attacking cultural property. Indeed, it is inconceivable today that a party would cite the nature of cultural property to this end, scarcely imaginable that it would cite its purpose, and highly unlikely that it would cite its location.

9. It is crucial to note in all of the above cases that, whatever contribution cultural property may make to military action, an attack against it is lawful only when its total or partial destruction, capture, or neutralization, in the circumstances ruling at the time, offers a definite military advantage. '[A]nd even then attacks on it may not be necessary'.[64] For example, as Rogers points out, if enemy snipers have installed themselves in cultural property, it may be possible simply to bypass it.[65] Equally, it may be possible to surround it and wait, while pursuing a peaceful resolution through negotiation and reliance on diplomatic good offices, as the Israel Defence Forces did for over a month in 2002 at the Church of the Nativity in Bethlehem, in which a large number of armed Palestinian militants had taken up position. In short, there must be no feasible alternative method for dealing with the situation before an attack on cultural property can be held permissible.[66]

10. The prohibition on attacks against cultural property is backed up by two mandatory precautions in attack deriving from Article 57, para. 2, AP I, Article 7 Prot2CultPropConv and customary international law. AP II makes no mention of such precautions.

903   **The parties to the conflict shall take all feasible precautions in the choice of means and methods of attack with a view to avoiding, and in any event minimizing, incidental damage to cultural property (Article 57, para. 2, lit. a(ii), AP I; Article 7, lit. b, Prot2CultPropConv). They shall refrain from deciding to launch any attack which may be expected to cause incidental damage to cultural property which would be excessive in relation to the concrete and direct military advantage anticipated (Article 57, para. 2 lit. a(iii), AP I; Article 7, lit. c, Prot2CultPropConv). They shall cancel or suspend an attack if it becomes apparent that it may be expected to cause incidental damage to cultural property which would be excessive in relation to the concrete and direct military advantage anticipated (Article 57, para. 2, lit. b, AP I; Article 7, lit. d(ii), Prot2CultPropConv).**

1. The three rules stated here apply during both international and non-international armed conflict, and apply to all attacks, whether by land, sea, or air. In the context of international armed conflict, all three accord with customary international law. In the context of non-international armed conflict, the first is probably consonant with custom, but evidence for the second and third is not yet conclusive.

---

[62] See also *ICRC Commentary*, para. 2078. For example, the defending German forces can be taken to have made passive or *de facto* use of the abbey of Monte Cassino in the Second World War.

[63] See also J. M. Henckaerts, 'New rules for the protection of cultural property in armed conflict' (1991) 81 *IRRC* 593, at 602–6. Indeed, *UK Manual*, para. 5.26.3 n. 120, goes so far as to state that waiver under Article 4, para. 2, CultPropConv 'only arises where the enemy unlawfully uses such property for military purposes'. See also Wolfrum (above, n. 21), para. 14.

[64] *UK Manual*, para. 5.26.3 n. 120.

[65] A. P. V. Rogers, *Law on the Battlefield*, 3rd edn (Manchester and New York: Manchester University Press, 2012), 186.

[66] *UK Manual*, para. 5.26.8; Rogers (above, n. 65), 186–7.

ROGER O'KEEFE

2. Incidental damage inflicted in the course of attacks against otherwise lawful targets has historically posed the single greatest threat to cultural property in armed conflict, at least since the rise of modern forms of bombardment. One of the most significant advances in the protection of cultural property in armed conflict came, therefore, with the adoption in Article 51, para. 5, lit. b, AP I, cross-referable to Article 51, para. 4, AP I, of a prohibition on attacks which may be expected to cause incidental loss of civilian life, injury to civilians, damage to civilian objects (including cultural property), or a combination thereof, which would be excessive in relation to the concrete and direct military advantage anticipated. The standard is one of proportionality. It is supported by the three obligatory precautions in attack found in Article 57, para. 2, lit. a(ii), Article 57, para. 2, lit. a(iii) and Article 57, para. 2, lit. b, AP I, reproduced in the specific context of cultural property in Article 7, lit. b, Article 7 lit. c, and Article 7, lit. d(ii), Prot2CultPropConv.

3. As applied to cultural property, proportionality in the context of incidental damage implicates qualitative as much as quantitative factors. The extent of incidental loss occasioned by damage to or destruction of cultural property is a question not just of square metres but also of the cultural value represented thereby. In this light, it is significant that cultural property is by definition of great importance to the cultural heritage of a people, and that the preamble to CultPropConv, as echoed in Resolution 20(IV) of the Diplomatic Conference of Geneva, declares that damage to cultural property belonging to any people whatsoever means damage to the cultural heritage of all mankind. Since elements of this heritage are often irreplaceable, only the anticipation of very considerable concrete and direct military advantage, in many cases overwhelming, will, in practice, suffice to justify an attack likely to cause incidental damage to cultural property. A textbook example of the application of the rule of proportionality came during the Gulf War in 1991, when Iraq positioned two fighter aircraft next to the ancient ziggurat of Ur. Coalition commanders decided not to attack the aircraft 'on the basis of respect for cultural property and the belief that positioning of the aircraft adjacent to Ur (without servicing equipment or a runway nearby) effectively had placed each out of action, thereby limiting the value of their destruction by Coalition air forces when weighed against the risk of damage to the temple'.[67]

> **All other acts of hostility against cultural property are prohibited unless impera-   904
> tively required by military necessity (Article 23, lit. g, HagueReg; Article 4, paras.
> 1 and 2, CultPropConv).**

1. The rule stated here is applicable to both international armed conflict and non-international armed conflict, and accords with customary international law in both contexts.

2. Article 23, lit. g, HagueRegs prohibits the destruction of enemy property unless it is imperatively demanded by the necessities of war. The rule is reiterated in the specific context of cultural property in Article 4, para. 1, CultPropConv, as qualified by Article 4, para. 2, CultPropConv, in accordance with which parties are obliged to respect cultural property by refraining from any act of hostility against it, unless military necessity imperatively requires otherwise. The term 'any act of hostility' is significant in forbidding

---

[67] Department of Defense, Report to Congress on the Conduct of the Persian Gulf War, Appendix O: The Role of the Law of War (1992) 31 *ILM* 626.

not just attacks against cultural property but also *inter alia* its demolition,[68] whether by way of explosives or bulldozers or other wrecking equipment, and whether to impede the progress of enemy columns, to clear a line of fire, to deny cover to enemy fighters or *a fortiori* for motives other than military. Since acts of hostility other than attacks are not amenable to an analysis based on the concept of a military objective, the latter being relevant only to attacks,[69] the rule stated here reflects the plain language of Article 4, paras. 1 and 2, CultPropConv and Article 23, lit. g, HagueRegs.

3. Article 53 AP I and Article 16 AP II similarly apply to any acts of hostility directed against cultural property, and thus encompass demolitions as much as attacks. It will be recalled that neither provision embodies a waiver in respect of military necessity. Nor, in the context of acts of hostility other than attacks, does Article 53 AP I interact with the concept of a military objective in Article 52, para. 2, AP I, since the latter applies only to attacks. The same goes *mutatis mutandis* for Article 16 AP II and the customary analogue of Article 52, para. 2, AP I applicable to non-international armed conflict. The result is that acts of hostility against cultural property other than attacks are absolutely prohibited by Article 53 AP I and Article 16 AP II. But Article 53 AP I and Article 16 AP II are without prejudice to CultPropConv, with the consequence that parties to both regimes are entitled to invoke the waiver in respect of imperative military necessity embodied in Article 4, para. 2, CultPropConv.

4. Imperative military necessity implies no feasible alternative for dealing with the situation. As emphasized by Eisenhower, military necessity is not the same as military convenience,[70] a view reiterated in 1997 by the third meeting of the parties to CultPropConv[71] and the following year by a meeting of governmental experts drawn from fifty-seven parties.[72] 'It is not sufficient that the objective could be more easily attained by endangering the protected object'; rather, 'an imperative necessity presupposes that the military objective cannot be reached in any other manner'.[73] Military necessity also serves to calibrate the extent of any damage or destruction compelled by military considerations: harm to cultural property occasioned by the invocation of the concept must be only to a degree that is imperatively necessary.

905   It is prohibited to make cultural property the object of reprisals (Articles 52, para. 1, and 53, lit. c, AP I; Article 4, para. 4 CultPropConv; see above, Section 488).

1. The rule stated here applies during both international and non-international armed conflict. In the context of international armed conflict, it accords with customary international law. The position is uncertain as regards non-international armed conflict.

---

[68] See also M. Bothe et al., *New Rules for Victims of Armed Conflicts* (The Hague/Boston/London: Nijhoff, 1982), para. 2.5.2; *ICRC Commentary*, para. 2070; Toman (above, n. 21), 389.

[69] Article 52, para. 2, AP I, as consonant with custom.

[70] Covering memorandum to General Order No. 68, 29 Dec. 1943, reproduced in *Hansard*, HC, Vol. 396, col. 1116, 1 February 1944.

[71] CLT-97/CONF.208/3, para. 5(ii).

[72] 155 EX/51, Annex, para. 14.

[73] Partsch (above, n. 33), 388. See also *UK Manual*, paras. 5.26.3 n. 120, 5.26.8; Rogers (above, n. 65), 186–7; R. Wolfrum, 'Protection of Cultural Property in Armed Conflict' 32 *IsrYHR* (2003) 305 at 325. See too H. Grotius, *De Jure Belli ac Pacis*, first published 1625, text of 1646 translated by F. W. Kelsey (Oxford: Clarendon Press, 1925), Book II, Ch. 22, s. 6 ('Advantage does not confer the same right as necessity').

ROGER O'KEEFE

2. Article 4, para. 4, CultPropConv obliges parties to refrain from any act directed by way of reprisals against cultural property, a prohibition to which the waiver in respect of imperative military necessity in Article 4, para. 2, CultPropConv is not applicable. This absolute prohibition is reiterated in Article 53, lit. c, AP I and, as regards civilian objects generally, in Article 52, para. 1, AP I. Article 16 AP II, on the other hand, makes no mention of reprisals.

> It is prohibited to make any use of cultural property likely to expose it to destruction or damage in the event of armed conflict unless no choice is possible between such use and another feasible method for obtaining a similar military advantage (Article 4, paras. 1 and 2 CultPropConv and Article 6, lit. b, Prot2CultPropConv).

906

1. The rule stated here is applicable to both international and non-international armed conflict, and accords with customary international law in both contexts.

2. The first limb of Article 4, para. 1, CultPropConv obliges parties to respect cultural property by refraining from any use of the property and its immediate surroundings for purposes which are likely to expose it to destruction or damage in the event of armed conflict. The wording makes this provision more than a prohibition on the use of cultural property for hostile purposes. The reference to 'its immediate surroundings' and to any use 'for purposes which are likely to expose it to destruction or damage' means that the prohibition extends to its *de facto* or passive use in any manner likely to draw fire on it.[74] Article 4, para. 1, CultPropConv therefore prohibits the deliberate interposition of cultural property in the line of fire, for example by retreating to a position obscured by a monument from the opposing party's view. The provision also serves to forbid the effective incorporation of a monument into a defensive line, as with the German 'Gustav line' around the abbey at Monte Cassino in the Second World War. Nor is it only use in combat that the rule prohibits. If it is foreseeable that the use of a protected building as a field headquarters or barracks, for example, will expose it to attack, such use is forbidden. The first limb of Article 4, para. 1, CultPropConv would also prohibit parking military aircraft in the immediate surroundings of cultural property,[75] as Iraq did in the Gulf War of 1991. Nor, indeed, need such use expose the property in question to attack for it to fall foul of the rule: the provision forbids any use likely to expose cultural property to damage during armed conflict (which, as per Article 18, para. 2, CultPropConv, includes belligerent occupation), with the result that the likelihood of more than *de minimis* deterioration in the fabric of a monument, and *a fortiori* the risk of vandalism, through its use as a headquarters, barracks, or the like is enough to render such use impermissible. It is important to note too that the first limb of Article 4, para. 1, CultPropConv prohibits the use of cultural property and its surroundings in any manner likely to expose it to damage or destruction 'in the event of armed conflict'. In other words, if such use in peacetime is likely to expose cultural property to attack on the outbreak of hostilities, it is not permitted.[76]

---

[74] Partsch (above, n. 33), 385, speaks in this respect of 'indirect' use.

[75] Rogers (above, n. 65), 188 n. 101.

[76] So, for example, the former Ukrainian SSR reported that, even in peacetime, Soviet armed forces were not allowed to be quartered, to stock arms or to install military targets in the immediate surroundings of historic monuments or groups of historic monuments, 'as stated in Article 4, paragraph 1 of the Convention': CC/MD/11, 38. That certain provisions of the CultPropConv apply in peacetime is made clear in Article 18, para. 1.

ROGER O'KEEFE

3. But Article 4, para. 1, CultPropConv is qualified by the waiver as to military necessity in Article 4, para. 2, CultPropConv. As such, if military necessity imperatively requires the use of cultural property and its surroundings for purposes likely to expose it to attack, such use is not prohibited. An example of one of the '*rare* cases where it is essential to use cultural property for military purposes' is a historic bridge which constitutes the only available river crossing.[77] A further example is the positioning of an artillery piece in the immediate vicinity of cultural property if that is the only point from which an enemy stronghold dominating the battlefield can be attacked.[78]

4. It should be emphasized that a party's use of cultural property and its surroundings in any manner likely to expose it to destruction or damage does not as such make it lawful for an opposing party to attack it. That is, a party's breach of the first limb of Article 4, para. 1, CultPropConv does not *ipso facto* relieve an opposing party from its obligation under the second limb of the provision, as stressed by the Legal Committee during the drafting of the Convention.[79] Cultural property put to such use may be attacked only if it makes an effective contribution to military action and its total or partial destruction, capture, or neutralization, in the circumstances ruling at the time, offers a definite military advantage.

5. Article 53, lit. b, AP I and Article 16 AP II prohibit parties from using cultural property in support of the military effort. The concept of 'the military effort' is arguably wider than the notion of 'military action' referred to in the definition of a military objective in Article 52, para. 2, AP I. According to the *ICRC Commentary*, the military effort is 'a very broad concept, encompassing all military activities connected with the conduct of a war'.[80] For example, the use of the cellars of a historic castle a long way behind the front line to store rations may be considered supportive of the military effort but may not be thought to make an effective contribution to military action. The same may go for the billeting of non-front-line troops there. Such use may be held to violate Article 53, lit. b, AP I or Article 16 AP II but would arguably not render the castle a military objective. Since neither Article 53, lit. b, AP I nor Article 16 AP II contains an exception in respect of military necessity, their respective prohibitions on the use of cultural property in support of the military effort are absolute. But as these provisions are without prejudice to CultPropConv, parties to both regimes may invoke the waiver as to military necessity in Article 4, para. 2, CultPropConv.

6. Article 6, lit. b, Prot2CultPropConv provides that a waiver on the basis of imperative military necessity pursuant to Article 4, para. 2, CultPropConv may be invoked to use cultural property for purposes which are likely to expose it to destruction or damage only when, and for as long as, no choice is possible between such use of the cultural property and another feasible method for obtaining a similar military advantage. The provision is no more than a codified statement of the proper application of Article 4, para. 2, CultPropConv as it applies to the use of cultural property.

---

[77] *UK Manual*, para. 5.25.3, original emphasis.
[78] *Der Schutz von Kulturgut bei bewaffneten Konflikten*, Federal Ministry of Defence publication ZDv 15/9, 15 July 1964, 16, cited in Rogers (above, n. 65), 187.
[79] Records 1954, para. 1170. See also Toman (above, n. 21), 70, 75; *UK Manual*, paras. 5.26.3 n. 120, 5.26.8.
[80] *ICRC Commentary*, para. 2078.

ROGER O'KEEFE

> All forms of theft, pillage, misappropriation, confiscation or vandalism of cultural   907
> property are prohibited. The parties to the conflict shall prohibit, prevent and, if
> necessary, put a stop to all such acts. They shall refrain from requisitioning mov-
> able cultural property situated in the territory of an opposing party (Article 4, para.
> 3, CultPropConv).

1. The first two rules stated here apply during international and non-international armed conflict alike; the third by definition only during international armed conflict. In the context of international armed conflict, all three accord with customary international law. The first two are also more likely than not to be consonant with custom in non-international armed conflict.

2. The undertaking in Article 4, para. 3, CultPropConv to prohibit, prevent, and, if necessary, put a stop to all forms of theft, pillage, misappropriation, confiscation, or vandalism of cultural property is not limited to the commission of such acts by a party's own armed forces but extends to commission by the local populace and by remnants of the opposing armed forces. This explains why the first limb of the provision is formulated as an obligation to prohibit, prevent, and, if necessary, put a stop to the relevant conduct, instead of merely an obligation to refrain from it, as is the case with the second limb of the provision and with Art 4, paras. 1 and 4, CultPropConv. Indeed, somewhat curiously, Article 4, para. 3, does not in terms oblige a party to refrain from theft, pillage, misappropriation, confiscation, or vandalism of cultural property. But a prohibition to this effect must be implied, reasoning *a fortiori*.[81] Any other outcome would fly in the face of the Article's object and purpose. The implication is strengthened by the adoption of Article 15, para. 1, lit e, Prot2CultPropConv, which recognizes as a war crime, when committed intentionally and in violation of CultPropConv, theft, pillage, or misappropriation of, or acts of vandalism directed against, cultural property protected under CultPropConv. Article 4, para. 3, CultPropConv is not subject to Article 4, para. 2's waiver in respect of military necessity.

> The parties to the conflict shall take the necessary precautions to protect cul-   908
> tural property under their control against the dangers resulting from mili-
> tary operations (Article 58, lit. c, AP I). They shall, to the maximum extent
> feasible, remove cultural property from the vicinity of military objectives
> (Article 58, lit. a, AP I; Article 8, lit. a, Prot2CultPropConv) or provide for
> adequate *in situ* protection (Article 8, lit. a, Prot2CultPropConv), and they
> shall avoid locating military objectives near cultural property (Article 8, lit. b,
> Prot2CultPropConv).

The first rule stated here applies only to international armed conflict, the following two rules to both international and non-international armed conflict. The customary status of all three is unclear in either context.

2. Special Protection

> Contracting parties may request that a limited number of refuges for movable   909
> cultural property and of centres containing monuments and a limited amount of

---

[81] For the use of identical *a fortiori* reasoning to read a prohibition on commission into an obligation to prevent, see Application of the Convention on the Prevention and Punishment of the Crime of Genocide (*Bosnia and Herzegovina v Serbia and Montenegro*), Merits, Judgment, *ICJ Reports 2007*, 43 at para. 166.

ROGER O'KEEFE

immovable cultural property of very great importance be placed under special protection (Article 8, para. 1, CultPropConv).

1. Chapter II CultPropConv (Articles 8–11) establishes a regime of 'special protection' applicable over and above the general protection provided for in Chapter I CultPropConv. This supplementary regime is designed to provide a higher standard of protection in respect of a narrower range of property, a higher standard which relates specifically to the obligation to refrain from using cultural property and its surroundings for military purposes and the obligation to refrain from directing acts of hostility against it. These twin obligations aside, all the obligations otherwise applicable to movables and immovables which satisfy the definition of cultural property under Article 1 CultPropConv are equally applicable to property which additionally qualifies for special protection under Article 8 CultPropConv. Special protection is available only in respect of refuges intended to shelter movable cultural property, centres containing monuments, and other immovable cultural property. It is not available for movable cultural property as such. Moreover, refuges, centres containing monuments, and other immovable cultural property are entitled to special protection only if they satisfy strict criteria.

2. The difference between the standards imposed during armed conflict by the regime of special protection and the respect owed to cultural property under general protection is extraordinarily minor. Although labelled 'immunity', the additional restraints mandated in relation to specially protected property amount to no more than a slight tightening of the conditions under which the waiver as to military necessity may be invoked. Any greater substantive protection that such property may stand to enjoy effectively derives from the regime's criteria for eligibility, which prescribe a *cordon sanitaire* around the property.

3. The success of the arrangements for special protection 'has proved very limited'.[82] Putting it less delicately, Chapter II CultPropConv is a white elephant. Only one centre containing monuments, the Vatican City, and eight refuges for movable cultural property (six of them in the Netherlands) have ever been entered in the International Register of Cultural Property under Special Protection, and the Vatican City's entry was possible only thanks to a special undertaking by Italy ostensibly under Article 8, para. 5, CultPropConv. Four of the refuges have since been removed at the request of the respective parties, leaving the Register to comprise now four refuges (three in the Netherlands and one in Germany), and a lone centre containing monuments.[83] The reasons for this underwhelming uptake are obvious: the criteria of eligibility for special protection are cripplingly difficult to satisfy, while the procedure by which such protection is granted is potentially tortuous, time-consuming, and, with precious little reward for success, hardly worth the effort.

4. The regime of special protection is now also, in effect, a dead letter, since it has, for all intents and purposes, been replaced by the regime of 'enhanced protection' under Chapter 3 Prot2CultPropConv. But it has not been formally abolished, making a bare outline of its rules a necessity.[84]

---

[82] Toman (above, n. 21), 108.
[83] See CLT/CIH/MCO/2008/PI/46 (December 2000), as manually amended.
[84] For a full account, see O'Keefe (above, n. 18), 140–62.

ROGER O'KEEFE

5. The rules stated in Sections 910–915 apply only during international armed conflict, and do not reflect customary international law.

The grant of special protection is subject to the following criteria: 910
— The cultural property must be situated at an adequate distance from any large industrial centre or from any important military objective constituting a vulnerable point (e.g. an aerodrome, broadcasting station, major port, railway station, or main line of communication) (Article 8, para. 1, lit. a, CultPropConv). Cultural property not so situated may, nonetheless, be placed under special protection if the contracting party requesting such protection undertakes, in the event of armed conflict, to make no use of the military objective in question and, in the case of a port, railway station, or aerodrome, to divert all traffic therefrom (Article 8, para. 5, CultPropConv). A refuge for movable cultural property not so situated may, nonetheless, be placed under special protection if it is designed in such a way that it will not, in all probability, be damaged in the event of attack (Article 8, para. 2, CultPropConv).
— The cultural property must not be used for military purposes (Article 8, para. 1, lit. b, CultPropConv). A centre containing monuments shall be deemed to be used for military purposes whenever it is used for the movement of military forces or material, even by way of transit, or whenever activities directly connected with military operations, the stationing of military forces or the production of military material take place within the centre (Article 8, para. 3, CultPropConv). The guarding of cultural property by specially authorized armed custodians or the presence in the vicinity of police forces responsible for the maintenance of public order shall not be deemed to be use for military purposes (Article 8, para. 4, CultPropConv).

Special protection is granted to cultural property by its entry in the International Register of Cultural Property under Special Protection (Article 8, para. 6, CultPropConv) maintained by the Director General of UNESCO (Articles 12–16 RegExCultPropConv).

If during an armed conflict a contracting party is induced by unforeseen circumstances to set up an improvised refuge for movable cultural property, and if in the view of the Commissioner General for Cultural Property accredited to that party (Articles 2, 4, 6, 8–10 RegExCultPropConv) the refuge fulfils the criteria for special protection, the refuge may, subject to the consent of the delegates of the protecting powers accredited to the opposing parties (Articles 2, 3, 5, 8–10 RegExCultPropConv), be granted special protection by its entry in the International Register of Cultural Property under Special Protection (Article 11 RegExCultPropConv).   911

Contracting parties shall ensure the immunity of cultural property under special protection by refraining from any act of hostility against such property, except in exceptional cases of unavoidable military necessity (Articles 9 and 11, para. 2, CultPropConv).   912

Contracting parties shall ensure the immunity of cultural property under special protection by refraining from any use of such property or its surroundings for military purposes, except in exceptional cases of unavoidable military necessity (Articles 9 and 11, para. 2, CultPropConv).   913

Unavoidable military necessity can be established only by the commander of a division or higher-ranking officer. When circumstances permit, the opposing   914 party shall be notified a reasonable time in advance of the decision (Article 11, para. 2, CultPropConv). The contracting party taking the decision shall, as soon as possible, and in writing, inform the Commissioner General for Cultural Property accredited to it of the decision, giving reasons (Article 11, para. 3, CultPropConv).

915   If a contracting party violates one of its obligations towards cultural property under special protection, the opposing party shall, for as long as the violation persists, be released from its obligation to ensure the immunity of the property concerned, although whenever possible the latter party shall first request the cessation of the violation within a reasonable time (Article 11, para. 1, CultPropConv). The contracting party taking the decision shall, as soon as possible, and in writing, inform the Commissioner General for Cultural Property accredited to it of the decision, giving reasons (Article 11, para. 3, CultPropConv). The cultural property in question shall remain protected by the general rules on respect for cultural property.

3. Enhanced Protection

916   Contracting parties may request that cultural property be placed under enhanced protection (Article 10 Prot2CultPropConv).

1. The predominant view during the review of CultPropConv was that the regime of special protection had been a failure. At the same time, although doubts were expressed as to the utility of maintaining two different levels of protection, it was generally agreed that the distinction should be kept. In the event, the effective replacement of special protection by the new regime of enhanced protection emerged as one of the core rationales of Prot2CultPropConv, as underscored in the first preambular recital.

2. Enhanced protection, unlike special protection, is available for immovable and movable cultural property alike. Its conditions of eligibility are intended to be more realizable than those for special protection, with the absence of any requirement that the property in question be situated an adequate distance from military objectives. The procedure by which enhanced protection is granted is designed to be more objective and transparent, with the final decision being taken by the Committee for the Protection of Cultural Property in the Event of Armed Conflict established under Article 24 Prot2CultPropConv. The immunity afforded is more substantial than is the case under special protection: cultural property under enhanced protection and its immediate surroundings may never be used in support of military action, it may never be subject to acts of hostility other than attacks, such as demolitions, and it may be attacked only if its use renders it a military objective.

3. The relationship between enhanced and special protection is outlined in Article 4, lit. b, Prot2CultPropConv: as between parties to Prot2CultPropConv, where cultural property has been granted both special and enhanced protection, the rules on enhanced protection alone apply.

4. Article 4, lit. a, Prot2CultPropConv states that Chapter 3 Prot2CultPropConv is without prejudice to Chapter I CultPropConv and Chapter 2 Prot2CultPropConv. What this means is that cultural property under enhanced protection enjoys the benefit of the general provisions regarding protection laid down in CultPropConv and Prot2CultPropConv, except to the extent that the rules on enhanced protection constitute *lex specialis*. The upshot

is that cultural property under enhanced protection is protected not only by Article 12 Prot2CultPropConv, as refined by Article 13, but also by Article 3, Article 4, paras. 3–5 and Article 5 CultPropConv and by Articles 5, 7, 8, and 9 Prot2CultPropConv. It also has the consequence that cultural property under enhanced protection is protected by Article 4, para. 1, CultPropConv to the extent that the expression 'act of hostility' used in that provision is more compendious than the term 'attack' used in Articles 12 and 13 Prot2CultPropConv.

> The grant of enhanced protection is subject to the following criteria: 917
> — The cultural property must be cultural heritage of the greatest importance for humanity (Article 10, lit. a, Prot2CultPropConv).
> — The cultural property must be protected by adequate domestic legal and administrative measures recognizing its exceptional cultural and historic value and ensuring the highest level of protection (Article 10, lit. b, Prot2CultPropConv).
> — The cultural property must not be used for military purposes or to shield military sites, and the party having control over the cultural property must make a declaration that it will not be so used (Article 10, lit. c, Prot2CultPropConv).
>
> Enhanced protection is granted to cultural property by its entry in the International List of Cultural Property under Enhanced Protection (Article 11, para. 10, Prot2CultPropConv) maintained by the Committee for the Protection of Cultural Property in the Event of Armed Conflict (Articles 11, 24, and 27, para. 1 lit. b, Prot2CultPropConv).

1. The conditions of eligibility for enhanced protection are laid down in Article 10 Prot2CultPropConv, which provides that cultural property may be placed under enhanced protection if it meets the three cumulative criteria stated here. Such property enjoys enhanced protection, however, only if entered in the International List of Cultural Property under Enhanced Protection (Article 11, para. 10, Prot2CultPropConv) maintained by the Committee for the Protection of Cultural Property in the Event of Armed Conflict (Articles 11, 24, and 27, para. 1, lit. b, Prot2CultPropConv), which decides upon any request for inclusion in the List (Article 11, para. 5, Prot2CultPropConv).

2. The requirement in Article 10, lit. a, Prot2CultPropConv that the cultural property in question constitute 'cultural heritage of the greatest importance to humanity' is stricter than the requirement in Article 8 CultPropConv, which speaks of 'very great importance'. This tough threshold criterion was the *quid pro quo* for the freeing up of what might be called the objective criteria for enhanced protection. It does not, however, represent a quantifiable legal standard. The open-textured formulation, reached by consensus, appears a means of accommodating both inclusivist and exclusivist schools of thought, deferring the debate to the case-by-case deliberations of the Committee. The term 'heritage', as distinct from 'property', and the word 'humanity', as compared with the draft text 'all peoples', were settled on for purely rhetorical reasons, the former to connote intergenerational ethical responsibilities of a fiduciary character, the latter to emphasize 'the common interest in safeguarding important cultural heritage'.[85]

3. The reference in Article 10, lit. b, Prot2CultPropConv to 'cultural and historic' value, where 'cultural' alone would have sufficed, wrongly implies that the adjectives

---

[85] Diplomatic Conference on the Second Protocol to the Hague Convention for the Protection of Cultural Property in the Event of Armed Conflict (The Hague, 15–26 March 1999), Summary Report, <http://unesdoc.unesco.org/images/0013/001332/133243eo.pdf> (June 1999), para. 15.

ROGER O'KEEFE

are mutually exclusive, is inconsistent with Article 10, lit. a, Prot2CultPropConv, which uses 'cultural' only, and sits uncomfortably with Article 1 CultPropConv, which employs 'cultural' as a catch-all term for 'historical', 'artistic', 'archaeological', 'scientific', and even bibliographical and archival.

4. The first entries in the International List of Cultural Property under Enhanced Protection were made by the Committee for the Protection of Cultural Property in Armed Conflict in November 2010. All four—namely Choirokoitia, the Painted Churches of the Troodos region and Paphos (both site I, Kato Paphos town, and site II, Kouklia village) in Cyprus and Castel del Monte in Italy—are inscribed on the World Heritage List.[86] To these were added in December 2011 the Kernavé Achaeological Site (Cultural Reserve of Kernavé) in Lithuania, which is also on the World Heritage List.[87]

918   The parties to the conflict shall ensure the immunity of cultural property under enhanced protection by refraining from making such property the object of attack (Article 12 Prot2CultPropConv). Cultural property under enhanced protection may, however, be made the object of attack if:
— it becomes, by its use, a military objective (Article 13, para. 1 lit. b, Prot2 CultPropConv);
— the attack is the only feasible means of terminating such use (Article 13, para. 2 lit. a, Prot2CultPropConv);
— all feasible precautions are taken in the choice of means and methods of attack, with a view to terminating such use and avoiding, or in any event minimizing, damage to the cultural property (Article 13, para. 2, lit. b, Prot2CultPropConv);
— unless circumstances do not permit owing to requirements of immediate self-defence, the attack is ordered at the highest operational level of command, effective advance warning is issued to the opposing forces requiring the termination of the use, and reasonable time is given to the opposing forces to redress the situation (Article 13, para. 2 lit. c, Prot2CultPropConv).

1. The rules stated here apply during both international and non-international armed conflict, but do not reflect customary international law.

2. For no obvious reason, Article 12 Prot2CultPropConv uses the phrase 'by refraining from making such property the object of attack' in preference to the more compendious 'by refraining... from any act of hostility directed against such property', the latter being employed in Article 9 CultPropConv (special protection), as well as *mutatis mutandis* in Article 4, para. 1, CultPropConv and Article 6 Prot2CultPropConv (general protection) and in Article 53, lit. a, AP I and Article 16 AP II. As a result of this more restrictive formulation, Article 12 Prot2CultPropConv does not encompass acts of hostility other than attacks, such as demolitions. But where the rules on enhanced protection does not constitute *lex specialis*, cultural property under enhanced protection benefits from the general provisions regarding protection in CultPropConv and Prot2CultPropConv. In

---

[86] See Article 11, para. 2, 1972 Convention concerning the Protection of the World Cultural and Natural Heritage, 1037 *UNTS* 151.

[87] For its part, the UK currently proposes to request enhanced protection for its twenty-two cultural sites on the World Heritage List. In the case of movable cultural property, in the absence of any internationally agreed criteria for designating the collections of museums, galleries, or archives, the UK proposes to request enhanced protection for the contents of twenty-six museums and galleries, as well as of the National Record Offices and the country's five legal deposit libraries. See Department of Culture, Media and Sport (above, n. 25), 30–3.

ROGER O'KEEFE

this light, the prohibition on demolitions inherent in the obligation in Article 4, para. 1, CultPropConv to refrain from acts of hostility against cultural property applies to cultural property under enhanced protection.

3. Article 13, para. 1, Prot2CultPropConv specifies two circumstances in which cultural property under enhanced protection can 'lose such protection', in the words of the chapeau. The wording is unfortunate, since what the cultural property is better characterized as losing in the second of the two circumstances is its immunity, rather than its enhanced protection as such. It is, however, a distinction without a difference, given the exact formulation of Article 13, para. 1, lit. b.

4. The first situation in which enhanced protection can be lost, as spelled out in Article 13, para. 1, lit. a, Prot2CultPropConv, is if such protection is suspended or cancelled in accordance with Article 14 Prot2CultPropConv. This eventuality is not included in the rule stated here, for the simple reason that, where enhanced protection is suspended or cancelled, the property in question is not cultural property under enhanced protection.

5. The other circumstance in which cultural property can lose its enhanced protection, or more accurately in this case its immunity, is if and for as long as it has, by its use, become a military objective (Article 13, para. 1, lit. b, Prot2CultPropConv). Two crucial implications are to be drawn from this provision. First, provided it is not suspended or cancelled, enhanced protection can be lost only in relation to attacks, since it is only attacks which depend on whether an object is a military objective. In other words, in contrast to the immunity of specially protected cultural property under CultPropConv, but no different from the protection afforded cultural property more generally by Article 53 AP I and Article 16 AP II, the immunity of cultural property under enhanced protection is absolute when it comes to acts of hostility other than attacks, such as demolitions. Military necessity can never justify such acts. Second, whereas cultural property under general protection can become a military objective through any one of its nature, location, purpose, or use, cultural property under enhanced protection, like cultural property under Article 53 AP I and Article 16 AP II, can become a military objective only through its use. It was this that a majority of delegates to the 1999 Hague diplomatic conference saw as the main difference in the protection afforded by general and enhanced protection respectively.[88]

> **The parties to the conflict shall ensure the immunity of cultural property under**   **919**
> **enhanced protection by refraining from any use of such property or its immediate**
> **surroundings in support of military action (Article 12 Prot2CultPropConv).**

1. The rule stated here applies during both international and non-international armed conflict, but does not reflect customary international law.

2. Article 12 Prot2CultPropConv uses the expression 'in support of military action', as found in Article 52, para. 2, AP I, rather than 'in support of the military effort', as contained in Article 53, lit. b, AP I and Article 16 AP II. The concept of 'military action', referring to military operations, is arguably more restrictive than the notion of 'the military effort', which is 'a very broad concept, encompassing all military activities connected with the conduct of a war',[89] with the result that the protection granted by

---

[88] Diplomatic Conference on the Second Protocol, Summary Report (above, n. 85), para. 22. See also Toman (above, n. 55), 231.
[89] *ICRC Commentary*, para. 2078.

ROGER O'KEEFE

Article 12 Prot2CultPropConv against military use, generically speaking, is possibly narrower than that provided by Article 53, lit. b, AP I and Article 16 AP II. The term 'military action' is also possibly narrower than 'military purposes', as used in Article 11, para. 2, CultPropConv.

3. The only[90] situation in which enhanced protection, or more accurately immunity, can be lost is if the cultural property has, by its use, become a military objective (Article 13, para. 1, lit. b, Prot2CultPropConv), and this is applicable only to attacks against such property. The result is that the immunity of cultural property under enhanced protection is absolute when it comes to its use in support of military action. Military necessity can never justify such use.

920   Where cultural property under enhanced protection no longer meets any of the criteria for such protection, the Committee for the Protection of Cultural Property in the Event of Armed Conflict may suspend this protection or may cancel this protection by removing the cultural property from the International List of Cultural Property under Enhanced Protection (Article 14, para. 1, Prot2CultPropConv). The Committee may also suspend the enhanced protection granted to cultural property in the case of a serious violation of the immunity of that property through its use in support of military action. Where such violation is continuous, the Committee may exceptionally cancel the enhanced protection granted to the property by removing the property from the List (Article 14, para. 2, Prot2CultPropConv). The Committee shall afford an opportunity to the contracting parties to make their views known before taking a decision to suspend or cancel enhanced protection (Article 14, para. 3, Prot2CultPropConv).

III. Safeguarding of Cultural Property

921   Contracting parties shall prepare in time of peace for the safeguarding of cultural property situated within their own territory against the foreseeable effects of an armed conflict, by taking such measures as they consider appropriate (Article 3 CultPropConv). Such measures shall include, as appropriate, the preparation of inventories, the planning of emergency measures for protection against fire or structural collapse, the preparation for the removal of movable cultural property or the provision of adequate *in situ* protection of such property, and the designation of competent authorities responsible for the safeguarding of cultural property (Article 5 Prot2CultPropConv).

1. The rule stated here does not reflect customary international law.

2. For the purposes of CultPropConv, the protection of cultural property is defined to comprise both the safeguarding of and respect for cultural property (Article 2 CultPropConv), the latter referring to restraints on methods of warfare, the former referring to so-called 'material' protection, that is practical measures, prepared in advance in peacetime, against the foreseeable effects of armed conflict. The obligation to safeguard cultural property is laid down in Article 3 CultPropConv, which obliges parties to prepare in time of peace for the safeguarding of cultural property situated within their own

---

[90] Leaving aside, that is, Article 13, para. 1, lit. a, Prot2CultPropConv, not considered here.

territory against the foreseeable effects of an armed conflict by taking such measures as they consider appropriate. What the drafters had in mind were '[s]pecial measures of an architectonic nature' designed to protect immovable cultural property, 'particularly against the dangers of fire and collapse'; special measures designed to protect movable cultural property 'in the building where it is generally to be found or in the immediate neighbourhood of the latter (organization, stocking of packing material, etc.)'; the establishment of refuges for movables and the organization of transport to them in the event of armed conflict; and the institution of a civilian service to execute such measures.[91] But the text of Article 3 leaves the choice of measures to be adopted to the complete discretion of the party in whose territory the cultural property is situated, and the ordinary meaning of the key phrase 'such measures as they consider appropriate' is capable of encompassing all conceivable sorts of measures.

3. Since the obligation is to take such measures as they consider appropriate, the parties are not compelled to undertake equally rigorous preparations in relation to each item of cultural property in their territory. The wording of Article 3 CultPropConv takes into account financial and technical constraints, leaving it to the parties to prioritize their resources as they see fit.[92] In the case of immovables, the drafters themselves foresaw that measures of safeguard would be taken only in relation to 'a certain number of buildings of great value and of buildings containing collections of cultural property (museums, archives, libraries, etc.)',[93] and this likelihood is acknowledged in Article 4, para. 5, CultPropConv, which provides that no party may evade the obligations of respect for cultural property incumbent upon it by reason of the fact that the opposing party has not applied the measures of safeguard referred to in Article 3. This selectivity has been borne out in the parties' practice. Those parties which in principle apply CultPropConv to the whole or a large proportion of their national cultural heritage seem generally to take fully fledged measures of safeguard in relation to only a very small fraction of immovables. For example, the Netherlands has instituted such measures for between 70 and 100 of the 43,000 immovables in the country to which it considers CultPropConv to apply.[94] As regards movables, many parties make provision for the evacuation in the event of armed conflict of only the most important artworks and antiquities, as effected in Croatia in 1991.[95]

4. Given that Article 1 CultPropConv leaves it to each party to determine the applicability of CultPropConv to specific cultural property in its territory, the measure *sine qua non* that a party can and should take in pursuance of the obligation laid down in Article 3 CultPropConv is the identification of the property in question. Linked to this, a useful practical measure of peacetime preparation undertaken in the past by some parties is the compilation and submission to UNESCO, as CultPropConv's depositary, of updated inventories of immovable cultural property and of collections of movable cultural property in their territories, for dissemination among the parties.[96] The drafters of

---

[91] 7 C/PRG/7, Annex I, 8.
[92] 7 C/PRG/7, Annex I, 8.
[93] 7 C/PRG/7, Annex I, 8, emphasis omitted.
[94] CC/MD/11, 28.
[95] CLT-95/WS/13, 22.
[96] See, e.g., CC/MD/11, 15 (FRG). See also, in this light, Article 4 RoerichPact, providing for an obligatory system of this nature.

ROGER O'KEEFE

CultPropConv themselves recognized that the encouragement of a standard practice of notification had, 'to a very large extent, become the essential factor in identifying property and facilitating its protection'.[97] Even better still, in the spirit of the drafters' view that cultural property will not be safe from bombardment unless its location is known,[98] Switzerland has previously sent to the Director General of UNESCO a map showing the location of cultural property in its territory and in Liechtenstein.[99] In turn, the Director General transmitted copies of the map to all the parties.[100] An updated topographic map showing 1,500 high-priority objects in Swiss territory and an inventory of the complete 8,000 'cultural items that Switzerland wished to protect and have protected' were subsequently circulated.[101] For their part, after an artillery attack in July 1991 on the town of Erdut damaged its medieval fortress, the Croatian authorities sent lists of cultural monuments marked with CultPropConv's distinctive sign to the Yugoslav Federal Defence Secretariat and to all headquarters of the Yugoslav National Army.[102]

5. There was general agreement during the review of CultPropConv that Article 3 CultPropConv was unhelpfully impressionistic. A more programmatic provision was needed, 'listing steps to be taken in peacetime to ensure overall risk-prevention'.[103] As a result, Article 5 Prot2CultPropConv puts flesh on the bare bones of Article 3 CultPropConv by providing that preparatory measures taken pursuant to Article 3 shall include, as appropriate, the preparation of inventories, the planning of emergency measures for protection against fire or structural collapse, the preparation for the removal of cultural property or the provision for its adequate *in situ* protection, and the designation of competent authorities responsible for the safeguarding of cultural property. The measures listed are merely indicative.[104]

IV. Protection of Cultural Property during Occupation

922   All acts of hostility against cultural property are prohibited during belligerent occupation unless imperatively demanded by military necessity (Articles 56 and 23, lit. g, HagueReg; Article 53 GC IV; Article 4, paras. 1 and 2, CultPropConv).

1. The rule stated here applies only during international armed conflict, and accords with customary international law.

2. Article 23, lit. g, HagueRegs prohibits the destruction of enemy property unless it is imperatively demanded by the necessities of war. In the specific context of belligerent

---

[97] CL/484, Annex, 14.

[98] CL/484, Annex, 11.

[99] SHC/MD/1, 34. See also the recommendation to this end in Final Communiqué of the NATO-Partnership for Peace (PfP) Conference on Cultural Heritage Protection in Wartime and in State of Emergency (21 June 1996), para. 3.5, and the analogous suggestion in M. Dutli (ed.), *Protection of Cultural Property in the Event of Armed Conflict: Report on the Meeting of Experts (Geneva, 5–6 October 2000)* (Geneva: ICRC, 2002), 178.

[100] SHC/MD/1, para. 13.

[101] CLT-95/WS/13, 43.

[102] CLT-95/WS/13, 22.

[103] CLT/CH/94/608/2, 6.

[104] CLT/CH/94/608/2, 6.

occupation, and as specifically regards cultural property, Article 56 HagueRegs lays down an absolute prohibition on the destruction and wilful damage of the latter. It is important to appreciate, however, that what Article 56 HagueRegs forbids is destruction and wilful damage to cultural property unconnected with military operations. Insofar as any destruction or damage is for the purpose of furthering military operations, it is governed under HagueRegs not by Article 56 but by Article 23, lit. g, regulating the destruction of enemy property in the context of hostilities. This accords with Article 53 GC IV, which provides that any destruction by the occupying power of real or personal property is prohibited, except where such destruction is rendered absolutely necessary by military operations.

3. The provisions of Article 4 CultPropConv apply as much to belligerent occupation as to active hostilities. As a consequence, all acts of hostility against cultural property are prohibited during belligerent occupation unless imperatively demanded by military necessity (Article 4, paras 1 and 2, CultPropConv) (see above, Section 904).

4. Reasoning along the lines of the rule stated here was relied on by the Supreme Court of Israel (sitting as the High Court of Justice) in *Hess v Commander of the IDF in the West Bank*,[105] where the Court, referring to HagueRegs, GC IV and CultPropConv without citing provisions, upheld an order of the commander of Israeli occupation forces in the West Bank to demolish, *inter alia*, a structure forming part of the historic streetscape of the Old City of Hebron in order to prevent armed attacks by Palestinian militants. The commander had revised his original order, which would have involved the destruction of twenty-two Ottoman and Mameluke buildings, some dating from the fifteenth century, in response to an earlier interim decision of the Court.[106] Although eventually upholding the order to demolish one building comprising cultural property, the Court ruled that the demolition had to be supervised by an expert in the preservation of historic buildings and an archaeologist, so as to protect as much heritage value as possible.

> **All forms of theft, pillage, misappropriation, confiscation, or vandalism of cultural**   923
> **property are prohibited during belligerent occupation (Article 56 HagueReg; Article**
> **4, para. 3, CultPropConv). The occupying power shall prohibit, prevent and,**
> **if necessary, put a stop to all such acts (Article 4, para. 3, CultPropConv). It shall**
> **refrain from seizing or requisitioning cultural property situated in the occupied ter-**
> **ritory (Article 56 HagueReg; Article 4, para. 3, CultPropConv).**

1. All three rules stated here apply only during international armed conflict, and accord with customary international law.

2. Article 56 HagueRegs lays down an absolute prohibition on all seizure of cultural property during belligerent occupation.

3. Article 4, para. 3, CultPropConv (see above, Section 907) is applicable as much to belligerent occupation as to active hostilities.

> **The occupying power shall as far as possible support the competent authorities of**   924
> **the occupied country in safeguarding and preserving cultural property (Article 5,**
> **para. 1, CultPropConv). Should it prove necessary to take measures to preserve**

---

[105] 58(3) PD 443 (2004).
[106] *Hess v Commander of the IDF in the West Bank*, HCJ 10356/02, Interim decision, 12 February 2003.

cultural property situated in occupied territory and damaged by military operations, and should the competent authorities be unable to take such measures, the occupying power shall, as far as possible, and in close co-operation with these authorities, take the most necessary measures of preservation (Article 5, para. 2, CultPropConv).

1. The two rules stated here apply only during international armed conflict, and accord with customary international law.

2. Article 5 CultPropConv is to be read against the backdrop of the pre-existing customary law of belligerent occupation, especially the rule reflected in Article 43 HagueRegs, which obliges the occupying power (unless absolutely prevented from doing so, and within the parameters set by the powers vested in and obligations imposed on it by specific rules[107]) to leave existing administrative authority intact and free to operate. In this light, the task of preserving cultural property under belligerent occupation continues to fall to the competent national authorities.

3. The obligation in Article 5, para. 1, CultPropConv goes beyond the obligation to refrain from hampering the competent national authorities to include, as far as possible, assistance. At the same time, the drafters made it clear that Article 5, para. 1, does not require the occupying power to take measures *proprio motu* to preserve (as distinct from to respect) cultural property in the territory, since such measures remain the responsibility of the competent national authorities.[108]

4. The words 'safeguarding' and 'preserving' in Article 5, para. 1, CultPropConv denote two distinct things. The former refers to the measures of safeguard mandated by Article 3 CultPropConv. The concept of 'preserving' refers to measures taken after the cessation of active hostilities to conserve and protect cultural property in the occupied territory—measures which, but for the state of belligerent occupation, would be considered peacetime measures. This second element of Article 5, para. 1, obliges the occupying power to support the competent national authorities, as far as possible, in implementing the legislative and administrative regime in force in the occupied territory for the preservation of cultural property, such as local planning laws requiring permits for construction on sensitive sites and laws regulating the upkeep of historic buildings.

925   The occupying power shall prohibit and prevent in relation to the territory any illicit export, other removal or transfer of ownership of cultural property (Article 5 CultPropConv; Section 1 Prot1CultPropConv; Article 9, para. 1, lit. a, Prot2CultPropConv; Article 2, para. 2, and Article 11 IllicitImpExpTransConv).

1. The rule stated here applies only during international armed conflict, and accords with customary international law.

2. Section 1 Prot1CultPropConv,[109] inspired by the systematic removal by Germany and the Soviet Union of artworks and antiquities from some of the countries occupied

---

[107] An example is the obligation under Article 4, para. 3, CultPropConv to prohibit, prevent and, if necessary, put a stop to all forms of theft, pillage, misappropriation, or vandalism of cultural property in the territory (see above, Section 923).

[108] 7 C/PRG/7, Annex I, 9.

[109] While the provisions of binding international agreements are usually called 'articles', Prot1CultPropConv refers to its provisions as 'paragraphs'.

ROGER O'KEEFE

by them during the Second World War, requires each party to prevent the export of cultural property from territory occupied by it during armed conflict. The obligation imposed on an occupying power goes beyond ensuring that its own occupation authorities or military forces do not export cultural property from the territory: para. 1 encompasses a duty to prevent private parties from doing so. Nor is the obligation limited to export contrary to local law: para. 1 obliges a belligerent occupant to prevent all export of cultural property.

3. In Article 2, para. 2, IllicitImpExpTransConv, parties undertake to oppose with the means at their disposal the illicit export and transfer of ownership of movable cultural property, and Article 11 IllicitImpExpTransConv provides that the export and transfer of ownership of cultural property under compulsion arising directly or indirectly from the occupation of a country by a foreign power shall be regarded as illicit.

4. Article 9, para. 1, lit. a, Prot2CultPropConv requires an occupying power, in respect of the occupied territory, to prohibit and prevent any illicit export, other removal or transfer of ownership of cultural property. The provision's generic reference to 'cultural property' comprehends not only movables (even if, in practice, the acts of export and removal can relate only to these) but also immovables, so that an occupying power is obliged to prohibit and prevent the illicit transfer of ownership not only of antiquities, works of art and the like but also of buildings, monuments, in the narrow sense, and archaeological sites in the territory. Like Article 4, para. 3, CultPropConv, Article 9 Prot2CultPropConv obliges parties to prohibit and prevent the impugned acts not only when committed by their own forces and occupation authorities but also, and this is the thrust of both provisions, when committed by private persons. Indeed, like Article 4, para. 3, CultPropConv, Article 9 Prot2CultPropConv does not, on its face, prohibit a party from engaging in such activities itself; but just as with Article 4, para. 3, CultPropConv, a prohibition to this effect must be read into Article 9 Prot2CultPropConv, reasoning *a fortiori*. The term 'illicit' for the purposes of Article 9 Prot2CultPropConv is defined in Article 1, lit. g, Prot2CultPropConv to mean under compulsion or otherwise in violation of the applicable rules of the domestic law of the occupied territory or of international law.

> A contracting party in occupation of the whole or part of the territory of another   926
> contracting party shall prohibit and prevent any archaeological excavation in the occupied territory, save where this is strictly required to safeguard, record, or preserve cultural property (Article 9, para. 1, lit. b, Prot2CultPropConv). The same shall apply in respect of any alteration to, or change of use of, cultural property which is intended to conceal or destroy cultural, historical, or scientific evidence (Article 9, para. 1, lit. c, Prot2CultPropConv). Any archaeological excavation of, alteration to, or change of use of, cultural property in the occupied territory shall, unless circumstances do not permit, be carried out in close co-operation with the competent authorities of that territory (Article 9, para. 2, Prot2CultPropConv).

1. The rules stated here apply only during international armed conflict, and do not reflect customary international law.

2. No provision in CultPropConv deals with archaeological excavations in occupied territory. The suggested insertion in RegExCultPropConv of an article on the question was rejected at the Hague intergovernmental conference in 1954, although only just

and partly on procedural grounds.[110] It had subsequently been hoped by its drafters that Article 32 of UNESCO's Recommendation on International Principles Applicable to Archaeological Excavations,[111] a hortatory provision on point adopted by the Organization's General Conference in 1956, would be incorporated, along with implementing regulations, in an addendum to CultPropConv, but this was never to be the case. The absence of binding rules on digs in occupied territory, and on the alteration of cultural property in this context, was exposed as a serious lacuna after 1967 by Israel's controversial activities in the occupied West Bank, particularly East Jerusalem. In the event, the 1999 Hague diplomatic conference reached consensus on three interrelated provisions, namely Article 9, para. 1, lits. a and b, and Article 9, para. 2.

3. The obligation imposed on an occupying power by Article 9, para. 1, lit. b, Prot2CultPropConv to prohibit and prevent any archaeological excavation in the occupied territory, save where this is strictly required to safeguard, record, or preserve cultural property, extends on its face to digs authorized by the competent national authorities, including digs in progress. At first blush this seems odd, and it is unclear if this is what was intended. On the one hand, with the exception of those matters falling expressly or necessarily within the rights ceded to and duties imposed on the occupying power by specific rules, the regulation of cultural property in occupied territory remains the province of these competent national authorities, and there seems no reason why they should not be free to authorize whatever archaeological excavations they see fit. On the other hand, it is possible that the provision is a precautionary one, premised on the calculation that the only way to prevent illicit excavations in occupied territory is to ban all excavations for the duration of the occupation. Either way, it may be that the exception in respect of excavations strictly required to safeguard, record or preserve cultural property would permit the continuation of digs in progress insofar as this is necessary to enable the recording of finds already unearthed and to prepare the site for suspension of the work.

V. Transport of Cultural Property

927 Means of transport engaged exclusively in the transport of cultural property may, at the request of the contracting party concerned, be placed under special protection (Article 12, para. 1, CultPropConv and Article 17, paras. 1 and 2, RegExCultPropConv). Such transport shall take place under international supervision (Article 12, para. 2, CultPropConv and Article 17, para. 3, RegExCultPropConv). All acts of hostility directed against such means of transport are prohibited (Article 12, para 3, CultPropConv).

1. The three rules stated here apply only during international armed conflict, and do not reflect customary international law.

2. The mass relocation of movable cultural property for protective purposes during the Second World War inspired the drafters of CultPropConv to make special provision for the transport of cultural property during armed conflict of an international

---

[110] Records 1954, paras. 1912–15.
[111] Records of the General Conference, Ninth Session, New Delhi 1956: Resolutions, 40. Article 32 provides that, in the event of armed conflict, any member state of UNESCO occupying the territory of another state should refrain from carrying out archaeological excavations in the occupied territory.

ROGER O'KEEFE

character. The rules eventually adopted in Chapter III CultPropConv and Chapter III RegExCultPropConv are applicable without distinction to transport by land, sea, or air. The gist of these rules is the absolute immunity of duly authorized transports of cultural property.

3. CultPropConv's regime for the transport of cultural property has never formally been put to use, although during the international armed conflict in Cambodia in 1972, to which CultPropConv did not actually apply, many treasures were transported from Angkor to Phnom Penh on trucks displaying the distinctive emblem and driven by personnel wearing the armlet provided for in Article 21 RegExCultPropConv.[112] It is also extremely unlikely that it ever will be formally put to use. For a start, *in situ* protection of movable cultural property has, from the point of view of conservation, always been preferable to relocation. In fact, a group of experts convened at the first meeting of the parties to CultPropConv in 1962 considered that 'the principle of the protection of cultural property by removing it to safety should be abandoned in favour of the more realistic principle of immediate if incomplete protection on the spot'.[113] Added to this, the procedure under RegExCultPropConv for obtaining immunity for the transport of cultural property is unduly complicated and cedes an element of veto to the relevant Commissioner General for Cultural Property with which parties may be uncomfortable. Finally, the regime for the transport of cultural property depends on there having been appointed a Commissioner General for Cultural Property, delegates of the protecting powers and, indeed, protecting powers in the first place (Article 17 RegExCultPropConv). In short, it depends on the functioning as intended of CultPropConv's regime of control. But CultPropConv's regime of control has never functioned as intended. In this light, only the bare outline of the relevant provisions is given here.

> Where, in the view of the contracting party concerned, the transport of cultural property is a matter of such urgency that the procedure for the grant of special protection cannot be followed, the opposing parties shall take, as far as possible, the necessary precautions to avoid directing acts of hostility such transport. The contracting party concerned shall, as far as possible, notify the opposing parties in advance of such transport (Article 13 CultPropConv).   928

> Contracting parties shall grant immunity from seizure, placing in prize and capture to cultural property transported under special protection or transported in urgent cases, as well as to the means of such transport (Article 14, para. 1, CultPropConv).   929

This rule does not limit the right of visit and search (Article 14, para. 2, CultPropConv).

VI. Personnel Engaged in the Protection of Cultural Property

> Personnel engaged in the protection of cultural property shall, as far as is consistent with the interests of security, be respected. Should such personnel fall into the hands of the opposing party, they shall be allowed to continue to carry out their   930

---

[112] E. Clément and F. Quinio, 'The role of the 1954 Hague Convention in protecting Cambodian cultural property during the period of armed conflict' (2004) 854 *IRRC* 389 at 394.
[113] CUA/120, 9.

duties whenever the cultural property for which they are responsible has also fallen into the hands of the opposing party (Article 15 CultPropConv).

1. The two rules stated here apply only during international armed conflict, and do not reflect customary international law.

2. It may be the case that, pursuant to Article 3 CultPropConv, a party designates competent authorities responsible for the safeguarding of cultural property against the foreseeable effects of armed conflict, a possibility expressly mentioned in Article 5 Prot2CultPropConv. Moreover, Article 7, para. 2, CultPropConv obliges parties to plan or establish in peacetime, within their armed forces, services or specialist personnel whose purpose will be to secure respect for cultural property and to co-operate with the civilian authorities responsible for safeguarding it. This second provision was inspired by German corps in both World Wars and by the monuments, fine arts, and archives officers in both the US and UK armies in the Second. Both categories of personnel engaged in the protection of cultural property are covered by the rule in Article 15 CultPropConv.

3. Should the specialist military personnel envisaged in Article 7, para. 2, CultPropConv fall into the hands of the opposing party, they are entitled to the protection of GC III. Their status is like that of medical personnel in the armed forces.[114]

4. RegExCultPropConv further provides for the involvement of a range of individuals in CultPropConv's regime of control, namely representatives for cultural property (Article 2, lit. a, RegExCultPropConv), delegates of Protecting Powers (Articles 2, 3, 5, and 8 RegExCultPropConv), Commissioners General for Cultural Property (Articles 2, 4, 6 and 8 RegExCultPropConv), inspectors of cultural property (Articles 7, para. 1, and 8 RegExCultPropConv), and experts (Articles 7, para. 2, and 8 RegExCultPropConv). These five categories of persons are not 'personnel engaged in the protection of cultural property' within the meaning of Article 15 CultPropConv. They are 'the persons responsible for the duties of control', as per Article 17, para. 2, lit. c, CultPropConv.

5. On the only occasion when Commissioners General for Cultural Property have been appointed, in the wake of the Six-Day War in 1967, the Executive Board of UNESCO invited the Director General of the organization to make the necessary arrangements to enable them to enjoy the privileges and immunities granted to senior officials of UN specialized agencies under the Convention on the Privileges and Immunities of the Specialized Agencies.[115]

931   Personnel engaged in the protection of cultural property may wear an armlet bearing the distinctive emblem of cultural property, issued and stamped by the competent authorities of the contracting party concerned (Article 17, para. 2, lit. c, CultPropConv and Article 21, para. 1, RegExCultPropConv). They shall carry a special identity card bearing the distinctive emblem (Article 21, para. 2, RegExCultPropConv). Such personnel may not, without legitimate reason, be deprived of their identity card or of the right to wear the armlet (Article 21, para. 4, RegExCultPropConv).

1. The three rules stated here apply only during international armed conflict, and do not reflect customary international law.

---

[114] Rogers (above, n. 65), 190.
[115] 77 EX/Decision 4.4.4, para. 5, lit. a, referring to 33 UNTS 261.

ROGER O'KEEFE

2. In contrast with Article 15 CultPropConv, the rules stated here apply also to the persons responsible for the duties of control (Article 17, para. 2, lit. b, CultPropConv and Article 21 RegExCultPropConv).

VII. Distinctive Marking of Cultural Property

The distinctive emblem of cultural property takes the form of a shield, pointed   932
below, per saltire blue and white (Article 16, para. 1, CultPropConv; see below,
Annex 'Distinctive Emblems' No. 8).

1. The emblem described here is the so-called 'distinctive emblem' of CultPropConv. What the technical heraldic language means is explained parenthetically in Article 16, para. 1, CultPropConv, namely a shield consisting of a royal-blue square, one of the angles of which forms the point of a shield, and of a royal-blue triangle above the square, the space on either side being taken up by a white triangle.

2. While in practice it cannot be said to matter, it is not ideal that CultPropConv's distinctive emblem differs from the 'visible signs' stipulated by Article 5 HC IX ('large, stiff rectangular panels divided diagonally into two colored triangular portions, the upper portion black, the lower portion white') and from the 'distinctive flag' prescribed by Article 3 RoerichPact ('red circle with a triple red sphere in the circle on a white background'). As between parties to both CultPropConv and HC IX, however, the distinctive emblem of the former replaces the signs prescribed by the latter (Article 36 CultPropConv). The same goes *mutatis mutandis* for CultPropConv and RoerichPact (Article 36 CultPropConv).

Contracting parties may, so as to facilitate its recognition, mark cultural   933
property with the distinctive emblem used once (Articles 6 and 17, para. 2,
CultPropConv).

1. As the wording of Article 6 CultPropConv makes clear, the marking of protected cultural property with the distinctive emblem is not obligatory.

2. In principle, the emblem, used once, may be displayed on both immovable and movable cultural property, although practicality militates against the latter. The placing of the distinctive emblem and its degree of visibility is left to the discretion of the competent authorities of each party, and it may be displayed on flags, painted on an object or represented in any other appropriate form (Article 20, para. 1, RegExCultPropConv).

3. In practice, the peacetime distinctive marking of cultural property under general protection is rare among parties to CultPropConv. It may be, however, that the relevant authorities have in place plans for distinctive marking if and when hostilities are imminent, as was the case with the Croatian authorities in 1991.[116] It is clear that some parties supply emblems to owners or curators of protected buildings with instructions to affix them in the event of armed conflict.

4. There are several possible reasons for the apparent unpopularity of distinctive marking. Given the numbers of buildings typically protected by CultPropConv in each state,

---

[116] CLT-95/WS/13, 22.

marking is an expensive business, although, as regards parties to Prot2CultPropConv, the Fund for the Protection of Cultural Property in the Event of Armed Conflict would now be authorized to provide financial or other assistance in this regard (Article 29, para. 1, Prot2CultPropConv). Marking is also laborious, especially when one takes into account the requirement in Article 17, para. 4, CultPropConv of an authorization duly dated and signed by the competent authority each time the emblem is used. Ironically, a concern for the preservation, not to mention aesthetics, of cultural property can also contraindicate marking.[117] The use of the distinctive emblem has been criticized by curators of museums, galleries, and monuments. Nor do the benefits seem to outweigh the costs: the effectiveness of a small plaque in the event of an attack must seriously be questioned in the age of high-altitude bombing, ship-launched cruise missiles, and long-range artillery, and no less so when military objectives are identified by satellites and very high-altitude spy planes. In 1996, the NATO-Partnership for Peace Conference on Cultural Heritage Protection in Wartime and in State of Emergency suggested incorporating new technology into the emblem,[118] by which it presumably meant a microchip or transmitter 'visible' electronically, but the bill for installation and upkeep would surely be prohibitive.

5. Nonetheless, the marking of cultural property can scarcely undermine its protection from attack, even if the fanciful fear was expressed during the drafting of CultPropConv that it could help an attacking force to get its bearings,[119] and despite the fact that Iraq defended its failure to mark cultural property during the Iran–Iraq War by claiming that the emblem might be seen by the Iranian aircraft, missile batteries, and artillery positions which were attacking Iraqi towns.[120] Moreover, marking may help to prevent the use of such property for purposes likely to expose it to damage or destruction. There are also foreseeable advantages when it comes to belligerent occupation.

6. If a party does opt to mark cultural property in its territory, reason suggests that it should be all or nothing. While the absence of the distinctive emblem does not, as a matter of law, denote the absence of protection under CultPropConv, the assumption made in practice by an opposing party may well be *expressio unius exclusio alterius*. In this way, the selective use of the emblem, which seems not uncommon,[121] poses a threat to the protection of the property it is meant to facilitate.

934　　During international armed conflict, contracting parties shall mark cultural property under special protection with the distinctive emblem repeated three times in triangular formation with one shield below (Articles 10, 16, para. 2, and 17, para. 1, lit. a, CultPropConv; see below, Annex 'Distinctive Emblems' No. 9). The same shall apply in respect of means of transport engaged exclusively in the transport of cultural property (Articles 12, para. 2, 13, para. 1, 16, para. 2 and 17, para. 1, lit. b, CultPropConv) and improvised refuges for cultural property (Articles 16, para. 2, and 17, para. 1, lit. c, CultPropConv and Article 11, para. 2, RegExCultPropConv).

---

[117] See, e.g., 7 C/PRG/7, Annex I, 12; Records 1954, para. 399 (Greece).
[118] NATO-PfP Conference on Cultural Heritage Protection, Final Communiqué, para. 3.4.
[119] 6 C/PRG/22, Annex, 13; 7 C/PRG/7, Annex I, 12.
[120] CC/MD/11, 20.
[121] For example, in 1991, the Croatian authorities affixed the emblem to 794 historic buildings, a fraction of the total immovable cultural heritage in the republic: CLT-95/WS/13, 22.

ROGER O'KEEFE

1. The three rules stated here apply only during international armed conflict, and do not reflect customary international law.

2. As remarked upon at the fourth meeting of the parties to CultPropConv, Prot2CultPropConv makes no provision for the distinctive marking of cultural property under enhanced protection.[122]

> **During international armed conflict, the deliberate misuse of the distinctive**   935
> **emblem is prohibited (Article 38, para. 1, AP I; Article 17, para. 3, CultPropConv),**
> **as is the use for any purpose whatsoever of a sign resembling the distinctive emblem**
> **(Article 17, para. 3, CultPropConv).**

1. The rule stated here applies only during international armed conflict. It is unclear whether the first limb reflects customary international law. The second does not.

2. The abuse of the distinctive emblem in peacetime and the peacetime use of a sign resembling the emblem are both unregulated.

---

[122] CLT-99/CONF.206/4, para. 10(v).

ROGER O'KEEFE

10

THE LAW OF ARMED
CONFLICT AT SEA

Introductory Remarks

Naval warfare has never been limited to the military subjugation of the enemy. Its over-all aim is sea denial and sea control. Methods necessary for sea control do not merely affect the parties to an international armed conflict but also states that are neutral or states not parties to the conflict. If the weakening of the enemy's economy is also consid-ered a legitimate goal, the law would be incomplete if it lacked rules relating to measures taken against neutral merchant shipping. Such rules are necessary since a state party to the conflict could otherwise shift its sea trade to third states' merchant shipping, and the adversary would be unable to prevent the supply of arms and war material to its opponent.

Measures against neutral merchant shipping are not dealt with in the present chap-ter, which is confined to the legal relationship between the parties to an armed conflict at sea. The rules governing the relationship between belligerents and states not parties to the conflict or their vessels are contained in Chapter 11 on the law of neutrality. However, in the present chapter the laws of neutrality cannot be ignored completely. They are relevant for the delimitation of the geographic region of naval warfare and for the determination of the enemy character of merchant vessels.

Moreover, two caveats seem to be necessary in view of an increasingly sceptical posi-tion vis-à-vis the law of naval warfare. First, the international law of the sea as embodied in the 1982 UN Law of the Sea Convention[1] has not resulted in a demilitarization of the oceans or in a prohibition of armed hostilities at sea. It is important to bear in mind that the list of high seas freedoms in Article 87(1), lit. a–f, UNCLOS is not exhaus-tive ('*inter alia*') and that the freedom of the high seas may be exercised also 'by other rules of international law'. Accordingly, the legality of the use of methods and means of naval warfare, including prize measures, is to be established under the law of naval warfare (and of maritime neutrality), not in the light of the international law of the sea. Second, both, operators and lawyers, criticize the law of naval warfare as outdated and as an unreasonable obstacle to the success of their operational or strategic goals. They, *inter alia*, refer to the provisions on measures short of attack (prize measures) and on methods and means of naval warfare, especially on blockade and operational zones. In their view those provisions do neither meet the necessities of modern operations, as for

---

[1] United Nations Convention on the Law of the Sea of 10 December 1982; entry into force on 16 November 1994, UN Doc. A/CONF.62/122 of 7 October 1982 (hereinafter referred to as 'UNCLOS'). See also the Agreement relating to the Implementation of Part XI of the Convention, UN Doc. A/RES/48/263 of 17 August 1994; entry into force on 28 July 1994.

WOLFF HEINTSCHEL VON HEINEGG

example maritime interception operations (MIO) or non-military enforcement measures decided upon by the UN Security Council, nor do they offer operable solutions
to the naval commander. This criticism is based upon an erroneous understanding of
the law of naval warfare and of its scope of applicability. Maritime interception operations aimed at combating transnational terrorism,[2] piracy (and armed robbery at sea),
or the proliferation of weapons of mass destruction[3] and related components do have a
legal basis that is independent from the law of naval warfare. The same holds true with
regard to enforcing an embargo—either with or without the authorization of the UN
Security Council.[4] Therefore, the law of naval warfare does not pose an insurmountable
obstacle to such operations. Its provisions apply exclusively to situations of international
armed conflicts.[5] MIO and other maritime security operations have to be based upon
that body of law only if they occur in the course of an armed conflict between two or
more States.

Finally, it must be borne in mind that the present chapter deals with international
armed conflicts only. Since long ago the law of naval warfare has been considered to exclusively apply to such conflicts.[6] However, it is far from clear whether the law of naval warfare would not, at least in some respects, apply to non-international armed conflicts that
involve the military use of the oceans.[7] In any event, the applicability of the law of naval
warfare to non-international armed conflicts is a highly contentious issue. This became
evident in the Algerian Crisis and during the Sri Lankan armed conflict. In the context
of the blockade established by Israel off the coast of Gaza, some argued that, in view of
the allegedly non-international character of the armed conflict, Israel was not entitled
to establish and enforce a naval blockade.[8] However, the Palmer Report has concluded
that 'the conflict should be treated as an international one for the purposes of the law of
blockade'.[9] The unique characteristics of the Gaza conflict should, however, not distract
from the fact that there seems to be wide agreement that the law of naval warfare *in toto*

---

[2] See Heintschel von Heinegg, 'Current Legal Issues in Maritime Operations: Maritime Interception
Operations in the Global War on Terrorism, Exclusion Zones, Hospital Ships and Maritime Neutrality'
(2004) 34 *IsrYHR* 151–78.

[3] See Heintschel von Heinegg, 'The Proliferation Security Initiative—Security vs. Freedom of Navigation?'
(2005) 35 *IsrYHR* 181–203.

[4] In that case the legal basis is the respective Security Council's decision based on Chapter VII of the
Charter. While some navies, in their rules of engagement, also refer to rules and principles of the law of
naval warfare this is due to the fact that there exists no specific rules on the conduct of enforcement measures
authorized by the Security Council. Therefore, they rely on the law of naval warfare as a general guidance
only. This practice does not give evidence of an opinion juris that the respective states consider the law of
naval warfare to be applicable in a formal sense.

[5] See *San Remo Manual*, para. 1.

[6] See also the Explanations to the *San Remo Manual* in L. Doswald-Beck (ed.), *San Remo Manual on
International Law Applicable to Armed Conflicts at Sea*, at 73 (Cambridge, 1995): '[…] although the provisions of this Manual are primarily meant to apply to international armed conflicts at sea, this has intentionally not been expressly indicated [...] in order not to dissuade the implementation of these rules in
non-international armed conflicts involving naval operations.'

[7] Cf. Heintschel von Heinegg, 'Methods and Means of Naval Warfare in Non-International Armed
Conflicts' (2011) 42 *IsrYHR* (forthcoming).

[8] Cf. Guilfoyle, 'The Mavi Marmara Incident and Blockade in Armed Conflict' (2011) 81 *BYIL* 171–223;
Sanger, 'The Contemporary Law of Blockade and the Gaza Freedom Flotilla' (2010) 13 *YIHL* 397–446;
Buchan, 'The International Law of Naval Blockade and Israel's Interception of the Mavi Marmara' (2011)
58 *Netherlands International Law Review* 209–41.

[9] Report of the Secretary General's Panel of Inquiry on the 31 May 2010 Flotilla Incident (September
2011), UN Doc. A/HRC/1521, para. 73.

only applies to international armed conflicts. Of course, this does not rule out that some parts of that law may be applied to non-international armed conflicts as well.

I. General

1. Definitions

> **'Ship' means manned surface and submarine vessels. 'Aircraft' means all manned**   **1001**
> **means of transport that are or can be used in the air above sea or land.**

The qualification that vessels must be manned is meant to exclude from the definition surface and submarine vehicles that have no personnel on board and are remotely controlled, such as 'drones' employed in mine countermeasures or other unmanned seagoing vehicles (USVs). Under this rule, similar considerations are valid for aircraft. It is, however, questionable whether and to what extent the rule continues to reflect customary international law. We will return to this issue in the commentary accompanying Section 1002.

Vessels exclusively employed in inland navigation are not 'ships' within the meaning of this definition. They are governed not by the rules of naval warfare but by those of land warfare. However, if such vessels are seaworthy and employed, for example, in coastal navigation they are to be considered 'ships' in the sense of Section 1001.

> **'Warships' are ships belonging to the (naval) armed forces of a state bearing the**   **1002**
> **external marks distinguishing warships of its nationality, are under the command**
> **of an officer duly commissioned by the government whose name appears in the**
> **appropriate service list or its equivalent, and manned by a crew which is under**
> **regular armed forces discipline. Warships need not be armed.**

1. *Warships.* The definition of warships[10] has its legal basis in Article 29 UNCLOS. It differs from the definition in Article 8, para. 2 of the Convention on the High Seas 1958[11] in that it also covers ships not belonging to the naval forces of a state. A further difference is that the name of the commanding officer need not necessarily appear in the Navy List. While it is generally agreed that the 1958 definition is customary in character, it is open to doubt whether this is also true as regards the 1982 definition. Still, the latter is here taken as the legal basis because it better meets the practical requirements of naval armed forces who then need not distinguish between warships operated by the enemy's naval forces and those belonging to other units. According to the present definition a vessel need not be armed in order to qualify as a warship. Hence tenders, troop transporters, and supply ships are covered as soon as they meet the requirements.[12] Merchant vessels converted into warships in accordance with the 1907 Hague Convention No. VII are also covered.[13]

---

[10] See Heintschel von Heinegg, *MPEPIL*, Vol. X, 790–802. The same definition is used in the *San Remo Manual*, para. 13(g).

[11] Signed on 29 April 1958, UN Doc. A/CONF.13/L.53 (hereinafter: HSC 1958). This Convention will, however, become obsolete in so far as states parties to UNCLOS are concerned.

[12] Cf. C. J. Colombos, *The International Law of the Sea*, 5th edn (London: Longmans, 1962), paras. 530 *et seq.*; D. P. O'Connell, *The International Law of the Sea*, 2 vols edited by I. A. Shearer (OUP, 1984), Vol. II, 1106 *et seq.*

[13] See Section 1005.

2. *Submarines.* It follows from the inclusion of submarine vessels in Section 1001 that submarines are warships in the sense of Section 1002. Although especially Great Britain, at the beginning of the twentieth century,[14] endeavoured to outlaw submarines, today they are generally considered legitimate means of naval warfare.[15]

3. *Civilian mariners on board warships.* There is a tendency in state practice to crew warships with civilians or at least to make use of civilian contractors who work on board warships.[16] In many cases, the contribution of civilian contractors is essential for the operation of the ship or of its weapons systems. Hence, the question arises whether the presence of civilian mariners or of civilian contractors affects the legal status of the ship concerned. The ability to exercise belligerent rights remains reserved for warships.[17] Warships are authorized to engage in offensive military activities, including visit and search, blockade, interdiction, and convoy escort operations. Auxiliary vessels are expressly prohibited from exercising belligerent rights. There are convincing arguments according to which civilians on board warships should perform neither crew functions nor other functions related to the operation of the ship and its weapons or electronic systems. Such activities should indeed remain reserved for state organs proper. It should be noted, however, that the definition of warships in this section and in customary international law does not necessarily rule out the use of civilian mariners and of civilian contractors. According to that definition the warships must be manned by '*a* crew that is under regular armed forces discipline'. In contrast, the 1907 Hague Convention VII Relating to the Conversion of Merchant Ships into Warships, in Article 4, provides that '*the* crew' of a converted merchant ship 'must be subject to military discipline'. While the use of the definite article in Hague Convention VII rules out the (further) use of civilian mariners the indefinite article in the definition of warships justifies the conclusion that not necessarily all crew members must be under regular armed forces discipline. Leaving aside the ensuing question of the permissible proportion of civilian mariners (or private contractors) in comparison with sailors and officers proper it thus becomes clear that the manning of warships with civilian mariners does not affect the legal status of the ship as long as the other criteria are met and as long as a certain portion of the crew remains under regular armed forces discipline. Of course, these findings are without prejudice to the legal status of civilian mariners and of civilian contractors. If captured they could, with good reasons, be considered unlawful combatants and prosecuted for direct participation in hostilities. The latter problem could be solved by conferring a special legal status on civilian mariners and private contractors.

4. *Unmanned vehicles.* Neither the present nor other sections of this Handbook contain definitions of unmanned—aerial or seagoing—vehicles. At first glance, such vehicles do

---

[14] Cf. Colombos, paras. 531 *et seq.*; O'Connell, Vol. II, 1131 *et seq.*; W. S. Anderson, 'Submarines and Disarmament Conferences' (1927) 53 *USNIP* 50 *et seq.*

[15] Cf. Heintschel von Heinegg, 'The International Legal Framework of Submarine Operations' (2009) 39 *IsrYHR* 331–56.

[16] For a long time, the Royal Navy has used civilian personnel to provide ship's services including food service, cleaning, and laundry. The US Navy also experimented with the concept of augmenting warship crews with civilian mariner supplied by Military Sealift Command (MSC). Three years ago MSC identified fleet command and control ships as platforms that can be transferred to MSC and staffed with civilian mariners. The *USS Coronado* had been chosen as the 'pilot program' for this initiative. In addition, there is very often a considerable number of private contractors on board warships who are maintaining and/or operating electronic and weapons systems.

[17] *UK Manual (2004)*, paras. 13.5 and 13.91. *See also NWP 1–14M*, paras. 2.2.1 and 7.6.

WOLFF HEINTSCHEL VON HEINEGG

not qualify as warships simply because they are not manned by a crew. It should not be left out of consideration, however, that very often USVs are either integral components of a warship's weapons systems or otherwise controlled from a military platform. If that military platform is a warship or a military aircraft the USV could be considered as sharing the legal status of the controlling platform. If, however, USVs are not part of, or controlled by, a warship, especially if they operate autonomously on a pre-programmed course, it is impossible to follow that approach. Of course, if operated by the armed forces or by another governmental institution, they constitute state craft enjoying sovereign immunity.[18] That, however, does not necessarily mean that they are 'warships' within the definition and thus entitled to the exercise of the entire spectrum of belligerent rights and of independent passage rights. Some of the problems could be solved if the scope of applicability of the rule on the exercise of belligerent rights could be limited to prize measures taken against neutral merchant vessels and neutral civil aircraft. Another solution could be to interpret the definition of 'warship' in a more liberal way as in the case of the definition of 'military aircraft' that comprises unmanned aerial vehicles.[19] At present, however, there is no sufficient state practice that would justify either approach.

> 'Government ships' are ships owned or operated by a state and used only in   1003
> governmental non-commercial service (e.g. customs and police vessels, state
> yachts).

1. *Government ships.* There is at present no generally accepted definition of government ships or of state ships. However, the elements contained in Section 1003 should not give rise to objections.[20] In times of peace, the vessels covered by this definition, for example customs and police vessels or state yachts, enjoy complete immunity from the jurisdiction of any state other than the flag state. This follows from Article 9 of the Convention on the High Seas 1958 (HSC 1958). They must, however, be exclusively employed in public or government service. It goes without saying that in times of armed conflict, belligerent government ships are not immune or specially protected against measures by the enemy. Rather, they may be captured and they will become booty of war, that is property passes to the capturing state immediately without the necessity of a prior decision by a competent prize court.

2. *Government ships operated for commercial purposes.* It follows from Section 1003, as well as from the Brussels Convention on the Unification of Rules on the Determination of the Immunity of Government Ships of 10 April 1926,[21] that government ships operated for commercial purposes are to be treated in the same manner as privately owned merchant vessels and their cargoes.[22]

> 'Merchant vessels' are ships other than warships as defined in Section 1002 and used   1004
> for commercial or fishery purposes or profit passenger transport (whether private
> or owned or controlled by the state) or private ships of non-commercial character

---

[18] See *NWP 1–14M*, para. 2.3.6.

[19] *HPCR Manual*, Rule 1(x).

[20] See *inter alia* G. C. Rodriguez Iglesias, 'State Ships', *MPEPIL*.

[21] This Convention never entered into force but, on 24 May 1934, was amended by an additional protocol. See E. Beckert/G. Breuer, *Öffentliches Seerecht* (Berlin, New York: de Gruyter, 1991), para. 428.

[22] Rodriguez Iglesias (*supra*, n. 20).

WOLFF HEINTSCHEL VON HEINEGG

(e.g. yachts). The mere fact that a merchant vessel is armed does not change its legal status, unless it fulfils the conditions described below in Section 1025.

1. *Merchant vessels.* In international law there exists no generally accepted definition of 'merchant vessel'. This term can, however, be defined negatively, that is in contradistinction to other vessels. In order for a vessel to qualify as a merchant vessel it needs to be employed for commercial or fishery purposes or transporting passengers for profit.[23] The attribute 'commercial' means that the use of such vessels has to be aimed at obtaining profits. Hence, government ships operated for commercial purposes, and deep-sea and coastal fishing vessels and passenger liners, are merchant vessels within the meaning of Section 1004. In this context it is, however, important to emphasize that vessels used exclusively for fishing along the coast, small boats employed in local trade, and passenger liners enjoy protected status under the law of naval warfare.[24] Also covered by the present definition are seagoing private vessels not used for commercial purposes, for example yachts and pleasure boats.

2. *Arming.* Traditionally, scholars differentiated between offensively and defensively armed merchant vessels, but were unable to agree on the relevant criteria.[25] Altogether, there never existed a generally accepted prohibition of arming merchant vessels.[26] Still, according to the *US Naval Manual* (2007) and the *Canadian Manual*, merchant vessels qualify as legitimate military objectives if they are armed 'with systems or weapons beyond that required for self-defense against terrorist, piracy or like threats'.[27] In view of the various difficulties involved, the *German Manual* has taken a different approach, stressing that the mere fact that a merchant vessel is armed does not change its legal status, and that it may only be attacked if it meets the conditions of the definition of 'military objectives'.[28]

1005   Merchant ships converted into warships in accordance with the VIIth Hague Convention of 1907, thus fulfilling the conditions of the definition of warships described in Section 1002, have the same status as warships. The state which converts a merchant ship into a warship has to publish this as soon as possible in its list of warships.

The conversion of merchant vessels into warships is governed by the rules laid down in the 1907 Hague Convention VII.[29] The commanding officer must be duly commissioned by the government and his name must appear in the Navy List (Article 3). The crew must be under regular armed forces' discipline (Article 4). The conversion must as soon as possible be notified on the list of warships (Article 5). Hence, all those conditions must be fulfilled that are contained in the definition of warships proper. However, the

[23] Cf. R. Lagoni, 'Merchant Ships', *MPEPIL*. See also *San Remo Manual*, para. 13(i) defining merchant vessel as 'a vessel, other than a warship, an auxiliary vessel, or a State vessel such as a customs or police vessel, that is engaged in commercial or private service'.
[24] See Section 1034 and the accompanying commentary.
[25] Cf. K. Zemanek, 'Armed Attack', *MPEPIL*.
[26] Colombos (*supra*, n. 12), para. 548.
[27] *NWP 1–14M*, para. 8.6.2.2; *Canadian Manual, Law of Armed Conflict at the Operational and Tactical Level* (Ottawa: National Defence Headquarters, Office of the Judge Advocate General, 2004), <http://www.forces.gc.ca/jag/publications/oplaw-loiop/loac-ddca-2004/index-eng.asp>, para. 834(2f).
[28] See below, Section 1025.
[29] For an overview, see G. Venturini, 'Commentary on the 1907 Hague Convention VII', in N. Ronzitti (ed.), *The Law of Naval Warfare* (Dordrecht: Nijhoff, 1988), 120–8, at 120 *et seq.*

WOLFF HEINTSCHEL VON HEINEGG

rules of Hague Convention VII leave a number of unresolved problems. On one hand, it is silent on the question of whether a merchant vessel maybe converted only in the flag state's territorial waters or also on the high seas. On the other hand, it lacks rules on the reconversion of warships to merchant vessels. In the legal literature those questions are hotly disputed.[30] In the absence of any express prohibitions, conversion on the high seas as well as reconversion should be considered permissible.[31]

> **'Support ships' are ships with civilian crew owned or operated by the government— that is government ships as defined in Section 1003—and which perform support services for the naval forces without being warships.**   **1006**

The domestic legislation of the majority of Western states provides for the incorporation of their merchant fleets into the naval armed forces in times of armed conflict or a state of emergency.[32] It is sometimes difficult to distinguish such support ships from converted merchant vessels.[33] For example, during the Falklands/Malvinas conflict, Great Britain, in accordance with the Requisitioning of Ships Order 1982[34] requisitioned a number of merchant vessels. Their masters and crews were subject to armed forces' discipline and to instructions by the Royal Navy. Thus, it was open to doubt whether those ships were converted merchant vessels, that is warships proper, or civilian.[35] In any event, however, even if supply ships do not qualify as warships because of their function (supplying naval forces) they meet the requirements of the definition of military objectives and may be attacked without prior warning.[36]

> **'Military aircraft' are all aircraft belonging to the armed forces of a state and bearing external marks distinguishing such aircraft of their nationality. The commanding soldier must be a member of the armed forces, and the crew must be subject to military discipline. Military aircraft need not be armed.**   **1007**

As regards the details of this definition, reference is made to the commentary on Section 1002.[37] Military aircraft are state or government aircraft within the meaning of Section 1008. It is important to emphasize that in view of contemporary state practice unmanned aerial vehicles (UAVs) may qualify as military aircraft.[38]

> **'State aircraft' are all aircraft belonging to or used by the state and serving exclusively state functions (e.g. in customs or police service).**   **1008**

Although there exists no generally accepted definition of state or government aircraft in international law,[39] it is agreed that aircraft employed in customs and police services

---

[30] See, *inter alia*, G. Schramm, 'Die Umwandlung von Kauffahrteischiffen in Kriegsschiffe auf hoher See während eines Krieges' (1911) 22 *Marine Rundschau* 1255 *et seq.*, 1539 *et seq.*

[31] See only Venturini, (*supra*, n. 29), 122 *et seq.*

[32] Note, however, that inland merchant vessels and maritime fishing vessels may not be required so to act.

[33] Cf. H. G. Helm, 'Die rechtliche Stellung der Troßschiffe einer Kriegsmarine' (1957) 54 *Marine Rundschau* 152–6.

[34] Order in Council of 4 April 1982, reprinted in Villar, 8.

[35] Lagoni, in Fleck (ed.), *The Gladisch Committee on the Law of Naval Warfare, 5 Bochumer Schriften zur Friedenssicherung und zum Humanitären Völkerrecht* (Bochum: Brockmeyer, 1990), 66.

[36] See below Section 1025.

[37] A similar definition of military aircraft is given in the *Canadian Manual* (*supra*, n. 27), Section 704; and in the *San Remo Manual*, para. 13(j).

[38] *HPCR Manual*, Rules 1(x), (dd), and (ee).

[39] See, however, Article 3(b) of the 1944 Chicago Convention on Civil Aviation (15 *UNTS* 295).

as well as those transporting heads of state are to be considered as state or government aircraft.[40]

1009 'Civilian aircraft' are all aircraft other than military aircraft as described in Section 1007 and state aircraft as described in Section 1008, serving exclusively civilian transport of passengers or cargo.

Again, there is no definition of civilian aircraft in international law. Hence, they have to be distinguished negatively from military and other government aircraft.[41]

2. Scope of Application

1010 The geographical scope of application of the law of armed conflict at sea, that is the area in which acts of naval warfare within the meaning of Section 1014 may be performed, comprises:
  — the territory of the parties to the conflict accessible to naval forces;
  — inland waters, archipelagic waters, and territorial sea of the parties to the conflict;
  — the high seas including exclusive economic zones; and
  — the airspace over these land and sea areas,
  with the exception of demilitarized zones as mentioned above in Section 216.

1. *Preliminary remarks.* In contrast to earlier times, it is now difficult to determine the scope of application of the law of naval warfare, or the region of naval warfare. The Third United Nations Conference on the Law of the Sea has progressively developed the law and contributed to the emergence of multiple differing regimes, some of which are now customary in character. Problems arise not so much in relation to the sea areas of the belligerents as to those sea areas that traditionally belonged to the high seas (and thus to the area of naval warfare) and in which states not parties to the conflict now enjoy certain sovereign rights. While the laws of neutrality are not dealt with in detail in the present chapter, it is necessary to describe the principles of the international law of the sea governing neutral coastal states' rights in order to explain the delimitation of areas of naval warfare.[42]

2. *Neutral territory and neutral territorial waters.* The land territory, inland waters, archipelagic waters, and the territorial sea of states neutral or not parties to the conflict are, in principle, excluded from the area of naval warfare. Belligerents are obliged to respect the inviolability of these areas. Special rules apply to neutral states' rights in their archipelagic waters and in international straits. These matters are, however, dealt with in Chapter 11. With regard to exclusive economic zones and continental shelves of neutral states, see Sections 1012 and 1013 and the accompanying commentaries. With regard to other sea areas exempt from acts of naval warfare, see Section 216. It should be noted in this context that the Montreux Convention of 20 July 1936 provides special restrictions for the Dardanelles in times of armed conflict.[43]

---

[40] See also *HPCR Manual*, Rule 1(cc).

[41] See also the *Canadian Manual* (*supra*, n. 27), Section 704; *San Remo Manual*, para. 13(1); Fischer in K. Ipsen, *Völkerrecht*, 5th edn (Munich: C. H. Beck, 2004), § 55, para. 29.

[42] For an overview, see O'Connell (*supra*, n. 12). In the context of naval warfare, see E. Rauch, *The Protocol Additional to the Geneva Conventions for the Protection of Victims of International Armed Conflicts and the United Nations Convention on the Law of the Sea: Repercussions on the Law of Naval Warfare* (Berlin: Duncker & Humblot, 1984), 31 *et seq.*; *San Remo Manual*, paras. 10, 14, *et seq.*

[43] Text in 31 *AJIL* (1937), Suppl., 1–18; see also Vignes, 'Commentary on the 1936 Montreux Convention', in Ronzitti (*supra*, n. 29), 468–82.

WOLFF HEINTSCHEL VON HEINEGG

'Internal waters' are waters on the landward side of the baseline of the territorial sea. 'Archipelagic' waters are waters on the landward side of archipelagic baselines. The 'territorial sea' comprises the waters on the seaward side of the baseline or archipelagic baseline in a breadth not exceeding twelve nautical miles. The so-called 'contiguous zone' does not belong to the territorial sea.

1. *Baselines.* In order to be legally effective baselines must be drawn in accordance with Articles 3 *et seq.* of the Geneva Convention on the Territorial Sea and the Contiguous Zone of 29 April 1958 (hereinafter: TSC 1958) and Articles 5 *et seq.* UNCLOS. According to these provisions, which are customary in character, the normal baseline is the low-tide line along the coast. In localities where the coastline is deeply indented and cut into, or if there is a fringe of islands along the coast in its immediate vicinity, the method of straight baselines joining appropriate points may be employed in drawing the baseline. Straight baselines may also be drawn in mouths of rivers and to and from low-tide elevations if lighthouses or similar installations have been built on them which are permanently above sea level. The drawing of straight baselines must not depart to any appreciable extent from the general direction of the coast, and the areas lying within the lines must be sufficiently closely linked to the land to be subject to the regime of internal waters.[44]

2. *Internal waters.* Waters on the landward side of the baselines form part of the internal waters of a state.[45] Also included are mouths of rivers where a straight baseline is drawn across the mouth between points in the low-water line of the river's banks.[46] Bays are internal waters only if they belong to a single state and if further qualifications are met.[47] According to UNCLOS, a bay is a well-marked indentation whose penetration is in such proportion to the width of its mouth as to contain land-locked waters and constitute more than a mere curvature of the coast. An indentation shall not, however, be regarded as a bay unless its area is as large as, or larger than, that of the semi-circle whose diameter is a line drawn across the mouth of that indentation. If the distance between the low-water marks of the natural entrance points of a bay does not exceed 24 nautical miles, a closing line may be drawn between these two low-water marks, and the waters enclosed thereby shall be considered as internal waters. From this it follows that, for example, the Gulf of Sidra is not a bay in the legal sense. Nor can it—despite Libya's assertions—be considered an 'historic' bay.[48] Outermost permanent harbour works which form an integral part of the harbour system are regarded as forming part of the coast. Off-shore installations and artificial islands shall not, however, be considered as permanent harbour works.[49]

---

[44] Cf. O'Connell (*supra*, n. 12) Vol. I, 171 *et seq.* For (allegedly) excessive baseline claims, see US Department of State, *Limits in the Seas No. 112, United States Responses to Excessive National Maritime Claims*, 17 *et seq.* (Washington, DC, 9 March 1992); J. A. Roach/R. W. Smith, *Excessive Maritime Claims*, 66 *International Law Studies* (Newport, RI: Naval War College, 1994).

[45] Article 5 TSC 1958; Article 8 UNCLOS.

[46] Article 9 UNCLOS.

[47] Article 7 TSC 1958; Article 10 UNCLOS. Note, however, that the following rules do not apply to so-called 'historic' bays.

[48] For a general overview, see O'Connell (*supra*, n. 12), Vol. I, 353 *et seq.*, 389 *et seq.* With regard to the Gulf of Sidra, see F. Francioni, 'The Gulf of Sidra Incident (*United States* v. *Libya*) and International Law', (1980/1981) 5 *ItalYIL* 85 *et seq.*, and 'The Status of the Gulf of Sirte in International Law' (1984) 11 *Syracuse Journal of International Law & Commerce* 311 *et seq.*

[49] Article 8 TSC 1958; Article 11 UNCLOS.

WOLFF HEINTSCHEL VON HEINEGG

3. *Territorial sea and international straits.* The breadth of territorial seas was the subject of a number of international conferences, all of which failed to agree upon a concrete rule. Now, according to Article 3 UNCLOS, every state has the right to establish the breadth of its territorial sea up to a limit not exceeding twelve nautical miles. Some states claim a territorial sea of less than 12 nautical miles (e.g. Greece and Palau); others claim a territorial sea of up to 200 nautical miles (e.g. some African and South American states). Still, in view of 135 states claiming a territorial sea of twelve nautical miles,[50] the rule laid down in Article 3 UNCLOS can be considered as declaratory of a corresponding rule of customary international law.[51] Roadsteads which are normally used for the loading, unloading, and anchoring of ships, and which would otherwise be situated wholly or partly outside the outer limit of the territorial sea, are included in the territorial sea.[52] Within the territorial sea, ships of all states enjoy the suspendable right of innocent passage.[53] In times of armed conflict, enemy ships, be they warships or merchant vessels, may be prohibited from entering the territorial sea.

In international straits, be they overlapped by the territorial sea of neutrals or of the belligerents, the non-suspendable right of transit passage continues to apply in times of armed conflict. Therefore, in those parts of the territorial sea of a belligerent that form part of an international strait the right of transit passage enjoyed by the shipping and aviation of third states may not be suspended, hampered, or otherwise impeded.[54]

4. *The contiguous zone* is the sea area bordering the territorial sea. It may not extend beyond 24 nautical miles from the baselines from which the territorial sea is measured. The sovereignty of the coastal state does not extend to the contiguous zone. Rather, the coastal state's rights are limited to the control necessary to prevent infringement of its customs, fiscal, immigration, or health and safety laws and regulations within its territory or territorial sea, and to punish infringements of such laws and regulations committed within its territory or territorial sea.[55]

5. *Archipelagic waters.*[56] An 'archipelagic state' is a state comprised entirely of one or more archipelagos and may include other islands. An 'archipelago' is a group of islands, including parts of islands, interconnecting waters, and other natural features which are so closely interrelated that such islands, waters, and other natural features form an intrinsic geographical, economic, and political entity, or which historically have been regarded as such. An archipelagic state may draw straight archipelagic baselines joining the outermost points of the outermost islands and drying reefs of the archipelago provided that within such

---

[50] See the references in United Nations, *Law of the Sea Bulletin* No. 54 (2004), 132 *et seq.*

[51] C. Gloria in Ipsen, *Völkerrecht (supra,* n. 41), § 52, paras. 3 *et seq.*; O'Connell (*supra,* n. 12) Vol. 1, 165 *et seq.*

[52] Article 9 TSC 1958; Article 12 UNCLOS.

[53] As regards the right of peaceful passage in general, see Articles 17 *et seq.* UNCLOS; O'Connell, Vol. II, 867 *et seq.*, 959 *et seq.* In times of armed conflict, the right of passage of belligerent warships and prizes through a neutral territorial sea is restricted to 24 hours. It may even, on a non-discriminatory basis, be restricted or suspended. With regard to the right of peaceful passage in cases where a belligerents mines its territorial sea, see Section 1041 and accompanying para. 2.

[54] *San Remo Manual,* paras. 27 *et seq.* See also *Canadian Manual* (*supra,* n .27), *para. 818; NWP 1–14M, para. 7.3.6.*

[55] Article 24 TSC 1958; Article 33 UNCLOS.

[56] For the exclusion of neutral archipelagic waters from the area of naval warfare see *San Remo Manual,* paras. 14 *et seq.* Special rules apply where third states enjoy the right of archipelagic sea passage. See ibid., paras. 23 *et seq.*

WOLFF HEINTSCHEL VON HEINEGG

baselines are included the main islands and an area in which the ratio of the area of the water to the area of the land, including atolls, is between 1:1 and 9:1. Only a few countries, such as the Philippines and Indonesia, qualify as archipelagic states. Within such archipelagic waters the archipelagic state exercises full sovereignty. Third states enjoy the right of archipelagic sea lanes passage[57] and of innocent passage. While the former may never be suspended[58] the right of innocent passage may only be suspended temporarily in specified areas if such suspension is essential for the security of the archipelagic state.

> Exclusive economic zones may not be extended more than 200 nautical miles from   1012
> the baselines which are relevant for the landward limitation of the territorial sea.
> While coastal states and archipelagic states exercise full sovereignty within their
> internal waters, archipelagic waters, and territorial sea, they have only certain sov-
> ereign rights in exclusive economic zones. The latter do not belong to the high seas,
> but third states also enjoy freedom of navigation and overflight and certain other
> freedoms within them. Hence, as a matter of principle for naval warfare purposes,
> the exclusive economic zones of neutral or non-belligerent states belong to the high
> seas. The rights of coastal and archipelagic states must, however, be taken into due
> consideration.

1. *Legal basis of the exclusive economic zone.* The right to proclaim an exclusive economic zone (EEZ) was for the first time laid down in Articles 55 *et seq.* UNCLOS. Although that Treaty entered into force only on 16 November 1994, at the time of writing 104 states have already proclaimed such a zone with a breadth of 200 nautical miles.[59] Despite some original doubts with regard to the customary character of the right to proclaim an EEZ, there have so far been no significant protests against such proclamations. Hence, it follows that today it has become a customary right.[60]

2. *Rights in the EEZ.* In the EEZ, the coastal state has sovereign rights to explore and exploit, conserve, and manage the natural resources, whether living or non-living, of the waters superjacent to the sea bed and of the sea bed, and its subsoil, and to undertake other activities for the economic exploitation and exploration of the zone, such as the production of energy from the water, currents, and wind. For these purposes the coastal state may establish and use artificial islands, installations, and structures.[61]

3. *Neutral EEZ.* The EEZ of states not parties to the conflict is not excluded from areas of naval warfare per se. However, it cannot be ignored that those states enjoy certain sovereign and exclusive rights in their economic zones. Hence, even though the belligerents are not barred from taking naval warfare measures within a neutral EEZ[62] they are

---

[57] UNCLOS Articles 46 *et seq.* See also O'Connell (*supra*, n. 12), Vol. I, 237 *et seq.*; H. P. Rajan, 'The Legal Regime of Archipelagos' (1986) 29 *GYIL* 137–53.

[58] This holds true in peacetime and in wartime. Moreover, the prohibition of suspending archipelagic sea lanes passage applies equally to neutral and belligerent states. See *San Remo Manual*, para. 27 *et seq.*

[59] See the references in United Nations, *National Legislation on the Exclusive Economic Zone*, New York 1993; United Nations, *Law of the Sea Bulletin* No. 54 (2004), 132 *et seq.*

[60] D. J. Attard, *The Exclusive Economic Zone in International Law* (OUP, 1987); R. Wolfrum, 'The Emerging Customary Law of Marine Zones: State Practice and the Convention on the Law of the Sea' (1987) *NethYIL* 121 *et seq.* See also O'Connell (*supra*, n. 12), Vol. I, 553 *et seq.*

[61] Article 56 UNCLOS. For a general overview, see Gloria in Ipsen (*supra*, n. 51), § 53; O'Connell, Vol. I, 553 *et seq.*

[62] See Heintschel von Heinegg, 'The United Nations Convention on the Law of the Sea and Maritime Security Operations' (2005) 48 *GYIL* 151–85 [158 *et seq.*]. See also *Canadian Manual*, para. 821; *NWP 1–14M*, para. 7.3.8.

obliged to pay due regard to the coastal state's sovereign rights. Accordingly, if hostile actions are conducted within the EEZ of a neutral state, belligerent states shall, in particular, have due regard for artificial islands, installations, structures, and safety zones established by the coastal state.[63] The duty to pay due regard to the coastal states' rights in their EEZs is, however, subject to considerations of military necessity.

1013   The 'high seas' comprise all parts of the sea which do not belong to the EEZ, the territorial sea, the internal waters, or archipelagic waters. The high seas also comprise the continental shelf of neutral or non-belligerent states. The rights of coastal and archipelagic states must, however, be taken into due consideration.

1. *Belligerent rights on the high seas.* Traditionally, the high seas belong to the region of naval warfare.[64] In view of the practice of the parties to the Israeli–Egyptian, Korean, and Vietnam conflicts, some international lawyers endeavoured to restrict the areas of naval warfare to the territorial waters of the belligerents.[65] They argued that under the UN Charter, the freedoms of the high seas, especially the freedom of navigation and overflight of states not parties to the conflict, may not be interfered with by states that were either unwilling or unable to refrain from the use of armed force. This position has never been generally shared by the international community. The freedom of the high seas has always been subject to the law of naval warfare. Hence, it is not seriously disputed that on the high seas belligerents are entitled to visit and search neutral merchant vessels or to attack enemy forces.[66] Of course, in the above-mentioned conflicts, the belligerents restricted their measures to their respective territorial waters. This practice, however, does not meet the qualifications required for a rule of customary law to come into being ('widespread', 'uniform', 'duration'). Moreover, it is not reflective of an *opinio juris* to the effect that those states felt obliged to refrain from committing acts of naval warfare on the high seas. Rather, those abstentions were merely deliberate self-limitations due to the special circumstances ruling at those times.[67] This is the sole possible understanding. Nothing else follows from the fact that, according to Article 136 UNCLOS, the so-called 'area', that is the sea bed and ocean floor and subsoil thereof beyond the limits of national jurisdiction,[68] and its resources are 'the common heritage of mankind'. The resulting rights and duties of states do not apply to the water column or the air space above the 'area'.[69] However, hostile actions on the high seas shall be conducted with due regard for the exercise by neutral states of rights of exploration and exploitation of the natural resources of the sea bed, the ocean floor, and the subsoil

---

[63] For a provision to the same effect, see para. 34 of the *San Remo Manual*. The *San Remo Manual*, in para. 35, provides for the laying of mines in a neutral EEZ: 'If a belligerent considers it necessary to lay mines in the exclusive economic zone… of a neutral state, the belligerent shall notify that state, and shall ensure, *inter alia*, that the size of the minefield and the type of mines used do not endanger artificial islands, installations, and structures, nor interfere with access thereto, and shall avoid so far as practicable interference with the exploration or exploitation of the zone by the neutral state. Due regard shall also be given to the protection of the marine environment.'

[64] See, *inter alia*, Colombos, para. 558.

[65] O'Connell, 'International Law and Contemporary Naval Operations' (1970) XLIV *BYIL* 28 *et seq.*

[66] With regard to state practice since the end of World War II, see R. Ottmüller, *Die Anwendung von Seekriegsrecht in militärischen Konflikten seit 1945* (Hamburg: Forschungsstelle für Völkerrecht, 1978), 47 *et seq.*

[67] W. A. Fenrick 'The Exclusion Zone Device in the Law of Naval Warfare' (1986) XXIV *CYIL* 115.

[68] Article 1, para. 1(1) UNCLOS.

[69] Rauch (*supra*, n. 42), 53 *et seq.*

thereof.[70] Finally, the reservation of the high seas for peaceful purposes in Articles 88 and 301 UNCLOS is also without prejudice to the legality of acts of naval warfare.[71] These provisions merely repeat the fundamental prohibition of the threat or use of force in Article 2(4) UN Charter.

2. *The continental shelf* of a coastal state comprises the sea bed and the subsoil of the submarine areas that extend beyond its territorial sea; it does not comprise the superjacent water column.[72] According to the 1958 Geneva provisions, the term 'continental shelf' is used as referring to the sea bed and subsoil of the submarine areas adjacent to the coast but outside the area of the territorial sea, to a depth of 200 metres or, beyond that limit, to where the depth of the superjacent waters admits of the exploitation of the natural resources of the said areas.[73] According to UNCLOS, the continental shelf comprises the said submarine areas throughout the natural prolongation of the land territory to the outer edge of the continental margin, or to a distance of 200 nautical miles where the outer edge of the continental margin does not extend up to that distance.[74] The coastal state exercises exclusive sovereign rights over the continental shelf for the purpose of exploring it and exploiting its natural resources. Hence, the same considerations apply here as with regard to neutral EEZs. Belligerents are obliged to pay due regard to those rights, subject to military necessity.

3. Acts of Naval Warfare, Competences, and Principles

Acts of naval warfare within the meaning of this chapter are the use of weapons   **1014**
including the (special) methods of naval warfare and the following measures of
economic warfare at sea:
— visiting and searching,
— ordering to take a specific course,
— capturing,
— requisitioning of cargo,
— bringing in, and
— confiscation.

1. *Preliminary remarks.* This enumeration of acts of naval warfare is rather general and far from exhaustive. It is meant to supplement the provisions of Sections 1015 and 1016 on competences. Hence, for the present purposes it is sufficient to give a short overview of the different acts of naval warfare and merely to refer to the use of weapons generally. Special legal aspects relating to the use of certain methods of naval warfare are dealt with in Sections 1039 *et seq.*[75] Further legal restrictions on the use of weapons follow from the principles laid down in Sections 1017 *et seq.* and 1021 *et seq.* As regards the so-called 'prize measures', the following should be taken into consideration: prize measures and measures of economic warfare at sea are respectively aimed at cutting off the

---

[70] To the same effect: *San Remo Manual,* para. 36.

[71] Heintschel von Heinegg (*supra,* n. 62).

[72] Geneva Convention on the Continental Shelf of 29 April 1958 (hereinafter: CSC 1958); Articles 76 *et seq.,* UNCLOS. See also O'Connell (*supra,* n. 12), Vol. I, 467 *et seq.*

[73] Article 1, lit. a, CSC 1958.

[74] Article 76, para. 1 UNCLOS. According to Article 76, paras. 5 and 6, UNCLOS, under certain conditions the breadth of the continental shelf may extend to 350 nautical miles.

[75] Those methods and means comprise blockades even though a blockade is generally considered a measure of economic warfare at sea.

WOLFF HEINTSCHEL VON HEINEGG

enemy's supplies by sea and rendering impossible, or at least difficult, further enemy war efforts.[76] As long as these measures affect enemy merchant vessels and their cargoes the mentioning of prize measures in the present chapter seems to be reasonable. However, legal problems only arise with regard to specially protected vehicles and goods. Of far more practical relevance are, of course, prize measures taken against neutral merchant vessels and their cargoes. Visit, search, diversion, and capture of neutral vessels and goods are dealt with in Chapter 11. Accordingly, the commentaries on the following sections are restricted to those rules that apply to the relationship between the parties to the conflict (including their respective merchant shipping). It may be added, however, that the competences dealt with in Sections 1015 and 1016 are also valid if prize measures are taken against neutral merchant vessels and their cargoes.

2. *Prize measures in detail.* National implementation of international law rules on prize measures is effected in so-called Prize Rules or Prize Ordinances. As regards the Federal Republic of Germany, one may argue that the 1939 Prize Ordinance[77] is of continuing validity as pre-constitution law. In view of the many uncertainties involved, the Federal Ministry of Defence had issued Standing Order No. 10 which was to remain in force until a formal revision of the law. Even though that Standing Order is no longer in force, it is worthwhile referring to the following definitions on prize measures given therein:[78]

— Visit comprises the procedure of ordering a vessel to stop and of examining the ship's papers.[79]
— Search means the interrogation of a ship's master, its crew, and its passengers as well as the examination of a ship and its cargo.[80]
— Diversion is an order to take a specific course in order to be visited and searched in an appropriate area or port.[81]
— Capture is exercised by sending a prize crew on board another vessel and assuming command over the ship.[82]
— Seizure of cargo is effected by the capture of a vessel. However, cargo may be seized independently, that is without capture of the vessel.
— Bringing in means to escort a vessel to a port of the captor or of an ally. This includes ports under the captor's or its allies' power.
— Confiscation of captured vessels is effected by a prize court decision. With the prize court's decision, ownership of the vessel and its equipment passes to the captor state.

1015   The following vessels and units are competent to perform acts of naval warfare:
— warships and other units of naval forces,
— military aircraft, and
— units of land and air forces.

---

[76] With respect to economic warfare at sea, see R. Tucker, *The Law of War and Neutrality at Sea* (Washington, DC: US Government Printing Office, 1957), 74 *et seq.*; Colombos (*supra*, n. 12), paras. 635 *et seq.*; J. Kraska, 'Prize Law', *MPEPIL*; Heintschel v. Heinegg/M. Donner 'New Developments in the Protection of the Natural Environment in Naval Armed Conflicts' (1994) XXXVII *GYIL* 281–314.
[77] Prisenordnung vom 28 August 1939, Reichsgesetzblatt 1939 I, 1585.
[78] Blockade is dealt with in Sections 1051 *et seq.*
[79] See also J. Kraska, 'Prize Law', *MPEPIL*.
[80] Ibid.
[81] See also U. Scheuner, II *Wörterbuch des Völkerrechts* (Berlin: de Gruyter, 1962), 385.
[82] See also C. G. Phillips, 'Capture at Sea in Perspective' (1965) 91 *USNIP* 60 *et seq.*

WOLFF HEINTSCHEL VON HEINEGG

1. Section 1015 clarifies that only warships and military aircraft *strictu sensu* are entitled to take the measures enumerated in Section 1014. It is self-evident that methods of naval warfare (including the use of weapons) may only be employed by units under military command and subject to military discipline. Section 1015 is of particular importance with regard to measures of economic warfare at sea. According to the ParisDecl 1856[83] and customary international law, 'privateering is, and remains, abolished'. Hence, such measures may be ordered by commanders of warships and of military aircraft as well as by other units of armed forces. They may also be ordered and carried out by other departments if specially authorized. However, in view of the abolition of privateering, private individuals or entities are never authorized to take prize measures at sea.

2. Recently, the question has arisen whether the exercise of belligerent rights is indeed limited to warships (and to military aircraft), that is to ships (or aircraft) meeting all the requirements of the definitions contained in Sections 1004 and 1007. Indeed, as regards the relationship between the belligerents' naval forces, it may seem rather odd if a lawful target, such as an enemy warship, could only be attacked by a warship and not by another state ship. Therefore, it could be argued that, in view of the object and purpose of the rule—that is transparency vis-à-vis neutral navigation by the prohibition of privateering—its scope of applicability is limited to the exercise of belligerent rights against neutral vessels and aircraft. Then, hostile acts against enemy naval forces could be taken by any state ship. However, it is far from settled whether the formal approach underlying the traditional law of naval warfare has been abandoned by states.

> The following vessels and persons may not perform acts of naval warfare: **1016**
> — state ships other than warships, even when carrying out support services for the naval forces;
> — state aircraft other than military aircraft;
> — merchant ships;
> — fishing boats and other civil ships;
> — civil aircraft; and
> — prize crews of captured ships.
>
> The crews of all ships and aircraft are, however, entitled to defend themselves against attacks by enemy forces.

Section 1016 re-emphasizes the rule laid down in Section 1015 that the categories of persons entitled to take measures of naval warfare are limited. In view of the characteristics of naval warfare, it is important to refer expressly to those units that, on one hand, are particularly affected but, on the other hand, are not allowed to take such measures. Of course, Section 1016 is without prejudice to the right to convert merchant vessels into warships.[84] In this context it should be stressed that according to Section 1025 merchant vessels visiting, searching, or attacking enemy merchant vessels are legitimate military objectives, and thus liable to attack on sight, without prior warning. To a certain extent, therefore, Section 1025 formulates the consequences resulting from a breach of Section 1016. Although the vessels and aircraft enumerated here are not entitled to

---

[83] For a general overview, see H. Fujita, 'Commentary on the 1856 Paris Declaration', in Ronzitti (*supra*, n. 29), 68.

[84] Colombos (*supra*, n. 12), paras. 536 *et seq.*

WOLFF HEINTSCHEL VON HEINEGG

take measures of naval warfare, they may defend themselves against enemy attacks.[85] This is a well-founded principle of customary international law. However, such self-defence measures may legitimately be countered by the enemy. If, for example, a merchant vessel resists capture the enemy warship may either break that resistance by force or, if the resisting merchant vessel qualifies as a legitimate military objective, it may even be attacked and sunk.

1017   Without prejudice to other conditions described in this chapter the following principles shall be observed in all acts of naval warfare, in particular those involving the use of arms:
— The right of the parties to the conflict to adopt methods of warfare is not unlimited.
— Neither the civilian population nor individual civilians may be the object of attacks.
— The parties to the conflict shall at all times distinguish between combatants and civilians.
— Attacks shall be limited strictly to military objectives. The definition of military objectives (see above, Sections 442–444) is applicable also in naval warfare.
— In planning or deciding upon acts of war at sea or in the air, all parties to the conflict shall ensure that all feasible precautions are taken in accordance with international law applicable in armed conflicts to avoid losses of civilian lives and damage to civilian objects.
— Ships and aircraft which surrender, for example by turning down the flag, communicating their intention on a common radio channel such as a distress frequency, or by any other means of clear surrender, shall not be attacked any longer.
— After each battle, the parties to the conflict shall without delay take all feasible action to search for and rescue the shipwrecked, wounded, and sick, to protect them against deprivation and maltreatment, to ensure necessary care, as well as to search for the dead and to protect them from pillage.

1. *Preliminary remarks.* The validity of the principles enumerated in Section 1017 follows from international treaty and customary law.[86] Despite the heading of this section, these principles are not peculiar to naval warfare. They are expressly mentioned in the present chapter to stress that the fundamental principles of the laws of armed conflict apply equally in naval warfare. The principles are not absolute in character but have to be weighed against considerations of military necessity.[87] However, such considerations do not render these principles obsolete. Such considerations justify deviations only if the norm in question expressly refers to military necessity. On the other hand, the principles are rather general in character. It is, therefore, difficult to determine specific duties beforehand and in the abstract. Such duties can be formulated only if the said principles are applied to a concrete case.[88]

---

[85] O'Connell (*supra*, n. 12), Vol. II, 1108; Colombos, para. 553.

[86] Evidence of the respective legal basis will be given in the commentaries to the individual principles. For a first overview, see G. J. F. van Hegelsom, 'Methods and Means of Combat in Naval Warfare', in W. Heintschel v. Heinegg (ed.), *Methods and Means of Combat in Naval Warfare, 8 Bochumer Schriften zur Friedenssicherung und zum humanitären Völkerrecht* (Bochum: Brockmeyer, 1992), 1–59, at 11 *et seq.*; H. B. Robertson, 'Modern Technology and the Law of Armed Conflict at Sea', in Robertson (ed.), *The Law of Naval Operations*, 64 *International Law Studies* (Newport, RI: Naval War College, 1991), 362–83, *at* 363 *et seq.*; *NWP 1–14M*, chapter 8; *Canadian Manual* (*supra*, n. 27) para. 825.

[87] Cf. G. I. A. D. Draper, 'Military Necessity and Humanitarian Imperatives' (1973) XII *RDMilG* 129 *et seq.*

[88] O'Connell (*supra*, n. 12), Vol. II, 1105 *et seq.*; Colombos (*supra*, n. 12), paras. 524 *et seq.*

WOLFF HEINTSCHEL VON HEINEGG

2. *The problem of the applicability of AP I to naval warfare.* According to Article 49, para. 3, AP I the provisions of Part IV, Section I (Articles 48–67) 'apply to any land, air or sea warfare which may affect the civilian population, individual civilians, or civilian objects on land. They further apply to all attacks from the sea or from the air against objectives on land but do not otherwise affect the rules of international law applicable in armed conflict at sea or in the air.' As regards the applicability to naval warfare of the rules of AP I dealing with the civilian population, this provision as well as Article 49, para. 4, AP I have been cited in support of contradictory positions.[89] Today, there is general agreement on the following solution: Article 49, para. 3, AP I merely excludes the application of Articles 48–67 AP I to naval warfare proper. The other provisions of AP I, especially Articles 35–41, are applicable. Section I governs methods of naval warfare 'which may affect the civilian population on land' and is moreover applicable to attacks from the sea against objectives on land. The second sentence of Article 49, para. 3, AP I is restricted to attacks against military objectives on land. Attacks against civilian objects are already dealt with in the first sentence. Hence, Section I is applicable to ship-to-ship, ship-to air, or air-to-ship operations only if the civilian population, individual civilians, or civilian objects may be affected. In other words: those operations are covered by Section I if there is or may be collateral damage to human beings or civilian objects on land. Therefore, Articles 51 and 52 AP I are not applicable to attacks on merchant vessels or to mine warfare. These operations are subject to 'the rules of international law applicable in armed conflict at sea'. That is made clear by the second sentence of Article 49, para. 3, and by Article 49, para. 4, AP I.[90] It follows from the preceding that the provisions of AP I may also be taken into consideration when it comes to the identification of principles and rules applicable in armed conflicts at sea.

3. *No unlimited right to choose methods of warfare.* This fundamental principle, first codified in Article 22 of the 1907 Hague Regulations, was reaffirmed in Article 35 AP I. As concerns the latter provision, its applicability to naval warfare as part of Section I, Part III follows from the interpretation of Article 49, para. 3, AP I favoured here. Moreover, it is applicable to all methods of naval warfare *qua* customary law.[91] The fact that the wording of the Hague Regulations differs from that of AP I is without prejudice to the principle's customary character as codified in Article 35, para. 1, AP I. The formulation in AP I is merely an adaptation to modern conditions.[92] In view of its relatively abstract wording, this principle, as such, allows no conclusions as to the extent of the limitations on the right to choose methods of warfare. These limitations are specified in the following principles as well as in the other rules laid down in the present chapter.

4. The customary prohibition of making the civilian population or individual civilians the object of attack is for the first time codified in Article 51, para. 2, AP I.[93] This

---

[89] E. Rauch, *The Protocol Additional to the Geneva Conventions for the Protection of Victims of International Armed Conflicts and the United Nations Convention on the Law of the Sea: Repercussions on the Law of Naval Warfare,* (Berlin: Duncker & Humblot, 1984) 57 *et seq.*; H. Meyrowitz 'Le Protocole Additionnel I aux Conventions de Genève de 1949 et le droit de la guerre maritime' (1985) 89 *RGDIP* 243 *et seq.*

[90] For the applicability of AP I to naval warfare and for further references, see Bothe, 'Commentary on the 1977 Geneva Protocol I', in N. Ronzitti (*supra,* n. 29), 761 *et seq.*

[91] W. A. Solf, in Bothe/Partsch/Solf, *New Rules for Victims of Armed Conflicts* (The Hague/Boston/London: Nijhoff, 1982), 193 *et seq.*; Robertson (*supra,* n. 86), at 363. See also *San Remo Manual,* para. 38.

[92] Hegelsom (*supra,* n. 86), 11.

[93] Solf, in Bothe/Partsch/Solf, 299 *et seq.*

WOLFF HEINTSCHEL VON HEINEGG

provision is directly applicable to measures of naval warfare 'which may affect the civilian population, individual civilians, or civilian objects on land'.

5. *The principle of distinction.* Also customary in character, and thus valid in naval warfare, is the principle of distinction, now codified in Article 48 AP I. Of course, Article 48 AP I, as such, is applicable to naval warfare only within the limits mentioned above. Still, the applicability of the principle of distinction to naval warfare *qua* customary law is undisputed.[94] Hence, it is prohibited to employ in naval warfare methods that are not, or cannot be, directed against a specific military objective or whose effects cannot be limited to such objectives. However, the principle does not prohibit attacks that result in collateral damage which has to be tolerated in the light of the principle of proportionality.

6. *The definition of military objectives.*

a) Validity. In view of Article 49, para. 3, AP I the definition of military objectives laid down in Article 52, para. 2, AP I is not directly applicable to naval warfare. Despite the differences between land and naval warfare there is, however, general agreement that this definition is also valid in the context of naval warfare *qua* customary law. For example, the Round Table of Experts of International Law Applicable to Armed Conflicts at Sea, at its Bochum session (1989), affirmed its applicability to naval warfare.[95] Accordingly, in land as well as in naval warfare, only military objectives may be attacked. The fact that the 1974–1977 Diplomatic Conference agreed on excluding naval warfare proper from the applicability of Part III, Section I does not justify a position to the contrary. In their military manuals, Canada[96] and the US[97] expressly acknowledge the validity of the definition of military objectives for naval warfare. As concerns the US, this is of particular significance since they have, so far, felt unable to ratify AP I.

b) Legal consequences arising from the validity of the definition of military objectives. It follows from the validity of the definition of military objectives that, in naval warfare too, military objectives are not merely those which, according to present day language, qualify as genuinely 'military'. A contribution to military action is 'effective' not only if there is a direct connection between action and object; indirect contributions are also sufficient as long as they conduce to (specific) military actions. Moreover, the total or partial destruction, capture, or neutralization of such an object must offer a definite military advantage. It is impossible to determine in advance and in the abstract when an attack will offer such a definite military advantage. Accordingly, multiple military considerations will have to be taken account of, especially the object of the military operation in question. 'Definite' does not mean that the advantage anticipated must be obvious or that it has to be effected

---

[94] *NWP 1–14M*, para. 8.1; *San Remo Manual*, para. 39.

[95] For the commentaries, the discussions, and the Bochum results see Heintschel v. Heinegg (ed.), *The Military Objective and the Principle of Distinction in the Law of Naval Warfare. Report, Commentaries and Proceedings of the Round Table of Experts on International Humanitarian Law Applicable to Armed Conflicts at Sea, Ruhr-Universität Bochum, 10–14 November 1989*, 7 *Bochumer Schriften zur Friedenssicherung und zum Humanitären Völkerrecht* (Bochum: Brockmeyer, 1991), 45 *et seq.*, 141 *et seq.*, 170 *et seq.* The 1994 *San Remo Manual*, in para. 40, now states: 'In so far as objects are concerned, military objectives are limited to those objects which by their nature, location, purpose or use make an effective contribution to military action and whose total or partial destruction, capture or neutralization, in the circumstances ruling at the time, offers a definite military advantage.'

[96] *Canadian Manual* (*supra*, n. 27), para. 825.

[97] *NWP 1–14M*, para. 8.2.

directly. It means rather that the advantage must be not merely hypothetical but concrete and discernible. 'In the circumstances ruling at the time' is meant to exclude advantages that materialize sometime during the course of hostilities; they must be ascertainable at the time of the attack. This presupposes the ability to base the selection of targets upon reliable and up-to-date information. If there remain doubts as to the military character of an objective non-military character must be presumed unless the omission to take military measures would entail significant dangers.[98]

7. *Precautions in attack.* The obligation to take appropriate precautions before launching or ordering an attack is codified in Article 57 AP I. However, its validity *qua* customary law follows implicity from the preceding principles.[99] If belligerents are obliged to limit attacks strictly to military objectives and to spare, as far as possible, civilians and civilian objects they are also obliged to take the appropriate precautions. Otherwise, the definition of military objectives and the principle of distinction are meaningless.

8. *No attacks on ships and aircraft that have surrendered.* The obligation to suspend attacks upon vehicles that have surrendered follows from the customary rules codified in Article 41 AP I and Article 23, lit. c, HagueReg.[100] The protective scope of this prohibition is limited to the people on board such vehicles. Consequently, a ship that has surrendered may, for example, be sunk after its passengers and crew have been taken to a place of safety.[101] Traditionally, hoisting the flag was considered a clear indication of surrender. While this rule has not become obsolete its practical relevance has certainly decreased because in modern armed conflicts at sea there will, in most instances, be no visual contact at all. While it is envisaged in this section that there may be other ways of 'clear surrender' it must be doubted whether that is indeed the case. So far, there is no other conduct than hoisting the flag that is generally recognized as clearly indicating surrender and that would entail an obligation to refrain from an attack. Radio or electronic signals are not considered sufficient proof for surrender. This also holds true for every other conduct, like stopping the engines, manoeuvring in a way that would make it impossible for the ship to effectively defend itself against attacks, or switching off the ship's systems.

9. *Search for and rescue of survivors.* After each engagement the parties to the conflict shall take all possible measures to search for and collect the shipwrecked, wounded, and sick. This obligation is codified in Article 18, para. 1, GC II. It follows from the principle of humanity and is applicable to naval warfare *qua* customary law.[102] It needs to be stressed that, in contrast to land warfare, the parties to an armed conflict at sea are not obliged to search for and collect survivors 'at all times, and particularly after an engagement'[103] but only 'after each engagement'. Thus, the special circumstances of naval

---

[98] For this and the preceding commentaries, see Solf, in Bothe/Partsch/Solf (*supra*, n. 91), 323 *et seq.*; Heintschel v. Heinegg, 'Das "militärische Ziel" im Sinne von Art. 52 Abs. 2 des I. Zusatzprotokolls', *HuV-I* (1989, 3) 51. For legitimate military objectives in naval warfare, see Sections 1021 *et seq.*

[99] See also *Canadian Manual* (*supra*, n. 27), para. 825; *NWP 1–14M*, para. 8.1; *San Remo Manual*, para. 46.

[100] See, *inter alia*, Colombos (*supra*, n. 12), para. 519.

[101] Note, in this context, that special rules apply for the destruction of captured merchant vessels.

[102] For further references, see W. T. Mallison, *Studies in the Law of Naval Warfare: Submarines in General and Limited Wars*, International Law Studies Vol. LVIII (Washington, DC: US Government Printing Office, 1968), 134 *et seq.*

[103] This is the wording of Article 15, para. 1, GC I.

WOLFF HEINTSCHEL VON HEINEGG

warfare, especially the vulnerability of ships engaged in rescue operations, is taken into account.[104] Of course, an omission to search for and collect the shipwrecked, wounded, and sick is justified only if such measures, in view of considerations of military necessity or of the circumstances ruling at the time, are not feasible. The formulation 'after each engagement' is, therefore, not restricted to major naval hostilities but covers all situations of hostilities at sea that have caused victims.[105]

1018   **Ruses of war are permissible also in naval warfare. Unlike land and aerial warfare, naval warfare permits the use of false flags or military emblems (Article 39, para. 3, AP I). Before opening fire, however, the true flag shall always be displayed.**

1. *State practice.* A famous example of flying false flags in naval warfare is the case of the German cruiser *Emden.* In 1914, the *Emden* while flying the Japanese flag entered the port of Penang. Before attacking the Russian cruiser *Shemtshug,* the *Emden* displayed the German Navy's war flag. Another example is the case of the German ship *Kormoran.* After it had been stopped by the Australian destroyer HMS *Sydney,* the *Kormoran* pretended to be registered in the Netherlands. Before the *Sydney* could verify the true character, the *Kormoran* displayed the German flag and sank the Australian warship.[106] No cases of ruses are reported from state practice during the post-World War II conflicts.

2. *Legitimate ruses in naval warfare.* In contrast to land warfare, the use of false flags and markings has always been considered a legitimate ruse in naval warfare. This has been expressly reaffirmed by Article 39, para. 3, AP I. It should be noted, however, that such ruses may be performed only by warships and the other ships and aircraft enumerated in Section 1015. It is hotly disputed whether merchant vessels are also entitled to fly false flags.[107] Be that as it may; for the present purposes this problem needs no further consideration. Its relevance is restricted to the determination of the enemy character of merchant vessels. As will be shown, the flag flown by a merchant vessel is only *prima facie* evidence of its true character.[108] In view of the technological development (over-the-horizon targeting, etc.) the use of false flags has almost become a negligible issue. The true character of a vessel will only in rare cases be determined by visual means. It is more likely that in future the use of civilian radar equipment by warships will be of practical relevance. Other electronic means of misleading the enemy may also be taken into consideration in the present context; for example, a transponder with an 'identification of friend or foe' (IFF) code whose use is intended to make the enemy believe that the ship or aircraft in question belongs to his allies. As regards their legitimacy, these and other ruses are legally restricted only by the prohibition of perfidy. Other legitimate ruses are, for example, the use of camouflage, decoys, mock operations, and misinformation.[109]

[104] J. S. Pictet, *The Geneva Conventions of 12 August 1949. Commentary* Vol. II (Geneva: ICRC, 1960), GC II, 132.
[105] Ibid.
[106] For further cases that occurred during the World Wars, see Colombos (*supra,* n. 12), paras. 520 *et seq.*
[107] Cf. Colombos, para. 522.
[108] See Section 1022.
[109] Article 37, para. 2, AP I. See also *San Remo Manual,* paras. 109 *et seq.* For an overview of ruses and perfidy in naval warfare, see M. Gimmerthal, *Kriegslist und Perfidieverbot im Zusatzprotokoll vom 10. Juni 1977 zu den vier Genfer Rotkreuz-Abkommen von 1949,* 4 Bochumer Schriften zur Friedenssicherung und zum Humanitären Völkerrecht (Bochum: Brockmeyer, 1990), 54 *et seq.,* 173 *et seq.*; G. P. Politakis, 'Stratagems and the Prohibition of Perfidy with a Special Reference to the Law of War at Sea' (1993) *Austrian Journal of*

The *San Remo Manual*'s rules on deception are too vague and, thus, do not provide the necessary guidance for naval commanders. On the one hand, it is rather difficult to distinguish 'active simulation'[110] from 'passive simulation'. The capabilities of modern technologies could open a vast grey area and, consequently, could render the provision obsolete. It needs to be emphasized in this context that it is not always sufficient to draw the necessary conclusions from the prohibition of perfidy. For example, actively feigning the status of a protected vessel is prohibited by paragraph 110 of the *San Remo Manual* and the corresponding customary law.[111] This finding, however, is without prejudice to the admissibility of feigning neutral status by the use of civilian radars or other electronic equipment. According to the position taken here, the use of civilian navigational radars (and thus taking advantage of the respective emissions) is to be considered a permissible ruse of naval warfare if the radar is switched off immediately prior to the launching of an attack. It may well be, however, that this position is not shared by all. It should be recalled that, in 1983, the World Administrative Conference for the Mobile Services adopted Resolution No. 18[112] on the identification of vessels and aircraft of states not participating in an international armed conflict, recommending the use of adequate transponders and that 'the frequencies specified in No. 3021 of the Radio Regulations may be used by ships and aircraft of States not parties to an armed for self-identification and establishing communications. The transmission will consist of the urgency or safety signals, as appropriate, described in Article 40 followed by the addition of the single group "NNN" in radiotelegraphy and by the addition of the single word "NEUTRAL" pronounced as in French "neutral" in radiotelephony. As soon as practicable, communications shall be transferred to an appropriate working frequency [...]' It would, of course, be a considerable progress if the protection of neutral vessels were enhanced. However, that proposal is not suited for achieving that aim. As *Fenrick* has rightly pointed out, the resolution 'appears to have been issued by a forum unfamiliar with law of armed conflict issues and without consultation with national officials responsible for such matters. Ships and aircraft using such procedures may assume they are entitled to protection when in fact they are not. The fact that a ship or aircraft is registered in a state not party to the conflict does not, in and of itself, mean that it is not a legitimate military objective.'[113]

> Perfidy is prohibited also in naval warfare. In particular, it is prohibited to misuse the emblem of the Red Cross or to give a ship, in any other way, the appearance of a hospital ship for the purpose of camouflage. It is also prohibited to make improper use of other distinctive signs equal in status with that of the Red Cross (Article 45 GC II; Article 37 AP I) and of the flag of truce, or to feign surrender or distress by sending a distress signal or by the crew taking to life-rafts. In addition, the principles described in Section 472 apply.   **1019**

Public International Law 45 253 *et seq.* For a general overview, see Fleck, 'Ruses of War and Prohibition of Perfidy' (1974) XIII *RDMilG* 269 *et seq.*

[110] *San Remo Manual*, para. 110.
[111] *UK Manual*, para. 13.83; *NWP 1–14M*, para. 12.1.
[112] Reprinted in (1984) 238 *IRRC* 58 *et seq.*
[113] W. J. Fenrick, 'Military Objectives in the Law of Naval Warfare' in Heintschel v. Heinegg (ed.), *The Military Objective and the Principle of Distinction in the Law of Naval Warfare*, 7 Bochumer Schriften zur Friedenssicherung und zum humanitären Völkerrecht (Bochum: Universitätsverlag N. Brockmeyer, 1991), 1–44, at 40.

As regards the prohibition of perfidy, see first Articles 37, para. 1, and 38 AP I as well as the commentary in Chapter 4 above. The example of the use of a transponder in the commentary to Section 1018 is to be considered an act of perfidy if, for example, one of the electronic means of identification for medical aircraft (Article 8 Annex I to AP I) is used. It would also be perfidious to use one of the other internationally recognized marks, signs, or signals which indicate a right to special protection.[114]

1020   **It is prohibited to employ weapons or warfare which are intended, or may be expected, to cause widespread, long-term, and severe damage to the natural environment (Article 35, para. 3, AP I).**

This provision hardly allows conclusions as to concrete obligations, nor legal evaluation of specific behaviour. In view of the obscure meaning of the terms used in Article 35, para. 3, AP I, like 'natural environment', 'widespread', and 'long-term', one can only think of extreme and exceptional cases in which this prohibition would cover the use of methods and means of naval warfare. That would, presumably, be the case if the belligerents massively employed weapons in an enclosed or semi-enclosed sea (like the Baltic Sea) and if the resulting severe damage to the flora and fauna in the entire eco-system would last for decades. The events during the second Gulf War (Kuwait–Iraq)[115] have made evident the difficulties of a proper legal evaluation of the effects of the use of methods of naval warfare on the natural environment.[116] In any event, it is incorrect to characterize the Iraqi conduct as war crimes or 'ecological terrorism'.

Similar difficulties of interpretation are involved when it comes to the application of the 1977 ENMOD Convention. However, this Convention has to be strictly distinguished from Article 35, para. 3, AP I. The prohibition of using the modified environment as a means of warfare does not seem to reflect existing technologies. Obviously, only in exceptional cases will states dispose of the technical means massively to modify the natural environment.[117]

Finally, it is noted that at least those states bound by AP I are obliged to take into consideration the natural environment when it comes to the use of methods and means of naval warfare.[118] Measures which may be expected to have an impact on the natural environment should not be taken if the resulting damage would be excessive in relation to the military advantage anticipated.[119] In any event, damage to, or destruction of, the

[114] For example, those agreed upon in the International Telecommunication Convention of 25 October 1973; see also Solf, in Bothe/Partsch/Solf (*supra*, n. 91), 207 *et seq.*; Gimmerthal, 173 *et seq.*

[115] Iraq had set fire to oil wells in Kuwait, and parts of the Persian Gulf had been polluted by oil. See US Department of Defense, *Conduct of the Persian Gulf War*—Appendix on the Role of the Law of War; N. A. Robinson, 'International Law and the Destruction of Nature in the Gulf War', (1991) 21 *Environmental Policy & Law* 216 *et seq.*

[116] It should be noted in this context that the reports and articles published either during the conflict or in its aftermath were highly exaggerated and, in many cases, based on deliberate misinformation. For a recent legal evaluation of the law applicable to the protection of the environment in naval armed conflicts, see Heintschel v. Heinegg/M. Donner, 'New Developments in the Protection of the Natural Environment in Naval Armed Conflicts' (1994) XXXVII *GYIL* 281–314.

[117] For an evaluation of the ENMOD Convention, see Sanchez Rodriguez, 'Commentary to the ENMOD Convention', in Ronzitti (*supra*, n. 29), 661 *et seq.*

[118] It is questionable whether there already exists a corresponding duty in customary international law, especially because some states have expressly excluded the applicability of Article 35, para. 3, AP I. Note, however, that para. 44 of the *San Remo Manual* states: 'Methods and means of warfare should be employed with due regard for the natural environment taking into account the relevant rules of international law.'

[119] This follows from the fundamental principles of the laws of war.

WOLFF HEINTSCHEL VON HEINEGG

natural environment not justified by military necessity, or carried out wantonly, is prohibited.[120] However, the mere fact that the use of methods and means of warfare may
have an impact on the natural environment, whether marine or coastal, does not imply
a legal duty on the parties of the conflict to refrain from their employment.[121]

II. Military Objectives and Protected Objects in Armed Conflicts at Sea

1. Enemy Warships and Military Aircraft

> Without prejudice to the principles applicable in the law of armed conflict at sea,   **1021**
> enemy warships and military aircraft may be attacked, sunk, or seized at any time
> without warning. Upon seizure, such ships and the cargo on board become war
> booty and property of the seizing state, as they do not fall under prize law. Members
> of the crew falling into the hands of the adversary become prisoners of war. The
> same applies to persons on board who accompany the armed forces.

1. *Military objectives.* Enemy warships, including converted merchant ships, and military
aircraft are entitled to perform acts of naval warfare. They are, thus, military objectives
by nature that may be attacked, sunk, or captured without prior warning anywhere and
at any time within the region of naval warfare.[122]

2. *The principles of naval warfare*, that is those peculiar to naval warfare as well as the
general principles of the laws of armed conflict, continue to be applicable. In the case
of warships and military aircraft—military objectives by nature, purpose, *and* use—
there is almost no situation conceivable, other than surrender, in which they would be
immune from attack on sight. Therefore, the special mentioning of the principles in the
first sentence is to be understood as a reference to the rules on target identification and
to the prohibition of excessive collateral damage.

3. *Booty of war.* According to customary international law, enemy warships and military
aircraft, as well as other state ships not merchant vessels, are not subject to the law of
prize. As soon as capture is completed they are to be considered war booty. Property
upon capture automatically passes to the captor state.[123] Cargo on board such vehicles
owned by the enemy state is also considered to be booty of war. Private property is subject to the laws of prize.[124]

4. *Prisoners of war.* The crews of warships, converted merchant vessels, and military
aircraft are combatants within the meaning of Article 43 AP I. They therefore become

---

[120] See also *San Remo Manual*, para. 44.

[121] One possible way of protecting the natural environment is an agreement of the parties to the conflict
to this effect. Accordingly, para. 11 of the *San Remo Manual* encourages them 'to agree that no hostile
actions will be conducted in marine areas containing . . . rare or fragile ecosystems or... the habitat of
depleted, threatened or endangered species or other forms of marine life'.

[122] See only Fenrick, 'The Exclusion Zone Device in the Law of Naval Warfare' (1986) XXIV *CYIL* 91
et seq.

[123] H. Lauterpacht (ed.), *Oppenheim's International Law*, Vol. II: *Disputes, War and Neutrality*, 7th edn (New
York: David McKay, 1952), 474 *et seq.*; W. G. Downey Jr, 'Captured Enemy Property, Booty of War and Seized
Enemy Property' (1950) *AJIL* 488 *et seq.*; A. P. Higgins, 'Ships of War as Prize' (1925) *BYIL* 103 *et seq.*

[124] See the provisions on capture and seizure of enemy and neutral cargoes in Sections 1027 *et seq.*

prisoners of war as soon as they fall into the power of an adverse party according to Article 4 A, No. 1, GC III and Article 44, para. 1, AP I. As regards persons who accompany the armed forces, this follows from Article 4 A, No. 4, GC III. Civilian mariners as well as private contractors on board warships do fall into that category. However, if not members of the regular armed forces or if not integrated into the regular armed forces and if they have directly taken part in the hostilities, for example by operating the ship's weapons systems, they are liable to criminal prosecution by the capturing state. It should be emphasized in this context, that despite the liability to criminal prosecution under the domestic law of the capturing state according to the law of naval warfare there is no prohibition of making use of civilian mariners or of civilian contractors.

2. Enemy Merchant Ships, their Cargo, Passengers, and Crew

a. *Enemy merchant ships*

1022   In principle, the enemy character of a merchant ship is determined by the flag which the ship is entitled to fly (Article 57 LondonDecl 1909).

Flying the enemy's flag has always been considered sufficient proof of the enemy character of merchant vessels.[125] Hence, in such cases the commander of a warship need not bother with questions of proper registration or ownership. This does not mean, however, that only those merchant vessels flying the enemy's flag have enemy character. The fact that a merchant vessel is flying the flag of a neutral state or a state not party to the conflict is only *prima facie* evidence of its neutral character.[126] If search of the ship's papers, or other information available to the commander, reveal that there has been a transfer of flag in order to evade the consequences to which an enemy vessel is exposed, then a vessel flying a neutral flag may be treated as an enemy merchant vessel.[127] If, however, there has been a transfer of one neutral flag to another neutral flag the vessel concerned may not be considered as enemy in character even if the transfer was made with a view to the ongoing hostilities.[128] Moreover, according to the international laws of armed conflict, the enemy character of merchant vessels flying neutral flags may be presumed if there exist reasonable grounds for suspicion that it in fact belongs to the enemy.[129] These cases

---

[125] Heintschel v. Heinegg, 'Visit, Search, Diversion and Capture: Conditions of Applicability' (1991) XXIX *CYIL* 283–329, at 300. See also *San Remo Manual*, para. 112.

[126] Heintschel v. Heinegg, *loc. cit.*, 301; *San Remo Manual*, para. 113.

[127] Article 55 of the—unratified—London Declaration of 1909. According to this provision there is, however, a rebuttable 'presumption, if the bill of sale is not on board a vessel which has lost her belligerent nationality less than six days before outbreak of hostilities, that the transfer is void.... Where the transfer was effected more than thirty days before the outbreak of hostilities, there is an absolute presumption that it is valid if it is unconditional, complete, and in conformity with the laws of the countries concerned, and if its effect is such that neither the control of, nor the profits arising from the employment of the vessel remain in the same hands as before the transfer.' According to Article 56 of the 1909 London Declaration the 'transfer of an enemy vessel to a neutral flag, effected after the outbreak of hostilities, is void unless it is proved that such transfer was not made in order to evade the consequences to which an enemy vessel, as such, is exposed. There is, however, an absolute presumption that a transfer is void: (1) if the transfer has been made during a voyage or in a blockaded port; (2) if a right to repurchase or recover the vessel is reserved to the vendor; (3) if the requirements of the municipal law governing the right to fly the flag under which the vessel is sailing, have not been fulfilled.'

[128] That was the case when, during the Iran–Iraq conflict Kuwaiti tankers were reflagged by the US. See M. H. Nordquist/M. G. Wachenfeld, 'Legal Aspects of Reflagging Kuwaiti Tankers and Laying of Mines in the Persian Gulf' (1988) XXXI *GYIL* 138–64.

[129] For further details, see Heintschel v. Heinegg (*supra*, n. 125), at 301. The fact that a merchant vessel is flying a flag of convenience is as such no sufficient reason for suspicion.

WOLFF HEINTSCHEL VON HEINEGG

are, however, of no relevance for the naval commander. He may regularly rely upon the information made available to him by higher authorities. The final determination of the enemy character of vessels lies with the competent prize court which has to decide on the legality of capture and other acts in any event.

> In relation to enemy merchant ships, all acts of economic warfare at sea may be **1023** performed, without consideration of the cargo and its owner. The same applies in principle to other seagoing private vessels, such as yachts and pleasure-boats, subject to particular provisions of protection. Prize law also applies to wrecks and to ships still in construction. After the capture of an enemy merchant vessel it must be decided in a prize court procedure whether the capture was lawful. Upon confirmation by the prize court the ship becomes property of the capturing state.

1. *Protection of enemy private property in naval warfare.* In contrast to the position in land warfare, enemy private property is not exempt from capture in naval warfare.[130] The traditional rule according to which enemy private property is liable to capture and confiscation has not been modified by the definition of military objectives that is also applicable in naval warfare. According to that definition, the capture of objects is permissible only if capture 'offers a definite military advantage' and if the objects concerned 'make an effective contribution to military action'. This does not, however, imply that according to the law of prize only objects qualifying as military objectives are liable to capture. The laws of prize on capture and confiscation of enemy private goods have not been altered by the validity of the definition of military objectives. The reference to 'capture' in that definition is merely a clarification of the principle of proportionality, as set out in Section 1021.[131]

2. *Procedure.* Whereas neutral merchant vessels may, in principle, be captured only after prior visit and search, that is not the case for enemy merchant vessels.[132] That does not mean that they may not be visited and searched. Visit and search should be exercised in order to verify whether a vessel belongs to a category of specially protected vessels. Property of a captured enemy merchant vessel does not pass to the captor automatically on assuming command over the ship. It only passes if the competent prize court decides upon confiscation.[133] The decision of the prize court on confiscation is without prejudice to the legality of capture.[134]

---

[130] During the nineteenth and early twentieth centuries, the US persistently endeavoured to exempt, with the exception of contraband and breach of blockade, private property from capture. Although they were supported by a number of other states, proposals to this effect were rejected by the respective majorities. See Articles 33 *et seq.* of the *Oxford Manual*; O'Connell (*supra*, n. 12), Vol. II, 1112 *et seq.*; Heintschel v. Heinegg, (*supra*, n. 125), at 305 *et seq.*

[131] See commentary to Section 1021, para. 2. According to para. 135 of the *San Remo Manual*, 'enemy vessels, whether merchant or otherwise, and goods on board such vessels may be captured outside neutral waters', unless they are exempt from capture.

[132] According to the traditional law this also applies to wrecks. See J. A. Roach, 'Sunken warships and military aircraft' (July 1996) 20 No. 4 *Marine Policy* 351–4.

[133] Colombos (*supra*, n. 12), para. 925; H. Lauterpacht (*supra*, n. 123), 474 *et seq.*; F. Berber, *Lehrbuch des Völkerrechts*, Vol. II (Munich: C. H. Beck, 1962), 195 *et seq.*

[134] Capture is permissible and legal if there are sufficient reasons for suspecting that the vessel concerned is either enemy or has committed acts rendering it a legitimate military objective. Confiscation is legal only if the facts justifying such confiscation have been proved in prize court proceedings.

WOLFF HEINTSCHEL VON HEINEGG

1024   A merchant ship belonging to one of the parties to the conflict located in an enemy
         port at the commencement of the hostilities shall be allowed to depart freely within
         a reasonable time. It may be furnished with a pass permitting it to proceed to its
         port of destination or any other port indicated (Article 1 HC VI). Merchant ships
         unable, owing to circumstances of *force majeure*, to leave the enemy port within
         the period fixed, or which have not been allowed to leave, cannot be confiscated.
         The belligerent may only detain such ships subject to the obligation to return them
         after the armed conflict or requisition them on payment of compensation (Article 2
         HC VI). These rules do not affect merchant ships whose design shows that they are
         intended for conversion into warships (Article 5 HC VI).

During the Crimean War, it was common practice to capture and confiscate, upon the declaration of war, enemy merchant vessels in one's own port.[135] Hague Convention VI of 1907
then took into account the practice of states during the second half of the nineteenth century.
During the two World Wars, HC VI was of no practical relevance.[136] On 14 November
1925, Great Britain and, on 13 July 1939, France denounced that Convention. Germany
took the Convention into consideration when it passed its Prize Ordinance of 1939, whose
applicability was, however, made subject to strict reciprocity. The US never ratified Hague
VI. Today the provisions of Hague VI, probably apart from those referring to *force majeure*,
are of even less practical relevance. Only in rare and exceptional cases will merchant vessels travel to an enemy port without knowledge of the outbreak of hostilities. Moreover, in
modern armed conflicts at sea the belligerents will certainly not wish to release ships likely
to make an effective contribution to the enemy's war efforts. For these and other reasons the
exception in the last sentence of Section 1024 will be interpreted widely.

1025   Without prejudice to the principles applicable in the law of armed conflict at sea,
         enemy merchant ships are military objectives and may be attacked at any time
         without warning, if they are:
         — engaging in acts of war (e.g. laying mines; mine-sweeping; cutting submarine
            cables and pipelines; visiting, searching, or attacking other merchant ships);
         — making an effective contribution to military action (e.g. by carrying military
            material, troop-carrying, or replenishing);
         — incorporated into or assisting the enemy's intelligence system, subject to, where
            necessary, a prior political determination;
         — sailing in convoy with enemy warships or military aircraft;
         — refusing an order to stop or actively resisting visit, search, or capture;
         — armed to an extent that they could inflict damage on a warship; or
         — engaging in any other activity bringing them within the definition of a military
            objective.

1. *Preliminary remarks.* According to the LondonProt 1936, warships are allowed to sink
merchant vessels whether enemy or neutral only if certain preconditions are fulfilled.[137]
At first sight the provisions of that agreement could be interpreted restrictively. The
sinking of a merchant vessel without prior warning and without first taking passengers, crews, and ship's papers to a place of safety would be permissible only if the vessel

---

[135] O'Connell (*supra*, n. 12), Vol. II, 1124 *et seq.*
[136] A. de Guttry, 'Commentary on the 1907 Hague Convention VI', in Ronzitti (*supra*, n. 29), 108;
A. P. Higgins, 'Enemy Ships in Port at the Outbreak of War' (1922/23) *BYIL* 55 *et seq.*
[137] As regards the continuing validity of the 1936 London Protocol, see the preliminary remarks in the
commentary on Sections 1046 *et seq.*

WOLFF HEINTSCHEL VON HEINEGG

concerned persistently refused to stop on being duly summoned or if it actively resisted visit and search. However, this would be a too simplistic way of looking at the 1936 Protocol. The rules laid down in that document formed part of the 1922 Washington Treaty and were reaffirmed by the 1930 London Conference. During that conference a committee of legal experts presented a report in which the matter was clarified as follows: 'The Committee wish to place it on record that the expression "merchant vessel", where it is employed in the declaration, is not to be understood as including a merchant vessel which is at the moment participating in hostilities in such a manner as to cause her to lose her right to the immunities of a merchant vessel.' Whereas it remains unclear what is meant by 'participating in hostilities' it is obvious that merchant vessels are not in all circumstances protected by the LondonProt 1936. This was confirmed by the judgment of the Nuremberg Tribunal.[138] Hence, enemy merchant vessels that, by their conduct, qualify as legitimate military objectives[139] are not protected by the LondonProt 1936 and may—as an exceptional measure—be attacked and sunk.[140] As made clear above, this applies only if sinking offers a definite military advantage and there are no other means available. The last sentence shows that the enumeration in Section 1025 is not exhaustive. Hence, enemy merchant vessels may also be attacked if they commit acts other than those mentioned here.[141] Such cases should, however, be treated with utmost care. If an enemy merchant vessel does *not* commit one of the acts expressly enumerated in Section 1025, the responsible commander will have to prove that the vessel in question did effectively contribute to military action and that destruction was the only possible reaction.

2. *Engagement in acts of war*, especially the exercise of visit, search, and capture, is a breach of the prohibition laid down in Section 1016. In this context, it is stressed that measures of self-defence against attacks of enemy forces are not considered to be engagement in acts of war. On the other hand, under the laws of armed conflicts at sea, warships are not prohibited from breaking resistance by force. Self-defence by an enemy merchant vessel is, therefore, not prohibited but entails considerable risks because it conflicts with the warship's right of capture. The distinction between permissible measures of self-defence and illegal engagement in hostilities is not always an easy task. For example, in 1916 Charles Fryatt, captain of the unarmed British merchant vessel *Brussels*, tried to ram the German submarine *U 23*. Captain Fryatt was sentenced to death and executed.[142]

3. *Effective contribution to military action* is regularly fulfilled by the acts enumerated.[143] Since Section 1025, as an exceptional provision, has to be interpreted narrowly, the term

---

[138] For details, see the commentary on Section 1047.

[139] Note that mere arming is not a sufficient reason for rendering a merchant vessel a military objective. See para. 2 of the commentary on Section 1004.

[140] Cf. Fenrick (*supra*, n. 122), at 105 *et seq.*; Mallison, (*supra*, n. 102), 106 *et seq.*

[141] For example, breach of blockade. See also *San Remo Manual*, para. 60, but note that, according to the position taken here, mere arming does not render an enemy merchant vessel a military objective.

[142] The sentence of the German War Tribunal of 27 July 1916 was considered in conformity with the law by a commission chaired by Schücking. Others characterized it as 'simple murder, bare of any military necessity', as a 'violation of the fundamental right of self-defence', and as 'inconsistent with the rules of the laws of war'. See, *inter alia*, J W. Garner, *International Law and the World War* (London: Longmans, 1920), Vol. 1, 413; Colombos (*supra*, n. 12), para. 557. For the *Fryatt* case generally, see I. Dischler, *Wörterbuch des Völkerrechts* (Berlin: de Gruyter, 1962), 606 *et seq.*

[143] See also *NWP 1–14M*, para. 8.6.2.2; *Canadian Manual* (*supra*, n. 27), para. 834; *San Remo Manual*, para. 60(b).

WOLFF HEINTSCHEL VON HEINEGG

'war material' may not be understood as comprising goods which have some tenuous relevance for the enemy's war efforts. Rather, the objects concerned must be directly apt for use by the enemy's armed forces. If that is not the case, enemy merchant vessels and goods on board such vessels are subject to the laws of prize only. With regard to the exceptional permissibility of the destruction of captured enemy merchant vessels,[144] see Section 1026.

4. *Incorporation into or assisting the enemy's intelligence system.* Even during the World Wars this was considered sufficient ground for attack without prior warning. In its sentence against Admiral Dönitz, the Nuremberg Tribunal ruled that such vessels lose the protection of the 1936 London Protocol.[145] Attacks on vessels incorporated into the enemy's intelligence system may, however, be undertaken only after a prior political decision to that effect. This reservation was deemed necessary to avoid an escalation of relatively low-scale conflicts.

5. *Convoy.* Sailing in convoy with enemy warships and military aircraft, too, has always been considered a sufficient justification for attacking enemy merchant vessels on sight. By travelling under convoy the merchant vessel concerned manifests its readiness to actively resist—with the help of the accompanying warship—visit, search, and capture.[146]

6. *Refusal to stop on being duly summoned or active resistance to visit, search, and capture.* These exceptions were acknowledged in the 1936 London Protocol. It is emphasized that resistance to visit, search, and capture must be 'active'. Enemy merchant ships are under no legal obligation to facilitate such measures.[147] The legitimacy of attack in such cases is in no way affected by the right of self-defence of enemy merchant vessels against attacks or other belligerent acts of the enemy, as laid down in Section 1016. The right of self-defence conflicts with the warship's right of capture and right to enforce capture whenever necessary.

1026   **Enemy merchant ships may only be destroyed if it is impossible to bring them into a port of one's own or that of an ally, and without having first brought the passengers, crews, and ships' papers to a safe place (Article 2 LondonProt 1936). The ship's boats are not regarded as a safe place unless the safety of the passengers and crew is assured, in the existing sea and weather conditions, by the proximity of land, or the presence of another vessel which is in a position to take them on board (Article 2 LondonProt 1936). Where possible, the personal belongings of the passengers and crew shall also be recovered.**

Enemy merchant vessels are often not legitimate military objectives because they do not commit any of the acts enumerated in Section 1025. However, they are always subject to capture according to the laws of prize. If military circumstances preclude taking or sending an enemy merchant vessel for adjudication as an enemy prize it may become necessary to destroy it. This situation is covered in Section 1026. The legality of the

---

[144] Cf. Mallison (*supra*, n. 102), 122 *et seq.*

[145] See commentary on Section 1047, including the references given. Further: Mallison, 122 *et seq.*; *NWP 1–14M*, para. 8.6.2.2; *Canadian Manual*, paras. 834 and 835; *San Remo Manual*, para. 60(c). In the *San Remo Manual*, the following examples are given: engaging in reconnaissance, early warning, surveillance, or command, control, and communications missions.

[146] *NWP 1–14M*, para. 8.6.2.2; *Canadian Manual*, para. 835(1e); *San Remo Manual*, para. 60(d).

[147] Cf. W. Schönborn, 'Der Widerstand feindlicher Handelsschiffe gegen Visitationen und Aufbringung' (1918) *Archiv für öffentliches Recht* 161 *et seq.*

WOLFF HEINTSCHEL VON HEINEGG

destruction of a (captured) enemy merchant vessel as an exceptional belligerent right follows from the LondonProt 1936.[148] However, before destruction passengers, crew, and ship's papers must be taken to a place of safety. The 1936 Protocol contains no further restrictions on the right of destroying enemy prizes.[149] However, such destruction may never take place for its own sake. It is an exceptional right, to be strictly distinguished from the destruction of enemy merchant vessels qualifying as legitimate military objectives. In the majority of cases it will suffice to destroy the cargo or simply to divert the vessel.[150] The destruction of passenger vessels carrying only civilian passengers is prohibited at sea. For the safety of the passengers, such vessels must be diverted to an appropriate area or port in order to complete capture.[151]

b. *Cargo of enemy merchant ships*

The enemy or neutral character of cargo is determined by the nationality of the owner or, if the owner is a stateless person, by his residence (Article 57 LondonDecl 1909). In the case of corporations and companies, their registered office is relevant. Where after the outbreak of hostilities enemy ownership of goods is transferred in transit they retain their enemy character until they reach their destination (Article 60 LondonDecl 1909).

This provision stems from the 1909 London Declaration which never entered into force. As far as the rules laid down in that treaty are here taken into consideration they are, however, reflective of customary international law. Many of the provisions of the LondonDecl 1909 have been implemented in national legislation and in prize regulations. The enemy character of the cargo's[152] owner is determined by his nationality.[153] Contrary to Anglo-American doctrine and jurisprudence, his residence is of relevance only if he is a stateless person. If cargo is owned by a corporation its head or registered office is decisive. The nationality of owners and/or shareholders is irrelevant unless the so-called 'control test' applies.[154] If, according to the preceding criteria, a determination of enemy or neutral character is impossible there is a rebuttable presumption that goods on board enemy vessels are of enemy character.[155] Transfers of title effected in the course of the vessel's journey do not have to be recognized. If, however, such transfer has been effected before the commencement of a journey, neutral cargo of enemy origin remains immune from seizure.[156]

---

[148] For its continuing validity and for further details see the preliminary remarks to Sections 1046 *et seq.*

[149] See, however, para. 139 of the *San Remo Manual* which is more specific.

[150] It is interesting to note in this context that para. 138 of the *San Remo Manual* provides that 'as an alternative to capture, an enemy merchant vessel may be diverted from its declared destination'.

[151] *San Remo Manual*, para. 140. See also commentary on Section 1034.

[152] Note that the ship's equipment does not belong to its cargo but is an integral part of and shares the same destiny as the ship. Personal belongings of passengers and crews are also not part of the cargo.

[153] Nationality is, however, only one criterion. Anglo-American prize courts always based their decisions on the owner's residence. Thus, even British or US nationals could be characterized as enemies if their residence was in enemy or enemy occupied territory. See Heintschel v. Heinegg (*supra*, n. 125), at 305 *et seq.*

[154] According to the 'control test' a corporation not based in enemy or enemy-controlled territory may be deemed enemy in character if it is controlled by individuals who are enemy subjects. See Berber (*supra*, n. 133), 200.

[155] This is the well-known maxim '*robe d'ennemi confisque robe d'ami*'. It can be traced back to Hugo Grotius (*De jure belli ac pacis*, Lib. III, Ch. VI, para. VI) and was acknowledged in Article 59 LondonDecl 1909. During the World Wars it was the basis of a significant number of prize court decisions. See Colombos (*supra*, n. 12), para. 616.

[156] Article 60, para. 1, LondonDecl 1909. See also Tucker (*supra*, n. 76), 86.

1028   Enemy cargo on board enemy ships may be requisitioned and confiscated no matter
               whether such cargo is contraband or whether it is state or private property.

In international treaties or drafts there is no express rule that enemy cargo on board
enemy vessels is liable to capture and confiscation. The validity of the rule follows,
however, from international customary law[157] and, indirectly, from the ParisDecl 1856.
According to that Declaration only neutral goods and enemy goods on board neutral
merchant vessels are exempt from capture. In principle, seizure of goods is effected by
capturing the vessel carrying them. If the vessel's master consents or if the vessel concerned can neither be captured nor diverted or destroyed, only its cargo may be seized.
Confiscation of seized cargo is subject to a confirmatory prize court decision.

1029   Neutral cargo on board enemy ships is exempt. Such cargo may, however, be requi-
               sitioned and confiscated if:
               — the cargo is contraband, for example goods designated for the adversary and apt
                 to be used for war purposes;
               — the ship is breaching a blockade, unless the shipper proves that at the time of
                 loading he neither knew nor should have known of the intention to breach the
                 blockade; or
               — the ship is sailing in convoy with enemy warships or engaging in any other
                 activity bringing it within the definition of a military objective.

1. According to the ParisDecl 1856 and international customary law, neutral goods are
exempt from seizure.[158] The exceptions to that principle enumerated in the present section are also part of customary law.[159]

2. Neutral goods are not exempt from seizure if they are contraband. If contraband
goods on board neutral merchant vessels are not exempt, *a fortiori* they are not protected
when on board enemy merchant vessels. The classification of goods as contraband is
closely related with prize measures taken against neutral shipping. Therefore, reference is
made to the commentaries on Sections 1142 and 1143. In the present context it suffices
if the goods in question are contained in a belligerent's contraband list.[160]

3. The provision on breach of blockade is based upon Article 21 LondonDecl 1909
which—despite doubts as to the continuing validity of the Declaration—is generally
accepted as customary law.[161]

4. Neutral cargo on board enemy merchant vessels travelling in convoy or qualifying
in some other way as a legitimate military objective is liable to seizure and confiscation.
This is consistent with the legality of attacking such vessels without prior warning. In
such cases the cargo shares the destiny of the vessel.

---

[157] Tucker, 74 *et seq.*; H. Lauterpacht, (*supra*, n. 123), 462 *et seq.*; Y. Dinstein, 'The Laws of War at Sea'
(1980) *IsrYHR* 38–69, at 40.
[158] See, *inter alia*, Heintschel v. Heinegg (*supra*, n. 125), at 306 *et seq.*
[159] Articles 21 and 63 LondonDecl 1909.
[160] *San Remo Manual*, para. 148, defines contraband as 'goods which are ultimately destined for territory under
the control of the enemy and which may be susceptible for use in armed conflict'. Note that under the present law
of prize, contraband lists may vary according to the particular circumstances of the armed conflict.
[161] See, *inter alia*, F. Kalshoven, 'Commentary on the 1909 London Declaration', in Ronzitti (*supra*, n.
29), 262, 269 *et seq.*

WOLFF HEINTSCHEL VON HEINEGG

Private and official postal correspondence found on board enemy ships is invio-   1030
lable. If a ship conveying such postal correspondence is captured the captor shall
ensure that the correspondence is forwarded without delay (Article 1 HC XI).
Before sinking a ship postal correspondence shall as far as possible be recovered
and forwarded. The enemy ship itself, even a mail ship, shall be liable to capture.
The prohibition relating to the seizure of postal correspondence does not apply to
postal consignments destined for or proceeding from a blockaded port. Parcels are
exempt from seizure if they are destined for neutral persons and do not contain any
contraband. The captor shall be entitled to open mail bags and inspect their contents. Inviolability shall not apply to contraband contained in letter post.

The inviolability of postal correspondence (except parcels) and the captor's duty to forward
it if the ship is detained follow from Article 1 HC XI.[162] In view of the practice of the two
World Wars and of modern military manuals, the continuing validity of HC XI is open to
severe doubt. Still, for practical reasons its provisions should be maintained.[163]

The following objects shall not be confiscated: 1031
— objects belonging to the passengers or crew of a captured ship and intended for
  their personal use;
— material exclusively intended for the treatment of the wounded and sick, the
  prevention of disease, or religious purposes, provided that the transport of such
  materiel has been approved by the capturing party (Article 35 GC I; Article 38
  GC II);
— instruments and other material belonging to relief societies;
— cultural property;
— postal correspondence of the national Prisoner of War Information Bureaux
  (Article 122 GC III) and the Central Prisoners of War Information Agency
  (Article 123 GC III);
— postal consignments and relief shipments destined for prisoners of war and civilian internees as well as postal consignments dispatched by these persons;
— relief shipments intended for the population of occupied territory, provided
  that the conditions attached by the capturing party to the conveyance of such
  shipments are observed (Article 59 GC IV); and
— relief shipments intended for the population of any territory under the control of
  a party to the conflict other than occupied territory (Article 70 AP I).

1. *Personal effects.* According to customary international law, personal effects of the passengers and crew of captured vessels are not liable to seizure. Such personal effects are
objects, including money, of the type usually taken on a voyage. Other objects or large
amounts of money that do not serve personal needs may be seized.

2. *Medical and religious equipment.* Equipment intended exclusively for the treatment
of wounded and sick, for the prevention of disease, or for religious purposes are exempt
from seizure if their shipment has been approved by the belligerents. It should be noted
that such equipment is regularly shipped on ships specially chartered for that purpose.[164]
If their voyage has been approved by the belligerents then their cargo has the same protected status as the ship in question.

---

[162] Cf. I. A. Shearer, 'Commentary on the 1907 Hague Convention XI', in Ronzitti (*supra*, n. 29), 183 *et seq.*
[163] Ibid. 189.
[164] See Article 38 GC II.

WOLFF HEINTSCHEL VON HEINEGG

3. *Equipment of relief societies.* Instruments and other equipment of recognized relief societies are also exempt from capture. Otherwise such societies would be unable to fulfil their tasks.

4. *Cultural property.* The specially protected status of cultural property follows from CultPropConv and Article 53 AP I.[165]

5. *Postal correspondence* of the national Prisoner of War Information Bureaux and the Central Prisoners of War Information Agency are specially protected under Articles 122 and 123 GC III. Such postal correspondence continues to be exempt from capture even if it contains goods covered by a belligerent's contraband list. It is irrelevant whether the sender is a relative, a third person, or an organization.

6. *Relief shipments intended for the population of occupied territory or intended for the population of any territory under the control of a party to the conflict other than occupied territory.* The exemption from capture of relief shipments intended for the population of occupied territory follows from Article 59 GC IV. As regards relief shipments intended for the population of any territory under the control of a party to the conflict other than occupied territory, their protected status follows from Article 70 AP I. The AP I contains no provisions on contraband. However, in view of its applicability to acts of naval warfare affecting the civilian population on land, such relief shipments may neither be declared contraband nor seized.[166]

c. *Crews and passengers of enemy merchant ships*

1032
> The captains, officers, and crews of enemy merchant ships, if they are nationals of the enemy state, become prisoners of war (Article 4 A, No. 5, GC III) unless they promise in writing not to undertake, while hostilities last, any service connected with the armed conflict (Article 6 HC XI). If they prove that they are nationals of a neutral state, they do not become prisoners of war (Article 5 HC XI). The provisions on releasing crew members do not apply if the ship has been engaging in any activity bringing it within the definition of a military objective.

In principle, members of crews, including masters, pilots, and apprentices of a merchant navy, according to Article 4 A, No. 5, GC III, become prisoners of war if they fall into the power of the enemy. Article 4 A, No. 5, GC III, however, prevents such persons from becoming prisoners of war if they would 'benefit by more favourable treatment under any other provisions of international law'. This is a clear reference to Article 6 HC XI.[167] Since release of those persons on the high seas will in most cases not be feasible they will normally be released in the port to which their vessel has been diverted or taken. It may, however, be doubted whether Article 6 HC XI can still be considered as according with the realities of modern armed conflicts. Hence, this provision will prevail over Article 4 A, No. 5, GC III only if reciprocity is guaranteed. In any event, release must in fact result in 'more favourable treatment'.

[165] See the commentary in Chapter 9.
[166] Bothe, 'Commentary on the 1977 Geneva Protocol I', in Ronzitti *(supra,* n. 29), 764 *et seq.*
[167] Cf. Shearer *(supra,* n. 29), 187.

WOLFF HEINTSCHEL VON HEINEGG

If, however, a merchant vessel has been engaged in acts rendering it a legitimate military objective, those members of the crew responsible for such acts may be considered to have directly taken part in the hostilities. Hence, while maintaining the status of prisoner of war they may be subjected to criminal prosecution under the domestic law of the capturing state.

> Passengers of enemy merchant ships shall, in general, be released. Passengers who   1033
> have taken part in hostilities or are travelling to join the enemy armed forces may
> be detained. They become prisoners of war if they belong to one of the categories
> enumerated in Article 4 of the Third Geneva Convention. Should any doubt arise as
> to whether they belong to any of these categories, they enjoy the protection of pris-
> oners of war until such time as their status has been determined by the competent
> tribunal (Article 5 GC III). Passengers who are members of enemy armed forces
> shall become prisoners of war.

Passengers on board enemy merchant vessels may only be made prisoners of war if they meet the conditions in Article 4 A GC III. This is the case if they are members of the enemy's armed forces.[168] If they belong to none of the categories enumerated in that provision they must, in principle, be released. The practical relevance of this rule is of minor interest since passengers of enemy nationality may be interned after they have been taken to an enemy port.[169]

3. Protected Enemy Vessels (Except Hospital Ships and Ships Under Similar Protection)

> The following enemy ships enjoying special protection may neither be attacked nor   1034
> seized:
> — vessels carrying material intended exclusively for the treatment of wounded
>   and sick or for the prevention of disease, provided that the particulars regard-
>   ing the consignment have been approved (Article 38 GC II);
> — vessels carrying relief goods for the civilian population of an occupied territory,
>   provided that the conditions connected with the transport are fulfilled (Article
>   23 GC IV);
> — vessels that, with the consent of the belligerent parties, are carrying relief con-
>   signments for the civilian population of territory under the control of a party to
>   the conflict other than occupied territory (Article 70 AP I);
> — vessels used exclusively for fishing along the coast or small boats employed in
>   local trade (Article 3 HC XI);
> — vessels charged with religious, non-military scientific, or philanthropic mis-
>   sions (Article 4 HC XI);
> — vessels engaged exclusively in the transfer of cultural property (Article 14
>   CultPropConv);
> — vessels used exclusively for the transport of parlementaires or exchanging pris-
>   oners of war (cartel ships);
> — vessels furnished with an acknowledged letter of safe conduct, provided that
>   they observe the restrictions imposed on them; and
> — without prejudice to the right of capture, passenger ships on the high seas used
>   exclusively for the transport of civilians while engaged in such transport.
>
> The right to stop and search such ships remains unaffected.

[168] Article 4 A, No. 1, GC III.
[169] Cf., *inter alia*, O'Connell (*supra*, n. 12), Vol. II, 1117.

WOLFF HEINTSCHEL VON HEINEGG

1. *Transport of certain material and goods.* A precondition for the special protection accorded to the first three categories of vessels enumerated in Section 1034 is that the material and goods they carry must exclusively serve humanitarian purposes. However, the particulars regarding their voyage must either be notified to and approved by the enemy or there must be an agreement to this effect.[170]

2. *Coastal fishing vessels and small boats engaged in local trade.* The exemption from capture of such vessels and boats, including their appliances, rigging, tackle, and cargo,[171] was codified in Article 3 HC XI. According to customary international law they are exempt not only from capture but also from attack.[172] High seas fishing vessels are not protected by this provision.[173] The object and purpose of exemption is to guarantee sufficient supply of fish for the population.[174] This does not, however, mean that the activities of coastal fishing boats have to be limited to the enemy's territorial sea. Fishing may also take place off the coasts of a third state.[175] As regards small boats engaged in local trade, it is widely agreed that it is not the boats' size but the extent of the economic factors involved, that is the trade, which determines their right to protection.[176] Hence, vessels engaged in general coastal trade are not exempt from attack and capture.[177]

3. *Vessels charged with religious, scientific, or philanthropic missions.* According to Article 4 HC XI and customary law, these are likewise exempt from capture and attack.[178] In contrast to the wording of Article 4 HC XI, today vessels charged with scientific missions

---

[170] See Article 38 GC II; Article 23 GC IV; Articles 69 and 70 AP I; *San Remo Manual*, paras. 47(c)(ii) and 136(c)(ii). With regard to the famous case of the Japanese ship *Awa Maru*, see the references in M. Whiteman, *Digest of International Law* 10 (Washington, DC: US Government Printing Office, 1962), 628 *et seq.*; Mallison (*supra*, n. 102), 126. In the case of relief shipments for the civilian population according to Article 70 AP I the adversary is not free to deny approval. See Bothe, in Bothe/Partsch/Solf (*supra*, n. 91), 434 *et seq.*

[171] Cf. O'Connell (*supra*, n. 12), Vol. II, 1122 *et seq.*

[172] For the famous case of the *Paquete Habana*, see I. v. Münch, II *Wörterbuch des Völkerrechts* (*supra*, n. 142), 736 *et seq.* For state practice during the World Wars, see H. Lauterpacht (*supra*, n. 123), 478; C. Rousseau, *Le droit des Conflits Armés* (Paris: Pedone, 1983), 291. With regard to the Korean conflict, see the references in Cagle/Manson, *Sea War in Korea* (Tiptree/Essex: Barbarossa Books, 1957), 296 *et seq.*; Mallison (*supra*, n. 102), 127. During the Vietnam conflict the US Navy respected Vietnamese coastal fishing boats although Vietnam was not bound by HC XI. The US attitude only changed after those boats had been abused for the transport of ammunition and so on. Still, naval commanders were obliged to verify such abuse before taking measures. See D. P. O'Connell, *The Influence of Law on Sea Power* (Manchester and New York: Manchester University Press, 1975), 177. For the general protection of coastal fishing boats, see also *NWP 1–14M*, para. 8.6.3; *Canadian Manual* (*supra*, n. 27), para. 828(1g); *San Remo Manual*, paras. 47, lit. g, and 136, lit. f; Colombos (*supra*, n. 12), paras. 656, 658; Shearer (*supra*, n. 29), 185 *et seq.*; Tucker (*supra*, n. 76), 96.

[173] Cf. Shearer (*supra*, n. 29), 186; H. Lauterpacht (*supra*, n. 123), 477; Colombos, para. 657.

[174] At the 1907 Hague Conference the Fourth Committee gave the following explanation in its report: 'La raison d'être de cette exemption est, et a toujours été, une raison d'humanité. Le régime de faveur est fait non pas à l'industrie de la pêche, mats aux pauvres gens qui s'y adonnent; il n'a pas pour but de protéger un commerce maritime particulier, plus qu'un autre, mais seulement d'éviter de causer à des individus pauvres, spécialement dignes d'interet, un dommage sans utilité pour le belligérant.'

[175] Cf. Colombos, para. 657; E. Castrén, *The Present Law of War and Neutrality* (Helsinki: Suomalaisen Kirjallisuuden Seuran Kirjapainon Oy, 1954), 339.

[176] Colombos, para. 658; Shearer, *Commentary*, 186 *et seq.*; J. Stone, *Legal Controls of International Conflict* (London: Stevens, 1954), 586; Castrén, 340 *et seq.* For the opposing view, see H. Lauterpacht (*supra*, n. 123), 478, who regards the boats' size as relevant. Rousseau (*supra*, n. 172), 292, merely states: 'Quant à la notion de petite navigation locale, c'est une question d'espèce à déterminer dans chaque cas.'

[177] See references given by Whiteman (*supra*, n. 170), Vol. 10, 642 *et seq.*

[178] *NWP 1–14M*, para. 8.6.3; *Canadian Manual* (*supra*, n. 27), para. 828(1f); *San Remo Manual*, paras. 47(f) and 136(e); Shearer, *Commentary*, 189 *et seq.*

are specially protected only if those missions do not serve military purposes.[179] It will not always be easy to distinguish between military and non-military scientific research. Hence, in practice, such vessels should commence their voyage only after notifying and obtaining approval from the adversary.[180] Vessels charged with philanthropic missions will usually already be protected by GC II and AP I or as one of the other categories enumerated in the present section. Today, this category is, therefore, of minor practical relevance.[181] This also holds true for vessels on religious missions. Formerly, missionary vessels would have fallen into that category.[182] Vessels transporting pilgrims will be classified as passenger ships.

4. *Transfer of cultural property.* Vessels engaged in this task are protected in accordance with Articles 12, 13, and 14 CultPropConv.[183] This presupposes that the transfer has been approved by the adversary in advance. In the absence of such approval, vessels may carry the protective emblem only if the transfer of cultural property takes place within the territory of one single state.

5. *Cartel vessels and vessels granted safe conduct.* Cartel vessels are usually designated for and engaged in the exchange of prisoners of war, or in the transport of parlementaires and of certain messages. As the term 'cartel' implies, agreement between the parties to the conflict is a precondition for their special protection. In the majority of cases they are then granted safe conduct. Hence, the difference between cartel vessels and vessels granted safe conduct is in the special mission for which those ships are designated.[184] The document granting safe conduct may always be examined. In case of falsification the special protection ceases, according to Section 1035.

6. *Passenger vessels.* According to Section 1004, these are merchant vessels. Hence, they are subject to visit, search, and capture. However, if such vessels are exclusively engaged in carrying civilian passengers a warship will only in rare cases be in a position to take passengers to a place of safety. They may, therefore, neither be attacked nor destroyed as prize in accordance with Section 1026 unless they lose their protected status because not innocently employed in their normal role.[185]

7. *Visit and search.* It is made clear in the last sentence of Section 1034 that the vessels enumerated are only exempt from attack and capture. Outside of neutral waters they may therefore be visited and searched any time. This follows from the restricted scope of protection. Especially, belligerents must be able to verify whether the vessels concerned are innocently employed in their normal role and that they comply with the conditions for exemption. Belligerents should, however, refrain from exercising the right of visit and

---

[179] *NWP 1–14M*, para. 8.6.3; *San Remo Manual*, paras. 47(f) and 136(e).

[180] Cf. Mallison (*supra*, n. 102), 128; Tucker (*supra*, n. 76), 97.

[181] As regards state practice during World War I, see Rousseau (*supra*, n. 172), 292 *et seq.*; H. Lauterpacht (*supra*, n. 123) 476; Tucker, 96 *et seq.*

[182] With regard to the Prussian missionary ship *Palme* captured during the Franco-Prussian War of 1870/71, see references in H. Lauterpacht, 476 n. 2; Rousseau, 292.

[183] Cf. *San Remo Manual*, paras. 47(d) and 136(d).

[184] Cf. Colombos, para. 660; H. Lauterpacht, 542; Tucker, 97 *et seq.*; Castrén, 339; *NWP 1–14M*, para. 8.6.3; *Canadian Manual*, para. 828(1c); *San Remo Manual*, paras. 47(c) and 136(c).

[185] Besides the well-known but still disputed case of the *Lusitania*, the case of the *Athenia* is worth mentioning. The Nuremberg Tribunal characterized the sinking of the unarmed *Athenia* by the German submarine *U30* on 3 September 1939 as a war crime; see *NWP 1–14M*, para. 8.6.3(6); *San Remo Manual*, para. 47(e).

WOLFF HEINTSCHEL VON HEINEGG

search if it is provided for otherwise that such vessels are not abused (e.g. by the presence of neutral observers on board).

1035   **The special protection ends if such vessels do not comply with conditions lawfully imposed upon them, if they abuse their mission, or engage in any other activity bringing them within the definition of a military objective.**

According to Article 3 HC XI, the vessels protected 'cease to be exempt as soon as they take any part whatever in hostilities'. Under customary international law the same applies to the other vessels enumerated in Section 1034.[186] They are all protected because of the special functions they serve. Hence, as soon as they are no longer innocently employed in their normal role, or if they are in some other way employed for purposes unrelated with their original function, they may be subject to measures of naval warfare. This is also the case if they do not submit to identification and inspection or to orders to stop or move out of the way. After loss of exemption they may be captured and confiscated. Moreover, if they make a direct contribution to military action, for example by participating in hostilities, they may be attacked on sight and sunk, provided that destruction offers a definite military advantage. In any event, the abuse must be clearly established before attack. Passenger vessels engaged in carrying civilian passengers as well as members of the enemy armed forces, contraband, or war material lose exemption and may be captured. Destruction is permissible only if the safety of passengers, crews, and ship's papers is ensured. If that is impossible the ship must be diverted to an appropriate port. The special protection of passenger vessels is, however, restricted to those cases in which they are carrying civilian passengers. In other cases they may be attacked and sunk if they meet the criteria laid down in the definition of military objectives.

4. Protected Enemy Aircraft (Except Medical Aircraft)

1036   **The provisions of Sections 1034 and 1035 are also relevant for enemy aircraft serving the enumerated purposes and operating exclusively in established corridors. Such aircraft may be requested to put down on land or water to be searched.**

1. *General.* The special status of the vessels listed in Section 1034 results from the functions they serve. Aircraft serving the same functions are similarly exempted from attack and capture. In view of the manifold difficulties involved in the identification of aircraft they are, however, obliged to operate exclusively in established corridors. In order to verify whether such aircraft are innocently employed in their normal role and whether they comply with conditions legitimately imposed upon them they may be requested to put down on land or water for the purpose of inspection.[187] If it is clearly established that exempt aircraft do not comply with the conditions imposed upon them or that they are not innocently employed in their normal role, they lose their special status and may be captured. Also, if they commit acts rendering them legitimate military objectives they may be attacked.

---

[186] See, *inter alia*, *San Remo Manual*, para. 48: 'Vessels listed in Section 47 are exempt from attack only if they: (a) are innocently employed in their normal role; (b) submit to identification and inspection when required; and (c) do not intentionally hamper the movement of combatants and obey orders to stop or move out of the way when required.' A rule to the same effect (para. 137) applies to vessels exempt from capture.

[187] See also *San Remo Manual*, paras. 53 *et seq.*

WOLFF HEINTSCHEL VON HEINEGG

2. *Civil airliners.* These are civil aircraft, clearly marked, and engaged in carrying civilian passengers in scheduled or non-scheduled services along air traffic routes.[188] Civil airliners are exempt from attack only if they are innocently employed in their normal role, do not intentionally hamper the movements of combatants, and operate exclusively along air traffic routes. The fact that a clearly identifiable civil airliner does not operate within a designated corridor does not in itself justify an attack. It may, however, be intercepted and forced to land. The prohibition of destruction does not apply to civil airliners on the ground, unless there is good reason to believe that there are civilian passengers on board. They are even then liable to capture, and may be intercepted and forced to land. As regards crews and passengers Sections 1032 and 1033 apply. Identification is one of the major problems involved in the implementation of the rules protecting civil airliners. The *Vincennes* incident during the Gulf War between Iran and Iraq made that evident. Even the use of transponders identifying an aircraft as a civil airliner does not guarantee absolute protection. It is therefore crucial that the parties to the conflict promulgate and adhere to safe procedures for identifying and intercepting civil aircraft. The Recommendations issued by the ICAO can in this regard prove helpful.[189] According to the *San Remo Manual* 'civil aircraft should file the required flight plan with the cognizant Air Traffic Service, complete with information as to registration, destination, passengers, cargo, emergency communication channels, identification codes and modes, updates en route, and carry certificates as to registration, airworthiness, passengers and cargo. They should not deviate from a designated Air Traffic Service Route or flight plan without Air Traffic Control clearance unless unforeseen conditions arise, for example, safety or distress, in which case, appropriate notification should be made immediately.'[190] Moreover, 'belligerents and neutrals concerned, and authorities providing air traffic services, should establish procedures whereby commanders of warships and military aircraft are continuously aware of designated routes assigned and flight plans filed by civil aircraft in the area of military operations, including information on communication channels, identification modes and codes, destination, passengers, and cargo'.[191]

5. Other Protected Objects

> Submarine cables and pipelines connecting occupied territory with neutral territory shall not be seized or destroyed. Submarine cables and pipelines connecting different parts of the territory of one party to the conflict, or connecting the territories of parties to the conflict and neutrals, may be interrupted within the law of naval warfare in case of military necessity.

1037

Submarine cables were internationally protected by the Convention on the Protection of Submarine Cables of 14 March 1884.[192] Today, the laying of submarine cables and pipelines, according to Article 2 HSC 1958 and Article 87, para. 1, lit. c, UNCLOS, is one of the freedoms of the high seas generally recognized as customary law. Hence, submarine cables and pipelines connecting neutral states may not be interfered with in naval armed conflict. As regards the laws of armed conflict at sea, there is no express prohibition on

---

[188] This definition is taken from para. 13(m), *San Remo Manual.*
[189] Printed in *AJIL* (1989), 335.
[190] *San Remo Manual,* para. 129.
[191] *San Remo Manual,* para. 130.
[192] Text in <http://www.austlii.edu.au/au/other/dfat/treaties/1901/1.html>.

WOLFF HEINTSCHEL VON HEINEGG

the destruction of submarine cables and pipelines.[193] The 1884 Convention, in Article XV, expressly stated that its stipulations did not restrict the freedom of action of belligerents. Therefore, in case of military necessity submarine cables connecting enemy territory with neutral territory may be cut outside of neutral territorial waters.[194] This does not mean, as mentioned above, that considerations of military necessity alone justify such action.

6. Targets on Land

1038
The following rules apply to targets on land subject to the provisions on the protection of the civilian population and the general principles of the law of naval warfare:
  a) The bombardment of defended localities, ports, and buildings situated on hostile coasts is permitted.
  b) The mining of ports and coastal installations alone does not justify bombardment (Article 1 HC IX).
  c) Military objectives located within undefended localities or ports may be bombarded if there are no other means available to destroy these objectives and when the local authorities have not complied with a summons within a reasonable period of time (Article 2 HC IX). The absence of such summons may be justified by urgent military reasons. If there is a possibility that these objectives could be destroyed by landing forces, bombardment shall not be permissible.

1. *The relevance of the 1907 Hague Convention IX.*[195] In view of the progressive development and the reaffirmation of international humanitarian law by AP I, the provisions of HC IX concerning bombardment by naval forces in time of war have become largely obsolete. The obligations in the latter can easily be derived from the provisions of Part IV, Section I of AP I.[196] It should be kept in mind, however, that not all states are bound by the Protocol. Then the question arises whether the provisions of the HC IX constitute customary international law. Even if that question is answered in the affirmative,[197] it remains unsettled how to deal with aircraft launched from warships attacking targets on land. According to Article XLI HRAW 1923 'aircraft on board vessels of war, including aircraft-carriers, shall be regarded as part of such vessels'. This could imply that the rules applicable to warships engaged in naval bombardment also apply to aircraft launched from them. Then, however, such aircraft would be allowed to attack military objectives in non-defended localities.[198] While Article 59, para. 1, AP I prohibits attacks of such localities 'by any means whatsoever', that is including aircraft, that would not be prohibited under Articles 1 and 2 of HC IX. *Castrén* states that HC IX 'must probably be understood to concern warships only, and not aircraft even when collaborating with

---

[193] According to Article 54 HagueReg, submarine cables connecting occupied territories with neutral territories are protected. The scope of this provision is, however, restricted to land warfare.
[194] Lagoni, 'Cables, Submarine', *Encyclopedia of Public International Law I* (Amsterdam: Elsevier, 1992), 516–9.
[195] Cf. Robertson, in Ronzitti (*supra*, n. 29), 161 *et seq.*
[196] Cf. Ipsen, 'Die "offene Stadt" und die Schutzzonen des Genfer Rechts', in Fleck (ed.), *Beiträge zur Weiterentwicklung des humanitären Völkerrechts für bewaffnete Konflikte* (Hamburg: Hanseatischer Gildenverlag, 1973), 149–210.
[197] See, *inter alia*, E. Spetzler, *Luftkrieg und Menschlichkeit* (Göttingen: Musterschmidt, 1956) at 127 *et seq.*
[198] This is the position taken by J. M. Spaight, *Air Power and War Rights*, 3rd edn (London: Longmans, 1947) at 221 *et seq.* For an early criticism, see M. W. Royse, *Aerial Bombardment* (New York: Hoover, 1928) at 162 *et seq.*

WOLFF HEINTSCHEL VON HEINEGG

them'.[199] If, however, Article XLI HRAW 1923 is a correct statement of customary law warships and military aircraft launched from warships would be bound by the same rules. Apart from the wording of the provisions mentioned a further argument in favour of that view is the ability of modern aircraft to discriminate and to conduct surgical strikes by means of high precision ammunition. Still, it should not be left out of consideration that for a locality to be entitled to protection against attacks Article 59, para. 2, AP I, and the probably corresponding rule of customary law, provides that four conditions must be met. Accordingly, even if fixed military installations or establishments remain in the respective port or town this would not justify an attack 'by any means whatsoever' if no hostile use is made of them. Then, regardless of the binding force of AP I, an attack would probably be contrary to the law of armed conflict because the object in question would not make an effective contribution to military action and its neutralization would not offer a definite military advantage. Be that as it may. A clarification of the rules applicable to naval bombardment including the use of aircraft and missiles launched from warships should be taken into consideration.

2. *Specific obligations.* The introductory sentence clarifies that, when attacking targets on land, naval forces are obliged to ensure the protection of the civilian population as laid down in AP I.[200] Accordingly, 'without prejudice to the provisions of the Hague Convention for the Protection of Cultural Property in Event of Armed Conflict of 14 May 1954...it is prohibited...to commit any acts of hostility directed against historic monuments, works of art or places of worship'.[201] Moreover, when attacking land targets, naval forces shall take care 'to protect the natural environment against widespread, long-term, and severe damage'.[202] 'Works or installations containing dangerous forces, namely dams, dykes and nuclear electrical generating stations, shall not be made the object of attack, even where these objects are military objectives, if such attack may cause the release of dangerous forces and consequent severe losses among the civilian population.'[203] Also worth mentioning are the provisions of Article 59 (non-defended localities) and of Article 60 (demilitarized zones) AP I.[204]

III. Special Provisions Concerning Methods of Naval Warfare

1. Mine Warfare

Introductory remarks

1. *Hague Convention VIII as the basis for legal evaluation of mine warfare at sea.* The extensive use of mines during the Russo-Japanese War (1904–1905) and the damage caused to innocent shipping even after the end of hostilities led to the inclusion of naval mines in the agenda of the Second Hague Peace Conference.[205] Even by HC VIII, which resulted from the Conference's deliberations, was considered a meagre compromise between the

---

[199] Castrén (*supra*, n. 175), at 402.
[200] Other conventions of relevance are: the GasProt, ENMOD, and Protocols I to III of the Inhumane WeaponsConv.
[201] For further details, see Article 53 AP I.
[202] Article 55, para. 1, AP I.
[203] Ibid.
[204] As regards the so-called 'hunger blockade' and relief shipments for the civilian population, see para. 5 of the commentary on Section 1051.
[205] See Verzijl, *International Law in Historical Perspective.* Vol. IX (Sijthoff, 1978), 297.

interests of the great sea powers on one hand, and of states with only small naval forces on the other.[206] Great Britain had urged the prohibition of automatic contact mines in sea areas beyond the belligerents' territorial seas.[207] The reason was that it considered their use in the high seas as prejudicial to its naval supremacy. The majority of states represented at the Hague, however, were unwilling to refrain from the use of this most effective means of naval warfare.[208]

Hence, HC VIII contains neither a general prohibition nor a specific geographical limitation of the use of automatic contact mines. Especially, it lacks a rule on mining of international straits which are overlapped by the territorial seas of the belligerents. Despite several proposals on the prohibition of mining such straits submitted by the Netherlands,[209] the majority held that questions related to straits were not covered by the mandates of either the Committee or of the Conference.[210] The existing treaty regimes for certain straits was not to be jeopardized by general rules on mining. Hence, the Netherlands' proposals were rejected.[211] The only provision referring to the area of mine-laying is Article 2, which prohibits the laying of automatic contact mines 'off the coast

[206] Hence, in the Preamble, the contracting parties deplored that 'the existing state of affairs makes it impossible to forbid the employment of automatic submarine contact mines'. They also expressed their hope that, in the future, it would be possible 'to formulate rules on the subject which shall ensure to the interests involved all the guarantees desirable'.

[207] Article 4 of the British proposal which served as a basis for discussion, (Annex 9) provided: '*Les belligérants ne pourront se servir de mines sous-marines automatiques de contact que dans leurs eaux territoriales ou celles de leurs ennemis.*'

[208] Especially, the US and Germany were in favour of an explicit rule on the use of mines in the high seas. Hence, Germany proposed the following amendment to Article 4 of the British proposal: 'La pose des mines automatiques de contact sera aussi permise sur le théâtre de la guerre; sera considéré comme théâtre de la guerre l'espace de mer sur lequel se fait ou vient de se faire une opération de guerre ou sur lequel une pareille opération pourra avoir lieu par suite de la présence ou de l'approche des forces armées des deux belligérants.' At first, the *Comité d'Examen*, in Article 2 of its draft, had been in favour of the British proposal. After the US delegate Sperry had made clear the US standpoint, the Third Committee dispensed with any spatial limitation of the use of mines. In its report of 9 October 1907, the Third Committee explained this as follows: 'Cette solution n'a pas obtenu, devant la Commission, la majorité absolue des suffrages. L'alinéa 2 de l'article 4, qui établissait la différence mentionnée entre 'attaque et la defense, fut même rejeté, n'ayant obtenu que 10 voix contre 12 et 10 abstentions.'

[209] The proposals by the Netherlands (Annex 12 and 22) provided: 'En tous cas les détroits qui unissent deux mers libres ne peuvent pas être barrés.' 'Dans aucun cas la communication entre deux mers libres ne peut être barrée entièrement et le passage ne sera permis qu'aux conditions qui seront indiquées par les autorités compétentes.'

[210] Thus, the Third Committee in its report to the plenary stated: 'Après discussion, il fut jugé préférable de ne rien ajouter au texte du Règlement, mais de modifier le passage du Rapport qui parle de la résolution prise sur cette question par le Comité d'Examen; on établirait dans le Rapport que les détroits sont restés en dehors des délibérations de la présente Conférence et, tout en réservant expressément les déclarations faites au sein du Comité par les Délégations des Etats-Unis d'Amérique, du Japon, de la Russie et de la Turquie, on indiquerait la conviction de voir appliquer sur les mines dont on pourrait se servir dans les détroits les conditions techniques adoptées par le présent Règlement.'

[211] In the report of the Comité d'Examen these statements are summarized as follows: '... la Délégation du Japon...qui, tout en déclarant qu'il n'avait pas d'objection, si la règle s'appliquait seulement aux pays neutres, avait fait observer...que' amendement néerlandais...lui paraissait pouvoir s'adapter peut-être aux conditions géographiques des Etats continentaux, mais pas toujours à celles des Puissances insulaires. En raison de la configuration particulière du Japon...détroits qui sont partie intégrante de son territoire, mais qui tomberaient néanmoins sous le coup de la définition inscrite dans le dit amendement, la Délégation Japonaise ne pourrait adhérer à cette disposition.... le Contre-Admiral Sperry déclara, au nom de la Délégation des Etats-Unis d'Amérique, que 'prenant en considération le grand nombre d'îles qui composent le groupe des Philippines, et l'incertitude des résultats que pourrait avoir la stipulation en question, envisageant en outre les stipulations de traités comprises dans l'alinéa ajouté, il ne pourrait pas prendre part à la

and ports of the enemy, with the sole object of intercepting commercial shipping'.[212] The material scope of HC VIII is limited to automatic submarine contact mines (and torpedoes).[213] To this effect the Convention differentiates between anchored and unanchored mines. According to Article 1, para. 1, the latter may not be laid 'except when they are so constructed as to become harmless one hour after the person who laid them ceases to control them'. The one-hour limit is designed to enable warships to escape pursuing enemy units by planting mines.[214] According to Article 1, para. 2, anchored mines must 'become harmless as soon as they have broken loose from their moorings'. Furthermore, the belligerents must take 'every possible precaution...for the security of peaceful', that is neutral,[215] shipping (Article 3, para. 1). Finally, they should 'undertake to do their utmost to render these mines harmless within a limited time, and, should they cease to be under surveillance, to notify the danger zones as soon as military exigencies permit, by a notice addressed to ship owners, which must also be communicated to the Governments through the diplomatic channel' (Article 3, para. 2).

In view of the unrestricted mine warfare of the two World Wars and of the technical development of naval mines,[216] the continued legal relevance of HC VIII has become a matter of dispute.[217] Indeed, it is open to doubt whether its provisions are applicable to bottom mines, modern anchored mines,[218] or to remote-controlled minefields activated by means of, for example, VLF transmissions. These sophisticated and highly accurate mines are not covered by the wording of the Convention because they react to magnetic and acoustic signals or to changes in water pressure, not to mere physical contact.[219]

---

discussion comme, à son avis, la matière sort des limites de ses instructions'.... la Délégation Ottomane... exposa que: 'La Délégation Impériale Ottomane croit de son devoir de déclarer qu'étant donné la situation exceptionnelle créé par les traités en vigueur aux détroits des Dardanelles et du Bosphore, détroits qui sont partie intégrante du territoire, le Gouvernement Impérial ne saurait, d'aucune façon, prendre un engagement quelconque tendant à limiter les moyens de défense qu'il pourrait juger nécessaire d'employer pour ces détroits, en cas de guerre ou dans le but de faire respecter sa neutralité'.... La Délégation de Russie estime que le régime de certains détroits étant réglé par des traités spéciaux, basés sur des considérations politiques, les stipulations concernant ces détroits ne peuvent faire l'objet d'une discussion. Quant à créer un régime special pour une partie des détroits en exceptant les autres, ce procédé lui paraîtrait inconséquent et très dangereux. La diversité du régime qui en résulterait tant pour les neutres que pour les belligérants, serait inévitablement une nouvelle source de conflits entre eux.'

[212] With regard to the difficulties in establishing the subjective element see Dinstein (*supra*, n. 157), at 45. Stone (*supra*, n. 176), 583 *et seq.* states: 'The escape from this prohibition provided by the reference to the *object* of the operation largely frustrated it from the first Article'.

[213] The use of torpedoes is regulated by Article 1, para. 3. Originally, the Conference's agenda was restricted to torpedoes. 'Torpedo' used to be the general designation that also covered mines. However, in view of the existence of self-propelling destructive devices, as early as 1907 the Conference agreed on the notion of 'mines'.

[214] See Dinstein, at 44; J. S. Cowie, *Mines, Minelayers and Minelaying* (OUP, 1949), 170.

[215] See Dinstein, ibid.; Cowie, 175.

[216] See H. S. Levie, *Mine Warfare at Sea* (Nijhoff, 1992), 97 *et seq.* With regard to the current technological state, see *Jane's Underwater Warfare Systems*, <http://torrentz.eu/48402b17e5b2116fef155ddaef89bc142e28 4a28>.

[217] Especially, R. R. Baxter, 'Treaties and Custom' (1970 I) 129 *RdC* 25–104, at 97, considers HC VIII to have become obsolete by desuetude. See also Stone (*supra*, n. 176), 584 *et seq.*

[218] Since modern anchored mines may be employed at greater depths than bottom mines, they are a highly effective means of naval warfare.

[219] According to a minority opinion, Hague Convention VIII may be applied to modern mines by analogy. See E. Rauch (*supra*, n. 89), 116. However, according to the view taken here, it is not possible to apply an international treaty by way of analogy to subjects not expressly regulated therein.

WOLFF HEINTSCHEL VON HEINEGG

However, it should not be overlooked that the old automatic contact mine is still used by most of the world's navies.[220] During armed conflicts since 1945, the belligerents only in rare cases employed modern sophisticated mines.[221] Hence, apart from the problem of whether HC VIII is of significance for modern mines, it seems to be the correct view that HC VIII *qua* customary law remains a valid legal yardstick for the use of automatic contact mines.[222]

HC VIII has, therefore, acquired the status of customary international law governing the use of automatic contact mines. However, its provisions are not applicable as such to other modern mines. These are, it is submitted, governed by rules and principles of customary international law, which also provide norms regulating the area where naval mines—whether antiquated or sophisticated—may be employed. These principles are elaborated in Sections 1040 and 1043.

2. *'Mines'.* International law still lacks a generally agreed definition of naval mines. The Hague Conference at first used the term 'torpedo' to include mines. In the course of the deliberations, mines were distinguished from torpedoes.[223] Still, the delegates did not agree on a definition. It merely follows from the wording that HC VIII is applicable to 'submarine automatic contact mines', which explode on physical contact. Hence, its provisions on mining are applicable to contact mines as well as to more modern mines. Thus, the difficulties involved with regard to the applicability of HC VIII to modern mines are avoided. For a better understanding it is, however, useful to refer to NATO practice according to which naval mines are defined as 'an explosive device laid in the water, on the seabed or in the subsoil thereof, with the intention of damaging or sinking ships or of deterring shipping from entering an area'.[224]

Since that definition is also employed in Article 2 of the Swedish proposal for amending the 1980 Inhumane WeaponsConv,[225] it can be taken as a basis for the present Handbook. Hence, the following means of naval warfare are not, or not exclusively, covered by the provisions on mining:

— anti-aircraft systems launched from submarines, such as the French *SM Polyphem*;
— devices attached to the bottom of ships or to harbour installations by personnel operating underwater;[226] and
— devices like the 'encapsulated torpedo' (CAPTOR) that are usually designated as mines[227] but are in fact torpedoes.

3. *Special treaty provisions.* Before elaborating the rules and principles of international law governing modern conventional mines, brief reference to two important treaties is

---

[220] Allegedly, the former Soviet Union still disposes of a vast number of automatic contact mines of the World War II type. Other states, such as Iraq, were supplied with these mines.

[221] See Levie (*supra*, n. 216), 135 *et seq.*

[222] For example, during the Iraq–Kuwait conflict, the US expressly referred to Hague Convention VIII. See US Dept. of Defense, *Conduct of the Persian Gulf War: Final Report to Congress (1992)*, Appendix O. With regard to the customary status of the Convention, see also Levie (*supra*, n. 216), 177 *et seq.*; *NWP 1–14M*, paras. 9.2 and 9.2.3; *Canadian Manual* (*supra*, n. 27), paras. 828 *et seq.*

[223] Cf. Levie (*supra*, n. 216), 24 *et seq.*

[224] See Hegelsom (*supra*, n. 86), 27.

[225] UN Doc. A/CN.10/141 of 8 May 1990.

[226] Cf. Hegelsom, 28.

[227] See, e.g., *Jane's Underwater Warfare Systems* (*supra*, n. 216).

necessary. The use of nuclear mines is subject to the 1971 Sea-bed Treaty.[228] Although an arms control treaty, its provisions are binding not only in peacetime but also in times of armed conflict.[229] Accordingly, a belligerent may not, in sea areas beyond its own 12 nautical miles territorial sea,[230] 'emplant or emplace on the sea bed and the ocean floor and in the subsoil thereof . . . any nuclear weapons', including nuclear mines.[231] This prohibition also covers tethered[232] tactical low-yield nuclear mines used for anti-submarine purposes.[233] The contrary view taken by Professor O'Connell[234] is incompatible with the wording ('nuclear weapons') as well as with the object and purpose of the Sea-bed Treaty.[235] Article 1 Protocol II of the 1980 Inhumane WeaponsConv[236] refers *inter alia* to 'mines laid to interdict beaches'. In some cases such mines are laid in waters less than 5 metres deep. However, Protocol II does not apply to naval warfare. The scope of that Protocol is restricted to anti-personnel mines and to land warfare.[237]

4. *Minelaying in times of crisis prior to the outbreak of hostilities.* The provisions of the present section are not restricted to the employment of naval mines in times of armed conflict. Sections 1041 and 1042 deal with minelaying prior to the outbreak of an international armed conflict. This is justified by the following consideration. In view of a possible escalation of a given situation it may become necessary to secure one's territorial sea and ports in times of crisis. However, the minelaying state must respect a number of legal restrictions stricter than the rules applicable in times of armed conflict.

a. *Types of mine warfare: principles*

In laying mines the following purposes are distinguished: 1039
 — protective mining, that is in friendly territorial and internal waters;
 — defensive mining, that is in international waters for the protection of passages, ports, and their entrances; and
 — offensive mining, that is in hostile territorial and internal waters or in waters predominantly controlled by the adversary.

---

[228] Treaty on the Prohibition of the Emplacement of Nuclear Weapons and Other Weapons of Mass Destruction on the Sea bed and the Ocean Floor and in the Subsoil Thereof, London, Moscow, Washington, 11 February 1971. For the text, see (1970) *UN Juridical Yearbook* 121–4.

[229] See *NWP 1–14M*, para. 10.2.2.1.

[230] According to Article II, the 12 nautical miles limit applies even when the breadth of the territorial sea is less than 12 nautical miles.

[231] On 7 October 1969, the US delegate declared: 'The Treaty would therefore prohibit, *inter alia*, mines that were anchored to or emplaced on the sea bed.'; *Documents on Disarmament* 479 (1969). See also Thorpe, (1987) 18 *Ocean Development and International Law* 255–78, 262.

[232] Drifting or floating mines are neither 'emplanted' nor 'emplaced' in the sense of Article I. See Rauch (*supra*, n. 89), 131; A. G. Y. Thorpe, 'Mine Warfare at Sea—Some Legal Aspects of the Future' (1987) 18 *Ocean Development and International Law* 255–78, at 262.

[233] Ibid.

[234] O'Connell (*supra*, n. 172), 157.

[235] See T. A. Clingan Jr, '*Submarine Mines* in International Law', in Robertson (*supra*, n. 86), 351–61, at 354 *et seq.*; Thorpe, *loc. cit.*, 262.

[236] Convention on Prohibitions or Restrictions on the Use of Certain Conventional Weapons Which May Be Deemed to Be Excessively Injurious or to Have Indiscriminate Effects, Geneva, 10 October 1980; Protocol on Prohibitions or Restrictions on the Use of Mines, Booby Traps and Other Devices (Protocol II).

[237] See Levie (*supra*, n. 216), 138.

WOLFF HEINTSCHEL VON HEINEGG

The distinction between different types of minelaying laid down in Section 1039 is not reflective of customary international law. It does, however, reflect the practice of NATO member states.[238]

1040   **Any mode of minelaying, whether before or after the beginning of an armed conflict, shall be subject to the principles of effective surveillance, risk control, and warning (HC VIII). In particular, all feasible measures of precaution shall be observed for the safety of peaceful navigation.**

1. *Legal basis.* As stated above, the provisions of HC VIII are applicable neither as such nor by analogy to mines other than automatic contact mines. Nevertheless, there is a general consensus, in practice as well as in the literature, that the customary principles derived from Articles 1, 2, 3, and 5 of the Convention must be taken into account when laying modern naval mines.[239] The duties derived from these principles may vary according to the circumstances of each case.

2. *Legal obligations of minelaying states.*

a) Basic considerations. The provisions of Section 1040 should not be considered an exhaustive enumeration of the duties incumbent on the minelaying state. The general principles of the (maritime) *jus in bello* also apply;[240] in particular, the principle of distinction.[241] Any indiscriminate use of mines, that is that are not or cannot be directed against a military objective, is contrary to international law. Moreover, naval mines may in principle only be employed against military objectives.

b) The principle of effective surveillance. This is designed to secure the principle of warning and the duty of clearing mined areas after the cessation of hostilities. It can therefore be deduced from Articles 3 and 5 HC VIII. In particular, it implies that the minelaying belligerent is obliged carefully to record the location of minefields.[242] Otherwise, the duties on warning and mine-clearance would be rendered obsolete. Moreover, belligerents are obliged to ensure, for example by random tests, that their mines are programmed correctly and will not react to other than the anticipated stimuli.

c) Risk control. Closely related to the foregoing is the principle of risk control, which can be deduced from Articles 1 and 3 HC VIII. Risk control does not mean that the minelaying party is obliged permanently to exercise surveillance over a minefield; it is sufficient if that party is able effectively to manage the dangers which minefields

---

[238] Cf. W. Ide, 'Der Minenkampf in Nordsee und Ostsee' (1989/7) *Europäische Wehrkunde* 447 *et seq.*; R. F. Hoffmann, 'Offensive Mine Warfare: A Forgotten Strategy' (1977) 103 *USNIP* 142 *et seq.*

[239] Thus, the *NWP 1–14M*, para. 9.2, provides: 'the general principles of law embodied in the 1907 Convention continue to serve as a guide to lawful employment of naval mines'. See also *Canadian Manual* (*supra*, n. 27), paras. 836 *et seq.*; Dinstein (*supra*, n. 157), 46; Thorpe (*supra*, n. 232), 259 *et seq.*; P. J. Rowe, *Defence. The Legal Implications. Military Law and the Laws of War* (London: Brasseys, 1987), 128; Clingan (*supra*, n. 235), 353; O'Connell (*supra*, n. 172), 157.

[240] See *NWP 1–14M*, para. 9.2; Rauch (*supra*, n. 89), 130.

[241] Article 3 of the Swedish proposal provides: 'The indiscriminate use of mines is prohibited. Indiscriminate use is (a) any use of mines which is not or cannot be directed against a military objective; (b) any laying of mines which may be expected to cause incidental loss of civilian life, injury to civilians, or a combination thereof which would be excessive in relation to the concrete and direct military advantage anticipated.'

[242] *NWP 1–14M*, para. 9.2.3 (5) provides: 'The location of minefields must be carefully recorded to ensure accurate notification and to facilitate subsequent removal and/or deactivation.' See also para. 84 of the *San Remo Manual*: 'Belligerents shall record the locations where they have laid mines.' Also Article 7, para. 1 of the Swedish proposal: 'The parties to a conflict shall record all zones where they have laid mines.'

constitute for peaceful shipping. The concrete duties resulting from the principle of risk control may, therefore, vary according to the type of mine used. Controlled mines, and especially remote-controlled minefields designed for anti-submarine warfare purposes, do not generally pose much threat to peaceful surface shipping.[243] Therefore, the minelaying state will normally comply with the principle of risk control by equipping the minefield with a remote control device. It needs to be stressed that in practice remotely controlled minefields will only be laid if the control system is nearly infallible. Otherwise, the military advantage envisaged (long duration, flexibility) cannot be achieved. The control systems depending on VLF transmissions from land require a considerable amount of energy and will probably not be absolutely immune from failure.[244] Hence, additionally, the mines must be equipped with a deactivation device. If the control system breaks down the belligerent is, of course, obliged to issue an appropriate warning. If other than (remotely) controlled mines are used, anchored mines must become harmless as soon as they break loose from their moorings.[245] They must be equipped with a self-destruction or deactivation device.[246] If Article 1, para. 1, HC VIII applied to bottom mines, designed to explode upon magnetic, acoustic signatures and/or changes in water pressure, then they would have to become harmless 'one hour at most after the person who laid them ceases to control them'.[247] Customary international law, however, has not developed in that direction. Modern bottom mines are highly sophisticated weapons systems that can be programmed to react to specific types of ships or even to one single ship only if sufficient data are available.[248] Hence, these mines need not become harmless within one hour after they have reached their position on the ocean floor. Only when it is not possible to ensure by programming that the mine will be directed at military objectives alone must it be equipped with some kind of deactivation device.[249] However, if drifting or floating mines are used the dangers which they pose

---

[243] In *NWP 1–14M*, para. 9.2.1, the differences between controlled and armed mines is explained as follows: 'Armed mines are either emplaced with all safety devices withdrawn or are armed following emplacement, so as to detonate when preset parameters (if any) are satisfied. Controlled mines (including mines possessing remote control activation devices) have no destructive capability until affirmatively activated by some form of controlled arming order (whereupon they become armed mines).' See also Dinstein (*supra*, n. 157), at 46.

[244] See *Jane's Underwater Warfare Systems* (*supra*, n. 216).

[245] Article 1, para. 2, HC VIII; *NWP 1–14M*, para. 9.2.3; Article 4 of the Swedish proposal: 'It is prohibited to lay anchored mines which do not become harmless as soon as they have broken loose from their moorings.'

[246] While the mines used for the blockade of Haiphong were equipped with such devices, the mines laid by Iran in the Gulf war (1980–8) did not become harmless after they had broken loose from their moorings.

[247] Dinstein (*supra*, n. 157), at 46, seems to be in favour of a rule to that effect: 'The rule must be that the use of any mine—antiquated or sophisticated—is permissible only if they are anchored (even though the anchor may enable them to home in on a ship within a given range), and on condition that they become harmless as soon as they are disconnected from their moorings.' For the contrary view, see H. S. Levie, 'Means and Methods of Combat at Sea', 14 *Syracuse Journal of International Law and Commerce* (1988), 727–39, at 732 *et seq.*; Thorpe (*supra*, n. 232), 260 *et seq.*

[248] See *Jane's Underwater Warfare Systems* (supra, n. 216).

[249] *NWP 1–14M*, para. 9.2.3: 'Unanchored mines otherwise affixed or imbedded in the bottom must become harmless within an hour after loss of control over them.' Article 4, para. 3 of the Swedish proposal provides: 'It is prohibited to lay mines, unless an effective neutralizing mechanism is used on each mine, that is to say, a self-actuating or remotely controlled mechanism which is designed to render a mine harmless or cause it to destroy itself when it is anticipated that the mine will no longer serve the military purpose for which it was placed in position, or at the latest 2 years after such emplacement.'

WOLFF HEINTSCHEL VON HEINEGG

to peaceful shipping (sometimes overestimated)[250] mean that they still have to be made harmless within one hour.[251]

d) Warning. The duty to warn arises as soon as effective control of the risk involved is lost. The duty to issue warnings of armed or dangerous minefields is not, however, absolute. The belligerent is obligated to notify danger zones or the position of a minefield only if 'military exigencies permit'.[252] This does not mean that the belligerent may refrain from issuing effective warnings only because there is still a potential military advantage. Rather, according to the general principles of the (maritime) *jus in bello*, the military advantage anticipated must, in the circumstances ruling at the time, be definite.[253] In case of doubt, the limits of the mined areas must be notified at least roughly. Judge Schwebel in his dissenting opinion to the *Nicaragua* judgment has summarized these duties in a way that may also be applied in times of armed conflict: 'However, as against third states whose shipping was damaged or whose nationals were injured by mines laid by or on behalf of the United States, the international responsibility of the United States may arise. Third States were and are entitled to carry on commerce with Nicaragua and their ships are entitled to make use of Nicaraguan ports. If the United States were to be justified in taking blockade-like measures against Nicaraguan ports, as by mining, it could only be so if its mining of Nicaraguan ports were publicly and officially announced by it and if international shipping were duly warned by it about the fact that mines would be or had been laid in specified waters; international shipping was not duly warned by it in a timely, official manner.'[254] The form in which these warnings must be issued depends on the circumstances of each case. In general, it will suffice to inform international shipping by the usual means, for example the 'Notices to Mariners'. If, however, a vessel that may not legitimately be considered a military objective is about to enter a mined sea area, the belligerent must use all means to prevent it from proceeding, *inter alia* by making use of internationally recognized emergency frequencies. Article 3, para. 2, HC VIII

---

[250] In the course of the proceedings of the *Corfu Channel* case it became evident that drifting automatic contact mines were less dangerous than generally believed. Cowie states: 'Incidentally, the legend has grown up that all drifting mines are dangerous to shipping, but this is by no means the case. When moored, mines are normally kept dangerous due to the tension in the mooring rope, and if they break adrift the tension is relaxed and a strong spring takes charge, so opening a switch in the circuit between the firing battery and the detonator. If a mine breaks adrift with a length of mooring trailing from it, that mooring may get caught up on rocks, pier structures, and so forth; the mine in effect becomes moored once more and so liable to detonate if one of the horns is struck.... Finally, it is extremely difficult to ram a mine or any small object floating freely on the surface of the sea. The chances of a ship being sunk or damaged by a mine which has broken adrift from its moorings are in fact remote, but none the less the prudent seaman will give them a clear berth.' Cowie (*supra*, n. 215), 188 *et seq.*

[251] *San Remo Manual*, para. 82 provides: 'It is forbidden to use free-floating mines unless: (a) they are directed against a military objective; and (b) they become harmless within an hour after loss of control over them.' See also Article 4, para. 4 of the Swedish proposal: 'It is prohibited to use drifting mines.'

[252] Article 3, para. 2, HC VIII; *NWP 1–14M*, para. 9.2.3(1). Article 6, para. 1 of the Swedish proposal provides: 'Effective warning, through notification of danger zones, of any use of activated mines which may affect neutral or non-belligerent shipping or vessels protected under Article 4, shall be given as soon as military considerations permit.' Para. 83 of the *San Remo Manual* reads: 'The laying of armed mines or the arming of prelaid mines must be notified unless the mines can only be exploded by ships which are military objectives.' This implies that sophisticated and discriminating mines need not be notified.

[253] This formulation stems from Article 52, para. 2, AP I. The definition of military objectives contained in that provision is today generally accepted as customary international law and thus applicable in naval warfare. See commentary on Section 1017; *NWP 1–14M*, para. 8.2.; *Canadian Manual*, para. 825.

[254] *ICJ Reports 1986*, 379 *et seq.*

WOLFF HEINTSCHEL VON HEINEGG

obliges the belligerents also to communicate danger zones to the 'Governments through the diplomatic channel'. In view of the technical state of modern means of communication it is, however, doubtful whether such formal notification is still necessary.[255]

e) Precautionary measures. In principle, a belligerent is required to allow peaceful shipping to leave the sea area that is, or is about to be, mined.[256] Since this is not an absolute duty the belligerent may refrain from granting such a period of grace if the military advantage anticipated would thereby be jeopardized. If the safety of peaceful shipping cannot be ensured by any of the means described above the belligerent is obliged to take additional precautionary measures.[257] This may include the duty to designate safe passages or to provide piloting.

b. *Minelaying prior to the beginning of an armed conflict*

Protective mining is permissible even in times of crisis, subject to the right of innocent passage of foreign ships through territorial waters. If it is indispensable for the protection of its security and if the ships have been appropriately warned, the coastal state may temporarily prohibit innocent passage through specific parts of its territorial waters. In the case of straits serving international navigation there is no right of protective mining in times of crisis.

1041

1. *Prior to the outbreak of an international armed conflict.* Only protective minelaying is permissible. It is self-evident that prior to the outbreak of an international armed conflict it is prohibited to lay mines in the territorial waters of a foreign state.[258] Rights and duties of states are governed by the law of peace. They are, therefore, obliged to respect the freedom of navigation beyond their territorial sea[259] and to use the high seas (including EEZs) for peaceful purposes only.[260] Violation of these obligations by the use of mines may be justified as self-defence, according to Article 51 UN Charter.[261] This presupposes an armed attack. If, however, an armed attack occurs then Section 1042 on wartime mining comes into operation. In such cases the question of mining prior to the outbreak of an international armed conflict is no longer of relevance. The question remains whether it is also prohibited to lay mines in sea areas beyond the outer limit of the territorial sea. The laying of mines in international waters, whether armed or remotely controlled, is contrary to international law. According to the *US Manual*, mining of international waters is considered legitimate under the following conditions: 'Controlled mines ... may be emplaced in international waters beyond the territorial sea

---

[255] According to the judgment of the ICJ in the *Nicaragua* case obviously any form of information may be considered sufficient as long as it is effective; see *ICJ Reports 1986*, para. 292.

[256] The US, when mining Haiphong, employed mines that were activated three days after they had been laid. Thus, innocent shipping was able to leave Haiphong unmolested; see Levie, *Mine Warfare*, 147. The *San Remo Manual*, para. 85, provides: 'Mining operations in the internal waters, territorial sea or archipelagic waters of a belligerent State should provide, when the mining is first executed, for free exit of shipping of neutral States.'

[257] Article 6, para. 2, of the Swedish proposal provides: 'When mines are employed, all feasible precautions shall be taken for the safety of vessels and shipping protected under Article 4. Feasible precautions are those precautions which are practicable or practically possible taking into account all circumstances ruling at the time, including humanitarian and military considerations.'

[258] See *NWP 1–14M*, para. 9.2.2. In the *Nicaragua* case the ICJ held: 'In peacetime for one state to lay mines in the internal or territorial waters of another is an unlawful act'; *ICJ Reports 1986*, 112.

[259] See Articles 87 and 58 UNCLOS.

[260] See, *inter alia*, Clingan (*supra*, n. 235), 356.

[261] *NWP 1–14M*, para. 9.2.2. See also Thorpe (*supra*, n. 232), 267.

if they do not unreasonably interfere with other lawful uses of the oceans. The determination of what constitutes an "unreasonable interference" involves a balancing of a number of factors including the rationale for their emplacement (i.e., the self-defense requirements of the emplacing nation), the extent of the area to be mined, the hazard (if any) to other lawful ocean uses, and the duration of their emplacement. Because controlled mines do not constitute a hazard to navigation, international notice of their emplacement is not required. Armed mines may not be emplaced in international waters prior to the outbreak of armed conflict, except under the most demanding requirements of individual or collective self-defense. Should armed mines be emplaced in international waters under such circumstances, prior notification of their location must be provided and the anticipated date of their complete removal must be clearly stated. The nation emplacing armed mines in international waters during peacetime also assumes the responsibility to maintain an on-scene presence in the area sufficient to ensure that appropriate warning is provided to ships approaching the danger area. All armed mines must be expeditiously removed or rendered harmless when the imminent danger that prompted their emplacement has passed.'[262] Even though there is some support in the literature for the US position, especially by those who acknowledge a right of preventive self-defence,[263] the rules laid down in the *US Naval Manual* (2007) are not covered by existing international law. Prior to the outbreak of an international armed conflict, the rights and duties of states are exclusively governed by the law of peace: in the present context, by the international law of the sea. Hence, the freedom of navigation as well as the duty of peaceful use of the high seas have to be observed. An infringement of these rules and principles is only justified if an armed attack occurs. It may be that according to the *US Naval Manual* the scope of self-defence is broader. Even then it is open to doubt whether a case of 'most demanding requirements of individual or collective self-defence' is still governed by the law of peace.[264]

2. Minelaying in one's own territorial waters. In times of crisis the laying of mines is permissible in the territorial sea, in the internal waters, and in the archipelagic waters of the minelaying state. The question arises whether and to what extent these rules are compatible with the international law of the sea, as far as the territorial sea is concerned. Even though the coastal state's sovereignty extends to the territorial sea it is not free to suspend the right of innocent passage.[265] Innocent passage may—temporarily—be suspended in exceptional cases only.[266] The ICJ in the *Nicaragua* case emphasized that 'if a State lays mines in any waters whatever in which the vessels of another State have rights of access or passage, and fails to give any warning or notification whatsoever, in disregard of the security of peaceful shipping, it commits a breach of the principles of humanitarian law

---

[262] *NWP 1–14M*, para. 9.2.2.

[263] See, *inter alia*, Thorpe, *loc. cit.*, 267 *et seq.*; Rowe (*supra*, n. 239), 128. D. W. Bowett, *Self Defence in International Law* (Manchester: Manchester University Press, 1958), 71, states: 'It can scarcely be contemplated that a state must remain passive while a serious menace to its security mounts on the high seas beyond its territorial sea. It is accordingly maintained that it is still permissible for a state to assume a protective jurisdiction, within the limits circumscribing every exercise of the right of self defence on the high seas in order to protect its ships, its aircraft and its right to territorial integrity and political independence from an imminent danger or actual attack.'

[264] See Clingan (*supra*, n. 235), 356.

[265] Ibid. 355 *et seq.*

[266] See Article 25, UNCLOS.

WOLFF HEINTSCHEL VON HEINEGG

underlying the specific provisions of Convention No. VIII of 1907'.[267] Hence, if mines are laid in the territorial sea peaceful shipping must be effectively warned if the mines form a threat. The rules laid down in the *US Naval Manual* do, however, comply with these principles. Mining of one's own territorial waters is said to be permissible only when either peaceful shipping remains unaffected or when it is demanded by fundamental security considerations.[268] If states, like Sweden, lay controlled minefields in their territorial waters in peacetime, they are not obliged to give notice of the minefield, nor are they obliged to issue warnings.[269] Only when the minefield is activated does the right temporarily to suspend innocent passage presuppose a prior warning.[270]

3. *International straits.* Prior to the outbreak of an international armed conflict the coastal state is not entitled to suspend the right of transit passage through international straits. In the *Corfu Channel* case, the ICJ held that 'unless otherwise prescribed in an international convention, there is no right for a coastal state to prohibit such passage through straits in time of peace'.[271] Since controlled minefields do not interfere with transit passage there is no reason for denying the coastal state the right to employ them within international straits. The foregoing commentary applies *mutatis mutandis* to archipelagic shipping lanes.

c. Minelaying during armed conflicts

> During an armed conflict protective mining is permissible without the limitations applicable before it begins. As a matter of principle, defensive mining is permissible only after the beginning of the armed conflict; the shipping lanes of neutral and non-belligerent states shall be kept open to an appropriate extent, if military circumstances so permit. Acts of aggression not amounting to armed attacks do not suffice as a motive. Offensive mining may not be undertaken solely to interdict merchant shipping.

1042

1. *Protective mining.* In the course of an international armed conflict this is a generally acknowledged belligerent right.[272] With the outbreak of hostilities the relationship between the belligerents is no longer governed by the rules of the international law of the sea concerning innocent passage, transit passage, or archipelagic shipping lane passage. The relationship of the parties to the conflict with neutral states or those not parties to the conflict must be differentiated. Whereas, for security reasons, the right of innocent passage may be denied to neutral shipping at least temporarily, this is not the case with regard to transit (and archipelagic shipping lanes) passage. In view of the provisions of UNCLOS III guaranteeing an inalienable right of transit passage, such mining constitutes a violation of international law if the belligerents do not provide for safe alternative routes of similar convenience.[273] It may be added in this context that at least in the first

---

[267] *ICJ Reports 1986*, 112.

[268] *NWP 1–14M*, para. 9.2.2.

[269] *NWP 1–14M*, para. 9.2.2 provides: 'Emplacement of controlled mines in a nation's own archipelagic waters or territorial sea is not subject to such notification or removal requirements.'

[270] *NWP 1–14M*, para. 9.2.2: 'If armed mines are emplaced in archipelagic waters or the territorial sea, appropriate international notification of the existence and location of such mines is required.'

[271] *ICJ Reports 1949*, 28. See also R. R. Baxter, 'Passage of Ships Through International Waterways in Time of War' (1954) XXXI *BYIL* 187–216.

[272] H. Lauterpacht (*supra*, n. 123), 471 *et seq.*; Colombos (*supra*, n. 12), paras. 562 *et seq.*; *NWP 1–14M*, para. 9.2; *Canadian Manual* (*supra*, n. 27), paras. 836 *et seq.*

[273] *NWP 1–14M*, para. 9.2.3 (6) provides: 'Naval mines may be employed to channelize neutral shipping, but not in a manner to impede the transit passage of international straits or archipelagic sea lanes passage

months of World War II free passage through international straits as well as piloting services were provided by the belligerents.[274] The conditions under which the right of transit passage may be exercised will depend on the circumstances ruling at the time. Probably, vital security interests will entitle a belligerent temporarily to close an international strait. This question is, however, far from settled. In any event such closure will only be legitimate in exceptional cases and may not last indefinitely.

2. *Defensive mining.* This presupposes the existence of an international armed conflict. The admissibility of mining international waters follows from the fact that the high seas belong to the areas of naval warfare. Mines may only be laid within the general area of naval operations.[275] Accordingly, the territorial seas[276] and internal waters of states not parties to the conflict are exempt. This is also true of archipelagic waters[277] since they are covered by the sovereignty of the archipelagic state. In addition, mining must not have the practical effect of preventing passage between neutral waters and international waters. In principle, the EEZs and continental shelf areas of neutral states are part of the general area of naval operations.[278] However, the belligerents shall have due regard for the rights of the coastal state concerning the exploration and exploitation of the natural resources in such sea areas. In particular, artificial islands, installations, structures, and safety zones may not be interfered with. In any event, if mines are laid within the EEZ or on the continental shelf of a neutral state the belligerent is obliged to give notice of the mined areas.[279]

As regards the mining of high seas areas there seem to exist no significant restrictions. Especially, Article 3 HC VIII suggests that 'belligerents may sow anchored automatic contact mines anywhere upon the high seas'.[280] It should, however, not be overlooked that according to the Preamble the contracting states were '[i]nspired by the principle of the freedom of sea routes, the common highway of all nations'. The generally accepted rules on treaty interpretation laid down in Article 31 of the Vienna Convention on the Law of Treaties would allow the Preamble to be taken into consideration. It would, therefore, be possible to deduce a prohibition of unrestricted mining in the high seas.

---

of archipelagic waters by such shipping.' Para. 89, *San Remo Manual* reads as follows: 'Transit passage through international straits and passage through waters subject to the right of archipelagic sea lanes passage shall not be impeded unless safe and convenient alternative routes are provided.' See also L. M. Alexander, 'International Straits', in Robertson (*supra*, n. 86), 91–108, at 94 *et seq.*

[274] According to secret documents prepared by the German Naval High Command, in the following straits free passages and piloting services were provided by the belligerents: Skagerrak, the Sound and the Great Belt, the Kattegat, the Dover Strait, and the Firth of Forth. See Oberkommando der Kriegsmarine, *Urkundenbuch zum Seekriegsrecht* (1 Sept. 1939 to 31 Aug. 1940), document nos. 340, 345, 346, 348, 354, 361. See also Levie, *Mine Warfare*, 77 *et seq.*

[275] For the 'general area of naval operations', see Sections 1010 *et seq.*; Colombos, paras. 558 *et seq.*

[276] It may be added that according to military manuals the 12 nautical miles territorial sea is generally accepted as in accordance with international law and has to be respected in times of armed conflict. See *NWP 1–14M*, para. 7.3.5; *Canadian Manual*, para. 802 *et seq.*

[277] See *NWP 1–14M*, para. 7.3.7; *Canadian Manual*, para. 804(1a).

[278] *Canadian Manual*, para. 804(1c).

[279] Ibid. para. 1509(1). See also para. 35, *San Remo Manual* which provides: 'If a belligerent considers it necessary to lay mines in the exclusive economic zone or the continental shelf of a neutral State, the belligerent shall notify that State, and shall ensure, *inter alia*, that the size of the minefield and the type of mines used do not endanger artificial islands, installations and structures, nor interfere with access thereto, and shall avoid so far as practicable interference with the exploration or exploitation of the zone by the neutral State. Due regard shall also be given to the protection and preservation of the marine environment.'

[280] Tucker (*supra*, n. 76), 303.

WOLFF HEINTSCHEL VON HEINEGG

On the other hand, this result may be doubted in view of the practice of the two World Wars.[281] If, however, recent statements on the law of naval warfare are taken into account it becomes obvious that even though international law still lacks a general and comprehensive prohibition, the right of belligerents to lay mines in the high seas is not unlimited.[282] The *US Naval Manual* (2007), for example, expressly states: 'Mining of areas of indefinite extent in international waters is prohibited. Reasonably limited barred areas may be established by naval mines, provided neutral shipping retains an alternate route around or through such an area with reasonable assurance of safety.'[283] Hence, unless free and safe passages for peaceful shipping are provided for, the mining of the high seas is contrary to international law.[284] Of course, during an international armed conflict at sea the freedom of navigation is not absolute.[285] Still, the parties to the conflict are not entitled to treat it as obsolete.

3. *Offensive mining.* During an international armed conflict this is also legitimate as long as the principles laid down in Section 1040 are observed. Its admissibility also follows from the provisions on the areas of naval warfare. Still, as is shown by paragraphs 3–5 of the present section, the mere existence of (armed) hostilities is not considered sufficient to justify the mining of enemy territorial waters. In accordance with the right of individual or collective self-defence of Article 51 UN Charter it is made subject to an 'armed attack'.[286] These provisions are, however, of minor relevance for the naval commander. They are rather addressed to political and high military decision-makers. On the justification of mining enemy territorial waters as an act of collective self-defence, the judgment of the ICJ in the *Nicaragua* case is of considerable significance. The ICJ ruled that the use of force, including the mining of another state's territorial waters, is to be considered a legitimate act of collective self-defence only if the following criteria are met: 'At all events, the Court finds that in customary international law, whether of a general

---

[281] Tucker states: 'Indeed, the severe condemnation of war zones from which neutral shipping is barred under threat of destruction from submarines and aircraft has not infrequently been accompanied by the acquiescence to zones from which neutral shipping is barred by means almost equally destructive'; Tucker, 303.

[282] See Thorpe, *loc. cit.*, 264.

[283] *NWP 1–14M*, para. 9.2.3(8).

[284] See Levie, *Mine Warfare*, 41 *et seq.*, 177. The corresponding *opinio juris* can also be deduced from the practice of states during the Iran–Iraq war. States not parties to that conflict, by deploying naval units in the Persian Gulf, made abundantly clear that they were not willing to acquiesce in a restriction of the freedom of navigation by unrestricted mine warfare. *San Remo Manual*, para. 88, provides: 'The minelaying States shall pay due regard to the legitimate uses of the high seas by, *inter alia*, providing safe alternative routes for shipping of neutral States.'

[285] See Thorpe, *loc. cit.*, 257. G. Schwarzenberger, *International Law as Applied by International Courts and Tribunals. Vol. II: The Law of Armed Conflict* (London: Stevens & Sons, 1968), 417, holds: 'On the high seas, fields of anchored automatic contact mines, even if announced and supervised, amount to a purported occupation of a portion of the high seas of indefinite duration. It appears impossible to square pretensions of this character with the rules underlying the principles of the freedom of the seas; for they deny the free use of the mined area of the high seas not only to the enemy, but also to neutral shipping at large.' However, this position finds no foundation in state practice.

[286] For the term 'armed attack' see, *inter alia*, Ipsen (*supra*, n. 41), § 59, paras. 28 *et seq.* 'Aggression' is defined in UN GA Res. 3314 (XXIX) of 14 Dec. 1974 that is meant to help the UN Security Council in determining the existence of such aggression. Certain kinds of direct force (open military attack, occupation of foreign territory, blockade, and attacks on foreign armed forces, ships, aircraft, etc.) are declared acts of aggression. That enumeration is not exhaustive; see Verdross/Simma, s. 233; Ipsen, § 59, paras. 10 *et seq.* Despite the non-binding character of UN GA Resolutions, Res. 3314 (XXIX) is widely considered as declaratory of customary international law.

WOLFF HEINTSCHEL VON HEINEGG

kind or that particular to the inter-American legal system, there is no rule permitting the exercise of collective self-defence in the absence of a request by the State which regards itself as the victim of an armed attack. The Court concludes that the requirement of a request by the State which is the victim of the alleged attack is additional to the requirement that such a State should have declared itself to have been attacked.'[287] If there is no such declaration and request offensive mining is not justified by the right of collective self-defence.

4. *The prohibition against laying mines with the sole object of intercepting commercial shipping.* According to a widely held view the prohibition of Article 2 HC VIII also applies to modern mines.[288] It is thus forbidden to lay mines 'off the coast and ports of the enemy, with the sole object of intercepting commercial shipping'. In practice, a violation of this prohibition is unlikely to be established. In any event, mining activities will only in exceptional cases be exclusively motivated by considerations of economic warfare.[289] However, even under conditions of modern naval warfare this prohibition is not meaningless. It implies that the offensive use of mines for the sole object of conducting economic warfare at sea is strictly forbidden.[290] Of course, mines may be employed for establishing and enforcing a naval blockade. Mines may not, however, be the only means employed for that purpose. If mines are used for blockade purposes the belligerent is obliged to deploy warships or other units of its armed forces near the blockaded area. The rationale behind that obligation is to ensure that ships in distress can reach a place of safety.

d. Duties after the cessation of hostilities

1043   At the close of hostilities the conflicting parties must do their utmost to remove, for the sake of safe shipping, the mines they have laid (Article 5 HC VIII).

1. *Removal of mines by the former belligerents.* At the close of the armed conflict the former belligerents must make every effort to remove the mines which they have laid.[291] This duty is generally accepted as a rule of customary international law.[292] Accordingly, each belligerent is obliged to remove the mines it has laid in its own territorial waters and in the high seas. As regards those mines laid in a belligerent's own territorial waters,

---

[287] *ICJ Reports 1986*, 105.

[288] See *NWP 1–14M*, para. 9.2.3; *Canadian Manual*, paras. 836 *et seq.*; Dinstein (*supra*, n. 157), 45.

[289] See Levie, *Mine Warfare*, 32 *et seq.*; Dinstein, *loc. cit.*, 45; Stone, *Legal Controls* (*supra*, n. 176), 583–4. For an evaluation of Article 2 from a purely military point of view, see Heintschel v. Heinegg, in Fleck (ed.), *Gladisch Committee* (*supra*, n. 35), 46 *et seq.*

[290] See *NWP 1–14M*, para. 9.2.3 (7); Dinstein, *loc. cit.*, 45.

[291] Article 5, para. 1, HC VIII; *NWP 1–14M*, para. 9.2.3(5); *Canadian Manual*, para. 842. Para. 90, *San Remo Manual* provides: 'After the cessation of active hostilities, parties to the conflict shall do their utmost to remove or render harmless the mines they have laid, each party removing its own mines. With regard to mines laid in the territorial seas of the enemy, each party shall notify their position and shall proceed with the least possible delay to remove the mines in its territorial sea or otherwise render the territorial sea safe for navigation.'

[292] In one of the Protocols of the US–North Vietnamese Agreement of 27 Jan. 1973, the US accepted international responsibility for the removal of approximately 8,000 mines it had laid in North Vietnamese coastal waters. 'Operation End Sweep' started in Feb. 1973 and was completed in July 1973. Egypt, after the end of the Yom Kippur War (1973) also accepted its responsibility for the removal of mines it had laid in the Suez Canal and in the Red Sea. During the Gulf War (1980–8), Iran, on 13 August 1987, announced it would sweep mines in international waters of the Persian Gulf; *The Times* (London) 1 September 1987, 6. For further references see Levie, *Mine Warfare*, 49 *et seq.*, 75, 88, 122, 149 *et seq.*

WOLFF HEINTSCHEL VON HEINEGG

it is sufficient merely to render them harmless. Remotely controlled minefields must only be switched off. Mines laid in the territorial waters of the (former) adversary may be removed only with the latter's express consent. A mine-clearing operation within the territorial sea without permission by the coastal state is a violation of its territorial sovereignty.[293] If the coastal state is unwilling to permit mine-clearing operations by the other state the latter is, in principle, obliged to notify the former of the position of the mines.[294] In practice, the performance of this duty may cause considerable difficulties. The mine-laying state may, for security reasons, not be willing to provide its former adversary with information on the construction of the mines it uses. International law provides no rules for such cases except for the general duty to resolve international disputes by peaceful means. Finally, if a state is unable to remove the mines it has laid because it does not have the necessary technical means it shall ask other states for assistance.[295]

2. *Removal of mines by neutrals.* The parties to an ongoing international armed conflict at sea do not, of course, always comply with the above requirements. Drifting mines are laid in sea areas with a high traffic density. In many cases, the mines used can neither be directed at military objectives nor are they equipped with effective deactivation devices. In such cases the question arises whether neutral states are entitled to protect their shipping by removing the illegally laid mines. The practice of states during the Iran–Iraq War has, it is submitted, contributed to the emergence of a confirmatory rule of international law. On 24 July 1987, the reflagged tanker *Bridgeton* hit a mine 18 nautical miles off the Iranian island of Farsi. Almost immediately the US sent mine experts to assist Saudi Arabia and Kuwait in removing the mines off their respective coasts and ports. It soon became clear, however, that the mines could be removed only if the necessary equipment was available. Therefore, the US started deploying its 'airborne mine countermeasure units' (AMCM) in the area.[296] At the request of the US, Great Britain and France also deployed naval units in the Gulf region to protect peaceful shipping and to remove mines in international shipping lanes.[297] On 21 September 1987, two US helicopters detected an Iranian landing craft, the *Iran Ajr*, approximately 50 nautical

---

[293] This follows from the judgment of the ICJ in the *Corfu Channel* case, *ICJ Reports 1949*, 4 *et seq.*

[294] See Swedish proposal, Article 7, para. 2: 'All such records shall be retained by the parties who shall: (a) as soon as possible, by mutual agreement, provide for the release of information concerning the location of activated mines, particularly in agreements governing the cessation of hostilities; (b) immediately after the cessation of active hostilities take all necessary and appropriate measures, including the use of such records, to protect civilians from the effects of mines; and make available to each other and to the Secretary-General of the United Nations all information in their possession concerning the location of activated mines.'

[295] After the end of the Yom Kippur War, for example, Egypt asked the US for assistance. Within three months (April to June 1973) the waters were cleared of the mines. See Levie, *Mine Warfare*, 157 *et seq.*; H. Kowark/S. M. Taylor 'Die Räumung des Suezkanals' (1974) 71 *Marine-Rundschau* 724–36. India, after the close of the 1971 conflict with Pakistan, removed the mines it had laid with the assistance of the former Soviet Union. See C. H. Petersen, 'Die Operationen der sowjetischen Marine für die Wiedereröffnung der Häfen in Bangladesh. März 1972–Juni 1974' (1975) 72 *Marine Rundschau* 665–76. Swedish proposal, Article 8: 'After the cessation of active hostilities, the parties shall endeavour to reach agreement both among themselves and, where appropriate, with other States and with international organizations, on the provision of information and technical and material assistance—including, in appropriate circumstances, joint operations—necessary to remove or otherwise render ineffective mines placed in position during the conflict.' An identical rule is laid down in para. 91, *San Remo Manual.*

[296] See Levie, *Mine Warfare*, 167 *et seq.*

[297] See A. Gioia/N. Ronzitti, 'The Law of Neutrality; Third States' Commercial Rights and Duties', in I. Dekker/H. Post (eds), *The Gulf War of 1980–1988* (Dordrecht: Nijhoff, 1992), 221–42, at 223 *et seq.*, 237 *et seq.*; Levie, *Mine Warfare*, 168.

miles to the north-east of Bahrain. After they had verified that the *Iran Ajr* was engaged in mining activities they opened fire. Five members of the Iranian crew were killed, the other twenty-six were captured.[298] While the Iranian government accused the US of having killed innocent seamen, the Legal Adviser of the Department of State, Judge A. Sofaer, justified the attack on the *Iran Ajr* as follows: 'Where, as here, a government engages in manifestly illegal use of armed force, international law entitles the victim to act in self-defense. The response must be necessary and proportionate. The United States' action plainly comported with these requirements. The United States acted to stop the unlawful act itself, and an imminent threat to US shipping was thereby avoided. The US immediately reported this action to the Security Council pursuant to Article 51 of the UN Charter and stated its hope and intention that the incident not be followed by additional hostilities.'[299]

As regards the removal of mines in areas beyond the territorial seas of the belligerents, there is unanimous agreement in the literature that the activities were in compliance with international law.[300] State practice supports this view since even the parties to the conflict in the Gulf War acquiesced in the removal of mines by neutral states.[301] Possible justifications are either the inherent right of self-defence[302] or the right to enforce the freedom of navigation against illegal interference by belligerent mining.[303]

A far more difficult question is whether neutral states are entitled to remove mines illegally laid in international straits. So far the only precedent is the *Corfu Channel* case.[304] The facts are well known. On 13 November 1946 Great Britain removed twenty-two mines from the Corfu Channel because Albania had refused to clear the mines itself or give permission to Great Britain. The ICJ held Albania responsible for damage caused to two British warships that struck mines when passing through the Corfu Channel.[305] The British action, however, was also considered illegal because it constituted a violation of Albania's sovereignty. The Court was not prepared to accept any justification for the British action. If the Corfu Channel decision were still considered as valid law the removal of mines in international straits overlapped by the territorial sea of a coastal state would be contrary to international law. Whether the mines were laid in accordance with the maritime *jus in bello* would make no difference. In view of the new rules on non-suspendable transit passage and of the importance of international straits for international commerce it is open to doubt whether the mere reference to the sovereignty of the belligerent coastal state suffices to render the removal of illegally laid mines by neutral states a violation of international law. The right of transit passage may only be infringed by measures that comply with the maritime *jus in bello*. Therefore, if the

---

[298] See Peace, (1988) 82 *Proceedings of the American Society of International Law* 151.

[299] Quoted in T. Meron, 'Neutrality, The Right of Shipping and the Use of Force in the Persian Gulf—Remarks' (1988) 82 *Proceedings of the American Society of International Law* 164–9.

[300] See Ronzitti, 'La guerre du Golfe, le déminage et la circulation des navires' (1987) XXXIII *Annuaire Français de Droit International* 647–62, at 651; Nordquist/Wachenfeld (*supra*, n. 128), at 162 *et seq.*; Gioia/Ronzitti, *loc. cit.*, 237; Meron, *loc. cit.*, 168.

[301] Originally, Iran had denied having laid mines for other purposes than coastal defence against US (!) attacks. When mines were detected in Omani waters, however, Iran proposed to remove them from Omani territorial waters. See Levie, *Mine Warfare*, 168.

[302] Nordquist/Wachenfeld, *loc. cit.*, at 162–4; Meron, *loc. cit.*, 167 *et seq.*

[303] Ronzitti, *loc. cit.*, at 651.

[304] *ICJ Reports 1949*, 4 *et seq.*

[305] Ibid. 22.

---

belligerents are not willing to observe these rules and if there exist no alternative routes of similar convenience, third states are entitled to remove mines in international straits in order to enforce their right of transit passage.[306]

2. Torpedoes

> **Torpedoes which have missed their mark must become harmless (Article 1 HC VIII). When using torpedoes, action shall be taken in accordance with the principles of naval warfare to ensure that only military objectives and not other ships and objects are damaged.**   1044

This provision stems from Article 1, para. 3, HC VIII[307] and is today generally accepted as part of customary international law.[308] In general, torpedoes presently in use by naval armed forces meet the requirements laid down in the first sentence. The provisions of the second sentence, in view of the accuracy of modern torpedoes,[309] pose no serious problems either. In this regard it makes no difference whether torpedoes are employed against surface or against subsurface vessels. However, torpedoes guided by wire during the initial phase seek their target independently during the final phase of their run. Hence they may hit other targets than those originally aimed at. It is the object and purpose of the second sentence to remind naval commanders of their duty to ensure that only military objectives are attacked.

3. Missiles

> **For the use of missiles at sea, including cruise missiles, the general principles of the law of naval warfare apply.**   1045

The inclusion of a special provision on missiles is meant to take account of modern naval warfare. Short-range missiles were successfully employed during the 1967 Arab–Israeli conflict,[310] the Falklands/Malvinas conflict,[311] and during the two Gulf Wars.[312] No specific rules on the use of cruise or other missiles have yet been included in the law of naval armed conflict. Hence, Section 1045 clarifies that when belligerents employ missiles (cruise or other) they are obliged to ensure that they are directed exclusively at military objectives.[313] In general, the technical state of modern missiles enables belligerents to conform with the fundamental principles of the laws of naval armed conflicts, especially

---

[306] Accordingly, the *San Remo Manual*, para. 92, provides: 'Neutral States do not commit an act inconsistent with the laws of neutrality by clearing mines laid in violation of international law.'

[307] Cf., *inter alia*, Levie, *Commentary*, 143 with further references.

[308] See *NWP 1–14M*, para. 9.4; *Canadian Manual*, paras. 836 *et seq*. *San Remo Manual*, para. 79 provides: 'It is prohibited to use torpedoes which do not sink or otherwise become harmless when they have completed their run.'

[309] For the technical aspects see *Jane's Underwater Warfare Systems* (*supra*, n. 216).

[310] Cf. O'Connell (*supra*, n. 172), 86 *et seq*.

[311] Cf. A. L. Zuppi, *Die bewaffnete Auseinandersetzung zwischen dem Vereinigten Königreich und Argentinien im Südatlantik aus völkerrechtlicher Sicht* (Köln/Berlin/Bonn/München: Heymanns, 1990), 200 *et seq*.

[312] For the Iran–Iraq conflict (1980–8), see R. Danziger, 'The Persian Gulf Tanker War' (1985) 111 *USNIP* 160 *et seq*.

[313] *San Remo Manual*, para. 78, provides: 'Missiles and projectiles, including those with over-the-horizon capabilities, shall be used in conformity with the principles of target discrimination as set out in Sections 38–46.'

WOLFF HEINTSCHEL VON HEINEGG

with the principle of distinction. However, there still exist problems with regard to identification and targeting.[314] If the use of missiles and projectiles depends upon over-the-
horizon targeting, belligerents are obliged to take precautionary measures to ensure that
anything other than military objectives is spared.[315] Provided that, if necessary, such
measures are taken the legality of the use of missiles cannot be doubted.[316] Modern missiles are highly discriminate weapons that will not usually miss their targets. In the light
of the fundamental principles of naval armed conflict, it is, therefore, not necessary to
equip them with self-destruction or similar devices.[317]

4. Submarine Warfare

Preliminary remarks. The rules on submarine warfare result from a development beginning in 1899. This development was to a considerable extent influenced by Great Britain's
endeavours to outlaw the submarine as a legitimate means of naval warfare.[318] These
endeavours (made during international codification and disarmament conferences)
failed in the face of resistance by other states, especially of France.[319] Already during
World War I the principal legitimacy of the submarine as a means of naval warfare was
not seriously doubted. It became evident, however, that it would be at least difficult to
reconcile the use of submarines with the rules of naval warfare. Despite allegations to the
contrary, submarines, because of their poor speed, could only be employed to a limited
extent against enemy warships. Hence, from the very beginning their importance lay
with measures against enemy merchant shipping. However, if submarines were to capture a merchant vessel they had to comply with the regular procedure of visit and search.
This exposed them to serious dangers since, once surfaced, they could be rammed or otherwise attacked. Moreover, during World War I, for example Great Britain had armed
its merchant shipping and ordered it to fly false flags and to ram German submarines
if possible. Hence, after initial compliance with the rule on visit, search, and capture,
Germany turned to a policy of 'unrestricted submarine warfare'. Vessels encountered
within the limits of a predeclared so-called 'war zone' were sunk without prior warning.[320] A further difficulty resulting from compliance with the rules of naval warfare was
the lack of space on board submarines. They were unable to take crews, passengers, and
ship's papers to a place of safety if a captured merchant vessel had to be destroyed. It was
also nearly impossible to take shipwrecked and wounded on board. In addition, rescue

---

[314] Cf. Robertson (*supra*, n. 86), 371 *et seq.*; Hegelsom (*supra*, n. 86), 35.

[315] See also *NWP 1–14M*, para. 9.10.

[316] Hegelsom, 36; S. C. Truver, 'The Legal Status of Submarine Launched Cruise Missiles' (1977) 103
USNIP 82 *et seq.*; W. H. Parks, 'Submarine-Launched Cruise Missile and International Law: A Response'
(1973) 103 *USNIP* 120 *et seq.* For the opposing view, see O'Connell (1972) *AJIL* 785 *et seq.*

[317] In any event a self-destruction device would not mean any improvement. The time period between
launching and reaching the target is too short to achieve any modifications. The flight time of the missile
fired by *USS Vincennes* against the Iranian Airbus took only 17 seconds from launching to impact. Cf. n.
Friedman, 'The Vincennes Incident' (1989) 115 *USNIP* 76.

[318] For a general overview of the law of submarine warfare, see Mallison, *Submarines*, 12 *et seq.*; J. L.
Jacobson, 'The Law of Submarine Warfare Today', in Robertson (*supra*, n. 86), 205 *et seq.*; J. Gilliland,
'Submarines and Targets: Suggestions for New Codified Rules of Submarine Warfare', *Georgetown Law
Journal* 1985, 976 *et seq.*; H. Sohler, 'U-Bootkrieg und Völkerrecht', *Marine Rundschau* (Sept. 1956), 1;
Heintschel von Heinegg (*supra*, n. 15).

[319] Cf., *inter alia*, Mallison, *Submarines*, 31 *et seq.*

[320] Ibid. 62 *et seq.*

operations, in view of the vulnerability of surfaced submarines, caused severe problems. Still, it was agreed at the 1922 Washington Conference that submarines were subject to the same rules of naval warfare as surface vessels and that non-compliance constituted an act of piracy. The Washington Treaty never entered into force but the same rules concerning the use of submarines were laid down in the 1930 London Agreement on Naval Armaments. When that Treaty expired the same rules were reaffirmed in the LondonProt 1936[321] that became binding law for the majority of the belligerent states of World War II. State practice during World War II, however, did not differ from that of World War I.[322] From the beginning all belligerents, including the US, conducted unrestricted submarine warfare directed at enemy merchant shipping and caused tremendous losses.

Shortly after its adoption the provisions of the LondonProt 1936 were criticized on the ground that they disregarded the differences between surface and subsurface vessels, and overlooked the impossibility for submarines to comply with the rules on visit and search.[323] Still, in its judgment on Admiral Dönitz, the Nuremberg Tribunal affirmed the continuing validity of the Protocol. The Tribunal did not, however, find Dönitz guilty of unrestricted submarine warfare against British merchant shipping.[324] In its reasoning the Tribunal did not refer to the dangers involved in the compliance with the procedure of visit and search. Rather, it considered British merchant vessels that had been incorporated into Britain's war efforts to have lost the protection of the LondonProt 1936.[325] Neither was Dönitz sentenced for having ordered attacks on neutral merchant vessels, especially within 'war zones'. The Tribunal qualified those attacks as violations of the LondonProt 1936 but refrained from a sentence in view of the similar practice of the Allies, especially of the US in the Pacific.

International lawyers have drawn quite different conclusions from practice during World War II and from the Nuremberg judgment. Whereas some consider the LondonProt 1936 to have been abrogated on grounds of desuetude,[326] others emphasize its continuing and unmodified validity.[327] The view according to which the LondonProt 1936 has been abrogated, according to the position taken here is not tenable. The conduct of states during World War II can hardly be considered a practice based upon an *opinio iuris* that has contributed to the development of a new rule of customary international law. In the vast majority of cases states justified their conduct by reference to reprisals.[328] Hence, they were convinced of the basic illegality of their measures. Therefore, state practice and the fact that measures of unrestricted submarine warfare were characterized as violations of the law are evidence of the *opinio iuris* of states that they have continuously been bound by the LondonProt 1936. Of course, post-World War II practice

---

[321] Worth mentioning are also the so-called Nyon Arrangements of 1937 that contain similar provisions; cf. L. F. E. Goldie, 'Commentary on the 1937 Nyon Agreements', in Ronzitti (*supra*, n. 29), 489 *et seq.*

[322] Cf. Mallison, *Submarines*, 75 *et seq.*; Sohler, *loc. cit.*

[323] Cf. the references given by Gilliland, *loc. cit.*, at 978–9.

[324] Judgment of 1 October 1946, Vol. 1, 350 *et seq.*

[325] See also E. I. Nwogugu, 'Commentary on Submarine Warfare', in Ronzitti (*supra*, n. 29), 358.

[326] This view is especially taken by D. P. O'Connell, 'International Law and Contemporary Naval Operations' (1970) LXIV *BYIL* 52. See also Gilliland, *loc. cit.*

[327] Cf. Fleck, 'Topical Approaches Towards Developing the Laws of Armed Conflicts at Sea', in Delissen/Tanja (eds), *Essays in Honour of Frits Kalshoven* (The Hague: Nijhoff, 1990), 407–23, at 420; Jacobson (*supra*, n. 318), 214 *et seq.*

[328] Cf. *inter alia*, Whiteman (*supra*, n. 170), Vol. X, 660 *et seq.*

WOLFF HEINTSCHEL VON HEINEGG

gives less testimony. The only known case of an employment of submarines during an international armed conflict was the attack by the British submarine HMS *Conqueror* on the Argentine *General Belgrano* that is of no relevance as regards the continuing validity of the 1936 Protocol. However, the provisions of the Protocol are referred to in recent military manuals[329] (even though the rules on submarine warfare sometimes differ from those on surface warfare).[330] Neither is the Nuremberg judgment authority for the abrogation of the LondonProt 1936. Rather, it has contributed to a clarification of the law in so far as enemy merchant vessels participating in hostilities are not covered by the Protocol's protective scope and may therefore be attacked and sunk without prior warning or prior exercise of visit and search. It needs to be emphasized in this context that, according to the Nuremberg judgment, an attack may not take place in cases of doubt as to the qualification of a merchant vessel as a legitimate military objective. The Nuremberg judgment merely lacks clarification of the status of neutral merchant vessels. According to the Tribunal, all neutral merchant vessels are protected by the Protocol regardless of the fact that under certain circumstances they become legitimate military objectives (e.g. if they are transporting enemy troops or if they are integrated into the enemy's intelligence system).[331] Attacks on neutral merchant vessels are, however, not the subject of the present chapter.

Finally, the continuing validity of the LondonProt 1936 is questioned because it allegedly does not meet the practical requirements of naval armed forces engaged in active hostilities. Its provisions would, therefore, not be observed during armed conflict. Submarines, by using their sonar equipment, could distinguish between different types of vessels but could not verify their respective functions. (One may add that communication with operational control is almost impossible because of the danger of detection.) A naval commander would not expose his submarine to the dangers involved in visit and search merely to realize after surfacing that the supposed merchant vessel is really a warship in disguise.[332] Such practical difficulties, however, are not sufficient proof for the validity of the allegation that, under international law, there are only two types of ships: submarines and targets. On one hand, the effective employment of submarines in modern armed conflict is not jeopardized by the continuing validity and applicability of the Protocol. Its protective scope only covers merchant vessels proper. It does not cover warships and merchant vessels that are legitimate military objectives. Today, submarines are neither exclusively nor predominantly employed against merchant shipping. Because of the technological development since the end of World War II their velocity and operability have increased considerably. They can thus be entrusted with specific military tasks, like protective mining for coastal defence purposes, and attacks on enemy warships and enemy territory.[333] In view of the fundamental principles of naval armed conflict and the overall principle of humanity, it would, on the other hand, be difficult to justify the

---

[329] The *Canadian Manual*, para. 826, expressly repeats the wording of the Protocol and states that merchant vessels meeting the requirements of the definition of military objectives are not protected.

[330] *NWP 1–14M*, para. 8.7.1, provides an enumeration of those conditions relieving submarines of the obligation to first, that is before attack, take crews, passengers, and ship's papers to a place of safety. Those conditions, however, do not differ from those applicable to surface ships. There are, for mere practical reasons, different provisions in order to differentiate between surface and subsurface warfare.

[331] See, *inter alia*, Mallison, *Submarines*, 80 *et seq.*; *San Remo Manual*, paras. 67 *et seq.*

[332] This position is taken by esp. Gilliland, *loc. cit.*, 987.

[333] Cf. K. Lautenschläger, 'The Submarine in Naval Warfare, 1901–2001' (1986–87) 11 *International Security* 94 *et seq.*

existence of different sets of rules for surface and subsurface forces by mere reference to practical considerations. In any event, attacks by submarines as well as by surface vessels must be restricted to military objectives. Only if an object is clearly identified as of military character may it be attacked. In cases of doubt there is a presumption of the non-military character of an object and attacks must be terminated. If, in such cases, the commander is unwilling to expose his submarine to the dangers involved in visit and search he can only leave the vessel concerned to pass unmolested above his periscope. It may be added that many of the concerns raised against the continuing validity of the LondonProt 1936 lose much of their weight in view of the endorsement of maritime exclusion zones.[334]

> **Submarines are subject to the same rules of international law as surface vessels**   1046
> **(Article 1 LondonProt 1936).**

As stated in the preliminary remarks, in view of the continuing validity of the LondonProt 1936 and since no rule of customary law to the contrary has developed, submarines are subject to the same rules as surface ships.[335] Apart from measures against enemy merchant vessels (dealt with in the commentary on Section 1047) this implies that when a submarine launches attacks on targets at sea, in the air, or on land, the fundamental principles of the law of naval armed conflict, as well as the rules on specific methods of naval warfare, must be strictly observed. Hence, despite their restricted technical capabilities, submarines are also subject to the rules on target discrimination. In principle, submarines are equally obliged to rescue shipwrecked and wounded. As already mentioned,[336] this obligation is subject to considerations of military necessity and to the circumstances prevailing at the time.[337] Hence, a submarine may refrain from rescue operations if the risks involved are too high. This will be the case, for example, if the submarine, after surfacing, could be attacked by aircraft. Nor will rescue be feasible if there is not sufficient space available to take shipwrecked and wounded on board. However, the commander is obliged to transmit the position of those who need help as long as this is possible without exposing his ship to attacks.

> **Merchant ships which meet the requirements of a military objective may also be**   1047
> **attacked and sunk by submarines without prior warning. A submarine intend-**
> **ing to capture a hostile merchant ship which does not meet the requirements of**
> **a military objective must first surface. It may not sink a merchant ship without**
> **having first brought the passengers, crew, and ship's papers to a safe place (Article**
> **2 LondonProt 1936). If the merchant ship refuses to stop on being duly summoned**
> **or puts up active resistance to visit or search, the submarine shall be allowed to**
> **attack without warning.**

1. *Merchant vessels meeting the requirements of the definition of military objectives.* These may be attacked anywhere within the areas of naval warfare, without prior warning. This is reaffirmed in the first sentence of the present section. Still, submarines are bound by the same rules as surface ships. Hence, they may not attack if under the prevailing

[334] The same view is taken by Gilliland, *loc. cit.*, 991 *et seq.*
[335] *San Remo Manual*, para. 45, provides: 'Surface ships, submarines and aircraft are bound by the same principles and rules.'
[336] See para. 8 of the commentary on Section 1017.
[337] See also *NWP 1–14M*, para. 8.7.1.

WOLFF HEINTSCHEL VON HEINEGG

circumstances the sinking of an enemy merchant vessel offers no definite military advantage, if less severe means are available, or if the military character of the vessel concerned cannot be clearly established.[338]

2. *Capture and destruction of other enemy merchant vessels.* The dangers connected with surfacing do not release a submarine from compliance with the obligations laid down in the LondonProt 1936. Enemy merchant vessels not qualifying as legitimate military objectives may therefore only be destroyed if after capture passengers, crews, and ship's papers have been taken to a place of safety. If this is not feasible, destruction is illegal.

5. Maritime Exclusion Zones

1. *Preliminary remarks.* The validity of the term 'exclusion zone' as well as the particular rules laid down in the present section can only to a limited extent be based upon state practice. On the one hand, there is neither a uniform usage of that term nor a general consensus as to the details of the concept. On the other hand, the majority of 'zones' established and enforced during armed conflicts at sea have been considered illegal by both, international courts and the legal literature. Still, in view of the growing recognition of 'exclusion' or 'operational zones' in military manuals, including the *San Remo Manual*, today such zones may be considered a generally recognized method under customary international law. However, there still is no consensus on either the such zones are to serve or on the specific rules that have to be observed if a belligerent makes use of an 'exclusion zone'. Therefore, the provisions of Sections 1048 *et seq.* still have to be considered a contribution to the progressive development of international law. It will be seen whether they will meet the general acceptance of the community of states necessary for a rule of customary international law to come into existence.

2. *State practice.*[339]

   a) *State practice until 1945.* Before and during the two World Wars, exclusion/war zones were established primarily to attack any vehicle encountered there, without prior warning. Exclusion zones for merely defensive purposes were for the first time proclaimed during the Russo-Japanese War of 1904/1905.[340] As regards World War I, Great Britain established a war/exclusion zone on 2 November 1914;[341] followed by Germany on 4 February 1915.[342] Because of the inferiority of its surface forces, Germany felt compelled steadily to increase the areas covered by its war zones.[343] Great Britain could confine itself to the originally proclaimed areas because it had already conducted a very successful economic war by means of a long-distance blockade.[344] In view of the fact that the belligerents justified their zones as reprisals and of the severe impact upon neutral merchant shipping, international lawyers in the aftermath of World War I almost

---

[338] See para. 1 of the commentary on Section 1025.

[339] For an excellent overview of the development of this method of naval warfare, see Fenrick (*supra*, n. 122); Goldie, *loc. cit.*, 156 *et seq.*

[340] Cf. Garner (*supra*, n. 142), Vol. I, 351 *et seq.*; Goldie, *loc. cit.*, 158 *et seq.*; M. N. Schmitt, in von Heinegg/Epping (eds), *International Humanitarian Law Facing New Challenges. Symposium in Honour of Knut Ipsen* (Berlin/Heidelberg: Springer, 2007), 11–48 [15].

[341] Cf. Garner, Vol. 1, 333 *et seq.*

[342] *Kriegsgebietserklärung*, published in *Reichs-Marine-Amt, Seekriegsrecht im Weltkriege*, Nos. 117, 135.

[343] J. W. Garner, 'War Zones and Submarine Warfare' (1915) *AJIL* 594; Fenrick, *loc. cit.*, at 94 *et seq.*

[344] For British economic warfare during World War I, see L. Guichard, *The Naval Blockade 1914–1918* (New York: Appleton, 1930), 22 *et seq.*

unanimously agreed on the illegality of such war/exclusion zones.[345] During World War II, Great Britain established a war/exclusion zone in the Skagerrak: by day all German vessels and by night all vessels regardless of their nationality were liable to attack on sight.[346] At the beginning of hostilities the German naval forces were obliged to comply with the rules of the LondonProt 1936, as implemented in the Prize Ordinance of 28 August 1939. Soon, however, they were released from those restrictions. Consequently, a comprehensive war zone around the British Isles was proclaimed. It was gradually increased in the course of the war.[347] In the Pacific Ocean, the US also made use of the exclusion zone device and conducted unrestricted submarine warfare against Japan.[348] After the end of World War II, the Nuremberg Tribunal characterized the establishment of war/exclusion zones as a violation of the LondonProt 1936. The Tribunal held that the Treaty had been ratified in knowledge of the practice of World War I. However, there were no exceptions on war/exclusion zones in the Protocol.[349] In this context, it is emphasized that the Tribunal reached its decision merely upon the ground that, within the German war zones, neutral merchant vessels had been sunk without prior warning. The Tribunal did not base its judgment upon attacks on enemy merchant vessels that had lost the protection of the Protocol by having been integrated into Great Britain's war efforts. Nevertheless, Admiral Dönitz was not sentenced for that violation of the Protocol, because Great Britain (in the Skagerrak) and the US (in the Pacific) had also established war zones in which neutral merchant vessels had been attacked on sight. It therefore remained an open question whether and to what extent neutral merchant vessels—whether within or outside exclusion zones—could be attacked. Obviously, the Nuremberg Tribunal did not take that possibility into consideration in order not to divest itself of the only legal yardstick available: the LondonProt 1936.[350] Hence, from the reasons given one may draw the conclusion that maritime exclusion zones are probably not illegal if measures taken there either serve purely defensive purposes or are directed solely at enemy military objectives. Still, state practice of the two World Wars is without prejudice to the legality of exclusion zones as laid down in the present Section. The World War zones had a quite different object and purpose.

b) State practice since 1945. This also does not justify the conclusion that, under customary international law, maritime exclusion zones are a legitimate method of naval warfare. The number of precedents—the Falklands/Malvinas conflict[351] and the first Gulf War[352]—is far from sufficient.[353] Moreover, there are considerable differences between

---

[345] For this and further references, see J. A. Hall, *The Law of Naval Warfare*, 2nd edn (London: Chapman, 1921), 246 *et seq.*

[346] Cf. Mallison, *Submarines*, 36 *et seq.*

[347] Cf. Fenrick, *loc. cit.*, 100. The order to attack all enemy vessels in the Channel was issued on 4 and 17 October 1939. On 24 November 1939, neutral merchant shipping was advised to refrain from travelling in the sea areas around the British Isles.

[348] This is evidenced by the statement of Admiral Nimitz before the Nuremberg Tribunal; see Vol. 17, 414 *et seq.* It should be added that other states participating in World War II proclaimed similar zones often labelled 'danger zones'.

[349] I *IMT*, 350 *et seq.*

[350] See also O'Connell (*supra*, n. 326), 52.

[351] Cf. Zuppi (*supra*, n. 311), 190 *et seq.*

[352] Cf. R. Leckow, 'The Iran–Iraq Conflict in the Gulf: The Law of War Zones' (1988) *ICLQ* 629 *et seq.*; Fenrick, *loc. cit.*, 116 *et seq.*

[353] During the Korean conflict the US Navy proclaimed something similar to an exclusion zone. According to the Rules of Engagement the 7th Fleet was entitled to attack any submarine contact in certain specified sea areas. Cf. O'Connell (*supra*, n. 172), 167.

WOLFF HEINTSCHEL VON HEINEGG

the exclusion zones established in the South Atlantic and those established in the Persian Gulf. However, the reactions of third states as well as statements in the legal literature justify the conclusion that the exclusion zone device may become a generally accepted method of naval warfare if certain criteria are met. On 28 April 1982, Great Britain proclaimed a 'Total Exclusion Zone' (TEZ) in the South Atlantic.[354] Beside deterring the Argentine naval forces from leaving their ports, its main purpose was to facilitate the early identification of military objectives and to prevent vessels flying neutral flags from conveying information to Argentina. Argentina, on 11 May 1982, proclaimed a war zone covering the whole South Atlantic and announced that any British vessel would be attacked. On one hand, the British TEZ covered an area of 200 nautical miles measured from the centre of the main island.[355] On the other hand, the TEZ was situated far from any main shipping lanes. Moreover, its duration was comparatively short. It did not serve economic warfare purposes but was aimed at facilitating military operations, including identification. Vessels and aircraft flying flags of states not parties to the conflict suffered no damage whatsoever.[356] For these reasons, only the former USSR officially protested against the British TEZ. During the 1980–1988 Gulf conflict, neither Iran nor Iraq seem to have been led by legal considerations when establishing their respective exclusion zones.[357] Iraq mainly concentrated on shipping (largely neutral) serving Kharg Island. It made no difference whether those tankers were travelling in convoy, armed or unarmed. Iraq's measures were generally condemned, as were similar measures taken by Iran against neutral merchant vessels travelling to and from other coastal states of the Persian Gulf.[358] During the recent Operation Iraqi Freedom, the US established 'zones' or 'exclusion zones' in order either to restrict sea and air traffic in a given area or to protect certain high value targets, like oil platforms, against possible (terrorist) attacks. That practice reveals that, according to the US position, the establishment of an exclusion zone for the said purposes is legal, especially if the area affected is limited in space. Of course, it should not be left out of consideration that if such zones are established for the purpose of countering terrorist threats the legal basis is not to be found in the law of armed conflict bur rather in the law governing the right of self-defence.

---

[354] Text in (1982) LIII *BYIL* 542. Already on 7 April 1982 Great Britain had proclaimed a 200 nautical miles 'Maritime Exclusion Zone' around the Falklands to the effect that 'any Argentine warship and Argentine naval auxiliaries found within this zone will be treated as hostile and are liable to attack by British forces' (*loc. cit.* 556). In its proclamation of the TEZ, the British government declared: 'The exclusion zone will apply not only to Argentine warships and naval auxiliaries but also to any other ship, whether naval or merchant vessel, which is operating in support of the illegal occupation of the Falkland Islands by Argentine forces. The zone will also apply to any aircraft, whether military or civil, which is operating in support of the Argentine occupation. Any ship and any aircraft, whether military or civil, which is found within the zone without authority from the Ministry of Defence in London will be regarded as operating in support of the illegal occupation and will therefore be regarded as hostile and will be liable to be attacked by British forces.'

[355] On 7 May 1982, Great Britain extended the TEZ to all sea areas 12 nautical miles off the Argentine coast. Consequently, 'any Argentine warship or military aircraft which is found more than 12 nautical miles from the Argentine coast will be regarded as hostile and is liable to be dealt with accordingly' (*loc. cit.* 549).

[356] However, in June 1982 the tanker *Hercules* flying the Liberian flag was attacked by Argentine aircraft outside the British TEZ and was severely damaged. Cf. 79 *ILR*, 1 *et seq.*

[357] For the belligerents' practice, see Danziger (*supra*, n. 312), 162 *et seq.*; Leckow, *loc. cit.*, 636 *et seq.*; Fenrick, *loc. cit.*, 118 *et seq.*; Politakis, (*supra*, n. 109), 148; D. L. Peace, 'Major Maritime Events in the Persian Gulf War' (1988) 82 *Proceedings of the American Society of International Law* 147.

[358] See the references given by Fenrick, *loc. cit.*, 121 *et seq.*

WOLFF HEINTSCHEL VON HEINEGG

c) Military manuals. A growing number of states, according to their military manuals, consider exclusion zones to be in conformity with the law of armed conflict. Thus, the *UK Manual* provides: 'Maritime exclusion zones and total exclusion zones are legitimate means of exercising the right of self-defence and other rights enjoyed under international law. However, in declaring the zones, the exact extent, location, duration and risks associated should be made clear... Should a belligerent, as an exceptional measure, establish such a zone: a. the same body of law applies both inside and outside the zone; b. the extent, location and duration of the zone and the measures imposed shall not exceed what is strictly required by military necessity and the principle of proportionality; c. due regard shall be given to the rights of neutral states to legitimate uses of the seas; necessary safe passage through the zone for neutral vessels and aircraft shall be provided: (1) where the geographical extent of the zone significantly impedes free and safe access to the ports and coasts of a neutral state; (2) in other cases where normal navigation routes are affected, except where military requirements do not permit; and d. the commencement, duration, location and extent of the zone, as well as the restrictions imposed, shall be publicly declared and appropriately notified.'[359] The *US Naval Manual* also considers the establishment of an exclusion zone in accordance with the law of naval warfare: '. . . To the extent that such zones serve to warn neutral vessels and aircraft away from belligerent activities and thereby reduce their exposure to collateral damage and incidental injury ..., and to the extent that they do not unreasonably interfere with legitimate neutral commerce, they are undoubtedly lawful. However, the establishment of such a zone does not relieve the proclaiming belligerent of the obligation under the law of armed conflict to refrain from attacking vessels and aircraft which do not constitute lawful targets...an otherwise protected platform does not lose that protection by crossing an imaginary line drawn in the ocean by a belligerent.'[360] Similar rules are recognized in the *Canadian Manual.*[361]

The *San Remo Manual* provides: '(105) A belligerent cannot be absolved of its duties under international humanitarian law by establishing zones which might adversely affect the legitimate uses of defined areas of the sea. (106) Should a belligerent, as an exceptional measure, establish such a zone: (a) the same body of law applies both inside and outside the zone; (b) the extent, location and duration of the zone and the measures imposed shall not exceed what is strictly required by military necessity and the principles of proportionality; (c) due regard shall be given to the rights of neutral States to legitimate uses of the seas; (d) necessary safe passage through the zone for neutral vessels and aircraft shall be provided: (i) where the geographical extent of the zone significantly impedes free and safe access to the ports and coasts of a neutral State; (ii) in other cases where normal navigation routes are affected, except where military requirements do not permit; and (e) the commencement, duration, location and extent of the zone, as well as the restrictions imposed, shall be publicly declared and appropriately notified.'

The 'Helsinki Principles of the Law of Neutrality in Relation to Warfare at Sea' adopted by the 67th Conference of the International Law Association in 1996, have acknowledged this practice: '3.3 *Special Zones.* Subject to Principle 5.2.9 [visit and search vis-à-vis neutral commercial ships] and without prejudice to the rights of commanders in the zone of

---

[359] *UK Manual (2004)*, paras. 13.77.1 and 13.78.
[360] *NWP 1–14M*, para. 7.9.
[361] Canadian Manual (*supra*, n. 27), paras. 852 *et seq.*

immediate naval operations, the establishment by a belligerent of special zones does not confer upon that belligerent rights in relation to neutral shipping which it would not otherwise possess. In particular, the establishment of a special zone cannot confer upon a belligerent the right to attack neutral shipping merely on account of its presence in the zone. However, a belligerent may, as an exceptional measure, declare zones where neutral shipping would be particularly exposed to risks caused by the hostilities. The extent, location and duration must be made public and may not go beyond what is required by military necessity, regard being paid to the principle of proportionality. Due regard shall also be given to the rights of all states to legitimate uses of the seas. Where such a zone significantly impedes free and safe access to the ports of a neutral state and the use of normal navigation routes, measures to facilitate safe passage shall be taken.'[362]

d) Statements in the legal literature. In the post-World War II era, the issue of the legality of exclusion zones is addressed in a far more differentiated way than in the post-World War I period.[363] There seems to be a tendency to acknowledge the legality of exclusion zones in principle if the interests of neutral shipping are duly taken into account and if they are not intended to serve as 'free-fire zones', where vessels are attacked indiscriminately, regardless of the fundamental principles of the law of naval warfare, and without prior warning.[364]

3. *Conclusions.* In some respects the provisions of the *San Remo Manual* on 'zones' lack the necessary clarity. On the one hand, there is no statement on the legitimate purpose a 'zone' may serve. On the other hand, it is difficult to distinguish such 'zones' from similar concepts, like warning zones/areas, security zones/areas, defensive zones, or the 'immediate vicinity of naval operations'. A comparison between paras. 105–108 and paragraph 75 of the *San Remo Manual* makes it possible to distinguish a 'zone' from the 'immediate vicinity of naval operations' or from an 'area of military activities potentially hazardous to civil aircraft'. Obviously, a belligerent is entitled to temporarily impose air traffic restrictions in the latter areas, including an absolute prohibition of overflight for neutral civil aircraft.[365] In view of the hazards a merchant vessel or a civil aircraft will be exposed to if they approach or enter an area of military activities a belligerent is (or rather: should be) entitled to temporarily establish and enforce a 'zone'. Moreover, as laid down in Article 34 HRAW 1923, enemy civil aircraft are liable to be fired upon in the immediate vicinity of military operations. All this, however, presupposes that military operations/activities in fact occur in the area in question. Similar considerations apply with regard to 'safety zones' that serve the sole purpose of protecting high value or extremely hazardous targets, like oil platforms or nuclear reactors.[366] The space affected would, of

---

[362] The International Law Association, Report of the 67th Conference (Helsinki 1996), Committee on Maritime Neutrality, Final Report, 367–400 [374–389].

[363] Cf. Colombos (*supra*, n. 12), paras. 559 *et seq.*; Tucker (*supra*, n. 76), 302; Mallison (*supra*, n. 102), *Submarines*, 91 *et seq.*; Whiteman (*supra*, n. 170), Vol. X, 607 *et seq.*; Goldie (*supra*, n. 321), *Maritime War Zones*, 156 *et seq.*; Gilliland, *loc. cit.*, 991 *et seq.*; Fenrick, *loc. cit.*, 91 *et seq.*

[364] Gilliland, *loc. cit.*, 991 *et seq.*; Fenrick, *loc. cit.*, 91 *et seq.*

[365] See also Article 30 HRAW 1923 which provides: 'In case a belligerent commanding officer considers that the presence of aircraft is likely to prejudice the success of the operations in which he is engaged at the moment, he may prohibit the passing of neutral aircraft in the immediate vicinity of his forces or may oblige them to follow a particular route. A neutral aircraft which does not conform to such directions, of which it has had notice issued by the belligerent commanding officer, may be fired upon.'

[366] For the most recent practice of such security zones, see broadcast warnings promulgated by the Worldwide Navigational Warnings Service (WWNWS), <http://msi.nga.mil/NGAPortal/MSI.portal?_nfpb=true&_pageLabel=msI_portal_page_63>.

WOLFF HEINTSCHEL VON HEINEGG

course, be rather limited. Still, the legitimate purpose of 'zones' remains unclear. Neither the *San Remo Manual* nor recent military manuals (e.g. of the UK) provide an answer to that question.[367] Thus, it is rather difficult to establish which measures a belligerent will be allowed to take against merchant vessels or civil aircraft. Probably, an answer can be deduced from the *US Naval Manual (2007)*. While there is general agreement that a 'zone' may never be a 'free-fire zone' and while it would be in accordance with the law to establish a zone for the purpose of limiting the geographic area of naval warfare a 'zone', according to the *US Naval Manual*, could also serve the protection of neutral aviation and shipping. Then, however, the question arises as to the distinction of a 'zone' from the 'area of military activities'/'immediate vicinity of naval operations'.

4. *Distinction from other concepts.* Accordingly, before establishing the legitimate purposes a belligerent may pursue with the establishment of an exclusion zone, such zones have to be distinguished from related concepts under the law of armed conflict.[368]

a) Naval mining. Although some of the zones established and enforced during the World Wars were nothing but extensive (and probably excessive) minefields, there is today general agreement that mine areas are to be distinguished from exclusion zones because the use of naval mines is governed by a specific legal regime.

b) Blockade. The latter also holds true with regard to blockades. According to the well-established rules and principles of the law of armed conflict on blockades, a blockade is a belligerent operation aimed at preventing vessels and/or aircraft of all nations, enemy as well as neutral, from entering or exiting specified ports, airfields, or coastal areas belonging to, occupied by, or under the control of an enemy nation. The purpose of establishing a blockade is to deny the enemy the use of enemy and neutral vessels or aircraft to transport personnel and goods to or from enemy territory. If effective and if properly declared the legality of a blockade is beyond any doubt. In short, the difference between a zone and a blockade can be described as follows: 'With blockades, the focus lies on the line (or "curtain") marking the outer limit of the blockaded area. The area/space within that line is of minor interest. By contrast, the focal point of "exclusion zones" ... is the three dimensional area/space within the declared borderline'.[369]

c) No-fly zones. A no-fly zone is the 'three dimensional airspace by which [a] Belligerent Party restricts or prohibits aviation in its own or in enemy national' airspace.[370] In contrast, an exclusion zone, while applicable to ships and aircraft, is established in areas beyond the territorial sovereignty of the parties to the conflict.

d) Immediate vicinity of naval operations. Special rules also apply within the immediate vicinity of operations.[371] Accordingly, the *US Naval Manual* (2007), para. 7.8, provides: 'Within the immediate area or vicinity of naval operations, a belligerent may establish special restrictions upon the activities of neutral vessels and aircraft and may prohibit altogether such vessels and aircraft from entering the area. The immediate area or vicinity of naval operations is that area within which hostilities are taking place or

---

[367] The *UK Manual* is most ambiguous on the subject. In Chapter 12 on air operations there is a general paragraph on 'war zones restrictions'. In Chapter 13 on maritime warfare the zones are termed 'security zones' but under the very same heading the *UK Manual* also refers to 'maritime and total exclusion zones'.

[368] An excellent overview of the different concepts made use of by belligerents is given by R. Jaques (ed.), *Maritime Operational Zones* (Naval War College, 2006).

[369] *HPCR Manual*, introduction to Section P.

[370] Ibid.

[371] Cf. Fenrick, *loc. cit.*, at 93.

belligerent forces are actually operating. A belligerent may not, however, purport to deny access to neutral nations, or to close an international strait to neutral shipping, pursuant to this authority unless another route of similar convenience remains open to neutral traffic.' Similar or identical rules are contained in the *UK Manual* (para. 13.82) and the concept is also recognized in the *San Remo Manual* (para. 108) and in the ILA Helsinki Principles (para. 3.3). The recognition of special belligerent rights in the immediate vicinity of operations is due to the fact that the presence of vessels and aircraft in that area will legitimately be considered a high threat, both for the vehicles concerned and for the belligerent units operating in the area in question. They therefore serve a twofold protective purpose and, if not excessive in character, are considered in accordance with the law of armed conflict.

e) 'Defensive bubbles' and other warning zones. Closely related to the former concept are 'defensive bubbles' and other warning zones that are designed to warn others of certain dangers caused by lawful uses of the seas (e.g. weapons exercises), by measures of force protection (e.g., defensive bubbles and a 'cordon sanitaire'[372]), or by actions to be taken in order to accomplish a particular mission or objective. Their legality seems to be undisputed, regardless of whether they are being made use of in time of peace or in times of international armed conflict.[373]

f) Neutral defensive zones. Of course, neutral states are entitled to deny belligerent warships the use of their territorial sea areas on a non-discriminatory basis. Since neutral territory, including neutral airspace, may never be used by belligerent warships and military aircraft such defensive zones established by a neutral state and aimed at the protection against the negative effects of an ongoing international armed conflict, will always be in accordance with the applicable law.

g) Safety zones. Safety zones will regularly be established around high-value installations or around installations containing dangerous material. If situated in high seas areas, both belligerent and neutral states are entitled to enforce such safety zones. Of course, the respective enemy will not be obliged to respect a safety zone, especially if the object concerned qualifies as a legitimate military objective.

h) Spatial self-restrictions. Spatial restrictions a belligerent may observe during an armed conflict may not be mistaken for an exclusion zone. For instance, if prize measures are taken in specified sea and air spaces only, this by no means implies the establishment of a zone. Such measures will remain legal everywhere within the area of aerial and naval operations as soon as the belligerent concerned decides to enlarge the area of such operations.

i) Humanitarian zones. The *San Remo Manual*, in para. 160, provides that the belligerents 'may agree, for humanitarian purposes, to create a zone in a defined area of the sea in which only activities consistent with those humanitarian purposes are permitted'. This paragraph is inspired by the so-called 'Red Cross Box' established during the 1982 Falklands/Malvinas conflict. The details of such a 'humanitarian zone'—location, extent, duration, and permissible measures—are subject to an agreement between the belligerents. Therefore, one may be inclined not to elaborate on this issue in great depth. It would, however, according to the position taken here, be helpful if reasonable

---

[372] Cf. S. F. Gilchrist, 'The Cordon Sanitaire: Is It Useful? Is It Practical?' (1982) 35 *Naval War College Review* 60 *et seq.*

[373] Cf. Gilliland, *loc. cit.*, 991 *et seq.*; Fenrick, *loc. cit.*, 110 *et seq.*

measures of protection were addressed. As already stated there is a realistic probability of illegal attacks against protected platforms. If gathered in a relatively limited sea area they would be exposed to an even higher risk.

j) Flight information regions and air defence identification zones, while genuinely peace-time concepts, may continue to play a role during an international armed conflict. Their legality can not be doubted under either the law of peace or the law of war.

> **A belligerent may establish an exclusion zone as an exceptional measure in pursu-**   **1048**
> **ance of one of the following aims, or a combination thereof:**
> — **to identify the geographic area of military operations;**
> — **to subject civil navigation and aviation to restrictions, especially in the immedi-**
>   **ate vicinity of military operations; or**
> — **to enhance the protection of:**
>   **(i) works and installations containing dangerous forces;**
>   **(ii) objects indispensable for the survival of the civilian population;**
>   **(iii) objects and installations for the medical treatment of wounded and sick**
>   **civilians or combatants;**
>   **(iv) persons and objects protected under international humanitarian law; or**
>   **(v) other objects and installations of high value.**

1. *Exceptional right.* The wording of Section 1048, especially the emphasis on the excep-tional character of the right to establish an exclusion zone, makes it clear that belligerents are not entitled to use such zones as they will. Rather, an exclusion zone may only be established if necessary for legitimate reasons of national security and of military necessity. Its geographical scope, its duration, and the restrictions imposed upon neutral shipping and air traffic must be kept within the limits of proportionality. It is, therefore, not pos-sible to state in advance and in the abstract the legal limitations which the belligerents will have to observe. It will depend upon the circumstances of each case whether an exclusion zone is acceptable under international law.[374] Accordingly, a zone established in remote sea areas may be legal; a zone in areas of high marine traffic density may not, because of its greater interference with neutral shipping. Subject to the prevailing circumstances, the interests of neutral shipping and air traffic must be taken into due consideration by provid-ing safe passage through the zone. Reasons of military convenience alone do not justify the establishment of an exclusion zone. In any event they may not be made 'free-fire zones' where all objects are indiscriminately attacked. The proclaiming belligerent is obliged to take all militarily feasible precautions to ensure that the use of weapons is confined to the minimum necessary for self-defence. For example, if prize measures can be expected to be equally effective, the use of weapons is prohibited. Moreover, naval armed forces are not released from the duty to ensure proper target identification. Within exclusion zones, too, only legitimate military objectives may be attacked. However, the demands resulting from the principle of distinction are less strict than outside an exclusion zone. In sum, exclusion zones exclusively serving economic warfare purposes or where the proclaiming belligerent disregards the principle of distinction are illegal.

2. *Purpose.* The use of the exclusion zone device in twentieth-century armed conflicts has often be misinterpreted as having contributed to the emergence of an exceptional right allowing the respective belligerent to target any object encountered in a given area ('free-

---

[374] A similar approach is taken in the *San Remo Manual*, paras. 105 *et seq.* See also *Canadian Manual*, para. 853.

fire zone'). However, as emphasized in Sections 1049 and 1050, by the establishment of an exclusion zone a belligerent is not absolved of its obligations under the law of naval warfare and of neutrality at sea. Accordingly, if the concept is to have a meaning of its own, the purpose an exclusion zone may serve needs to be specified.

a) Identification of the area of military operations. At least in theory a belligerent may wish to limit its military operations to a given geographical area and therefore declare that it will not make use of the full spectrum of methods and means of naval warfare outside that area. For example, it may continue to target enemy military objectives everywhere in the legitimate 'region of operations' but may limit its exercise of prize measures to the close vicinity of the enemy's and its own coast lines. The shipping and aviation of third states would thus remain unmolested outside the exclusion zone. This, however, presupposes a clear commitment on behalf of the belligerent. The mere fact that a zone is limited to a certain geographical area is not sufficient.[375]

b) Restrictions for civil navigation and aviation. Closely related to the former is the purpose of subjecting civil navigation and aviation to special restrictions. Especially in the vicinity of military operations belligerents have a legitimate right to limit the movement of merchant vessels and of aircraft. However, this may not be confused with the establishment of a warning zone for force protection purposes which is always in accordance with international law both in peacetime and in wartime. Rather, the restrictions covered by the present section aim at protecting a military operation or the overall military mission. If justified by considerations of military necessity they may include the prohibition of entering the zone. This does not mean that any vessel or aircraft encountered within the zone would be liable to attack on sight. However, they may ordered to leave the area, they may be subjected to extensive control measures and they would, in any event, navigate at their own risk.

c) Enhancing protection. From an operational perspective the protection of the high value targets enumerated in lit. c is of overall importance. The fact that those objects and persons are in principle already protected by other rules of the law of naval warfare should not distract from the threats posed by all forms of asymmetric warfare. While asymmetries are not a new phenomenon of war today non-state actors dispose of highly effective capabilities outreaching those of the past. Moreover, transnational terrorists will not confine their attacks on military objectives or combatants. Rather, they will target persons and objects with a view to destabilizing the political situation. Therefore, the principle of reciprocity that guarantees respect for protected persons and objects in the relation between belligerent states can no longer be relied upon. The means by which the enhancement of protection could be achieved will therefore depend upon the threat posed by non-state actors. This may result in attacks against any vessel or aircraft that approaches one of the high value targets without clearly indicating its intentions. Such attacks will regularly be justified in view of the special protection such persons and objects enjoy under the law of naval warfare.

3. *Effectiveness.* Since the establishment of an exclusion zone is an exceptional belligerent right, it has to meet strict legal requirements. It cannot be expected that so-called 'paper

---

[375] For example, the TEZ established around the Falkland Islands was, by some, misinterpreted as limiting attacks to the area covered by the zone. As the wording of the British declaration contained no such intention the Argentine warship *General Belgrano*—beyond any doubt a legitimate military objective—could be attacked and sunk although it was outside the British TEZ.

WOLFF HEINTSCHEL VON HEINEGG

exclusion zones', not enforced by a sufficient number of naval and air forces, will be accepted by the international community.[376] This, however, does not mean that a large number of armed forces must be present in the area concerned. It is sufficient if the area is surveyed by radar and if naval and air forces units are able to reach any point situated within the zone quickly.

4. *Time limits and notification.* A grace period sufficient for all interested vessels and aircraft to leave the area covered by a proclamation is as essential for a zone's legality as the official notification of its commencement, duration, location, and extent, and the restrictions imposed. Restrictions on neutral air and sea traffic must be confined to what is necessary to serve the proclaiming state's security interests.

> **Should a belligerent establish an exclusion zone, both inside and outside the zone**   1049
> **the same legal norms would apply.**

Section 1049 is an emphasis of the prohibition to establish a 'free-fire zone' by clarifying that the establishment of an exclusion zone does not imply the applicability of a special set of rules. Rather, the respective belligerent remains bound by the law of naval warfare and of neutrality at sea. Section 1050 restates that obligation in a more specific way.

> (1) **A belligerent is not absolved of its duties under the international law of armed**   1050
>   **conflict by establishing exclusion zones.**
> (2) **The establishment of an exclusion ('no-fly') zone does not diminish the obligation**
>   **to respect within the zone the protection of civilians and civilian objects.**
> (3) **Nothing in Sections 1048–1049 should be deemed to derogate from the right**
>   **of a party to an armed conflict to control navigation and civil aviation in the**
>   **immediate vicinity of military operation.**

1. *No modification of the applicable law.* The first paragraph of Section 1050 restates the prohibition in Section 1049 of establishing a 'free-fire zone'. Accordingly, the belligerent establishing an exclusion zone remains bound by the rules of the law of naval warfare on the conduct of hostilities at sea and on specially protected persons and objects. Attacks must be limited to military targets, that is enemy combatants, persons directly taking part in the hostilities, and objects contributing to the enemy's military action and whose neutralization offers a definite military advantage. Moreover, the rules on proper target identification as well as on precautions in attack remain applicable inside an exclusion zone. Specially protected vessels and aircraft may not be attacked as long as they are engaged in their innocent role.

2. *Protection of civilians and of civilian objects.* Civilians and civilian objects, even when encountered within an exclusion zone continue to be protected under the law of naval warfare and neutrality at sea. Therefore, in principle any direct attack against these persons and objects is illegal. However, this presupposes that they are engaged in their innocent role. If an exclusion zone has been established with a view to protecting high-value targets an attack against a merchant vessel or civilian aircraft will therefore be in accordance with the law if there are reasonable grounds for suspicion that it intends to

---

[376] Even though the term 'paper exclusion zone' is an allusion to the term 'paper blockade' it is emphasized that the legal basis of exclusion zones is not the law of blockade.

WOLFF HEINTSCHEL VON HEINEGG

attack or otherwise jeopardize the protected persons or objects. Such reasonable grounds will regularly exist if the vessel or aircraft remains on its course although it has been warned and ordered to change its course.

3. *Immediate vicinity of naval operations.* Paragraph 3 emphasizes that the provisions on exclusion zones are without prejudice to the well-established belligerent right to subject merchant navigation and civil aviation to control measures if they enter the immediate vicinity of naval operations. Within the immediate area or vicinity of naval operations, a belligerent may establish special restrictions upon the activities of neutral vessels and aircraft and may prohibit altogether such vessels and aircraft from entering the area. The immediate area or vicinity of naval operations is that area within which hostilities are taking place or belligerent forces are actually operating. A belligerent may not, however, purport to deny access to neutral nations, or to close an international strait to neutral shipping, pursuant to this authority unless another route of similar convenience remains open to neutral traffic.

Moreover, belligerent vessels continue to enjoy the right to take all measures necessary for effective force protection. During the Falklands/Malvinas conflict, Great Britain established 'defence bubbles' around its naval units.[377] Defensive measures were to be restricted to cases in which the approach of vessels or aircraft constituted a threat.[378] There were no protests by third states. Legal commentators apparently did not question their legality.[379] It is self-evident that in the case of the proclamation of a 'defence bubble' the belligerent is not obliged publicly to notify the unit's course and/or destination. Otherwise, the units concerned would be too easy a target for, for example, over-the-horizon attacks by the enemy. It is, therefore, sufficient if the declaration contains information about the extent of the zone and about what will be perceived as hostile intent. The permissible extent will depend upon the defence needs in the prevailing circumstances. It may be up to 5 nautical miles[380] but may also exceed that limit if otherwise the approach of vessels or aircraft would constitute an unbearable risk. The restrictions imposed and measures to be taken must be limited to that degree of force necessary to ensure effective self-defence. The use of weapons will be permissible if an approaching vessel or aircraft qualifies as a legitimate military objective and if less severe means are not available.

6. Blockade

1051   A blockade is a method of naval warfare that aims at preventing all vessels or aircraft from entering or exiting enemy coastal areas or ports. The purpose of blockades is to block supplies to the adversary without directly meaning to occupy territory. Starvation of the civilian population as a method of warfare is prohibited (Article 49, para. 3 in connection with Article 54, para. 1, AP I). It is also prohibited to hinder relief shipments for the civilian population (Article 70 AP I).

1. *Introduction.* Blockade is one of the oldest methods of naval warfare. In the nineteenth and in the first half of the twentieth century it was regarded a method of economic

[377] See the declaration of 23 April 1982 in *The Times*, 26 April 1982; Fenrick, *loc. cit.*, 110.
[378] A similar 'defence bubble' was proclaimed by the US Navy during the Iran–Iraq War. However, the US was not a party to that conflict.
[379] Cf. Gilliland, *loc. cit.*, 991 *et seq.*; Fenrick, *loc.cit.*, 110 *et seq.*
[380] During the Iran–Iraq War the US Navy considered 5 nautical miles as sufficient because the main threat was expected from the Iranian *Pasdaran*.

warfare at sea. In recent state practice, for example in the Israel–Lebanon conflict (2006), such economic blockades have been the exception. Today the establishment of a blockade is very often an integral part of a military operation that is not directed against the enemy's economy but against its armed forces.[381] But even if an economic blockade in the strict sense were established, there would always be a strategic element: cutting off the enemy's trade links and weakening its economy will also weaken its military power of resistance. No matter which purpose is pursued by the establishment of a blockade, it always involves the use of military force directed against the enemy's coastline and ports. Accordingly, a blockade is a method of naval warfare to which the general principles and rules of the law of naval warfare apply.

The conditions for its legality were laid down in the ParisDecl 1856. The fact that none of the 1907 Hague Conventions contains provisions on blockade is due to the fact that the time then available was limited. In 1909, blockade was regulated in the LondonDecl.[382] Although it never entered into force, the main features of its provisions on blockade are today generally recognized as customary in character.[383] However, the practice of the two World Wars made evident that only in exceptional cases can naval armed forces maintain a blockade in accordance with the relatively strict preconditions of the traditional law. Today, the maintenance of a naval blockade in accordance with the traditional law will only be feasible if the sea area in question is almost completely under the control of the blockading power.[384] Often the blockaded state will have intermediate or long-range missiles and will, thus, be able to keep its enemy forces far away from its coastline.[385] Hence, today the preconditions for a legal blockade are less strict, as will be shown in the commentary on Section 1053.

2. No limitation to vessels. There is today general agreement that a blockade need not be enforced exclusively against seagoing vessels but that it may also be enforced against aircraft.[386] Moreover, and in view of the importance of aerial reconnaissance, a blockade may be maintained and enforced 'by a combination of legitimate methods and means of warfare',[387] including military aircraft.[388] The *San Remo Manual*'s provisions on blockade, however, lack any express reference to aircraft. Of course, an interpretation of paras. 96[389] and 97 justifies the conclusion that a blockade may be enforced and maintained by military aircraft, too. In most cases will these aircraft belong to a warship that will serve

[381] For a comprehensive legal, operational, and historical evaluation of blockades, see the contributions in B. A. Elleman/S. C. M. Paine (eds), *Naval Blockades and Seapower* (London/New York: Routledge, 2006).

[382] For these provisions, see Fleck, 'London Naval Conference (1908–1909)', *MPEPIL*; Kalshoven (*supra*, n. 161), 257 *et seq.*

[383] Cf. C. J. Colombos, 'The Actual Value of the Declaration of London of 1909' (1959) 12 *Revue Héllenique de Droit International* 10 *et seq.*; *NWP 1–14M*, para. 7.7.5; *Canadian Manual*, paras. 844 *et seq.*

[384] This was the case during the Iraq–Kuwait conflict in which the Allied forces were able to cut off all imports by sea and air destined for Iraq.

[385] See also O'Connell (*supra*, n. 12), Vol. II, 1154 *et seq.*

[386] See, *inter alia*, *NWP 1–14M*, para. 7.7.1; H. Lauterpacht (*supra*, n. 123), at 781; Castrén (*supra*, n. 175), at 301. Further Tucker (*supra*, n. 76), at 283 n. 1: 'The extension of blockades to include the air space over the high seas remains a development for the future. It is next to impossible to declare with any degree of assurance what procedures may govern blockade by air. Certainly, there are grave difficulties in assuming that the practices of naval blockade can be applied readily, by analogy, to aerial blockade.' Note, however, that *Tucker* does not doubt the legality of a blockade if applied and enforced against air traffic.

[387] *San Remo Manual*, para. 97.

[388] H. Lauterpacht, *op. cit.*, 780–1; Castrén, at 300 *et seq.*

[389] 'The force maintaining the blockade may be stationed at a distance determined by military requirements.' The term 'force' is broad enough to also cover military aircraft.

as their base.[390] It is, however, also possible that the aircraft entrusted with the enforcement of a blockade are deployed on airfields on land. Still, while there seems to be general agreement on the lawfulness of the enforcement of a blockade by military aircraft, two questions remain unanswered: (1) Is the presence of a warship or its operational control of the military aircraft necessary for a blockade to be lawful or may a blockade be enforced by aircraft (and mines) alone? (2) What criteria have to be met in order for the blockade to be effective if it is maintained and enforced by aircraft?

In most cases the aircraft entrusted with the enforcement of a blockade need not be dependent upon a warship, that is they are not necessarily under the operational control of a warship. However, the answer to the first question becomes a little complicated if one takes into consideration the following scenario: a merchant vessel or a neutral warship may be damaged or in another distress situation. Therefore it will have to access the blockaded coast or port but the blockade is maintained by mines and aircraft only. How will the blockading power be able to comply with its obligation to allow ships in distress entry into the blockaded coastline if no warship is in the near vicinity?[391] Accordingly, there is at least one argument against the legality of a blockade that is enforced and maintained without any surface warship present in, or in the vicinity of, the blockaded area.

As regards the second question, one may be inclined to point at the well-established rule according to which the 'question whether a blockade is effective is a question of fact'.[392] While it is clear that 'effectiveness' can no longer be judged in the light of the state of technology of the nineteenth century[393] and while the view is widely held that effectiveness continues to be a constitutive element of a legal blockade[394] it may not be left out of consideration that there are no criteria that would make possible an abstract determination of the effectiveness of all blockades. In this context, *Castrén* postulates: 'Aircraft in the blockaded area may leave the area when there are other aircraft on patrol duty so that the blockade remains in force the whole time. The activities of aircraft even in connexion with a naval blockade are effective only to the extent that they do in fact dominate the air.'[395] It is maintained here that this position is correct. In any event, aircraft will be used for the enforcement of a blockade only if the respective belligerent has gained air superiority. Otherwise the use of aircraft would be too dangerous.

A further aspect regarding blockade as dealt with in the *San Remo Manual* is whether this method of naval warfare is necessarily restricted to vessels or whether it may also be enforced vis-à-vis aircraft. Again, the provisions of the *San Remo Manual* are silent on this issue. The 'explanations' reveal that the legal and naval experts, in the context of the

---

[390] See Castrén, at 409 *et seq.*

[391] See also the *San Remo Manual*—Explanations, para. 97.1, at 178.

[392] *San Remo Manual*, para. 95.

[393] Kalshoven (*supra*, n. 161), at 274 maintains: '[…] developments in the techniques of naval and aerial warfare have turned the establishment and maintenance of a naval blockade in the traditional sense into a virtual impossibility. It would seem, therefore, that the rules in the Declaration on blockade in time of war are now mainly of historical interest.' This position is certainly not shared by those states having published manuals for their respective navies or by other authors. See Stone, at 508: 'The realities of the present century require the British long distance blockade to be viewed as a long term transformation of the traditional law of blockade, rather than as mere reprisals, or mere breach of the traditional law.' Further, H. Lauterpacht, *op. cit.*, at 796–7.

[394] See *NWP 1–14M*, para. 7.7.2.3; *UK Manual*, para. 13.67.

[395] Castrén, at 409.

effectiveness of a blockade, considered that question only indirectly.[396] While it may be correct that a (purely) naval blockade may not be considered to have lost its effectiveness for the sole reason that a very small number of aircraft continue to land within the blockaded area this is but one aspect. Although traditionally blockades have been viewed upon as a method of naval warfare proper there is no reason why it may not be extended (or even restricted) to aircraft. In this context the argument that 'transport by air only constitutes a very small percentage of bulk traffic'[397] is not absolutely convincing. The blockaded belligerent state, either alone or together with its allies, may dispose of a considerable air fleet. As the example of the 'blockade of Berlin' shows—although the cargoes only served humanitarian purposes—a considerable percentage of bulk traffic can be transported by air over a considerable period of time.

3. *Impartiality.* In principle, a blockade must be applied impartially to the vessels and aircraft of all nations.[398] This duty also applies to vessels flying the flag of the blockading power. Apart from relief shipments, only in exceptional cases is it permissible to exempt neutral warships and military aircraft by permitting them to enter and leave a blockaded port or coastline.[399] Neutral merchant vessels and civil aircraft in distress may also be allowed to enter and leave the blockade area, provided they have neither discharged nor loaded any cargo there.[400]

4. *Free access to neutral ports and coastlines.* A blockade must not extend beyond the ports and coasts belonging to or controlled or occupied by the enemy.[401] It must not prevent access to ports or coasts of neutral states since this would violate their neutrality.[402]

5. *'Starvation blockade' and relief actions.* If a blockade has the effect of starving the civilian population it becomes illegal according to Article 49, para. 3, and Article 54, para. 1, AP I. During the Diplomatic Conference the Third Committee took the view that Article 54 AP I had no impact on naval blockades.[403] That view, it is argued here, is untenable. Article 54 AP I applies to naval blockades if they 'may affect the civilian population, individual civilians, or civilian objects on land' (Article 49, para. 3, AP I).[404] If the establishment of a blockade causes the civilian population to be inadequately provided with food and other objects essential for its survival, the blockading party must provide for free passage for such essential supplies.[405] It is questionable in this context

---

[396] *San Remo Manual*—Explanations, at 177: 'The Round Table considered whether the fact that aircraft could still land within the territory of the blockaded belligerent would affect the effectiveness of a sea blockade. This was found not to be the case, as, on the one hand, transport of cargo by air only constitutes a very small percentage of bulk traffic and, on the other hand, the fact that transport over land could take place without affecting this criterion.'

[397] *San Remo Manual—Explanations*, at 177.

[398] Article 5, LondonDecl 1909.

[399] Ibid. Article 6.

[400] Ibid. Article 7. See also *NWP 1–14M*, para. 7.7.3.

[401] Article 1, LondonDecl 1909.

[402] Article 18, LondonDecl 1909. See also para. 99, *San Remo Manual*.

[403] CDDH/215/Rev. 1, para. 73.

[404] See also Bothe, *Commentary*, 764. *San Remo Manual*, para. 102, provides: 'The declaration or establishment of a blockade is prohibited if (a) it has the sole purpose of starving the civilian population or denying it other objects essential for its survival; or (b) the damage to the civilian population is, or may be expected to be, excessive in relation to the concrete and direct military advantage anticipated from the blockade.'

[405] Article 70 AP I. See also *San Remo Manual*, para. 103.

WOLFF HEINTSCHEL VON HEINEGG

whether the blockading power is to be considered a 'party concerned' whose permission is necessary. In any event, the blockading power is under an obligation to provide for and permit free passage of goods essential for the survival of the civilian population.[406] That permission may be denied only temporarily for the reason of overwhelming security concerns.[407] Of course, the obligation to provide for and to permit free passage of relief shipments is subject to the right to prescribe the technical arrangements, including search, under which such passage is permitted.[408]

1052   A blockade shall be declared and notified by the government of the party to the conflict concerned or by a commander authorized by that government (Article 8 LondonDecl 1909). It shall also be notified to the neutral powers (Article 11 LondonDecl 1909). Any extension and lifting of the blockade shall be declared and announced in the same manner (Article 12 LondonDecl 1909). A declaration of blockade shall contain the following details:
— the date on which the blockade begins;
— geographical boundaries of the blockaded coastal strip;
— the period granted to neutral ships for departure (Article 9 LondonDecl 1909).

The provisions on notification, competences, content, and announcement follow from Articles 8, 9, 11, 12, and 13 LondonDecl 1909, which are generally recognized as customary law.[409] The requirement to inform neutral powers, that is states not parties to the conflict, is justified by the fact that, according to the principle of impartiality, a blockade must be applied to all vessels and aircraft regardless of their nationality. The declaration must contain the details enumerated in order to enable vessels of neutral states to leave the blockaded coastline in time or to refrain from entering it.

1053   A blockade, in order to be binding, must be effective (Article 4 ParisDecl 1856). It must be maintained by armed forces sufficient to prevent access to the blockaded coast. Long-distance blockades are also permissible, that is the obstruction and control of the blockaded coast or ports by armed forces keeping a longer distance from the coastline. A naval blockade shall be considered to be effective if ship-to-shore supplies are cut off. Air transport need not be stopped. A barricade achieved by other means, for example by ships scuttled in the entrance, does not constitute a blockade. Neither will the mining of coasts and ports compensate for the absence of warships even if all movements are temporarily stopped by mines. The effectiveness of a blockade is not suspended if the blockading force is temporarily withdrawn on account of bad weather (Article 4 LondonDecl 1909) or in pursuit of a blockade-runner. A blockade which ceases to be effective is no longer binding. The blockade shall end with the repulse of the blockading forces by the enemy or with their complete or partial destruction, even if new forces are charged with this task without delay. In this case the blockade must be declared and notified anew (Article 12 LondonDecl 1909).

1. *Traditional law.* Originally, blockades were applied to coastal forts, never to a coastline as a whole. Hence, the former rules on blockade were taken from the law of siege.

---

[406] According to para. 104, *San Remo Manual* the 'blockading belligerent shall [also] allow the passage of medical supplies for the civilian population or for the wounded and sick members of armed forces, subject to the right to prescribe technical arrangements, including search, under which such passage is permitted.'
[407] Bothe (*supra*, n. 166), 764. For the opposite view, see Rauch (*supra*, n. 89), 91 *et seq.*
[408] *San Remo Manual*, para. 103.
[409] *NWP 1–14M*, para. 7.7.2; *Canadian Manual*, paras. 844 *et seq.*; *San Remo Manual*, paras. 93, 94, and 101.

During the Dutch–Spanish War the purpose of a blockade changed for the first time from siege to obstruction of traffic to and from the enemy's coastline.[410] Since then blockades, in order to be legal, have to be effective. This means, according to the 1856 Paris Declaration, they must be maintained by a force sufficient to prevent access to the enemy coastline.[411] Hence, naval forces had to be stationed within sight of the blockaded port or coastline.

2. *Effectiveness.*

a) Shortly after the adoption of the LondonDecl 1909 many realized that, in view of the probable employment of submarines, mines, and aircraft, the establishment of an effective blockade was nearly impossible. This is one of the reasons why Great Britain was not prepared to ratify the Declaration. During the two World Wars the principle of effectiveness was generally disregarded. Instead of effective blockades in the traditional sense, Great Britain proclaimed so-called 'long-distances blockades'. Germany declared a number of 'war zones'. However, the principle of effectiveness was never officially declared void. Rather, the belligerents justified their excessive methods as reprisals.[412]

b) In view of the practice of the World Wars and of the technological development of modern weapons systems the principle of effectiveness had been modified. It is, therefore, now sufficient that within the area specified in the declaration any import of goods is cut off. It makes no difference if the blockade is maintained by air or by naval forces stationed at a distance determined by military requirements or by both.[413] It must, however, be probable that vessels (and aircraft) will be prevented from entering or leaving the blockaded area.[414] A blockade may be restricted to vessels. Its effectiveness is not negated on the sole ground that it does not apply to aircraft.

c) It is a matter of dispute whether during the maintenance of a blockade the presence of surface naval forces or other units of the armed forces is an indispensable condition for its legality. The US, in particular, has taken the view that a blockade may also be established merely by mining the enemy's ports and coasts,[415] as was done in the case of Haiphong. The following considerations, however, speak against that approach: on one hand, it is still forbidden to lay mines off the coast and ports of the enemy with the sole object of attacking commercial shipping.[416] The mining of Haiphong can hardly be considered a sufficient practice to give rise to the development of a rule of customary law to the contrary. On the other hand, it must be recalled that certain vessels may or even must be exempted from the restrictions imposed by a blockade.[417] That is especially true for vessels in distress. The provisions on the protected status of such vessels would not make much sense if the rule on the compulsory presence of surface naval forces or other

---

[410] Cf. O'Connell (*supra*, n. 12), Vol. II, 1150.

[411] See also Article 2, LondonDecl 909.

[412] Cf. O'Connell, Vol. II, 1153 *et seq.*

[413] *San Remo Manual,* para. 96.

[414] This result can—to a certain extent—be founded upon Article 3 of the 1909 London Declaration according to which the 'question whether a blockade is effective is a question of fact'. See also *San Remo Manual,* para. 95. Effectiveness is, therefore, dependent upon the circumstances of each case. See also Kalshoven (*supra*, n. 161), 260.

[415] Cf. *NWP 1–14M*, para. 7.7.5. See also van Hegelsom (*supra*, n. 86), 46. A more cautious approach is taken in the *San Remo Manual,* para. 97: 'A blockade may be enforced and maintained by a combination of legitimate methods and means of warfare provided this combination does not result in acts inconsistent with the rules set out in this document.'

[416] Article 2 HC VIII. See also para. 3 of the commentary on Section 1042.

[417] See para. 2 of the commentary on Section 1051.

units were renounced. Hence, it is not forbidden to enforce and maintain a blockade *also* by naval mines. In any event, units of naval or other forces must be present in the vicinity of the blockaded areas in order to ensure that protected vessels and aircraft, especially those in distress, can reach a place of safety.

d) In spite of many technological improvements naval forces may still be forced to leave the blockade area temporarily because of bad weather. Since vessels intending to enter the blockade area will also be affected, the temporary withdrawal of the blockading force does not prejudice the blockade's effectiveness.[418] The same holds true with regard to a temporary absence due to pursuit of a blockade-runner. If, however, entry and exit are no longer generally prevented the blockade becomes ineffective. Measures connected with the enforcement of a blockade then automatically become illegal. In particular, neutral merchant vessels entering the area may no longer be captured or attacked. The blockading party must confine itself to visit and search.

IV. Hospital Ships

1. General

1054   The following ships and boats enjoy special protection in naval warfare in accordance with the following provisions, so that they shall not be attacked, sunk, or captured under any circumstances:
— military hospital ships (Article 22 GC II);
— hospital ships operated by national Red Cross and Red Crescent societies, officially recognized relief societies, or private persons, whether or not they are members of a party to the conflict, or citizens of a state not party to the conflict (Articles 24, 26 GC II);
— coastal rescue craft operated by a state or by officially recognized relief societies, as far as military necessity permits (Articles 22, 24 GC II); and
— ships specially designed to transport wounded and sick civilians (Article 21 GC IV; Article 22).

1. *Legal basis.* Hospital ships were dealt with at the Hague Peace Conferences of 1899 and 1907. The results of these conferences, the provisions of HC X, were revised in 1949.[419] The treaty law forming the basis of the present section is to be found in Chapter III of the Second Geneva Convention of 1949, as amended by Articles 21 *et seq.* AP I.

2. *Protected vessels.*

a) Military hospital ships. The protected status of military hospital ships is closely linked to the protection of wounded, sick, and shipwrecked according to Article 12 GC II. However, their special status remains unchanged whether or not such persons are in fact on board. It is not the transport of wounded, sick, and shipwrecked that is decisive but the ship's function, whose fulfilment must be guaranteed. The protection of military hospital ships, including their lifeboats,[420] does not cease simply because they are transporting wounded, sick, and shipwrecked civilians.[421] Protected status means that such vessels 'may in no circumstances be attacked or captured'. In view of their special

---

[418] Article 4 LondonDecl 1909.
[419] As to the minor modifications of HC X by GC II, see Pictet (*supra*, n. 104), 156.
[420] Article 26 GC II; Article 22, para. 1, lit. b, AP I.
[421] Article 22, para. 1, AP I.

functions, however, that alone would not suffice. They must at all times be respected and protected. Hence, hospital ships may not be hampered in fulfilling their tasks. This may amount to an obligation on the part of belligerents actively to support hospital ships.[422]

b) Other hospital ships. Hospital ships utilized by national Red Cross societies, officially recognized relief societies, or private persons, and their lifeboats,[423] are accorded the same protection as military hospital ships by Article 24 GC II. This presupposes that 'the Party to the conflict on which they depend has given them an official commission',[424] that they are 'provided with certificates from the responsible authorities, stating that the vessels have been under their control while fitting out and on departure',[425] and that 'their names and descriptions have been notified to the Parties to the conflict ten days before those ships are employed'.[426] Subject to those requirements, the protection provided by Articles 22 and 24 GC II also extends to hospital ships made available for humanitarian purposes to a party to the conflict by either a neutral state or other state not party to the conflict[427] or by an impartial international humanitarian organization.[428]

c) Tonnage. In principle, the specially protected status of all hospital ships, including military hospital ships, is not dependent upon the ships' tonnage.[429] However, during the Second World War smaller vessels were not recognized as legitimate hospital ships.[430] The delegates of the 1949 Geneva Conference, while unable to agree upon a minimum tonnage, therefore laid down in the second sentence of Article 26 GC II that the parties to the conflict 'shall endeavour to utilize... only hospital ships of over 2,000 tons gross'.

d) Coastal rescue craft. Under the conditions laid down in Articles 22 and 24 GC II, small coastal rescue craft employed by the state or by officially recognized lifeboat institutions enjoy the same protection as hospital ships.[431] The notification envisaged in Articles 27 and 22 GC II is not necessary for their protection. Article 22, para. 3, AP I now provides that they 'shall be protected even if the notification... has not been made'. Nevertheless, the parties to the conflict are 'invited to inform each other of any details of such craft which will facilitate their identification and recognition'. The area of operation of small coastal rescue craft need not be confined to waters near the coast.[432] The special status of such craft is subject to 'operational requirements'. This restriction is due to the fact that such craft travel at high speed, cannot easily be identified, and are often perceived as dangerous.

e) Other medical ships and craft. The protection of vessels designed for the transport of wounded, sick, and shipwrecked civilians can be derived from Article 21 GC IV. It is now made clear in Article 22, para. 1, AP I that the protected status of hospital ships is not prejudiced if they carry 'civilian wounded, sick and shipwrecked who do not belong

[422] Pictet, *Commentary* GC II, 157.
[423] Articles 24 and 26 GC II.
[424] Article 24, para. 1, GC II.
[425] Article 24, para. 2, GC II.
[426] Article 24, para. 2, in conjunction with Article 22 GC II.
[427] Article 22, para. 2, lit. a, AP I.
[428] Article 22, para. 2, lit. b, AP I.
[429] Article 26, first sentence GC II.
[430] Cf. J. C. M. Mossop, 'Hospital Ships in the Second World War' (1947) XXIV *BYIL* 160 *et seq.*, 398 *et seq.*, 403 *et seq.*; Tucker, *op. cit.*, 125 n. 92.
[431] Article 27 GC II.
[432] Cf. Pictet, *op. cit.*, 173.

to any of the categories mentioned in Article 13 of the Second Convention'. A well-known example of such a hospital ship is the case of the *Helgoland* which operated in the waters off Vietnam from August 1966 until January 1972. The German Red Cross sent the *Helgoland* to Vietnamese waters in order to care for wounded and sick civilians after the Federal Republic of Germany and Vietnam, on 28 March 1966, concluded an agreement[433] to this effect.[434] Medical ships and craft other than those referred to in Article 22 AP I and Article 38 GC II now enjoy special protection under Article 23 AP I. This provision covers all means of transportation by water fulfilling the following conditions:[435]

— they must be exclusively assigned, for the duration of their assignment (which may be short), to medical transportation;
— they must be placed under the control of a party to the conflict.

They do, however, remain subject to the laws of war, which means that they are subject to capture unless one of the exceptions of Article 23, para. 2, applies.

3. *'In accordance with the following provisions'.* The following provisions of Sections 1055 to 1064, according to their wording, refer to hospital ships. Unless there is an express reservation, those provisions also apply to the other vessels referred to above.

2. Conditions for Protection and Identification

1055   **Hospital ships are ships exclusively designed to assist, treat, and transport the wounded, sick, and shipwrecked. Their names and descriptions shall be notified to the parties to the conflict not later than ten days before they are employed for the first time (Article 22 GC II).**

1. *Function.* The function of hospital ships and the other vessels dealt with in the present section is the essential condition of their protected status. This does not mean that they must have been specially built solely for the purpose of assisting the wounded, sick, and shipwrecked.[436] All vessels solely and definitely assigned to service as hospital ships or to serve one of the other functions mentioned above are protected. Thus, it is permissible to transform a merchant vessel or a passenger vessel into a hospital ship. Transformed vessels may not, however, be put to any other use throughout the duration of hostilities.[437]

2. *Notification.* The notification shall include details of registered gross tonnage, length from stem to stern, and numbers of masts and funnels.[438] The parties to the conflict are, of course, free to notify further details. According to Article 23, para. 4, AP I a party to the conflict 'may notify any adverse Party as far in advance of sailing as possible of the name, description, expected time of sailing, course and estimated speed of the medical ship or craft, particularly in the case of ships of over 2,000 gross tons, and may provide other information which would facilitate identification and recognition'.

---

[433] Bundesgesetzblatt 1966 II, 323.
[434] Cf. A. Schlögel, 'Völkerrechtliche Aspekte des Einsatzes des Hospitalschiffes "Helgoland" ', *Jahrbuch für Internationales Recht* 1973, 92 *et seq.*
[435] Cf. Sandoz, in *ICRC Commentary*, para. 885.
[436] Cf. Pictet, *op. cit.*, 159.
[437] Article 33 GC II.
[438] Article 22, para. 2, GC II.

WOLFF HEINTSCHEL VON HEINEGG

The notification according to Article 22 GC II must be made ten days before those ships are employed.[439] The object and purpose of that time limit is to increase the safety of hospital ships (and of small coastal rescue craft) by enabling the adverse party to pass the information to armed forces. In peacetime the notification will normally be transmitted directly. After the outbreak of hostilities the parties to the conflict will usually make use of the assistance of protecting powers.

> Hospital ships shall be distinctively marked as follows: **1056**
> — all exterior surfaces shall be white;
> — the distinctive emblem of the Red Cross shall be painted once or several times on each side of the hull and on the horizontal surfaces, as large as possible, so as to be clearly visible from sea and air;
> — a white flag with a red cross shall be flown as high as possible, visible from all sides.
> — In addition, all hospital ships shall fly their national flags; neutral ships shall further hoist the flag of the party to the conflict whose direction they have accepted (Article 43 GC II). As far as possible, their painting and distinctive emblems shall be rendered visible at night. Other identification systems, for example internationally recognized light, radio, and electronic signals, are also permissible (Articles 5–6, Annex I, AP I). Lifeboats of hospital ships, coastal rescue boats, and all small craft used by the medical service shall be marked in the same manner as hospital ships (Article 43, paras. 3 and 4, GC II; Article 23, para. 1, AP I).

1. *Visual marking.* For hospital ships and small coastal rescue craft these are not an essential condition of their special protection. Such markings do not, of themselves, confer protected status but are intended only to facilitate identification.[440] In place of the red cross on a white ground the parties to the conflict can use the red crescent or the red lion and sun on a white ground.[441] In principle, the distinctive emblem as well as the national flag must be hoisted permanently.[442] Only hospital ships temporarily detained in accordance with Section 1061 lower the flag of the state in whose service they are employed or under whose control they have placed themselves. The obligation to fly the distinctive emblem at the mainmast as high as possible[443] is because that part of the ship will first be visible on the horizon. There are no specific obligations as to visual marking at night. Hence, all means appropriate to facilitate identification, especially lights, are permissible. Visual means of identification also include flashing lights.

2. *Other kinds of identification.* Already in 1949 the delegates of the 1949 Geneva Conference were aware of the insufficiency of visual signs and markings in modern naval wars. Hence, Article 43, para. 8, GC II provides that 'parties to the conflict shall at all times endeavour to conclude mutual agreements, in order to use the most modern methods available to facilitate the identification of hospital ships'. There was, however, no agreement on specific and universally binding methods. A first improvement was then brought about by the regulations concerning identification in Annex I to AP I. Now the parties to the conflict

---

[439] Originally, a period of thirty days was envisaged. After a proposal of the ICRC to this effect that period was reduced to ten days which was considered sufficient. Cf. Pictet, *op. cit.*, 161.

[440] See also *San Remo Manual*, para. 173.

[441] Article 43, para. 7, and Article 41, para. 2, GC II.

[442] Article 43, para. 2, GC II.

[443] Article 43, para. 2, GC II.

WOLFF HEINTSCHEL VON HEINEGG

can, by agreement, supplement visual methods of identification of hospital ships and other medical transports by light signals,[444] radio signals,[445] or electronic identification.[446] In modern warfare, which is characterized by the use of electronic means of warfare, these additional technical means of identification are essential for minimizing the danger of mistaken attacks.[447] Provisions on special means of underwater acoustic identification of hospital ships[448] have now been included in the revised Annex I to AP I. In 1990, the ICRC tried to optimize the provisions of Annex I by publishing its *Manual for the Use of Technical Means of Identification*.[449] In view of modern weapons technology the methods recommended therein are, however, only a first step in the right direction.[450]

3. Rights and Obligations

1057   Hospital ships shall afford assistance to all wounded, sick, and shipwrecked without distinction of nationality (Article 30 GC II). They shall by no means be employed for any military purposes.

1. *Obligation to afford relief and assistance impartially.* This is laid down in Article 30, para. 1, GC II, but also follows from Articles 12 and 22 GC II. Nationality is not the only unlawful criterion for discrimination. Others are sex, race, religion, and political opinion.[451]

2. *The prohibition against using these vessels for any military purpose.* (Article 30, para. 2, GC II.) Prohibited purposes include intelligence activities and transport of troops, weapons, and ammunition.[452] This provision is closely linked to Section 1062 concerning loss of protection. It is self-explanatory, and was inspired by the experience of the World Wars.[453]

1058   Hospital ships may be equipped with radio systems. They may not, however, possess or use a secret code for their wireless or other means of communication (Article 34 GC II). Also permissible is (Article 35 GC II):
— the use of apparatus designed to facilitate navigation or communication;
— the transport of medical supplies and personnel over and above the ship's requirements (Article 35 GC II);
— the use of portable arms by the personnel of a hospital ship for the maintenance of order, for their own defence, or for that of the wounded and sick;
— the carrying of portable arms and ammunitions taken from the wounded, sick, or shipwrecked and not yet handed over to the proper service; and

---

[444] Article 6, Annex I to AP I.
[445] Article 7, Annex I to AP I.
[446] Article 8, Annex I to AP I.
[447] Cf. R. Feist, 'Manual for the Use of Technical Means of Identification' (1990) *HuV-I* 212.
[448] Cf. P. Eberlin, 'Underwater acoustic identification of hospital ships' (1988) 267 *IRRC* 505–28.
[449] Geneva 1990.
[450] Feist, *loc. cit.*, 212, stating that 'the only achievement was to start a discussion of the problem under the competent guidance of the ICRC'.
[451] Cf. Pictet, *op. cit.*, 179.
[452] Cf. O'Connell, *op. cit.*, Vol. II, 1120.
[453] For example, in World War I the German hospital ship *Ophelia* was condemned because it had not afforded assistance and because it had transmitted encrypted messages that had not been properly documented. Moreover, the *Ophelia* was equipped with a radio system; then unusual for a hospital ship. The radio installations were destroyed by the crew prior to capture. Cf. O'Connell, *op. cit.*, Vol. II, 1120.

WOLFF HEINTSCHEL VON HEINEGG

— the taking on board of wounded, sick, or shipwrecked civilians (Article 22,
para. 1, AP I).

1. *Radio and communications systems.* In contrast to some delegates of the 1907 Hague
Conference, the delegates of the 1949 Geneva Conference considered the equipment of
hospital ships necessarily to include a radio. This is made evident by Article 35, para. 2,
GC II. According to Article 34, para. 2, GC II hospital ships may not, however, 'possess or
use a secret code for their wireless or other means of communication'. Despite the differences between the French (*pour leurs émissions*) and the English wordings of that provision
it is a widely held view that hospital ships may neither send nor receive messages in other
than generally known codes. In view of the fact that equally authentic texts are to be taken
into consideration when interpreting a treaty provision this view is untenable. Therefore,
according to the wording of Article 34, para. 2, GC II, hospital ships are allowed to use
encryption for receiving messages.[454] This is, moreover, in accordance with the object and
purpose of the provisions on hospital ships. If prohibited to receive encrypted messages
they would be unable to fulfil their humanitarian mission because the respective belligerent
would refrain from informing its hospital ships of possible areas of operation.[455] Moreover,
Article 34, para. 2, GC II can be considered to have become obsolete by the subsequent
practice of the states parties. Today, hospital ships, like all warships and the majority of
merchant vessels, communicate via satellite. The use of satellite communications implies
encryption for both sending and receiving messages. The only two remaining hospital
ships—the USS *Comfort* and the USS *Mercy*—do not dispose of traditional radio equip-
ments but communicate over satellite communications only. This fact is known to the
states parties to GC II. Still, there have been no protests so far. Hence, there are good
reasons to believe that the other states parties have acquiesced in the US practice. Again,
it should not be left out of consideration that abandoning the prohibition of using encryption for emissions would better serve the humanitarian purposes hospital ships are to serve.
In order to fulfil their humanitarian mission most effectively, hospital ships should—it
is maintained here—be permitted to use cryptographic equipment. Otherwise, neither
belligerents nor neutrals will any longer make use of hospital ships but rather follow the
British example of designating a warship as a 'fighting hospital ship' that, of course, does
not enjoy any special protection under the law.

2. *Other permissible equipment and actions.* Apparatus intended exclusively to facilitate
navigation is nowadays part of the essential equipment of modern vessels. Hence, its
presence on board will not prejudice the protected status of hospital and other ships.[456]
Also permissible is the transport of equipment and personnel intended exclusively for
medical duties above the normal requirements.[457] This helps avoid the difficulties arising
from the transport of equipment and personnel that do not belong to the usual equipment and personnel of a hospital ship but are intended for a specific area of operations.
Finally, as stated above, the mere fact that a hospital ship is carrying wounded, sick, and
shipwrecked civilians does not deprive it of its special protection.[458]

---

[454] Also provided in para. 171, *San Remo Manual.*
[455] As was the case during the Falklands/Malvinas conflict. Instead, hospital ships were made to stay in a
so-called 'Red Cross Box' established by *ad hoc* agreement between the belligerents.
[456] Article 35, No. 2, GC II.
[457] Article 35, No. 5, GC II.
[458] Article 35, No. 4, GC II; Article 22, para. 1, AP I.

WOLFF HEINTSCHEL VON HEINEGG

3. *Arms on board hospital ships.* The crews of hospital ships, according to Article 35, No. 1, GC II, are entitled to carry small ('portable') arms and to use them either for the maintenance of order, for their own defence, or for that of the sick and wounded. Military hospital ships and infirmaries are usually subject to military discipline. Guards are necessary to prevent patients from leaving without permission. They must also be in a position to hinder unauthorized persons from entering. For these purposes small-arms are necessary. Moreover, it is not uncommon that wounded, sick, and shipwrecked at the time of their rescue still possess weapons and ammunition. Such weapons and ammunitions must be taken away and delivered to the competent authority. Delivery, however, will take some time because the competent authority is situated on land. Therefore, the presence of such weapons and ammunition on board a hospital ship does not jeopardize its protected status.

According to GC II, weapons and weapons systems with the capability of repulsing a military attack may not be placed on board the vessels protected under the present section. If such an (illegal!) attack occurs, the crews of a hospital ship would be limited to warning the attacking ship or aircraft.

These rules are based on the assumption that an attack on a hospital ship will in most cases be rather accidental than intentional. Indeed, in a traditional international armed conflict the principle of reciprocity will regularly guarantee observance of the protected status. In such a conflict there is no necessity of equipping a warships with offensive weapons. In view of the probability of an unintentional attack, especially by a misguided missile, there is, however, general agreement that hospital ships may be equipped with deflective means like chaff and flares.[459]

However, in an asymmetric conflict situation—either because of the participation of non-state actors or because of a simultaneous threat by non-state actors unrelated to an ongoing conflict—reciprocity will hardly work. Therefore the question remains whether the prohibition of arming a hospital ship with, for example, larger guns is absolute in character or whether it depends upon the threat a hospital ship is exposed to in a given situation. According to the position taken here, such arming is in accordance with the law if there are reasonable grounds for suspicion that non-state actors may intentionally attack a hospital ship. Accordingly, the recent US practice of arming hospital ships with large calibre guns for defence against terrorist attacks seems to be no violation of the law.

1059   **Any hospital ship in a port which falls into the hands of the adversary shall be authorized to leave the said port (Article 29 GC II). During and after an engagement, hospital ships will act at their own risk. Hospital ships shall not hamper the movements of the combatants (Article 30 GC II).**

1. *The right to leave a port.* The ability to leave a port which is in the hands of the enemy (Article 29 GC II) is a consequence of the general protection of hospital ships. It also follows indirectly from the provisions on the exceptional and temporary detention of hospital ships. However, it was considered necessary to restate that principle in a separate provision.

2. *Acting at their own risk.* This refers to the entering of areas of operation in order to assist the victims of armed conflict. Hospital ships may not be attacked. However, belligerents cannot be held responsible for accidentally hitting a hospital ship. This also

[459] *San Remo Manual*, para. 170.

holds true for damage suffered during entrance to the area of naval operations shortly after the cessation of active hostilities.[460]

3. *The prohibition against hampering the movements of combatants.* (Article 30, para. 3, GC II.) This corresponds with the basic rule that hospital ships may not be employed for any military purpose (Article 30, para. 2, GC II). The exemption from attack ceases according to Section 1062 if a hospital ship breaches these conditions. Otherwise, a party to the conflict could position its hospital ships in such a way as to render impossible any self-defence measures by the enemy.

> While hospital ships are not liable to capture, they are subject to the right of control and visit accorded to the parties to the conflict (Article 31 GC II). Any warship may request the handing over of the wounded, sick, and shipwrecked by hospital or other ships, no matter which nationality such ships have, provided that the state of health of the wounded and sick allows such action and that the receiving warship can provide the facilities necessary for medical treatment (Article 14 GC II; Article 30 AP I).

1060

1. *Control and search.* According to Article 31, para. 1, GC II the parties to the conflict are entitled to control the vessels protected under this section. Control and search serve to verify whether the adverse party is complying with its duty not to use hospital and other vessels for military purposes. Control and search may also be conducted in order to examine the condition of the wounded on board. This right comprises search of the whole ship, its equipment, and cargo, as well as control of the list of patients and the establishment of the identity of the members of the crew.

2. *Handing over.* All warships of a belligerent are entitled to demand that wounded, sick, or shipwrecked persons on board hospital and other ships shall be surrendered, whatever their nationality.[461] This right is conferred on the belligerents to meet their interest in preventing those persons from joining the hostilities after recovery. If they are members of the armed forces or if they belong to any of the categories of Article 4 A GC III they become prisoners of war as soon as they fall into the enemy's hands.[462] If they are not in a fit state to be moved and if the warship cannot provide adequate facilities for necessary medical treatment, surrender of those persons may not be demanded. Surrender of merchant vessel crew members who have promised in writing not to undertake any service connected with the armed conflict while hostilities last may not be required.

> The belligerents are not obliged to accept assistance from hospital ships. They may order them off, make them follow a certain course, control the use of their means of communication, and, if the gravity of the circumstances requires, detain them for a period of up to seven days (Article 31, para. 1, GC II). A commissioner may temporarily be put on board to monitor the execution of such orders (Article 31, para. 2, GC II). For the purpose of control, the parties to the conflict may also send neutral observers on board (Article 31, para. 4, GC II).

1061

1. *Orders of belligerents to hospital ships.* For reasons of military security the parties to the conflict may refuse assistance from hospital ships, order them off, or make them take a

---

[460] See also Pictet, *op. cit.*, 180.
[461] Article 14 GC II.
[462] Article 16 GC II.

certain course.[463] The right to control the use of their radio or of other means of communication is to ensure that a hospital ship is not abused for military purposes.

2. *Detention of hospital ships.* According to Article 31 para. 1, GC II this is an exceptional right. It may be exercised only if necessary, for example to ensure the secrecy of important military operations that have come to the knowledge of the hospital ship.[464] The time limit of seven days runs from the detention order. Even if the reasons for detention continue to exist, that time limit may not be extended. This is meant to prevent belligerents from effectively capturing hospital ships. If the reasons for detention cease to exist before seven days have passed, the hospital ship must be released immediately.

3. *Commissioners and neutral observers.* The sole task of commissioners temporarily put on board a hospital ship is to see that legitimate orders are carried out. If the commissioner is a naval officer he may be captured by enemy armed forces, not by the hospital ship's crew and personnel. If he is also a member of the medical or hospital personnel he continues to be protected.[465] The sending of a non-neutral commissioner has often led to problems. According to Article 31, para. 4, GC II it is, therefore, also possible to place (either unilaterally or by particular agreements) neutral observers on board hospital ships who shall verify the strict observation of the provisions of GC II.

4. Discontinuance of Protection

1062
> If such ships are misused for military purposes or act in any other way contrary to their obligations, in particular by clearly resisting an order to stop, to turn away, or to follow a distinct course, they lose their protected status, after due warning has been given (Article 34 GC II).

Article 34 GC II provides that the 'protection to which hospital ships... are entitled shall not cease unless they are used to commit, outside their humanitarian duties, acts harmful to the enemy'. The following acts, *inter alia*, constitute an abuse for military purposes: transmission of military/intelligence information to the enemy,[466] transport of military material or enemy troops, intentionally hampering the movements of naval forces, or any of the acts rendering a vessel a legitimate military objective.[467] It is emphasized in the present context that, in view of modern weapons technology, hospital ships may be equipped with purely deflective means of defence, such as chaff and flares. The presence of such equipment should, however, be notified.[468] Abuse does not automatically lead to loss of exemption. In view of the humanitarian function of such vessels their protection may cease only after due warning has been given, allowing in all appropriate cases a reasonable time limit, and after such warning has remained unheeded. The extent of the time limit will depend upon the circumstances prevailing at the time. The aggrieved belligerent is not obliged to name a time limit if that would be inappropriate, for example

---

[463] Article 31, para. 1, GC II.
[464] Cf. Pictet, *op. cit.*, 183.
[465] Cf. Pictet, *op. cit.*, 185.
[466] Article 34, para. 2, GC II.
[467] According to the *San Remo Manual*, para. 49, hospital ships and other protected vessels lose their exemption if they (a) are not innocently employed in their normal role; (b) do not submit to identification and inspection when required; and (c) intentionally hamper the movements of combatants and do not obey orders to stop or move out of the way when required.
[468] See *San Remo Manual*, para. 170.

if the hospital ship participates in the hostilities or if its crew fires at the warship. If after due warning a hospital ship persists in breaking a condition of its exemption, it renders itself liable to capture or other necessary measures to enforce compliance.[469] It may only be attacked as a last resort if: (a) diversion or capture is not feasible; (b) no other method is available for exercising military control; (c) the circumstances of non-compliance are sufficiently grave that the hospital ship has become, or may reasonably be assumed to be, a military objective; and (d) collateral casualties or damage will be proportionate to the military advantage gained or expected.[470] If feasible, before destruction the wounded, sick, and shipwrecked shall be taken to a place of safety.

5. Personnel and Crew

> The religious, medical, and hospital personnel of hospital ships and their crews   1063
> shall be respected and protected; they may not be captured during the time they are
> in the service of the hospital ship, whether there are wounded and sick on board or
> not (Article 36 GC II; see above, Sections 613–619 and 818–826).

This provision guarantees a far-reaching protection because it also covers crew members. This is justified because hospital ships will only be able to fulfil their humanitarian function if they are equipped with a crew able to handle the ship. 'During the time they are in service' does not mean that the personnel must be actively engaged in the assistance and care of wounded, sick, and shipwrecked. It is sufficient if they are assigned such duties. Therefore, it makes no difference whether there are wounded and sick on board or not. A temporary absence of patients from the ship does not prejudice their protected status. It is emphasized that personnel and crew on board coastal rescue craft, according to Article 37 GC II, are protected only while engaged in rescue operations.[471]

> The personnel of hospital ships, including the crew, shall wear a white armlet bear-   1064
> ing the distinctive emblem. Their armlets or identity cards may not be taken away
> from them (Article 42 GC II).

The obligation of personnel on board hospital ships to wear an armlet bearing the distinctive emblem follows from Article 42, para. 1, GC II. According to Article 42, para. 2, GC II the identity card shall be worded in the national language, shall mention at least the full name, date of birth, rank, and service number of the bearer, and shall state in what capacity he is entitled to the protection of GC II. The card shall bear the photograph of the owner and also his signature or fingerprints or both. The prohibition in Article 42, para. 4, GC II of depriving said personnel of their insignia, identity cards, or armlets is intended to guarantee permanent protection for such personnel. In case of loss the owner is entitled to receive duplicate or replacement cards and insignia.

---

[469] Ibid. para. 50.
[470] Ibid. para. 51.
[471] See also *San Remo Manual*, para. 162; Pictet, *op. cit.*, 205.

WOLFF HEINTSCHEL VON HEINEGG

11

THE LAW OF NEUTRALITY

I. General

Neutrality (derived from the Latin neuter: neither of each) is defined in interna-   1101
tional law as the status of a state which is not participating in an armed conflict
between other states. Neutral status gives rise to rights and duties in the relationship between the neutral state on one hand and the parties to the conflict on the
other.

1. 'Neutrality' describes the particular status, as defined by international law, of a state
not party to an armed conflict.[1] This status entails specific rights and duties in the relationship between the neutral and the belligerent states. On one hand, there is the right
of the neutral state to remain apart from, and not to be adversely affected by, the conflict. On the other hand there is the duty of non-participation and impartiality.[2]

2. The right not to be adversely affected means that the relationship between the neutral and belligerent states is governed by the law of peace, which is modified only in
certain respects by the law of neutrality. In particular, the neutral state must tolerate
certain controls in the area of maritime commerce.[3] The duty of non-participation and
impartiality are a necessary corollary to the right not to be adversely affected. The duty
of non-participation means, above all, that the state must abstain from supporting a
party to the conflict. This duty not to support also means that the neutral state is under
a duty not to allow one party to the conflict to use the resources of the neutral state
against the will of the opponent. Therefore, the defence of neutrality is part of the duty
of non-participation. The scope of those duties is described in more detail in the following provisions.

3. The duty of impartiality does not mean that the state is bound to treat the belligerents in exactly the same way. It entails a prohibition of discrimination, that is it forbids
only differential treatment of the belligerents which in view of the specific problem of
the armed conflict is not justified. This duty of impartiality, too, will be defined more
precisely below.

---

[1] M. Bothe, 'Neutrality, Concept and General Rules', *MPEPIL*; E. Kussbach, 'La neutralité permanente
et les Nations Unies; nouvelles perspectives après les changements fondamentaux en Europe de l'Est' (1991)
35 *Annales de droit international médical* 82 *et seq.*; I. Seidl-Hohenveldern, 'Der Begriff der Neutralität in den
bewaffneten Konflikten der Gegenwart', in *Zum Recht und Freiheit. Festschrift für Friedrich August Freiherr
von der Heydte* (Duncker & Humblot, 1977) Vol. 1, 593–613; J. Köpfer, *Die Neutralitätim Wandel der
Erscheinungsformen militärischer Auseinandersetzung* (München: Bernhard & Graefe, 1975), 50–64.
[2] W. Heintschel von Heinegg, *Seekriegsrecht und Neutralität im Seekrieg* (Duncker & Humblot, 1995),
501 *et seq.*
[3] J. A. Roach, 'Neutrality in Naval Warfare', para. 16 *et seq.*, *MPEPIL*.

MICHAEL BOTHE

4. As impartiality does not entail a duty of exactly equal treatment, a neutral state is under no duty to eliminate differences in the commercial relations between itself and each of the parties to the conflict existing at the time of the outbreak of the armed conflict. The neutral state is entitled to continue existing commercial relations (the principle of the so-called *courant normal*). A change in commercial relationships favouring one of the belligerents would, however, constitute taking sides in a manner incompatible with the status of neutrality. In more general terms, impartiality means that the neutral state must apply the specific measures it takes on the basis of the rights and duties deriving from its neutral status in a substantially equal way as between the parties to the conflict (Article 9 HC V, Article 9 HC XIII). This regime of rights and duties of the neutral state is an important international legal tool for restraining conflicts. By establishing a clear distinction between neutral states and states parties to the conflict, international law prevents more states from being drawn into the conflict. Neutral states may help parties to a conflict to maintain or establish relations which may mitigate the suffering of victims (e.g. by conducting relief operations or exchanging information) and which may finally smooth the path to peace (e.g. by arranging ceasefires). It is incompatible with this conflict-restraining function of neutrality that states should try to evade the duties flowing from their neutral status by styling themselves non-belligerents.[4] This, however, has often happened in the past.

5. The US considered itself as a non-belligerent before entering the Second World War, but not as neutral because it supported Great Britain in a way which was incompatible with the duty of non-participation under the law of neutrality.[5] More recently, during the 2003 US–British intervention in Iraq, Italy issued a proclamation of non-belligerency.[6] Other European states also gave assistance to the intervening states which were incompatible with the law of neutrality[7] without becoming parties to the conflict (e.g. Germany), but they did not make a similar declaration—leaving a legal explanation of their behaviour open. Although there are, thus, a number of cases of declared or undeclared non-belligerency, there is no sufficiently uniform general practice which would justify the conclusion that non-belligerency has become a notion recognized by customary international law. The cases of non-belligerency either arose in the absence of a conflict of sufficient scope to require the application of the law of neutrality (or in a conflict which was not considered as such) or were simply violations of the law of neutrality. If a 'non-belligerent' state violates the law of neutrality it must bear the consequences, for instance reprisals. A claim of non-belligerent status may not be used as a justification for a breach of the laws of neutrality. The consequences of such violations are discussed below.[8] Even support given to the victim of aggression may constitute a violation of the law of neutrality, and even when it does not amount to participation in the conflict. It

[4] Bothe, *supra*, n. 1, *para. 5*.
[5] G. P. Politakis, *Modern Aspects of the Law of Naval Warfare and Maritime Neutrality* (Geneva: IUHEI/Kegan Paul International, 1998), 458 *et seq.*
[6] N. Ronzitti, 'Italy's Non-Belligerency During the Iraqi War', in Ragazzi (ed.), *International Responsibility Today* (Nijhoff, 2005), 201.
[7] Heintschel v. Heinegg, 'Wider die Mär vom Tode des Neutralitätsrechts', in H. Fischer/U. Froissart/W. Heintschel von Heinegg/C. Raap (eds), *Krisensicherung und Humanitärer Schutz—Crisis Management and Humanitarian Protection: Festschrift für Dieter Fleck* (Berliner Wissenschafts-Verlag, 2004), 221–41, at 231.
[8] See commentary to Section 1107.

MICHAEL BOTHE

may, thus, be answered by countermeasures.[9] Neutrality is not optional, in the sense that each state is free to violate single duties of the law of neutrality as it will, or to declare them irrelevant, without having to fear a countermeasure taken by the adversely affected state.

6. The situation is different if and to the extent that the law of neutrality is modified by the Charter of the United Nations, in particular by a binding decision of the Security Council (see Section 1103). In this case, it is meaningful and correct that newer treaties use the term 'neutral or other states not party to the conflict' (Article 2, lit. c, AP I). Such a formulation clarifies that a provision is to be applied to any state not participating in the conflict, without the need to enter into any controversy over the status of neutrality, and also where there is a conflict not sufficiently great in scope to trigger the application of the law of neutrality.[10]

> The sources of the international law of neutrality are customary law and, for cer-   **1102**
> tain questions, international treaties (HC V; HC XIII).

1. The essential aspects of neutrality have been developed through state practice in modern times.[11] As a legal status of non-participation, its basic scope was fixed by the end of the eighteenth century. The development continued during the nineteenth century in two ways. On one hand, greater protection of neutral commerce from belligerent acts was achieved. On the other hand, a legal duty of permanent neutrality as an essential element of the maintenance of peace and the balance of powers in Europe was established (by the recognition of the neutrality of Switzerland, Belgium, and Luxembourg). During the First and Second World Wars, and also in a number of later conflicts, the law of neutrality retained its significance.[12] The development of the international legal prohibition of the use of force, however, offered reasons to differentiate between the aggressor and the victim of aggression, a fact which calls into question the classical principle of the impartiality of the neutral state. In addition, the political polarization after the Second World War, which had an impact on many conflicts, made the impartiality of the neutral state a politically doubtful rule. Some details of this development are discussed below. The development of the earlier state practice gave rise to customary law which is still an essential source of the law of neutrality. Following a modification of state practice, this customary law too underwent changes and introduced distinctions. This change, however, has produced only modifications of single specific rules of the law of neutrality, not a general revocation of this whole body of law.

2. Essential parts of the law of neutrality were codified during the nineteenth and the early twentieth centuries. Important steps in this development were the Paris Declaration of 1856[13] and the Hague Conventions of 1907, namely Conventions V respecting the rights and duties of neutral powers and persons in case of war on land and XIII concerning

---

[9] D. Schindler, 'Transformations in the Law of Neutrality since 1945' in A. J. M. Delissen/G. J. Tanja (eds), *Humanitarian Law of Armed Conflict—Challenges Ahead: Essays in Honour of Frits Kalshoven* (Nijhoff, 1991), 373.

[10] See commentary to Section 1106.

[11] Bothe, *loc. cit.*, n. 1, paras. 7 *et seq.*; E. Castrén, *The Present Law of War and Neutrality* (Helsinki: Annales Academiae Scientiarum Fennicae, 1954), 421 *et seq.*

[12] Heintschel von Heinegg, n. 7, at 222, 238.

[13] D. Schindler/J. Toman (eds), *The Law of Armed Conflict*, 4th edn (Nijhoff, 2004), 1065 *et seq.*

the rights and duties of neutral powers in naval warfare. Other treaties relating to the laws of war contain specific provisions concerning the rights and duties of neutral states, in particular the four Geneva Conventions of 1949 and Protocol I Additional thereto of 8 June 1977. There has, however, been no comprehensive codification of the law of neutrality since the Hague Conventions of 1907. These rules of 1907 have in part been rendered obsolete by later practice. The need for a new codification is urgent. The different bases of the rules of the law of neutrality will be indicated in the commentaries below. An important part of the law of neutrality, namely neutrality in naval warfare, has recently been formulated in private restatements, namely in the *San Remo Manual on International Law Applicable to Armed Conflict at Sea*, adopted in 1994 by a group of experts convened by the International Institute of Humanitarian Law,[14] and in a set of rules formulated by a committee of the International Law Association.[15]

1103   **The Charter of the United Nations and decisions of the Security Council based on the Charter may in certain circumstances modify the traditional law of neutrality. Therefore enforcement measures taken by the United Nations are governed by particular rules different from the traditional law of neutrality. The general law of neutrality, however, has not been revoked by the Charter of the United Nations.**

1. The Charter of the United Nations completed the development of the international legal prohibition of the use of force and established a system of collective security, by the reaction of the international community against breaches of peace. The traditional law of neutrality with its duty of impartiality, that is the prohibition of discrimination between the parties to the conflict, seems to be incompatible with this development which outlaws the aggressor. However, this is not generally the case. Also under the UN Charter, neutrality during international armed conflicts is permissible and possible.[16] States expressly rely on the law of neutrality.[17] The International Court of Justice[18] as well as national courts[19] have recently upheld the continued validity of the law of neutrality. The International Law Commission, in its 2011 Draft articles on the effects of armed conflicts on treaties, also treats the law of neutrality as a valid and relevant body of law.[20] The impartiality of the neutral state retains its important functions at least as long as there is no possibility of a binding decision concerning the question of who in a given conflict is the aggressor and who is the victim. Although the Charter provides for a binding decision by the Security Council on the question of whether there has

---

[14] *San Remo Manual.*
[15] Final Report of the Committee on Maritime Neutrality, in International Law Association, *Report of the Sixty-eighth Conference* (Taipeh Conference 1998), 496–521. As these rules had already been accepted in substance by the previous ILA Conference held in Helsinki, they were adopted under the name of 'Helsinki Principles on the Law of Maritime Neutrality'.
[16] K. Ipsen, in Ipsen, *Völkerrecht*, 5th edn (München: Beck, 2004), 1112; Bothe, in Graf Vitzthum (ed.), *Völkerrecht*, 5th edn (Berlin: de Gruyter, 2010), 724 *et seq.*
[17] Schindler, in Delissen/Tanja (eds), *loc. cit.*, n. 8, 367 *et seq.*
[18] Legality of the Use or Threat of Nuclear Weapons, Advisory Opinion, *ICJ Reports 1996*, 66 (paras. 88 *et seq.*).
[19] *Hogan v An Taoiseach et al.*, High Court of Ireland, Judgment of 28 April 2003, [2003] 468, 2 I.R., at 504 *et seq.*; Bundesverwaltungsgericht (German Federal Administrative Court), Judgment of 21 June 2005, 59 *Neue Juristische Wochenschrift* (2006), 77, at 96, affirmatively quoting the preceding edition of this *Handbook.*
[20] Art. 17, *Yearbook of the International Law Commission 2011*, Vol. II, Part Two.

MICHAEL BOTHE

been an armed attack and which state is the aggressor, decisions of this kind have long been politically impossible in view of the polarization between the superpowers. After the end of the East–West conflict, the Security Council is in a better position to take decisions, but it has very often refrained from legally characterizing situations as breach of the peace or act of aggression from designating a state as being an aggressor. It can thus not be taken for granted that the Security Council will always exercise its powers in this respect.

2. Furthermore, it is stressed that the UN Charter provides a right of collective self-defence, that is a right of all states to assist a victim of aggression, but not a duty to do so. Thus, it is by no means unlawful if a state abstains from supporting a victim of aggression, that is remains impartial and neutral.[21] The situation is different only if and to the extent that the Security Council uses its powers under Chapter VII of the Charter to oblige states to conduct enforcement measures (Articles 41, 42, 43, and 48 UN Charter). This means that the traditional duty of non-participation and impartiality has not in a general way been excluded by the Charter, but only that it may in particular cases be suspended by a binding decision of the Security Council. When taking such a decision, the Security Council may also differentiate the duties of support imposed upon particular states.[22] In this respect, one has to distinguish between enforcement measures *stricto sensu* undertaken by the United Nations under the direction of the Security Council and military operations undertaken by one or more states and authorized by the Security Council. Many commentators considered the military operation to liberate Kuwait as not constituting an enforcement action undertaken by the United Nations, but simply as collective self-defence authorized by the Security Council. A distinction must be made, however, between the authorization to conduct military operations against Iraq, an authorization given only to the states 'co-operating with the government of Kuwait', which clearly implies the legal admissibility of non-participation, and non-military enforcement measures against Iraq, in particular the interruption of commercial relations and of monetary transactions imposed as a duty on all members of the United Nations. In this case, states were clearly under a duty to deviate from the principle of *courant normal*,[23] to that extent there was a modification of the rules of neutrality. The authorization given by the Security Council to take military action against Iraq also modified the duty of non-participation, but it did not exclude the possibility of neutrality, as no state was obliged to make use of that authorization. But in the light of this authorization, it could not be considered unlawful to grant to the states taking military action assistance which otherwise would be a violation of neutrality. In the case of the US–British intervention in Iraq 2003, the intervening states also claimed that they acted under an authorization by the Security Council, which however, is subject to controversy. The assistance given to the intervening states by a number of other states, including Germany, could be justified under the law of neutrality if the US–British justification of the intervention was correct.[24] If not, the law of neutrality had to be applied and the assistance was unlawful.

---

[21] Schindler, *loc. cit.*, n. 8, 373.

[22] See M. Torrelli, 'La neutralité' (1991) 35 *Annales de droit international médical* 25–59, at 38 *et seq.*

[23] See above, commentary to Section 1101.

[24] In this sense apparently R. Wedgwood, 'The Fall of Saddam Hussein: Security Council Mandates and Pre-emptive Self-Defense' (2003) 97 *AJIL* 576–85, at 582.

MICHAEL BOTHE

3. The duty of non-participation as well as that of impartiality may, thus, be restricted by decisions of the Security Council.[25] But it must be ascertained in each particular case how far this has been the case.

1104   **Every state is free to participate in an armed conflict, but only on the side of the victim of an armed attack (collective self-defence), not on that of the aggressor.**

1. Traditional international law left to each state the sovereign decision of whether, at the outbreak of a conflict between other states, it would participate or remain neutral. Thus neutrality, as a matter of principle, was a question to be decided ad hoc by each state when a conflict broke out. Therefore, there was a practice of pronouncing 'declarations of neutrality' at the outbreak of a conflict.

2. As explained above, this is still true but only in a limited sense. At the outbreak of a conflict between two other states, a state is still free to participate or to remain neutral. Modern international law, however, limits the freedom of decision as to the side on which a state may become involved. Support granted to an aggressor is illegal, participation on the side of the victim of aggression, being collective self-defence, is permissible.

3. The decision to participate or to remain neutral is a political, not a military, decision. Where the law of neutrality requires decisions to be taken by military command, the government concerned must give political guidance and clarify the position which it takes in relation to a particular conflict.

1105   **Permanent neutrality is a status under which a state undertakes in peacetime a legal obligation to remain neutral in case of an armed conflict between two other states. This status requires the neutral state in peacetime not to accept any military obligations and to abstain from acts which would render the fulfilment of its obligations of neutrality impossible should the armed conflict occur. A distinction must be made between such a legal obligation to remain neutral and a neutrality policy.**

1. The legal neutralization of certain states was one of the political tools used to maintain a balance of power in Europe under the European Concert during the last century. The states which still possess a legally based status of permanent neutrality are Switzerland and Austria.[26] The permanent neutrality of Switzerland is based on mutual unilateral declarations made by Switzerland and by the most important European powers, in connection with the Vienna Congress in 1815. The international legal basis of the permanent neutrality of Austria is also a unilateral act, namely the Austrian notification of the Federal Constitution Act of 26 October 1955. Whether, and to what extent, both states are under an international legal duty to maintain this status of permanent neutrality is not clear.

2. A permanently neutral state may not, in time of peace, accept any obligation which would render it impossible to fulfil, in times of armed conflict, its duties of neutrality. Therefore, a permanently neutral state may not become a member of a military alliance. In relation to Austria, there was a lively discussion as to whether the economic obligations involved in Austrian membership of the EC would be incompatible with its status

---

[25] Schindler, in Delissen/Tanja (eds), *loc. cit.*, n. 8, at 372.
[26] Bothe, *loc. cit.*, n. 1, para. 16.

MICHAEL BOTHE

of permanent neutrality. Whether this was true in the context of the division of Europe into two blocs is a question which no longer needs an answer. The political changes in Europe have rendered the question of the significance of economic ties for the status of permanent neutrality irrelevant in the European context.[27]

3. In a more general way, permanent neutrality means a renunciation of the right of collective self-defence, that is the right to grant assistance, but not a renunciation of the right to accept help from others if the permanently neutral state is itself attacked. In most other cases where states declared themselves as permanently neutral, the declarations were not of a legal, but of a political nature. Legal acts establishing permanent neutrality of the kind adopted by Switzerland and Austria are lacking in the case of states which during the past years had followed a policy of neutrality (Sweden, Finland, Ireland). In these cases, there may have been some legal underpinning of neutrality in the principle of estoppel, namely where political declarations had created a situation of confidence in which other states may have relied on the state making such a declaration to remain neutral and where, due to that reliance, they had abstained from making defence preparations in relation to that state. Such situations are, however, subject to progressive development.[28]

> **Except for those rules which, in a legally based permanent neutrality, apply in**   **1106**
> **times of peace, neutrality begins with the outbreak of an armed conflict of signifi-**
> **cant scope between two other states.**

1. The status of neutrality as defined by international law becomes effective with the outbreak of an armed conflict between two other states.[29] Thus, the question arises of what constitutes an armed conflict within the meaning of the law of neutrality; in other words, what is the threshold of application of the law of neutrality? The law of neutrality leads to considerable modifications in the relationships between the neutral and the belligerent states, for instance as to the admissibility of exports, the sojourn of warships of the parties to the conflict in neutral waters, and the control of neutral trade. These fundamental changes are not triggered by every armed incident, but require an armed conflict of a certain duration and intensity. Thus, the threshold of application of the law of neutrality is probably higher than that for the rules of the law of war relating to the conduct of hostilities and the treatment of prisoners, which are applicable also in conflicts of less intensity.

2. There is a traditional thesis, still defended in literature and by state organs, to the effect that the application of the law of neutrality requires the existence of 'a war in the legal sense'.[30] Whether and to what extent this thesis is a correct statement of the current

---

[27] F. Cede, 'Staatsvertrag und Neutralität aus heutiger Sicht', in M. Rauchensteiner/R. Kriechbaume (eds), *Die Gunst des Augenblicks: neuere Forschungen zu Staatsvertrag und Neutralität*, 2nd edn (Wien: Böhlau, 2006).

[28] See, e.g., for the current Swedish foreign policy: 'Sweden will not take a passive stance if another EU Member State or other Nordic country suffers a disaster or an attack. We expect these countries to act in the same way if Sweden is affected. Sweden should therefore have the capability to provide and receive military support.' (<http://www.government.se/sb/d/3103/a/116839>.)

[29] Bothe, 'Neutrality at Sea', in I. Dekker/H. Post (eds), *The Gulf War of 1980–1988*, (Nijhoff, 1992), 205 *et seq.*

[30] Castrén, *op. cit.*, n. 10, 34 *et seq.*; C. Greenwood, 'Neutrality at Sea: Comments', in Dekker/Post (eds), *op. cit.*, n. 29, 212 *et seq.*; Schindler, in Delissen/Tanja (eds), *loc. cit.*, n. 8, 375 *et seq.*

MICHAEL BOTHE

state of customary law depends on the definition of 'war in the legal sense' under current international law. There is still a widespread opinion that, in addition to the objective existence of armed hostilities, there must be a subjective element: the intent to conduct a war (*animus belligerendi*). If this were correct a state could, simply by declaring that it did not intend to conduct a war, evade all the restraints imposed upon a party to the conflict by the law of neutrality. For states not party to the conflict this construction would provide an excuse not to respect the prohibition of supporting a belligerent. It is exactly in this sense that the construction has been used time and time again. However, the threshold of the application of the law of neutrality must be prevented from becoming in this way a question for the subjective discretion of the states involved. Therefore, the threshold must be determined according to the object and purpose of the law of neutrality. This means that the law of neutrality must be applied in any conflict which has reached a scope which renders its legal limitation by the application of the law of neutrality meaningful and necessary. It is, however, impossible to establish this threshold in a general way. One can only say that there must be a conflict of a certain duration and intensity.

3. On closer analysis, all those defending a 'subjective' notion of war come to a similar result if and to the extent that they tie the intent to conduct a war to a series of objective criteria relevant for the character of the relationships between the parties to a conflict as well as between these parties and neutral states. For them, the decisive question is whether and to what extent states use legal instruments typical for the existence of a state of war; for instance the severance of diplomatic relations, the treatment of nationals of the other party as enemy aliens, the exercise of control over the commerce of third states, and similar measures.

4. It is apparent from the above that the determination of whether a particular conflict has reached the threshold of application of the law of neutrality is a matter of complex legal construction both for the parties to the conflict and for third states. In the interest of legal clarity, it is therefore desirable that states expressly clarify their position in this respect. This legal construction is a matter to be decided by governments, not by military command. Therefore, declarations and notifications of a state's construction of the status of the conflict are relevant, but by no means constitutive for the characterization of the conflict. The law of neutrality is applicable without a specific declaration on the part of the state not party to the conflict being necessary. The difficulties described, however, have frequently led to situations in which different states evaluated the legal status of the same conflict in a different way (e.g. the Gulf War between Iran and Iraq[31]), a fact which has led to considerable legal insecurity.

5. States not parties to a conflict which has not reached the threshold of application of the law of neutrality are not neutral in the legal sense, that is they are not bound by the particular duties of the law of neutrality. In those fields where the rules of international humanitarian law have a lower threshold of application than the law of neutrality, the use of the term 'other state not party to a conflict' is the logical consequence of this situation.[32]

---

[31] See, e.g., Bothe, *loc. cit.*, n. 28, on the one hand, and Greenwood, *loc. cit.*, n. 30, on the other.
[32] See commentary to Section 1101.

MICHAEL BOTHE

6. The application of the law of neutrality requires the existence of an international conflict. There is no neutrality in relation to non-international conflicts. On the other hand, third states are subject to certain legal restrictions in relation to internal armed conflicts. According to a traditional rule of international law, support given to insurgents constitutes unlawful interference in the internal affairs of another state. If it reaches a certain intensity, this support is considered equivalent to an unlawful armed attack. Support given to an established government, in whatever form, was in former times generally considered as legal, each state being free to request the assistance of other states for the purpose of maintaining its internal order. This, however, is no longer uncontroversial, in particular because there have been a number of cases where the legitimacy of the government requesting the assistance was subject to doubt (e.g. Afghanistan,[33] Vietnam[34]). Whether the assistance given to parties to a civil war, even in the form of an 'intervention by invitation', is admissible still is a matter of controversy.[35] A prohibition of interference of this kind must not be confused with the duty of non-participation under the law of neutrality. Foreign intervention, whether lawful or not, can change the status of an internal conflict and render it an international one. In this case, the law of neutrality is, indeed, applicable.

Neutral status ceases with the end of an armed conflict or by the neutral state becoming a party to the conflict. However, neither limited actions of armed defence of neutrality nor breaches of single duties of neutrality by the state alone necessarily result in that state becoming a party to the conflict.   1107

1. The status of neutrality (except, of course, those rules of permanent neutrality which apply in times of peace) ends with the armed conflict. This obvious rule raises a number of practical problems similar to those concerning the beginning of neutral status. Under today's conditions, the end of a conflict can not always be clearly determined. The actual cessation of hostilities does not always lead to a modification in the relations between the parties to the conflict which would render the law of neutrality inapplicable. Restraints imposed by the law of neutrality remain relevant in this situation, as for instance the resumption of arms exports during an armistice might even prompt the resurgence of the armed conflict and thus render futile a positive effect of the law of neutrality. On the other hand, an armistice may lead to the pacification of the situation which, after several years, can no longer be distinguished from normal peacetime relations. For this question, too, there are no sufficiently clear criteria of general validity. Within the meaning of the law of neutrality, a conflict must be considered as terminated where, after the cessation of active hostilities, there is a certain degree of normalization of the relations between the parties to a conflict. There are specific rules for certain norms of the law of neutrality (e.g. Article 111 GC III).

2. In the course of the conflict, a neutral state may become a party to the conflict. Whether and under what circumstances this occurs is not always easy to determine. Different cases must be distinguished.

[33] The Afghan government requesting Soviet help in 1979.
[34] The South Vietnamese government co-operating with the US since the mid-1950s was not universally recognized as the government of a separate state of South Vietnam, nor was the state as such. That government had to face an internal rebellion by the 'Vietcong', which was actively supported by North Vietnam. Thus, the armed conflict had both an internal and an international aspect. For an analysis of the status of the conflict, see Q. Wright, 'Legal Aspects of the Vietnam Conflict' (1966) 60 *AJIL* 750–69.
[35] Nolte, 'Intervention by invitation', *MPEPIL* (n. 1).

MICHAEL BOTHE

3. The first possibility is that either a party to the conflict or the neutral state by une-quivocal acts or declarations change the existing status, for example Germany and Italy during the Second World War by their declaration of war against the US (which was neutral, but not behaving according to the law of neutrality) or Germany by its invasion of Norway. The question of whether this triggering of an armed conflict is or is not a violation of international law is irrelevant for the other question of whether the neutral status is ended. As long as states do not legally characterize their acts by declarations, the mere fact that hostilities are present between a neutral state and a party to the conflict must be evaluated in a differentiated way. Thus, the massive support given by the US to the states at war with Germany did not render the US a party to the conflict until the declaration of war just mentioned. Only where a hitherto neutral state participates to a significant extent in hostilities is there a change of status.

4. This becomes obvious if the duty of the neutral state to defend its neutrality, if neces-sary by the use of arms, is also considered. Where a party to a conflict tries to occupy parts of the neutral territory for use as a base for hostilities, the neutral state is bound to take military countermeasures. If it complies with this obligation, it cannot be consid-ered as losing all the advantages of neutral status. It remains neutral despite the fact that it is engaged in hostilities with one of the parties of conflict.

5. The question of whether a change of a neutral status is effected where a hitherto neu-tral state is drawn into the conflict must be distinguished from the different question of whether or not this change of status is brought about lawfully. In this respect, the change of status effected by a party to the conflict and by the neutral state itself must be distinguished. In addition, two levels of legal evaluation must be differentiated, namely the evaluation under the law of neutrality and that under the law relating to the inter-national prohibition of the use of force.[36] Where a hitherto neutral state violates the law of neutrality by supporting a party to the conflict or in any other way, the affected party to the conflict is entitled to take reprisals, which are then subject to the general rules concerning reprisals, in particular the principle of proportionality.[37] According to tra-ditional international law, reprisals could have involved the use of military force against the state violating the law. In this respect, the Charter of the United Nations requires a differentiated view. Armed reprisals are generally unlawful.[38] As a consequence, a reac-tion against violations of neutrality which would involve the use of force against another state is permissible only where the violation of the law triggering that reaction itself constitutes an illegal armed attack. If this rule is applied in the context of an existing armed conflict, the question arises of whether the violation of neutrality is to the advan-tage of the aggressor or the victim. Support of the aggressor is illegal not only under the law of neutrality, but also under the law prohibiting the use of force. Illegal support for an aggressor, however, is not necessarily equivalent to an armed attack. Therefore, the victim of aggression reacting to a non-neutral service in favour of the aggressor is still subject to the prohibition of the use of force.[39] In this case, it is therefore not necessarily

---

[36] Concerning the problem of the parallel application of different levels of legal regulation, see Schindler, in Delissen/Tanja (eds), *loc. cit.*, n. 9, 374 *et seq.*

[37] M. Ruffert, 'Reprisals', para. 10, *MPEPIL*.

[38] Ibid. 332; Schindler, in Delissen/Tanja (eds), *loc. cit.*, n. 9, 381 *et seq.*

[39] For example, during the Iran–Iraq War, the unneutral services rendered to Iraq by the US, Saudi Arabia, and Kuwait did not entitle Iran to adopt measures against those states involving the use of military force.

MICHAEL BOTHE

legal to attack a state violating the law of neutrality and to make it, by that attack, a party to the conflict.

6. If a neutral state renders its support to the victim of aggression, this is contrary to the law of neutrality, but not a breach of the prohibition of the use of force. The neutral state could claim the right of collective self-defence and thus become a party to the conflict without violating the international prohibition of the use of force. The question then arises of whether the right of collective self-defence serves as a justification also for the purposes of the law of neutrality, thus excluding the lawfulness of a countermeasure otherwise lawful under the law of neutrality. Such a conclusion would be contrary to a general principle of the law of war, namely the principle of equality of the parties regardless of the justification of the conflict.[40] Like international humanitarian law, the law of neutrality can effectively fulfil its function of restraining conflicts only if the question of which party is the aggressor and which the victim remains irrelevant for the evaluation of certain acts in the light of the law of neutrality. Therefore, reprisals taken against the state supporting the victim of aggression are admissible under the law of neutrality. Whether or not this support is legal under the rules relating to the prohibition of the use of force is reserved to a different level of analysis, for example where the question of the duty of the aggressor to pay damages is raised after the conflict.

II. The Rights and Duties of Neutral States

1. General Provisions

> **The territory of a neutral state is inviolable. It is prohibited to commit any act of hostility whatsoever on such territory (Article 1 HC V).**   1108

1. This rule formulates the fundamental right of the neutral state to remain outside the armed conflict and not to be adversely affected by it. Above all, this means that the armed forces of the parties to the conflict may not enter neutral territory. They may not in any way use this territory for their military operations, or for transit or similar purposes. It must again be stressed that this rule applies regardless of whether a party to the conflict is the aggressor or the victim of aggression. The right of self-defence does not legitimize the use of any means contrary to the laws of war. Nor does it legitimize military measures against states which have not themselves committed aggression, even if the use of their territory were useful or necessary for the exercise of the right of self-defence to be militarily effective. The right of self-defence does not constitute a comprehensive right of self-help against innocent third states. The inviolability of neutral territory applies not only to neutral land but also to neutral waters (internal waters, territorial sea, see Section 1117) and airspace (see Section 1149). As far as sea areas are concerned, this right is limited by the right of innocent passage. As far as the right of flight over sea areas is concerned, a distinction must be made between the territorial sea generally (no right of overflight) and international straits and shipping lanes through archipelagic waters, for both of which there is a right of overflight.

---

[40] See above, Section 101. Therefore, Schindler's theory of optional neutrality (in Delissen/Tanja (eds), *loc. cit.*, n. 8, 373 *et seq.*) is problematic. Any attempt to mix in this way the law relating to the prevention of war and that relating to its conduct (and the law of neutrality is part of the latter) would negatively affect the functioning of the principle of reciprocity which is also the basis of the law of neutrality.

MICHAEL BOTHE

2. The inviolability of neutral territory also means that the neutral states must not be affected by collateral effects of hostilities. The parties to the conflict have no right to cause damage to neutral territory through hostilities themselves. Therefore, there is no rule of admissible collateral damage to the detriment of the neutral state (for collateral damage generally, see Section 455). If the effects of attacks directed against targets on the territory of a party to the conflict are felt on neutral territory, they are unlawful. Recognizing this rule, Allied governments paid compensation for damage occurring during the Second World War in Switzerland caused by attacks on targets in Germany which had an impact in Switzerland. Also in this respect, the principle that the relations between the neutral states and the parties to the conflict are generally governed by the law of peacetime applies.[41] An exception to this rule applies only where, as for example in maritime warfare, customary law recognizes a certain impact of hostilities on a neutral interest, in particular on neutral navigation, as being lawful (see Sections 1138 *et seq.*). As to land warfare, there is no similar rule of customary law which would lower the normal standard of peacetime protection against transboundary impact. The fact that the use of weapons yielding high explosive power, in particular nuclear weapons, would thus be rendered illegal under the law of neutrality may render respect for this rule difficult in the case of an armed conflict. However, this fact has so far clearly not resulted in a change of practice and legal opinion which would have modified the traditional rule of the inviolability of the neutral territory.

1109   **The neutral state is bound to repel any violation of its neutrality, if necessary by force (Article 5 HC V; Articles 2, 9, 24 HC XIII). This obligation, however, is limited by the international legal prohibition of the use of force. The use of military force outside the neutral state's own territory for the purpose of defending its neutrality is permissible only if it is legitimate self-defence against an armed attack.**

1. The duty of the neutral state to prevent its territory from being used by one of the parties to the conflict as a base for military operations is the corollary of the neutral's right not to be adversely affected by the conflict. Therefore it must prevent any attempt by a party to the conflict to use its territory for military operations, through invasion or in transit, by all means at its disposal.[42] This duty, however, is limited to the defence feasible for the neutral state under the circumstances. A neutral state is not obliged to destroy itself (see in particular the commentary to Section 1115).

2. In connection with the duty to defend neutrality, it has been debated whether and to what extent neutrality obliges the neutral state to undertake military efforts. The Austrian and Swiss concept is that of armed neutrality,[43] based on the idea that neutral states are indeed obliged to undertake military efforts in order to repel a violation of neutrality by the use of armed force. The neutrality policy of Costa Rica, on the other hand, is based on unarmed neutrality. This is certainly unobjectionable as long as no party to the conflict attempts to use the territory of the unarmed neutral state. In the absence of

---

[41] Bothe, 'The Protection of the Environment in Times of Armed Conflict' (1991) 34 *GYIL* 54–62, 59 *et seq.*

[42] P. Hostettler/O. Danai, 'Neutrality in Land Warfare', *MPEPIL* n. 1.

[43] L. Wildhaber, 'Muss die dauernde Neutralität bewaffnet sein?', in W. Haller/A. Kölz/G. Müller/D. Thürer (eds), *Im Dienst an der Gemeinschaft. Festschrift für Dietrich Schindler* (Basel: Helbing & Lichtenhahn, 1989), 423, esp. 434 *et seq.*

MICHAEL BOTHE

any effort by the neutral state to react to a violation of its territory, however, that state risks no longer being considered neutral by the party to the conflict adversely affected.

3. If the neutral state defends its neutrality it must respect the limits which international law imposes on military violence. There is no specific need for international legal justification of military measures which the state takes on its own territory, for instance if it drives troops out which have invaded its territory. The specific justification as self-defence is only necessary if military measures are employed outside the neutral state's own territory. In this case, they are admissible only to the extent that the preceding violation constitutes an armed attack within the meaning of Article 51 of the UN Charter and if the countermeasure taken constitutes a necessary and proportional reaction to that attack. Article 51 of the Charter, thus, always marks the limits of counter-force the neutral state may legally use.[44] In other words: the Charter of the United Nations grants a right to use counter-force; the law of neutrality may, under certain circumstances, impose an obligation to exercise this right.

> **A neutral state must not assist a party to the conflict. It is especially prohibited**   **1110**
> **to supply warships, ammunition, or other war materials (Article 6 HC XIII).**
> **Humanitarian assistance for victims of the conflict does not constitute a violation**
> **of neutrality even where it is for the benefit of only one party to the conflict (Article**
> **14 HC V).**

1. This rule formulates in a general way the principle of non-participation. The neutral state must abstain from any act which may have an impact on the outcome of the conflict. The second sentence names only a few examples of such forbidden assistance. Massive financial support for a party to the conflict also constitutes non-neutral service. This was the case with a number of Arab states during the conflict between Iran and Iraq who gave substantial financial support to the war effort of Iraq. The arms supplies by Western states to Iraq, too, were objectionable under the law of neutrality. The prohibition is absolute, and applies also where assistance is given to both parties. Section 1110 constitutes a concretization not of the duty of impartiality, but of the duty of non-participation. Therefore, it is unlawful for a neutral state to compensate an uneven relation of strength between the parties to the conflict by supplying arms or similar support.

2. The supply of any war material is forbidden (as to the definition, see comments to Section 1112, also Article 44 HRAW). This rule, however, is among those which lend themselves to be modified where the Security Council adopts measures for the maintenance of peace.

3. As far as the humanitarian protection of the victims of the conflict is concerned, the only criterion for such assistance is need, and not equal benefit for the parties to the conflict. This idea was for the first time clearly formulated in Article 70 AP I which states that humanitarian assistance may not be considered as an interference in the conflict. Humanitarian assistance, however, is subject to its own requirements of neutrality. Any assistance whose purpose is not to mitigate the need of victims, but to provide a

---

[44] C. Greenwood, 'Self-Defence and the Conduct of International Armed Conflict', in Dinstein/Tabory (eds), *International Law at a Time of Perplexity. Essays in Honour of Shabtai Rosenne* (Nijhoff, 1989), 273 at 275 *et seq.*; R. Lagoni, 'Gewaltverbot, Seekriegsrecht und Schifffahrtsfreiheit im Golfkrieg', in *Festschrift für Wolfgang Zeidler* (Berlin: de Gruyter, 1987), 1833, at 1847 *et seq.*

MICHAEL BOTHE

military advantage to one party is not humanitarian. On the other hand, inequalities of assistance based on a difference in need and requirements do not violate the principle of humanitarian impartiality.

1111   **A neutral state may in no circumstances participate in acts of war by a party to the conflict.**

This rule names a further example of assistance forbidden according to Section 1110. It may be questionable what is considered to be forbidden participation in a particular case. If the neutral state takes part by engaging its own military forces, this is a clear example. Another example might be the supply of military advisors to the armed forces of a party to the conflict.

1112   **State practice has modified the former rule of both customary and treaty law that a neutral state is not bound to prohibit export and transit of war material by private persons for the benefit of one of the parties to the conflict (Article 7 HC V). To the extent that arms export is subject to control by the state, the permission of such export is to be considered as a non-neutral service.**

1. The traditional law of neutrality distinguished between unlawful assistance by the neutral state and assistance by private persons or private enterprises belonging to a neutral state. The latter was not attributed to the neutral state and there was no obligation on this state to prevent it. This rule has resulted in the private arms industry of neutral states supplying armaments in a relatively unimpeded way to a party to the conflict, and frequently to both sides.

2. The separation of the state and the private armaments industry is nowadays artificial and does not correspond with political reality. Arms production and arms trade are in many ways managed, promoted, and controlled by the state. Therefore it would simply be unrealistic if one did not attribute to the state the exports of that state's 'official' arms industry. Modern state practice accords with the rule of non-separation. Where states took the view that the law of neutrality applied, they did not permit arms exports by private enterprise, nor did they rely on the artificial separation between state and private enterprise. According to the current state of customary law, the correct view is that a state's permission to supply war material constitutes a non-neutral service.[45]

3. In addition to the question of the scope of application of the law of neutrality discussed above, this raises two additional questions. First, what kind of effort must a state make to prevent the export of war material, and second, what kinds of material constitute war material within the meaning of the rule. As to the first question, one has to assume that besides arms exports controlled by the state, there is a black market which evades state controls. The more stringent the controls, the greater the incentive to undertake transfers to circumvent them. Discussions about the supply of equipment for the production of chemical weapons in Libya and Iraq are examples. As to this question, there is no sufficient practice to produce an *opinio iuris*. In the field of chemical weapons, the 1993 convention on their prohibition entails specific duties of export control. Nonproliferation regimes, in particular the Non-Proliferation Treaty require export controls which have the effect of buttressing export restraints based on neutrality rule.

---

[45] S. Oeter, *Neutralität und Waffenhandel* (Berlin: Springer, 1992), esp. at 216 *et seq.*; for a discussion see Politakis, *op. cit.*, n. 5, 506 *et seq.*

MICHAEL BOTHE

4. As to the definition of war materials which may not be supplied to the parties to the conflict, the problem must be distinguished from that of the definition of contraband. There is apparently no state practice to the effect that the rule of neutrality prohibiting supply covers more than weapons *stricto sensu*, that is material which is capable of being used for killing enemy soldiers or destroying enemy goods. Non-proliferation regimes in the field of arms control usually cover related materials (technology, construction plans etc.).

5. Another open question is whether the permission given to an export/import enterprise to grant sub-licences or the non-prevention of re-exports are equivalent to the permission of exports. Arms exports may have the effect of instigating a conflict. For Germany, Article 26 of the Basic Law has established a constitutional duty to restrict the export of weapons. This duty was implemented by the War Weapons Control Act. In addition, the export of materials relevant for armament may be restricted under the Foreign Economic Transactions Act. Both acts empower the Federal government to prevent exports which are prohibited under the law of neutrality.[46]

> **Citizens of neutral states may, at their own risk, enter into the service of one of**   **1113**
> **the parties to the conflict (Article 6 HC V). In such a case, they must be treated**
> **as nationals of the respective party to the conflict (Article 17 HC V). The prohibi-**
> **tion against recruiting, using, financing, or training mercenaries must be respected**
> **(Article 47 AP I; Mercenary Convention; see above, Section 303).**

> **It is prohibited to recruit and raise troops on neutral territory to assist one of the**   **1114**
> **parties to the conflict (Article 4 HC V).**

1. While the troops of a neutral state may not take part in any war operations (see Section 1111), it cannot and is not required that the neutral state prevents its nationals from entering the service of a party to the conflict on their own initiative and responsibility. This distinction between private and governmental assistance may, however, be misused. If the state tolerates the establishment of so-called volunteer corps, a not uncommon practice, this amounts to a non-neutral service. The same applies where the neutral state tolerates publicity for the establishment of troops by the parties to the conflict. All acts and omissions of the neutral state are prohibited which further the military effort of a party to the conflict.

2. Further duties of prevention result from the Convention against recruitment, use, financing, and training of mercenaries, opened for signature and ratification by the General Assembly of the United Nations on 4 December 1989. The parties to this Convention are bound to punish the recruitment of mercenaries. It must be taken into account, however, that the members of regular armed forces of a party to the conflict are not mercenaries within the meaning of the Convention. Recruitment for activities within the regular armed forces of another state thus does not constitute an activity which must be punished according to the Mercenaries Convention.

3. Still greater duties of prevention may apply when the Security Council imposes an obligation to abstain from any assistance to an aggressor. This may imply an obligation

---

[46] Act implementing Article 26, para. 2, of the Basic Law (*Gesetz über die Kontrolle von Kriegswaffen*) of 20 April 1961, as promulgated on 22 November 1990 (BGBl I 2506); Foreign Economic Transaction Regulation of 18 December 1986 (BGBl I 2671).

MICHAEL BOTHE

to prevent private assistance which does not exist under the general law of neutrality nor under the Mercenaries Convention.

2. War on Land

1115   **Troop or supply movements must not be carried out on neutral territory (Article 2 HC V). The neutral state may allow the transit of wounded persons and relief goods (Article 14 HC V).**

1. This provision is a consequence of the prohibition of non-neutral services set out in Sections 1110 and 1112, and also of the prohibition against using neutral territory for the military purposes of a party to the conflict.[47] Prohibited transport across neutral territory includes cases where a party to the conflict is granted landing rights for supply flights, a case which has considerable practical importance.[48]

2. During the Second World War, the prohibition of transit was in some cases not respected by neutral states under the pressure of circumstances. Neutral states have granted transit rights to belligerents in different ways. In most cases, this was the first step towards a neutral state being drawn into the conflict. On the other hand, states refusing transit rights were attacked.

3. The exact definition of forbidden supply movement presents difficulties. Transport of weapons belongs to this category. On the other hand, the movement of medical supplies or of raw materials for the war industry would be considered as permitted.

4. The second sentence establishes an exception to the rule for the transport of wounded persons and relief supplies. There is a general principle of the law of war behind this rule (also expressed in Section 1110, second sentence) namely that humanitarian assistance to the victims of conflict, as a rule, does not constitute a non-neutral service.

1116   **It is not considered a non-neutral service if a neutral state permits the use by a party to the conflict of generally accessible means of communications on its territory. The neutral state must not, however, install or permit on its territory special means of communication for a party to the conflict (Article 3 HC V).**

1. In view of the great importance of telecommunications for modern high-technology warfare, the rules of the law of neutrality relating to neutral telecommunication installations are of particular significance. The relevant rules of Hague Convention V do not address modern problems of telecommunication with the necessary clarity, but they contain principles which remain valid and applicable today. Another element of the delimitation between permissible and impermissible use of neutral telecommunication installations is the idea of *courant normal*, which is of general importance for neutral commercial relations. The outbreak of an armed conflict does not result in an obligation for the neutral state to prevent the use of its telecommunication installations by a party to the conflict which used them or which had access to them before. Existing non-military telecommunication infrastructure, in particular that owned by a public

---

[47] Hostettler/Danai, *loc. cit.*, n. 42.

[48] This was a major issue during the US–British intervention in Iraq 2003. See the decisions of the Irish High Court of 28 April 2003, *Horgan v An Taoiseach* [2003] 468, 2 I.R. and of the German Federal Administrative Court, quoted above n. 19; see above, commentary to Section 1103.

MICHAEL BOTHE

telecommunications enterprise or administration of the neutral state, may be used by the parties to the conflict. In this sense, the Global Positioning System (GPS) is a generally available means of communication. The same holds true for data communication infrastructure, in particular hardware components of the Internet, for example servers situated on neutral territory or under the jurisdiction or control of a neutral state. A neutral state is not obliged to bar the use of such components of the Internet by the parties to a conflict even if that use is of a military nature.

2. Thus, the parties may rent fixed lines for voice and data communication of a military nature and may be granted access from such lines to satellite communications. On the other hand, it is a non-neutral service for a neutral state to place at the disposal of a party to the conflict telecommunication installations not available to it under normal conditions (e.g. its own military telecommunication infrastructure) or if it creates, or acquiesces in the creation of, new telecommunication infrastructure for the particular purposes of a party to the conflict. Furthermore, it is a violation of neutrality if a neutral state provides one party to a conflict satellite imagery containing valuable military information concerning the other party.

> **Neutral states must intern forces of the parties to the conflict trespassing on neutral territory (Articles 11 and 12 HC V). Escaped prisoners of war who are allowed to remain in the territory of the neutral state may be assigned a specific place of residence (Article 13 HC V).**   **1117**

1. The treatment of military personnel and war material of the parties to the conflict which are found on neutral territory is unclear in many respects.

2. If whole units of the armed forces of a party to the conflict arrive on neutral territory, it would be a violation of the duty of non-participation if the neutral state permitted them to take part again in hostilities. Therefore, those troops must be interned (Article 11 HC V). War material, too, has to be withheld until the end of the conflict (e.g. the military aircraft brought into Iran during the Gulf War, if the law of neutrality is applicable in that case).

3. A logical consequence of this rule would be that the neutral state had to prevent escaped prisoners arriving on its territory from taking further part in the hostilities. Article 13 HC V expressly states that such escaped prisoners must remain free. Certain authors conclude from this that they must be permitted to go back to their home country.[49] However, this is by no means clear. The provisions of the Third Geneva Convention provide for repatriation of prisoners of war on neutral territory only in certain cases and do not regulate the question comprehensively (see Articles 110 and 111 GC III). This question should, whenever possible, be regulated by a specific agreement between the states concerned.

3. Naval Warfare

a. General

> **The internal waters, archipelagic waters, and territorial sea of neutral states must be respected (Article 1 HC XIII). It is prohibited to commit any act of war in such waters (Article 2 HC XIII).**   **1118**

---

[49] Castrén, *op. cit.*, n. 11, 468.

MICHAEL BOTHE

1119   **The parties to the conflict may not use neutral ports or territorial waters as a base for naval operations (Article 5 HC XIII).**

1120   **Acts of war are prohibited in neutral waters to the same extent as on neutral territory (Article 2 HC XIII). The acts of war which are forbidden include stop, visit, and search, orders to follow a specific course, the exercise of the law of prize, and capture of merchant ships (Article 2 HC XIII).**

1. Sections 1118–1120[50] constitute the maritime aspect of the general principle (formulated in Section 1108) that the territory of a neutral state is inviolable and may not be used for the purpose of conducting hostilities. This rule, however, is somewhat modified for neutral territorial sea, as compared to the rule in land warfare, in that there is a right of innocent passage (Section 1126).[51] The jurisdictional waters to be respected consist of the territorial sea and the internal waters belonging to the sea, that is sea areas on the landward side of the base line from which the territorial sea is measured (see Article 8 of the United Nations Convention on the Law of the Sea). The exclusive economic zone and the sea area above the continental shelf do not constitute neutral waters within the meaning of Sections 1118–1120.[52]

2. The status of the waters superjacent the continental shelf is not affected by the exclusive rights of the coastal state over the resources of the shelf (Article 78 UNCLOS). They may thus belong to the high seas or the EEZ. As to the EEZ, third states enjoy all the freedoms of the high seas (Article 58 UNCLOS) except the rights specifically reserved to the coastal state by Part V UNCLOS. Article 88 UNCLOS, which reserves the use of the high seas and the EEZ for peaceful purposes is generally interpreted in the sense that it excludes belligerent activities only to the extent that they violate the Charter of the United Nations, in particular the prohibition of the use of force.[53] The parties to the conflict must, however, in conducting hostilities have due regard to rights and duties of the neutral coastal state in whose EEZ hostilities are taking place.[54] On the high seas, the belligerents must also conduct hostilities with due regard to the relevant rights of neutral states.[55]

3. The acts of war prohibited in neutral waters are not defined with any precision. Mere passage is not a forbidden act of war. Acts of war include shooting at enemy ships, take-off by military aircraft from aircraft carriers, laying mines, and also transmission of intelligence. Section 1120 clarifies that the exercise of the right of prize is also a prohibited act of war.

1121   **When a ship has been captured by a party to the conflict in the waters of a neutral state, the latter must, as long as the prize is still within its waters, use all means at its disposal to obtain the release of the prize and its crew. The prize crew must be interned (Article 3, para. 1, HC XIII).**

---

[50] See *San Remo Manual*, *supra* n. 14, paras. 14–36; Helsinki Principles, *supra* n. 15, para. 1.4.; see Heintschel von Heinegg, *op. cit.*, n. 2, 509 *et seq.*

[51] *San Remo Manual*, paras. 31–3.

[52] *San Remo Manual*, paras. 14, 34–5, Helsinki Principles, para. 1.1.

[53] R. Wolfrum, 'Military Activities on the High Seas: What are the Impacts of the U.N. Convention on the Law of the Sea?', in M. N. Schmitt/L. C. Green (eds), *The Law of Armed Conflict Into the Next Millennium. International Law Studies* Vol. 71 (Naval War College, 1998) 501–13, at 502 *et seq.*; A Proelß, 'Peaceful Purposes', para. 12 *et seq.*, MPEPIL.

[54] *San Remo Manual*, para. 34.

[55] *San Remo Manual*, para. 36.

MICHAEL BOTHE

Section 1121 reflects the duty to defend neutrality. If the right of prize is exercised in neutral waters contrary to the laws of neutrality, the neutral state must make an effort to undo this violation by freeing the prize captured in its waters. This liberation of the prize is not inconsistent with the prohibition of the use of force, since it constitutes an exercise of sovereign rights in the state's own jurisdictional area where the justification of self-defence is not required.

> **A neutral state may demand the release of a ship captured within its waters even if the ship has already left those neutral waters (Article 3, para. 2, HC XIII).**   1122

This rule clarifies the rights of the neutral state in case of an illegal taking of a prize in its waters. It is a secondary obligation derived from the primary rule in Section 1120: the situation must be re-established as if the violation of neutral waters had not occurred. Thus, the respective party to the conflict must render the prize illegally taken.

> **If a ship of a neutral state takes wounded, sick, or shipwrecked persons on board, it must, to the extent required by international law, ensure that these persons take no further part in hostilities (Article 15 GC II).**   1123

1. Section 1123 is the maritime aspect of Section 1117. As a matter of principle, combatants who fall into the power of a neutral state must be prevented from taking further part in hostilities. The reference in Article 15 GC II to general international law is, however, somewhat problematic.

2. In land warfare, the transit of wounded and sick persons through neutral territory is permitted (Article 14, para. 1, HC V). If one were to equate the situation of taking such persons aboard with their transit, it would be lawful to permit them to return to their own party. As a matter of principle, however, one would compare the situation rather with that of reception on neutral territory. Then, the general rule applies that any further participation of military personnel in hostilities must be prevented (Article 14, para. 2, HC V). Only those seriously sick or heavily wounded whose complete recovery is unlikely may be repatriated. These rules for disabled prisoners of war (Article 110 GC III) may be applied by analogy.

> **As regards the laying of sea mines, neutral states are subject to the same safety regulations as the parties to the conflict (Article 4, para. 1, HC VIII). They must notify the location of minefields to the government of maritime states without delay (Article 4, para. 2, HC VIII).**   1124

The neutral state which is bound to defend its neutrality may, as a matter of principle, do so by using the same means of warfare which the parties to the conflict can use. Defensive laying of sea mines therefore constitutes a lawful protective measure. However, the neutral state must then take the same precautionary measures in the interest of third parties which the parties to the conflict are required to take.

> **A neutral state is bound to use all means at its disposal to prevent the fitting out or arming of any vessel within its jurisdiction which it has reason to believe is intended to be engaged in acts of war against the party to a conflict. It is also bound to prevent the departure of any vessel that has been adapted entirely or partly within its jurisdiction for use in war (Article 8 HC XIII).**   1125

MICHAEL BOTHE

Section 1125 is the maritime version of the general prohibition of assisting parties to the conflict in their military effort. It has to be noted that in the field of naval warfare, the distinction between assistance by the state and by private persons or entities, which had formerly limited the prohibition as far as land warfare is concerned, has never been made. To that extent, the broader prohibition in the field of naval warfare corresponds to modern trends concerning the general regulation of arms exports.

b. *Innocent passage through territorial sea and archipelagic waters; transit passage*

1126

> Passage through the territorial sea and archipelagic sea lanes of a neutral state by warships belonging to and prizes taken by a party to the conflict does not consti-tute a violation of neutrality (Article 10 HC XIII). While transit passage through international straits and archipelagic sea lanes passage include the right of over-flight (Articles 38 and 53 of the United Nations Convention on the Law of the Sea) and the right of submarine navigation, there are no such rights of innocent passage outside those waterways. The right of transit or innocent passage is subject to the provisions set out in Sections 1127–1137.

1. The principle of innocent passage constitutes an exception to the general rule of land warfare that a neutral state may not acquiesce in the presence of armed forces of a party to the conflict in areas subject to its jurisdiction. On the other hand, it confirms the rule that the relation between the neutral state and the parties to the conflict is as a matter of principle subject to the law of peacetime relations which also provides for such rights of passage. This principle entails greater rights of innocent passage than those expressly provided for in Hague Convention XIII. The parties to the conflict also enjoy rights of transit passage through international straits and archipelagic shipping lanes passage granted to their warships in times of peace (see Articles 37 and 53 of the United Nations Convention on the Law of the Sea).[56]

2. The right of transit or innocent passage is subject to a number of specific limita-tions designed to prevent the exercise of those rights from developing into the use of neutral jurisdictional areas for the purpose of conducting war contrary to the law of neutrality.

1127

> Warships of the parties to the conflict are, as a matter of principle, not permitted to remain in neutral ports, roadsteads, or territorial sea for more than twenty-four hours. The neutral state may prolong this period, but may also altogether prohibit such vessels from remaining in its waters (Article 12 HC XIII). Warships of the parties to the conflict may not extend their stay beyond the permissible time except on account of damage or bad weather. They must depart as soon as the cause of the delay has ceased to exist (Article 14 HC XIII).

1. The 'twenty-four hour rule' is the most important exception to the rule that the rights of passage or transit existing in peacetime apply equally in times of armed conflict.[57] The rationale is to prevent a party to the conflict from using neutral waters as a refuge from enemy ships. According to the text of the Hague Convention, the twenty-four hour rule applies to the 'stay'. Taking into account the object and purpose of this provision,

---

[56] Heintschel von Heinegg, *op. cit.*, n. 2, 512 *et seq.*
[57] Helsinki Principles, *supra* n. 15, para. 2.2.

MICHAEL BOTHE

however, any passage is also covered. This became controversial during the Second World War in the *Altmark* case, where a German auxiliary warship had spent two days passing through the coastal waters of Norway, which at the time was still neutral, in order to avoid being captured by the British fleet. At that time, Norway claimed that the twenty-four hour rule did not apply to mere passage. That view has not prevailed.[58]

2. The twenty-four hour rule does not apply to the passage through neutral international straights or archipelagic sea lanes. That passage must proceed without delay.[59] Neutral waters is not possible within twenty-four hours. This will be the case particularly for archipelagic shipping lane passage. In that case, the rule is modified to the effect that the time required for the shortest possible passage is permitted.

> In neutral ports and roadsteads, warships of the parties to the conflict may only carry out such repairs as are absolutely necessary to restore their seaworthiness. Restoring the combat readiness of these ships is no cause for extending the permissible duration of their stay. Activities to increase their fighting capability are also prohibited (Article 17 HC XIII).   1128

> Warships of the parties to the conflict may neither complete their crews nor replenish or increase their armament or their military supplies in neutral waters (Article 18 HC XIII).   1129

> Warships of the parties to the conflict may only revictual in neutral ports and roadsteads to bring up their supplies to a normal peacetime level (Article 19 HC XIII).   1130

> In neutral ports and roadsteads, warships of the parties to the conflict may only ship sufficient fuel to enable them to reach the nearest port in their own country (Article 19 HC XIII). These ships may not again replenish their fuel supplies in a port of the same neutral state before three months have passed (Article 20 HC XIII).   1131

Sections 1128–1131 clarify the assistance permissible during a stay of ships of a party to the conflict in neutral waters. They constitute a compromise between the prohibition of assisting armed forces of the belligerents and the requirements of seafaring solidarity. Seafaring solidarity requires granting such help to a ship which is necessary, taking into account the seaworthiness of the ship, navigational difficulty caused by weather, and provision of food and fuel. Assistance must be strictly limited to those essential seafaring requirements.

> If a warship of a party to the conflict stays in a neutral port without being entitled to do so and does not leave this port notwithstanding notification, the neutral state may detain the ship and prevent it from departing for the duration of the armed conflict (Article 24 HC XIII). The crew of the detained ship may also be detained. Its members may be left on the ship or brought either to another vessel or ashore. In any case, a number of personnel sufficient to look after the vessel must be left on board.   1132

A warship of the party to the conflict which stays longer than the time permissible according to the rules stated above (i.e. over twenty-four hours or over the time required

---

[58] *San Remo Manual*, para. 21.
[59] *San Remo Manual*, para. 30.

MICHAEL BOTHE

in view of the condition of either the ship or the sea) violates the laws of neutrality. The duty to defend neutrality then applies. The neutral state must detain the ship and ensure that it can take no further part in any hostilities.

1133   **A prize may only be brought into a neutral port if it is absolutely necessary on account of unseaworthiness of the prize, bad weather, or want of fuel or provisions. It must leave as soon as the circumstances which justified its entry are at an end (Article 21 HC XIII).**

1134   **If, after the cause for a stay has ceased to exist, a prize does not leave even after it has been ordered to do so by the neutral authorities, the neutral state must seek to release the prize and its crew. The prize crew must be interned (Article 21 HC XIII). The same rule applies when a prize has entered a neutral port without authorization (Article 22 HC XIII).**

Sections 1133 and 1135 clarify the preceding rules concerning the stay of prizes in neutral waters. As a general rule, the right of passage also applies to prizes, subject to the twenty-four hour rule. Prizes may not, however, be brought into neutral ports except for reasons of navigational stress. A violation of this rule (as in the cases discussed before) gives rise to the duty of the neutral state to defend its neutrality and to free the prize.

1135   **When warships of several parties to the conflict are present simultaneously in a neutral port or roadstead, a period of not less than twenty-four hours must elapse between the departure of the ships belonging to one party and the departure of the ships belonging to the other party (Article 16 HC XIII).**

This rule is a variation of the requirement that no assistance must be given which affects the outcome of the conflict, and also reflects the principle of impartiality. The requirement of a fixed period between the departure of warships belonging to different parties prevents confrontations between them immediately after they leave neutral waters. Otherwise, the order of departure may influence the outcome of the conflict.

1136   **A neutral state may allow warships of a party to the conflict to employ its pilots (Article 11 HC XIII). It is bound to prevent, within the means at its disposal, any violation of the rules of neutrality within its waters and to exercise such surveillance as is required for this purpose (Article 25 HC XIII).**

This rule further clarifies the limits of the prohibition of non-neutral service. In this case, the prohibition is modified in the interests of navigational safety.

1137   **A neutral state must apply impartially to all parties to the conflict any conditions, restrictions, or prohibitions which it imposes on admission into its ports, roadsteads, or waters of warships or prizes belonging to the parties to the conflict (Article 9 HC XIII). A neutral state may forbid a warship which has failed to comply with its directions or which has violated its neutrality to enter its ports or roadsteads (Article 9 HC XIII).**

Again, this rule clarifies the neutral duty of impartiality. Even in times of peace, but especially in times of armed conflict, the neutral state may regulate passage through its waters and any stay therein by imposing its own rules. In particular, it may limit passage rights. To the extent that it makes such rules, it is bound by the duty of equal treatment, and may not create more advantageous conditions for one party than for another.

MICHAEL BOTHE

Nevertheless, in specific geographic circumstances, one party to the conflict may benefit from such rules more than another.

c. *Control by the parties to the conflict*

> **Warships of a party to the conflict are entitled to stop, visit, and search merchant**   **1138**
> **ships flying the flag of a neutral state on the high seas and control the contents and**
> **destination of their cargo.**

1. The control of neutral commercial shipping by the parties to the conflict was traditionally a very important question until the recent past. The state of international customary law is controversial in many details concerning the extent of this control. The London Declaration of 1909 which codified these rights of control was never ratified, but is considered at least largely to constitute an expression of customary law.

2. In more recent conflicts, too, such rights of control were exercised without objection, although certain specific measures and the status of some conflicts were controversial.[60]

3. The control by the parties to the conflict of neutral shipping constitutes an essential exception to the principle that the neutral state may not be adversely affected by the existence of an armed conflict. These rights of control, however, are limited, although during the Second World War a tendency to expand those rights was evident.

4. The purpose of such control is to impede the provision of goods important for the war effort to the other party to the conflict. A key position is taken by the right of visit and search, that is the right of warships of a party to the conflict to stop neutral commercial ships and to search them in order to find out whether they have goods aboard which could assist the war effort of another party to the conflict.

> **Warships of a party to the conflict may use only such force as is necessary against**   **1139**
> **neutral merchant ships to exercise such control. In particular, neutral merchant**
> **ships which, although subject to control by a party to the conflict, resist inspec-**
> **tion may be damaged or destroyed if it is not possible to prevent them from**
> **continuing their voyage by other means. The captain of the neutral ship shall**
> **be warned in an appropriate manner. Rescue of shipwrecked persons must be**
> **ensured.**

As a last resort, the right of control described in Section 1137 may be exercised by using force.[61] However, this is limited by a strict principle of necessity. Only such force is permissible which is indispensable to enforce the right of control, in particular to prevent a merchant ship from evading such control. The destruction of the neutral merchant ship is permissible only in exceptional circumstances, because a warship will generally have other means at its disposal to enforce its right of control.

> **To simplify inspection, a party to the conflict may, subject to the approval of the**   **1140**
> **neutral state concerned, issue an inspection document (navicert) to the neutral**

---

[60] *San Remo Manual, supra* n. 14, para. 146; Helsinki Principles, *supra* n. 15, para. 5.2.1. N. Ronzitti, 'Armed Conflict at Sea and the Need for its Revision', in N. Ronzitti (ed.), *The Law of Naval Warfare* (Nijhoff, 1988), 1–58, 7 *et seq.*; A. Gioia/N. Ronzitti, 'The Law of Neutrality: Third States' Commercial Rights and Duties', in Dekker/Post (eds), *op. cit.*, n. 29, 221, 231 *et seq.*; M. Donner, *Die neutrale Handelsschiffahrt im begrenzten militärischen Konflikt* (Kehl: Engel-Verlag, 1994) 261 *et seq.*
[61] *San Remo Manual*, paras. 151 and 152.

MICHAEL BOTHE

vessel in the port of loading. A navicert issued by one party to the conflict is not binding on the other party. The fact that the ship carries a navicert of another party to the conflict does not justify any more far-reaching measures of control.

1. The 'navicert system' has often been used in practice.[62] The navicert makes it possible for the neutral ship to prove, in the case of control by a warship of a party to the conflict, by a document issued at the port of loading by that party to the conflict (usually by its diplomatic representative) that it is not carrying contraband. A navicert is only accepted by the party which issued it.

2. During the Second World War, it was argued that carrying a navicert, which places a neutral merchant ship under the partial control of one belligerent, constitutes a non-neutral act because it favours the belligerent exercising this control. If this were so, neutral commerce would be unreasonably endangered because it could not protect itself against conflicting control claims of the parties.[63] In the end, however, that argument did not prevail, as clearly stated in the last sentence of Section 1140. It is noteworthy in this connection that the *San Remo Manual*[64] does not mention the navicert.

1141   The right of control shall not apply to merchant ships flying neutral flags and escorted by a neutral warship (convoy). In this case, however, a warship of a party to the conflict may request the commander of the neutral warship to specify the type and destination of the cargo.

1. The right of convoy was long controversial.[65] The effect of the rule is that warships of the parties to the conflict may control neutral merchant ships but not neutral warships. The question then arises of whether the fact that certain neutral merchant ships are placed under the protection of neutral warships limits the right of control of the belligerents. In the Gulf conflict between Iran and Iraq, convoys of merchant ships flying neutral flags were indeed placed under the protection of warships of neutral states. In that case, the neutral states did not accept the rights of control of the parties to the conflict, essentially of Iran, which they otherwise tolerated. This practice seems to be a last step in the development which has led to the recognition of the right of neutral convoy.[66] In a lawful convoy, control is exercised by requiring the commander of the neutral warship to provide information concerning the type and destination of the cargo to the warship of the party to the conflict.

2. Whether a neutral state may place only neutral ships flying its own flag under the protection of its warships or whether it may grant such protection to the ships of other neutral states is less clear.[67] The latter is probably the case. This practice may not, however, be used in order to disguise non-neutral service. Thus, it is problematic if a neutral state allows ships of another state, which has rendered non-neutral service to a party to

---

[62] C. Schaller, 'Contraband', *MPEPIL*; W. Meng, 'Contraband', *Encyclopedia of Public International Law* (Amsterdam: Elsevier, 1992), 809, at 812.
[63] Heintschel von Heinegg, *op. cit.*, n. 2, 573.
[64] *Supra*, n. 14.
[65] I. Venzke, 'Convoy', *MPEPIL*.
[66] *San Remo Manual, supra* n. 14, para. 120(b); Helsinki Principles, para. 5.2.8., 6.1; Ronzitti, in Ronzitti (ed.), *Armed Conflict at Sea loc. cit.*, n. 60, 9; Bothe, in Delissen/Tanja (eds), *loc. cit.*, n. 9, 387, 394.
[67] Roach, 'Neutrality in Naval Warfare', *loc. cit.*, n. 3, para. 22.

MICHAEL BOTHE

the conflict, to fly its own flag and places reflagged merchant ships under the protection of its own warships.

> If the cargo contains goods essential for war which are destined for the port of an   1142
> adversary, such goods may be captured by the warship of the party to the conflict
> ('absolute contraband'). The parties to the conflict may notify to the neutral states
> lists of the goods which they deem to be essential for war. Any goods destined for
> the administration or the armed forces of the opposing party to the conflict will
> likewise be deemed contraband ('conditional contraband').

As stated above, the rules concerning the control of neutral shipping are intended to prevent essential war goods from reaching the adversary. If control reveals essential war goods destined for the enemy aboard the ship, their further transportation may be prevented, subject to certain procedural rules. The first question arising in this connection is: what kinds of essential war goods are subject to this power to prevent further transportation ('contraband').[68] A distinction must be made between absolute and conditional contraband.[69] Absolute contraband comprises all essential war goods. Parties to the conflict have some discretion as to the determination of what is to be considered as essential for war. That distinction must always take into account the specific circumstances of the conflict. If the parties to the conflict set out their construction of goods essential for war in lists notified to the adversary, legal clarity is achieved. On the other hand, such lists have tended to be unacceptably wide. Absolute contraband is goods which must by their very nature be considered as essential for war, and must be distinguished from conditional contraband which comprises those goods destined for the administration and armed forces of the adversary, whether or not they otherwise serve essential purposes of war. Thus, equipment which would otherwise not be considered as war essential belongs to this category. Article 24 of the London Declaration of 1909 refers also to food and clothing as conditional contraband. To the extent that such items are shipped for the purpose of humanitarian relief actions (Articles 23, 59 GC IV; Article 70 AP I), they may, of course, not be considered as contraband. Contraband may be captured by the controlling warship.

> A ship carrying contraband is also subject to capture.   1143

As well as the cargo, the ship carrying such contraband is also subject to capture. Whether and to what extent this applies where only part of the cargo constitutes contraband is somewhat controversial.

> A captured ship (prize) must be brought as safely as possible to a port of a party to   1144
> the conflict or of a state allied with that party. In that port the permissibility of the
> capture of ship and cargo are to be reviewed by a prize court. Ship and cargo may
> be confiscated by the order of a prize court.

Capture is a provisional measure only. The legality of the capture must be reviewed in a judicial procedure as soon as possible. The principle *'toute prise doit être jugée'* applies. Only if the prize court finds that the ship was indeed carrying contraband a final

---

[68] *San Remo Manual*, n. 14, para. 148; Ronzitti, in Ronzitti (ed.), *Armed Conflict at Sea, op. cit.*, n. 60, 7 *et seq.*
[69] Roach, *loc. cit.*, n. 3, para. 17.

MICHAEL BOTHE

determination concerning the ship and cargo is permissible. Cargo may be confiscated only after a prize court judgment.[70] The same is true of the ship carrying that cargo and only if the contraband constituted more than half of the cargo, whether by value, weight, volume, or freight (Articles 39 and 40 of the London Declaration of 1909). Bringing the prize to the port of a territory occupied by a party to the conflict is also permissible. The prize court may be established anywhere on the territory of the party to the conflict, in a territory occupied by it, or on the territory of an ally of that party.

1145   **If suspicion that a ship is carrying contraband, which led to control measures, proves unfounded, and if the neutral ship has not given rise to that suspicion, the party to the conflict is obliged to compensate for any damage caused by the delay.**

If the capture is not upheld by the prize court, and the cargo not confiscated, the control measure was unjustified. Delay of the shipping may have caused a considerable financial damage. Such expense must be paid by the party which exercised the control.

1146   **The parties to the conflict may not hold prize court proceedings on neutral territory or on a vessel in neutral waters (Article 4 HC XIII).**

This rule adds further precision to the principle that neutral territory may not be used for any act which causes damage to the enemy. The establishment of a prize court belongs to this category of activities.

d) Protection of neutral merchant shipping

1147   **Warships of neutral states may escort merchant ships flying the flag of the same or another neutral state.**

1. Freedom of neutral shipping, limited only by the rights of control just described, is by no means unchallenged. Recent experiences in the conflict between Iran and Iraq proved this. From a political point of view, impeding neutral shipping, especially oil tankers, has obvious benefits because the adversary will benefit from this shipping, although according to the rules just described those ships were not subject to capture and confiscation. Fuel constitutes contraband only if it is destined for a party to the conflict, not if it comes from a party to the conflict which uses revenue from sales of fuel to finance its war effort.[71] Nevertheless, in such a situation the temptation for the disadvantaged party to the conflict to impede navigation is great. In this or similar situations, the question arises of how neutral shipping can be protected.

2. The formation of convoys has proved an efficient means of protection. The advantage of convoys in relation to the rights of control concerning cargo and destination have already been described. The formation of convoys also means that those convoys, in a manner of speaking, represent the state, so that attacks against them constitute attacks against a neutral state which trigger its right of self-defence.[72]

3. It is understood that convoys operate within the applicable law of the sea and, in particular, must respect the rules concerning innocent passage and transit passage. The fact

[70]   *San Remo Manual*, Commentary to para. 146.
[71]   Helsinki Principles, *supra* n. 15, para. 5.2.5; Bothe, in Dekker/Post (eds), *loc. cit.*, n. 29, 211.
[72]   Donner, *op. cit.*, n. 60, 285 *et seq.*

MICHAEL BOTHE

that the formation of a convoy also demonstrates military power does not mean that it constitutes a violation of the prohibition of the use of force. This was confirmed by the judgment of the ICJ in the *Corfu Channel* case.[73]

4. The formation of convoys may constitute a non-neutral service if merchant ships of a party to the conflict are placed under the protection of a neutral warship.

5. It is doubtful whether it is possible to place merchant ships of a neutral state under the protection of a neutral warship if the flag state of the merchant ship renders non-neutral services to a party to the conflict. This was the case with the passage of Kuwaiti tankers through the Gulf. Kuwait was certainly guilty of non-neutral services in favour of Iraq. This would have justified the taking of reprisals by Iran against Kuwaiti navigation. The US placed Kuwaiti tankers under their protection, but only after reflagging the tankers with the American flag. Whether such reflagging could shield ships which would otherwise be a permissible object of reprisals is open to doubt.[74]

> On international shipping routes and on the high eas, warships of neutral states   1148
> may sweep mines to the extent necessary to protect and maintain neutral shipping.
> Such minesweeping operations do not constitute a non-neutral service for the benefit
> of the adversary of the minelaying party.

1. Sweeping mines on the high seas and in sea areas subject to transit rights is a means for neutral states to protect themselves, which attained considerable practical significance during the conflict between Iran and Iraq. For the purpose of legal evaluation, minesweeping in the jurisdictional waters of a party to the conflict and similar activities on the high seas must be distinguished. On the high seas, the first aspect to be considered is the law of the sea. Conducting hostilities is a lawful use of the high seas, although this is not explicitly stated in the Law of the Sea Convention. Minesweeping, therefore, constitutes a kind of self-help against a lawful activity. On the other hand, the high seas should be free for shipping, and this right has a great weight. The conduct of hostilities also limits the freedom of navigation of other states. Minesweeping, therefore, involves balancing two freedoms, similar to the conflicting interests involved in the conduct of hostilities on the high seas. Minesweeping undertaken to protect a state's freedom of shipping does not constitute an unacceptable limitation of the freedom of the parties to the conflict to conduct hostilities at sea.[75]

2. From the point of view of the law of neutrality, minesweeping by neutral states constitutes an activity which benefits the adversary of the party which laid the mines. However, from the point of view of social significance, it is not the support for one of the parties which is the essential point, but the protection of the neutral state. Therefore, a minesweeping operation intended only to protect neutral shipping does not constitute a non-neutral service.

3. Unilateral minesweeping operations in the waters of a party of the conflict constitute a violation of the prohibition of the use of force. As a rule, they are illegal. However,

[73] *ICJ Reports 1949*, 4, 28.

[74] Ronzitti, in Ronzitti (ed.), *Armed Conflict at Sea, op. cit.*, n. 60, 9; Bos, in Dekker/Post (eds), *op. cit.*, n. 29, 219 *et seq.*

[75] The *San Remo Manual* (para. 92) only recognizes a right of mine sweeping where the mines have been laid in violation of international law. This is too restrictive. Para. 6.2. of the Helsinki Principles is somewhat more open.

MICHAEL BOTHE

there is no violation where a party to a conflict has laid mines in shipping lanes through which transit rights exist and which the minesweeping state is bound to keep open. This was confirmed by state practice during the conflict between Iran and Iraq.[76]

4. Aerial Warfare

1149   **The airspace of a neutral state is inviolable (Article 40 HRAW 1923; Rules 170 and 171 *HPCR Manual*).**

1. Section 1149 formulates the application to airspace of the general rule of inviolability of neutral territory. This rule is of particular importance because, in the era of modern air warfare and missile technology, violations of airspace are easily committed.

2. The territorial jurisdiction of a neutral state extends to the limits of the atmosphere. Outer space above neutral territory is not subject to the neutral state's jurisdiction. Overflights by satellites and missiles moving in outer space therefore do not constitute a violation of neutrality.

3. The delimitation between airspace and outer space is still controversial. In both practice and theory, there are two main trends which, however, possess a number of variations. Functional theories focus on the kind of activity for which the delimitation is relevant. According to this view, satellites in orbit are typical space objects. Crossing a specific territory or stationing a satellite on a fixed point over the territory of a state does not constitute a violation of the territorial sovereignty of the respective states. Missiles only constitute typical space vehicles where they are at least partially brought into orbit around the earth where the centrifugal force and the attraction of the earth balance each other. Theories based on spatial concepts try to draw the line between airspace and outer space at a particular altitude, of roughly 100 kilometres.[77]

1150   **Parties to a conflict are forbidden to send military aircraft, missiles, or unmanned aerial vehicles into neutral airspace (Article 40 HRAW 1923; Rule 170 *HPCR Manual*). This is without prejudice to the right of transit passage through straights used for international navigation or archipelagic sea lanes passage and to the entry by military aircraft in distress (Rules 170, 172 *HPCR Manual*; see above, Section 1126).**

1. As a consequence of the inviolability of neutral airspace, the parties to the conflict are not allowed to penetrate by aircraft or other flight objects the airspace of neutral states. For aircraft attacking targets over large distances this may involve significant detours.

2. Overflight by civilian aircraft does not constitute a violation of neutrality. The neutral state must, however, exercise all necessary controls in order to prevent civilian overflight from being used for military purposes. Under air traffic rules, this is rendered possible by the so-called 'war clause' of the Chicago Convention.

3. The prohibition of overflight extends to neutral territorial waters. Overflight is, however, permissible over neutral international straights and archipelagic sea lanes.

---

[76] Ronzitti, in Ronzitti (ed.), *Armed Conflict at Sea, op. cit.*, n. 60, 5.
[77] V. Vereshchetin, 'Outer Space', paras. 8–17, *MPEPIL*; Hostettler/Danai, 'Neutrality in Air Warfare', para. 18, *MPEPIL*.

MICHAEL BOTHE

A neutral state is bound to prevent violations of its airspace. Aircraft which enter   1151
such space must be forced to leave or to put down. The crews of military aircraft of
a party to the conflict who have been brought down must be interned (Article 42
HRAW 1923; Rules 168 and 172, lit. b, *HPCR Manual*).

1. The dangers for neutral airspace described in the commentary to Section 1149 lead
to the question: what must a neutral state do in order to prevent such violations of its
airspace? It is difficult to determine the effort required for this purpose.[78] There is an
obligation of observation and of using force if necessary. The neutral state must exercise
surveillance to the extent that the means at its disposal allow, in order to ascertain violations of its air space.[79] This includes at least simple radar observation of its airspace. It
must also use all means at its disposal to prevent or terminate such violations.[80] A neutral state must take economically feasible measures in order to create an aerial defence
capacity. On the other hand, it may not be required that each state possess the latest
missile technology in order to protect its neutrality.

2. The defence must be feasible for the neutral state. In this respect, defence against missiles possessing nuclear warheads, which may after interception fall on neutral territory
and cause damage therein, cannot be required.

3. Interception of aircraft by the air force of a neutral state is undoubtedly among the
measures which the neutral state is required to take. Aircraft entering its airspace must
be forced to turn back or land. The obligation to intern their crews derives from the
general principle described above.

Medical aircraft may be allowed to overfly the territory of a neutral state and to   1152
land therein (Article 37 GC I; Article 40 GC II; Article 31 API; Article 17 HRAW
1923).

A neutral state may allow medical aircraft of a party to a conflict to overfly its territory or
to land therein; this does not constitute non-neutral service. On the contrary, it is a form
of humanitarian assistance, subject to rules similar to those concerning land warfare.

Overflight and stopover require permission. A neutral state may place conditions   1153
and restrictions on overflight (Article 37, para. 2, GC I; Article 40, para. 2, GC II;
Article 31 AP I).

1. Section 1153 regulates the procedure to be respected in overflights authorized in
accordance with Section 1152. Even medical aircraft are not permitted to penetrate into
neutral airspace without authorization. On the contrary, they require specific authorization, the granting of which is in the discretion of the neutral state.

2. If a neutral state grants such permission it may be subject to conditions, especially
as to routes which must be followed and necessary stopovers. At a stopover an aircraft
may be inspected to verify that it is medical transport (Article 31, para. 3, AP I). If the
neutral state grants authorization to and imposes conditions on medical flights, the duty
of impartiality applies. Both sides must be treated equally. In this case also identical

---

[78] Hostettler/Danai, *loc. cit.*, n. 77; A. S. Millet, 'La neutralité aerienne' (1991) 35 *Annales de droit international médical* 63, 69; Torrelli, *loc. cit.*, n. 22, 44.
[79] *HPCR Manual*, para. 170(b).
[80] *HPCR Manual*, para. 170(c).

MICHAEL BOTHE

treatment is not required. Often, geographic factors will result in one party using such transit flights, and the other not. The fact that the possibility of transit favours one party more than the other does not constitute a violation of the requirement of impartiality.

3. The neutral state is not bound to tolerate flights which are not authorized or which violate conditions lawfully imposed. It may attack a medical aircraft flying illegally if there is no other means to prevent it from continuing the flight, or subject it to scrutiny. Given the risk of abuse of medical flights, it may even be concluded that the neutral state has a duty not to tolerate unauthorized medical flights over its territory, and to take appropriate countermeasures.

1154   **The right of neutral aircraft to overfly the territory of the parties to the conflict is regulated by the general rules of international law on the protection of national airspace and the rules of international air traffic.**

1. Under general international law applicable in times of peace, there is no general right for foreign aircraft, whether private or state-owned, to overfly the territory of another state or to land therein. For private non-scheduled air services, the Chicago Convention provides certain rights of overflight and landing. However, these rights do not apply in armed conflicts. According to the 'war clause' of the Chicago Convention on International Civil Aviation of 7 December 1944 (Article 89), the provisions of the Convention do not affect the freedom of action of the contracting parties in a war, be they belligerent or neutral. Traffic rights for scheduled air services are, as a rule, derived from bilateral agreements. Whether and to what extent these rights are affected by the fact that one of the contracting parties is a party to a conflict with a third state is a question to be regulated by the relevant agreement. Generally speaking, the legal situation is that a state which is party to a conflict is relatively free to grant or not to grant rights of overflight to aircraft flying neutral flags, subject, in particular, to the provisions of bilateral air transport agreements.

2. Special rules apply to airspace above specific types of jurisdictional waters. As stated above, the right of innocent passage over territorial sea does not comprise overflight. As far as overflight is concerned, territorial sea is treated in the same way as the land areas around it. An exception to this rule applies to international straits and archipelagic waters. In this case, the right of transit or passage (Articles 38 and 53 of the United Nations Convention on the Law of the Sea) includes a right of overflight (see commentary to Section 1108).[81] It is submitted that these rules are now customary law.

1155   **The relevant rules of naval warfare apply to the control, capture, and confiscation of neutral aircraft above sea areas and to the treatment of their passengers and crew (Article 35 HRAW 1923). An aircraft which does not carry clearly visible neutral national emblems may be treated as enemy aircraft.**

The increase in air traffic raised the question (originally rather theoretical) of the control of neutral air commerce. The analogy to neutral shipping offered itself. When the Hague Rules of Air Warfare were elaborated, the rules concerning the control of neutral shipping were imported comprehensively. There is, however, relatively little state practice in this matter. As it can only be applied by analogy, not every detail of the rules concerning the control of neutral shipping applies. The special character of air traffic must be

---

[81] See above.

taken into account. As far as air traffic over the high seas is concerned, account must be taken of the fact that aircraft constitute a considerable threat to warships of the parties to the conflict. Thus, those ships will be inclined to react to a perceived threat where the identity of an aircraft is not beyond doubt. The shooting down of an Iranian civilian airbus by a US warship during the conflict between Iran and Iraq shows the kind of tragic errors which may result. The principle must be maintained that both belligerent and neutral warships, as in the case just mentioned, must endeavour to ascertain the nationality and category of an aircraft before it is attacked. This is only possible where neutral aircraft and civilian aircraft of the parties to the conflict do everything feasible to facilitate their identification. An aircraft which is not identifiable and does not carry any exterior emblem of nationality must be considered as an enemy military aircraft and may therefore be attacked.

5. Military Uses of Outer Space

Where military activities conducted in outer space relate to an armed conflict, the   **1156**
general rules of the law of neutrality must be observed.

1. There are various military uses of outer space, including uses in armed conflict. Military uses of outer space are not per se unlawful. Only the Moon and other celestial bodies are demilitarized.[82] For instance, attacks launched from outer space must respect the inviolability of neutral territory.[83] In this connection, it may be relevant that destroying telecommunication or observation satellites belonging to a party to a conflict may have serious consequences for third, that is neutral states which may depend on the commercial services of these satellites. Although the law of neutrality prohibits attacks, even though directed against the adversary, which cause incidental damage on neutral territory, that safety guaranty for the neutral state does probably not go as far as a guaranty of uninterrupted telecommunication or other services provided by a belligerent in peacetime.

2. Parties to a conflict may not use neutral air space for overflight, nor may neutral states allow them to do so.[84] There seems to be general agreement that this duty ends where the airspace over neutral territory ends—at whatever altitude one places the dividing line between air space and outer space. Passing over neutral territory above that altitude, that is in outer space, does not constitute a violation of neutrality. Yet, the space activities of neutral states must abide by duties of impartiality and abstention which are imposed on neutral states. In this connection, the question arises whether and to what extent a neutral state may allow the use of its satellites, for purposes of observation and communication, by a belligerent. In the case of telecommunication satellites,[85] the situation is not clear. Arguably, Article 8 of Hague Convention V of 1907 constitutes the applicable law, although it is found in a treaty on land warfare:

A neutral Power is not called upon to forbid or restrict the use on behalf of belligerents of telegraph or telephone cables or of wireless telegraphy apparatus belonging to it or to companies or private individuals.

---

[82] Art. IV(2) Outer Space Treaty.
[83] See above, Sections 1108 *et seq.*
[84] See above, nos. 1149 and 1150.
[85] See above, no. 1116.

MICHAEL BOTHE

Article 9 HC V requires the impartial application of any restrictions. The conclusion as to space warfare is this: states not parties to a conflict are not obliged to bar belligerents from the use of their communication satellites, but they may not grant access to one party while barring access for the other.

3. Similar questions arise with regard to access to satellite imagery, which can be of high military value. Giving such imagery to one party and denying it to the other certainly is a violation of the duties of abstention and impartiality, that is of fundamental rules of the law of neutrality.

MICHAEL BOTHE

12

THE LAW OF NON-INTERNATIONAL ARMED CONFLICT

I. General

Many armed conflicts today take place largely within the boundaries of a state   1201
and involve confrontations between the authorities of a state and armed groups or
among armed groups that do not operate under state authority at all. Such armed
conflicts are referred to as non-international and although, by definition, they
do not occur between sovereign states, there is a body of international law which
applies to them nonetheless.

1. *The notion of non-international armed conflict.* While civil wars have frequently taken
place throughout history, after the end of the Second World War such conflicts have
exceeded wars between states, not only in numbers and duration, but often also in the
level of atrocities. After the end of the Cold War, even more wars were fought within
states, both with and without outside interventions. These 'new wars' resembled former
forms of partisan warfare, but they have clearly reached new dimensions. If it was ever
realistic to expect during armed conflict that warring parties generally treat each other
equally, voluntarily accept rules of fair fighting and make effective efforts to minimize
suffering, the opposite is often shown in internal wars. Armed opposition groups may
be aiming at denying state control, changing political leadership, or securing resources
(oil, diamonds, gold, tropical wood, etc.). While it is typical for non-international armed
conflicts that the size, equipment, training, and tactics of the warring parties are very
different, this asymmetric nature is a constant challenge for the application of humanitarian law (see below, Section 1219).

2. *Recognition of belligerency and its disuse.* At some occasions before the beginning of
the twentieth century, states have recognized the existence of civil wars in other states
to avow a determination to remain neutral; in other cases insurgents have been recognized by their own governments as belligerents, to secure application of the laws of war.[1]
This practice dates back to times when the prohibition of war as a means of protecting
national interests had not yet emerged and there prevailed a general perception that in
the relationship between belligerent powers the law of peace is fully replaced by the
law of war. That perception is no longer correct (see above, Sections 253 and 254). The
application of the modern law of armed conflict is not dependent on recognition of belligerency by the state against which an insurgency is directed. Recognition of belligerency by a third state, however, whether expressly declared or implied by its activities,

---

[1] Anthony Cullen, *The Concept of Non-International Armed Conflict in International Humanitarian Law*
(CUP, 2010), 14–23.

would trigger obligations under the law of neutrality (see above, commentary para. 6 to Section 1106).

3. *Borderline situations in non-international armed conflicts.*

a) Third-state intervention will not necessarily change the non-international character of an armed conflict, if it is performed on invitation by the government of the territorial state. This principle applies also to multinational armed forces intervening on the side of a host state, and whether or not the armed forces of that state are involved in military operations against the insurgents.

b) Ancillary cross-border operations by or against armed groups will still qualify as non-international armed conflicts, provided that no armed forces of another state are involved.

4. *Internationalized armed conflicts.* Certain armed conflicts may be considered as internationalized, even if not all parties to the conflict are sovereign states. In such cases the law of international armed conflicts applies.

a) Outside control of and support for insurgents. Interventions by states in support of armed opposition groups in another state will internationalize the armed conflict if the intervening state is itself conducting military operations or controlling operations performed by the armed opposition group. Both these conditions do not necessarily come together. Where the intervening state is fighting to support an insurgence without exercising control of the armed opposition groups, two different types of conflict are taking place at the same time. This applies to the war between Libyan opposition fighters and the Ghaddafi government in 2011 and the air and sea campaign by NATO Allies and Partners in Libya which was started in March 2011 pursuant to SC Resolution 1973 (2011), paras. 4–5, and concluded on 31 October 2011 in accordance with SC Resolution 2016 (2011), para. 5. Two different types of armed conflict have also been assumed by the ICJ in the armed conflict in Nicaragua during the early 1980s.[2]

The level of control by intervening states may be controversial. In 1999, the ICTY Appeals Chamber in *Tadić*, after extensive discussion of the ICJ's more restrictive judgment in *Nicaragua*,[3] accepted the evidence of *'overall control* [of insurgents in Bosnia and Herzegovina (the Bosnian Serb Army) by the Federal Republic of Yugoslavia] going beyond the mere financing and equipping of such forces and involving also participation in the planning and supervision of military operations' as sufficient for qualifying the ongoing armed conflict as international; the Appeals Chamber held that 'international rules do not require that such control should extend to the issuance of specific orders or instructions relating to single military actions, whether or not such actions were contrary to international humanitarian law'.[4] Although the general point of departure was the same for both courts, that is to ascertain the conditions on which under international

---

[2] ICJ, *Military and Paramilitary Activities in and against Nicaragua (Nicaragua v US)*, Judgment of 27 June 1986, para. 219: 'The conflict between the contras' forces and those of the Government of Nicaragua is an armed conflict which is "not of an international character". The acts of the contras towards the Nicaraguan Government are therefore governed by the law applicable to conflicts of that character; whereas the actions of the United States in and against Nicaragua fall under the legal rules relating to international conflicts.' See also Andreas Paulus and Mindia Vashakmadze, 'Asymmetrical war and the notion of armed conflict—a tentative conceptualization' (2009) 91 *IRRC* 95–125.

[3] ICJ, ibid. para. 115.

[4] ICTY, *The Prosecutor v Tadić*, Case No. IT-94–1-AR72, Appeals Chamber, Merits Judgment of 15 July 1999, paras. 99–145, at 145.

law an individual may be held to act as an organ of another state, both decisions were made in different context. The ICJ had decided with the view to determine the international responsibility of the respondent state, whereas the ICTY had to establish the necessary precondition for the grave breaches regime of the Geneva Conventions to apply.[5] The purpose for the ICTY Appeals Chamber to qualify the armed conflict in Bosnia-Herzegovina was not to decide on a matter of state responsibility, but to determine whether the appellant was guilty of grave breaches.[6] The ICTY, when critically discussing the 'effective-control test' used by the ICJ, did not acknowledge that difference; but the ICJ has later observed that while the 'overall-control test' may be applicable and suitable to a determination of the nature of a conflict, it was not suitable for making determinations on state responsibility, as 'a State is responsible only for its own conduct, that is to say the conduct of persons acting, on whatever basis, on its behalf'.[7]

b) National liberation wars. Article 1, para. 4, AP I provides that international armed conflicts include situations 'in which peoples are fighting against colonial domination and alien occupation and against racist régimes in the exercise of their right of self-determination, as enshrined in the Charter of the United Nations and the Declaration on Principles of International Law concerning Friendly Relations and Co-operation among states in accordance with the Charter of the United Nations'. A formal international recognition of the legitimacy of the movement involved in a national liberation war is not a condition for application of Article 1, para. 4.[8] Under Article 96, para. 3, AP I the authority representing a people engaged in a war of national liberation may undertake to apply the Geneva Conventions and AP I in relation to that conflict by means of a unilateral declaration addressed to the depositary.[9] It should be taken

---

[5] Meanwhile, war crimes committed in non-international armed conflicts are penalized under Art. 8(2) (c) and (e) ICC Statute which is, however, not applicable to the ICTY.

[6] See ILC, Report on the work of its fifty-third session, Chapter IV 'Responsibility of states for internationally wrongful acts', UN Doc. A/56/10 (2001), 106–7.

[7] ICJ, *Case Concerning the Application of the Convention on the Prevention and Punishment of the Crime of Genocide (Bosnia and Herzegovina v Serbia and Montenegro)*, Judgment of 26 February 2007, paras. 402–6. For a differing view, see Antonio Cassese, 'The Nicaragua and Tadić Tests Revisited in Light of the ICJ Judgment on Genocide in Bosnia' (2007) 18 *EJIL* 649–68.

[8] The *UK Manual*, para 3.4.2, requires 'as a minimum recognition by the appropriate regional intergovernmental organization'. This would go too far. As the *ICRC Commentary* to Art. 1(4) AP I, para. 105, correctly explains, this idea was advanced during the negotiations but was not adopted.

[9] The *UK Manual*, para. 3.4.2(c) and para. 15.2.2, states that the Protocol only applies if the authority representing the peoples engaged in the armed conflict makes a special declaration in accordance with Article 96, para. 3, AP I. While declarations in accordance with Article 96, para. 3, are in the interest of humanitarian protection, it appears from the text of Art. 1, para. 4, AP I that its applicability results from the very fact of fighting for national liberation, irrespective of declarations made and of the communication of such declarations to the state party. The *ICRC Commentary* (para. 3767) confirms that the authority representing a people engaged in a struggle *may* make a declaration (para. 116), the effect of which would be that the Conventions and AP I would immediately come into force between the parties. The text of the AP I, however, does not make such declaration a condition for evaluating the conflict as international, neither does it pronounce itself on procedures under which the depositary should handle a declaration made by a national liberation movement. It may be considered that any requirement of formal acceptance by the state party to the conflict would lead to political problems, as no government will readily offer status to insurgents, whereas special acts of acknowledgement would be inevitable with the acceptance of declarations communicated by the depositary. As spelled out in Article 96, para. 3, lit. a, the effect of a declaration made by an authority representing a people fighting a national liberation war is that the Conventions and AP I are brought into force 'for the said authority', while their applicability for the state parties even to this conflict is a result of their ratification. For practical purposes this discussion may be left aside, as in the numerous armed conflicts which are currently fought Art. 1, para. 4, AP I does not apply.

DIETER FLECK

into consideration, however, that humanitarian protection may not be made subject to reciprocity;[10] yet, the expectation of reciprocity may be a driving force to motivate for better compliance.[11] Articles 1, para. 4, and 96, para. 3, AP I are relevant only for the application of international humanitarian law, without, however, exempting insurgents from criminal prosecution under the law of the state.[12]

c) Armed conflicts between states and transnational armed groups. To the extent that a 'war on terror' can be qualified as an armed conflict (see above, Section 209), this conflict may be internationalized when military operations are conducted against a transnational group acting on behalf of a foreign state, such as the Taliban in Afghanistan 2001. From the time, however, the state is no longer controlled by the group, ongoing hostilities between the group and regular armed forces operating with the consent of the territorial state are part of a non-international armed conflict.[13] A position by the US administration in 2004, characterizing the conflict with al-Qaeda as an armed conflict with a non-party to the Geneva Conventions, in which even common Article 3 did not apply,[14] was characterized as 'erroneous' and rejected by the US Supreme Court in 2006.[15] The internationalization of an armed conflict has also been assumed when a state is engaged in military operations against a transnational group on the territory of a foreign state without the agreement of the latter, such as during the Israeli–Hizbollah War in Lebanon 2006.[16] Similar arguments were used for military operations of the Israel Defense Forces against other Palestinian groups both within Israel and in areas no longer claimed by Jordan. The conflict between Israel and Palestinian groups which is lasting now for decades, was originally characterized by Israel as an international armed conflict. In a response to a petition against targeted killings the government of Israel claimed that the classification of the conflict is a complicated question, with characteristics that point

---

[10] See above, Section 206 and below, Section 1219; cf. George Abi-Saab, 'Wars of National Liberation in the Geneva Conventions and Protocols' (1979 IV) 165 *RdC* 353–445, at 434–5.

[11] See below, Section 1404.

[12] For this aspect, see below, Section 1220.

[13] The ICRC has stated in an aide-memoire submitted on 18 November 2002 to Permanent Missions in Geneva that following the convening of the Loya Jirga in Kabul in June 2002 and the subsequent establishment of an Afghan transitional government on 19 June 2002—which not only received unanimous recognition by the entire community of states but could also claim broad-based recognition within Afghanistan through the Loya Jirga process—the ICRC no longer views the ongoing military operations in Afghanistan directed against remnants of Taliban or al-Qaeda forces as an international armed conflict.

[14] Associate Press, *Prisoner Abuse Bush Order*, 22 June 2004, § 2: 'I accept the legal conclusion of the Department on Justice and determine that none of the provisions of Geneva apply to our conflict with al-Qaida in Afghanistan or elsewhere throughout the world because, among other reasons, al-Qaida is not a High Contracting Party to Geneva. . . . I also accept the legal conclusion of the Department of Justice and determine that common Article 3 of Geneva does not apply to either al-Qaida of Taliban detainees, because, among other reasons, the relevant conflicts are international in scope and common Article 3 applies only to "armed conflict not of an international character".'

[15] US Supreme Court, *Hamdan v Rumsfeld et al.*, 29 June 2006, 67–72, stating that Art. 3 is applicable here and emphasizing that 'the Executive is bound to comply with the rule of Law that prevails in this jurisdiction'.

[16] Marco Sassòli, *Transnational Armed Groups and International Humanitarian Law* (Harvard: HPCR, Occasional Paper Series, 2006), 5, considering that the military operations of Hizbollah were not attributable to Lebanon, as the Lebanese government has not authorized and was unable to stop them, although Hizbollah was represented in the Lebanese Cabinet; Report of the Commission of Enquiry on Lebanon pursuant to Human Rights Council Resolution S-2/1, UN Doc. A/HRC/3/2 (23 November 2006), paras. 8–9 and 57; for detailed consideration, see Andreas Zimmermann, 'The Second Lebanon War: *Jus ad bellum, Jus in bello and the Issue of Proportionality*', in (2007) *Max Planck Yearbook of United Nations Law* 99–141, at 110–15.

in different directions. The Supreme Court of Israel has stated that according to all of the various classifications the laws of armed conflict apply; these laws allow striking at persons who are party to the armed conflict and take an active part in it, whether it is an international or non-international armed conflict, and even if it belongs to a new category of armed conflict, that is conflicts between states and terrorist organizations.[17] This judgment convincingly underlines that a differentiation between international and non-international armed conflicts is not really relevant for the conduct of hostilities (see below, Section 1203). Yet, important distinctions, most especially for the status of fighters, remain (see below, Sections 1213–1215). Discussions whether 'transnational armed conflicts', that is conflicts between states and non-state groups outside the territory of the state would *de lege ferenda* require a new legal regime to regulate the application of combat power and the treatment of non-combatants[18] should not overlook that armed conflicts may be either international or non-international and that in the latter case the same legal regime applies to conflicts between governmental armed forces and forces of armed groups as to conflicts between such groups. Efforts to develop a more specific regulatory framework for 'transnational armed conflicts' must respect all existing legal obligations.[19] The introduction of wars against terrorist organizations as a new legal category for a new type of armed conflict is not convincing. The non-international or international character of an armed conflict depends on the question whether or not a responsible territorial government has given its consent to military operations performed by the intervening state. Thus, it is still true that armed conflicts can be determined as international only in a case in which states (or at least national liberation movements fighting against colonial domination and alien occupation and against racist régimes) are involved as parties to the conflict.

5. *The applicability of international law in non-international armed conflicts.* The general issue of whether international legal principles and provisions apply in non-international armed conflicts cannot lightly be set aside. As the late Antonio Cassese correctly stated decades ago: 'In practice, insurgents are not willing to live up to international standards they have not accepted. What is even more important, States engaged in an internal armed conflict do not readily concede that civil strife calls for the application of international regulations.'[20] It may be more widely accepted today that international law is binding states even in their internal affairs, a consideration that applies not only to human rights obligations of states towards their own citizens, but also to norms of international humanitarian law applicable in non-international armed conflicts. The

---

[17] Supreme Court of Israel, *1. The Public Committee Against Torture in Israel, 2. Palestinian Society for the Protection of Human rights and the Environment v The Government of Israel et al.*, Judgment of 13 December 2006, HCJ 769/02, para. 11.

[18] Geoffrey S. Corn and Eric Talbot Jensen, 'Transnational Armed Conflict: A "Principled" Approach to the Regulation of Counter-Terror Combat Operations' (2009) 42(1) *Israel Law Review* 46–80, at 57–80. See also Michael N. Schmitt, 'Classification in Future Conflict', in Elizabeth Wilmshurst (ed.), *International Law and the Classification of Conflicts* (OUP, 2012), 455–77.

[19] ICRC, 'How is the Term "Armed Conflict" Defined in International Humanitarian Law?', Opinion Paper, March 2008, available at <http://www.icrc.org/eng/resources/documents/article/other/armed-conflict-article-170308.htm>; ICTY *The Prosecutor v Haradinaj, Balaj, and Brahimaj*, IT-04-84-T, Trial Chamber Judgment, 3 April 2008, paras. 49, 60; see also Sandesh Sivakumaran, *The Law of Non-International Armed Conflict* (OUP, 2012), 234.

[20] Antonio Cassese, 'The Status of Rebels under the 1977 Geneva Protocol on Non-International Armed Conflict' (1981) 30 *ICLQ* 416–39, at 425.

DIETER FLECK

more controversial question as to how non-state actors—insurgents or armed opposition groups—may be bound by rules of international law which have been adopted not by themselves, but by states including the state these groups are fighting against, has for a long time been perceived as overly complicating the fundamental principle that international treaties are not concluded on behalf of governments, but on behalf of states lawfully representing all their citizens. But is it fully convincing to assume that an acceptance of obligations by the government of the state is binding also armed groups fighting on its territory?[21] In that case it could be argued that universal acceptance and recognition of international principles and rules by the international community is binding not only states but also armed opposition groups.[22] This would include customary international law which is based on practice and *opinio juris* of states. The doctrine of legislative jurisdiction of a state transforming international law into domestic law and enforcing self-executing provisions[23] may have particular relevance for rules on humanitarian protection, but it needs to be combined with voluntary elements, thus to ensure that principles and rules imposed by a cogent legal system are accepted by all actors and implemented in a responsible manner. While non-state actors are often unable or unwilling to accept pertinent obligations, mechanisms such as Geneva Call[24] which encourage such commitments may support compliance with existing obligations.

a) The law of non-international armed conflict. The law of armed conflict, as it has developed in the last part of the nineteenth and the first part of the twentieth century, deals predominantly with wars between states. Its basic principles and rules are, however, likewise relevant for non-international armed conflicts: in all armed conflicts elementary considerations of humanity must be respected under all circumstances, in order to protect victims, to reduce human sufferings, and to minimize damages to objects vital for survival. Therefore, the parties to the conflict do not have an unlimited choice of the means and methods of conducting hostilities, nor of selecting the targets to be attacked, and they must protect the victims from the effects and consequences of war. This concept is reflected in the principles and rules of international humanitarian law, to be respected by all and, while taking military necessity into account, limiting the use of force for humanitarian reasons. Parties to the conflict respecting these principles and rules are considered as respecting the international order, while those seriously violating them will commit internationally wrongful acts and perpetrators are liable to punishment.

b) Human rights. The applicability of the law of human rights is not limited to times of peace, unless and to the degree a state has used possibilities of derogation;[25] yet, it is a difficult task to ensure respect for human rights in armed conflicts. The state whose armed forces are engaged in hostilities is not always able to exercise jurisdiction with respect to enemy fighters and victims, so that conventional human rights obligations

---

[21] Michael Bothe, 'Conflits armés internes et droit international humanitaire' (1978) *RDGIP* 82, at 92–3.

[22] Constitutional Court of Colombia in Case No. C-225/95, Constitutional Review of AP II, decision of 18 May 1995, partly reproduced in M. Sassòli, A. Bouvier, and A. Quintin (eds), *How Does Law Protect in War? Cases, Documents and Teaching Materials on Contemporary Practice in International Humanitarian Law*, 3rd edn (ICRC, 2011), Vol. III, 2240–55, paras. 7, 14.

[23] Sandesh Sivakumaran, 'Binding Armed Opposition Groups' (2006) 55 *ICLQ* 369–94, at 381.

[24] See <http://www.genevacall.org/>.

[25] Article 4 ICCPR, Article 15 ECHR, Article 27 ACHR, Article 4 Arab Charter on Human Rights. There is no derogation clause in the African Charter on Human and Peoples' Rights.

might not apply (see above, Section 245). With respect to people held in detention, however, the exercise of jurisdiction is not seriously disputable. Armed opposition groups, in turn, are often unaware of their human rights obligations, even if those obligations have binding effects also on non-state actors (see above, Section 256). Yet, adherence to human rights obligations is mandatory under existing law and essential for reconciliation in the long term. The complex relationship between humanitarian law and human rights law (see above, Sections 251–253) is of particular practical relevance in non-international armed conflicts.[26]

6. *Different thresholds for the application of treaty law.* Treaty law has established different thresholds for its application in non-international armed conflicts.

a) Article 3 common to the Geneva Conventions, without giving any specific definition, simply refers to 'the case of armed conflict not of an international character occurring in the territory of one of the High Contracting Parties' (for the negotiating history see below, Section 1205). This definition does not require that armed groups are fighting against the government of the territory in which operations are conducted, rather the conflict may be fought between armed groups or between an armed group and the state outside the territory of the latter. As the threshold for application of common Article 3 is not further specified, it has been argued that according to its current understanding that threshold might be lower today than what was expected during the negotiations in the Diplomatic Conference 1949, when many proposals had referred to situations displaying the characteristics of civil war.[27] An interpretation as to the text and its contents and purpose has to acknowledge that the Article was deliberately confined to a few minimum rules which should receive the widest scope of application. This limitation in substance enabled states to avoid a more specific definition of the scope of application which otherwise would have been controversial. The notion of 'armed conflict not of an international character' thus in itself reflects the dynamics of war and its changing character. The *ICRC Manual*, too, does not attempt to define that term too precisely.[28]

b) A much higher threshold of application was deliberately introduced in AP II. According to its Article 1, para 1, the Protocol shall apply 'to all armed conflicts [not covered by AP I] which take place in the territory of a High Contracting Party between its armed forces and dissident armed forces or other organized armed groups which, under responsible command, exercise such control over a part of its territory as to enable them to carry out sustained and concerted military operations and to implement this Protocol'. By establishing such a high threshold, in particular with the requirement of territorial control held by insurgents against a government, the exclusion of military operations against insurgents outside the state's own territory, and the exclusion of conflicts which do not involve governmental armed forces, the range of applicability of AP II is extremely reduced in modern armed conflicts.[29]

c) Article 8(2e) ICC Statute, which enumerates a number of serious violations of the laws and customs of non-international armed conflict, is limited by virtue of the second

---

[26] See Hans-Peter Gasser, 'International Humanitarian Law and Human Rights Law in Non-International Armed Conflict: Joint Venture or Mutual Exclusion?' (2002) 45 *GYIL* 149–65.
[27] Cf. Cullen, above (n. 1), 158.
[28] *ICRC Manual*, Part B, Chapter 23, para. 503.4 ('. . . as a matter of common sense, before it can be said that there is an armed conflict, there has to be a certain level of violence').
[29] See below, Section 1209.

sentence of sub-para. f to 'armed conflicts that take place in the territory of a State when there is protracted armed conflict between governmental authorities and organized armed groups or between such groups'. This limitation to 'protracted armed conflict' is not mentioned in sub-paras. c and d with respect to serious violations of Article 3 common to the Geneva Conventions, hence different thresholds could be construed for the application of sub-paras. e and f. The negotiating history might suggest that such difference was initially intended, as China, Russia, and other states wanted to limit the field of application of sub-para. f at a time when sub-para. e had been settled. A proposal was first made for sub-para. f to refer to conflicts as defined in Article 1, para. 1, AP II,[30] but the final text falls short of such extreme limitation. The ICRC and others had pointed out that a threshold as for AP II would exclude many existing armed conflicts involving dissident armed groups fighting against each other and also armed groups fighting against the established government without having a proper chain of command or exercising control of part of the territory.[31] This led to the adoption of sub-para. f as it stands today, while the text of sub-para. e was not reconsidered. Drafters of the ICC Statute may have been unable to agree on the full amount of customary law existing for non-international armed conflicts. But they were also unable to settle the matter in clear treaty language. The use of the word 'protracted' is redundant in sub-para. f; it was deliberately taken from the 1995 *Tadić* decision, where the term 'protracted armed violence' was first used, although not in an effort of describing a higher threshold than that of common Article 3 common to the Geneva Conventions, but just to explain the notion of armed conflict as opposed to internal disturbances (for the latter see below, Section 1205).[32] Sierra Leone had initially proposed a reference to 'protracted armed violence' in this context, but this was changed by the conference into 'protracted armed conflict' in an effort which was essentially the same in *Tadić*, to describe a situation which has clearly reached armed conflict level.[33] For a textual interpretation it is difficult to find a common sense argument for this distinction, as the crimes listed in sub-paras. c and e respectively are fully comparable and any distinction would counter a fundamental humanitarian principle which was stressed by the ICTY in the following terms: 'What is inhumane, and consequently proscribed, in international wars, cannot but be inhumane and inadmissible in civil strife.'[34] With the strange distinction in the texts of sub-paras. c and e an example of careless drafting was given, as with the use of the term 'protracted' an element is stressed which is already inherent in the term 'armed conflict' itself, that is an armed violence which is sufficiently intense. The word 'protracted' thus refers more to the intensity of the armed violence than to its duration; it does not require 'sustained'

[30] Bureau Proposal, UN Doc. A/CONF/.183/C.1/L.59.

[31] ICRC memorandum conveyed by New Zealand, UN Doc. A/CONF/.183/INF/11 (13 July 1998).

[32] ICTY, *The Prosecutor v Tadić*, Appeals Chamber Decision on Defence Motion for Interlocutory Appeal on Jurisdiction of 2 October 1995, para. 70: '. . . an armed conflict exists whenever there is a resort to armed force between States or protracted armed violence between governmental authorities and organized armed groups or between such groups within a State'. See also ICTY, *The Prosecutor v Delalić et al. (Celebici)*, Case No. IT-96–21-A, Appeals Chamber Judgment of 20 February 2001, para. 184.

[33] Machteld Boot, *Genocide, Crimes Against Humanity, War Crimes. Nullum Crimen Sine Lege and the Subject Matter Jurisdiction of the International Criminal Court*, 12 School of Human Rights Research Series (Intersentia, 2002), 573–5; Knut Dörmann, *Elements of War Crimes under the Rome Statute of the International Criminal Court. Sources and Commentary*, with contributions by Louise Doswald-Beck and Robert Kolb (CUP, 2003), 441; Andreas Zimmermann, in Otto Triffterer (ed.), *Commentary on the Rome Statute of the International Criminal Court. Observers' Notes, Article by Article* (Nomos, 1999), Art. 8, no. 333.

[34] Above, (n. 23), para. 119. For further discussion of this principle see below, Section 1212.

military operations, or even operations that are conducted in a continuous manner.[35] If this understanding can be accepted, the level of application of Article 8, para. 2, lit. c and e, ICC Statute is substantially the same as in Article 3 common to the Geneva Conventions (see below, Section 1211). It should also be considered that the contents of Article 8, para. 2, lit. c and e, ICC Statute is not based on an analytically convincing structure and does not fully reflect the current state of customary law.[36]

7. Policy considerations and operational needs. Military operators, legal experts, and policy-makers have argued over the years that humanitarian protection should be the same for all types of armed conflicts. While 'the law on different types of conflicts has pursued different courses to the prejudice of a common core of humanitarian principles',[37] considerations of sound policy and military effectiveness are strongly speaking in favour of applying similar rules to the conduct of hostilities in all armed conflicts (see below, Section 1216). Yet, there remain certain legal distinctions between international and non-international armed conflicts, most especially in respect of the status of fighters (see below, Sections 1213–1215).

> To better understand the law of non-international armed conflict, it is important to consider how two separate bodies of law for armed conflict—international and non-international—originally arose. Throughout the course of twentieth-century international lawmaking, many states took the position that a number of the rules applicable in international armed conflict—particularly those associated with the status of combatants—would limit their rights of action if applied in non-international armed conflicts. The concern that the application of the law applicable in international armed conflict to internal situations could obstruct the state's ability to pursue the conflict was not fundamentally based on concern about restrictions related to the conduct of hostilities. It was based, instead, on uneasiness about the legal implications for the status of parties to the conflict, and, in particular, on states' concerns about restrictions on their ability to prosecute and punish individuals under domestic law for their belligerent acts which constituted crimes under that law. These considerations gave rise to the legal conclusion that the application of provisions on humanitarian protection should not affect the legal status of the parties to the conflict.

1202

1. Historical context. The principal instruments in the law of armed conflict address, and distinguish between, armed conflicts of international and non-international character. Their provisions governing non-international armed conflicts are less extensively developed than those governing international armed conflicts. While non-international armed conflicts, and rules regarding their conduct, received little focus in these instruments, certain fundamental principles applicable to non-international conflict find expression in Article 3 common to the Geneva Conventions. It sets out a basic set of protections that apply in all non-international armed conflicts, and are confirmed and supplemented by rules of customary law.

[35] *Tadić*, above, (n. 32); ICTY, *The Prosecutor v Haradinaj, Balaj, and Brahimaj*, IT-04–84-T, Trial Chamber Judgment, 3 April 2008, paras. 37–49; Cullen, above, (n. 1), 127–30.
[36] Claus Kress, 'War Crimes Committed in Non-International Armed Conflict and the Emerging System of International Criminal Justice' (2001) 30 *IsrYHR* 103–77, at 130–42, 175.
[37] Richard R. Baxter, 'Some Existing Problems of Humanitarian Law' (1975) XIV *RDMilG* 297–303, at 301.

2. *Reluctance of states to apply rules of international law in internal armed conflict.* All states have legal frameworks which privilege their own police and armed forces as against insurgents who oppose them. In many cases it was held that a number of the rules applicable in international armed conflict—particularly those associated with the status of detained combatants—would limit a state's freedom of action if applied in non-international armed conflicts. Many governments did not want to accept any body of international law to apply domestically within their own sovereign territory. Importantly, the concern that the application of the laws of war in internal situations would or could obstruct the government's ability to prosecute the conflict was *not* fundamentally based on anxiety about restrictions related to methods and means of conflict. The concern was based, instead, on uneasiness about the laws' implications for the status of parties to the conflict, and, in particular, on states' concerns about restrictions on their ability to sanction individuals under domestic law for their belligerent acts. The 'fear'—this is the word the ICRC used in describing the concern—that application of international law to civil conflicts might somehow confer protected belligerent status to rebel forces gave rise to Article 3, para. 4, common to the Geneva Conventions, which provides that '[t]he application of the preceding provisions shall not affect the legal status of the Parties to the conflict'.[38] The committee developing common Article 3 referred to the 'enormous practical difficulties' that were seen to be associated with applying the international rules to civil conflicts.[39] It is still true today that states are reluctant to apply the laws of war in internal conflicts. They would not want to imply that their own armed forces are legitimate targets in a civil war. They rather maintain a legal framework which privileges there own police and armed forces against those who oppose them. There are not just concerns about according a legal status to insurgents but also other difficulties of applying the laws of war in a civil war: maintaining the key distinction between civilian and military is notoriously difficult in civil wars.

3. *The relevance of status.* The question of status in the law of armed conflict is one of central importance. The law of armed conflict recognizes combatants as having a right to participate directly in hostilities. There are two benefits of profound consequence which flow from this right. First, those who hold it are entitled to prisoner-of-war status and its attendant rights and protections. Second, and perhaps more importantly, they are held immune from criminal prosecution for their belligerent acts—acts that would otherwise constitute serious crimes under domestic law. Combatants who are thus privileged have what is referred to as 'combatant immunity' which is, in effect, a limited licence to take life and cause destruction.[40] Those who participate in hostilities without combatant status may be prosecuted under relevant criminal law for their belligerent actions. States facing domestic insurgencies or threats from armed groups who fail to meet the criteria for combatant status have an obvious interest in ensuring that their rights to prosecute

---

[38] Jean S. Pictet, *The Geneva Conventions of 12 August 1949. Commentary, Vol. IV* (ICRC, 1958), 44: 'This clause is essential. Without it neither Article 3, nor any other Article in its place, would ever have been adopted. It meets the fear—always the same one—that the application of the Convention, even to a very limited extent, in cases of civil war may interfere with the de jure Government's lawful suppression of the revolt, or that it may confer belligerent status, and consequently increased authority and power, upon the adverse Party.'

[39] Report drawn up by the Joint Committee and presented to the Plenary Assembly, *Final Record of the Diplomatic Conference of Geneva of 1949*, Volume II, Section B, at 129.

[40] This licence is limited in the sense that the denial of life and destruction caused must be consistent with international humanitarian law.

DIETER FLECK

and sentence opponents for acts which may constitute murder and destruction remain uncompromised by the concept of combatant immunity. Thus, a line was drawn in order to avoid chaos of unaccountable groups claiming a right to lawfully use force.

4. *The principle of distinction in non-international armed conflicts.* The fundamental legal distinction between fighters and civilians and between military objectives and civilian objects may be difficult to apply in non-international armed conflicts, as armed opposition groups are often not well organized and equipped and they are conducting their operations with civilian support. It is applicable nevertheless, as '[t]he basic rule of protection and distinction . . . is the foundation on which the codification of the laws and customs of war rests'[41] and 'the prohibition of attacks against the civilian population as such, and against individual civilians, remains valid, even if the adversary has committed breaches'[42] (see below, Section 1203, para. 1).

> **Certain general principles of conduct underpin all military operations, regardless**   **1203**
> **of the nature of the conflict. These principles are:**
> — **the distinction between fighters and civilians, as well as between military objectives and civilian objects;**
> — **the prohibition of superfluous injury or unnecessary suffering; and**
> — **humane treatment without discrimination.**

1. *General observation.* The three principles referred to in this section are inherent to international humanitarian law in general. They have the same meaning in international and non-international armed conflicts. All military operations must comply with these principles.

2. *The principle of distinction.* This principle protects civilians from the effects of military operations (see above, Section 401) and it also requires that civilians taking direct part in hostilities lose protection against the effects of hostilities for the duration of each specific act amounting to direct participation, whereas persons assuming a permanent combatant function for a party to the conflict lose civilian protection for the duration of such conflict (see above, Section 517). The application of this principle in non-international armed conflicts is based on customary law,[43] irrespective of the disputed practice of targeted killings by some states.[44] For civilians in conflicts of a higher threshold it is confirmed in Article 13 AP II. The term 'fighters' does not appear in treaty law and is used to avoid any misunderstanding as to the status of the persons concerned. It comprises combatant members of regular armed forces (see above, Chapter 3) and members of armed groups fighting against the government or against each other. The term 'military objectives' is 'limited to those objects which by their nature, location, purpose or use make an effective contribution to military action and whose total or partial destruction, capture or neutralization, in the circumstances ruling at the time, offers a definite military advantage'.[45]

---

[41] *ICRC Commentary* to Art. 48 AP I, para. 1863.

[42] *ICRC Commentary* to Art. 13(2) AP II, para. 4784.

[43] Rules 6 and 7 *CIHL; ICRC, Interpretive Guidance on the Notion of Direct Participation in Hostilities* (ICRC, 2009), *33–6.*

[44] See, e.g., Israel Supreme Court, *1. The Public Committee Against Torture in Israel, 2. Palestinian Society for the Protection of Human Rights and the Environment v The Government of Israel et al.,* Judgment of 13 December 2006, HCJ 769/02.

[45] Art. 52, para. 2, AP I; Art. 2, para. 6 of the amended MinesProt; Art. 1 Prot2CultPropConv; Rule 8 *CIHL.*

3. *The prohibition of superfluous injury or unnecessary suffering.* This principle applies to the use of weapons, projectiles and material, and to methods of warfare of a nature to cause superfluous injury or unnecessary suffering,[46] irrespective whether this effect was 'calculated' or not; the expression 'superfluous injury or unnecessary suffering', covers simultaneously the sense of moral and physical suffering (see above, Sections 401, 402).[47]

4. *The principle of humane treatment.* The principle of humane treatment without adverse distinction is a legal obligation which calls for actively reducing needless suffering and accepting humanitarian imperatives as obstacles to a supposed right of doing whatever is needed to win a war.[48] It is expressly stated in Article 3, para. 1, common to the Geneva Conventions with respect to persons *hors de combat*, but humanity requires to refrain from cruelties and perfidious acts also against fighters. Various distinct aspects of humane treatment are also addressed in human rights conventions.[49]

1204   There is an important trend in the law towards expanding the scope of application of the rules related to the conduct of hostilities originally contained only in the law of international armed conflict to situations of non-international armed conflict, while, at the same time, respecting the distinction which continues to exist in these two types of conflicts on matters of status of the fighters.

1. *Historical origin.* This trend was visible already in the work of Hugo Grotius (1583–1645), some of whose main ideas in *De Jure Belli ac Pacis* were first developed in defence of private and mercenary wars.[50] In the eighteenth century, Emmerich de Vattel held that a sovereign has to observe the ordinary laws of war towards rebellious subjects who openly take up arms against him.[51] A century later, the first modern codification of the laws of war was developed by Francis Lieber during the American Civil War, at a time when there was no actual involvement of US forces in international armed conflicts.[52] The Lieber Code expressly refers to situations '[w]hen humanity induces the adoption of the rules of regular war toward rebels, whether the adoption is partial or entire'. It facilitates such adoption by expressly stating that 'it does in no way whatever imply a partial or complete acknowledgement of [the rebels'] government, if they have set up one, or of them, as an independent and sovereign power'. To avoid any misunderstanding in this matter, Lieber even added the sentence: 'Neutrals have no right to make the adoption of the rules of war by the assailed government toward rebels the ground of their own acknowledgement of the revolted people as an independent power.'[53]

---

[46] Art. 35, para. 2, AP I.

[47] *ICRC Commentary*, Art. 35, para. 2, AP I, para. 1426.

[48] Yves Sandoz, 'International Humanitarian Law in the Twenty-First Century' (2006) 6–2003 *YIHL* 3–40, at 7–8.

[49] Art. 2, para. 1, ICCPR, Art. 14 ECHR, Art. 1, para. 1, 5 ACHR; Lindsay Moir, *The Law of Internal Armed Conflict* (CUP, 2002), 197–8.

[50] Karma Nabulsi, *Traditions of War: Occupation, Resistance, and the Law* (OUP, 2005), 129.

[51] Emer de Vattel, *Le Droit des Gens ou Principes du Droit Naturel* (first published Neuchâtel, 1758), *The Law of Nations* (J. B. Scott (ed.) (Washington, DC: Carnegie Institute, 1916)), 238.

[52] Michael H. Hoffman, 'The customary law of non-international armed conflict. Evidence from the United States Civil War' (1990) 277 *IRRC* 322–44, at 326; Silja Vöneky, 'Der Lieber's Code und die Wurzeln des modernen Kriegsvölkerrechts' (2002) 62 *ZaöRV* 423–60.

[53] Art. 152 of the Lieber Code.

2. *Influences from other branches of law.* The trend to overcome the traditional distinction between rules of conduct for international and non-international armed conflicts was supported by the development of standards of protection in other fields of law. Human rights instruments apply not only in peacetime, but in general also during armed conflict. Protections of civilians, even of those who are indicted for having committed crimes, are part of constitutional guarantees in many states today.

3. *Present meaning.* The clear trend in customary humanitarian law towards expanding the scope of application of the rules governing the conduct of hostilities to non-international armed conflicts has become manifest in state practice and *opinio iuris*.[54] This trend carries implications for how and which weapons are used in warfare, for the protection of victims of armed conflict, and for the criminalization of violations of these rules. While more progressive trends in literature towards full convergence of the law of international and non-international armed conflicts[55] are not always supported by practice, it is also fair to state that restrictive attempts to limit international legal obligations in non-international armed conflicts to 'rudimentary' or 'minimum' protection rules that still characterize the attitude of states at diplomatic conferences do not fully reflect the interest of parties in military operations and were in fact overtaken by developments of customary international law (see below, Section 1212).

> **International humanitarian law generally does not apply to internal disturbances   1205
> and tensions, such as riots, isolated and sporadic acts of violence or other acts of a
> similar nature.**

1. *Relevant treaty provisions.* Non-international armed conflicts are distinct from international armed conflicts on the one hand (see above, Section 1201, paras. 1–3) and internal disturbances and tensions on the other. The principle that international humanitarian law generally does not apply to internal disturbances and tensions, such as riots, isolated and sporadic acts of violence, or other acts of a similar nature was first stated in Article 1, para. 2, AP II. While AP II has a range of application much smaller than common Article 3 (see above, Section 1201, para. 6), the principle stated here is generally applied to all non-international armed conflicts. It was reaffirmed in Article 8, sub-paras. 2(d) and 2(f), ICC Statute which expressly excludes violations committed in internal disturbances and tensions from the Court's jurisdiction for war crimes. While sub-para. 2(d) is related to serious violations of common Article 3, a number of other serious violations of the laws and customs of non-international armed conflict are enumerated in sub-para. 2(e), and are limited to 'armed conflicts that take place in the territory of a State when there is protracted armed conflict between governmental authorities and organized armed groups or between such groups', by virtue of the second sentence of sub-para. 2(f). For the contents and meaning of these provision see above, Section 1201, para. 6(c), and below, Section 1211.

---

[54] Theodor Meron, 'The Humanization of Humanitarian Law' (2000) 94 *AJIL* 239–78, at 260–3. The existing trend towards equal application on rules of means and methods of fighting in both types of armed conflict is, although reluctantly, widely conceded today, see Kenneth Watkin and Andrew J. Norris (eds), *Non-International Armed Conflict in the Twenty-first Century*, Vol. 88 *International Law Studies* (Newport, RI: Naval War College, 2012), in particular the contributions by William H. Boothby (197–210), Wolff Heintschel v. Heinegg (211–36), and Richard B. Jackson (237–59).

[55] See, e.g., James Stewart, 'Towards a Single Definition of Armed Conflict in International Humanitarian Law: A Critique of Internationalised Armed Conflict' (2003) 85 *IRRC* 313; Emily Crawford, *The Treatment of Combatants and Insurgents under the Law of Armed Conflict* (OUP, 2010).

2. *General considerations.* The distinction between non-international armed conflicts and internal disturbances and tensions is not expressly addressed in common Article 3 to the Geneva Conventions, which applies to 'the case of armed conflict not of an international character occurring in the territory of one of the High Contracting Parties'. While no definition of 'armed conflict' was included in the Conventions (see above, Section 201), Pictet's Commentary lists the following 'different conditions, although in no way obligatory', constituting convenient criteria in this context: (1) that the party in revolt against the *de iure* government possesses an organized military force, an authority responsible for its acts, acting within a determinate territory and having the means of respecting and ensuring respect for the Geneva Conventions; (2) that the legal government is obliged to have recourse to the regular military forces against insurgents organized as military and in possession of a part of the national territory; (3) that the *de iure* government has: (a) recognized the insurgents as belligerents; or (b) claimed for itself the rights of a belligerent; or (c) accorded the insurgents recognition as belligerents for the purposes only of the Geneva Conventions; or (d) that the dispute has been admitted to the agenda of the Security Council or the General Assembly of the United Nations as being a threat to international peace, a breach of the peace, or an act of aggression; (4)(a) that the insurgents have an organization purporting to have the characteristics of a state; (b) that the insurgent civil authority exercises *de facto* authority over persons within a determinate portion of the national territory; (c) that the armed forces act under the direction of an organized authority and are prepared to observe the ordinary laws of war; (d) that the insurgent civil authority agrees to be bound by the provisions of the Convention.[56] Stressing the descriptive character of this list which obviously summarizes discussions at the Diplomatic Conference, Pictet gave the following explanation which is still relevant today: 'The above criteria are useful as a means of distinguishing a genuine armed conflict from a mere act of banditry or an unorganized and short-lived insurrection. Does this mean that Article 3 is not applicable in cases where armed strife breaks out in a country, but does not fulfil any of the above conditions (which are not obligatory and are only mentioned as an indication)? We do not subscribe to this view. We think, on the contrary, that the scope of application of the Article must be as wide as possible. There can be no drawbacks in this, since the Article in its reduced form, contrary to what might be thought, does not in any way limit the right of a State to put down rebellion, nor does it increase in the slightest the authority of the rebel party. It merely demands respect for certain rules, which were already recognized as essential in all civilized countries, and embodied in the municipal law of the States in question, long before the Convention was signed. What Government would dare to claim before the world, in a case of civil disturbances which could justly be described as mere acts of banditry, that, Article 3 not being applicable, it was entitled to leave the wounded uncared for, to torture and mutilate prisoners and take hostages? However useful, therefore, the various conditions stated above may be, they are not indispensable, since no Government can object to observing, in its dealings with internal enemies, whatever the nature of the conflict between it and them, a few essential rules which it in fact observes daily, under its own laws, even when dealing with common criminals.'[57] Arguing eloquently for the

---

[56] Pictet, above, (n. 38), *Commentary* (IV), 35–6, with reference to the *Final Record of the Diplomatic Conference of Geneva of 1949*, Volume II, Section B, at 121.
[57] Pictet, ibid.

DIETER FLECK

application of the humanitarian protection standards of Article 3 also in situations of internal 'armed strife', Pictet at the same time endorsed existing national limitations relevant for law enforcement operations, as, indeed, Article 3 does not authorize states to treat a riot like an armed conflict or to use lethal force and detention without trial (see, in particular, Article 3, para. 1, no. 1, lit. a and d). Similar considerations are included in the *ICRC Commentary* to Art. 1 AP II.[58] Consequently, the 'Turku Declaration'[59] affirmed minimum humanitarian standards which are applicable in all situations, including internal violence, disturbances, tensions, and public emergency, and which cannot be derogated from under any circumstances.

3. *Remaining legal distinctions.* It has been suggested that a 'unified use of force rule' that unifies the law of armed conflict for international and non-international conflicts and even for military operations other than war, such as robust peacekeeping and law enforcement operations, has emerged as a customary international legal norm, hence the degree of force permitted and the notion of military necessity should not be interpreted differently in international and non-international armed conflicts.[60] While this opinion seems convincing in certain respect, a critical reservation must be made with respect to the conduct of hostilities during armed conflict. It may still be held that in all armed conflicts international humanitarian law provides a more liberal regime for the use of force than human rights law. Pertinent rules, in particular those requiring the protection of civilians and persons *hors de combat*, avoidance and in any event minimization of incidental deaths, injuries, and destruction, are still less restrictive for military operations under the *lex specialis* rules of international humanitarian law than for law enforcement operations in peacetime. In the conduct of hostilities enemy combatants may be targeted and attacked with lethal force, regardless of whether they could be captured or arrested. On the other hand, in law enforcement operations police forces may be entitled to seek some advantages in exceptional situations by feigning civilian status or using tear gas or dum-dum bullets, practices that are prohibited in hostilities. Law enforcement operations in internal disturbances will generally follow specific rules which are not fully comparable to military operations in an armed conflict. The use of riot control agents such as tear gas (CS), prohibited as a method of warfare under Article I, para. 5, Chemical WeaponsConv,[61] is not prohibited for law enforcement including domestic riot control purposes, as expressly stated in Article II(9) Chemical WeaponsConv. For

[58] *ICRC Commentary*, paras. 4475–8.

[59] Declaration of Minimum Humanitarian Standards (Turku Declaration) of 2 December 1990 (Annex to UN Doc. E/CN.4/1996/80); No. 282 *IRRC* (1991), 328; reprinted in (1995) 89 *AJIL* 215; see Alan Rosas/Theodor Meron, 'Combatting lawlessness in grey zone conflicts through minimum humanitarian standards' (1995) 89 *AJIL* 215.

[60] Franciso F. Martin, 'Using International Human Rights Law for Establishing a Unified Use of Force Rule in the Law of Armed Conflict' (2001) 64 *Saskatchewan Law Review* 347–96; see also the discussion by Martin, Jordan J. Paust, L. C. Green, and Martin in (2002) 65 *Saskatchewan Law Review* 405–10, 411–25, 427–50, and 451–68; William Abresch, 'A Human Rights Law of Internal Armed Conflict: The European Court of Human Rights in Chechnya' (2005) 16 *EJIL* 741–67.

[61] This provision has removed controversies on the question whether such prohibition already derived from the 1925 GasProt and customary law. Riot control agents are defined in Art. II, para. 7 of the Chemical WeaponsConv as chemicals 'which can produce rapidly in humans sensory irritation or disabling physical effects which disappear within a short time following termination of exposure'. While many states considered the use of riot control agents for military purposes as unacceptable, the UK had stated in 1970 that CS and other such gases were outside the scope of the GasProt. The US, on ratification of the GasProt in 1975, reserved the right to use riot control agents and chemical herbicides and declared that, as a matter of policy, such use would be restricted, see *UK Manual (2004)*, para 1.27.2.

DIETER FLECK

riot control CS is a means of last resort, to avoid the use of deadly fire. The employment in certain police operations of dum-dum bullets which have been generally outlawed for armed conflicts,[62] may be permissible to lessen the risk to civilians, in particular within buildings where the use of fully jacketed projectiles might have a 'billiard' effect on concrete walls, thus jeopardizing the lives of hostages and police officers in action. Both prohibitions apply in international as in non-international armed conflicts today,[63] but not in law enforcement operations.

4. *The law applicable in internal disturbances.* Even in the absence of specific treaty provisions of international humanitarian law, clear legal protections apply in internal disturbances and tensions, such as riots, isolated and sporadic acts of violence, or other acts of a similar nature. These are derived from human rights and national laws. States may decide, and have done so sometimes as a matter of policy, that even if a particular situation is not an armed conflict under international law, the relevant principles and rules of international humanitarian law will be applied.[64] There may be situations where below the threshold of the conduct of hostilities law enforcement operations are executed by armed forces. In such cases a strict line must be drawn between these two different tasks both with respect to the goals and the methods and means to be used.[65]

1206   **Even in cases not covered by existing rules, the principles of humanity must guide all parties.**

1. *General.* The origin of this rule dates back to the Martens Clause (see above Section 131) which has been reaffirmed in Article 1, para. 2, AP I, and, in a shorter form, also referred to in the Preamble (para. 4) of AP II. The legal effect of this rule lies in its limitations of possible denunciations of treaty obligations, as expressly recognized in Articles 63, para. 4, GC I; 62, para. 4, GC II; 142, para. 4, GC III; and 158, para. 4, GC IV, but even more importantly in its role as a guide for conduct in situations which are not fully addressed by existent treaty law.

2. *'Cases not covered by existing rules'.* These cases include acts not expressly addressed in this Handbook and situations below the level of an armed conflict.

3. *'Principles of humanity'.* As a matter of logic, principles not covered by the law in force derive from unwritten rules inherent to existing law. Principles of humanity are inherent

---

[62] Dum-Dum Bullets HagueDecl 1899; see Louise Doswald-Beck, 'Implementation of International Humanitarian Law in Future Wars' in Michael N. Schmitt and L. C. Green (eds), *The Law of Armed Conflicts: Into the Next Millennium, Vol. 71 International Law Studies* (Newport, RI: Naval War College, 1998) 39–75, at 41 and note 7.

[63] See Rules 75 and 77 *CIHL*. The use of dum-dum bullets is listed in Art. 8(2)(b)(xix), ICC Statute as a war crime in international armed conflicts, but not in Art. 8(2)(e) for non-international armed conflicts, as this latter list does not include prohibited weapons altogether. Michael Schmitt/Charles Garraway/Yoram Dinstein, 'The Manual on the Law of Non-International Armed Conflict. With Commentary' (2006) 36 *IsrYHR* Special Supplement, 35–6, consider it doubtful whether the prohibition of dum-dum bullets can be regarded as applicable in non-international armed conflicts, but the examples given by them clearly relate to law enforcement against terrorists and hostage-takers rather than military operations, that is to situations which could also arise in international armed conflicts and should not be treated differently.

[64] *UK Manual*, Section 15.2.1.

[65] Fleck, 'Law Enforcement and the Conduct of Hostilities: Two Supplementing or Mutually Excluding Legal Paradigms?' in Andreas Fischer-Lescano/Hans-Peter Gasser/Thilo Marauhn/Natalino Ronzitti (eds), *Frieden in Freiheit. Peace in liberty. Paix en liberté. Festschrift für Michael Bothe zum 70. Geburtstag* (Nomos, DIKE, 2008), 391–407.

to international humanitarian law and human rights law. Both AP I and AP II refer to 'the principles of humanity and the dictates of public conscience' in the same context, thus reinforcing their obligatory character. While in contrast to Article 1, para. 2, AP I, no reference to 'established custom' was made in the Preamble to AP II, it was rightly stressed soon after the Protocols' adoption, that 'the existence of customary norms in internal armed conflicts should not be totally denied'.[66] Today, the existence of customary international law for non-international armed conflicts is fully acknowledged (see above, Section 1204, para. 3, and below, Section 1212).

4. *Operational relevance.* Principles of humanity, whether or not these are covered by conventional law or custom, are essential for reaching the aim of the law of all armed conflict: to maintain the rule of law by protecting victims of violence. Their full observance is of both tactical and strategic importance, as it will be decisive for conducting convincing operations, winning the hearts and minds of the people and establishing a stable peace (see below, Section 1402).

II. Applicable Law

Specific conventional rules on humanitarian protection in non-international armed conflicts have first been developed with Article 3 common to the Geneva Conventions. They provide for fundamental protections of persons taking no part or no longer an active part in hostilities, a right of initiative of impartial humanitarian bodies, such as the International Committee of the Red Cross, and an encouragement to the parties to the conflict to bring into force, by means of special agreements, all or part of the other provisions of the Geneva Conventions.   1207

1. *General.* The rules contained in Article 3 common to the Geneva Conventions provide fundamental standards of protection stemming from the right to life and principles of humanity in all armed conflicts. These rules have been recognized by the ICJ as an emanation of 'elementary considerations of humanity' constituting 'a minimum yardstick' applicable to all armed conflicts.[67] The fundamental importance of common Article 3 was reconfirmed many times.[68]

2. *Obligations of non-state actors.* The law of non-international armed conflicts is binding upon all parties, both states and non-state actors (see above, Section 1201, para. 5). For international legal obligations to apply, recognition of armed opposition groups by the state they are fighting against or by a third state is not required. Non-state actors as nationals of the state that has made the international commitment under conventional or customary law are direct addressees of the relevant norms and fully bound by them. They cannot successfully claim that they could not participate in the lawmaking process and may be

---

[66] *ICRC Commentary* to the Preamble of AP II, para. 4435.

[67] ICJ, *Military and Paramilitary Activities in and against Nicaragua (Nicaragua v US)*, Judgment of 27 June 1986 (para. 218). Because of a reservation made by the US in accepting the jurisdiction, the ICJ could not apply multilateral treaties to the facts of this case, but had to rely on the customary nature of the relevant rules.

[68] ICJ, ibid.; ICTY, *The Prosecutor v Tadić*, Appeals Chamber Decision on Defence Motion for Interlocutory Appeal on Jurisdiction of 2 October 1995, paras. 89, 98; *The Prosecutor v Kunarac et al.*, Judgment of 22 February 2001, para. 68; *CIHL* Vol. I, xliv.

fighting the legal order of their nation state. Whereas the binding effect of international humanitarian law on non-state actors was never seriously disputed, the extent to which this would also apply to underlying human rights norms was shadowed by a widely believed myth according to which human rights could be claimed against the state, but not against individuals. That myth may have been supported by a limited textual understanding of human rights conventions, but it was never keeping with custom, neither with practice, and cannot be upheld.[69] Non-state actors have included human rights commitments in their policy statements and codes of conduct. The UN has secured such commitments on many occasions. Human rights breaches by individuals were never excused with failing obligations. It is logical to state that non-state actors may not only claim rights, but have also to comply with obligations under existing humanitarian law and human rights law.

3. *Legal status of the parties.* As expressly stated in Article 3, para. 4, these rules do not affect the legal status of the parties to the conflict.

4. *Right of initiative.* The right of initiative of impartial humanitarian bodies enables them to offer services to the parties to the conflict. The ICRC, which is expressly mentioned in this context, has a unique role to play in armed conflicts (see below, Section 1424). It is supplemented today by activities of the UN (see below, Sections 1425–1431), international and regional organizations, states, and NGOs (see below, Sections 1432–1433).

5. *Special agreements.* Special agreements relating to all or part of the other provisions of the Geneva Conventions are encouraged to supplement the fundamental rules contained in Article 3. It will be difficult to conclude such agreements during an ongoing non-international armed conflict, although this was possible in some cases.[70] A general forum for humanitarian engagement of armed non-state actors is provided by Geneva Call.[71] It remains an important task to support implementation of applicable rules of humanitarian law and human rights law for the protection of victims of armed conflicts.

1208   Certain subsequent treaties also provide for fundamental protections in non-international armed conflicts (Article 19 CultPropConv).

1. Following the example of Article 3 common to the Geneva Conventions, the 1954 CultPropConv provides in Article 19 that in a non-international armed conflict 'the

---

[69] Andrew Clapham, *Human Rights Obligations of Non-State Actors* (OUP, 2006), 58, 280; August Reinisch, 'The Changing International Legal Framework for Dealing with Non-State Actors', in Philip Alston (ed.), *Non-State Actors and Human Rights* (OUP, 2005), 37–89 [69–72]; Christian Tomuschat, 'The Applicability of Human Rights Law to Insurgent Movements' in Horst Fischer/Ulrike Froissart/Wolff Heintschel v. Heinegg/Christian Raap (eds), *Krisensicherung und Humanitärer Schutz—Crisis Management and Humanitarian Protection* (Berliner Wissenschafts-Verlag, 2004), 573–91 [588–91].

[70] See, e.g., Agreement of 22 May 1992 concluded at the invitation of the ICRC between the Parties to the Bosnian conflict, Marco Sassòli/Antoine Bouvier/Anne Quintin (eds), *How Does Law Protect in War? Cases, Documents and Teaching Materials on Contemporary Practice in International Humanitarian Law*, 3rd edn (ICRC, 2011), 1112; Agreement between UNICEF and Sudan People's Liberation Movement-United (SPLM-United) on Ground Rules for Operation Lifeline Sudan, May 1996, <http://www.c-r.org/accord-article/operation-lifeline-sudan>. For further information on humanitarian negotiations with armed groups in Afghanistan, Angola, Bosnia and Herzegovina, Burma/Myanmar, Burundi, Colombia, Democratic Republic of Congo, Liberia, Sierra Leone, Sri Lanka, Sudan, Tadjikistan, Turkmenistan, Uganda, and Uzbekistan, see <http://ochaonline.un.org/humanitariannegotiations/Documents/Bibliography%20docs/AnnexII.htm>. Similar practices were relevant for the conflicts in Yemen 1962, Nigeria 1967, El Salvador (FMNL) 1990; and The Philippines (NDFP) 1998.

[71] <http://www.genevacall.org/>.

provisions of the present Convention which relate to respect for cultural property' should apply. With this formula not much of the Convention's core provisions were left outside. Any practical limitation which might derive from this formula was removed by Prot2CultPropConv (see below, Section 1210).

2. It may be recalled that the 1935 Roerich Pact has no such limitation at all; its declared purpose is 'that the treasures of culture be respected and protected in time of war and in peace'.

> An attempt to develop and supplement Article 3 common to the Geneva   1209
> Conventions led to controversial negotiations from 1970 to 1977 and had to be
> reduced to a number of provisions applicable to armed conflicts which take place
> in the territory of a contracting party between its armed forces and 'dissident
> armed forces or other organized armed groups which, under responsible com-
> mand, exercise such control over a part of its territory as to enable them to carry
> out sustained and concerted military operations and to implement' the rules so
> achieved (AP II).

1. For the threshold of application of AP II, as defined in its Article 1, see above, Section 1201, para. 6, lit. b. Due to this high threshold, AP II is technically inapplicable to the many armed conflicts in disintegrated states in which the government has become largely ineffective and warring parties are fighting against each other.[72]

2. The contents of AP II is limited to rudimentary provisions of humane treatment, humanitarian protection of the wounded, sick, and shipwrecked, and the civilian population and individual civilians against the dangers arising from military operations. All of its basic provisions are reflected in customary international law today. By virtue of customary law, practically all substantial provisions of AP II are also applicable in non-international armed conflicts of much lower threshold.[73]

3. AP II, its clear deficiencies notwithstanding, has supported an educational process which has enhanced awareness of existing rules of humanitarian protection in non-international armed conflicts.

> For some treaties the scope of applicability was subsequently expanded to include   1210
> armed conflicts not of an international character (Blinding WeaponsProt; MinesProt
> as of 1996; Prot2CultPropConv; Article 1, paras. 2–6, Inhumane WeaponsConv as
> of 2001). Other treaties were enacted with a broad scope right from their first entry
> into force (LandMinesConv; ClusterConv).

1. There have been a number of successful efforts to formally expand the scope of rules of conventional international law originally designed for international armed conflicts in order to ensure their application also in non-international armed conflicts. The Prot2CultPropConv, adopted on 26 May 1999, extended all provisions of the CultPropConv to non-international armed conflicts, thus further amplifying its scope of application (see above, Section 1208). In 2001, at the Second Review Conference on

---

[72] Dino Kritsiotis, 'International Humanitarian Law and the Disintegration of States' (2001) 30 *IsrYHR* Special Supplement, 17–35, at 22.
[73] ICTY, *The Prosecutor v Tadić*, Appeals Chamber Decision on Defence Motion for Interlocutory Appeal on Jurisdiction of 2 October 1995, para. 117.

DIETER FLECK

the 1980 InhumaneWeaponsConv,[74] its Article 1 was amended to cover non-international armed conflicts,[75] due to a successful US initiative[76] which followed similar earlier developments under the 1995 BlindingWeaponsProt and the 1996 MinesProt. The latter also prohibits 'the transfer of any landmines to any recipient other than a State or a State agency authorised to receive such transfers' (Article 8, para. 1, lit. b).

2. Under Article 1, para. 1 of the 1997 LandMinesConv, each state party undertakes 'never under any circumstances' to use, produce, acquire, or stockpile anti-personnel mines and destroy or ensure destruction of such weapons, irrespective of their use in international or non-international conflicts. States are likewise obliged not to 'transfer to anyone' or 'assist, encourage or induce, in any way, anyone to engage in any activity prohibited to a State Party under this Convention'. The latter obligations also prohibit states from providing anti-personnel mines to any non-state actors, such as armed opposition groups.[77] Similar provisions are contained in Article I of the 1993 Chemical WeaponsConv, which provides that state parties 'never under any circumstances' develop, produce, otherwise acquire, stockpile, or transfer, 'directly or indirectly, chemical weapons to anyone'. That Convention further prohibits to use chemical weapons, to engage

---

[74] Report of the Second Review Conference of the States Parties to the Convention on Prohibitions or Restrictions on the Use of Certain Conventional Weapons Which May be Deemed to be Excessively Injurious or to Have Indiscriminate Effects, CCW/CONF.II/MC.I/CRP. 1/Rev. 1, 20 December 2001, <http://www.icrc.org/eng/resources/documents/misc/59kc84.htm>.

[75] The Conference decided to amend Article 1 of the Convention to read as follows:

'1. This Convention and its annexed Protocols shall apply in the situations referred to in Article 2 common to the Geneva Conventions of 12 August 1949 for the Protection of War Victims, including any situation described in paragraph 4 of Article I of Additional Protocol I to these Conventions.

2. This Convention and its annexed Protocols shall also apply, in addition to situations referred to in paragraph 1 of this Article, to situations referred to in Article 3 common to the Geneva Conventions of 12 August 1949. This Convention and its annexed Protocols shall not apply to situations of internal disturbances and tensions, such as riots, isolated and sporadic acts of violence, and other acts of a similar nature, as not being armed conflicts.

3. In case of armed conflicts not of an international character occurring in the territory of one of the High Contracting Parties, each party to the conflict shall be bound to apply the prohibitions and restrictions of this Convention and its annexed Protocols.

4. Nothing in this Convention or its annexed Protocols shall be invoked for the purpose of affecting the sovereignty of a State or the responsibility of the Government, by all legitimate means, to maintain or re-establish law and order in the State or to defend the national unity and territorial integrity of the State.

5. Nothing in this Convention or its annexed Protocols shall be invoked as a justification for intervening, directly or indirectly, for any reason whatever, in the armed conflict or in the internal or external affairs of the High Contracting Party in the territory of which that conflict occurs.

6. The application of the provisions of this Convention and its annexed Protocols to parties to a conflict which are not High Contracting Parties that have accepted this Convention or its annexed Protocols, shall not change their legal status or the legal status of a disputed territory, either explicitly or implicitly.

7. The provisions of Paragraphs 2–6 of this Article shall not prejudice additional Protocols adopted after 1 January 2002, which may apply, exclude or modify the scope of their application in relation to this Article.'

The Conference also recognized the right of a state party to take legitimate measures to maintain or re-establish law and order in accordance with paragraph 4 of amended Art. 1 of the Convention. It encouraged all states parties to deposit as soon as possible their instrument of ratification, acceptance, approval, or accession of the amendment to Art. 1 with the UN Secretary General as Depositary of the Convention.

[76] David Kaye/Steven A. Solomon, 'The Second Review Conference of the 1980 Convention on Certain Conventional Weapons' (2002) 96 *AJIL* 922–36.

[77] Stuart Maslen, *Commentaries on Arms control Treaties, Vol. I, The Convention on the Prohibition of the Use, Stockpiling, Production, and Transfer of Anti-Personnel Mines and on their Destruction* (OUP, 2004), 75.

DIETER FLECK

in any military preparations for such use, and 'to assist, encourage or induce, in any way, anyone to engage in any activity prohibited to a State Party under this Convention'. This prohibition likewise includes any assistance for or encouragement of non-state actors to acquire or use chemical weapons. Article I, para. 5, Chemical WeaponsConv prohibits the of use riot control agents as a method of warfare, as one of the rare provisions that may illustrate different conduct in armed conflict and law enforcement operations (see above, Section 1205, para. 3).

Article 8(2)(e) of the Rome Statute on the International Criminal Court confirms   1211
the existence of rules limiting methods and means of combat in non-international
armed conflicts.

Article 8(2)(e) ICC Statute enumerates twelve serious violations of rules concerning the conduct of hostilities in non-international armed conflicts as 'war crimes'. This list supplements the violations of Article 3 common to the Geneva Conventions which are listed in Article 8(2)(c) ICC Statute. The fact that the application of sub-para. e is expressly limited to 'armed conflicts that take place in the territory of a State when there is protracted armed conflict between governmental authorities and organized armed groups or between such groups' (see sub-para. f, second sentence), does not establish a higher threshold than that of common Article 3 (see above, Section 1201, para. 6(c)).

As confirmed by current customary international humanitarian law, many rules on   1212
means and methods of fighting and protection are likewise applicable in interna-
tional as in non-international armed conflicts.

1. *Current law.* After adoption of AP II, and despite severe controversies during its negotiations (see above Section 1209), practice has lead to the creation of rules parallel to those in AP I, and applicable as customary law to non-international armed conflicts.[78] This applies to the rules on the conduct of hostilities,[79] and the respect for specifically protected persons and property.[80] Customary rules so confirmed may be derived from common sense, as stated by the ICTY in the following terms: 'What is inhumane, and consequently proscribed, in international wars, cannot but be inhumane and inadmissible in civil strife.'[81] Hence an attempt to summarize the law of non-international armed conflicts in an enumerative form remains a questionable undertaking, as any comprehensive list[82] can be understood as excluding the applicability of further rules. Whether intended or not, this would create the wrong perception that in non-international armed conflicts only minimum rules would apply. It may be true that there are often little restraints on the armed engagements of government forces and rebels;[83] but such attitude does not reflect existing law. It also ignores that states still have an interest to maintain the rule of law vis-à-vis rebels, even if today it seems to be more difficult to understand this than for example during the American Civil War, for which the Lieber Code had been adopted. Rebels in turn have an interest in winning support from civilians, which

---

[78] Jean-Marie Henckaerts, 'Study on customary international humanitarian law: A contribution to the understanding and respect for the rule of law in armed conflict' (2005) 87 No. 857 *IRRC* 175–212, at 189.
[79] Rules 1–2, 5–6, 7–24, 46–8, 50, and 52–105 *CIHL*.
[80] Rules 25–45, 55–6, 109–113, 115–129, and 131–8 *CIHL*.
[81] See above, (n. 20), para. 119.
[82] See, e.g., Schmitt/Garraway/Dinstein, above (n. 63).
[83] Antonio Cassese, *International Law*, 2nd edn (OUP, 2005), 430.

DIETER FLECK

could hardly be achieved by denying their protection under international humanitarian law. While a comprehensive approach remains necessary to identify relevant rules, it must concentrate on a full description of rules applicable in all armed conflicts, a comprehensive evaluation of existing differences between international and internal conflicts, and a realistic assessment of special issues of compliance and enforcement.

2. *Human rights influence.* The UN project on 'Fundamental Standards of Humanity'[84] is a significant contribution to evaluating human rights law and international humanitarian law in its application to situations of internal violence. The adoption in 2001 of a General Comment on Article 4 ICCPR with respect to the application of human rights norms in situations of national emergencies[85] and the International Law Commission's Articles on State Responsibility for Internationally Wrongful Acts.[86] It also drew attention to recent rulings of the ICTY and ICTR that have helped to clarify the definition of crimes and contributed to the alignment of international humanitarian law norms applicable in international and non-international armed conflicts.[87] Although final results of this project were not formally adopted, the study may facilitate an assessment of principles of humanitarian protection which apply to all human beings in all situations. It may also contribute to a better understanding of the accountability of armed groups and other non-state actors.

3. *Security Council support.* UN Security Council activities on the protection of civilians in armed conflicts have underlined the need for developing substantial rules including procedural structures and mechanisms for better protection. As civilians must be protected in all armed conflicts, not many differences can be made between international and internal conflicts in this context. Based on reports of the Secretary General,[88] the Security Council has taken first steps to alert political interest, encourage consensus among states, and develop a plan for further action.[89] Closer co-operation between the Office for the Coordination of Humanitarian Affairs (OCHA), the Department of Peacekeeping Operations (DPKO), and the Department of Political Affairs is envisaged,

---

[84] Reports of the Secretary General on Fundamental Standards of Humanity: UN Doc. E/CN.4/1998/87 (5 January 1998); E/CN.4/1999/92 (18 December 1998); E/CN.4/2000/94 (27 December 1999); E/CN.4/2001/91 (12 January 2001); E/CN.4/2002/103 (20 December 2001); see also Report of the Expert Meeting on Fundamental Standards of Humanity (Stockholm, 22–4 February 2000); E/CN.4/2000/145 (4 April 2000); for a critical review in retrospect, see Emily Crawford, 'Road to Nowhere? The Future for a Declaration on Fundamental Standards of Humanity' (14 April 2011) <http://papers.ssrn.com/sol3/papers.cfm?abstract_id=1810151>.

[85] General Comment No. 29 on Article 4 of the International Covenant on Civil and Political Rights (CCPR/C/21/Rev. 1/Add.11).

[86] UN Doc. A/56/10; James Crawford, Alain Pellet, Simon Olleson (eds) *The Law of International Responsibility* (OUP, 2010).

[87] ICTY, *Prosecutor v Kordić and Cerkez*, Judgment of 26 February 2001; *Prosecutor v Krstić*, Judgment of 2 August 2001; *Prosecutor v Delalić et al. (Celebici)*, Judgment of 20 February 2001; *Prosecutor v Kunarac et al.*, Judgment of 22 February 2001; *Prosecutor v Furundzija*, Judgment of 10 December 1998; *Prosecutor v Tadić*, Decision on Defence Motion for Interlocutory Appeal on Jurisdiction of 2 October 1995. See also ICTR, *Prosecutor v Kambanda*, Judgment of 19 October 2000.

[88] Reports of the Secretary General to the Security Council on the protection of civilians in armed conflict (UN Doc. S/1999/957 of 8 September 1999 and S/2001/331 of 30 March 2001); Report of the Secretary General on prevention of armed conflict (UN Doc. A/55/985–S/2001/574 of 7 June 2001).

[89] SC/RES/1265 (1999) and SC/RES/1296(2000), see also Minutes of the 4312th meeting of the Security Council on 23 April 2001 (UN Doc. S/PV.4312 and Resumption 1) and of the 4334th meeting of the Security Council on 21 June 2001 (UN Doc. S/PV.4334 and Resumption 1); Letter dated 21 June 2001 from the President of the Security Council addressed to the Secretary-General (UN Doc. S/2001/614). 4424th meeting of the Security Council on 21 November 2001 (UN Doc. S/PV.4424).

DIETER FLECK

to effectively support these activities. The Security Council has adopted an aide-memoire for addressing issues of protection of civilians in armed conflict on a more systematic and consistent basis.[90]

4. *Support from civil society.* Non-governmental organizations (NGOs) have an important role to play in conflict prevention, conflict resolution, and post-conflict reconstruction.[91] The influence of NGOs has been supported by the courage, devotion, and compassion of individuals and in turn the role of individuals for the implementation and development of international humanitarian law has clearly been increased by NGOs during their activities. This role has been indispensable already in the past and it is challenging states at present and in the foreseeable future.[92]

5. *Prevailing limits.* It must be borne in mind, however, that certain legal distinctions between international and non-international armed conflicts still remain (see below, Sections 1213–1215).

III. Legal Distinction between International and Non-International Armed Conflicts

A distinction between international and non-international armed conflict remains part of the law of armed conflict, most especially in respect of the status of fighters.   **1213**

The right to participate in armed hostilities is generally limited to combatants of a state who meet the requisite elements. Such right may be exercised only by forces sufficiently organized within a system of international accountability to ensure to the maximum extent possible its responsible exercise.   **1214**

In non-international armed conflicts, fighters cannot claim status as prisoners of war upon detention, neither are their actions exempt from criminal prosecution.   **1215**

1. *Treaty law.* There is still a significant distinction between international and internal conflicts in current treaty law. The treaty provisions of international humanitarian law applicable to conflicts between states do not apply to non-international armed conflicts, unless particularly specified.

2. *Customary law.* The progressive development of customary law has not led to a complete amalgamation between rules for international and non-international armed

---

[90] Statement by the President of the Security Council with Annex: Aide Memoire for the consideration of issues pertaining to the protection of civilians in armed conflict, UN Doc. S/PRST/201/25 (22 November 2010).

[91] Carsten Stahn, 'NGOs and International Peacekeeping—Issues, Prospects and Lessons Learned' (2001) 61 *ZaöRV* 379–401.

[92] Fleck, 'Humanitarian Protection Against Non-State Actors', in Jochen Abr. Frowein/Klaus Scharioth/ Ingo Winkelmann/Rüdiger Wolfrum (eds), *Verhandeln für den Frieden/Negotiating for Peace. Liber Amicorum Tono Eitel* (Springer, 2003), 69–94; Fleck, 'The Role of Individuals in International Humanitarian Law and Challenges for States in Its Development', in Michael N. Schmitt & Leslie C. Green (eds), *The Law of Armed Conflict: Into the Next Millennium* (*International Law Studies*, Vol. 71, Newport, RI, 1998), 119–39; Tomuschat, 'The Applicability of Human Rights Law to Insurgent Movements', in H. Fischer/ U. Froissart/W. Heintschel v. Heinegg/C. Raap (eds), *Krisensicherung und Humanitärer Schutz—Crisis Managment and Humanitarian Protection* (Berliner Wissenschafts-Verlag, 2004), 573–91.

DIETER FLECK

conflicts. Specific distinctions still remain. They apply to the status of fighters,[93] public property,[94] the time of release of persons deprived of their liberty,[95] and belligerent reprisals[96] (see below, paras. 3–4).

3. *Specific distinctions.* Prevailing distinctions between the law of international and non-international armed conflict may be described as follows:

a) Status of combatants/fighters. In international armed conflicts combatants enjoy significant protection upon capture, as they are entitled to prisoner-of-war status and may neither be tried for their participation in hostilities nor for acts that do not violate international humanitarian law.[97] Armed opposition groups in a non-international armed conflict cannot claim prisoner-of-war protection for their fighting members,[98] but fundamental procedural principles and safeguards under human rights do apply.

b) Public property. The parties to an international armed conflict may seize military equipment belonging to an adverse party as war booty.[99] In occupied territory, they may take public property that can be used for military operations, without the obligation to compensate the state to which it belongs.[100] In a non-international armed conflict, the seizure of such equipment is not regulated under international law.[101]

c) Release of persons deprived of their liberty. While under the law of international armed conflicts, prisoners of war must be released and repatriated without delay after the cessation of hostilities[102] and civilian internees must be released as soon as the reasons which necessitated internment no longer exist, but at the latest as soon as possible after the close of active hostilities,[103] there is no universal treaty provision on the release of persons deprived of their liberty in non-international armed conflicts. It may be concluded from numerous peace accords and from resolutions of the Security Council and regional organizations that such detainees must be released as soon as the reasons for the deprivation of their liberty cease to exist.[104] A clear regulation will depend on the question, whether an amnesty for participation in hostilities has been proclaimed (see below, Section 1220).

d) Belligerent reprisals. Where not expressly prohibited, parties to an international armed conflict may in extreme cases resort to reprisals, subject to stringent conditions.[105] Parties to an non-international armed conflict do not have the right to resort to belligerent reprisals.[106]

4. *Controversial distinctions.* Certain rules well accepted in international armed conflict may be disputed in internal conflicts.

---

[93] Rules 3–4, 106–8 *CIHL*.
[94] Rules 49 and 51 *CIHL*.
[95] Rule 128 *CIHL*.
[96] Rules 145–8 *CIHL*.
[97] *CIHL*, Vol. I, 384.
[98] Waldemar A. Solf, 'The Status of Combatants in Non-International Armed Conflicts Under Domestic Law and Transnational Practice' (1983) 33 *American University International Law Review* 53.
[99] Rule 49 *CIHL*.
[100] Rule 51 *CIHL*.
[101] *CIHL*, Vol. I, 174.
[102] Art. 118 GC III.
[103] Art. 132, 133 GC IV.
[104] Rule 128 *CIHL*.
[105] Rules 145–147 *CIHL*; see above, Sections 485–8.
[106] Rule 148 *CIHL*.

a) The law of belligerent occupation. As the rules of occupation law have been developed in situations of foreign occupation as a result of a clear and lasting victory, important preconditions for their application are absent in a non-international armed conflict. Yet, essential standards for the protection of civilians and persons *hors de combat* are essentially the same in internal armed conflict.[107] Hence, it would not be correct to deny the applicability of rules of occupational law in non-international armed conflicts altogether.

b) Military objectives. Some have argued that in non-international armed conflicts the notion of 'military objectives' is in effect more limited than in international armed conflicts.[108] This argument is based on US objections against certain aspects of the definition set forth in Article 52, para. 2, AP I. It ignores that the same definition was confirmed for all armed conflicts in Article 2, para. 6, MinesProt and Article 1, lit. f, Prot2CultPropConv, which limits military objectives to those objects which 'by their nature, location, purpose or use make an effective contribution to military action and whose total or partial destruction, capture or neutralization, in the circumstances ruling at the time, offers a definite military advantage'. Different interpretations of this rule are discussed above (Section 401). The US has interpreted it as including objects that contribute to the enemy's 'war-fighting or war sustaining capability', but has referred to the issue solely in the context of international armed conflicts.[109] It should be accepted, however, that similar considerations could become relevant for the conduct of parties to a non-international armed conflict. Hence the more convincing view is that in all armed conflicts a similar interpretation of 'military objectives' should be applied.

IV. Compliance

Armed forces should comply with the rules applicable in international armed conflicts in the conduct of their operations in all armed conflicts; however, such conflicts are characterized (see above, Section 209).   1216

1. The policy rule to comply with the rules of international humanitarian law in the conduct of any armed conflict, irrespective of whether the conflict is characterized as internal or international serves not only humanitarian interests but also operational requirements.[110] The rule avoids confusion on the side of troops and their commanders, as regular armed forces are normally trained for military operations in international armed conflicts and not for law enforcement purposes. Also, the character of an armed conflict is not always clear, sometimes it may even change during operations.

2. The policy to comply with the law of war during all armed conflicts, however such conflicts are characterized, was first stated for the US Forces[111] and for the German

---

[107] Rules 87–105, 112–38 *CIHL*.

[108] Schmitt/Garraway/Dinstein, above (n. 63).

[109] *US Naval Manual*, 402–3: 'Economic targets of the enemy that indirectly but effectively support and sustain the enemy's war fighting capability may also be attacked.' This opinion is controversial in itself, see *San Remo Manual*, 117: 'The Round Table considered whether or not it should include the expression "military action" or some alternative expression such as "war effort" or "war sustaining effort" and eventually decided that these alternative expressions were too broad.'

[110] See above, Section 209, para. 6.

[111] DoD Directive 5100.77 of 10 July 1979, restated in DoD Directive 2311.01E of 9 May 2006, DoD Law of War Program, Section 4.1. See also US Army, Judge Advocate General's Legal Center and School, *Operational Law Handbook* (2011), Chapter 2 III.

DIETER FLECK

Bundeswehr.[112] It was vigorously endorsed by international consensus,[113] and may be considered today as indicating a progressive development of the law. Its quite obvious meaning is not to encourage any disregard for the legal distinction between the two different forms of armed conflict, as they are explained above (Sections 1213–1215), but rather to fully apply the rules related to the conduct of hostilities also in a non-international armed conflict (see above, Section 1204, para. 3). Thus, soldiers are professionally trained to comply with international humanitarian law fully and any misunderstanding as to the applicability of more than rudimentary (or 'minimum') rules in an non-international armed conflict shall be avoided.

1217   **Also unprivileged fighters must be treated humanely.**

1. *Fundamental principle.* Humanitarian protection is essential for all victims of violence. This is underlined by fundamental human rights obligations, as deriving from the ICCPR, as from the ECHR, ACHR, the African Charter on Human and Peoples' Rights or the Arab Charter on Human Rights. These obligations apply also in military operations, unless they are lawfully derogated in cases of emergency (see above, Section 1201, para. 5(b)) or their application is excluded by *lex specialis* rules of humanitarian law (see above, Sections 251–253). Both exceptions are seldom fulfilled in reality. Furthermore, even beyond treaty law, there are fundamental standards of protection which have been generally accepted and must be respected as guidelines for best practice in the treatment of prisoners (see above, Section 704).

2. *Restrictions in a state of emergency.* It is to be deplored that even minimum protection was denied in recent counter-terrorist operations. Fundamental human rights must be respected without exemption. Even in a state of emergency *habeas corpus* may not be completely suspended, although in extreme cases the right to liberty and security may be limited to the effect that in case of arrests or detentions the reasonable time to implement *habeas corpus* may be longer than twenty-four hours.[114] Under existing law detainees do not lose the right of legal protection altogether.

3. *Good governance and effective policy.* In armed conflicts, as in peacetime, humanitarian protection of victims is not only a technical legal issue. It must be considered in broader terms of good governance and effective policy. Long-term perspectives may lead to the introduction of protections which are not strictly required under existing law. If states participating in a multinational operation have taken differing policy decisions in this respect, interoperability problems must be solved (see below, Section 1403). This may include the application of humanitarian law standards by analogy. Unilateral statements to that effect may be made by the detaining power.

---

[112] *German Manual*, Section 211.

[113] International Institute of Humanitarian Law, 'Declaration on the Rules of International Humanitarian Law Governing the Conduct of Hostilities in Non-International Armed Conflicts' (1990) 278 *IRRC* 404–8.

[114] England and Wales Court of Appeal, *Abbasi et al. v Secretary of State for the Foreign and Commonwealth Office* [2002] EWCA Civ. 1598, para. 29. See also IACtHR, *Habeas Corpus in Emergency Situations*, Advisory Opinions OC-8/87 of 30 January 1987, Series A No. 8 (1987), para. 42, and OC-9/87 of 6 October 1987, Series A No. 9 (1987), para. 1: ' "writs of habeas corpus" [. . .] are among those judicial remedies that are essential for the protection of various rights whose derogation is prohibited [. . .] and that they serve, moreover, to preserve legality in a democratic society'. The arguments of the IACtHR, developed in implementation of Article 27 and Article 7 ACHR, are fully applicable to Article 4 ICCPR.

DIETER FLECK

All fighters in non-international armed conflicts must comply with the rules applicable in such conflicts.

1. *Obligation of states and non-state actors.* The law of non-international armed conflicts is not only binding upon states but also upon non-state actors. This principle was first recognized with the adoption of Article 3 common to the Geneva Conventions, which established fundamental rules of humanitarian protection binding all parties to a non-international armed conflict, notwithstanding the fact that the application of these rules shall not affect the legal status of any of them.[115]

2. *Policy considerations.* Many have argued that compliance with the law contributes to effective and efficient conduct of operations, while violations by one side would be likely to encourage reciprocal misconduct by the other side; that harsh and inhumane behaviour will alienate potential allies, both on the domestic and international level; that compliance will facilitate ending the hostilities and promote resolution of the conflict, while misconduct in military operations would frustrate such endeavours; and 'winning the peace' in the long term presupposes national reconciliation which can only come about if the parties believe they can live and work together.[116] Considering the duration of and atrocities committed in many non-international armed conflicts, such assumptions fall deploringly short of existing realities. Neither the parties to the conflict, nor the victims can rely on benevolent considerations. They must take convincing initiatives to make such principles work. Strategies must be developed to engage armed groups on humanitarian issues, to build pressure on relevant groups, and to support them in their capacity as administrative organizations.[117] To do this effectively, states and civil society must take positive action to investigate the root causes for violations of the law, develop incentives for compliance, and ensure respect for its fundamental principles. This also includes the prosecution of war crimes committed in non-international armed conflicts.[118]

3. *The obligation of states.* All states have a legal obligation to respect and ensure respect for international humanitarian law (Common Article 1 GC I–IV; Article 1, para. 1, AP I). The applicability of this provision to non-international armed conflicts, initially denied in 1949,[119] has been subject to a dynamic interpretation during the last decades

---

[115] For an instructive description of the progressive development of binding obligations of non-state actors with respect to humanitarian assistance, see Mary Ellen O'Connell, 'Humanitarian Assistance in Non-International Armed Conflict, The Fourth Wave of Rights, Duties and Remedies' (2002) 31 *IsrYHR* 183–217.

[116] Schmitt/Garraway/Dinstein, above (n. 63).

[117] Olivier Bangerter, 'Reasons why armed groups choose to respect IHL or not' (2011) 93 No. 882 *IRRC* 1–32; Marco Sassòli, 'Taking Armed Groups Seriously: Ways to Improve their Compliance with International Humanitarian Law' (2010) 1 *International Humanitarian Legal Studies* 5–51; Claude Bruderlein, 'The Role of Non-State Actors in Building Human Security: The Case of Armed Groups in Intra-State Wars' (Geneva: Centre for Humanitarian Dialogue, 2000), <https://www.google.de/search?q=Claude+Bruderlein%2C+%E2%80%98The+Role+of+Non-State+Actors+in+Building+Human+Security%3A.+The+Case+of+Armed+Groups+in+Intra-State+Wars%E2%80%99&rlz=1C1AVSX_EnDE406DE410&aq=f&oq=Claude+Bruderlein%2C+%E2%80%98The+Role+of+Non-State+Actors+in+Building+Human+Security%3A.+The+Case+of+Armed+Groups+in+Intra-State+Wars%E2%80%99&aqs=chrome.0.57j60.3113j0&sourceid=chrome&ie=UTF-8>, 10, Sandesh Sivakumaran, 'Binding Armed Opposition Groups', (2006) 55 *ICLQ* 369–94.

[118] Kress, above (n. 36).

[119] Pictet, above, (n. 38); *Commentary* I (1952), Article 1, 28; *Commentary* II (1960), Article 1, 26; *Commentary* III (1960), Article 1, 18; *Commentary* IV (1958), Article 1, 16.

and is now widely accepted.[120] It marks the responsibility of a state for acts committed by its armed forces and other persons and groups acting in fact on its instructions, or under its direction or control,[121] but it also extends to acts of third states, not directly involved in an armed conflict, in their relations to state and non-state parties to the conflict. The modern understanding of existing obligations under Article 1 clearly goes beyond traditional perceptions of national sovereignty, which in the past had strictly excluded any interference in domestic matters of another state. Measures to be taken under this obligation by states together with international organizations and civil society are essential to convince parties of an armed conflict of the advantages of compliance with the law. This calls for an extended spectrum of activities to influence the relevant actors (see below, Chapter 14). In non-international armed conflicts, special agreements between the parties may help to further compliance with international humanitarian law (see above, Section 1207). Unilateral declarations by armed opposition groups may include commitments to international humanitarian law. They may even be requested by the ICRC or other organizations, such as Geneva Call, addressing the party's interest to comply with the law (see above, Section 1201, para. 5). Codes of conduct for armed groups may induce their members to fight according to the rules. An inclusion in cease-fire agreements of commitments to ensure respect for international humanitarian law may not only support observance of those rules that continue to apply after the cessation of hostilities, but remind parties of their obligations if hostilities are renewed. Last but not least, the parties to the conflict must consider offering incentives for compliance. For making such offers states will be in a better position than insurgents, even if recognition of belligerency is not considered as an option (see below, Section 1220).

1219   **Reciprocal compliance with international humanitarian law should be encouraged, but in no case may humanitarian protection be made subject to compliance by the other side.**

1. Due to the asymmetric nature of non-international armed conflicts it is difficult for states to influence the operations of armed opposition groups by setting examples in the interest of reciprocity. Yet, political contacts are essential even while fighting is continued and signals must be given to create and support understanding for the importance of compliance with legal standards of protection. This underlines the importance of civil–military co-operation even during military operations.

2. The obligation to respect and ensure respect for international humanitarian law does not depend on reciprocity.[122] Hence, compliance with international humanitarian law must not be enforced by denying protection to victims.

---

[120] See Frits Kalshoven, 'The Undertaking to Respect and Ensure Respect in All Circumstances: From Tiny Seed to Ripening Fruit' (1999) 2 *YIHL* 3–61, at 54; Birgit Kessler, *Die Durchsetzung der Genfer Abkommen von 1949 in nicht-internationalen bewaffneten Konflikten auf Grundlage ihres gemeinsamen Art. 1*, 132 Veröffentlichungen des Walther-Schücking-Instituts für Internationales Recht an der Universität Kiel (Duncker & Humblot, 2001); Kessler, 'The Duty to "Ensure Respect" Under Common Art. 1 of the Geneva Conventions: Its Implication in International and Non-International Armed Conflicts' (2001) 44 *GYIL*, 498–516.

[121] Rule 139 *CIHL*.

[122] Rule 140 *CIHL*. Bruno Simma, 'Reciprocity', *MPEPIL*, paras. 6 and 8, seems to deny this, questioning the absolute character of human rights and humanitarian obligations. Yet, a difference should be made between 'normative' treaties and 'contract' treaties essentially codifying a *quid pro quo* between two categories of states parties; it should be considered that general participation clauses are no longer part of

3. Parties to an armed conflict must encourage respect for international humanitarian law by the adversary through their own behaviour, thus creating a climate of compliance.

The detaining state must endeavour to grant amnesties for mere participation in hostilities.   1220

1. Article 6, para. 5, AP II provides that '[a]t the end of hostilities, the authorities in power shall endeavour to grant the broadest possible amnesty to persons who have participated in a non-international armed conflict, or those deprived of their liberty for reasons related to the armed conflict, whether they are interned or detained'. Such amnesties should also be possible after conflicts below the threshold set forth in Article 1, para. 1, AP II.[123] The Security Council and competent UN and regional bodies have encouraged and many states have granted such amnesty to members of armed opposition groups.[124] During the conflict and even after the end of hostilities it may be difficult if not impossible to balance competing interests in achieving or denying amnesties. Yet, without a clear perspective for their own individual treatment as detainees, fighters will hardly adapt their conduct to humanitarian principles and rules.[125]

2. As amnesties are related to the mere participation in hostilities, they apply to certain offences under domestic law connected with such participation, but not to war crimes and crimes against humanity. An amnesty which would not observe this principle would hardly help to stabilize a post-conflict situation.

V. Termination of Hostilities

The termination of hostilities in non-international armed conflicts is often a complex process in which rules of international humanitarian law continue to exist and may influence post-conflict peacebuilding (see above, Section 223).   1221

1. As in international armed conflicts, the termination of hostilities between armed opposition groups and the government or between various armed groups requires more than a mere cessation of hostilities. While factual fighting may be brought to an end with the intensity of violence falling below the threshold of protracted armed confrontation (see above, Section 1201, para. 6) or even terminating armed activities temporarily or permanently, this does not automatically mark the end of the state of armed conflict. Parties may not find themselves in agreement on whether and under which terms the hostilities have been brought to an end. There may be continuing mistrust and there may be fighting and peaceful co-operation going on at the same time.

2. Unlike the beginning of an armed conflict which often challenges other states, the Security Council, the ICRC, or other international organizations to formally react on its existence, its termination in practice is often left to the parties themselves. Formal

---

international humanitarian law; and the potential impact of behaviour should not be confused with the existence of a legal obligation.

[123] See above, Section 1201, para. 5, lit. c.
[124] Rule 159 *CIHL*; Vol. I *CIHL*, 611–14; Vol. II/2 *CIHL*, 4017–44.
[125] Fleck, 'International Humanitarian Law After September 11: Challenges and the Need to Respond', 6–2003 *YIHL*, 41–71, at 65–7.

DIETER FLECK

agreements to end a non-international armed conflict are rather rare[126] and if concluded, as recently in the case of Sudan,[127] a continuation of fighting is a frequent phenomenon. A recent research project dealing with the matter concluded that international law contains no rule as to how long the cessation of hostilities needs to last for an armed conflict to be considered legally at the end.[128]

3. While it may be difficult to identify a clear point in time when an armed conflict has ended, for practical purposes such definition may not be desirable, as important principles of international humanitarian law continue to apply even after the end of hostilities and it is essential for parties to the (former) conflict, to communicate with each other, establish working relationships between each other, and improve the living conditions of the victimized population.

---

[126] Christine Bell, *On the Law of Peace: Peace Agreements and the Lex Pacificatoria* (OUP, 2008); Bell, *Peace Agreements and Human Rights* (OUP, 2000).

[127] See above, Section 1301, (n. 21).

[128] ILA Committee on the Use of Force, 'Final Report on the Meaning of Armed Conflict in International Law', ILA (ed.), *Report of the Seventy-Fourth Conference* (The Hague, 2010), 676–721, at 712.

DIETER FLECK

13

THE LAW OF INTERNATIONAL
PEACE OPERATIONS

I. General

International peace operations comprise all peacekeeping operations and peace   1301
enforcement operations conducted in support of diplomatic efforts to establish and
maintain peace. The modern concept of peace operations goes beyond traditional
peacekeeping, as it combines elements of peacekeeping with peacemaking and
peacebuilding.

1. *Introduction.* The international community is engaged worldwide in operations in
which armed forces and other governmental agencies, such as police are deployed to
establish, maintain, and secure peace. A clear distinction could be made between operations led by the United Nations and missions led by regional or sub-regional organizations. Most of the operations today are deployed with complex mandates to support
national authorities to rebuild a nation after often lengthy periods of conflict. Peace
operations are mandated to assist in providing security and public order to host populations but also to support the introduction or restoration of basic essential services, such
as governmental structure in which democratic representation take place, an independent, impartial justice delivery system, and to help begin to tackle the root causes of
conflict essential in achieving sustainable peace and development.[1]

2. *Peace operations, historical development.* Peacekeeping is a technique pioneered and
developed by the United Nations that defies simple definition. It is based on the principle
that an impartial presence of multinational troops on the ground can ease tensions and
allow negotiated solutions in a conflict situation. Peacekeepers have patrolled buffer
zones between hostile parties, monitored ceasefires and helped defuse local conflicts,
allowing the search for durable, political settlements to continue. Lightly armed troops
or unarmed military observers from around the world were sent to observe ceasefire
agreements. The 'entry strategy' and decisions leading to deployment was straightforward: war, ceasefire, invitation to monitor ceasefire compliance and deployment of military observers or units to do so, while efforts continued for a political settlement.

3. *United Nations peace operations, period 1948–1988.* In May 1948, the Security Council
decided to establish a field operation to assist the United Nations Mediator and the
Truce Commission in supervising the observance of the truce in Palestine. Two weeks

---

[1] See T. D. Gill and D. Fleck, *The Handbook of the International Law of Military Operations* (OUP, 2010).
For an overview of national peacekeeping practices and legal implications, see the General Report and
Recommendations on 'The Rule of Law in Peace Operations' (2006) XVII *Recueils de la Société de Droit
Militaire et de Droit de la Guerre*, Scheveningen Congress 108–57, 416–7.

later, an initial group of 36 unarmed military observers arrived in the Middle East as the first United Nations peacekeepers establishing UNTSO.[2] Soon after, the conflict between India and Pakistan over Kashmir led to the establishment of UNMOGIP[3] with functions of monitoring ceasefires and reporting on the situation. UNEF I[4] was the first armed mission and the first to be labelled peacekeeping. Until 1988, missions were established usually in a stable environment with limited means and a limited mandate, maintaining a neutral position and essentially with the sole function of monitoring the situation. Peacekeepers were not authorized to use force to fulfil their mandate; force was only to be used in self-defence. An important exception was the 1961 intervention in Congo. ONUC[5] had been the largest operation until the 1990s. It was the first intervention under conditions of violent civil conflict and the first case of peacekeeping combined with peace enforcement, authorized by the UN Security Council. Because of the violence involved, and the ambiguity concerning the mandate of the operation, for a long time ONUC was also an example of how peacekeeping should not work. All subsequent missions were limited in number and scope, and no new operation was established between 1978 and 1988.

4. *United Nations peace operations (1989–2003).* With the end of the Cold War, the Security Council looked to UN peacekeeping as the instrument of choice for international conflict management. UN peacekeeping successfully transformed itself into a mechanism for not only observing ceasefire agreements, but also for implementing comprehensive peace agreements.[6] In Namibia, El Salvador, and Mozambique, this newly retooled instrument of UN peacekeeping was quite successful. In these more complex and dangerous missions, peacekeepers were regularly authorized to use force in the context of their mandate. The humanitarian mission in Northern Iraq[7] was the first mission authorized to use force, not as a measure of peace enforcement but to guarantee the protection of the population and the delivery of assistance. Traditional UN peacekeeping operations have shifted in the course of an evolving conflict from Chapter VI to Chapter VII, such as the case of Somalia.[8]

---

[2] United Nations Truce Supervision Organization, SC Res. 50 (1948), 29 May 1948. Since then, UNTSO has performed various tasks, including the supervision of the General Armistice Agreement of 1949 and the observation of the ceasefire in the Suez Canal area and the Golan Heights following the Arab–Israeli War of June 1967.

[3] United Nations Military Observer Group in India and Pakistan, SC Res. 91 (1951), 20 March 1951.

[4] United Nations Emergency Force, SC Res. 118 (1956) of 13 October 1956, established to monitor the withdrawal of British, French, and Israeli forces from the Suez Canal. Peacekeeping missions were generally composed of small military contingents, lightly armed, from contributions of many different, mostly neutral or non-aligned countries, following principles of balanced geographic distribution.

[5] United Nations Operation in Congo, SC Res. 143 (1960) of 17 July 1960.

[6] Namibia, El Salvador and Mozambique, Cambodia. <http://www.un.org/Depts/dpko/dpko/intro/1.htm>.

[7] SC Res. 688 (1991) of 5 April 1991.

[8] United Nations Operation in Somalia (UNOSOM I) was established as a humanitarian relief operation by SC Res. 751 (1992) of 21 April 1992. The Security Council welcomed the US offer to help create a secure environment for the delivery of humanitarian aid in Somalia and authorized, under Chapter VII, the use of 'all necessary means' to do so. President George H. Bush responded to the resolution with a decision to initiate *Operation Restore Hope*, under which the US would assume the unified command UNITAF/Restore Hope, SC Res. 794 (1992) of 3 December 1992. Following a transition period, UNOSOM II was established under Chapter VII, SC Res. 814 (1993) of 26 March 1993.

BEN F. KLAPPE

5. *United Nations peace operations (2004–2006)*. In 2004–2006, nine UN peace operations have been launched or expanded: Burundi (ONUB), Côte d'Ivoire (UNOCI), the Democratic Republic of Congo (MONUC), Haiti (MINUSTAH), Iraq (UNMI), Lebanon (UNIFIL), Liberia (UNMIL), Sudan (UNMIS) and Timor Leste (UNMIT), while four have drawn-down or closed: Burundi (ONUB), Kosovo (UNMIK), Sierra Leone (UNAMSIL), and, in the context of the previous UN peacekeeping operation in that country, Timor Leste (UNMISET).[9] The UN Secretariat has been further tasked to undertake assessments and, in some cases, preplanning, for potential future operations in the Central African Republic, Chad, Darfur, and Nepal. In parallel, the Department of Peacekeeping Operations has increased its administrative and logistics support to special political missions managed by the Department of Political Affairs, and was supporting fifteen such field operations. DPKO became increasingly engaged in assisting regional actors to develop their peacekeeping capabilities, in particular providing substantial support to the African Union's mission in Sudan (AMIS) and the African Union's mission in Somalia (AMISOM). As 2006 drew to a close, more than 100,000 men and women were deployed in eighteen peace operations around the world, of which approximately 82,000 were troops, police, and military observers provided by 115 contributing countries.[10] This adds up to a broad range of mandated tasks, each of which demands appropriate—and often significant—focus, expertise, and resources in the field and in headquarters. It also demands a much higher degree of mission integration at every level and phase. Such expanded activity takes place in environments that are often volatile and insecure and where, despite the establishment of a peace agreement, the presence of UN peacekeepers may be resisted by factions and armed groups that remain outside of a peace process. In these unstable contexts, UN field missions are required to operate at high levels of sensitivity and risk, complicating the implementation of complex tasks and engagement with those local populations most in need of support. Even where political and security conditions are favourable, the operational challenges for peace operations are daunting.[11]

6. *United Nations peace operations (2007–2012)*. From 2007 to May 2012, in total five new UN peace operations have been launched: three were launched[12] and one concluded[13] in Sudan, one was launched and concluded in Chad and the Central African Republic,[14] and one was launched in Syria.[15] In the Democratic Republic of Congo, MONUC transformed into a stability mission.[16] Peacekeepers withdrew from Eritrea

---

[9] UN Doc. A/61/668, 13 February 2007, Report of the Secretary General, Implementation of the recommendations of the Special Committee on Peacekeeping Operations, para. 7.

[10] Ibid. para. 6.

[11] The modern peacekeeping environment is often remote and difficult, with little infrastructure or communications. The largest UN peacekeeping operation, the mission in the Democratic Republic of Congo (MONUSCO) is deployed in a country the size of Western Europe that has only 300 miles of paved road. Most UN field missions face practical challenges, such as limited or severely weakened local markets for goods and services, lack of housing stock, potable water, or sufficient fresh-food supply. The logistic and supply challenges facing many missions make deployment a highly complex issue.

[12] African Union–United Nations Hybrid Operation in Darfur (UNAMID) 2007, United Nations Organization Interim Security Force Abyei (UNISFA) 2011, United Nations Mission in the Republic of South Sudan (UNMISS) 2011.

[13] UNMIS 2011.

[14] MINURCAT in 2007 and concluded in 2010.

[15] UNSMIS United Nations Supervision Mission in Syria.

[16] MONUSCO.

and Ethiopia in 2008 after UNMEE had monitored the tense border between the two countries for seven-and-a-half years after restrictions placed on it by Eritrea undermined its ability to carry out its mandate.[17] The Observer Mission in Georgia concluded in 2009. The newest addition to field operations in 2009 was the UN Support Office for AMISOM (African Union Mission in Somalia). UNSOA is a unique operation in that it is removed from the theatre, and headquartered in Kenya.[18] UNSOA is mandated to deliver a support package to AMISOM similar to that of a traditional UN peacekeeping mission. In 2009, there were just over 5,000 troops from Burundi and Uganda in AMISOM. UNSOA's logistical support is an element of the UN's three-phase plan in Somalia—to strengthen the Transitional Federal government's security sector, to create a 'light footprint' for the UN, and when conditions allow, to transition from AMISOM to a UN peacekeeping operation, pending Security Council approval.[19] In July 2007, the Department of Peacekeeping Operations was restructured into two separate departments: DPKO focuses on providing strategic direction, management, and guidance to peacekeeping operations, while the new Department for Field Support (DFS) is to provide operational support and expertise in the areas of personnel, finance and budget, and communications.[20] One of the key innovations within the DPKO in 2007 has been the creation of the Office of Rule of Law and Security Institutions (OROLSI), which is to provide an integrated and forward-looking approach to UN assistance in the area of rule of law and security. Established by the General Assembly as part of the Secretary General's wider reform of peacekeeping, the new pillar brings together a wide range of DPKO entities: the police division; judicial, legal and correctional units; mine action; disarmament, demobilization and reintegration (DDR), as well as security sector reform (SSR) functions. It builds on key reform recommendations from the Brahimi Report of 2000, emphasizing the significance of the rule of law for sustainable peace and security.[21]

7. *Regional- and sub-regional-based organizations.* Since the mid-1990s, there has been a trend towards a variety of regional- and sub-regional-based peacekeeping missions.[22] This trend holds the promise of developing regional capacity to address shortfalls in the numbers of peacekeepers, and it should augment and not detract from the ability of the United Nations to respond when blue helmets are requested. This poses a challenge for the Security Council and regional organizations to work closely with each other and mutually support each other's efforts to keep the peace and ensure that regional operations are accountable to universally accepted human rights standards. Regional and other partners that have collaborated politically or co-deployed with United Nations peacekeeping operations include the African Union in Burundi, Ethiopia, and Eritrea; the Democratic Republic of the Congo and the Sudan; the Economic Community of West African States (ECOWAS) in Côte d'Ivoire, Sierra Leone and Liberia; the European Union in Bosnia-Herzegovina, the Former Yugoslav Republic of Macedonia; and the Democratic Republic of the Congo, performing a variety of tasks, from law enforcement and ceasefire monitoring to security

[17] United Nations Peace Operations, Year in Review 2008, 3.
[18] United Nations Peace Operations, Year in Review 2009, 37.
[19] Ibid. 38.
[20] United Nations Peace Operations, Year in Review 2007, 4.
[21] Ibid. 30.
[22] This role is envisaged in Chapter VIII of the UN Charter.

BEN F. KLAPPE

and humanitarian crisis management; the Commonwealth of Independent States and OSCE in Georgia; the North Atlantic Treaty Organization in Bosnia-Herzegovina and Kosovo;[23] and currently leading the International Security Assistance Force (ISAF) in Afghanistan.[24] NATO concluded its training activities in Iraq in 2011 and is providing assistance to the AU Mission in Somalia and capacity-building support to its long-term peacekeeping capabilities, in particular the African Standby Force. NATO also provided support to the AU Mission in Sudan, at the request of the AU, from mid-2005 to end 2007. Furthermore, operational co-operation has taken place in many diverse ways. In some cases, such as in Liberia in 2003, a transition took place from a regional operation—in that case ECOWAS—to a United Nations operation. In other contexts, such as Kosovo or the Democratic Republic of the Congo, coordinated separate operations took place side by side. In Haiti, OAS has provided support within the context of a United Nations-led mission. In Darfur, ongoing United Nations/African Union peacekeeping co-operation has taken a new dimension in the context of United Nations support for an African Union-led operation, the African Union Mission in the Sudan (AMIS). The Security Council expressed its determination[25] to take appropriate steps to the further development of co-operation between the United Nations and regional and sub-regional organizations in maintaining international peace and security. The resolution reflects the growth of interaction between the United Nations and partner organizations. This includes annual high-level meetings of the UN Secretary General with regional and other intergovernmental organizations, along with recent meetings of the Security Council with regional organizations. The opportunities lie in the establishment of a more effective partnership operating in close co-operation with the Security Council, based on a clear division of labour that reflects the comparative advantage of each organization.

8. *Peace enforcement.* Peace enforcement operations in principle lack consent of states involved and are based on a strong Chapter VII mandate addressing serious human rights violations and threats against international peace and security of a certain state. Enforcement operations are usually conducted by a multinational force and as a rule commanded by a lead-nation. Examples include Korea (1950) carried out by a group of states on the invitation of the state concerned, and Kuwait (1990),[26] authorized by the Security Council. A distinction could be made between full-scale enforcement operations (a factual armed conflict situation between the coalition of the willing and a state)

---

[23] SC Res. 1244 (1999) of 10 June 1999, 'Acting under Chapter VII, Decides on the deployment in Kosovo, under United Nations auspices, of international civil and security presences, with appropriate equipment and personnel as required, and welcomes the agreement of the Federal Republic of Yugoslavia to such presences; authorizes Member States and relevant international organizations to establish the international security presence in Kosovo [. . .] with all necessary means to fulfil its responsibilities [. . .].'

[24] SC Res. 1386 (2001) of 20 December 2001, to assist the Afghan Interim Authority in the maintenance and security in Kabul and its surrounding areas so that the Afghan Interim Authority as well as personnel of the UN can operate in a secure environment.

[25] SC Res. 1631 (2005) of 17 October 2005.

[26] Operation Desert Storm (Second Gulf War; coalition forces led by US), SC Res. 661 (1990) of 6 August 1990 and SC Res. 678 (1990) of 29 November 1990. The Security Council first made reference to 'the inherent right of individual or collective self-defence, in response to the armed attack by Iraq on Kuwait' later authorized 'Member States cooperating with the Government of Kuwait . . . to use all necessary means to uphold and implement resolution 660 (1990) and all subsequent relevant resolutions and to restore international peace and security in the area', acting under Chapter VII. This construction, combining elements of self-defence and collective security, can be interpreted as the exercise of collective self-defence under the authorization of the Security Council, or as an enforcement action under Article 42 of the Charter.

BEN F. KLAPPE

and relatively small-scale actions to enforce peace during a UN-led peacekeeping operation. Such enforcement actions are sometimes necessary to protect the mission or to protect civilians under imminent threat of physical violence. In the Democratic Republic of Congo, robust UN military operations based on Chapter VII, including cordon and search operations and pre-emptive action against militias, illustrate the intertwining of peacekeeping and peace-enforcing.

1302   Deployments in peace operations should be negotiated with the receiving state.

This would naturally flow from the consensual character of peace operations. Ultimately, receiving states have a final say as to what countries, units, and equipment enter the territory. Where assistance is solicited, the host state is in a position to determine the terms and conditions of the personnel it will receive. During negotiations on the status of mission agreement between the international or regional organization/contributing states and the host state, sensitive issues need to be disclosed, discussed, and cleared.[27] Whether and to what extent this host state consent entails the consequence that the military operation cannot be considered as an enforcement action is difficult to decide. An authorization to unilateral use of force may constitute an enforcement action even where the host state has consented to this use.

1303   At all times the functional immunity of military and civilian personnel of a sending state must be observed.

The Convention on the Privileges and Immunities of the United Nations of 1946 is the agreement that provides legal status to the United Nations and its subsidiary bodies. The Convention provides certain privileges and immunities to the United Nations and its officials for the fulfilment of the organization's purpose and to allow its personnel to conduct their official duties without interference. Such provisions are to be specified in any agreement the United Nations concludes with the country regarding its hosting of a peace operation.

1304   Immunities and privileges of peacekeepers solely apply to the performance of their mission in the receiving state and in transit states. They do not exclude or limit individual and collective responsibilities for wrongful acts.

1. This notion is referred to as 'functional immunity' for acts that form part of the official duties. For all other actions, peacekeepers can be prosecuted under both civil and criminal law in the host country. For military members of contingents troop-contributing countries usually retain exclusive criminal jurisdiction. Military members of a contingent who commit a crime must be repatriated to their own country and undergo judicial process there; they cannot be tried in the host country. Such an exception to host-country criminal jurisdiction applies not to military observers, police officers, or civilian staff of a peace operation. The Secretary General has the right and the obligation to waive even the functional immunity of United Nations personnel if such immunity impedes the course of justice. Therefore, respect for the law of the host country is an essential obligation of all peacekeepers. The relevant status of mission or forces agree-

---

[27] See also Michael Bothe/Thomas Dörschel in Fleck (ed.), *The Handbook of the Law of Visiting Forces* (OUP, 2001), 491.

BEN F. KLAPPE

ment (SOMA or SOFA) includes the obligations of United Nations personnel to respect the law of the country where they are deployed.

2. Following allegations of misconduct by UN peacekeepers in 2004, the United Nations released a report entitled 'A comprehensive strategy to eliminate future sexual exploitation and abuse in United Nations peacekeeping operations'.[28] In formulating recommendations, the drafter drew on extensive consultations with representatives of troop and police contributing countries that provide the most military and police personnel and the Secretariat as well as insights from a visit to the United Nations peacekeeping operation in the Democratic Republic of Congo in late 2004. *First*, the report recommends that rules against sexual exploitation and abuse be unified for all categories of peacekeeping personnel so that civilian, civilian police, and military personnel are all held to the same standard. This would involve amending the current Memorandum of Understanding between the UN and troop- and police-contributing countries. *Second*, it recommends establishment of a professional investigative capacity staffed by experts who have experience in investigating sex crimes, particularly those involving young children. This would entail having access to modern techniques of forensic identification (e.g. fibre analysis and DNA testing). *Third*, it recommends a series of organizational, managerial, and command measures to address sexual exploitation and abuse. For instance, it proposes improving welfare and recreational facilities to off-set increased restrictions on peoples' personal lives such as curfews and wearing of military uniforms at all times. It also proposes recovering from member states the 'troop costs' for soldiers and commanders found to have engaged in sexual exploitation and abuse and to pay that money into a trust fund for victims. A similar provision is proposed for civilians. *Last*, it makes a number of recommendations to ensure that peacekeeping personnel who commit acts of sexual exploitation and abuse are held:

— individually accountable through appropriate disciplinary action. For instance, there is a recommendation for expedited disciplinary procedures for sexual exploitation and abuse cases involving civilians;
— financially accountable for the harm they have done to victims. For instance, it proposes that existing rules be amended to compel civilians to make child support payments; and
— criminally accountable if the acts of sexual exploitation and abuse committed by them constitute crimes under applicable law.

3. A group of legal experts[29] has made a number of recommendations that are designed to overcome the obstacles that exist in holding UN peacekeeping personnel accountable for crimes committed during peacekeeping operations. The group recommends that priority be given by the UN to facilitating the exercise of jurisdiction by the host state. The UN should not readily assume that the host state is unable to exercise jurisdiction merely because a peacekeeping operation is carried out in a post-conflict area. If the host state is unable, even with UN assistance, to exercise all aspects of criminal jurisdiction, there

---

[28] Report of the Secretary General's adviser on sexual exploitation and abuse by UN peacekeeping personnel, HRH Prince Zeid Ra'ad Zeid Al-Hussein, Permanent Representative of Jordan (UN Doc. A/59/710 of 24 March 2005).

[29] UN Doc. A/60/980 of 17 August 2006, Report of the Group of Legal Experts on ensuring the accountability of UN staff and experts on mission with respect to criminal acts committed in peacekeeping operations.

BEN F. KLAPPE

will be a need to rely on other states to do so. However, even in these circumstances, the host state may be able to provide some assistance to enable the exercise of criminal jurisdiction by another state, including by gathering evidence or arresting alleged offenders. Jurisdiction is not an indivisible concept and the host state and other states may be involved in different but mutually supportive aspects of the overall exercise of criminal jurisdiction. The exercise of jurisdiction by states other than the host state presents many challenges that are not unique to the peacekeeping environment. These include the extradition of persons and securing admissible evidence for use in another jurisdiction. To provide a sound legal basis for the exercise of jurisdiction by states other than the host state, the group recommends the development of a new international convention to address jurisdiction and related issues. Administrative investigations conducted by the UN for disciplinary purposes may be relevant to holding a person criminally accountable as they may be the only means of gathering evidence of the alleged crime. UN administrative investigators therefore need to be cognizant of the fact that the material they collect may be used to support not only disciplinary action but also criminal proceedings. The group makes a number of recommendations designed to ensure that administrative investigations are carried out to the highest possible standard.

II. Applicable Law

1305

In peace operations today, a complex legal regime comprising peacetime rules of international law, international humanitarian law, and national law must be adhered to and properly implemented.

1. Peace operations will derive their legitimacy from the authority of the Security Council. In establishing a peace operation, the Security Council follows the Charter of the United Nations, exercising its primary responsibility for maintaining international peace and security. The fundamental legitimacy of a peace operation ensures that it commands the respect and support of all member states in implementing its mandate. International legitimacy and recognition is all-important for the day-to-day work of peacekeepers. Member states contribute personnel, equipment, and other resources to a peace operation because of its legitimacy. Furthermore, legitimacy confers a privileged legal status on a peace operation and its personnel that is essential in implementing its mandate.

2. The rules of engagement[30] for the operation, which form the legal authority for the use of force, specify how and when peacekeepers are authorized to use force, including deadly force. Other international legal instruments and norms guide the activities of peacekeepers and define the relationship between the operation and the host country. Altogether the apparatus of authority and law composes the legal framework for peace operations. All peacekeepers must have a sound understanding of the legal framework of their operation so that they know their own obligations and responsibilities in the implementation of their mandate. Legal norms must be considered in the conduct of their official duties as well as their personal life. In fulfilling their duties, peacekeepers also need to be aware of other legal agreements, including the peace agreement or ceasefire

---

[30] See below, Sections 1316–33.

agreement if such exists, other national laws, and international treaties and conventions that can guide their activities in support of the peace process.

> **Where peace operations are mandated by the Security Council in accordance with**   1306
> **Chapter VI or VII of the UN Charter, or by a regional arrangement under Chapter**
> **VIII, participating states will operate on the basis of relevant international resolu-**
> **tions. These resolutions may flow from ceasefire agreements, peace agreements,[31] and**
> **assessments and reports such as those from the UN Secretary General.**

The United Nations Secretary General reports frequently to the Security Council. In 2006, more than one hundred reports were sent to the Security Council. An example of the latter is the Report of the Secretary General on the situation in Afghanistan and its implications for international peace and security.[32] The report reviews the activities of the United Nations Assistance Mission in Afghanistan with a view to extend the mission. Such a report will usually contain an assessment of the current security situation, including the security institutions and the international military assistance, political developments, including governance at national regional and local levels. It furthermore assesses human rights, rule of law developments, and economic and social developments. In the case of Afghanistan, separate paragraphs are reserved for counter-narcotics, the Joint Coordination and Monitoring Board[33] and the Afghanistan Compact.[34]

> **In peace operations, the significance of human rights obligations may be seen**   1307
> **under three different aspects:**
> **— Ideally, there would be an express mandate by the Security Council and/or a**
> **regional organization requesting not only all parties to the conflict, but also the**
> **peacekeeping force to protect human rights.**

[31] An example is an excerpt of the Agreements and Protocols related to the peace process in Sudan. An overview and the full texts are available online at <http://www.c-r.org/our-work/accord>. N'Djamena Humanitarian Ceasefire Agreement on the Conflict in Darfur between the Government of Sudan, the SLM/A and the JEM, N'Djamena, 8 April 2004; Protocol between the Government of Sudan and the SPLM/A on the Resolution of Conflict in Southern Kordofan/Nuba Mountains and Blue Nile States, Naivasha, 26 May 2004; Protocol between the Government of Sudan and the SPLM/A on the Resolution of the Abyei Conflict, Naivasha, 26 May 2004; Protocol on Power Sharing between the Government of the Sudan and the SPLM/A, Naivasha, 26 May 2004; Agreement on Permanent Ceasefire and Security Arrangements Implementation Modalities during the Pre-Interim and Interim Periods between the Government of the Sudan and the SPLM/A, Naivasha, 31 December 2004; The Comprehensive Peace Agreement between the Government of the Sudan and the SPLM/A, Naivasha, 9 January 2005; *Cairo Peace Agreement* with the National Democratic Alliance (16 June 2005), <http://www.goss-brussels.com/agreements/gov_south/cairo_agreement_between_gos_nda.pdf>; Darfur Peace Agreement between the Government of Sudan and the Sudan People's Liberation Movement/Army (SLM/A) and the Justice and Equality Movement, Abuja, 5 May 2006, <http://www.globalsecurity.org/military/world/para/darfur.htm>, <http://www.reliefweb.int/rw/RWB.NSF/db900SID/EVIU-6AZBDB?OpenDocument>; Declaration of Principles for the Resolution of the Conflict in Eastern Sudan between the Government of Sudan and the Eastern Front, Asmara, 19 June 2006; Eastern Sudan Peace Agreement between the Government of Sudan and the Eastern Front, Asmara, 14 October 2006, <http://www.sd.undp.org/doc/Eastern_States_Peace_Agreement.pdf>.

[32] UN Doc. A/61/799-S/2007/152 of 15 March 2007.

[33] See *supra* (n. 22), at 14, Principal mechanism for facilitating co-operation between the Government of Afghanistan and the international community under the Afghanistan Compact.

[34] The Compact is the result of consultation between the Government of Afghanistan, the UN and the international community, and represents a framework for co-operation for the next five years. The agreement affirms the commitment of the Government of Afghanistan and the international community to work towards conditions where the Afghan people can live in peace and security under the rule of law, with good governance and human rights protection for all, and can enjoy sustainable economic and social development. The Compact follows the formal end of the Bonn Process in September 2005, with completion of the parliamentary and provincial elections. The Compact was launched on 31 January 2006 (<http://www.fco.gov.uk>).

BEN F. KLAPPE

— Even where such commitment has not been expressly stated, peace operations are to respect the law of the receiving state including its obligations under international law of which human rights are an important part.
— Finally, the human rights obligations of the sending state apply extraterritorially for acts committed within their jurisdiction (see above, Section 245).

1. *Human rights in peace operations.* As large-scale human rights violations are both a root cause as well as an outcome of many modern conflicts, addressing human rights issues has become an integral part of UN-led or UN-mandated peace operations. Depending on the mandate of a peace operation, human rights work may include:

— reporting human rights violations and working to prevent future abuse;
— investigating and verifying past human rights violations;
— promoting and protecting civil, cultural, economic, political, and social rights;
— conducting capacity-building initiatives with local governmental agencies and non-governmental organizations (NGOs), including national and local human rights institutions;
— assisting relevant judicial and truth and reconciliation processes to foster a culture of accountability and address impunity;
— collaborating with UN and international development and emergency relief organizations on human rights issues;
— designing and conducting human rights training programmes for UN peacekeeping personnel and local and national institutions, such as the military and police forces;
— providing advice and guidance on human rights to all peacekeeping components;
— working to address the human rights aspects of problems associated with most modern conflicts, including massive movements of refugees and internally displaced persons (IDPs), the increasing conscription of child soldiers, and the sexual exploitation and trafficking of women and children; and
— identifying and integrating a human rights perspective into programmes to disarm, demobilize, and reintegrate combatants.[35]

2. *Human rights component.* Peace operations have addressed human rights issues by including a human rights component[36] in operations. A memorandum of understanding (MoU)[37] may govern how human rights components function within peacekeeping operations. The MoU provides, among other things, for dual reporting lines to both the Special Representative to the Secretary General and the Office of the High Commissioner for Human Rights and joint responsibilities for the recruitment of human rights officers for peacekeeping operations. Although the human rights component has the lead role on human rights issues in a peacekeeping operation, human rights work is everyone's responsibility. All peacekeeping personnel should be aware of human rights

---

[35] See Chapter VII, UN Handbook on Multidimensional Peacekeeping Operations (2005), <http://www.peacekeepingbestpractices.unlb.org/Pbps/library/Handbook%20on%20UN%20PKOs.pdf>.

[36] The human rights component would normally act under the authority of the Special Representative of the Secretary General (SRSG) who can also provide guidance on how to most effectively pursue a human rights agenda within the particular circumstances of a mission.

[37] See for example the MoU concluded between the Department of Peacekeeping Operations (DPKO) and the Office of the United Nations High Commissioner for Human Rights (OHCHR), November 2002.

BEN F. KLAPPE

issues and, through their work and conduct, be ready to promote human rights values with their colleagues and counterparts in the host society. Human rights information and analysis should systematically inform the mission's strategic thinking and policymaking at all levels. The early involvement of human rights experts in the planning of human rights activities of peacekeeping operations can contribute to the effectiveness and full integration of such activities within the mission, as well as to their sustainability after the withdrawal of the mission. Specifically, the inclusion of human rights experts in an integrated mission task force (IMTF), which is established at UN Headquarters for the planning of future missions, is essential. Similarly, the early deployment of human rights officers in the first phase of mission deployment is important.

3. *International standards and codes of conduct.* International humanitarian organizations and other actors, when providing assistance, should give due regard to the protection needs and human rights of internally displaced persons and take appropriate measures in this regard.[38] In so doing, these organizations and actors should respect relevant international standards and codes of conduct. The need for military forces conducting humanitarian or military operations outside their own countries to respect human rights standards is strengthened by the possibility that increasingly they may be subject to national and regional human rights scrutiny in respect of their conduct. Increasingly, courts in a number of countries are showing a willingness to exercise jurisdiction over actions which occurred outside their territory but which have a connection with it. Human rights provisions should be reflected in the rules of engagement and codes of conduct of military forces engaged in providing forms of humanitarian assistance.

4. *International versus state responsibility in case of alleged human rights violations by peace-keepers.* Two cases involving NATO peacekeepers in Kosovo were declared inadmissible by the European Court of Human Rights. The first case involved two Kosovar brothers who found a number of undetonated cluster bombs.[39] While playing, one bomb detonated and killed one and seriously injuring wounding the other. The applicants (the surviving brother and his father) alleged that the death and injuries were caused by the failure of French KFOR troops to mark and/or defuse the undetonated cluster bombs which KFOR had known to be present on the side in question. They referred on the right to life under Article 2 ECHR. In the second case,[40] the applicant complained under Article 5 (right to liberty and security) and Article 13 (right to an effective remedy) about his detention by KFOR. He further complained under Article 6 (right to fair trial) and under Article 1 (obligation to respect human rights) that France, Germany, and Norway had failed to guarantee the Convention rights of individuals living in Kosovo. The Court considered whether it was competent to review the acts of the states in question carried out on behalf of the UN and, more generally, as to the relationship between the Convention and the UN acting under Chapter VII of its Charter. The Court argued that Chapter VII allowed the Security Council to adopt coercive measures in relation to an identified conflict considered to threaten peace, in case UN SC Res. 1244, establishing UNMIK and KFOR. The Court further found that since operations established under

---

[38] 1998 Guiding Principles on Internal Displacement.

[39] ECtHR, *Behrami and Behrami v France* (application no. 71412/01), admissibility decision of 31 May 2007.

[40] ECtHR, *Saramati v France, Germany and Norway* (application no. 78166/01), admissibility decision of 31 May 2007.

BEN F. KLAPPE

Chapter VII of the Charter were fundamental to the mission of the UN and since they relied for their effectiveness on support from member states, the Convention could not be interpreted in a manner which would subject the acts and omissions of contracting partners to the scrutiny of the Court. To do so would be to interfere with the fulfilment of the UN's key mission in the field including the effective conduct of its operation.

5. *State responsibility for peacekeepers.* In 2007, a civil claim[41] was filed at the Hague District Court against the state of the Netherlands and the United Nations. The complainants were family members (partially organized in a foundation) of the 8,000–10,000 persons killed during the Dutch military presence in the enclave of Srebrenica. Plaintiffs held the defendants jointly responsible for the fall of the enclave Srebrenica and the consequences thereof. In these proceedings, plaintiffs and the foundation sought a judicial declaration that the state of the Netherlands and the UN, due to a failure to perform their undertakings and obligations, acted unlawfully with respect to plaintiffs and the murdered members of their family. Plaintiffs further claimed an advance of EUR 25,000 per person for the loss and injury suffered and yet to be suffered, as well as damages yet to be determined by the Court. The claims of plaintiffs and the foundation rest upon the alleged actions, or omissions, of the state of the Netherlands and the UN, within the framework of the implementation of, *inter alia*, UN SC Resolutions 819, 824, and 836, to protect the enclave of Srebrenica (declared by the UN as a 'Safe Area') and the civilians who found themselves there, against attacks by the Bosnian Serbs.

The Hague District Court[42] in deciding the matter of whether or not the UN enjoys immunity in this case first considers how the immunity, enshrined in Article 105, subsection 1 of the UN Charter and developed in Article II, para. 2 of the Convention on the Privileges and Immunities of the United Nations is interpreted and applied to prevailing law in international practice. The Court concludes that in international-law practice, absolute immunity of the UN is the standard and is respected, and that the interpretation of Article 105 of the UN Charter offers no basis for restriction of the immunity of the UN. The Hague Court of Appeals[43] dismissed the argument of the District Court that the UN enjoys an absolute immunity. The Court ruled that there has to be a balancing of interests between the immunity of jurisdiction of the UN on the one hand and the protection of the fundamental rights of the plaintiffs to have access to an effective judicial review on the other. The Court of Appeals decided that—even in this exceptional case—the immunity of jurisdiction of the United Nations prevails as plaintiffs have alternative means to bring their claims to justice and therefore upholding the UN's immunity would be proportionate. Because the perpetrators as well as the Dutch state can be sued, the general interest of the UN not to be forced to appear in national courts would prevail. Plaintiffs have appealed to the Court of Cassation in the Netherlands pleading to reject UN-immunity or refer the case to the Court of Justice of the European Union.

---

[41] Van Diepen en Van der Kroef advocaten, Writ of summons Srebrenica, <http://www.vandiepen. com>.

[42] District Court of The Hague, Judgment of 10 July 2008, *The Association et al. v The State of The Netherlands*, LJN: BD6796.

[43] Court of Appeal of The Hague, Judgment of 30 March 2010, *The Association et al. v The State of The Netherlands*, LJN: BL8979.

BEN F. KLAPPE

a) In two related cases, the Civil Chambers of the Court of Appeal of The Hague held the state of the Netherlands responsible for the death of three Muslim men after the fall of Srebrenica.[44] In July 1995, a Dutch battalion under the command of the UN had the task of protecting the Muslim enclave Srebrenica in Bosnia-Herzegovina. The enclave was surrounded by the Bosnian Serbian Army under the command of General Mladic. On 11 July 1995, the Bosnian Serbian Army occupied Srebrenica. The Dutch battalion (Dutchbat) withdrew all troops to a nearby compound. A stream of thousands of refugees from Srebrenica soon began. 5,000 of these refugees were admitted into the Dutch compound, among whom 239 were able-bodied men (i.e. 16–60 years of age). Among the refugees who had sought refuge to the compound were the families of the interpreter (father, mother, and younger brother) and the electrician (wife and children) for Dutchbat. The brother of the interpreter and the electrician were sent by Dutchbat from the compound at the end of 13 July 1995. The father of the interpreter went with them. Subsequently, they were murdered by the Bosnian Serbs. In a proceeding before the Court of Appeal, their next of kin (hereinafter complainants) sought compensation from the state. The District Court of The Hague had rejected their claims in the first instance.

b) The Court of Appeal first had to make a decision about the defence of the state that the Dutchbat military acted under the auspices of the UN and that the state, therefore, was not responsible for the actions of Dutchbat. As to what criterion applies for state versus UN responsibility, the Court noted that the question that should be answered is who exercised 'effective control', not who exercised 'command and control', as considered by the District Court.[45] Both in international public law literature[46] and in works of the International Law Commission, in situations in which a state contributes troops to the UN for the execution of a peace operation, the question of who should be held accountable for specific actions of these troops depends on who exercises 'effective control' over those actions. This opinion has also been expressed in the draft articles on responsibilities of international organizations of the International Law Commission, Article 6 of which reads: 'The conduct of an organ of a State or an organ or agent of an international organization that is placed at the disposal of another international organization shall be considered under international law an act of the latter organization if the organization exercises effective control over that conduct.' Although 'effective control' in this provision only refers to the accountability of the acquiring international organization, it is accepted that the same criterion applies to the question of whether acts by individual troops shall be considered as acts of the state that contributed the troops. The question of whether the state exercised 'effective control' over actions of Dutchbat should be answered bearing in mind the specific circumstances at hand. Not only is it relevant

---

[44] Court of Appeal of The Hague, Judgment of 5 July 2011, *Nuhanovic v State of The Netherlands*, LJN: BR0133 and Judgment of 5 July 2011, *Mustafic c.s. v. State of The Netherlands*, LJN: BR0132.

[45] Court of Appeal of The Hague, *Mustafic c.s. v State of The Netherlands*, Judgment of 5 July 2011, LJN: BR0132, para. 5.8.

[46] The Court refers to M. Hirsch, *The Responsibility of International Organizations Towards Third Parties: Some Basic Principles* (Nijhoff, 1995), 64; F. Messineo, 'The House of Lords in Al-Jedda and Public International Law: Attribution of Conduct to Un-authorized forces and the Power of the Security Council to displace Human Rights' (2009) 65 *Netherlands International Law Review* 35–61, at 41–2; Aurel Sari, 'Jurisdiction and International Responsibility in Peace Support Operations: The Behrami and Saramati Cases' (2008) *Human Rights Law Review* 151–70, at 164; T. Dannenbaum, 'Translating the Standard of Effective Control into a System of Effective Accountability: How Liability Should be Apportioned for Violations of Human Rights by Member State Troop Contingents Serving as United Nations Peacekeepers' (2010) *Harvard International Law Journal* 113–92, at 140–1.

to consider if the underlying actions were the result of specific instruction by the UN or the state, but also if no specific instruction exists, whether the UN or state were in a position to prevent such actions.[47] The Court considers it generally accepted that more than one party exercises 'effective control', so it cannot be excluded that applying the criterion results in the accountability of more than one party. This leads the Court only to investigate whether the state exercises effective control over the alleged actions and sets aside the question of whether the UN also exercised effective control. The Court considered it relevant to point to the highly differing circumstances of the alleged actions by Dutchbat from a normal situation where a state contributes troops to UN Operations as was the case in *Behrami v France*[48] and *Saramati v France, Germany, and Norway*.[49] The Court further argued that after 11 July 1995 the mission to protect Srebrenica had failed. Srebrenica fell that day and there was no discussion that Dutchbat, or United Nations Protection Force (UNPROFOR) in any other composition, would continue the mission. On the evening of 11 July 1995, a meeting between the UN Force Commander, the Dutch Chief of Defence Staff, and the Deputy Commander of the Dutch Army took place and resulted in the conclusion that use of force would be useless. The aim was to evacuate the refugees and Dutchbat. The Court considered the outcome of the meeting was a consensual decision to evacuate between the UN Force Commander on behalf of the UN and the two Dutch generals on behalf of the Dutch government, the implication also being that after completion of the evacuation Dutchbat would be redeploying.[50] As of 11 July 1995, an interim period started and one important task of Dutchbat was to support the evacuation of refugees. During this period, the Dutch government had separate authority from the UN as it related to the preparations for the overall redeployment of Dutchbat from Bosnia-Herzegovina. The highest Dutch senior-ranking officer acted in a dual-hatted capacity on behalf of the UN, being chief-of-staff of HQ UNPROFOR in Sarajevo and on behalf of the Dutch government. In that capacity he instructed the Dutchbat commander on the evacuation, confirmed by the latter in a message to Mladic: '... I did receive a message from the authorities of the Netherlands through HQ UNPROFOR in Sarajevo concerning the evacuation of Dutchbat. I have been ordered...'.[51] The Court concluded there is no doubt that the Dutch government was closely involved in the evacuation and the preparations thereof and was in a position to prevent the alleged actions, provided it was timely informed. The facts left no other conclusion than if the government had ordered not to have M. leave the compound or to take him along with the unit when redeploying, this order would have been executed. The Court emphasized that the alleged actions violated UN orders issued by the acting commander of HQ UNPROFOR to protect refugees and that the authority to take disciplinary measures against such violations resided with the state. The alleged actions for which the complainants blame Dutchbat are directly linked to decisions and orders of the Dutch government. The complaint that Dutchbat ordered M. to leave the

[47] Court of Appeal of The Hague, Judgment of 5 July 2011, *Mustafic c.s. v. State of The Netherlands*, LJN: BR0132, LJN: BR0132, para. 5.9.

[48] ECtHR, *Behrami and Behrami v France* (application no. 71412/01), admissibility decision of 31 May 2007.

[49] ECtHR, *Saramati v France, Germany, and Norway* (application no. 78166/01), admissibility decision of 31 May 2007.

[50] Court of Appeal of The Hague, Judgment of 5 July 2011, *Mustafic c.s. v. State of The Netherlands*, LJN: BR0132, para. 5.17.

[51] Ibid. para. 5.16.

compound and did not prevent the separations of M. and his wife and children is linked to the way in which the evacuation and orders of the Dutch Minister of Defence were executed. The same is true for the complaint that Dutchbat did not immediately report the separations of men and women and other human rights violations the battalion witnessed.[52] The Court ultimately concluded the state exercised 'effective control' over the alleged actions by Dutchbat and, therefore, could be held accountable.[53] The Court was of the opinion that Dutchbat should not have sent the electrician and the interpreter's brother from the compound and they had to have anticipated that the interpreter's father would follow his son. Dutchbat had witnessed in the meantime more than one incident in which Bosnian Serbs had beaten up or killed male refugees outside the compound. Therefore, at the end of the afternoon of 13 July 1995, Dutchbat knew that the men would run a great risk when they would leave the compound. The Court considered explicitly that its judgment in this case was exclusively related to the specific situation of these individuals. No judgment was given about the situation of the other refugees. The position of the other refugees, which differs in certain aspects from the case at hand, is not at issue in this procedure.

**When peace operations include elements of peace enforcement, international   1308
humanitarian law must be applied.**

1. Peace operations traditionally encompass a wide range of activities where military units are used for purposes other than the large-scale combat operations. They have monitored ceasefire agreements and manned observation posts in buffer zones. But the idea of a peacekeeper seen as an international policeman has changed due to the often more volatile and complex character of operations. The changing character necessitated appropriate action: a powerful and broad mandate and a flexible and responsive approach towards parties or elements that obstructed peace. The approach has led to questions related to the use of force and have triggered a discussion on the applicability of international humanitarian law.

2. In an attempt to address the issue and for the purpose of setting out fundamental principles and rules of international humanitarian law that apply to forces conducting operations under UN command and control, the UN Secretary General has issued a Bulletin.[54] Section 1 of the Bulletin states that the fundamental principles and rules of international humanitarian law set out in the Bulletin are applicable to United Nations forces when in situations of armed conflict they are actively engaged therein as combatants, to the extent and for the duration of their engagement. They are accordingly applicable in enforcement actions, or in peacekeeping operations when the use of force is permitted in self-defence.[55] Shortly after its promulgations, the Bulletin triggered questions in the military and legal community on the threshold for the 'situation of armed conflict'. A practical solution for the applicability of the Bulletin may be found by declaring the fundamental principles specified in the Bulletin to be applicable at all

[52] Ibid. para. 5.19,
[53] Ibid. para. 5.20.
[54] Secretary General's Bulletin Observance by United Nations forces of international humanitarian law, UN Doc. ST/SGB/1999/13 of 6 August 1999.
[55] The Bulletin does not affect the protected status of members of peacekeeping operations under the 1994 UN SafetyConv or their status as non-combatants, as long as they are entitled to the protection given to civilians under the international law of armed conflict.

BEN F. KLAPPE

times. To adhere to such fundamental principles as humane treatment of the wounded, women, children and detainees should be a matter of standard policy, regardless of the situation at hand.

1309   **Specific rules of international humanitarian law may apply in all peacekeeping missions (see above, Sections 208, 420).**

Rules of engagement typically may refer to international humanitarian law provisions. The argument being that the rules referred to are perceived customary international law, and regardless the factual situation, the rules should be adhered to in any case.

III. Mandates

1310   **Mandates for peace operations should be issued by the Security Council in the exercise of its primary responsibility for the maintenance of international peace and security. In the absence of a Security Council mandate, operations must be based on another international legal basis, for example host-state consent. The drafters of mandates should consider that the relevant provisions are to be implemented at different levels and for different purposes.**

1. All peace operations operate under a mandate which provides both a legal basis under public international law for the deployment of military forces by the participating states on the territory of the state(s) where the operation is conducted and sets out the basic objectives and purposes of the operation in question.[56] These in turn serve as the parameters and framework for the implementing instruments, such as the agreements by which the participating states commit elements of their armed forces to the operation and the rules of engagement (ROE) under which the operation is conducted.[57] It goes without saying that such instruments of implementation derive their authority from the mandate itself and as such must reflect the terms, objectives, and purposes of the mandate.

2. Unlike traditional peacekeeping operations, modern peacekeeping operations support post-conflict efforts to preserve and consolidate peace by helping to rebuild the basic foundations of a secure, functioning state. To this end, missions will undertake a broad range of Security Council-mandated tasks to support the implementation of an agreed peace process. Such multidimensional operations have become the dominant form of peacekeeping operations in recent years. In contrast to traditional peacekeeping operations, multidimensional operations have been deployed in the dangerous aftermath of an intrastate conflict, normally at the request of the parties, to assist in the implementation of a comprehensive peace agreement.

3. Numerous actors provide humanitarian assistance and support long-term peacebuilding efforts with local institutions. Post-conflict activities undertaken in collaboration with or alongside a UN peacekeeping operation may include:

— humanitarian relief;
— economic governance and anti-corruption;

---

[56] See *inter alia* H. McCoubrey and N. D. White, *The Blue Helmets: Legal Regulation of United Nations Military Operations* (Hants: Aldershot, 1996), 69 *et seq.*; T. Findlay, *The Use of Force in UN Peace Operations* (OUP/SIPRI, 2002), 7–9.
[57] Findlay, ibid. 9–14.

— investment in infrastructure reconstruction;
— human capacity-building;
— long-term rule of law support;
— institution-building and technical assistance; and
— poverty alleviation.

4. In situations where no central state authority has ever existed, the UN may be required to play a dual administrative and capacity-building role for an extended period. Consequently, in addition to the functions fulfilled by multidimensional peacekeeping operations, a UN interim or transitional administration may be required to assume temporary authority over the executive and legislative structures in a given territory or country.[58]

The term 'mandate' should be used to refer exclusively to the authorization and   **1311**
tasks under public international law.

1. Depending on the nature of the peace agreement and its own assessment of the measures required to support the peace process, the term mandate refers exclusively to tasks under public international law such as:

— monitor a ceasefire or cessation of hostilities to allow space for political negotiations and a peaceful settlement of disputes;
— protect civilians;
— provide operational support to law enforcement agencies;
— assist in the restructuring and reform of the armed forces;
— facilitate the implementation of the peace agreement through the provision of good offices, mediation support, and other confidence-building measures;
— assist with the disarmament, demobilization, and reintegration (DDR) of former combatants;
— support the delivery of humanitarian assistance;
— supervise and assist with the organization of elections;
— strengthen the rule of law, including assistance with judicial reform and training of civilian police;
— promote respect for human rights and investigate alleged violations;
— assist with post-conflict recovery and rehabilitation;
— assist with mine action; and
— promote national dialogue and reconciliation.

2. National authorities when providing personnel (military or police) to peacekeeping operations may have restrictions on how and where there units will deploy and what tasks will not be supported by them. These so-called *caveats* may be based upon national policy, national legislation, or factual (operational or logistic) limitations of the units.

Mandates have to be rather broad to cover evolving scenarios. There is a clear need   **1312**
for realistic objectives and a reasonable degree of specificity in order to provide a
precise legal framework for the mission.

1. An increasing number of UN operations are multifunctional in nature. Mandates range from immediate stabilization and protection of civilians to supporting humanitarian

---

[58] Examples of such UN Transitional Administrations include Kosovo (1999–present), Timor Leste (1999–2002), Eastern Slavonia (1996–8), and West Papua (1962–3).

assistance; organizing elections; assisting the development of new political structures; engaging in security sector reform; disarming, demobilizing, and reintegrating former combatants; and laying the foundations of a lasting peace.[59] The UN frequently works with other global institutions, regional organizations, donor countries, NGOs, and host governments, in trying to achieve these ends. The Secretary General, however, still refers to a 'gaping hole' in the UN system's institutional machinery when it comes to meeting the challenge of helping countries with the transition from war to lasting peace effectively.[60] While performance is improving, the success rate in long-term stabilization is still too low, and many countries relapse into conflict after an initial period of stabilization. This conclusion can in part be ascribed to a lack of strategic, coordinated, and sustained international efforts. An Integrated Mission is an instrument with which the UN seeks to help countries in the transition from war to lasting peace, or to address a similarly complex situation that requires a system-wide UN response, through subsuming actors and approaches within an overall political-strategic crisis management framework.[61] At least three dilemmas are raised in relation to integration: the humanitarian dilemma reflects a tension between the partiality involved in supporting a political transition process and the impartiality needed to protect humanitarian space. The human rights dilemma relates to the tension that arises when the UN feels compelled to promote peace by working with those who may have unsatisfactory human rights records, while still retaining the role of an 'outside critic' of the same process. The local ownership dilemma relates to the need to root peace processes in the host country's society and political structures without reinforcing the very structures that led to conflict in the first place.[62]

2. Realistic long-term objectives and an exit strategy must be based on an all-encompassing vision. As part of a broader UN peacebuilding strategy, the Secretary General has endorsed guidelines for a comprehensive and inclusive UN system approach to the planning of integrated peace support operations or integrated missions.[63] An Integrated Mission is one in which there is a shared vision among all UN actors as to the strategic objective of the UN presence at country level. This strategic objective is the result of a deliberate effort by all elements of the UN system to achieve a shared understanding of the mandates and functions of the various elements of the UN presence at country level and to use this understanding to maximize UN effectiveness, efficiency, and impact in all aspects of its work. An Integrated Mission is one in which structure is derived from an in-depth understanding of the specific country setting; of the evolving security, political, humanitarian, human rights, and development imperatives in that particular country; and of the particular mix of assets and capacities available and/or required to achieve the desired impact through mutually supportive action. In other words, form (mission structure) should follow function and be tailored to the specific characteristics of each country setting.

---

[59] Report on Integrated Missions, Practical Perspectives and Recommendations, Independent Study for the Expanded UN ECHA Core Group, Executive summary, Espen Barth Eide, Anja Therese Kaspersen, Randolph Kent, Karen von Hippel, 19 May 2005, <http://www.regjeringen.no/upload/UD/Vedlegg/FN/report_on_integrated_missons.pdf>.

[60] In Larger Freedom: towards development, security and human rights for all, 21 March 2005, UN Doc. A/59/2005, para. 114.

[61] Ibid. at n. 33.

[62] Ibid. at n. 33.

[63] Endorsed by the Secretary General on 13 June 2006, <https://ochanet.unocha.org/p/Documents/UN%20IMPP%20Guidelines%20(2006).pdf>.

BEN F. KLAPPE

Decision-makers should consider the adoption of a mandate allowing the international military force to intervene in cases of illegal use of force against civilians in
the area of operations. When doing so, they should take the means and capabilities
of the international military force into account.

1. *Protection of civilians.* Many peace operations involve an element of the protection
of internally or externally displaced persons. It is important that military personnel
are aware of the human rights of the persons they are assigned to protect. The origins of the concept of a 'responsibility to protect' are to be found in the debate in the
1990s about humanitarian intervention. At that time, the Security Council showed
itself willing, in some circumstances at least, to characterize egregious human rights
abuses as a threat to international peace and security, thus opening up the possibility
of enforcement action under Chapter VII of the UN Charter. The problem was a gap
between theory and practice, often with tragic consequences, as the genocidal acts in
both Rwanda and Srebrenica showed. In addition, humanitarian intervention was, and
remains, a politically charged and divisive concept—a fact which did not contribute to
its positive reception or use. The Report of the Secretary General's High-Level Panel on
Threats Challenges and Change set out its proposals for 'a more secure world'.[64] In it, the
Panel endorsed what it called 'the emerging norm of a responsibility to protect civilians
from large-scale violence'. The UN Secretary General, likewise urged all to 'embrace the
responsibility to protect, and, when necessary, . . . act on it'.[65] This was further endorsed
in the outcomes of the September UN Summit, convened by the Secretary General to
review progress with implementation of the UN Millennium Goals. It is recognized that
this responsibility rests first and foremost with each individual state; however, where the
state is unable or unwilling, the international community shares a collective responsibility to act—through, for example, humanitarian operations, monitoring missions,
diplomatic pressure, and, ultimately as a last resort, with force.

2. At the end of 2009, there were an estimated 27 million internally displaced persons (IDPs) around the world and UNHCR was helping about 14.7 million of them
in twenty-two countries, including the three with the largest IDP populations—Sudan,
Colombia, and Iraq,[66] far outnumbering the world's 10.5 million refugees.[67] Their access
to protection and assistance has been seriously impeded both by the absence of an agreed
and implemented international law framework to guarantee access, and by the fact that
no one international organization has the mandate to intervene on their behalf. This
has in fact now been recognized as a serious gap in the international protection system,
necessitating a range of activities to fill it. The 1998 Guiding Principles on Internal
Displacement, which purport to set out the basic normative framework, were a first
step. At the institutional level, there has also been tentative progress with making the
UN response more 'collaborative'. UNHCR sees promise in the model for collaboration
being developed, which is built around so-called 'clusters' of activities, and has indicated
its preparedness to coordinate the protection, camp management, and emergency shelter

---

[64] 'A more secure world: our shared responsibility—Report of the High-level Panel on Threats, Challenges
and Change', UN Doc. A/59/565 of 2 December 2004. See also the earlier Report of the International
Commission on Intervention and State Sovereignty, 'The Responsibility to Protect', December 2001, and
UNHCR, 'Note on International Protection', UN Doc. A/AC.96/1008 of 4 July 2005, paras. 35 and 72.
[65] Ibid.
[66] UNHCR, Internally displaced people, <http://www.unhcr.org/pages/49c3646c146.html>.
[67] UNHCR, Refugee numbers at a glance, <http://www.unhcr.org/pages/49c3646c11.html>.

BEN F. KLAPPE

clusters, albeit in situations of internal displacement caused by conflict. Today, there is some real progress towards closing the protection gap for IDPs. At the same time, how-ever, there are complex issues still to resolve, one being whether it will always be realistic to build protection around categories of people. More specifically, the question being asked is whether it is artificial, in a complex emergency, to make a distinction between persons actually displaced and the broader population of the country, who may well be just as vulnerable. This is illustrated well by the situation in the eastern provinces of the Democratic Republic of Congo (DRC)—one of the countries where the new 'cluster' approach is to be piloted. It is exceedingly difficult there to distinguish between IDPs and the population at large. Humanitarian access is lacking; the population as a whole faces constant harassment by armed elements; sexual and gender-based violence is rife; there is no rule of law; and corruption is endemic and rampant.

3. Often, military units will be the first people who come into contact with people flee-ing persecution. Especially in view of the growth of international criminal jurisdiction for human rights abuses, it is important that military personnel either document such evidence themselves (if they have the requisite skills and resources) or create the condi-tions where human rights workers can receive such testimony. Military personnel will increasingly be regarded as having a duty to contribute to the effective prosecution of human rights abuses.

4. *Protection of civilians, limitations.* Most mission mandates routinely include three caveats which limit the protection of civilians to those under imminent threat, in line with the mission's capacity and capability, and according to its geographical deploy-ment. While the first allows for subjective (and partisan) interpretations about what exactly constitutes an imminent threat, the other two are clearly a function of param-eters determined prior to deployment. All three are conceptually vague enough to be used as escape clauses which serve to explain *post facto* why effective protection could not be provided in a given situation.[68]

5. There is significant variation in the use of the term 'protection'. The Office for the Coordination of Humanitarian Affairs uses it as an umbrella concept to advocate for a number of otherwise unrelated interventions (child protection, refugee security, humanitar-ian access, etc.), whereas DPKO responds to it as an additional mandated task, usually with-out the additional resources it would warrant. This only increases the need for continuous and ambiguous prioritization between competing and under-resourced mission objectives. As a result, some protection interventions are pursued intermittently and therefore lose their effectiveness. There is an inherent difficulty in correlating, in quantifiable terms, a given protection situation with an appropriate military response (how many troops are needed to protect a spontaneous refugee settlement?). Furthermore, there are no benchmarks in civilian protection such as the crude mortality rate in a camp situation which tracks improvements (or a worsening) in the welfare of a given population over time. This methodological void raises some hard questions about, for instance, the level of violence that should be considered as normal or what would constitute a real improvement in the protection situation.

6. The geographical limitation brings to light a classical dilemma of humanitarian triage: is it morally just to focus only on those pockets of threatened civilians which are within

---

[68] Internal note, June 2006, based on a DPKO meeting between Mr D. Barth and the author.

BEN F. KLAPPE

the sphere of influence of a given military unit's area of responsibility when it is known that gross abuses take place just beyond it? 'Better some protection than none at all' may not be an appropriate answer here because an uneven protection environment produces multiple push and pull factors, including population movements which in turn create their own protection dynamics.

> **Peace operations have an inherent role in the protection of human rights and the restoration of justice, whether expressly declared or not. The mandate should provide a framework for the role of the international military presence.**   1314

The role of the international military presence primarily is the restoration of peace and stability. The mandate may include tasks for which the military component is suitable. This may include the monitoring of the human rights situation, taking appropriate actions when confronted with violations of human rights, and reporting on violations and actions taken. In the mandate, a delineation of responsibilities with respect to the protection of human rights should be provided for the various actors and entities such as UNHCHR, UNHCR, UNICEF, NGOs, police, and military.

> **When appropriate, mandates should address co-operation with designated competent criminal tribunals.**   1315

Increasingly, in Security Council resolutions reference is made to co-operation with the International Criminal Court (ICC). The United Nations has concluded a framework agreement with the ICC for the provision of documents that may help to build a case against suspects and for operational support in the field.[69] Furthermore, implementing agreements on these issues are being concluded between field missions and the ICC.

IV. Rules of Engagement (ROE)

> **Rules of engagement (ROE) are directives to operational commanders, which delineate the parameters within which force may be used by designated international peace operations personnel. They should be founded on Security Council resolutions and must be issued and implemented in accordance with the provisions of international law. ROE should be established for each peace operation. They should be clear and simple.**   1316

1. ROE, in general, are no new phenomenon. Rules for the use of force or directives for opening fire have existed for ages to avoid early escalation of a conflict and to guarantee unity of doctrine when it comes to the most visible and potentially destructive part of warfare.[70] Increasingly, the use of force during peace operations will be a sensitive matter for a variety of reasons. The changing character of peace operations—patrolling streets in built-up areas and in crowded slums instead of patrolling in deserted buffer zones between nation states—inevitably will lead to an increased risk of civilian casualties once peacekeepers use force as a last resort. Civilian casualties as a result of

---

[69] Relationship Agreement between the International Criminal Court and the United Nations of 4 October 2004, <http://www.icc-cpi.int/iccdocs/asp_docs/Publications/Compendium/Compendium.3rd.03.ENG.pdf>.

[70] See above, n. 1.

peacekeepers' actions may rapidly jeopardize the operation and may lead to demonstrations and revenge or have other far-reaching political consequences. It is, therefore, of extreme importance that ROE are developed thoroughly and carefully, within an operational, legal, and political framework.[71]

2. The Security Council resolution for a new peacekeeping operation is a compromise of the deliberations of the fifteen members of the Council. The mandate therefore leaves much room for interpretation by mission planners when developing an initial concept of operations. Second, a concept of operations will leave the necessary operational space for planners at force headquarters level, adjusting plans to situations as they occur. Despite the necessary room for interpretation, clarity is needed when it comes to the authority to use force. Not only will this clarity protect individuals against excessive use of force, it also protects peacekeepers from prosecution when force is used within the parameters of the ROE.

3. ROE traditionally are developed for military personnel. Police forces are using ROE or similar directives for the use of force. Specific ROE are often developed for maritime operations and interception and engagement of aircraft. As private (military) contractors are increasingly participating during peace operations, similar rules on the use of force may exist for such personnel.

In peacekeeping operations, small groups of soldiers rather than large formations of military units are deployed to execute tasks. Often, junior leaders will have to make decisions on the use of force. No commander or superior when monitoring the situation from headquarters or a command post with live-camera images can substitute for the common sense of the leader on the scene. Only they are able to make a final analysis and assessment and decide how best to defuse or control the situation on the ground. Hence, rules should be clear and simple, understandable for junior leaders and soldiers.

1317   **Where issued as prohibitions, ROE are orders not to take specific actions. Where issued as permissions, they are the authority for commanders to take certain specific actions if they are judged necessary to achieve the objectives of the mission.**

An example is the general prohibition to indiscriminately point weapons in the direction of any person. Such a prohibition underlines the peaceful character of a mission and contributes to the acceptability by the civilian population of foreign peacekeepers on their territory. An example of permission is the authorization to use force, up to and including deadly force, to protect civilians under imminent threat of physical violence, when competent local authorities are not in a position to render immediate assistance. It should be clearly understood at all levels that this is at the heart of the *raison d'être* of peacekeeping. The subsequent question that will arise is: how imminent is the threat and who will determine the imminence, the available means to respond to a situation, and prioritization in case of conflicting responsibilities? How imminent is imminent? Should it be instant and overwhelming or do we need to wait for a smoking gun? The answer will have to be given by commanders on the ground as the situation develops, in line with the overall mission strategy and the mandate, worked out in operation plans and

---

[71] Guidelines for the Development of Rules of Engagement for UN Peacekeeping Operations, UN Department of Peacekeeping Operations, March 2002.

BEN F. KLAPPE

in line with the ROE. If intelligence reveals plans and credible evidence armed elements are mounting an attack on civilians in villages nearby, the commander may conclude the threat is imminent: within hours killing may start. No time should be lost and the armed elements should be engaged, if necessary by using deadly force. Radio stations, broadcasting inciting language, and ordering violence should be stopped as well. This may eventually include the use of force, proportionate and necessary. When information reveals the location of weapon caches, commanders are supposed to act and not wait until the weapons are distributed and used against the population. Although the present approach may deviate from peace operations a decade ago, the mandates and rules have not changed that much, although it should be noted that language in resolutions today is more explicit. The authority to act is in the resolution and the permission to use force is in the ROE. What is new is the awareness at both political and military levels based on dramatic experiences and failures in the past that peacekeepers cannot stand idle when civilians are threatened.

> **When and where possible, permission to use force should be sought from the immediate superior commander.**   1318

During military operations, this is more or less a standard doctrine and based on the fact that higher up in the chain-of-command more information is available and a better assessment of the situation and courses of action and consequences is possible. Moreover, in peacekeeping the use of force should be the exception, not the rule.

At the same time it is essential to point at the individual's responsiveness to situations. Soldiers as a result of proximity of their commanders or the availability of high-tech communication means are sometimes connected with their superiors twenty-four hours a day and may tend to wait for their instant responses and decisions. Various soldiers during a peacekeeping exercise were confronted with an opponent-trainer, who apparently was about to throw a hand grenade, responded to the trainer that they would warn their commander instead of using force to quell the situation. They argued that they were trained to be reluctant when using force, trying to defuse violent situations rather than escalate. This approach, however, is a dangerous one. Soldiers should be trained and prepared to use deadly force instantly if the need arises. Sometimes, force can be used in order to remove certain hostile elements from theatre, diffusing a developing volatile situation.

> **While remaining predominantly defensive in nature, the ROE allow for the potential need for offensive action if necessary, in order to ensure the implementation of the tasks assigned. The ROE also provide a definition of the circumstances under which the use of force may be justified.**   1319

Nothing in ROE excludes a commander's right and obligation to take all necessary and appropriate action for self-defence. All personnel may exercise the inherent right of self-defence. Measures to protect personnel, premises, and property of the mission and to guarantee freedom of movement of peace operations personnel should be clearly addressed in ROE. The ROE should allow peacekeepers to use up to deadly force, to defend oneself and other peacekeeping or international personnel against a hostile act or a hostile intent. Moreover, it accepts the use of force, under circumstances, deadly force, to protect peacekeeping installations and areas or goods designated by the force commander, against a hostile act. Rules would normally also allow up to and including deadly force against any person and/or group that limits or intends to limit freedom of movement.

1320   **The ROE define the degree and the manner in which force may be applied and are designed to ensure that the application of force is controlled and legal. They inform commanders of the constraints imposed and the degrees of freedom they have, in the course of carrying out their mission.**

Force can be defined as the use of, or threat to use, physical means to achieve an objective. In peacekeeping, minimum force[72] aims to use force only as a means of last resort. As the host country has accepted peacekeepers on its territory, use of force with a view to collateral damage should be minimized. If peacekeepers as a result of their actions cause the death of innocent spectators, alienation of the civilian population comes closer. Therefore, less lethal means should be employed if possible. Commanders should, where appropriate, consider the use of alternatives to the use of physical force such as deception, psychological methods, negotiation, and other non-lethal means, which may include the deployment or manoeuvre of larger forces in order to demonstrate resolve. This could be unarmed force: physical force, short of the use of 'armed force'. Stop, search, and apprehension is a form of unarmed and physical force, and although weapons may be present at the scene or at hand, armed force[73] as such may not be used in the situation. If unarmed force is inappropriate, two distinct levels of armed force could be applied: deadly force or non-deadly force. Non-deadly force is the level of force which is neither intended nor likely to cause death regardless of whether death actually results.[74] It entails the use of batons, and the use of firearms firing warning shots or shots aimed at lower body parts. Non-deadly force would be appropriate if the opponent is not carrying firearms and poses a non-deadly threat to peacekeepers or to those under their protection. The ultimate degree of force of peacekeepers would be deadly force, the level of force, which is intended, or is likely to cause death regardless of whether death actually results.[75] This generally will be applied if no other means or methods are available to react to a hostile act or hostile intent of armed opponents.

1321   **The ROE are to be translated in a clear and concise way into the language(s) of each participating nationality. Throughout the conduct of military operations, where armed force is to be used, peace operations personnel must comply with the international legal principles of proportionality, the minimum use of force and the requirement to minimize the potential for collateral damage.**

Once the ROE are finalized and signed by the appropriate authorities, a translation should be available at short notice to enable commanders and troops to get familiar with the rules and to continue predeployment training or update training in the mission area. As mission-specific rules are largely based on a generic set of rules, basic definitions and principles for the use of force do not change much. Translations should be clear and concise. It is relevant to have the final language checked by commanders and junior

---

[72] Ibid. minimum force is defined as the minimum degree of authorized force, which is necessary and reasonable in the circumstances, to achieve the objective. The minimum degree of force is applicable whenever force is used. Minimum force can be deadly force if appropriate.

[73] Ibid. armed force is defined as the actual use of weapons, including firearms and bayonets.

[74] Ibid.

[75] Ibid.

BEN F. KLAPPE

troop leaders, as mistakes in the pocket card (soldier's card) made by translators may have unintended consequences when it comes to applying the rules.

> **Whenever the operational situation permits, every reasonable effort must be made**   1322
> **to resolve any hostile confrontation by means other than the use of force (e.g.**
> **through negotiations). Any force used must be limited in its intensity and duration**
> **to what is necessary to achieve the objective. In some circumstances, operational**
> **urgency may dictate the immediate use of deadly force. The use of force must be**
> **commensurate with the level of the threat and all necessary measures are to be**
> **taken to avoid collateral damage.**

Proportionality in peace operations is directly linked to winning hearts and minds in peace operations. Civilian deaths among the local population will immediately reflect on the attitude and behaviour of the local population against peacekeepers. This is especially the case in operations where units and soldiers will continue to work in the same area of operations. They will be confronted on a daily basis with the negative effects of their actions. Warnings of the civilian population may be an effective measure to limit collateral damage and need to be balanced with operational security and the element of surprise. It appears that in peacekeeping operations priority should be given at all times to the protection of civilians and the avoidance of collateral damage, even if this may lead to delays in daily operations.

> **During peace operations, use of force beyond self-defence may only be used in the**   1323
> **circumstances as specified in the ROE.**

Pre-emptive self-defence against an anticipated attack must be supported by compelling evidence (in the prevailing context) that hostile units or persons are committed to an immediate attack. See below, Section 1324.

> **Decision-makers should adopt specific ROE authorizing the use of force to ensure**   1324
> **the protection to civilians under imminent threat of physical violence. When doing**
> **so, they should take the means and capabilities of the international military force**
> **into account.**

Peacekeepers who witness violence against civilians should be authorized to stop it, using deadly force if necessary. These rules may seem relatively easy, but when it comes to application in the field, soldiers may be confused. What constitutes a hostile act? How to recognize hostile intent? Even with clear-cut definitions, simple answers are not always possible in given situations. A hostile act is defined as: 'An attack or other use of force, intended to cause death, bodily harm or destruction.'[76] On first sight this may seem quite clear, but how will the individual soldier make his split-second decisions when an action is likely to demonstrate hostile intent? Hostile intent may be defined as: 'The threat of imminent use of force, which is demonstrated through an action which appears to be preparatory to a hostile act.' The soldier will be backed by the remainder of the definition, namely: 'only a reasonable belief in the hostile intent is required, before the use of force is authorized'. Whether or not hostile intent is being demonstrated must be judged by the on-scene commander, on the basis of one or a combination of factors, including: the capability and preparedness of the threat, the available evidence which

---

[76] *Ibid.*

indicates an intention to attack, and the historical precedent within the mission's area of responsibility.

1325   The implementation of the ROE is a command responsibility. The ROE are normally addressed to the force commander, who is then responsible for issuing them to all subordinate commanders. All commanders have an obligation to seek clarification, if the authorized ROE are considered to be unclear or inappropriate for the military situation.

1. Subordinate commanders are not authorized to alter the ROE. They may propose changes to the existing rules if they believe such is necessary for the adequate execution of their tasks.

2. It is the responsibility of the commanders of all national contingents to ensure that all those under their command understand these ROE. To assist in this process, they must issue an ROE aide-memoire or pocket card, translated into the language(s) appropriate for their own contingent, to each individual. This is to be done before the contingent can be considered to be effective.

1326   Training in the application of ROE is the responsibility of commanders at all levels. ROE training sessions should be conducted on a regular basis and as a minimum, once per month and whenever personnel, including individual replacements or reinforcements are deployed into the mission area.

Training is best conducted in the field. Scenarios would include actors/colleagues involved in realistic role-play, simulating hostile acts and hostile intent against peacekeepers, and against civilians under their protection. Commanders subsequently evaluate and assess the appropriateness of the use of force or the lack thereof in the situations.

1327   Troop-contributing nations should co-operate in the common development and implementation of ROE.

The 2002 Guidelines for the Development of Rules of Engagement for UN Peacekeeping Operations were developed during lengthy consultations at New York between staff members of the Department of Peacekeeping Operations, the Office of Legal Affairs and more than fifty troop-contributing countries through their military representatives to the UN, commencing in 2000. The rules reflect the common vision on use of force standard.

1328   Policymakers should consider publishing relevant elements of those ROE that should be publicly known in the area of operation.

In wartime, opponents are not supposed to be familiar with the rules for the use of force as this would run counter with elementary principles of combat: deception and surprise. In peacetime, surprise as an operational principle is the exception, not the rule. Patrolling in the mission area by peacekeepers results in daily interaction with civilians. Clarifying the role and responsibility of peacekeepers in general and raising awareness related to the use of force and the authority to act in self-defence would help to improve the acceptance of the peacekeeping force by the civilian population.

1329   There is a need for common doctrine and training in the area of maintenance of public order and law enforcement.

BEN F. KLAPPE

Although maintenance of public order is a highly specialized task, necessitating the presence of trained police and law enforcement officials, reality indicates that military peacekeepers occasionally deploy in situations where national or local law enforcement authorities have ceased to function. It is in such situations that military units arrive and have to play a role. Basic training in the area of maintenance of public order will contribute to the preparedness for dealing with these situations. Ideally, initial entry units have received full training in crowd and riot control and the detention and treatment of detainees; two sensitive and visible areas with a high potential for failure.

> **For the drafting process of ROE the utilization of legal advisors at different levels should be obligatory.**   1330

Developing and drafting ROE is a command responsibility at various levels. At all times, operation officers and legal advisors at the different levels are to be involved in the process. The task of the legal advisor could best be described as a facilitating one. He should be intimately familiar with the general situation on the ground, proposed courses of action, the position of own forces, and the position of opponents. He will review the courses of action, taking into consideration the legal constraints based on international law obligations.

> **To enhance interoperability, continuous information-sharing between legal advisors at all levels, including field level, should be encouraged.**   1331

Legal advisors today are deployed with peacekeeping forces. They often function in the operations room or nearby, participate actively in staff briefings, and ideally have direct access to the commander. Legal advisors share information with legal advisors from higher headquarters and subordinate headquarters in a technical chain of command. To enhance interoperability, a database containing treaties, legal codes, rules, and regulations should be available. A lessons-learned manual of situations with legal ramifications that have been dealt with in the past should be readily available.

> **National caveats on the ROE should be limited to the minimum extent necessary.**   1332

A list of national *caveats* should be available at force headquarters level. The list should be taken into consideration when headquarters is developing plans. Operation officers and legal advisors will assess to what extent national caveats will restrict certain units in the execution of plans.

> **In the context of lessons learned studies, a database on the use of force should be developed and made available for future planning.**   1333

Although to date no comprehensive database on the use of force is available, such a tool would assist troops to prepare for new deployments. Although no situation will be identical, some common lessons from the use of force may be learned. Particular countries that so far have not been active in peace operations would benefit tremendously from an overview of best practices when applying force in peace operations.

V. Search, Apprehension, and Detention

> **ROE will determine under what circumstances search, apprehension, and detention operations may take place.**   1334

BEN F. KLAPPE

In peacetime, search, apprehension, and detention measures are the exclusive domain of law enforcement officials. The measures, as a rule, infringe on individual rights by entering the private domain of an individual and restraining his freedom of movement. Human rights provisions to guarantee minimum standards are translated and incorporated into directives for law enforcement officials. During peace operations, the same measures may be applied by peacekeepers in situations where law enforcement agencies of the host country are unable to take appropriate action or when individuals are about to commit hostile acts or have shown hostile intent against peacekeepers or those under the protection of the mission. The principles of proportionality and minimum use of force require peacekeepers to consider apprehension and detention first, even in cases where the use of up to and including deadly force is authorized. Situations will be specified in ROE and may vary, depending on the mandate and status quo of national law enforcement agencies.

1335   **The following minimum principles must be observed during all search procedures: the purpose of the search must be clearly stated in the orders and to the individuals to be searched; searchers are not to humiliate, nor embarrass persons being searched; the search procedure must take into account gender and be sensitive to other factors such as race, religion, etc.**

Detainees must be searched by using minimum necessary force. Ideally, the search is to be conducted in the presence of at least one witness, and preferably is to be conducted by a person of the same gender. The on-scene commander must ensure that all confiscated items are recorded properly.

1336   **Persons may not be apprehended other than in accordance with the authorization given in the ROE. All apprehended persons are to be handed over to appropriate local authorities, as soon as possible. Until handover takes place, such individuals may be detained.**

Regular peacekeeping forces are usually neither trained nor programmed to deal with civilian detainees. Therefore, straightforward procedures should be established to act rapidly and hand over to units and levels that are better equipped and prepared to guarantee safety of the unit and the detained individual. Strict adherence to ROE and detention procedures based on accepted human rights norms and standards[77] and promulgated by peacekeeping forces should guarantee a minimum standard for detained individuals.

1337   **Wherever possible, detainees are to be informed of the reason for their apprehension or detention.**

This rule, based on the Universal Declaration and various treaties,[78] should not cause too much difficulty, provided that language assistants or interpreters are readily available. If this is not the case, peacekeepers could anticipate by preparing translated written statements including a caution and detention grounds referring to language derived from the ROE. A ground for detention could be: (attempted) use of armed force against a peacekeeper.

[77] An example is the Professional Training Series No. 5/Add.3, Human Rights Standards and Practice for the Police, Geneva/New York 2004, <http://www.ohchr.org/Documents/Publications/training5Add3en.pdf>.
[78] Article 9 of the Universal Declaration of Human Rights; Article 9 ICCPR.

Peace operations personnel are fully responsible for the safety and well-being   1338
of persons whom they apprehend or detain, as long as those persons are in their
charge.

1. The authority to detain and the subsequent handover to appropriate national authorities is based on an agreement with the host state and based on the notion that the host state itself is not always in a position to apprehend and detain individuals whenever there may be a need.

2. A recent phenomenon is the perceived responsibility of peacekeepers for detainees once they are handed over to appropriate national authorities. Claims based on violations of human rights obligations against peacekeepers may come up by relatives or next of kin of a detained person if that person disappears after handover. Sometimes, an agreement is concluded between troop-contributing states and the host state to stress the mutual obligation to respect basic standards of international humanitarian law, human rights law, and national law, such as the right to life, to a fair trial, and the protection against torture. The agreement may include an obligation for the host state to allow full access to detainees after their transferral to the host state by representatives of a national human rights commission, the ICRC, or relevant human rights institutions within the UN system. The agreement may also include the responsibility for keeping an accurate account of all persons transferred to national authorities, making records available upon request, notifying the transferring state prior to the initiation of legal proceedings involving individuals and prohibiting detainees to be subjected to the execution of the death penalty.

Detainees must not be subjected to torture, to cruel, inhuman or degrading treat-   1339
ment or punishment or to intimidation, deprivation, humiliation, mistreatment,
or any form of abuse.

At no time in history, wrongful treatment of detainees has been more scrutinized by the international community based on photographs taken by perpetrators. It is, therefore, necessary to avoid ambiguity about the applicable rules or their interpretation. Mixed messages are not well understood by soldiers on the ground. A clear example is the ambiguity about the applicability of the Geneva Conventions. On 7 February 2002, the US President issued a memorandum stating that he determined the Geneva Conventions did not apply to the conflict with al-Qaeda, and although they did apply in the conflict with Afghanistan, the Taliban were unlawful combatants and therefore did not qualify for prisoner-of-war status. Nonetheless, the Secretary of State, Secretary of Defense, and the Chairman of the Joint Chiefs of Staff were all in agreement that treatment of detainees should be consistent with the Geneva Conventions.[79] In the memorandum, the President ordered accordingly that detainees were to be treated 'humanely and, "to the extent appropriate" and consistent with military necessity, in a manner consistent with the principles of Geneva'. This phrase will cause trouble in the field and may leave commanders and soldiers with the questionable notion that treatment of detainees consistent with the Geneva principles is conditional. Earlier, the Department of State

---

[79] Final Report of the Independent Panel to Review DoD Detention Operations, 24 August 2004, <http://www.defenselink.mil/news/Aug2004/d20040824finalreport.pdf>.

BEN F. KLAPPE

supported by the Chairman Joint Chiefs of Staff, his legal advisor, and many of the military lawyers had argued that the Geneva Conventions in their traditional application provided a sufficiently robust legal construct under which the global war on terror could effectively be waged.[80] A related example of ambiguity inevitably contributed to the Abu Ghraib scandal in 2004 and 2005. In two memoranda, US lawyers argued that there may be some situations where the Geneva Conventions do not apply and that anything less than 'the pain accompanying serious physical injury such as organ failure, impairment of bodily function, or even death' does not violate the UN Convention Against Torture. Around the same time, the Secretary of Defense and the then-commander in Iraq, approved limited use of harsh interrogation techniques. Although the memoranda and the approval were later rescinded, the abuses at Abu Ghraib occurred while they were in force. The memoranda suggest that the diminution of standards at Abu Ghraib was endorsed through the chain of command.[81]

1340   **Detainees must be treated in a humane manner and with respect for the inherent dignity of the human person. Full respect is to be shown for their gender, race, and religious beliefs and for the customs and practices of the group to which they belong. Particular care is to be taken to ensure the protection and well-being of women and children.**

Whenever peacekeepers are holding persons in detention, the following are the fundamental standards which should be applied:

a) Presumption of innocence. Guilt or innocence of the detainee will be decided by a court of law according to a process respectful of fair-trial guarantees. Until that time, the detainee is to be presumed innocent and treated as such (Article 14, para. 2, ICCPR; Rule 84 of the Standard Minimum Rules for the Treatment of Prisoners; Principle 6 of the Body of Principles for the Protection of All Persons under Any Form of Detention or Imprisonment).

b) Officially recognized places of detention. As a protective measure against the risk of disappearances and other abuses, detainees must be kept in appropriately designated places of detention (Principles 12 and 16 of the Body of Principles for the Protection of All Persons under Any Form of Detention or Imprisonment; Rules 7 and 44, para. 3 of the Standard Minimum Rules for the Treatment of Prisoners; Article 10 of the Declaration on the Protection of All Persons from Enforced Disappearance; Principle 6 of the Principles on the Effective Prevention and Investigation of Extra-legal, Arbitrary and Summary Executions).

c) Contact with the outside world. Access to family members, legal counsel, and other relevant organizations (e.g. human rights staff) must be allowed (Principles 16, 18, and 19 of the Body of Principles for the Protection of All Persons under Any Form of Detention or Imprisonment; Rules 37, 44, para. 3, and 92 of the Standard Minimum Rules for the Treatment of Prisoners).

d) Separation. Different categories of detainees must be kept separately. Men and women must be detained in separate buildings or at least separate premises; women should have separate sanitary facilities; young persons must be separate from adults

[80] Ibid.
[81] Ibid.

(Article 10 ICCPR; Rules 8, lit. a and d of the Standard Minimum Rules for the Treatment of Prisoners).

e) Registration. All detainees must be registered. In addition to the details related to the arrest, the register must include the day and time of entry into the detention centre, the release or handover to another detaining authority, for example civilian international or local police, and the date and time of the person's first appearance before a judicial authority (Principle 12 of the Body of Principles for the Protection of All Persons under Any Form of Detention or Imprisonment; Rule 7 of the Standard Minimum Rules for the Treatment of Prisoners).

f) Personal effects. All money, valuables, clothing, and other personal effects belonging to detainees, which they cannot keep, must be recorded in an inventory signed by the detainee, placed in safe custody, and returned upon release (Rule 43 of the Standard Minimum Rules for the Treatment of Prisoners).

g) Discipline. Measures for discipline and order should be clearly set out in regulations and shall not be inhumane. Corporal punishment for disciplinary offences committed by detainees is prohibited, and so is the use of dark cells (Rules 29–31 of the Standard Minimum Rules for the Treatment of Prisoners).

Detainees must be protected against all acts or threats of violence, insults, and public curiosity.   1341

1. Detainees must be treated at all times humanely and with respect for their dignity. Torture is always prohibited, with no exceptions, and so are other forms of ill-treatment (Article 5 of the 1948 Universal Declaration of Human Rights; Article 7 ICCPR; Article 2 of the 1984 Convention against Torture; Rule 31 of the Standard Minimum Rules for the Treatment of Prisoners, Principle 6 of the Body of Principles for the Protection of All Persons under Any Form of Detention or Imprisonment).

2. Instruments of restraint such as handcuffs, chain, irons, and straitjackets must never be applied as a punishment, and chains and irons cannot be used as restraints either. Other instruments of restraint may only be used in the following circumstances: as a precaution against escape during transfer; on medical grounds if directed by a medical officer; as a last resort, if other methods fail, to prevent detainees from injuring themselves or others or damaging property (Rule 33 of the Standard Minimum Rules for the Treatment of Prisoners).

Detainees are to be given rations, shelter, and access to medical care.   1342

1. *Humane conditions of detention.* Detainees shall be kept in facilities, designed to preserve health, and shall be provided with adequate food, water, shelter, clothing, medical services, hygiene items, and sanitary facilities (Article 10 ICCPR; Principles 1, 22, 24, 25, and 26 of the Body of Principles for the Protection of All Persons under Any Form of Detention or Imprisonment; Rules 9–14, 15–16, 17–19, 20, 21, and 22–26 of the Standard Minimum Rules for the Treatment of Prisoners).

2. *Medical care.* Detainees must be offered a medical examination promptly after admission to the place of detention, and medical care must be provided whenever necessary (Principle 24 of the Body of Principles for the Protection of All Persons under Any Form of Detention or Imprisonment).

BEN F. KLAPPE

VI. Child Soldiers

1343   International humanitarian law and the UN Convention on the Rights of the Child set fifteen as the minimum age for military recruitment and participation in armed conflict (Article 77, para. 2, AP I; Article 38 ChildConv; see above, Sections 306 and 505). The Optional Protocol to the UN Convention on the Rights of the Child on the involvement of children in armed conflict states that governments and armed groups are prohibited from using children under the age of eighteen years in armed conflict. It also bans compulsory recruitment of children under the age of eighteen years and it bans voluntary recruitment of children under the age of eighteen years by armed groups.

Children are uniquely vulnerable to military recruitment and manipulation into violence because they are ignorant and impressionable. They are forced or enticed to join armed groups. Regardless of how they are recruited, child soldiers are victims, whose participation in conflict bears serious implications for their physical and emotional well-being. They are commonly subject to abuse and most of them witness death, killing, and sexual violence. Many participate in killings, sometimes committing the very worst atrocities and most suffer serious long-term psychological consequences. Fighting groups have developed brutal and sophisticated techniques to separate and isolate children from their communities. Children are often terrorized into obedience, consistently made to fear for their lives and well-being. They quickly recognize that absolute obedience is the only means to ensure survival. Sometimes, they are compelled to participate in the killing of other children or family members, because it is understood by these groups that there is 'no way back home' for children after they have committed such crimes.

1344   A child soldier is any person under eighteen years of age who is part of any kind of regular or irregular armed force or armed group in any capacity, including but not limited to cooks, porters, messengers, and anyone accompanying such groups, other than family members. The definition includes girls recruited for sexual purposes and for forced marriage. It does not, therefore only refer to a child who is carrying or has carried arms.

The definition may have significant consequences once the disarmament phase starts. When child soldiers are financially compensated when handing in weapons or ammunition, formerly unarmed family members may suddenly possess weapons or parts of weapons, potentially blurring anticipated numbers and eligibility criteria. The eligibility criteria should be sufficiently broad and based upon the 'Cape Town Principles' for children associated with armed forces or groups.[82] Children should, therefore, not be required to hand in weapons in order to participate in disarmament, demobilization, and reintegration programmes, and there should be no cash remuneration for weapons relinquished. Unfortunately, even where disarmament, demobilization, and reintegration planning has incorporated these widely accepted principles, as in the case of

---

[82] Principles and Guidelines on Children Associated with Armed Conflicts or Armed Groups ('Paris Principles') of February 2007, drafted under UNICEF auspices, which update the 'Cape Town Principles' of 1979, <http://www.diplomatie.gouv.fr/en/article-imprim.php3?id_article=8638>.

BEN F. KLAPPE

Liberia, their application has been uneven[83] and there was increased evidence that the payment of cash allowances to demobilized children adversely affected their acceptance and reintegration into the community.

> **The considerable challenges in healing and reintegrating children into their com-**   1345
> **munities in the aftermath of conflict is sometimes further compounded by severe**
> **addiction and dependency of children to drugs.**

Drugs may result in the reckless and brutal behaviour of children who are sometimes committing the very worst atrocities. Therefore, reintegration is often a complex process of community healing and atonement, and negotiation with families to accept their children back. All these dimensions of the experience of child combatants carry significant implications and challenges in terms of design and resources needs for psychosocial and other reintegration programming. The demobilization of children should be sought at all times, and separate and child-specific programmes should be organized for demobilized children.[84] Peacekeeping missions and United Nations agencies should seek to benefit from local expertise and NGO child-protection capacity in developing and implementing such comprehensive child-specific disarmament, demobilization, and reintegration programmes. Issues that require further attention and consideration include the duration of hosting and types of activities undertaken in care centres, appropriate ways to approach child drug abuse and options for assisting children without families.

> **Monitoring, documentation, and advocacy are fundamental to eliminating child**   1346
> **recruitment and to informing programmes to this end. Special protection measures**
> **are needed to prevent recruitment of children in camps for refugees and internally**
> **displaced persons.**

1. Peacekeepers, ideally, would identify recruitment processes and areas where recruitment takes place in an early stage. Subsequently, advocacy and other tactics targeting recruiters and their adult leaders will assist in eliminating the recruitment of children.

2. Children associated with armed forces who have crossed into a country of asylum should be accorded a legal status, protection, and assistance that promotes their rehabilitation and reintegration. Refugee status should be accorded to children who flee armed conflict due to their well-founded fear of being subjected to forced military recruitment, sexual slavery, or other serious child rights violations. From 2002 to 2004, 168

---

[83] Some children associated with armed forces or groups in Liberia were actually prevented from entering demobilization sites because they were not armed. The promise of a cash allowance upon presentation of a weapon has also proved problematic in Liberia; reports indicate that commanders have posed as guardians to former child soldiers, or have taken arms away from them and given the weapons to their own children, in order to obtain the cash payments. Commanders have even sold weapons to children so they could enter the disarmament, demobilization, and reintegration programme. Alternatives to cash allowances should be employed in order to prevent these practices and should contribute directly to the education and sustainable livelihood of former child soldiers.

[84] In Burundi, approximately 2,260 children were demobilized from armed forces and groups ahead of adult combatants, through the Child Soldiers National Structure. However, many children formerly associated with armed groups were cantoned in assembly areas where they waited for over eight months to return to their families; this delay was due to the lack of commitment of some leaders, lengthy negotiations over global demobilization and inadequate disarmament, demobilization, and reintegration resources. In Liberia, child-specific programmes, including literacy classes, psychosocial care, and recreational activities, were organized by NGOs through interim care centres, where demobilized child soldiers could stay for up to three months.

BEN F. KLAPPE

disarmed Liberian child soldiers were granted *prima facie* refugee status in Sierra Leone and were placed in camps for Liberian refugees; children whose families were traced were voluntarily repatriated. This process incorporated child-protection elements such as proper identification of children immediately upon entry to the country of asylum; prompt separation from commanders; accommodation in a civilian environment conducive to rehabilitation (instead of together with adult foreign combatants in internment camps); sensitization of refugee communities to facilitate community-based integration; access to education, counselling and other psychosocial programmes; and community-based interim care, tracing, family reunification, and voluntary repatriation in safety and dignity. Reintegration activities should adopt an integrated community approach, and interventions should avoid singling out former child soldiers. Both of these practices were employed in Afghanistan.[85] In order to support community reintegration activities for children formerly associated with armed forces or groups, long-term donor support is required.[86] Children who escape, are released, or are captured from any armed force or group should not be considered or treated as enemy combatants.[87]

1347   **While it is standard practice for peacekeepers to defend themselves against hostile acts or hostile intent, complications are to be expected when they are confronted with threats from child soldiers. Peacekeepers should realize that armed children can be more volatile and unpredictable than adults, even if they are poorly trained.**

Although permitted to use force in self-defence, use of force against children will raise moral questions and may have far-reaching consequences when situations are reported worldwide. Failure to act adequately and appropriately may also result in extreme reactions in the mission area as well as from public opinion. Commanders should raise awareness at all levels of the existence of child soldiers in the mission area. The collection of information is key to successful and peaceful disarmament of child soldiers. Adequate scenario-driven training of troops for encounters with armed children could save lives on all sides.

VII. Humanitarian Assistance by Armed Forces

1348   **In planning peace operations, the provision of humanitarian assistance should be considered, having regard to the expected role of other actors in this field and the principles set out below.**

---

[85] Demobilized child soldiers were provided the same services as other war-affected children through the Afghanistan New Beginnings Programme, and communities played a central role in demobilization efforts by participating in the screening of eligible child participants.

[86] The Government of Sierra Leone requested continuing assistance for the reintegration of demobilized children through the Community Education Investment Programme, which provided educational materials to schools whose enrolment included demobilized children and children returning from neighbouring countries. This support facilitated the reintegration of more than 3,000 former child combatants and returnee children.

[87] In accord with this principle, and in implementation of Article 6 of the Optional Protocol on the Involvement of Children in Armed Conflict, a group of children associated with a Colombian armed group and arrested by the Venezuelan authorities was immediately offered protection and reintegration assistance. The Government of Colombia established legal and administrative procedures ensuring that children who leave armed groups are handed over to the Colombian Institute for Family Welfare national disarmament, demobilization, and reintegration programme.

BEN F. KLAPPE

Military components of peacekeeping operations assist humanitarian organizations and agencies when such support is requested. Furthermore, most contingents that carry out community support projects are not only focused on pragmatically building good relationships with the local population or generating positive publicity but are genuinely committed to improving the living conditions of and making a positive contribution to their host communities.[88] The quality and effectiveness of those activities varies greatly and, in some instances, will lead to unintended consequences that hamper support for humanitarian organizations and agencies and confidence-building with the local population. Effective military involvement in humanitarian assistance should begin with coherent planning and strategy development.

> **Although peacekeepers in many operations have successfully implemented humanitarian projects (hearts and mind projects, quick impact projects), humanitarian assistance by armed forces have drawn criticism from the humanitarian community, arguing that any humanitarian assistance should not be the responsibility of the military component. In cases where the humanitarian and development communities are closely involved in planning and designing of such humanitarian assistance projects, there have been less problems.**   1349

1. Humanitarian organizations and agencies have argued that in volatile situations and during robust peacekeeping or peace enforcement, other parties to the conflict and beneficiaries of assistance may be neither willing nor able to differentiate between assistance provided by the military and that provided by humanitarian agencies. A contributing factor is the grey zone, being a beneficiary of assistance and party to the conflict at the same time. Besides the necessity for close coordination within the military component, proper coordination and liaison with the humanitarian community through the humanitarian coordinator or his/her representative would help contingents to concentrate on projects with the highest impact, to address the needs of the target population and, most of all, to harmonize their initiatives with the overall humanitarian and rehabilitation activities in an area.

2. However, such coordination rarely occurs with regard to community support projects. Lack of coordination may lead to grave consequences, as pointed out by humanitarian organizations and agencies. This very serious concern makes close consultation between the military component and humanitarian organizations and agencies essential to ensure that lives are not endangered and that access to the affected population remains open. The provision of support to humanitarian activities requires early coordinated planning to ensure that adequate resources and coordination capacity are available to carry out effective support tasks, such as infrastructure work. Support for local communities should be based on a clear strategy and an understanding of the needs of the affected population in order to achieve mission objectives and complement other civil activities in an area of operations.

3. Thorough consultation and coordination with humanitarian organizations and agencies is necessary to identify the highest-impact projects based on the needs of the local population and to avoid duplication and irrelevant or conflicting activities. In particular,

---

[88] UN Doc. A/60/588 of 13 December 2005, Report of the Office of Internal Oversight Services on the review of military involvement in civil assistance in peacekeeping operations.

existing coordination and liaison functions, such as the civil–military coordination positions staffed by military and civilian personnel in peacekeeping operations, need to be strengthened and better aligned. Furthermore, the development, revision, distribution, and follow-up of relevant policies are needed to ensure that the military component has a clear understanding of what proper military involvement in civil assistance entails and how the military can make a positive contribution to the affected population and support the mission as a whole. Adequate resources and personnel qualified to provide support to humanitarian activities or local communities are needed to make military involvement more effective.

1350　　**In cases where humanitarian assistance is not made available from civilian sides, humanitarian assistance should be provided by armed forces.**

Military reconnaissance teams visiting the mission area prior to deployment will assess the humanitarian situation and the possible presence of humanitarian organizations and agencies. When no humanitarian organizations are in place the force should anticipate and plan for humanitarian assistance.

1351　　**In order to enhance the effectiveness of humanitarian action, states should ensure that humanitarian assistance is coordinated as effectively as possible by a responsible coordinator, such as the United Nations Office for the Coordination of Humanitarian Affairs (OCHA).**

1. In most countries in the process of concluding ceasefire and peace agreements, humanitarian organizations and agencies are already present before a peacekeeping force deploys. Their activities, ideally, are controlled by a (UN) humanitarian or resident coordinator. When transforming the existing humanitarian operation in an integrated mission including military and police elements, the resident coordinator may assume the role of Deputy Special Representative of the Secretary General. As the military component possesses means to provide humanitarian assistance, the development and coordination of humanitarian assistance is a shared responsibility for the humanitarian coordinator and the force commander who may set priorities for the use of military assets.

The main military entity responsible for coordinating humanitarian assistance is the civil–military coordination and liaison function at force headquarters. Staff officers responsible for civil–military coordination and liaison at force headquarters are primarily tasked with advising the force commander on civil–military issues and operations, and participating in coordination mechanisms.

2. Community-support projects are generally approved by contingent commanders, sometimes in consultation with the force commander, and should be consulted with the humanitarian coordinator or his/her representative because such projects may have a serious impact on humanitarian activities. In order to maximize effects of humanitarian actions, a coordination mechanism should be reliable, and it is essential to have established points of contact and clear authorization channels and procedures for dealing with requests for support.

1352　　**The above-mentioned principles also apply to humanitarian assistance outside peace operations, for example in rescue missions or natural disasters.**

14

IMPLEMENTATION AND ENFORCEMENT OF INTERNATIONAL HUMANITARIAN LAW

Introductory Remarks

1. *Implementation and enforcement in general.* In every legal order there are actions or omissions that violate legal rules and obligations. This is true in regard to the international legal order and the rules of international humanitarian law as well. Such violations do not mean that the international legal order or international humanitarian law is not the law; but it does mean that there is—as in a national legal order—the need for a lawful counterreaction in order to show that the violation of a certain humanitarian rule is a violation of the *law*.[1] However, one of the peculiarities of international law is that its legal rules are not implemented and enforced through a central body or hierarchical institutions. In this respect it differs fundamentally from domestic law.[2] This general feature of the international legal order as an order of coordination does not exclude elements of hierarchy or constitutionalization in some areas of international law.[3] Such elements can be seen in the proliferation of international courts and tribunals,[4] and in the area of the preservation of international peace and security. Within the latter, the Security Council, acting under Chapter VII Charter of the United Nations, has the main competences.[5] Apart from this, enforcement of international law lies with individual members of the international community, which have recourse to different enforcement methods.

---

[1] In general to the 'reaffirmation of the commitment to the rule of law and its fundamental importance for political dialogue and cooperation among all States and for the further development of the three main pillars upon which the United Nations is built: international peace and security, human rights and development', cf. UN GA Res. A/67/L.1*, *Declaration of the High-level Meeting of the 67th Session of the General Assembly on the rule of law at the national and international levels*, 24 September 2012, No. 20, available at <http://unrol.org/files/Official%20Draft%20Resolution.pdf>.

[2] Cf. Torsten Stein, 'Decentralized International Law Enforcement', in Jost Delbrück (ed.), *Allocation of Law Enforcement Authority in the International System* (Duncker & Humblot, 1995), 107–26.

[3] Cf. D. J. Elazar, *Constitutionalizing Globalization, The Postmodern Revival of Confederal Arrangements* (Lanham, MD: Rowan and Littlefield, 1998).

[4] Cf. Fausto Pocar, 'The International Proliferation of Criminal Jurisdictions Revisited: Uniting or Fragmenting International Law?' in Holger P. Hestermeyer, Doris König, Nele Matz-Lück, Volker Röben, Anja Seibert-Fohr, Peter-Tobias Stoll, Silja Vöneky (eds), *Coexistence, Cooperation and Solidarity: liber amicorum Rüdiger Wolfrum* (Nijhoff, 2012), 1705 *et seq.*; Tullio Treves, 'Cross-Fertilization between Different International Courts and Tribunals: The Mangouras Case', in *op. cit.*, 1787 *et seq.*

[5] See below, Sections 1427–31.

2. There are certain positive and negative structural features of this decentralized implementation: (1) Flexibility: there is no per se limited number of means of implementing in international law and international humanitarian law (no *numerus clausus*); therefore, different means of implementation can be modified and combined. (2) Power-sensibility: the *de facto* power of the subject (i.e. the state) implementing international humanitarian law is often decisive. This can be called the power-sensibility of the different means of implementation. (3) Overlapping norms and competences: due to the lack of a clear hierarchy of rules, there is the problem of overlapping branches of international law and overlapping competences of courts and tribunals. (4) Implementation deficits of rules protecting common values: there is a structural problem in the implementation of common values and concerns, especially in regard to obligations *erga omnes* and to *jus cogens* norms.

3. But apart from these general problems of decentralized implementation, there is an additional underlying problem in implementing and enforcing international humanitarian law. International humanitarian law has a *telos* which points in two different directions: on the one hand, there is the clear aim of international humanitarian law, especially after World War II (WWII), to not allow any kind of total warfare. The main aim of international humanitarian law is to restrict the methods and means of warfare and to protect certain persons and objects, above all to protect civilians and civilian objects. On the other hand, there is the need to not prohibit the use of weapons altogether, since states are allowed to use military means in order to exercise their right of self-defence as confirmed in Article 51 UN Charter. Hence, humanitarian law tries to humanize an area which is per se inhumane. Implementing and enforcing law in such circumstances is one of the greatest efforts a legal order has to cope with.

4. In order to classify the various lawful reactions to violations of international law and international humanitarian law, the following differentiation seems to be convincing: first, there are so-called bilateral confrontative forms of implementation and enforcement of international legal obligations. This is mainly an implementation by lawful countermeasures, that is retorsions and reprisals.[6] They are regarded as classic forms of the national enforcement of international law obligations (see below, Section 1408). Second, there are non-confrontative means of implementation and enforcement in a general sense. This includes, for instance, the international law of state responsibility.[7] Part of these non-confrontative means are all means of peaceful settlement according to Article 33 UN Charter (see below, Section 1432). Third, there are non-confrontative means of implementation and enforcement by decisions and opinions of courts and tribunals: most importantly, the decisions and opinions of the International Court of Justice (ICJ) implement international humanitarian law; apart from this, human rights bodies and courts are important in implementing the law applicable to armed conflicts (see below, Section 1426). A special kind of this way of implementing international humanitarian law is the criminal prosecution of certain individuals by national or international or hybrid courts or tribunals. The punishment of individuals as war criminals seems essential for the effective enforcement of international humanitarian law (see

---

[6] Thomas Giegerich, 'Retorsion', in *MPEPIL*.

[7] See, for instance, for a breach of Art. 1 GC, ICJ, *Military and Paramilitary Activities in and against Nicaragua (Nicaragua v US)*, Merits, 27 June 1986, *ICJ Reports 1986*, para. 220.

SILJA VÖNEKY

below, Sections 1411–1418).[8] Fourth, there are special forms of implementation and enforcement which can be found only in regard to certain branches of international law. A special form of the implementation of international humanitarian law is the system of collective security, with the Security Council acting under Chapter VII Charter of the United Nations (see below, Sections 1427–1431). International humanitarian law itself has developed specific instruments to secure both interstate and domestic enforcement. These support the institutions of protecting powers and substitutes (Article 5 AP I, see below, Sections 1420–1421) and the International Fact-Finding Commission (Article 90 AP I, see below, Section 1422).

5. Within each individual state, continuous efforts are required to implement international humanitarian law effectively. Activities of states, international organizations, courts and tribunals, NGOs, and individuals remain essential for the success of these efforts. The competence and responsibilities of the various actors and the interplay of their activities to ensure respect of international humanitarian law shall be discussed in this chapter.

I. General

Violations of international humanitarian law have been committed by parties to nearly every armed conflict. However, both published reports and internal findings show that the protective provisions of international humanitarian law have prevented or reduced great suffering in many cases.   **1401**

Rules of law that are valid must be generally obeyed and must be effectively accepted as a common standard of official behaviour.[9] International law faces the same problems concerning violations as every other legal system. This is not to be understood as an excuse for violations, but it stresses that the realization of legal obligations is to a great extent dependent on the effectiveness of law enforcement and implementation. One necessary condition for the effective implementation of humanitarian law is that its contents be known by persons involved in a conflict, especially the combatants, that those persons be aware that violations carry disciplinary or penal consequences, and that they realize that persistent breaches may lead to an escalation of the conflict. In this regard, compliance with humanitarian law is in the interest of every individual party to an armed conflict. The developments in many recent conflicts indicate that public opinion, particularly the mass media and information via the Internet, can be in a position to keep conflicts under surveillance and to document breaches of international humanitarian law to a certain extent.[10] Furthermore, there is a growing tendency to use the spectre of public

---

[8] John Alan Appleman, *Military Tribunals and International Crimes* (Indianapolis: Bobbs-Merrill Company, 1954; Westport, Connecticut: Greenwood Press, 1971), 53; Antonio Cassese, 'On the Current Trends towards Criminal Prosecution and Punishment of Breaches of International Humanitarian Law' (1998) 9 *EJIL* 2–17.

[9] For a national legal order, see on these conditions H. L. A. Hart, *The Concept of Law*, 1st edn (OUP, 1961), 113 *et seq.*

[10] However, the non-international armed conflict in Syria in 2012 shows that without a free press the possibilities to document breaches of international humanitarian law are diminished to a great extent and that mass media and the Internet are misused for propaganda purposes. See also A. Lustgarten and F. Debrix, 'The Role of the Media in Monitoring International Humanitarian Law during Military Interventions: The Case of Kosovo' (2005) 3 *Peace & Change* 359–97, at 359.

SILJA VÖNEKY

documentation as a weapon to deter abuses as well as to lay the foundations for later prosecutions. The inquiries of the Security Council and the Commission on Human Rights in the case of the Former Yugoslavia may be seen in this light.[11] Apart from this, military leaders and responsible political organs are themselves under an obligation to investigate possible breaches of humanitarian law, to suppress them, and to document corresponding investigations and measures taken (for duties in relation to war crimes and violations of human rights, see below, Sections 1410–1418).

1402   **Each party to the conflict must respect and ensure respect for international human-itarian law by its armed forces and other persons or groups acting in fact on its instructions, or under its direction or control (Article 1 common to the Geneva Conventions; Article 1, para. 1, AP I; Rule 139 *CIHL*).**

1. The wording of Article 1 common to the Geneva Convention and Article 1, para. 1, AP I states that the parties of the Geneva Conventions 'undertake *to respect and ensure respect* for the present Convention in all circumstances'. These unconditional obligations do not depend on reciprocity;[12] they are valid in regard to international armed conflicts covered by the GC and the AP I, and in regard to those duties in non-international armed conflicts that are embodied in Article 3 GC[13] or spelled out in more detail, for example in AP II,[14] Article 1 GC forms part of customary international law.[15] According to this, a state is obliged to ensure that the rules of the GC and AP I are not violated by its organs or by any subjects under its jurisdiction (persons acting under the command and effective control of the state without belonging to its armed forces)[16] and to do everything within its possibilities to ensure universal compliance with the 'humanitarian principles underlying the Conventions'.[17] Hence, it cannot be argued that violations of the GC, of the AP I and of customary law with the same content are lawful because of recourse to certain circum-stances precluding wrongfulness, as for instance self-defence, consent of the victim state, a state of necessity, and so on. Article 1 GC rejects the *tu quoque*- or *do-ut-des*-principle: the obligations of the GC and the AP I are not based on reciprocity.[18]

2. The obligation to ensure respect for international humanitarian law in all circum-stances entails, for instance, using all possibilities of diplomatic action, resorting to the

---

[11] M. Cherif Bassiouni, 'Former Yugoslavia: Investigating Violations of International Humanitarian Law and Establishing an International Criminal Tribunal' (1994) 4 *Fordham International Law Journal* 1191–211, 1202 *et seq.*; B. G. Ramcharan, *Human Rights and U.N. Peace Operations: Yugoslavia* (Brill, 2011).

[12] In contrast to Art. 2 HC IV (1907), which states: 'The provisions contained in the Regulations referred to in Article 1, as well as in the present Convention, do not apply except between Contracting powers, and then only if all the belligerents are parties to the Convention.'

[13] ICJ, *Military and Paramilitary Activities in and against Nicaragua (Nicaragua v US)*, Merits, 27 June 1986, *ICJ Reports 1986*, para. 220 *et seq.*

[14] Duties spelled out in AP II are indirectly covered by Art. 1 GC insofar as AP II is an elaboration of Art. 3 GC, cf. Art. 1, para. 1, AP II, see Laurance Boisson de Chazournes/Luigi Condorelli, 'Common Article 1 of the Geneva Conventions revisited: Protecting collective interests' (2000) 837 *IRRC* 1–14, available at <http://www.icrc.org/eng/resources/documents/misc/57jqcp.htm>.

[15] ICJ, *Military and Paramilitary Activities in and against Nicaragua (Nicaragua v US)*, Merits, 27 June 1986, *ICJ Reports 1986*, para. 220.

[16] ICTY Appeals Chamber, *The Prosecutor v Dusko Tadić*, Judgment, The Hague, 15 July 1999, Case No. IT-94-1. Cf. G. D. Solis, *The Law of Armed Conflict* (CUP, 2010), 142.

[17] Cf. in regard to the *travaux préparatoires* Jean S. Pictet (ed.), *Commentary, Geneva Convention relative to the Protection of Civilian Persons in Time of War* (ICRC., 1958), 21.

[18] ICTY Trial Chamber, *The Prosecutor v Zoran Kupreskić et al.*, Judgment, 14 January 2000, Case No IT-95-16-T, para. 517.

SILJA VÖNEKY

protecting powers institution and its substitutes, enforcing the system of prosecution and extradition of war criminals, calling upon the Fact-Finding Commission or using the naming and shaming of parties that breach the *jus in bello*.

3. These obligations have to be fulfilled by a state even if the Security Council authorizes the use of military means, as the armed forces remain under the command and control of that state; additionally, it is the UN's duty to ensure respect for international humanitarian law.[19] That the obligations of states and the UN to respect and to ensure respect of humanitarian law have to be combined is expressly laid down in Article 89 AP I, which states a duty of co-operation for certain serious violations.[20]

4. It is debatable whether it is convincing that Article 1 GC and Article 1, para. 1, AP I additionally obliges all parties of the GC and the AP I to take all possible steps at all times to ensure that these rules applicable in armed conflicts are respected by all other states. According to this reading, states and international organizations would have to take an active part in ensuring compliance and would also have to react against violations of these laws.[21] This interpretation would mean that Article 1 GC imposes a universal obligation for states and international organizations that does not derive from other provisions of the Geneva Conventions.[22]

> States engaged in military co-operation must ensure legal interoperability in the event of any difference in legal obligations that may become relevant for certain operations. While such a difference would not exclude military co-operation as such, no state may request any act or omission which would contravene any legal obligation of the requesting state or even the requested state. States bearing certain legal obligations may be obliged to encourage other states to accept them (Article 21 ClusterConv).   1403

In armed conflicts, where a coalition of states against an adversary is involved, the difference in legal obligations can make co-operation difficult. If a coalition of states is using military means, often some of the states are parties to the AP I and AP II, but others are only bound by the Hague and Geneva Conventions and the relevant customary humanitarian law.[23] This gap between different *jus in bello* obligations is especially relevant in non-international armed conflicts, as the AP II entails much more detailed norms and obligations than Article 3 GC and the customary law applicable in non-international armed conflict. Different obligations from international human rights treaties and other peacetime law applicable in armed conflicts[24] make it necessary to find a common legal ground for military co-operation as well. Military co-operation is not excluded because of such differences. However, no state may request anything from another state in a coalition which contravenes any legal obligation of the two states. This limitation can

[19] In regard to UN forces conducting operations under United Nations command and control, the practice of the UN Secretary-General is decisive, cf. UN SG, Observance by United Nations forces of international humanitarian law, 6 August 1999, UN Doc. ST/SGB/1999/13.

[20] Art. 89 AP I states: 'In situations of serious violations of the Conventions or of this Protocol, the High Contracting Parties undertake to act jointly or individually, in co-operation with the United Nations and in conformity with the United Nations Charter.'

[21] L. B. de Chazournes/L. Condorelli (above, n. 14).

[22] Some argue in favour of this, ibid.

[23] Many states are not parties of the AP I and/or AP II, for instance India, Indonesia, Iran, Israel, Pakistan, Somalia, South Sudan, Turkey, and the US.

[24] S. Vöneky, 'Armed Conflict, Effect on Treaties', *MPEPIL*.

SILJA VÖNEKY

be deduced from general rules of international treaty law: according to these rules, every state party to a treaty may not act contrary to the treaty obligations and has to do everything possible so that the treaty obligations are fulfilled.[25] Additionally, a treaty applicable in armed conflicts—because of its wording, object and purpose—can lay down the duty of states parties to encourage other states to accept the treaty obligations.

1404   The following factors can induce the parties to an armed conflict to ensure compliance with and counteract breaches of international humanitarian law:
— consideration for public opinion,
— reciprocal interests of the parties to the conflict,
— maintenance of discipline,
— fear of reprisals,
— penal and disciplinary measures,
— liability for compensation,
— activities of protecting powers,
— international fact finding,
— the activities of the International Committee of the Red Cross (ICRC),
— the activities of the United Nations,
— diplomatic activities,
— activities of non-governmental organizations,
— national implementing measures,
— dissemination of humanitarian law, and
— the personal conviction and responsibility of the individual.

The obligation to observe international humanitarian law addresses itself both to states parties to the conflict and to individuals, mainly combatants and civilians directly participating in hostilities. The incentives for states and individuals to comply with the law are diverse.

1. *Public opinion.* In the days of mass media, and the present possibility to spread information via the Internet across borders, the role which public opinion plays in humanitarian law enforcement is growing both within states parties to a conflict and in other countries. There are many examples of this. An important one is the US entry into WWII after breaches of international humanitarian law committed in territories of, and occupied by, the German Reich. The course of the Vietnam conflict was clearly influenced by public opinion both from within the US and from outside. Pictures broadcast from Iraq, the Former Yugoslavia, Somalia, and information via the Internet about the civil war in Libya contributed substantially to the willingness of the community of states to attempt to contain these conflicts (see below, para. 8). However, that public opinion can be manipulated through false information can be shown, for instance, in regard to incidents after the invasion of Kuwait.[26] Apart from this, in non-international armed conflicts in undemocratic societies, as in Syria in 2012, it can be difficult to distinguish information about breaches of humanitarian law by state troops or insurgents from pure

---

[25] Such obligations are not in conflict with Art. 34 *et seq.* 1969 Vienna Convention of the Law of Treaties (UNTS Vol. 1155, 331), limiting treaty obligations and treaty rights in regard to non-treaty parties without their consent.

[26] It was falsely asserted by a witness that after the Iraqi invasion of Kuwait, Iraqi soldiers caused the death of babies by taking them out of incubators in a Kuwaiti hospital, cf. M. Kunczik, 'Transnational Public Relations by Foreign Governments', in Krishnamurthy Sriramesh/Dejan Vercic (eds), *The Global Public Relations Handbook: Theory, Research, and Practice* (Taylor & Francis, 2009), 863 *et seq.*

propaganda.[27] If there is no free press in a country where an armed conflict takes place, NGOs may help to find out objective information about violations of humanitarian law and human rights and spread them.[28]

2. *Reciprocal interests of the parties.* An important element in guaranteeing respect for humanitarian law results from the idea of reciprocity.[29] No party to a conflict can expect its opponent to observe rules of warfare which it does not itself respect. The expectation of mutual advantages is one of the guarantees for the implementation of international law in general[30] as well as international humanitarian law specifically (see below, Section 1406). Therefore, implementation and enforcement of international humanitarian law in all those armed conflicts, where one party decides not to obey humanitarian law at all, becomes extremely difficult. This is true in regard to so-called asymmetric armed conflicts, where insurgents or terrorist groups fight against a state and want to obtain a military advantage or reach a political aim by breaking the relevant rules, as for instance by attacking civilians.

3. *Fear of reprisals.* A breach of international humanitarian law can be countered by the opponent through an act normally contrary to international law (reprisal). This responding violation of international law finds its justification in the principle of reciprocity. Here, in particular, exists a real danger of further escalation. International humanitarian law after WWII, particularly AP I, human rights law applicable in armed conflicts, and norms of *jus cogens,* limits the permissibility of reprisals.[31] The protection of certain persons and objects in all circumstances is an important feature of the present humanitarian law.

4. *Penal and disciplinary measures.* Fear of criminal or disciplinary punishment, in addition to the deterrent effect of past convictions, is another means by which adherence to humanitarian law can be guaranteed. The evolution of international criminal law and the establishment of the ICC, post-conflict international criminal courts, and tribunals, where war crimes can be prosecuted, are important and necessary improvements for the implementation of humanitarian law when states themselves are not willing or not able to prosecute war criminals. However, these repressive measures, after a violation of humanitarian law, alone are not sufficient. Rather, as a preventive measure, it is the duty of superiors to make their troops aware that the conduct of war is subject to limitations and that adherence to the rules of warfare is in the interest of every single combatant. A precondition for this is that international humanitarian law has been implemented

---

[27] *CIHL*, Practice Relating to Rule 144, para 16.10.2. <http://www.icrc.org/customary-ihl/eng/docs/v2_rul_rule144>. See on Syria, Nathan Smith, 'Propaganda, truth and lies in Syria', The National Business Review, 23 September 2012 <http://www.nbr.co.nz/>.

[28] In regard to the armed conflict in Syria, see, for instance, 'Save the Children, Untold atrocities, the story of Syria's children', 2012 <http://www.savethechildren.org.uk/sites/default/files/images/untold_atrocities.pdf>.

[29] See Bruno Simma, 'Reciprocity', *MPEPIL* for further supporting evidence. For an interdisciplinary general theory on reciprocity, see Elionor Ostrom/James Walker (eds), *Trust and Reciprocity, Interdisciplinary Lessons from Experimental Research* (Russell Sage, 2003).

[30] A. Verdross/B. Simma, *Universelles Völkerrecht: Theorie und Praxis,* 3rd edn (Berlin: Duncker & Humblot, 1984), 49.

[31] See above, Sections 410, 476, 479, 1215 (para. 3, lit. c), and below, Section 1406. Cf. A. R. Albrecht, 'War Reprisals in the War Crimes Trials and in the Geneva Conventions of 1949', in Michael N. Schmitt/Wolff Heintschel von Heinegg (eds), *The Implementation and Enforcement of International Humanitarian Law* (Ashgate, 2012), 1 *et seq.*; Frits Kalshoven, 'Belligerent Reprisals Revisited', *op. cit.,* 27 *et seq.*

in national law and is made generally known to the troops,[32] for instance, by military manuals.

5. *Liability for compensation. Non-confrontative means of implementation.* International law recognizes the possibility of allowing a state to claim compensation for breaches of international law.[33] This instrument is not fully standardized, but could be a useful means of guaranteeing application of humanitarian law.[34] The claims for compensation made against Iraq—however, because of the breach of *jus ad bellum*—are an example.[35] For international armed conflicts, Article 3 HC IV,[36] reaffirmed by Article 91 AP I, provides that states are liable to pay compensation for violations of international humanitarian law committed by their armed forces. These provisions, which are part of customary law, confirm obligations of states to make payments if the case demands. However, after armed conflicts full compensation can be a heavy burden for the economy of a state.[37] On the other hand, payments shall only be made for *violations* of international humanitarian law: if a state acts mainly in conformity with the *jus in bello*, no or only minor compensation has to be paid. Apart from this, many states have not implemented this obligation as is required.[38] The legal evaluation of unlawful actions of states has been facilitated by the completion and final adoption in 2001 of the International Law Commission's Articles on Responsibility of States (ARS).[39] These Articles are not part of a lawmaking treaty, yet they have exerted considerable influence, and are rightly used today in jurisprudence and legal literature as an important reference document reiterating many rules of customary international law.[40] The basic rule stresses the obligation of Article 3 HC IV, Article 91 AP I, that every unlawful act, which can be attributed to a state, obliges that state to pay compensation for the damages caused. Furthermore, the fundamental character of certain humanitarian standards[41] as obligations *erga omnes*

---

[32] See below, Sections 1408–16.

[33] See below, Section 1417.

[34] Cf. Georg Dahm/Jost Delbrück/Rüdiger Wolfrum, *Völkerrecht*, Vol. I/3 (Berlin: de Gruyter, 2002) 956–90.

[35] E.g. the UN Compensation Commission was established in 1991 as a subsidiary organ of the Security Council in order to process claims and pay compensation for losses resulting from Iraq's invasion and occupation of Kuwait: 'Iraq... is liable under international law for any direct loss, damage, including environmental damage and the depletion of natural resources, or injury to foreign Governments, nationals and corporations, as a result of Iraq's unlawful invasion and occupation of Kuwait' (SC Res. 687 (1991)).

[36] Article 3: 'A belligerent party which violates the provisions of the said Regulations shall, if the case demands, be liable to pay compensation. It shall be responsible for all acts committed by persons forming part of its armed forces.'

[37] The payments of Iraq because of the illegal invasion of Kuwait included, up to 2012, US $37.7 billion (see <http://www.uncc.ch/status.htm>).

[38] On the problematic but crucial implementation of victims' rights in several European countries, see Marion E. Brienen and Ernestine H. Hoegen, *Victims of Crime in 22 European Criminal Justice Systems* (Nijmegen: Wolf Legal Productions, 2000), at 27 *et seq.*

[39] Articles on Responsibility of States for Internationally Wrongful Acts, United Nations, International Law Commission, Report on the Work of its Fifty-third Session (23 April–1 June and 2 July–10 August 2001), General Assembly, Official Records, Fifty-fifth Session, Supplement No. 10 (A/56/10), <http://untreaty.un.org/ilc/texts/instruments/english/commentaries/9_6_2001.pdf>, UN Doc. A/56/10.

[40] James R. Crawford, 'State Responsibility', in *MPEPIL*; D. Bodansky/J. R. Crook, 'Symposium: The ILC's State Responsibility Articles. Introduction and Overview', 93 *AJIL* 2002, 773–91, at 790.

[41] For example, crimes against humanity *East Timor (Portugal v Australia), ICJ Reports* 1995, 90 *et seq.*, at 102, para. 29; the prohibition of torture contained in common Art. 3(1)(a) common to the Geneva Conventions is part of *jus cogens*; 'basic rules of international humanitarian law applicable in armed conflict' (*Legality of the Threat or Use of Nuclear Weapons, ICJ Reports* 1996, 226 *et seq.*, at 257, para. 79); rights and obligations enshrined by the Genocide Convention are rights and obligations *erga omnes* (ICJ, *Application*

underlines that all states can be held to have a legal interest in their protection.⁴² The ICJ has again confirmed this principle,⁴³ but the exact consequences that the *erga omnes* principle might have in this context are not yet clear.⁴⁴ While state practice and jurisprudence seem still to deny that international law offers rights to individuals corresponding to the duties of states to comply with international humanitarian law, remedies to ensure compliance with international humanitarian law widely depend on individual initiatives within the executive branches of states and within civil society.⁴⁵ Nevertheless, a national legal order may provide a legal basis so that individuals can claim monetary compensation from that state because of violations of international humanitarian law, which caused damages or injuries.⁴⁶

6. *The role of protecting powers.* One institution to secure enforcement of international humanitarian law is that of protecting powers. It has not been implemented in many recent conflicts, but Article 5 AP I reaffirms the duty of the parties to international armed conflicts to secure the supervision and implementation of the Geneva Conventions and AP I by the application of the system of protecting powers.⁴⁷

7. *The International Committee of the Red Cross.* The ICRC provides protection and assistance to victims of armed conflict and acts as a guardian of international humanitarian law. It has the task of ensuring observation of the rights of protected persons (prisoners of war, wounded and shipwrecked persons, civilians, etc.) and may also assume the role of a substitute of a protecting power.⁴⁸ The work of the ICRC is important not only in 'classical' international armed conflicts, but also in non-international armed conflicts and the so-called 'war against Al-Qaida'.⁴⁹,⁵⁰

of the Convention on the Prevention and Punishment of the Crime of Genocide, Preliminary Objections, *ICJ Reports 1996*, 595 *et seq.*, at 616, para. 31).

⁴² ICJ, *Barcelona Traction, Light and Power Company Limited, ICJ Reports 1970*, para. 33. Article 26 '(Compliance with peremptory norms): Nothing in this chapter precludes the wrongfulness of any act of a State which is not in conformity with an obligation arising under a peremptory norm of general international law.'

⁴³ ICJ, *Legal Consequences of the Construction of a Wall in the Occupied Palestinian Territory*, Advisory Opinion of 9 July 2004, General List No. 131, *ICJ Reports 2004*, ILM 43 (2004), 1009 *et seq.*, paras. 155–7; *Legality of the Threat or Use of Nuclear Weapons*, Advisory Opinion of 8 July 1996, *ICJ Reports 1996*, 226, ILM 35 (1996), 809, para. 79.

⁴⁴ D. Fleck, 'International Accountability for Violations of the Ius in Bello: The Impact of the ICRC Study on Customary International Humanitarian Law' (2006) 11 *Journal of Conflict and Security Law* 179–99, at 181.

⁴⁵ D. Fleck, 'Individual and State Responsibility for Violations of the Ius in Bello: An Imperfect Balance', in W. Heintschel von Heinegg/V. Epping (eds), *International Humanitarian Law Facing New Challenges* (Berlin: Springer, 2007), 171–93.

⁴⁶ See, for instance, the decision of the German Federal Court of Justice (civil division) in the case of *Varvarin* of 2 November 2006: this lawsuit is based upon the bombing of a bridge in Serbia during the NATO operation Allied Force. The Court repudiated claims for compensation but did not negate the possibility that the German national law of state liability gives everybody the legal ground to claim compensation if a German combatant is violating the ius in bello and causing damages, cf. BGHZ 169, 349; Helmut Philipp Aust, 'Bridge of Varvarin Case', *Oxford Reports on International Law/International Law in Domestic Courts* 887 (DE 2006). Thereupon a constitutional complaint was lodged with the German Federal Constitutional Court, which is pending.

⁴⁷ See below, Sections 1418–19.

⁴⁸ See below, Section 1422.

⁴⁹ For this notion of the Obama-Administration (after the 'war on terror'-notion of the Bush administration) since 2009, cf. <http://www.washingtontimes.com/news/2009/aug/06/white-house-war-terrorism-over/?page=all>; Trevor McCrisken, 'Ten years on: Obama's war on terrorism in rhetoric and practice' (2011) 4 *International Affairs* 781–801.

⁵⁰ See for instance the ICRC report on its visits to detainees being held in US facilities in Afghanistan, Guantanamo, and Iraq: 'Persons detained by the US in relation to armed conflict and the fight against

8. *The United Nations.* Various UN bodies have stressed the need to strengthen the protection of victims of armed conflicts and to ensure compliance with international humanitarian law.[51] A special form of implementing international humanitarian law can be seen at the activities of the *Security Council.* The Security Council plays a special role in the implementation and enforcement of international humanitarian law. The Security Council is a quasi-central body, although the international legal order entails only certain elements of a hierarchy. Chapter VII of the UN Charter grants the Security Council the competence to employ coercive measures against a threat to or breach of the peace or against an act of aggression (Article 39 *et seq.* UN Charter). As every armed conflict, which is covered by international humanitarian law, is *prima facie* a situation falling under Article 39 UN Charter, the Security Council Competence of Chapter VII can and has to be[52] an enforcement mechanism in regard to the rules of humanitarian law if the Security Council decides to act in regard to a conflict. Since 1989, this coercive competence of the Security Council has come to practical existence.[53] Armed conflicts, serious and continuous human rights violations, acts of terrorism, and the proliferation of weapons of mass destruction have been considered to constitute threats to the peace by the Council. The Security Council has, in particular, called on parties to international or non-international armed conflicts to ensure the safety of civilian populations and to fully respect human rights *and international humanitarian law.* Invoking its responsibility for world peace, the Security Council condemned—for instance—the attacks of 9/11,[54] supported the fight against terrorists and Taliban in Afghanistan,[55] and passed a resolution in regard to the civil war in Libya.[56] In the Libyan conflict, as during the conflict in the Former Yugoslavia,[57] the Security Council prohibited military flights in Libyan airspace and authorized enforcement of control and aid measures by armed force to ensure the protection of civilians. In the Yugoslav conflict, it appointed an impartial commission of experts to investigate reports of violations of international human rights provisions.[58] In this and other conflicts, the Security Council has also endorsed the prosecution of war crimes and crimes against humanity.[59] In the Darfur conflict in Sudan and in the non-international armed conflict in Libya, the Council even transferred the case to the

terrorism—the role of the ICRC', 9 January 2012, available at <http://www.icrc.org/eng/resources/documents/misc/united-states-detention.htm>; cf. BBC News South Asia, 'Red Cross in Afghanistan gives Taliban first aid help', 26 May 2010, available at <http://www.bbc.co.uk/news/10161136>.

[51] See below, Sections 1423–9. In regard to the civil war in Libya 2011, see SC Res. 1970 (2011); SC Res. 1973 (2011). On the conflict in Syria in 2012, see, for instance, SG/SM/14490, GA/11271, 5 September 2012; Report of the Secretary-General, Implementation of General Assembly resolution 66/253 B on the situation in the Syrian Arab Republic, UN Doc. A/66/889, 21 August 2012.

[52] For the duty of co-operation between states and the UN, cf. Art. 89 AP I.

[53] Marco Roscini, 'The UN Security Council and the enforcement of international humanitarian law' (2010) 43(2) *Israel Law Review* 330–59. Laurence Boisson de Chazournes, 'The collective responsibility of States to ensure respect for humanitarian principles', in A. Bloed et al. (eds), *Monitoring Human Rights in Europe* (Kluwer, 1993), 247–60.

[54] SC Res. 1368 (2001).

[55] See, for instance, SC Res. 1707 (2006); SC Res. 1776 (2007); SC Res. 1943 (2010).

[56] SC Res. 1973 (2011).

[57] SC Res. 816 (1993) on Yugoslavia; SC Res. 1973 (2011) on Libya. M. N. Schmitt, 'Clipped Wings—Effective and Legal No-fly Zone Rules of Engagement' (1997–98) 20 *Loyola of Los Angeles International & Comparative Law Review* 727.

[58] SC Res. 780 (1992), UN Doc. S/25274 of 10 February 1993 (Report of the Commission).

[59] See n. 57 above.

International Criminal Court (ICC).[60] These actions were based upon Chapter VII of the UN Charter.[61] In regard to general questions[62] and at critical stages, these activities were supported by the General Assembly. The General Assembly, for example, requested the Secretary-General to submit a comprehensive report after the fall of Srebrenica.[63] They are supported as well by the Secretary-General, who, for example, appointed an independent inquiry into the action of the United Nations during the 1994 genocide in Rwanda.[64] In many cases, however, as in Syria in 2012, grave atrocities remained without sanctions, as the Security Council did not find the necessary support from some of its members for forceful actions.[65] If one looks at the activities of the Security Council acting under Chapter VII before, during or after an armed conflict covered by international humanitarian law, one has to conclude that the Council helps to implement and enforce international humanitarian law *inter alia* by stressing the responsibility of all parties of a conflict to obey these rules, by reiterating that both human rights law and international humanitarian law has to be obeyed, by establishing certain no-fly zones and weapon embargos, and by establishing post-conflict international or internationalized criminal courts or tribunals, where war crimes can be prosecuted. Other important means used by the SC are the offer of good offices, the dispatch of observer missions, and the initiation of operations of peacekeeping, peace-enforcement, or peacebuilding. Acting under Chapter VII, the SC can resort—and has resorted—to a great variety of peaceful measures and to different military means to promote respect for humanitarian principles.

This practice confirms that serious and continuing violations of human rights and international humanitarian law by a state are no longer considered an internal affair, and that the community of states can intervene through its co-operative organs. However, sufficient political will on the part of the world community remains necessary for the effective use of available instruments.

---

[60] SC Res. 1593 (2005); Res. 1970 (2011); cf. Art. 13, lit. b, ICC Statute.

[61] For other similar SC Resolutions after 1989 see e.g. SC Res. 770 (1992), 781 (1992), 794 (1992), 816 (1993), 819 (1993), 859 (1993), 1003 (1995), 1264 (1999), 1272 (1999), 1291 (2000).

[62] Cf. UN GA Res. A/67/L.1*, *Declaration of the High-level Meeting of the 67th Session of the General Assembly on the rule of law at the national and international levels*, 24 September 2012, No. 20, available at <http://unrol.org/files/Official%20Draft%20Resolution.pdf>.

[63] *Report of the Secretary-General pursuant to General Assembly Resolution 53/35. The fall of Srebrenica*, UN Doc. A/54/549 of 15 November 1999.

[64] *Report of the Independent Inquiry into the Actions of the United Nations During the 1994 Genocide on Rwanda*, 15 December 1999 [S/PV.4127 of 14 April 2000, SC/6843]. In regard to the occupied Palestinian territories and the call of SC and GA upon the Secretary-General to convene a meeting of the High Contracting Parties to the Fourth Geneva Convention, cf. S/RES/681 (1990) of 20 December 1990. The UN Secretary-General has dealt with problems of compliance with international humanitarian law in many different contexts, see e.g. *Uniting against terrorism: recommendations for a global counter-terrorism strategy*. Report of the Secretary-General, UN Doc. A/60/825 (27 April 2006); Report of the Secretary-General to the Security Council on the protection of civilians in armed conflict, UN Doc. S/2005/740 (28 November 2005); *In larger freedom: towards development, security and human rights for all*. Report of the Secretary-General, UN Doc. A/59/2005 (21 March 2005); Secretary-General's keynote address to the Closing Plenary of the International Summit on Democracy, Terrorism and Security—*A Global Strategy for Fighting Terrorism* (Madrid, 10 March 2005); Report of the Secretary-General's High-level Panel on Threats, Challenges and Change, *A more secure world: Our shared Responsibility* (New York: United Nations, 2004).

[65] SC Res. 2042 (2012), 2043 (2012), 2052 (2012), 2059 (2012); GA Res. 66/253 A (2012), 66/253 B (2012).

SILJA VÖNEKY

9. *Third states.* States not party to the original conflict may intervene against grave breaches[66] of international humanitarian law. The protection of individuals, according to modern international law, is no longer the internal affair of a state, and the possibility exists for intervention by international organizations (UN) or regional organizations or arrangements.[67]

10. *Non-governmental organizations.* In addition to the ICRC, NGOs have increased activities in assisting victims of armed conflicts during the recent decades. Some NGOs have exerted considerable influence on public opinion and developed professional services in the political arena and at field level.[68]

11. *National implementing measures.* In implementing their obligations under international humanitarian law,[69] many states have issued military manuals, enacted legal provisions, and developed national activities supporting a system of compliance.[70]

II. Public Opinion

1405

Public reports on violations of international law may render an essential contribution to enforcing behaviour in compliance with international law. To this end, considering the global information network, the media (press, radio broadcasting, television, Internet) can be employed today in an incomparably better way and thus more efficient manner than has been the case in previous armed conflicts. When offences against international law become known, each party to the conflict must expect that truthful reports on its violations of international law will impair the fighting morale of its forces and support by its own population.

Reference has already been made to the increasing significance of public opinion for enforcement of international humanitarian law.[71] Public opinion has initiated political decision-making on international peace operations, supported the prosecution of war crimes and influenced humanitarian assistance at a worldwide scale. The Internet today makes it easier and faster for information about massacres and other violations of humanitarian law to cross borders. In comparison with mass media, Internet communication makes it possible that sometimes even real-time information is available worldwide and that private individuals and non-state groups can spread their information nearly as successful as a

---

[66] Cf. Yves Sandoz, 'The History of the Grave Breaches Regime', in M. N. Schmitt/W. Heintschel von Heinegg (eds), *The Implementation and Enforcement of International Humanitarian Law* (Ashgate, 2012), 209 *et seq.*; Gary D. Solis, above, n. 16, 93 *et seq.*, 121 *et seq.*, 301 *et seq.*

[67] Thomas G. Weiss, 'RtoP Alive and Well after Libya' (2011) 3 *Ethics & International Affairs* 1–6; Alex J. Bellamy, 'Libya and the Responsibility to Protect: The Exception and the Norm' (2011) 3 *Ethics & International Affairs* 263–9. See below, Section 1430.

[68] See below, Section 1431. Claudia Hofmann, 'Reasoning with Rebels. International NGOs' Approaches to Engaging Armed Groups', SWP research paper, September 2012, p. 10, available at <http://www.swp-berlin.org/fileadmin/contents/products/research_papers/2012_RP11_hof.pdf>; Philippe Ryfmann, 'Non-governmental organizations: an indispensable player of humanitarian aid' (2007) 865 *IRRC* 21 *et seq.*

[69] See UN GA Res. A/67/L.1*, Declaration of the High-level Meeting of the 67th Session of the General Assembly on the rule of law at the national and international levels, 24 September 2012, No. 20, available at <http://unrol.org/files/Official%20Draft%20Resolution.pdf>.

[70] See below, Sections 1432, 1433.

[71] See above, Section 1402, para. 2.

SILJA VÖNEKY

state can via the traditional tools of mass media.[72] Through the Internet, more information can be distributed and more transparency could be reached in regard to violations of humanitarian law; however, new kinds of propaganda[73] and delusion have been developed and spread by this medium as well.[74]

III. Reciprocal Interests of the Parties to the Conflict

Only those who themselves comply with the provisions of international humanitarian law can expect the adversary to observe the dictates of humanity in an armed conflict. No one shall be guided by the suspicion that soldiers of the other party to the conflict might not observe these rules. Soldiers must treat their opponents in the same manner that they themselves wish to be treated.   1406

Although humanitarian protection may not be made subject to reciprocity,[75] the expectation of reciprocal behaviour should be and will be a driving force to motivate for better compliance. Therefore, in conflicts where it is clear that one party, for instance a terrorist group or a militarily weak state party, is deliberately or regularly committing war crimes and other violations of humanitarian law as a means of warfare, special efforts are necessary by the other parties so that their combatants uphold their duties in respect to the law. The negative psychological effects of the non-fulfilment of the relevant rules have to be answered with special support and measures motivating the adversary combatants to comply with the legal standards. Such support can be expressed at the international level by Security Council Resolutions naming the violations and war crimes, and by stressing the need to comply with humanitarian and human rights law for all sides;[76] even more important measures and support have to be given by the national states that are parties to a conflict: they have to train and to instruct combatants in regard to those special circumstances when the adversary is willing to break all legal rules.

IV. Maintenance of Discipline

Ordering or tolerating violations of international law leads to subordinates' doubts as to the justification of their own side's activities. It can also undermine the authority of the military leader giving such an order and can jeopardize the discipline of the forces.   1407

Violations of the law of warfare have a negative influence on subordinates in many regards. They can lead to relaxation of discipline, as they may favour a propensity among subordinates to disregard international humanitarian law. A superior who acts contrary

---

[72] James Reynolds, 'The view from inside Syria's propaganda machine', *BBC News Middle East*, 5 July 2012, <http://www.bbc.co.uk/news/world-middle-east-18717647>.

[73] See for a general overview of propaganda in the light of international law: Eric de Brabandere, 'Propaganda', in *MPEPIL*.

[74] Cf. Aiem El Difraoui, jihad.de-Jihadistische Online-Propaganda; *SWP 2012*, available at <http://www.swp-berlin.org/fileadmin/contents/products/studien/2012_S05_dfr.pdf>; Yochi J. Dreazen, 'The Taliban Is Winning the Propaganda War', *The Atlantic*, 2 November 2011, available at <http://www.theatlantic.com/international/archive/2011/11/the-taliban-is-winning-the-propaganda-war/247747>.

[75] Rule 140 *CIHL*; see above, Section 1219.

[76] See above, Section 1404, para. 8.

to international law endangers his own authority. He undermines the law in general and cannot expect that his orders will be followed unquestioningly in the future.

V. Reprisals

1408   The use of reprisals can cause an adversary, who is contravening international law, to cease that violation. Reprisals are permissible only in exceptional cases and for the purpose of enforcing compliance with international law. They require a decision at the highest political level (see Sections 485–488).

1. Reprisals are a means of enforcement of international law in general and of international humanitarian law. Reprisals are countermeasures that justify the infringement of the rights of a subject of international law, which itself is violating the law; this justification is given if and only if certain conditions are met: reprisals are aimed to stop the ongoing unlawful conduct; to this aim, any resort to reprisals must be necessary and proportional in regard to the ongoing unlawful conduct and the caused damage; reprisals must end if the unlawful conduct of the adversary ends.[77] They may not be used if there exists a prohibition or limitation: such prohibitions and limitations are norms of *jus cogens* and self-contained regimes,[78] or can be laid down in an international treaty or customary law.[79] Since WWII, international humanitarian law has expressly prohibited reprisals against protected persons and objects, that is the wounded, sick, and shipwrecked (Article 46 GC I; Article 47 GC II; Article 20 AP I), prisoners of war (Article 13, para. 3, GC III), civilians (Article 33, para. 3, GC IV; Article 51, para. 6, AP I;[80] Article 3, para. 2, MinesProt) and civilian objects (Article 52, para. 1, AP I), cultural property (Article 4, para. 4, CultPropConv; Articles 52, para. 1, and 53, lit. c, AP I), objects indispensable to the survival of the civilian population (Article 54, para. 4, AP I), and the natural environment (Article 55, para. 2, AP I) as well as works and installations containing dangerous forces (Article 56, para. 4, AP I). The express prohibitions of reprisal secure the protection of the named persons and objects, as far as possible. They state the core of the humanization of humanitarian law and are an important protection against the psychological *do-ut-des*[81] effect:[82] there is no justification for the violation of such protected persons or objects to become a means of enforcement. The prohibitions in humanitarian law against damaging persons in situations where reprisals would be lawful, according to general international law, is in accordance with the concept of human dignity.[83] If no prohibition of reprisals is part of humanitarian law or other branches of international law, the general conditions, outlined above, have to be met.

---

[77] Matthias Ruffert, 'Reprisal', in *MPEPIL*.

[78] Self-contained regimes are those parts of international law which limit the possible reactions to violations, cf. Eckart Klein, 'Self-Contained Regime', in *MPEPIL*.

[79] Georg Dahm/Jost Delbrück/Rüdiger Wolfrum, *Völkerrecht*, Vol. 1/1 (Berlin: de Gruyter, 1989), 92; Alfred Verdross/Bruno Simma, *Universelles Völkerrecht*, 3rd edn (Berlin: Duncker & Humblot, 1984), 909; Bruno Simma, in Jost Delbrück (ed.), *The Future of International Law Enforcement. New Scenarios—New Law?* (Berlin: Duncker & Humblot, 1993), 125, 136 *et seq.*

[80] However, the UK has entered a reservation to that rule; it is questionable whether such reservation is compatible with the object and purpose of AP I. Cf. K. Dörmann, 'Article 8, war crimes', in Otto Triffterer (ed.), *Commentary on the Rome Statute of the International Criminal Court*, (Munich: Beck, 2008), 324.

[81] Lat.: 'I give so that you will give.'

[82] See above, Section 1406.

[83] Nils Petersen, 'Human Dignity, International Protection', in *MPEPIL*.

2. In any case, the decision to take retaliatory measures lies at the political level. A military leader does not have the right to decide to answer an unlawful act of his opponent with an unlawful act of his own. Such measures constitute violations or grave breaches of humanitarian law and may result in disciplinary or criminal proceedings (see above, Sections 485–488).

VI. Command Responsibility

The command responsibility of superiors is not only relevant for the conduct of military operations (see above, Sections 139–146), but likewise for criminal and disciplinary procedures.

1409

Military commanders are responsible for the conduct of operations by their units and subordinates. This includes the obligation to ensure the lawful conduct of the mission. The behaviour of military commanders invokes state responsibility and also individual responsibility under (international and national) criminal law and under disciplinary law (see below Sections 1410–1418).

VII. Penal and Disciplinary Measures

Each member of the armed forces who has violated the rules of international humanitarian law must be aware of the fact that he or she can be prosecuted according to penal or disciplinary provisions.

1410

1. This provision refers to every violation, both grave breaches,[84] that is war crimes,[85] and others. The consequences of a grave breach are always of a penal nature—there is the duty to prosecute or extradite; other violations may be punished through disciplinary procedures.

2. The development of international criminal law is decisive for the implementation and enforcement of international humanitarian law. International law norms for the punishment of war crimes have evolved along with the development of international humanitarian law. They are understood primarily as a means of enforcement of the latter. However, the development of international treaty law on the punishment of war criminals has limped along behind the developmental pace of rules on warfare.[86] The

---

[84] See below, Sections 1409–11.

[85] For an overview, cf. Solis, above, n. 16, 301.

[86] Regarding prosecution of war crimes in the Middle Ages, cf. M. Keen, *The Laws of War in the Late Middle Ages* (Routledge, 1965); L. S. Sunga, *Individual Responsibility in International Law for Serious Human Rights Violations* (Nijhoff, 1992), 18. Punishment was already discussed for Napoleon following his return from Elba. In a statement made on 13 March 1815 in Vienna by the powers which had defeated Napoleon, the countries alleged that Napoleon had placed himself above the law, exposing himself to public retribution as an enemy of world peace. After his defeat, however, no criminal proceedings were initiated against him. Instead, by agreement of the great powers, he was treated as both a prisoner of war and a security risk and accordingly interned on St Helena. For rules on criminal sanction included in the first military manual, the so-called Lieber Code, see Arts. 37, 44, 47 Lieber Code 1863 [Instructions for the Government of Armies of the United States in the Field, General Order No 100]; cf. S. Vöneky, 'Der Lieber Code und die Wurzeln des modernen Kriegsvölkerrechts', 62 *ZaöRV* (2002), 423–60, available at <http://www.zaoerv.de/62_2002/62_2002_1_a_423_460.pdf>. See above, Section 117.

SILJA VÖNEKY

punishment of war criminals by the injured state was thus based primarily upon customary international law, disregarding the amnesty clauses of peace treaties pre-dating WWI that concerned the punishment of war crimes.[87] The Hague Conventions of 1899 and 1907 contained no express regulation of individual responsibility for offences against the laws and practices of war. However, specific indications of the right or possibility of criminal prosecution for war crimes are to be found in Articles 30, 41, and 56, para. 2, HagueReg. Article 41 HagueReg addresses the violation of ceasefire terms by private individuals and provides that compensation from and punishment of the accused parties can be demanded. Pursuant to Article 56, para. 2, HagueReg, all seizure, destruction, or wilful damage to common and institutional property, historic monuments, or works of art and science is prohibited and punishable. A comparable rule is found in Article 28 of the Geneva Convention of 1906, pursuant to which the states parties agreed 'to repress, in time of war, individual acts of robbery and ill-treatment of the sick and wounded of the armies, as well as to punish, as usurpations of military insignias, the wrongful use of the flag and brassard of the Red Cross'. These provisions assume the right or obligation to punish individuals, but fail to incorporate detailed regulations for prosecution. Thus, although a series of treaties governing the rules of warfare already existed before WWI, an international treaty securing an enforcement mechanism for punishment of war criminals was lacking and recourse to customary international law was necessary.

3. At the end of WWI, the punishment of those who had violated customary or treaty-made rules of warfare was considered at the preparatory meeting for the Paris Peace Conferences. This meeting established a Commission whose task was to investigate responsibility for the outbreak of the war. More specifically, the Commission was responsible for determining offences against the rules of warfare committed by Germany and its allies, and was mandated to establish a criminal court for the prosecution of responsible individuals. The Commission listed thirty-two war crimes.[88] The

---

[87] R. Lesaffer/M. van der Linden, 'Peace Treaties after World War I', *MPEPIL*; M. Lachs, *War Crimes: An Attempt to Define the Issues* (London: Stevens, 1945) emphasizes the Martens Clause in the Preamble (para. 8) HC IV: 'Until a more complete code of the laws of war has been issued, the High Contracting Parties deem it expedient to declare that, in cases not included in the Regulations adopted by them, the inhabitants and the belligerents remain under the protection and the rule of the principles of the law of nations, as they result from the usages established among civilized peoples, from the laws of humanity and the dictates of public conscience.' See above, Section 131.

[88] '(1) Murders and massacres; systematic terrorism. (2) Putting hostages to death. (3) Torture of civilians. (4) Deliberate starvation of civilians. (5) Rape. (6) Kidnapping of girls and women for the purpose of enforced prostitution. (7) Deportation of civilians. (8) Internment of civilians. (9) Forced labour of civilians in connection with the military operations of the enemy. (10) Usurpation of sovereignty during military occupation. (11) Compulsory enlistment of soldiers among the inhabitants of occupied territory. (12) Attempts to denationalize the inhabitants of occupied territory. (13) Pillage. (14) Confiscation of property. (15) Exactions of illegitimate contributions and requisitions. (16) Debasement of currency and issue of spurious currency. (17) Imposition of collective penalties. (18) Wanton devastation and destruction of property. (19) Deliberate bombardment of undefended places. (20) Wanton destruction of religious, charitable, educational, and historic buildings and monuments. (21) Destruction of merchant ships and passenger vessels without warning and without provision for the safety of passengers and crew. (22) Destruction of fishing boats and of relief ships. (23) Deliberate bombing of hospitals. (24) Attack on and destruction of hospital ships. (25) Breach of other rules relating to the Red Cross. (26) Use of deleterious and asphyxiating gases. (27) Use of explosive or expanding bullets, and other inhumane appliances. (28) Directions to give no quarter. (29) Ill-treatment of the wounded and prisoners of war. (30) Employment of prisoners of war on unauthorized works. (31) Misuse of flags of truce. (32) Poisoning of wells.' (1920) 14 *AJIL* 114–5; reprinted also in United Nations War Crimes Commission, *History of the United Nations War Crimes Commission and the Development of the Laws of War* (London: His Majesty's Stationery Office, 1948), at 34 *et seq.*

Treaty of Versailles[89] planned for punishment of individuals who had violated rules of warfare through the military tribunals of the Allied and Associated Powers (Articles 228–230), whereby offenders were to be handed over by the German Reich. This form of prosecution broke down when the German government[90] refused to surrender individuals accused of having committed war crimes. Instead, punishment of war criminals was undertaken, although inadequately, by the Supreme Court of the German Reich (*Reichsgericht*) on the basis of a law passed on 18 December 1919.[91] After the establishment of the League of Nations, the Commission entrusted with the preparation of a statute for the Permanent International Court of Justice made an attempt to develop a code on international criminal law. The proposals submitted in 1920 proposed punishment of violations of international law through an international court. However, the recommendation was not pursued further in the League of Nations.[92] Proposals for punishment of war crimes are found in the Geneva Conventions of 1929.[93] Despite these first steps, at the outbreak of WWII no general international law codification existed concerning the prosecution of war crimes. Nevertheless, the various attempts and proposals for regulation of this problem made it clear that there were three possible types of tribunal for punishment of war crimes: an international criminal court, the courts of the injured state, or the courts of the war criminal's home state. If punishment is to be pursued by the home state, the prosecution of war criminals can only be regarded as an effective means of enforcement of the law of war if this state is under an obligation to prosecute (i.e. Article 56, para. 2, HagueReg).

4. Already during WWII, the intention was voiced to punish German and Japanese war criminals. In 1942, stepping into the place of older institutions, a United Nations War Crimes Commission was set up and entrusted with preparation to that end.[94] At the end of 1943, a programme for the prosecution of war criminals was agreed upon at the Moscow Conference between the major powers (the US, the UK, and the former USSR).[95] On 8 August 1945, the US, the UK, France, and the former USSR signed

---

[89] Treaty of Versailles, RGBl. 1919, 687 *et seq.*

[90] Article 227 of the Treaty of Versailles considered the establishment of an international tribunal against Kaiser Wilhelm II; charges were to be brought against him for violation of international law and of sanctity of the contracts. The provision stipulated that the court 'should decide [pursuant to the] applied principles of international policy'. However, the execution of the trial foundered on the Netherlands' refusal to extradite. Article 230 of the Treaty of Sèvres provided for the sentencing of those responsible for the crimes against the Armenians. However, this treaty was not ratified and stipulations of this sort were absent from the later Treaty of Lausanne.

[91] Of the 901 persons against whom proceedings were initiated, only thirteen were convicted. The penalties were deemed to be too light, and they were not fully executed. The fact that the punishment of war criminals following WWI was considered unsatisfactory led to the establishment of the International Military Tribunal after WWII.

[92] International Law Commission, Historical Survey of the Question of International Criminal Jurisdiction—Memorandum submitted by the Secretary-General, UN Doc. A/CN.4/7/Rev. 1.

[93] Article 30: 'On the request of a belligerent, an enquiry shall be instituted, in a manner to be decided between the interested parties, concerning any alleged violation of the Convention; when such violation has been established the belligerents shall put an end to and repress it as promptly as possible.' See J. S. Pictet, *Humanitarian Law and the Protection of War Victims* (Institut Henry Dunant, 1975), at 68.

[94] Cf. *History of the UN War Crimes Commission* (above, n. 88); E. Schwelb, 'Crimes against Humanity' (1946) 23 *BYIL* 363–76.

[95] The Moscow Declaration reads: 'Those German officers and men and members of the Nazi party who have been responsible for, or have taken a consenting part in the above atrocities, massacres, and executions, will be sent back to the countries in which their abominable deeds were done in order that they may be judged and punished according to the laws of these liberated countries and of the free governments which

the Agreement for the Prosecution and Punishment of the Major War Criminals of the European Axis Powers, which nineteen other states ratified before the conclusion of the Nuremberg Trials. An integral part of this Agreement is the Charter of the International Military Tribunal, located in an addendum.[96] According to Article 6, lit. a, of its Statute, the Tribunal was competent to try crimes against the peace, war crimes, and crimes against humanity, which constitute three different offences.[97] Article 6 of the Statute defines the concept of war crimes as: 'violations of the laws or customs of war. Such violation shall include, but not be limited to, murder, ill-treatment or deportation to slave labour or for any other purpose of civilian population of or in occupied territory, murder or ill-treatment of prisoners of war or persons on the seas, killing of hostages, plunder of public or private property, wanton destruction of cities, towns or villages, or devastation not justified by military necessity.' To prove the legitimacy of punishment based upon this agreement the Tribunal stated that these acts had long been recognized as war crimes, either as customary or treaty law. Reference was made in this respect to Articles 46, 50, 52, and 56 HagueReg and to Articles 2, 3, 4, 46, and 51 of the 1929 Geneva Convention Relative to the Treatment of Prisoners of War.[98] In addition to the Germans, Japan's political and military decision-makers were also subjected to criminal prosecutions after WWII. Through a proclamation by the chief commanding officers of the Allied armed forces on 19 January 1946, an International Military Tribunal for the Far East was established and the Statute of the Tribunal was appended to it. Japan accepted the judgments passed by the International Military Tribunal in the San Francisco Peace Treaty.[99] The International Military Tribunals of Nuremberg and Tokyo conducted trials and imposed penalties against a number of German and Japanese actors. Further trials against groups of German persons were carried out by American military courts on the basis of Control Council Law No. 10, which followed the provisions of the Nuremberg Statutes with modifications. Similar war crimes trials took place against Japanese military personnel before courts in the US, the UK, Australia, Canada, and the Netherlands.[100]

5. A substantial number of war crimes are covered by the Four Geneva Conventions of 1949 and the two Additional Protocols. Although the Red Cross has not succeeded

will be created therein. […] The above declaration is without prejudice to the case of the major criminals, whose offences have no particular geographical location and who will be punished by the joint decision of the Governments of the Allies.' Cf. *A Decade of American Foreign Policy: Basic Documents, 1941–49 prepared at the request of the Senate Committee on Foreign Relations by the Staff of the Committee and the Department of State* (Washington, DC: Government Printing Office, 1950).

[96] Printed at 39 *AJIL* (1945), Suppl. 258.

[97] These three different offences had already been provided for in the proposals of the Commission on the Responsibility of the Authors of War and on Enforcement of Penalties appointed by the Preliminary Peace Conference of 1919; (1920) 14 *AJIL* 95. According to Morris Greenspan, *The Modern Law of Land Warfare* (New York: Columbia University Press, 1959), at 419, on the other hand, the term war crimes is to be understood generically as including conventional war crimes, crimes against humanity, and crimes against peace, as well as genocide. See C. Kreß, 'International Criminal Law', in *MPEPIL*.

[98] For the trials before the Nuremberg Military Tribunal, see J. Fuchs/F. Lattanzi, 'International Military Tribunals', in *MPEPIL*. See also the thorough study by K. J. Heller, *The Nuremberg Military Tribunals and the Origins of International Criminal Law* (OUP, 2011).

[99] For a comprehensive analysis see Yuki Tanaka, Tim McCormack, Gerry Simpson (eds), *Beyond Victor's Justice?: The Tokyo War Crimes Trial Revisited* (Nijhoff, 2011).

[100] Edward Drea, Introduction, in National Archives and Records Administration for the Nazi War Crimes and Japanese Imperial Government Records Interagency Working Group (eds), *Researching Japanese War Crimes Records: Introductory Essays*, 2006, at 7.

SILJA VÖNEKY

in developing its own 'Model Law' for punishing war criminals, which would serve as a model for the legislation,[101] the Geneva Conventions contain rules governing the prosecution of grave breaches of the Conventions (Articles 49–50 GC I; Articles 50–51 GC II; Articles 129–130 GC III; Articles 146–147 GC IV). Specific abuses committed against persons or goods protected by the Convention are defined here as falling into this category. These rules offer national legislatures sufficient grounds for prosecution. A number of breaches named in the Conventions had already previously been recognized as war crimes by customary international law. The contents of GC II address in principle the same issues as GC I. The second Convention contains special provisions resulting from the problems posed by naval warfare.[102] The same holds true for GC III, which rewrites individual standards of conduct in an effort to protect prisoners of war, and makes violations of these provisions a grave breach of the Convention.[103] GC IV also expands the scope of obligations, thus expanding the meaning of 'grave breach'.[104] These provisions circumscribe the necessary elements of a criminal offence, yet without the precision of a national penal code; concrete statements about the range of punishments are nowhere to be found. An exception is made regarding prosecution of criminal offences against prisoners of war (Articles 82–108 GC III). However, the parties to the treaty are only obliged to enact 'all legislation necessary to provide effective penal sanctions' (Article 129, para. 1, GC III). With this provision the Geneva Conventions decided on the third of the named prosecution methods, namely prosecution of war criminals by the state to which the transgressor belongs. Corresponding obligations to investigate and prosecute exist in Article 49, para. 2, GC I; Article 50, para. 2, GC II; Article 129, para. 2, GC III; and Article 146, para. 2, GC IV. This duty does not create any monopoly on investigation and prosecution on the side of the home state. The ability to investigate and prosecute is left fully open to other states. In this respect, other states interested in prosecuting war crimes are as much empowered to do so as the custodial state (for prisoners of war or internees).

6. In accordance with Article 49, para. 2, GC I, the home state of the offender, instead of conducting a prosecution itself, can hand such a person over for trial to another state interested in the prosecution, provided that sufficient incriminatory evidence is produced. The principle *aut dedere aut judicare* is thus valid. The extent to which such extradition is possible is regulated by the domestic law of the home state. Normally, the state interested in prosecution will most likely be either the injured state or the home state of the accused. However, extradition is not limited to these states. A request for extradition can be made by all parties to the Conventions, even by states neutral in the conflict, as long as they demonstrate an interest in the prosecution of the grave breaches committed and produce corresponding incriminating evidence. With this, international humanitarian law secures the prosecution of war criminals by all states.[105] The punishment of prisoners of war in the custodial state for grave breaches can occur under the terms of either the custodial state's domestic law or international (and thus also international

---

[101] Cf. Jean Pictet, *Humanitarian Law and the Protection of War Victims* (Stevens, 1975), at 70.
[102] Articles 22, 24, 25, and 27 GC II.
[103] Article 13 GC III.
[104] Article 147 GC IV.
[105] Hans-Heinrich Jescheck, 'War Crimes', IV *Encyclopedia of Public International Law* (Amsterdam: Elsevier, 2002), 1349–54, at 1351.

SILJA VÖNEKY

humanitarian) law.[106] The above-mentioned lack of precision in the Geneva Conventions is balanced by the fact that Articles 84–108 GC III contain a list of guarantees for the criminal proceedings as well as limits to sentences. Equally, the ICTY Statute is based on the prosecution of war criminals in accordance with international law.[107]

7. No explicit regulation is to be found in the Geneva Conventions governing the prosecution of war criminals in instances where the accused individual acted under orders.[108] Article 49, para. 2, GC I makes it clear, however, that both the person who acts and that person's commander may have committed a grave breach. The practice of the trials against war criminals immediately following WWII is consistent with this language. The Geneva Conventions deny a war criminal's claim that he acted as an organ of state and that his behaviour is therefore attributable to the state and not to him personally.[109] However, no indication is given of the extent to which following orders can exonerate a subordinate. The Conventions do not provide that grave breaches can also be committed through acts of omission, although the International Military Tribunals immediately following WWII have recognized these as violations. AP I lists further grave breaches. Article 11, para. 4 and Article 85, paras. 3 and 4, are examples. The Geneva Conventions are also expanded by Articles 86–87 AP I in that both acts and omissions can produce grave breaches. AP II does not mention grave breaches. Article 6 AP II, nevertheless, regulates prosecution and punishment of criminal offences connected with armed conflict. AP II presumes application of domestic criminal law, whereby the domestic power of sentence is subordinate to the demands of the Protocol.

8. Beyond these rules of the Geneva Convention and AP I and AP II, efforts were made in the United Nations to create a comprehensive international criminal law modelled on the London Agreement of 8 August 1945. These endeavours have remained unsuccessful for a long time. The International Law Commission in particular had increased its efforts to create a Code of Crimes Against the Peace and Security of Mankind.[110] These efforts were influenced by violations of the prohibition on war and of international humanitarian law committed in the international and non-international armed conflicts during the 1980s and 1990s.[111] Today, a broad *opinio iuris* exists that individuals who commit

---

[106] See Article 99, para. 1, GC III.

[107] UN Doc. S/25704 of 3 May 1993. Cf. Sascha-Dominik Bachmann, in Noelle Quénivet/Shilan Sha-Davis (eds), *International Law and Armed Conflict, Challenges in the 21st Century* (The Hague: Asser Press, 2010), 289–301.

[108] Proposals of some kind of immunity on the grounds of coercion or mistake of law were submitted during the drafting process of the Geneva Conventions, but the negotiating states could not reach any consensus (Final Record of the Diplomatic Conference of Geneva of 1949, Vol. II, Section B, at 115; 6 Official Records, at 307 *et seq.*).

[109] Cf. Dieter Matthei, 'Befehlsverweigerung aus humanitären Gründen' (1980) XIX *RDMilG* 257–90, at 259 *et seq.* Negotiations during the formulation of the 1977 Protocols to the 1949 Geneva Conventions illustrated that the former communist states and many developing countries offered their soldiers full immunity when they obeyed unlawful orders, even if they could not demonstrate that they mistakenly believed that the orders were lawful. 'Despite lengthy negotiations to draft a provision limiting the defense of superior orders, the effort was unsuccessful due to objections by some African and Asian states.' Cf. Solis, 'Obedience of Orders and the Law of War: Judicial Application in American Forums' (1999) 15 *American University International Law Review* 481–526, at 523. For an analysis of historical as well as recent developments, see Hiromi Sato, 'The Defense of Superior Orders in International Law: Some Implications for the Codification of International Criminal Law' (2009) 9 *International Criminal Law Review* 117–37.

[110] UN Doc. A/CN.4/457 of 15 February 1994, 6 *et seq.*

[111] Rosemary Rayfuse, 'The Draft Code of Crimes against the Peace and Security of Mankind: Eating Disorders at the International Law Commission' (1997) 8 *Criminal Law Forum* 43, at 47 *et seq.*; G. Acquaviva/F. Pocar, 'Crimes against Humanity', in *MPEPIL*.

war crimes, crimes against peace, or crimes against humanity can be held responsible for those acts under national or international criminal law.[112] This proposition has been supported by the decisions of the Security Council, the first in 1992 and 1994, to create for instance the ICTY and the ICTR, in order to prosecute those who have committed serious violations of international humanitarian law in the Former Yugoslavia and in Rwanda.[113]

9. The creation of the ICC in 1998 was a breakthrough in this development.[114] The Court came into being on 1 July 2002 and has jurisdiction on genocide, crimes against human-ity, and war crimes,[115] and it may act according to clear provisions on the responsibility of commanders and other superiors.[116] Its jurisdiction is limited to 'the most serious crimes of concern to the international community as a whole'[117] and it is complementary to that of national criminal justice systems.[118] Co-operation with the Security Council is secured by the fact that the latter, by means of a resolution adopted under Chapter VII of the UN Charter, may block the 'commencement or continuation of investigations for a period up to 12 months'.[119] The US has even entered into a series of bilateral treaties to ensure that no US servicemen serving in UN-authorized operations will be transferred to the jurisdiction of the Court.[120] While it remains questionable whether such a step was necessary to avoid situations in which the Court would be faced with cases moti-vated by political hostility,[121] the ICC has proven in its present practice to be impartial, fair, and free from political influence as far as possible.[122] In 2012, ten years after coming to force, the ICC issued its first decision against Lubanga Dyilo who was found guilty of the war crimes of enlisting and conscripting of children under the age of fifteen years and using them to participate actively in hostilities.[123]

10. Apart from this, to strengthen national criminal jurisdiction, internationalized or mixed criminal courts or tribunals have been established in Sierra Leone, East Timor,

---

[112] Ian Brownlie, *Principles of Public International Law*, 7th edn (OUP, 2008), 559–75; Y. Dinstein, 'International Criminal Law' (1985) 20 *Israel Law Review* 206–42; Georg Dahm/Jost Delbrück/Rüdiger Wolfrum, *Völkerrecht*, Vol. I/3, 2nd edn (Berlin: de Gruyter, 2002), 993–1002.

[113] Fausto Pocar, 'International Criminal Tribunal for the Former Yugoslavia (ICTY)'; F. Pocar, 'International Criminal Tribunal for Rwanda'; G. Acquaviva and F. Pocar, 'Crimes against Humanity', in *MPEPIL*. See also S-D Bachmann, above, n. 107.

[114] Statute of the International Criminal Court (ICC Statute), 17 July 1998, 37 *ILM* 1002.

[115] Articles 5–9 ICC Statute.

[116] Article 28 ICC Statute.

[117] Preamble, para. 4, ICC Statute.

[118] Article 17 ICC Statute.

[119] Article 16 ICC Statute.

[120] Attila Bogdan, 'The United States and the International Criminal Court: Avoiding Jurisdiction through Bilateral Agreements in Reliance on Article 98' (2008) 8 *International Criminal Law Review* 1–54; Markus Benzing, 'U.S. Bilateral Non-Surrender Agreements and Article 98 of the Statute of the International Criminal Court: An Exercise in the Law of Treaties' (2004) 8 *Max Planck Yearbook of United Nations Law* 181–236.

[121] D. Fleck, 'Are Foreign Military Personnel Exempt from International Criminal Jurisdiction under Status of Forces Agreements?' (2003) 1/3 *Journal of International Criminal Justice* 651–70.

[122] In 2012, sixteen cases in seven so-called situations have been brought before the ICC. Three states parties to the Rome Statute, Uganda, the Democratic Republic of the Congo, and the Central African Republic, have referred situations occurring on their territories to the Court. Cf. <http://www.icc-cpi.int/EN_Menus/icc/Pages/default.aspx>: Situations and Cases.

[123] Cf. ICC, Judgment of 14 March 2012, Trial Chamber I, ICC-01/04–01/06, Case *The Prosecutor v Thomas Lubanga Dyilo*, Situation in Democratic Republic of the Congo, available at <http://www.icc-cpi.int/iccdocs/doc/doc1379838.pdf>. Lubanga was sentenced, on 10 July 2012, to fourteen years of imprisonment.

SILJA VÖNEKY

Kosovo, and Cambodia.[124] They may be seen as transitional means in a development to ensure the prosecution of genocide and other serious violations of international humanitarian law, which is still incomplete.

11. The primary duty in prosecuting violations of humanitarian law lies within the hands of the state the offender belongs to. That state has the main opportunity and, therefore, the first duty to punish. The aim of the punishment is twofold: the effectiveness of the international law of war shall be secured and the discipline of the troops shall be maintained. The influential 1863 so-called Lieber Code,[125] the first national military manual,[126] states that, for prosecution, military jurisdiction can be based on statute or on the common law of war (Article 13 Lieber Code). However, for a conviction, certain procedural rights and the principle of proportionality have to be observed according to that Code.[127] State practice supports the view that the *right* to bring an individual of the enemy troops before a court because of violations of the laws of war was part of customary international law, even during the time the Lieber Code was published. Whether there has been an equivalent *duty* of states to punish violations of the laws of war is more doubtful; state practice and the writings of the academics of that time, however, seem to indicate so.[128]

12. Today, in accordance with Article 49, para. 2, GC I, and likewise Article 50, para. 2, GC II; Article 129, para. 2, GC III; Article 146, para. 2, GC IV, every state party is under an obligation to investigate persons accused of the commission or ordering of a grave breach. The provisions of the Geneva Conventions explicitly state that the commission of a grave breach and an order which leads to one are equally serious. The commander and the subordinate who acts on the command are equally responsible. No possibility exists for the subordinate to escape penal responsibility through reference to his orders. The same conclusion can be inferred from the objective and purpose of the indicated provisions. In this respect, again, the 1863 Lieber Code[129] and early

---

[124] Cf. Bachmann, above, n 107; Cesare Romano/André Nollkaemper/Jann K. Kleffner (eds), *Internationalized Criminal Courts* (OUP, 2004).

[125] Cf. Solis, above n. 16, 39 *et seq.*

[126] On behalf of US President Lincoln, Francis Lieber prepared the General Order No. 100 containing the Instruction for the Government of the Armies of the United States in the Field of 24 April 1863, reprinted at Leon Friedman (ed.), *The Law of War, A Documentary History*, Vol. 1 (Random House, 1972), 187, 264. It has since become known as the Lieber Code. The Lieber Code consists of 157 articles and was adopted by the US to inform the military personnel of the armed forces of the Union during the American Civil War (1861–5) about the rules of the law of wars. Hence, the code was an internal, non-binding code of conduct and the first national manual on the laws of armed conflict. However, the Code, which became the military manual of the US until 1914 and was the model for many military manuals in Europe, had a major influence on the further development of the laws of war in general: the Code was the model for the Geneva Convention of 1864, followed by the Declaration of St Petersburg of 1868, and the 1874 Brussels International Declaration on the Laws of War, which was never adopted but influenced the 1899 Hague Rules of Land Warfare. Not only the emergence of international humanitarian law is linked to the Code, but also the history of modern codes of conduct in general, see Jürgen Friedrich, 'Codes of Conduct', in *MPEPIL*.

[127] Art. 4 Lieber Code: 'Martial Law is simply military authority exercised in accordance with the laws and usages of war. Military oppression is not Martial Law. It is the abuse of the power which that law confers. As Martial Law is executed by military force, it is incumbent upon those who administer it to be strictly guided by the principles of justice, honour and humanity—virtues adorning a soldier even more than other men, for the very reason that he possesses the power of his arms against the unarmed.'

[128] Cf. S. Vöneky, above, n. 86, at 445 *et seq.*

[129] See above n. 126.

international agreements can also be invoked. Article 11, para. 3, Lieber Code states: 'Offences to the contrary *[i.e. violations of the laws of war]* shall be severely punished, and *especially so if committed by officers*.'[130] Article 11 exemplifies the principles and fundamentals of the Code and of the embodied modern or civilized laws of war;[131] it does not only codify the limits of the right to harm the enemy, but stipulates also an individual criminal responsibility if the rules of the laws of war are not obeyed. The defence of superior order was not recognized by the Code. The 1922 Washington Treaty Relating to the Use of Submarines and Noxious Gases in Warfare (which never entered into force), already intended to eliminate the defence of following orders for violations committed under higher command.[132] A similar regulation is found in the Charter of the International Military Tribunal of 8 August 1945.[133] Whether a subordinate has the right to refuse an order in such cases has not yet been dealt with in international treaties. Attempts to enshrine the right to refuse an order violating international humanitarian law in AP I failed.[134]

13. In accordance with Article 86, para. 2, AP I, superiors whose subordinates violate the Convention will not be relieved of criminal or disciplinary responsibility if they were aware, or under the circumstances should have been aware, that the subordinate was committing or was going to commit such a violation. The superior will be liable if he or she has failed to take all possible measures to foreclose or repress such violation, and if the person committing such violation was under his or her command.[135] Article 86, para. 2, AP I is to be read in connection with Article 87 AP I (Duties of Military Leaders). It underlines that a failure to act is as culpable as an action, if both a duty and possibility to act exist.[136]

14. The superior's responsibility for actions is a logical consequence of Article 1 HagueReg, according to which militia and volunteer corps fall under the HagueReg only if they are commanded 'by a person responsible for his subordinates'.[137] The same notion is to be found in Article 39 GC III, according to which each prisoner-of-war

---

[130] *My italics.* Art. 11, paras. 1 and 2 read as follows: 'The law of war does not only disclaim all cruelty and bad faith concerning engagements concluded with the enemy during the war, but also the breaking of stipulations solemnly contracted by the belligerents in time of peace, and avowedly intended to remain in force in case of war between the contracting powers. It disclaims all extortions and other transactions for individual gain; all acts of private revenge, or connivance at such acts.'

[131] For an interpretation, cf. S. Vöneky, above, n. 86, at 445 *et seq.*

[132] See Article 3: 'The Signatory Powers [...] further declare that any person in the service of any Power who shall violate any of those rules, whether or not such a person is under orders of a government superior, shall be deemed to have violated the laws of war and shall be liable to trial and punishment as if for an act of piracy and may be brought to trial before the civil or military authorities of any Power within the jurisdiction of which he may be found' (1922) 16 *AJIL* Suppl. 58.

[133] Article 8: 'The fact that the Defendant acted pursuant to order of his Government or of a superior shall not free him from responsibility, but may be considered in mitigation of punishment if the Tribunal determines that justice so requires.'

[134] Cf. D. Matthei, above, n. 109, at 266 *et seq.*

[135] Cf. *ICRC Commentary*, Article 86, para. 3543.

[136] Article 86, para. 2, AP I is based largely on the decision in the war crime proceedings against General Yamashita. He was sentenced by the US Military Commission in Manila for war crimes his troops had committed in the Philippines. A petition was submitted to the US Supreme Court. *Trial of General Tomoyuki Yamashita*, US Military Commission, Manila (8 October–7 December 1945) and the US Supreme Court (Judgments Delivered on 4 February, 1946), in *Law Reports of Trials of War Criminals*, Vol. IV, 1–96 [43], reprinted in L. Friedman (ed.), above, n. 126, Vol. 2, 1596–1623 [1605].

[137] Also Article 4 A 2 GC III; Article 43 AP I.

camp is placed under the immediate authority of a responsible commissioned officer. From that responsibility results the superior's specific accountability for violations by his or her subordinates.

15. Article 49, para. 2, GC I[138] obliges states to take action if they receive knowledge of grave breaches having been committed. Such obligation does not only come into existence if states are exhorted by other states to initiate investigations. Investigations must be made in any case. Further, it is of no consequence who has committed a breach. Investigations and eventual prosecutions must be initiated against nationals and citizens of allies, as well as citizens of opponent states.

16. Even if the home state does not itself undertake the investigation and ensuing prosecution, it is obliged under Article 49, para. 1, GC I to *extradite* alleged violators to another interested state party for trial, as long as such state party can produce a *prima facie* case against the suspects. In this regard, the general principle of international law is clearly reflected, in which the state having custody over the accused person is itself under an obligation either to prosecute or to extradite the suspect. Article 49, para. 2, GC I does not contain a further specification of the potential states which may ask for extradition if they are interested in prosecuting.[139] The only restrictions provided by the Geneva Conventions in this respect are the reference to the domestic law of the extraditing state and the requirement of sufficient incriminating evidence.

1. War Crimes at National Courts

1411   The four Geneva Conventions and Additional Protocol I oblige the contracting parties to make grave breaches of the protective provisions liable to punishment and to take all suitable measures to ensure compliance with international humanitarian law (Articles 49, 50 GC I; Articles 50, 51 GC II; Articles 129, 130 GC III; Articles 146, 147 GC IV; Article 85 AP I).

1. These provisions impose a twofold obligation on the contracting states. They must shape their domestic law, in particular their criminal law and military codes of discipline, so that the punishment of grave breaches[140] of international humanitarian law is ensured.[141] This assumes that both the elements constituting the offence and the range of punishment are established for each offence. Such obligation already exists in times of peace. In addition, the contracting parties must employ further measures to ensure that the additional protective provisions of the Convention are observed and that offences which do not constitute grave breaches are prosecuted according to domestic law. This follows primarily from Article 49, para. 3, GC I.

2. Article 85, para. 1, AP I ensures that the provisions of the four Geneva Conventions for punishment of violations and grave breaches are applied to the punishment of corresponding breaches of AP I. Apart from that, Article 85, paras. 2 and 4, AP I elaborate

---

[138] Also Article 50 GC I.

[139] Critical of this is Howard S. Levie, *The Code of International Armed Conflict*, Vol. 2 (New York: Oceana, 1986), 892.

[140] See Section 1410.

[141] For an overview see S-D Bachmann, above, n. 107.

SILJA VÖNEKY

and expand the provisions of the four Geneva Conventions concerning protected persons and objects.[142]

3. In accordance with Article 49, para. 4, GC I, parties are not entirely free in organizing the legal procedure. Minimum standards of international law, as stated in Articles 99–108 GC III and Article 75 AP I, must be respected.

> **States shall make the following grave breaches of international humanitarian law liable to punishment and prosecution (Article 49 GC I; Article 50 GC II; Article 129 GC III; Article 146 GC IV; Article 85 AP I).**

1412

1. The indicated provisions list the grave breaches. They are tailored to the objectives of the Geneva Conventions, as supplemented by Article 85, paras. 2–4, AP I. Rulings of the ICTY and ICTR have helped to clarify the definition of crimes and contributed to the alignment of international humanitarian law norms applicable in international and non-international armed conflicts.[143] Further clarifications are given by the ICC.[144] For the description of war crimes according to the ICC Statute, see Article 8, para. 2, lit. a, b, c, and e, ICC Statute.[145] Article 8(2) lit. a lists the grave breaches of humanitarian law which is contained in the GC. It is an important step forward that Article 8 ICC Statute entails the prohibition of war crimes in international and non-international armed conflicts, even though the threshold in non-international conflicts is still too high.[146]

> **— Indictable offences against protected persons (wounded, sick, medical personnel, chaplains, prisoners of war, inhabitants of occupied territory, other civilians), such as wilful killing, mutilation, torture, or inhuman treatment, including biological experiments, wilfully causing great suffering, serious injury to body or health,**

---

[142] For the term 'grave breach' see above, Section 1410, para. 1.

[143] See, e.g., ICTY, *Prosecutor v Kordić and Cerkez*, Case No. IT-95–14/2-T, Judgment of 26 February 2001; *Prosecutor v Krstić*, Case No. IT-98–33-T, Judgment of 2 August 2001; *Prosecutor v Delalić et al. (Celebici)*, Case No. IT-96–21-A, Judgment of 20 February 2001; *Prosecutor v Kunarac et al.*, Case Nos. IT-96–23-T and IT-96–23/1-T, Judgment of 22 February 2001; *Prosecutor v Furundzija*, Case No. IT-95–17/1, Judgment of 10 December 1998; *Prosecutor v Tadić*, Judgments of 2 October 1995 and 15 July 1999; *Prosecutor v Krstić*, Case No. IT-98–33-A, Appeals Chamber Judgment of 19 April 2004; *Prosecutor v Milan Martić*, Case No. IT-95–11-T, Judgment of 12 June 2007; *Prosecutor v Ramush Haradinaj et al.*, Case No. IT-04–84-T, Judgment of 3 April 2008; *Prosecutor v Gotovina et al.* Vols. 1 and 2, Vol. 1, Case No. IT-06–90-T, Judgment of 15 April 2011; ICTR, *Prosecutor v Kambanda*, Case No. 97–23, Appeals Chamber Judgment of 19 October 2000; *Prosecutor v Bagilishema*, Case No. 95-IA-A, Appeals Chamber Judgment of 2 July 2002; *Prosecutor v Callixte Kalimanzira*, Case No. 05–88-T, Judgment of 22 June 2009; see for a comprehensive compilation of seminal judgments of the ICTR Human Rights Watch, *Genocide, War Crimes and Crimes Against Humanity. A Digest of the Case Law of the International Criminal Tribunal for Rwanda* (New York: Human Rights Watch, 2010), available at <http://www.hrw.org/sites/default/files/reports/ictr0110webwcover.pdf>.

[144] At the time of writing the ICC has opened investigations into seven situations in Africa (Democratic Republic of the Congo, Uganda, Central African Republic, Darfur/Sudan, Republic of Kenya, Libyan Arab Jamahiriya, Republic of Côte d'Ivoire), see above, n. 122. In March 2012 the Court has delivered its first decision ever by finding the accused Lubanga guilty. For a case analysis, see K. Ambos, 'The First Judgment of the International Criminal Court (Prosecutor v. Lubanga): A Comprehensive Analysis of the Legal Issues', 2 *International Criminal Law Review*, 115–53.

[145] For elements of crimes see Knut Dörmann, *Elements of War Crimes under the Rome Statute of the International Criminal Court: Sources and Commentary* (CUP, 2003), 38–80.

[146] For an overview, cf. Michael Cottier, 'Article 8, war crimes' in O. Triffterer (ed.), *Commentary on the Rome Statute of the International Criminal Court* (Munich: Beck, 2008), 297 *et seq*. For the difference, see Art. 8(2), lit. a and b, and Art. 8(2), lit. c and e ICC Statute. In non-international armed conflicts, for instance, intentional causing of excessive collateral damage is not a war crime. However, for international armed conflicts, see Art. 8(2), lit. b(iv) ICC Statute.

SILJA VÖNEKY

taking of hostages (Articles 3, 49–51 GC I; Articles 3, 50, 51 GC II; Articles 3, 129, 130 GC III; Articles 3, 146, 147 GC IV; Articles 11, para. 2, and 85, para. 3, lit. a, AP I).

2. Protected persons include the injured and sick (Article 13 GC I)[147] as well as shipwrecked[148] (Article 13 GC II), prisoners of war (Article 4 GC III), and civilians (Article 4 GC IV; Article 85, paras. 3 and 4, AP I). This category includes as well persons who have participated in military operations and fallen into enemy hands (Articles 44, 45 AP I);[149] injured, sick, and shipwrecked of the opposing party (Article 8 AP I);[150] medical and religious personnel (Article 8 AP I);[151] and persons *hors de combat*[152] (Article 85, paras. 2–4, AP I).

3. The term 'wilful killing' covers all cases in which a protected person is killed, that is the death of a protected person is caused[153] and the perpetrator meant to kill the person or was aware that the death would occur (Article 30(2) ICC Statute). 'Wilful killing' includes active deeds as well as omissions, if the omission was committed with intent to cause the death of a protected person. Hence, the reduction of rations for prisoners of war resulting in their starvation falls into the category of wilful killing.

4. 'Mutilation' comprises any serious invasion of physical integrity that causes residual damage. The scope of this grave breach of international humanitarian law overlaps with that of serious injury of physical body or health.[154]

5. 'Torture' or 'inhumane treatment' refers to cases in which suffering is inflicted upon persons, for example in order to extract confessions or information from them or from other persons. For a more accurate interpretation of this provision, the 1984 Convention against Torture and other Cruel, Inhumane or Degrading Treatment or Punishment can be applied as there is no definition of torture in a humanitarian law treaty. This provides that torture comprises any treatment by which great physical or mental pain or suffering is inflicted.[155]

6. The prohibition of 'inhumane treatment' refers to Article 12 GC II and Article 27 GC IV. All protected persons must be treated humanely. The obligation of humane treatment is practically a guiding theme for the four Geneva Conventions.[156] The principle

---

[147] Also belonging to this category are persons accompanying the armed forces without being members, such as civilian crew members of military aircrafts, war correspondents, army contractors, members of work units, or services responsible for the care of military personnel; cf. H. S. Levie, above, n. 139, 6 *et seq.*

[148] It is irrelevant whether or not the shipwrecked persons have fallen into the hands of the detaining state. For example, *Admiral Dönitz* was accused before the Nuremberg Military Tribunal of having given the command that shipwrecked persons of hostile nations were not to be rescued. He was not convicted on this charge, as a similar command on the side of the Allies had been given to the commanding officers of British and American submarines, see *Trial of Doenitz* in *Judgment of the International Military Tribunal for the Trial of German Major War Criminals (1 October 1946)*, 107–10. Yet, a British military tribunal convicted the crew members of a German submarine that had opened fire on the crew of a sinking Greek ship after they had climbed into lifeboats. Pursuant to the 1936 LondonProt, the commanding officer of a submarine is not allowed to sink a civilian merchant vessel if he is not in a position to save the crew.

[149] See above, Sections 301–31; 601; this term is broader than the notion of prisoners of war in GC III.

[150] More far-reaching than GC I; see Sections 603, 605, as well as H. S. Levie, above, n. 139, 7 *et seq.*

[151] See above, Sections 801–5.

[152] Cf. M. Cottier, above, n. 146, 344 *et seq.*

[153] M. Cottier, *op. cit.*, 305, para. 17.

[154] See above, Section 606.

[155] Gary D. Solis, above, n. 16, 436; Knut Dörmann, above, n. 80, 306 *et seq.*

[156] In accordance with Article 13 GC III prisoners must be treated humanely.

originates from The Hague and was also contained in both Geneva Conventions of 1929. The word 'treatment' must be understood in the broadest possible sense, involving acts or omissions. It principally prohibits any use of force or intimidation which cannot be justified by military necessity or a legitimate desire for security. On this basis, the term is not limited to the physical condition of the concerned person. On the contrary, any treatment, which substantially injures human dignity, constitutes a violation.[157] Complete isolation from the external world or from family members would fall under this category.

7. The prohibition of 'biological experiments' refers to experiments on the human body or health (cf. Articles 12 GC I, 13 GC II). This means that the use of prisoners of war or protected persons for medical or scientific experiments is strictly prohibited.[158] Such experiments are given, if the intent of the experiment was non-therapeutic and it was neither justified by medical reasons nor carried out in the person's interest. Hence, medical care is not forbidden, even when it entails new medical procedures. But it is then at all times essential that the sole purpose of such treatment is to improve the state of health of the person concerned. In practice, the differentiation between medical care and medical experimentation may cause difficulties. In consequence, special significance is attached to the free consent of the person in question to the medical treatment.[159] Lastly, only medical treatment, given to the civilian population of the host state, may be employed on protected persons under its custody.

8. The prohibition of the wilful imposition of 'great suffering' corresponds in essence with the prohibition of torture and inhumane treatment, including biological experimentation. This includes both infliction of suffering as punishment or revenge and that brought about by other motives, for example through unmitigated cruelty, torture, or biological experiments. Pursuant to the wording of the four Conventions, this prohibition does not refer exclusively to physical suffering, but it applies equally to mental suffering.[160] Thus, solitary confinement and penal measures may also fall within the notion of 'inhumane treatment'.

9. The prohibition of causing 'serious detriment to physical integrity or health' covers the physical side of this rule.

10. A wilful attack directed in violation of the Protocol against the civilian population or individual civilians not taking direct part in hostilities, which results in death or grave detriment to body or health, constitutes a grave breach according to Article 85, para. 3, lit. a, AP I (see also Article 147 GC IV; Article 8, para. 2. lit. a(i), ICC Statute). A prohibition of attacks upon the civilian population or individual civilians is contained in Article 51, para. 2, AP I.[161] In this context, the terms 'civilian population', 'civilians', and 'attack' are defined in Article 50 AP I. The terms 'civilian population' and 'civilians'

---

[157] Cf. Knut Dörmann, above, n. 80, 308.

[158] Cf. Arts. 13 GC III, 32 GC IV, 11 AP I. In this respect Geneva Convention Law refers to earlier decisions in the trials of war criminals following WWII, e.g. *Trial of Erhard Milch*, US Military Tribunal at Nuremberg (20 December 1946–17 April 1947), in *Trials of War Criminals before the Nuernberg Military Tribunals*, Vol. II, 355–888, and *Law Reports of Trials of War Criminals*, Vol. VII, 27–66. Field Marshall Milch was cleared of this charge.

[159] See above, Sections 606–8.

[160] Cf. Knut Dörmann, above, n. 80, 310.

[161] Cf. Howard S. Levie, *The Code of International Armed Conflict*, Vol. I (Oceana, 1986), 67 *et seq.*

SILJA VÖNEKY

are defined negatively. Civilians are all those persons who are not members of the armed forces in accordance with Article 43 AP I or members of the regular or irregular forces according to Articles 13 GC I (apart from the organized militias and volunteer corps belonging to a state party to the conflict, the organized militias and volunteer corps belonging to organized resistance movements, and inhabitants of an unoccupied territory who, on the approach of the enemy, spontaneously take up arms to resist). In any case of doubt, a person is presumed to be a civilian. The civilian population is the sum of all civilians (Article 50, para. 2, AP I), but this group does not lose its civilian status if individuals, who are not civilians or are offensive civilians, are found among its numbers. However, civilians are protected only as long as they do not take direct part in hostilities.[162] Direct participation in hostilities is given if an act by a civilian is, by its nature or purpose, likely to cause actual harm to the armed forces.[163]

11. The term 'attacks' includes both offensive and defensive use of force against the opponent, whether by land, air, or sea, in the opponent's state territory or in the territory of a party to the conflict controlled by the opponent (Article 49(1) AP I), that is any combat action. A grave breach of AP I is committed if an attack is directed against the civilian population or individual civilians of such areas.[164] Such an attack may be obviously directed against civilians, as certain weapons are used without a degree of error in targeting and if military objectives are not located close to the civilians. Attacks, which incidentally harm the civilian population, do not fall under the prohibition of Article 85, para. 3, lit. a AP I, but may be a war crime according to Article 8(2), lit. b(iv) ICC Statute if they are excessive.

12. The prerequisite for a grave breach, and a war crime, is intent; the attack must be intentionally directed at the civilian population or individual civilians, and the intent must embrace physical consequences. If this is not the case, there is no grave breach, but rather a violation of the Protocol, which gives rise to disciplinary proceedings.

13. In accordance with Article 51, para. 1, AP I, even a threat made with the primary goal of spreading fear throughout the civilian population is forbidden. Such offences are breaches, but not grave breaches, of the Protocol.

— **Compelling prisoners of war and civilians to serve in the forces of the adversary (Articles 129–131 GC III, 147 GC IV).**

14. This prohibition derives from Article 130 GC III, which forbids the pressing of prisoners of war into such service and the compulsion of a prisoner of war to serve in the fighting forces of the detaining power and is included in Article 8, para. 2, lit. a(v), ICC Statute.[165] In accordance with Article 23 HagueReg, it is forbidden for the belligerent country to enlist nationals of the opposing party to participate in the conduct of war against their own country. This is also true in the case where they were enlisted before the outbreak of war. It is likewise prohibited to impose an obligation on the civilian

[162] Cf. Art. 51(3) AP I. Cf. Gary D. Solis, above, n. 16, 543 *et seq.*
[163] Cf. K. Dörmann, above, n. 80, 324.
[164] Cf. Karl J. Partsch, in Michael Bothe/Karl J. Partsch/Waldemar A. Solf (eds), *New Rules for Victims of Armed Conflicts, Commentary on the Two 1977 Protocols Additional to the Geneva Conventions of 1949* (Nijhoff, 1982), 516; W. A. Solf, ibid. 300 *et seq.*
[165] See K. Dörmann, *Elements of War Crimes*, above, n. 145, 97–9.

SILJA VÖNEKY

population of an occupied area to serve in the occupier's forces or to work for military purposes.[166] The rationale, according to Article 52 of Hague IV, is that the population should not be obliged to participate in the conduct of war against its homeland. In the war crime trials after WWII, several judgments condemned offences against this principle.[167]

— Deportation, illegal transfer, or confinement of protected civilians (Articles 146–148 GC IV; Articles 50, 51, 57, 85, para. 4, lit. a, AP I).

15. The prohibition of deportation and illegal transfer of civilians[168] results from Article 147 GC IV and is laid down in Article 8, para. 2, lit. a(vii), ICC Statute.[169] It includes breaches of Articles 45 and 49 GC IV. A transfer of the population is allowed only if it serves the security of the population involved. Deportation for the deployment of labour is forbidden, whether or not such labour is of military or civilian significance.[170] A number of war criminals were convicted of violations against this principle after WWII.[171] Today, Article 49 GC IV contains the necessary clarification. Individual or mass deportations, as well as displacement of protected persons from occupied areas to territories of the occupying power or elsewhere, is forbidden, regardless of the reasons underlying such displacement. Article 45 GC IV also forbids the delivery of protected persons to another power.

16. A special provision on the protection of children is contained in Article 78 AP I which provides that evacuation of children, who are not nationals of the evacuating power, is acceptable only for medical treatment and with the written consent of the parents or those primarily responsible for the care of children. Evacuation of children from an occupied area is permitted for reasons of safety. A violation of Article 78 AP I constitutes a breach of the prohibition of 'illegal transfer'.[172]

17. The prohibition of illegal confinement of civilians creates practical problems. The occupying power has the right to take prisoners under certain conditions, for its security or for criminal prosecution. However, confinement or internment is forbidden without legitimate reason.

— Starvation of civilians by destroying, removing, or rendering useless objects indispensable to the survival of the civilian population, for example foodstuffs, means for the production of foodstuffs, drinking water installations and supplies, and irrigation works (Article 54 AP I; Article 14 AP II).

18. In accordance with Article 51 AP I and Article 13 AP II, the civilian population and individual civilians enjoy general protection from dangers arising from military

---

[166] Morris Greenspan, *The Modern Law of Land Warfare* (Berkeley: University of California Press, 1959), 177.

[167] Cf. the proceedings against Milch, *loc. cit.*, 39.

[168] For reference to the term 'civilians', see above, Section 502.

[169] See K. Dörmann, *Elements of War Crimes*, above, n. 145, 106–23.

[170] The Hague Law does not contain a particular prohibition of this sort, but in the aftermath of WWI, the deportation of sections of the Belgian civilian population to Germany for compulsory work was already seen as unlawful, even by the German *Reichstag*.

[171] Cf. *The I. G. Farben Trial*, US Military Tribunal, Nuremberg (14 August 1947–29 July 1948), in *Law Reports of Trials of War Criminals*, Vol. X, 1–68; *The Krupp Trial*, US Military Tribunal, Nuremberg (17 November 1947–30 June 1948), *op. cit.*, Vol. X, 69–177 [142]; *Trial of Erhard Milch*, US Military Tribunal, Nuremberg (20 December 1946–17 April 1947), *op. cit.*, Vol. VII, 27–66, at 39.

[172] K. Dörmann, above, n. 80, 321.

action. This principle is enforced by Article 54, paras. 1 and 2, AP I and Article 14 AP II, which prohibit the starvation of the civilian population as a method of warfare. The objective is to preserve facilities, institutions, and objects indispensable for the survival of the civilian population. This is laid down as well in Article 8, para. 2, lit. b(xxv), ICC Statute.[173]

19. Even though these codifications were introduced into international humanitarian law by the Additional Protocols, their foundation was laid in Articles 23 and 53 GC IV. Pursuant to these provisions, passage is to be guaranteed for shipments of medicines and medical supplies, objects necessary for religious services, and essential foodstuffs, clothing, and medicines for those in special need of protection. Article 53 GC IV prohibits unnecessary destruction of movable and immovable property.[174]

20. The catalogue of grave breaches contained in Article 85 AP I does not expressly mention the violation of Article 54 AP I. However, starvation of a population through destruction of facilities, institutions, and objects necessary for survival always constitutes an attack on the civilian population (Article 85, para. 3, lit. a, AP I).

— **Destruction or appropriation of goods, carried out unlawfully and wantonly without any military necessity (Article 50 GC I; Article 147 GC IV).**

21. This prohibition summarizes a number of grave breaches of the Geneva Conventions (see as well Article 8, para. 2, lit. b(xiii), ICC Statute.)[175] In accordance with Article 50 GC I, the destruction and appropriation of protected goods constitutes a grave breach if it is not justified by military necessity, and if protected goods are taken on a large scale, unlawfully, and arbitrarily. The term 'protected goods' is defined in Articles 33–36 GC I. Medical institutions, whether fixed or mobile, come within the ambit of this provision. Other goods protected under GC II include mobile medical units, coastal rescue craft, hospital ships, transport ships for the wounded, and air ambulances (Articles 22, 23, 24, 25, 27, 28, 38, and 39). Finally, GC IV prohibits the destruction of property within the occupied territory by an occupying power (Article 53), unless destruction is clearly necessary to fulfil military objectives. Not included in this prohibition is the destruction of property in the battlefield.

22. The expropriation of protected objects is also forbidden unless the special requirements of the Geneva Conventions for such types of appropriations are met.

— **Launching an indiscriminate attack in the knowledge that it will have adverse effects on civilian life and civilian objects (Article 85, para. 3 lit. b, AP I).**

23. See Article 8, para. 2, lit. b(i), ICC Statute.[176] The prohibition, and punishment as a grave breach, of an 'indiscriminate attack in the knowledge that such attack will have adverse effects on civilian life and civilian objects' (collateral damage) corresponds with Article 85, para. 3, lit. b, and Article 51, para. 4, AP I. This prohibition is a concretization

---

[173] See K. Dörmann, *Elements of War Crimes*, above, n. 145, 363–74.
[174] Article 13 AP II acquires greater significance since the rules of AP II lack a clause regarding general protection of objects such as that found in Article 52 AP I. See above, Sections 448–60.
[175] See K. Dörmann, *Elements of War Crimes*, above, n. 145, 249–62.
[176] See K. Dörmann, *Elements of War Crimes*, above, n. 145, 130–48.

SILJA VÖNEKY

of the obligations enshrined in Articles 48 and 52 AP I.[177] The regulation of Article 85, para. 3, lit. b, AP I serves to reinforce the general principle that military actions against combatants must be aimed at military objects (Articles 48 and 52 AP I). The term 'civilian objects' is defined in Article 52 AP I.

24. The regulation of Article 85, para. 3, lit. b, AP I contains two qualifications: the indiscriminate attack must be intentional and it must be known in advance that this attack will lead to a disproportionately high loss of life, wounding of civilians, or damage to civilian property.

25. Specification of which collateral damage is considered 'disproportionate' can be found in Article 57, para. 2, lit. a(iii), AP I.[178] This provides that a balance is required between concrete, direct military advantage, and the requirement that the civilian population be protected. However, Article 57, para. 2, lit. a, AP I is broader in regard to the situations covered than the penal standard in Article 85, para. 3, AP I. Article 57, para. 2, lit. a(i) and (ii), AP I require particular precautionary measures when planning and carrying out attacks. An attack, however, will only be considered illegal when the prerequisites of Article 57, para. 2(iii), AP I are fulfilled, that is when the precautionary measures were manifestly insufficient. A serious breach of AP I is committed. however, when knowledge of the disproportionality of collateral damage exists.[179]

26. An attack on civilians with the 'primary goal' of spreading terror throughout the civilian population constitutes a grave breach (Article 85, para. 2, lit. a, AP I). Pursuant to Article 51, para. 2 (second sentence), AP I this is strictly forbidden, although in practice these types of terror attacks were frequently committed. Two of the most prominent examples since WWII are the Iraqi attacks on Israeli cities during the Gulf War (1991) and the bombardment by the Yugoslav Army and Serbian militia during the Yugoslav conflict (1991–1992).[180]

— Launching an attack against works or installations containing dangerous forces (dams, dykes, and nuclear electricity-generating stations), expecting that such an attack will cause excessive loss of life, injury to civilians, or damage to civilian objects (Article 85, para. 3 lit. c, AP I; Article 15 AP II).

27. This regulation is based on Article 85, para. 3, lit. c, AP I. Reference is made to Article 56 AP I, by which some institutions enjoy absolute protection. Institutions of this sort must also not be attacked if they are of military significance to the extent that the attack can lead to the release of dangerous forces (overflow, radioactivity), which would lead to grievous injury of the civilian population. This holds equally true whether the attack on such facilities is deliberate or the incidental result of strikes on other military objects.

28. A comparable rule is found in Article 15 AP II. AP II, however, does not recognize the concept of grave breaches, and prosecution of breaches is by domestic criminal law.

— Launching an attack against an undefended locality, demilitarized zone, or neutralized zone (Article 85, para. 3, lit. d, AP I; Article 15 AP II).

---

[177] See above, Sections 448–60.
[178] Ibid.
[179] K. J. Partsch, above, n. 164, at 516; *ICRC Commentary*, Article 85, para. 3479.
[180] See Section 454.

SILJA VÖNEKY

29. Undefended localities are described in Article 59 AP I.[181] Localities of this sort may not be attacked by the parties to the conflict for any reason. The same is true for demilitarized zones, according to Article 60 AP I.[182] A grave breach of international humanitarian law is committed if an undefended locality or demilitarized zone is intentionally made the object of attack, which results in death or serious harm to the physical integrity or health of persons in the area.

— **Launching an attack against defenceless persons (Article 85, para. 3, lit. e, AP I).**

30. See Article 8, para. 2, lit. b(v) and (vi), ICC Statute.[183] The category of defenceless persons is defined by Article 41 AP I. This notion covers persons who find themselves under the control of a hostile party, who unmistakably announce their intention to surrender, or who are unconscious or otherwise unable to defend themselves due to injury or sickness, as long as they refrain from hostile actions and do not attempt to escape. A grave breach is committed if the attacker knows that the person is incapable of fighting. It is not enough, however, to say that the attacker was obliged to infer this from the circumstances.[184]

— **Unjustifiable delay in the repatriation of prisoners of war and civilians (Article 85, para. 4, lit. b, AP I).**

31. In accordance with Article 109 GC III, seriously wounded or seriously ill prisoners of war must be repatriated to their own countries even during a military conflict. In addition, after the termination of the hostilities, an obligation exists to immediately release and repatriate prisoners of war. Unjustifiable delay in repatriation constitutes a grave breach. A delay is unjustifiable when there are no objective reasons for it and when the delay furthers none of the reasons which the custodian state has invoked.

32. The situation concerning the civilian population differs from that of prisoners of war. In accordance with Article 35 GC IV, all protected persons, who wish to leave the conflict area during the course of the conflict, have the right to do so, as long as their departure does not conflict with national interests. In other words, a grave breach is committed if civilians are denied departure without sufficient reason.[185]

33. A grave breach is also committed according to Article 85, para. 4, lit. b, AP I if a civilian population, lawfully displaced in accordance with Article 49 GC IV, is not allowed to return promptly. This should be differentiated from the rule contained in Article 85, para. 4, lit. a, AP I, which provides that a grave breach is committed if the occupying power either uses a portion of its own civilian population to colonize an occupied territory (in violation of Article 49 GC IV) or expatriates segments of the civilian population native to an occupied territory (in violation of Article 49 GC IV). Article 49 GC IV sets strict limits on the resettlement of civilian populations native to occupied territories. Violations of these constitute grave breaches under Article 147 GC IV. In this respect, Article 85, para. 4, lit. a, AP I has a merely repetitive character.

[181] See Sections 4461–3.
[182] See Sections 464–6.
[183] See K. Dörmann, *Elements of War Crimes*, above, n. 145, 177–92.
[184] K. J. Partsch, above, n. 164, at 517; *ICRC Commentary*, Article 85, para. 3493.
[185] *ICRC Commentary*, Article 85, para. 3509.

SILJA VÖNEKY

34. On the other hand, the classification of the colonization of an occupied territory by the occupying power's civilian population as a grave breach is new to humanitarian law. The reasons underlying this reclassification (Article 49, para. 6, GC IV) as a grave breach are recent experiences in the Middle East, as well as the desire to protect established populations from foreign infiltration and control. In addition, this provision is intended to prevent the creeping annexion of occupied territories. It has gained greatly in significance in the light of the Yugoslav conflict.

— **The practice of apartheid and other inhumane and degrading practices based on racial discrimination (Article 85, para. 4, lit. c, AP I).**

35. See Article 8, para. 2, lit. b(xxi), ICC Statute.[186] Examples of such serious breaches include segregation on the basis of race within prisoner-of-war camps, or bad treatment (or worse) handling of specific ethnic groups. Most of the practices condemned here fall under the category of 'inhumane practices'. The notion of 'apartheid' is defined by the International Convention on the Suppression and Punishment of the Crime of Apartheid.[187] The term 'racial discrimination' is from Article 1 of the International Convention on the Elimination of all Forms of Racial Discrimination, GA Res. 2106 A (XX) of 21 December 1965.

— **Extensive destruction of cultural property and places of worship (Article 85, para. 4, lit. d, AP I; Article 16 AP II).**

36. See Article 8, para. 2, lit. b(ix), ICC Statute.[188] Articles 53 AP I and 16 AP II, without prejudice to the Protection of Cultural Property in the Event of Armed Conflict,[189] forbid all acts of hostility directed against historical monuments, works of art, or places of worship which constitute the cultural or intellectual heritage of peoples and which have been given special protection based upon specific conventions, for example within the framework of a competent international organization.[190] More specifically, it is forbidden to use such articles to attain military objectives.[191]

37. According to Article 85, para. 4, lit. d, AP I, a breach of the duty to protect cultural property constitutes a grave breach of the Protocol if the attack was directed at such a protected object, if the object was plainly protected, and if it suffered extensive damage. No violation occurs if the object attacked was being used primarily to support military objectives (Article 53, lit. b, AP I) or was located in the immediate vicinity of a military facility. The violation can be attributed to any military leader, even one in charge of a small unit, as long as that leader was competent to decide upon the target of the attack concerned.

— **Prevention of a fair and regular trial (Article 3, para. 3, lit. d, GC I; Article 3, para. 1, lit. d, GC III; Article 85, para. 4, lit. e, AP I).**

38. See Article 8, para. 2, lit. a(vi), ICC Statute.[192] GC Article 3, para. 1, lit. d, prohibits the passing of sentences and the carrying out of executions without previous judgment

---

[186] See K. Dörmann, *Elements of War Crimes*, above, n. 145, 314–24.
[187] GA Res. 3068 (XXVIII) of 30 November 1973.
[188] See K. Dörmann, *Elements of War Crimes*, above, n. 145, 215–28.
[189] See above, Chapter 9.
[190] See Section 901.
[191] See Section 903.
[192] See K. Dörmann, *Elements of War Crimes*, above, n. 145, 100–5.

SILJA VÖNEKY

pronounced by a regularly constituted court, affording all the judicial guarantees which are recognized as indispensable by civilized people. Article 50 GC I does not classify this violation as a grave breach of the Convention. The situation in GC III and GC IV is different.

39. Articles 99–108 GC III and Articles 71–75 and 126 GC IV contain corresponding procedural guarantees, as does Article 75 AP I.[193]

40. According to Article 130 GC III and Article 147 GC IV, the wilful deprivation of a prisoner of war's right to a fair and impartial trial, as described in GC III and IV, is a grave breach. This principle is also found in Article 85, para. 4, lit. e, AP I, where it is expanded to encompass all protected peoples.

> — Perfidious (Article 37 AP I) use of recognized protective signs (Article 53, para. 1, GC I; Article 45 GC II; Article 185, para. 3, lit. f, AP I; Article 12 AP II).

41. See Article 8, para. 2, lit. b(vii), ICC Statute.[194] The improper use of the Red Cross or Red Crescent emblem or any other emblems, signs, or signals which create such illusion was originally forbidden by Article 53, para. 1, GC I. Article 45 GC II prohibits the misuse of emblems designated for hospital ships. Article 38 AP I expands this prohibition to include improper use of the Red Cross and misuse of all other symbols, markings, or signals adopted by the Geneva Conventions and Protocols.[195] The abuse of any other international symbols, markings, or signals, such as the flag of truce, is also prohibited.

42. According to Article 85, para. 3, lit. f, AP I, perfidious use of the distinctive emblems of the Red Cross in violation of Article 37 AP I is a grave breach, if it is wilfully committed and leads to death or serious injury. The word 'perfidious', as used in Article 85, para. 3, lit. f, makes clear that the action must be intended to deceive the opponent. Unintentional use of these symbols does not constitute a grave breach.

> — Use of prohibited weapons.

43. See Article 8, para. 2, lit. b(xvii)–(xx), ICC Statute.[196] This prohibitive norm is based upon Article 23 HagueReg and specific international treaties. Forbidden weapons include particularly those which cause superfluous injury and unnecessary suffering.[197]

44. Neither the Geneva nor the Hague Law sees the infringement of this provision as a grave breach. Its characterization as a war crime in national laws is nonetheless allowed. This supports the special significance placed upon these prohibitions for humanitarian purposes.[198]

---

[193] See Sections 714–26.
[194] See K. Dörmann, *Elements of War Crimes,* above, n. 145, 193–207.
[195] Counted among these are the individual indications and identifying features in accordance with Article 38 GC I; GC IV, Annex I, Article 6; Article 66 AP I and Annex I; see Section 473.
[196] See K. Dörmann, *Elements of War Crimes,* above, n. 145, 281–313.
[197] Article 35, para. 1, AP I; cf. also the Biological Weapons Convention as well as the St Petersburg Declaration of 1868 and the Declaration of 1899 on the prohibition of dum-dum bullets; see Section 402.
[198] Also, Morris Greenspan, *The Modern Law of Land Warfare* (Berkeley: University of California Press, 1959), 317.

SILJA VÖNEKY

Serious violations of international humanitarian law are covered by the general sub-   1413
ject matters in national penal codes, which particularly include offences against:
— life;
— body and health;
— personal liberty;
— personal property;
— offences constituting a public danger; and
— offences committed in execution of official duties.

1. The regulations concerning all the grave breaches listed in Section 1411 are part of most national criminal law statutes. The injury and killing of civilians as well as the seizure or destruction of property during armed conflicts breach numerous penal provisions. The actions may be justified if committed within the framework of a military conflict. However, there is no justification for violations of international humanitarian law.

2. Crimes involving death, that is offences of which the collective shame lies in the killing of one or more individuals, normally include offences causing the death of protected persons, for example by starving persons to death, through indiscriminate attacks, through assaults on facilities containing dangerous forces, through aggression against undefended localities, through perfidious and unauthorized use of recognized protective symbols, or through the use of forbidden weapons.

3. If the above-mentioned actions lead to non-fatal personal injury, then the violations will be termed offences against the bodily integrity of others. These provisions protect the bodily integrity and health of all persons, where the effects of violations can be either physical or psychological in nature.

4. Compelling prisoners of war and civilians to serve in the armed forces of the adversary falls under a statutory crime. The same applies to hostage-taking, deportation, illegal transfer, or confinement of protected civilians and to unjustifiable delay in the repatriation of prisoners of war and civilians.

5. The destruction of public and private property as well as its unjust expropriation, neither of which is permissible under the law of war, is likewise punishable under national law.

The misuse of the emblem of the Red Cross, the Red Crescent, or the Red Crystal or   1414
of the heraldic emblem of Switzerland should constitute an offence under national
penal law, liable to a fine (see above Section 637).

States must prevent and repress any misuse of the emblem of the Red Cross, Red Crescent, or Red Crystal (Article 53 GC I; Article 45 GC II; Article 6 AP III). This obligation includes the Swiss coat of arms by reason of the tribute paid to Switzerland by the adoption of the reversed Federal colours and of the confusion, which may arise between the arms of Switzerland and the distinctive emblems under the Geneva Conventions (Article 53, para. 2, GC I). The proper use of the distinctive emblems is regulated by states parties to the Geneva Conventions together with the Red Cross and Red Crescent movements in their International Conferences.[199] It is punishable as a grave breach if

---

[199] See Regulations adopted at the 20th International Conference (1965), Text in No. 289 *IRRC* (1992), 339–62, to be revised at the 30th International Conference (Geneva, 2007). See also ICRC

wilfully committed and causing death or serious injury. An administrative offence is committed whenever the Red Cross or Red Crescent are used without authorization, if the conditions required in Section 1410 have not occurred.

1415   The abuse of distinctive emblems and names which, according to the rules of international law, are equal in status to the Red Cross should also be prosecuted.

Distinctive emblems other than the Red Cross, Red Crescent, or Red Crystal include the UN emblem, the emblem of the CultPropConv, and the emblems marking hospital and safety zones, internment camps, civil defence, and prisoner-of-war camps (see Annex).

2. War Crimes at International Courts

1416   War crimes and crimes against humanity, which are not properly prosecuted in national penal procedures, may be brought to the International Criminal Court (ICC) or an ad hoc tribunal established for such purpose.

The jurisdiction of the ICC, which is complementary to national criminal jurisdictions, is limited to the most serious crimes of concern to the international community as a whole (Article 5 ICC Statute).[200] International ad hoc tribunals were established after WWII to prosecute crimes committed by German and Japanese actors and more recently for war crimes committed in the Former Yugoslavia and in Rwanda. Internationalized criminal courts (mixed courts) were created in Sierra Leone, East Timor, Kosovo, and Cambodia.[201]

3. Disciplinary Action

1417   National disciplinary measures against members of the armed forces (see above, Section 151) remain unaffected.

The maintenance of military discipline, which is important for any armed forces, should be used for ensuring compliance with international humanitarian law. This may lead to measures additional to and independent from penal prosecution.

1418   A disciplinary superior, who learns about incidents substantiating suspicion that international law has been violated, shall clarify the facts and consider whether disciplinary measures are to be taken. If the disciplinary offence constitutes a criminal offence, the case shall be referred to the appropriate criminal prosecution authority.

Advisory service, Model Law concerning the use and the protection of the emblem of the red cross, the red crescent and the red crystal, available at <http://www.icrc.org/eng/assets/files/other/model-law-emblem-0107-eng-.pdf>.

[200] At the High-Level Meeting of the General Assembly on the Rule of Law on 24 September 2012, world leaders called on all states to recommit to the rule of law as a fundamental factor in preventing war at a United Nations summit that stressed the universality of humanitarian law and the importance of the ICC, see the *Draft Declaration of the High-Level Meeting of the 67th Session of the General Assembly on the rule of law at the national and international levels* (<http://www.unrol.org/files/Draft%20Declaration%20of%20 the%20High-level%20Meeting%20of%20the%2067th%20Session.pdf>).

[201] Cf. Romano, Nollkaemper, and Kleffner (eds), above, n. 124.

1. Not only can criminal responsibility attach to superiors for a grave breach by their subordinates, but the officers themselves are generally under an obligation to prevent such injuries, to report the violations if necessary,[202] and further to impose disciplinary or criminal punishment.[203]

2. The question of whether disciplinary punishment is sufficient or whether the case should be referred to criminal prosecutors is decided by national (military) law. The possibility of disciplinary punishment by the military remains even after a case has been handed over to the prosecutor (Article 87, para. 3, AP I).

VIII. Reparation

A party to a conflict, which does not comply with the provisions of international humanitarian law, shall be liable to make reparation. It shall be responsible for all acts committed by persons forming part of its armed forces (Article 91 AP I; Article 3 HC IV). Forms of reparation include restitution, compensation, rehabilitation, satisfaction, and guarantees of non-repetition.   1419

1. The obligation to compensate can be traced to Article 91 AP I, which copies Article 3 HC IV *verbatim*.[204] At the time that this norm was written, it was considered as an effective tool for making reparation in the case of breaches of the HagueReg. It corresponds with the principle, as developed both in state practice and jurisprudence, that a breach of international law caused by an individual state will invoke its responsibility. But not in each single case of wrongful personal conduct is responsibility of states or international organizations involved.[205] Where such responsibility exists, not only compensation, but also other forms of reparation including restitution, rehabilitation, satisfaction, and guarantees of non-repetition must be considered.

2. The obligation to provide compensation for violations of international humanitarian law applies equally to each party to the conflict, whether aggressor or defender. Pursuant to the object and purpose of Article 91 AP I, compensation must be paid if the violation of international humanitarian law causes compensatable damages (personal injuries, material and property damage, etc.). The sentence of Article 3 HC IV and Article 91 AP I is clear on the point that every act of a member of the armed forces, whether or not committed under orders, and whether or falling within the realm of military duties, is attributable to the relevant state. Thus liability is strict.

3. In practice, state responsibility for breaches of international humanitarian law has widely been neglected. Almost always, victor states have demanded reparation without ensuring compensation for each individual violation.[206] In some cases, states have

---

[202] Article 87, para. 1, AP I.

[203] Article 87, para. 3, AP I.

[204] Cf. Frits Kalshoven, 'State Responsibility for Warlike Acts of the Armed Forces: From Art. 3 of Hague Convention IV of 1907 to Article 91 of AP I of 1977 and Beyond', in M. N. Schmitt/W. Heintschel von Heinegg (eds), above, n. 31, 177 *et seq.*

[205] Knut Ipsen, *Völkerrecht*, 5th edn (Munich: C. H. Beck, 2004), 616, for further supporting evidence.

[206] This tendency is countered by the Geneva Conventions. Under Article 51 GC I, Article 52 GC II, Article 131 GC III, and Article 148 GC IV, all states must face their obligation to ensure effective penal

arranged for the payment of compensation for accidental damage.[207] Also, beyond such incidental cases, there is an encouraging practice of claims commissions established by states willing or persuaded by other states or ordered by the Security Council under Chapter VII to bring redress in specific situations of a breach of *ius in bello* or *jus ad bellum*.[208]

4. The completion and final adoption in 2001 of the International Law Commission's Articles on Responsibility of States (ARS)[209] has confirmed that state responsibility extends to breaches of international humanitarian law which may be attributed to the state. This attribution may be made to acts committed by regular armed forces (Articles 4–9 ARS),[210] irrespective of whether the act was committed in an international or non-international armed conflict. It may also be made *ex post facto* to acts of members of armed opposition groups, if their insurrectional movement was successful (Article 10 ARS). In all these cases, individual crimes and other violations of international law—as they are internationally wrongful acts of a state—entail state responsibility.

5. State practice and jurisprudence have so far denied that international law offers rights to individuals, corresponding to the duties of states, to comply with international humanitarian law. After several years' debate, the UN Commission on Human Rights has prepared 'Basic Principles and Guidelines on the Right to a Remedy and Reparation for Victims of Gross Violations of International Human Rights Law and Serious Violations of International Humanitarian Law', adopted by the General Assembly in December 2005.[211] According to this document, the obligation to respect, ensure respect for and implement international human rights law and international humanitarian law includes, *inter alia*, the duty: (a) to take appropriate measures to prevent violations; (b) to investigate violations effectively, promptly, thoroughly, and impartially and, where appropriate, take action against those allegedly responsible in accordance with domestic and international law; (c) to provide victims with equal and effective access to justice; and (d) to provide effective remedies to victims, including reparation. Adoption of this document, which confirms the responsibility of states to provide remedies and reparation for gross violations, has been facilitated by avoiding the controversial question of individual rights, except for the plea that states should provide equal and effective access to justice, adequate, effective, and prompt reparation for harm suffered, and access to

---

sanction for grave breaches. This obligation includes the prosecution of perpetrators belonging to victorious armed forces. States cannot free themselves or another state from this responsibility.

[207] Thus, when the Chinese Embassy in Belgrade was erroneously bombed by US forces during the Kosovo campaign on 8 May 1999, a US senior official offered 'sincere apologies' in Beijing and stated that the attack was 'completely unintended'. Compensation to the victims and their families were settled in a Memorandum of Understanding of 30 July 1999, cf. Memorandum of Understanding between the Delegation of the United States of America and the Delegation of the People's Republic of China, as of 30 July 1999, full text available at <http://www.state.gov/documents/organization/6526.doc>.

[208] See, e.g., the UN Compensation Commission on claims against Iraq 'as a result of Iraq's unlawful invasion and occupation of Kuwait', established under SC Res. 687 (1991) of 8 April 1991; but also practice (*inter alia* by Bosnia and Herzegovina, Canada, Germany, Iran, the US) and other states, documented by Fleck, in Wolff Heintschel von Heinegg/Volker Epping (eds), *International Humanitarian Law Facing New Challenges* (Springer, 2007), 171–206, [193–7].

[209] See above, n. 39.

[210] See Crawford, above, n. 40.

[211] UN GA Res. 60/147 (16 December 2005), UN Doc. A/RES/60/147 (2006); Annex to Human Rights Resolution 2005/35, adopted by the Commission on Human Rights on 19 April 2005.

SILJA VÖNEKY

relevant information concerning violations and reparation mechanisms. Thus, states are called on to close gaps which continue to exist in current international law.

6. The International Law Association established a Committee on Compensation for Victims of War[212] and issued a 'Declaration of International Law Principles on Reparation for Victims of Armed Conflict (Substantive Issues)' in 2010.[213] The Declaration is an important step forward in further stressing and clarifying the rules of international humanitarian law and general international law in this field. The main rule is the right to reparation, as '[v]ictims of armed conflict have a right to reparation from the responsible parties' (Article 6). The concepts and notions of restitution, compensation, satisfaction, victim, responsible party, and so on are clarified by the Committee. The Commentary to the 2010 Articles rightly states that there is a notable trend towards recognizing an individual right to reparation.[214] This is in line with Article 75 ICC Statute, as the ICC may award reparation and such an order can be requested by the victim. The question of collective reparation is addressed as well,[215] and the duty of states is included as an assurance that victims have a right to reparation under national law (Article 13).[216] Along these lines, states may develop practical solutions for different situations.

7. In some non-international armed conflicts and situations of counterinsurgency, warfare condolence payments (compensation *ex gratia*) are seen by some states as a tool 'to win the peace', that is to create trust in situations where a civilian is inadvertently killed by a combatant of another state.[217] These payments are not seen by the states as an admission of liability and they are not required by international law. However, the payments may reflect an indigenous custom of financial compensation. Moral and strategic reasons can justify such payments, if they can be seen in the context of a broader reconciliative process.[218]

IX. Protecting Powers and their Substitutes

At the beginning of a conflict, the parties to the conflict have the duty to appoint   1420
protecting powers, which safeguard their interests (Article 5, para. 1, AP I). For this
purpose, each party to the conflict shall designate a protecting power (Article 8, para.
1, GC I; Article 8, para. 1, GC II; Article 8, para. 1, GC III; Article 9, para. 1, GC

---

[212] Cf. <http://www.ila-hq.org/en/committees/index.cfm/cid/1018>.

[213] ILA, Declaration of International Law Principles on Reparation for Victims of Armed Conflict (Substantive Issues), Resolution No. 2/2010, The Hague, 15–20 August 2010.

[214] Cf. ILA, The Hague Conference (2010), Draft Declaration of International Law Principles on Reparation for Victims of Armed Conflict, 30 pp., <http://www.ila-hq.org/en/committees/index.cfm/cid/1018>.

[215] ILA, Arts. 1–14, Draft Declaration of International Law Principles on Reparation for Victims of Armed Conflict, 19 *et seq.*

[216] However, there is no specification as regards the content of the right to reparation and the standard to be observed. For the procedural standards for reparation mechanisms for victims of armed conflict, see the outcome of the ILA Sofia Conference (2012), <http://www.ila-hq.org/en/committees/index.cfm/cid/1018>.

[217] For instance, as of 2004, a victim's family in Iraq can apply for a condolence payment of up to $2,500 if an Iraqi non-combatant civilian is inadvertently killed by a combatant of the US. Cf. J. Joseph, 'Winning Hearts and Minds in Iraq Through Mediated Condolence Payments', Vol. 25, No. 5, *Alternatives to the High Cost of Litigation* (May 2007), 85 *et seq.* In regard to *ex gratia* payments of $5,000 for a family of one or more victims of the Kunduz incident by Germany, cf. BT Drs. 17/3723 and BT Drs. 17/8120, 12.12.2011.

[218] To questions of 'Muslim conflict resolution', cf. J. Joseph, above, n. 217.

IV). The party involved shall, without delay and for the same purpose, permit the activities of a protecting power, which has been acknowledged by it as such, after designation by the adverse party. The International Committee of the Red Cross may assist in the designation of protecting powers (Article 5, para. 3, AP I).

1. A protecting power is an important tool for the implementation of humanitarian law during an international armed conflict. A protecting power has to implement humanitarian law by supervision, inspection, assistance, and transmissions. It has the right to inspect prisoner-of-war camps, to assist in judicial proceedings, to deliver notes to the belligerents, and to render good offices.[219] Through a protecting power, a kind of neutral supervision is created that functions as a tool for the implementation of international humanitarian law, even though the protecting power is obliged to advocate the interests of the party to the conflict that it represents. However, a state has to agree to be a protecting power. The state has to be neutral or not party to the conflict, and must be designated by a party to the conflict and accepted by the adverse party as a protecting power. Usually, there is an agreement between the protected state, the protecting power, and the host state with regard to the special tasks of the protecting power. The duties of the protecting power end with the demise of the protected state or with the restoration of diplomatic relations between the warring states. If no state agrees to be a protecting power, the ICRC can act as a substitute. The same is true in regard to non-international armed conflicts: the ICRC offers to perform the function of a protecting power; however, the parties to a non-international armed conflict have to accept such offers.

2. The institution of the protecting power developed during the Franco-Prussian War of 1870–1871 and was incorporated—after WWI—into an international agreement for the first time in Article 86 of the 1929 Geneva Convention relative to the Treatment of Prisoners of War.[220] During WWII, most belligerents party to the 1929 Convention appointed protecting powers. The 1949 Geneva Conventions all contain provisions regarding protecting powers (Articles 8–10 GC I; Articles 8–10 GC II; Articles 8–10 GC III; and Articles 9–11, 30 GC IV). According to this, the parties to an armed conflict are obliged to appoint protecting powers. They regulate the procedure of appointment and the functions of the protecting powers and try to fill in the lacunae of the 1929 Convention. Rules concerning protecting powers are further improved in Article 5 AP I with regard to international armed conflicts. Additionally, the 1961 Vienna Convention on Diplomatic Relations is applicable as there is an overlap between the law of diplomacy and international humanitarian law after an armed conflict has begun (Article 5(6) AP I).[221] Special regulations[222] bind states parties to the 1999 Second Protocol[223] of the 1954 Convention for the Protection of Cultural Property[224] in the Event of Armed Conflict. Apart from this treaty law, the institution of a protecting power is an established rule of customary international law.

---

[219] Cf. for an overview Hans-Joachim Heintze, 'Protecting Power', *MPEPIL*.
[220] 1929 Convention, entered into force 19 June 1931, 118 LNTS 343.
[221] Cf. Art. 45 *et seq.* 1961 Vienna Convention on Diplomatic Relations; the two kinds of protecting powers (Vienna mandate and Geneva mandate) can exist simultaneously, cf. Heintze, above, n. 219.
[222] Arts. 2–4 Annex Regulations for the Execution of the Convention.
[223] Entered into force 9 March 2004, (1999) 38 *ILM* 769.
[224] Entered into force 7 August 1956, 249 UNTS 240.

SILJA VÖNEKY

3. There are four possibilities for the appointment of a protecting power: *first*, appointment may be made through trilateral agreement between the determining party, the opposing party, and the protecting power. In this case, a belligerent appoints a state not party to the conflict to safeguard its interests in view of the other parties engaged in the conflict. The prospective protecting power, as well as the state with which the party is engaged in armed conflict, must agree to this selection. The *second*, and more likely, possibility is that the appointment of protecting powers will be accomplished through the mediation efforts of the ICRC, if the trilateral method has no success. The reasons why states could not agree in the appointment of protecting powers are irrelevant for the involvement of the ICRC. In order to achieve the appointment of protecting powers, the ICRC can summon a party— here the *third* procedure comes into play—to present it with a list of at least five states that it judges to be acceptable to act as a protecting power against the hostile party. Each opposing party can be called concurrently to submit a list of at least five states which they would recognize as protecting powers. The ICRC then compares both lists and requests the consent of a state specified on both lists to act as a protecting power. If no appointment of a protecting power is reached through this method, *fourth*, the possibility exists that the parties will designate the ICRC or another international organization, which offers all guarantees of impartiality and efficacy, to act as substitute.[225]

4. The functions of the protecting powers are not completely defined. As follows from the Geneva Conventions, it is the duty of the protecting powers to safeguard the interests of the party to the conflict which has designated them (Article 8, para. 1, 1st sentence, GC I) and to encourage compliance with international humanitarian law in an impartial manner. According to Article 126, paras. 1–3, GC III, the representatives or delegates of the protecting powers have a free right of access to the places of internment of prisoners of war.[226] According to Article 143, paras. 1–4, GC IV, they have the right to enter all places where protected persons may be. This is particularly true for places of internment, confinement, or work. In accordance with Article 30 GC IV, protected persons can appeal to the protecting powers of the ICRC and of any other aid organization. According to Article 105, para. 5, GC III, the representatives of protecting powers have the right to attend trials of war criminals. The same holds true for trials of civilians in occupied territories (Article 74, para. 1, GC IV). Finally, in accordance with Article 55, para. 3, GC IV, it can be determined by protecting powers whether sufficient foodstuffs and medical supplies are available in the occupied territories. In addition, according to Article 5 CultPropReg, protecting powers can also verify violations of cultural property.

5. The system of protecting powers was reaffirmed in Article 5, para. 1, AP I, but in many recent armed conflicts no protecting powers were designated.[227]

> **If there is no protecting power, the parties to the conflict are obliged to accept an**   1421
> **offer of the International Committee of the Red Cross or of any other impartial and**
> **efficient organization to act as a substitute (Article 5, para. 4, AP I).**

If no protecting power has been designated, the parties to the conflict shall recognize the ICRC or another impartial organization as a substitute (Article 10 GC I; Article 5,

---

[225] See below, Section 1421.
[226] See above, Sections 714–26.
[227] For the reasons, see Heintze, above, n. 219.

para. 4, AP I). Despite ambiguous wording in Article 5, para. 4, AP I, it seems that a corresponding obligation to accept exists. Only this interpretation of the duties contained in Article 5, para. 1, AP I allows parties of an armed conflict to avail themselves of the system of protecting powers (see above, Section 706).

X. International Fact-Finding

1422   **The International Humanitarian Fact-Finding Commission—IHFFC—(Article 90 AP I) was established in 1991. It is comprised of fifteen independent members and shall investigate any incident alleged to be a grave breach or a serious violation of the rules of international humanitarian law within states, which have recognized the competence of the Commission.**

1. Whereas fact-finding and enquiry is—in general terms—a recognized form of international dispute settlement through the process of elucidating facts,[228] there are the special rules of Article 52 GC I, Article 53 GC II, Article 132 GC III, and Article 149 GC IV in international humanitarian law. Those rules provide for the creation of a fact-finding commission upon the request of one party to a conflict.[229] Although the *ICRC Commentary* has always seen this provision as binding,[230] such an investigation has never yet been conducted. The probability for this is also slight, as the accused party can escape simply by refusing to permit an international investigation of the incident.

2. Article 90 AP I is a considerable step forward in supporting impartial investigations as it establishes the International Humanitarian Fact-Finding Commission (IHFFC), and creates a special tool for the implementation of AP I. Composed of fifteen individuals, acting in their personal capacity, the IHFFC is a permanent, impartial, and independent body with its seat in Berne/Switzerland.[231] The IHFFC has to investigate allegations of grave breaches and serious violations of international humanitarian law (Article 90(2c) AP I). A party can declare, by or after signing or ratifying AP I, that it recognizes the competence of such a fact-finding commission vis-à-vis every other contracting party, which accepts the same obligation. Such declarations of acceptance of the Commission's competence have presently been submitted by seventy-four states (as of January 2014);[232] the IHFFC was constituted in 1991. The main functions of the Commission are fact-finding and conciliation in international armed conflicts: the investigation of all activities alleged to constitute a grave breach or other serious violation of the Geneva Conventions or AP I; good offices contributing to adherence to the Geneva Conventions and AP I; other investigations at the request of one party to a conflict and with the agreement of the other. The last function means that even states not party to AP I can ask for the help of the Commission; if all parties to the conflict agree then the Commission shall accept to

---

[228] See Art. 33 *et seq.* UN Charter; cf. Agnieszka Jachec-Neale, 'Fact-Finding', *MPEPIL*.

[229] Cf. Heike Spieker, 'International (Humanitarian) Fact-Finding Commission', *MPEPIL*.

[230] Jean S. Pictet (ed.), *Commentary to the Geneva Convention Relative to the Treatment of Prisoners of War*, Vol. III (ICRC, 1960), 632.

[231] Spieker, above, n. 229.

[232] See for a list of current states parties: <http://www.ihffc.org/index.asp?Language=EN&page=states parties_list&listfilter=off> and <http://www.icrc.org/IHL.nsf/(SPF)/party_main_treaties/$File/IHL_and_ other_related_Treaties.pdf>. For a concise history of negotiations, see K. J. Partsch, International Fact-Finding Commission, in Bothe/Partsch/Solf, above, n. 164, at 537 *et seq.*

make enquiries into alleged violations of international law in non-international armed conflicts as well.[233] Hence, although the Commission cannot enquire into any facts unless it has been seized by the relevant party to the conflict, it may take initiatives within its mandate and offer its services. Such offers can also be rightly made in conflicts not of an international character.

3. In accordance with Article 90, para. 5, lit. c, AP I, the Commission does not publicly communicate the results of its fact-finding, unless all parties to the conflict so request. This provision may, in effect, strengthen the initiative of states to take necessary measures within their own responsibility, without pressure from outside. As the results of other fact-finding activities, in particular those by UN bodies, are by nature available for public discussion, states might see a national interest in seizing the Commission rather than any other fact-finding mechanism. In practice, however, the services of the Commission have not been used so far.[234]

> **In the case of serious violations, states are further bound to act, jointly or indi-**   1423
> **vidually, in co-operation with the United Nations and in conformity with the UN**
> **Charter (Article 89 AP I).**

1. Article 89 AP I is the result of a long debate over whether to prohibit all reprisals or to allow them only under strictly limited conditions.[235] Article 89 AP I does not explain which actions states or the United Nations respectively may take to ensure observance of international humanitarian law. This may be deplored, as mechanisms agreed under the 1949 Geneva Conventions have not been used so far: Articles 52 GC I, 53 GC II, 132 GC III, 149 GC IV provide for formal inquiries at the request of a party to the conflict concerning any alleged violation. Even procedural aspects, including the choice of an umpire, are addressed in these provisions, but states have never put them into practice. It may be preferable to states to convene a meeting for consideration of general problems concerning the application of international humanitarian law. This possibility is provided for in Article 7 AP I, but procedural thresholds are rather high: Switzerland, as depositary of AP I, shall convene such meeting 'at the request of one or more of [the parties to AP I] and upon the approval of the majority of [all parties]'. Thus, each request made must find the approval by a majority of all (presently 172)[236] states parties, before states may be convened for its consideration.

2. The most likely measures may arise from fact-finding by competent UN bodies, as has been the case for instance in the Former Yugoslavia, and from Security Council action under Chapter VII of the UN Charter, that is economic and military measures.[237] The Security Council has taken this path in recent years, in particular in the cases of Iraq

---

[233] The wording of Art. 90 AP I is no limitation, as the object and purpose of international humanitarian law calls for an effective implementation of that law in all situations where the law of armed conflict is applicable; see as well H. Spieker, above, n. 229.

[234] E. Mikos-Skuza, 'The International Humanitarian Fact-Finding Commission: An Awakening Beauty?' in A. Fischer-Lescano/H-P Gasser/T. Marauhn/N. Ronzitti (eds), *Frieden in Freiheit. Peace in Liberty. Paix en liberté. Festschrift für Michael Bothe zum 70.* Geburtstag (Baden-Baden: Nomos, 2008), 481 *et seq.*

[235] See Section 1408.

[236] October 2012, cf. <http://www.icrc.org/IHL.nsf/(SPF)/party_main_treaties/$File/IHL_and_other_related_Treaties.pdf>.

[237] For an overview of the activities of the SC, see Michael Wood, 'United Nations, Security Council', *MPEPIL.*

(1991), Somalia (1992), and the Former Yugoslavia (1991–1995), East Timor (1999), Kosovo (1999), Afghanistan (2000–2002), Sierra Leone (2003), Liberia (2003), Haiti (2004), Sudan (2005), and Libya (2011). For further discussion see below, Sections 1427–1433.

3. Since the end of the so-called Cold War, with Security Council Resolution 688 of 5 April 1991, serious violations of human rights are classified as a threat to the peace and security of the region, thus clearing the way for Security Council activities based on Chapter VII of the Charter. Until that time, no Security Council Resolution had taken so serious a step.[238] The line adopted in Resolution 688 was also pursued by the Security Council in the case of Somalia: Resolution 794 of 3 December 1992 focuses exclusively on serious human rights violations which justify measures pursuant to Chapter VII. The Security Council entered the case of the Former Yugoslavia as a result of violations of international humanitarian law. Resolutions 764 of 13 July 1992 and 780 of 6 October 1992 emphasized the obligation of parties to the conflict to obey international humanitarian law and initiated steps towards the prosecution of war criminals. Even if the action taken pursuant to Chapter VII relied mainly on the violation of Bosnia-Herzegovina's territorial integrity, the serious violations of international humanitarian law also legitimized the enforcement measures.

XI. The International Committee of the Red Cross

1424   The International Committee of the Red Cross (ICRC) is an impartial, neutral, and independent humanitarian organization whose exclusively humanitarian mission is to protect the lives and dignity of victims of armed conflict and other situations of violence and to provide them with assistance. The ICRC is an organization based in Swiss law. The members of its governing board (the Committee) are Swiss citizens, yet the delegates acting in its name are of various nationality. The Geneva Conventions and their Additional Protocols recognize the special status of the ICRC at the international level and assign specific tasks to it, including visiting prisoners of war, civilian internees and detainees, carrying out its activities in occupied territories, providing relief to persons in need, selecting and transmitting information concerning missing persons (Central Tracing Agency), and offering its good offices to facilitate the establishment of hospital and safety zones. The ICRC's mission is to promote the faithful application of the principles and rules of international humanitarian law by the parties to an armed conflict, whether international or not, and, in general, to strengthen the protection of victims of armed conflicts through international law. In humanitarian matters, it serves as a neutral intermediary between belligerents and has a general right of initiative. Owing to its humanitarian activities in situations of violence, which are guided by the principles of humanity, impartiality, neutrality, independence, voluntary service, unity, and universality, the ICRC enjoys high respect and deserves support.

1. The ICRC—established in 1863—is, in practice, the organ which serves as guardian of international humanitarian law.[239] It is an independent humanitarian organization

---

[238] The Security Council had addressed serious human rights violations in South Rhodesia in Resolutions 217 of 20 November 1965 and 221 of 19 April 1966, but its measures were justified by the danger of military conflict between South Rhodesia and neighbouring states.

[239] See for instance, Hans-Peter Gasser, 'International Committee of the Red Cross (ICRC)', *MPEPIL*.

that has a status of its own and is recognized as a privileged non-state actor with a limited personality under international law.[240] It monitors observance of the four Geneva Conventions and their Additional Protocols and directs the International Red Cross and Red Crescent Movement. Due to the nature of its organization, it is assured that the ICRC performs its duties independently of government influence (including the Swiss government). The ICRC has continuous or temporary delegations in foreign countries which represent its interests to the host state's authorities.

2. According to its own Statutes[241] and the Statutes of the Movement,[242] the duties of the ICRC are *inter alia*: to secure observation of the basic principles of the Red Cross; to work towards the strengthening of international humanitarian law; to enforce humanitarian measures in civil wars and domestic conflicts; and to serve as protection and aid for military and civilian victims in such conflicts and as a mediator in humanitarian questions between parties to the conflict. In addition, the ICRC performs duties assigned to it by the Geneva Conventions and Additional Protocols.[243] Among these, the visiting of prisoners of war and interned civilians,[244] the protection of the rights of those living in occupied territories,[245] as well as the maintenance of the International Tracing Service and the rights to take any humanitarian initiative that it deems necessary are of importance. Additionally, the ICRC is a possible substitute for a protecting power (see above Section 1421). The duties and rights of the ICRC are not limited to international armed conflicts; common Article 3, para. 2, GC states that the ICRC can offer its services to each party of a non-international conflict as well.

3. It is generally recognized that the ICRC monitors observance of international humanitarian law and has to react to serious breaches of international law.[246] The ICRC may notify one party of violations complained of by another party and in this way initiate dialogue between the two conflicting parties.[247] ICRC activities in case of violations of international humanitarian law are generally based on confidential and bilateral representations. They are aimed at influencing states and non-state actors through persuasion. It is only under very exceptional and strict conditions that the ICRC resorts to a public denunciation of violations of international humanitarian law.[248]

---

[240] The Statutes of the International Red Cross and Red Crescent Movement were adopted in 1986; they form one legal basis of the ICRC. Article 5, Statutes of the International Red Cross and Red Crescent Movement.

[241] Article 4, Statutes of the International Committee of the Red Cross.

[242] Article 5, para. 1, Statutes of the International Red Cross and Red Crescent Movement.

[243] Cf. common Arts. 9, 10, and 11 Geneva Conventions; Art. 81(1) AP I.

[244] Art. 126(1), (4) GC III.

[245] Art. 143(1), (5) GC IV.

[246] See for instance, Gasser, above, n. 239.

[247] P. Boissier, *Histoire du Comité international de la Croix-Rouge. De Solférino à Tsoushima* (Paris: Librairie Plon, 1963), reprinted in Geneva: Institute Henry Dunant, *1978*; Hans Haug, *Rotes Kreuz. Werden, Gestalt, Wirken* (Bern/Stuttgart: Verlag Hans Huber, 1966), 13–32; Anton Schlögel, 'IRC—International Red Cross', in R. Wolfrum (ed.), *United Nations: Law, Policies and Practice*, Vol. 2 (Berlin: Springer, 1995), 814 *et seq.*

[248] Hans-Peter Gasser, above, n. 239. Cf. as well Action by the International Committee of the Red Cross in the event of violations of international humanitarian law or of other fundamental rules protecting persons in situations of violence, (2005) 858 *IRRC* 393–400; Hans-Peter Gasser/Nils Melzer, *Humanitäres Völkerrecht. Eine Einführung*, 2nd edn (Zürich: Schulthess, 2012), 238–47.

SILJA VÖNEKY

XII. Implementation Roles of the UN

1425   Competent organs of the United Nations shall promote universal respect for, and observance of, human rights and fundamental freedoms, in peacetime as in times of armed conflict.

The UN is committed 'to reaffirm faith in fundamental human rights, in the dignity and worth of the human person' and 'to establish conditions under which justice and respect for the obligations arising from treaties and other sources of international law can be maintained' (Preamble, paras. 2 and 3, UN Charter). Much more than a mere political programme, commitment is an essential element for maintaining and restoring international peace and security. It is mandatory of all competent organs of the United Nations and fully includes the task to promote universal respect for, and observance of, human rights and fundamental freedoms. Compliance with international humanitarian law is a necessary element of this task and this entails particular responsibilities for the General Assembly, the Security Council, and the Secretary-General, in peacetime as in times of armed conflict.

1426   The competence of human rights bodies and courts established under human rights conventions is generally limited to the determination of whether a given act was in violation of the relevant human rights norm. This does not preclude, however, taking into consideration provisions of international humanitarian law in order to interpret such norm. It may also be considered that human rights bodies have a responsibility to investigate those limitations of human rights in armed conflicts, which may apply under the *lex specialis* role of international humanitarian law (see above, Sections 252–256). Hence, international humanitarian law may be dealt with even by human rights organs, which can thus provide support to ensure respect for international humanitarian law.

1. *Non-confrontative means of implementation by courts and tribunals: human rights bodies.* References to human rights and fundamental freedoms, which are made in Articles 1, para. 3, 55, lit. c, and 56 UN Charter, must be understood today as determinations establishing firm legal commitments for states.[249] Many states are parties to universal and/or regional human rights treaties.[250] The core of the human rights obligations form part of *jus cogens.*[251] Accordingly, international bodies, supported by states, NGOs, and individuals, have lent their voice for strengthening the protection of human rights in armed conflicts. The ICJ has stated that human rights are applicable during armed conflict.[252] The former Commission on Human Rights has initiated an assessment and a documentation

---

[249] Christian Tomuschat, *Human Rights: Between Idealism and Realism*, 2nd edn (OUP, 2008), 115–31.

[250] International Covenant on Civil and Political Rights, 999 UNTS 171 and 1057 UNTS 407; International Covenant on Economic, Social and Cultural Rights, 993 UNTS 2; European Convention on Human Rights, 213 UNTS 222; African Charter on Human and Peoples' Rights, 1001 UNTS 45; American Convention on Human Rights, 1144 UNTS 123.

[251] Jochen A. Frowein, 'Ius cogens', in *MPEPIL*; A. Bianchi, 'Human Rights and the Magic of Jus Cogens' (2008) 19 *EJIL* 491–508; Myres S. McDougal/Harold D. Lasswell/Chen Lung-Chu, *Human Rights and World Public Order: the Basic Policies of an International Law of Human Dignity* (Yale University Press, 1980), at 345.

[252] ICJ, Advisory Opinion, *Legality of the Threat or Use of Nuclear Weapons, ICJ Reports 1996*, 226, at para. 25.

SILJA VÖNEKY

of human rights violations committed during fighting in the Former Yugoslavia (mass shootings, torture, rape, ethnically motivated expulsions) and authorized criminal prosecution for these actions in its special session in August 1992.[253] Specialized bodies, such as the Committee Against Torture (CAT) and the Committee on the Elimination of Racial Discrimination (CERD), have also been invoked to deal with situations in armed conflicts. Considering the close interrelationship between human rights in armed conflicts and international humanitarian law (see above, Sections 252–256), human rights bodies are to apply norms of international humanitarian law in certain circumstances. In any event, human rights bodies have a responsibility to investigate those limitations of human rights in armed conflicts which may apply under the *lex specialis* rule of international humanitarian law. Notwithstanding this situation, it may be suggested that human rights bodies acting fully within their mandate may provide support to ensure respect not only for human rights, but also for international humanitarian law.

2. The competence of human rights bodies for violations of international humanitarian law is an indirect one, as each of these bodies works under a particular mandate that is distinct from the responsibility of states to respect and ensure respect for international humanitarian law. The competence of human rights bodies for violations of international humanitarian law depends on the applicability of human rights during armed conflicts[254] and—if the military measures take place in another state—on the question of extraterritorial jurisdiction of the states parties.[255]

3. Regional human rights bodies have effectively supported this development. The relationship between human rights and international humanitarian law has been dealt with *inter alia* in the jurisprudence under the ECHR[256] and the ACHR. Already in 2001, the IACtHR stated that it did not have the competence to determine whether a given act was in violation of the Geneva Conventions or treaties other than the ACHR;[257] but it has also confirmed that this does not preclude the taking into consideration of provisions of international humanitarian law in order to interpret the ACHR.[258] The ECtHR ruled in several cases on the violation of human rights during armed conflict.[259] In

---

[253] Resolution 1992/S–1/1 of 14 August 1992, at para. 9.

[254] For further evidence, see S. Vöneky, 'Armed Conflict, Effect on Treaties', in *MPEPIL*.

[255] Cf. for instance Art. 1 ECHR; one has to differentiate between the state's acts occurring within the treaty space but outside the state's own territory and the state's acts occurring outside the treaty space (state forces acting abroad); for the former, see *Loizidou v Turkey* (23 March 1995, No. 15318/89); *Cyprus v Turkey* (10 May 2001, application no. 25781/94); for the latter, see *Al-Saadoon and Mufdhi v UK* (2 March 2010, No. 61498/08); *Al-Skeini et al. v UK* (7 July 2011); *Al-Jedda v UK* (7 July 2011); *Mansur PAD et al. v Turkey* (28 June 2007, no. 60167/00); *Marković et al. v Italy* (14 December 2006, application no. 1398/03); *Banković et al. v Belgium* (19 December 2001, application no. 52207/99); *Issa et al. v Turkey* (16 November 2004, no. 31821/96); *Saddam Hussein v Coalition Forces* (14 March 2006, No. 23276/04); *Behrami and Behrami v France* (31 May 2007, no. 71412/01).

[256] Ibid.

[257] IACtHR, *Las Palmeras v Colombia*, Judgment of 6 December 2001, Series C No. 67, paras. 17 n. 1, 24 n. 2.

[258] IACtHR, *Bámaca-Velásquez v Guatemala*, Series C No. 70 (2000), Judgment of 16 November 2000, paras. 205–9.

[259] See, e.g., ECtHR, *Korbely v Hungary*, (application no. 9174/02), Judgment of 19 September 2008; *Al-Skeini et al. v UK*, (application no. 55721/07), Judgment of 7 July 2011; *Al-Jedda v UK*, (application no. 27021/08), Judgment of 7 July 2011; *Al-Saadoon and Mufdhi v UK*, (application no. 61498/08), Judgment of 2 March 2010. For a review of the case law of the ECtHR referring to situations of armed conflict, see Magdalena Forowicz, *The Reception of International Law in the European Court of Human Rights* (OUP, 2010), 313–51.

SILJA VÖNEKY

earlier cases—concerning Northern Ireland, Cyprus, and Chechnya (where operations had been conducted by armed forces although the existence of an armed conflict was denied by the state concerned)—the Court applied human rights law directly and *lex specialis* rules of international humanitarian law were not yet considered relevant.[260]

XIII. The Security Council and International Humanitarian Law

1427   The Security Council may emphasize the direct responsibility of states and armed groups under international humanitarian law.

1. Under Chapter VII of the UN Charter, the Security Council is empowered to take far-reaching decisions to maintain or restore international peace and security. In doing so, the Council enjoys considerable discretion and, while its decisions are binding on member states in accordance with Article 25 UN Charter, no judicial control is expressly provided.[261] Whereas in the many years between 1945 and 1990, enforcement measures under Chapter VII could be agreed upon only very occasionally (North Korea 1950–1953, Southern Rhodesia 1965–1970, and South Africa 1966–1990), the historical change marked by the end of the Cold War in 1989 has provided better conditions for the Council's decision-making (see above, Section 1423).

2. With SC Res. 688 (1991), serious violations of human rights in many parts of Iraq have expressly been classified as a threat to the peace and security of the region, thus clearing the way for activities based on Chapter VII of the Charter. The Security Council had addressed serious human rights violations in South Rhodesia in Resolutions 217 (1965) and 221 (1966), but its measures were justified by the danger of military conflict between South Rhodesia and neighbouring states caused by the flow of refugees.

3. The line adopted in Res. 688 was also pursued by the Security Council in the cases of Liberia and Somalia. Resolution 788 (1992) determined that 'the deterioration of the situation in Liberia constitutes a threat to international peace and security, in particular in West Africa as a whole'. Resolution 794 (1992) focuses exclusively on 'the magnitude of the human tragedy caused by the conflict in Somalia, further exacerbated by the obstacles being created to the distribution of humanitarian assistance', to constitute a threat to international peace and security justifying measures pursuant to Chapter VII.

4. The Security Council entered the case of the Former Yugoslavia as a result of violations of international humanitarian law. Resolutions 764 (1992) and 780 (1992) emphasized the obligation of parties to the conflict to obey international humanitarian law and initiated steps towards the prosecution of war criminals. Even if the measures enforced,

[260] See, e.g., ECtHR, *McCann et al. v UK*, Judgment of 27 September 1995, Series A 324, 21 EHRR 97; *Ergi v Turkey*, (application no. 23818/94), Judgment of 28 July 1998; *Khashiyev and Akayeva v Russia* (applications nos. 57942/00 and 57945/00), Judgment of 24 February 2005; *Medka Isayeva, Yusupova and Bazayeva v Russia*, (applications nos. 57947/00, 57948/00, and 57949/00), Judgment of 24 February 2005; *Zara Isayeva v Russia*, (application nos. 57947/00, 57950/00), Judgment of 24 February 2005; *Saramati v France, Germany, and Norway* (application no. 78166/01), Admissibility Decision of 31 May 2007; Abresch, (2005) 16 *EJIL* 741–67.
[261] See M. Wood, 'United Nations, Security Council', *MPEPIL*.

pursuant to Chapter VII, relied mainly on the violation of Bosnia-Herzegovina's territorial integrity, the serious violations of international humanitarian law also legitimized these measures.

5. Traditionally, it was assumed that the Security Council could act under Chapter VII of the UN Charter only in cases of a military breach of peace and could uphold the respect of international humanitarian law as well as human rights only in this context. But this connection between military breach of peace and violation of international humanitarian law is not necessary to trigger actions of the Security Council based on Chapter VII of the UN Charter. For example, in the case of Darfur, the Security Council has condemned the violation of international humanitarian law and invoked Chapter VII of the UN Charter, although the situation had not developed out of an act of aggression.[262] The same is true in regard to Libya. The responsibility of states and armed groups under international humanitarian law and applicable human rights law remains an important element for the restoration of peace and security and is an important element in the deliberations of the Security Council.

> **The Security Council may take action if the safe and unimpeded access of humani-**   1428
> **tarian personnel to civilian populations in need is denied.**

Access to civilian populations is an essential prerequisite for assisting them in armed conflicts and post-conflict situations. The Security Council underlines 'the importance of safe and unhindered access of humanitarian personnel to civilians in armed conflict'.[263] As host-nation consent to such access must not be withheld arbitrarily,[264] ad hoc decisions should also be considered, where necessary.

> **The Security Council should initiate fact-finding missions to conflict areas**   1429
> **with a view to identifying the specific requirements for humanitarian assist-**
> **ance, and in particular obtaining safe and meaningful access to vulnerable**
> **populations.**

Specific requirements for humanitarian assistance must be identified at field level to ensure that assistance can be provided in an effective manner. Today, such fact-finding is widely dependent on initiatives of states, the ICRC, NGOs, and individuals. The Security Council should seek objective advice on existing needs and base its decisions on a more regular fact-finding in this respect.

> **The Security Council should take effective measures to bring perpetrators of grave**   1430
> **violations of international humanitarian and human rights law to justice.**

Even before the ICC was established, the Security Council was instrumental in establishing some ad hoc tribunals for the purpose of prosecuting persons responsible for genocide and other serious violations of international humanitarian law. Thus, the Council

---

[262] See SC Res. 1755 (2007) and S/Res. 1672 (2006) in which sanctions have been taken against particular persons responsible for such violations. In SC Res. 1593 (2005), the Security Council has declared the situation in Sudan to constitute a threat to peace and has referred the case to the Prosecutor of the ICC. On that basis, on 2 May 2007 two arrest warrants have been issued by the Pretrial Chamber of the ICC.

[263] See for instance, SC Res. 1265 (1999).

[264] See above, Section 525; Mary Ellen O'Connell, 'Humanitarian Assistance in Non-International Armed Conflict, The Fourth Wave of Rights, Duties and Remedies' (2001) 31 *IsrYHR* 183–217, at 217.

SILJA VÖNEKY

adopted the Statutes for the ICTY[265] and the ICTR.[266] It also paved the way for the Agreement for and Statute of the Special Court for Sierra Leone of 16 January 2002.[267] Serious Crimes Panels in the District Court of Dili (East Timor)[268] and 'Regulations 64' Panels in the Courts of Kosovo[269] have contributed to a practice of the courts which was, and still is, supported by the international community.[270]

1431   The Security Council may consider the establishment of arrangements addressing post-conflict peacebuilding and reconciliation.

Truth and reconciliation commissions of different types have been established to consolidate the peace process after recent conflicts in *inter alia* Argentina, Uganda, Chile, Chad, El Salvador, East Timor, Haiti, Liberia, Morocco, Nepal, Panama, Paraguay, Peru, Philippines, Serbia and Montenegro, Sri Lanka, Sierra Leone, South Africa, South Korea, Ghana, Guatemala, Nigeria, and Uruguay.[271] Truth commissions are institutions established to collect the facts of a prior conflict and they aim for reconciliation. Their competences vary and can include the making of recommendations, even in regard to reparations and amnesties, yet they have no binding legal consequences.[272] While each of them was created by an international treaty, especially peace agreements, national legislation, or decree, some of them have been successfully brokered by the UN, using persuasion rather than enforceable action. This is true for instance in regard to El Salvador's Commission on the Truth about the 12-Year War in El Salvador; its members were appointed by the UN in consultation with the parties.[273] The extent to which this process could be supported by peace operations on a more regular basis deserves consideration, although there are several legal problems in connection with Truth Commissions.[274]

XIV. Diplomatic Activities

1432   Compliance with international law may be ensured by using protest, good offices, mediation, investigation, and diplomatic intervention, whether by neutral states, international bodies, religious organizations, or humanitarian organizations, as well as by sanctions decided upon by the United Nations Security Council.

1. When violations of international humanitarian law reach a certain gravity, they can and have to trigger reactions from other states.[275] Apart from measures taken by the

---

[265] SC Res. 827 (1993) and Report of the Secretary-General (UN Doc. S/25704 and Add. 1).
[266] SC Res. 955 (1994), and request of the government of Rwanda (UN Doc. S/1994/1115).
[267] SC Res. 1315 (2000).
[268] SC Res. 1272 (1999), para. 16.
[269] SC Res. 1244 (1999), and UNMIK Reg. 2000/64.
[270] Romano, Nollkaemper, and Kleffner (eds), above, n. 124.
[271] Priscilla B. Hayner, 'Truth commissions: a schematic overview' (2006) 862 *IRRC* 295–310.
[272] Andreas O'Shea, 'Truth and Reconciliation Commissions', *MPEPIL*.
[273] See SC Res. 693 (1991) and Mexico Peace Agreements, Art. 12. For the Clarification Commission in Guatemala, see Christian Tomuschat, 'Clarification Commission in Guatemala' (2001) 23 *Human Rights Quarterly* 233–58.
[274] For instance, the relationship between these Commissions and the pursuit of prosecution and the courts; see for further details O'Shea, above, n. 272.
[275] See above, Section 1423.

United Nations,[276] it is quite possible that individual states, the ICRC, or humanitarian organizations engage in diplomatic intervention. With this intervention, in addition to the influence of bad publicity, diplomatic pressure can be brought to bear on the state to adhere to humanitarian provisions. Examples can be found in the recent history of international law, in which states have countered massive breaches of international law with sanctions, although they themselves were not directly involved in the conflict. One example involves sanctions imposed by the community of states in response to the taking of hostages at the US Embassy in Teheran.[277] The International Court upheld this concerted action in its later decision.[278]

2. Such reaction can be based on the obligation of states to ensure respect of international humanitarian law, as stated in Article 1 common to the Geneva Conventions and Article 1, para. 1, AP I.[279] They may include preventive measures to promote compliance and states should act jointly to achieve this goal. An example is the 2005 'EU Guidelines on promoting compliance with international humanitarian law',[280] stressing the obligation of states and non-states actors, as well as the political and humanitarian interest in improving compliance with international humanitarian law throughout the world. The Guidelines call for an early identification of situations where international humanitarian law may apply, for monitoring, and for appropriate actions including political dialogue, general public statements, demarches, restrictive measures/sanctions, co-operation with other international bodies, crisis management operations, measures to stress individual responsibility, training, and a responsible arms export policy in full consideration of compliance with humanitarian standards by importing countries. The ICRC has welcomed these Guidelines in a Circular Note dated 23 November 2006 and described modalities of ICRC support for their implementation.

XV. The Role of Non-Governmental Organizations

Non-governmental organizations (NGOs) have an important role to play in conflict prevention, conflict resolution, and post-conflict reconstruction. The influence of NGOs has been supported by the courage, devotion, and compassion of individuals, and in turn, the role of individuals for the implementation and development of international humanitarian law has clearly been increased by NGOs during their activities. This role has already been indispensable in the past and it is challenging states at present and in the foreseeable future.   **1433**

---

[276] See above, Sections 1425–31.

[277] On 22 April 1980, the European Community Foreign Ministers resolved, in the framework of European political co-operation, to carry out measures necessary for the imposition of sanctions against Iran. *EC Bulletin* 1980, No. 4, 26 *et seq.*

[278] *ICJ Reports* 1980, 3, 43 *et seq.*

[279] See above Section 1402. Cf. Frits Kalshoven, 'The Undertaking to Respect and Ensure Respect in All Circumstances' (1999) 2 *YIHL* 3–61, at 54; Birgit Kessler, 'The Duty to "Ensure Respect" Under Common Art. 1 of the Geneva Conventions: Its Implication in International and Non-International Armed Conflicts' (2001) 44 *GYIL* 498–516.

[280] General Affairs and External Relations Council of the European Union, European Union Guidelines on promoting compliance with international humanitarian law, Official Journal of the European Union, 2005/C 327/04 (23 December 2005).

NGOs have an important role in addition to and independent from governments, international organizations, and the ICRC.[281] Although not all NGOs serve strictly humanitarian purposes, many of them, including Amnesty International,[282] Human Rights Watch,[283] Médecins sans Frontières,[284] and others, may offer professional services, which may be indispensable for the victims of armed conflicts and should be accepted and supported by states. NGOs may help to publish violations of humanitarian law, even in non-international armed conflicts, and can stabilize post-conflict situations, for instance in initiating truth commissions (see above, Section 1431). In this context as well, the role of individuals for the implementation of humanitarian law and human rights law cannot be underestimated.[285]

XVI. National Implementing Measures

1434   **The relative weakness of international measures to secure the performance of obligations under humanitarian law calls for national implementing efforts, among which legislative measures, education programmes, and military manuals are of particular importance.**

International humanitarian law must be made an integral part of any national law system,[286] binding upon individuals as a set of norms which is in most cases directly applicable. In any national legal system, a number of legislative and administrative activities must be taken to implement international legal obligations effectively. First of all, states need to make sure, by military manuals and educational measures, that every member of the armed forces of a state knows the relevant norms and principles of humanitarian law and human rights law applicable in armed conflicts. Besides, states shall consult the Advisory Service of the ICRC that provides excellent information on the implementation of international humanitarian law. In addition to legislative, administrative, and political measures, military regulations are of particular significance in this context, as they translate humanitarian rules into the military sphere and may support their application in daily practice.[287]

XVII. Dissemination of Humanitarian Law

1435   **Effective implementation is dependent upon the dissemination of humanitarian law. Providing information about it is the necessary basis from which to educate and to further the attitude of people towards a greater acceptance of these principles as an achievement of social and cultural development.**

---

[281] Carsten Stahn, 'NGOs and International Peacekeeping—Issues, Prospects and Lessons Learned', 61 *ZaöRV* (2001), 379–401.

[282] See http://www.amnesty.org/.

[283] See <http://www.hrw.org/>.

[284] See <http://www.msf.ch/>.

[285] D. Fleck, 'The Role of Individuals in International Humanitarian Law and Challenges for States in Its Development' in M. N. Schmitt and L. C. Green (eds), *The Law of Armed Conflict: Into the Next Millennium*, 71 *International Law Studies* (Naval War College, 1998), 119–39.

[286] For the complexity of this task, see D. Fleck, 'Implementing International Humanitarian Law: Problems and Priorities' (1991) *IRRC* 140–53.

[287] Cf. Michael Bothe/Peter Macalister-Smith/Thomas Kurzidem (eds), *National Implementation of International Humanitarian Law* (Nijhoff, 1990).

The observance of international humanitarian law can only be expected if all authorities, armed forces, and peoples are made familiar with its contents. Military manuals and regular education programmes for all members of armed forces are useful tools and necessary first steps.

XVIII. Personal Responsibility of the Individual

Each individual shall be responsible for realizing the ideals of international humani-   1436
tarian law and observing its provisions. Military leaders shall highlight this by
their own behaviour. They shall make clear that everyone is required by his or her
conscience to stand up for the preservation of the law.

Customary international humanitarian law is binding on every state and each individual; treaty obligations of international humanitarian law are binding on the states parties and the individuals of those parties, especially the combatants of states parties. In addition to these legal obligations, a moral obligation flows from the realization that the objective of international law is to reduce, as far as possible, the human suffering caused by military conflicts. There is an individual responsibility for each person realizing the ideals of international humanitarian law and observing its provisions. Military leaders, with their outstanding position, shall stress that every combatant is required to stand up for the preservation of the law. However, the consequences of a command, given by a superior, that violates international humanitarian law or other norms of international law, have not been fully settled.[288] Generally speaking, a soldier is obliged to obey his or her superior. This is an important general rule because only with a clear hierarchy and a clear command structure can the implementation of humanitarian law be reached.[289] However, to reach the implementation of humanitarian law standards, it has to be forbidden that a soldier be obliged to obey a command if that command requires him or her to commit a punishable offence. From the object and purpose of international humanitarian law, it can be derived that the soldier is obliged not to obey a command that requires him or her to commit a punishable offence.[290] This is very obvious in regard to orders that constitute an international crime; they must not be obeyed. According to Article 33 ICC Statute, the criminal responsibility of a person obeying an order is not relieved if this order is manifestly unlawful, namely an order to commit genocide or crimes against humanity. When the order is not manifestly unlawful, the criminal responsibility concerning war crimes is only relieved if and only if the soldier was under a legal obligation to obey the order *and* did not know that the order was unlawful.[291] Orders, which are obviously a violation of international law without constituting an international crime, are non binding. For instance, such violations of international law are intentional violations of the main principles of humanitarian law that do

---

[288] Cf. for instance Chantal Meloni, *Command Responsibility in International Criminal Law* (Asser Press, 2010); Solis, above, n. 16, 341 *et seq.*, 381 *et seq.*

[289] See in regard to this hierarchical structure for armed groups in non-international armed conflicts, Art. 1(1) AP II.

[290] Cf. Georg Nolte/Heike Krieger, 'European Military Law Systems—Summary and Recommendation', in Nolte (ed.), *European Military Law Systems* (Berlin: de Gruyter, 2003), 10.

[291] It is questionable whether Art. 33 ICC Statute departs from customary international law, cf. Christopher Staker, 'Defence of Superior Orders Revisited' (2005) 79 *Australian Law Journal* 431 *et seq.*:

not constitute war crimes, and intentional violations of main principles of human rights laws that do not constitute genocide or crimes against humanity. Apart from this, it is questionable whether it is sound to argue that a combatant is not obliged to obey illegal orders at all.[292] The drawback of such a rule would be that the command structure could be undermined; the positive side effect could be that illegal actions might be stopped without the personal risk of disciplinary sanctions. However, there does not seem to be enough state practice to support this view as a rule of customary law.[293] More convincing is the view, which is laid down in some national laws as well,[294] that such orders, which are not given for an official purpose, are non-binding and that every combatant has a duty to disobey a *manifestly unlawful* order (see above, Sections 144–147).[295]

'[A]lthough a defence of superior orders is now expressly recognised in Art 33 of the ICC Statute, that defence does not yet form part of customary international law. Rather, in customary international law, the Nuremberg principle still prevails, according to which superior orders is no defence but may be taken into account in mitigation of sentence' (446). Yoram Dinstein, 'International Criminal Courts and Tribunals, Defences', in *MPEPIL* states, that '[u]nder customary international law, the fact that an accused acted in obedience to superior orders does not constitute a defence *per se*, but is a factual element that may be taken into account—in conjunction with other circumstances—within the scope of an admissible defence based on lack of mens rea, specifically, duress or mistake.'

[292] See G. Nolte/H. Krieger, above, n. 290.
[293] H. Sato, 'The Defense of Superior Orders in International Law: Some Implications for the Codification of International Criminal Law' (2009) 9 *International Criminal Law Review* 117–37, at 133.
[294] Cf. § 11(1) Soldatengesetz der Bundesrepublik Deutschland [German Soldiers Law].
[295] Cf. *CIHL*, Rule 154. See as well separate and dissenting Opinion of President Antonio Cassese, Judgment, *Erdemović*, Case No. IT-96-22-A, Appeals Chamber, 7 October 1997, § 15: 'Duress is commonly raised in conjunction with superior orders. However there is no necessary connection between the two. Superior orders may be issued without being accompanied by any threats to life or limb. In these circumstances, if the superior order is *manifestly illegal* under international law, the subordinate is under a duty to refuse to obey the order. If, following such a refusal, the order is reiterated under a threat to life or limb, then the defence of duress may be raised, and superior orders lose any legal relevance.'

SILJA VÖNEKY

Annex

DISTINCTIVE EMBLEMS

1.		**Military Medical and Religious Services Components of the International Red Cross and Red Crescent Movement Civilian Medical Services** (under strict conditions) 1949 Geneva Convention I, Arts. 38, 44 1949 Geneva Convention II, Art. 41 1977 Additional Protocol I, Art. 18 1977 Additional Protocol II, Art. 12 2005 Additional Protocol III, Art. 1 Reproduced by kind permission of the International Committee of the Red Cross
2.		**Hospital and Safety Zones and Localities** 1949 Geneva Convention IV, Art. 14 and Annex I, Art. 6
3.		**Prisoner-of-War Camp** 1949 Geneva Convention III, Art. 23(4)
4.		**Internment Camp** 1949 Geneva Convention IV, Art. 83
5.		**Civil Defence** 1977 Additional Protocol I, Art. 66(4), Annex I, Art. 16
6.		**Works and Installations Containing Dangerous Forces** 1977 Additional Protocol I, Art. 56(7), Annex I, Art. 17

7.

Warning Sign for Areas Containing Mines

Technical Annex of the 1980 Protocol on Prohibitions or Restrictions on the Use of Mines, Booby-Traps and Other Devices, as amended on 3 May 1996, 1997 Ottawa Convention on the Prohibition of Anti-personnel Mines, Art. 5(2)

Signs shall be utilized in the marking of minefields and mined areas to ensure their visibility and recognition by the civilian population:
1. *Size and Shape*: a triangle or square no smaller than 28 centimetres (11 inches) by 20 centimetres (7.9 inches) for a triangle and 15 centimetres (6 inches) per side for a square.
2. *Colour*: red or orange with a yellow reflecting border.
3. *Symbol*: the symbol illustrated above, or an alternative readily recognizable in the area in which the sign is to be displayed as identifying a dangerous area.
4. *Language*: the sign should contain the word 'mines' in one of the six official languages of the Convention (Arabic, Chinese, English, French, Russian, and Spanish) and the language or languages prevalent in that area.
5. *Spacing*: signs should be placed around the minefield or mined area at a distance sufficient to ensure their visibility at any point by a civilian approaching the area.

8.

Cultural Property

1954 Hague Cultural Property Convention, Art. 16 and Regulations, Art. 20

9.

Cultural Property Under Special Protection

1954 Hague Cultural Property Convention, Arts. 16, 17

10.

Artistic and Scientific Institutions and Historic Monuments in the Organization of American States

1935 Roerich Pact, Art. III

11.

Flag of Truce

1907 Hague Regulations, Art. 32

12.

United Nations Emblem and Flag

General Assembly Resolutions 92(I) of 7 December 1946 and 167(III) of 19 December 1947, (UN Doc. ST/SGB/132, 1967)
Reproduced by kind permission of the United Nations

Index

Bold faced figures refer to Sections, normal figures to paragraphs of the commentaries.